TORT LAW

TORT LAW

Text, Cases, and Materials

FOURTH EDITION

Jenny Steele

Professor of Law, University of York

OXFORD
UNIVERSITY PRESS

OXFORD
UNIVERSITY PRESS

Great Clarendon Street, Oxford, OX2 6DP,
United Kingdom

Oxford University Press is a department of the University of Oxford.
It furthers the University's objective of excellence in research, scholarship,
and education by publishing worldwide. Oxford is a registered trade mark of
Oxford University Press in the UK and in certain other countries

Public sector information reproduced under Open Government Licence v3.0
(http://ww.nationalarchives.gov.uk/doc/open-government-licence/open-government-licence.htm)

Published in the United States of America by Oxford University Press
198 Madison Avenue, New York, NY 10016, United States of America

British Library Cataloguing in Publication Data
Data available

Library of Congress Control Number: 2017943294

ISBN 978-0-19-876880-7

Printed in Great Britain by
Bell & Bain Ltd., Glasgow

This book is dedicated to the memory of Thomas Steele

PREFACE

As a textbook enters its fourth edition, the challenges of updating become rather different from the challenges of writing the first or even the second edition. The overriding challenge is to keep track not only of updates, but also of shifts in the shape and emphasis of the law. I have always tried to ask myself, if this was the first edition, what aspects of the older law, or what interesting illustrations in the lower courts, would have to be overlooked in order to make way for the most helpful explanation of the current law? If some useful material has been cut, I hope this has been made worthwhile by giving newer developments the space and attention that they need.

In the Preface to the third edition, I noted that the most significant developments had occurred away from what students of twenty or thirty years ago might have thought of as the 'doctrinal core' of the law of tort, such as evolutions in the recoverability of economic losses in negligence; or in the general approach to the 'duty of care'. That same point can be made once more about this fourth edition; and once again, this seems to me to justify one of the key decisions made when writing the original text, namely to include a sufficiently wide range of torts to give a genuine sense of the shape of the subject. Certainly, there have been some significant decisions concerning the tort of negligence, but the most significant of these are perhaps *Montgomery v Lanarkshire Health Board* dealing with standard of care rather than duty of care; and a series of cases about tort defences: three of them relating to illegality; and one to contributory negligence. Also significant is the 'duty' case of *Michael v Chief Constable of South Wales*, but this also illustrates the untidy relationship between negligence duties, and positive duties to protect human rights. Other key changes incorporated into this edition have concerned judicial developments in the intentional torts and particularly the action in *Wilkinson v Downton*; recognition of an action for malicious *civil* prosecution; further evolution in the notion of 'material contribution' as a causal link; the application of the new 'serious harm' test in the law of defamation; the Supreme Court's decision to maintain a privacy injunction despite widespread publication elsewhere; and the same court's reflections on the correct approach to interpreting Parliamentary intent for the purposes of the action for breach of statutory duty. This follows the trend of earlier editions, and these developments are far removed from questions about the duty of care in negligence. Legislative developments have continued to have a strong influence, with the Defamation Act 2013 now being litigated in the courts, and the Social Action, Responsibility and Heroism Act 2015 bringing uncertain potential effects into the law relating to breach of duty.

I would like to thank the team at Oxford University Press for bearing with me through the familiar delays in the writing process, and particularly to thank Natasha Ellis-Knight for her encouragement and support. With the guidance of Oxford University Press, I have also added a brief 'Conclusions' section to each chapter, drawing together the threads, and with a focus on the most recent developments. It is intended that these will build on the existing 'Central Issues' theme at the start of each chapter, and offer students an opportunity to consolidate and a sense of progression. Finally, watching someone prepare a manuscript is doubtless less than exciting and almost certainly quite trying, especially at Christmas, and so I would like to thank Nick, Joe, and Theo, for accepting the need to share my attention. Special thanks go to Nick for being a prize motivator, as well as a rock of support this time around.

I have done my best to state the law as it stood in December 2016. Inevitably, there will have been some developments between the writing of this Preface, and publication. But help is at hand: as was the case with the second and third editions, the text is now also accompanied by an Online Resource Centre, where updates and additional materials and links are available.

Jenny Steele

York

January 2017

NEW TO THIS EDITION

Key new materials and cases covered in this fourth edition include:

- The Supreme Court's endorsement of 'informed consent', overruling *Sidaway v Bethlem Royal Hospital*, and acknowledging the significance of the patient's right to autonomy in *Montgomery v Lanarkshire Health Board*, and consequent ousting of the *Bolam* test for negligence when advising of the risks of medical treatment (Chapters 2 and 6);

- The Supreme Court's ruling in *Willers v Joyce*, in agreement with the Privy Council in *Crawford Adjusters v Sagicor*, that English law recognizes an action for malicious *civil* prosecution (Chapter 2);

- The decision of the Supreme Court in *OPO v Rhodes*, confining the tort in *Wilkinson v Downton* to the wilful infliction of physical or psychiatric harm, and rejecting an injunction to restrain publication of autobiographical details that could cause harm to the claimant (Chapter 2);

- The Court of Appeal's ruling in *Dunnage v Randall* that the objective standard of care applies notwithstanding mental impairment in the nature of schizophrenia (Chapter 3);

- The provisions of the Social Action, Responsibility and Heroism Act 2015, requiring courts to consider certain criteria when deciding when there has been a breach of duty (Chapter 3);

- The decision of the Supreme Court in *IEG v Zurich*, reasserting that damages under *Fairchild v Glenhaven* are, at common law, proportionate, and dealing with related issues of insurance liability in a jurisdiction to which section 3 of the Compensation Act 2006 does not apply; and the extension of the *Fairchild* enclave to lung cancer in *Heneghan v Manchester Dry Docks Ltd* (Chapter 4);

- The Privy Council's discussion of 'material contribution' to injury in a medical context in *Williams v Bermuda Hospital* (Chapter 4);

- Consideration of the principles of apportionment in contributory negligence in the Supreme Court, in *Jackson v Murray* (Chapter 5);

- Further developments in the Supreme Court in relation to the defence of illegality, through the decisions in *Hounga v Allen*; *Les Laboratoires Servier v Apotex*; and *Mirza v Patel*, the latter setting out the approach to be taken in future cases (Chapter 5);

- The notable decision of the Supreme Court in *Michael v CC of South Wales Police* that there was no duty to protect a murder victim whose 999 call had allegedly been negligently handled; and contrasting decision in *Michael* itself that a claim for damages under the Human Rights Act should proceed to trial, as well as the decision to award HRA damages where there had been failures in investigation in *DSD v Commissioner of Police of the Metropolis* (Chapter 6);

- The decision of the Supreme Court concerning the requirements for accessory liability as joint tortfeasors, in *Fish & Fish v Sea Shepherd* (Chapter 7);

- The decision of the Supreme Court in *Coventry v Lawrence* (*No 3*), concerning the compatibility of the 1999 costs regime with the ECHR (Chapter 8);

- The Supreme Court's decisions in *Cox v Ministry of Justice* and *Mohamud v Morrison Supermarkets*, concerning vicarious liability (Chapter 9);

- The Court of Appeal's decision in *Cocking v Eacott* that a licensor of premises is liable for nuisances created by her licensee (Chapter 10);

- The implications of the Consumer Rights Act 2015 for Occupiers' Liability (Chapter 12);

- Judicial interpretation of the 'serious harm' requirement in section 1 Defamation Act 2013, including *Lachaux v Independent Print Limited* (Chapter 13);

- The Supreme Court's decision to continue a privacy injunction despite the publication of information on the internet and in some other jurisdictions, in *PJS v News Group Newspapers* (Chapter 14);

- The Court of Appeal's decision that as a matter of law, the action for misuse of private information is categorized as a tort, in *Vidal-Hall v Google* (Chapter 14);

- The damages awards in phone hacking cases, considered in *Gulati v Mirror Group Newspapers* (Chapter 14);

- The Supreme Court's decision in *Campbell v Peter Gordon Joiners*, that there is no action against an individual company director for breach of the company's statutory duty to insure against liability to its employees, and the implications for the approach to breach of statutory duty cases (Chapter 16).

ACKNOWLEDGEMENTS

Grateful acknowledgement is made to all the authors and publishers of copyright material which appears in this book, and particularly to the following for permission to reprint material from the sources indicated.

AMERICAN LAW INSTITUTE: extract from Restatement (3rd) Torts: Liability for Physical Harm, section 1 (including comment). Copyright by the American Law Institute, reprinted with permission. All rights reserved.

STANFORD UNIVERSITY PRESS: extract from Stephen Guest, *Ronald Dworkin* (3rd edn, Stanford Law Books, 2013); Copyright (c) 2013 by the Board of Trustees of the Leland Stanford Jr. University. All rights reserved. Used by permission of the publisher, Stanford University Press, sup.org.

HART PUBLISHING, an imprint of Bloomsbury Publishing Plc: extract from P. Cane, *The Anatomy of Tort Law* (Hart Publishing, 1997), (c) author.

HARVARD LAW REVIEW ASSOCIATION: extracts from Dean Thayer, 'Liability Without Fault' (1916) 29 Harvard Law Review 801–15; Warren and Brandeis, 'The Right to Privacy' (1890) 4 Harvard Law Review 193; republished with permission of Harvard Law Review Association; permission conveyed through Copyright Clearance Center, Inc.

A. J. E. JAFFEY: extract from A. J. E. Jaffey, '*Volenti non fit injuria*' (1985) 44 Cambridge Law Journal 87.

OXFORD UNIVERSITY PRESS: extracts from D. Feldman, *Civil Liberties in England and Wales* (2nd edn, Oxford University Press, 2002); D. Ibbetson, *A Historical Introduction to the Law of Obligations* (Oxford University Press, 1999); R. Merkin and J. Steele, *Insurance and the Law of Obligations* (2013); A. W. B. Simpson, *Leading Cases in the Common Law* (Oxford University Press, 1995).

RELX (UK) LIMITED, TRADING AS LEXISNEXIS: extracts M. Millner, *Negligence in Modern Law* (Butterworths, 1967), *All England Law Reports* (All ER) and *Family Law Reports* (FLR).

A. W. B. SIMPSON: extract from A. W. B. Simpson, *Leading Cases in the Common Law* (Oxford University Press, 1995).

THE INCORPORATED COUNCIL OF LAW REPORTING: extracts from *Appeal Court Reports* (AC), *Queen's Bench Reports* (QB), *King's Bench Reports* (KB), and *Weekly Law Reports* (WLR).

SWEET & MAXWELL LTD: extracts from A. Ruck Keene and C. Dobson, 'At What Price Liberty? The Supreme Court Decision in Lumba and Compensation for False Imprisonment' (2012) PL 628 and *Road Traffic Reports* (RTR).

Every effort has been made to trace and contact copyright holders but this has not been possible in every case. If notified, the publisher will undertake to rectify any errors or omissions at the earliest opportunity.

OUTLINE TABLE OF CONTENTS

CONTENTS

TABLE OF CASES

STATUTORY INSTRUMENTS

TABLE OF EUROPEAN MATERIAL

TABLE OF TREATIES AND CONVENTIONS

PART I

INTRODUCTORY

1

INTRODUCTION: THE SHAPE OF TORT LAW TODAY

CENTRAL ISSUES

i) In this introduction, we begin by mapping out the diverse torts which will be considered in this text, identifying in broad terms the nature of the 'wrongs' with which they are concerned.

ii) Tort law has significant social and economic impact. Over many years, legislation has particularly improved the ability of tort law to compensate for accidental harm and to spread the risks of such harm. Recently however, there has been a sustained period of political concern with over-extensive liability, and with the costs of tort. Caution surrounds the costs of tort litigation and the possible impact on defendants, including not only public bodies but also enterprises and ultimately the wider public. Tangible effects on the law and its operation have followed.

iii) A new era in tort was also signalled by the enactment of the Human Rights Act 1998; but it was not clear exactly what difference the Act would make. At the end of this chapter, we introduce the statute and its effects to date where tort law is concerned. Some such effects have been subtle and some have been unexpected. The unfolding influence of the Human Rights Act is still in progress and will be seen in many chapters of this book.

1. TORTS AS WRONGS, AND THE MAP OF TORT LAW

Torts are 'wrongs'. To be slightly more precise, torts are civil wrongs for which law will provide a remedy. This remedy will be enforceable against one party, to the benefit of the other, and it will reflect (and perhaps correct) the wrong committed. There are other civil wrongs which are not torts, notably breaches of contract and of equitable obligation. Torts make up the most diverse bunch of civil wrongs in English law, protecting a wide range of interests against different types of invasion.

Unfortunately, we cannot go much further than this in defining the law of tort. There is no widely accepted definition of a 'tort' which would distinguish clearly between torts, and all other civil wrongs (although the word 'tort' is considered clear enough in its meaning to be used in a statute).[1]

The following extract considers the proper categorization of tort alongside other elements of the law, and identifies some of its key features.

Peter Cane, *The Anatomy of Tort Law* (Oxford: Hart Publishing, 1997), 11–13; by permission of Hart Publishing, an imprint of Bloomsbury Publishing Plc.

The law of tort is part of a larger body of civil (as opposed to criminal) law sometimes called 'the law of obligations'. Other parts of the law of obligations are the law of contract, the law of restitution and the law of trusts. The law of obligations may be contrasted with the law of property. The law of property consists of rules (which we might call 'constitutive rules') which establish (proprietary) rights and interests which the law of obligations protects by what might be called 'protective rules'. For example, tort law protects real property through the tort of trespass: to enter someone's land without their permission and without legal justification is to commit the tort of trespass to land. Property law defines who owns what land, and tort law protects the rights of the owner against unwanted intruders.

Although contract law and the law of trusts may be treated as part of the law of obligations, in fact these bodies of law contain both constitutive and protective rules. The law of contract not only establishes an obligation to keep contracts, but also lays down rules about how contracts are formed or, in other words, about what constitutes a binding contractual undertaking which there is a legal obligation to fulfil. … By contrast, tort law and the law of restitution terms is that civil law organizes relationships between individuals on a one to one basis. In are purely protective—they establish obligations designed to protect interests created by constitutive rules of the law of property, trusts or contracts or which arise in some other way.

Both the law of obligations and the law of property are part of what we call 'civil law' as opposed to criminal law. Civil law is a social institution by which we organize and interpret human conduct in a particular way. A central feature of civil (or, as it is sometimes called, 'private') law is 'bilateralness' or (more euphoniously) 'correlativity'.[2] What this means in simple the law of obligations, for instance, one person's obligation corresponds ('is correlative' to another person's right. …

The idea of correlativity provides the framework within which I will analyze the law of tort. Every cause of action in tort and, therefore, every principle of tort liability, has two basic (sets 1 of) elements, one concerned with the position of one party to a bilateral human interaction (the 'victim' of the tortious conduct) and the other concerned with the position of the other party to that interaction (the perpetrator of the tortious conduct, or the 'injurer'). …

The aim of this 'correlative analysis' is to understand and explain the law of tort as a system of ethical principles of personal responsibility or, in other words, a system of precepts about how people may, ought and ought not to behave in their dealings with others.

[1] Private International Law (Miscellaneous Provisions) Act 1995: see *Douglas v Hello! (No 3)* [2006] QB 125 (Chapter 14).

[2] We have omitted a lengthy footnote here which contrasts Cane's analysis of correlativity *between the parties* with a different and more challenging idea—expounded by Ernest Weinrib in *The Idea of Private Law* (Harvard University Press, 1995)—to the effect that rights and obligations are *themselves* 'correlative' (an obligation is inherent in the existence of the right).

The view of tort law above makes a valuable starting point for our present project. Torts are wrongs, and the wrongs in question are defined by reference to the relationship between the parties.

Having said that, the existence of a liability in tort does not always mean that the defendant ought not to have behaved as he or she did. Admittedly it *will* mean this on many occasions. For example, one should not be negligent if one can help it, and one certainly should not engage in deliberate acts of deceit. But sometimes, there is liability even though it cannot be said that the defendant is to be blamed for not behaving differently. For example, the negligent party may be a learner driver who simply could not have driven better; or the defendant may have carefully accumulated a dangerous thing, which has escaped through no fault of the defendant, causing harm to the claimant; or the defendant may have honestly believed that the umbrella they took home was their own, and not the claimant's. In all of these examples, there may be liability in tort, despite the fact that the defendant is not to be blamed for the way that they acted.[3] But in each of the three illustrations, the reason for imposing liability irrespective of blame may be quite different. The learner driver is held to an objective standard of care from which all road users can expect to benefit, despite her personal shortcomings. Failure to attain that standard is considered to amount to 'fault' for the purposes of the tort of negligence. It might be argued that the neighbour whose accumulated things escape and cause damage thereby takes responsibility for the outcomes of his or her own activity, despite their general reasonableness: the risk should be that of the accumulator, not of the victim.[4] The honest taker of an umbrella must compensate the owner in order to vindicate the latter's right over the property: this is a question of the definition and protection of proprietary rights. The difficulty perhaps is in squaring these different justifications with the notion of a 'wrong', or with the notion of a 'breach of duty'. Not all wrongs are 'conduct-based'; and 'duties' may be 'strict', in that their breach need not involve fault.[5]

Parties and Terminology

We should at this point introduce the parties and explain the applicable terminology.

Since 1999, the wronged party or 'victim' of the tort who brings an action has been referred to in England and Wales as the **claimant**. Previously, this party would have been referred to as the **plaintiff**, and that is the term still used in other common law jurisdictions. Since this book reproduces extracts from cases, statutes, and academic commentary, many of which predate this change, and some of which derive from other common law jurisdictions, the reader will encounter both sets of terminology.

The alleged wrongdoer (the party who is said to have committed a tort) is referred to as the **tortfeasor**. The tortfeasor is not necessarily a party to the action. The appropriate term for the person who is on the receiving end of the claim in tort (who is generally *but not always* the tortfeasor) is **defendant**. In Scotland, where the subject is not tort but **delict**, the terms are **pursuer** and **defender**. A number of Scottish cases are extracted in this volume, not least the most famous of all UK tort cases, *Donoghue v Stevenson* [1932] AC 562.

We have just mentioned that the defendant will not always be the tortfeasor (the person who actually committed the tort). This is an important feature of the law of tort. The

---

[3] The torts in question are negligence, the action in *Rylands v Fletcher*, and conversion (respectively).

[4] As we will see, *which* risks are placed with the accumulator in such cases have been steadily reduced, so that common law does not use this logic very often (Chapter 11).

[5] See for example the discussion of limitation periods in relation to trespass to the person, in Chapters 2 and 7: trespass generally is a breach of duty, but does not require fault.

defendant will not be the tortfeasor where the action is brought on the basis of **vicarious liability** for the torts of employees and agents (Chapter 9), or against an insurer pursuant to the Third Parties (Rights against Insurers) Act 1930 or 2010 (Section 4). In each case, it must be established that the *tortfeasor* (and not the defendant) has committed a tort. In a much larger group of claims, the named defendant *is* the tortfeasor, but the defence is paid for, conducted, and where appropriate settled by the defendant's **liability insurer**,[6] who will also be paying for any damages that may be awarded.

For the benefit of relative newcomers to the study of law, or readers who are not familiar with the legal system of the UK, it should also be mentioned that the most senior court in the UK has undergone a change, as part of significant constitutional reorganization.[7] The UK's highest court was, until its final judgments in 2009, the **Judicial Committee of the House of Lords** (generally simply referred to as the 'House of Lords'). From October 2009, that role has been taken by the **UK Supreme Court** (generally referred to here simply as 'the Supreme Court'). Decisions both of the House of Lords and of the Supreme Court will be encountered in this book: both are of the highest authority.

Torts

Some years ago, Bernard Rudden argued that (at the time of counting) there were 70 identifiable torts.[8] In fact, the boundaries are fluid and it is not impossible for new torts to be recognized, or old ones to be revived. For example, the action for misfeasance in a public office (Chapter 2, Section 8.2) has undergone a revival in recent years, having been presumed extinct, though it must be admitted that the volume of litigation involving this tort has not been translated into success for claimants.[9] From time to time, wholly new torts have been urged. Recent (unsuccessful) examples include a proposed tort of 'unlawful exile' (*Chagos Islanders v Attorney General* [2003] EWHC 2222), and of unlawful interference with body parts (*In re Organ Retention Litigation* [2005] QB 506). A new tort of publishing private information or images seems to have emerged, influenced by close analysis of the Human Rights Act 1998 (explained in Section 4.2). (The Court of Appeal has said that the action is *not* a tort; while some members of the House of Lords have clearly referred to it as a tort.) More recently, the Privy Council opened the door to actions for malicious *civil* (as opposed to criminal) prosecution, which was rejected by the House of Lords only just over a decade previously; and the Supreme Court has ruled that this change represents domestic law.[10] The terrain of tort law is apt to change.

---

[6] A *liability insurer* agrees to indemnify the insured party for civil liability that they may incur to others. A *first party insurer* agrees to indemnify the insured party for losses they suffer directly, not through liability to others.

[7] Part 3, Constitutional Reform Act 2005. The aim was to create a clear and secure division between the legislative and judicial branches. Previously, the Lord Chancellor has been a political appointment who could nevertheless sit as a judge of the House of Lords, for example. For debate, prior to implementation of the change, see the special edition of *Legal Studies* edited by Derek Morgan, *Constitutional Innovation: the creation of a Supreme Court for the United Kingdom* (Butterworth, 2004).

[8] B. Rudden, 'Torticles' (1991–2) 6/7 Tulane Civil Law Forum 105.

[9] There may be no recent case where a claimant has been awarded damages in this tort, and where they would not have secured damages in some other tort. Yet it is clear that claimants continue to assert misfeasance claims, and it is possible that this influences settlements. In *Amin v Imran Khan & Partners* [2011] EWHC 2958 (QB), a court accepted that solicitors' failure to add a claim for misfeasance amounted to actionable negligence in the circumstances, as it was likely to have weakened the claimants' bargaining position.

[10] *Crawford Adjusters and others v Sagicor General Insurance (Cayman) Limited and another* [2013] UKPC 17, an appeal from the Cayman Islands; *Willers v Joyce* [2016] UKSC 43; [2016] 3 WLR 477. The issues are discussed in Chapter 2, Section 8.

2. THE NATURE OF TORTS: DEFINING THE 'WRONGS'

In *The Anatomy of Tort Law* (extracted in Section 1), Peter Cane argues that the ethical nature of the law of tort, which he considers to be based upon responsibility, will be best understood by breaking down the various torts into certain components. These components are **protected interests** on the part of the claimant; **sanctioned conduct** on the part of the tortfeasor; and **remedies** for the wrong. Between them, these three components strike a balance, in each case, between the claimant and the tortfeasor. They express the nature of tort law as concerned with what Cane calls 'correlativity' (the relationship between the parties). Cane argues that this approach is better than a more traditional exposition, which simply adopts and applies the existing requirements of recognized torts as 'legal formulae', without reflection on the ethical underpinnings of the wrongs concerned. On that approach, the structure of the law of tort is presented, uncritically, as largely the product of historical accident, and as though there is no more to be said about it than this.

Spelling out the various elements of different torts in this way can help us to map the diverse ways in which conduct of one party may interfere with interests of another party, so as to amount to an actionable wrong. In other words, this is a way of expressing the diversity of the terrain that is covered by tort law.

Cane goes on to argue against too much adherence to legal categories such as distinct causes of action in the form of different torts, or even 'tort' and 'contract'. He suggests that different causes of action with different criteria should not be available on the same facts, and that the ethical principles of personal responsibility discovered by unpacking the various torts in this way will be better applied without excessive reference to these categories.[11] But there are reasons to hesitate about this prescription. If the various torts describe different ways in which an interaction may be 'wrong', why and indeed how should we decide that a single way of approaching the facts is valid? *Which* way should those facts be approached? This sort of thinking has contributed to the near demise of strict liability under the rule in *Rylands v Fletcher*, for example (Chapter 11). It has also led to the classification of trespass to the person as an 'intentional' tort (explained further in Chapter 2), while other forms of trespass are categorized as 'strict'. For example, the significant differences between the implications of a finding of trespass to the person (unlawfulness); misfeasance in a public office (damage caused by abuse of power); and negligence (damage caused through the defendant's lack of care), all potentially existing on the same facts, are highlighted by the litigation in *Ashley v Chief Constable of Sussex Police*.[12] Legal concepts should not be 'mapped' in too restrictive a way; and the field of tort is a dynamic and changing one.

The Structure of Our Map of Tort

Table 1.1 sets out key components of a number of torts. The dimensions of our map are similar to the first two of Cane's categories, namely protected interests, and relevant 'conduct'. We also include a column specifying whether the tort requires 'actual' or 'material' damage, since this criterion provides a very important division between different torts. In torts

[11] It is sometimes said that the argument on the basis of different torts should no longer happen since we have done away with the 'forms of action'. But rather the reverse is true: since claimants no longer have to choose the right procedure ('form'), they are free to argue the substantive merits in alternative ways ('cause').

[12] [2008] UKHL 25; (2008) 2 WLR 975. See further Chapter 2, Section 2.

which do not require damage, the invasion of the claimant's interest is 'actionable per se' (without more); although it seems that in the absence of damage, only 'nominal' damages are likely to be awarded (*Walumba Lumba v Secretary of State for the Home Department* [2011] UKSC 12; [2012] 1 AC 245, Chapter 2). There is no column relating to Cane's third element, remedies. Issues about remedies are hard to capture in this general table, since it is not possible to tie remedies very neatly to causes of action, and they are therefore left for later chapters.

Table 1.1 An introductory map

Tort(s)	Protected interests	Need to show 'damage'? ('DAMAGE-BASED'?)	Relevant 'wrongdoing': what must the tortfeasor do? (STANDARD OF LIABILITY)
1. Trespass to the person: a. Battery b. Assault c. False imprisonment	Bodily integrity/ right of self-determination	No	Battery: unlawful interference with bodily integrity Assault: immediate threat which deliberately puts C in fear of a battery False imprisonment: total unlawful restraint of claimant's liberty *Contact, threat, or restraint must be intended.* Unlawfulness or harm need not be either intended, or careless INTENTIONAL AND STRICT ELEMENTS
2. 'The action in *Wilkinson v Downton*'	Freedom from mental harm	Yes	Intention to inflict mental harm; intention may be imputed where likelihood of such harm is obvious INTENTION TO HARM, BUT INTENT MAY BE IMPUTED; NEED NOT BE ACTUAL
3. Action for harassment under Protection from Harassment Act 1997	Freedom from harassment	No	Course of conduct amounting to harassment; constructive knowledge that this conduct would amount to harassment CONSTRUCTIVE KNOWLEDGE OF HARASSMENT

Table 1.1 (*cont.*)

Tort(s)	Protected interests	Need to show 'damage'? ('DAMAGE-BASED'?)	Relevant 'wrongdoing': what must the tortfeasor do? (STANDARD OF LIABILITY)
4. 'Unlawful means' economic torts and simple conspiracy	Economic interests	Yes	Intention to harm the claimant's interests; generally (and apart from simple conspiracy), unlawful means INTENTION TO HARM IN STRONG SENSE
5. Inducing breach of contract	Contractual interests	Yes	Intention to procure the breach of contract INTENTION IN A STRONG SENSE
6. Deceit	Economic interests (and perhaps others)	Yes	Giving a false statement with: Intention that C should rely; and Knowledge of (or recklessness as to) the falsity of the statement INTENTION IN TWO SENSES
7. Malicious falsehood	Reputation and economic interests	Yes, except where defined by statute as actionable per se	Malicious publication of *falsehoods*: '*malice*' comprises either Intent to harm; or Lack of belief in truth of statement INTENT TO HARM OR LACK OF BELIEF (BAD FAITH)
8. Malicious prosecution and analogous torts	Freedom from prosecution/ intrusion through criminal or civil process;[13] liberty/economic losses/reputation?	Yes	Initiating prosecution/ obtaining search warrant (etc.) with: subjective malice, criminal process, and lack of reasonable cause BAD FAITH AND UNREASONABLENESS
9. Misfeasance in a public office	Economic/ personal?	Yes	Exercise of power by a public official with targeted malice (intent to harm the claimant); or Intentional or reckless abuse of power INTENT TO HARM, OR RECKLESSNESS

[13] This tort has been expanded to embrace civil process, as well as criminal: *Crawford Adjusters v Sagicor* [2013] UKPC 17; *Willers v Joyce* [2016] UKSC 43.

Table 1.1 (*cont.*)

Tort(s)	Protected interests	Need to show 'damage'? ('DAMAGE-BASED'?)	Relevant 'wrongdoing': what must the tortfeasor do? (STANDARD OF LIABILITY)
10. Negligence	Personal, property, or economic interests (from damage)	Yes	Careless conduct, but only if this amounts to breach of a duty to take care, owed to the claimant NEGLIGENCE
11. Private nuisance	Relevant interests in land (Use and enjoyment; easements)	No	Unreasonable interference with relevant interests. Careless conduct not required in most cases UNREASONABLE INTERFERENCE; MAY BE STRICT IN TERMS OF CONDUCT
12. Public nuisance	Personal and property interests	Yes	Interference with comfort or convenience of a class of Her Majesty's subjects UNREASONABLENESS; STRICT AS TO CONDUCT
13. The action in *Rylands v Fletcher*	Interests in land	Yes	Accumulation of a dangerous thing; non-natural user of land STRICT; SUBJECT TO NON-NATURAL USER
14. Occupiers' liability	Personal and (for visitors) property	Yes	Breach of occupancy duty: failing to ensure that premises are 'reasonably safe' REASONABLENESS—NEGLIGENCE?
15. Defamation: a. Libel b. Slander	Reputation	No? (libel); Yes (most forms of slander)	Publication of a defamatory statement referring to the claimant (No need for intention or carelessness) STRICT
16. Publication of private information and images	Privacy in respect of information and images	No	Publication of information or images where there is a reasonable expectation of privacy STRICT

Table 1.1 (*cont.*)

Tort(s)	Protected interests	Need to show 'damage'? ('DAMAGE-BASED'?)	Relevant 'wrongdoing': what must the tortfeasor do? (STANDARD OF LIABILITY)
17. Product liability under the Consumer Protection Act 1987	Personal and property interests (against damage)	Yes	Manufacture or first supply of a product containing a defect STRICT
18. Breach of statutory duty	Various: as the statute prescribes	Yes/no depending on what is protected by the statute	Breach of the statutory duty: may be strict or fault-based VARIABLE: MAY BE STRICT
19. Trespass to land	Possession of land	No	Interference with right to possession. Entering land must not be 'involuntary', but trespass may be entirely inadvertent STRICT
20. Conversion	Right to possession of goods	No	Action inconsistent with the rights of the claimant. Intent to assert dominion over the goods. Bona fide acts (without knowledge of C's rights) may amount to conversion STRICT

Conduct and the Special Case of Negligence

It will be noticed that there are many torts of strict liability and several torts requiring intention, but only one general tort which truly depends on 'negligence'.[14] This invites a number of comments.

First, most undergraduate courses in the law of tort are substantially concerned with the tort of negligence. This is understandable given the practical importance of negligence and the sheer volume of case law it generates,[15] but it means that, typically, courses in tort law

[14] Occupiers' liability may be described as a special case of negligence where the duty relates specifically to *keeping premises reasonably safe*, rather than (more generally) acting in a reasonable way.

[15] The part of this book dealing with negligence is also the longest; but many of the most actively developing areas lie in other torts. For example, major changes have occurred across the diverse range of 'intentional torts' since the first edition in 2007 (see Chapter 2).

are not particularly representative of the whole subject. Second, 'negligence'—in the sense of the careless infliction of harm—has been broadened into a very general principle, while other 'wrongs' have remained confined in their scope. Indeed, we will see that 'fault-based' thinking has tended to affect the interpretation of other torts also. This feature of the law of tort—the generalization of a negligence principle—may reflect the fact that liability on the basis of fault is considered to express a suitable approach to the relationship between the parties; alternatively, it may reflect the fact that such liability is thought to pursue a relevant and appropriate objective.

On the other hand, the progress of the tort of negligence can also be used to illustrate the *dangers* of a general approach. A great deal of difficult case law is generated by the need to set limits to the tort of negligence. One of the most abstract ideas in the law of tort is the 'duty of care in negligence'. The ambit of negligence is confined largely by considering whether it is appropriate for such a duty to be imposed.[16]

Protected Interests

Protected interests could be defined in very broad terms (dignitary interests, interests in the person, economic interests, property interests). But this would give us little detailed information concerning the precise ambit of some of the torts above, and may actually be misleading.

'Property interests' provide a good illustration of the detailed differences between protected interests. Property interests *of different sorts* are protected *against invasion of different types* by various torts. So **negligence** protects against **damage** to property; **private nuisance** overlaps with negligence but more broadly protects against **interference with use and enjoyment** of land; **trespass to land** protects against **interference with possession of** land, and need not involve any diminution in value at all; and **conversion** title to chattels against actions which are actually *inconsistent with* the claimant's rights (most particularly, where the defendant *treats the chattel as their own*). When comparing these four actions, one must bear in mind the different property interests protected *and* the difference this variation may make to the remedies awarded.

The Structure of this Book

There are different ways of structuring the law of tort. This text follows a broad and general progression from the torts which require intention; through those which require carelessness or other unreasonableness; to those which are broadly strict (requiring no fault). It is not claimed that this direction is entirely without anomalies or controversies. 'Intention' appears to be the very antithesis of strict liability (liability irrespective of fault) when it takes the form of intentional causation of harm (as in the tort of deceit); yet elements of intention and strict liability combine in trespass to the person: physical contact must be intentional; but the wrongfulness of that contact may even be unknown to the defendant. The approach is selected because it offers the best chance of understanding the broad spectrum of the wrongs involved in the law of tort, whilst not oversimplifying the rights and interests that various torts protect. In other words, this approach has been chosen as a means of organizing and indeed revealing the diversity of torts.

[16] See Chapter 6, which is entirely concerned with application of the 'duty of care' idea—and is by far the longest chapter in this book.

There is also some essential material common to all torts. This material is included in Chapters 7, 8, and 9. The reason for presenting this material in the centre of the text, rather than leaving it to languish at the end as is more traditional, is that the issues are at least as important as the substantive rules of liability. The majority of undergraduate courses in tort law will be primarily concerned with the tort of negligence, although very few, if any, are restricted to negligence. Since no understanding of negligence is complete without considering issues concerning recoverable damages and potential remedies, contribution between parties, and vicarious liability, it is important that these issues should not be separated too far from the substantive principles of negligence. But these issues also have much broader application. To the extent that other torts raise different or distinctive issues concerning remedies, those issues are considered in appropriate chapters. This way of organizing the material is chosen in order to enliven and make more immediate the issues surrounding remedies, costs, limitation, and distribution of liability between different parties.

An obvious alternative to the present approach is to group torts according to protected interests (though if done consistently, this would require certain torts, including negligence, to be broken down into different pieces). A 'protected interests' approach is particularly valuable if the goal is to set out the remedies available through tort law alongside other potential sources of remedies, protection, or compensation (industrial injuries schemes, social security benefits, insurance schemes, and so on).[17] For some years, that functional approach was in the ascendancy, whereas a new interest in the contours of private law as a whole has heralded a shift away from functional analysis. Although this text does not adopt a 'protected interests' approach, it is still important that some of the insights of such an approach should be retained. In particular, it should not be assumed that the *only* goal of tort law is to remedy wrongs perceived in terms of the relationship between two parties; or that the real-world *impact* of tort liability is unimportant.

3. TORT LAW AND SOCIAL PURPOSE

So far, we have discussed the shape of tort law in terms of its principles of liability and the approach taken to the interaction between parties. The idea that tort law might also have a 'function' outside remedying of wrongs is less widely accepted and perhaps less fashionable at present than it once was. But the evidence is overwhelming that in some instances the law of tort is used in order to distribute losses and compensate injuries.

Peter Cane, *Atiyah's Accidents, Compensation and the Law* (8th edn, Cambridge: Cambridge University Press, 2013), 32

… there have been many legal developments in the last eighty years or so which have been designed to facilitate the operation of the fault-based tort system of accident compensation. These include the system of compulsory third-party insurance to cover liability for road accidents, and of compulsory insurance to cover liability of employers to their employees. There is also a body called the Motor Insurers' Bureau (MIB) which is designed to fill the gap in the

---

[17] The leading work in this tradition is *Atiyah's Accidents, Compensation and the Law*, now in its eighth edition, which is extracted in Section 3.

compulsory motor insurance system caused by failure of vehicle owners to insure in accordance with the legal requirements; in addition, the MIB accepts liability in some hit-and-run cases and in cases where the party at fault was insured but the insurer has become insolvent.

The operation of tort law as a compensation mechanism has been expanded in various other ways by legislation. The Law Reform (Miscellaneous Provisions) Act 1934 allows actions to be brought against the estate of a deceased negligent person; the Law Reform (Contributory Negligence) Act 1945 changed the law to allow claimants to recover some damages despite having contributed by their own negligence to the injuries suffered; the Law Reform (Personal Injuries) Act 1948 abolished the doctrine of common employment and enabled employees to sue their employers where they suffered injury as a result of the negligence of a fellow-employee; and the Occupiers' Liability Acts of 1957 and 1984, among other things, simplified the law by making the occupier of premises liable for negligence.

The first part of this extract points out that legislators have in some of the 'core' areas of tort law aimed to provide a route to compensation through liability insurance; while the second points to a much broader set of statutory developments. As to the first of these, in the case of road traffic accidents (which currently make up around 80 per cent of personal injury claims), and in relation to claims against employers, liability insurance is compulsory. The next extract continues this theme, explaining that there is more to the observable desire to compensate victims of tort, than simply a legislative provision requiring insurance.[18]

R. Merkin and J. Steele, *Insurance and the Law of Obligations* (Oxford University Press, 2013), Chapter 9, 'Compulsory Liability Insurance', 256–7; by permission of Oxford University Press[19]

Compulsory insurance necessarily represents a legislative choice. Generally speaking behind the choice is a decision to ensure (to one degree or another) that a person suffering harm receives indemnity or compensation. In the UK, the only existing instances of compulsory insurance by legislation (referring here to private rather than national insurance) relate to liabilities. The choice of compulsory liability insurance also amounts in some sense to choosing *liability*. Where liability is delivered through the law of tort and analogous regimes, with the choice of liability comes not only a reliance on breach of duty (defining the risks to be distributed), but also, unless it is adapted by legislation, a choice of the tort measure of damages.

The introduction of compulsory liability insurance, assuming that both liability and the tort measure of damages are to be retained, nevertheless brings with it further legislative choices. Apart from compulsion itself, will further legal resources be deployed to ensure that insurance *does* mean cover? In this respect, a first question surrounds policy defences. As a matter of ordinary insurance contract law, insurers may have one of many defences to a claim, including breach of the duty of utmost good faith, lack of coverage or failure by the assured to comply with policy terms, and the operation of these defences may remove the source of funds for compensation. An important question is whether legislation allows the insurers to rely upon their defences or whether it modifies rights under the policy so that the proceeds are payable to meet a third party claim even though they are not so available in respect of first party loss. Where this occurs, it is plainly a further step away from the idea

---

[18] The interaction of different factors in shaping tort claiming is elaborated in the next extracted source.

[19] Footnote references have been removed from this extract.

that insurance relationships are 'fortuitous', and that they are a matter between assured and insurer, not concerning the tort claimant. It is a step which has clearly been taken in the UK. As will be seen below, compulsory policies issued in respect of road traffic losses and injury at work both modify policy terms. Partial relief is also given under the Third Parties (Rights against Insurers) Acts 1930 and 2010 to a claimant who brings an action against an insolvent assured when the assured has failed to comply with his post-claim obligations under the policy. The latter point is not confined to compulsory insurance. This in turn illustrates a general point, that legal actors and policy-makers have learned progressively through the interactions of tort and insurance against the backdrop of evolving social policy. Component parts of different solutions—themselves sometimes pragmatically oriented to grasping the advantages of existing market responses—have been translated to and absorbed by new contexts, increasing the cross-fertilisation to which we have already referred.

In their book, Merkin and Steele explore a number of dimensions of the relationship between tort and insurance,[20] emphasizing the complexity of this interaction and citing the suggestion by Baker and Siegelman that 'little or nothing makes sense in Tort law except in the light of liability insurance'.[21] However, the answer to the question of *how* liability insurance affects tort will vary from one context to another and its implications may be complex.

4. TWO CURRENT CHALLENGES

Here we consider two continuing challenges to the law of tort. Both illustrate that political controversy and questions of public interest surround the operation of private law, though in quite different ways.

4.1 'COMPENSATION CULTURE' AND THE COSTS OF TORT

Tort law has been the subject of renewed political debate over the last few years. Part of this debate has invoked the spectre of a 'compensation culture'. Critics of the (supposed) 'compensation culture' suggest that there is an unhealthy preoccupation with seeking compensation for any loss, insult, or disappointment that is suffered; and sometimes that this is tending to sap the moral fibre of the nation, to disrupt the provision of public services, and to deny individuals and the economy the benefit of healthy risk-taking. More prosaically, the 'compensation culture' is said to be driving up the costs of tort to an unhealthy and unnecessary level, as well as creating undesirable incentives to avoid risk.

The rise of a 'compensation culture' rhetoric is often associated with a particular idea of individual responsibility, emphasizing that victims of accidents do to some extent have responsibility for their own safety, and perhaps also for making financial provision in relation to the risks they face. That debate continues across national boundaries. In Australia, a 'crisis' was experienced in the availability and cost of liability insurance, and was itself

---

[20] A sustained analysis of the interplay between tort law and liability insurance in the United States can be found in K. Abraham, *Liability Century: From the Progressive Era to 9/11* (Harvard University Press, 2008).
[21] T. Baker and P. Siegelman, 'The Law and Economics of Liability Insurance: A Theoretical and Empirical Review', citing T. Dobhanzy, 'Nothing in Science Makes Sense Except in the Light of Evolution' (1973) 35 *American Biology Teacher* 125. Examples are illegality; duty questions; vicarious liability; and the funding of litigation.

precipitated by the fall of a major insurer, HIH. Whether tort law, or other factors, were to blame for this state of affairs is debatable. A Committee was set up and instructed to consider how best to restrict tort liability in order to avoid such problems in the future. The end result has been extensive legislative adjustment to the principles of tort law in Australia.[22]

UK tort law has not endured quite the same pressure for thorough and extensive change to the principles of liability in order to stem the tort tide, although there are some important exceptions (Chapters 13; 16). But the idea of a pervasive 'compensation culture' is still used—by government ministers, amongst others—despite empirical reviews suggesting that the overall level of claiming has not, in fact, been rising in the short or long term.[23] It might be said, however, that concerns surrounding the cost and impact of tort have become more specific. For example, there has been a particular focus in recent years on the need to control the costs of litigation; on the costs of health and safety duties for businesses; and on the rising costs of motor insurance.

On this last theme, in the article extracted next, Richard Lewis and Annette Morris explain that increased claiming is indeed a hallmark of one particular category of personal injury claims, namely road traffic ('RTA')[24] claims; but emphasize that this is an exceptional case. In this particular category, a compulsory liability insurance regime facilitates recovery where liability is established. The point made by Lewis and Morris is that the regime also facilitates and encourages claiming.

R. Lewis and A. Morris, 'Tort Law Culture in the United Kingdom', (2012) 3 Journal of European Tort Law, 230, 263

Overall, … The process of encouraging, processing and resolving RTA claims is heavily institutionalized when compared to other types of claim. In addition, given their financial attractiveness, RTA claims have become more of a commodity. Whilst the impact of advertising is unclear, CFAs and payments for referral have certainly played a role in increasing our propensity to claim after an RTA. A circular process has occurred whereby demand has driven supply and supply has driven demand. It is clear that our propensity to claim compensation depends as much on institutionalized ways of handling different types of dispute as upon broader cultural propensities to litigate. Practices of claiming encouraged by this institutionalization inevitably, however, feed into and become embedded in our wider culture. With claiming after an RTA becoming increasingly common, the experiences of other people may encourage us to claim because we feel they are no more deserving. We may naturally think about compensation after an accident and even come to expect it. The overall result is that a stronger 'cultural link' has developed between RTAs, injury and compensation.

22 See B. MacDonald, 'Legislative Intervention in the Law of Negligence: The Common Law, Statutory Interpretation and Tort Law in Australia' (2005) 27 Syd Law Rev 443; J. Goudkamp, 'Statutes and Tort Defences', in Arvind and Steele, *Tort Law and the Legislature: Common Law, Statute, and the Dynamics of Legal Change* (Hart, 2013).

23 For a review of the response to the evidence and nature of the debate see A. Morris, 'The "Compensation Culture" and the Politics of Tort', in T. T. Arvind and J. Steele, *Tort Law and the Legislature* (Hart Publishing, 2013).

24 The compulsory insurance regime is currently enshrined in the Road Traffic Act 1998. It originated in the Road Traffic Act 1930.

The nature of the specific RTA claims environment has produced an increase in claims, some of them unmeritorious and fraudulent, but this is at odds with the general picture in relation to tort.

Costs

Focus has shifted in recent years to the costs and burdens of tort litigation. The need to protect potential defendants from the threat of litigation is a common theme, whether potential defendants are public authorities (where the perception is that public services may be put at risk by tort), enterprises (where the threat is of red tape as much as excessive liability), insurers (where the fear is of inflated insurance premiums), or publishers of statements of one sort or another (where the fear is of disincentives to publication). There has been considerable legislative activity aimed at curtailing the costs of litigation, and the perceived negative impact of tort claiming. The most notable change is a wide-ranging overhaul of the costs regime applicable to civil litigation, with implications at least as significant for the operation of the law of tort as any change to the principles of liability or of damages. These changes are reviewed in Chapter 8. The Justice Secretary directly linked these changes with the assault on 'compensation culture', announcing the reforms with the comment that: 'We are turning the tide on the compensation culture. It's pushing up the cost of insurance, and making it more expensive to drive a car or organize an event. It's time the whole system was rebalanced.'[25]

Legislative Changes to Liability

There have also been specific, but important legislative changes designed to moderate the impact of the law of tort by adjusting specific principles of liability. The Defamation Act 2013 includes both substantive and procedural elements, and is designed to moderate the threat of defamation actions and to 'rebalance' the law of defamation. This move has attracted all-party support in Parliament,[26] and would perhaps have been undertaken quite independently of 'compensation culture' debate. Nevertheless, the idea that the threat of litigation may have adverse effects is in harmony with the prevailing political outlook on the law of tort more generally. In a different context, further significant change is effected by section 69 of the Enterprise and Regulatory Reform Act 2013, part of the last government's war on 'red tape' and a striking reversal of well over a century of development in strict liability of employers to their employees.[27] This provision was passed with relatively little consultation and has not attracted much comment by comparison with reform of defamation. Both are considered in depth in later chapters. The government has also brought into force the Social Action, Responsibility and Heroism Act 2015, extracted in Chapter 3. This statute does not seek to change the general framework for determining whether there has been a breach of duty, but aims to ensure that the merits of deserving defendants' actions will be taken into account. The goal is to avoid the perceived deterrent effect of potential tort liability.

The overriding impression is that policy-makers are currently either defendant-centred, or at least wary of the possible impact on defendants and on society not only of tort liability, but of tort litigation. While tort liability may be a tool to be deployed in the public interest, it is also perceived as a danger. In the courts too, a number of cases have indicated a renewed

[25] <https://www.gov.uk/government/news/turning-the-tide-on-compensation-culture>.
[26] Defamation Act 2013, discussed in Chapter 13.
[27] Chapter 16.

culture of restraint in the law of tort.[28] In such a context, whether or not the label 'compensation culture' eventually begins to fade away, the concerns that lie behind it seem to have achieved a secure foothold at the level of legal policy, both legislative and judicial.

4.2 THE HUMAN RIGHTS ACT 1998

The Human Rights Act 1998 (HRA) has significantly changed the contours of English law. It gives a new status to the rights guaranteed by the European Convention on Human Rights, so that they are not solely accessible by bringing a case against the state itself in an international court. Rather, they play a role in domestic litigation in domestic courts. Naturally, the influence of the HRA is far broader than the law of tort, with which we are concerned here. So far as tort law is concerned however, it is significant that the HRA makes violation of applicable rights by a public authority actionable in domestic courts (rather than merely in Strasbourg): it therefore makes it possible to pursue a public authority, such as a Chief Constable or local education authority, directly in relation to violations of such rights. It also obliges all public authorities to respect the specified Convention rights, and defines 'public authorities' in such a way as to include courts and tribunals. The impact on private law (including tort) is still unfolding.

Human Rights Act 1998 (c. 42)

The Convention Rights

1. (1) In this Act the Convention rights means the rights and fundamental freedoms set out in

    (a) Articles 2 to 12 and 14 of the Convention,

    (b) Articles 1 to 3 of the First Protocol, and

    (c) Articles 1 and 2 of the Sixth Protocol,

    as read with Articles 16 to 18 of the Convention.

    (2) Those Articles are to have effect for the purposes of this Act subject to any designated derogation or reservation (as to which see sections 14 and 15).

    (3) The Articles are set out in Schedule 1….

Interpretation of Convention Rights

2. (1) A court or tribunal determining a question which has arisen in connection with a Convention right must take into account any

    (a) judgment, decision, declaration or advisory opinion of the European Court of Human Rights,

    (b) opinion of the Commission given in a report adopted under Article 31 of the Convention, decision of the Commission in connection with Article 26 or 27(2) of the Convention, or

---

[28] Prime examples are *Tomlinson v Congleton* (Chapter 12) and *Michael v Chief Constable of South Wales* (Chapter 6). Of course there are counter-examples where liability has expanded, notably *Willers v Joyce* (above) and *Montgomery v Lanarkshire Health Board* [2015] UKSC 11; [2015] AC 1430 (Chapter 3).

...

(d) decision of the Committee of Ministers taken under Article 46 of the Convention,

whenever made or given, so far as, in the opinion of the court or tribunal, it is relevant to the proceedings in which that question has arisen.

... Public Authorities

Acts of Public Authorities

6. (1) It is unlawful for a public authority to act in a way which is incompatible with a Convention right.

(2) Subsection (1) does not apply to an act if

(a) as the result of one or more provisions of primary legislation, the authority could not have acted differently or

(b) in the case of one or more provisions of, or made under, primary legislation which cannot be read or given effect in a way which is compatible with the Convention rights, the authority was acting so as to give effect to or enforce those provisions.

(3) In this section public authority includes

(a) a court or tribunal, and

(b) any person certain of whose functions are functions of a public nature,

but does not include either House of Parliament or a person exercising functions in connection with proceedings in Parliament.

(4) In subsection (3) Parliament does not include the House of Lords in its judicial capacity.

(5) In relation to a particular act, a person is not a public authority by virtue only of subsection (3)(b) if the nature of the act is private.

Proceedings

7. (1) A person who claims that a public authority has acted (or proposes to act) in a way which is made unlawful by section 6(1) may—

(a) bring proceedings against the authority under this Act in the appropriate court or tribunal, or

(b) rely on the Convention right or rights concerned in any legal proceedings,

but only if he is (or would be) a victim of the unlawful act.

(2) In subsection (1)(a) "appropriate court or tribunal" means such court or tribunal as may be determined in accordance with rules; and proceedings against an authority include a counterclaim or similar proceeding.

... (5) Proceedings under subsection (1)(a) must be brought before the end of—

(a) the period of one year beginning with the date on which the act complained of took place; or

(b) such longer period as the court or tribunal considers equitable having regard to all the circumstances, but that is subject to any rule imposing a stricter time limit in relation to the procedure in question.

(6) In subsection (1)(b) "legal proceedings" includes—

(a) proceedings brought by or at the instigation of a public authority; and

(b) an appeal against the decision of a court or tribunal.

(7) For the purposes of this section, a person is a victim of an unlawful act only if he would be a victim for the purposes of Article 34 of the Convention if proceedings were brought in the European Court of Human Rights in respect of that act.

Judicial Remedies

8. (1) In relation to any act (or proposed act) of a public authority which the court finds is (or would be) unlawful, it may grant such relief or remedy, or make such order, within its powers as it considers just and appropriate.

(2) But damages may be awarded only by a court which has power to award damages, or to order the payment of compensation, in civil proceedings.

(3) No award of damages is to be made unless, taking account of all the circumstances of the case, including—

(a) any other relief or remedy granted, or order made, in relation to the act in question (by that or any other court), and

(b) the consequences of any decision (of that or any other court) in respect of that act, the court is satisfied that the award is necessary to afford just satisfaction to the person in whose favour it is made.

(4) In determining—

(a) whether to award damages, or

(b) the amount of an award,

the court must take into account the principles applied by the European Court of Human Rights in relation to the award of compensation under Article 41 of the Convention.

...

(6) In this section—

"court" includes a tribunal;

"damages" means damages for an unlawful act of a public authority; and

"unlawful" means unlawful under section 6(1).

... Freedom of Expression

12. (1) This section applies if a court is considering whether to grant any relief which, if granted, might affect the exercise of the Convention right to freedom of expression.

(2) If the person against whom the application for relief is made ('the respondent') is neither present nor represented, no such relief is to be granted unless the court is satisfied—

(a) that the applicant has taken all practicable steps to notify the respondent; or

(b) that there are compelling reasons why the respondent should not be notified.

(3) No such relief is to be granted so as to restrain publication before trial unless the court is satisfied that the applicant is likely to establish that publication should not be allowed.

(4) The court must have particular regard to the importance of the Convention right to freedom of expression and, where the proceedings relate to material which the respondent claims, or which appears to the court, to be journalistic, literary or artistic material (or to conduct connected with such material), to—

the extent to which—

    (i) the material has, or is about to, become available to the public; or

    (ii) it is, or would be, in the public interest for the material to be published;

any relevant privacy code.

(5) In this section—

    "court" includes a tribunal; and

    "relief" includes any remedy or order (other than in criminal proceedings).

We have not extracted the relevant Convention rights here. They are extracted in later chapters as and when they are appropriate to particular issues.

Actions under Sections 7 and 8

The HRA creates free-standing rights of action in cases where a Convention right has been violated *by a public authority* (section 7).[29] A 'public authority' may be a 'person certain of whose functions are functions of a public nature' (section 6(3)(b)),[30] a possibility captured in the idea of 'hybrid' public authorities (which are 'public' when performing some functions, but not otherwise). A civil remedy may be available in an action under section 7, by virtue of section 8. An action under section 7 is not an action in tort. There is a shorter limitation period, of one year,[31] although this may be extended if the court thinks it equitable to do so. Further, the damages remedy is subject to restrictions which are not present in the law of tort. Courts will consider whether damages are necessary and appropriate, and must consider the principles applied by the European Court of Human Rights when determining both *whether* to grant damages, and what the *quantum* of those damages should be (section 8(4)). In some circumstances, only a declaration may be awarded; or damages may be set at a relatively low level. On the other hand, it is significant that the HRA may offer a remedy in circumstances where tort will not.

The Influence on Tort Law

Here we identify three broad questions.

---

[29] Some guidance on the meaning of 'public authority' is set out in section 6 itself. It is a much analysed expression. In *YL v Birmingham City Council* [2007] UKHL 27, it was held not to include a private care home providing accommodation for people funded by a local authority (see M. Elliott, '"Public" and "Private": Defining the Scope of the Human Rights Act' (2007) 66 CLJ 485–7). The effect of this case has been reversed on its facts by statute (Health and Social Care Act 2008, s 145).

[30] For example in *R (Weaver) v London & Quadrant Housing Trust* [2009] EWCA Civ 587; [2010] 1 WLR 363, a registered housing association was held to be carrying out a public function when it terminated a tenancy. See S. Handy and J. Alder, 'Housing Associations: "Sufficient Public Flavour"' (2009) JHL 101.

[31] The limitation periods applicable in tort claims are explored in Chapter 7.

(a) *Horizontal Effect*

When the statute was enacted, the chief controversy among private lawyers was whether it would have 'horizontal effect'. Clearly, the statute is intended to have 'vertical effect', creating new actions and remedies against public authorities. But is it intended to affect private law in cases where the defendant is not a 'public authority'?

One potential trigger for such an effect is section 6. Section 6 specifies that 'it is unlawful for a public authority to act in a way which is inconsistent with a Convention right'. By section 6(3), 'public authority' *includes* 'a court or tribunal'. Therefore, it is unlawful for a court or tribunal to act inconsistently with a Convention right. There has been considerable discussion of what this should be taken to mean for the future development of private law.

Widely divergent views were initially expressed as to whether section 6 would give 'horizontal effect' to Convention rights. Sir William Wade argued that the Convention rights would have *direct* horizontal effect after the HRA, becoming applicable even in disputes between private parties ('Horizons of Horizontality' (2000) 116 LQR 217, supported by J. Morgan, 'Questioning the "True Effect" of the Human Rights Act' (2002) 22 LS 259). Others denied that the rights would be directly applicable in this way, but conceded that the Convention rights would have 'indirect' horizontal effect.

A 'weak' interpretation of indirect horizontal effect would mean that courts would be in some way influenced by the Convention rights in their interpretation of the law. (See for example H. Beale and N. Pittam, 'The Impact of the Human Rights Act 1998 on English Tort and Contract Law', in Friedmann and Barak-Erez, *Human Rights in Private Law* (Hart Publishing, 2001).) A stronger interpretation of indirect horizontal effect holds that courts will consider themselves under a duty to interpret, apply, and develop the common law in such a way as to ensure that the Convention rights are protected. This 'strong' interpretation of indirect horizontal effect would suggest that existing common law doctrines would come to be transformed, and was supported for example by Murray Hunt. In the following extract, he summarizes a 'strong indirect' position.

Murray Hunt, 'The Effect on the Law of Obligations', in B. Markesinis (ed.), *The Impact of the Human Rights Bill on English Law* (Oxford: Clarendon Press, 1998), 180

The case law of the Convention, the text of the Bill, the purpose disclosed by the White Paper and in the Parliamentary debates, together with the current practice of our courts all point irresistibly towards the Convention being horizontally applicable when the Human Rights Act comes into effect, save that it will not give rise to an independent cause of action for breach of Convention rights. This does not necessarily mean to say that the Human Rights Act will immediately confer new causes of action against private parties where none previously existed. But it does mean that the private law of obligations will be developed by courts so as to be compatible with Convention rights, and that is likely to mean, over time, the metamorphosis of existing causes of action so as to fulfil the State's international obligation to secure the rights contained in the Convention and fulfil the clear intention of both Government and Parliament that enactment of the Human Rights Act will ensure that nobody will any longer be without a remedy in domestic law for breach of their Convention rights.

After thirteen years, what does experience suggest about the horizontal effect of the Convention rights in tort law in particular?

In Chapter 14, we will explain that the House of Lords has indeed denied that *new causes of action will be recognized* as a result of the HRA (*Campbell v MGN* [2004] 2 AC 457). But we will also note that that case endorsed change in the rules of an existing cause of action (following the Court of Appeal in *Douglas v Hello!* [2001] QB 967) to protect 'privacy' in its own right. This was certainly influenced by the requirements of Article 8 ECHR. In the law of defamation, too, the terms of debate have changed considerably since enactment of the statute, and both reputation and speech are recognized to be associated with protected rights. Article 10 and freedom of expression had been mentioned before the HRA in relation to defamation, but the discourse now is of 'balance' and 'proportionality' between rights. Nevertheless, the transformation to the law of privacy wrought in the name of the Convention rights does not suggest general, theoretical acceptance of a 'strong' form of horizontality.[32] The developments in this area of the law have not been replicated elsewhere.

(b) Tort Developing New Rights Protection?

The availability of an action under the Human Rights Act has on a number of occasions influenced the development of tort law in 'vertical' cases. However, the existence of a Human Rights Act remedy has on some important occasions been considered a reason *not* to develop the common law.

An early case is *JD v East Berkshire NHS Trust* [2004] 2 WLR 58, where the Court of Appeal decided not to follow an earlier decision of the House of Lords (*X v Bedfordshire* [1995] 2 AC 633). Since an action would lie in future under section 7 of the HRA, the policy issues which had led the House of Lords to decide that no duty of care was owed *in tort* in respect of the claim were considered to be no longer tenable. It is highly unlikely that such a move would be made by the Court of Appeal today (see Chapter 6); and the correctness of *JD* is currently the subject of an appeal: *CN v Poole BC* [2016] EWHC 569 (QB) (appeal pending). On the other hand, the Court of Appeal has on one recent occasion suggested that it would have been prepared to depart from a decision of the Supreme Court and adopt a *more recent* interpretation of the Convention delivered by the Strasbourg Court, on the basis that the Supreme Court would of course follow Strasbourg where interpretation of the Convention was concerned.[33] This, however, was not a route it felt compelled to take, because the Supreme Court's interpretation was not considered inconsistent with Strasbourg decisions. (Ironically, the Supreme Court itself on appeal disagreed with this last point, and reversed its own earlier position (and therefore the Court of Appeal)). The episode underlines that the power of the Convention rights—here, their power to affect the operation of precedent—is still by no means permanently settled.

In a number of important cases, courts have taken the view that tort law ought *not* to develop in order to reflect Convention rights, since sections 7 and 8 provide a more appropriate and proportionate means of vindicating such rights in the manner envisaged by the statute. This view was articulated by the House of Lords in *Watkins v Home Office* [2006]

---

[32] G. Phillipson, 'Privacy: The Development of Breach of Confidence—The Clearest Case of Horizontal Effect?', in D. Hoffman (ed.), *The Impact of the UK Human Rights Act on Private Law* (Cambridge University Press, 2011).

[33] *Smith v Ministry of Defence* [2013] UKSC 41. This related to Art 1 ECHR, on territorial extent of the Convention. Here there was no scope for a local 'margin of appreciation' in interpretation.

UKHL 17, and reiterated by Lord Brown in *Chief Constable of Hertfordshire Police v Van Colle; Smith v Chief Constable of Sussex Police* [2008] UKHL 50, at [138]. In *Michael v Chief Constable of South Wales* [2015] UKSC 2, a claim for compensation under the HRA proceeded to trial in a case where no duty of care was recognized. In all of these cases, the House of Lords and Supreme Court have emphasized the difference in *remedies* between these actions, proposing that they reflect the different purposes of the actions themselves. That difference, however, is very difficult to establish with precision, since tort remedies may very well be said to 'vindicate rights'.[34] 'The existence of new remedies under the HRA focuses attention on the extent to which tort protects and vindicates rights, either as an inherent part of, or in addition to its more widely recognized function in redressing losses.[35]

A particularly striking indication of the varied ways in which the HRA might be exerting an influence over the law of tort can be seen in the following statement of Lord Kerr. The case from which we briefly extract here marked a significant step in recognition of patients' right to autonomy and the influence of this on a doctor's duty to disclose risks associated with medical treatment: for extended discussion, see Chapter 3. Lord Kerr here points to the broader, perhaps deeper *influence* of the HRA; and its effect on the 'consciousness' of judges in relation to fundamental values. There is a marked difference between this, and the decisions in cases such as *Michael* (in which Lord Kerr dissented).

Lord Kerr, *Montgomery v Lanarkshire Health Board*
[2015] UKSC 11

80 In addition to these developments in society and in medical practice, there have also been developments in the law. Under the stimulus of the Human Rights Act 1998, the courts have become increasingly conscious of the extent to which the common law reflects fundamental values. As Lord Scarman pointed out in *Sidaway's case* [1985] AC 871, these include the value of self-determination.... As well as underlying aspects of the common law, that value also underlies the right to respect for private life protected by article 8 of the European Convention for the Protection of Human Rights and Fundamental Freedoms. The resulting duty to involve the patient in decisions relating to her treatment has been recognised in judgments of the European Court of Human Rights, such as *Glass v United Kingdom* (2004) 39 EHRR 341 and *Tysiąc v Poland* (2007) 45 EHRR 947, as well as in a number of decisions of courts in the United Kingdom.

(c) *Tort-like Remedies Against Public Authorities under the HRA?*

If tort as a whole is not to be adjusted to protect the Convention rights, to what extent does the HRA nevertheless allow for distinctly 'tort-like' remedies, in circumstances where tort does not? There are some areas where remedies for breach of Convention rights on the part of public authorities have been developed in such a way as to resemble tort actions.

The most evident instance concerns positive duties to protect rights to life under Article 2. More than one positive duty under Article 2 has been recognized. We are most concerned here not with the broad 'framework' duty on states to protect citizens (from violent crime, for example), but with an *operational* duty, which resembles the tort of negligence, requiring

---

34 For an analysis of tort in general in terms of the protection of primary rights, see R. Stevens, *Torts and Rights* (Oxford: Oxford University Press, 2007).

35 See K. Barker, 'Private and Public: the Mixed Concept of Vindication in Torts', in Pitel, Neyers and Chamberlain (eds), *Tort Law: Challenging Orthodoxy* (Hart Publishing, 2013).

steps to be taken to protect particular individuals from imminent danger. However, remedies are available to a wider range of parties than would be the case in tort, because a claimant need only show they are a 'victim' of a rights violation. Remedies may also be available in a broader range of circumstances, for example where courts have decided *not* to recognize tort remedies for policy reasons.[36] The implication is that restraints imposed on tort law may be 'circumvented'. The operational duty has been referred to as creating what is essentially a tort remedy, emanating not from the domestic courts, but from Strasbourg jurisprudence.[37]

In two recent cases, the UK Supreme Court has afforded an HRA remedy in circumstances where the Strasbourg court has not yet ruled that a remedy should be available.[38] Both concerned 'tort-like' liabilities. It is not yet clear how far these cases open a new chapter in the relationship between the law of tort and Convention rights, in which English court are prepared to develop rights protection ahead of developments in Strasbourg. But they do illustrate how hard it is to be sure whether—and when—principles in this context have become truly settled. Given that the current Prime Minister, Theresa May, has made clear her preference for repeal of the HRA, the question emerges of where tort law would stand without the HRA. If repealed, would tort law need to expand to secure some of the rights currently protected by HRA damages? Or would the courts be at least less content with restricting tort liability in certain areas, since there may no longer be a more suitable remedy? These questions of course are speculative; but the complexity of recent developments makes them all the more interesting.

5. CONCLUSIONS

i. Tort law is a diverse category, encompassing a number of different torts. This chapter has 'mapped' the range of torts according to the interests that they protect; whether they require damage or are actionable 'per se', and what form of 'wrongdoing' they require. Torts in this book are loosely ordered around the nature of wrongdoing or standard of liability, from 'intentional' torts, through negligence liabilities, to stricter liabilities. Each of these categories contains quite a diversity of causes of action, with their own purpose and logic. The temptation to see negligence as 'the' modern law of tort should not lead us to neglect other significant areas of liability. Indeed, in each new edition, some of the most important developments in the law do not take place within the realm of negligence at all. Indeed, some of them are concerned not with substantive legal principles, but with process.

ii. We have also noted two contemporary challenges for the law of tort, both of which have influenced the shape of the subject. First, there has been growing political concern with the economic burden of the law of tort, both in relation to liabilities, and in relation to the cost of the process itself. These fears are sometimes encapsulated in the notion of 'compensation culture', a notion which also suggests that tort law may become over-protective, and that individuals should be less quick to blame others. There is much dispute over whether compensation culture really exists; but the costs of tort litigation are undoubtedly real. For the most part, UK courts have effectively confined the growth of

---

[36] For example, in order to protect police functions in investigating and suppressing crime: *DSD v Commissioner of Police of the Metropolis* [2015] EWCA Civ 646.
[37] *Rabone v Pennine Care NHS Trust* [2012] UKSC 2; [2012] 2 WLR 381, [121]).
[38] *Rabone* (n 37); *Smith v Ministry of Defence* (n 33). See further Chapter 6.

tort law, and wide-ranging 'tort reform' has been unnecessary. The costs regime applicable to civil litigation has, however, been the subject of significant reform.

iii. The second challenge is the embedding of 'Convention rights' in domestic law through the Human Rights Act 1998. This raises a multifaceted challenge for the law of tort, and unsurprisingly, the judicial response has not been uniform. On the whole, the early case law saw a greater willingness to change the common law to reflect the Convention rights, while later tort cases have been more circumspect. But by no means is this a consistent pattern. When interpreting the HRA itself, the courts have shown themselves willing to recognize and indeed expand the range of 'tort-like' liabilities to protect Convention rights. The relationship between common law and the Convention is thus still unfolding, and affects many aspects of the law explored in this work.

FURTHER READING

Atiyah, P., *The Damages Lottery* (Oxford: Hart Publishing, 1997).

Atiyah, P., 'Personal Injuries in the Twenty-First Century: Thinking the Unthinkable', in P. Birks (ed.), *Wrongs and Remedies in the Twenty-First Century* (Oxford: Oxford University Press, 1996).

Campbell, D., 'Interpersonal Justice and Actual Choice as Ways of Determining Personal Injury Law and Policy' (2015) 35 LS 430.

Cane, P., 'Reforming Tort Law in Australia: A Personal Perspective' [2003] MULR 26.

Commission on a Bill of Rights, *A British Bill of Rights: The Choice Before Us* (December 2012)

Gearty, C., *Principles of Human Rights Adjudication* (Oxford: Oxford University Press, 2004), chapter 8.

Hedley, S., 'Making Sense of Negligence' (2015) 36 LS 491.

Keren-Paz, T., *Torts, Egalitarianism and Distributive Justice* (Dartford: Ashgate, 2007).

Klug, F., 'A Bill of Rights: do we need one or do we already have one?' (2007) PL 701.

Lewis, R., 'Compensation Culture Reviewed: Incentives to Claim and Damages Levels' (2014) JPIL 209.

Morris, A., 'Spiralling or Stabilising? The Compensation Culture and our Propensity to Claim Damages' (2007) 70 MLR 349.

Mullender, R., 'Blame Culture and Political Debate—finding our way through the fog' (2011) 27 Professional Negligence 64.

Sedley, S., 'Bringing Rights Home: Time to Start a Family?' (2008) 28 LS 327.

Steele, J., '(Dis)owning the Convention in the Law of Tort', in J. Lee (ed.), *From House of Lords to Supreme Court* (Hart Publishing, 2010).

Sunkin, M., 'Pushing Forward the Frontiers of Human Rights Protection: the Meaning of Public Authority under the Human Rights Act' [2004] PL 643.

Varuhas, J., *Damages and Human Rights* (Hart Publishing, 2016).

Wright, J., *Tort Law and Human Rights*, 2nd edn. (Hart Publishing, 2017).

Young, A., 'Mapping Horizontal Effect', in Hoffman, D., *The Impact of the UK Human Rights Act on Private Law* (Cambridge University Press, 2011).

PART II

INTENTIONAL INTERFERENCES

In this Part, we explore the diversity of torts requiring intention. Three points can be made at the outset about these causes of action.

First, the very diversity of the intentional torts is worthy of note. The idea of 'intention' itself is not identical in respect of different torts (what counts as 'intending' something?), but there is also large variation in what must be intended (a breach of contract? Physical contact? Actual harm to the claimant?) More than this, in terms of our mapping exercise in Chapter 1, intentional torts exist to protect a wide variety of different interests, ranging from personal integrity to economic harm. Some intentional torts require material damage to be shown, as does negligence, while others are actionable per se or without proof of damage.

Second, intention—even intentional harm—is not in itself enough to justify liability. Confining our attention to material damage, there is no broad and general duty to avoid causing loss intentionally, but a series of causes of action whose requirements must be satisfied for a remedy to lie. The temptation to expand liability for intentional harm in a general way has been resisted. This being the case, why should it be expected that a broad general duty to avoid carelessly causing loss could ever be developed? There are lessons here for the study of the tort of negligence (Part III).

This brings us to the third point. Despite the rise of negligence, and recognition of wider duties of care, the torts collected here have not lost their relevance. Indeed, this chapter has been one of the most changed over successive editions. The use of tort to secure and protect civil liberties has a long history, but cases such as *Austin v Commissioner of Police of the Metropolis*; *Watkins v Home Secretary*; and *R (Lumba) v Secretary of State for the Home Department*, underline the continuing importance of this role of the law of tort. All of these decisions, though in different ways, raise particularly clearly the question of how tort law compares with the protection of Convention rights through the HRA, raised in Chapter 1. What, given the restrictive approach in all of these cases, is the role of torts such as these in protecting fundamental 'constitutional' rights?

Other areas of the topic have also been subject to important development. The action in *Wilkinson v Downton* has been restricted in order to avoid interference with the right to freedom of expression. Principles drawn from the tort of battery have been progressively developed and have been codified and adapted in the Mental Capacity Act 2005. The restrictive principles of the tort of negligence in respect of economic losses—and particularly the need for proximity—leaves ample space for the intentional 'economic torts' to operate. Turning to malicious prosecution, the Privy Council and Supreme Court have greatly expanded the reach of the tort, allowing its use in respect of civil proceedings and in relation to a wider range of harms. And the boundary between trespass to the person and negligence has been decisively altered by the decision of the House of Lords in *A v Hoare*, with the result that trespass to the person in the context of sexual abuse is resurgent. This in turn has helped to bring about the real transformations in vicarious liability outlined in Chapter 9. There is ample reason not to overlook the 'intentional' torts.

2

TORTS OF INTENTION

CENTRAL ISSUES

i) This chapter explores the 'intentional torts'. The intentional torts arise in a wide variety of different contexts, but in all those contexts the law has been on the move in recent years.

ii) We begin by exploring intention itself. We will note considerable variation within the intentional torts. This variation affects both the required **target** of intention (*what* must be intended?), and the required **level** of intention (what does it mean to *intend* something?).

iii) We then break down the 'intentional torts' into a number of groups. The first of these, **trespass to the person**, comprises three torts: battery, assault, and false imprisonment. Trespass to the person has been confined in modern law to acts which are in some sense 'intentional' (*Letang v Cooper*). Even so, trespass torts do *not* depend on showing intentional infliction of harm. Rather, they concern acts whose *intended consequences* (for example, physical contact, or physical restraint) are judged to be unlawful. Trespass torts remain significant in situations where the 'lawfulness' of physical intervention or restraint is in issue. The potential overlap with issues of civil liberties and human rights is therefore considerable. What is the 'constitutional' role of tort in protecting from abuse of power?

iv) The action in *Wilkinson v Downton* is a damage-based tort of intention. A remedy may lie for physical and psychiatric harm which is 'intentionally' caused, and not through any physical impact. In England, courts have resisted academic argument that *Wilkinson v Downton* should be developed in order to provide remedies for injury falling short of psychiatric or physical illness, particularly in the form of 'anxiety and distress.' However, the **Protection from Harassment Act 1997** now provides civil remedies (as well as setting out criminal offences) in respect of a course of conduct that amounts to harassment.

v) The **intentional economic torts** require a higher level of intention than *Wilkinson v Downton*. Even so, in virtually all of the economic torts, intentional harm is not enough. Something additionally 'unlawful' or otherwise 'wrongful' about the defendant's acts is required. No uniform meaning of 'unlawful means' has emerged.

vi) Finally, we turn to torts concerning intentional abuse of process (**malicious prosecution**) and of power (**misfeasance in a public office**). The 'gist' of the latter tort is injurious *abuse of power*. Power exercised recklessly is power abused. Both, however, are damage-based torts. Again, intention alone does not suffice.

1. 'INTENTION'

There is considerable diversity in the meaning of 'intention' in the torts considered in this chapter. Intention has two dimensions:

1. The **target** of intention

   Here we ask, *what* must be intended? For example, in trespass to the person (assault, battery, and false imprisonment), neither harm nor unlawfulness needs to be intended. In battery, the target of intention is simply physical contact. In *Wilkinson v Downton* by contrast, the target of intention is harm: it must be shown that the tort-feasor intended to cause harm to the claimant.

2. The **level** of intention required

   Once we have answered the first question (what must be intended?) we still have to ask, *what is the relevant state of mind?* What do we mean by 'intending' something? This is a more difficult question to answer. For example, must the outcome be a (or the) *goal of the defendant's action?* Or is it enough that it is almost certain to follow? Again the answer varies. In *Wilkinson v Downton*, it was thought until the decision of the Supreme Court in *OPO v Rhodes* [2015] UKSC 32 that a strong degree of likelihood was sufficient for intention to be 'imputed by law': it appears that it must now be the subjective intention of the defendant that harm should be caused, and degrees of likelihood, if relevant at all, will be relevant as evidence of intention. In the economic torts by contrast, it has long been understood that harm to the claimant must generally be a *goal or purpose* of the action, or at least a necessary means to the intended goal.

Is a General Definition of Intention Possible—or Desirable?

It follows from the above examples that no general definition of intention is shared by the English torts of intention. We will have to spell out the relevant meaning of intention in respect of each tort. In its 'Restatement' of the law of torts, the American Law Institute set out a general statement of the meaning of intention in American tort law as a whole. The project of 'restating' tort law in the United States has become more complex, and the Third Restatement is being published in volumes covering particular areas, rather than tort law as a whole. A Third Restatement on causing physical and emotional harm was published in 2010, and is extracted next; while work is under way on a further volume dealing with Intentional Torts to the Person: a First Tentative Draft was published in April 2015.

Section 1 Intent

A person acts with the intent to produce a consequence if:

(a) the person acts with the purpose of producing that consequence; or

(b) the person acts knowing that the consequence is substantially certain to result.

Comment:

a. *The dual definition.* For a variety of reasons, tort law must distinguish between intentional and nonintentional consequences and harms (including harms that may be negligent, reckless, or without fault). Harms that are tortious if caused intentionally may not be tortious if caused unintentionally; affirmative defences available in negligence cases may not be available when the underlying tort is intentional; the limitation period may vary depending on whether the tort is one of intent or instead one of negligence.

…

There are obvious differences between the actor who acts with the desire to cause harm, and the actor who engages in conduct knowing that harm is substantially certain to happen. There is a clear element of wrongfulness in conduct whose very purpose is to cause harm. While there are circumstances in which acting in such a way is appropriate, tort law can fashion affirmative defences (such as necessity and defence of self and property) that take those circumstances into account.…

b. *Intentional consequences and intentional harms.*…when tort-liability rules do attach significance to intended consequences, most of the time the consequence in question is the fact of harm, and it is the intention to cause such harm that under ordinary tort discourse renders the actor liable for an intentional tort.…

Comparing this statement of US law with the law outlined in this chapter shows how far the tort law of England and Wales and of the United States have diverged, despite their common roots. The first point to make is that no such general comment could summarize the full range of torts referred to by English courts as 'intentional'. Comment b suggests that so far as *the target of intention* is concerned, 'intentional torts' in the US will generally involve an intention to bring about harm. This is by no means the case with all those torts described in English law as 'intentional', as is made clear by *Letang v Cooper* [1965] 1 QB 232, extracted in Section 2.3. English law may recognize a wrong where there is no intention to cause harm, or even to violate rights. However, there are torts where intention to cause harm is part of the definition of the tort: deceit provides an example (requiring intent that the claimant should rely to his or her detriment). English tort law does not begin with a defined approach to intent which can then be applied in a range of torts; rather, each tort in this chapter has its own intention requirement. This is certainly untidy, and there are signs that it may lead to confusion if principles are read across from one tort to another.[1] But it might nevertheless

---

[1] Note the discussion of contributory negligence as a defence to the torts of battery, and of deceit, in Sections 3.4, and 7.6.

be justifiable, to the extent that the torts collected here protect a range of interests, and do so in different ways. For example, protecting against *unlawful* interferences—including interferences in excess of public law powers—has become the hallmark of some aspects of the English law of trespass to the person. By contrast, in the tort of misfeasance in a public office, requirements as to a public officer's mental state are added to the notion of excess of power. This tort focuses on egregious conduct, where false imprisonment focuses on unlawful states of affairs.

In respect of the *level* of intention (our second question of intention, above), the US Restatement seems to be broader and less demanding than at least a number of English intentional torts. It includes some results which are merely the side-effects of action (though they must be 'substantially certain' to result) and not the actor's *purpose*. This is enabled by the 'dual definition', reflected in parts (a) and (b) of Section 1.[2] On the other hand, the definition excludes recklessness, which *is* sufficient to amount to intention at least in the English tort of misfeasance in a public office and (in respect of some of their elements) in deceit and malicious falsehood. Recklessness is separately defined in another section of the Restatement just extracted (Section 2). In US law, the implications of recklessness are quite separate from the implications of intent.

The Insufficiency of 'Intention'

The Restatement makes clear that the core meaning of intention in US tort law is intention to cause harm. No such general point can be made about English 'intentional torts'. But at the same time, it is also stated that it is generally easy to justify liability based on such intention. English law however often declines to treat even intentional harm as a *sufficient* 'wrong-making factor'.[3] A key case to this effect is *Allen v Flood* [1898] AC 1,[4] in which the House of Lords decided that bad motive did not suffice to render an otherwise lawful act 'unlawful'. American courts rejected *Allen v Flood* and the law took a different path still reflected in the Restatement: *Tuttle v Buck* 119 NW 946 (Minn 1909). In the case of battery and false imprisonment (both aspects of 'trespass to the person'), the key 'wrong-making factors' lie not in intent nor fault, but in the unlawful or non-consensual nature of the physical interference.

Intentional infliction of harm is rarely a sufficient basis for liability in the English law of tort. At the same time, intention may be targeted at something other than the infliction of harm, yet tortious liability may follow. Intention does not have the same general significance as a 'wrong-making factor' in English tort law as it does in American tort law. Nevertheless, the torts included in this chapter are very significant and, in many cases, are still in the process of development despite their long history.

---

[2] The previous Restatement, Section 8, also contained a dual definition. The present version makes this more apparent.

[3] The term 'wrong-making factor' is used by John Finnis, 'Intention in Tort Law', in D. Owen (ed.), *Philosophical Foundations of Tort Law* (Oxford: Clarendon Press, 1995), 229–47, supporting generalization of liability for truly 'intended' harms. The general picture in this chapter by contrast is one of 'wrong-making recipes': there are many ways to make a wrong.

[4] Discussed in Section 7 of the present chapter.

2. TRESPASS TO THE PERSON

2.1 THE RELEVANT TORTS AND THEIR GENERAL FEATURES

There are three torts which together make up 'trespass to the person'. These are **battery**, **assault**, and **false imprisonment**. In this section, we outline their basic features; more detailed discussion of each tort follows.

Battery

Battery requires an act of the defendant which directly and intentionally brings about contact with the body of the claimant, where the contact exceeds what is lawful. Battery is actionable without proof of damage (though see *R (Lumba) v Secretary of State for the Home Department* [2011] UKSC 12, considered in Section 4.1 of this chapter). There need not be an intent to harm, nor even an intent to act unlawfully. In battery, the necessary intention is to bring about the physical contact. The unlawfulness of that contact creates the wrong. It is for this reason that very similar torts—battery, and false imprisonment—have been referred to as an 'intentional tort' and a 'strict liability tort' respectively,[5] without inaccuracy. Liability is strict because it does not require fault; at the same time, it is based on intention to the extent that an important aspect of the tort (the interference complained of) must be intended.

It has been argued that battery does not need even this limited intentional element and that it may be committed recklessly or even carelessly.[6] This would enable trespass to the person to be reunited with trespass to land and goods. We will see that the legacy of *Letang v Cooper* has been a requirement that the contact must be intentional. A major change would be needed to resurrect 'negligent trespass to the person' in English law; and it is likely the courts would be reluctant to allow trespass to emerge as an alternative to negligence in cases of careless personal injury.

Directness

The idea that the contact must be **direct** is a legacy of history. As Hale LJ put it in *Wong v Parkside* [2003] 3 All ER 932:

> [7] As every law student knows, the common law distinguished between an action in trespass and an action on the case. Trespass to the person consisted in the direct infliction of harm (or the threat of the immediate infliction of such harm) upon the claimant. But the law recognised that physical harm might be inflicted indirectly. If intentional, this was the tort recognised by the High Court in *Wilkinson v Downton* [1897] 2 QB 57. . . . If negligent, it was eventually recognised as the tort of negligence in *Donoghue v Stevenson* [1932] AC 562.

---

[5] As to the former see Aikens LJ in *Pritchard v Co-operative Group* [2011] EWCA Civ 329; as to the latter see Lord Hope in *R v Deputy Governor of Parkhurst Prison, ex p Hague* [1992] 1 AC 58 (both extracted later in the present chapter).

[6] F. A. Trindade, 'Intentional Torts: Some Thoughts on Assault and Battery' (1982) 2 OJLS 211–37, finds evidence that this used to be the case but also emphasizes that, these days, battery is confined to cases of intentional contact.

M. J. Prichard, 'Trespass, Case and the Rule in *Williams v Holland*' (1964) CLJ 234–53, places the origins of the tort of negligence (liability for carelessly caused harm outside a particular relationship) at a much earlier date than *Donoghue v Stevenson*, with the case of *Mitchil v Alestree* (1676). Prichard too particularly notes that trespass was limited by the need for directness or 'immediacy'. *Mitchil v Alestree* involved the dangers created by breaking unruly horses in Lincoln's Inn fields: when the horses bolted, they were no longer controlled by the defendant, and the damage was not directly or 'immediately' caused by the defendant's act.

F. A. Trindade, 'Intentional Torts: Some Thoughts on Assault and Battery' (1982) 2 OJLS 211, at 216–17

The first ingredient of the tort of battery is that whatever has to be done to the plaintiff by the defendant to make the activity actionable as a battery must be done *directly*. It is an ingredient which is common to all three torts of trespass to the person, assault, battery and false imprisonment but it is not sufficiently emphasised in the textbooks. . . .

The example given by Fortescue CJ in *Reynolds v Clarke*[7] of tumbling over a log left unlawfully on the highway (consequential) and being hit by a log being thrown unlawfully onto the highway (direct) emphasised the element of immediate contact with which 'direct' acts came to be associated. But it was not only hits by something thrown at you which were regarded as 'direct'. An act which set in motion an unbroken series of continuing consequences, the last of which ultimately caused contact with the plaintiff was still regarded as sufficiently 'direct' for the purposes of trespass. So when the defendant rode his motorcycle into B who collided with the plaintiff who was thrown to the ground, it was held that the facts constituted a 'direct' act for an action in trespass.[8]

F. A. Trindade, 'Intentional Torts: Some Thoughts on Assault and Battery' (1982) 2 OJLS 211, at 220

Intention

The target of intention in the tort of battery is *physical contact*.

A consequence of the 'directness' requirement is that although the tort of battery might justify an action against a party who is generally 'blameless' (for example, a surgeon who carries out surgery having been falsely informed that a patient has consented), it does not tend to allow actions against 'peripheral parties' (for example, a local authority which does not spot that a builder has not complied with the approved plans; or a mother who fails to report criminal acts of abuse on the part of her husband). In particular, it does not appear to allow a claim for 'nonfeasance' (or failure to act).[9]

Intention

. . . In battery what is required is intentional contact not an intention to do harm—and it is not correct to say that trespass can be brought 'only for the direct physical infliction of *harm*'.

---

7 (1725) 1 Stra 634, 636.

8 *Hillier v Leitch* [1936] SASR 490.

9 In relation to false imprisonment, see *Iqbal v Prison Officers Association* in Section 4. . . .

As Talbot J said in *Williams v Humphrey* [*The Times* 13 February 1975; p. 20 (transcript)]: 'it was argued that for the act to be a battery, there must be an intent to *injure*. I do not accept this contention. The intention goes to the commission of an act of force. This seems to be the principle in many cases of trespass to the person'.

Assault

Assault requires no physical contact but is a direct threat by the defendant which intentionally places the claimant in reasonable apprehension of an imminent battery.

Assault is, therefore, a 'secondary' tort, which is defined in terms of apprehension of battery. The target of intention in assault is not entirely clear. In *Read v Coker* the requirement is said to be intent to commit a battery. In *Bici v Ministry of Defence* it was intent to put in fear of violence. The latter is more consistent with *R v Ireland* [1998] AC 147 (discussed later).

In *Stephens v Myers* (1830) 4 C & P 349, 172 ER 735, a member of the audience at a parish meeting threatened to hit the chairman. No assault was established because the defendant was at some distance from the plaintiff and surrounded by others, and was considered to have no 'present means' of executing his threat. By contrast, in *Read v Coker* (1853) 13 CB 850; 138 ER 1437, the plaintiff was threatened by a group of workmen who said they would break his neck if he did not leave the premises. An assault *was* established since they had the means of carrying out their threat.

The threat may of course take the form of words. But what of silence? In *R v Ireland* [1998] AC 147, a case of criminal assault occasioning psychiatric harm, the House of Lords held that a menacing *silence* could amount to an assault, provided it put the victim in reasonable fear of immediate violence. This is not inconsistent with the requirement for a positive act: a series of phone calls, consisting of silence, is what provided the occasion with its menace.

In *Bici v Ministry of Defence* [2004] EWHC 786, Elias J maintained that the defendant must *intend* to put the claimant in fear of imminent violence. In this particular case, although there was an intention to commit a battery, which it was held could be transferred to the unintended victim,[10] there was *no* intention to put anyone *in fear of violence*. This being the case, a claim in assault failed.

False Imprisonment

False imprisonment is unlawful and total bodily restraint of the claimant, by the defendant.

Lord Bridge of Harwich, *R v Deputy Governor of Parkhurst Prison, ex p Hague* **[1992] 1 AC 58, 162**

The tort of false imprisonment has two ingredients: the fact of imprisonment and the absence of lawful authority to justify it.

Despite this very simple statement, false imprisonment also retains the elements of directness and intention referred to in relation to battery, discussed earlier.

---

[10] This conclusion has been criticized by A. Beever, 'Transferred Malice in Tort Law?' (2009) 29 LS 400.

Intention

The target of intention is physical restraint of the claimant:

Smith LJ, *Iqbal v Prison Officers Association*
[2009] EWCA Civ 1312

[72] . . . with false imprisonment, the loss of liberty is the essence of the tort and, in my view, the claimant must show not merely an intentional act or omission (to the extent that an omission will suffice . . .) but also an intention to deprive the claimant of his liberty. I can illustrate the point as follows. If a security guard in an office block locks the door on the claimant's room believing that the claimant has gone home for the night and not realizing that he is in fact still inside the room, he has committed a deliberate act. However, he did not intend to confine the claimant. He may well be guilty of negligence because he did not check whether the room was empty but he would not be guilty of false imprisonment.

Intention therefore is different from 'volition' (intentional action), and relates to a significant component of the tort.

Other Features

All trespass torts are actionable without proof of damage. 'Consent' is a vital defence to each of them. Available remedies reflect the fact that trespass is not solely concerned with compensation. They include compensatory damages; punitive damages in appropriate circumstances (particularly if the tort is committed by a public official);[11] or a declaration that the contact, threat, or restraint is *unlawful*.[12] The role of such a declaration may perhaps be performed by an award of nominal damages, but not it seems by a substantial sum unless some harm flows from the trespass (as a consequence of the decision in *Lumba*, Section 4). In some circumstances, courts may issue a declaration that a planned intervention is lawful.[13]

The breadth of recoverable damages in trespass is not truly settled. Logically, recovery of 'all' harm flowing from a trespass could be extreme and one would expect some sort of remoteness rule to be applied, the question being which one? In *Smith New Court Securities v Citibank* [1997] AC 254, the 'foreseeability' test for recoverable damage, which applies in the tort of negligence, was not applied to another tort of intention, namely an action in deceit. We explain why not in Section 7.5 of the present chapter. The reasons for applying the more generous 'directness' rule in a case of deceit do not translate especially easily to trespass to the person, where there needs to be an 'unlawful' act but need not be any bad motive nor intentional harm. On the other hand, the fact that the interference is judged unlawful may itself be a good enough reason for all the *direct* consequences of the act to be attributed to the defendant.

It has been said that the main purpose of trespass torts is not to compensate for injury, but to identify and respond to actions of the defendant which transgress the acceptable

---

11   Chapter 8.
12   *Ashley v Chief Constable of Sussex Police* [2008] UKHL 25; [2008] 1 AC 962.
13   Declarations of lawfulness have often been used in medical cases although the basis for this is not straightforward: see *Re F* [1990] 2 AC 1 (Section 2.4 of the present chapter).

boundaries of physical interference. In the following extract, Tony Weir relates the trespass torts to excess of authority and the vindication of constitutional rights:

Tony Weir, *A Casebook on Tort* (10th edn, London: Sweet & Maxwell, 2004), 322–3

The law of tort does not have one function only: few things do. It is true that most tort claimants want compensation for harm caused to them by someone else and that in this sense (and in this sense only) the main function of tort law is to ordain such compensation. It has another function, however, which, though traditional, has rarely been more important than now, namely to vindicate constitutional rights. Not every infraction of a right causes damage. That is precisely why the law of trespass does not insist on damage. But if jurists believe that damage is of the essence of a tort claim, they will regard trespass as anomalous, deride it as antiquated, ignore the values it enshrines and proceed to diminish the protection it affords to the rights of the citizen. When constitutional rights are in issue what matters is whether they have been infringed, not whether the defendant can really be blamed for infringing them. But if jurists think of negligence as the paradigm tort (and they do so for no better reason than that a great many people are mangled on the highway) they will regard it as the overriding principle of the law of tort that you do not have to pay if you were not at fault (and, equally, that you always have to pay if you were at fault....If a defendant can say that he acted reasonably, a negligence lawyer will let him off, without bothering to distinguish the reasonable but erroneous belief that the projected behaviour was *authorised* from the reasonable but erroneous belief that it was *safe*.

Weir's analysis explains why the focus of the trespass torts is not 'damage'; *and also why* these torts are not (despite their 'intentional' label) centrally concerned with the quality of the defendant's *conduct*. It is the unlawfulness of the intended outcome that matters, not the unreasonableness of the intention itself. Nevertheless, the Supreme Court in *Lumba* appears to have decided that in a case not involving harm, this unlawfulness is insufficient basis for an award of more than nominal damages. In terms of the function outlined by Weir, this is something of a disappointment.

The *distinctness* of trespass from negligence clearly emerges from the decision of the House of Lords in *Ashley v Chief Constable of Sussex Police* [2008] UKHL 25; [2008] 1 AC 962. The claimants were relatives of an individual (J) who had been fatally shot by the police during an armed raid. In a criminal prosecution, the police constable who had fired the shot was acquitted of J's murder. The claimants turned to civil law, suing the police commissioner (S) in a number of torts: false imprisonment (during the raid); negligence in the planning and execution of the raid; misfeasance in a public office for conduct after the event; assault and battery in respect of the shooting.[14] S admitted liability in negligence and in false imprisonment, but defended the other claims. Because S had admitted liability in negligence, success in the claim for assault and battery could not increase compensatory damages payable to the claimants. They would not stand to be compensated twice merely because more than one cause of action was applicable to the loss.

The House accepted that although the defendant had accepted liability to compensate the claimant in full, the claim based on trespass to the person could still proceed to trial. The

[14] Some of these claims relate to wrongdoing on the part of the police authorities; others propose that the commissioner is liable 'vicariously' for a tort on the part of the police constable (see Chapter 9). The specific claims against S in assault and battery are claims for *vicarious* liability.

judges differed substantially in the reasons that they gave for finding legitimate space for the action in trespass; but the majority of judges accepted that 'vindication' was a legitimate aim to pursue through the trespass action. A finding of trespass would add distinctively to a finding of negligence.

In short, trespass is centrally concerned with the boundaries of legitimate physical interference. While the 'intentional' aspect of trespass torts is weak, the 'unlawfulness' element may lead defendants—particularly those exercising public functions—to resist a finding of liability more strongly than in the case of negligence, for example. That was the case in *Ashley*. However, we should note the conclusions of the Supreme Court in *Lumba v Secretary of State for the Home Department*, addressed in relation to false imprisonment (Section 4). Substantial, as opposed to nominal, damages will not be awarded to 'vindicate' rights, where no damage is suffered.

2.2 TRESPASS IN HISTORY AND MODERN LAW: FORMS OF ACTION AND CAUSES OF ACTION

During the medieval period, trespass *was* the law of (what would now be called) 'tort'. 'Trespass' meant little more specific than 'wrong'.

S. F. C. Milsom, *Historical Foundations of the Common Law* (2nd edn, Oxford: Oxford University Press, 1981), at 305

Had some lawyer in the late fourteenth century undertaken to write a book about what we should call tort, about actions brought by the victims of wrongs, he would have called his book 'Trespass'.

The *substantive* requirements of the law at this stage are shrouded in mystery, largely because the majority of issues, other than procedural issues, were treated as matters of fact to be determined by the jury. Also obscuring the nature of trespass is the habit of claiming that harm had been occasioned *vi et armis* (with force and arms), even if it clearly had not.[15] Whatever the reason for this (and it may have been perceived to be a necessary feature of a claim in trespass in the royal courts),[16] trespass became associated with *forcible* wrongs.[17]

The more directly relevant period of history for our purposes was to follow. A new form of action, 'the action on the case', began to develop, outside the jurisdiction of the royal courts. There were two forms of trespass, denoting different *forms of action*, and the two could not

[15] D. Ibbetson, *A Historical Introduction to the Common Law* (Oxford University Press, 2001), at 44, gives the example of *Rattlesdene v Grunestone* (1317). Here it was claimed that the defendant, having sold the plaintiff a barrel of wine but before delivery, removed the cap 'by force of arms, with swords bows and arrows etc', and replaced some of the wine with salt water. As Ibbetson says, 'It is hard not to suspect that the true basis of the claim was a shipping accident'.

[16] See also S. Douglas, *Liability for Wrongful Interferences with Chattels* (Hart Publishing, 2011), Chapter 6.

[17] This is not because the only 'wrongs' understood in medieval times were 'forcible'. Ibbetson points out that defamation (harm to reputation) was recognized at an early stage but was hived off to the ecclesiastical courts. Likewise, an action in 'covenant' was developed which broadly concerned contractual wrongs, leaving 'trespass' to deal (primarily at least) with forcible interventions.

be mixed. The one was simply 'trespass'; the other was 'trespass on the case'. It was the action on the case which flourished, and from which the tort of negligence evolved.

Initially, the main distinctions between the forms of action called trespass and case were procedural. The drafting of writs was the principal skill of English civil lawyers. But actions 'on the case' also became distinct from trespass in substantive terms. On the one hand they required 'damage' to be shown (not a necessary feature of trespass then or now); on the other hand they allowed remedies for *indirect* or *consequential* harm, rather than purely for *direct* and *forcible* interference, as in trespass. The distinction between the action in trespass, and the action 'on the case', seems to have focused upon these principles of directness and force.

The following extract outlines the situation which was reached by the eighteenth century, and which still leaves its mark today.

S. F. C. Milsom, *Historical Foundations of the Common Law* (2nd edn, Oxford: Oxford University Press, 1981), 283–4

By the eighteenth century almost all litigation at common law was being conducted in *ostensurus quare* actions of trespass and case. Trespass was now a term of art referring to *ostensurus quare* writs alleging a breach of the king's peace, which had become common during the thirteenth century. Although these writs covered various harms to persons, goods and land, they were understood as representing a single entity: the essence of trespass was direct forcible injury. . . .

Actions on the case by the eighteenth century covered the remainder of our law of torts and almost the whole of our law of contract; and by contrast with the direct forcible injury of trespass they were identified with consequential harm. They were begun by *ostensurus quare* writs which did not allege a breach of the king's peace, but did describe the factual background more fully in a preamble. . . . Their full name 'trespass on the case' seemed to show that they were a development from trespass, a conscious reaching out from the central idea of direct forcible injury. . . .

The procedural implications of the different 'forms of action' were eventually abolished by the Judicature Acts of 1873 and 1875. It is often said that courts should now be free to respond to *the merits of the case*. This does not mean however that it should make no difference which tort is argued. Torts are not forms of action (a procedural idea); but they do have different substantive principles. If this had not been misunderstood in the case of *Letang v Cooper* [1965] 1 QB 232 (extracted and discussed later in this chapter), the modern history of the trespass torts might have been quite different.

2.3 THE LIMITED ROLE OF TRESPASS IN ACTIONS FOR PERSONAL INJURY

Three modern cases progressively limited the role of trespass *in personal injury law*. The last of the three has now been 'departed from' by the House of Lords (which is to say, in effect, overruled, since it is no longer to be followed), preparing the way for growth in the use of trespass claims for harm caused by deliberate abuse and assault. This avenue is particularly relevant for claims of historic abuse, including sexual abuse.

Fowler v Lanning [1959] 1 QB 426

The statement of claim, which was expressed in terms of trespass to the person, asserted simply that 'the defendant shot the plaintiff'. No particulars of negligence (nor of intention) were set out. The defendant argued that this statement of claim 'disclosed no cause of action', and that the plaintiff must at least allege negligence, setting out facts which would support such a finding.

Diplock J interpreted the issue at stake in terms of burden of proof. In a trespass action, was the burden on the defendant to show that the injury was caused by 'inevitable accident'? This would treat 'due care' as (in effect) a *defence* to the action. Alternatively, was the burden on the plaintiff to show that the shooting was either intentional, or negligent? Diplock J decided the latter was the case, and the burden of alleging and showing carelessness was on the plaintiff.

Trespass had to be either intentional, or negligent, and the plaintiff had to establish that this was so. (It is important to note that *Letang v Cooper*, below, went a step further, and said that battery was an *intentional* tort.)

Diplock J, *Fowler v Lanning*, at 439

I think that what appears to have been the practice of the profession during the present century is sound in law. I can summarise the law as I understand it from my examination of the cases as follows:

(1) Trespass to the person does not lie if the injury to the plaintiff, although the direct consequence of the act of the defendant, was caused unintentionally and without negligence on the defendant's part.

(2) Trespass to the person on the highway does not differ in this respect from trespass to the person committed in any other place.

(3) If it were right to say with Blackburn J. in 1866 that negligence is a necessary ingredient of unintentional trespass only where the circumstances are such as to show that the plaintiff had taken upon himself the risk of inevitable injury (i.e., injury which is the result of neither intention nor carelessness on the part of the defendant), the plaintiff must today in this crowded world be considered as taking upon himself the risk of inevitable injury from any acts of his neighbour which, in the absence of damage to the plaintiff, would not in themselves be unlawful—of which discharging a gun at a shooting party in 1957 or a trained band exercise in 1617 are obvious examples....

Glanville Williams, noting this case at [1959] CLJ 33, wondered why this should not be an appropriate case for invoking the maxim '*res ipsa loquitur*' which applies in the tort of negligence (Chapter 3, Section 1.4): an injury of this nature would not generally occur *without* negligence. It might be argued that the mere fact of being shot by the defendant *does* disclose a cause of action, unless the defendant brings some evidence supporting an innocent explanation.[18]

Diplock J seemed to suggest that in trespass, the relevant *intention* or *carelessness* (if it exists) is intention or carelessness *as to the injury*. He argues that trespass does not lie 'if the

[18] *Res ipsa loquitur* places on the defendant the task of showing *some* evidence weighing against an inference of negligence.

injury to the plaintiff … was caused unintentionally and without negligence on the plaintiff's part' (emphasis added). We have already proposed that the relevant intention relates only to *contact*.

It is suggested that not too much should be read into Diplock J's words in this respect, since the issue was not crucial to *Fowler v Lanning*. The case involved a shooting incident, and in such a case intention to injure or carelessness as to injury are ordinarily identical with the intention to have physical contact (i.e., to shoot C). If there is intention to shoot C then there typically is intention to injure;[19] if there is carelessness as to shooting, then there is surely carelessness in respect of injury. The same goes for accidents on the highway. The next case extracted effectively removed trespass from the law of 'accidents'.

Letang v Cooper [1965] 1 QB 232

It may be wondered why anyone would frame their action in terms of trespass, if the facts could also be said to support a claim in negligence. One reason is that the claimant may not have any knowledge at all about the incident and why it happened, so that they cannot prove lack of care. This probably explains the claim in *Fowler v Lanning* (extracted earlier in this section), but since Diplock J's decision in that case trespass torts will be unable to assist a claimant in these circumstances. Another, more technical reason explains our next case although, as we will go on to explain, the incentive to prefer trespass for this reason no longer exists.

In *Letang v Cooper*, the plaintiff alleged that she was sunbathing in the grounds of a Cornish hotel when the defendant drove his car over her legs, causing her personal injury. She brought her action in trespass to the person, rather than negligence, for the simple reason that she had run out of time to bring the negligence action. The claim was 'time barred'. To understand this case, we must therefore say something about 'limitation of actions'.

Limitation of Actions: the Problem in Letang v Cooper

In general, tort actions must be brought within a period of six years from the time that the action 'accrues' (in this case, the time of the impact and consequent injury).[20] However, according to the legislation in place at the time of this incident, the available time was reduced to a period of three years 'in the case of actions for damages for negligence, nuisance or breach of duty … where the damages claimed by the plaintiff … consist of or include damages in respect of personal injuries to any person'.[21]

A period of over three years had elapsed, so an action in negligence was plainly out of time, but what of an action in trespass to the person? This sort of action was not mentioned by name in the relevant statutory provision quoted above, and the first instance judge held that the action in trespass attracted the general six-year limitation period. The Court of Appeal reversed this decision.

---

[19] This point may be debated in those relatively rare cases where there is an intention to disarm, for example.

[20] The rules of 'limitation' and their rationale are explained in Chapter 7.

[21] Law Reform (Limitation of Actions, etc) Act 1954, s 2(1). As we will see, the limitation period for personal injury is no longer so inflexible.

Lord Denning MR, *Letang v Cooper*, at 238–40

The truth is that the distinction between trespass and case is obsolete. We have a different sub-division altogether. Instead of dividing actions for personal injuries into trespass (direct damage) or case (consequential damage), we divide the causes of action now according as the defendant did the injury intentionally or unintentionally. If one man intentionally applies force directly to another, the plaintiff has a cause of action in assault and battery, or, if you so please to describe it, in trespass to the person. "The least touching of another in anger is a battery," *per* Holt C.J. in *Cole v. Turner*. [(1704) 6 Mod. 149] If he does not inflict injury intentionally, but only unintentionally, the plaintiff has no cause of action today in trespass. His only cause of action is in negligence, and then only on proof of want of reasonable care. If the plaintiff cannot prove want of reasonable care, he may have no cause of action at all. Thus, it is not enough nowadays for the plaintiff to plead that "the defendant shot the plaintiff." He must also allege that he did it intentionally or negligently. If intentional, it is the tort of assault and battery. If negligent and causing damage, it is the tort of negligence.

The modern law on this subject was well expounded by Diplock J. in *Fowler v. Lanning*, with which I fully agree. But I would go this one step further: when the injury is not inflicted intentionally, but negligently, I would say that the only cause of action is negligence and not trespass. If it were trespass, it would be actionable without proof of damage; and that is not the law today.

In my judgment, therefore, the only cause of action in the present case, where the injury was unintentional, is negligence and is barred by reason of the express provision of the statute.

It is plain that Lord Denning sought to make trespass to the person depend upon 'intention'. This being the case, it is unfortunate that he slips here between references to 'inflicting injury intentionally', and 'intentionally applying force directly to another'. These two approaches specify different 'targets of intention'. The correct approach was clarified by a later Court of Appeal, in *Wilson v Pringle*.[22]

Croom-Johnson LJ, *Wilson v Pringle*
[1987] QB 237, at 249–50

The judgment of Lord Denning M.R. [in *Letang v Cooper*] was widely phrased, but it was delivered in an action where the only contact between the plaintiff and the defendant was unintentional.... In our view,... [I]t is the act and not the injury which must be intentional. An intention to injure is not essential to an action for trespass to the person. It is the mere trespass by itself which is the offence.

To return to *Letang v Cooper*, Lord Denning turned next to the statutory wording. This part of his reasoning was subsequently disapproved by the House of Lords in *Stubbings v Webb* [1993] AC 498; but his approach has now been vindicated by the House of Lords in *A v Hoare* [2008] UKHL 6.

22 This aspect of the judgment in *Wilson v Pringle* is not called into doubt by the developments in cases such as *Re F* [1990] 2 AC 1, also extracted later.

Lord Denning MR, *Letang v Cooper*, at 241–2

So we come back to construe the words of the statute with reference to the law of this century and not of past centuries. So construed, they are perfectly intelligible. The tort of negligence is firmly established. So is the tort of nuisance. These are given by the legislature as sign-posts. Then these are followed by words of the most comprehensive description: "Actions for...breach of duty (whether the duty exists by virtue of a contract or of a provision made by or under a statute or independently of any contract or any such provision)." Those words seem to me to cover not only a breach of a contractual duty, or a statutory duty, but also a breach of any duty under the law of tort. Our whole law of tort today proceeds on the footing that there is a duty owed by every man not to injure his neighbour in a way forbidden by law. Negligence is a breach of such a duty. So is nuisance. So is trespass to the person. So is false imprisonment, malicious prosecution or defamation of character. Professor Winfield indeed defined "tortious liability" by saying that it "arises from the breach of a duty primarily fixed by the law: this duty is towards persons generally and its breach is redressible by an action for unliquidated damages": See Winfield on Tort, 7th ed. (1963), p. 5.

In my judgment, therefore, the words "breach of duty" are wide enough to comprehend the cause of action for trespass to the person as well as negligence....

I come, therefore, to the clear conclusion that the plaintiff's cause of action here is barred by the Statute of Limitations. Her only cause of action here, in my judgment, where the damage was unintentional, was negligence and not trespass to the person. It is therefore barred by the word "negligence" in the statute. But even if it was trespass to the person, it was an action for "breach of duty" and is barred on that ground also.

Diplock LJ took a different route to the conclusion that trespass and negligence were mutually exclusive.

Diplock LJ, *Letang v Cooper*, at 244–5

The factual situation upon which the plaintiff's action was founded is set out in the statement of claim. It was that the defendant, by failing to exercise reasonable care, of which failure particulars were given, drove his motor car over the plaintiff's legs and so inflicted upon her direct personal injuries in respect of which the plaintiff claimed damages. That factual situation was the plaintiff's cause of action. It was the cause of action for which the plaintiff claimed damages in respect of the personal injuries which she sustained. That cause of action or factual situation falls within the description of the tort of negligence and an action founded on it, that is, brought to obtain the remedy to which the existence of that factual situation entitles the plaintiff, falls within the description of an action for negligence. The description "negligence" was in fact used by the plaintiff's pleader; but this cannot be decisive for we are concerned not with the description applied by the pleader to the factual situation and the action founded on it, but with the description applied to it by Parliament in the enactment to be construed. It is true that that factual situation also falls within the description of the tort of trespass to the person. But that, as I have endeavoured to show, does not mean that there are two causes of action. It merely means that there are two apt descriptions of the same cause of action. It does not cease to be the tort of negligence because it can also be called by another name. An action founded upon it is nonetheless an action for negligence because it can also be called an action for trespass to the person.

It is not, I think, necessary to consider whether there is today any respect in which a cause of action for unintentional as distinct from intentional trespass to the person is not equally aptly described as a cause of action for negligence. The difference stressed by Elwes J. that actual damage caused by failure to exercise reasonable care forms an essential element in the cause of action for negligence, but does not in the cause of action in trespass to the person, is, I think, more apparent than real when the trespass is unintentional; for, since the duty of care, whether in negligence or in unintentional trespass to the person, is to take reasonable care to avoid causing actual damage to one's neighbour, there is no breach of the duty unless actual damage is caused. Actual damage is thus a necessary ingredient in unintentional as distinct from intentional trespass to the person. But whether this be so or not, the subsection which falls to be construed is concerned only with actions in which actual damage in the form of personal injuries has in fact been sustained by the plaintiff. Where this factor is present, every factual situation which falls within the description "trespass to the person" is, where the trespass is unintentional, equally aptly described as negligence. I am therefore of opinion that the facts pleaded in the present action make it an action "for negligence... where the damages claimed by the plaintiff for the negligence... consist of or include damages in respect of personal injuries to" the plaintiff, within the meaning of the subsection, and that the limitation period was three years.

As we saw, Lord Denning proposed that 'trespass' is only an apt description where the act in question is 'intentional.' Diplock LJ (a little more obscurely) said that the facts should only be *described* in one way. If the contact was careless rather than deliberate, the facts should be described in terms of negligence, even if they could also be said to disclose a trespass; and the rules of negligence should apply. There should be no overlap between different torts with different reasoning. (He did not explain why it was the *negligence* reasoning that should prevail.)

The Diplock approach was pertinently criticized by J. A. Jolowicz in the following note. Jolowicz pointed out that the abolition of the 'forms of action' was meant only to banish *procedural* consequences. Indeed, the abolition of 'forms of action' was meant to have precisely the opposite of the effect proposed by Diplock LJ. It should now be possible to argue alternative torts *with different substantive rules* alongside one another, instead of choosing a single *procedure* and being restricted accordingly.

J. A. Jolowicz, 'Forms of Action—Causes of Action—Trespass and Negligence' [1964] CLJ 200, at 202

It is...true, or should be true, that no *procedural* consequences flow from the pleader's choice of description for his cause of action. It is not true, however, that no consequences flow from the fact that more than one description is appropriate for a given factual situation. If the *substantive* rules appropriate to one description entitle the plaintiff to succeed it is no answer for the defendant to say that according to the rules appropriate to a different but equally apt description the plaintiff's action fails. If for example I say that X, a trader, is selling goods which he knows to have been stolen, my words may be described as 'slander of title' (or 'injurious falsehood'), a tort in which actual malice is required. But they are also aptly described as slander actionable *per se* and therefore, if the words are in fact untrue, it is no defence for me to prove that I honestly believed what I said. This, indeed, is the principal consequence of the so-called abolition of the forms of action. It is not necessarily true that only one description of the factual situation is apt. And if the court proceeds to confine itself to one set of rules only where more than one apply, it is, in effect, restoring to the forms of action—these "ghosts of the past"—much of their former prominence, not passing through them undeterred.

A host of recent cases could be cited to prove Jolowicz's point. They allow a number of substantive torts to be argued on the same set of facts, leading to success in one and failure in others. For example, it is clear that a claimant may succeed in negligence or malicious falsehood while failing, or being otherwise unable to proceed, in libel: *Spring v Guardian Assurance* [1985] 2 AC 296 (Chapter 6); *Kaye v Robertson* [1991] FSR 92 (Chapter 14). The judgment of Diplock J in *Letang v Cooper* appears to state that negligence and trespass are mutually exclusive: the facts should give rise to a claim in negligence, or in trespass, but not both. This, however, is not the case, as is clearly illustrated by *Ashley v Chief Constable of Sussex* (discussed earlier).

Summary: Trespass and Negligence in Personal Injury Cases

In the case of direct and *intentional* contact, both trespass and negligence can apply to the same facts, provided that (for the negligence action) a 'duty of care' was owed and breached. In the case of merely *negligent* contact, however, the effect of *Letang v Cooper* is that any action will be governed by the rules of negligence. In effect, only the negligence action may be pursued.

Stubbings v Webb [1993] AC 498

We have seen that in *Letang v Cooper*, Lord Denning argued that trespass involves a 'breach of duty' so that, in a case involving personal injury, it could not attract a more generous limitation period than negligence.

In *Stubbings v Webb* the House of Lords had to decide which limitation period applied to a case of alleged sexual abuse occasioning lasting psychiatric harm. The relevant acts, if proven, would clearly amount to trespass to the person as the physical contact was 'intentional'. But the impact of treating trespass the same as negligence would now be beneficial. This is because the applicable limitation period in *Stubbings v Webb* was determined by the Limitation Act 1980. This allows certain actions to benefit from extensions to the standard limitation period as of right (on conditions set out in section 14), or through exercise of the court's discretion (section 33). Section 11(1) of this Act, which defines those actions to which sections 14 and 33 will apply, used the same wording as the earlier statutory provision considered in *Letang v Cooper* to define the actions which must be brought within three years. The plaintiff in *Stubbings v Webb* argued that the requirements of section 14 had not been satisfied in her case until some years after the acts of abuse themselves, which took place during childhood.

The House of Lords held however that trespass to the person in the form of rape and sexual abuse did *not* fall within section 11. Therefore, section 14 was also not applicable.

Trespass was subject to a non-extendable limitation period of six years, which would begin to run when the victim reached adulthood; whereas a negligence claim would have been extended *at least* until three years from the plaintiff's date of knowledge. The claim was out of time. Lord Griffiths accepted an argument which had been rejected by Lord Denning in *Letang v Cooper*.[23] By reference to the recommendations of the Tucker Committee,[24] Lord Griffiths argued that the 'date of knowledge' qualifications applicable from 1954 onwards were *intended* (by their drafters) only to cover what he called 'accident cases', not *intentional* assaults. He also considered that Lord Denning had been wrong to say that 'trespass to the person' involves a 'breach of duty'.

Stubbings v Webb further limited the reach of trespass in cases of *actual personal injury*. While it can be argued that in an accident case such as *Letang* the job will be done instead by the tort of negligence, this argument does not help in the case of deliberate sexual assaults. In a case of sexual abuse, it is unlikely that a court would accept that the defendant has acted 'negligently'.[25] The problem is illustrated by cases where there is also a claim in negligence against a third party who *fails to prevent* abuse. A claim against such a person may benefit from an extended limitation period, thanks to section 14 and section 33.

This was notoriously illustrated in *S v W* [1995] 1 FLR 862. The plaintiff had been abused by her father (the first defendant) during childhood. Her father had been convicted on several charges of incest. The plaintiff brought civil actions both against her father (in trespass), and against her mother, the second defendant, for failing to protect her or to report the acts of abuse. The Court of Appeal held that the action against the mother was an action in negligence and was not out of time. The action against the father was statute-barred on the authority of *Stubbings v Webb*. Millett LJ criticized the reasoning in *Stubbings v Webb* but the Court of Appeal could not, of course, depart from a House of Lords decision.

The anomaly was removed by the House of Lords in *A v Hoare* [2008] UKHL 6, which is discussed in Chapters 7 and 9. For present purposes, we need only note that the conclusion in *Letang v Cooper* [1965] 1 QB 232 was reaffirmed. After *A v Hoare*, trespass will still only assist a claimant where the physical contact was intentional; but actions against deliberate abusers will no longer be time-limited where a claim in negligence would not be. Since the demise of *Stubbings v Webb*, many such cases have been argued in trespass. In this context at least, no longer does trespass appear to be a relic of a bygone age. Removal of this limitation problem has, indeed, opened the door to some large changes in the principles of vicarious liability for deliberate acts such as sexual abuse, explored in Chapter 9.

2.4 BATTERY: THE NATURE OF THE REQUIRED CONTACT

So far, we have said that intentional and direct touching of the claimant amounts to a battery. Consent, necessity, or self-defence will render lawful what would otherwise be a

[23] He did so on the basis that courts were now free, following the decision in *Pepper v Hart* [1993] AC 593, to consult the record of parliamentary debates through *Hansard*, in order to construe the intentions of the proposer of a statute. This is a supplement to interpretation of the words of the statute themselves, and was not an accepted technique at the time of *Letang*.

[24] Report of the Committee on the Limitation of Actions 1949 (Cmd. 7740).

[25] In fact there is no definitive reason to think that the tort of negligence *only* applies to unintended harms. For example, a person who deliberately drives into another vehicle would surely be in breach of the duty of care owed to other road users.

battery. But even so, this definition is very broad. How have the courts limited the scope of the tort?

Collins v Wilcock [1984] 1 WLR 1172

The claimant police officer had cautioned the defendant prostitute. When the defendant walked away, the officer took hold of her arm. The defendant scratched the officer's restraining arm. In the Court of Appeal, the *defendant* argued that the police officer had committed a battery in holding her. The Court of Appeal accepted the defendant's argument. There was no implied power upon the officer to detain the defendant for the purpose of the caution. The touching went beyond conduct which is generally accepted. It was a trespass, so that the officer could not be said to have been acting in the course of her duty. The conviction was quashed.

Robert Goff LJ analysed the older case law and presented it in an updated and clarified form. His formulation is adapted to define the limits of appropriate intervention by public officials such as police officers.

Robert Goff LJ, at 1177

We are here concerned primarily with battery. The fundamental principle, plain and incontestable, is that every person's body is inviolate. It has long been established that any touching of another person, however slight, may amount to a battery. So Holt C.J. held in *Cole v. Turner* (1704) 6 Mod. 149 that "the least touching of another is anger is a battery." The breadth of the principle reflects the fundamental nature of the interest so protected. As Blackstone wrote in his *Commentaries*, 17th ed. (1830), vol. 3, p. 120:

"the law cannot draw the line between different degrees of violence, and therefore totally prohibits the first and lowest stage of it; every man's person being sacred, and no other having a right to meddle with it, in any the slightest manner."

The effect is that everybody is protected not only against physical injury but against any form of physical molestation.

But so widely drawn a principle must inevitably be subject to exceptions. For example, children may be subject to reasonable punishment; people may be subjected to the lawful exercise of the power of arrest; and reasonable force may be used in self-defence or for the prevention of crime. But, apart from these special instances where the control or constraint is lawful, a broader exception has been created to allow for the exigencies of everyday life. Generally speaking consent is a defence to battery; and most of the physical contacts of ordinary life are not actionable because they are impliedly consented to by all who move in society and so expose themselves to the risk of bodily contact. So nobody can complain of the jostling which is inevitable from his presence in, for example, a supermarket, an underground station or a busy street; nor can a person who attends a party complain if his hand is seized in friendship, or even if his back is, within reason, slapped: see *Tuberville v. Savage* (1669) 1 Mod. 3. Although such cases are regarded as examples of implied consent, it is more commonly nowadays to treat them as falling within a general exception embracing all physical contact which is generally acceptable in the ordinary conduct of daily life. We observe that, although in the past it has sometimes been stated that a battery is only committed where the action is "angry revengeful, rude, or insolent" (see *Hawkins, Pleas of the Crown*, 8th ed. (1824), vol. 1, c. 15, section 2), we think that nowadays it is more realistic, and indeed more accurate, to state the broad underlying principle, subject to the broad exception. . . .

'Wrongful' touching, amounting to a battery, is here defined as touching which goes beyond that which is generally acceptable. It does not need to be hostile or (certainly) to be aimed at injuring the claimant. In *Wilson v Pringle* [1987] QB 237, a case of physical injury sustained in horseplay between schoolboys, a differently constituted Court of Appeal thought the above formulation too wide and impractical in application.

Croom-Johnson LJ, *Wilson v Pringle*, at 252–3 (giving the judgment of the court)

...it is not practicable to define a battery as "physical contact which is not generally acceptable in the ordinary conduct of daily life."

In our view, the authorities lead one to the conclusion that in a battery there must be an intentional touching or contact in one form or another of the plaintiff by the defendant. That touching must be proved to be a hostile touching. That still leaves unanswered the question "when is a touching to be called hostile?" Hostility cannot be equated with ill-will or malevolence. It cannot be governed by the obvious intention shown in acts like punching, stabbing or shooting. It cannot be solely governed by an expressed intention, although that may be strong evidence. But the element of hostility, in the sense in which it is now to be considered, must be a question of fact for the tribunal of fact. It may be imported from the circumstances.... Where the immediate act of touching does not itself demonstrate hostility, the plaintiff should plead the facts which are said to do so.

In the next case extracted, Lord Goff (now in the House of Lords) restored the authority of the views he had set out in *Collins*. This case has been central to the development of aspects of medical law and to the modern law of trespass to the person.

Re F (Mental Patient: Sterilization) [1990] 2 AC 1

The patient, who had the mental age of a small child, had formed a sexual relationship with a male patient. It was thought undesirable to prevent the relationship from being conducted, but it was also thought that the patient would be unable to cope with pregnancy or childbirth should she conceive. Sterilization was judged to be in her best interests, but since she was unable to comprehend the procedure or its purpose (and therefore could not validly consent) could the proposed operation be carried out without committing a trespass?

Lord Goff, at 72–3

I start with the fundamental principle, now long established, that every person's body is inviolate. As to this, I do not wish to depart from what I myself said in the judgment of the Divisional Court in *Collins v Wilcock...*, and in particular from the statement, at p. 1177, that the effect of this principle is that everybody is protected not only against physical injury but against any form of physical molestation.

Of course, as a general rule physical interference with another person's body is lawful if he consents to it; though in certain limited circumstances the public interest may require that his consent is not capable of rendering the act lawful. There are also specific cases where physical interference without consent may not be unlawful—chastisement of children, lawful arrest, self-defence, the prevention of crime, and so on. As I pointed out in *Collins v. Wilcock* [1984] 1 W.L.R. 1172, 1177, a broader exception has been created to allow for the exigencies of everyday life—jostling in a street or some other crowded place, social contact at parties, and such like. This exception has been said to be founded on implied consent, since those who go about in public places, or go to parties, may be taken to have impliedly consented to bodily contact of this kind. Today this rationalisation can be regarded as artificial; and in particular, it is difficult to impute consent to those who, by reason of their youth or mental disorder, are unable to give their consent. For this reason, I consider it more appropriate to regard such cases as falling within a general exception embracing all physical contact which is generally acceptable in the ordinary conduct of everyday life.

In the old days it used to be said that, for a touching of another's person to amount to a battery, it had to be a touching "in anger" (see *Cole v. Turner* (1794) 6 Mod. 149, *per* Holt C.J.); and it has recently been said that the touching must be "hostile" to have that effect (see *Wilson v. Pringle* [1987] Q.B. 237, 253). I respectfully doubt whether that is correct. A prank that gets out of hand; an over-friendly slap on the back; surgical treatment by a surgeon who mistakenly thinks that the patient has consented to it—all these things may transcend the bounds of lawfulness, without being characterised as hostile. Indeed the suggested qualification is difficult to reconcile with the principle that any touching of another's body is, in the absence of lawful excuse, capable of amounting to a battery and a trespass. Furthermore, in the case of medical treatment, we have to bear well in mind the libertarian principle of self-determination which, to adopt the words of Cardozo J. (in *Schloendorff v. Society of New York Hospital* (1914) 105 N.E. 92, 93) recognises that:

> "Every human being of adult years and sound mind has a right to determine what shall be done with his own body; and a surgeon who performs an operation without his patient's consent commits an assault…"

…It is against this background that I turn to consider the question whether, and if so when, medical treatment or care of a mentally disordered person who is, by reason of his incapacity, incapable of giving his consent, can be regarded as lawful. As is recognised in Cardozo J.'s statement of principle, and elsewhere (see e.g. *Sidaway v. Board of Governors of the Bethlem Royal Hospital and the Maudsley Hospital* [1985] A.C. 871, 882, *per* Lord Scarman), some relaxation of the law is required to accommodate persons of unsound mind. In *Wilson v. Pringle* [1987] Q.B. 237, the Court of Appeal considered that treatment or care of such persons may be regarded as lawful, as falling within the exception relating to physical contact which is generally acceptable in the ordinary conduct of everyday life. Again, I am with respect unable to agree. That exception is concerned with the ordinary events of everyday life—jostling in public places and such like—and affects all persons, whether or not they are capable of giving their consent. Medical treatment—even treatment for minor ailments—does not fall within that category of events. The general rule is that consent is necessary to render such treatment lawful. If such treatment administered without consent is not to be unlawful, it has to be justified on some other principle.

The case raised a fundamental question for medical law. Given that valid consent could not be obtained, was there an *alternative justification* for treatment, which would render it *not unlawful*?

One possible alternative was that treatment could not be performed on the basis of 'necessity' (a recognised defence to trespass). But necessity is not a sufficiently generous principle: it would only justify a narrow range of emergency treatment. This might be adequate for those suffering a *temporary* lack of consciousness. But what of those suffering long-term or permanent lack of capacity? Lord Bridge pointed out a significant problem that might arise if only necessary treatment could lawfully be carried out:

Lord Bridge, *Re F*, at 52

...it seems to me of first importance that the common law should be readily intelligible to and applicable by all those who undertake the care of persons lacking the capacity to consent to treatment. It would be intolerable for members of the medical, nursing and other professions devoted to the care of the sick that, in caring for those lacking the capacity to consent to treatment they should be put in the dilemma that, if they administer the treatment which they believe to be in the patient's best interests, acting with due skill and care, they run the risk of being held guilty of trespass to the person, but if they withhold that treatment, they may be in breach of a duty of care owed to the patient. If those who undertake responsibility for the care of incompetent or unconscious patients administer curative or prophylactic treatment which they believe to be appropriate to the patient's existing condition of disease, injury or bodily malfunction or susceptibility to such a condition in the future, the lawfulness of that treatment should be judged by one standard, not two. It follows that if the professionals in question have acted with due skill and care, judged by the well known test laid down in *Bolam* v. *Friern Hospital Management Committee* [1957] 1 W.L.R. 582, they should be immune from liability in trespass, just as they are immune from liability in negligence.

The solution was to say that all treatment which was *in the best interests of the patient* would be lawful.

Broadly this approach was codified by the Mental Capacity Act 2005. The Act does not repeal the principles of common law but aims to set out clearly the guiding principles which will apply. Even so these principles may be slightly different from those accepted at common law. The statute also expressly states that compliance with the approach set out in the Act will provide a defence to a civil action at common law, in the absence of negligence (s 5), and in this sense it takes priority over any common law principles. As Dyson LJ pointed out in *H v Commissioner of Police of the Metropolis* [2013] EWCA Civ 69, where section 5 is concerned, 'reasonableness' is the prevalent idea and there is no room for strict liability. The actions of the police officers in that particular case, which involved the restraint of a severely autistic and epileptic teenager at a swimming pool, were found comprehensively unreasonable. Damages were awarded in battery, in false imprisonment, and under the HRA.

The general principles are set out in section 1. Section 1(5) states the 'best interests' principle.

Mental Capacity Act 2005

1 The principles

The following principles apply for the purposes of this Act.

(1) A person must be assumed to have capacity unless it is established that he lacks capacity.

(2) A person is not to be treated as unable to make a decision unless all practicable steps to help him to do so have been taken without success.

(3) A person is not to be treated as unable to make a decision merely because he makes an unwise decision.

(4) An act done, or decision made, under this Act for or on behalf of a person who lacks capacity must be done, or made, in his best interests.

(5) Before the act is done, or the decision is made, regard must be had to whether the purpose for which it is needed can be as effectively achieved in a way that is less restrictive of the person's rights and freedom of action.

Persons who 'lack capacity' are defined by section 2, the key idea being that through mental impairment or disturbance in the functioning of the mind or brain, the person cannot make a decision for themselves. The meaning of 'best interests' is set out by section 4:

4 Best interests

(1) In determining for the purposes of this Act what is in a person's best interests, the person making the determination must not make it merely on the basis of—

    (a) the person's age or appearance, or

    (b) a condition of his, or an aspect of his behaviour, which might lead others to make unjustified assumptions about what might be in his best interests.

(2) The person making the determination must consider all the relevant circumstances and, in particular, take the following steps.

(3) He must consider—

    (a) whether it is likely that the person will at some time have capacity in relation to the matter in question, and

    (b) if it appears likely that he will, when that is likely to be.

(4) He must, so far as reasonably practicable, permit and encourage the person to partici-pate, or to improve his ability to participate, as fully as possible in any act done for him and any decision affecting him.

(5) Where the determination relates to life-sustaining treatment he must not, in considering whether the treatment is in the best interests of the person concerned, be motivated by a desire to bring about his death.

(6) He must consider, so far as is reasonably ascertainable—

    (a) the person's past and present wishes and feelings (and, in particular, any relevant writ-ten statement made by him when he had capacity),

    (b) the beliefs and values that would be likely to influence his decision if he had capacity, and

    (c) the other factors that he would be likely to consider if he were able to do so.

. . .(9) In the case of an act done, or a decision made, by a person other than the court, there is sufficient compliance with this section if (having complied with the requirements of subsec-tions (1) to (7)) he reasonably believes that what he does or decides is in the best interests of the person concerned.

(10) "Life-sustaining treatment" means treatment which in the view of a person providing health care for the person concerned is necessary to sustain life.

(11) "Relevant circumstances" are those—

    (a) of which the person making the determination is aware, and

    (b) which it would be reasonable to regard as relevant.

Analysis of these provisions and their origins is not possible within the constraints of space available here. But it should be noted that section 4(6) incorporates a range of considerations based not only on the objective welfare of the patient, but also on their likely views or wishes so far as these can be estimated or ascertained. In this, it seems to differ from the 'objective' best interests test at common law: see P. Bartlett, *Blackstone's Guide to the Mental Capacity Act 2005*, 2nd edn, chapter 3, both for this point and for a general overview of the statute. On the other hand, the common law position had become more nuanced in the years leading up to the statutory reforms.[26]

To return to *Re F*, the decision was also significant because of the order made by the court. The House of Lords found that where incompetent *adults* were concerned, the court had no jurisdiction to 'consent to' or 'approve' a particular operation as being in the patient's best interests.[27] However, the House of Lords decided that under the inherent jurisdiction of the High Court, it could make **a declaration** to the effect that the operation *was lawful*. Declarations of lawfulness have subsequently been widely used and were still developing at the time of the statutory reforms.

By section 4(9) of the Mental Capacity Act 2005, a 'reasonable belief' that the decision made is in the patient's best interest will now suffice to give the defendant the benefit of section 5 and thus to avoid civil liability (other than where there is negligence: section 5(3)). These provisions are also of importance in relation to false imprisonment and in contexts other than medical treatment. We return to this point later.

3. DEFENCES TO ASSAULT AND BATTERY

3.1 CONSENT

It will be clear from *Re F* (Section 2.4) that consent is a defence of the first importance in trespass to the person. Indeed, battery could potentially be defined as a direct, intended and non-consensual physical invasion. This difference would be of some practical importance, because it is generally for a *defendant* to show that a defence is made out, while a claimant must establish the main elements of a tort. To treat 'lack of consent' as part of the definition of trespass would shift the burden of proof regarding consent from defendant, to claimant. Surprisingly perhaps, there is limited English authority on this point; though there is also some parallel discussion of proof of 'unlawfulness' in relation to false imprisonment (Section 4).

In *Freeman v Home Office (No 2)* [1984] QB 524, McCowan J (at first instance) ruled that the burden is on the *claimant* to establish his or her own *lack* of consent. His ruling seemed to contradict the various authorities he cited on the point (gleaned both from Commonwealth case law[28] and English textbooks). He was persuaded by an attractive argument put by counsel for the Home Office, to the effect that these authorities were

---

[26] An accessible overview of the common law position, the gaps in it, and the new possibilities presented by the Mental Capacity Act (particularly as regards participation by the incapacitated person) is provided by M. Donnelly, 'Best interests, patient participation and the Mental Capacity Act 2005' (2009) 17 Med L Rev 1.

[27] For the position with children (minors) who are incompetent to consent, see the discussion of *Re A (Conjoined Twins)*, below. Powers under the Mental Capacity Act 2005 do not apply where the person who lacks capacity is under the age of 16 (s 2(5)).

[28] Particularly *Reibl v Hughes* (1980) 114 DLR (3d) 1.

principally concerned not with consent in the context of trespass, but with the rather different defence of *volenti* which can also be called 'willing acceptance of risk' (Chapter 5). It is true that 'consent' and *volenti* are separate defences, but this does not justify the conclusion that lack of consent is therefore not a defence at all. Therefore, we could accept the first three sentences of the following extract, while doubting the last four (presented here in italics).

McCowan J, *Freeman v Home Office (No 2)*, at 539–40

Mr. Laws submits that volenti is consent to the risk of injury and is accordingly a defence most apt to a claim in negligence. What a plaintiff consents to in a case of alleged battery is not risk but a specific intrusion on his body. Therefore, consent to a surgical operation is not properly an example of volenti. *The action fails not because of volenti but because there is no tort. Volenti, he submits, does not arise at all unless the tort of battery, which he defines as "the unconsented to intrusion of another's bodily integrity" is made out. That definition, he says, meets the vice at which the tort is aimed. I accept Mr. Laws' submission and rule that the burden of providing absence of consent is on the plaintiff.*

If the definition of trespass accepted by McCowan J was right, there would be no obvious reason why other issues which go to lawfulness—including self-defence—should not also be a part of the definition of trespass. In *Ashley v CC Sussex* [2006] EWCA Civ 1985, the Court of Appeal noted this controversy (at para [31]). The court declined to say whether it regarded *Freeman* as correct, but held that whatever the correct position with consent, *self-defence* was for the *defendant* to establish (a conclusion also reached by the House of Lords (above)). Similarly in *Austin v Commissioner of Police of the Metropolis* [2007] EWCA Civ 989; [2008] QB 660, an action in false imprisonment, the Court of Appeal held that the defence of 'necessity' was for the defendant to establish (though they imposed an onerous burden on claimants who wanted to say that in their particular case, the general necessity of the situation did not require their continued detention). The House of Lords did not consider this point as the appeal related only to a claim in respect of Article 5 ECHR. Both decisions are extracted in Section 4.1.

In *Freeman* too, this particular point did not fall for decision on appeal. It was treated as clear that the plaintiff *had indeed consented to* the administration of drugs.[29] However, Lord Donaldson pointed out that consent and *volenti* are separate, and may both arise in a trespass action.

Consent to Medical Treatment: Two Types of Problem Case

Consent to medical treatment has been a significant issue in two very different types of case. The first type of case concerns the lawfulness of treatment in the absence of consent. In fact this category is further divided into cases where treatment is *refused*; and other cases where valid consent simply cannot be obtained. The second type of case concerns treatment where

[29] The decision in *Sidaway v Bethlem Royal Hospital* [1984] QB 493 had meanwhile made it clear that only broad knowledge of the treatment is required for consent to be valid and effective; it remains the case after *Montgomery v Lanarkshire Health Board* [2015] UKSC 11; [2015] AC 1430, that questions as to disclosure of risks to a patient will be approached as questions of negligence, rather than consent.

consent is given, but that consent is not based on sufficient knowledge about the treatment or its likely consequences.

Type 1: Treatment without Consent

Refusal

The starting point is that where a competent adult refuses treatment, it is unlawful (amounting to the tort of battery and also potentially to a criminal offence against the person) to inflict that treatment upon him or her. This is the case even if the likely or inevitable result of refusal is the patient's death.[30] The patient does not need to have any rational grounds for refusal, nor any grounds for refusal at all. In other words, the *right of self-determination* (which is underpinned by the value of autonomy) is a trump card, which overrides the patient's best interests. Even sanctity of life does not outweigh the patient's right to self-determination. At least, that is the principle.

The role of autonomy as a trump card has been stated many times by English courts. In *Re T*, it was held that the refusal of treatment was not effective because of undue influence from the patient's mother. In *St George's Healthcare NHS Trust v S* [1999] Fam 26, it was determined that it *had been* a trespass to impose treatment (in this case, a caesarean section) not only in order to save the life of a competent mother who refuses treatment, but also to save her unborn child. The interests of the foetus do not weigh against the competent mother's autonomy. In this case, the caesarean had already been carried out, and the mother sought an order that this was unlawful. There was no longer an emergency.

No Possibility of Consent or Refusal: 'Best Interests' vs Sanctity of Life?

In 'refusal' cases, sanctity of life *and* best interests of the patient are in principle trumped by autonomy or self-determination. What of the case where there is *neither consent nor refusal*, because the patient is permanently unable to give or withhold consent? Here, the trump card of 'autonomy' cannot come into play.[31] In the next case extracted the House of Lords held that in such a case, given that the best interests of the patient prevail, even life-saving or life-sustaining treatment need not be offered or maintained if it is judged not to be in the best interests of the patient to receive it. It is important to note that this is an application of *Re F*.

Airedale NHS Trust v Bland [1993] AC 789

The patient had been in a 'persistent vegetative state' for three years. He was judged to have no prospect of recovery. A declaration was sought that it would be lawful to withdraw the artificial feeding which was maintaining his life. Without such a declaration, the medical

---

[30] This should now be read subject to the provisions of the Mental Capacity Act 2005 extracted in Section 2.4.

[31] Difficult questions surround the status of *advance* expressions of a patient's wishes (to have treatment at all costs, or to have treatment withdrawn in specified circumstances). These questions were inconclusively discussed by the Court of Appeal in *R v GMC, ex p. Burke* [2004] 3 FCR 579. Sections 24–26 of the Mental Capacity Act 2005 now govern the validity and effect of advance decisions to *refuse* particular treatment. These sections allow (amongst other things) for declarations as to the validity and effect of such refusal.

team which withdrew treatment might be open to civil proceedings for trespass and criminal prosecution for murder.[32]

The House of Lords held that the 'best interests of the patient' required that treatment to prolong his life should be discontinued. The patient had not expressed any advance wishes as to what should happen if he should be in such a state, so that there was *no consent to the treatment*. (Equally, of course, there was no *refusal* of treatment.) Applying the reasoning in *Re F*, the lack of consent to treatment could make the treatment a trespass, if it was not judged to be *in the patient's best interests*. This is the only sense in which *Bland* is a case about trespass. The medical team sought a declaration that they could *cease to treat*, and Lord Goff explained that non-treatment (even if it involves some physical steps) is essentially an omission; and an omission cannot amount to a battery. Larger concerns in respect of withdrawal of treatment were raised concerning the criminal law, but these are beyond the scope of this book. The following passage is particularly germane to the role of consent.

Lord Goff, at 864

First, it is established that the principle of self-determination requires that respect must be given to the wishes of the patient, so that if an adult patient of sound mind refuses, however unreasonably, to consent to treatment or care by which his life would or might be prolonged, the doctors responsible for his care must give effect to his wishes, even though they do not consider it to be in his best interests to do so . . . : Moreover the same principle applies where the patient's refusal to give his consent has been expressed at an earlier date, before he became unconscious or otherwise incapable of communicating it; though in such circumstances especial care may be necessary to ensure that the prior refusal of consent is still properly to be regarded as applicable in the circumstances which have subsequently occurred: see, e.g., *In re T. (Adult: Refusal of Treatment)* [1993] Fam. 95. I wish to add that, in cases of this kind, there is no question of the patient having committed suicide, nor therefore of the doctor having aided or abetted him in doing so. It is simply that the patient has, as he is entitled to do, declined to consent to treatment which might or would have the effect of prolonging his life, and the doctor has, in accordance with his duty, complied with his patient's wishes.

But in many cases not only may the patient be in no condition to be able to say whether or not he consents to the relevant treatment or care, but also he may have given no prior indication of his wishes with regard to it. In the case of a child who is a ward of court, the court itself will decide whether medical treatment should be provided in the child's best interests, taking into account medical opinion. But the court cannot give its consent on behalf of an adult patient who is incapable of himself deciding whether or not to consent to treatment. I am of the opinion that there is nevertheless no absolute obligation upon the doctor who has the patient in his care to prolong his life, regardless of the circumstances. Indeed, it would be most startling, and could lead to the most adverse and cruel effects upon the patient, if any such absolute rule were held to exist. It is scarcely consistent with the primacy given to the principle of self-determination in those cases in which the patient of sound mind has declined to give his consent, that the

[32] In fact, a declaration does not in theory preclude a future criminal prosecution: *Airedale NHS Trust v Bland* [1993] AC 789, at 862.

law should provide no means of enabling treatment to be withheld in appropriate circumstances where the patient is in no condition to indicate, if that was his wish, that he did not consent to it.

Several members of the House of Lords appeared to say in *Bland* that the best interests of the patient outweigh the sanctity of life itself. It is important to note that this has been doubted. John Keown, 'Restoring Moral and Intellectual Shape to the Law After *Bland*' (1997) 113 LQR 482–503, argued that the sanctity of life should *not* be regarded as 'giving way' to best interests in such a case. On the other hand, sanctity of life does not on his view require the continuation of life at all costs (this would be a doctrine which Keown calls 'vitalism'). On this account, life-saving treatment can indeed be withheld *while respecting the sanctity of life*, provided that attention focuses on *whether the treatment is of any therapeutic benefit*, rather than on the question of *whether the patient's life is no longer of value*. In other words, treatment may be judged futile, but no person's *life* should ever be judged futile.

Keown's analysis has prompted a large literature.[33] It was adopted by Ward LJ in the next case considered.

Re A (Children) (Conjoined Twins: Surgical Separation) [2001] Fam 147

In deciding whether to approve treatment of an incompetent minor, a court must be guided by 'the best interests of the child': section 1(1) of the Children Act 1989. Therefore, the wishes of *parents* may clearly be overridden. Indeed, there is no question of starting with the parents' wishes and determining whether they are 'reasonable': the welfare of the child is paramount.

Re A was a case of conjoined twins. It posed an acute problem for a 'best interests' approach because surgery to separate the twins would result inevitably in the death of one of them, Mary. On the other hand, not to proceed with surgery would inevitably lead to the death of both twins. Jodie, the twin who would be expected to survive surgery, was sustaining Mary's life and could not do so for very long. The parents withheld their consent, but their refusal was overridden by the court.

Much of the crucial argumentation in *Re A* concerned criminal law. The Court of Appeal held that the separation would not amount to murder because it could be said to be 'necessary'.[34] But on what basis could the court validly approve the operation on the basis of *civil* law, given the ruling principle that they must give effect to the best interests of the child?

Ward LJ and Brooke LJ conceded that they could not apply the thinking in *Bland* directly to this case. The operation could not be considered as being *in the best interests of Mary*.[35]

[33] D. Price, 'Fairly Bland: an Alternative View of a Supposed New "Death Ethic" and the BMA Guidelines' (2001) 21 LS 618; A. McGee, 'Finding a Way Through the Legal and Ethical Maze: Withdrawal of Treatment and Euthanasia' (2005) 13 Med LR 357; J. Keown, 'Restoring the Sanctity of Life and Replacing the Caricature: A Reply to David Price' (2006) 26 LS 109. Similarly—and controversially—the Mental Capacity Act 2005, s 4(5) (extracted in Section 2.4) provides that decisions as to life-sustaining treatment *must not be* motivated by a desire to bring about death. For discussion see J. Coggon, 'Ignoring the Moral and Intellectual Shape of the Law After *Bland*' (2007) 27 LS 110–25.

[34] The court therefore distinguished the case of a cabin boy killed to maintain the life of fellow shipwrecked crew members, who were duly convicted of murder: *R v Dudley and Stevens* (1884–85) 14 QBD 273.

[35] Robert Walker LJ disagreed on this point.

Ward LJ, at 190

The question is whether this proposed operation is in Mary's best interests. It cannot be. It will bring her life to an end before it has run its natural span. It denies her inherent right to life. There is no countervailing advantage to her at all. It is contrary to her best interests. Looking at her position in isolation and ignoring, therefore, the benefit to Jodie, the court should not sanction the operation on her.

On the other hand, the court could not, consistently with its duty to act in the best interests of the child, simply refuse consent for the operation. This would lead to the death of Jodie, as well as Mary. Instead, Ward LJ explained that the court must act *in the best interests of both twins*. This meant engaging in a balancing act but, applying Keown's analysis of 'sanctity of life', this would not mean weighing the *value* of the two lives against one another, as all lives are of equal value; rather it would depend on the *worthwhileness of the treatment* (or withholding the treatment) to each of the twins. Since in Jodie's case the treatment was expected to lead to a reasonably fulfilling life in future, and in Mary's case withholding treatment could only delay death for a short time, this approach led to the conclusion that *in the best interests of the twins* (taken together and balanced in this way), consent to the operation should be granted.

Type 2: 'Uninformed Consent'

The doctrine of 'informed consent' originated in the United States. This doctrine holds that consent to medical treatment is real and valid only if it is based on sufficient information about the risks involved. Generally speaking, sufficiency of information would be judged, for the purposes of this doctrine, according to the requirements of a 'prudent patient'.

The doctrine of informed consent in the context of the tort of battery was rejected by the House of Lords in *Sidaway v Bethlem Royal Hospital* [1985] AC 871, holding that questions of *information* and *advice as to risks* should be addressed solely through the tort of negligence, not through trespass to the person. In *Sidaway*, the relevant question was held to be what information *the reasonable doctor would have given*. This test appeared inconsistent with informed consent, although in the negligence case of *Chester v Afshar*, the House of Lords treated informed consent as part of English law. Scholars proposed that *Chester* was part of a more general trend to appreciate the need to respect the decision-making autonomy of patients in the context of the tort of negligence, and this was very clearly confirmed by the Supreme Court in *Montgomery v Lanarkshire Health Board* [2015] UKSC 11.[36] However, *Montgomery* too was argued in negligence, and it appears the doors have not been reopened to actions in trespass. The issue of 'which tort' (battery or negligence) was more or less settled in *Chatterton v Gerson* [1981] QB 432: so long as consent was 'real'—which required that the patient knew the general 'nature of the operation'—it would operate as a defence to an action in trespass.

---

[36] R. Heywood, 'Medical Disclosure of Alternative Treatments' (2009) CLJ 30 (noting the decision in *Birch v University College Hospital NHS Foundation Trust* [2008] EWHC 2237 (QB)).

Bristow J, *Chatterton v Gerson*

[1981] QB 432 (emphasis added)

In my judgment what the court has to do in each case is to look at all the circumstances and say "Was there a real consent?" I think justice requires that in order to vitiate the reality of consent there must be a greater failure of communication between doctor and patient than that involved in a breach of duty if the claim is based on negligence. When the claim is based on negligence the plaintiff must prove not only the breach of duty to inform, but that had the duty not been broken she would not have chosen to have the operation. Where the claim is based on trespass to the person, once it is shown that the consent is unreal, then what the plaintiff would have decided if she had been given the information which would have prevented vitiation of the reality of her consent is irrelevant.

In my judgment once the patient is informed in broad terms of the nature of the procedure which is intended, and gives her consent, that consent is real, and the cause of the action on which to base a claim for failure to go into risks and implications is negligence, not trespass. Of course if information is withheld in bad faith, the consent will be vitiated by fraud. Of course if by some accident, as in a case in the 1940's in the Salford Hundred Court where a boy was admitted to hospital for tonsilectomy and due to administrative error was circumcised instead, trespass would be the appropriate cause of action against the doctor, though he was as much the victim of the error as the boy. But in my judgment it would be very much against the interests of justice if actions which are really based on a failure by the doctor to perform his duty adequately to inform were pleaded in trespass.

3.2 NECESSITY

It is a defence to battery that the defendant applied only such force as a reasonable person would consider 'necessary' in the circumstances. Similar defences apply in assault (threatening a battery in order to achieve an appropriate goal, such as the safety of others) and false imprisonment (imprisoning someone to protect them, or others).

Evidently, for a defence of necessity to apply, the relevant circumstances must create a genuine *need* for the trespass. Through the standard of the 'reasonable person', the defence of 'necessity' introduces a 'reasonableness' element into the trespass torts.[37]

We have seen that in a medical case where the patient is suffering a transient inability to consent, the defence of necessity will be vitally important. It is an important defence in cases of emergency and in cases, such as *Re A*, where a choice must be made between the interests of two or more people. But as *Re F* made clear, necessity is not a sufficient guiding principle in cases of long-term incompetence to consent. It will also be noted that section 4 of the Mental Capacity Act 2005 (extracted in Section 2.4) provides that the 'best interests' principle will apply even where the incapacity is temporary; however, the likely length of incapacity and likely views of the patient, so far as these can be ascertained, will be relevant. Necessity is also overridden by a *refusal* of consent to be treated (or, presumably, rescued) more generally.

[37] Note however that in the special circumstances set out in Criminal Justice Act 2003, s 329 an honest belief suffices: see Chapter 5.

3.3 SELF-DEFENCE

Earlier in this chapter, we outlined the facts of *Ashley v Chief Constable of Sussex*, and explored its implications for the nature of trespass torts. Another crucial question to arise in this case was the boundary between trespass torts, and criminal trespass, given that a criminal prosecution of the officer who had shot the deceased had failed. In particular, could it be said that the tort claim stood a chance of success if the officer had successfully argued self-defence in connection with the *criminal* charge?

The House of Lords concluded that there was still room for the claim in tort. Self-defence is a recognized defence to civil trespass, just as it is to criminal trespass, but the content of these two defences differs. In criminal law, the defendant needs to show an honest belief in the necessity of his actions. There is no need to show that this belief is reasonable. Not so in civil law: the actor's belief must be both honestly held, and reasonable. This difference is not arbitrary, but reflects the different purposes of the criminal and civil law.

3.4 NO REDUCTION FOR CONTRIBUTORY NEGLIGENCE

Under the Law Reform (Contributory Negligence) Act 1945, damages are reduced by the court to reflect the relative 'responsibility' of claimant and defendant. This replaces the previous defence of contributory negligence, where causative fault on the part of the claimant operated as a complete bar. The defence is explored in relation to negligence in Chapter 5. It was determined by the Court of Appeal in *Pritchard v Co-operative Group Ltd* [2011] EWCA Civ 329, [2012] QB 320, that contributory negligence does not operate in cases of trespass to the person. Here we consider the reasons behind this position.

First, we should reject any simple idea that the defence does not apply because the tort of battery is 'intentional'. It had previously been *suggested* by one member of the House of Lords that the defence of contributory negligence would not apply to any case where *harm is intentionally caused* (Lord Rodger, *Standard Chartered Bank v Pakistan Shipping* [2003] 1 AC 959).[38] And indeed, in a case where harm was *intended*, there is an argument that the defendant's liability for the harm should not be affected by contributory fault on the part of the claimant. But this thinking cannot be coherently applied to trespass to the person as a whole, since intent to cause harm is not an element of these torts. The judgment of Aikens LJ in *Pritchard* made reference to battery as an 'intentional wrong'. But there is no requirement that the *wrongful* element of trespass should be intended.

A different aspect of the reasoning in *Standard Chartered Bank* holds the key to the decision in *Pritchard*. Both Lord Hoffmann and Lord Rodger took the view that the 1945 Act introduced apportionment *only* in those torts to which the old defence of contributory negligence applied. This was the case both because of the precise wording of the Act, and because of the broader intention indicated by that wording.

As to the wording, damages are to be reduced where the claimant suffers injury 'as the result partly of his own fault and partly of the fault of any other person . . .' (section 1(1)). 'Fault' is defined in section 4:

---

[38] This was a case in deceit. It was unanimously held by the House of Lords that the defence of contributory negligence is not available in deceit: see Section 7.

Law Reform (Contributory Negligence) Act 1945

4 Interpretation

... 'fault' means negligence, breach of statutory duty or other act or omission which gives rise to a liability in tort or would, apart from this Act, give rise to the defence of contributory negligence.

In *Standard Chartered Bank*, it was concluded that this definition of fault should be read as having two separate limbs. The first (acts or omissions etc which give rise to liability in tort) applies to defendants; and the second ('would, apart from this Act, give rise to the defence of contributory negligence') to claimants. On this basis, the reduction in damages required by section 1(1) applies only in those torts where the claimant's conduct would have given rise to a defence of contributory negligence before 1945; and this was not the case with the tort of deceit. Lord Hoffmann thought this was also in line with the intentions of the legislature, which were not to reduce lower damages than would otherwise have been recovered.

In *Pritchard*, the Court of Appeal applied this reasoning to trespass to the person. On a review of the authorities, Aikens LJ concluded that contributory negligence had not operated to bar claims in trespass to the person before the reform; and that the statute could not be read as extending to such claims. It is important to note that the reasoning in *Standard Chartered Bank* is not restricted to intentional torts; and should in principle apply to *any* tort to which the defence of contributory negligence did not apply before 1945.

The decision in *Pritchard* means that suggestions in a number of earlier cases, to the effect that contributory negligence is available in relation to battery, are now to be regarded as incorrect. In one of these, the claimant had been participating in a riot, and had been hit by a plastic baton round: *Wasson v Chief Constable of Northern Ireland* [1987] NI 420. In another, Lord Denning MR suggested that damages might be reduced where the deceased had been involved in a violent affray.[39] These authorities will not now be followed.

It has been suggested by James Goudkamp that in a case such as *Pritchard* itself, the better solution is to reduce damages pursuant to the doctrine of 'provocation'.[40] Goudkamp concedes however that the precise status of provocation in tort law is unclear, particularly in relation to compensatory damages.[41]

4. FALSE IMPRISONMENT

False imprisonment consists of unlawful and total physical restraint of the liberty of the claimant, brought about by the defendant. This may be very fleeting, and in *Walker v Commissioner of Police for the Metropolis* [2014] EWCA Civ 897, being confined to a doorway for a few seconds was a false imprisonment. Damages, however, will reflect the

---

[39] *Murphy v Culhane* [1977] QB 94. Alternatively, there may be no damages in such a case, on grounds of illegality: see Chapter 5.

[40] J. Goudkamp, 'Contributory Negligence and Trespass to the Person' (2011) 127 LQR 519.

[41] If provocation is grounds for reducing an award of *punitive* damages, by contrast, this would be unsurprising. Such damages reflect a judgment that the defendant's conduct has been particularly egregious; and the claimant's part in provoking that conduct would naturally affect this judgment.

seriousness of the restraint: in *Walker*, they were assessed at £5. Like the other trespass torts, false imprisonment is actionable per se; and the claimant need not even have been aware of the detention (*Murray v Ministry of Defence* [1988] 2 All ER 521 (a decision of the House of Lords)). However, in the absence of any harm to the claimant, only nominal damages will be available.

In *Bird v Jones* (1845) 7 QB 742, a plaintiff who was prevented by an obstruction from crossing Hammersmith Bridge was *not* 'falsely imprisoned', because he was free to turn back. Equally, it seems that a 'reasonable condition' may be placed on exit from a place which the claimant has voluntarily entered—at least if they have done so in pursuance of a contract and the 'contractual route out' is still open. In *Robinson v Balmain New Ferry* [1910] AC 295, the plaintiff had paid to gain entry to a wharf in order to catch a boat but had changed his mind and sought to make his way out through the turnstile through which he had come in. It was considered reasonable for the defendant to charge a penny for him to leave the wharf.

In *Iqbal v Prison Officers Association* [2009] EWCA Civ 1312; [2010] QB 732, a claim in false imprisonment against a trade union whose members had undertaken an unlawful one-day strike failed. The claimant had been confined to his cell as a consequence of the strike. Members of the Court of Appeal concluded that there was no positive act on the part of the trade union members, Lord Neuberger MR and Smith LJ arguing that this was an essential component of the tort unless there was some particular affirmative duty, in particular where there was a right to be released at the end of a lawful sentence.[42] Equally, the union and its members were not directly responsible for the additional imprisonment of the claimant, despite the fact that it was plainly foreseeable as a result of the strike, and directness too was required; nor did the union or its members wish or intend that the additional confinement would follow. Therefore, the reasoning illustrates the criteria of positive act; direct causation of result; and intention, in relation to this tort.

Smith LJ, *Iqbal v Prison Officers Association*

80 In summary, it appears to me that, although the act required for false imprisonment does not have to be that of physically depriving the claimant of his freedom, it must be an intentional or at least reckless (see above) positive act or, in limited circumstances, omission (see above) and it must be the direct and immediate cause of the loss of liberty.

Lord Neuberger MR suggested that claims involving additional periods of confinement due to the inaction of prison officers would be better confined to the tort of misfeasance in a public office, which we consider at the end of this chapter, and therefore to cases where the inaction was 'deliberate or dishonest'.

In contemporary law, the tort of false imprisonment is most used where police officers are said to have exceeded their powers or where detention in prison exceeds lawful limits.[43] The relationship between trespass to the person and 'unlawfulness' is particularly clear in such cases, and this tort has a strong 'constitutional' element acknowledged by the Supreme

[42] This dealt with the case of *ex p Evans*, extracted in Section 4.1, where there was a false imprisonment consisting of failure to order the claimant's release.

[43] However, a very serious case of false imprisonment in the form of sexual enslavement (forced prostitution) is discussed in Chapter 8 in connection with remedies: *AT v Dulghieru* [2009] EWHC 225 (QB).

Court in *Lumba*. Two elements to the constitutional role of false imprisonment should be noted:

1. The definition of 'lawfulness' of detention will frequently depend upon analysis of powers of arrest and/or detention;

2. Where the defendant is a 'public authority' within the terms of the Human Rights Act 1998, the tort of false imprisonment may coexist with an action for damages in respect of a violation of the Convention right to liberty (Article 5 ECHR): HRA, sections 7 and 8. The scope of Article 5 is broader than the scope of false imprisonment in certain respects, applying for example to failures to *review* imprisonment.

4.1 THE ELEMENTS OF THE TORT

It is generally accepted that, since *Letang v Cooper*, this form of trespass to the person—like the others—must be confined to intentional conduct on the part of the defendant.[44] *Iqbal*, extracted earlier, suggests that the *target* of intention is 'imprisonment', and this would well reflect the position in battery, where the target of intention is the physical contact which is complained of. At the same time, there need be no intention, nor even knowledge, in relation to the unlawfulness of the detention. The next case powerfully illustrates this.

In *R v Governor of Brockhill Prison, ex p Evans* [2001] 2 AC 19, Ms Evans had been sentenced to two years' imprisonment. The governor of Brockhill Prison calculated her release date in a manner which was clearly consistent with judicial decisions interpreting relevant statutory provisions. Doubt was then cast on the judicial rulings, and Ms Evans applied for an order for her release. A subsequent judicial ruling confirmed that the doubts were correct, and an order was made. By this time, the claimant had spent 59 days too long in captivity. The House of Lords held that the prison governor was liable in damages for false imprisonment. The gist of the tort is unlawfulness, *not* inappropriate conduct. Detention for those additional days was now known to have been unlawful, even if the governor could not have been aware of that at the time.

Ex p Evans was distinguished by the Court of Appeal in the case of *Quinland v Governor of Swaleside Prison and Others* [2003] QB 306, applying the (pre-*Evans*) case of *Olutu v Home Office* [1997] 1 WLR 103. In each of these cases, a prison governor detained a prisoner pursuant to a court order requiring detention. By these orders, the governor was not permitted to release the prisoner until the stated date. In *ex p Evans* by contrast, the governor himself had calculated the release date. In *Quinland* and *Olutu*, the existence of the court order was found to 'justify' the continued detention of the prisoner, by the governor. He did not commit a tort.

R (Lumba) v Secretary of State for the Home Department [2011] UKSC 12; [2012] 1 AC 245 provides a contrast with *ex p Evans*. Its background is the adoption by the Secretary of State of an unlawful, blanket policy of detention for all foreign nationals at the end of their prison terms. No change in the published policy was made to reflect this, from its adoption in 2006 until 2008, and it remained not only undisclosed, but also concealed, as officers were instructed to give false reasons (consistent with the published policy) for their decisions.[45]

---

[44] F. A. Trindade, 'The Modern Tort of False Imprisonment', in N. J. Mullaney (ed.), *Torts in the Nineties* (LBC, 1997), contrasts English with Australian and New Zealand law in this respect.

[45] This is highlighted as the 'most disturbing' feature of the case by Baroness Hale in her judgment, who nevertheless had some sympathy with the government in light of tabloid complaints about release of foreign nationals at the end of their term of imprisonment.

Its existence was revealed only as the consequence of judicial review proceedings brought by two of the tort claimants. Applying a policy inconsistent with the published policy was unlawful. Two further questions of law arose in relation to claims in false imprisonment.

First, is there a false imprisonment where a claimant is unlawfully detained, but where (on the balance of evidence) they *would have remained in prison even if the lawful policy had been applied*? This goes to the requirements of the tort of false imprisonment and can be called the 'liability question'.

Second, if there is a false imprisonment here, what damages are available to the claimant? This may be called the 'damages question'.

It is only when these questions are looked at together that we can really answer the question of whether the tort of false imprisonment protects against arbitrary and unlawful decisions and actions (consistent with its alleged character as a 'constitutional tort'); or whether it simply protects against deprivations of liberty. As a preliminary point, it should be pointed out that it is well settled that detention *itself* is sufficient 'harm' to form the subject of a claim for damages.[46] The fact that there is no simple way of calculating how much money to award for deprivation of liberty per se is not to the point. The question was, rather, whether detention pursuant to an unlawful process could be the subject of damages where *lawful* detention would otherwise have followed, so that the unlawful action had not 'caused' a loss of liberty at all.

It is for this reason that the court considered the possibility of 'vindicatory' damages. These are not necessarily needed as a separate head of damages in a case of loss of liberty, because the compensatory award will also vindicate the claimant's right. The question is whether damages, whether they are called 'compensatory' or 'vindicatory', are available to protect against *arbitrary* detention in its own right. Quite simply, does common law compensate violations of rights, or does it only compensate for consequent harm, including deprivation of liberty?

Understanding the decision in *Lumba* is made more difficult by the way that the nine-judge panel split in relation to the key questions. On the liability question, six of the nine judges decided that a false imprisonment may be committed even where, as here, the unlawful action is not causative of imprisonment: false imprisonment is actionable *per se*. On the damages question, a different six judges might appear to have agreed that in these circumstances, only nominal damages were recoverable for the false imprisonment. But this is not the case. Three of these six judges thought there was no false imprisonment at all, and two of them (Lord Brown, and Lord Rodger) expressly rejected the idea of nominal damages for a false imprisonment. In fact they argued that such damages would 'devalue the tort'. They joined the majority in refusing the damages claimed, but for reasons which are actually inconsistent with the supposed ratio.[47] Since they also rejected the idea of nominal damages, it seems *there was no majority* on the damages question. Only three of the nine judges supported both aspects of the result.

---

[46] This can be illustrated by reference to the torts of both malicious prosecution and misfeasance in a public office, discussed later. Both of these are torts which require damage, and in each case imprisonment itself may clearly be the relevant damage.

[47] Readers may find it interesting to refer to A. Burrows, 'Numbers Sitting in the Supreme Court' (2013) 129 LQR 305. The article seeks the thinking behind the growing practice of using panels of more than five judges in the highest court, and is sceptical of its value. One of the reasons reviewed is that where decisions are reached by a bare majority, there may be a feeling that with a different panel, a different result might have followed. The presence of a nine-judge panel in *Lumba* appears to have exacerbated this problem, rather than resolving it.

Lord Kerr, Lumba. Lord Kerr was in the majority both on the liability question, and on the damages question—there was a false imprisonment, but only nominal damages would be awarded.

239 False imprisonment is established if there has been a detention and an absence of lawful authority justifying it. The question whether lawful authority exists is to be determined according to an objective standard. It either exists or it does not. It is for this elementary—but also fundamental—reason that a causation test can have no place in the decision whether imprisonment is false or lawful. By a "causation test" in this context I mean a test which involves an examination of whether the persons held in custody could have been lawfully detained. The fact that a person *could have been lawfully* detained says nothing on the question whether he was lawfully detained.

240 The Court of Appeal in the present case decided that, since the claimants could have been detained lawfully had the published policy been applied to them, the fact that an unpublished and unlawful policy was in fact applied was immaterial. With great respect, this cannot be right. The unpublished policy was employed in the decision to detain the appellants. It was clearly material to the decision to detain. Indeed, it was the foundation for that decision. An ex post facto conclusion that, had the proper policy been applied, the appellants would have been lawfully detained cannot alter that essential fact.

...

242 It is, I believe, important to recognise that lawful detention has two aspects. First the decision to detain must be lawful in the sense that it has a sound legal basis and, secondly, it must *justify* the detention. This second aspect has found expression in a large number of judgments, perhaps most succinctly in the speech of Lord Hope in *R v Governor of Brockhill Prison Ex p Evans (No 2)* [2001] 2 AC 19, 32 d where he said "it is of the essence of the tort of false imprisonment that the imprisonment is without lawful justification". It seems to me to be self evident that the justification must relate to the basis on which the detainer has purported to act, and not depend on some abstract grounds wholly different from the actual reasons for detaining. As Mr Husain put it, the emphasis here must be on the right of the detained person not to be detained other than on a lawful basis which justifies the detention. Detention cannot be justified on some putative basis, unrelated to the actual reasons for it, on which the detention might retrospectively be said to be warranted. Simply because some ground for lawfully detaining may exist but has not been resorted to by the detaining authority, the detention cannot be said, on that account, to be lawful.

...it is nothing to the point in this case that if the decision had been taken on the basis of the published policy, it would have been immune from challenge. As Professor Cane put it in "The Temporal Element in Law" (2001) 117 LQR 5, 7 "imprisonment can never be justified unless *actually* [as opposed to hypothetically] authorised by law". (The emphasis and the words enclosed in square brackets are mine.)

...

256 ...The defendant's failures have been thoroughly examined and exposed. A finding that those failures have led to the false imprisonment of the appellants constitutes a fully adequate acknowledgement of the defendant's default. Since the appellants would have been lawfully detained if the published policy had been applied to them, I agree that no more than a nominal award of damages is appropriate in their cases.

Baroness Hale, *Lumba*. Baroness Hale was in the majority on the liability question, but in the minority on the damages question: she would have awarded more than nominal damages.

217 ...no one can deny that the right to be free from arbitrary imprisonment by the state is of fundamental constitutional importance in this country. It is not the less important because we do not have a written constitution. It is a right which the law should be able to vindicate in some way, irrespective of whether compensatable harm has been suffered or the conduct of the authorities has been so egregious as to merit exemplary damages. Left to myself, therefore, I would mark the false imprisonment in these cases with a modest conventional sum, perhaps £500 rather than the £1,000 suggested by Lord Walker JSC, designed to recognise that the claimant's fundamental constitutional rights have been breached by the State and to encourage all concerned to avoid anything like it happening again. In reality, this may well be what was happening in the older cases of false imprisonment, before the assessment of damages became such a refined science.

The final point made by Baroness Hale is instructive. Any idea of 'vindicatory' damages here may well be a distraction, suggesting some form of *additional* head of damages to reflect constitutional impropriety. Instead, damages for torts actionable per se may inherently vindicate rights, a fact which is less evident because generally the tort *does* lead to a loss of liberty.

Lord Brown (with whom Lord Rodger agreed), *Lumba*. Lords Brown and Rodger dissented on the liability question, and would have awarded no damages.

341 "Freedom from executive detention is arguably the most fundamental right of all". Thus Lord Bingham of Cornhill in his 2002 Romanes lecture. The tort of false imprisonment is, of course, the remedy provided by law for the violation of this freedom, for the unlawful deprivation of a person's liberty. The outcome of the appeals proposed by the majority of the court is to hold the appellants—and, indeed, a large number of others similarly placed—to have been unlawfully detained, in many instances for a period of years, and yet to compensate them by no more than a nominal award of damages. They are to be held unlawfully detained because, in his (or her) exercise of the undoubted power to detain them, the Secretary of State breached certain public law duties. But they are to be awarded only nominal damages because, whatever approach had been taken to the exercise of the detaining power, the appellants must inevitably have been detained in any event.

342 Whilst I share to the full the majority's conclusion that it would be quite wrong in the circumstances of these cases to award the appellants any substantial compensation in respect of their detention, for my part I would reach that conclusion by a very different route. I would hold that a public law breach of duty in the course of exercising an executive power of detention does not invariably, and did not here, result in the subsequent detention itself being unlawful—in short, that these appellants were not the victims of false imprisonment.

343 ...Why should someone imprisoned without lawful justification be paid nominal damages only? If the answer is that they would have been imprisoned anyway, under the same power and in just the same way, then in reality the court is saying that the tort may be committed merely in a technical way. I have to say that such an approach would to my mind seriously devalue the whole concept of false imprisonment.

Lord Brown refers to a merely 'technical' false imprisonment, where no additional detention results. But it is arguable that to be subject to an arbitrary exercise of power is not merely a technical 'wrong.' If comparing torts actionable per se with liability under the HRA, it is arguable that the decision is a missed opportunity to reassert the traditional capacity of common law torts to remedy invasions of fundamental rights. We return to this comparison at the end of the section. First however, we should note some objections to the decision in *Lumba*.

A Ruck Keene and C Dobson, 'At What Price Liberty?' The Supreme Court Decision in *Lumba* and Compensation for False Imprisonment' (2012) PL 628

… Understanding that the right to freedom from executive detention is a right to procedural protections against arbitrary detention rather than a right to liberty itself is key to determining what relief ought to be available in order to vindicate that right.

If that approach is taken, then at the very least relief must be such as to acknowledge that harm is caused where there has been a failure strictly to adhere to the procedural requirements for detention, regardless of whether the decision to detain would have been the same if taken in accordance with the law. To suggest that an individual suffers no harm where the decision to detain would have been the same if taken in accordance with the law might be said to erode a fundamental distinction between arbitrary and lawful detention.

Access to the courts to challenge the legality of executive detention is also critical to the vindication of the right to liberty. The cause of action in false imprisonment is the principal means for an individual to challenge the legality of historic detention once released. The ability to bring an action in false imprisonment often depends on the availability of public funding. Our experience already is that claims that would previously had been brought in the mental health field are no longer being advanced because of the likelihood that only nominal damages could be recovered, such that they cannot now satisfy the cost-benefit criteria established by the Legal Services Commission. (The Administrative Court has already indicated that individuals should not pursue claims in false imprisonment unless they are likely to achieve substantive damages: see *R. (on the application of Betteridge) v The Parole Board* [2009] EWHC 1638 (Admin); *R. (on the application of Degainis) v The Secretary of State for Justice* [2010] EWHC 137 (Admin) at [15] and [22].)

Furthermore, it is not fanciful, we suggest, that devaluing the cost of non-compliance in monetary terms carries with it the risk that procedural rules will not be respected. (In this regard, see *Law Commission Consultation Paper No.187, Administrative Redress: Public Bodies and the Citizen, Appendix B*, particularly at para.B.10.) The potential chilling effect on litigation combined with the fact that public bodies may now be able to avoid an award of substantial damages risks creating a culture in which arbitrary detention can occur with impunity…

Further Limits to False Imprisonment, and Comparison with HRA Remedies

As we have seen, *Sidaway* confirmed the view that consent based on broad understanding of the nature of medical treatment was sufficient to exclude a claim in battery. In *Hague v Deputy Governor of Parkhurst Prison and Others* [1992] 1 AC 58, the House of Lords held that a lawful detention did not become unlawful when the *conditions* of detention were in breach of applicable Prison Rules.[48] False imprisonment is not the proper route to take in order to gain compensation where conditions of detention are unacceptable. That does not mean that there is no source of compensation in such a case. There may be an action for breach of statutory duty; in negligence; for misfeasance in a public office; or under the HRA. For example in *Karagozlu v Commissioner of Police for the Metropolis* [2006] EWCA Civ 1691, loss of 'residual' liberty was held to be actionable damage for the tort of misfeasance in a public office (Section 8.2 of this chapter: here the claimant was transferred from open to closed prison).

The right to 'liberty' is also protected by Article 5 ECHR. Article 5 is a complex provision with more than one aspect. We extract Article 5(1), which is the most general of the provisions, when we discuss *Austin v Saxby* later in this section. Further provisions relate to the conduct of arrest and detention, while Article 5(5) appears to set out a general right to compensation for violation of the Article. Of immediate interest is Article 5(4):

Article 5(4), European Convention on Human Rights

4. Everyone who is deprived of his liberty by arrest or detention shall be entitled to take proceedings by which the lawfulness of his detention shall be decided speedily by a court and his release ordered if the detention is not lawful.

Article 5 therefore includes certain *procedural* rights in relation to liberty. In *Lumba*, as we have seen, application of an unlawful procedure did not justify an award of more than nominal damages at common law, unless it led to a loss of liberty. But in a series of decisions relating to claims by prisoners, not only have *damages* been awarded under the HRA in circumstances where there would clearly be no action for false imprisonment at common law, but this has included cases of delay in relation to parole hearings, irrespective of any loss of residual liberty. These claims have given rise to awards of relatively modest, but not purely 'nominal' damages, both in cases involving a change in the conditions of detention ('residual liberty' cases), and in cases where it is not established that any difference to the period or nature of detention resulted. The remedy is not for the unlawful delay itself, but for the impact of that delay on the claimant.[49] This impact may include feelings of stress and frustration, which would not ground a compensation claim at common law. Taking into account both the limits on false imprisonment set out in cases such as *Hague*, and the application of a causation test to compensatory damages in *Lumba*, it has become much harder to maintain that false imprisonment operates satisfactorily as a constitutional tort, protecting against abuse of power—despite Lord Walker's reference to 'the pride that English law has taken for centuries in protecting the liberty of the subject against arbitrary executive action'.[50] Being subject to such action is not itself a harm to be remedied by damages. It is certainly not that the common law is unable to accommodate 'conventional' awards.[51] But *Lumba* suggests that tort compensates only for a certain

---

[48] See also *Cullen v Chief Constable of RUC* [2003] 1 WLR 1763: detention lawful at its inception would not become unlawful through breach of codes of conduct.

[49] *R (Faulkner) v Parole Board* [2013] UKSC 23; [2013] 2 WLR 1157, on the proper approach to damages in such cases, is discussed in Chapter 8.

[50] *Lumba*, [181].

[51] Apart from *ex p Evans* (Section 4.1), and other false imprisonment cases, see the discussion of *Rees v Darlington* (Chapter 6); and of damages for death (Chapter 8).

range of consequences, and not for breaches of rights per se. For many, this will be a disappointing conclusion.

We further explore the question of HRA damages, and of vindicatory damages, in Chapter 8.

Lawfulness and Justification

The cases in the previous section turn on lawfulness of detention, and justification for detention. In *ex p Evans*, Lord Hope said (at 32):

> The tort of false imprisonment is a tort of strict liability. But the strict theory of civil liability is not inconsistent with the idea that in certain circumstances the harm complained of may have been inflicted justifiably. This is because it is of the essence of the tort of false imprisonment that the imprisonment is without lawful justification.

Lord Hope describes lack of 'lawful justification' as being 'of the essence of the tort'. This recalls our discussion of consent in respect of the tort of battery, where we noted that in *Freeman v Home Office (No 2)*, it was held that lack of consent, being central to the definition of the tort of battery, was for the claimant to establish.[52] Is the same true of lack of 'lawful justification' in false imprisonment? Must the *claimant* show that the imprisonment was unjustified?

In *Austin and Saxby v Commissioner of Police of the Metropolis* [2005] EWHC 480, a case where police officers had detained a number of protestors for seven hours in Oxford Circus in an attempt to preserve order and prevent violence, Tugendhat J suggested otherwise:

> **157** In a claim for false imprisonment the burden of proof clearly rests upon the claimant to prove the imprisonment, and (subject to one point) upon the defendant to prove the justification for it. . . .

This seems to suggest that justification is to be treated as a defence.

The 'one point' which qualifies this was important, however. Here the officers 'detained' the claimants without arresting them, on the basis of a reasonable suspicion of a threat which might justify that detention. The burden of proof was then regarded as falling on the claimant to show that this *exercise of discretion was unreasonable*.[53] The Court of Appeal agreed with Tugendhat J on these points: *Austin & Saxby v Commissioner of Police of the Metropolis* [2007] EWCA Civ 989, at [70]. The relevant defence was referred to in terms of 'necessity'. In this case, necessity was established.

There was a further appeal to the House of Lords ([2009] UKHL 5; [2009] 1 AC 564). The appeal was occupied solely with Article 5 ECHR, though this was treated as relevant to the tort claim because of a concession on the part of the claimant, mentioned at para [11] of the House of Lords' judgment: 'the appellant accepts that, if her detention did not amount to an unlawful deprivation of liberty contrary to article 5(1), she was contained within the cordon in the lawful exercise of police powers'. This does not seem to be at all consistent

52 We also suggested that the approach in *Freeman* may have been wrong.
53 On this point, Tugendhat J followed *Al Fayed v Metropolitan Police Commissioner* [2004] EWCA Civ 1579.

with the analysis of the Court of Appeal, and it may be that it was made for tactical reasons.[54] The Article 5 claim, like the false imprisonment claim, failed. We will extract the judgments of the Court of Appeal, and then the House of Lords. The relevance of the House of Lords' decision for tort law depends on the validity of the concession, and this is doubtful. Therefore, the Court of Appeal's judgment continues to be of relevance.

Austin & Saxby in the Court of Appeal: False Imprisonment

Austin & Saxby v Commissioner of Police of the Metropolis [2007] EWCA Civ 989 (CA)

The Court of Appeal considered that for the purposes of the tort of false imprisonment, the claimants clearly had been 'imprisoned' in a relevant sense: they were kept behind a cordon for seven hours with no opportunity to leave. The court also took the view that necessity could provide a defence to a claim for false imprisonment. In this case, the limits of necessity would be equated with the limits to the power to act to prevent a breach of the peace. This power had been strictly defined by the House of Lords shortly before in *R (Laporte) v Chief Constable of Gloucestershire Constabulary* [2006] UKHL 55; [2007] 2 AC 105, and required that the anticipated breach must be 'imminent'.[55]

Sir Anthony Clarke MR, Austin v Commissioner of Police of the Metropolis

62 ... If the claimants did not appear to be about to commit a breach of the peace, was their containment lawful?

63 The judge held that the answer to this question was "No". He did so on the basis to which we have already referred, namely that, unless the question whether a particular claimant was about to commit a breach of the peace was answered in the affirmative, the case against that claimant based on powers to prevent a breach of the peace must fail: para 520.

64 Mr Pannick nevertheless invites an affirmative answer to this question. He does so on the basis of the obiter reasoning in *Laporte*'s case [2007] 2 AC 105 discussed above, which was not of course available to the judge. He submits that on the judge's findings of fact a breach of the peace was reasonably thought by the police to be imminent, that the police had taken all the steps which they possibly could to avoid a breach of the peace by those likely to cause it by arrest or other action directed at them and that, in all the circumstances, if a breach of the peace was to be avoided, there was no alternative but to contain everyone within a police cordon. As to release, no alternative strategy was possible, or indeed suggested, other than that adopted by the police and, in these circumstances, the containment of some innocent people such as the claimants was inevitable and lawful in accordance with the principles discussed earlier and summarised, at para 35 above. In short, Mr Pannick submits that, on the findings of fact made by the judge, the situation was wholly exceptional and that the police had no alternative but to do what they did in order to avoid the imminent

---

[54] Perhaps the claimant wished to narrow the range of issues to be determined, in order to smooth her path to Strasbourg and the European Court of Human Rights; or perhaps this was simply a question of reciprocal concessions.

[55] False imprisonment was not considered by the House of Lords in *Laporte*, in which passengers on a coach were prevented from joining a demonstration (see the discussion of *Bird v Jones*, earlier in Section 4). But the police action in preventing attendance at the demonstration was held to be unlawful.

risk of serious violence, with its consequent risk of serious injury and perhaps death, quite apart from damage to property.

....

67 While we see the force of the points made by Mr Starmer, especially his point that the containment of the crowd for hours without any or any sufficient toilet facilities and in many cases without food or drink was intolerable, with consequent risk to the health and safety of innocent members of the public, and we can well understand that being in Oxford Circus for so long without any idea when one would be released would have been very unpleasant, we see no realistic alternative but to accept Mr Pannick's submission in response. It is that the judge properly held that the police could not reasonably have foreseen what happened or that it would have been necessary to have contained people for so long. The judge held that the police took action to avoid or minimise the risk of crushing: paras 371 and 376.

68 For these reasons, we conclude that in this very exceptional case, on the basis of the judge's finding that what the police did in containing the crowd was necessary in order to avoid an imminent breach of the peace, the actions of the police were lawful at common law in accordance with the principles discussed above. On that basis, we answer the question whether the containment was lawful in the affirmative, even though the police did not reasonably suspect that the individual claimants were about to commit a breach of the peace. In our judgment that was the case, both when the cordon was imposed at about 2.20 p m and throughout the time the cordon was maintained. On the judge's findings of fact, the conditions of necessity remained throughout because no one had or has suggested an alternative release policy.

In effect, dicta in *Laporte* which were intended to define very narrowly the circumstances in which 'bystanders' (people not themselves threatening a breach of the peace) could have their freedom of movement curtailed, were used to create and define a defence of necessity, equated with lawful exercise of police powers, to an action in tort on the part of such individuals. The claimants then faced an insuperable hurdle: they could only succeed by showing that in their own individual cases, the failure to release them was '*Wednesbury* unreasonable'. This is a public law concept and is much more demanding than the idea of reasonableness ordinarily applied in the law of tort.

The following extract sets out the circumstances in which the Court of Appeal took it that people could be detained:

Sir Anthony Clarke MR, *Austin v Commissioner of Police of the Metropolis* (CA)

35 As we read the speeches of Lord Rodger and Lord Brown [in *Laporte*] they give some support for the following propositions: (i) where a breach of the peace is taking place, or is reasonably thought to be imminent, before the police can take any steps which interfere with or curtail in any way the lawful exercise of rights by innocent third parties they must ensure that they have taken all other possible steps to ensure that the breach, or imminent breach, is obviated and that the rights of innocent third parties are protected; (ii) the taking of all other possible steps includes (where practicable), but is not limited to, ensuring that proper and advance preparations have been made to deal with such a breach, since failure to take such steps will render interference with the rights of innocent third parties unjustified or unjustifiable; but (iii) where (and only where) there is a reasonable belief that there are no other means whatsoever whereby a breach or imminent breach of the peace can be obviated, the lawful exercise by third parties of their rights may be curtailed by the police; (iv) this is a test of necessity which it is to be expected can only be justified in truly extreme and exceptional circumstances; and (v) the action taken must be both reasonably necessary and proportionate.

The reference to necessary and proportionate action is familiar from the ECHR, though the Court of Appeal preferred to separate discussion of tort and Convention rights. The approach to the issues relating to Article 5 was itself controversial. As we have seen, it was thought that 'imprisonment' for the purposes of tort was established, but justified by necessity. Yet where Article 5 ECHR was concerned, the court found that there was no 'deprivation of liberty' at all. This finding was challenged before the House of Lords; but was upheld.

Austin and Article 5: The House of Lords and European Court of Human Rights
Austin v Metropolitan Police Commissioner [2009] 1 AC 564 (HL)

The conclusion of both Court of Appeal and House of Lords that for the purposes of Article 5(1) there was no 'deprivation of liberty' in this case (rather than a deprivation of liberty that required justifying) may seem very strange. The key to understanding it lies in the lack of any general exception to the Article 5 right.

Article 5 ECHR

(1) Everyone has the right to liberty and security of person. No one shall be deprived of his liberty save in the following cases and in accordance with a procedure prescribed by law: (a) the lawful detention of a person after conviction by a competent court; (b) the lawful arrest or detention of a person for non-compliance with the lawful order of a court or in order to secure the fulfilment of any obligation prescribed by law; (c) the lawful arrest or detention of a person effected for the purpose of bringing him before the competent legal authority on reasonable suspicion of having committed an offence or when it is reasonably considered necessary to prevent his committing an offence or fleeing after having done so; (d) the detention of a minor by lawful order for the purpose of educational supervision or his lawful detention for the purpose of bringing him before the competent legal authority; (e) the lawful detention of persons for the prevention of the spreading of infectious diseases, of persons of unsound mind, alcoholics or drug addicts or vagrants; (f) the lawful arrest or detention of a person to prevent his effecting an unauthorised entry into the country or of a person against whom action is being taken with a view to deportation or extradition.

Article 5(1) lists exhaustively the reasons why an individual may be deprived of their liberty. None of these would cover the case in hand. Therefore, a police action which had been found to be 'necessary' at common law within the terms of *Laporte* would violate Article 5 unless the House of Lords held—as it did—that the Article was simply not engaged in circumstances where the action was justified. The Article was said to be aimed only at 'arbitrary' deprivations of liberty. Otherwise, Lord Hope argued, there would be a conflict with competing rights, such as those in Article 2 (right to life),[56] and a need to ensure 'fair balance' between individual and collective interests was read into the Article on the basis that this is

[56] The state, and the police force, are under a positive duty to act to protect the life of citizens, including protection from the crimes of others: *Osman v UK* (Chapter 6, Section 3).

inherent to the Convention as a whole. Pragmatism and fair balance were seen as relevant factors even here, where there is no indication to this effect in the wording of the Article.

Lord Hope, *Austin v Metropolitan Police Commissioner* (HL)

34 I would hold therefore that there is room, even in the case of fundamental rights as to whose application no restriction or limitation is permitted by the Convention, for a pragmatic approach to be taken which takes full account of all the circumstances. No reference is made in article 5 to the interests of public safety or the protection of public order as one of the cases in which a person may be deprived of his liberty. This is in sharp contrast to article 10(2), which expressly qualifies the right to freedom of expression in these respects. But the importance that must be attached in the context of article 5 to measures taken in the interests of public safety is indicated by article 2 of the Convention, as the lives of persons affected by mob violence may be at risk if measures of crowd control cannot be adopted by the police. This is a situation where a search for a fair balance is necessary if these competing fundamental rights are to be reconciled with each other. The ambit that is given to article 5 as to measures of crowd control must, of course, take account of the rights of the individual as well as the interests of the community. So any steps that are taken must be resorted to in good faith and must be proportionate to the situation which has made the measures necessary. This is essential to preserve the fundamental principle that anything that is done which affects a person's right to liberty must not be arbitrary. If these requirements are met however it will be proper to conclude that measures of crowd control that are undertaken in the interests of the community will not infringe the article 5 rights of individual members of the crowd whose freedom of movement is restricted by them.

The decision of the House of Lords has been strongly criticized. In particular, David Feldman suggests that pragmatism and individual rights are not so easily reconciled and often 'pull in opposite directions': D. Feldman, 'Containment, Deprivation of Liberty and Breach of the Peace' (2009) 68 CLJ 243–5. One would have thought that this is indeed part of the point of statements of fundamental rights and freedoms—the most fundamental of them are stated without general exceptions because they should be respected irrespective of pragmatism. Balance and proportionality have been used in the developing 'privacy tort' (Chapter 14), but proportionality and balance are inherent in Articles 8 and 10 as we will see; and not, on the face of it, to Article 5. On this point, the necessity of balancing other Convention rights, employed by Lord Hope, is of particular significance.

Despite these criticisms, in *Austin and Others v UK* (3692/09), 15 March 2012, the Grand Chamber of the European Court of Human Rights reached a decision that was largely consistent with the approach taken by the House of Lords. The Chamber agreed that outside the paradigm case of confinement in a cell, Article 5 must be applied within the context of the Convention as a whole. Especially pertinent are the positive obligations imposed upon states to protect safety within Articles 2 and 3. On this basis, where action was taken in order to protect other Convention rights, there had been no violation of Article 5(1). The decision was a majority one; the minority judges thought they detected illegitimate recourse to 'public interest' arguments in the approach of the majority. The truth is, weighing rights of other members of the public, and restricting rights pursuant to a public interest, are not easily distinguished.[57]

---

[57] For criticism of the Grand Chamber's decision, see N. Oreb (2013) 76 MLR 735. A balancing approach has also been taken in justifying a use of tort remedies against protestors who are interfering with the

People Lacking Capacity

The Mental Health Act 2007 introduced a number of amendments and additions to the Mental Capacity Act 2005 (MCA), dealing with the deprivation of liberty of people who lack capacity. Once again, Convention rights were an influencing factor: the amendments were provoked by the decision of the European Court of Human Rights in *HL v UK* (2005) 40 EHRR 32, finding the UK in violation of Article 5 where an adult lacking capacity and who was notionally free to leave a psychiatric facility had nevertheless been unlawfully deprived of his liberty. His movements were closely tracked; those outside with whom he had had contact were discouraged from visiting him in case he attempted to leave; and he would be 'sectioned' if he tried to do so. The House of Lords had previously held in *R(L) v Bournewood Community and NHS Trust* [1999] 1 AC 458 that this did not amount to a false imprisonment under domestic law, so that there was clearly a shortfall in protection. The new provisions are lengthy and complex (indeed they have been described as 'hideously and needlessly complicated').[58] In essence, they apply to people lacking capacity and deprived of their liberty in hospitals or care homes.[59] They provide that a supervisory body or local authority will need to be informed of the deprivation of liberty so that it can ensure that the provisions of the MCA are followed, and that individuals will be appointed to be consulted on the best interests of the individual concerned, and to maintain contact with and represent that person, respectively. Since these provisions are essentially designed to ensure compatibility with the state's obligations under Article 5 ECHR, their detailed operation lies beyond the reach of this text. However, it is worth noting that courts have found it particularly challenging to set the boundary between deprivation of liberty (which would engage Article 5), and mere 'restriction' of liberty. For an account of where the law stands, see the decision of the Supreme Court in *Cheshire West and Chester Council v P* [2014] UKSC 19, holding that the living arrangements for certain mentally incapacitated adults *did* amount to a deprivation of liberty.

5. INTENTIONAL INFLICTION OF PHYSICAL OR MENTAL HARM

Wright J, *Wilkinson v Downton*
[1897] 2 QB 57

In this case the defendant, in the execution of what he seems to have regarded as a practical joke, represented to the plaintiff that he was charged by her husband with a message to her to the effect that her husband was smashed up in an accident, and was lying at The Elms at Leytonstone with both legs broken, and that she was to go at once in a cab with two pillows to fetch him home. All this was false. The effect of the statement on the plaintiff

Convention and other rights of landowners and the public: *Mayor of London v Samede* [2012] EWCA Civ 160 (clearing a protest camp in St Paul's churchyard). But such cases do not engage Art. 5.

[58] P. Bartlett, *Blackstone's Guide to the Mental Capacity Act 2005*, (2nd edn, 2008), at 4.05.
[59] For a case of false imprisonment outside this context, where the provisions of the Mental Capacity Act 2005 were applied and damages awarded, see *H v Commissioner of Police of the Metropolis* [2013] EWCA Civ 69.

was a violent shock to her nervous system, producing vomiting and other more serious and permanent physical consequences at one time threatening her reason, and entailing weeks of suffering and incapacity to her as well as expense to her husband for medical attendance. These consequences were not in any way the result of previous ill-health or weakness of constitution; nor was there any evidence of predisposition to nervous shock or any other idiosyncrasy.

... The defendant has, as I assume for the moment, wilfully done an act calculated to cause physical harm to the plaintiff—that is to say, to infringe her legal right to personal safety, and has in fact thereby caused physical harm to her. That proposition without more appears to me to state a good cause of action, there being no justification alleged for the act. This wilful injuria is in law malicious, although no malicious purpose to cause the harm which was caused nor any motive of spite is imputed to the defendant.

It remains to consider whether the assumptions involved in the proposition are made out. One question is whether the defendant's act was so plainly calculated to produce some effect of the kind which was produced that an intention to produce it ought to be imputed to the defendant, regard being had to the fact that the effect was produced on a person proved to be in an ordinary state of health and mind. I think that it was. It is difficult to imagine that such a statement, made suddenly and with apparent seriousness, could fail to produce grave effects under the circumstances upon any but an exceptionally indifferent person, and therefore an intention to produce such an effect must be imputed, and it is no answer in law to say that more harm was done than was anticipated, for that is commonly the case with all wrongs. The other question is whether the effect was, to use the ordinary phrase, too remote to be in law regarded as a consequence for which the defendant is answerable. Apart from authority, I should give the same answer and on the same ground as the last question, and say that it was not too remote ...

Wilkinson v Downton is our first example of an action which depends on showing *intentionally caused harm*. The target of intention in *Wilkinson v Downton* is harm (including distress) to the claimant. In fact, it is a tort both of *intention*, and of *damage*. The damage caused must be more than mere distress: physical injury or recognized psychiatric illness is required, so that the required damage and the target of intention do not match precisely: While the tort has for most of its career been named purely by reference to *Wilkinson v Downton*, the Supreme Court in *OPO v Rhodes* has referred to it as **the tort of wilful infringement of the claimant's right to personal safety**, emphasizing both of these requirements (Baroness Hale and Lord Toulson at [81]). Most of the 'economic torts' (Section 7) also require both intention and damage. That comparison was clearly in the mind of Wright J, since the claimant attempted to argue the case in 'deceit' (one of the economic torts). Deceit requires that the defendant made *a false statement, with the intention that the claimant should rely upon that statement to her detriment.* There was a false statement in this case, and the plaintiff was able to claim in deceit for her bus fare to the scene of the supposed accident. But the basis of liability in deceit is that *a person who makes a false statement intended to be acted on must make good the damage naturally resulting from its being acted on.* The plaintiff's physical injury flowed from *believing* the statement, but *not* from acting upon it.

If the claim did not fall within the action for deceit, then the main obstacle to its success was the restrictive decision in *Victorian Railways Commissioners v Coultas* (1888) 13 App Cas 222. This decision had treated psychiatric harm suffered as a result of a railway accident as unrecoverable for being 'too remote'. That case, Wright J reasoned, could be distinguished because it did not concern a '*wilful*' act. In fact, change soon followed.[60] Arguably, it was the need to distinguish *Coultas* at the time of *Wilkinson v Downton* which explains Wright J's emphasis on the damage as 'wilful'.

In the recent case of *OPO v Rhodes* [2015] UKSC 32, the Supreme Court considered the action in *Wilkinson v Downton*. Success of the claimant before the Court of Appeal was considered problematic, partly because the claimant's goal was to prevent publication of the defendant's autobiography. Her argument was that its stark and hard-hitting style and its revelations about the author's early life would cause harm to their psychologically vulnerable son. The Supreme Court responded by emphasizing the value of freedom of speech and constraining the range of application of the tort in certain respects.

The elements of the tort were broken down by the Supreme Court into three: the conduct element; the required mental element (what form of 'intention' will suffice?); and the consequence element (what type of harm is required). The last of these was not in issue in *OPO*, but members of the Supreme Court commented on it nonetheless. The three elements are used here to explore the ambit of the tort.

The Conduct Element

As we have seen, in *Wilkinson v Downton*, a false statement was made, without justification, and directly to the claimant. However, Wright J seems to have categorized the conduct involved, in the extract above, as merely 'wilfully doing an act', though without justification. There is no sense that this should be confined to speech. *OPO* too involved words, but was a very different case, where a book was to be published to the world at large, whose contents were truthful and whose publication was clearly justified both in the sense that it concerned the author's own life; and in the sense that there were public interest reasons why it should be published. The book starkly detailed the abuse suffered by the author from the age of six, the impact this had on his life, and the way he had found salvation in music, forming a successful career as a concert pianist. The majority of the Supreme Court thought that 'words or conduct' could suffice; but the words in this instance did not fit the conduct element of the tort for two reasons. First, the words were not 'directed to' the child (though the book was dedicated to him and contained one passage addressing him); second, publication was far from unjustified.

Baroness Hale and Lord Toulson, *OPO v Rhodes*

74 The conduct element requires words or conduct directed towards the claimant for which there is no justification or reasonable excuse, and the burden of proof is on the claimant. We are concerned in this case with the curtailment of freedom of speech, which gives rise to its own particular considerations. We agree with the approach of the Court of Appeal in regarding the tort as confined to those towards whom the relevant words or conduct were directed, but they may be a group. A person who shouts "fire" in a cinema, when there is no

[60] *Bell v Great Northern Railway Company of Ireland* (1890) 26 LR Ir 428, mentioned by Wright J, had already declined to follow *Coultas* in Ireland; within a few years, a barmaid put in fear for her safety was able to claim for the consequences in English law: *Dulieu v White* [1901] 2 KB 669 (see further Chapter 6, Section 1). In *OPO v Rhodes*, however, Baroness Hale pointed out that *Dulieu* would not have covered the outcome in *Wilkinson v Downton*, as it would have required the trigger to be fear for oneself.

fire, is addressing himself to the audience. In the present case the Court of Appeal treated the publication of the book as conduct directed towards the claimant and considered that the question of justification had therefore to be judged vis-à-vis him. In this respect we consider that they erred.

75 The book is for a wide audience and the question of justification has to be considered accordingly, not in relation to the claimant in isolation. In point of fact, the father's case is that although the book is dedicated to the claimant, he would not expect him to see it until he is much older. Arden LJ said that the father could not be heard to say that he did not intend the book to reach the child, since it was dedicated to him and some parts of it are addressed to him. We have only found one passage addressed to him, which is in the acknowledgments, but more fundamentally we do not understand why the father may not be heard to say that the book is not intended for his eyes at this stage of his life. Arden LJ also held that there could be no justification for the publication if it was likely to cause psychiatric harm to him. That approach excluded consideration of the wider question of justification based on the legitimate interest of the defendant in telling his story to the world at large in the way in which he wishes to tell it, and the corresponding interest of the public in hearing his story.

76 When those factors are taken into account, as they must be, the only proper conclusion is that there is every justification for the publication. A person who has suffered in the way that the father has suffered, and has struggled to cope with the consequences of his suffering in the way that he has struggled, has the right to tell the world about it. And there is a corresponding public interest in others being able to listen to his life story in all its searing detail. Of course vulnerable children need to be protected as far as reasonably practicable from exposure to material which would harm them, but the right way of doing so is not to expand *Wilkinson v Downton* [1897] 2 QB 57 to ban the publication of a work of general interest. But in pointing out the general interest attaching to this publication, we do not mean to suggest that there needs to be some identifiable general interest in the subject matter of a publication for it to be justified within the meaning of *Wilkinson v Downton*.

77 Freedom to report the truth is a basic right to which the law gives a very high level of protection (see, for example, *Napier v Pressdram Ltd* [2010] 1 WLR 934, para 42.) It is difficult to envisage any circumstances in which speech which is not deceptive, threatening or possibly abusive, could give rise to liability in tort for wilful infringement of another's right to personal safety. The right to report the truth is justification in itself. That is not to say that the right of disclosure is absolute, for a person may owe a duty to treat information as private or confidential. But there is no general law prohibiting the publication of facts which will cause distress to another, even if that is the person's intention. The question whether (and, if so, in what circumstances) liability under *Wilkinson v Downton* [1897] 2 QB 57 might arise from words which are not deceptive or threatening, but are abusive, has not so far arisen and does not arise for consideration in this case.

78 The Court of Appeal recognised that the father had a right to tell his story, but they held for the purposes of an interlocutory injunction that it was arguably unjustifiable for him to do so in graphic language. The injunction permits publication of the book only in a bowdlerised version. This presents problems both as a matter of principle and in the form of the injunction. As to the former, the book's revelation of what it meant to the father to undergo his experience of abuse as a child, and how it has continued to affect him throughout his life, is communicated through the brutal language which he uses. His writing contains dark descriptions of emotional hell, self-hatred and rage, as can be seen in the extracts which we have set out. To lighten the darkness would reduce its effect. The reader gains an insight into his pain but also his resilience and achievements. To lighten the darkness would reduce its effect. The court has taken editorial control over the manner in which the father's story is expressed. A right to convey information to the public carries with it a right to choose the language in which it is expressed in order to convey the information most effectively: see *Campbell v MGN Ltd* [2004] 2 AC 457, para 59, and *In re Guardian News and Media Ltd* [2010] 2 AC 697, para 63.

Although the passage above is concerned with speech, the majority of the Supreme Court did not confine the relevant conduct in *Wilkinson* to speech: the 'words or conduct' must be directed at the claimant, and be unjustified. Lord Neuberger by contrast referred to the action as 'the tort of making distressing statements'. It is suggested that the majority approach better captures the essence of the action.

The Mental Element

What form of intention is required for the action in *Wilkinson v Downton*? As we saw in our first extract, Wright J did not claim that the defendant actually *desired* the plaintiff to suffer harm. Rather, he said that the law here *imputes* intention to the defendant. Arguably, *Wilkinson v Downton* fitted the *second* form of intention mentioned in the US Restatement on Torts (extracted in Section 1), by which a party is held to intend consequences which are substantially 'certain' to follow from his or her actions. It makes no claim that this is *the same thing as* desiring the result. Indeed, Wright J may even be read as saying that in the absence of any other motive, the virtual certainty of the result is *evidence* that the outcome was desired.

The Supreme Court did not however see Wright J's discussion in this way. Rather, they looked at *Wilkinson* in its historical context, and argued that 'imputed intention' was by no means a creation of Wright J, but a familiar aspect of the law at the time of the decision. In criminal law, it has been removed by section 8 of the Criminal Justice Act 1967; and it was best for it to be removed from civil law also.

Baroness Hale and Lord Toulson, *OPO v Rhodes*

81 There is a critical difference, not always recognised in the authorities, between imputing the existence of an intention as a matter of law and inferring the existence of an intention as a matter of fact. Imputation of an intention by operation of a rule of law is a vestige of a previous age and has no proper role in the modern law of tort. It is unsound in principle. It was abolished in the criminal law nearly 50 years ago and its continued survival in the tort of wilful infringement of the right to personal safety is unjustifiable. It required the intervention of Parliament to expunge it from the criminal law, but that was only because of the retrograde decision in *Director of Public Prosecutions v Smith* [1961] AC 290. The doctrine was created by the courts and it is high time now for this court to declare its demise.

82 The abolition of imputed intent clears the way to proper consideration of two important questions about the mental element of this particular tort.

83 First, where a recognised psychiatric illness is the product of severe mental or emotional distress, (a) is it necessary that the defendant should have intended to cause illness or (b) is it sufficient that he intended to cause severe distress which in fact results in recognisable illness? . . .

84 Secondly, is recklessness sufficient and, if so, how is recklessness to be defined for this purpose? Recklessness is a word capable of different shades of meaning. In everyday usage

it may include thoughtlessness about the likely consequences in circumstances where there is an obvious high risk, or in other words gross negligence....

...

87 Our answer to the first question is that of option (b): para 83 above. Our answer to the second question is not to include recklessness in the definition of the mental element. To hold that the necessary mental element is intention to cause physical harm or severe mental or emotional distress strikes a just balance. It would lead to liability in the examples in para 85 but not in the example in para 86. It means that a person who actually intends to cause another to suffer severe mental or emotional distress (which should not be understated) bears the risk of legal liability if the deliberately inflicted severe distress causes the other to suffer a recognised psychiatric illness. A loose analogy may be drawn with the "egg shell skull" doctrine, which has an established place in the law of tort. This formulation of the mental element is preferable to including recklessness as an alternative to intention. Recklessness was not a term used in *Wilkinson v Downton* [1897] 2 QB 57 or *Janvier v Sweeney* [1919] 2 KB 316 and it presents problems of definition.

Clearly, the mental element has been defined here to exclude both 'imputed' intention, and recklessness. Lord Neuberger agreed that recklessness should not suffice; but maintained (with reference to *Wilkinson v Downton* itself) that:

Lord Neuberger, *OPO v Rhodes*

112 ... There are statements (and indeed actions) whose consequences and potential consequences are so obvious that the perpetrator cannot realistically say that those consequences are unintended...

It is suggested that this is correct, and it is compatible with the approach taken by the US Restatement and extracted in Section 1 of this chapter. Indeed, it may be compatible with the judgment of the majority, who made a distinction between imputing at law and 'inferring' as a matter of fact. The door may therefore remain open to acceptance of Lord Neuberger's comments above; and indeed Lord Neuberger's statement was applied in the case of *C v WH* [2015] EWHC 2687 (QB). This was a case in which a senior member of staff at a special school was found to have groomed a pupil and actively encouraged him to send indecent photographs to him. A claim under *Wilkinson v Downton* was successful: the emotional harm suffered was considered such an obvious consequence that it was 'intended', even though the trigger for this was the fact that it was discovered.

Sir Robert Nelson, *C v WH*
[2015] EWHC 2687 (QB)

89 ... The mental element requires the claimant to establish that Mr Whillock intended to cause severe mental or emotional distress to her. There are however, as was said in Rhodes, para [112] actions whose 'consequences or potential consequences are so obvious the perpetrator cannot realistically say that those consequences were unintended'. It was obvious that the illicit relationship would in the end cause nothing but harm to the vulnerable claimant

some 39 years younger than her groomer and those consequences must have been entirely clear and obvious to Mr Whillock. The consequence element is also established. As I have found under the heading of causation she suffered from an adjustment disorder after the disclosure in January 2010 with an acute exacerbation of her mental health problems when the abuse became public.

So far as the 'target' of intention is concerned, the Supreme Court in *OPO* held that it should suffice to intend to cause severe distress. But did the Court consider that distress could suffice for the 'consequence' element?

The Consequence Element

There has been considerable academic support for a development of *Wilkinson v Downton* to cover less tangible injuries, such as distress or anxiety.[61] In the United States, *Wilkinson* has indeed developed into an action in respect of the consequences of 'harassing and outrageous acts', provided the product of such acts amounts to 'severe emotional distress'. In *Wong v Parkside Health NHS Trust* [2003] 3 All ER 932, the Court of Appeal rejected an argument that *Wilkinson v Downton* had been similarly extended in English law. This was a case of bullying at work which would, if the events occurred now, give rise to claims under the Protection from Harassment Act 1997.[62] Hale LJ concluded that English common law had not developed an action for harassment before the Protection from Harassment Act 1997.

In *Wainwright v Home Office*, a decision of the House of Lords, Lord Hoffmann did not entirely rule out a remedy for intentionally caused anxiety and distress in its own right under *Wilkinson v Downton*. In his view, if such a claim were to be recognized, it would depend on much stronger 'intention' than the sort of intention which he thought was referred to by Wright J. No such strong intention was present in that case. In *OPO*, the Supreme Court has of course rejected 'imputed intention' as the basis of liability under *Wilkinson* generally, and was critical of the analysis in the extract below, which it considered a 'reconstruction' ([62]); but it did not choose to expand the forms of damage that would thereby become recoverable.

Lord Hoffmann, *Wainwright v Home Office*

[2004] 2 AC 406

44 I do not resile from the proposition that the policy considerations which limit the heads of recoverable damage in negligence do not apply equally to torts of intention. If someone actually intends to cause harm by a wrongful act and does so, there is ordinarily no reason why he should not have to pay compensation.[63] But I think that if you adopt such a principle, you have

---

[61] See J. Bridgeman and M. Jones, 'Harassing Conduct and Outrageous Acts: A Cause of Action for Intentionally Inflicted Mental Distress?' (1994) 14 LS 180. Generally, this form of damage is not sufficient to ground an action in negligence per se, but may be recoverable sometimes as a head of consequential loss: P. Giliker, A "New" Head of Damages: Damages for Mental Distress in the English Law of Torts' (2000) 20 LS 19–41.

[62] The events predated the Act. Although the claimant had been physically assaulted by one of the defendants, a claim in battery on the basis of this attack was ruled out. By statute, battery cannot be the subject both of a successful private prosecution (as was the case here) *and* of a further civil claim.

[63] It is doubtful whether this comment fits with the economic torts, considered in Section 7.

to be very careful about what you mean by intend. In *Wilkinson v Downton* Wright J wanted to water down the concept of intention as much as possible. He clearly thought, as the Court of Appeal did afterwards in *Janvier v Sweeney*, that the plaintiff should succeed whether the conduct of the defendant was intentional or negligent. But the *Victorian Railway Comrs* case prevented him from saying so. So he devised a concept of imputed intention which sailed as close to negligence as he felt he could go.

45 If, on the other hand, one is going to draw a principled distinction which justifies abandoning the rule that damages for mere distress are not recoverable, imputed intention will not do.

In *OPO*, the question of which damage would suffice did not arise for determination, and discussion on the point was brief. Nevertheless, the Court stated its conclusions on all three elements, and on the ambit of the tort, as follows:

Baroness Hale and Lord Toulson, *OPO v Rhodes*

88 It would be possible to limit liability for the tort to cases in which the defendant's conduct was "extreme, flagrant, or outrageous", as in Canada. But this argument has not so far been advanced in this country, and, although Arden LJ adverted to it as a possibility, the father has not sought to pursue it. We are inclined to the view, which is necessarily obiter, that the tort is sufficiently contained by the combination of (a) the conduct element requiring words or conduct directed at the claimant for which there is no justification or excuse, (b) the mental element requiring an intention to cause at least severe mental or emotional distress, and (c) the consequence element requiring physical harm or recognised psychiatric illness.

For the time being, this is the authoritative statement of the boundaries of the tort of 'wilful infringement of another's right to personal safety'.

6. STATUTORY ACTION FOR HARASSMENT

Protection from Harassment Act 1997[64]

1 Prohibition of harassment

(1) A person must not pursue a course of conduct—

  (a) which amounts to harassment of another, and

  (b) which he knows or ought to know amounts to harassment of the other.

...

(3) Subsection (1) does not apply to a course of conduct if the person who pursued it shows—

  (a) that it was pursued for the purpose of preventing or detecting crime,

---

[64] The statute as a whole has been considerably amended so far as it relates to criminal offences: for example, recently, the Protection of Freedoms Act 2012 has added new offences. Here we focus solely on the provisions relating to civil liabilities and therefore omit these provisions.

(b) that it was pursued under any enactment or rule of law or to comply with any condition or requirement imposed by any person under any enactment, or

(c) that in the particular circumstances the pursuit of the course of conduct was reasonable.

…

3 Civil Remedy

(1) An actual or apprehended breach of [section 1(1)] may be the subject of a claim in civil proceedings by the person who is or may be the victim of the course of conduct in question.

(2) On such a claim, damages may be awarded for (among other things) any anxiety caused by the harassment and any financial loss resulting from the harassment.

…

7 Interpretation of this group of sections

(1) This section applies for the interpretation of sections 1 to 5.

(2) References to harassing a person include alarming the person or causing the person distress.

[(3) A "course of conduct" must involve—

(a) in the case of conduct in relation to a single person (see section 1(1)), conduct on at least two occasions in relation to that person…]

…

(4) "Conduct" includes speech.

[(5) References to a person, in the context of the harassment of a person, are references to a person who is an individual.]

Protected Interests

Clearly, by section 3(1) and (2), the available remedies include compensation for harm suffered, and this harm may include 'anxiety and distress'. That is already more flexible than the common law. However, this form of harm is not a *requirement* of the civil action under the Act which, quite simply, protects *against harassment*. Where physical or mental injuries flow from the harassment, these too may be recoverable (see *Jones v Ruth*, below).

In *Levi v Bates* [2015] EWCA Civ 206, the Court of Appeal considered the important question of *whose* interests were protected by the civil liabilities created by the Act, and found that it was not only the 'target' of the conduct who was protected. Here, a wife was also the victim of harassment directed at her husband:

Briggs LJ, *Levi v Bates*
[2015] EWCA Civ 206

33 I agree that alarm or distress suffered out of nothing more than sympathy for the targeted victim of harassment is insufficient to found a claim under the Act. The claimant must be

harassed by it, in the sense that the conduct complained of must have some direct effect on the claimant (in terms of causing foreseeable harm, usually, but not limited to, alarm and distress). This is because section 3(1) of the Act confers a right to bring a civil claim on persons who are or may be the victim of the course of conduct in question, and because section 1(1) requires that course of conduct to amount to harassment of another. My view that the harm to the claimant must be foreseeable arises from section 1(1)(b) because of the requirement that the perpetrator knows or ought to know that the relevant course of conduct amounts to harassment.

34 The result of that analysis is that the ability to bring a harassment claim extends beyond the targeted individual only to those other persons who are foreseeably, and directly, harmed by the course of targeted conduct of which complaint is made, to the extent that they can properly be described as victims of it.

States of Mind

Liability under the 1997 Act is based on actual or constructive knowledge that conduct is likely to amount to harassment. This requirement may be fulfilled without any actual realization on the part of the defendant that he or she is 'harassing' the claimant. There is certainly no need for the defendant to *wish* to have the effect of making the claimant feel 'harassed', or to suffer anxiety. The following case goes further: a claimant was entitled to damages for personal injury brought about as a result of the defendants' conduct during building works on neighbouring property, irrespective of whether personal injury was a *foreseeable consequence* of the conduct:

Patten LJ, *Jones v Ruth*
[2011] EWCA Civ 804

32 . . . Conduct of the kind described in section 1(1) is actionable under section 3 in respect of anxiety or injury caused by the harassment and any financial loss resulting from the harassment. There is nothing in the statutory language to import an additional requirement of foreseeability. Nor is the foreseeability of damage the gist of the tort. Section 1(1) is concerned with deliberate conduct of a kind which the defendant knows or ought to know will amount to harassment of the claimant. Once that is proved the defendant is responsible in damages for the injury and loss which flow from that conduct. There is nothing in the nature of the cause of action which calls for further qualification in order to give effect to the obvious policy objectives of the statute.

There must however be a 'course of conduct', and a single incident will therefore not suffice, no matter how serious. The primary remedy is an injunction, but damages are also available. The Act also creates criminal offences of harassment.

Section 1(3)(a) creates a defence for conduct pursued for the purpose of combating crime. Plainly, the provision is not subject to a 'reasonableness' criterion, and is generally 'subjective' in nature. However, the Supreme Court has concluded that it contains implicit limits. In particular, it does not protect a party whose pursuit of justice is 'irrational'.

Lord Sumption JSC, Hayes v Willoughby

[2013] UKSC 17 (*Lord Neuberger and Lord Wilson agreeing*)

[14] ... Rationality is not the same as reasonableness. Reasonableness is an external, objective standard applied to the outcome of a person's thoughts or intentions. The question is whether a notional hypothetically reasonable person in his position would have engaged in the relevant conduct for the purpose of preventing or detecting crime. A test of rationality, by comparison, applies a minimum objective standard to the relevant person's mental processes. It imports a requirement of good faith, a requirement that there should be some logical connection between the evidence and the ostensible reasons for the decision, and (which will usually amount to the same thing) an absence of arbitrariness, of capriciousness or of reasoning so outrageous in its defiance of logic as to be perverse. For the avoidance of doubt, I should make it clear that, since we are concerned with the alleged harasser's state of mind, I am not talking about the broader categories of *Wednesbury* unreasonableness (*Associated Provincial Picture Houses Ltd v Wednesbury Corpn* [1948] 1 KB 223), a legal construct referring to a decision lying beyond the furthest reaches of objective reasonableness.

Lord Mance agreed in the result, but clearly wished to leave open the content of the applicable criterion:

[23] ... On the judge's finding, Mr Willoughby's state of mind took his course of conduct outside paragraph (a), whether one describes it as irrational, perverse or abusive or as so grossly unreasonable that it cannot have been intended to be covered by that head of justification.

Lord Reed, who dissented, was more sceptical about the irrationality criterion, and concerned about the introduction of such a criterion where both criminal liabilities, and civil liberties, were potentially involved. He could not bring to mind 'any example, in any context, of a statutory requirement not of reasonableness but of rationality, the latter being understood as conceptually distinct from the former' (at [26]), and plainly did not think that the comparison with public law notions of 'irrationality' was clear. Moreover, he was concerned about the potential use of the statute against those involved in the prevention or detection of crime, including investigative journalists, and on this basis wary of limiting the protection that Parliament had included in the relevant provision ([29]).

Vicarious Liability

The House of Lords has accepted that an employer may be *vicariously liable* for harassment under the Act: *Majrowski v Guy's and St Thomas's NHS Trust* [2006] UKHL 34. On the other hand, in *Daniels v Commissioner of Metropolitan Police* [2006] EWHC 1622, it was made clear that an employer will not be vicariously liable under the Act for a series of individual acts of bullying where the employees concerned are acting independently. For the employer to be vicariously liable for the statutory torts of their employees under this Act, the acts of the employees must amount to a *course of conduct*, with a common purpose. Equally, courts have emphasized that the conduct in question must not be merely unpleasant or unreasonable.

Lord Nicholls, *Majrowski*

…Courts are well able to recognize the boundary between conduct which is unattractive, even unreasonable, and conduct which is oppressive and unacceptable. To cross the boundary from the regrettable to the unacceptable the gravity of the misconduct must be of an order which would sustain criminal liability under Section 2.

Corporate Defendants

A corporate defendant sued in its own right (rather than vicariously) may have the necessary mental element. In *Ferguson v British Gas Trading* [2009] EWCA Civ 46, the Court of Appeal declined to strike out an action against British Gas for alleged harassing conduct taking the form of a host of computer-generated bills, reminders, and threats (including threats of disconnection and of reporting to a credit agency) to a previous customer who had terminated her contract with the company. The alleged persistent and unwarranted threats were the kind of course of conduct which Parliament had intended the Act to cover, and the fact that the defendant was a corporation (and there was alleged to be no individual with an intention to make the threats or cause distress, only a computer) did not mean it necessarily lacked the mental element: the statute refers to what the defendant 'ought to know'.

Similar issues arose in *Roberts v Bank of Scotland plc* [2013] EWCA Civ 882, in which an individual account-holder gained damages under the Act against her bank, having made it plain that she did not wish to be telephoned about the modest arrears on her accounts with Halifax. The bank's response to her arrears was to subject her to what Jackson LJ described as a 'monstrous system of 547 automated phone calls followed by a series of futile conversations' ([56]). Again, this is a form of harassment by computer. The bank's own records revealed the monstrous number of calls generated, so that the knowledge requirement (which is based on what the defendant *ought to know*) was plainly satisfied.

7. INTENTIONAL INTERFERENCE WITH ECONOMIC INTERESTS

Most undergraduate law courses omit coverage of the important torts collected here. On the other hand, two very significant House of Lords decisions have fundamentally altered the shape of the law in this area since the first edition (albeit without simplifying its structure as might have been hoped). This section is designed to operate as an introduction and over-view, though no such overview can be entirely straightforward given the twists and turns of the law. Certainly, the role of intention in English tort law cannot be properly understood without some attention to the economic torts.

These torts require intention to cause loss to the claimant, except for the tort of inducing breach of contract, where the target of intention is the breach, rather than the loss which may often follow. The kind of intention they require is stronger than the form of intention we saw in *Wilkinson v Downton*, and they are genuinely based upon intentional harm. Yet at the same time, in (nearly) all the economic torts, this strong form of intention *is not enough*. Something more is needed before there is said to be an actionable wrong—though the nature of that 'something more' is not identical between the different torts. The 'abstentionist' approach to liability to be seen in the economic torts is an important element in the general understanding of tort law.

The economic torts continue to defy any simple framework. While the House of Lords in *OBG v Allan* [2007] UKHL 21; [2008] 1 AC 1 appeared to have clarified the area (while emphasizing that the principles of the various torts were not unified), the subsequent decision of a differently constituted House of Lords in *Total Network v Revenue and Customs Commissioners* [2008] UKHL 19; [2008] 2 WLR 711 would appear to have restored the previous piecemeal position and appears to contradict some of the details—and possibly the spirit—of *OBG*. It seems therefore that the decision in *OBG* dealt only with part of the field. A particularly helpful and detailed analysis of the whole field since *OBG* and *Total Network* can be found in H. Carty, 'The Economic Torts in the 21st Century' (2008) LQR 641; and a proposal to reorganize the torts in a more rational and coherent way (concentrating in part on the interests that are protected by the torts) is developed by S. Deakin and J. Randall, 'Rethinking the Economic Torts' (2009) 72 MLR 519–53.

We will group the economic torts into two categories:

(a) Group A economic torts, involving actions or threats;

(b) Group B economic torts, involving misrepresentation.

With one exception, the economic torts selected here[65] require *intentional causation of economic harm*. The one exception—inducing breach of contract—still requires intention, but intention to induce breach (rather than cause harm) is the focus.

Equally, in all or nearly all of these torts, *intention is not enough*. Otherwise, there would simply be a tort of 'intentionally causing economic loss'.[66] Such a tort would be very awkward in a competitive market economy (even more so in a society which still recognizes the legitimacy of trade union activity). Generally speaking (and with exceptions), the torts in Group A also require some 'unlawful means', while the torts in Group B require false representations.

7.1 THE STARTING POINT: INTENTIONALLY CAUSING LOSS IS NOT A SUFFICIENT BASIS FOR LIABILITY

All of our economic torts require intention. But our starting point is that intentionally causing economic harm is not in itself sufficient to justify liability. This is very important when comparing these torts with the tort of negligence. In negligence, there has been some temptation to say that *carelessly causing foreseeable harm* is sufficient to justify liability, unless there is some sufficient reason why not.[67] This broad approach (in terms of general principles of foreseeability, carelessness, and causation) is now not generally adopted, and has been resisted particularly strongly in the case of *economic losses*.[68]

The economic torts help to illustrate why the search for such reasons is important. Most of the cases we will consider in this chapter involve damage inflicted *between competitors*

[65] We do not include passing off in this chapter. It primarily protects against damage to goodwill, not against economic losses, and is not dependent on intention.

[66] See our discussion of the US case *Tuttle v Buck*, Section 1 in the present chapter.

[67] This was broadly the *Anns v Merton* test for the duty of care, since superseded by the more detailed *Caparo* approach: Chapter 3, Section 3.3.

[68] We explore some of the reasons for this in Chapter 6, Section 2.

or (if this is genuinely different) *between trade unions and their targets*. There is no general duty to avoid harming one another's interests intentionally, and (therefore) certainly no duty to avoid doing so carelessly. No general obligation (moral or legal) to 'keep safe' from economic harm' exists between parties, who are in a competitive or antagonistic relationship.

Although the history of the 'economic torts' goes back much further, an important point of reference in understanding the present law is the decision of the House of Lords in *Allen v Flood*. Where action was not in itself 'unlawful' but was motivated by a dominant motive to *harm* (called, rather imprecisely, 'malice'),[69] could this motive in itself make the harm actionable? Or was it necessary to show *both* unlawful means, *and* ulterior purpose? A specially constituted panel of nine judges was assembled to decide this question, indicating how important it was perceived to be. The answer, given by a 6–3 majority, was that economic harm was not actionable, no matter what the intention of the defendant, unless some independent unlawfulness was present.

Allen v Flood [1898] AC 1

The plaintiffs (respondents) were shipwrights employed on repairs to the woodwork of a ship. The association of which they were members allowed them to work on both wood and iron. The boilermakers association (whose members worked with iron alone) took exception to this arrangement. They felt that shipwrights should be confined to working with wood. Ironworkers on the ship discovered that the respondent shipwrights had previously worked on the ironwork of another ship.

The ironworkers called for their delegate (Allen, the defendant), and told him they planned to walk out. He spoke to the employers and secured the dismissal of the shipwrights. The shipwrights sued Allen for maliciously causing them economic loss. Crucially, the employers were within their rights to dismiss the shipwrights and did so with no breach of any contractual term; equally, the ironworkers were not contractually obliged to continue their work. As a result, no breach of contract was either threatened, or procured. Had Allen *procured* a breach of the employer's contract, then the shipwrights would have been able to sue the employer for breach; and would also have had an action against Allen on the authority of *Lumley v Gye* (1853) 2 E & B 216 (discussed below).

Allen v Flood has been criticized *both* for an unduly restrictive approach to recovery of intentional harm,[70] *and* for a lack of clarity in the idea of 'malice'.[71] Whether the first criticism is well placed is a matter for debate. The second criticism however is not unfair. It is not at all clear that Allen's motive really *ought* to be described as malicious, or as really different from the motive of a competitor out to win the entire market (and thereby to put his rivals out of business). He was trying to protect the interests of his trade association at the expense of another; and the reason for doing this was not predominantly to cause harm to shipwrights, even if this was a necessary corollary. It was to benefit boilermakers. Indeed this point was (briefly) made explicit by Lord Herschell at 132: the object which the defendant, and those he represented, had in view throughout was what

69 The expression 'malice' is now generally avoided in describing the relevant intention: but a strong form of intention is clearly required. See our discussion of *OBG v Allan*, below.
70 J.D. Heydon, *The Economic Torts* (2nd edn, Sweet & Maxwell, 1978). Sir John Salmond was also a noted critic of *Allen v Flood*.
71 Finnis, 'Intention in Tort Law', extracted later.

they believed to be the interest of the class to which they belonged; the step taken was a means to that end.

This may be compatible with the approach to intention accepted by the Court of Appeal in *Douglas v Hello (No 3)* [2006] QB 125, but that approach appears to have been disapproved by the House of Lords: *OBG v Allan* [2007] UKHL 21. We explore these developments later.

Perhaps, though, it is unwise to scour the judgments in *Allen v Flood* closely for analysis of the motives involved. The essence of the majority decision was that Allen's motive did not matter. No form of malice or ill-will (if present) would have sufficed to make his actions into an actionable wrong. The headnote to *Allen v Flood* clearly states:

An act lawful in itself is not converted by a bad motive into an unlawful act so as to make the doer of the act liable to a civil action. . . .

. . . the appellant had violated no legal right of the respondents, done no unlawful act, and used no unlawful means, in procuring the respondents' dismissal; . . . his conduct was therefore not actionable however malicious or bad his motive might be . . .

The main question for those who take a philosophical approach to intention is not so much whether *Allen v Flood* was clear enough about the nature of 'malice' (it would almost certainly fail that test), but whether it took intention seriously enough as a 'wrong-making factor'.

J. Finnis, 'Intention in Tort Law', in D. Owen (ed.), *Philosophical Foundations of Tort Law*, at 238

. . . One's conduct will be right only if *both* one's means *and* one's ends are right; therefore, *one* wrong-making factor will make one's choice and action wrong, and *all* the aspects of one's act must be rightful for the act to be right. The acting person's intentions must be right all the way down (or up).

But the question to be addressed was not whether Allen's actions were *right*. It was whether they were wrong in such a way as to attract legal liability. Finnis concedes that intentional harm will not *always* justify legal liability; but, following J. B. Ames ('How Far an Act May be a Tort Because of the Wrongful Motive of the Actor' (1905) 18 Harv L Rev 411), he contends that a defendant may *escape* liability for intentional harm only for particular reasons such as legal privilege, or because the defendant only compels the claimant to do what he has a duty to do, or because the defendant's malevolence only extended to an omission or non-feasance (where there was no positive duty to act). This implies that intentionally caused harm *ought always* to attract a remedy. This is at odds with the 'abstentionist' approach (to use the word applied by Hazel Carty)[72] that may be argued to operate in respect of the economic torts generally.[73]

[72] H. Carty, *An Analysis of the Economic Torts* (see Further Reading to Section 7), at 6.

[73] One of the key tensions between *OBG v Allan* and *Total Network* is that the former clearly expresses an abstentionist approach to the economic torts, while the latter appears to embrace an 'interventionist' approach. The question of course is whether this is merely the superficial appearance given where the court was dealing with different issues—or whether it betrays underlying differences in approach. See Lee and Morgan, Further Reading to Section 7 for a suggestion that it is the latter.

This approach is to be contrasted with the position in the US Restatement (extracted at the start of this chapter).

7.2 GROUP A: ECONOMIC TORTS INVOLVING ACTIONS OR THREATS

One indication of the difficulties in this area is that there is still no uncontroversial way even of listing the 'economic torts' that exist. *OBG v Allan* clarified the nature of two entries on the list; but *Total Network* (see below) did not facilitate its easy completion.

Causing Loss by Unlawful Means

This is the largest economic tort and while it has enjoyed a number of different names (even in *OBG v Allan* itself), its nature and essential ingredients are relatively clear (albeit with some areas of uncertainty). It has in the past been called the 'genus' tort, with the implication that other economic torts are species of it. But it is clear that not all economic torts fall within its principles.

In *OBG v Allan*, Lord Hoffmann made clear that this tort requires intention to cause loss to the claimant through unlawful means. He preferred to define the relevant unlawful means closely, but may have intended to loosen the restrictive approach to intention which had become accepted before this decision. He also clarified that the nature of the tort involved striking at the claimant's interests through another. Thus one uncertainty that remained was whether unlawful means aimed *directly* at the claimant would count for this tort. Some remarks of Lord Hoffmann about 'two-party intimidation' (where the defendant directly intimidates the claimant, rather than intimidating someone else into not trading with the claimant, for example) imply that direct use of unlawful means against the claimant would not fall within the tort.

We address the elements of this tort, and the meaning of unlawful means, in the next section.

Inducing Breach of Contract

OBG v Allan confirmed the consensus of view that had surrounded the action in *Lumley v Gye*, 'inducing breach of contract'. That is, it confirmed that this is not a species of the 'causing loss by unlawful means' tort, but a separate tort in which the defendant intentionally causes a third party to breach its contract with the claimant. In keeping with the abstentionist approach of the decision as a whole, the House of Lords tightly defined the criteria of this tort in *OBG v Allan*.

Conspiracy

Before *OBG v Allan*, it had been thought that there were two forms of actionable conspiracy. 'Unlawful means' conspiracy involved conspiring to use unlawful means, and seemed consistent with the broader action of causing loss by unlawful means. It could be seen to be a species of the genus tort. 'Simple conspiracy' always seemed anomalous because it did not require unlawful means, so that it imposed liability on parties acting together, where an individual acting alone would not incur liability. This was particularly onerous where trade unions were concerned, since their activities could often be said to involve 'combination'. These two torts will, since *Total Network*, continue to be separate. But in *Total Network* the House of Lords considered the basis and nature of **unlawful means conspiracy** afresh, and decided that the unlawful means which might suffice to give rise to the action were broader than the unlawful means required for the purpose of the tort of 'causing loss by unlawful means' (above). There was no requirement that the unlawful means used should be capable of giving rise to a civil action in their own right. In this case, the alleged 'unlawfulness' was the common law criminal offence of 'cheating the revenue'—which is not a tort. But it sufficed to provide the 'unlawful means' required. 'Unlawful means' conspiracy is clearly not an element in a broader tort of causing loss by unlawful means. This is untidy, and means that there is wider liability in conspiracy than where acting alone. No convincing justification has yet been found.

The economic torts after these two decisions of the House of Lords are therefore neither unified, nor coherently differentiated.

7.3 INTENTION AND MEANS IN THE GROUP A ECONOMIC TORTS

In this section, we will briefly explore each of the torts according to the **nature of the intention** required (what does it mean to cause loss intentionally in this context?), and the **relevant unlawful means** (or other equivalent factor). For a fuller grasp of the area, it is also now necessary to consider the nature of the interests protected by each of the torts, since there is some difference in the way that the torts were analysed in the two lengthy recent decisions of the House of Lords.[74]

Causing Loss through Unlawful Means/Unlawful Interference with Trade/the 'Genus' Tort

Causing loss by unlawful means (the expression used by Lord Hoffmann in *OBG v Allan*) requires that the defendant should have used unlawful means with the intention of causing harm to the claimant. Actual harm to the claimant must flow from the defendant's acts. Lord Hoffmann explained that this tort imposes liability where the defendant has used unlawful means towards a third party, which would be actionable on the part of that third party. (An exception to this would arise where there are threats of unlawful action, rather than action as such: this is the case of 'intimidation', below). 'Unlawful means' were defined by Lord Hoffmann (though not by Lord Nicholls in the same case) as being confined to those actions which are capable of giving rise to a civil action on the part of the third party. Two other members of the House agreed with Lord Hoffmann, therefore his is the majority approach. The ambit of the tort is therefore restricted (though note the less restrictive approach to intention, below).

---

[74] For a proposed way forward after *OBG* and *Total Network* which focuses on the interests protected, see Deakin and Randall (earlier, and Further Reading for Section 7). For a very different exploration of whether analysis of protected rights may provide the basis for a coherent exposition of what is now called 'causing loss by unlawful means', see J. Neyers, 'Rights-based Justifications for the Tort of Unlawful Interference with Economic Relations' (2008) 28 LS 215–33.

Unlawful Means

Lord Hoffmann, *OBG v Allan*

47 The essence of the tort…appears to be (a) a wrongful interference with a third party in which the claimant has an economic interest and (b) an intention thereby to cause loss to the claimant.…

49 In my opinion, and subject to one qualification, acts against a third party count as unlawful means only if they are actionable by that third party. The qualification is that they will also be unlawful means if the only reason why they are not actionable is because the third party has suffered no loss. In the case of intimidation, for example, the threat will usually give rise to no cause of action by the third party because he will have suffered no loss. If he submits to the threat, then, as the defendant intended, the claimant will have suffered no loss. If he submits to the threat, then, as the defendant intended, the claimant will have suffered loss instead. It is nevertheless unlawful means. But the threat must be to do something which would have been actionable if the third party had suffered loss.…

51 Unlawful means therefore consists of acts intended to cause loss to the claimant by interfering with the freedom of a third party in a way which is unlawful as against that third party and which is intended to cause loss to the claimant. It does not in my opinion include acts which may be unlawful against a third party but which do not affect his freedom to deal with the claimant.

The rationale for this restricted approach to unlawful means was not explored at length, but may be located in the idea that there is existing civil liability (or would be, if the harm was not visited upon the claimant, rather than upon the person against whom the unlawful means is directed). In other words, this approach means that the economic torts (or at least this economic tort) operate to extend liability for existing wrongs to provide an action for the person whom the defendant intended to be the target. As we have already said, Lord Nicholls took a different view, from a different vantage point: if a civil wrong such as a tort or breach of contract is sufficient 'unlawful means', then surely the more serious wrong represented by a criminal offence ought, obviously, to suffice? The abstentionist's answer might be that criminal offences are not intended in themselves to create civil liability or rights of action. To extend the 'unlawful means' tort to criminal wrongs would create new civil liabilities, rather than extending existing ones. But Lord Hoffmann also briefly mentioned a variation of this reason: '…other writers have wondered whether it would be arbitrary and illogical to make liability depend upon whether the defendant has done something which is wrongful for reasons which have nothing to do with the damage inflicted on the claimant: see Roderick Bagshaw's review of Weir in "Can the Economic Torts be Unified?" (1998) 18 OJLS 729–739, at p 732. I agree.'

Intention

Where the required intention is concerned, Lord Hoffmann felt able to relax the restrictive view adopted by the Court of Appeal—presumably because of the tightening of the definition of 'unlawful means'. The Court of Appeal in *Douglas v Hello!* had set out a series of possible meanings of intention, in each case avoiding excessive concentration on the 'state of mind' of the defendant. It is suggested that this had been a valuable exercise in articulating what is meant by the expression 'targeted malice'—frequently considered the required type of intent for at least the majority of economic torts in Group A.

Lord Phillips MR, *Douglas v Hello! (No 3)*
[2006] QB 125 (giving the judgment of the court)[75]

159 There are a number of contenders for the test of the state of mind that amounts to an "intention to injure" in the context of the tort that we have described as "unlawful interference". These include the following:

(a) an intention to cause economic harm to the claimant as an end in itself;

(b) an intention to cause economic harm to the claimant because it is a necessary means of achieving some ulterior motive;

(c) knowledge that the course of conduct undertaken will have the inevitable consequence of causing the claimant economic harm;

(d) knowledge that the course of conduct will probably cause the claimant economic harm;

(e) knowledge that the course of conduct undertaken may cause the claimant economic harm coupled with reckless indifference as to whether it does or not.

A course of conduct undertaken with an intention that satisfies test (a) or (b) can be said to be "aimed", "directed", or "targeted" at the claimant. Causing the claimant economic harm will be a specific object of the conduct in question. A course of conduct which only satisfies test (c) cannot of itself be said to be so aimed, directed or targeted, because the economic harm, although inevitable, will be no more than an incidental consequence, at least from the defendant's perspective. None the less, the fact that the economic harm is inevitable (or even probable) may well be evidence to support a contention that test (b), or even test (a), is satisfied.

Nothing less than intention of forms (a) or (b)—both described by Lord Phillips as 'aimed', 'directed', or 'targeted' at the claimant—would be sufficient for any of the economic torts considered by the Court of Appeal in this case. The stronger of these forms of intention—category (a)—was required for the tort of simple conspiracy.

Lord Hoffmann took a different view from the Court of Appeal in respect of the case of *Douglas v Hello!*, in that he thought the defendant did have the required intent (though he thought the other aspects of the tort were not made out because there was no interference with the claimants' freedom to contract with the relevant third party: there was merely an impact on the value of their contract). The difficulty is that it is unclear whether he thought

---

[75] In this case, the defendants *Hello!* had failed to acquire the exclusive right to publish photographs of the Douglases' wedding, which had gone to their rival, *OK!* So they appear to have infiltrated the wedding and taken illicit photographs, and published them, fully aware that they did not have permission to do so, and that this would interfere with the contractual rights of their rival, *OK!* Actions were brought against them by both the Douglases (breach of confidence) and *OK!* The latter's claim failed before the Court of Appeal because their contract was made less profitable: this did not fit the definition of any of the economic torts. *OK!* later succeeded before the House of Lords on the basis of confidence: see Chapter 14.

that the above dissection of the meaning of intent was incorrect (perhaps doubting the possibility of drawing a line drawn between (b) and (c)), or whether he simply understood the facts differently. It may be thought that he was doubting the distinction between (b) and (c), because he compared (b) (means to a desired end) directly with something like (d) or (e) (foreseeability). True intention included necessary means to desired ends, and this was stronger than mere foreseeability.

Lord Hoffmann, *OBG v Allan*

134 . . . the position of Senor Sanchez Junco was that he wished to defend his publication against the damage it might suffer on account of having lost the exclusive. But that, it seems to me, is precisely the position of every competitor who steps over the line and uses unlawful means. The injury which he inflicted on "OK!" in order to achieve the end of keeping up his sales was simply the other side of the coin. His position was no different from Mr Gye saying that he had no wish to injure Mr Lumley and had the greatest respect for Her Majesty's Theatre but his intention was to improve attendance at his own theatre. . . .

The injury to "OK!" was the means of attaining Senor Sanchez Junco's desired end and not merely a foreseeable consequence of having done so.

135 The analysis of intention by the Court of Appeal in my opinion illustrates the danger of giving a wide meaning to the concept of unlawful means and then attempting to restrict the ambit of the tort by giving a narrow meaning to the concept of intention. The effect is to enable virtually anyone who really has used unlawful means against a third party in order to injure the plaintiff to say that he intended only to enrich himself, or protect himself from loss. The way to keep the tort within reasonable bounds is to restrict the concept of unlawful means to what was contemplated in *Allen v Flood*, not to give an artificially narrow meaning to the concept of intention.

The comment in para [135] suggests that Lord Hoffmann did intend to adopt a different *approach* to intention, rather than simply judging the case differently on its facts. However, there must be some doubt whether his alternative approach is sufficiently clearly set out to establish a general alternative. The consequence is that the nature of the required intention will probably return to the courts for further consideration.

Inducing Breach of Contract

In the tort of **inducing breach of contract**, the defendant must have deliberately and with knowledge of the contract persuaded, procured, or induced a contracting party to breach a contract with the claimant. **Breach of contract** and **harm to the claimant** must both result.

Lumley v Gye [1853] 2 E & B 216

Johanna Wagner was an opera star. The plaintiff was manager of Her Majesty's Theatre and the defendant had a rival opera house at Covent Garden. Johanna Wagner had contracted to sing exclusively at the plaintiff's theatre. The defendant persuaded Johanna Wagner to breach her contract, and to sing for him instead. The court agreed that there was a case to be argued at trial—it was not a claim doomed to fail for not disclosing a cause of action.[76]

This tort has inspired a considerable amount of academic comment for two reasons. One is that it has appeared difficult to fit within the general schema of economic torts suggested by *Allen v Flood*. The decision in *OBG v Allan* has determined that it does not, thereby resolving this set of problems. The other is that the effect of this tort is to extend the impact of contractual rights and duties *to third parties*. It uses *tort* in order to protect *contractual* interests against all comers. In *OBG v Allan*, bounds were set on the tort by requiring that there be *knowledge* that a breach of contract is being induced; and *intention* to bring about the breach. While the 'target' of intention is different in this tort from the 'causing loss' tort, the actual nature of intention is the same. What counts as intention is as set out above. It is not enough that the breach should be foreseeable; but it is enough that it is a necessary means to a desired end.

'Unlawful Means' Not Required

The House of Lords, while confirming that breach of contract can be sufficient unlawful means for the 'causing loss' tort, has also said that 'inducing breach of contract' does not require separately unlawful means. This concludes (perhaps?) a long academic debate. The tort does however require knowledge and intention.

Knowledge and Intention

In requiring knowledge of the likely breach, and adopting the same standard of intention in this tort as in the 'causing loss' tort, though with a different target of intention (the breach of contract), the House of Lords in *OBG v Allan* has departed from a much-criticized case.

Miller v Bassey [1994] EMLR 44

In *Miller v Bassey*, the defendant (singer Shirley Bassey) was sued for inducing breach of contract when *she* decided not to perform. The plaintiffs were musicians who would have been paid for performing at the recording studio, had she not been in breach; the recording studio seems to have been forced to breach its contract with them when she withdrew her services. Beldam LJ thought it arguable that the singer should be liable for inducing breach of their contracts, despite the fact that she would not have had their contracts at the forefront of her mind (if indeed she was aware of them).

Peter Gibson LJ dissented:

Peter Gibson LJ, *Miller v Bassey* (dissenting)

The conduct of the defendant [must] be aimed directly at the plaintiff, the contracting party who suffers the damage, in the sense that the defendant intends that the plaintiff's contract should be broken [and it is not] sufficient that the conduct should have the natural and probable consequence that the plaintiff's contract should be broken.

This dissenting approach has now been accepted as correct.

---

[76] In fact, the claim did ultimately fail at trial.

OBG v Allen and 'Abstentionism'

Responding to the ostensibly 'abstentionist' theme of the decision in *OBG v Allan*, the author of the next extract observes that in this area restraint on the part of the common law has been the exception rather than the rule. He is sceptical whether the same restraint would be shown in a case where the inducement to breach of contract was done on the part of a trade union, at least if the issues were seen to be still of genuine importance. In *OBG v Allan*, the House treated union issues as effectively dealt with through legislation and beyond the reach of common law, but the completeness of this was overstated.[77] This extract deals with the tort of inducing breach of contract, but places the tort within the broad frame of labour law and policy more generally.

Lord Wedderburn, 'Labour Law 2008: 40 Years On'
(2007) 36 ILJ 397–424

Why did the Law Lords suddenly rein in this tort rather than expand it, differing from the judicial habit of extending tort liability as Lord Denning had so blatantly done, thereby blocking the trade dispute immunities essential for lawful industrial action? Several factors give us a clue to the explanation.

First, the new cases in 2006 all raised economic tort liabilities in relation to commercial activity, so trade union activities were seen merely as background, parallel as judges like to make it to commercial law liabilities. Second, trade unions did not appear in 2007 to be as dangerous an engine of power of social disturbance as they were taken to be in 1901 [when *Quinn v Leatham* was decided] or in 1964. Expanding on these thoughts, Lady Hale of Richmond explained why the court must restrict the economic tort:

[Lord Hoffmann's reasoning] is also consistent with legal policy to limit rather than to encourage the expansion of liability in this area. In the modern age Parliament has shown itself more than ready to legislate to draw the line between fair and unfair trade competition or between fair and unfair trade union activity. This can involve major economic and social questions which are often politically sensitive and require more complicated answers than the courts can devise. Such things are better left to Parliament.

This kills two birds with one legal formula. Legally it sets another brick in the wall built by the decision in *Johnson v Unisys*, limiting the development of implied contractual terms in territory already occupied by rules enacted by Parliament. Second, it is no accident that this concept that liability in the economic torts should be limited and not expanded was advanced in a case involving not a trade union or labour relations at all but between commercial parties. . . . The contradiction in what is put forward as new judicial restraint is plain. Lady Hale adds that the courts must develop the common law only 'with the grain of legal policy'. But that policy 'grain' of collective labour law was set by, and still reflects, the restrictive anti-union legislation which satisfied the advocates of the new market capitalism . . .

---

[77] B. Simpson, 'Trade Disputes Legislation and the Economic Torts', in T. T. Arvind and J. Steele (eds), *Tort Law and the Legislature: Common Law, Statute, and the Dynamics of Legal Change* (Hart Publishing, 2013), traces the role of the courts in resisting defences to liability created by statute for the unions, and argues that the courts' resistance in this respect has shaped the economic torts.

For his part, Lord Hoffmann has made plain his view that abstentionism in the economic torts should be general, and that he hopes they will now be of little significance: L. Hoffmann, 'The Rise and Fall of the Economic Torts', in S. Degeling, J. Edelman, and J. Goudkamp (eds), *Torts in Commercial Law* (Sweet and Maxwell, 2010).

Intimidation

In the tort of **third party intimidation**, the defendant deliberately threatens a third party in order to compel that third party to harm the claimant. The threat itself must be unlawful, so this tort is consistent with the requirement of 'unlawful means' in *Allen v Flood*. Lord Hoffmann seems to have treated it in *OBG v Allan* as part of the 'causing loss through unlawful means' tort, though an exceptional instance given that the unlawful means may not cause harm to the third party, and therefore may not be actionable. Lord Hoffmann also mentioned, in *OBG v Allan*, that there may be an action for 'two-party intimidation', but thought such an action would 'raise different issues'. Presumably then it would not be part of the 'causing loss' tort, which requires some wrong directed at a third party.

Rookes v Barnard [1964] AC 1129

The plaintiff brought an action against members of a union from which he had resigned. The union threatened to withdraw labour unless the plaintiff was removed from his job. The defendants were individuals who spoke in favour of this action at a union meeting. Agreements between BOAC (the employer) and the union provided that there would be 100 per cent union membership, and no strikes. It was conceded by the defendants' counsel (perhaps unwisely) that the threatened strike would therefore be in breach of an implied term of the employment contracts.

The House of Lords decided that a threat to breach contract could amount to a tort, despite the absence of any threat of force or violence. For a critical review of this case in its context, see Wedderburn, 'Intimidation and the Right to Strike' (1964) 27 MLR 257–81 (especially at 257–8).

Conspiracy Torts

OBG v Allan did not deal with conspiracy, since none of the cases on appeal raised the issue. But unlawful means conspiracy was the key issue soon afterwards in *Total Network v Customs & Excise Commissioners* [2008] UKHL; [2008] 2 WLR 711.[78]

Unlawful means conspiracy requires that two or more persons combine together to use unlawful means in order to harm the claimant. There must be a common design aimed at the claimant; and *action* in concert (not just agreement). On the other hand, only one of the conspirators needs to have used unlawful means. Actual loss by the claimant must be shown. As we have seen, the House of Lords in *Total Network* defined 'unlawful means' in this tort more broadly than in the tort of 'causing loss by unlawful means'.

---

[78] For discussion see J. Lee and P. Morgan, 'The Province of *OBG v Allan* Determined: The Economic Torts Return to the House of Lords' (2008) King's Law Journal 338–46; J. O'Sullivan, 'Unlawful Means Conspiracy in the House of Lords' (2008) 67 CLJ 459–61.

Simple conspiracy requires two or more persons to act in combination for the predominant purpose of causing injury to the claimant. There is no need for the acts performed to be unlawful in themselves.

Simple conspiracy has long been recognized to be an exception to the clear principle in *Allen v Flood*, that intentional harm, without unlawful means, is not actionable in itself. The only explanation for this tort (though the explanation has been almost universally recognized as rather weak, until it was adopted in respect of unlawful means conspiracy by the House of Lords in *Total Network*) is that the *fact of combination* is so wrong or so threatening in itself that it stands in for the use of unlawful means. This tort was recognized in *Quinn v Leatham* [1901] AC 495.

The idea behind simple conspiracy seems to be that individual self-interest is fine, provided one stops short of unlawful means, but that collective self-interest and combination are bad in themselves. In *Lonrho v Shell Petroleum (No 2)* [1982] AC 173, Lord Diplock identified the flaws in this reasoning:

Lord Diplock, *Lonrho v Shell Petroleum (No 2)*
[1982] AC 173

. . . Why should an act which causes economic loss to A but is not actionable at his suit if done by B alone become actionable because B did it pursuant to an agreement between B and C? An explanation given at the close of the 19th century by Bowen L.J. in the *Mogul* case when it was before the Court of Appeal (1889) 23 Q.B.D. 598, 616, was:

> "The distinction is based on sound reason, for a combination may make oppressive or dangerous that which if it proceeded only from a single person would be otherwise."

But to suggest today that acts done by one street-corner grocer in concert with a second are more oppressive and dangerous to a competitor than the same acts done by a string of supermarkets under a single ownership or that a multinational conglomerate such as Lonrho or oil company such as Shell or B.P. does not exercise greater economic power than any combination of small businesses, is to shut one's eyes to what has been happening in the business and industrial world since the turn of the century and, in particular, since the end of World War II. . . .

Lord Diplock went on to say that the tort is too well established to ignore. The only solution was to confine its ambit through a particularly demanding intention requirement.

Lord Diplock, *Lonrho v Shell Petroleum (No 2)*, at 189

This House, in my view, has an unfettered choice whether to confine the civil action of conspiracy to the narrow field to which alone it has an established claim or whether to extend this already anomalous tort beyond those narrow limits that are all that common sense and the application of the legal logic of the decided cases require. My Lords, my choice is unhesitatingly the same as that of Parker J and all three members of the Court of Appeal. I am against extending the scope of the civil tort of conspiracy beyond acts done in execution of an agreement entered into by two or more persons for the purpose not of protecting their own interests but of injuring the interests of the plaintiff.

Given the strength of these comments, it has been seen as surprising that the House of Lords in *Total Network* was prepared to extend the range of unlawful means that would suffice for 'unlawful means conspiracy' to make it broader than the range of unlawful means that will suffice in respect of other 'unlawful means' torts. The opportunity to distinguish *OBG v Allan* was provided by some comments of Lord Hoffmann, where he said that two-party intimidation raised entirely separate issues from the three-party torts with which he was dealing. This was then generalized to conspiracy. But the underlying rationale seems to be that here, the defendant strikes at the claimant, not through a third party, but directly. It is this directness, together with the fact of combination (itself implying that the defendant is not pursuing his or her own interests), which the House of Lords has used to distinguish between the two torts.

Lord Hope, whose judgment is extracted below, differed from the majority as to the outcome of the case, on the basis that the applicable statutory scheme barred the Commissioners from claiming damages in the tort of conspiracy. But he agreed with all the other judges on the question of whether unlawful means for the purposes of conspiracy could include criminal acts. That is the point considered in this extract. If the means used had to be actionable by the claimant, then the claimant would by definition have no need of an action in conspiracy: two-party intimidation and conspiracy are in fact outside the range of situations to which the thinking in *OBG v Allan* can be said to apply.

Lord Hope, *Total Network*

43 In OBG Ltd v Allan [2008] 1 AC 1, para 56 Lord Hoffmann said that the courts should be cautious in extending the tort of causing loss by unlawful means beyond the description given by Lord Watson in *Allen v Flood* [1898] AC 1, 96 and Lord Lindley in *Quinn v Leathem* [1901] AC 495, 535, which was designed only to enforce standards of civilised behaviour in economic competition between traders or between employers and labour. I entirely appreciate the point that he makes that caution is needed where the unlawful act is directed against a third party at whose instance it is not actionable because he suffers no loss. There the claimant's cause of action is, as Hazel Carty, *An Analysis of the Economic Torts*, p 274 puts it, parasitic on the unlawful means used by the defendant against another party. As to that situation I would prefer to reserve my opinion. But in this case there was no third party. The means used by the conspirators were directed at the claimants themselves. This is a case where the claimants were persuaded by the unlawful means to act to their own detriment which, in para 61 of *OBG*, Lord Hoffmann said raises altogether different issues. One has to ask why, in this situation, the law should not provide a remedy.

44 The situation that is contemplated is that of loss caused by an unlawful act directed at the claimants themselves. The conspirators cannot, on the commissioners' primary contention, be sued as joint tortfeasors because there was no independent tort actionable by the commissioners. This is a gap which needs to be filled. For reasons that I have already explained, I do not accept that the commissioners suffered economic harm in this case. But assuming that they did, they suffered that harm as a result of a conspiracy which was entered into with an intention of injuring them by the means that were deliberately selected by the conspirators. If, as Lord Wright said in *Crofter Hand Woven Harris Tweed Co Ltd v Veitch* [1942] AC 435, 462, it is in the fact of the conspiracy that the unlawfulness resides, why should that principle not apply here? As a subspecies of the tort of unlawful means conspiracy, the case is virtually indistinguishable from the tort of conspiracy to injure. The fact that the unlawful means were not in themselves actionable does not seem, in this context at least, to be significant. As Professor Joe Thomson put it in "An island legacy—The delict of conspiracy", *Comparative and Historical Essays in Scots Law*, ed Carey Miller and Meyers (1992), p 148, the rationale of the tort is conspiracy to injure. These factors indicate that a conspiracy is tortious if an intention of the conspirators was to harm the claimant by using unlawful means to persuade him to act to his own detriment, even if those means were not in themselves tortious.

45 I would hold that the decision of the Court of Appeal in *Powell v Boladz* [1998] Lloyd's Rep Med 116 was erroneous and that it should be overruled. I would also hold, in agreement with all your Lordships that criminal conduct at common law or by statute can constitute unlawful means in unlawful means conspiracy. Had it been open to the commissioners to maintain a civil claim of damages the tort of unlawful means would have been available to them, even though the unlawful means relied upon were not in themselves actionable.

7.4 GROUP B: FALSE STATEMENTS

Deceit requires that the defendant should knowingly make a false representation to the claimant, with the intention that the claimant should rely upon it. The claimant must rely upon the representation, to his or her detriment.

Unlike most of the Group A torts, *and* unlike malicious falsehood (below), deceit typically applies in a 'two-party' situation. The person *relying upon the statement* is the claimant. A clear statement of the 'intention' requirements in the tort of deceit is as follows:

Jackson LJ, *EC03 Capital Ltd and others v Ludson Overseas Ltd*
[2013] EWCA Civ 413

77 . . . What the cases show is that the tort of deceit contains four ingredients, namely:

i)   The defendant makes a false representation to the claimant.

ii) The defendant knows that the representation is false, alternatively he is reckless as to whether it is true or false.

iii) The defendant intends that the claimant should act in reliance on it.

iv) The claimant does act in reliance on the representation and in consequence suffers loss.

Ingredient (i) describes what the defendant does. Ingredients (ii) and (iii) describe the defendant's state of mind. Ingredient (iv) describes what the claimant does.

In *Derry v Peek* (1889) 14 App Cas 337, the House of Lords strictly limited the ambit of deceit by holding that misrepresentations giving rise to harm were not actionable except in the presence of 'fraud' or contractual breach. 'Fraud' generally means that the defendant *knows* that the statement is false, or is *reckless* as to its truth or falsity; and relates only to (ii) above. 'Recklessness' involves *neither knowing nor caring whether the statement is true or false*.

An exception to the fraud requirement was carved out for cases of 'fiduciary relationship' (or relationships close to this) in *Nocton v Lord Ashburton* [1914] 2 AC 932. Much later, in *Hedley Byrne v Heller* [1964] AC 465, this exception was developed to allow claims *in the tort of negligence* for merely negligent misrepresentation, in defined circumstances. A large body of case law now exists in respect of liability under *Hedley Byrne*, and is reviewed in Chapter 6. Not only does the action in negligence require no fraud, it also requires no *intention* that C should rely. (On the other hand, knowledge of the purpose for which C will use the information or advice given does appear to be essential.) And yet, despite the growth of negligence liability, deceit retains utility because it allows for recovery of a broader range of loss than negligence; and the defence of contributory negligence is not available.

Malicious falsehood requires that the defendant should maliciously publish falsehoods concerning the claimant or his or her property. Except where statutory exceptions apply, there must also be 'special damage'.

'Malice' in Malicious Falsehood

Hazel Carty, *An Analysis of the Economic Torts* (Oxford University Press, 2nd edn, 2010), 211–12

The real issue has become to pinpoint the definition of malice applied by the courts. A review of case law reveals that malice can be proved in various ways, summarized by Heydon [*The Economic Torts*, p. 83] as either personal spite, or an intention to injure the plaintiff without just cause or excuse or knowledge of the falsity of the statement. However, it is difficult to separate personal spite from the related concepts of improper motive and intention to injure without lawful excuse.… It is simpler and consistent with leading modern case law to define malice as either 'motive' malice (*mala fides* means that an honest belief will not negative liability) or 'deceit' malice (lies where indifference as to the effect on the claimant will not negate liability). The absence of good faith is, therefore, due to either the knowledge of falsity or the malicious intention. So, 'if you publish a defamatory statement about a man's goods which is injurious to him, honestly believing that it is true, your object being your own advantage and no detriment to him, you obviously are not liable' [Stable J in *Wilts United Dairies v Robinson* 57 RPC 220, p. 237].

Either 'deceit malice' or 'motive malice' will suffice:

- If there is intent to harm (motive malice), honest belief in truth will not assist the defendant.

- If there is no belief in truth (deceit malice), lack of intent to harm will not assist the defendant.

7.5 MEASURE OF DAMAGES

The House of Lords has ruled that damages for **deceit** in particular are not confined to damage that is *foreseeable* (which is the case in a claim for negligence). Rather, all those losses that were the *direct consequence* of reliance on the false representation are recoverable. Furthermore, damages in respect of a *negligent* misstatement are limited to those damages which are regarded as 'within the scope' of the particular duty of care that was owed. Thus if the duty is only one to give information, and not to 'advise' in a general way, then only damage that can be fairly attributed to the incorrectness of the information can be recovered in negligence. In deceit, however, because there is an intention that the claimant should rely *and* fraud in respect of the statement, *all* direct consequences of the statement (subject to a duty to mitigate) can be recovered.

Lord Steyn, *Smith New Court Securities v Citibank NA*
[1997] AC 254, at 283

The context is the rule that in an action for deceit the plaintiff is entitled to recover all his loss directly flowing from the fraudulently induced *transaction*. In the case of a negligent misrepresentation the rule is narrower: the recoverable loss does not extend beyond the consequences flowing from the negligent *misrepresentation*: see *Banque Bruxelles Lambert SA v Eagle Star Insurance Co Ltd* [1997] AC 191.

'Directness' is clearly intended to be distinct from 'foreseeability'. The impact of the directness test and the contrast with negligence liability can be illustrated by reference to *Nationwide Building Society v Dunlop Haywards (DHL) Ltd* [2009] EWHC 254 (Comm). Here there were two liable parties in respect of a mortgage fraud. The first defendant was liable in deceit for the fraud. The second defendant, the solicitors of the first defendant, had negligently failed to notice the fraud. Quite apart from the fact that the first defendant bore a greater share of the 'responsibility' for the claimant's losses, the court emphasized clearly that damages in deceit cover a range of losses which in negligence would be regarded as 'too remote' a consequence of the breach. So the second defendant had to pay a 20 per cent share of *negligence* damages; *deceit* damages were higher. The amount for which the first defendant was liable in deceit was £15,464,106, including the net amount advanced on the basis of the fraudulent over-valuation; lost interest on other advances that would have been made; cost of staff time exploring the fraud; additional funding costs; and loss of opportunity to make mortgage loans. Staff time, lost opportunities, and additional costs were not included in the calculation of *negligence* damages.

In *Parabola Investments Ltd and another v Browallia Cal Ltd (formerly Union Cal Ltd) and others* [2010] EWCA Civ 486, the Court of Appeal applied the *Smith New Court* approach to hold that a trader whose fund had been significantly depleted by the defendant's fraud was entitled to compensatory damages encompassing not only the initial losses suffered through the defendants' fraud, but also, on the basis of his exceptional and consistently successful record as a trader on the London markets, for lost gains that he was unable to make because of the depletion of his funds. In assessing 'direct' consequences, the date of discovery of the fraud would be an artificial cut-off point, since the impact of the fraud continued to affect the claimant. This result needs to be compared with the approach taken within the tort of negligence in relation to economic loss, where damages are limited by interpretation of the relevant duty to take care: see Chapter 3.

Should the *Smith New Court* approach be applicable to all those torts where harm to the claimant is actually intended? Lord Steyn placed considerable emphasis on the element of 'fraud' in an action for deceit. This particular element is not present in the other economic torts.

7.6 DEFENCES

Justification

The tort of inducing breach of contract is clearly qualified by a defence of 'justification'. It seems that the defence requires some 'compelling reason' for inducing the breach. In those torts which, unlike inducing breach of contract, require some independently unlawful means, it has been wondered whether these unlawful means could ever be 'justified'. In respect of the tort of 'causing loss by unlawful means', Carty argues that any such defence (if it exists) would be 'very residual'.[79] Arguably, because the tort of intimidation has been developed to include a threatened breach of contract (*Rookes v Barnard*), intimidation—like inducing breach of contract—should benefit from a justification defence. It seems less likely that there could be 'justification' for a fraud or malicious falsehood (Group B), but this is not out of the question.

Contributory Negligence

In *Standard Chartered Bank v Pakistan National Shipping Corpn* [2003] 1 AC 959, the House of Lords clearly decided that fault on the part of the claimant did *not* give rise to a defence of contributory negligence in the tort of deceit. This defence requires the court to reduce damages to reflect fault on the part of both parties and is fully explored in relation to negligence in Chapter 5. The essential reason why it was held not to apply in deceit is that no such defence to deceit was recognized before 1945. The Law Reform (Contributory Negligence) Act 1945 did not *introduce* a defence of contributory negligence, it only converted it from a total defence (no damages at all) to a partial one (damages reduced). We visited this reasoning in relation to battery in an earlier section of this chapter (Section 3.4).

8. INTENTIONAL ABUSE OF POWER AND PROCESS

8.1 MALICIOUS PROSECUTION AND ANALOGOUS TORTS

The tort of malicious prosecution is committed where the defendant has maliciously and without reasonable or probable cause 'prosecuted' the claimant, and where the prosecution has ultimately ended in the claimant's favour. In *Crawford Adjusters v Sagicor General Insurance (Cayman) Limited and another* [2013] UKPC 17 (an appeal from the Cayman Islands), the Privy Council determined that the tort should be applicable where the prosecution is a civil one. The result was surprising because only a few years earlier, in *Gregory v Portsmouth City Council* [2000] 1 AC 419, the House of Lords had heard full argument on the subject of malicious prosecution of civil proceedings and confirmed quite authoritatively that the tort did not extend to such proceedings. This also put lower courts in a difficult position: should they treat *Gregory* as binding upon them, or follow a more recent Privy Council decision which was plainly based on an interpretation of English law? In *Willers v Joyce* [2016] UKSC 43; [2016] 3 WLR 477, the Supreme Court reached the same conclusion in an English appeal; and thus the scope of malicious prosecution has been markedly expanded.

[79] Carty, *An Analysis of the Economic Torts*, 101.

Prosecution

The defendant need not be a public 'prosecutor'. So far as criminal prosecution is concerned, the activity of 'prosecuting' for the purposes of this tort is plainly broad enough to incorporate the role of the Crown Prosecution Service *and* of police officers who are responsible for charging the claimant and assembling evidence, but it may also include a private individual who instigates a prosecution and offers to give evidence, if they alone can attest to the truth of the charge: see *Martin v Watson* [1996] AC 74. More recently however, in *H v AB* [2009] EWCA Civ 1092, the Court of Appeal emphasized that only if the public prosecutor's discretion is 'overborne' in some way will such a complainant be considered as a prosecutor. Plainly, an individual who instigates a *private prosecution* will also be treated as having 'prosecuted' the claimant; and it appears from *Willers v Joyce* that an individual pursuing a civil claim will also be a 'prosecutor'. The range of individuals susceptible to a claim in civil malicious prosecution is much broader than in the case of criminal prosecution, because there is no public body which typically pursues civil claims—the category may potentially include all claimants.

Reasonable and Probable Cause and Malice

'Lack of reasonable and probable cause' and 'malice' are two separate requirements. The tort is committed only when there is a subjective type of 'malice', combined with an *objective* lack of reasonable or probable cause. The subjective form of malice may involve any sort of 'improper motive' in launching the prosecution, not confined to 'spite and ill will' towards the claimant.

Damage

Unlike the trespass torts with which this chapter started, the tort of malicious prosecution is 'damage-based', and not actionable 'per se'. The kinds of damage against which it protects are generally thought to be those captured in the following summary of the damage which may be caused to an individual by a malicious prosecution:

Holt CJ, *Savill v Roberts*
(1698) 12 Mod 208

First, damage to his fame if the matter whereof he be accused be scandalous. Secondly, to his person, whereby he is imprisoned. Thirdly, to his property, whereby he is put to charges and expenses.

In *Crawford Adjusters v Sagicor*, the Privy Council warned that this dictum is not to be read as restricting the range of damage that can be compensated through the tort. In particular, purely economic losses, which as we will see in Chapter 6 are problematic in the tort of negligence, are recoverable in broader circumstances than those implied by Holt CJ. Nor should the idea of 'scandalous' matters be read too restrictively. Even a civil prosecution may threaten the claimant's reputation.

It will be evident that malicious prosecution deals with a combination of damage, 'malice', and lack of reasonable and probable cause. In *Crawford Adjusters*, Lord Wilson and

Baroness Hale in particular regarded the existence of the relevant forms of damage, together with malicious use of the legal system, not merely as essential *requirements* of the action, but as between them giving the recipe for a 'wrong' which would require a remedy unless principled reasons could be given to the contrary. Their very presence justified an expansion in liability.

Baroness Hale of Richmond, *Crawford Adjusters*
[2013] UKPC 17

81 It is always tempting to pray in aid what Sir Thomas Bingham MR referred to as "the rule of public policy which has first claim on the loyalty of the law: that wrongs should be remedied": *X (Minors) v Bedfordshire County Council* [1995] 2 AC 633, 663. But by itself that wise dictum does not tell us what the law should define as a wrong. Some conduct is wrongful whether or not it causes any damage—that is the essence of the tort or torts of trespass; other conduct is only wrongful if it causes particular types of damage—that was the essence of the action on the case; but not all conduct which causes such damage is wrongful. The tort or torts of wrongfully bringing legal proceedings are actions on the case and therefore can only lie if there is damage of the kinds specified in *Savile v Roberts* (1698) 1 Ld Raym 374. But that is not enough. Instigating legal proceedings in good faith and with reasonable cause, even if they fail and even if they do damage in the *Savile v Roberts* sense, is not wrongful. Even maliciously instigating legal proceedings is not always, or even often, wrongful. So how is the wrong done by instituting legal proceedings to be defined?

Baroness Hale later answered the closing question as follows. The passage begins by referring to a negligence case (*Jain*), discussed in Chapter 6, where there was no liability; and also confronts the problem that expansion of malicious prosecution would contrast with the culture of abstentionism already noted in relation to the economic torts, even in the presence of malice. Baroness Hale concludes that the combination of *malice* and *damage*, both present in the economic torts, with *misuse of the legal system*, justified a less restrained approach to malicious prosecution. This was despite the fact that she had already noted that it would 'not be surprising' if there were no such tort at all, given the need to protect the integrity of the legal process by deterring relitigation (at [82]). She was willing to set aside that consideration on the basis that there already is such a tort; and on that basis, its limits ought to be principled.

Baroness Hale, *Crawford Adjusters v Sagicor*
[2013] UKPC 17

88 In *Jain v Trent Strategic Health Authority* [2009] AC 853, Mr and Mrs Jain were ruined when their business was closed down in an ex parte procedure brought by the regulator without good cause. The House of Lords held that there was no duty of care, partly because the parties to litigation do not generally owe one another a duty of care and partly because regulators do have a duty of care towards the vulnerable people whom they are protecting, which could conflict with a duty of care to the people they are regulating. All that makes sense, although the Jains undoubtedly suffered a grievous injustice. But had the regulator been malicious, why should they not have had a cause of action in malicious prosecution? It is one thing to say that the regulator should not be liable for carelessness, and quite another to say that they should not be liable for malice.

89 The Jains, of course, suffered from an ex parte remedy of the sort which has previously given rise to liability for malicious prosecution. They also suffered at the hands of a body performing public functions, which is a distinction favoured by Lord Sumption JSC. But it cannot be accepted that malice only turns right into wrong when public officials are concerned. Intentionally causing physical or psychological harm is a tort which can be committed by any one. Intentionally causing economic damage is not a tort, because that is the object of most business competition. But intentionally abusing the legal system is a different matter. That is not simply doing deals to damage the competitors' business. It is bringing claims which you know to be bad in order to do so.

Torts Analogous to Malicious Prosecution

Malicious prosecution is an old tort and there exist a number of potential variations on its theme.

Malicious Procurement of an Arrest Warrant

In *Roy v Prior* [1971] AC 470, the defendant was a solicitor acting for a man accused of a criminal offence. The defendant sought to serve the plaintiff with a witness summons. When the plaintiff did not appear at trial, the defendant secured a warrant for his arrest, and he was kept in custody for several hours. The House of Lords held that these facts might disclose a cause of action, provided the plaintiff could show *both* malice, *and* lack of reasonable and probable cause.

Malicious Procurement of a Search Warrant

Malicious procurement of a search warrant may be actionable on the same principles: *Gibbs v Rea* [1998] AC 786. The harm against which this tort protects appears slightly different from the harm in the last two torts, in that the procurement of the warrant will lead primarily to disruption, anxiety, and invasion of privacy (and consequential harm) rather than loss of liberty or the threat of it.

Abuse of Civil Process

An action may be an 'abuse of civil process' if it is brought for some improper, collateral purpose, outside the legal claim itself. For example, it may be brought with the intention of forcing the other party's hand on a different matter, or in other words in order to coerce. In *Grainger v Hill* (1838) 4 Bing NC 212, the defendant's purpose in arresting the claimant was essentially extortion. In *Crawford Adjusters*, the defendant's employee pursued civil actions against the claimant because he wanted to ruin him. This was malicious, and in the absence of reasonable and probable cause it formed the foundation for the malicious prosecution action. But the way in which the employee wished to ruin the claimant was to succeed in the civil actions against him. The Privy Council considered that this purpose could not be called 'collateral'; and declined to expand this tort as it had expanded malicious prosecution itself.

8.2 MISFEASANCE IN A PUBLIC OFFICE

The tort of misfeasance in a public office is distinctive because unlike any other tort, it can be committed only by a public officer exercising a power. The tort is committed when a public officer exercising his or her power *either*:

(a) does so with the intention of injuring the claimant; *or*

(b) acts (or decides not to act)[80] in the knowledge of, or with reckless indifference to, the illegality of his or her act or failure to act and in the knowledge of, or with reckless indifference to, the probability of causing injury to the claimant or to persons of a class of which the claimant was a member.

The claimant must suffer damage as a consequence.

The existence of two very different forms of this tort captured as (a) and (b) above was accepted by the House of Lords (except Lord Millett, who argued that they really come down to the same thing) in *Three Rivers District Council v Bank of England (No 3)* [2003] 2 AC 1. This litigation arose from the collapse of BCCI (a bank). The claimants were depositors who lost money when the bank collapsed; they claimed that the Bank of England either wrongly (with the requisite mental element) granted a licence to the bank; or wrongly (with the requisite mental element) failed to revoke the licence when it was clear that BCCI was likely to collapse.[81]

The tort encompasses acts *and* failures to act, but not *all* failures to act will suffice. According to Lord Hobhouse (at [230]), in the case of an omission (such as the failure to *revoke* licences in *Three Rivers* itself), there must be an actual *decision* not to act, rather than a mere failure to consider whether or not to do so. If there is a mere failure to think about it, then the only cause of action is negligence. Lord Hope would go one step further, to include 'wilful or deliberate failure' to take a decision whether to act. In what follows, we will refer to 'acts' to include the relevant sort of 'intended' omission.

The Mental Element

Variation (a)—Targeted Malice

In variation (a), there is no need to show that, apart from the intention to harm the claimant, the act of the official was 'unlawful'. Exercise of public power with intent to harm is *in itself unlawful*. The intent to harm provides the abuse of power.

In *Three Rivers* itself, it was accepted that the acts and omissions of the Bank of England could not be said to have been performed with 'targeted malice'. The only possibility was that variation (b) might be established.

Variation (b)—Intentional or Reckless Abuse of Power

The second variation requires knowledge or 'reckless indifference' in respect of two different things.

First, the official must either know that, or be reckless whether, his or her act is illegal (in excess of the power conferred). Second, the official must *also* know that, or

---

[80] Or perhaps, according to Lord Hope, wilfully fails to decide whether to act.
[81] The expensively litigated claim eventually collapsed in its turn. So also did the claim for misfeasance brought by shareholders in Railtrack, *Weir v Secretary of State for Transport* [2005] EWHC 2192.

be reckless whether, injury would be caused to the claimant as a result of the illegal act. Since the concept of 'recklessness' has caused significant difficulties in *criminal* law, there was some discussion of what 'recklessness' might mean in this context. In particular, is it a *subjective* state of mind, by which is meant that the official considered the matter and genuinely did not care whether the action was in excess of power, and would cause the claimant harm (the *Cunningham* test)?[82] Or, is it sufficient that there was an obvious risk, which the official failed to consider in terms of the likely impact on the claimant (the *Caldwell* test)?[83] According to Lord Steyn, whatever the position in criminal law, in this tort recklessness is to be judged subjectively, in terms of what the official actually *thought*.

Lord Steyn, at 193

Counsel argued for the adoption of the *Caldwell* test in the context of the tort of misfeasance in public office. The difficulty with this argument was that it could not be squared with a meaningful requirement of bad faith in the exercise of public powers which is the raison d'être of the tort. But, understandably, the argument became more refined during the oral hearing and counsel for the plaintiffs accepted that only reckless indifference in a subjective sense will be sufficient. This concession was rightly made. The plaintiff must prove that the public officer acted with a state of mind of reckless indifference to the illegality of his act: *Rawlinson v Rice* [1997] 2 NZLR 651.

As we have seen, reckless indifference does not suffice for the economic torts, which clearly require *intent*. The difference in mental element between the torts is explained by their different focus. The 'gist' of misfeasance is abuse of power.[84]

The Damage Requirement

When we mapped torts in Chapter 1, we specified that misfeasance in a public office is actionable only where there is damage to the claimant. Unlike the trespass torts, but like malicious prosecution, it is not a tort 'actionable per se'. This was confirmed by the House of Lords in *Watkins v Secretary of State for the Home Department and Others* [2006] UKHL 17; [2006] 2 AC 395, a case where prison officers had unlawfully interfered with a prisoner's mail. Importantly, the House of Lords rejected an argument that the action in misfeasance should also be available, in the absence of actual damage, where a 'fundamental right' or 'constitutional right' was interfered with. We have seen how the Supreme Court in *Lumba* continued to limit common law's protection of such rights, on that occasion in the context of a tort actionable *per se*. Lord Bingham argued that if the right in question is not protected in relevant circumstances by the law of tort, then the claimant should have recourse to an action under section 7 of the Human Rights Act 1998, and should not seek to rewrite the fundamental principles of an action in tort to accommodate their claim. Established torts themselves express a balance between claimants, defendants, and other interests, and

---

[82] *R v Cunningham* [1957] 2 QB 396.
[83] *R v Caldwell* [1982] AC 341.
[84] Lord Phillips MR commented specifically on this point in *Douglas v Hello!* (*No 3*), at [222].

core features of this balance should not be cast aside in response to arguments based on Convention rights. These rights may be appropriately protected in other ways.[85]

Subsequently, in *Karagozlu v Commissioner of Police of the Metropolis* [2006] EWCA Civ 1691, the Court of Appeal held that loss of liberty is itself capable of amounting to 'material or special damage' in the sense required by the House of Lords' decision in *Watkins*. The category of material damage is therefore broader than 'financial loss or physical or mental injury' (the terminology used by Lord Bingham in *Watkins* at para [1])—or, perhaps, loss of liberty is closely analogous to physical injury. The Court of Appeal reasoned to this conclusion partly by reference to the tort of malicious prosecution. Lord Steyn clearly said in *Gregory v Portsmouth City Council* [2000] 1 AC 419, at 426 (a case argued in malicious prosecution) that '[d]amage is a necessary ingredient of the tort'; and it is plain that loss of liberty is considered sufficient 'damage' for the purposes of that tort. The Court of Appeal also argued that there was nothing in the House of Lords' judgment in *Watkins* to contradict the idea that loss of liberty was damage.

The Court of Appeal also argued that the decision in *R v Deputy Governor of Parkhurst Prison, ex p Hague* [1992] 1 AC 58 was no impediment to their conclusion. In *ex p Hague* the House of Lords ruled that change in the conditions in which a prisoner is kept did not render the imprisonment—which was generally lawful—unlawful for the purposes of an action in false imprisonment. We have already said that false imprisonment is primarily concerned with unlawfulness not with wrongful damage, and we have contemplated the significance of *Lumba* in relation to the integrity of the tort of false imprisonment. Since the claimant in *Karagozlu* argued that he had been wrongly transferred from open prison to more confined conditions in a closed prison, it appears that loss of 'residual liberty' constitutes damage for the purposes of an action in misfeasance, but will not suffice to render imprisonment unlawful for an action in false imprisonment.

The Court of Appeal gave further consideration to the damage requirement in *Hussain v Chief Constable of West Mercia* [2008] EWCA Civ 1205. The claimant taxi driver alleged a campaign of racial discrimination against him. He suffered stress-related conditions including some physical discomfort and irritability, but no recognized psychiatric damage. The Court was unanimous that this was insufficient damage for the tort, but expressed different views on whether the damage requirement in misfeasance is the same as in negligence, which is itself of course a tort requiring damage. Kay LJ, in particular, did not discount the idea that in this 'tort of obloquy', mental distress falling short of psychiatric damage should suffice. That issue, however, did not fall to be resolved in this case.

Recoverable Damage/Remoteness

In *Three Rivers* Lord Steyn also considered the **extent of recoverable damage** in the tort of misfeasance in a public office. We have already noted that in the case of deceit, all *directly* caused damage can be recovered. The defendant does not gain 'the benefit' of the foreseeability test which, in the tort of negligence and in private nuisance, limits the recoverable damages to those of a type which the defendant could have foreseen. Lord Steyn concluded that even the foreseeability test was too generous to the claimant in this particular tort, even

[85] The position in *D v East Berkshire*, a case mentioned by Lord Bingham in the passage above, is quite different. The argument there concerned policy considerations affecting the application of the tort of negligence. There was no question of fundamentally altering the nature of the tort.

though it is an intentional tort. Only the damage *actually foreseen* by the defendant as likely or probable should be recoverable (Lord Steyn at 195–6).

In support of this view, it can be argued that misfeasance in a public office is different from the intentional economic torts discussed earlier, as they in turn are different from the torts of trespass to the person and the action in *Wilkinson v Downton*. There is no reason to say that all torts of intention, given their considerable and often justified variations, should be subject to the same remoteness rule; and the solution reached was deliberately aimed at achieving balance in protection of different interests and policy goals. On the other hand, against Lord Steyn's solution is the practical difficulty that proving what damage a *recklessly indifferent* official *actually had in mind* may prove to be far from straightforward.

Although misfeasance in a public office is in a sense a resurgent tort, it is hedged in by significant restrictions relating to state of mind; damage; and remoteness. The Law Commission, in its Consultation Paper, *Administrative Redress: Public Bodies and the Citizen* (LCCP 187, 2008) invited views on the abolition of the tort, as part of a package including introduction of a new form of liability where there is serious fault in a 'truly public' activity—although its consultation is now closed and the proposals withdrawn. It is fair to say that the resurgence of the tort raises the possibility of expensive and unfounded litigation against public bodies, on the part of those with a grievance. The boundaries of the tort are not policed by a 'duty' concept in the same way as the tort of negligence. On the other hand, successful claims are not unheard of, even if rare, and it is the seriousness of the abuse of power established in these successful claims which may be thought to justify the risks and expense of unfounded claims.

9. CONCLUSIONS

i.   The diverse array of intentional torts in English law should serve as a contrast to the wide, sprawling tort of negligence addressed in the next section. Negligence is certainly the dominant tort; but it has by no means driven out other torts nor deprived all of them of their significance.

ii. There is however no unifying principle which underlies torts of intention in English law. Some, such as malicious prosecution, require damage or harm in the same way as negligence, though the range of harms covered may be different. As we saw in Chapter 1, torts have different 'ingredients', and there is no specific recipe for a tort of intention in English law. Even the 'economic torts' are hard to unify; certainly, no attempt to unify all the torts in this chapter is likely to succeed. Rather, the possibilities can be 'mapped' and compared.

iii. Most undergraduate law courses pay minimal attention to intentional torts, yet many of them continue to develop and successive editions of this book have seen significant developments both through statute and appellate decisions of the courts, for example in *OPO v Rhodes*. Intentional torts may have uses which are very different from the core of negligence, for example by restraining *unlawful* (rather than damaging) acts, and in this sense protecting certain core fundamental rights. In such instances, intention may vary from weak (false imprisonment) to strong (misfeasance in a public office) as an element of the cause of action. This function of the common law is far older than the Human Rights Act 1998, but coexistence with the action for damages under that statute undoubtedly poses challenges.

iv. At the same time, it is clear that intention alone is not enough to justify liability. The economic torts illustrate this clearly, since strong intention must be accompanied by unlawfulness of action. Perhaps the closest the law has come to a general principle of liability for intentionally caused harm is through the tort in *Wilkinson v Downton*, now renamed as the tort of wilfully endangering another's personal safety. This too has been confined however, and the trend towards containment is further continued by the Supreme Court in *OPO v Rhodes*, with particular care being paid to the need for unjustified conduct; actual intention; and causation of personal injury or psychiatric harm.

v. An obvious instance of an expanding intentional tort is malicious prosecution. This tort requires both a malicious motive, and actual harm to the claimant. By recognizing the possibility of liability for malicious *civil* prosecution, the Supreme Court has expanded the potential ambit of this tort exponentially. Many of the limiting factors which have confined the operation of malicious criminal prosecution—for example, the existence of a public prosecutor and police force—will simply not operate to limit the civil version of the tort.

FURTHER READING

Intention

Atiyah, P., 'American Tort Law in Crisis' (1987) 7 OJLS 279.

Finnis, J., 'Intention in Tort Law', in D. Owen (ed.), Philosophical Foundations of Tort Law (Oxford: Clarendon Press, 1995).

Trespass to the Person

Bartlett, P., *Blackstone's Guide to the Mental Capacity Act 2005* (2nd edn, Oxford University Press, 2008).

Brazier, M., 'Patient Autonomy and Consent to Treatment: the Role of the Law?' (1987) 7 LS 169.

Donnelly, M., 'Best Interests, Patient Participation and the Mental Capacity Act 2005' (2009) 17 Med L Rev 1–29.

Donnelly, M., 'Capacity Assessment under the Mental Capacity Act: Delivering on the Functional Approach?' (2009) 29 LS 464–91.

Donnelly, M., *Healthcare Decision-Making and the Law* (Cambridge University Press, 2010)

Feldman, D., 'Containment, Deprivation of Liberty and Breach of the Peace' (2009) 68 CLJ 243–5.

Feldman, D., 'Consequences of Administrative Unlawfulness' (2012) 71 CLJ 11

Ibbetson, D., *A Historical Introduction to the Law of Obligations* (Oxford: Oxford University Press, 1999), chapter 3.

Keown, J., 'Restoring Moral and Intellectual Shape to the Law After *Bland*' (1997) 113 LQR 482–503.

Tan Keng Feng, 'Failure of Medical Advice: Trespass or Negligence?' (1987) 7 LS 149–68.

Mead, D., 'Of Kettles, Cordons and Crowd Control—Austin v Commissioner of Police for the Metropolis and the Meaning of "deprivation of liberty"' (2009) EHRLR 376–94.

Michaelowski, S., 'Advance Refusals of Life-sustaining Medical Treatment: The Relativity of an Absolute Right' (2005) 68 MLR 958–82.

Trindade, F., 'Intentional Torts: Some Thoughts on Assault and Battery' (1982) 2 OJLS 211–37.

Trindade, F., 'The Modern Tort of False Imprisonment', in N. J. Mullaney (ed.), *Torts in the Nineties* (Sydney: LBC Information Services, 1997).

Intentional Infliction of Physical or Mental Harm and Statutory Action for Harassment

Bridgeman, J., and Jones, M., 'Harassing and Outrageous Acts' (1994) 14 LS 180.

Conaghan, J., 'Harassment and the Law of Tort: *Khorasandjian v Bush*' (1993) Fem LS 189.

Conaghan, J., 'Gendered Harms and the Law of Tort: Remedying (Sexual) Harassment' (1996) 16 OJLS 407.

Handford, P., '*Wilkinson v Downton* and Acts Calculated to Cause Physical Harm' (1985) 16 UWAL Rev 31.

Trindade, F., 'The Intentional Infliction of Purely Mental Distress' (1986) 6 OJLS 219.

Witting, C., 'Tort Liability for Intended Mental Harm' (1998) 21 UNSWLJ 55.

Economic Torts

Bagshaw, R., 'Can the Economic Torts be Unified?' (1998) 18 OJLS 729–39.

Bagshaw, R., 'Inducing Breach of Contract', in J. Horder (ed.), *Oxford Essays in Jurisprudence*, Fourth Series (Oxford: Oxford University Press, 2000).

Carty, H., *An Analysis of the Economic Torts* (Oxford: Oxford University Press, 2nd edn, 2010).

Carty, H., 'The Economic Torts in the 21st Century' (2008) 124 LQR 641–74.

Carty, H., 'The Modern Functions of the Economic Torts: Reviewing the English, Canadian, and New Zealand Positions' (2015) 74 CLJ 261.

Deakin, S., and Randall, J., 'Rethinking the Economic Torts' (2009) 72 MLR 519–53.

Hoffmann, L., 'The Rise and Fall of the Economic Torts', in S. Degeling, J. Edelman, and J. Goudkamp (eds) *Torts in Commercial Law* (Thomson Reuters, 2010)

Howarth, D., 'Against *Lumley v Gye*' (2005) 68 MLR 195–232.

Lee, J., 'Restoring Confidence in the Economic Torts' (2007) 15 Tort L Rev 172–6.

Murphy, J., 'Understanding Intimidation' (2014) 77 MLR 33.

Neyers, J., 'Rights-based Justifications for the Tort of Unlawful Interference with Economic Relations' (2008) LS 215–33.

Neyers, J., 'Economic Torts as Corrective Justice' (2009) Torts Law Journal 162.

Sales, P., and Stilitz, D., 'Intentional Infliction of Harm by Unlawful Means' (1999) 115 LQR 411.

Simester, A., and Chan, W., 'Inducing Breach of Contract: One Tort or Two?' [2004] CLJ 132–65.

Simpson, B., 'Economic Tort Liability in Labour Disputes: The Potential Impact of the House of Lords' Decision in *OBG v Allan*' (2007) 36 ILJ 468–79.

Simpson, B., 'Trade Disputes Legislation and the Economic Torts', in T. T. Arvind and J. Steele (eds), *Tort Law and the Legislature: Common Law, Statute, and the Dynamics of Legal Change* (Hart Publishing, 2013).

Waddams, S., 'Johanna Wagner and the Rival Opera Houses' (2001) 117 LQR 431.

Weir, T., *Economic Torts* (Clarendon Press, 1997).

Misfeasance in A Public Office

Aronson, M., 'Misfeasance in Public Office: A Very Peculiar Tort' (2011) 35 *Mel ULR* 1.

Chamberlain, E., *Misfeasance in a Public Office* (2016, Carswell).

Vines, P., 'Misfeasance in Public Office: Old Torts, New Tricks?', in S. Degeling, J. Edelman, and J. Goudkamp (eds), *Torts in Commercial Law* (2010, Sweet and Maxwell).

PART III

THE TORT
OF NEGLIGENCE

In this Part of the book, we begin to explore the tort of negligence. Our exploration will not be complete until the end of Part IV. In this Part, we consider the requirements for liability in negligence.

Chapter 3 introduces and explores the key components of the tort. There is negligence liability only if the claimant can show that the tortfeasor fell short of the degree of care expected of 'the reasonable person': negligence requires 'fault' in this particular sense. This however is not enough. Only lack of care which amounts to a *breach of a duty owed to the claimant* will give rise to liability in negligence.

It is all too easy for students to be lured into thinking that duty of care—difficult concept as it is—is all there is to a claim in negligence. Chapters 3, 4, and 5 introduce other elements of the tort before we turn to the detailed application of 'duty' ideas in more difficult contexts, in Chapter 6. Because negligence is a tort requiring damage, it must be shown that the breach of duty has caused material damage to the claimant. In the most elusive of the negligence criteria, that damage must also be attributable to—or not too remote from—the defendant's breach of duty. In one variation of this, the damage must fall within the scope of the duty.

Identifying the principles by which a sufficient causal link may be established has been one of the most problematic issues for negligence law in recent years. In Chapter 4, we explore some of the most difficult problems of causation to have arisen, which have implications for the nature of the tort itself. In Chapter 5, we explore a range of defences to negligence. Available defences are as important for understanding the reach of liability as the principles of liability themselves, and defences provide important background for Chapter 6. The idea that no duty is owed (Chapter 6), and the idea that the risk for some other reason should fall wholly or partly on the claimant (Chapter 5), are overlapping.

Finally in Chapter 6 we turn to the duty concept in more detail. The inherent flexibility of the tort of negligence has contributed to its success, but has also made it difficult to identify its boundaries. Such are the difficulties thrown up by the varied contexts in which negligence operates, Chapter 6 is easily the longest of the book. Even so, it is important to bear in mind that negligence is not the whole of tort; and duty is not the whole of negligence.

3

ESSENTIALS OF NEGLIGENCE: ESTABLISHING LIABILITY

CENTRAL ISSUES

i) Negligence dominates the modern law of tort. One of the reasons for this is the broad appeal, and potential broad application, of the fault principle on which it is based. Liability under the fault principle depends on showing that the defendant's conduct has **fallen short of an objective standard**.

ii) The fault principle or negligence standard has a positive and a negative implication. The **negative** implication is that there is 'no liability without fault'. But the negligence standard does not require personal fault in the fullest sense. The objective standard does not vary in order to fit the particular abilities of defendants.

iii) The **positive** implication of the fault principle is that where there is faulty conduct which foreseeably causes damage, the defendant *ought* to make good the damage caused. But this aspect of the negligence standard, together with the range of damage which it will compensate, raises the spectre of virtually limitless liability. The duty of care plays a key role in limiting the reach of the tort of

negligence. There will be liability only if the tortfeasor breached a **duty of care owed to the claimant.**

iv) In Section 3, we track the development of the duty of care. In *Donoghue v Stevenson* [1932] AC 562, Lord Atkin argued that the existing examples of duties to take care could be seen as aspects of a single tort. Through the 'neighbour principle', he sought to state what these 'duty situations' had in common. In *Anns v Merton* [1978] AC 728, Lord Wilberforce went further and stated a single, universal test for the duty of care in negligence. A duty would arise on the basis of 'neighbourhood', unless there was some distinct reason to deny a duty. This generalizing trend has since been reversed. Since *Caparo v Dickman* [1990] 2 AC 605, a tortfeasor will be subject to a duty of care only if there are *positive reasons* for holding the defendant responsible for the claimant's loss.

v) **Negligent omissions** raise distinct issues in respect of duty, but also potentially of breach, causation, and remoteness. We consider such issues at the end of the section on duty of care, identifying particular categories of case where the omissions issue will be found to be relevant, and considering the general question of negligent omissions and the problems they pose.

vi) Negligence is a damage-based tort, and the claimant must show that appropriate damage was caused by the defendant's breach of duty. Traditionally, there have been two distinct questions of causation. The first is known as **'cause in fact'**. On the face of it, this states a simple factual test. But as we will begin to discover in Section 3, this impression is not accurate. We defer the most complex questions of 'cause in fact' to Chapter 4.

vii) There is also a second question about the connection between the breach of duty, and the damage. Controversy persists over whether this question (traditionally called **'cause in law'** or **'remoteness'**) is really a question of causation at all. In *The Wagon Mound* (1961), the Privy Council attempted to establish that there was only one causal question ('cause in fact'), and that the remaining question of remoteness was best expressed in terms of foreseeability. That attempt was never wholly successful, and elements of causal language persisted. A more recent interpretation of remoteness questions is to ask whether the damage is 'within the scope of the duty' owed by the defendant to the claimant. 'Scope of duty' analysis thus brings together issues of duty and of damage, while attempting to avoid the language of causation.

1. STANDARD OF CARE: WHAT IS 'NEGLIGENCE'?

In order to succeed in a claim in negligence, the claimant must show that the following criteria are met:

1. The defendant owes the claimant a duty to take care.
2. That duty has been breached.
3. The defendant's breach of duty has caused the claimant to suffer loss or damage of a relevant sort.
4. That damage is caused in law by the defendant's negligence/is not too remote/is within the scope of the duty.

It is easy to see why the majority of texts begin with the first question, whether a duty of care is owed. It appears to be the logically prior question. And yet, 'duty of care' is a relatively abstract and difficult notion, which does not have an exact parallel in any other tort, and whose purpose is open to argument. By contrast, the standard of care is more easily grasped, and it is of equal importance.[1] The standard of care defines what conduct will count in law as negligence or lack of care, and in this sense it defines the 'content' of the tort.

[1] D. Nolan, 'Deconstructing the Duty of Care' (2013) 129 LQR 559, goes further and argues that many questions currently dealt with as 'duty' questions could be answered instead using notions of standard of care and of causation.

Historically too, lack of care (together with damage) could be said to be the prime mover in the development of the tort. According to David Ibbetson, a series of 'innominate' (unnamed) tort actions involving loss to the claimant were redefined during the nineteenth century as components of a tort of negligence. What they had in common was the nature of the defendant's conduct, and thus 'carelessness' was the key feature of the emerging tort:

David Ibbetson, *A Historical Introduction to the Law of Obligations* (Oxford University Press, 1999), 169

The law of torts at the beginning of the nineteenth century was still recognizably medieval. It was characterized by a division between the action of trespass and the action on the case, the latter of which was subdivided into a number of nominate forms and a large residual group linked together by nothing stronger than that the defendant was alleged to have caused loss to the plaintiff. In the nineteenth century a substantial part of this residual group coalesced as the tort of negligence. This brought about a wholesale realignment of the law of torts, as this tort, defined by reference to the quality of the defendant's conduct, cut across the previously existing categorisation of torts.

While some other torts (for example the actions in defamation) are defined according to the interest they protect, the tort of negligence was and is defined primarily according to the 'quality of the defendant's conduct'. In this text, we will therefore begin our exploration of negligence with the standard of care, but readers may of course use sections of this chapter in whichever order suits them.

'Mapping' Torts and the Negligence Standard

In Chapter 1, we discussed the way that torts may be 'mapped' according to their essential elements. These elements included the nature of the protected interests, and the nature of the defendant's 'wrong'. We noted that in some torts, such as libel, there is no required element of fault on the part of the defendant. In the case of negligence, however, there clearly is a requirement that the defendant's conduct should be defective (and that damage must be caused). In negligence, conduct is judged according to whether it falls short of a relevant objective standard of care.

This distinctive negligence standard has tended to infiltrate other torts, sometimes displacing existing and different standards of liability: see for example Chapter 11 on *Rylands v Fletcher*. This may be because the idea of liability based on fault has intuitive appeal. But on the other hand, the 'objective' standard, which we introduce in the section that follows, is quite adaptable, and its exact link with personal fault is open to question.

The relevant standard peculiar to negligence is that of the 'reasonable person'. In general, we must judge the defendant by the standards of a reasonable person who is undertaking the task or activity in the course of which the negligence is said to arise.[2] The 'reasonable person'

---

[2] Most cases until very recently referred not to reasonable 'persons' but to reasonable 'men'. We will assume that this terminology makes no substantive difference, and that the 'reasonable man' is no different from the 'reasonable woman'. Some writers have doubted this. See generally Mayo Moran, *Rethinking the Reasonable Person* (Oxford University Press, 2003).

test is generally an objective one, which is not adjusted to fit the particular qualities of the defendant. Therefore, although negligence is concerned with 'falling short' of a relevant standard, it does not necessarily involve actions for which we would 'blame' an individual defendant. In the sense that it sets standards which are sometimes not reasonably attainable for particular defendants, negligence does indeed involve an element of 'strict' liability of a certain sort. This is inherent in the 'objective' standard.

1.1 THE OBJECTIVE STANDARD

Nettleship v Weston [1971] 2 QB 691

In *Nettleship v Weston*, the defendant was a learner driver. She was given driving lessons by the plaintiff, a family friend. She 'froze' at the wheel, so that her car mounted the pavement and struck a lamp post. This caused injury to the plaintiff instructor. The plaintiff and defendant were in joint control of the car, since the instructor was operating the gear stick and handbrake while the defendant was steering.

The Court of Appeal held that the defendant's conduct fell below the required standard of care, which was the same objective standard owed by every driver. One of the judges, Salmon LJ, dissented on this point. There was a reduction of damages on account of the instructor's own fault in respect of the accident.

In Chapter 5, we will consider this case again in respect of defences, in particular the failed defence of *volenti non fit injuria* (acceptance of risk). For the time being, we concentrate on those elements of the case that relate to the standard of care.

Lord Denning MR

The Responsibility of the Learner Driver Towards Persons on or near the Highway

Mrs. Weston is clearly liable for the damage to the lamp post. In the civil law if a driver goes off the road on to the pavement and injures a pedestrian, or damages property, he is prima facie liable. Likewise if he goes on to the wrong side of the road. It is no answer for him to say: "I was a learner driver under instruction. I was doing my best and could not help it." The civil law permits no such excuse. It requires of him the same standard of care as of any other driver. "It eliminates the personal equation and is independent of the idiosyncrasies of the particular person whose conduct is in question": see *Glasgow Corporation v. Muir* [1943] A.C. 448, 457 by Lord Macmillan. The learner driver may be doing his best, but his incompetent best is not good enough. He must drive in as good a manner as a driver of skill, experience and care, who is sound in wind and limb, who makes no errors of judgment, has good eyesight and hearing, and is free from any infirmity …

The Responsibility of the Learner Driver in Criminal Law

Mrs. Weston was rightly convicted of driving without due care and attention. In the criminal law it is no defence for a driver to say: "I was a learner driver under instruction. I was doing my best and could not help it." Such a plea may go to mitigation of sentence, but it does not go in exculpation of guilt. The criminal law insists that every person driving a car must attain an objective standard measured by the standard of a skilled, experienced and careful driver. …

The high standard thus imposed by the judges is, I believe, largely the result of the policy of the Road Traffic Acts. Parliament requires every driver to be insured against third party risks. The reason is so that a person injured by a motor car should not be left to bear the loss on his own, but should be compensated out of the insurance fund. The fund is better able to bear it than he can. But the injured person is only able to recover if the driver is liable in law. So the judges see to it that he is liable, unless he can prove care and skill of a high standard: see *The Merchant Prince* [1892] P. 179 and *Henderson v. Henry E. Jenkins & Sons* [1970] A.C. 282. Thus we are, in this branch of the law, moving away from the concept: "No liability without fault." We are beginning to apply the test: "On whom should the risk fall?" Morally the learner driver is not at fault; but legally she is liable to be because she is insured and the risk should fall on her.

The Responsibility of the Learner Driver towards Passengers in the Car

… The driver owes a duty of care to every passenger in the car, just as he does to every pedestrian on the road: and he must attain the same standard of care in respect of each. If the driver were to be excused according to the knowledge of the passenger, it would result in endless confusion and injustice. One of the passengers may know that the learner driver is a mere novice. Another passenger may believe him to be entirely competent. One of the passengers may know that he has had only two drinks. Another passenger may know that he has had a dozen. Is the one passenger to recover and the other not? Rather than embark on such inquiries, the law holds that the driver must attain the same standard of care for passengers as for pedestrians. The knowledge of the passenger may go to show that he was guilty of contributory negligence in ever accepting the lift—and thus reduce his damages—but it does not take away the duty of care, nor does it diminish the standard of care which the law requires of the driver: see *Dann v. Hamilton* [1939] 1 K.B. 509 and *Slater v. Clay Cross Co. Ltd.* [1956] 2 Q.B. 264, 270 ….

Comments

Lord Denning had three reasons for holding the learner driver to the same standard as an experienced driver. First, she had already been convicted of driving without due care and attention, illustrating that the criminal law did not excuse the learner driver who was doing her 'incompetent best'. It would be strange if tort law, which in these circumstances has as its consequence the payment of compensation from an insurance fund, should *more* readily accept excuses than does the criminal law, whose sanctions here are generally punitive.

Lord Denning's second reason is practicality. It would be inappropriate, and confusing, for the driver of a car to owe different duties to different passengers in the car, and to different individuals outside the car, depending on what they knew or did not know about the driver's competence.

Lord Denning's third reason concerns insurance. We should consider this reason with care. Lord Denning states very clearly that the law in this area, governed by the Road Traffic Acts, is less concerned that there should be 'no liability without fault', and more concerned with the distributive question, 'on whom should the risk fall?' This effectively flags up a continuing dispute within the tort of negligence, concerning the purpose and nature of the tort as a whole. It is clear that negligence liability attempts to shift loss to a person whose conduct is defective, from a person who has suffered injury as a consequence—though only in those circumstances where the defective conduct amounts to a breach of duty owed to the injured party. It is less clear why it does so, particularly where there is compulsory insurance. Is the shifting of losses justified by the faulty conduct of individual defendants? If so, why do we require them to insure, since this will make sure that they do not bear the loss themselves? Alternatively, is the shifting of loss justified through more distributive questions concerning the most effective or fairest means of spreading loss, ensuring (as Lord Denning put it) that no individual has to bear the loss alone?

The insurance context was introduced in Chapter 1, and similar questions will be encountered in various chapters of this book. But it would be wrong to assume that the background insurance position has only one effect on the case law, namely that judges will 'see to it' (in Lord Denning's blunt expression) that those who carry liability insurance will be liable for losses they cause. This is by no means always the case. English courts have on many occasions been eager to prevent claimants from pursuing those with deep pockets (including insurance companies) simply in order to transfer losses from themselves. An example is *Transco v Stockport MBC* [2003] UKHL 61; [2004] 2 AC 1, a case concerning the limits of strict liability for escapes, which is considered in Chapter 11. It needs to be remembered that on some occasions the claimant against whom the compensation paid. In such a case, the practical outcome of a negligence claim will be to determine which of two insurers will ultimately bear the burden of compensating (or indemnifying) the injured party or, if the defendant has no valid insurance, it may even shift the loss to an uninsured party. This is not limited to situations of *compulsory* liability insurance as we will see below; but these situations (road traffic, and employer liability) have the important special feature that insurance is predictable.

A case raising essentially the same issues as *Nettleship v Weston* reached the High Court of Australia in *McNeilly v Imbree* [2008] HCA 40. Prior to this case, the High Court of Australia had decided that the standard of care of an inexperienced driver should be varied in relation to a passenger who knows of the relative lack of experience and has voluntarily taken on the role of supervising or instructing the driver (*Cook v Cook* (1986) 162 CLR 376). In *McNeilly*, the variable standard applicable within such 'relationships' was abandoned and a position akin to the English approach was adopted. The outcome was unanimous, but the reasoning was not. The 'plurality' (a term used in Australia to refer to a group of judges whose joint reasoning represents the majority in a case) explained that *Cook v Cook* had been decided at a time when the existence of a duty of care was thought to respond primarily to 'proximity' between the parties—and had extended this thinking to the content of the duty. That general approach had since been rethought. Kirby J on the other hand went out of his way to emphasize that the insurance position had played not only a role, but a decisive role in his reasoning. The particular feature of the insurance position in this case was that liability insurance for drivers was not merely commonplace, but also compulsory, throughout Australia. This, he argued, was a vital piece of information in deciding whether it was appropriate to hold an inexperienced driver to a higher standard of care than was justified by his or her particular level of skill and experience, in respect of a supervising passenger. The policy of compulsory insurance legislation made it appropriate to measure that lack of care objectively.

Kirby J, *Imbree v McNeilly*

[2008] HCA 40

169 Compulsory insurance: a special case:

...

171 The availability and existence of voluntary liability insurance is one thing. The compulsory provisions for universal statutory third party insurance of all motor vehicles registered for use on Australian roads is quite another. The latter form of insurance exists to provide coverage against "fault" on the part of drivers of motor vehicles. It does so because of the recognition, by the 1930s, that the use of vehicles would inevitably occasion a toll of death and injury, for which a system of compulsory insurance was essential. That system was necessary to prevent intolerable burdens of unrecoverable losses falling upon persons injured in consequence of the ever-increasing use of motor vehicles on Australian roads of varying conditions. Such persons would otherwise often have been thrown back upon social security entitlements, welfare agencies or their families. Instead, a statutory insurance fund was provided from subventions paid by *all* motorists. That is the context in which the applicable principle of the common law falls to be determined.

172 Another way in which the existence of compulsory third party motor vehicle insurance operates in this area of tort law concerns the applicability of the second purpose of tort law, namely to encourage care to avoid personal liability and thereby to modify potentially harmful behaviour. Where, as in this context, the payment of a compulsory (but relatively small) premium exempts the driver or owner from personal liability for negligence in all but the most exceptional of cases, it is hard to see how the second objective of the common law is attained. This simply serves to reinforce the conclusion that the common law liability in issue is not "pure". It is a hybrid form of liability in which the common law is inescapably affected by the presence of compulsory statutory insurance.

Of the other members of the High Court, only one mentioned insurance, and this was in order to state explicitly that the insurance position *could not be* a step in the court's reasoning toward a result. Even so, he emphasized the enormous significance of insurance in making sure that the law did not operate with 'intolerable harshness' in this area.

Gleeson CJ, *McNeilly v Imbree*

[2008] HCA 40

23 ... If it were not for insurance, the common law would operate with intolerable harshness in its application to driving. That is a sound reason in public policy for legislative intervention. If it were not for third party insurance, it may be assumed that the first respondent would not have been permitted, and (at least if well informed) would not have dared, to drive at all on the occasion in question. Such insurance does not, however, provide a step in a process of reasoning towards an answer to the particular question that arises for decision in this appeal.

Kirby J goes as far as to say that tort is really a 'hybrid', so that some of its principles and rules can make sense only when viewed in tandem with the insurance position. Gleeson CJ does not go so far, and merely describes the principles of tort as having an 'overlay' of statutory intervention.

Mental and Physical Impairment

In the following decision, the Court of Appeal decided that the standard of care was not varied to reflect mental or physical impairment; only if actions were involuntary would there be no liability; and this was not apparently treated as an aspect of the standard of care.

Dunnage v Randall [2015] EWCA Civ 673; [2016] QB 639

The claimant, whose intervention was recognized by the judge as heroic, had tried to stop a visitor to his house from setting fire to himself with petrol. The visitor died as a consequence, and the claimant was badly burned. The claimant brought an action in negligence against the visitor, who was retrospectively diagnosed as affected by schizophrenia. His goal was to obtain damages from the defendant's insurers through a household policy which covered liability for 'accidental' personal injury. As is typically the case, the insurance policy excluded liability arising from 'wilful or malicious' actions on the part of the insured. Thus there were two questions: had the defendant breached his duty of care and acted negligently, despite the effect of his schizophrenia? And if he had, was the liability excluded from the insurance policy because it was 'wilful and malicious'?

The Court of Appeal unanimously held for the claimant. On the first question, the Court emphatically stated that the standard of care applicable in negligence is objective; and this means that it does not vary to reflect the capacity and state of mind of an individual defendant. No distinction is to be made between mental and physical incapacity in this regard; and the sole exception was said to be the case of children (considered below), where the objective standard is set according to age. The situation would be different only if it could be said that the defendant 'had not acted at all': in such an extreme case, for example where a driver suffers an unforeseen attack and 'blacks out' at the wheel of a vehicle (*Mansfield v Weetabix* [1998] 1 WLR 1263), the defendant is simply not responsible. On the analysis in *Dunnage*, this is not a question of departing from the objective standard, but a recognition that the defendant has done nothing that could amount to a breach of duty.[3]

Vos LJ, *Dunnage v Randall*

130 ... is there some principle that requires the law to excuse from liability in negligence a defendant who fails to meet the normal standard of care partly because of a medical problem. In my judgment, there is and should be no such principle. The courts have consistently and correctly rejected the notion that the standard of care should be adjusted to take account of personal characteristics of the defendant. The single exception in respect of the liability of children should not, I think, be extended. People with physical and mental health problems should not properly be regarded as analogous to children, even if some

---

[3] The attempt to distinguish *Mansfield* in this way is criticized by J. Goudkamp and M. Ihouma, 'A Tour of the Tort of Negligence' (2016) 32 PN 137, arguing that the Court of Appeal in *Mansfield* plainly thought it was varying the standard of care—though not declaring a preference between the two approaches. See also (before *Dunnage*) D. Nolan, 'Varying the Standard of Care in Negligence' (2013) 72 CLJ 651.

commonly and inappropriately speak of adults with mental health problems as having a "mental age of five".

131 In my judgment, only defendants whose attack or medical incapacity has the effect of entirely eliminating any fault or responsibility for the injury can be excused. It is only defendants in that category that have not actually broken their undoubted duty of care. The actions of a defendant, who is merely impaired by medical problems, whether physical or mental, cannot escape liability if he causes injury by failing to exercise reasonable care.

132 What then does it mean to say that a medical condition entirely eliminates any fault or responsibility for the injury? It simply means that the defendant himself did nothing to cause the injury. Mr Michael Davie QC, leading counsel for the first defendant, gave the example of a person whose arm is holding a knife and who is overcome by another forcing him to stab a victim. The person holding the knife cannot have broken his duty of care because he did nothing himself.

133 In my judgment, however, at all intermediate stages where the defendant does something himself he risks being liable for failing to meet the standards of the reasonable man. This approach avoids the need for medical witnesses to become engaged with difficult and undefined terms such as volition, will, free choice, consciousness, personal autonomy and the like. It is only if the defendant can properly be said to have done nothing himself to cause the injury that he escapes liability. . . .

134 This approach also has the attraction of not requiring any fine distinction to be made between the effects of physical health problems and mental health problems. Such a distinction seems to me, in the light of modern science, to be outdated and inappropriate. Even mental health problems often have some physical cause or manifestation. There is neither a logical nor a societal reason why the law should differentiate in this area between the two.

The Court of Appeal has clearly stated therefore that the standard of care is not varied to take into account mental or physical conditions suffered by the defendant. It is strongly hinted by Vos LJ here, and by Arden LJ in her judgment, that part of the appeal of the objective standard in such cases is that there is no need for experts to be asked to make complex judgments which could complicate and extend the process of litigation.

As to the second question, the Court of Appeal held that the damage did fall within the terms of the insurance policy.

Arden LJ, *Dunnage v Randall*

156 The next question is whether damages payable to the claimant fall within Vince's householder policy. The critical matter is whether the injury suffered by the claimant was accidental bodily injury. In my judgment, the injury was accidental because on the evidence Vince had clearly lost control of his ability to make choices and therefore he could not be said to have intended to cause injury to the claimant (see the cases already cited, and see per Lord Clarke of the Outer House of the Court of Session in *Howie v CGU Insurance plc* [2005] CSOH 110, at para 11) . . .

The strength of support for the objective standard of care in this case is illustrated by the answers given to the two questions. On the negligence question, the defendant was in law 'negligent', in the sense that he fell short of the objective standard of care. The fact that his will was overborne was irrelevant since he did act, and the events were not 'involuntary'. On the insurance question however, it was said that the capacity to make choices had been lost. Thus, the acts were not wilful. It seems then that to avoid liability in negligence, there must be more than lost capacity to make meaningful choices: there must be a loss of capacity to act. It is hard to resist the conclusion that in this case too, the fact that the defendant is not the person who is to pay the damages has an impact on the policy of the law. In the absence of a suitable insurance policy however, the burden of paying damages might otherwise have fallen on the widow of the deceased.

Variations of the Objective Standard

Children

Where children are concerned, it is recognized that the applicable standard of care will be varied to suit the defendant's age. This is not intended to be an exception to the objective standard. A child will not be judged according to his or her particular level of maturity or ability. Rather, the approach is an application of the objective standard, but it is adjusted to the case in hand in the manner that was rejected for those with medical conditions in *Dunnage v Randall*. Children will be held to the standard of the 'typical' child of their own age.

Mullin v Richards [1998] 1 WLR 1304 (CA)

The claimant suffered an injury to her eye when a plastic ruler broke during a mock sword-fight at school. Her claim against the education authority (based on alleged failures of supervision) was unsuccessful, but the judge awarded damages against her fellow pupil, subject to a reduction of 50 per cent for contributory negligence. The Court of Appeal reversed the decision to award damages. Both schoolgirls were 15 years of age, and the extract below deals with the question of whether the injury could be said to have been foreseeable. In answering this, age was a relevant factor.

Hutchison LJ, at 1308–9

The argument centres on foreseeability. The test of foreseeability is an objective one; but the fact that the first defendant was at the time a 15-year-old schoolgirl is not irrelevant. The question for the judge is not whether the actions of the defendant were such as an ordinarily prudent and reasonable adult in the defendant's situation would have realised gave rise to a risk of injury, it is whether an ordinarily prudent and reasonable 15-year-old schoolgirl in the defendant's situation would have realised as much. In that connection both counsel referred us to, and relied upon, the Australian decision in *McHale v. Watson* (1966) 115 C.L.R. 199 and, in particular, the passage in the judgment of Kitto J., at pp. 213–214. I cite a portion of the passage ...

"The standard of care being objective, it is no answer for him, [that is a child] any more than it is for an adult, to say that the harm he caused was due to his being abnormally slow-witted, quick-tempered, absent-minded or inexperienced. But it does not follow that he cannot rely in his defence upon a limitation upon the capacity for foresight or prudence, not as being personal to himself, but as being characteristic of humanity at his stage of development and in that sense normal. By doing so he appeals to a standard of ordinariness, to an objective and not a subjective standard."

Mr. Stephens also cited to us a passage in the judgment of Owen J., at p. 234: "the standard by which his conduct is to be measured is not that to be expected of a reasonable adult but that reasonably to be expected of a child of the same age, intelligence and experience." I venture to question the word "intelligence" in that sentence, but I understand Owen J. to be making the same point essentially as was made by Kitto J. It is perhaps also material to have in mind the words of Salmon L.J. in *Gough v. Thorne*:

> "The question as to whether the plaintiff can be said to have been guilty of contributory negligence depends on whether any ordinary child of 13½ can be expected to have done any more than this child did. I say 'any ordinary child.' I do not mean a paragon of prudence; nor do I mean a scatter-brained child; but the ordinary girl of 13½."

Sporting Events and Playtime Dangers

In certain circumstances, decisions have to be made and actions taken when time is short. The law continues to require that the defendant must exercise reasonable care, but it is accepted that 'reasonable care' may be different in these circumstances.

Wooldridge v Sumner [1963] 2 QB 43

The plaintiff, a photographer, was seriously injured when the defendant, a participant in a horse show, rode his horse too fast around a corner and veered into the area where the photographer was standing.

Diplock LJ, at 67–8

A reasonable spectator attending voluntarily to witness any game or competition knows and presumably desires that a reasonable participant will concentrate his attention upon winning, and if the game or competition is a fast-moving one, will have to exercise his judgment and attempt to exert his skill in what, in the analogous context of contributory negligence, is sometimes called "the agony of the moment." If the participant does so concentrate his attention and consequently does exercise his judgment and attempt to exert his skill in circumstances of this kind which are inherent in the game or competition in which he is taking part, the question whether any mistake he makes amounts to a breach of duty to take reasonable care must take account of those circumstances.

The law of negligence has always recognised that the standard of care which a reasonable man will exercise depends upon the conditions under which the decision to avoid the act or omission relied upon as negligence has to be taken. The case of the workman engaged on repetitive work in the noise and bustle of the factory is a familiar example.... a participant in a game or competition gets into the circumstances in which he has no time or very little time to think by his decision to take part in the game or competition at all. It cannot be suggested that the participant, at any rate if he has some modicum of skill, is, by the mere act of participating, in breach of his duty of care to a spectator who is present for the very purpose of watching him do so. If, therefore, in the course of the game or competition, at a moment when he really has not time to think, a participant by mistake takes a wrong measure, he is not, in my view, to be held guilty of any negligence.

Furthermore, the duty which he owes is a duty of care, not a duty of skill. Save where a consensual relationship exists between a plaintiff and a defendant by which the defendant impliedly warrants his skill, a man owes no duty to his neighbour to exercise any special skill beyond that which an ordinary reasonable man would acquire before indulging in the activity in which he is engaged at the relevant time. It may well be that a participant in a game or competition would be guilty of negligence to a spectator if he took part in it when he knew or ought to have known that his lack of skill was such that even if he exerted it to the utmost he was likely to cause injury to a spectator watching him. No question of this arises in the present case. It was common ground that Mr. Holladay was an exceptionally skilful and experienced horseman.

The practical result of this analysis of the application of the common law of negligence to participant and spectator would, I think, be expressed by the common man in some such terms as these: "A person attending a game or competition takes the risk of any damage caused to him by any act of a participant done in the course of and for the purposes of the game or competition notwithstanding that such act may involve an error of judgment or a lapse of skill, unless the participant's conduct is such as to evince a reckless disregard of the spectator's safety."

It could be argued that Diplock LJ was over-elaborate in his argument here. Why should we need to introduce the idea of 'consent' on the part of the spectator, when we could simply say that the standard of care varies with the circumstances, reflecting the fact that even the reasonable person will be less able to take precautions in those circumstances? Diplock LJ makes two separate points about the standard of reasonable care:

1. in the heat of the moment, a reasonable person may be unable to avoid causing injury; *and*

2. reasonable care varies with the expectation of a person in the position of the claimant.

While this case dealt with spectators, it is clear that duties may also be owed to fellow participants and the standard of care owed will be similarly judged. In *Condon v Basi* [1985] 1 WLR, a local league footballer broke the leg of the claimant, an opposing player, with a tackle. The Court of Appeal accepted the authority of *Rootes v Shelton* [1968] ALR 33, a decision of the High Court of Australia. Sir John Donaldson MR pointed out that there were two different approaches to the standard of care in the case of *Rootes v Shelton*. One of these (the approach taken by Barwick CJ) takes up the second point derived from *Wooldridge v Sumner* because it refers to the level of risk that has been accepted by fellow participants. The other, the judgment of Kitto J, was more straightforward, concentrating simply upon reasonableness 'in relation to the special circumstances of the conduct'; this is the first point from *Wooldridge v Sumner* above. Sir John Donaldson MR said that he would prefer the more straightforward approach of Kitto J, but that it did not matter on the facts of *Condon v Basi* itself, where the defendant through his foul play showed 'reckless disregard' of his opponent's safety.

In *Blake v Galloway* [2004] EWCA Civ 814; [2004] 1 WLR 2844, the Court of Appeal reviewed the sporting authorities in order to determine the right approach to an injury suffered in the course not of sport but of simple 'horseplay'. Five teenagers were throwing bark and twigs at one another for amusement when one of them suffered an eye injury. The Court of Appeal concluded that there had been no breach of duty. Participation in the game was thought to make its tacit 'rules' consensual. Applying the case law on sporting injuries, this meant that the test for breach of duty would require something more than a simple 'error of judgment or lack of skill' (Dyson LJ at [17] quoting Diplock LJ) in *Wooldridge*).

Dyson LJ, *Blake v Galloway*

15 I recognise that the participants in the horseplay owed each other a duty to take reasonable care not to cause injury. What does that mean in the context of play of this kind? ... I consider there is a sufficiently close analogy between organised and regulated sport or games and the horseplay in which these youths were engaged for the guidance given by the authorities to which I have referred to be of value in the resolution of this case. The only real difference is that there were no formal rules for the horseplay. But I do not consider that this is a significant distinction. The common features between horseplay of this kind and formal sport involving vigorous physical activity are that both involved consensual participation in an activity (i) which involves physical contact or at least the risk of it, (ii) in which decisions are usually expected to be made quickly and often as an instinctive response to the acts of other participants, so that (iii) the very nature of the activity makes it difficult to avoid the risk of physical harm.

16 I would, therefore, apply the guidance given by Diplock LJ in *Wooldridge*, although in a slightly expanded form, and hold that in a case such as the present there is a breach of the duty of care owed by participant A to participant B only where A's conduct amounts to recklessness or a very high degree of carelessness.

The decision in *Blake v Galloway* makes clear that the different approach to breach in sporting cases is not simply a question of what expectation is reasonable 'in the heat of the moment', since the pressure and speed referred to in the sporting cases did not exist. In this particular case, a less demanding standard imposed on the defendant is justified by the consensual nature of the game.

Domestic Settings

Mullins v Richards illustrates the propensity of tort claims to arise in as wide a range of circumstances as there are opportunities to cause one another harm. This raises the question of what burdens may appropriately be placed on ordinary citizens, where they are exercising no particular expertise and not pursuing an enterprise or business. In *Perry v Harris* [2008] EWCA Civ 907, a very serious injury was suffered by a child on a bouncy castle which had been hired for a birthday party. The Court of Appeal ruled that the relevant standard was that of the reasonable parent, so that knowledge of the detailed contents of 'official' documents and guidance relating to the equipment was not assumed. The domestic setting was therefore very important to the outcome.[4]

Thus, a 'reasonable parent' would not necessarily have kept the children under constant surveillance; nor stopped the children from somersaulting; nor prevented children of different sizes from using the bouncy castle at the same time, even though these were touched upon in the instructions supplied.

The Ordinary Skilled Person Professing to Have a Special Skill

Just as the applicable standard of care is lowered in the case of children, and adjusted for actions taken 'in the heat of the moment', so also it will be higher if the defendant is performing actions which require special skill. In the leading case of *Bolam v Friern Hospital*

[4] Contrast *Hall v Holker Estate* [2008] EWCA Civ 1422, where a goal fell on the claimant at a campsite. In this commercial setting, emphasis was placed on the manufacturer's safety literature supplied with the equipment.

Management Company [1957] 1 WLR 582, McNair J advised the jury that the question of 'negligence' in a medical procedure should be approached as follows:

> In the ordinary case which does not involve any special skill, negligence in law means a failure to do some act which a reasonable man in the circumstances would do, or the doing of some act which a reasonable man in the circumstances would not do; and if that failure or the doing of that act results in injury, then there is a cause of action. How do you test whether this act or failure is negligent? In an ordinary case it is generally said you judge it by the action of the man in the street. He is the ordinary man. In one case it has been said you judge it by the conduct of the man on the top of a Clapham omnibus. He is the ordinary man. But where you get a situation which involves the use of some special skill or competence, then the test as to whether there has been negligence or not is not the test of the man on the top of a Clapham omnibus, because he has not got this special skill. The test is the standard of the ordinary skilled man exercising and professing to have that special skill. A man need not possess the highest expert skill; it is well established law that it is sufficient if he exercises the ordinary skill of an ordinary competent man exercising that particular art.

McNair J went on to discuss how the law should approach differences of opinion among medical practitioners, and we return to this element of his judgment later in this section.

Wilsher v Essex Area Health Authority [1987] QB 730 (CA)

In this case, Mustill and Glidewell LJJ explained that there would be no exception to the 'objective' standard of care where an inexperienced or newly qualified medical professional was concerned. Rather, the applicable standard would be set according to the post that is filled by the defendant. Where the plaintiff was cared for in a specialist unit, in this case a neonatal unit, the applicable standard of care was a high one. This standard would be variable according to the post held within the team providing care for the plaintiff, but it would not be variable according to the level of experience held by the particular individual member of staff. (There was an appeal to the House of Lords from this case on the issue of causation, but the House of Lords did not reconsider the issue of standard of care.)

The standard of care to be applied in any given case will depend upon the activity being performed by the defendant. It is clear that the relevant standard will in some cases also depend on the kind of skill that the defendant professes to have (as opposed to their level of experience, which should be irrelevant; see for example *Phillips v William Whiteley* [1938] 1 All ER 566, where a jeweller who pierced ears was held to the standards of care and hygiene to be expected of a reasonable jeweller, not to the standards of a qualified medical practitioner; and *Luxmoore-May v Messenger May Baverstock* [1990] 1 WLR 1009, where provincial auctioneers and valuers were on analogy with medical cases subjected to a standard of care appropriate to a 'general practitioner', which was lower than the standard applied to 'one of the leading auction houses' (at 1020). There are limits to this relativism, and in *Shakoor v Situ* [2000] 1 WLR 410, a practitioner of Chinese traditional medicine was held to the standard of an 'orthodox' general practitioner where patient safety was concerned. These cases determine which objective standard to select, reflecting the activity undertaken by the defendant: thus, they are not in conflict with *Dunnage v Randall* [2015] EWCA Civ 673, extracted earlier, where the standard of care was indeed set according to the reasonable person engaged in the same activity as the defendant.

Assessing Professional Skill and Care: Practice and Opinion

Earlier, we extracted a statement by McNair J, in the case of *Bolam v Friern Hospital Management Committee* [1957] 1 WLR 583, concerning the correct approach to the standard of care in respect of activities which require special skill. Another important aspect of his summary of the law concerned *differences of opinion* among practitioners. How should the law approach a case of alleged negligence against a professional person where that person's conduct is supported by some, but perhaps not all, fellow professionals? Should the court be free to choose which opinion to prefer? Indeed, should the existence of settled professional practice be decisive at all? The words used by McNair J on this point have become known as 'the *Bolam* test'. This test has been applied on numerous occasions.

McNair J, at 587

... he is not guilty of negligence if he has acted in accordance with a practice accepted as proper by a responsible body of medical men skilled in that particular art.... Putting it the other way round, a man is not negligent, if he is acting in accordance with such a practice, merely because there is a body of opinion who would take a contrary view.

This approach could remove the final judgment on carelessness from the court, in cases where a defendant adheres to a recognized professional practice. In an article published soon after *Bolam*, J. L. Montrose pointed out that there is no reason to take issue with the second sentence in the statement by McNair J reproduced above: certainly a 'man' is not to be held negligent *merely* because there is a body of opinion against his practice. It is the first sentence which, according to Montrose, appears to make due care synonymous not with what *should* be done, but with what is generally done—or at least with what is defended by a responsible body of appropriately skilled professionals. Montrose gives some powerful reasons why courts should not defer to those with expertise too readily:

J. L. Montrose, 'Is Negligence an Ethical or a Sociological Concept?' (1958) 21 MLR 259, at 263

It is surely negligent not to provide against risks which ought to have been known. The fact that it was not appreciated by men experienced in the particular province is, of course, strong evidence that it could not reasonably have been guarded against, but not conclusive evidence. Experts may blind themselves by expertise. The courts should guard the citizen against risks which professional men and others may ignore.

Bolam in the Medical Context

The application of the *Bolam* test within the medical context has led to accusations of a protectionist stance towards doctors. Two broad problems have been identified with the courts' interpretation of the *Bolam* test in such cases, at least up until the decisions in *Bolitho* and *Montgomery* (later in the present chapter). In the specific case of disclosure of risks associated with medical procedures, it was held by the Supreme Court in *Montgomery* that the *Bolam* test is no longer regarded as the correct approach: *Montgomery v Lanarkshire Health Board* [2015] AC 1430.

A first problem was that *Bolam* has been applied in medical cases in such a way that the court's judgment is replaced with the judgment of the defendant's medical expert, as long as the expert is found to be honest and respectable. Brazier and Miola explain this effect, while also proposing that it is particular to medical cases:

M. Brazier and J. Miola, 'Bye-Bye Bolam: A Medical Litigation Revolution?' (2000) 8 Med L Rev 85–114

What distinguishes medical litigation from other areas of professional liability is in part that a series of judgments (or maybe a gloss on those judgments) have given rise to a perception that all *Bolam* requires is that the defendant fields experts from his or her medical speciality prepared to testify that they would have followed the same course of management of the patient-plaintiff as did the defendant. If such experts can be identified, are patently honest and stand by their testimony vigorously, neither they nor the defendant will be asked to justify their practice . . . Yet in other professional negligence claims, time after time, judges have made it clear that expert opinion must be demonstrably responsible and reasonable.

Second, it has been suggested that many aspects of medical negligence litigation have been inappropriately 'Bolamized'.[5] In other words, wherever a tricky issue arises concerning the standard of care in a medical context, the habitual response of the courts has been to reach for the *Bolam* test, and to resist making their own judgments. Brazier and Miola, in the article quoted above, suggest in particular that three aspects of medical ethics had been treated in this way: advice of patients and consent to medical treatment (particularly through the judgment of Lord Diplock in *Sidaway v Royal Bethlem Hospital*); the treatment of medically incapacitated patients; and the treatment of mature minors as considered in *Gillick v West Norfolk Area Health Authority* [1985] 3 All ER 402. As already noted, *Bolam* no longer holds sway in relation to consent to medical treatment, and we return to this important point below. Against this general background however, the judgment of the House of Lords in the following case was significant.

Bolitho v City of Hackney Health Authority [1998] AC 232

In principle, this case clarified that the *final* judgment on breach of duty lies with the court, not with medical practitioners. In relation to informed consent, that step was taken more clearly in the later case of *Montgomery*; and *Bolitho* may therefore be seen as a step in the development of the law away from deference to medical practitioners. Certain of Lord Browne-Wilkinson's comments, including his approval of dicta in *Hucks v Cole* (a case from 1968 reported at [1993] 4 Med LR 393), show the importance of this clarification of the *Bolam* test.

In *Bolitho*, a 2-year-old boy suffered brain damage, and later died, as a result of cardiac arrest following respiratory failure. He was in the care of hospital staff and had suffered two severe episodes of respiratory difficulties before the final attack. On both occasions the nurses caring for the little boy called for a doctor to attend, but on neither occasion did a doctor attend. It was the claimant's case that the doctor should have attended the little boy; that he should have been intubated following the first two episodes; and that if this had been

5 M. Davies, 'The "New *Bolam*" Another False Dawn for Medical Negligence?' (1996) 12 PN 10.

done then this would have prevented the respiratory failure and cardiac arrest. It was the doctor's case that even if she had attended, she would not have intubated the child, so that her failure to attend had not, she argued, caused the injury.

Causation issues arising from this case are discussed in Section 5 of this chapter. The following extract deals with the standard of care of a medical professional. In particular, the question arose of whether it would have been negligent of the doctor not to intubate the child, had she attended him after the two initial attacks. If this course of inaction would have been negligent, then her defence to the negligence claim would fail.

Lord Browne-Wilkinson, at 241–3

The *Bolam* test—should the judge have accepted Dr. Dinwiddie's evidence?

…

Mr. Brennan…submitted that the judge had wrongly treated the *Bolam* test as requiring him to accept the views of one truthful body of expert professional advice even though he was unpersuaded of its logical force. He submitted that the judge was wrong in law in adopting that approach and that ultimately it was for the court, not for medical opinion, to decide what was the standard of care required of a professional in the circumstances of each particular case.

My Lords, I agree with these submissions to the extent that, in my view, the court is not bound to hold that a defendant doctor escapes liability for negligent treatment or diagnosis just because he leads evidence from a number of medical experts who are genuinely of opinion that the defendant's treatment or diagnosis accorded with sound medical practice. In the *Bolam* case itself, McNair J. [1957] 1 W.L.R. 583, 587 stated that the defendant had to have acted in accordance with the practice accepted as proper by a "*responsible* body of medical men." Later, at p. 588, he referred to "a standard of practice recognised as proper by a competent *reasonable* body of opinion." Again, in the passage which I have cited from *Maynard's* case [1984] 1 W.L.R. 634, 639, Lord Scarman refers to a "*respectable*" body of professional opinion. The use of these adjectives—responsible, reasonable and respectable—all show that the court has to be satisfied that the exponents of the body of opinion relied upon can demonstrate that such opinion has a logical basis. In particular in cases involving, as they so often do, the weighing of risks against benefits, the judge before accepting a body of opinion as being responsible, reasonable or respectable, will need to be satisfied that, in forming their views, the experts have directed their minds to the question of comparative risks and benefits and have reached a defensible conclusion on the matter.

There are decisions which demonstrate that the judge is entitled to approach expert professional opinion on this basis. For example, in *Hucks v. Cole* [1993] 4 Med. L.R. 393 (a case from 1968), a doctor failed to treat with penicillin a patient who was suffering from septic spots on her skin though he knew them to contain organisms capable of leading to puerperal fever. A number of distinguished doctors gave evidence that they would not, in the circumstances, have treated with penicillin. The Court of Appeal found the defendant to have been negligent. Sachs L.J. said, at p. 397:

"When the evidence shows that a lacuna in professional practice exists by which risks of grave danger are knowingly taken, then, however small the risk, the court must anxiously examine that lacuna—particularly if the risk can be easily and inexpensively avoided. If the court finds, on an analysis of the reasons given for not taking those precautions that, in the light of current professional knowledge, there is no proper basis for the lacuna, and that it is definitely not reasonable that those risks should have been taken, its function is to state that fact and where necessary to state that it constitutes negligence. In such a case the practice will no doubt thereafter be altered to the benefit of patients. On such occasions the fact that other practitioners would have done the same thing as the defendant practitioner is a very weighty matter to be put on the scales on his behalf; but it is not, as Mr. Webster readily conceded, conclusive. The court must be vigilant to see whether the reasons given for putting a patient at risk are valid in the light of any well-known advance in medical knowledge, or whether they stem from a residual adherence to out-of-date ideas."

Again, in *Edward Wong Finance Co. Ltd. v. Johnson Stokes & Master* [1984] A.C. 296, the defendant's solicitors had conducted the completion of a mortgage transaction in "Hong Kong style" rather than in the old fashioned English style. Completion in Hong Kong style provides for money to be paid over against an undertaking by the solicitors for the borrowers subsequently to hand over the executed documents. This practice opened the gateway through which a dishonest solicitor for the borrower absconded with the loan money without providing the security documents for such loan. The Privy Council held that even though completion in Hong Kong style was almost universally adopted in Hong Kong and was therefore in accordance with a body of professional opinion there, the defendant's solicitors were liable for negligence because there was an obvious risk which could have been guarded against. Thus, the body of professional opinion, though almost universally held, was not reasonable or responsible.

These decisions demonstrate that in cases of diagnosis and treatment there are cases where, despite a body of professional opinion sanctioning the defendant's conduct, the defendant can properly be held liable for negligence (I am not here considering questions of disclosure of risk). In my judgment that is because, in some cases, it cannot be demonstrated to the judge's satisfaction that the body of opinion relied upon is reasonable or responsible. In the vast majority of cases the fact that distinguished experts in the field are of a particular opinion will demonstrate the reasonableness of that opinion. In particular, where there are questions of assessment of the relative risks and benefits of adopting a particular medical practice, a reasonable view necessarily presupposes that the relative risks and benefits have been weighed by the experts in forming their opinions. But if, in a rare case, it can be demonstrated that the professional opinion is not capable of withstanding logical analysis, the judge is entitled to hold that the body of opinion is not reasonable or responsible.

I emphasise that in my view it will very seldom be right for a judge to reach the conclusion that views genuinely held by a competent medical expert are unreasonable. The assessment of medical risks and benefits is a matter of clinical judgment which a judge would not normally be able to make without expert evidence. As the quotation from Lord Scarman makes clear, it would be wrong to allow such assessment to deteriorate into seeking to persuade the judge to prefer one of two views both of which are capable of being logically supported. It is only where a judge can be satisfied that the body of expert opinion cannot be logically supported at all that such opinion will not provide the benchmark by reference to which the defendant's conduct falls to be assessed.

Lord Browne-Wilkinson went on to explain that this was not 'one of those rare cases' where there were grounds to dismiss the body of expert opinion as illogical. In particular, he was mindful that intubation was by no means a routine or risk-free procedure.

Informed Consent

In *Sidaway v Bethlem Royal Hospital* [1985] AC 871, the House of Lords appeared to close the door to a doctrine of informed consent in English law. However, courts did not rest easy with this, and the position has now been resoundingly reversed. In *Sidaway*, with the exception of Lord Scarman, the House of Lords thought that the content of a medical practitioner's duty to advise a patient of the risks of medical procedure was to be determined by considering *the steps the reasonable medical practitioner should take*. There was some variation between their Lordships' judgments, and Lord Bridge in particular proposed that a reasonable doctor would respond honestly to questions asked by an inquisitive patient. However, the general position was that the reasonableness of disclosure and advice was to be approached by reference to the *Bolam* test. As we have seen, the interpretation of this test appeared to offer little space for courts to reach their own judgments, since the question would be one of accepted practice.

We saw above how *Bolitho* built on earlier decisions of the courts to qualify the *Bolam* test. *Bolitho* however was not a case of advice or disclosure; and it described the case where the court would substitute its own judgment as 'rare'. Some years after *Bolitho*, in *Chester v Afshar* [2004] UKHL 1; [2005] 1 AC 134, the House of Lords treated patient autonomy as a well-established and significant value protected by the law. In *Chester*, the defendant seems to have conceded that the patient should have been warned of a small risk of very significant injury associated with surgery. That risk did in fact come to pass, and the sole question was one of causation: given that the patient would most likely have had the same treatment if properly advised, albeit on a different occasion, was the failure to advise a cause of her injury?[6] Despite the fact that standard of care was not directly in issue, the emphasis placed on patient autonomy and on the right to self-determination appeared to mark a distinct change in approach.

Lord Steyn, *Chester v Afshar*

14 … The starting point is that every individual of adult years and sound mind has a right to decide what may or may not be done with his or her body. Individuals have a right to make important medical decisions affecting their lives for themselves: they have the right to make decisions which doctors regard as ill advised. Surgery performed without the informed consent of the patient is unlawful. The court is the final arbiter of what constitutes informed consent. Usually, informed consent will presuppose a general warning by the surgeon of a significant risk of the surgery

…

24 Standing back from the detailed arguments, I have come to the conclusion that, as a result of the surgeon's failure to warn the patient, she cannot be said to have given informed consent to the surgery in the full legal sense. Her right of autonomy and dignity can and ought to be vindicated by a narrow and modest departure from traditional causation principles.

25 On a broader basis I am glad to have arrived at the conclusion that the claimant is entitled in law to succeed. This result is in accord with one of the most basic aspirations of the law,

[6] For recent critique of the decision in relation to causation, see T. Clark and D. Nolan, 'A Critique of *Chester v Afshar*' (2014) 34 OJLS 631.

namely to right wrongs. Moreover, the decision announced by the House today reflects the reasonable expectations of the public in contemporary society.

26 The result ought to come as no surprise to the medical profession which has to its credit subscribed to the fundamental importance of a surgeon's duty to warn a patient in general terms of significant risks: Royal College of Surgeons, Good Surgical Practice (2002), ch 4, guidelines on consent.

In the final paragraph of this extract, Lord Steyn refers to changes in the medical profession's approach to advice of risks. This illustrates a significant factor in the evolving law here, namely a change in attitudes. In the following case, the Supreme Court reinterpreted *Sidaway*. As an exercise in interpretation, this may not be persuasive. But more importantly, it also noted change both in general expectations of the doctor-patient relationship; and in the nature of the law of tort. Tort law now, according to Lord Kerr, is more inclined to recognize fundamental values—here, the value of patient autonomy. After *Montgomery*, questions of disclosure are approached primarily in terms of the patient's right to be adequately informed, in order to make decisions about their treatment. Lord Kerr emphasizes that this also brings with it a share of decisional responsibility: the hope is that the involvement of patients in decision-making about their treatment may reduce litigation, by enhancing the patient's role.

Montgomery v Lanarkshire Health Board [2015] UKSC 11; [2015] AC 1430

The claimant's son suffered severe injury during birth, as a result of his shoulders being unable to pass through the pelvis. The claimant was diabetic, and 'shoulder dystocia' is a recognized risk for diabetic mothers, which would be placed at 9–10 per cent. There was a smaller, but recognized further risk that this would cause grave injury to the child. The claimant had expressed concern at her final scan about her ability to deliver the baby vaginally. Her doctor, employed by the defendants, had not advised of the risk of shoulder dystocia, nor of the further risk of injury to the child. Her reason was that if so advised, most diabetic mothers would opt for a caesarean delivery; and this was not in the maternal interest. The claimant argued that she would indeed have elected to have a caesarean delivery if advised of the risks. The Supreme Court held that *Bolam* did not offer the right approach to such a case. The leading judgment of Lord Kerr and Lord Reed JJSC does not shy away from general issues.

Lord Kerr and Lord Reed, *Montgomery v Lanarkshire Health Board*

74 The Hippocratic Corpus advises physicians to reveal nothing to the patient of her present or future condition, "for many patients through this cause have taken a turn for the worse". *Decorum*, XVI. Around two millennia later, in *Sidaway's case* [1985] AC 871 Lord Templeman said "the provision of too much information may prejudice the attainment of the objective of restoring the patient's health" (p 904) and similar observations were made by Lord Diplock and Lord Bridge. On that view, if the optimisation of the patient's health is treated as an overriding objective, then it is unsurprising that the disclosure of information to a patient should be regarded as an aspect of medical care, and that the extent to which disclosure is appropriate should therefore be treated as a matter of clinical judgment, the appropriate standards being set by the medical profession.

75 Since *Sidaway's* case, however, it has become increasingly clear that the paradigm of the doctor–patient relationship implicit in the speeches in that case has ceased to reflect the reality and complexity of the way in which healthcare services are provided, or the way in which the providers and recipients of such services view their relationship. One development which is particularly significant in the present context is that patients are now widely regarded as persons holding rights, rather than as the passive recipients of the care of the medical profession. They are also widely treated as consumers exercising choices: a viewpoint which has underpinned some of the developments in the provision of healthcare services. In addition, a wider range of healthcare professionals now provide treatment and advice of one kind or another to members of the public, either as individuals, or as members of a team drawn from different professional backgrounds (with the consequence that, although this judgment is concerned particularly with doctors, it is also relevant, mutatis mutandis, to other healthcare providers). The treatment which they can offer is now understood to depend not only on their clinical judgment, but on bureaucratic decisions as to such matters as resource allocation, cost-containment and hospital administration: decisions which are taken by non-medical professionals. Such decisions are generally understood within a framework of institutional rather than personal responsibilities, and are in principle susceptible to challenge under public law rather than, or in addition to, the law of delict or tort.

Their Lordships explored evidence of 'changes in society' reflected for example in professional practice and guidance offered to doctors by the General Medical Council, and continued:

81 The social and legal developments which we have mentioned point away from a model of the relationship between the doctor and the patient based on medical paternalism. They also point away from a model based on a view of the patient as being entirely dependent on information provided by the doctor. What they point towards is an approach to the law which, instead of treating patients as placing themselves in the hands of their doctors (and then being prone to sue their doctors in the event of a disappointing outcome), treats them so far as possible as adults who are capable of understanding that medical treatment is uncertain of success and may involve risks, accepting responsibility for the taking of risks affecting their own lives, and living with the consequences of their choices.

82 In the law of negligence, this approach entails a duty on the part of doctors to take reasonable care to ensure that a patient is aware of material risks of injury that are inherent in treatment. This can be understood, within the traditional framework of negligence, as a duty of care to avoid exposing a person to a risk of injury which she would otherwise have avoided, but it is also the counterpart of the patient's entitlement to decide whether or not to incur that risk. The existence of that entitlement, and the fact that its exercise does not depend exclusively on medical considerations, are important. They point to a fundamental distinction between, on the one hand, the doctor's role when considering possible investigatory or treatment options and, on the other, her role in discussing with the patient any recommended treatment and possible alternatives, and the risks of injury which may be involved.

83 The former role is an exercise of professional skill and judgment: what risks of injury are involved in an operation, for example, is a matter falling within the expertise of members of the medical profession. But it is a non sequitur to conclude that the question whether a risk of injury, or the availability of an alternative form of treatment, ought to be discussed with the patient is also a matter of purely professional judgment. The doctor's advisory role cannot be regarded as solely an exercise of medical skill without leaving out of account the patient's entitlement to decide on the risks to her health which she is willing to run (a decision which may be influenced by non-medical considerations). Responsibility for determining the nature and extent of a person's rights rests with the courts, not with the medical professions.

84 Furthermore, because the extent to which a doctor may be inclined to discuss risks with a patient is not determined by medical learning or experience, the application of the Bolam test to this question is liable to result in the sanctioning of differences in practice which are attributable not to divergent schools of thought in medical science, but merely to divergent attitudes among doctors as to the degree of respect owed to their patients.

...

86 It follows that the analysis of the law by the majority in *Sidaway's case* [1985] AC 871 is unsatisfactory, in so far as it treated the doctor's duty to advise her patient of the risks of proposed treatment as falling within the scope of the Bolam test, subject to two qualifications of that general principle, neither of which is fundamentally consistent with that test. It is unsurprising that courts have found difficulty in the subsequent application of *Sidaway*, and that the courts in England and Wales have in reality departed from it; a position which was effectively endorsed, particularly by Lord Steyn, in *Chester v Afshar* [2005] 1 AC 134. There is no reason to perpetuate the application of the *Bolam* test in this context any longer.

87 The correct position, in relation to the risks of injury involved in treatment, can now be seen to be substantially that adopted in *Sidaway* by Lord Scarman, and by Lord Woolf MR in *Pearce* [1999] PIQR P53, subject to the refinement made by the High Court of Australia in *Rogers v Whitaker* 175 CLR 479, which we have discussed at paras 67–73. An adult person of sound mind is entitled to decide which, if any, of the available forms of treatment to undergo, and her consent must be obtained before treatment interfering with her bodily integrity is undertaken. The doctor is therefore under a duty to take reasonable care to ensure that the patient is aware of any material risks involved in any recommended treatment, and of any reasonable alternative or variant treatments. The test of materiality is whether, in the circumstances of the particular case, a reasonable person in the patient's position would be likely to attach significance to the risk, or the doctor is or should reasonably be aware that the particular patient would be likely to attach significance to it.

88 The doctor is however entitled to withhold from the patient information as to a risk if he reasonably considers that its disclosure would be seriously detrimental to the patient's health. The doctor is also excused from conferring with the patient in circumstances of necessity, as for example where the patient requires treatment urgently but is unconscious or otherwise unable to make a decision. It is unnecessary for the purposes of this case to consider in detail the scope of those exceptions.

89 Three further points should be made. First, it follows from this approach that the assessment of whether a risk is material cannot be reduced to percentages. The significance of a given risk is likely to reflect a variety of factors besides its magnitude: for example, the nature of the risk, the effect which its occurrence would have on the life of the patient, the importance to the patient of the benefits sought to be achieved by the treatment, the alternatives available, and the risks involved in those alternatives. The assessment is therefore fact-sensitive, and sensitive also to the characteristics of the patient.

90 Secondly, the doctor's advisory role involves dialogue, the aim of which is to ensure that the patient understands the seriousness of her condition, and the anticipated benefits and risks of the proposed treatment and any reasonable alternatives, so that she is then in a position to make an informed decision. This role will only be performed effectively if the information provided is comprehensible. The doctor's duty is not therefore fulfilled by bombarding the patient with technical information which she cannot reasonably be expected to grasp, let alone by routinely demanding her signature on a consent form.

91 Thirdly, it is important that the therapeutic exception should not be abused. It is a limited exception to the general principle that the patient should make the decision whether to undergo a proposed course of treatment: it is not intended to subvert that principle by enabling the doctor to prevent the patient from making an informed choice where she is liable to make a choice which the doctor considers to be contrary to her best interests.

In order to update the law on disclosure of medical risks, the Supreme Court has made a decisive move away from application of *Bolam* in this context. While its more general remarks are particularly pertinent to questions of consent, the point that courts, rather than medical practitioners, should determine questions of law is of much broader application. It remains to be seen whether there will be further 'de-Bolamization' of other areas of medical law.[7]

Beyond the Medical Context

It should be emphasized that the *Bolam* test is not confined to the medical context, even if this is where it originated. Rather, it is applicable wherever the defendant is applying special skills which a court cannot appropriately assess for itself. In *Bolitho*, Lord Browne-Wilkinson referred to a case of solicitors' negligence—though here, courts may understandably feel in a better position to judge the practice itself. The same approach has been taken to assessing claims of negligence against social workers, for example: Chapter 6, Section 3.4.

1.2 RISKS AND 'DESIRABLE ACTIVITIES' Compensation Act 2006

1 Deterrent effect of potential liability

A court considering a claim in negligence or breach of statutory duty may, in determining whether the defendant should have taken particular steps to meet a standard of care (whether by taking precautions against a risk or otherwise), have regard to whether a requirement to take those steps might—

(a) prevent a desirable activity from being undertaken at all, to a particular extent or in a particular way, or

(b) discourage persons from undertaking functions in connection with a desirable activity.

---

[7] For an argument that *Bolam* will retain rather more relevance after *Montgomery* than appears at first sight, see C. Hobson, 'No (.) More Bolam Please: *Montgomery v Lanarkshire Health Board* (2016) 79 MLR 468–503.

The most curious thing about the above provision is that it was generally agreed from the start that courts already took into account the issues to which they are here directed. Indeed, the Explanatory Notes to the Compensation Act 2006 included the following statement concerning section 1:

Explanatory Notes to Compensation Act 2006

10. This provision is intended to contribute to improving awareness of this aspect of the law; providing reassurance to the people and organisations who are concerned about possible litigation; and to ensuring that normal activities are not prevented because of the fear of litigation and excessively adverse behaviour.

11. This provision is not concerned with and does not alter the standard of care, nor the circumstances in which a duty to take that care will be owed . . . .

Section 1 was intended to 'send out a message' that good risks should go ahead; and not to change the law.[8] This is an unusual goal for legislation (though see also the Social Action, Responsibility and Heroism Act, extracted in Section 1.3 of this chapter).

How has the section applied in practice? So far, courts have not found that it makes any difference. In *Sutton v Syston RFC* [2011] EWCA Civ 1182, the Court of Appeal noted that 'neither party suggested that the section in any way altered the common law position' (at [13]).

That common law position was set out in *Humphrey v Aegis Defence Services Ltd* [2016] EWCA Civ 11:

Moore-Bick LJ, *Humphrey v Aegis Services Ltd* [2016] EWCA Civ 11

10 . . . In paragraph 36 of his speech in *Tomlinson v Congleton Borough Council* [2003] UKHL 47; [2004] 1 AC 46, on which Mr. Weir placed much emphasis, Lord Hoffmann drew a distinction between cases such as *Jolley v Sutton London Borough Council* [2000] 1 WLR 1082, in which there was no social utility in leaving a derelict boat lying about, and *Bolton v Stone* [1951] AC 850, in which the cricket club was engaged in a socially useful activity which would have had to cease if it were to eliminate the risk of balls being hit into the garden of an adjoining property. His purpose in doing so, however, was simply to illustrate the point that the risk of harm, the nature and gravity of that harm and the social utility of the activity are all factors to be taken into account in determining the nature and scope of any duty of care. That is the point that Asquith L.J. was seeking to make in *Daborn v Bath Tramways Motor Co. Ltd* [1946] 2 All ER 333 when he said at page 336:

"In determining whether a party is negligent, the standard of reasonable care is that which is reasonably to be demanded in the circumstances. A relevant circumstance to take into account may be the importance of the end to be served by behaving in this way or that . . . The purpose to be served, if sufficiently important, justifies the assumption of abnormal risk."

This brings us to the general question of when it is 'reasonable' to take a risk.

1.3 ESTABLISHING BREACH: WHEN DOES THE REASONABLE PERSON TAKE RISKS?

As we have just seen, there are some circumstances in which the reasonable person *would* choose to run a foreseeable risk. No liability will attach to a defendant who acts reasonably in this sense.

The treatment of reasonable risk-taking differentiates negligence liability from strict liability. The negligence position is that only unreasonable behaviour gives rise to liability. This appears on the face of it to be fair. On the other hand, this means that defendants may therefore create risks to others for their own benefit, without accepting any legal consequences. This allows defendants to profit (in the loosest possible sense) at the expense of those who are put at risk. In some situations, then, there is an argument of fairness *against* the negligence standard, and in favour of stricter liability.[9]

Overseas Tankship (UK) Ltd v The Miller Steamship Co ('The Wagon Mound No 2') [1967] 1 AC 617

This was an appeal to the Privy Council from the Supreme Court of New South Wales.[10] The respondents had two ships at Sheerlegs Wharf in Sydney Harbour, undergoing repairs. The appellant was charterer of another ship, *The Wagon Mound*, which was taking on oil from the nearby Caltex Wharf. Because of the carelessness of *The Wagon Mound*'s engineers, a large quantity of oil overflowed on to the surface of the water and drifted towards Sheerlegs Wharf where it accumulated around the respondents' vessels. That oil was set alight, causing extensive damage to the two vessels.

There were two *Wagon Mound* cases arising from this incident. The difference between them turns on a question of fact. In *Overseas Tankship v Morts Dock & Engineering Co Ltd (The Wagon Mound No 1)* [1961] AC 688, an action was brought by the owners of Sheerlegs Wharf (whose welding activities had probably led to the ignition of the oil) for damage to their wharf. This action was unsuccessful because the ignition of the oil while it was on the surface of the water was found to have been unforeseeable. *The Wagon Mound (No 1)* is a leading authority on remoteness of damage, and is extracted in Section 6.2.

In the present case (*The Wagon Mound No 2*), the owners of the two damaged ships brought an action against the charterer of *The Wagon Mound*. This subsequent action was *successful*. This is what sometimes causes confusion. How can this claim have succeeded, if it was concluded in the first case that the ignition of the oil was unforeseeable? The answer is that in this case, there was a different finding of fact by the first instance court. This was an entirely separate action brought by different plaintiffs in respect of different damage. The finding of fact in the first *Wagon Mound* case was irrelevant. No doubt also the argument of the plaintiffs in this second case was more robustly advanced because the ship owners had played no role in causing the fire. In *The Wagon Mound No 1*, the wharf owners were in a difficult position. If they argued that the ignition of the oil was foreseeable, they might themselves be considered negligent in continuing their welding activities.

---

[9] See Chapters 9, 11, and 15.
[10] Note the discussion in this extract of *Bolton v Stone* [1951] AC 850, which we have not extracted separately.

In this second case, it was concluded that the ignition of the oil though unlikely was nevertheless foreseeable. The question was whether it was justifiable (not negligent) to create this particular risk by spilling the oil, given that the risk was so low.

The Privy Council held that the spillage of oil was negligent. The reasonable person will sometimes take foreseeable risks where this is worthwhile. But here, there was no benefit to be derived from spreading the oil on the water.

Lord Reid (delivering the judgment of the Board)

Bolton v. Stone posed a new problem. There a member of a visiting team drove a cricket ball out of the ground onto an unfrequented adjacent public road and it struck and severely injured a lady who happened to be standing in the road. That it might happen that a ball would be driven onto this road could not have been said to be a fantastic or far-fetched possibility: according to the evidence it had happened about six times in 28 years. And it could not have been said to be a far-fetched or fantastic possibility that such a ball would strike someone in the road: people did pass along the road from time to time. So it could not have been said that, on any ordinary meaning of the words, the fact that a ball might strike a person in the road was not foreseeable or reasonably foreseeable—it was plainly foreseeable. But the chance of its happening in the foreseeable future was infinitesimal. A mathematician given the data could have worked out that it was only likely to happen once in so many thousand years. The House of Lords held that the risk was so small that in the circumstances a reasonable man would have been justified in disregarding it and taking no steps to eliminate it.

But it does not follow that, no matter what the circumstances may be, it is justifiable to neglect a risk of such a small magnitude. A reasonable man would only neglect such a risk if he had some valid reason for doing so, e.g., that it would involve considerable expense to eliminate the risk. He would weigh the risk against the difficulty of eliminating it. If the activity which caused the injury to Miss Stone had been an unlawful activity, there can be little doubt but that *Bolton v. Stone* would have been decided differently. In their Lordships' judgment *Bolton v. Stone* did not alter the general principle that a person must be regarded as negligent if he does not take steps to eliminate a risk which he knows or ought to know is a real risk and not a mere possibility which would never influence the mind of a reasonable man. What that decision did was to recognise and give effect to the qualification that it is justifiable not to take steps to eliminate a real risk if it is small and if the circumstances are such that a reasonable man, careful of the safety of his neighbour, would think it right to neglect it.

In the present case there was no justification whatever for discharging the oil into Sydney Harbour. Not only was it an offence to do so, but it involved considerable loss financially. If the ship's engineer had thought about the matter, there could have been no question of balancing the advantages and disadvantages. From every point of view it was both his duty and his interest to stop the discharge immediately....

In their Lordships' view a properly qualified and alert chief engineer would have realised there was a real risk here and they do not understand Walsh J. to deny that. But he appears to have held that if a real risk can properly be described as remote it must then be held to be not reasonably foreseeable. That is a possible interpretation of some of the authorities. But this is still an open question and on principle their Lordships cannot accept this view. If a real risk is one which would occur to the mind of a reasonable man in the position of the defendant's servant and which he would not brush aside as far-fetched, and if the criterion is to be what that reasonable man would have done in the circumstances, then surely he would not neglect such a risk if action to eliminate it presented no difficulty, involved no disadvantage, and required no expense.

Some risks, though foreseeable, are very low in probability. The fact that a risk is small (in probability terms) does not justify us in ignoring it. There must, as Lord Reid says, be some valid reason for neglecting it. For example, the cost of precautions may be very high. In *The Wagon Mound* itself, there was no justification for releasing oil into the harbour, so that even if the risk of ignition was tiny, there was no good reason for having disregarded it.

The mention made in the extract above of 'weighing' the risk against the difficulty of avoiding it supports the view that English negligence law adopts something along the lines of the 'Learned Hand' test. This test is derived from the approach of the American judge Learned Hand in the case of *US v Carroll Towing Co* 159 F 2d 169 (1947), 173. The approach represents the test for whether a duty was breached in terms of formula:

if the probability be called P; the injury, L, and the burden [i.e., of precautions or avoidance], B; liability depends on whether B is less than L multiplied by P; i.e. whether B < PL.

The Learned Hand test is itself interpreted by some commentators as enshrining an economic approach to negligence law in which the optimum, which is to say most economically productive, level of risk and precautions will be encouraged.

Although all the elements mentioned in the Learned Hand test are important in English cases on breach of duty, there is no evidence that the question of breach is interpreted in a mathematical or purely economic fashion by English courts. The overriding question is not a mathematical one (which has the lower value, B or PL?). Rather, it is an evaluative one. The question is, as Lord Reid put it in the extract above, whether 'a reasonable man, careful of the safety of his neighbour, would think it right to neglect [the risk]'. Issues of probability and cost are merely elements in this judgment. In addition, English courts have been openly evaluative of the activities of defendants, as we saw in Section 1.2.

The **Social Action, Responsibility and Heroism Act 2015** requires courts to consider some specific factors when dealing with particular types of action on the part of defendants. The statute merely requires the court to *consider* these factors; and, as with section 1 of the Compensation Act 2006, it appears that these are factors which common law would already accommodate. However, by *requiring* courts to have regard to these factors, it is possible that the structure of judgments, at least, may change. The provisions were subject to considerable criticism at Bill stage, many suggesting that the overall purpose was unnecessary. For an extended argument that the statute may have unlooked for and unfortunate effects, see R. Mulheron, 'Legislating Dangerously: Bad Samaritans, Good Society, and the Heroism Act 2015' (2017) 80 MLR 88.

Social Action, Responsibility and Heroism Act 2015

1. When this Act applies

This Act applies when a court, in considering a claim that a person was negligent or in breach of statutory duty, is determining the steps that the person was required to take to meet a standard of care.

2. Social action

The court must have regard to whether the alleged negligence or breach of statutory duty occurred when the person was acting for the benefit of society or any of its members.

3. Responsibility

The court must have regard to whether the person, in carrying out the activity in the course of which the alleged negligence or breach of statutory duty occurred, demonstrated a predominantly responsible approach towards protecting the safety or other interests of others.

4. Heroism

The court must have regard to whether the alleged negligence or breach of statutory duty occurred when the person was acting heroically by intervening in an emergency to assist an individual in danger.

The goal of the legislation is set out in the accompanying 'Explanatory Note', extracted below; footnotes have been omitted from this extract.

6. There is some evidence that people are deterred from participating in socially useful activities due to worries about risk or liability. For example, 'Helping Out: A national survey of volunteering and charitable giving' in 2006/2007 found this was one of the main reasons cited by respondents to the survey who did not currently volunteer. The Act forms part of the Coalition Government's wider programme to encourage participation in civil society and the Coalition Agreement contained a specific commitment to 'take a range of measures to encourage volunteering and involvement in social action'.

A particular worry surrounds section 3: does this invite defendants to show evidence of their *overall* social responsibility? If so, what impact should this, or will this have? It is suggested that courts will not read the section as a broad invitation in this way; but the provisions do introduce greater uncertainty than section 3 of the Compensation Act 2006, extracted earlier.

1.4 *RES IPSA LOQUITUR* AND ABSENCE OF EVIDENCE OF FAULT

Generally speaking, it is for the claimant to establish that all elements of a cause of action are present.[11] In tort, the relevant standard of proof is the civil standard, 'balance of

[11] It is for the *defendant* on the other hand to establish that a relevant *defence* is made out (see further Chapter 5).

probabilities'. To establish breach, it must be shown that it is *more likely than not* that the defendant was careless. The claimant must also show, on balance, that the negligence caused the harm.

It is tempting to think that the maxim '*res ipsa loquitur*' ('the thing speaks for itself') reverses this burden of proof, placing the burden of showing *lack* of negligence on the defendant. But it does not. The maxim does not change the burden of proof at all. But it does mean that, sometimes, the circumstances themselves may be treated as evidence of carelessness.

If a claim in negligence is to disclose a good cause of action, evidence of carelessness must be pleaded. If no evidence of carelessness is provided, a defendant may apply for summary judgment (the claim will fail without further argument). This initial hurdle has nothing to do with the balance of probabilities.

Sometimes, it is very difficult for a claimant to get past this first 'evidentiary' stage, because all information about the defendant's *conduct* is simply outside their knowledge. The claimant may know nothing about the manufacturing processes of the defendant, knowing only that the goods they consumed were defective and led to illness. Or the claimant may know nothing about the way in which the defendant discharged his or her gun, knowing only that the end result was that they were shot.[12] On some such occasions, a court may decide that the circumstances 'speak for themselves'. The mere facts of the injury as recounted by the claimant *suggest* negligence.

The classic statement of this 'doctrine' is as follows.[13] Bags of sugar being loaded by the defendant's crane fell and struck the plaintiff:

Erle CJ, *Scott v The London and St Katherine Docks Company*
[1865] 3 H & C 596

But where the thing is shown to be under the management of the defendant or his servants, and the accident is such as in the ordinary course of things does not happen if those who have the management use proper care, it affords reasonable evidence, in the absence of explanation by the defendants, that the accident arose from want of care.

Where this is the case, the effect is that some evidence of *lack* of carelessness must be brought by the defendant. The burden of proving negligence lies on the claimant in the usual way, and must be discharged to the usual standard, namely on the balance of probabilities. If the circumstances *strongly* suggest negligence, then the claimant may have little else to do than state the facts. This is why it may *appear as though* the burden has shifted to the defendant.

These distinctions are well illustrated by the following case. The plaintiffs (and in one case the deceased relative of a plaintiff) were passengers in a light bus. They were injured (or killed) when the defendants' coach left its side of the road and ploughed across a central reservation into oncoming traffic. These basic facts were confirmed by a police report.

---

[12] In *Fowler v Lanning* [1959] 1 QB 426, *res ipsa* was not invoked in such circumstances. Perhaps it should have been: see Chapter 2.

[13] In fact, *res ipsa* is probably not a doctrine so much as a complex name for a common sense inference from the facts.

Lord Griffiths (giving the judgment of the court), *Ng Chun Pui v Lee Chuen Tat* **(Privy Council, on Appeal from the Court of Appeal of Hong Kong) [1988] RTR 298**

The plaintiffs called no oral evidence and relied upon the fact of the accident as evidence of negligence or, as the judge put it, the doctrine of *res ipsa loquitur*. There can be no doubt that the plaintiffs were justified in taking this course. In ordinary circumstances if a well-maintained coach is being properly driven it will not cross the central reservation of a dual carriageway and collide with on-coming traffic in the other carriageway. In the absence of any explanation of the behaviour of the coach the proper inference to draw is that it was not being driven with the standard of care required by the law and that the driver was therefore negligent. If the defendants had called no evidence the plaintiffs would undoubtedly have been entitled to judgment.

The defendants however did call evidence and gave an explanation of the circumstances ...

(The explanation offered was that a car in front of the coach had performed a dangerous manoeuvre. The driver was not negligent in his response.)

The judge however was of the view that ... because the plaintiffs had originally relied upon the doctrine of *res ipsa loquitur*, the burden of disproving negligence remained upon the defendants and they had failed to discharge it. In their Lordships' opinion this shows a misunderstanding of the so-called doctrine of *res ipsa loquitur*, which is no more than the use of a latin maxim to describe a state of evidence from which it is proper to infer negligence. Although it has been said in a number of cases it is misleading to talk of the burden of proof shifting to the defendant in a *res ipsa loquitur* situation ....

... in an appropriate case the plaintiff establishes a *prima facie* case by relying upon the fact of the accident. If the defendant adduces no evidence there is nothing to rebut the inference of negligence and the plaintiff will have proved his case. But if the defendant does adduce evidence that evidence must be evaluated to see if it is still reasonable to draw the inference of negligence from the mere fact of the accident. Loosely speaking this may be referred to as a burden on the defendant to show he was not negligent, but that only means that faced with a *prima facie* case of negligence the defendant will be found negligent unless he produces evidence that is capable of rebutting the *prima facie* case ... . In so far as resort is had to the burden of proof the burden remains at the end of the case as it was at the beginning upon the plaintiff to prove that his injury was caused by the negligence of the defendants.

No breach of duty could be established in this particular case. The defendant's account of the facts was accepted, and in the light of this he was judged according to the standard of a reasonable person placed in a position of peril. It should be noted that the maxim '*res ipsa loquitur*' was applicable in this case—the facts suggested negligence, so that the defendant had to give an explanation consistent with proper care having been taken. But the defendant successfully offered such an explanation. The burden of proof remained with the plaintiff throughout.[14]

[14] Note also *George v Eagle Air* (12 May 2009), where the Privy Council held that in the absence of evidence in respect of the cause of a light aircraft crash, the maxim assisted the claimant. Fault would be assumed unless some other explanation was advanced.

2. DUTY OF CARE: AN INTRODUCTION

The following section provides a general introduction to the 'duty of care', and particularly to the way in which this concept has evolved. There will be detailed consideration of some of its more complex areas of application in Chapter 6.

It must be established that the defendant owed to the claimant a duty to take care, so that it amounts to a breach of that duty. Furthermore, the breach of duty must be shown to have caused recoverable damage (Section 4), which is within the scope of the duty and/or not too remote a consequence of the lack of care (Section 5).

In the section that follows, we will:

1. consider the origins of the general duty of care in *Donoghue v Stevenson*, and its subsequent evolution through the defining cases of *Anns v Merton* and *Caparo v Dickman*; and

2. reflect briefly on the nature of the duty concept and the part it plays in the tort of negligence.

3. THE EVOLUTION AND CONTENT OF THE DUTY CONCEPT: *DONOGHUE* TO *CAPARO*

3.1 A GENERAL TORT OF NEGLIGENCE: *DONOGHUE V STEVENSON*

M'Alister (or Donoghue) v Stevenson [1932] AC 562

The appellant claimed damages for personal injuries from the respondent, a manufacturer of soft drinks. She alleged that a bottle of ginger beer manufactured by the defendants was bought for her by a friend in a café in Paisley, the bottle being made of dark opaque glass so that she could not see its contents. She further alleged that the café proprietor had poured some of the ginger beer into a glass, and she had drunk some of it, before her friend proceeded to pour out the remainder. At this point a decomposing snail floated out of the bottle. As a result of the nauseating sight of the snail, and in consequence of the impurities in the ginger beer that she had drunk, she claimed to have suffered shock and gastro-enteritis. The respondents argued that these alleged facts disclosed no valid action, and the House of Lords dealt with this purely legal question on the basis of assumed facts.[15] The best-known passage in UK tort law[16] appears in the judgment of Lord Atkin, and is highlighted in bold below. But a real flavour of the importance of this case will only be gained by comparing Lord Atkin's approach with the dissent of Lord Buckmaster.

---

[15] To this day, it is not known whether there was a decaying snail in the bottle of ginger beer.
[16] Although in Scotland the subject is not tort but 'delict'.

Lord Buckmaster (dissenting)

At 568

The case of *Winterbottom v. Wright* (10 M & W 109) is ... an authority that is closely applicable. Owing to negligence in the construction of a carriage it broke down, and a stranger to the manufacture and sale sought to recover damages for injuries which he alleged were due to negligence in the work, and it was held that he had no cause of action either in tort or arising out of contract. This case seems to me to show that the manufacturer of any article is not liable to a third party injured by negligent construction, for there can be nothing in the character of a coach to place it in a special category. It may be noted, also, that in this case Alderson B. said (10 M & W 115): "The only safe rule is to confine the right to recover to those who enter into the contract; if we go one step beyond that, there is no reason why we should not go fifty. ..."

At 578

In *Mullen v. Barr & Co.* [1929 S.C. 461, 479], a case indistinguishable from the present excepting upon the ground that a mouse is not a snail, and necessarily adopted by the Second Division in their judgment, Lord Anderson says this: "In a case like the present, where the goods of the defenders are widely distributed throughout Scotland, it would seem little short of outrageous to make them responsible to members of the public for the condition of the contents of every bottle which issues from their works. It is obvious that, if such responsibility attached to the defenders, they might be called on to meet claims of damages which they could not possibly investigate or answer."

In agreeing, as I do, with the judgment of Lord Anderson, I desire to add that I find it hard to dissent from the emphatic nature of the language with which his judgment is clothed. I am of opinion that this appeal should be dismissed, and I beg to move your Lordships accordingly.

Lord Atkin, at 578–83

My Lords, the sole question for determination in this case is legal: Do the averments made by the pursuer in her pleading, if true, disclose a cause of action? I need not restate the particular facts. The question is whether the manufacturer of an article of drink sold by him to a distributor, in circumstances which prevent the distributor or the ultimate purchaser or consumer from discovering by inspection any defect, is under any legal duty to the ultimate purchaser or consumer to take reasonable care that the article is free from defect likely to cause injury to health. I do not think a more important problem has occupied your Lordships in your judicial capacity: important both because of its bearing on public health and because of the practical test which it applies to the system under which it arises. The case has to be determined in accordance with Scots law; but it has been a matter of agreement between the experienced counsel who argued this case, and it appears to be the basis of the judgments of the learned judges of the Court of Session, that for the purposes of determining this problem the laws of Scotland and of England are the same.... The law of both countries appears to be that in order to support an action for damages for negligence the complainant has to show that he has been injured by the breach of a duty owed to him in the circumstances by the defendant to take reasonable care to avoid such injury.... We are solely concerned with the question whether, as a matter of law in the circumstances alleged, the defender owed any duty to the pursuer to take care.

It is remarkable how difficult it is to find in the English authorities statements of general application defining the relations between parties that give rise to the duty. The Courts are concerned with the particular relations which come before them in actual litigation, and it is sufficient to say whether the duty exists in those circumstances. The result is that the Courts have been engaged upon an elaborate classification of duties as they exist in respect of property, whether real or personal, with further divisions as to ownership, occupation or control, and distinctions based on the particular relations of the one side or the other, whether manufacturer, salesman or landlord, customer, tenant, stranger, and so on. In this way it can be ascertained at any time whether the law recognizes a duty, but only where the case can be referred to some particular species which has been examined and classified. And yet the duty which is common to all the cases where liability is established must logically be based upon some element common to the cases where it is found to exist. To seek a complete logical definition of the general principle is probably to go beyond the function of the judge, for the more general the definition the more likely it is to omit essentials or to introduce non-essentials. The attempt was made by Brett M.R. in *Heaven v. Pender* (11 QBD 503, 509), in a definition to which I will later refer. As framed, it was demonstrably too wide, though it appears to me, if properly limited, to be capable of affording a valuable practical guide.

At present I content myself with pointing out that in English law there must be, and is, some general conception of relations giving rise to a duty of care, of which the particular cases found in the books are but instances. The liability for negligence, whether you style it such or treat it as in other systems as a species of "culpa," is no doubt based upon a general public sentiment of moral wrongdoing for which the offender must pay. But acts or omissions which any moral code would censure cannot in a practical world be treated so as to give a right to every person injured by them to demand relief. In this way rules of law arise which limit the range of complainants and the extent of their remedy. The rule that you are to love your neighbour becomes in law, you must not injure your neighbour; and the lawyer's question, Who is my neighbour? receives a restricted reply. You must take reasonable care to avoid acts or omissions which you can reasonably foresee would be likely to injure your neighbour. Who, then, in law is my neighbour? The answer seems to be—persons who are so closely and directly affected by my act that I ought reasonably to have them in contemplation as being so affected when I am directing my mind to the acts or omissions which are called in question. This appears to me to be the doctrine of *Heaven v. Pender* (11 QBD 503, 509), as laid down by Lord Esher (then Brett M.R.) when it is limited by the notion of proximity introduced by Lord Esher himself and A. L. Smith L.J. in *Le Lievre v. Gould* ([1893] 1 QB 491, 497, 504). Lord Esher says: "That case established that, under certain circumstances, one man may owe a duty to another, even though there is no contract between them. If one man is near to another, or is near to the property of another, a duty lies upon him not to do that which may cause a personal injury to that other, or may injure his property." So A. L. Smith L.J. [said]: "The decision of *Heaven v. Pender* (11 QBD 503) was founded upon the principle, that a duty to take due care did arise when the person or property of one was in such proximity to the person or property of another that, if due care was not taken, damage might be done by the one to the other." I think that this sufficiently states the truth if proximity be not confined to mere physical proximity, but be used, as I think it was intended, to extend to such close and direct relations that the act complained of directly affects a person whom the person alleged to be bound to take care would know would be directly affected by his careless act. That this is the sense in which nearness of "proximity" was intended by Lord Esher is obvious from his own illustration in *Heaven v. Pender* of the application of his doctrine to the sale of goods. "This" (i.e., the rule he has just formulated) "includes the case of goods, etc., supplied to be used immediately by a particular person or persons, or one of a class of persons, where it would be obvious to the person supplying, if he thought, that the goods would in all probability be used at once by such persons before a reasonable opportunity for discovering any defect which might exist, and where the thing supplied would be of such a nature that a neglect of ordinary care or skill as to its condition or the manner of supplying it would probably cause danger to the person or property of the person for whose use it was supplied, and who was about to use it. It would exclude a case in which the goods are supplied under circumstances in which it would be a chance by whom they would be used or whether they would be used or not, or whether they would be used before there would probably be means of observing any defect, or where the goods would be of such a nature that a want of care or skill as to their condition or the manner of supplying them would not probably produce danger of injury to person or property." I draw particular attention to the fact that Lord Esher emphasizes the necessity of goods having to be "used immediately" and "used at once before a reasonable opportunity of inspection." This is obviously to exclude the possibility of goods having their condition altered by lapse of time, and to call attention to the proximate relationship, which may be too remote where inspection even of the person using, certainly of an intermediate person, may reasonably be interposed. With this necessary quali- fication of proximate relationship as explained in *Le Lievre v. Gould*, I think the majority of the Court in *Heaven v. Pender* were justified in thinking the principle was expressed in too general terms. There will no doubt arise cases where it will be difficult to determine whether the contemplated relationship is so close that the duty arises. But in the class of case now before the Court I cannot conceive any difficulty to arise.

Lord Macmillan, at 609–11

It humbly appears to me that the diversity of view which is exhibited in such cases as *George v. Skivington* on the one hand and *Blacker v. Lake & Elliot, Ld.*, on the other hand—to take two extreme instances—is explained by the fact that in the discussion of the topic which now engages your Lordships' attention two rival principles of the law find a meeting place where each has contended for supremacy. On the one hand, there is the well estab- lished principle that no one other than a party to a contract can complain of a breach of that contract. On the other hand, there is the equally well established doctrine that negligence apart from contract gives a right of action to the party injured by that negligence—and here I use the term negligence, of course, in its technical legal sense, implying a duty owed and neglected. The fact that there is a contractual relationship between the parties which may give rise to an action for breach of contract, does not exclude the co-existence of a right of action founded on negligence as between the same parties, independently of the contract, though arising out of the relationship in fact brought about by the contract. Of this the best illustration is the right of the injured railway passenger to sue the railway company either for breach of the contract of safe carriage or for negligence in carrying him. And there is no reason why the same set of facts should not give one person a right of action in contract and another person a right of action in tort. . . .

Where, as in cases like the present, so much depends upon the avenue of approach to the question, it is very easy to take the wrong turning. If you begin with the sale by the manu- facturer to the retail dealer, then the consumer who purchases from the retailer is at once seen to be a stranger to the contract between the retailer and the manufacturer and so dis- entitled to sue upon it. There is no contractual relation between the manufacturer and the consumer; and thus the plaintiff, if he is to succeed, is driven to try to bring himself within one or other of the exceptional cases where the strictness of the rule that none but a party to a contract can found on a breach of that contract has been mitigated in the public interest, as it has been in the case of a person who issues a chattel which is inherently dangerous or which he knows to be in a dangerous condition. If, on the other hand, you disregard the fact that the circumstances of the case at one stage include the existence of a contract of sale between the manufacturer and the retailer, and approach the question by asking whether there is evidence of carelessness on the part of the manufacturer, and whether he owed a duty to be careful in a question with the party who has been injured in consequence of his want of care, the circumstance that the injured party was not a party to the incidental contract of sale becomes irrelevant, and his title to sue the manufacturer is unaffected by that circumstance. The appellant in the present instance asks that her case be approached as a case of delict, not as a case of breach of contract. She does not require to invoke the exceptional cases in which a person not a party to a contract has been held to be entitled to complain of some defect in the subject-matter of the contract which has caused him harm. The exceptional case of things dangerous in themselves, or known to be in a dangerous condition, has been regarded as constituting a peculiar category outside the ordinary law both of contract and of tort.

At 618–19

The law takes no cognizance of carelessness in the abstract. It concerns itself with carelessness only where there is a duty to take care and where failure in that duty has caused damage. In such circumstances carelessness assumes the legal quality of negligence and entails consequences in law of negligence. What, then, are the circumstances which give rise to this duty to take care? In the daily contacts of social and business life human beings are thrown into, or place themselves in, an infinite variety of relations with their fellows; and the law can refer only to the standards of the reasonable man in order to determine whether any particular relation gives rise to a duty to take care as between those who stand in that relation to each other. The grounds of action may be as various and manifold as human errancy; and the conception of legal responsibility may develop in adaptation to altering social conditions and standards. The criterion of judgment must adjust and adapt itself to the changing circumstances of life. The categories of negligence are never closed. The cardinal principle of liability is that the party complained of should owe to the party complaining a duty to take care, and that the party complaining should be able to prove that he has suffered damage in consequence of a breach of that duty. Where there is room for diversity of view, it is in determining what circumstances will establish such a relationship between the parties as to give rise, on the one side, to a duty to take care, and on the other side to a right to have care taken.

There are three dimensions to the significance of this case.

1. It secured the independence of tort from contract. The judgment of Lord Macmillan was particularly important in this regard.

2. Through the judgment of Lord Atkin in particular, it recognized a *general* tort of negligence, not confined to specific duty situations.

3. It enabled negligence to emerge, albeit gradually, as the most flexible of torts, adapting to fill an ever-increasing range of claims. As Lord Macmillan put it, 'the categories of negligence are never closed'. Claimants have certainly turned to negligence in search of remedies.

Tort and Contract in *Donoghue*

Donoghue recognized that a remedy may be available through the tort of negligence, where 'privity of contract' would prevent the consumer from having any contractual claim. The doctrine of 'privity' restricts contractual remedies to those who are parties to the contract.

Since the consumer in this case had not entered into a contract with the defendant manufacturer of the goods (nor, indeed, with the retailer who sold the ginger beer to her friend), she had no contractual remedy. Even today under the Contracts (Rights of Third Parties) Act 1999, a non-contracting consumer in the position of Mrs Donoghue would not have a contractual remedy, as no rights of action are conferred upon her by the contracting parties. *Donoghue* is the key case establishing that the cause of action in tort for negligence is independent of contract, and is not bound by the rules of privity which restrict contractual remedies. Duties to take care are imposed quite independently of contractual duties, so that they may be owed to parties who are strangers to the contract.

The relationship between tort and contract dominated Lord Macmillan's judgment. He analysed tort and contract as providing two ways of looking at the same set of facts, so that tort duties may coexist with contractual duties without the need to have identical content.

The same step had already been taken in the United States in *MacPherson v Buick Motor Co* 217 NY 382 (1916) (a decision of the New York Court of Appeals which was adopted by most state jurisdictions). *MacPherson v Buick* is referred to in the majority judgments of both Lord Atkin and Lord Macmillan, although it appears that its authority was not pressed by counsel for Mrs Donoghue (see further A. Rodger, 'Lord Macmillan's Speech in *Donoghue v Stevenson*' (1992) 108 LQR 236). The extracts from Lord Buckmaster's dissenting judgment above, and especially the strength of his criticism, indicate how significant this aspect of *Donoghue v Stevenson* was felt to be, at the time of the judgment. Lord Buckmaster was primarily concerned to prevent the traditional rules of contract law, particularly privity, from being undermined by a developing law of negligence. The complex relationship between tort and contract has evolved further in recent years, and it is important to the discussion in Chapter 6.

The Duty of Care in *Donoghue*

Progressively over the succeeding years, attention began to focus on Lord Atkin's analysis of the duty concept. It is clear that the terminology of 'duty' existed in the case law prior to *Donoghue v Stevenson*. Then, as now, there could only be liability on the basis of negligence if the defendant owed a legal duty to the injured party to take care for his or her safety. The distinction marked by the duty concept was and is the distinction between carelessly inflicted damage which involves the breach of a duty of care, and carelessly inflicted damage in respect of which there is no duty and therefore no liability. But the law prior to *Donoghue v Stevenson* consisted of a series of instances where a 'duty to take care' was recognized, and these were not united by any general theory. Many of the situations were contractual or perceived to be similar to contract (for example, the position of carriers in respect of their passengers).

Lord Atkin was not the first judge to set out a general theory which sought to explain the particular instances of negligence liability. Brett MR (later Lord Esher) had propounded a broad test based on foreseeability in the case of *Heaven v Pender* ((1883) 11 QBD 503, 509):

> Whenever one person is by circumstances placed in such a position with regard to another that every one of ordinary sense who did think would at once recognise that if he did not use ordinary care and skill in his own conduct with regard to those circumstances he would cause danger of injury to the person or property of the other, a duty arises to use ordinary care and skill to avoid such danger.

He did not gain the agreement of his fellow judges in that case, and Lord Atkin agreed that the above statement is 'demonstrably too wide'. Lord Macmillan on the other hand thought that, with appropriate qualification, it could provide a useful practical guide, although not a formal definition. Later, Lord Esher and A. L. Smith LJ added the important qualification of 'closeness', 'directness', or 'proximity' (*Le Lievre v Gould* [1893] 1 QB 491, 497, 504).

Lord Atkin agreed that proximity was the necessary *additional* component which would restrict the circumstances in which a duty to take care could be said to arise. Equally importantly, he understood proximity to have a special meaning. This meaning would not be restricted to *physical* closeness, but could reflect a variety of aspects of the relationship between the parties in terms of closeness (see the second highlighted passage in his judgment, earlier in this section). In the particular case in hand, it was the fact that the goods were expected to reach the eventual consumer without intermediate tampering, and without inspection, that supplied the necessary closeness and 'directness'.

Foreseeability and **proximity** continue to be core elements in the test for the duty of care today.

Donoghue v Stevenson and the Unified Tort of Negligence

In 1957, looking back at the influence of *Donoghue v Stevenson*, R. V. F. Heuston argued that the neighbour principle had been over-emphasized. It was never intended by Lord Atkin to amount to a universal test for the existence of a duty of care in negligence, and had 'been called upon to bear a weight . . . manifestly greater than it could support': Heuston, '*Donoghue v Stevenson* in Retrospect' (1957) 20 MLR 1, 23. Heuston may well have been right in a narrow but important sense. Lord Atkin prefaced his broader remarks with a warning: to seek a 'complete logical definition is probably to go beyond the function of the judge'.[17]

However, to deny the validity of the neighbour principle as a *test* is perhaps to miss the historical contribution of *Donoghue v Stevenson*—though it is a point that Heuston would surely have wished to make more forcefully in the light of *Anns v Merton*, which is extracted and discussed in Section 3.2. Looking historically at the issue of negligence, the issue of the day at the time of *Donoghue* was one of generalization. Could there be said to be a general tort of negligence, or was there just a 'wilderness of single instances' (Ibbetson, *A Historical Introduction to the Law of Obligations*, 179) where a duty could be said to arise? Lord Atkin's explanation of the duty of care was significant because it treated those isolated single instances as aspects of a broad and integrated tort of negligence. It may not have occurred to him to worry whether his explanation could be used as a precise test. Historically, the

---

[17] This warning was noted by Lord Devlin in the key case of *Hedley Byrne v Heller* [1964] AC 465, and again by Lord Oliver in *Caparo v Dickman* (see Section 3.3).

important question was simply whether there was such a thing as a single tort of negligence. The alternative was that the law only recognized a series of distinct and separate duty situations, in which the defendant would be liable for losses caused should he or she act negligently in breach of the duty.

Donoghue v Stevenson is generally recognized as beginning the process through which a general tort of negligence emerged. This process had been encouraged by many of the tort scholars of the day (among them Winfield, 'The History of Negligence in the Law of Torts' (1926) 42 LQR 184; Pollock, *Torts* (13th edn, 1929)). In the next extract, Ibbetson traces this broader historical development up to about 1970, a few years before *Anns v Merton*. Subsequently, we will turn to the attempt to set out a universal 'test' for the duty of care in *Anns*.

David Ibbetson, *A Historical Introduction to the Law of Obligations* (1999), 190–3; by permission of Oxford University Press

The turning point came with the well-known decision in *Donoghue v Stevenson*. . . . In point of detail, this [decision] amounted to a reversal of the line of cases stemming from *Winterbottom v Wright*, it was never afterwards doubted that the person injured by a defectively manufactured product might in principle have an action against the negligent manufacturer.

There were three possible routes to this conclusion. Most minimally, it could simply have been said that the cases following *Winterbottom v Wright* had been overruled, and that a duty of care was in fact owed by the manufacturer to the ultimate consumer. This would have been sufficient to explain the decision in the case. It would not, however, have involved any qualification of the traditional analysis in terms of a multiplicity of duties of care; nor would it have involved any qualification of the traditionally conservative 'incremental' approach to liability whereby the plaintiff was expected to demonstrate the existence of a duty of care by showing that the case fell within an already recognised duty situation or was very closely analogous to one. Such a minimalist approach was consistent with the speeches of Lord Thankerton and Lord Macmillan, and was the favoured interpretation of the case by contemporary commentators. . . .

Secondly, *Donoghue v Stevenson* could have been treated as accepting an approach based upon a multiplicity of duty situations, but without any requirement that new duty situations could be recognized only by very close analogy to duty situations that had previously been recognised. This was implicit in Lord Macmillan's speech, and his central conclusion that 'the categories of negligence are never closed'. . . Such an approach inevitably involved some element of generalization, though Lord Macmillan himself was diffident about laying down any such principle. . . .[1932] AC 562, 619 . . .].

Finally, and most generally, *Donoghue v Stevenson* might have involved the wholesale rejection of the analysis dependent upon a multiplicity of duties of care in favour of a single requirement of taking reasonable care. This was, famously, the approach of Lord Atkin. . . .

In practice there was not a great deal of difference between the approaches of Lord Macmillan and Lord Atkin, for both of them allowed the law considerable flexibility to adapt to new situations. At a rhetorical level Lord Atkin's approach was particularly valuable, for it provided ready support for any conclusion that a judge wished to reach, and it provided a useful starting point for academic analysis. As a matter of reality, though, it was Lord Macmillan's more careful approach that was followed. . . . Text-book writers, while paying lip service to Lord Atkin's statement, still dealt with the law in terms of more or less discrete categories of duty situation, albeit that they were couched at a more general level... Judges, too, although less hide-bound by previous precedents, did not expand the law into a whole range of new situations simply on the grounds that the defendant had carelessly caused foreseeable harm to the plaintiff. Two types of case in particular stood in the way of the wholesale recognition of a general duty of care of the sort formulated by Lord Atkin: cases where a trespasser had been injured, and cases where financial loss had been suffered by reliance upon a negligent representation....[18]

After a brief flirtation in the late nineteenth century, the Common law had turned its face against allowing actions for negligent statements (as opposed to negligent acts or omissions).... The wider view of *Donoghue v Stevenson*, though, contained no such limitation, and by the early 1950s it was being argued (unsuccessfully) that liability should be imposed [*Candler v Crane Christmas & Co* [1951] 2 KB 164. But see the dissenting judgment of Denning L.J. based on the nineteenth century cases in the Court of Chancery ...]. As in the case of trespassers, this was at first rejected, but in 1963 the House of Lords laid down that there was no relevant difference between causing loss by negligent statement and causing loss in some other way [*Hedley Byrne & Co v Heller & Partners Ltd* [1964] AC 465]. Thus an action was held to lie in principle (though not on the facts of the case) against a bank that had negligently represented to the plaintiff that its customer was a good credit risk, as a result of which the plaintiff had allowed the customer's order to continue in place and had hence suffered loss.

Hedley Byrne v Heller and *Herrington v British Railways Board* [a case on trespassers] removed the two largest obstacles to the acceptance of Lord Atkin's broad approach. By around 1970 the law of negligence was beginning to be conceptualized in terms of an ocean of liability for carelessly caused foreseeable harm, dotted with islands of non-liability, ...rather than as a crowded archipelago of individual duty situations... .

Ibbetson's account is valuable for its analysis of the trend toward general principle, particularly taken together with his account of the historical origins of negligence law in a series of isolated instances. However, he perhaps overstates, in this particular passage, the generality both of the neighbour principle *and* of the *Hedley Byrne* decision. We have already noted the important role of proximity or directness in the neighbour principle. Although *Hedley Byrne v Heller* contributed greatly to the emergence of a general 'tort of negligence' and the recognition of novel categories of duty, it did so with attention to the special requirements of a particular relationship.

We will explore *Hedley Byrne* in Chapter 6, Section 2. For now, we will consider the 'ocean of liability' to which Ibbetson refers.

3.2 THE 'OCEAN OF LIABILITY': THE *ANNS* TEST AND THE PRIMA FACIE DUTY OF CARE

The trend toward generalization in the tort of negligence reached its peak with the case of *Anns v Merton LBC* [1978] AC 728, and a number of cases decided under its influence.[19] Here, we are not chiefly concerned with the facts of *Anns*, though they are briefly set out later

[18] Ibbetson here considers duties to trespassers, which we will debate in Chapter 12.
[19] For example *Ross v Caunters* [1980] Ch 297; *Junior Books v Veitchi* [1983] 1 AC 520; *Lawton v BOC Transhield* [1987] ICR 7.

in this section. The decision was overruled by the House of Lords in *Murphy v Brentwood District Council* [1991] 1 AC 398 (Chapter 6, Section 2). For now, we are more interested in the attempt made by Lord Wilberforce to express a universal test which would determine whether a duty of care is owed.

Lord Wilberforce's 'two-stage test' elevated the neighbour principle in *Donoghue v Stevenson* into a universal test. As will be explained later, many features of the two-stage test proved to be controversial, and this has prompted the emergence of a more complex approach (*Caparo v Dickman*, extracted and discussed in Section 3.3). It would be easy to identify *Caparo* with a return to the pre-*Donoghue* days of isolated duty instances. But that interpretation of *Caparo* is, as we will see, exaggerated. The truth is that the current approach to the duty of care exhibits a real tension between the recognition that negligence is a single tort, and the need to determine specific criteria which will guide decisions in different classes of case. A truly universal tort of negligence would have almost boundless potential to throw up new duty situations, and foreseeability is not a sufficient criterion to control this potential. Understanding the problems with *Anns v Merton* will be a useful step in helping us to appreciate the subtleties and the frustrations of the current law.

It is also important to note that, in principle, the rejection of *Anns* has not been universal. In Canada, *Anns* remains the leading authority on the duty of care. Nevertheless, the version of *Anns* applied in Canada has been considerably amended (*Cooper v Hobart* 2001 SCC 79; see J. Neyers, 'Distilling Duty: The Supreme Court of Canada Amends *Anns*' (2002) 118 LQR 221).

Anns v Merton LBC [1978] AC 728

The plaintiffs were lessees of flats in a two-storey block. The block began to suffer cracked walls and sloping floors, and the plaintiffs alleged that this was because the foundations of the block were too shallow. Statutory powers under the Public Health Act 1936 allowed the defendant local authority to approve plans, and to inspect foundations before they were covered up. Plans had duly been approved, specifying foundations to a depth of 3 feet or more. The eventual foundations were of a depth of only 2 feet 6 inches.

For the purposes of the House of Lords' decision, it was not determined whether any inspection of the foundations had been made. Thus the case proceeded on the basis of the two alternative claims that either (a) the local authority had negligently failed to inspect the foundations, or (b) the local authority had been responsible for negligently inspecting the foundations. Lord Wilberforce made the following general remarks about the duty of care in negligence.

Lord Wilberforce, at 751–2

Through the trilogy of cases in this House—*Donoghue v Stevenson* [1932] A.C. 562, *Hedley Byrne & Co. Ltd. v. Heller & Partners Ltd.* [1964] A.C. 465, and *Dorset Yacht Co. Ltd. v. Home Office* [1970] A.C. 1004, the position has now been reached that in order to establish that a duty of care arises in a particular situation, it is not necessary to bring the facts of that situation within those of previous situations in which a duty of care has been held to exist. Rather the question has to be approached in two stages. First one has to ask whether, as between the alleged wrongdoer and the person who has suffered damage there is a sufficient relationship of proximity or neighbourhood such that, in the reasonable contemplation of the former, carelessness on his part may be likely to cause damage to the latter—in which case a prima facie duty of care arises. Secondly, if the first question is answered affirmatively, it is necessary to consider whether there are any considerations which ought to negative, or to reduce or limit the scope of the duty or the class of person to whom it is owed or the damages to which a breach of it may give rise: see *Dorset Yacht* case [1970] A.C. 1004, *per* Lord Reid at p. 1027. Examples of this are *Hedley Byrne's* case [1964] A.C. 465 where the class of potential plaintiffs was reduced to those shown to have relied upon the correctness of statements made, and *Weller & Co. v. Foot and Mouth Disease Research Institute* [1966] 1 Q.B. 569; and (I cite these merely as illustrations, without discussion) cases about "economic loss" where, a duty having been held to exist, the nature of the recoverable damages was limited: see *S.C.M. (United Kingdom) Ltd. v. W. J. Whittall & Son Ltd.* [1971] 1 Q.B. 337 and *Spartan Steel & Alloys Ltd. v. Martin & Co. (Contractors) Ltd.* [1973] Q.B. 27.

Problems with the 'Anns Test'

Problem 1: The Disappearance of 'Proximity' as an Independent Criterion

Clearly, Lord Wilberforce considered himself to be encapsulating Lord Atkin's 'neighbour principle' as the first stage of his two-stage test. Yet there is a problem with the way in which he expressed the neighbour principle. He gave the impression that 'proximity or neighbourhood' is a *function of foreseeability: 'a sufficient relationship of neighbourhood or proximity such that, in the reasonable contemplation of the former, carelessness on his part may be likely to cause damage to the latter ...'.* In *Donoghue v Stevenson* as we have explained, proximity of relationship was deliberately added as a way of qualifying the foreseeability test, and was clearly intended to add extra *limits* to a test based on foreseeability. It was not simply another way of establishing foreseeability, which seems to have become its role in *Anns*.

This aspect of the *Anns* test was particularly criticized by Richard Kidner. Writing before the decision in *Caparo v Dickman* (Section 3.3), but in an article which largely anticipated that decision and specifically its rejection of *Anns*, Kidner suggested that to neglect proximity in this way was a significant error. It might lead courts to overlook some very significant policy (and other) reasons which had been decisive in the pre-*Anns* case law, including *Donoghue* itself, since such reasoning was often conducted under the heading of 'proximity'. Proximity had acquired a 'coded meaning' in these pre-*Anns* cases, and varied as between different categories of case.

R. Kidner, 'Resiling from the *Anns* Principle' (1987) 7 LS 319, at 323–4

... as a yardstick for the extension of old duties or the establishment of new duties the *Anns* principle does not advance the law very far, for outside the area of foreseeable physical damage the degree of proximity necessary to bring about a duty of care will and always has been an issue. *Anns* tends to obscure that fact by giving the impression that foresight is the dominant criterion ..., obscuring the need to apply historical and policy considerations to the question of other levels of proximity.

It is not clear whether the disappearance of proximity as an independent criterion was deliberate. In *Anns* itself, Lord Wilberforce mentioned proximity, but it seems he thought the proximity question was adequately resolved by the following passage:

Lord Wilberforce, *Anns v Merton*, 753–4

… One of the particular matters within the area of local authority supervision is the foundations of buildings—clearly a matter of vital importance, particularly because this part of the building comes to be covered up as building proceeds. Thus any weakness or inadequacy will create a hidden defect which whoever acquires the building has no means of discovering: in legal parlance there is no opportunity for intermediate inspection. So, by the byelaws, a definite standard is set for foundation work (see byelaw 18 (1) (b) referred to above): the builder is under a statutory (sc. byelaw) duty to notify the local authority before covering up the foundations: the local authority has at this stage the right to inspect and to insist on any correction necessary to bring the work into conformity with the byelaws. It must be in the reasonable contemplation not only of the builder but also of the local authority that failure to comply with the byelaws' requirement as to foundations may give rise to a hidden defect which in the future may cause damage to the building affecting the safety and health of owners and occupiers. And as the building is intended to last, the class of owners and occupiers likely to be affected cannot be limited to those who go in immediately after construction.

… as I have suggested, a situation of "proximity" existed between the council and owners and occupiers of the houses… [Lord Wilberforce went on to consider the nature of the statutory context and its influence on common law duties of care].

This passage draws upon Lord Atkin's discussion in *Donoghue v Stevenson* of proximity in the sense of absence of opportunity for intermediate inspection of goods. Lord Wilberforce makes the comparison directly: in *Donoghue*, the bottle was opaque and not likely to be opened before it reached the consumer; in *Anns* the foundations were bound to be covered and so were likely to lead to a hidden defect. But Lord Wilberforce has here run together the notions of proximity and foreseeability: it must be in the reasonable contemplation of the builder and of the local authority that failure to comply with the bye-laws would affect the health and safety of occupiers in the future, and thus the requirement that there should be 'proximity or neighbourhood' is satisfied. Lord Wilberforce did not consider, under the heading of 'proximity', issues concerning the nature of the relationship between local authority and subsequent purchasers. A more extensive range of issues, independent of foreseeability, would today be considered under this heading.

The impact of *Anns*, in some of the cases that followed, was indeed that 'proximity' was run together with foreseeability. In *Ross v Caunters* [1980] Ch 297, an intended beneficiary brought an action in negligence against solicitors for their role in an invalid will. Sir Robert Megarry V-C approached the question of proximity as if it was determined through foreseeability:

Sir Robert Megarry V-C, at 308

First, there is the close degree of proximity of the plaintiff to the defendants. There is no question of whether the defendants could fairly have been expected to contemplate the plaintiff as a person likely to be affected by any lack of care on their part, or whether they ought to have done so: there is no "ought" about the case. This is not a case where the only nexus between the plaintiff and the defendants is that the plaintiff was the ultimate recipient of a dangerous chattel or negligent mis-statement which the defendants had put into circulation. The plaintiff was named and identified in the will that the defendants drafted for the testator. Their contemplation of the plaintiff was actual, nominate and direct. It was contemplation by contract, though of course the contract was with a third party, the testator.

It was the fact that the beneficiaries were known, hence more than foreseeable, that made them proximate. Indeed, Sir Robert Megarry V-C felt able to justify a prima facie duty of care on the basis of 'obviousness' (a very strong version of 'foreseeability'), thanks to the decision in *Anns*:

Sir Robert Megarry V-C, at 310

If one approaches the present case in the manner indicated by Lord Wilberforce, I can see only one answer to the question that has to be asked at the first stage. Prima facie a duty of care was owed by the defendants to the plaintiff [the intended beneficiary] because it was obvious that carelessness on their part would be likely to cause damage to her.

The complex case law on recovery for economic losses was regarded as relevant only at the second stage, where it had to be considered whether there were any factors to negative the duty. This was consistent with the treatment of the economic loss cases in Lord Wilberforce's dictum, extracted earlier. In the later case of *White v Jones* [1995] 2 AC 207, it was observed by the House of Lords that the simple approach in *Ross v Caunters* could not withstand the change marked by *Caparo v Dickman* (Section 3.3). In particular, the absence of a direct relationship between the defendant solicitor, and the intended beneficiary, was perceived to give rise to problems of proximity, which is once again understood as a criterion independent of foreseeability. The decision in *White v Jones*, and the current approach to cases of negligence in respect of wills, are further considered in Chapter 6. *Ross v Caunters*, like *Anns v Merton* in this jurisdiction,[20] is now a part of legal history.

Problem 2: *The Universal Test and Prima Facie Duty of Care*

So far, we have been chiefly concerned with the content of the test. But the structure and scope of the test caused further problems.

It is clear that Lord Wilberforce expected his approach to apply to all cases where the court had to decide whether to recognize a duty of care in negligence. For a period of time, courts were ready to accept that this represented the correct way forward for negligence law. However, problems began to be noted in two directions. First, negligence law was likely to expand into unpredictable areas. The range of situations in which one's negligence is foreseeably likely to cause harm is very broad indeed. The 'ocean of liability' referred to by Ibbetson was a real possibility. Second, courts were tempted to reconsider established areas under the influence of *Anns*, questioning existing restrictions. Reasoning which had been applied to restrict liability in previously decided cases was prone to be swept aside or addressed only at the second stage.

[20] The last aspect of *Anns* to fall was its analysis of negligence in the context of statutory powers: *Gorringe v Calderdale* [2004] 1 WLR 1057 (Chapter 6, Section 3).

By the time this second stage was reached, a prima facie duty was already said to have arisen. Thus considerations at this stage appeared (literally) secondary when compared to the idea of 'neighbourhood' in the first stage. 'Prima facie duty' would be a simple matter of foreseeability, checked by the weak concept of proximity or directness referred to earlier in this section, rather than requiring detailed justification in each case. 'No duty' or 'no liability' cases would begin to require exceptional justification. In a number of cases, courts even used the language of 'immunity' to describe the denial of a duty of care at the second stage: *Hill v Chief Constable of West Yorkshire Police* [1989] 1 AC 53. This has led to difficulties of compatibility with the European Convention on Human Rights (ECHR), and particularly Article 6 (right of access to a court or tribunal). Adoption of the more nuanced approach under *Caparo*, which incorporates policy considerations on equal terms with foreseeability, has helped to resolve this problem.

All of this raises the difficult question of the relationship between the two stages of the two-stage test.

Anns v Merton and Legal Principle

The general or universal test in the first stage of *Anns* can be interpreted as being based on legal principle. Many judicial statements in recent tort cases make reference to the need to be 'principled' in developing the law. 'Principled' distinctions are contrasted with 'arbitrary' distinctions. An example can be found in Lord Nicholls' judgment in *Fairchild v Glenhaven Funeral Services* [2003] 1 AC 32:

> To be acceptable our law must be coherent. It must be principled. The basis on which one case, or one type of case, is distinguished from another should be transparent and capable of identification.

There has also been some judicial comment contrasting 'principle' with 'policy'. Certain judges have sought to explain that the type of 'policy' that is relevant to the determination of whether the defendant owes a duty of care is primarily 'legal' policy. In this section, we briefly outline the characteristics of principle and policy, and identify their relative roles in the cases of *Anns v Merton* and *Caparo v Dickman*.

According to Ronald Dworkin,[21] 'principles' have two characteristic features. First, principles can be generalized. Principles which have been employed in answering one question can be used to generate solutions to a different question, provided that the second question is similar in a relevant way. Decisions which are based on principled statements might be thought to exert 'gravitational force'—as Dworkin puts it—beyond the area in which they are formally binding, because they are capable of being generalized. *Donoghue v Stevenson* and *Anns v Merton* appear to be excellent examples of this. However, we will see that the later history of negligence displays a retreat back to analysis of specific facts. At the very least, 'principled' decisions should be reconcilable with one another when viewed with hindsight. In one or two areas of negligence, even the search for consistency (with hindsight) has been abandoned.[22] This, however, may have been a passing phase, as courts sought a new set of tools to deal with emerging concerns of over-extensive liability, while still attempting to

---

[21] See particularly *Taking Rights Seriously* (2nd edn, Duckworth, 1996), chapters 2 and 4.
[22] *White v Chief Constable of South Yorkshire Police* [1999] 2 AC 455; *McFarlane v Tayside* [2000] 2 AC 59.

'right wrongs'. In the most recent period, these areas have not been those which cause the greatest difficulty.

'Foreseeability', as a criterion, is easily generalized through the idea of the reasonable person. In any given situation, what would a reasonable person in the position of the defendant have foreseen? To promote foreseeability appears to be to promote simplicity, coherence, and fairness. Indeed the emergence of foreseeability as the key criterion both in duty of care analysis, and in other elements of the tort of negligence, is linked to a trend towards universal tests. Proximity on the other hand has traditionally been more sensitive to factual variations. The existence of a proximity test of this sort would not prevent the law from being *consistent*. But it means consistency must be sought at a very detailed level.

What is the other dimension of 'legal principle'? Dworkin argued that 'principles', as opposed to 'policies', have particular content. Their content must reflect the rights of the parties, and not broader policy goals. This is well summarized and explained in the following extract.

Stephen Guest, *Ronald Dworkin* (3rd edn, Stanford University Press, 2013), 90–1

Principles and Policies

Dworkin's well-known distinction between principles and policies serves several purposes. It is intended to characterize distinctions which lawyers actually use in describing what judges should do. I think he captures that discourse successfully.

principle and policy are terms of art for [Dworkin] and formal definitions are to be found in chapters 2 and 4 of *Taking Rights Seriously* ... He does not change his mind in *Law's Empire*, nor in *Justice for Hedgehogs*. Roughly, principles describe rights, and policies describe goals:

A 'principle' [is] a standard that is to be observed, not because it will advance or secure an economic, political or social situation deemed desirable, but because it is a requirement of justice or fairness or some other dimension of morality.

... principles describe rights which aim at establishing an *individuated* state of affairs. So, he says:

A political right is an individuated political aim. An individual has a right to some opportunity or resource or liberty if it counts in favor of a political decision that the decision is likely to advance or protect the state of affairs in which he enjoys the right, even when no other political aim is served and some political aim is disserved thereby, and counts against that decision that it will retard or endanger that state of affairs, even when some other political aim is thereby served.

Policies, on the other hand, describe goals which aim at establishing an *unindividuated* political state of affairs:

A 'policy' [is] that kind of standard that sets out a goal to be reached, generally an improvement in some economic, political, or social feature of the community.

We speak of making something a 'matter of principle' and mean that we should act in some way rather than another. Whatever the consequences are because fairness, or justice, or some other matter of morality demands it. Lawyers have no difficulty at all in speaking in this way about legal rights nor, indeed, do most people.... .

'Policy' is more ambiguous and is at times used loosely, sometimes even just to mean that the judge has run out of good arguments and is striking out on his own...More often, though, it is used in the way Dworkin says it is, that is, it is a reference to the consequences that would follow from deciding in favour of one of the parties. The usual example is where the judge decides one way because he would 'open the floodgates of litigation'. All law students are familiar with that sort of reasoning.

As Guest says, one of the hallmarks of 'principle' is supposed to be that it gives 'individuated' reasons for decisions. A principle does not aim at a state of affairs that will be of general benefit, but concentrates on the rights and responsibilities of the particular parties affected.

We can see that foreseeability fits the 'content' requirement for principles, just as it fitted the form of principle by being easily generalizable. It is based on reasons that relate to the *individual defendant*, and not to broader social policy goals. Proximity, as it has subsequently been developed, is a very different matter.

In *Law's Empire* (Fontana, 1986), Dworkin theorizes that law 'works itself pure', gradually casting aside detailed issues based on particular facts and aiming at a more universal respect for principle and right. The recent history of negligence suggests rather the reverse. In terms of both substance and form, negligence has become less 'principled' in both of Dworkin's senses. Recent cases, as we will see in Chapter 6, show greater attention to the impact on social goals such as economic welfare, and greater attention to the specific facts of individual situations. And yet, there is a continuing search for coherence in negligence law, albeit with greater tolerance of variation according to the specific context of a given case.

What seems untrue, in the case of negligence law at least, is that principle defined according to *content* is in any sense dominant over policy. Analysis of policy factors has become a dominant feature of duty of care questions.

The contrast between two aspects of the 'duty of care' enquiry—factors relating to foreseeability, and factors relating to policy—are conveniently summarized in the following extract.[23] Here, Millner suggests that the duty of care concept is essentially policy based. Were it not for policy questions, the duty of care would be 'dispensable'.

M. Millner, *Negligence in Modern Law* (Butterworths, 1967), 230

The duty concept in negligence operates at two levels. At one level it is fact-based, at another it is policy-based. The fact-based duty of care forms a part of the enquiry whether the defendant's behaviour was negligent in the circumstances. The whole enquiry is governed by the foreseeability test, and 'duty of care' in this sense is a convenient but dispensable concept.

On the other hand, the policy-based or notional duty of care is an organic part of the tort; it is basic to the development and growth of negligence and determines its scope, that is to say, the range of relationships and interests protected by it. Here is a concept entirely divorced from foreseeability and governed by the policy of the law. 'Duty' in this sense is logically antecedent to 'duty' in the fact-determined sense. Until the law acknowledges that a particular

23 For a similar description see D. Nolan, 'Deconstructing the Duty of Care' (2013) 129 LQR 559, referring to a 'factual' duty of care and a legal or 'notional' duty of care. Unlike Millner, Nolan suggests that 'duty' has become an impediment to understanding and development of the law, partly because this dual usage tends not to be noticed.

interest or relationship is capable in principle of supporting a negligence claim, enquiries as to what was reasonably foreseeable are premature. The syntheses achieved in *Donoghue v Stevenson* and the *Hedley Byrne* case were concerned with duty of care in this sense and show the duty concept as an antenna with which to probe delicately the novel categories of relationship and classes of injury which come before the courts for recognition. The dynamics of the duty of care are largely outside the conceptual framework of negligence. The social forces which favour stability and those which promote change interact in a profoundly complex and subtle manner to yield normative solutions in law and morals. For this reason, there is no simple explanation of the subtle shifts in the scope and character of the duty of care or the precise timing of such movements. No analysis is worth its salt which is not based upon a concrete and detailed study of the society in which the changes are generated.

Summary

It is one thing to say that there is a single unified tort of negligence. Lord Atkin in *Donoghue v Stevenson* did this, and when he did so he answered an important question which was widely asked at the time: did negligence exist as an independent tort? To say that there is a single test for establishing a duty of care in negligence is quite a different matter. Lord Wilberforce in the *Anns* case thought the time had come to attempt the latter, but with hindsight he was wrong. In Canada, where the *Anns* test is still approved, it seems not to operate as a universal test in this way.

The single universal test based primarily on foreseeability was unsuccessful for a number of reasons. It paid insufficient attention to the detailed reasons for decided cases in specific areas; it paid insufficient attention to the analysis of the relationship between the parties in those cases; and it did not give priority to questions of practical impact. Furthermore, it appeared to provide a 'hierarchy' of reasons, in which principle was more important than pragmatic reasons, and in which a prima facie duty arose on the basis of principle alone. As we have seen, commentators such as Millner (before *Anns*) and Kidner (some years after *Anns*) have objected that policy is inherent to the recognition of a duty of care. It should not be relegated to a role where it merely 'negatives' such duties on specific occasions. Although there may be a general tort of negligence, that does not mean there is a general test for a duty of care, based on foreseeability of damage. On the other hand, at the most basic level, legal decision-making should be 'principled' in the sense that the distinction between cases is based on sound reasoning. This essential feature applies just as strongly to 'policy' decisions as to any other.

3.3 AN 'IRRESISTIBLE FORCE'? *CAPARO*, THREE FACTORS, AND INCREMENTAL DEVELOPMENT

In the period of development surrounding *Donoghue v Stevenson* and the decades leading up to *Anns v Merton*, it might have seemed that generalization was the main force at work in the tort of negligence. But, as we discussed in Chapter 1, tort as a whole has proved resistant to generalization. In *Caparo v Dickman*, the 'irresistible force' described by Christian Witting later in this section is one that works *against* generalization and universality.

The incremental approach, which recommends the consideration of 'duty questions' through close scrutiny of 'established categories', was advocated in a number of cases prior to *Caparo v Dickman*. These cases are referred to in the first paragraph of the extract from

Lord Bridge's judgment, later in this section. But it was in the case of *Caparo* that the House of Lords made its decisive move, authoritatively stating that the *Anns* approach could no longer be supported as appropriate, and attempting to outline most fully what the new approach would be.

Caparo Industries plc v Dickman and Others [1990] 2 AC 605 (HL)

Defendant auditors had prepared an annual report in respect of a company, F plc. This they were obliged to do by virtue of sections 236 and 237 of the Companies Act 1985. The claimants had purchased shares in F plc both before and after the publication to shareholders of the audited accounts. The claimants argued that they had relied on the published accounts in deciding to purchase sufficient shares to take over the company. They alleged that the auditors had been negligent in their preparation of the accounts, and that they owed a duty of care to the claimants. It was foreseeable both that F plc would be susceptible to a take-over bid; and that any investor seeking to make such a bid would rely upon the accuracy of the accounts. The Court of Appeal decided that a duty of care was owed by the auditors to the claimants, not in their role as investors, but in their capacity as existing shareholders in F plc.

The House of Lords allowed the auditors' appeal. In preparing the annual accounts, no duty of care was owed to the claimants either as investors, or as shareholders. Foreseeability would not be sufficient to form the basis of such a duty. Since this was a case of economic loss caused by allegedly negligent statements, it would be essential to show that there was a 'special relationship' between the parties, as explained in the leading case of *Hedley Byrne v Heller and Partners Ltd* [1964] AC 465.

The extracts below concern the general approach to establishing whether a duty of care was owed.

Lord Bridge of Harwich, at 617–18

But since the *Anns* case a series of decisions of the Privy Council and of your Lordships' House, notably in judgments and speeches delivered by Lord Keith of Kinkel, have empha-sised the inability of any single general principle to provide a practical test which can be applied to every situation to determine whether a duty of care is owed and, if so, what is its scope: see *Governors of Peabody Donation Fund v. Sir Lindsay Parkinson & Co. Ltd.* [1985] A.C. 210, 239f–241c; *Yuen Kun Yeu v Attorney-General of Hong Kong* [1988] A.C. 175, 190e–194f; *Rowling v. Takaro Properties Ltd.* [1988] A.C. 473, 501d–g; *Hill v. Chief Constable of West Yorkshire* [1989] A.C. 53, 60b–d. What emerges is that, in addition to the foreseeability of damage, necessary ingredients in any situation giving rise to a duty of care are that there should exist between the party owing the duty and the party to whom it is owed a relationship characterised by the law as one of "proximity" or "neighbourhood" and that the situation should be one in which the court considers it fair, just and reasonable that the law should impose a duty of a given scope upon the one party for the benefit of the other. But it is implicit in the passages referred to that the concepts of proximity and fairness embodied in these additional ingredients are not susceptible of any such precise definition as would be necessary to give them utility as practical tests, but amount in effect to little more than convenient labels to attach to the features of different specific situations which, on a detailed examination of all the circumstances, the law recognises pragmatically as giv-ing rise to a duty of care of a given scope. Whilst recognising, of course, the importance of the underlying general principles common to the whole field of negligence, I think the law has now moved in the direction of attaching greater significance to the more traditional categorisation of distinct and recognisable situations as guides to the existence, the scope and the limits of the varied duties of care which the law imposes. We must now, I think, recognise the wisdom of the words of Brennan J. in the High Court of Australia in *Sutherland Shire Council v. Heyman* (1985) 60 A.L.R. 1, 43–44, where he said:

"It is preferable, in my view, that the law should develop novel categories of negligence incrementally and by analogy with established categories, rather than by a massive extension of a prima facie duty of care restrained only by indefinable 'considerations which ought to negative, or to reduce or limit the scope of the duty or the class of person to whom it is owed.'"

One of the most important distinctions always to be observed lies in the law's essentially different approach to the different kinds of damage which one party may have suffered in consequence of the acts or omissions of another. It is one thing to owe a duty of care to avoid causing injury to the person or property of others. It is quite another to avoid causing others to suffer purely economic loss.

Lord Oliver of Aylmerton, at 632–3

… it is now clear from a series of decisions in this House that, at least so far as concerns the law of the United Kingdom, the duty of care in tort depends not solely upon the existence of the essential ingredient of the foreseeability of damage to the plaintiff but upon its coincidence with a further ingredient to which has been attached the label "proximity" and which was described by Lord Atkin in the course of his speech in *Donoghue v. Stevenson* [1932] A.C. 562, 581 as:

"such close and direct relations that the act complained of directly affects a person whom the person alleged to be bound to take care would know would be directly affected by his careless act."

It must be remembered, however, that Lord Atkin was using these words in the context of loss caused by physical damage where the existence of the nexus between the careless defendant and the injured plaintiff can rarely give rise to any difficulty. To adopt the words of Bingham L.J. in the instant case [1989] Q.B. 653, 686:

"It is enough that the plaintiff chances to be [out of the whole world] the person with whom the defendant collided or who purchased the offending ginger beer."

The extension of the concept of negligence since the decision of this House in *Hedley Byrne & Co. Ltd. v. Heller & Partners Ltd.* [1964] A.C. 465 to cover cases of pure economic loss not resulting from physical damage has given rise to a considerable and as yet unsolved difficulty of definition. The opportunities for the infliction of pecuniary loss from the imperfect performance of everyday tasks upon the proper performance of which people rely for regulating their affairs are illimitable and the effects are far reaching. A defective bottle of ginger beer may injure a single consumer but the damage stops there. A single statement may be repeated endlessly with or without the permission of its author and may be relied upon in a different way by many different people. Thus the postulate of a simple duty to avoid any harm that is, with hindsight, reasonably capable of being foreseen becomes untenable without the imposition of some intelligible limits to keep the law of negligence within the bounds of common sense and practicality. Those limits have been found by the requirement of what has been called a "relationship of proximity" between plaintiff and defendant and by the imposition of a further requirement that the attachment of liability for harm which has occurred be "just and reasonable." But although the cases in which the courts have imposed or withheld liability are capable of an approximate categorisation, one looks in vain for some common denominator by which the existence of the essential relationship can be tested. Indeed it is difficult to resist a conclusion that what have been treated as three separate requirements are, at least in most cases, in fact merely facets of the same thing, for in some cases the degree of foreseeability is such that it is from that alone that the requisite proximity can be deduced, whilst in others the absence of that essential relationship can most rationally be attributed simply to the court's view that it would not be fair and reasonable to hold the defendant responsible. "Proximity" is, no doubt, a convenient expression so long as it is realised that it is no more than a label which embraces not a definable concept but merely a description of circumstances from which, pragmatically, the courts conclude that a duty of care exists.

There are, of course, cases where, in any ordinary meaning of the words, a relationship of proximity (in the literal sense of "closeness") exists but where the law, whilst recognising the fact of the relationship, nevertheless denies a remedy to the injured party on the ground of public policy. *Rondel v. Worsley* [1969] 1 A.C. 191 was such a case, as was *Hill v. Chief Constable of West Yorkshire* [1989] A.C. 53, so far as concerns the alternative ground of that decision. But such cases do nothing to assist in the identification of those features from which the law will deduce the essential relationship on which liability depends and, for my part, I think that it has to be recognised that to search for any single formula which will serve as a general test of liability is to pursue a will-o'-the wisp. The fact is that once one discards, as it is now clear that one must, the concept of foreseeability of harm as the single exclusive test—even a prima facie test—of the existence of the duty of care, the attempt to state some general principle which will determine liability in an infinite variety of circumstances serves not to clarify the law but merely to bedevil its development in a way which corresponds with practicality and common sense.

Lord Oliver quoted from Brennan J in *Sutherland Shire Council* and Lord Devlin in *Hedley Byrne* before continuing:

At 635

Perhaps, therefore, the most that can be attempted is a broad categorisation of the decided cases according to the type of situation in which liability has been established in the past in order to found an argument by analogy. Thus, for instance, cases can be classified according to whether what is complained of is the failure to prevent the infliction of damage by the act of the third party (such as *Dorset Yacht Co. Ltd. v. Home Office* [1970] A.C. 1004, *P. Perl (Exporters) Ltd. v. Camden London Borough Council* [1984] Q.B. 342, *Smith v. Littlewoods Organisation Ltd.* [1987] A.C. 241 and, indeed, *Anns v. Merton London Borough Council* [1978] A.C. 728 itself), in failure to perform properly a statutory duty claimed to have been imposed for the protection of the plaintiff either as a member of a class or as a member of the public (such as the *Anns* case, *Ministry of Housing and Local Government v. Sharp* [1970] 2 Q.B. 223, *Yuen Kun Yeu v. Attorney-General of Hong Kong* [1988] A.C. 175) or in the making by the defendant of some statement or advice which has been communicated, directly or indirectly, to the plaintiff and upon which he has relied. Such categories are not, of course, exhaustive. Sometimes they overlap as in the *Anns* case, and there are cases which do not readily fit into easily definable categories (such as *Ross v. Caunters* [1980] Ch. 297). Nevertheless, it is, I think, permissible to regard negligent statements or advice as a separate category displaying common features from which it is possible to find at least guidelines by which a test for the existence of the relationship which is essential to ground liability can be deduced.

Commentary

The Necessary Ingredients of the Duty of Care

It is clear from each of the judgments extracted that foreseeability of harm will not suffice, even in order to establish a 'prima facie' duty of care. The approach in *Anns v Merton* is rejected. Equally, all of the extracts specify that the following 'ingredients' are necessary:

1. harm to the plaintiff/claimant must be foreseeable;

2. the situation must be one of proximity or neighbourhood;

3. the situation must be one in which it is 'fair, just and reasonable' to impose a duty of care.

Clearly, 'proximity' has re-emerged as a distinct element in the analysis of the situation, separate from foreseeability. Equally importantly, each of the factors above is given equal status in determining whether a duty of care is owed. Since it is acknowledged that these factors include considerations of 'practical' reasons (which we might broadly categorize as 'policy'), policy is no longer restricted to a merely subsidiary role.

Although *Caparo* itself, like *Anns*, was a case of economic loss, the approach in *Caparo*, including the 'fair, just and reasonable' criterion, is nevertheless applicable to all categories of negligence claim. The Court of Appeal made this clear in *Robinson v CC West Yorkshire* [2014] EWCA Civ 15, a case in which the claimant had been caught up in the arrest of a drug dealer in the street, and physically injured. The claimant argued that the *Caparo* approach did not apply to cases of directly caused physical injury:

Hallett LJ, *Robinson v CC West Yorkshire*
[2014] EWCA Civ 15

Applicability of the Caparo test to claims for direct physical harm

40 ... the *Caparo* test applies to all claims in the modern law of negligence. The third stage of the test may have been triggered by the desire to constrain the development of the law of negligence in relation to claims which do not involve direct physical damage, but it has become part of the general law. In the vast majority of claims the answer to the question posed at the third stage of the test—whether it is fair just and reasonable to impose a duty— may be obvious but it still applies. I can see no justification in the case law or the textbooks for restricting its application to the more difficult areas. In any event, Miss Widdett accepts the first two stages of the *Caparo* test foreseeability and proximity apply to all claims and they will inevitably involve some examination of what might be called public policy. The court will only impose a duty where it considers it right to do so on the facts.

41 The idea that the Common Law would impose a duty, in circumstances where it is unfair unjust and or unreasonable to do so, is to my mind nonsensical. The court may not have used these words but the whole basis of the decision in *Donoghue v Stevenson* was that it was fair just and reasonable to impose a duty. The ginger beer was intended

for consumption and produced in such a way the contents could not be examined by the ultimate consumer. The consumer had no contract with the manufacturer and therefore no other remedy. The manufacturer was understandably held liable for the damage caused to her.

There is a sense in this extract that the 'fair, just and reasonable' 'test' is simply an inevitable aspect of the duty of care enquiry, whatever the formal approach adopted.

Although it is common to refer to *Caparo* as establishing a 'three-stage test', it does not operate in terms of distinct stages in the same way that the *Anns* test did. No factor takes priority. A duty of care will only arise if, in all the circumstances and taking into account the factors above, it seems appropriate that it should do so. Policy is part of the positive process of establishing a duty of care, rather than a merely limiting factor.

Ingredients Not Tests

To refer to a 'three-stage test' may be misleading in another sense, too. For it suggests that *Caparo* does in fact set out a 'test'. In stating the three 'ingredients' of the duty of care enquiry, Lords Bridge and Oliver both explain that these will not operate as 'tests' as such. Instead, words such as 'proximity' are only 'convenient labels', which summarize the reasons why the court has decided that the relationship is one that ought to give rise to a duty of care. The description of a particular relationship as 'proximate' is therefore a conclusion. It marks the court's judgment that the situation in question displays the hallmarks of 'proximity.' What this does not tell us is what the hallmarks of proximity actually are.

In what sense can a 'pragmatic' approach based on a court's judgment in all the circumstances, 'guided' only by concepts that turn out to be mere labels, be expected to steer future courts to coherent and predictable decision-making? The existence of important concepts which nevertheless appear not to operate as 'tests' has been a source of some frustration. At the same time, lower-level tests or (at least) common descriptors or groups of reasons have subsequently begun to emerge, suggesting that the three stages of *Caparo* may at least provide a workable framework of analysis for duty questions.

Categories

In theory, help should be at hand in the 'categories' of decided cases which are to be given attention under the *Caparo* approach. Guidance on what sort of considerations will be relevant for the determination of a novel case can, under *Caparo*, be gleaned from previously decided cases in similar categories. Of particular importance in *Caparo v Dickman* itself was that the damage caused was purely economic, involving no physical damage to property or the person; equally, that the damage was allegedly caused by negligent statements rather than acts. For both of these reasons, the simple version of 'proximity' to be found in *Donoghue v Stevenson* would not suffice. In theory, this idea of categories ought to aid the predictability of decision-making, because it ought to be relatively clear which sorts of reasons will be decisive in the novel case before the court.

Incrementalism

Associated with the role of categories is the idea of 'incremental development.' Incrementalism implies that duties of care should be recognized more easily in situations which are similar to previously recognized 'duty situations'. Negligence should develop step by step, allowing proper consideration of the practical impact of the extended duties, rather than allowing huge leaps into unknown territory. As the *Caparo* approach matures, it is also now clear that one of its most important implications is the reversal of any 'presumption' of duty which might have arisen from *Anns*. A duty of care will not only require the defendant to be careful, but also impose the risk of loss upon the defendant. There need to be positive reasons why a duty should be imposed in a novel case. Again, the shadow of potentially limitless liability (and, short of this, of potentially limitless litigation) can be discerned.

Before we evaluate the use of categories and of incremental development, we should dispose of one question. Does the emphasis on 'categories', together with the idea of 'incrementalism', return us to the 'wilderness of single instances', or separate duty situations, obtaining before the decision in *Donoghue*? It does not. It is true that Lord Oliver's remarks in some respects appear to reverse the effect of *Donoghue*. In particular, he observes that 'one looks in vain for some common denominator by which the existence of the essential relationship can be tested'. This directly, probably deliberately, contrasts with Lord Atkin's famous dictum, 'there must be, and is, some general conception of relations giving rise to the duty of care, of which the particular cases found in the books are but instances'. Even so, it is now recognized that all instances in which a duty of care is held to exist are aspects of a single tort.

In *Donoghue*, Lord Macmillan famously stated that the 'categories of negligence are never closed'. The categories of negligence are also not entirely separate. The recent case law on duty of care shows considerable generalization from one category to another. For example, the concept referred to as 'voluntary assumption of responsibility' has been relied upon in diverse situations such as negligent misstatement (*Hedley Byrne v Heller* [1964] AC 465), negligent professional services (*Henderson v Merrett* [1995] 2 AC 145), negligent failure to diagnose dyslexia (*Phelps v Hillingdon* [2001] 2 AC 619), and police failure to safeguard the interests of informants (*Swinney v Chief Constable of Northumbria* [1997] QB 464). More recently, it has been seen as the key to justifying liability for failure to warn (*Mitchell v Glasgow* [2009] UKHL 11; [2009] 1 AC 874). Does this cross-fertilization suggest the return of principle in a more cautious, more sophisticated, more pragmatic form? It all depends whether the concepts applied have at least some reasonably stable and identifiable meaning. The challenge is that if they do not, then the use of previous cases can only be of limited assistance, and 'cross-fertilization' will only be a matter of labels, rather than principles.

Evaluation

It will be apparent that where *Caparo* is applied to a truly novel case, the decision on whether a duty of care arises has the potential to be unpredictable. Since all of the component factors we listed earlier will enter into a decision which is finally made by a court on pragmatic grounds, it will be difficult to predict with confidence whether a duty of care will be said to arise, or not. On the other hand, this uncertainty is greater in some areas than in others; and efforts to head off the uncertainty (and generally, to limit the duties owed) are more satisfactory in some parts of the law than others.

We will have to address such issues through examination of the case law in Chapter 6. For the time being, we will address some arguments that have been put both for, and against, the *Caparo* approach. First, we will return to Millner for a very perceptive but possibly idealized statement of the nature of the duty of care enquiry as initiated by *Hedley Byrne v Heller*. Although this extract is taken from a work which is over forty years old, given our analysis of *Caparo v Dickman* (above) it can be argued that the *Anns* case simply took a wrong turning from *Hedley Byrne*. It is interesting to note that Millner's pre-*Anns* statement accords to a large extent with the aspirations of the *Caparo* approach.

M. Millner, *Negligence in Modern Law* (Butterworths, 1967), 236–7

… the controlled extension of negligence liability into novel fields demands solutions of great delicacy. How far and upon what conditions shall the law afford a remedy for careless invasions of interests which are as yet protected not at all, or not beyond deliberate or reckless infringement? At first glance, the abstraction achieved in *Donoghue v Stevenson* offers solutions of beguiling simplicity. But there is no such royal road. Outside the broad context of that case, the 'neighbour principle' falters. It yields not an answer but a point of departure for further and more particular enquiry. This phase in the evolution of negligence is specialised and sophisticated, and the crux of it is the formulation—in the *Hedley Byrne* manner—of *supplementary criteria* of a refined type. Thus the negligence principle works powerfully to rationalise the law, giving it a more coherent pattern of liability as diversified as befits the complex modern society which it serves.

Clearly, Millner's approach in this extract endorses diversity in approach, of a sort which the *Anns* test discouraged. It suggests that the appropriate response is to develop 'supplementary criteria'. But it also assumes that more diversified criteria can be more 'sophisticated', and that the courts' social antennae (to borrow a metaphor from our previous extract from the same book) can guide them to appropriate rules.

Some post-*Caparo* case law suggests that the last point is very much in doubt. For example, the law on psychiatric harm has given rise to a number of artificial and unprincipled restrictions whose connection to exact policy goals is obscure and which have been described at the highest judicial level as 'disfiguring' the law in this area (Lord Hoffmann, *Gregg v Scott* [2005] UKHL 2, para 87) (Chapter 4, Section 4). The case law on economic loss has been permeated by deep divisions over the appropriate 'test' or even 'label' to apply in problematic cases, with battle lines particularly being drawn up over the meaning and applicability of the concept of 'voluntary assumption of responsibility' and whether it is part of, or in competition with, the three-stage 'test' (Chapter 6, Section 2). On the other hand, it is arguable that the problems in this area are finally easing.

The next extract defends the *Caparo* approach against criticism by the Australian High Court in *Sullivan v Moody* (2001) 75 JLR 1570, and particularly defends the benefits of labels such as 'proximity'. In *Sullivan* and later cases, the High Court of Australia abandoned proximity and replaced it with a 'multi-factorial' or 'salient features' approach, treating a wide range of factors as potentially relevant. Witting doubts whether this is an advance over proximity, properly understood and applied.

C. Witting, 'The Three-Stage Test Abandoned in Australia—or Not?' (2002) 118 LQR 214, at 217–19

It is submitted that *each* element within the *Caparo Industries* three-stage test has a coherent function to play in determining whether a duty of care ought to be found to exist. The test for foreseeability is 'agent-general' in that it examines the ability to foresee an accident from the point of view of *any* reasonable person in the position of the defendant…. Foreseeability thus acts in a negative way by excluding from liability those persons who had no such minimal capacity to take action in order to avoid damage.

Proximity is the more difficult concept to explain. But explanation is assisted by keeping in mind the point that proximity is a concept which, ultimately, requires an evaluation of facts. . . . The essential function of the test for proximity is . . . to *identify* those persons (if any) who were most appropriately placed to take care in the avoidance of damage.

At 220–1

If the observations in this note are correct—it being possible to outline the essential functions played by each of the elements of the *Caparo Industries* three-stage test for duty—it would appear that the High Court of Australia has acted without due care in abandoning that test. It is difficult to conceive how duty issues can properly be analysed without resort to each of the three elements of the test. It is clear that courts must look for factors which indicate a minimum ability to avoid the causation of damage and for factors which identify particular persons as being appropriately placed to take care so as to avoid such damage. Foreseeability and proximity, respectively, serve these functions. But the decision whether or not to impose a duty will be, ultimately, a normative one—a question of legal policy, if you like. For this reason, *Caparo Industries* is likely to remain an irresistible force in the law of negligence. The High Court of Australia, in disapproving that case, is indeed, with respect, in error.

Do notions such as 'proximity' give any real guidance as to what we are 'looking for' when we evaluate the particular relationship in question? With the development of the 'categories' of case law, and of 'supplementary criteria' such as 'voluntary assumption of responsibility', is the duty of care enquiry under *Caparo* becoming more 'sophisticated' (to refer to Millner's aspiration in 1967), or more 'vacuous' (Hoyano, Further Reading)? Has it finally stabilized to a point where the courts can achieve gradual extension without fear of unforeseen effects across categories? These are the issues we must consider, along with the case law itself, in Chapter 6.

4. THE SPECIAL CASE OF OMISSIONS: POSITIVE DUTIES TO ACT

Here, we introduce the special case of omissions. Omissions are certainly capable of giving rise to liability in negligence, but special considerations apply to them. These special considerations may be expressed as questions of duty; of breach; of causation; or of remoteness. Because omissions typically raise complex policy questions about particular types of defendants (such as the police and public authorities), or the balance of risks (for example between occupiers and those entering the land they occupy), cases of omissions liability will be found represented in various parts of the book. The purpose of this section is simply to introduce the law's general approach to omissions as a category. The key to this general approach lies in the question of when a positive *duty* to act will, or will not, be recognized.

Omissions liability arises as an issue where the defendant's alleged negligence consists in *not doing something*. In *Anns v Merton* (earlier), this factor was not treated as particularly relevant, but *Anns v Merton* now seems isolated in this respect as in all others (*Gorringe v Calderdale* [2004] UKHL 15, Chapter 6). Although the status of omissions in negligence law has not been completely resolved, there has been recent clarification from the House of Lords in *Mitchell v Glasgow* [2009] UKHL 11; (2009) 1 AC 874. In the case of public authorities, the role of omissions has become particularly pertinent since there are recognized, but limited, obligations on states under the ECHR (and on public authorities under the Human Rights Act 1998) to take positive steps to protect Convention rights. These are explored in Chapters 1 and 6.

4.1 DISTINGUISHING ACTS FROM OMISSIONS

There is ambiguity in the very distinction between acts, and omissions. A 'mere' omission or 'pure' omission can be said to involve doing nothing at all (an expression used by Lord Hoffmann in the case of *Gorringe v Calderdale* [2004] UKHL 15, where a highway authority had not chosen to renew road markings advising motorists to slow down approaching the brow of a hill). We can certainly contrast this sort of case with omissions that occur *in the course of acting*. A clear example of an omission in the course of acting is where a driver fails to put his foot on the brake. Negligence law would have no difficulty in treating this as equivalent to an act. It is a case of driving inappropriately. At the other end of the scale, the 'classic' example of a pure omission attracting no liability is the failure to warn a stranger. If I see somebody about to walk over a cliff I am generally under no duty to shout a warning. On the other hand, we will see later in the present chapter that this outcome depends on who that person is and whether I have any pre-existing relationship with or duty in connection with that person. Alternatively, it may depend on whether I have any special role in connection with the danger itself, for example if it arises on land that I occupy, or if it is a danger that I have created.

4.2 LIABILITY FOR OMISSIONS: THE GENERAL APPROACH

The judgments extracted in this section are often treated as the starting point in this area.

Lord Diplock, *Dorset Yacht v Home Office*
[1970] AC 1004, at 1060

The branch of English law which deals with civil wrongs abounds with instances of acts and, more particularly, of omissions which give rise to no legal liability in the doer or omitter for loss or damage sustained by others as a consequence of the act or omission, however reasonably or probably that loss or damage might have been anticipated. The very parable of the good Samaritan (*Luke* 10, v. 30) which was evoked by Lord Atkin in *Donoghue v. Stevenson* illustrates, in the conduct of the priest and of the Levite who passed by on the other side, an omission which was likely to have as its reasonable and probable consequence damage to the health of the victim of the thieves, but for which the priest and Levite would have incurred no civil liability in English law. Examples could be multiplied. You may cause loss to a tradesman by withdrawing your custom though the goods which he supplies are entirely satisfactory; you may damage your neighbour's land by intercepting the flow of percolating water to it even though the interception is of no advantage to yourself; you need not warn him of a risk of physical danger to which he is about to expose himself unless there is some special relationship between the two of you such as that of occupier of land and visitor; you may watch your neighbour's goods being ruined by a thunderstorm though the slightest effort on your part could protect them from the rain and you may do so with impunity unless there is some special relationship between you such as that of bailor and bailee.

Lord Reid, at 1027

... when a person has done nothing to put himself in any relationship with another person in distress or with his property mere accidental propinquity does not require him to go to that person's assistance. There may be a moral duty to do so, but it is not practicable to make it a legal duty.

None of this implies that there is *never* a positive duty to act in negligence law. Lord Diplock went on to draw a parallel with Lord Atkin's question 'who is my neighbour?' in *Donoghue v Stevenson*:

Lord Diplock, at 1061

This appeal, therefore, also raises the lawyer's question: "Am I my brother's keeper?" A question which may also receive a restricted reply.

The question receives a restricted reply. It does not receive a *wholly negative* reply.

Mitchell v Glasgow City Council [2009] UKHL 11; (2009) 1 AC 874

The pursuer argued that the deceased ought to have been warned that his neighbour Drummond, who had previously threatened to kill him, had been called to a meeting at the Council to discuss, in part, his behaviour towards the deceased. The meeting left Drummond in an agitated state, and on returning home he carried out his earlier threat, attacking and killing the deceased.

Lord Hope, *Mitchell v Glasgow City Council* [2009] UKHL 11

15. Three points must be made at the outset to put the submission into its proper context. The first is that foreseeability of harm is not of itself enough for the imposition of a duty of care ... Otherwise, to adopt Lord Keith of Kinkel's dramatic illustration in *Yuen Kun Yeu v Attorney General of Hong Kong* [1988] AC 175, 192, there would be liability in negligence on the part of one who sees another about to walk over a cliff with his head in the air, and forebears to shout a warning. The second, which flows from the first, is that the law does not normally impose a positive duty on a person to protect others. As Lord Goff of Chieveley explained in *Smith v Littlewoods Organisation Ltd*, 76, the common law does not impose liability for what, without more, may be called pure omissions. The third, which is a development of the second, is that the law does not impose a duty to prevent a person from being harmed by the criminal act of a third party based simply upon foreseeability: *Smith v Littlewoods Organisation Ltd*, 77–83, per Lord Goff.

Mitchell was a case where the positive duty claimed was a duty to warn M about the potential criminal acts of another (in fact, at one remove: the claimed duty was to warn M about a meeting with the third party, which might be expected to make him angry, in the context of earlier threats to kill M). Related issues are explored in relation to 'remoteness' or 'novus actus' in Section 6.3 of this chapter. In *Mitchell*, Lords Hope, Scott, and Brown set out in broadly similar terms those circumstances where there may be liability in negligence for the criminal acts of another. Here we extract Lord Brown's version. The circumstances are:

1. where there is vicarious liability (Chapter 9);

2. where there is an obligation to supervise;

3. where the defendant creates the risk of danger (for example by giving off-duty employees access to firearms);

4. where there is an assumption of responsibility (Chapter 6).

Lord Brown, *Mitchell v Glasgow City Council* [2009] UKHL 11

81. Generally speaking, people are not liable for the crimes of others. A is not ordinarily liable to victim B for injuries (or damage) deliberately inflicted by third party C. In some situations, of course, where, for example, C is employed by A or otherwise acting on A's behalf, A may be vicariously liable for C's crime. But it cannot be said that a landlord is vicariously liable for his tenant's crimes and a consistent line of authority holds that landlords are not responsible for the antisocial behaviour of their tenants: *Smith v Scott* [1973] Ch 314, *O'Leary v London Borough of Islington* (1983) 9 HLR 83, *Hussain v Lancaster CC* [2000] QB 1, and *Mowan v Wandsworth LBC* [2001] LGR 228.

82. A may also be liable for C's crime where he is under an obligation to supervise C and fails to do so: *Dorset Yacht Co Ltd v Home Office* [1970] AC 1004, where Borstal boys escaped (and caused damage in the vicinity whilst escaping: important because proximity too is a necessary condition of liability in these cases) whilst their warders were asleep, is a good illustration of this. Similarly, if A specifically creates a risk of injury, by, for example, arming C with a weapon, he may be liable for the resulting damage, as in the particular circumstances of *Attorney General of the British Virgin Islands v Hartwell* [2004] 1 WLR . . .

83. Similarly, A may be liable if he assumes specific responsibility for B's safety but carelessly then fails to protect B: see, for example, *Costello v Chief Constable of Northumbria* [1999] 1 All ER 550. It cannot credibly be suggested, however, that any of these situations arise here. Landlords are under no obligation to supervise their tenants and prevent their committing criminal acts; by threatening a disruptive tenant with eviction a landlord cannot sensibly be said to be creating the risk of personal violence towards others in the same way as the British Virgin Islands police created a risk by arming an erratic probationer; and there can be no question of landlords assuming responsibility for the safety of neighbours (or, indeed, visitors) even if they know their tenants to be threatening them.

Among the positive duties to be explored in this text are the positive duties on states and, through the HRA, on 'public authorities' to secure certain Convention rights. These are dealt with in Chapters 1 and 6. Their conceptual basis is different from the categories referred to by Lord Brown as they flow from the provisions of the ECHR; but they create a parallel source of 'compensation' which has been described as notably tort-like (Chapter 1, Section 4.2).

5. CAUSATION AND REMOTENESS/ATTRIBUTION OF DAMAGE

5.1 INTRODUCTION: HOW MANY 'CAUSATION' QUESTIONS ARE THERE?

We have already seen that liability in negligence depends on showing that a duty of care has been breached. Negligence however is a tort requiring damage, and the claimant must therefore also establish that the defendant's breach caused the damage in respect of which a remedy is claimed. Further, there must be a relevant link between the breach, and the damage, so that the damage can properly and fairly be attributed to the breach.

The traditional analysis of causation in the law of tort holds that there are two distinct questions of causation involved in the tort of negligence and in those other torts that require damage. Here we set out the two generally recognized questions, known as 'cause in fact', and 'cause in law' or 'remoteness'. We will then explain the general problems of categorization and terminology which plague this aspect of the law of tort. Some say that only the first is a causation question, though their description of the second question varies; others that there are more than two questions of causation.

The Traditional Division: Two Questions

On a traditional approach, there are two basic questions of causation:

1. *Was the defendant's breach of duty or other tortious intervention a **factual cause** of the damage?* This question is addressed in an introductory fashion by Section 5.2. More difficult aspects of this question continue to arise and are debated in Chapter 4.

2. Is the damage **attributable** to the defendant's breach of duty (or other tortious conduct)? This is the more elusive question addressed in Section 6.

The first question is apparently rather simple. It seems to ask about facts. As we will see, it is often not simple at all. However, there is at least a recognized starting point for such questions, which is whether the breach of duty was a 'but for' cause of the harm. In other words, would the harm have come about 'but for' the tort? This test is sometimes not sufficient because too many factors pass this initial test. On other occasions it is inappropriate because factors which clearly are causes are unable to pass the test. So it is set aside. On other occasions still, there are difficulties of *proving* that it is satisfied, and what amounts to proof will be subject to consideration. Even so, 'but for' expresses a recognized test with a recognized purpose—to show whether the harm is historically linked (regarded as a test of cause and effect) with the damage.

The second question cannot be so easily identified.

'Remoteness' or 'Attribution': Causal or Not?

Remoteness Not a Causal Idea

There are those who argue that the only question of causation in the law of tort is the first, relating to factual causation. Other questions of attribution or remoteness are not about cause. Of these approaches, we can pick out two variations:

1. Some have argued that the second question of attribution is a purely legal question about 'the foreseeability of the harm', 'the scope of the duty', or 'the scope of the risk

against which the defendant had a duty to guard'. All these approaches try to align the question of attribution with the question of duty.

2. Others have argued that the second question is best expressed quite honestly and openly in terms of 'the scope of liability for consequences'.

The second of these two approaches is championed by Jane Stapleton, 'Cause in Fact and the Scope of Liability for Consequences' (2003) 119 LQR 388. It has the merit of being simple to state. There are two tests: one concerns factual causation, the other asks whether the harm is within the scope of the consequences for which there should be liability. But it has the disadvantage that the second stage is a very open enquiry and many factors could, in principle, be relevant.

Variations of the first of the two approaches above, aligning attribution with duty, will be encountered in the case law extracted in Section 6. In particular, the foreseeability approach was adopted in *The Wagon Mound (No 1)* [1961] AC 388; while the 'scope of duty' approach was adopted by Lord Hoffmann, in particular, in important cases such as *Reeves v Commissioner of Police for the Metropolis* [2000] 1 AC 360, and *South Australia Asset Management Corporation v York Montagu* [1997] AC 191. It has been continued in a number of more recent cases, as we will see.

Multiple Causal Questions

Not everyone agrees that the only question of causation encountered in the law is the question of factual causation. Hart and Honoré, in a highly influential work, argued that the test of 'but for' causation does not establish, as a matter of ordinary language, whether the factor in question is to be called a 'cause'.[24] Too many factors will satisfy the test. Even if the 'but for' test identifies those factors which pass a threshold of 'historical involvement', not all such factors deserve to be identified as 'causes'. Equally, Hart and Honoré argued that the remoteness test in law involves genuinely 'causal' elements, and that there are other causal questions in play apart from those we capture in terms of 'but for' cause and 'remoteness'.

Jane Stapleton has been critical of the Hart and Honoré approach, though that approach has clearly influenced some of our most senior judges.[25]

J. Stapleton, 'Occam's Razor Reveals an Orthodox Basis for Chester v Afshar' (2006) 122 LQR 426, at 426[26]

Lawyers across the common law world often find "causation" problematic. This is because we do not actually agree on what we mean by that and other causal terms. Sometimes by "causation" lawyers mean just the objective question of historical "fact": whether the defendant's breach of obligation had anything at all to do with the production of the claimant's injury. Other times lawyers use causal terminology not merely for this idea of historical involvement but for

[24] H. L. A. Hart and T. Honoré, *Causation in the Law* (2nd edn, Oxford University Press, 1985). In fact, Hart and Honoré defended a refined version of the 'but for' test known as the 'NESS' test (the condition must be a 'necessary element in a sufficient set'). This refinement almost certainly goes beyond what will be required of a student of tort law, and is not encountered in the case law. There is a brief introduction to 'NESS' in Chapter 4.

[25] Lord Hoffmann, 'Causation' (2005) 121 LQR 592.

[26] Footnotes omitted.

a separate notion of "causal connection" which, together with a third notion of "remoteness", concerns the normative evaluation of whether this particular consequence of the defendant's breach is one for which he should be held legally responsible. The most well known version of this three-step approach was that championed by Hart and Honoré.

For them, even where a factor is historically involved in the production of an outcome, or to use their terms, even when it is "a causally relevant factor" in relation to that outcome, it will not be a "cause" of it where there is no "causal connection" between the factor and outcome. Yet it is not at all clear what they mean by a "causal connection", what therefore beyond historical involvement they mean by a "cause", and where the line between "causal connection" and "remoteness" lies.

The three-step Hart and Honoré approach is both inconvenient and obfuscatory. Clarity in legal reasoning will not be improved in this area until it is abandoned in favour of a two-step analysis consisting of the factual issue of historical involvement and the normative question of whether a particular consequence of breach should be judged to be within the scope of liability for the breach.

It is true that the Hart and Honoré approach is inconvenient and subtle. Then again, they were seeking to describe a multi-faceted phenomenon. Given the influence of their work, we should spend a little space identifying some of its key features. We should then be better placed to consider, particularly in Section 6 of this chapter, to what extent ideas of 'cause' still make themselves felt in the second question of attribution ('remoteness', 'scope of liability for consequences', or whatever else it may be called) identified earlier.

Causation and Ordinary Language

Lord Hoffmann, *Environment Agency v Empress Car Co (Abertillery) Ltd* [1999] 2 AC at 29

The courts have repeatedly said that the notion of causing is one of 'common sense'. So in *Alphacell v Woodward* [1972] AC 824, 847 Lord Salmon said:

'what or who has caused an event to occur is essentially a practical question of fact which can best be answered by ordinary common sense rather than abstract meta-physical theory.'

H. L. A. Hart and T. Honoré, *Causation in the Law* (2nd edn, Oxford University Press, 1985), 1

... the assertion often made by the courts, especially in England, that it is the plain man's notions of causation (and not the philosopher's or the scientist's) with which the law is concerned, seems to us to be true.

The quotations above reinforce a common theme of English law in respect of causal enquiries. Law does not depend upon either science or philosophy for its notions of causation.

Rather, it employs 'common sense' notions which are inherent in the way that ordinary people talk about cause.

At first sight, this position appears naive. It would seem to deny the many problems associated with causation, taking refuge in a fictional 'shared understanding'. Common sense is, notoriously, not something on which people can commonly agree, so what hope is there for using this concept to arrive at solutions to difficult questions of causation?

According to Hart and Honoré, law's 'common sense' approach does not involve a denial of the complexities of causal statements, but is actually based on an appreciation of such complexities. Equally, and to the extent that it rejects scientific approaches, the law's approach does not do so through lack of understanding. Rather, according to Hart and Honoré, law relies on 'common sense' primarily because the concerns of the law in discussing cause are often similar to the concerns of everyday language, and different from the concerns of science or philosophy. As John Gardner has put it:

> 'Common sense [in Hart's work] does not have its popular Forrest Gump overtones. It has a technical oppositional meaning specific to philosophers . . .' (Book review of N. Lacey, *A Life of HLA Hart* in [2005] 121 LQR 329, 331).

A distinction between the concerns of science and the concerns of law is made in the following extract. Here, Hart and Honoré are concerned to distinguish some common scientific questions about cause from some 'everyday' attempts to *explain* particular events in terms of what caused them.

Hart and Honoré, *Causation in the Law*, 33–5

Abnormal and normal conditions

In the sciences causes are often sought to explain not *particular* occurrences but *types of* occurrence which usually or normally happen: the processes of continuous growth, the tides, planetary motions, senile decay. In ordinary life, by contrast, the particular causal question is most often inspired by the wish for an explanation of a *particular* contingency the occurrence of which is puzzling because it is a departure from the normal, ordinary, or reasonably expected course of events: some accident, catastrophe, disaster, or other deviation from the normal cause of events . . .

. . . What is normal and what is abnormal is, however, relative to the context of any given inquiry . . . If a fire breaks out in a laboratory or in a factory, where special precautions are taken to exclude oxygen during the manufacturing process, since the success of this depends on safety from fire, there would be no absurdity at all in *such* a case in saying that the presence of the oxygen was the cause of the fire. The exclusion of oxygen in such a case and not its presence is part of the normal functioning of the laboratory or the factory, and hence a mere condition . . .

. . . the distinction between cause and conditions may be drawn in different ways. The cause of a great famine in India may be identified by the Indian peasant as the drought, but the World Food authority may identify the Indian government's failure to build up reserves as the cause and the drought as a mere condition . . .

We can particularly highlight two implications of the above extract:

1. The answer to any question of causation in respect of the law will depend upon the reason for asking the question.

2. In isolating the factor or factors which we consider to deserve the title of 'cause', there is generally more attention paid, in everyday language as in law, to 'abnormal' events.

The influence of Hart and Honoré's work is clearly to be seen in the following extract. The case from which this passage is drawn concerned *criminal* liability under a particular statutory provision, but Lord Hoffmann's judgment has since been referred to in a number of crucial cases on causation in the tort of negligence:

Lord Hoffmann, *Environment Agency v Empress Car Co (Abertillery) Ltd* [1999] 2 AC 22, at 29

The first point to emphasise is that common sense answers to questions of causation will differ according to the purpose for which the question is asked. Questions of causation often arise for the purpose of attributing responsibility to someone, for example, so as to blame him for something which has happened or to make him guilty of an offence or liable in damages. In such cases, the answer will depend upon the rule by which responsibility is being attributed. Take, for example, the case of the man who forgets to take the radio out of his car and during the night someone breaks the quarterlight, enters the car and steals it. What caused the damage? If the thief is on trial, so that the question is whether he is criminally responsible, then obviously the answer is that he caused the damage. It is no answer for him to say that it was caused by the owner carelessly leaving the radio inside. On the other hand, the owner's wife, irritated at the third such occurrence in a year, might well say that it was his fault. In the context of an inquiry into the owner's blameworthiness under a non-legal, common sense duty to take reasonable care of one's own possessions, one would say that his carelessness caused the loss of the radio.

In everyday *explanations* as to what 'caused' a particular event, some events and states of affairs are reduced to the level of 'mere conditions' of the occurrences in question. Out of the many conditions which form the necessary history of an adverse event, we tend to select one (sometimes more than one) as 'causes'. As Hart and Honoré point out, this will generally be an 'abnormal' condition, although what is counted as abnormal will vary with the context. Human intervention will often be selected as a cause, particularly so if it is in some way 'faulty'. But as Lord Hoffmann explains, this depends on the reason for asking. If we want to know whether a car owner should have taken more precautions, even a deliberate criminal act on the part of another may become part of the general 'context' of the event, amounting perhaps even to a 'normal condition'. So one can, by an omission, 'cause' loss of a car radio, even though it is taken by someone else—at least if there is a positive duty to act.

This last point shows that for the purposes of 'cause in fact', we do not need to ask whether the defendant's breach of duty was *the* cause of accidental damage. Rather, the breach needs to be *a* cause of that damage. Lord Hoffmann also pointed out, in the *Empress Car* case, that an event may have *more than one cause*. However, 'mere conditions'—factors which we would most naturally treat as being essential to the history of the event, but which we would not select as a relevant 'cause' of the event—will *also* pass the 'but for' test. For Hart and Honoré, 'mere conditions' are *not* to be called 'causes'.

In summary, the idea of 'but for causation' is treated by Hart and Honoré as no more than a useful way of asking whether the defendant's breach of duty was effective in the history of events which led to the claimant's loss, while avoiding 'abstract metaphysics'. 'But for' causation is an important element in our common understanding of the nature of 'cause', particularly when causal questions are asked for the purposes of attribution of responsibility. 'But for' causation will, however, not always provide the tools that we need.

Hart and Honoré treat causation as a multilayered concept best understood through close analysis of the way in which we use language in everyday life and in law. The purpose of the enquiry into causation will help to determine the meaning of causation in a given case. There are many important 'causation' questions in law.

5.2 'BUT FOR' CAUSATION

It should be especially underlined that for the purposes of causation in the tort of negligence, it is not enough to show that the defendant's *conduct* has been the cause of the damage suffered by the claimant. Rather, it is the *breach of the duty of care* that must have caused the relevant damage.

In determining questions of factual causation, the starting point is 'but for' causation: would the claimant's injury have occurred 'but for' the defendant's negligence? If the same injury would have occurred even without the defendant's negligence, then that negligence is not a 'necessary cause' of the damage or loss to the claimant. The idea of necessary cause is also referred to in the Latin version as *causa sine qua non*.

Since tort is a civil action, the claimant must establish that the breach of duty is a 'but for' cause of his or her injury or loss *on the balance of probabilities*. That is to say, the claimant must convince the court that it is more likely than not that the injury would *not* have occurred *without* the negligence (or other tortious intervention) of the defendant. The following case provides a classic illustration of the 'but for' test.

Barnett v Chelsea and Kensington Hospital Management Committee [1969] 1 QB 428

Three nightwatchmen presented themselves at a casualty department provided and run by the defendants, complaining to the nurse that they had been vomiting for three hours after drinking tea. The nurse reported their complaints by telephone to the duty medical officer, who instructed her to tell the men to go home to bed and call in their own doctors. This, reportedly, is what the duty medical officer said:

Well, I am vomiting myself and I have not been drinking. Tell them to go home and go to bed and call in their own doctors, except Whittal, who should stay because he is due for an X-ray later this morning [at 431].

All of the men left. About five hours later, one of them died from poisoning by arsenic, which had been introduced into the tea. Nield J concluded that he would have died from the poisoning even if he had been admitted to the hospital and treated with all due care five hours earlier.

Nield J, at 433–4

My conclusions are: that the plaintiff, Mrs Bessie Irene Barnett, has failed to establish, on the balance of probabilities, that the death of the deceased, William Patrick Barnett, resulted from the negligence of the defendants, the Chelsea and Kensington Hospital Management Committee, my view being that had all care been taken, still the deceased must have died. But my further conclusions are that the defendant's casualty officer was negligent in failing to see and examine the deceased, and that, had he done so, his duty would have been to admit the deceased to the ward and to have treated him or caused him to be treated.

This case illustrates just how important the causation requirement is. It will no doubt have appeared to the plaintiff that the 'but for' test was an obstruction to justice in this case. There had been a proven breach of a duty of care in that there was a failure to diagnose and treat, and a man had died as a consequence of the condition for which he should have been treated. But causation is not a merely technical requirement. It is itself linked to questions of fairness and justice, primarily through the idea of responsibility. In this instance, where the arsenic was introduced to the tea with criminal intent, the defendants should not be held liable for consequences that they *could not have prevented.*

Further Illustrations of the 'But for' Test

Hypothetical Acts of the Claimant: *McWilliams v Sir William Arroll Co Ltd* [1962] 1 WLR 295 (HL, Scotland)

The appellant was the widow of a steel erector, who had been working at a height of 70 feet when he fell and was fatally injured. No safety belt had been provided. The appellant claimed damages both for breach of common law duties of care, and for breach of the duty contained in the following statutory provision:

Section 26(2), Factories Act 1937

Where any person is to work at a place from which he is liable to fall a distance of more than ten feet, then…means shall be provided, so far as is reasonably practicable, by fencing or otherwise for ensuring his safety.

The respondents argued successfully that because the deceased would not have worn a belt, even if it had been provided, their breaches of duty had not caused his death.

Viscount Simonds, at 301–2

The deceased was a steel erector of many years' experience and was employed by the first respondents in erecting a steel tower for a crane for the use of the second respondents in their shipbuilding yard at Port Glasgow. Whilst so employed he fell from a height of about 70 feet and was fatally injured. I need not describe in detail the nature of his work. It was dangerous work, as all such work must appear to a layman, but it was not specially dangerous work. It was the work he had been accustomed to do for many years. On the day of the accident he was not wearing a safety belt. It was proved that a safety belt was not on that day available for his use if he had wanted to use it. A belt had been available until two or three days before the accident but then had been removed, together with the but in which it had been stored, to another site. It is a matter of conjecture whether the deceased knew that it had been removed.

In these circumstances, the simple case was made that the respondents were in breach of their duty to provide a safety belt for the use of the deceased; he was not wearing one when he fell to his death; if he had been wearing one, he would not, or at least might not, have so fallen: therefore the respondents are liable.

To this simple case the respondents make answer. Let it be assumed that they were in breach of their duty in not providing a safety belt on the day of his accident and, further, that if he had then been wearing one, the accident would not have occurred. Yet there is a missing link: for it was not proved that the deceased was not wearing a belt because it was not provided; and alternatively, if any question of onus of proof arises, it was proved that if one had been provided, the deceased would not have worn it.

… The evidence showed conclusively that the deceased himself on this and similar jobs had except on two special occasions (about which the evidence was doubted by the Lord Ordinary) persistently abstained from wearing a safety belt and that other steel erectors had adopted a similar attitude. Nor was their attitude irrational or foolhardy. They regarded belts as cumbersome and even dangerous and gave good reason for thinking so. It was, however, urged that on this single occasion the deceased might have changed his mind and that the respondents did not and could not prove that he had not done so.

My Lords, I would agree that, just as a claim against a dead man's estate must always be jealously scrutinised, so also an inference unfavourable to him should not be drawn except upon a strong balance of probability. But there is justice to the living as well as to the dead, and it would be a denial of justice if the court thought itself bound to decide in favour of the deceased because he might, if living, have told a tale so improbable that it could convince nobody. That, my Lords, is this case and in my opinion the courts below were amply justified in receiving the evidence given (not only by the respondents' witnesses) as to the attitude adopted by the deceased and other steelworkers to the wearing of belts and acting upon it.

This case offers another illustration of the potency of 'but for' causation. Viscount Simonds' judgment is dominated by the perceived 'injustice' to the defendants if they should be held to be liable in negligence for damage that their actions, if careful, would probably not have prevented. Causation is, again, related to responsibility. The only 'responsibility' in question is responsibility for *consequences*. If no consequences flow from the breach of duty, then I am not responsible in tort for that breach. If there is an injury, but I could not have prevented that injury through proper conduct, then again I am not responsible, even if my behaviour is culpable. Even a clear breach of a statutory duty will give rise to no liability in tort if it is not shown to have caused the eventual damage.

We should pause here to point out that 'but for' has not always been found a satisfactory test for the first, 'factual' aspect of causation. Recently, Jane Stapleton has suggested that this is because not all factual scenarios are like the ones we have addressed so far. Some cases involve cumulative states of affairs, all of which play a role in bringing about an outcome: they do not resemble the binary 'either/or' world of these cases, and as a consequence, some interventions which should be called 'causes' are not in fact necessary to the result. An example is the case where two fires combine to destroy a building: either would be sufficient on its own, and neither passes the 'but for' test, with absurd results. The suggested solution is that the law contains an alternative to the 'but for' test for factual causation, which applies in those non-binary cases: Jane Stapleton, 'Unnecessary Causes' (2013) 129 LQR 39. We reserve discussion of these more difficult cases, and of the existence of alternatives to 'but for', until Chapter 4.

In any case, the 'but for' test has its own difficulties. Unavoidably, it deals in hypotheticals (also known as counter-factuals): what *would* have happened *if* the defendant had not breached their duty? Here we consider some variations of this hypothetical dimension.

Hypothetical Acts of the Defendant

Matters become more complex if the defendant's negligence has removed an opportunity for the *defendant* which might prevent the loss to the claimant. In assessing whether this negligence has 'caused' the claimant's injury, the court must try to determine what the defendant *would* have done, 'but for' his or her own original negligence. It seems obvious that the defendant will argue that he or she would not have acted so as to save the claimant from harm, even if the opportunity had arisen to do so. In accordance with the general approach to causation, the court must then assess this evidence for persuasiveness. On balance, what does the court think that the defendant would have done?

When we extracted *Bolitho* in Section 1.1 of this chapter, we noted the House of Lords' conclusion that if the defendant's hypothetical failure to save the claimant from harm *would in itself be negligent*, it cannot be relied upon by the defendant. In this instance, whether the hypothetical act or omission would be *negligent* must be answered by application of the *Bolam* test. This is clearly an application of the 'but for' test for causation, adjusted to the circumstances. However, it raises particular issues because the defendant's evidence as to his or her own likely actions will be crucial. That evidence will be scrutinized for persuasiveness, and it will also be measured against the relevant standard of care. But the defendant's own carelessness in such a case will nevertheless give that defendant the opportunity to present a hypothetical course of action and claim it to be the most likely. The claimant's problems are compounded because the *Bolam* test will apply to the hypothetical events. If the claimant cannot show that the defendant would have acted so as to avoid the harm (and here the defendant controls much of the evidence), then she or he will in effect have to show that *no competent doctor* would have acted so as to prevent the damage.

Hypothetical Acts of Third Parties

How does the situation differ where the hypothetical negligent acts are those not of the defendant, but of a third party? Generally (though an alternative scenario will be seen immediately below), this arises where that third party cannot be sued, because it has not in fact been negligent—the path of events has been altered by the defendant's negligence. In *Gouldsmith v Mid-Staffordshire General Hospitals Trust* [2007] EWCA Civ 397, the claimant ought to have been referred to a specialist unit, and failure to do so was a breach of duty. The question was whether a referral would have led to surgery which would have prevented the later need to amputate some of the claimant's fingers. Expert evidence persuaded the judge that a majority of specialist units would have carried out the surgery; but a minority would not have done. The trial judge applied *Bolitho* and held that since not operating would have been acceptable practice in a *Bolam* sense, causation was not established. The Court of Appeal pointed out an error in the approach. Because this case concerned hypothetical acts of third parties, not of the defendant, the judge did not need to ask about the negligence of not operating: it was enough to establish that on the balance of probabilities, in light of expert evidence about the practice of specialist centres generally, the surgery would have taken place. The *Bolam* test, therefore, did nothing to hinder the claim.

Oddly enough, it has proved to be more difficult to resolve a situation where the defendant's negligence results in a delay in medical treatment, which in fact *is* negligent. The 'hypothetical' issue here is whether the treatment received *would* also have been negligent even if referral had been more speedy. This was the situation in *Wright v Cambridge Medical Group Ltd* [2011] EWCA Civ 669, but it is unlikely to arise in just this form in too many other instances. That is because either the claimant, or the defendant, ought to have 'joined' the hospital to the litigation, so that there could be a proper analysis of all the evidence—the judges of the Court of Appeal expressed surprise and concern that this had not been done. In the absence of this obvious move, Lord Neuberger argued that the point in *Bolitho* discussed earlier, namely that a defendant cannot—as a matter of law—rely on his or her own hypothetical negligence to resist a claim, also applied to a *third party's* negligence: there was a presumption that a third party would act with due care, and this *could not* be rebutted by evidence. The other judges—one of whom dissented—did not reason in this way. Lord Neuberger explained the issue as embodying a principle which was not articulated in *Bolitho* in relation to the defendant's own hypothetical negligence, and which has not so far been accepted elsewhere in English law. That is, that the initial negligence removed an opportunity to sue the party who would have been negligent, for the consequences of their, *hypothetical* fault.

The essence of Lord Neuberger's solution was that a claim may be based on the removal of the opportunity for the third party to cause harm through their negligence, and with it, the opportunity of the injured party to claim against them. But it is capable of treating *all* claims as claims for economic loss. This argument was unnecessary in the case of *Wright* and, applied more broadly, it could be very problematic.[27] It is *unnecessary* in *Wright* because members of the Court of Appeal found no basis on which to conclude that the hospital would have been negligent in the event of an earlier referral. This was sufficient on its own to deal with the question of 'factual causation' in this case. It could be *problematic* because, as Lord Neuberger noted, it translates a claim for physical injury into a claim for economic loss. As we will see in relation to remoteness, courts are wary of extending liability to forms of damage which were not within the scope of the duty owed. More than that, as we will see in relation to 'loss of a chance' (in Chapter 4), it would lay the ground for lost chance claims in medical negligence and perhaps much more generally. That route has already been rejected by the House of Lords, though it seems that Lord Neuberger would welcome a reopening of the issue.

The decision in *Wright* raises the question of 'lost chances', explored in Chapter 4. But *Wright* also, evidently, raises the question of what happens when more than one negligent act or omission contributes to harm. That relates directly to our next issue for discussion.

Multiple Causes

Particular problems arise where multiple events contribute to the injury suffered by the claimant, most particularly where there are multiple torts. In this section, we introduce

27 More extensive review of the problems that might follow will be found in N. McBride and S. Steel, 'Suing for the Loss of a Right to Sue: Why *Wright* is Wrong' (2012) 28 PN 27.

only one aspect of such cases. Other aspects of 'multiple cause' are considered in respect of 'intervening acts' (later in the present chapter), in respect of proof of causation and contributing causes (Chapter 4), and in respect of contribution between tortfeasors (Chapter 7). We will indicate where appropriate how these other issues link with the causal question considered here. But the fact that we must return to different aspects of the problems raised by multiple causes indicates how difficult it is to categorize 'causal' questions.

Concurrent and Consecutive Torts

A first (and frequently difficult) question is whether the claimant's damage should be treated as 'divisible' or 'indivisible'. If it is indivisible, the general principle is that each tortfeasor who can be said to have contributed to the damage is held fully responsible for that damage, subject to any deduction for contributory negligence on the part of the claimant (Chapter 5, Defences): *Dingle v Associated Newspapers* [1961] 2 QB 162. A defendant who is held liable for causing injury may pursue contribution proceedings in order to recover a proportion of damages from a concurrent tortfeasor. Torts contributing to the same damage are *concurrent* torts. Where damage is considered to be *divisible*, the claimant in an action against any specific defendant will be awarded damages only for that part of the injury that is caused by the specific defendant's breach. It is not always obvious whether the injury is 'divisible'. Torts contributing distinct injuries are *consecutive* torts.

In the following cases, damage caused by the original tort seemed to have been swallowed up by the effects of the later event. What, if anything, is the continuing responsibility of the original tortfeasor?

Baker v Willoughby [1970] AC 467

The plaintiff suffered injury to his leg in a road traffic accident caused by the tort of the defendant. Shortly before his tort action was heard, he was shot in the same leg during an armed robbery and the leg had to be amputated. This was a case of consecutive torts, although there was no prospect of proceeding against the second tortfeasor. Equally, there was no question of holding the first tortfeasor liable for the loss of the leg—there was no meaningful causal link between the first and the second torts. The first tortfeasor had not put the plaintiff in danger, for example.

The House of Lords held that the first tortfeasor should pay for the damage he had 'caused' notwithstanding the intervention of the second incident. This makes perfect sense because, if the second tortfeasor had been available to be sued, he would have had to pay only for the *additional* pain, suffering, loss of amenity and loss of earnings that he had caused.

Lord Pearson, *Baker v Willoughby*, at 496

I think a solution of the theoretical problem can be found in cases such as this by taking a comprehensive and unitary view of the damage caused by the original accident.... The original accident caused what may be called a "devaluation" of the plaintiff, in the sense that it produced a general reduction of his capacity to do things, to earn money and to enjoy life. For that devaluation the original tortfeasor should be and remain responsible to the full extent, unless before the assessment of the damages something has happened which either diminishes the devaluation (e.g. if there is an unexpected recovery from some of the adverse effects of the accident) or by shortening the expectation of life diminishes the period over which the plaintiff will suffer from the devaluation. If the supervening event is a tort, the second tortfeasor should be responsible for the additional devaluation caused by him.

Jobling v Associated Dairies [1982] AC 794

Here the plaintiff suffered a back injury at work through the tort of the defendant. He later developed a disease to which he had a predisposition. The House of Lords held that the disease had to be taken into account in assessing damages. The award for lost earnings must be reduced to reflect the fact that such earnings would have stopped at a certain date in any event. From the point of view of the law of damages, this too makes perfect sense, because reductions will be made if there is a known *risk* of future incapacity independent of the tort, to avoid compensating for injuries that are not caused by a tort (they would have happened anyway). But there is an ugly clash with the *Baker* decision. Could they *both* be correct? Why should a second tort be different from a supervening *illness*? There really is no good answer to this and the House of Lords in *Jobling* expressed doubts about the solution reached in *Baker v Willoughby*.

The conflict between *Baker v Willoughby*, and *Jobling*, was considered by the House of Lords in the next case.

Gray v Thames Trains [2009] UKHL 33

The claimant had sustained minor physical injuries, but much more serious psychiatric injury, in the Ladbroke Grove rail crash, which was admitted to have been caused by the appellants' negligence. The appellants accepted liability for his physical and mental injuries including the reduction in his earnings to a lower level. The present case arose because, under the influence of his psychiatric condition, the claimant eventually armed himself with a knife and killed a man with whom he had had an altercation. He was convicted of manslaughter. The appellants denied that they were liable for the consequences of this crime (detention), and this aspect of their defence is considered in Chapter 5, 'illegality'. The appellants also denied that they were liable for the continuation of the existing diminished earning claim, into the period after the claimant's conviction for manslaughter. There was now, they argued, a more significant (perhaps 'supervening') reason why the claimant could not earn at all, which was that he had been convicted of a criminal offence. It should be noticed that this is different from the other 'concurrent causes' cases discussed earlier for two reasons, one of which counted decisively against the claimant, the other of which ought to have counted against the defendant, but seemed to impress only Lord Brown.[28] The first is that, evidently, the claimant here had committed a criminal offence which led to his detention. The second is that the supervening event (the criminal offence and detention) would itself not have come about without the fault of the defendants. The second event was, at least in this sense, caused by the defendants' breach of duty.

---

[28] Though the result was unanimous, the two judges who did not directly deal with the concurrent causes issue themselves (Lord Phillips and Lord Scott) expressed agreement with Lords Hoffmann and Rodger. They did not express agreement with Lord Brown, who was more sympathetic both to the claimant, and to the authority of *Baker v Willoughby*.

On this point, Lord Hoffmann simply applied *Jobling v Associated Dairies*, without commenting on the correctness or otherwise of *Baker v Willoughby*. Lord Rodger was more detailed in his remarks, and clearly seemed to doubt the correctness of *Baker*. He concluded though that *Baker* could not apply to the present case in any event, because of the first factor above (the claimant's criminal act).

Lord Rodger, *Gray v Thames Trains* [2009] UKHL 33

75. The immediately obvious objection to the claimant's formulation of his claim for loss of earnings is that it proceeds by ignoring what actually happened—he killed Mr Boultwood and was detained as a result. Yet it is well established that "the court should not speculate when it knows". In other words, the judge should base any award of damages on what has actually happened, rather than on what might have happened, in the period between the tort and the time when the award is to be made. So, even if the court were satisfied that the claimant would have continued to lose earnings after 19 August 2001, due to the PTSD [post-traumatic stress disorder] brought on by the accident, it would be highly artificial to ignore the fact that, by committing manslaughter, the claimant had created a new set of circumstances which actually made it impossible for him to work and to earn after that date. Why should the defendants pay damages on the basis that, but for his PTSD, the claimant would have been able to work after 19 August, when, as the court knows, because of the manslaughter, at all material times after that date he was actually in some form of lawful detention which prevented him from working?

76. The claimant's approach is, to say the least, unreal. If that were the worst that could be said against it, it might stand in the uncomfortable company of *Baker v Willoughby* [1970] AC 467. There the plaintiff was injured in a road accident which left him with a permanently stiff leg. About three years later, just before his action of damages was due to come on for trial, he was shot in the same leg, which had then to be amputated. This House held that the plaintiff's disability could be regarded as having two causes and, where the later injuries became a concurrent cause of the disabilities caused by the injury inflicted by the defendant, they could not reduce the amount of the damages which the defendant had to pay for those disabilities. So the defendants had to pay the same sum by way of damages for the plaintiff's stiff leg, even though it had actually been amputated. In *Jobling v Associated Dairies Ltd* [1982] AC 794, 806G, Lord Edmund-Davies described this approach as "unrealistic" and Lord Keith of Kinkel concluded, at p 814E, that "in its full breadth" the decision was "not acceptable". Happily, there is no need to review the merits of *Baker v Willoughby* in this case since there is a fundamental objection to this version of the claimant's claim for loss of earnings which, in my view, takes it well beyond any possible reach of the reasoning in that case. At this point I return to the desirability of different organs of the same legal system adopting a consistent approach to the same events.

The 'consistency principle' referred to in the final sentence requires that if criminal law treats the claimant as responsible, he cannot then seek compensation for the same act from the defendant. This would imply that he is not responsible after all, and would thus contradict the criminal law. The argument is not beyond criticism and is discussed in Chapter 5.

Lord Brown, ultimately, reached the same decision, also on grounds of consistency. But he seemed to accept the validity of *Baker v Willoughby* and also emphasized the role of the defendant in bringing about the criminal act of the claimant.

Lord Brown, *Gray v Thames Trains* [2009] UKHL 33

95. . . . two reasons are suggested why [the partial loss claim] too must fail. One is the basic principle that subsequent events affecting a loss of earnings claim have to be taken into account when assessing what loss is recoverable—see, for example, *Jobling v Associated Dairies Ltd* [1982] AC 794 . . . This I shall refer to as "the vicissitudes principle" (as it was called in *Jobling*) and, where the supervening event has already occurred, it applies in conjunction with a second principle, that the court will not speculate when it knows. The other reason is that the partial loss claim, no less than the total loss claim, falls foul of the consistency principle. Lord Hoffmann . . . emphasises the first of those reasons, Lord Rodger . . . the second.

96. For my part I question whether the first reason is in itself sufficient to dispose of the partial loss claim. *Baker v Willoughby* [1970] AC 467, where the claimant was injured by two successive tortfeasors . . . , demonstrates if nothing else that on occasion justice will require some modification of the vicissitudes principle. How precisely, in the case of successive torts, this modification is to be rationalised and applied—the subject of extensive discussion in the speeches in *Jobling* and some subsequent consideration by Laws LJ in the Court of Appeal in *Rahman v Arearose Ltd* [2001] QB 351 is not presently in point. Just as *Baker v Willoughby* was held to have no application in *Jobling* where "the victim is overtaken before trial by a wholly unconnected and disabling illness" (Lord Edmund-Davies at p809E), so too here, where the respondent ("the victim" of the appellant's tort) has been "overtaken before trial" by a continuing detention order disabling him from working, *Baker v Willoughby* cannot apply. Obviously neither *Jobling* nor the present case involved successive torts. But whereas the disabling subsequent event in *Jobling* (myelopathy) was "wholly unconnected", that can hardly be said of the manslaughter and the respondent's consequential detention here. But for the appellants' negligence there would have been no manslaughter and no detention. That here is a given.

97. All these cases raise in one form or another the question: on what disabling supervening events is the initial tortfeasor entitled to rely to reduce or extinguish the consequences of his tort? Put another way: from what further misfortunes of the claimant should the tortfeasor be held entitled to benefit?

98. It is perhaps instructive in this context to consider the recent decision of the House in *Corr v IBC Vehicles Ltd* [2008] AC 884.[29] Shift the facts and suppose that Mr Corr had in fact failed rather than succeeded in his suicide attempt but had further injured himself so as to turn a partial loss of earnings into a total one. It inevitably follows from the House's decision that, so far from such a supervening event bringing the claimant's partial earning loss to an end, he would have been found entitled to recover the whole. Why? Why would the continuing loss claim not fall foul of the vicissitudes principle? Essentially, as it seems to me, for two reasons: first, because the original tort remained causative of the suicide attempt (certainly the latter was not "wholly unconnected with the original injuries"), and, secondly, because there was no public policy reason for regarding the suicide attempt as a supervening vicissitude such as to extinguish the tortfeasor's liability for the continuing loss. The first of those reasons is common to this case too (which is why it seems to me that the vicissitudes principle is not sufficient in itself to defeat A's continuing loss claim). But what of the second reason, recognising of course that manslaughter, unlike suicide, *is* a criminal offence?

[29] In this case, the deceased committed suicide under the influence of depression, suffered in reaction to a workplace incident caused by the employer's breach of duty. The employer was liable for the claimant's death.

Ultimately, Lord Brown thought that this second reason—effectively, the consistency principle—was enough to distinguish this case from both *Baker and Corr v IBC*.

We will leave 'cause in fact' for now, but return in Chapter 4. There we will particularly consider cases where *proof* of causation has been problematic; the possibility that there are further routes to causation in addition to being a 'but for' cause; and the difficult issue of 'lost chances'.

6. 'CAUSE-IN-LAW'/REMOTENESS/SCOPE OF LIABILITY

6.1 INTRODUCTION: THREE VERSIONS OF THE REMOTENESS QUESTION

At the start of Section 5, we pointed out that there have been different interpretations of the 'remoteness' question, some more compatible than others with the idea that this is a question about 'causation'.

Imagine that the remoteness question is stated in the following three very different ways. This exercise will help us to understand diverging currents in the case law.

1. Is the full extent of the damage fairly attributable to the defendant's breach of duty or other tortious intervention?

This was the question adopted by the Privy Council in *The Wagon Mound (No 1)*, still the leading authority on remoteness of damage though now beginning to show its age, which is extracted in Section 6.2. Fairness of attribution was interpreted in terms of 'foreseeability'. In cases of negligence, this was meant to align remoteness with duty of care and breach. This has been the authoritative test since 1961, and as we will see later it was supposed to sweep away the problems associated with more 'causal' language. But it has failed to resolve all of the difficulties, and 'causal' language persists in certain areas. At the end of this section, we will address the possibility that duty and remoteness questions are now better aligned through analysis of the 'scope of the duty', since foreseeability is not a sufficient criterion upon which to establish a duty of care.

2. Is the damage a *direct* consequence of the defendant's breach, or has the chain of causation been broken?

This was the approach endorsed by the Court of Appeal in *Re Polemis and Furness Withy & Co* [1921] 3 KB 560. It appears to pose a factual question, but since the 'chain of causation' is not a real entity, it was never anything more than a metaphor. It was disapproved by the Privy Council in *The Wagon Mound*, yet vestiges of this approach tend to survive. In particular, some issues are framed in terms of 'new cause' or '*nova causa interveniens*' (or, in the case of human interventions, '*novus actus interveniens*'), even if analysis in terms of 'directness' is no longer expected to provide the answers.

3. Even if the defendant's breach is a condition of the damage suffered, so that it satisfies the 'but for' test, is it a 'cause' of that damage?

This formulation opens up a range of possibilities, based on common sense, ordinary language, and intuition. It is more like question 2 than question 1. Unlike *The Wagon Mound* variant of 1, it does not address questions of what the *defendant* might have been able to foresee, in order to establish what is 'fair'. Instead, it looks with hindsight at what has occurred in order to identify whether a particular condition can be treated as having 'caused' the damage. However, it is broader than 2, because 'a break in the chain of causation' is not the only reason why a condition may not be considered a cause; and it does not seek a solution in logical or (pseudo-)scientific analysis of events. This can be seen within the broad 'common sense causal approach' of Hart and Honoré.

The above possibilities can be used to explain some continuing inconsistencies in the case law, to which we now turn.

6.2 FORESEEABILITY OF THE TYPE OF HARM: *THE WAGON MOUND (NO 1)*

The Issue: *Re Polemis* and 'Direct Consequences'

In *The Wagon Mound (No 1)*, the Privy Council considered the correctness of a previous Court of Appeal decision, *Re Polemis and Furness Withy & Co* [1921] 3 KB 560 (generally known as *Re Polemis*). *Re Polemis* held that a defendant who is shown to have been at fault is liable for all *direct* consequences of that fault.

Re Polemis and Furness Withy & Co [1921] 3 KB 560

Through the negligence of stevedores employed by the defendant charterers, a board fell into the hold of a ship where tins of benzene and/or petrol were being shifted. The fall of the plank was followed by a rush of flames and the total destruction of the ship. On a claim against the charterers for the full value of the ship, arbitrators found that the fire which destroyed the ship was caused by a spark igniting vapour in the hold; that the spark was caused by the fall of the plank into the hold; and that the causing of the spark (and therefore the fire) could not reasonably have been anticipated from the falling of the board, though some mechanical damage to the ship might reasonably have been anticipated. The Court of Appeal held that the charterers were liable for all the direct consequences of the negligence of their servants, even though those consequences could not reasonably have been anticipated:

Warrington LJ, at 574

The presence or absence of reasonable anticipation of damage determines the legal quality of the act as negligent or innocent. If it be thus determined to be negligent, then the question whether particular damages are recoverable depends only on the answer to the question whether they are the direct consequence of the act.

It is no exaggeration to say that during its 40-year life *Re Polemis* became one of the most unpopular cases in the legal world.

Martin Davies, 'The Road From Morocco: Polemis Through Donoghue to No-Fault' (1982) 45 MLR 534–55, at 534

Davies argues that *Polemis* was, initially, a perfectly acceptable decision, popular in the shipping world and not at the time criticized for creating over-expansive liability to defendants.

Although he is critical of the later *Wagon Mound* decision, Davies does not seek to defend the general approach in *Re Polemis* as providing a better interpretation of causal questions. Rather, he argues that developments in the tort of negligence had, by the time of his article in 1982, created problems for both remoteness tests, and he simply points out that *Polemis* itself should be judged in terms of its effect at the time of the decision. In particular, having established that the successful claim was one in tort and not in contract,[30] Davies adds that the relevant *duty* which was breached by the negligence of the stevedores was necessarily a specific one, since the case predated the recognition of a generalized duty of care in *Donoghue v Stevenson*. The specific duty in question was owed by the charterer of the ship, hired (chartered) from the ship owner.

> Why is it so important to establish the source of the defendants' duty of care in *Re Polemis*? It is important because that duty was, like all pre-Donoghue duties of care, a particularised relational one. It was owed by the defendants to the plaintiffs alone, and it arose from the nature of the special relationship between the parties. To forget this is to misunderstand why the *Re Polemis* rule took the form it did. The true original intention behind the *Re Polemis* remoteness rule can only be recognised by seeing it in the context of a pre-1932 duty of care. A wide remoteness rule was unexceptionable when duty was narrowly conceived. Extensive liability of defendants is not a problem when those defendants can only be liable to a limited class of plaintiffs, or even a single plaintiff only....

We should notice that Davies here mentions only one reason why the *Polemis* rule was unpopular. He does not mention that Viscount Simonds also took exception to the very idea that such cases should be dealt with in terms of causation. In the extract below, Viscount Simonds refers to the 'never-ending and insoluble problems of causation'. Elsewhere in his judgment, he was more scathing, suggesting that courts 'were at times in grave danger of being led astray by scholastic theories of causation and their ugly and barely intelligible jargon' (at 419). Martin Davies suggests that the *Polemis* rule was 'self-applying', but in fact it threw up considerable difficulty. Nonetheless, the Privy Council was mistaken if it thought that the move to foreseeability would result in an easily applicable general test.

Overseas Tankship (UK) Ltd v Morts Dock and Engineering Co Ltd (The Wagon Mound (No 1)) [1961] AC 388

The facts of this case are set out in Section 1.3 of this chapter.

Viscount Simonds (delivering the judgment of the Board), at 422–6

> Enough has been said to show that the authority of *Polemis* has been severely shaken though lip-service has from time to time been paid to it. In their Lordships' opinion it should no longer be regarded as good law. It is not probable that many cases will for that reason have a different result, though it is hoped that the law will be thereby simplified, and that in some cases, at least, palpable injustice will be avoided. For it does not seem consonant with current ideas of justice or morality that for an act of negligence, however slight or venial, which results in some trivial foreseeable damage the actor should be liable for all consequences however unforeseeable and however grave, so long as they can be said to be

[30] Drawing on analysis by A. D. McNair, 'This Polemis Business' (1931) 4 CLJ 125.

"direct." It is a principle of civil liability, subject only to qualifications which have no present relevance, that a man must be considered to be responsible for the probable consequences of his act. To demand more of him is too harsh a rule, to demand less is to ignore that civilised order requires the observance of a minimum standard of behaviour.

This concept applied to the slowly developing law of negligence has led to a great variety of expressions which can, as it appears to their Lordships, be harmonised with little difficulty with the single exception of the so-called rule in *Polemis*. For, if it is asked why a man should be responsible for the natural or necessary or probable consequences of his act (or any other similar description of them) the answer is that it is not because they are natural or necessary or probable, but because, since they have this quality, it is judged by the standard of the reasonable man that he ought to have foreseen them. Thus it is that over and over again it has happened that in different judgments in the same case, and sometimes in a single judgment, liability for a consequence has been imposed on the ground that it was reasonably foreseeable or, alternatively, on the ground that it was natural or necessary or probable. The two grounds have been treated as coterminous, and so they largely are. But, where they are not, the question arises to which the wrong answer was given in *Polemis*. For, if some limitation must be imposed upon the consequences for which the negligent actor is to be held responsible—and all are agreed that some limitation there must be—why should that test (reasonable foreseeability) be rejected which, since he is judged by what the reasonable man ought to foresee, corresponds with the common conscience of mankind, and a test (the 'direct' consequence) be substituted which leads to no-where but the never-ending and insoluble problems of causation. "The lawyer," said Sir Frederick Pollock, "cannot afford to adventure himself with philosophers in the logical and metaphysical controversies that beset the idea of cause." Yet this is just what he has most unfortunately done and must continue to do if the rule in *Polemis* is to prevail. A conspicuous example occurs when the actor seeks to escape liability on the ground that the "chain of causation" is broken by a "nova causa" or "novus actus interveniens." ...

At an early stage in this judgment their Lordships intimated that they would deal with the proposition which can best be stated by reference to the well-known dictum of Lord Summer: "This however goes to culpability not to compensation." It is with the greatest respect to that very learned judge and to those who have echoed his words, that their Lordships find themselves bound to state their view that this proposition is fundamentally false.

Their Lordships conclude this part of the case with some general observations. They have been concerned primarily to displace the proposition that unforeseeability is irrelevant if damage is "direct." In doing so they have inevitably insisted that the essential factor in determining liability is whether the damage is of such a kind as the reasonable man should have foreseen. This accords with the general view thus stated by Lord Atkin in *Donoghue v. Stevenson*: 'The liability for negligence, whether you style it such or treat it as in other systems as a species of 'culpa', is no doubt based upon a general public sentiment of moral wrongdoing for which the offender must pay.' It is a departure from this sovereign principle if liability is made to depend solely on the damage being the "direct" or "natural" consequence of the precedent act. Who knows or can be assumed to know all the processes of nature? But if it would be wrong that a man should be held liable for damage unpredictable by a reasonable man because it was "direct" or "natural," equally it would be wrong that he should escape liability, however "indirect" the damage, if he foresaw or could reasonably foresee the intervening events which led to its being done: cf. *Woods v. Duncan*. Thus foreseeability becomes the effective test. In reasserting this principle their Lordships conceive that they do not depart from, but follow and develop, the law of negligence as laid down by Baron Alderson in *Blyth v. Birmingham Waterworks Co.* [(1856)11 Ex. 781]

Commentary

The Privy Council dismissed as an 'error' Lord Sumner's dictum in *Weld-Blundell v Stephens* [1920] AC 956, 999, that foreseeability 'goes to culpability, not to compensation'. On the face of it, *The Wagon Mound (No 1)* determines that there should no longer be different tests for the breach of duty, and the extent of the damage which is recoverable. This decision is not based on analysis of causation. In fact, the judgment shows a strong distaste for causal language, and in principle it ought to leave 'cause in fact' as the only remaining question of causation in tort law. This was precisely the interpretation of *The Wagon Mound* adopted by Glanville Williams, a strong supporter of a foreseeability-based approach, who saw *The Wagon Mound* as decisive.

G. Williams, 'The Risk Principle' [1961] 77 LQR 179–212, at 179

… If *The Wagon Mound* is accepted by the English courts, as surely it must be … [w]e shall be spared most of what the Board called "the never-ending and insoluble problems of causation," together with the subtleties of *novus actus interveniens*, and shall be left with a comparatively simple rule the application of which involves merely an adjudication of fact. In future, broadly speaking, there will not be two questions in the tort of negligence, a question of initial responsibility and one of "proximity," [by which Williams means 'proximate cause' or remoteness] but only one question—was the defendant negligent as regards this damage? He will not be liable to the "unforeseeable plaintiff," nor even to the foreseeable plaintiff in respect of unforeseeable damage. This amounts to a complete acceptance of what is conveniently called the risk principle, namely, that negligence is to be considered not in the abstract but only in relation to a particular risk.

The ambition was to replace two tests (duty and remoteness) with one (foreseeability). But it swiftly became clear that this was over-ambitious in both respects.

Although the change in the law effected by *The Wagon Mound* had wide academic support, there were large ambiguities in the decision itself. It is clear that Viscount Simonds expected his approach to appeal to the sense of fairness. It is argued to be *unfair* to make a defendant liable for very extensive damage which was unforeseeable, simply because some trivial damage *was* foreseeable. But what exactly did *The Wagon Mound* decide would be the relevant rule? Attention to the detail of the judgment shows that the Privy Council distinguished between foreseeable and unforeseeable *types* of damage: 'the essential factor in determining liability is whether the damage is of such a kind as the reasonable man should have foreseen' (final paragraph extracted above). If this is taken literally, then if the damage is unforeseeable in extent, but foreseeable in *type*, then all of the damage will in fact be recoverable. This was the understanding of the case which immediately followed (see for example R. W. M. Dias, 'Trouble on Oiled Waters' [1967] CLJ 62, 72), and indeed it is the way that the rule in *The Wagon Mound* has generally been interpreted (see the discussions of *Smith v Leech Brain* and *Hughes v Lord Advocate*, as well as more recent case law, in Section 6.3). But importantly, this means that the rule as expressed is not fully consistent with the idea that only foreseeable harm is fairly recoverable. Some harm which was not foreseeable will be recoverable, if it is of the appropriate type. This in turn is not consistent with the rhetoric of 'fairness' at the start of the extract.

There is a further ambiguity. The Privy Council held that damage by fouling was foreseeable in this case, but that damage by fire was not. Is this consistent with the distinction mentioned earlier in terms of different *kinds* of damage, or does it suggest a different distinction, in terms of damage done by a different *process*? The interpretation of *The Wagon Mound* in later cases such as *Hughes v Lord Advocate* has approached foreseeability in terms of type of damage and *not* in terms of the process by which it comes about.

How to Judge Foreseeability

According to the Privy Council, the view taken by the courts below that the damage was direct and therefore recoverable, depended upon hindsight. This, the court argued, was unfair to the defendant, since '[a]fter the event even a fool is wise. But it is not the hindsight of a fool; it is only the foresight of a reasonable man which alone can determine responsibility'. Instead, the Privy Council adopted a test of reasonable foresight, judged from the point of view of a reasonable person *in the position of the defendant at the time of the breach.*

This form of foreseeability is referred to by Hart and Honoré as 'foreseeability in a practical sense'. We will need this idea again in addressing the case law that follows. According to Hart and Honoré, normal *causal* statements are not like this. They are generally retrospective and are to do with attribution rather than fault. The adoption of foreseeability in a 'practical' sense is a sign that remoteness is aligned with duty and breach, rather than being guided by 'causal' ideas.

6.3 LINGERING PROBLEMS

Pre-existing Vulnerability: *Smith v Leech Brain and Co Ltd*
[1962] 2 QB 405

The plaintiff was the widow of a steel galvanizer employed by the defendants. Part of his job involved lowering articles by means of an overhead crane into molten metal. He was afforded inadequate protection against splashing by molten metal and suffered a burn on his lower lip. The burn promoted cancer, from which he died three years later. In this first instance decision, Lord Parker CJ considered whether he was permitted by the Privy Council decision in *The Wagon Mound* to depart from the directness rule in *Re Polemis*. *Re Polemis* was a Court of Appeal decision and in principle binding upon the lower court; the Privy Council decision had only persuasive authority.

He held that *The Wagon Mound* made no difference to a case such as this. The initial injury (the burn) was of a readily foreseeable type, and the subsequent cancer was treated as merely extending the amount of harm suffered.

Lord Parker CJ, at 413–15

... I find that the burn was the promoting agency of cancer in tissues which already had a pre-malignant condition. In those circumstances, it is clear that the plaintiff's husband, but for the burn, would not necessarily ever have developed cancer. On the other hand, having regard to the number of matters which can be promoting agencies, there was a strong likelihood that at some stage in his life he would develop cancer. But that the burn did contribute to, or cause in part, at any rate, the cancer and the death, I have no doubt.

The third question is damages. Here I am confronted with the recent decision of the Privy Council in *Overseas Tankship (U.K.) Limited v. Morts Dock and Engineering Co. Ltd. (The Wagon Mound)*. But for that case, it seems to me perfectly clear that, assuming negligence proved, and assuming that the burn caused in whole or in part the cancer and the death, the plaintiff would be entitled to recover....

For my part, I am quite satisfied that the Judicial Committee in the *Wagon Mound* case did not have what I may call, loosely, the thin skull cases in mind. It has always been the law of this country that a tortfeasor takes his victim as he finds him. It is unnecessary to do more than refer to the short passage in the decision of Kennedy J. in *Dulieu v. White & Sons* [1901] 2 KB 669], where he said [679]: "If a man is negligently run over or otherwise negligently injured in his body, it is no answer to the sufferer's claim for damages that he would have suffered less injury, or no injury at all, if the had not had an unusually thin skull or an unusually weak heart." ...

The Judicial Committee were, I think, disagreeing with the decision in the *Polemis* case that a man is no longer liable for the type of damage which he could not reasonably anticipate. The Judicial Committee were not, I think, saying that a man is only liable for the extent of damage which he could anticipate, always assuming the type of injury could have been anticipated. I think that view is really supported by the way in which cases of this sort have been dealt with in Scotland. Scotland has never, so far as I know, adopted the principle laid down in *Polemis*, and yet I am quite satisfied that they have throughout proceeded on the basis that the tortfeasor takes the victim as he finds him.

In those circumstances, it seems to me that this is plainly a case which comes within the old principle. The test is not whether these employers could reasonably have foreseen that a burn would cause cancer and that he would die. The question is whether these employers could reasonably foresee the type of injury he suffered, namely, the burn. What, in the particular case, is the amount of damage which he suffers as a result of that burn, depends upon the characteristics and constitution of the victim.

Lord Parker argued that *The Wagon Mound* decision did not alter the existing rule that the defendant must 'take his victim as he finds him'. He sought to make this rule compatible with *The Wagon Mound* by suggesting that the 'thin skull' or 'egg-shell skull' rule only operates so as to allow the defendant to be liable for *more extensive damage* than he might have foreseen. It does not allow defendants to be liable if, without the vulnerability, no damage (or no damage of the same type) would be foreseeable at all. Of course, acceptance of his approach depends on accepting that *The Wagon Mound* does not require the *extent* of the damage to be foreseeable.

Hart and Honoré argue that this attempt to reconcile the 'egg-shell skull' cases with *The Wagon Mound* is 'mere window dressing': 'the truth is that this aspect of common sense causal discourse has survived the *Wagon Mound*' (*Causation in the Law*, 2nd edn, 274). However, the decision in *Smith v Leech Brain* itself can be reconciled with the *Wagon Mound* if we accept Lord Parker's approach of treating the eventual damage suffered as the same in type as the damage that was foreseeable. Lord Parker argued that once the burn was foreseeable, the cancer only raised the issue of how extensive *damages* should be. Is cancer the same 'type' of damage as a burn? If cancer is the same type of damage as a burn, then it seems that personal physical injury is very generously treated for the purposes of this test, and it appears that the *Wagon Mound* does not do what it professed to do. On the other hand, if it is not the same type of damage, then the 'egg-shell skull' rule is a decisive departure from *The Wagon Mound*.

Glanville Williams, from whose important article we extracted earlier, also supported the retention of the egg-shell skull rule both for physical injury and for mental harm. He supported the rule on grounds of policy, justice, and fairness, and did not seek to make it compatible with the 'risk principle'. But this may be because he thought that *The Wagon Mound* would limit recovery to those damages that were foreseeable in *extent*.

Williams, 'The Risk Principle' [1961] 77 LQR 179, 196

It seems to me that, balancing one consideration with another, and expressing the opinion with considerable doubt, the thin skull rule is on the whole a justifiable exception to the risk principle. In a situation where our sympathy for the plaintiff conflicts with our sense of justice towards the defendant, the risk principle normally requires us to concentrate our attention upon justice to the defendant, acquitting him of consequences in respect of which he was not at fault. However, where the plaintiff has suffered bodily injury, it is difficult to maintain the cold logical analysis of the situation. Human bodies are too fragile, and life too precarious, to permit a defendant nicely to calculate how much injury he may inflict without causing more serious injury.

It is clear from subsequent cases that the egg-shell skull rule has been retained. Examples include *Robinson v Post Office* [1974] 1 WLR 1176 (allergic reaction leading to very extensive injuries, further discussed under 'third party interventions', later in this chapter) and *Malcolm v Broadhurst* [1970] 3 All ER 508 (exacerbation of a long-standing nervous condition by a car accident: 'there is no difference in principle between an egg-shell skull and an egg-shell personality', per Geoffrey Lane J), applied in *Page v Smith* (considered in Chapter 6). *Malcolm v Broadhurst* applied the pre-*Wagon Mound* authority of *Love v Port of London Authority* [1959] 2 Lloyd's Rep 541, illustrating that the Privy Council case had less immediate impact than might have been expected.

Lack of Funds: The Demise of *The Leisbosch Dredger*

In *The Leisbosch Dredger* [1933] AC 449, the plaintiffs' ship sank as the result of the defendant's negligence. The dredger was engaged in work under contract and a contractual penalty would be paid if the work was not completed on time. Because the plaintiffs were short of funds, they were unable to buy another dredger and had to hire one at great expense in order to avoid the contractual penalty. They claimed for the whole of their financial loss, but the House of Lords held that nothing attributable to the plaintiffs' own lack of funds or 'impecuniosity' could be recovered. This decision was approved by the Privy Council in *The Wagon Mound (No 1)*, presumably because it did not allow for 'all direct consequences' to be recovered. It did, however, employ causal language in expressing the view that the cost of the hire of a dredger was not an 'immediate physical consequence' of the defendant's negligence. In the words of Donaldson LJ in *Dodd Properties v Canterbury City Council* [1980] 1 WLR 433, 458, Lord Wright 'took the view that, in so far as the plaintiffs had in fact suffered more than the loss assessed on a market basis, the excess flowed directly from their lack of means and not from the tortious act'. This is a judgment as to cause.

The Leisbosch Dredger was taken to establish that the 'egg-shell skull rule' does not apply to financial vulnerability. The case was distinguished in a number of cases with strong disapproval (for example *Alcoa Minerals v Broderick* [2002] 1 AC 371, a decision of the Privy

Council; *Dodd Properties v Canterbury City Council* [1980] 1 WLR 433). *The Leisbosch Dredger* was finally departed from by the House of Lords in the case of *Lagden v O'Connor* [2004] 1 AC 1067. This amounts to an overruling of the older decision.

It is a peculiarity of the egg-shell skull rule that it has not only been accepted, but also now extended to financial vulnerability, without a clear determination of whether it is an application of the foreseeability principle, or an exception to it.

Causal Sequence and Type of Damage: *Hughes v Lord Advocate* [1963] AC 837

A manhole in a city street was left open and unguarded. It was covered with a tent and surrounded by warning paraffin lamps. An 8-year-old boy entered the tent and somehow knocked one of the lamps into the hole (or perhaps lowered it in). An explosion occurred causing him to fall in to the hole and be severely burned. On appeal to the House of Lords, it was held that the workmen breached a duty of care owed to the boy, and that the damage was reasonably foreseeable.

Lord Reid, at 845

It was argued that the appellant cannot recover because the damage which he suffered was of a kind which was not foreseeable. That was not the ground of judgment of the First Division or of the Lord Ordinary and the facts proved do not, in my judgment, support that argument. The appellant's injuries were mainly caused by burns, and it cannot be said that injuries from burns were unforeseeable. As a warning to traffic the workmen had set lighted red lamps round the tent which covered the manhole, and if boys did enter the dark tent it was very likely that they would take one of these lamps with them. If the lamp fell and broke it was not at all unlikely that the boy would be burned and the burns might well be serious. No doubt it was not to be expected that the injuries would be as serious as those which the appellant in fact sustained. But a defender is liable, although the damage may be a good deal greater in extent than was foreseeable. He can only escape liability if the damage can be regarded as differing in kind from what was foreseeable.

So we have (first) a duty owed by the workmen, (secondly) the fact that if they had done as they ought to have done there would have been no accident, and (thirdly) the fact that the injuries suffered by the appellant, though perhaps different in degree, did not differ in kind from injuries which might have resulted from an accident of a foreseeable nature. The ground on which this case has been decided against the appellant is that the accident was of an unforeseeable type. Of course, the pursuer has to prove that the defender's fault caused the accident, and there could be a case where the intrusion of a new and unexpected factor could be regarded as the cause of the accident rather than the fault of the defender. But that is not this case. The cause of this accident was a known source of danger, the lamp, but it behaved in an unpredictable way.

The decision to allow recovery in this case, in which a known source of danger behaves in an unforeseeable way and thereby creates damage which is more extensive than might have been expected, decisively qualifies the claim that *The Wagon Mound* limits liability to foreseeable damage. In lower courts, subsequent case law has been inconsistent. For example, in *Doughty v Turner* [1964] 1 QB 518, the Court of Appeal drew a distinction between burning caused by a splash of hot liquid (foreseeable) and burning caused by an explosion (unforeseeable). In *Tremain v Pike* [1969] 1 WLR 1556, a first instance decision, it was suggested that illness contracted through contact with rat's urine (which was thought to be unforeseeable) was different in type from illness suffered through a rat bite (which was foreseeable). However, the principal reason for the decision in *Tremain* was that because the risk of infection from rat's urine was not foreseeable, there was no reason why the employer in that case should have taken the additional precautions necessary to protect against infection by rat's urine. Thus there was no breach of duty and the judge's remarks about remoteness were *obiter dicta*. Crucially, the steps necessary to protect against the *unforeseeable* infection would have been different from those needed to protect against the known danger associated with rat bites. In the other cases we have examined here (including *Page v Smith*, *Hughes v Lord Advocate*, and *The Wagon Mound* itself), there is only one set of steps required to remove the risk, however broadly or narrowly it is defined.

The authority of *Hughes v Lord Advocate* has been reinforced through the following case.

Jolley v Sutton LBC [2000] 1 WLR 1082

A boat was left abandoned for about two years on land owned by the defendants. The council made plans to remove the boat, but these plans were not implemented. Two boys, the plaintiff and a friend, aged 13 and 14, used a car jack to prop up the boat and to repair it. The boat fell off the prop and crushed the plaintiff, who suffered serious spinal injuries leading to paraplegia. He brought an action against the council for negligence and breach of duty under the Occupiers Liability Act 1957, section 2(2)(3).[31] At first instance, judgment was given for the plaintiff subject to a reduction in damages of 25 per cent for contributory negligence (Chapter 5). The judge found that the presence of the boat would foreseeably attract children and that the type of accident and injury was reasonably foreseeable. The House of Lords agreed.

The judgment of Lord Steyn was chiefly concerned with examination of the facts of the case. He said that 'very little needs to be said about the law'. However, he defended the compatibility of *Hughes v Lord Advocate* (above) with *The Wagon Mound (No 1)* at 1090:

… The speech of Lord Reid in *Hughes v. Lord Advocate* [1963] A.C. 837 is … not in conflict with *The Wagon Mound No. 1*. The scope of the two modifiers—the precise manner in which the injury came about and its extent—is not definitively answered by either *The Wagon Mound No. 1* or *Hughes v. Lord Advocate*. It requires determination in the context of an intense focus on the circumstances of each case. …

The judgment of Lord Hoffmann is far more concerned with the question of which approach to take as a matter of law:

It is … agreed that the plaintiff must show that the injury which he suffered fell within the scope of the council's duty and that in cases of physical injury, the scope of the duty is determined by whether or not the injury fell within a description which could be said to have been reasonably foreseeable. *Donoghue v. Stevenson* [1932] A.C. 562 of course established the general principle that reasonable foreseeability of physical injury to another generates a duty of care. The further proposition that reasonable foreseeability also governs the question of whether the injury comes within the scope of that duty had to wait until *Overseas Tankship (U.K.) Ltd. v. Morts Dock and Engineering Co. Ltd. (The Wagon Mound)* [1961] A.C. 388 ("*The Wagon Mound No. 1*") for authoritative recognition. Until then, there was a view that the determination of liability involved a two-stage process. The existence of a duty depended upon whether injury of some kind was foreseeable. Once such a duty had been established, the defendant was liable for any injury which had been "directly caused" by an act in breach of that duty, whether such injury was reasonably foreseeable or not. But the present law is that unless the injury is of a description which was reasonably foreseeable, it is (according to taste) "outside the scope of the duty" or "too remote."

It is also agreed that what must have been foreseen is not the precise injury which occurred but injury of a given description. The foreseeability is not as to the particulars but the genus. And the description is formulated by reference to the nature of the risk which ought to have been foreseen. . . .

The short point in the present appeal is therefore whether the judge [1998] 1 Lloyd's Rep. 433, 439 was right in saying in general terms that the risk was that children would "meddle with the boat at the risk of some physical injury" or whether the Court of Appeal were right in saying that the only foreseeable risk was of "children who were drawn to the boat climbing upon it and being injured by the rotten planking giving way beneath them:" *per* Roch L.J. [1998] 1 W.L.R. 1546, 1555. Was the wider risk, which would include within its description the accident which actually happened, reasonably foreseeable?

. . . The council admit that they should have removed the boat. True, they make this concession solely on the ground that there was a risk that children would suffer minor injuries if the rotten planking gave way beneath them. But the concession shows that if there were a wider risk, the council would have had to incur no additional expense to eliminate it. They would only have had to do what they admit they should have done anyway. On the principle as stated by Lord Reid, the wider risk would also fall within the scope of the council's duty unless it was different in kind from that which should have been foreseen (like the fire and pollution risks in *The Wagon Mound No. 1*) and either wholly unforeseeable (as the fire risk was assumed to be in *The Wagon Mound No. 1*) or so remote that it could be "brushed aside as far-fetched:" see Lord Reid in *The Wagon Mound No. 2* [1969] 2 A.C. 617.

I agree with my noble and learned friend, Lord Steyn, and the judge that one cannot so describe the risk that children coming upon an abandoned boat and trailer would suffer injury in some way other than by falling through the planks. . . .

. . . In the present case, the rotten condition of the boat had a significance beyond the particular danger it created. It proclaimed the boat and its trailer as abandoned, res nullius, there for the taking, to make of them whatever use the rich fantasy life of children might suggest.

In the Court of Appeal, Lord Woolf M.R. observed, at p. 1553, that there seemed to be no case of which counsel were aware "where want of care on the part of a defendant was established but a plaintiff, who was a child, had failed to succeed because the circumstances of the accident were not foreseeable." I would suggest that this is for a combination of three reasons: first, because a finding or admission of want of care on the part of the defendant establishes that it would have cost the defendant no more trouble to avoid the injury which happened than he should in any case have taken; secondly, because in such circumstances the defendants will be liable for the materialisation of even relatively small risks of a different kind, and thirdly, because it has been repeatedly said in cases about children that their ingenuity in finding unexpected ways of doing mischief to themselves and others should never be underestimated. For these reasons, I think that the judge's broad description of the risk as being that children would "meddle with the boat at the risk of some physical injury" was the correct one to adopt on the facts of this case. The actual injury fell within that description and I would therefore allow the appeal.

We should notice two important features of the discussion by Lord Hoffmann above. First, at the beginning of the extract, Lord Hoffmann adopts terminology that was not present in *The Wagon Mound* but which he treats as compatible with that decision: was the damage within the scope of the duty owed by the defendants? Alternatively, was it 'within the risk' against which the defendant should protect the claimant? The language of 'within the risk' is familiar from Williams' article on 'The Risk Principle' (Section 6.2). But the language of 'scope of duty' is a relatively new development. Arguably, this development would allow us to interpret *The Wagon Mound*'s emphasis on foreseeability as just one aspect of a broader question, namely whether the damage suffered was within the scope of the duty. And that would reflect the fact that the test for a duty of care has become increasingly nuanced. This as we will see may pave the way for *The Wagon Mound* to be updated.

Second, and much less helpfully, Lord Hoffmann then merged the question of remoteness with the question of breach. Since the defendants should in any event have removed the boat in order to avoid the admittedly foreseeable danger of injury, he argues that there is no reason to suggest that the defendants were free to leave the boat in place because there was only a small possibility that the sort of events in question might happen. The truth is that such an approach, if applied without the 'kind of damage' limitation, would effectively do away with any separate question of remoteness based on foreseeability or scope of duty, and would simply ask whether avoidance of the damage would have required any other precautions than those already required by the need to avoid the *foreseeable* injury. For example, it would lead to reversal of the decision in *The Wagon Mound (No 1)* itself, on the basis that avoidance of the serious risk of damage by fire (unforeseeable) required no further precautions than avoidance of the trivial risk associated with fouling (foreseeable). The oil should not have been released. Since there is no obvious intention to depart from *The Wagon Mound* in this case, the idea that the avoidance of the wider risk would cost no greater precautions than avoidance of the lesser and more foreseeable risk should only operate *together with* the requirement that the damage suffered should be of a 'foreseeable type'. In this case the foreseeable risk posed by the rotten boat was held to be that children 'would meddle with the boat at the risk of some physical injury'. The risk is very broadly defined. Lord Hoffmann in his closing remarks invites the conclusion that this is a special approach adapted to known sources of hazard to children, since in such a case all manner of accidents are to be expected.

Intervening Acts: What is a *Novus Actus Interveniens*?

Cases involving a human act which intervenes between the defendant's breach of duty, and the claimant's loss, have traditionally been addressed through the expression '*novus actus interveniens*' ('new intervening act'). There are instances where no damage would have occurred at all but for the intervening act (for example *Home Office v Dorset Yacht, Reeves v Commr of Police*); but there are also certain other cases where the intervention of a third party (or of the claimant) *adds to* the damage suffered, where there was some initial harm (*Knightley v Johns; Robinson v Post Office; McKew v Holland & Hannen & Cubbitts; Wright v Cambridge Medical Group*). In some cases in both categories, the defendant is released from liability to the extent that the damage flows from the intervening act. In other cases, the defendant is held liable for the full extent of the damage.

Traditionally, the question in such cases has been whether the intervening act is to be held to amount to a 'new cause', 'breaking the chain of causation'. Clearly, this is a 'causal' idea, and it is the origin of the expressions *novus actus interveniens*, and *nova causa interveniens*. These expressions were singled out in *The Wagon Mound* as providing a 'conspicuous example' of the problems caused by the *Polemis* approach, leading (in words borrowed from Pollock) to the 'logical and metaphysical controversies that beset the idea of cause'. But here *The Wagon Mound* has singularly failed to replace the causal approach. In these cases, the language of *novus actus* continues to be employed more often than the language of foreseeability. Can these cases be decided *without* recourse to the 'logical and metaphysical controversies' associated with causation?

On several occasions, an attempt has been made to resolve cases in this area by reference to foreseeability. However, foreseeability in these cases was never used in the true *Wagon Mound* sense, where it was asked whether *the chain of events* was foreseeable. Could the intervention of the third party have been foreseen? Also, 'foreseeability' no longer, in such cases, referred to the question of whether the *defendant* could have foreseen the intervention of the third party. This was the 'practical' sense of foreseeability that we mentioned above in our commentary on *The Wagon Mound*. Instead, foreseeability was judged with hindsight. But even with this change, the 'foreseeability' approach has not proved successful and it is suggested below that it has now been abandoned.

What other possibilities are there? It is possible that the broader causal approach of Hart and Honoré can provide assistance. As we saw, this approach retains a focus on causal language, while denying that this might lead to highly technical or 'metaphysical' solutions. On this approach, the relevant distinction to be drawn would be between 'normal' and 'abnormal' interventions. This would not necessarily tally with the distinction between interventions that are foreseeable and unforeseeable, nor between those that are negligent and non-negligent, nor between those that are deliberate and accidental. All such factors may be relevant, but none decisive. This being so, much would be left to the opinion of the deciding tribunal. In some more recent cases, as well as a few older ones, a direct appeal to the purpose and extent of the relevant duty has been employed to resolve the issues. In some important respects, this emerging approach based on distinct duties and their scope is better suited to the more purposive and nuanced approach to establishing the duty of care to be found in current English law.

Intervening Acts of Third Parties

In some cases, such as *Knightley v Johns* or *Lamb v Camden*, the initial negligence of the defendant provides the conditions for another party to cause more extensive damage. The question is whether these further effects are recoverable against the original defendant. In other cases, such as *Dorset Yacht v Home Office*, the defendant's negligence may consist in doing nothing to *prevent* a third party from causing harm. In the latter type of case, there will be a question concerning the nature of any *positive duty* to prevent third party acts.

Intervening Deliberate Acts: *Dorset Yacht v Home Office* [1970] AC 1004

A number of trainees (young offenders) were sent, under the control of three officers, to Brownsea Island on a training exercise. The officers were under instruction to keep the trainees in custody. However, the officers simply went to bed, leaving the trainees to their own devices. During the night, the trainees attempted to escape from the island and in the course of doing so they damaged the respondents' yacht. The claim in negligence was for property damage (to the yacht) caused by breach of the duty to maintain control over the trainees, all of whom had offending records and several of whom had a record of attempting escape.

Lord Reid, at 1027

. . . it is said that the respondents must fail because there is a general principle that no person can be responsible for the acts of another who is not his servant or acting on his behalf. But here the ground of liability is not responsibility for the acts of the escaping trainees; it is liability for damage caused by the carelessness of these officers in the knowledge that their carelessness would probably result in the trainees causing damage of this kind. So the question is really one of remoteness of damage. And I must consider to what extent the law regards the acts of another person as breaking the chain of causation between the defendant's carelessness and the damage to the plaintiff.

. . .

What, then, is the dividing line? Is it foreseeability or is it such a degree of probability as warrants the conclusion that the intervening human conduct was the natural and probable result of what preceded it? There is a world of difference between the two. If I buy a ticket in a lottery or enter a football pool it is foreseeable that I may win a very large prize—some competitor must win it. But, whatever hopes gamblers may entertain, no one could say that winning such a prize was a natural and probable result of entering such a competition.

Lord Reid considered the case law and continued (at 1030):

These cases show that, where human action forms one of the links between the original wrongdoing of the defendant and the loss suffered by the plaintiff, that action must at least have been something very likely to happen if it is not to be regarded as novus actus interveniens breaking the chain of causation. I do not think that a mere foreseeable possibility is or should be sufficient, for then the intervening human action can more properly be regarded as a new cause than as a consequence of the original wrongdoing. But if the intervening action was likely to happen I do not think that it can matter whether that action was innocent or tortious or criminal. Unfortunately, tortious or criminal action by a third party is often the "very kind of thing" which is likely to happen as a result of the wrongful or careless act of the defendant. And in the present case, on the facts which we must assume at this stage, I think that the taking of a boat by the escaping trainees and their unskilful navigation leading to damage to another vessel were the very kind of thing that these Borstal officers ought to have seen to be likely.

The final paragraph extracted from Lord Reid's judgment is peppered by references to different ways of judging either foreseeability, or likelihood. A 'mere foreseeable likelihood' is dismissed as insufficient. Rather, the act of the third party 'must at least be very likely' to happen. Here, the attempted escape and consequent damage are treated as the 'very kind of thing' that the officers 'ought to have seen to be likely'.

This approach is ambiguous. It mentions not only foreseeability but also probability ('likelihood'). Alternatively, the expression 'the very kind of thing' that would be likely to happen could be taken to refer to the *reason* for imposing a positive duty of care to keep the trainees in custody. This would amount to a particular version of 'the risk principle'. The duty here is a particular and positive duty, to exercise control over a third party where the defendants had a specific responsibility in connection with that third party.

That the role of the expression 'the very kind of thing' might be better explained in terms of the purpose and scope of the duty, rather than in terms of degrees of foreseeability or likelihood, is reinforced by *Stansbie v Troman* [1948] 2 KB 48, decided well before *The Wagon Mound* but is generally accepted to be correct. A contractor carrying out decorations in the plaintiff's house was left alone and entrusted with a key; on going out, he left the door unsecured and burglars entered, stealing property. The case was one of breach of contract through negligent conduct, but the following explanation is of general importance to tort law:

Tucker LJ, at 51–2

[Counsel] referred to *Weld-Blundell v. Stephens* and, in particular, to the following passage in the speech of Lord Sumner: "In general (apart from special contracts and relations and the maxim respondeat superior), even though A. is in fault, he is not responsible for injury to C. which B., a stranger to him, deliberately chooses to do. Though A. may have given the occasion for B.'s mischievous activity, B. then becomes a new and independent cause." I do not think that Lord Sumner would have intended that very general statement to apply to the facts of a case such as the present where, as the judge points out, the act of negligence itself consisted in the failure to take reasonable care to guard against the very thing that in fact happened.

Perhaps the influence of *The Wagon Mound* led Lord Reid to superimpose on to this duty-oriented approach the confusing language of foreseeability and likelihood. In a sense, *Stansbie v Troman* vindicates a 'risk principle', but not a risk principle based on foreseeability. The purpose of the duty imposed is to prevent damage being done by a third party; therefore, such damage cannot be outside the risk for which the defendant is responsible.

Lamb v Camden LBC [1981] QB 625

The defendants were alleged to have been negligent in causing the bursting of a water main which led to the flooding of the plaintiff's house together with physical damage. Because of the need for repairs, the house remained empty for some time. It was eventually invaded by squatters who caused considerable damage. The plaintiff sought to recover damages from the council for the damage caused by the squatters. The judges in the Court of Appeal were agreed that the appeal by the owners of the house should be dismissed, but gave varying reasons. Oliver LJ attempted to apply a test of reasonable foreseeability to the case of third party acts. In his view, instead of holding that the damage was 'foreseeable but not likely', the official referee at first instance should have held that the damage was 'not reasonably foreseeable' at all. He proposed a *special* test—that the behaviour would be 'very likely to occur'—for use in determining the 'reasonable' foreseeability of a third party intervention.

There is no such requirement for foreseeability to be based on something 'very likely' in the general run of negligence cases. As exemplified by *Bolton v Stone* and *The Wagon Mound (No 2)*, some relatively low probability events are nevertheless treated as foreseeable. Can Lord Denning's judgment in the same case offer us an improved approach?

Lord Denning, at 636–8

A question of policy

… Looking at the question as one of policy, I ask myself: whose job was it to do something to keep out the squatters? And, if they got in, to evict them? To my mind the answer is clear. It was the job of the owner of the house, Mrs. Lamb, through her agents. That is how everyone in the case regarded it. It has never been suggested in the pleadings or elsewhere that it was the job of the council. No one ever wrote to the council asking them to do it. The council were not in occupation of the house. They had no right to enter it. All they had done was to break the water main outside and cause the subsidence.

… On broader grounds of policy, I would add this: the criminal acts here—malicious damage and theft—are usually covered by insurance. By this means the risk of loss is spread throughout the community. It does not fall too heavily on one pair of shoulders alone. The insurers take the premium to cover just this sort of risk and should not be allowed, by subrogation, to pass it on to others.

Lord Denning suggests that the 'remoteness' analysis in such cases is really a mechanism for addressing the policy issues associated with liability for third party actions. Policy is of course a matter of judgment and opinion and it will vary from case to case. So in a sense, this insight provides relatively little guidance to the likely outcome in future cases. On the other hand, the approach could be seen as consistent, not with open-ended and general 'policy', but with duty analysis wholly consistent with the modern approach to be found in *Caparo v Dickman*. As we saw, *Caparo* asks for positive reasons to hold the defendant responsible for the damage done, precisely including questions concerning the appropriateness of identifying the defendant as the person who ought to take precautions.

A duty-based approach is also encapsulated in the following extract.

Perl (Exporters) Ltd v Camden LBC [1984] 1 QB 342

The defendants left their premises unsecured because of a broken lock. Burglars gained access to the defendants' premises and, by knocking a hole in the wall, made their way into the adjoining premises. These premises were let by the defendants to the plaintiffs, who were retailers of knitwear. Garments were stolen.

Robert Goff LJ, at 360

It is of course true that in the present case the plaintiffs do not allege that the defendants should have controlled the thieves who broke into their storeroom. But they do allege that the defendants should have exercised reasonable care to prevent them from gaining access through their own premises; and in my judgment the statement of principle by Dixon J. is equally apposite in such a case. I know of no case where it has been held, in the absence of a special relationship, that the defendant was liable in negligence for having failed to prevent a third party from wrongfully causing damage to the plaintiff.… Indeed, the consequences of accepting the plaintiffs' submission in the present case are so startling, that I have no hesitation in rejecting the suggestion that there is a duty of care upon occupiers of property to prevent persons from entering their property who might thereby obtain access to neighbouring property. Is every occupier of a terraced house under a duty to his neighbours to shut his windows or lock his door when he goes out, or to keep access to his cellars secure, or even to remove his fire escape, at the risk of being held liable in damages if thieves thereby obtain access to his own house and thence to his neighbour's house? I cannot think that the law imposes any such duty.

It is an attractive feature of Goff LJ's approach that it does not suggest that any degree of foreseeability will generally justify liability for the deliberate acts of a third party. Rather, there is generally no duty to prevent their actions. I owe no duty to my neighbour that would prevent me from leaving a window open for my cat, even if it is 'foreseeable'—and perhaps 'reasonably foreseeable'—that someone will gain access through the window to my property and thus to my neighbour's. The approaches of Lord Reid in *Dorset Yacht*, and of Oliver LJ in *Lamb v Camden*, are a reflection of negligence law's experiment with foreseeability as a generalizing guide to liability in the period surrounding *The Wagon Mound* and, later, *Anns v Merton*, and it now seems clearer that they belong in the past.

As we have seen in Section 4.2, a 'no duty' approach was adopted by the House of Lords in *Mitchell v Glasgow City Council* [2009] UKHL 11, in the context of an omission to warn.

Attempted Rescues

A number of cases have arisen where third parties have attempted to ease a situation created by the negligence of the defendant, thereby inadvertently causing further damage either to themselves, or to others. These can be categorized as 'rescue' cases. In general, an attempted rescue will not amount to a *novus actus*, since it is in many cases both a foreseeable and a 'natural and probable' result of the negligently created situation. Even where the rescuer has behaved in a manner that could ordinarily be described as careless, the law will generally be reluctant to release a negligent party from his obligation to compensate a rescuer who is injured: see for example *Videan v BTC* [1963] 2 QB 650. There are limits to the law's protective stance. In *Cutler v United Dairies* [1933] 2 KB 297, the Court of Appeal found that the plaintiff's attempt to hold the head of an agitated horse amounted to a *novus actus interveniens*, and that he assumed the risk of injury, even though the driver of the horse had called for help. Soon after, however, in *Haynes v Harwood* [1935] 1 KB 146, a police officer's effort to hold a horse in a crowded street was held not to be a *novus actus*, so that he could recover from the defendants for his injuries.

Haynes v Harwood is more in tune with the general law on rescuers. In general, rescuers are treated as foreseeable; it is accepted that they are often acting in the heat of the moment so that the standard of care applied to them must take this into account; and it is recognized that they are often put in the position of deciding whether to attempt a rescue by the circumstances that confront them.[32] But in *Knightley v Johns* [1982] 1 WR 349, a rescue—or elements of it—were found to have been unreasonably executed. Stephenson LJ struggled to find any single description of the reasons for his conclusion, employing a wide variety

[32] On standard of care and rescuers, see also the provisions of the Social Action, Responsibility and Heroism Act 2015, extracted in Section 1.3 of this chapter.

of language in order to seek to explain why the chain of causation should be seen as having been broken. Among these is the language of foreseeability, but also of that which is 'natural and probable'—language that is equally associated with *Re Polemis* and which was supposed to be superseded by foreseeability as a result of *The Wagon Mound*. Also prominently featured was the language of 'chains of events'; and elsewhere the negligence of the fourth defendant was referred to as 'the real cause' of the accident. Clearly, this is 'causal' language. We can glean from this case that a very unusual sequence of events involving the carelessness of a third party rescuer (especially but not only if this involves an extended sequence of links) may be sufficient to make the damage too remote a consequence of the defendant's initial negligence; we can also be clear that it will not be sufficient simply to show some fault, carelessness, error, or perhaps even 'folly' on the part of third parties after the event, so simple negligence will not do. And it is also clear that the defendant must accept the risk of *some* 'expected mischances'. A complex series of unexpected events of this nature *may* however be sufficient to break the causal chain. As to when that will be the case, Stephenson LJ suggested that this will be a matter of opinion.

This messy solution in the case of *Knightley* is consistent with the prediction of Glanville Williams. In his article 'The Risk Principle', to which we have referred already in this chapter, Williams described cases like this one (where the initial harm of the defendant's negligence is added to in rather unexpected ways involving the acts of a third party) as cases of 'ulterior harm'. In respect of these cases, he conceded that the foreseeability approach is in effect seeking to replicate a more 'causal' approach. He also accepted that (just like the causal approach) foreseeability would not give a tidy answer:

In respect of ulterior harms . . . I think that Hart and Honoré are right in saying that the test of foreseeability is a way of distinguishing between normal and abnormal consequences . . . The question is whether the harm is within ordinary experience. I would add, however, that the distinction is governed to some extent not only by statistical considerations but by notions of policy. That this is an imprecise rule is shown by the divergent results obtained by different courts at different times. It is here that we reach the limits of predictability in determining the consequences for which a tortfeasor will be held liable. [p. 200]

Williams also predicted an important element of the approach in *Knightley v Johns*, which is that negligence or even 'folly' on the part of a third party will not *necessarily* lead to a break in the chain of causation. He suggested, in particular, that where it was foreseeable that the plaintiff would require medical treatment as a result of the defendant's negligence, even *negligent* medical treatment might sometimes be within the general risk and would not necessarily break the chain of causation (p. 200, n. 49).

Intervening Medical Negligence

In *Robinson v Post Office* [1974] 1 WLR 1176, the plaintiff slipped on an oily ladder, and suffered a grazed shin. This injury was treated as being caused through the defendant employer's breach of duty. A doctor administered an anti-tetanus injection which, due to a pre-existing susceptibility on the part of the plaintiff, resulted in encephalitis and permanent disability. It was found that although there was some negligence on the part of the doctor, that negligence was not an operating cause of the plaintiff's injuries because it did not pass the 'but for' test: even if the doctor had followed approved procedures, these would still not have indicated that the plaintiff's particular reaction was likely. This in turn was taken to be significant in holding that the employers were fully liable in that the chain of causation was not broken; the actions of the doctor in administering the injection were not a 'novus actus'.

However, it seems from the approach in *Knightley v Johns*, supported by the views of Glanville Williams, that even if medical negligence were to be established, this need not necessarily amount to a *novus actus*. This is compatible with the decision of the Court of Appeal in *Wright v Cambridge Medical Group* (Section 5.2). That was a different case because the defendant had not caused the need for medical treatment, but had delayed the claimant's access to that treatment and thus increased the risk that she would not be successfully treated. There, too, the negligent medical treatment did not break the chain of causation. Even Elias LJ, the dissenting judge, thought that in the normal sort of case, where the defendant's negligence creates the need for medical treatment, which proves to be negligent, the damage is generally not too remote. As Smith LJ put it, the defendant's initial negligence continues to be an 'operating cause'.

Intervening Act of the Claimant

Reeves v Commissioner of Police for the Metropolis [2000] 1 AC 360

The deceased was held in custody in a police cell. Police officers had been warned that he might commit suicide, although when attended by a doctor he was found not to be showing signs of clinical depression or other psychiatric disorder. He could be regarded as being at risk, but of sound mind. The deceased took advantage of the fact that the flap of his cell door had been left open, and hanged himself. The House of Lords held that his suicide did not constitute a *novus actus interveniens*, and that his death was caused by the officers' breach of their duty to protect him. Damages were reduced on account of his contributory negligence, which can only be the case if there is considered to be 'fault' on both sides (Law Reform (Contributory Negligence) Act 1945, s 1(1), see Chapter 5).

Lord Hoffmann, at 367–9

It would make nonsense of the existence of such a duty if the law were to hold that the occurrence of the very act which ought to have been prevented negatived causal connection between the breach of duty and the loss. This principle has been recently considered by your Lordships' House in *Environment Agency (formerly National Rivers Authority) v. Empress Car Co. (Abertillery) Ltd.* [1998] 2 W.L.R. 350. In that case, examples are given of cases in which liability has been imposed for causing events which were the immediate consequence of the deliberate acts of third parties but which the defendant had a duty to prevent or take reasonable care to prevent.

Mr. Pannick accepted this principle when the deliberate act was that of a third party. But he said that it was different when it was the act of the plaintiff himself. Deliberately inflicting damage on oneself had to be an act which negatived causal connection with anything which had gone before.

This argument is based upon the sound intuition that there is a difference between protecting people against harm caused to them by third parties and protecting them against harm which they inflict upon themselves. It reflects the individualist philosophy of the common law. People of full age and sound understanding must look after themselves and take responsibility for their actions. This philosophy expresses itself in the fact that duties to safeguard from harm deliberately caused by others are unusual and a duty to protect a person of full understanding from causing harm to himself is very rare indeed. But, once it is admitted that this is the rare case in which such a duty is owed, it seems to me self-contradictory to say that the breach could not have been a cause of the harm because the victim caused it to himself.

The approach taken here focuses on the particular duty in question, which was conceded by the police commissioner to be owed to the deceased. If a prisoner at risk who commits suicide is held solely responsible for the consequences of his actions in these circumstances, then the admitted duty to protect prisoners who are at risk of suicide would be entirely empty of content. The actions of the deceased were readily foreseeable, but this is not the reason given by Lord Hoffmann in the extract above, just as Lord Reid rejected foreseeability as sufficient to extend the defendant's liability in cases of first party intervening acts, in the *McKew* case. Rather, this is a case where the purpose of the duty is to protect the recipient of the duty against harm done to himself (See further Chapter 5).

Corr v IBC [2008] UKHL 13; (2008) 1 AC 884

In *Reeves*, the defendants owed a duty to take steps to prevent the deceased from committing suicide. Here, there had been an accident at work. The accident very nearly killed the deceased, but instead injured him quite seriously. The accident and injury led to clinical depression, which led to suicide. The question was whether the suicide was attributable to the initial breach of duty. The House of Lords held that it was. On the question of whether the suicide amounted to a 'novus actus', there was more than one possible approach to the question, though these approaches yielded the same answer. Lord Bingham took the view that although the deceased had made a choice (to take his own life), he had not made a free and voluntary choice because of the effect on his mind of the accident and its effects. The fact that he was not described as 'insane' (a term which Lord Bingham approached with some scepticism) was not decisive. Consistently with this, he would not support a reduction in damages for contributory negligence in such a case (we discuss this element in Chapter 5). Lord Scott approached the question through application of the 'egg-shell skull' principle, discussed earlier in this section, as extended to psychiatric harm by *Page v Smith*: the employer must take the employee as he finds him, even if his susceptibility is toward psychiatric injury. Lord Scott would have been prepared to reduce damages for contributory negligence, though in the event he thought there was insufficient evidence before the court to do this.

Lord Bingham, *Corr v IBC*

15. The rationale of the principle that a *novus actus interveniens* breaks the chain of causation is fairness. It is not fair to hold a tortfeasor liable, however gross his breach of duty may be, for damage caused to the claimant not by the tortfeasor's breach of duty but by some independent, supervening cause (which may or may not be tortious) for which the tortfeasor is not responsible. This is not the less so where the independent, supervening cause is a voluntary, informed decision taken by the victim as an adult of sound mind making and giving effect to a personal decision about his own future.…

16. In the present case Mr Corr's suicide was not a voluntary, informed decision taken by him as an adult of sound mind making and giving effect to a personal decision about his future. It was the response of a man suffering from a severely depressive illness which impaired his capacity to make reasoned and informed judgments about his future, such illness being, as is accepted, a consequence of the employer's tort. It is in no way unfair to hold the employer responsible for this dire consequence of its breach of duty, although it could well be thought unfair to the victim not to do so.

Lord Scott

27. ... The question in this case... is whether Mr Corr's deliberate act of jumping from a high building in order to kill himself, an apparent novus actus, albeit one that was causally connected, on a 'but-for' basis, to the original negligence, broke the chain of causative consequences for which Mr Corr's negligent employers must accept responsibility.

28. The answer to this question does not, in my opinion, require the application of a reasonable foreseeability test. To ask whether it was reasonably foreseeable that an accident of the sort that injured Mr Corr might have psychiatric as well as physical consequences and, if it did have psychiatric consequences, whether those consequences might include suicidal tendencies and an eventual suicide would be unlikely, on the facts of this case, to result in an affirmative answer.

...

29. Authority, however, discourages attempts to decide cases like the present by the application of a reasonable foreseeability test. The general rule is that in a case where foreseeable physical injuries have been caused to a claimant by the negligence of a defendant the defendant cannot limit his liability by contending that the extent of the physical injuries could not have been reasonably foreseen; the defendant must take his victim as he finds him.

... *Page v Smith* ... extended the rule as stated in *Smith v Leech Brain* so as to include psychiatric injury. If a duty of care to avoid physical injury is broken and psychiatric injury is thereby caused, whether with or without any physical injury being caused, the negligent defendant must accept liability for the psychiatric injury. He must take his victim as he finds him. That this is so is a consequence of the House's decision in *Page v Smith*. That decision has been the subject of some criticism but not in the present case. If Mr Corr's psychiatric damage caused by the accident at work is damage for which his employers must accept liability, it is difficult to see on what basis they could escape liability for additional injury, self-inflicted but attributable to his psychiatric condition. If Mr Corr had not suffered from the clinical depression brought about by the accident, he would not have had the suicidal tendencies that led him eventually to kill himself. In my opinion, on the principles established by the authorities to which I have referred, the chain of causal consequences of the accident for which Mr Corr's negligent employers are liable was not broken by his suicide. For tortious remoteness of damage purposes his jump from the multi-storey car park was not, in my opinion, a novus actus interveniens. Mrs Corr is entitled, in my opinion, to a Fatal Accidents Act claim against his employers.

Here, a voluntary act of the party to whom a duty was owed did not break the chain of causation and was not treated as a 'supervening event'. The suicide was, in this sense, 'caused by' the tort of the defendant. We have already seen that by contrast in *Gray v Thames Trains*, the House of Lords held that a criminal act by the person to whom the duty is owed does break the chain of causation, and/or is a supervening cause akin to the medical condition in *Jobling*. The decisive difference appears to be that the claimant's act in *Gray* is a criminal act, and the law of tort cannot be seen to hold people responsible for the acts of others in conditions where the criminal law is prepared to punish the actor, or otherwise hold him criminally responsible. It seems relatively clear that this is not altogether a claim about 'causation', independent of judgments about responsibility.

These difficult cases involve acts by claimants which bring about intended outcomes. In a wider range of cases, injured claimants may make poor decisions which result in their suffering further injury. One such case is *Spencer v Wincanton Holdings* [2009] EWCA Civ 1404. Here, the claimant had lost a leg through an accident for which the defendant was vicariously liable. His injuries were considerably exacerbated when he fell at a petrol station, having attempted to refuel his car without first securing his prosthetic leg. The Court of Appeal found that he had not acted so unreasonably as to break the chain of causation from the first accident. Rather, the burden of the additional injuries would be shared between the parties, by application of contributory negligence principles (Chapter 5).

Sedley LJ, *Spencer v Wincanton Holdings*
[2009] EWCA Civ 1404

13 It seems to me problematical, with respect, to try to explain remoteness in terms of foreseeability. If anything, it is foreseeability which has to be explained in terms of remoteness.... ...

In essence, the 'remoteness' question was defined as concerned with the *fairness* of extending liability to incorporate the injury. In the present case, that test was satisfied, subject to a reduction for contributory negligence. Fairness, not foreseeability, is the guiding principle. We may point out that the second accident was in no way coincidental: the claimant was at risk of further injury of this sort due to the consequences of the initial tort. A compatible case is *Dalling v Heale & Co* [2011] EWCA Civ 365, where responsibility for the claimant's newly excessive drinking after a head injury—leading to a fall and further injury—was shared between claimant and defendant. The claimant's failure to control his drinking was causally related to the tort.

Two of the judges in *Spencer v Wincanton* referred to the following summary, on the part of Lord Rodger, in the Scottish case of *Simmons v British Steel*. In this extract, Lord Rodger does not seek to explain the law, but provides a checklist of how the law currently stands:

Lord Rodger, *Simmons v British Steel*
2004 SC (HL) 94

67 ...once liability is established, any question of the remoteness of damage is to be approached along the following lines which may, of course, be open to refinement and development. (1) The starting point is that a defender is not liable for a consequence of a kind which is not reasonably foreseeable (*McKew v Holland & Hannen & Cubitts (Scotland) Ltd* (1970), per Lord Reid at p 25; *Bourhill v Young*, per Lord Russell of Killowen at p 85; *Allan v Barclay*, per Lord Kinloch at p 874). (2) While a defender is not liable for damage that was not reasonably foreseeable, it does not follow that he is liable for all damage that was reasonably foreseeable: depending on the circumstances, the defender may not be liable for damage caused by a *novus actus interveniens* or unreasonable conduct on the part of the pursuer, even if it was reasonably foreseeable (*McKew v Holland & Hannen & Cubitts (Scotland) Ltd* (1970), per Lord Reid at p 25;

Lamb v Camden London Borough Council; but see *Ward v Cannock Chase District Council*). (3) Subject to the qualification in (2), if the pursuer's injury is of a kind that was foreseeable, the defender is liable, even if the damage is greater in extent than was foreseeable or it was caused in a way that could not have been foreseen (*Hughes v Lord Advocate*, per Lord Reid at pp 38, 40). (4) The defender must take his victim as he finds him (*Bourhill v Young*, per Lord Wright at p 92; *McKillen v Barclay Curle & Co Ltd*, per Lord President Clyde at p 42). (5) Subject again to the qualification in (2), where personal injury to the pursuer was reasonably foreseeable, the defender is liable for any personal injury, whether physical or psychiatric, which the pursuer suffers as a result of his wrongdoing (*Page v Smith*, per Lord Lloyd of Berwick at p 197F–H).

Conclusion: Intervening Acts

Foreseeability does not provide a sufficient criterion for determining whether there is a *novus actus*—a point made very clearly through the last few extracts above. 'Common sense' causal principles along the lines suggested by Hart and Honoré may provide guidance by focusing our attention on 'normal' or 'abnormal' events, rather than the culpability or otherwise of those who intervene. As Glanville Williams concedes, this judgment will be a personal one on the facts of the case and in respect of these cases, 'the limits of predictability' may have been reached. In at least some of these cases, an alternative is to approach the question of *novus actus* in light of an analysis of the purpose and scope of the duty of care. The language used by Lord Reid in *Dorset Yacht*, where he described the incident as 'the very kind of thing' that would be foreseen, could be taken to reflect such an approach, as can the case of *Stansbie v Troman*. In *Dorset Yacht*, the approach was only obscured by the language of foreseeability and probability employed, and more recent cases have frankly acknowledged that such concepts will not provide the answers to remoteness questions. Duty analysis is also apparent in the cases of *Perl Exporters* (Goff LJ) and *Reeves v Commissioner of Police for the Metropolis* (Lord Hoffmann). Analysis of this type is more in tune with the *Caparo* approach since it is dependent on consideration of the nature, scope, and purpose of the duty owed by the defendant. This brings us conveniently to a compatible development in respect of a different category of remoteness case.

6.4 'SCOPE OF DUTY' ANALYSIS

In his article 'The Road From Morocco', extracted in Section 6.1, Davies contended that if there was any injustice created by the remoteness test in *Re Polemis*, it stemmed from the development of over-extensive and non-specific duties of care. *The Wagon Mound* could be said to be a response to this development; perhaps also it shared the general optimism of the period which led to a ground-swell of support for generalization in the law of tort and in the tort of negligence in particular. In more recent years, the concept of 'duty' has become more specific to particular circumstances. Perhaps it is time to update *The Wagon Mound*, to reflect this change in the approach to duty.

The following decision, like the cases of *Jolley* and *Reeves*, gives priority to analysis of the 'scope of the duty'. Unlike those cases, it marks a departure from traditional approaches in order to resolve a new problem. That problem is partly created by the evolution of duty analysis in the field of economic losses. For example, where information is relied upon, the duty is owed only in respect of reliance for certain defined purposes (*Caparo v Dickman*). The solution reached could be seen as a version of the 'risk principle', amended to take account of change in the nature of the duty of care.

South Australia Asset Management Corporation v York Montague Ltd ('SAAMCO') [1997] AC 191; on appeal from Banque Bruxelles Lambert SA v Eagle Star Insurance Co Ltd

This decision, which dealt with three appeals, raised important questions concerning losses of value in the UK property market during the early 1990s. In each of the cases, it was found at first instance that the defendants had negligently over-valued certain properties and that the plaintiffs in reliance on these valuations had advanced loans secured upon the properties. Subsequently, the borrowers defaulted and the lenders' security proved to be worth less than the sums advanced. A general fall in the market value of property had enhanced the losses suffered. Would the valuers be liable for the full extent of the losses suffered, or only for some portion of those losses?

Lord Hoffmann, at 210–13

My Lords, the three appeals before the House raise a common question of principle. What is the extent of the liability of a valuer who has provided a lender with a negligent overvaluation of the property offered as security for the loan? The facts have two common features. The first is that if the lender had known the true value of the property, he would not have lent. The second is that a fall in the property market after the date of the valuation greatly increased the loss which the lender eventually suffered.

The Court of Appeal (*Banque Bruxelles Lambert S.A. v. Eagle Star Insurance Co. Ltd.* [1995] Q.B. 375) decided that in a case in which the lender would not otherwise have lent (which they called a "no-transaction" case), he is entitled to recover the difference between the sum which he lent, together with a reasonable rate of interest, and the net sum which he actually got back. The valuer bears the whole risk of a transaction which, but for his negligence, would not have happened. He is therefore liable for all the loss attributable to a fall in the market. They distinguished what they called a "successful transaction" case, in which the evidence shows that if the lender had been correctly advised, he would still have lent a lesser sum on the same security. In such a case, the lender can recover only the difference between what he has actually lost and what he would have lost if he had lent the lesser amount. Since the fall in the property market is a common element in both the actual and the hypothetical calculations, it does not increase the valuer's liability.

The valuers appeal. They say that a valuer provides an estimate of the value of the property at the date of the valuation. He does not undertake the role of a prophet. It is unfair that merely because for one reason or other the lender would not otherwise have lent, the valuer should be saddled with the whole risk of the transaction, including a subsequent fall in the value of the property. Much of the discussion, both in the judgment of the Court of Appeal and in argument at the Bar, has assumed that the case is about the correct measure of damages for the loss which the lender has suffered ...

I think that this was the wrong place to begin. Before one can consider the principle on which one should calculate the damages to which a plaintiff is entitled as compensation for loss, it is necessary to decide for what kind of loss he is entitled to compensation. A correct description of the loss for which the valuer is liable must precede any consideration of the measure of damages. For this purpose it is better to begin at the beginning and consider the lender's cause of action.

The lender sues on a contract under which the valuer, in return for a fee, undertakes to provide him with certain information. Precisely what information he has to provide depends of course upon the terms of the individual contract. There is some dispute on this point in respect of two of the appeals, to which I shall have to return. But there is one common element which everyone accepts. In each case the valuer was required to provide an estimate of the price which the property might reasonably be expected to fetch if sold in the open market at the date of the valuation.

There is again agreement on the purpose for which the information was provided. It was to form part of the material on which the lender was to decide whether, and if so how much, he would lend. The valuation tells the lender how much, at current values, he is likely to recover if he has to resort to his security. This enables him to decide what margin, if any, an advance of a given amount will allow for a fall in the market, reasonably foreseeable variance from the figure put forward by the valuer (a valuation is an estimate of the most probable figure which the property will fetch, not a prediction that it will fetch precisely that figure), accidental damage to the property and any other of the contingencies which may happen. The valuer will know that if he overestimates the value of the property, the lender's margin for all these purposes will be correspondingly less.

On the other hand, the valuer will not ordinarily be privy to the other considerations which the lender may take into account, such as how much money he has available, how much the borrower needs to borrow, the strength of his covenant, the attraction of the rate of interest or the other personal or commercial considerations which may induce the lender to lend.

Because the valuer will appreciate that his valuation, though not the only consideration which would influence the lender, is likely to be a very important one, the law implies into the contract a term that the valuer will exercise reasonable care and skill. The relationship between the parties also gives rise to a concurrent duty in tort: see *Henderson v. Merrett Syndicates Ltd.* [1995] 2 A.C. 115. But the scope of the duty in tort is the same as in contract.

A duty of care such as the valuer owes does not however exist in the abstract. A plaintiff who sues for breach of a duty imposed by the law (whether in contract or tort or under statute) must do more than prove that the defendant has failed to comply. He must show that the duty was owed to him and that it was a duty in respect of the kind of loss which he has suffered. Both of these requirements are illustrated by *Caparo Industries Plc. v. Dickman* [1990] 2 A.C. 605. The auditors' failure to use reasonable care in auditing the company's statutory accounts was a breach of their duty of care. But they were not liable to an outside take-over bidder because the duty was not owed to him. Nor were they liable to shareholders who had bought more shares in reliance on the accounts because, although they were owed a duty of care, it was in their capacity as members of the company and not in the capacity (which they shared with everyone else) of potential buyers of its shares. Accordingly, the duty which they were owed was not in respect of loss which they might suffer by buying its shares ...

In the present case, there is no dispute that the duty was owed to the lenders. The real question in this case is the kind of loss in respect of which the duty was owed.

How is the scope of the duty determined? In the case of a statutory duty, the question is answered by deducing the purpose of the duty from the language and context of the statute: *Gorris v. Scott* (1874) L.R. 9 Ex. 125. In the case of tort, it will similarly depend upon the purpose of the rule imposing the duty. Most of the judgments in the *Caparo* case are occupied in examining the Companies Act 1985 to ascertain the purpose of the auditor's duty to take care that the statutory accounts comply with the Act. In the case of an implied contractual duty, the nature and extent of the liability is defined by the term which the law implies. As in the case of any implied term, the process is one of construction of the agreement as a whole in its commercial setting. The contractual duty to provide a valuation and the known purpose of that valuation compel the conclusion that the contract includes a duty of care. The scope of the duty, in the sense of the consequences for which the valuer is responsible, is that which the law regards as best giving effect to the express obligations assumed by the valuer: neither cutting them down so that the lender obtains less than he was reasonably entitled to expect, nor extending them so as to impose on the valuer a liability greater than he could reasonably have thought he was undertaking.

What therefore should be the extent of the valuer's liability? The Court of Appeal said that he should be liable for the loss which would not have occurred if he had given the correct advice. The lender having, in reliance on the valuation, embarked upon a transaction which he would not otherwise have undertaken, the valuer should bear all the risks of that transaction, subject only to the limitation that the damage should have been within the reasonable contemplation of the parties.

There is no reason in principle why the law should not penalise wrongful conduct by shifting on to the wrongdoer the whole risk of consequences which would not have happened but for the wrongful act. Hart and Honoré, in *Causation in the Law*, 2nd ed. (1985), p. 120, say that it would, for example, be perfectly intelligible to have a rule by which an unlicensed driver was responsible for all the consequences of his having driven, even if they were unconnected with his not having a licence. One might adopt such a rule in the interests of deterring unlicensed driving. But that is not the normal rule ...

Rules which make the wrongdoer liable for all the consequences of his wrongful conduct are exceptional and need to be justified by some special policy. Normally the law limits liability to those consequences which are attributable to that which made the act wrongful. In the case of liability in negligence for providing inaccurate information, this would mean liability for the consequences of the information being inaccurate.

I can illustrate the difference between the ordinary principle and that adopted by the Court of Appeal by an example. A mountaineer about to undertake a difficult climb is concerned about the fitness of his knee. He goes to a doctor who negligently makes a superficial examination and pronounces the knee fit. The climber goes on the expedition, which he would not have undertaken if the doctor had told him the true state of his knee. He suffers an injury which is an entirely foreseeable consequence of mountaineering but has nothing to do with his knee.

On the Court of Appeal's principle, the doctor is responsible for the injury suffered by the mountaineer because it is damage which would not have occurred if he had been given correct information about his knee. He would not have gone on the expedition and would have suffered no injury. On what I have suggested is the more usual principle, the doctor is not liable. The injury has not been caused by the doctor's bad advice because it would have occurred even if the advice had been correct.

Applying the approach set out in the above extract, Lord Hoffmann reasoned that in the first of the appeals, *SAAMCO v York Montague* itself, the plaintiffs could recover the entire loss caused by the fall in market value, subject to a deduction for contributory negligence (for an explanation of this defence, see generally Chapter 5). The property had been valued at £15 million, and the true value was £5 million; £11 million had been advanced. After the market fall, the property was sold for just under £2.5 million, a loss of just over £9.5 million. The plaintiffs were entitled to recover their full loss (subject to deduction for contributory negligence) because (at 222):

The consequence of the valuation being wrong was that the plaintiffs had £10 million less security than they thought. If they had had this margin, they would have suffered no loss. The whole loss was therefore within the scope of the defendants' duty.

In reaching this solution, the active question in Lord Hoffmann's analysis is what would have been the case if the valuation which *was* given had turned out to be correct? The plaintiffs would have had an extra £10 million security. Their loss was just over £9.5 million, which was within this bracket, so they were entitled, prima facie, to recover that amount. As Lord Hoffmann put it, if the information had been correct, there would have been no loss.

His language tends to obscure the novelty of the solution. Asking what was the 'consequence of the valuation being wrong' is not in this instance the same as asking what would have happened if the defendant had given a correct valuation. The latter is a question of 'but for' causation and it was the one asked by the Court of Appeal. The answer given was that the plaintiffs would not have entered into the transaction and so they would have suffered no loss on that property. The difference is made clear by the result of applying the approach to the other appeals.

In the other appeals, the valuations were less grossly inaccurate. The plaintiffs would still have suffered some loss if the valuation given had turned out to be correct, so they were awarded less than the full amount. For example, in the case of *Bank of Kuwait v Prudential Property Services Ltd* the lenders advanced £1.75 million on the security of a property valued at £2.5 million. The correct value was between £1.8 million and £1.85 million. After the market fall, it was sold for £950,000. According to Lord Hoffmann (at 222):

> In my view the damages should have been limited to the consequences of the valuation being wrong, which were that the lenders had £700,000 or £650,000 less security than they thought….
>
> I would therefore allow the appeal and reduce the damages to the difference between the valuation and the correct value.

Stapleton argues ([1997] 113 LQR 1) that in each case the effect is to place a 'cap' on damages so that they should not exceed the difference between the valuation given (which she calls *V*) and an accurate valuation at the time (*V**). The damages may of course be less than this amount, if the plaintiff's loss is lower than the misevaluation. This was the case in the *SAAMCO* appeal itself as explained above. But we should be careful to note that although this is the *effect* of the decision in these cases, the *method* is not to place a cap. Lord Hoffmann made this clear in *SAAMCO* (at 219–20):

> An alternative theory was that the lender should be entitled to recover the whole of his loss, subject to a "cap" limiting his recovery to the amount of the overvaluation. This theory will ordinarily produce the same result as the requirement that loss should be a consequence of the valuation being wrong, because the usual such consequence is that the lender makes an advance which he thinks is secured to a correspondingly greater extent…. But I would not wish to exclude the possibility that other kinds of loss may flow from the valuation being wrong and in any case, as Mr. Sumption said on behalf of the defendants York Montague Ltd., it seems odd to start by choosing the wrong measure of damages (the whole loss) and then correct the error by imposing a cap. The appearance of a cap is actually the result of the plaintiff having to satisfy two separate requirements: first, to prove that he has suffered loss, and, secondly, to establish that the loss fell within the scope of the duty he was owed.

The point is reinforced in a subsequent decision concerning calculation of interest.

**Lord Hoffmann, *Nykredit v Edward Erdman Ltd (No 2)*
[1997] 1 WLR 1627, at 1638–9**

... in order to establish a cause of action in negligence [the plaintiff] must show that his loss is attributable to the overvaluation, that is, that he is worse off than he would have been if it had been correct.

It is important to emphasise that this is a consequence of the limited way in which the House defined the valuer's duty of care and has nothing to do with questions of causation or any limit or "cap" imposed upon damages which would otherwise be recoverable. It was accepted that the whole loss suffered by reason of the fall in the property market was, as a matter of causation, properly attributable to the lender having entered into the transaction and that, but for the negligent valuation, he would not have done so. It was not suggested that the possibility of a fall in the market was unforeseeable or that there was any other factor which negatived the causal connection between lending and losing the money. There was, for example, no evidence that if the lender had not made the advance in question he would have lost his money in some other way. Nor, if one started from the proposition that the valuer was responsible for the consequences of the loan being made, could there be any logical basis for limiting the recoverable damages to the amount of the overvaluation. The essence of the decision was that this is not where one starts and that the valuer is responsible only for the consequences of the lender having too little security.

Proof of loss attributable to a breach of the relevant duty of care is an essential element in a cause of action for the tort of negligence. Given that there has been negligence, the cause of action will therefore arise *when the plaintiff has suffered loss in respect of which the duty was owed*... [Emphasis added]

Like Viscount Simonds in *The Wagon Mound*, Lord Hoffmann denies that his solution is related to causation. But it certainly depends on identifying which effects were 'the consequence' of the breach of duty, and it is hard to imagine discussion of consequences without any reference to causation. However, this is not an exercise in 'but for' causation. In terms of 'but for', it can be accepted that the breach was, as the Court of Appeal said, a cause of the loss. But that is not sufficient to establish that the loss is recoverable.

The reasoning is subtle, and the case has been hugely influential, so we will outline the ways in which it is controversial and distinctive.

The Reasoning

Scope of Duty

It will be apparent from the extracts above that Lord Hoffmann's reasoning turns on identifying 'the scope of the duty'. This is the first of two steps in his reasoning. At this first stage, Lord Hoffmann determined that the scope of the duty was to offer a correct valuation.

In relation to the 'scope of duty' analysis, Lord Hoffmann offers the analogy of a mountaineer who approaches a doctor for advice on the condition of his knee. If the doctor says that the knee is sound and this particular information is incorrect, it might lead the mountaineer to undertake an expedition when otherwise he would have stayed at home. If he then suffers a fall which is unrelated to the condition of the knee, then the doctor's misinformation will pass the 'but for' test: it will be a 'condition precedent' of the accident. Nevertheless, it would be wrong to attribute the injury to the incorrect information. The doctor's role was only in respect of the condition of the knee. In the course of criticizing the approach in *SAAMCO*, Jane Stapleton nevertheless accepts that this example illustrates effectively that issues of 'but for' causation do not provide all the answers in cases of this sort ((1997) 113 LQR 1, 2). She further suggests, however, that Lord Hoffmann is mistaken when he treats the nature of the 'wrong' in such cases as failure to give *accurate information*, rather than failure to give a *careful valuation* (at 5). But Lord Hoffmann gives clear reasons for suggesting that where a defendant is called upon only to give particular and specific *information* in relation to a transaction or other course of action, the only duty is to take care to give that information accurately. In other cases, there may be a broader duty to offer advice. In the latter sort of case, there may, for example, be a duty to advise on the possibility of a general market fall and loss of security. We can agree that there is room to differ in this interpretation of the scope of the duty. 'Scope of duty' analysis will be subjective at both stages. But for the same reason it seems too simplistic to describe it as mistaken. The greater controversy exists, it is suggested, at the next stage.

Identifying the 'Consequences'

At the next stage, Lord Hoffmann applied an unprecedented kind of 'but for' test. He asked what would have happened if the defendant's valuation (which is to say the valuation *actually given* by the defendants) had been correct. As we have already seen, this is not the same as asking what would have happened if the defendant had provided a correct valuation. That would have been a question of factual causation, and this is not. It is designed specifically to establish which losses will be treated as *attributable to* the breach of duty. Lord Hoffmann's approach can be regarded as a question of remoteness in the sense that it determines attribution. It does not, however, employ the language of foreseeability, which would also give too broad an answer. It identifies the scope and purpose of the duty with some precision (a subjective exercise) and then asks which aspects of the damage suffered are attributable to breach of the duty so understood. To express this second stage in terms of 'but for' causation is to use familiar language in an unfamiliar way.

Influence

The significance of *SAAMCO* as an updating of the 'risk principle' is illustrated by the decision of the Court of Appeal in *Haugesund Kommune v Depfa ACS Bank (No 2)* [2011] EWCA Civ 33. Here, the claimant bank had entered into 'swap' transactions with certain Norwegian 'kommunes' (the equivalent of local authorities). The bank first sought advice from the defendants as to whether it was within the powers of the kommunes to enter into such transactions. The defendants advised that it was. At a later date, it proved that this advice was wrong: the kommunes had no power to enter into the transactions. Since the contracts were therefore void, there was no prospect of a contractual remedy in respect of the sums advanced by the bank. However, the agreements were governed by English law, and there *was* a restitutionary claim for return of those sums. As a consequence, the invalidity of the transactions (which was the subject of the advice) did not *in itself* mean that the bank lost the sums advanced. As a matter of *law*, the bank was able to recover the sums. As a matter of fact, however, the kommunes were unable to return the money, having engaged in some disastrously unsuccessful investment activities, amongst other reasons.[33]

---

[33] There were public and political impediments to reducing expenditure in order to cover the debt.

On this basis, and applying *SAAMCO*, the Court of Appeal concluded that the loss of the sums advanced was not within the scope of the lawyers' duty to advise. Although the bank argued that it would not have entered into the transactions at all if it had known that the kommunes had no power to contract in this way, and that 'but for' causation was established, the reason why the funds could not be returned was the lack of creditworthiness of the kommunes—and this was a risk which the bank had knowingly retained. To put it another way, the risk of inability to pay was not the risk as to which the bank sought the defendants' advice; and it was inability to pay, not legal incapacity, which led to the loss. This depends upon identification of the risks retained by relevant parties and not, for example, on foreseeability. A shortcut to this solution, adopted by Rix LJ but not by Gross LJ, was to say that this was a 'category 1' case of advice (which is to say, advice as to a specific matter); not a 'category 2' case (more general advice on a transaction). But that division will not always point to the right answer and is merely a rule of thumb. Gross LJ identified the central point:

Gross LJ, *Haugesund Kommune v Depfa ACS Bank (No 2)*

[101] …whether this was a 'category 1' case or a 'category 2' case, losses attributable to enforcement and credit risks were outside the scope of Wikborg Rein's duty …

Or as Rix LJ encapsulated the same point:

Rix LJ, *Haugesund Kommune v Depfa ACS Bank (No 2)*

[87] …The inability to execute has always been a risk the responsibility for which lay on Depfa [the claimant], not on Wikborg Rein.

It may prove that *SAAMCO* has its most comfortable application in this sort of context, where the allocation of risks between parties is an important aspect of their relationship. Here, the relationship was advisory, and it also related to commercial risks. Questions of risk allocation are a natural part of the relationship. In other contexts, the basis of judgments reached in determining the 'scope of the duty' has sometimes been less clear;[34] yet it may still be the case that, in principle, liability should be fitted to the scope of the duty imposed or assumed. We can illustrate this by comparing *Haugesund Kommune*, with the case of *Bhamra v Dubb* [2010] EWCA Civ 13.

In *Bhamra v Dubb*, a guest at a Sikh wedding died after suffering an allergic reaction to egg. It was agreed that there is generally no duty on a caterer to warn consumers of the presence of egg (those with allergies should ask); but in this instance, there was clearly a duty not to serve egg for the different reason that the consumption of eggs is prohibited in the Sikh religion. The Court of Appeal found that in these circumstances, the damage fell within the scope of a duty owed by the defendant. If we were to superimpose the reasoning in *Haugesund*, one might think that the answer would be different: the caterer might not be

---

[34] See for example *Calvert v William Hill Credit* [2008] EWCA Civ 1427, where the Court of Appeal found that a bookmaker had assumed a responsibility to a compulsive gambler to honour a 'self-exclusion agreement'; but found that they had not assumed a duty to prevent him from gambling and therefore were not liable for the losses that he suffered.

thought to owe a duty in relation to the *particular* risk of allergic reaction, so that it was in the same position as the lawyer in that case. But the two decisions may be compatible nevertheless. It is not the case that the wedding guest knowingly retained the risk of a reaction to egg in the same way that the bank retained the risk of the kommunes' impecuniosity: the susceptible guest will have assumed that this is an occasion where no questions needed to be asked, because egg is in any case not present. This reflects the nature of the hazard, of the parties, and of their relationship.

Moore-Bick LJ (Judgment of the Court), *Bhamra v Dubb*

[42] ... Mr. Bhamra, who knew himself to be allergic to eggs, had every reason to rely without inquiry on Mr Dubb to supply food which did not contain egg, as would not have been the case if this had been anything other than an exclusively Sikh occasion. In our view this very unusual combination of circumstances is sufficient to extend the scope of Mr. Dubb's duty of care to harm in the form of personal injury suffered as a result of eating food containing eggs.

The Court of Appeal therefore thought that the duties of the caterer in this context *extended to* a warning, since egg would not be expected. The underlying difference between the two cases could be identified as the familiarity of multiple, specific questions of risk-bearing as a central feature of financial transactions; while the same is not true of the relationship between consumers, and caterers. On this basis, the usual expectation that allergy sufferers will guard against a risk was negated by the expectation that egg would not, for other reasons, be present.

6.5 REMOTENESS OF DAMAGE: SUMMARY

It cannot be argued that the problems of remoteness have been satisfactorily resolved, either by *The Wagon Mound* or subsequently. Although remoteness issues have typically received less attention than issues of duty, the case law on remoteness still presents an unsatisfactory mosaic of different approaches and apparent 'rules' depending on the type of case in hand. We have identified that 'foreseeability' has never wholly succeeded in displacing causal language, and we have also identified the emergence of a new emphasis on the scope and purpose of the duty of care. This new approach could be regarded as an updated interpretation of 'the risk principle', which holds that the defendant is liable only for those consequences falling within the scope of the risk created by his or her breach of duty. Because duty of care under *Caparo* is no longer addressed primarily in terms of foreseeability, so the identification of which consequences fall within the relevant risk will also need to be adjusted. *SAAMCO* shows an attempt to do just this, in circumstances where the problem of attribution was, in terms of justice and fairness as well as policy, one that needed to be addressed. The present author has argued that the new 'integrated' approach to duty and damage is true to the nature of the tort of negligence, and to *Donoghue* itself.[35]

---

[35] Steele, Further reading; see also R. Merkin and J. Steele, *Insurance and the Law of Obligations* (Oxford University Press, 2013), chapter 8.

7. CONCLUSIONS

i. The tort of negligence may be summarized as requiring a negligent breach of a duty of care owed by defendant to claimant, which results in damage that is not too remote from the breach of duty or, to put the point another way, which falls within the scope of the duty owed. Each element of this summary has required consideration over the years and the duty component in particular has led to such a volume of case law that it threatens to overwhelm an overall understanding of the tort. In this chapter, we have deferred consideration of specific instances of duty and causation, and explored the general principles and their evolution. As will be apparent, all elements of the tort raise issues of fundamental principle.

ii. The significance of breach of duty, also referred to in terms of the applicable 'standard of care', is often overlooked. In recent years however, there have been considerable developments in relation to standard of care. Courts have reemphasized the objective nature of the standard of care, and thus the tentative link between 'negligence', and any blameworthiness on the part of a particular defendant. While negligence is undoubtedly 'fault based', the meaning of fault is therefore in issue. Other developments in relation to breach of duty include legislative restatement of the significance of public interest factors and social utility when assessing the reasonableness of the defendant's actions; and a clear statement on the part of the Supreme Court that patient choice is the supreme consideration when assessing the reasonableness of risk disclosure on the part of medical professionals. The deeper significance of this last development is that the courts have therefore reclaimed their role as arbiters of whether or not reasonable care has been taken.

iii. Also outlined in this chapter is the general evolution of the duty of care in negligence. After the emergence of a general tort of negligence, there was a process of generalization in the applicable concepts and principles. This process however has now been reversed, and there is far more caution about recognizing novel duties. The notion of duty has emerged as a means of controlling, rather than simply expanding, liability in negligence, and the principles upon which the existence of a duty is to be determined will be sensitive to many different factors and circumstances. A degree of categorization therefore exists in the current law, which however is neither formal nor clearly settled. We will see in Chapter 6 how far this contributes to the complexity of the modern law of negligence.

iv. Just as evolution of the duty of care concept has moved from general principles, to more specific factors, so also the notion of remoteness can be seen to have defied any unifying principle, despite the apparent dominance of 'foreseeability'. Another attempt has been made, through the notion of 'scope of duty', to dovetail the issues of whether a duty is owed, and how far that duty extends. In both of these aspects of the tort of negligence, it is possible to recast the questions in terms of risk: whose risk is it that harm will result from the defendant's acts or omissions; and to which risks does responsibility extend?

FURTHER READING

Standard of Care

Bagshaw, R., 'Modernising the doctor's duty to disclose risks of treatment' (2016) 132 LQR 182.

Brazier, M., and Miola, J., 'Bye-Bye Bolam: A Medical Litigation Revolution?' (2000) 8 Med L Rev 85–114.

Charlish, P., 'Sports: Ordinary Negligence in the Final Furlong' (2005) JPIL 308–19.

Gardner, J., 'The Negligence Standard: Political Not Metaphysical' (2017) 80 MLR 1.

Grubb, A., 'Causation and the *Bolam* Test' (1993) 1 Med L Rev 241.

Kidner, R., 'The Variable Standard of Care, Contributory Negligence and *Volenti*' (1991) 11 LS 1.

McGrath, C.P., ' "Trust Me, I'm a Patient": Disclosure Standards and the Patient's Right to Decide' (2015) CLJ 211

Miola, J., 'The Standard of Care in Medical Negligence—Still Reasonably Troublesome' in J. Richardson and E. Rackley (eds), Feminist Perspectives on Tort Law (Routledge, 2012).

Mulheron, R., 'Legislating Dangerously: Bad Samaritans, Good Society, and the Heroism Act 2015' (2017) 80 MLR 88.

Norrie, K., 'Medical Negligence: Who Sets the Standard?' (1985) 11 JME 135.

Williams, K., '*Res ipsa loquitur* still speaks' (2009) 125 LQR 567–70.

Duty of Care

Buckland, W., 'The Duty to Take Care' (1935) 51 LQR 637.

Heuston, R., '*Donoghue v Stevenson* in Retrospect' (1957) 20 MLR 1.

Hoyano, L., 'Misconceptions About Wrongful Conception' (2002) 65 MLR 883.

McBride, N., 'Duties of Care in Negligence—Do They Really Exist?' (2004) 3 OJLS 417–41.

Nolan, D., 'Deconstructing the Duty of Care' (2013) 129 LQR 559.

Robertson, A., 'On the Function of the Law of Negligence' (2013) 33 OJLS 31.

Robertson, A., 'Policy-Based Reasoning in Negligence' (2013) 33 LS 119.

Rodger, A., 'Lord Macmillan's Speech in *Donoghue v Stevenson*' (1992) 108 LQR 236.

Steele, J., 'Duty of Care and Ethic of Care: Irreconcilable Difference?' in J. Richardson and E. Rackley (eds), *Feminist Perspectives on Tort* (Routledge, 2012)

Weir, T., 'The Staggering March of Negligence', in P. Cane and J. Stapleton (eds), *The Law of Obligations: Essays in Honour of John Fleming* (Oxford University Press, 1988), 97–140.

Winfield, P.H., 'Duty in Tortious Negligence' (1934) 34 Col LR 41.

Omissions

Honoré, T., 'Are Omissions Less Culpable?', in P. Cane and J. Stapleton (eds), *Essays for Patrick Atiyah* (Oxford University Press, 1992).

Lucy, W., *Philosophy of Private Law* (Oxford: Clarendon Press, 2007), chapter 5.

Smith, J. C., and Burns, P., '*Donoghue v Stevenson*—The Not So Golden Anniversary' (1983) 46 MLR 147.

Causation and Attribution or 'Remoteness'

Hart, H.L.A., and Honoré, T., *Causation in the Law* (2nd edn, Oxford University Press, 1985).

Hoffmann, Lord, 'Causation' (2005) 121 LQR 59.

Howarth, D., 'Complexity Strikes Back—Valuation in the House of Lords' (2000) 8 Tort L Rev 85.

Stapleton, J., 'The Gist of Negligence: Part II' (1988) 104 LQR 389.

Stapleton, J., 'Cause in Fact and the Scope of Liability for Consequences' (2003) 119 LQR 388.

Stauch, M., 'Risk and Remoteness of Damage in Negligence' (2001) 64 MLR 191.

Steele, J., 'Breach of Duty, Causing Harm? Recent Encounters Between Negligence and Risk' (2007) 60 CLP 296–337.

Williams, G., 'The Risk Principle' (1961) 77 LQR 179.

4

CAUSATION PROBLEMS

CENTRAL ISSUES

i) The second half of Chapter 3 introduced the essential elements of causation in relation to the tort of negligence. This chapter focuses on certain particularly vexed problems of causation, which have extended the courts and divided academic opinion. All concern multiple potential causes.

ii) The first issue relates to 'material contribution to damage'. Courts have clearly considered this a sufficient causal link under some circumstances. But the nature of the test remains in doubt. Some have argued that this is merely a response to difficulties of proof; others that it is a way of satisfying the 'but for' test; and others still that it captures a distinct form of causal connection.

iii) Courts have also considered what *evidence* of the relevant causal link will suffice. In *Fairchild v Glenhaven Funeral Services Ltd* [2002] UKHL 22; [2003] 1 AC 32, the House of Lords accepted that in certain circumstances, where even a material contribution cannot be shown, it will be sufficient for the claimant to show that a given breach has materially contributed to the *risk of injury*. This has unleashed a series of issues requiring attention in the highest court. Senior judges have spoken in terms of special principles

applying within the '*Fairchild* enclave'; but the boundaries of that enclave remain in some doubt.

iv) In *Barker v Corus* [2006] UKHL 20; [2006] 2 WLR 1027, the House of Lords decided that a defendant whose liability depends on contributing to the risk of injury should be liable only for a *proportion* of the injury suffered, to reflect their contribution. This proportionate approach was a marked departure for English law and appeared to treat the suffering of risk as the relevant damage. Section 3 of the Compensation Act 2006 ensures that in cases of mesothelioma, liability under *Fairchild* will be full, rather than proportionate; but the implications of *Barker* in jurisdictions where the statute does not apply, has been subject to further consideration by the Supreme Court; so too has the position in relation to insurers. Pursuing a just and practicable solution within the *Fairchild* enclave has required further innovation at the level of insurance law. Despite the unease of some judges, the Supreme Court has so far decided that, as the reasons for the *Fairchild* innovation are readily understandable, it is appropriate to 'keep digging', and to continue to innovate within the enclave.

v) A related problem is captured in the idea of **loss of chance**. In *Gregg v Scott* [2005] UKHL 2, the House of Lords refused to recognize increase in risk (or loss of opportunity) as damage in its own right. Traditional causal principles were applied, despite the then recent decision in *Barker v Corus*. The traditional 'all or nothing' approach was further reinforced by the House of Lords in *Rothwell Chemical and Insulating Company* [2007] UKHL 39, where increase in risk was held not to be actionable harm. The reinstatement of 'joint and several' (as opposed to proportionate) liability at common law within *Fairchild* referred to above means that there is no longer a need to reconcile these decisions with the proportional approach in *Barker*. However, the decision still seems to leave another anomaly in the law, since there are clearly cases where loss of the chance of *financial gain* will be compensated. The idea of liability based on contribution to risk or chance continues to recur.

1. MULTIPLE POTENTIAL CAUSES: SOME DIFFICULTIES

This chapter extends the analysis in the second half of Chapter 3. In that chapter, we introduced the traditional division of causal questions in tort into two stages. First, the defendant's breach must be a 'cause in fact' of the injury. Second, the law must determine whether the damage caused is 'too remote' from the breach. The first of these appears to be a 'filter', ensuring that all events designated by the law as causes have 'in fact' made a difference to the outcome suffered. The very description of this stage in terms of 'cause *in fact*' seems to make an appeal to something outside the law, whether that is philosophy, natural science, or ordinary language. In Chapter 3, we discussed various problems connected with 'intervening causes', and particularly the question whether the 'chain of causation' is broken. Here, our problems are concerned instead with multiple potential causes which may act either independently, or 'cumulatively', to cause damage to the claimant.

Traditionally, as we have seen, a 'cause in fact' is identified by asking what would have happened 'but for' the breach. The essence of the 'but for' question is that it seeks *necessary* causes, without which the damage would not have come about. In some cases, however, it is recognized that the 'but for' test does not yield satisfactory results. This is the case, for example, where more than one event would have been sufficient to cause the harm. Neither passes the 'but for' test, because in the absence of either of them, the harm would come about in any event through the intervention of the other. The law is, understandably, reluctant to conclude that neither event is a cause. In these circumstances, 'but for' is an unhelpful test, and the result is 'over-determined'. Maybe therefore not all 'causes' are 'necessary' causes.

What test can be used in place of 'but for' in such cases? One approach, which has been influential in academic circles but appears not to have been entertained by the courts, is to ask whether the breach of duty was a 'Necessary Element of a Sufficient Set' of factors leading to the harm: the 'NESS' test.[1] Since it has not been adopted by the courts, 'NESS' will not

---

[1] See particularly R. W. Wright, 'Causation in Tort Law' (1985) 73 Cal L Rev 1735.

be discussed at length here. However, we should note that it is designed to respond to cases where the result is 'over-determined', which is to say that there are 'duplicate' causes: for example, where two fires each reach a house and it is destroyed, and each fire would suffice to destroy it. The key to the NESS approach is to consider what would have occurred if one such duplicate cause was removed. Would the remaining factors, including the breach of duty, be *sufficient* to bring about the harm? If so, was the breach of duty a *necessary* element of that set of factors? NESS therefore maintains an element of necessity, but also incorporates an element of 'sufficiency'.

Continuing the focus on unnecessary causes, Jane Stapleton has suggested that as an overarching principle, the law should recognize as causes those factors which *contribute to* outcomes. This is designed to include both 'but for' causes, and causes that satisfy the 'NESS' criterion just sketched. Most recently, Stapleton has explained that some factors may properly be said to *operate upon* events (for example, D may literally exert force on an object which is also being subjected to other forces), without being either necessary, or sufficient, to bring about a result. These factors are properly called 'causes' of the events which lead to damage as, for example, where D pushes a car towards a cliff while several others do the same.[2] D's pushing is a cause of the car falling from the cliff because it contributes to the process by which this occurs. There need be no evidential difficulties for this to be selected as an appropriate analysis; and evidence that the other forces on the car would probably have sufficed without D's contribution does not displace its status as a part of the causal mechanism.

This opens up the possibility that the notion of a 'material contribution', which has been employed by the courts, is not merely a way of overcoming evidential difficulties. There is however a sting in the tail because Stapleton's approach reintroduces hypothetical reasoning to determine whether a contributory 'cause' of an event can *also* be said to have resulted in *damage* to the claimant. These are not questions which the law, so far, has dealt with separately. Rather, the question addressed by the law is, simply, whether the breach was a cause of relevant harm (which is within the scope of the duty, and/or not too remote). The new approach appears to introduce 'causal influence' ('cause in fact') as the first stage of three, rather than the traditional two, questions about causation of recoverable damage: 'causal influence'; 'but for' applied to damage suffered; and remoteness or, as Stapleton would prefer, 'scope of liability for consequences'.[3] We return to this account at the end of the next section, in relation to 'material contribution'.

Another possibility is to argue that far from there being three stages of enquiry, there are not even two stages in determining causation, one 'factual' and one 'legal'. Rather, there is only one enquiry, aimed at addressing whether the causal requirements of a specific legal rule have been satisfied. Writing in a non-judicial capacity, Lord Hoffmann has recently suggested that this is, in fact, how courts approach issues of causation; and that this explains why judges show little sign of sharing the concerns of academics who seek a general test for 'factual' causation.[4] Indeed, where the questions in this chapter are concerned, Lord Hoffmann has said that 'the concept of cause in fact seems to me to add nothing of value to the discussion'. When courts address causation, in his view, they simply seek to determine whether the particular requirements of a particular legal rule are satisfied. In other words,

[2] J. Stapleton, 'Unnecessary Causes' (2013) 129 LQR 39, includes this and a number of other examples; see also J. Stapleton, 'An "Extended But-for" Test for the Causal Relation' (2015) 35 OJLS 697.

[3] See the discussion in the final section of Chapter 3.

[4] Lord Hoffmann, 'Causation', in R. Goldberg (ed.) *Perspectives on Causation* (Hart Publishing, 2011).

it may not be going too far to say that the law does not adopt, and does not need, a theory of causation; though as Hart and Honoré proposed, it is influenced by the way that causal language and concepts are ordinarily used and understood.

2. 'MATERIAL CONTRIBUTION': BEFORE AND AFTER *FAIRCHILD*

In a number of cases, particularly when dealing with diseases caused by toxic agents, courts have determined that causation is established where the breach of duty can be shown to have made a 'material contribution' to the damage. The landmark case of *Fairchild v Glenhaven Funeral Services Ltd* [2002] UKHL 22; [2003] 1 AC 32 went further, holding that it would be sufficient *proof* of a causal link that the breach had made a material contribution to the *risk* of harm; but in doing this, it necessarily built upon and interpreted the idea of 'material contribution'. The starting point therefore is the 'material contribution' test itself.

2.1 MATERIAL CONTRIBUTION BEFORE *FAIRCHILD*

Bonnington Castings v Wardlaw [1956] AC 613

A steel dresser was exposed to silica dust at work, and as a result contracted pneumoconiosis. Part of his exposure (from use of swing grinders) was in breach of his employers' statutory duty under the Grinding of Metals (Miscellaneous Industries) Regulations 1925, because dust guards used with the grinders were not kept clear from obstruction. However, some of his exposure (caused by use of a pneumatic hammer) was treated as 'innocent' because no practicable precautions could have been taken to reduce the exposure.

Lord Reid, at 621–2

The medical evidence was that pneumoconiosis is caused by a gradual accumulation in the lungs of minute particles of silica inhaled over a period of years. That means, I think, that the disease is caused by the whole of the noxious material inhaled and, if that material comes from two sources, it cannot be wholly attributed to material from one source or the other. I am in agreement with much of the Lord President's opinion in this case, but I cannot agree that the question is: which was the most probable source of the respondent's disease, the dust from the pneumatic hammers or the dust from the swing grinders? It appears to me that the source of his disease was the dust from both sources, and the real question is whether the dust from the swing grinders materially contributed to the disease. What is a material contribution must be a question of degree. A contribution which comes within the exception de minimis non curat lex is not material, but I think that any contribution which does not fall within that exception must be material....

At 622

I think that the position can be shortly stated in this way. It may be that, of the noxious dust in the general atmosphere of the shop, more came from the pneumatic hammers than from the swing grinders, but I think it is sufficiently proved that the dust from the grinders made a substantial contribution. The respondent, however, did not only inhale the general atmosphere of the shop: when he was working his hammer his face was directly over it and it must often have happened that dust from his hammer substantially increased the concentration of noxious dust in the air which he inhaled. It is therefore probable that much the greater proportion of the noxious dust which he inhaled over the whole period came from the hammers. But, on the other hand, some certainly came from the swing grinders, and I cannot avoid the conclusion that the proportion which came from the swing grinders was not negligible. He was inhaling the general atmosphere all the time, and there is no evidence to show that his hammer gave off noxious dust so frequently or that the concentration of noxious dust above it when it was producing dust was so much greater than the concentration in the general atmosphere, that that special concentration of dust could be said to be substantially the sole cause of his disease.

The House of Lords held that there was no need to show that the contribution of the defendant's breach to the dust inhaled exceeded or even approached 50 per cent. It only had to make a 'material' contribution. In this case, it was recognized that more of the dust in the atmosphere came from the 'innocent' source, than from the breach of duty, but the defendants were still liable for the disease.

In the case of a progressive disease, greater exposure worsens the *disease*, not just the *risk* of the disease. Did the result in *Bonnington* depend on this? There is more than one potential answer. It may be that the House of Lords was simply saying that the greater exposure added to the harm suffered, by worsening the condition. That would make the notion of 'material contribution' entirely compatible with the 'but for' test: the tortious exposure is a 'but for' cause of some *part* of the harm. But alternatively, it may be that the tortiously created agent in the atmosphere was regarded as exerting a causal influence, regardless of whether the same harm *would* have been suffered without it. On that hypothesis, then 'material contribution' is an *alternative to* 'but for' causation, and making such a contribution is another way of being a 'cause' of an outcome. The fact that the defendant was liable in full to the claimant, rather than for a share in the damage suffered which would reflect the likely contribution of the tortious exposure, appears to point to the second interpretation. But this may simply reflect the fact that the defendants never raised the issue, and focused on resisting liability altogether. Because these issues were not addressed in *Bonnington*, it remains an ambiguous decision.

Non-progressive Diseases and Contribution to Risk of Harm: *McGhee v National Coal Board* [1973] 1 WLR 1

The plaintiff was employed emptying brick kilns in hot and dusty conditions, and developed dermatitis. He alleged that this was caused by the defendants' breach of duty in that he should have been provided with washing facilities, including showers. The plaintiff had been forced to cycle home caked in dust and sweat. The difficulty faced by the plaintiff was one of evidence. In the course of his judgment in *Fairchild v Glenhaven* (at [17]), Lord Bingham offered an extract from the first instance decision in *McGhee* on the part of the Lord Ordinary (Lord Kissen), which is reported at 1973 SC (HL) 37. It very effectively analyses the problem of evidence in *McGhee*.

In the House of Lords, Mr McGhee's appeal was allowed. But what exactly was the reason for that decision? Lord Reid appears to have decided to reject the very clear (and correct) distinction referred to by Lord Kissen (above). Lord Wilberforce on the other hand may have accepted that distinction, but decided that the particular facts of this case required that 'contribution to risk' was to be *treated* as being the same as contribution to injury. Lord Simon seems to have blurred the distinction altogether.

Lord Kissen

As I have maintained earlier, the pursuer, in order to succeed, must also establish, on a balance of probabilities, that this fault on the part of the defenders 'caused or materially contributed to his injury', that is to his contracting dermatitis. Dr Hannay's evidence was that he could not say that the provision of showers would probably have prevented the disease. He said that it would have reduced the risk materially but he would not go further than that. Dr Ferguson said that washing reduces the risk. Pursuer's counsel maintained that a material increase in the risk of contracting a disease was the same as a material contribution to contracting the disease and that Dr Hannay established this by his evidence. I think that defenders' counsel was correct when he said that the distinction drawn by Dr Hannay was correct and that an increase in risk did not necessarily mean a material contribution to the contracting of the disease. The two concepts are entirely different.…

Lord Reid, at 4–5

It has always been the law that a pursuer succeeds if he can show that fault of the defender caused or materially contributed to his injury. There may have been two separate causes but it is enough if one of the causes arose from fault of the defender. The pursuer does not have to prove that this cause would of itself have been enough to cause him injury. That is well illustrated by the decision of this House in *Bonnington Castings Ltd. v. Wardlaw* [1956] A.C. 613.…

In the present case the evidence does not show—perhaps no one knows—just how dermatitis of this type begins. It suggests to me that there are two possible ways. It may be that an accumulation of minor abrasions of the horny layer of the skin is a necessary precondition for the onset of the disease. Or it may be that the disease starts at one particular abrasion and then spreads, so that multiplication of abrasions merely increases the number of places where the disease can start and in that way increases the risk of its occurrence.

I am inclined to think that the evidence points to the former view. But in a field where so little appears to be known with certainty I could not say that that is proved. If it were, then this case would be indistinguishable from *Wardlaw's* case. But I think that in cases like this we must take a broader view of causation. The medical evidence is to the effect that the fact that the man had to cycle home caked with grime and sweat added materially to the risk that this disease might develop. It does not and could not explain just why that is so. But experience shows that it is so. Plainly that must be because what happens while the man remains unwashed can have a causative effect, though just how the cause operates is uncertain. I cannot accept the view expressed in the Inner House that once the man left the brick kiln he left behind the causes which made him liable to develop dermatitis.... Nor can I accept the distinction drawn by the Lord Ordinary between materially increasing the risk that the disease will occur and making a material contribution to its occurrence.

Lord Wilberforce, at 5–6

But the question remains whether a pursuer must necessarily fail if, after he has shown a breach of duty, involving an increase of risk of disease, he cannot positively prove that this increase of risk caused or materially contributed to the disease while his employers cannot positively prove the contrary. In this intermediate case there is an appearance of logic in the view that the pursuer, on whom the onus lies, should fail—a logic which dictated the judgments below. The question is whether we should be satisfied, in factual situations like the present, with this logical approach. In my opinion, there are further considerations of importance. First, it is a sound principle that where a person has, by breach of a duty of care, created a risk, and injury occurs within the area of that risk, the loss should be borne by him unless he shows that it had some other cause. Secondly, from the evidential point of view, one may ask, why should a man who is able to show that his employer should have taken certain precautions, because without them there is a risk, or an added risk, of injury or disease, and who in fact sustains exactly that injury or disease, have to assume the burden of proving more: namely, that it was the addition to the risk, caused by the breach of duty, which caused or materially contributed to the injury? In many cases, of which the present is typical, this is impossible to prove, just because medical opinion cannot segregate the causes of an illness between compound causes. And if one asks which of the parties, the workman or the employers, should suffer from this inherent evidential difficulty, the answer as a matter of policy or justice should be that it is the creator of the risk who, ex hypothesi must be taken to have foreseen the possibility of damage, who should bear its consequences.

Lord Simon of Glaisdale, at 8

... In my view, a failure to take steps which would bring about a material reduction of the risk involves, in this type of case, a substantial contribution to the injury.... .

McGhee treated contribution to the risk of a non-progressive disease as equivalent to material contribution to the disease, or to use Lord Reid's expression, to the 'development' of the disease. But the nature of the House of Lords' judgment did not clearly set out an intention to change the law. *McGhee* was a mystery at the time, as Smith LJ has recounted:

Smith, J, 'Causation—The Search for Principle' (2009) JPIL 101–13, at 106

Those of us who were in practice at the time were puzzled by that decision but we just had to see it as an extension of the usual rule on material contribution to the disease; no one had any idea when the extension would apply.

In the following case, the House of Lords confined the impact of *McGhee*, in a case concerning medical negligence.

Wilsher v Essex Area Health Authority [1988] AC 1078

A prematurely born baby suffered a condition known as RLF, which led to blindness. This condition may have been caused by the defendants' breach of duty in exposing the baby to excess oxygen. However, there were a number of other possible causes which were not related to the defendants' actions but were the natural consequence of premature birth. The House of Lords rejected an argument (accepted by the Court of Appeal) that *McGhee* should apply to assist the plaintiff, in that the defendants materially contributed to the risk that the baby would suffer RLF and could therefore be treated as materially contributing to the injury. The House of Lords endorsed the dissenting opinion of Sir Nicolas Browne-Wilkinson V-C in the Court of Appeal, as follows:

Sir Nicolas Browne-Wilkinson V-C

[1987] QB 730, at 771–2

There are a number of different agents which could have caused the RLF. Excess oxygen was one of them. The defendants failed to take reasonable precautions to prevent one of the possible causative agents (e g excess oxygen) from causing RLF. But no one can tell in this case whether excess oxygen did or did not cause or contribute to the RLF suffered by the plaintiff. The plaintiff's RLF may have been caused by some completely different agent or agents, e.g. hypercarbia, intraventricular haemorrhage, apnoea or patent ductus arteriosus. In addition to oxygen, each of those conditions has been implicated as a possible cause of RLF. This baby suffered from each of those conditions at various times in the first two months of his life. There is no satisfactory evidence that excess oxygen is more likely than any of those other four candidates to have caused RLF in this baby. To my mind, the occurrence of RLF following a failure to take a necessary precaution to prevent excess oxygen causing RLF provides no evidence and raises no presumption that it was excess oxygen rather than one or more of the four other possible agents which caused or contributed to RLF in this case. The position, to my mind, is wholly different from that in the *McGhee* case [1973] 1 WLR 1, where there was only one candidate (brick dust) which could have caused the dermatitis, and the failure to take a precaution against brick dust causing dermatitis was followed by dermatitis caused by brick dust. In such a case, I can see the common sense, if not the logic, of holding that, in the absence of any other evidence, the failure to take the precaution caused or contributed to the dermatitis . . . . A failure to take preventative measures against one out of five possible causes is no evidence as to which of those five caused the injury.

The House of Lords declined to extend *McGhee* to a case in which there were several possible causes for the injury other than exposure to the same substance or agent (on this occasion, excess oxygen; in the case of *McGhee*, coal dust) that is present through the breach of the defendant. This distinction is hard to explain. Indeed, no reason is given for supporting it. But it would preserve the authority of *McGhee* in single agent cases, and has been endorsed by a later House of Lords and by the Supreme Court in each of *Fairchild*, *Barker v Corus*, and *Sienkiewicz* (below).

In *Wilsher*, however, the House also cast doubt on the general authority of *McGhee*. Lord Bridge suggested (at 1090) that *McGhee* 'laid down no new principle of law whatever', and that the majority decision was based not on an adaptation of legal principle but on an 'inference of fact'. Thus considerable doubt surrounded the status of *McGhee*, until the case of *Fairchild* was heard in the House of Lords.

2.2 THE DECISION IN *FAIRCHILD*

Fairchild v Glenhaven Funeral Services Ltd [2002] UKHL 22; [2003] 1 AC 32

Fairchild restored the status of McGhee in single agent cases. It both (a) ensured that 'material contribution to damage' will be an important issue in future tort claims and (b) allowed the claimants to succeed although the only connection they could prove was a material contribution not to damage, but to the risk of damage. *Fairchild* is the key case around which the asbestos litigation in this chapter has developed.

The claimants had been exposed to asbestos dust by more than one employer in different periods of employment. All had developed mesothelioma, a fatal cancer. It was common ground that the mechanism initiating the genetic process which culminated in mesothelioma was unknown, and that the trigger might be a single, a few, or many fibres.[5] It was also accepted that once caused the injury was not aggravated by further exposure but that the greater the quantity of fibres inhaled the greater the risk of developing the disease. On the other hand, there is no known 'safe' level of exposure. The Court of Appeal, applying *Wilsher* rather than *McGhee*, concluded that the claimants had not established on the balance of probabilities which employer had caused their injury. The claimants therefore could not succeed in their actions. The House of Lords allowed appeals by the claimants.

Each of the five judges in *Fairchild* presented their views at substantial length. Our focus will be on the various ways in which their Lordships interpreted *McGhee*, and the ways in which they stated the limits within which the special approach to proof of causation derived from *McGhee* would be applied. Was it essential, for example, that this is a case where several *tortious* exposures each fails to pass the 'but for' test?

Lord Bingham of Cornhill

2 The essential question underlying the appeals may be accurately expressed in this way. If (1) C was employed at different times and for differing periods by both A and B, and (2) A and B were both subject to a duty to take reasonable care or to take all practicable measures to prevent C inhaling asbestos dust because of the known risk that asbestos dust (if inhaled) might cause a mesothelioma, and (3) both A and B were in breach of that duty in relation to C during the periods of C's employment by each of them with the result that during both periods C inhaled excessive quantities of asbestos dust, and (4) C is found to be suffering from a mesothelioma, and (5) any cause of C's mesothelioma other than the inhalation of asbestos

---

[5] The 'single fibre theory'—that one fibre can on its own cause the cancer—was not therefore essential to the outcome in *Fairchild*. Rather, it was essential that the disease was indivisible, and that medical science could not attach probabilities to the likelihood that the cancer was caused by any individual exposure. This is important now that the single fibre theory has been discredited. In *Durham v BAI (EL Trigger Litigation)* [2008] EWHC 1692 (QB), none of the experts who gave evidence accepted that theory.

dust at work can be effectively discounted, but (6) C cannot (because of the current limits of human science) prove, on the balance of probabilities, that his mesothelioma was the result of his inhaling asbestos dust during his employment by A or during his employment by B or during his employment by A and B taken together, is C entitled to recover damages against either A or B or against both A and B? To this question (not formulated in these terms) the Court of Appeal . . . gave a negative answer. It did so because, applying the conventional "but for" test of tortious liability, it could not be held that C had proved against A that his mesothelioma would probably not have occurred but for the breach of duty by A, nor against B that his mesothelioma would probably not have occurred but for the breach of duty by B, nor against A and B that his mesothelioma would probably not have occurred but for the breach of duty by both A and B together. So C failed against both A and B. The crucial issue on appeal is whether, in the special circumstances of such a case, principle, authority or policy requires or justifies a modified approach to proof of causation. . . .

Lord Bingham set out the facts of the case and analysed the relevant English case law on causation including *Bonnington* and *McGhee* (Section 2.1) before continuing:

21 This detailed review of *McGhee* permits certain conclusions to be drawn. First, the House was deciding a question of law. Lord Reid expressly said so, at p 3. The other opinions, save perhaps that of Lord Kilbrandon, cannot be read as decisions of fact or as orthodox applications of settled law. Secondly, the question of law was whether, on the facts of the case as found, a pursuer who could not show that the defender's breach had probably caused the damage of which he complained could none the less succeed. Thirdly, it was not open to the House to draw a factual inference that the breach probably had caused the damage: such an inference was expressly contradicted by the medical experts on both sides; and once that evidence had been given the crux of the argument before the Lord Ordinary and the First Division and the House was whether, since the pursuer could not prove that the breach had probably made a material contribution to his contracting dermatitis, it was enough to show that the breach had increased the risk of his contracting it. Fourthly, it was expressly held by three members of the House (Lord Reid at p 5, Lord Simon at p 8 and Lord Salmon at pp 12–13) that in the circumstances no distinction was to be drawn between making a material contribution to causing the disease and materially increasing the risk of the pursuer contracting it. Thus the proposition expressly rejected by the Lord Ordinary, the Lord President and Lord Migdale was expressly accepted by a majority of the House and must be taken to represent the ratio of the decision, closely tied though it was to the special facts on which it was based. Fifthly, recognising that the pursuer faced an insuperable problem of proof if the orthodox test of causation was applied, but regarding the case as one in which justice demanded a remedy for the pursuer, a majority of the House adapted the orthodox test to meet the particular case. The authority is of obvious importance in the present appeal since the medical evidence left open the possibility, as Lord Reid pointed out at p 4, that the pursuer's dermatitis could have begun with a single abrasion, which might have been caused when he was cycling home, but might equally have been caused when he was working in the brick kiln; in the latter event, the failure to provide showers would have made no difference. In *McGhee*, however, unlike the present appeals, the case was not complicated by the existence of additional or alternative wrongdoers.

Lord Bingham further outlined the facts and decision in *Wilsher v Essex Area Health Authority* (Section 2.1), and disapproved of the comments of Lord Bridge in relation to *McGhee*. Lord Bingham went on to explore 'the wider jurisprudence', considering case law from around the world on similar issues, before turning to policy issues:

Policy

33 The present appeals raise an obvious and inescapable clash of policy considerations. On the one hand are the considerations powerfully put by the Court of Appeal [2002] 1 WLR 1052, 1080, para 103 which considered the claimants' argument to be not only illogical but

"also susceptible of unjust results. It may impose liability for the whole of an insidious disease on an employer with whom the claimant was employed for quite a short time in a long working life, when the claimant is wholly unable to prove on the balance of probabilities that that period of employment had any causative relationship with the inception of the disease. This is far too weighty an edifice to build on the slender foundations of *McGhee v National Coal Board* [1973] 1 WLR 1, and Lord Bridge has told us in *Wilsher v Essex Area Health Authority* [1988] AC 1074 that *McGhee* established no new principle of law at all. If we were to accede to the claimants' arguments, we would be distorting the law to accommodate the exigencies of a very hard case. We would be yielding to a contention that all those who have suffered injury after being exposed to a risk of that injury from which someone else should have protected them should be able to recover compensation even when they are quite unable to prove who was the culprit...."

The Court of Appeal had in mind that in each of the cases discussed in paragraphs 14–21 above (*Wardlaw, Nicholson, Gardiner, McGhee*) there was only one employer involved. Thus there was a risk that the defendant might be held liable for acts for which he should not be held legally liable but no risk that he would be held liable for damage which (whether legally liable or not) he had not caused. The crux of cases such as the present, if the appellants' argument is upheld, is that an employer may be held liable for damage he has not caused. The risk is the greater where all the employers potentially liable are not before the court.... It can properly be said to be unjust to impose liability on a party who has not been shown, even on a balance of probabilities, to have caused the damage complained of.. On the other hand, there is a strong policy argument in favour of compensating those who have suffered grave harm, at the expense of their employers who owed them a duty to protect them against that very harm and failed to do so, when the harm can only have been caused by breach of that duty and when science does not permit the victim accurately to attribute, as between several employers, the precise responsibility for the harm he has suffered. I am of opinion that such injustice as may be involved in imposing liability on a duty-breaking employer in these circumstances is heavily outweighed by the injustice of denying redress to a victim. Were the law otherwise, an employer exposing his employee to asbestos dust could obtain complete immunity against mesothelioma (but not asbestosis) claims by employing only those who had previously been exposed to excessive quantities of asbestos dust. Such a result would reflect no credit on the law. It seems to me, as it did to Lord Wilberforce in *McGhee* [1973] 1 WLR 1, 7 that:

"the employers should be liable for an injury, squarely within the risk which they created and that they, not the pursuer, should suffer the consequence of the impossibility, foreseeably inherent in the nature of his injury, of segregating the precise consequence of their default."

Conclusion

34 To the question posed in paragraph 2 of this opinion I would answer that where conditions (1)–(6) are satisfied C is entitled to recover against both A and B. That conclusion is in

my opinion consistent with principle, and also with authority (properly understood). Where those conditions are satisfied, it seems to me just and in accordance with common sense to treat the conduct of A and B in exposing C to a risk to which he should not have been exposed as making a material contribution to the contracting by C of a condition against which it was the duty of A and B to protect him. I consider that this conclusion is fortified by the wider jurisprudence reviewed above. Policy considerations weigh in favour of such a conclusion. It is a conclusion which follows even if either A or B is not before the court. It was not suggested in argument that C's entitlement against either A or B should be for any sum less than the full compensation to which C is entitled, although A and B could of course seek contribution against each other or any other employer liable in respect of the same damage in the ordinary way. No argument on apportionment was addressed to the House.

I would in conclusion emphasise that my opinion is directed to cases in which each of the conditions specified in (1)–(6) of paragraph 2 above is satisfied and to no other case. It would be unrealistic to suppose that the principle here affirmed will not over time be the subject of incremental and analogical development. Cases seeking to develop the principle must be decided when and as they arise. For the present, I think it unwise to decide more than is necessary to resolve these three appeals which, for all the foregoing reasons, I concluded should be allowed.

Lord Hoffmann

61 What are the significant features of the present case? First, we are dealing with a duty specifically intended to protect employees against being unnecessarily exposed to the risk of (among other things) a particular disease. Secondly, the duty is one intended to create a civil right to compensation for injury relevantly connected with its breach. Thirdly, it is established that the greater the exposure to asbestos, the greater the risk of contracting that disease. Fourthly, except in the case in which there has been only one significant exposure to asbestos, medical science cannot prove whose asbestos is more likely than not to have produced the cell mutation which caused the disease. Fifthly, the employee has contracted the disease against which he should have been protected.

62 In these circumstances, a rule requiring proof of a link between the defendant's asbestos and the claimant's disease would, with the arbitrary exception of single-employer cases, empty the duty of content....

63 So the question of principle is this: in cases which exhibit the five features I have mentioned, which rule would be more in accordance with justice and the policy of common law and statute to protect employees against the risk of contracting asbestos-related diseases? One which makes an employer in breach of his duty liable for the employee's injury because he created a significant risk to his health, despite the fact that the physical cause of the injury may have been created by someone else? Or a rule which means that unless he was subjected to risk by the breach of duty of a single employer, the employee can never have a remedy? My Lords, as between the employer in breach of duty and the employee who has lost his life in consequence of a period of exposure to risk to which that employer has contributed, I think it would be both inconsistent with the policy of the law imposing the duty and morally wrong for your Lordships to impose causal requirements which exclude liability....

73 ...I would suggest that the rule now laid down by the House should be limited to cases which have the five features I have described.

74 That does not mean that the principle is not capable of development and application in new situations. As my noble and learned friend, Lord Rodger of Earlsferry has demonstrated, problems of uncertainty as to which of a number of possible agents caused an injury have required special treatment of one kind or another since the time of the Romans. But the problems differ quite widely and the fair and just answer will not always be the same. For example, in the famous case of *Sindell v Abbott Laboratories* (1980) 607 P 2d 924 the plaintiff had suffered pre-natal injuries from exposure to a drug which had been manufactured by any one of a potentially large number of defendants. The case bears some resemblance to the present but the problem is not the same. For one thing, the existence of the additional manufacturers did not materially increase the risk of injury. The risk from consuming a drug bought in one shop is not increased by the fact that it can also be bought in another shop. So the case would not fall within the *McGhee* principle. But the Supreme Court of California laid down the imaginative rule that each manufacturer should be liable in proportion to his market share. Cases like this are not before the House and should in my view be left for consideration when they arise. For present purposes, the *McGhee* principle is sufficient. I would therefore allow the appeals.

Lord Rodger of Earlsferry

168 … Following the approach in *McGhee* I accordingly hold that, by proving that the defendants individually materially increased the risk that the men would develop mesothelioma due to inhaling asbestos fibres, the claimants are taken in law to have proved that the defendants materially contributed to their illness.

Lord Nicholls of Birkenhead delivered a concurring judgment, also rejecting the idea that *McGhee* was based on a factual inference. Lord Hutton concurred in the result but thought *McGhee* was based on a factual inference.

The effect of *Fairchild* is that in certain circumstances, a claim is not defeated by the impossibility of proving that the breach of duty caused the injury suffered. But this works two ways: proof of causation must be *impossible*, for the claimant to benefit from the exceptional approach. In the course of reaching this conclusion, most members of the House of Lords (with the clear exception of Lord Hutton) accepted that the *McGhee* case laid down a principle of law, and did not rest purely on a 'robust' inference of fact. Lord Hope (who was Junior Counsel for the Coal Board in *McGhee*) has expressed the view that Lord Bingham in particular (at [21], extracted earlier) correctly interprets that case:

Lord Hope of Craighead, 'James McGhee—A Second Mrs Donoghue?' [2003] 62 CLJ 587–604, at 599

… Lord Bingham grasped the point of Lord Reid's judgment precisely when he said that, recognising that the pursuer faced an insuperable problem of proof if the orthodox test of causation was applied, but regarding the case as one in which justice demanded a remedy for the pursuer, a majority of the House adapted the orthodox test to meet the particular case. As Lord Rodger explained [para 142], what Lord Reid has done is to accept that the pursuer must prove that the defender's conduct materially contributed to the onset of the condition and then to hold, as a matter of law, that the proof that the defender's conduct materially increased the risk was sufficient for this onus to be discharged.

The House of Lords in *Fairchild* clearly noted that proof of material contribution to a *risk* of injury is not the same as proof of material contribution to the injury itself, particularly in the case of a non-progressive disease. This is the distinction that was blurred in *McGhee*. But the House accepted that *as a matter of law*, in certain circumstances proof of contribution to the risk will be sufficient evidence of causation. The pressing question was of course, 'in which circumstances?' The extracts above show that different members of the Court identified the relevant features in different ways.

2.3 APPLYING *FAIRCHILD*: UNCERTAINTY, SINGLE AGENTS, AND NON-TORTIOUS SOURCES

Immediately after *Fairchild*, what appeared to be the necessary features of a claim for the *Fairchild* approach to apply?

'Uncertainty'

First, it was plainly necessary to show that the state of scientific knowledge is such that proof of causation of damage is *impossible*. That was the 'rock of uncertainty', as Lord Bingham put it, on which the claim would otherwise founder. But the 'rock' of uncertainty is now the solid foundation on which a *Fairchild* claim must be based, for without it there can be no departure from the usual approach to proof of causation. Two challenges to this alleged impossibility have arisen. First, it has been suggested that understanding of mesothelioma has now developed to the point where the assumptions made in *Fairchild* are no longer correct. In particular, no experts now appear to accept the idea that a 'single fibre' can cause the cancer. The Supreme Court in *Sienkiewicz* (Section 2.4) decided that the essential element of uncertainty remains, because it cannot be established which fibres, and therefore which exposures, did in fact make such a contribution. Though some exposures may operate cumulatively, others may play no part at all in the causation of the disease (as opposed to, the risk).

In reaching this conclusion, the Supreme Court in *Sienkiewicz* dealt with a second challenge to the rock of uncertainty. To the extent that statistical estimates as to contribution to *risk* can be devised in order to determine contribution between liable parties, why can these same estimates not be used to demonstrate whether *or not* the usual 'but for' test has been passed, thus removing the very uncertainty on which *Fairchild* is built? This problem too was resolved in the claimants' favour in *Sienkiewicz*. The possibility of generating purely statistical estimates as to risks does not erode the rock of uncertainty on which a *Fairchild* claim is based.

Single Agents

It was also clear after *Fairchild* that the *McGhee*–*Fairchild* approach will not be applied to a case like *Wilsher*, in which the claimant is exposed to a variety of different risks. It will apply only where the claimant's injury was caused by exposure to the same type of risk (or the same 'noxious substance') to which the defendant exposed him or her. That position was approved in *Barker* and it is plain that it remains the case, even in the absence of a convincing explanation. Lord Phillips, in *Sienkiewicz* ([104]), floated the idea that whatever the initial reason for adopting it, the 'single agent' criterion is now justified by the information that mesothelioma is probably caused by the interaction of a number of asbestos fibres, potentially from different sources.

'Innocent' or Self-imposed Periods of Exposure

In *Fairchild*, Lord Rodger specifically reserved his judgment on one particular issue. This issue was of central importance to later developments.

> 170 . . . the principle applies where the other possible source of the claimant's injury is a similar wrongful act or omission of another person, but it can also apply where, as in *McGhee*, the other possible source of the injury is a similar, but lawful, act or omission of the same defendant. I reserve my opinion as to whether the other possible source of the injury is a similar but lawful act or omission of someone else or a natural occurrence.

This issue was not resolved in any of the judgments. But the remarks suggested that if there is a case where one former employer who exposed the claimant to asbestos dust can be shown to have been *not negligent* (for example because they took proper precautions, or because their exposure of the claimant took place before the date on which such exposure could be said to give rise to foreseeable harm), then the solution reached in *Fairchild* may not apply.

These issues were core to the litigation in both *Barker v Corus* and *Sienkiewicz v Greif* (below). In the latter case, the tortious exposure was at a very low level and was assessed by the judge to be much less likely to have caused the cancer than the background, non-tortious sources. In both *Barker* (where the answer was balanced by a proportionate approach to damages), and *Sienkiewicz* (where it was not), this question too has been answered in favour of claimants.

2.4 APPORTIONMENT AND NON-TORTIOUS POTENTIAL CAUSES

In neither *Bonnington*, *McGhee*, nor *Fairchild* was the House of Lords invited to address the issue of apportionment. This is specifically pointed out in the judgment of Lord Bingham, at [34]: 'no argument was addressed to the House that . . . there should be an apportionment of damages because the breaches of duty of a number of employers had contributed to cause the disease . . .' (the full paragraph is extracted in Section 2.2). But why should Lord Bingham have mentioned apportionment at all? As we have explained, mesothelioma (unlike asbestosis for example, or progressive deafness caused by occupational exposure)[6] is an indivisible disease. Successive defendants did not worsen the disease by further exposure, though they did add to the risk.[7] Once the cancer begins to form, further exposures do no further harm. This was not, therefore, a case like *Bonnington*.

---

[6] *Holtby v Brigham and Cowan* [2000] 3 All ER 423; *Thompson v Smith Shiprepairers* [1984] QB 405, respectively.
[7] As understanding of mesothelioma grows, it becomes harder to state with certainty what the role of a single fibre is. It seems that an accumulation of fibres may be required. That means that the product of a number of different exposures may interact. But this is not the same as individual defendants adding a particular proportion to the injury itself.

The controversy that would attach to apportionment in such a case is encapsulated in the following extract, which followed the Court of Appeal judgment in *Barker v Corus*, but pre-dates the House of Lords' judgment (extracted below). The author responds to the comment of Lord Bingham quoted above, and states the orthodox view which was later disturbed by *Barker*.

C. McCaul, '*Holtby* and the End Game' (2006) JPIL 6–11, 7

It is impossible to understand this observation [of Lord Bingham] in the light of legal principles as they currently stand. Apportionment of damage does not arise because there has been a breach of duty by a number of different defendants. To adopt such an approach is to look at the problem from the wrong end of the telescope. It is necessary to look at the damage, not the breach, in order to see whether apportionment is appropriate. If the damage is indivisible, then it matters not how many defendants' breaches of duty have caused it.

In *Barker v Corus* [2006] UKHL 20, the House of Lords stepped away from this orthodoxy. *Barker* appears to have been the first UK case to apportion an indivisible injury.[8] In fact, the majority of the court appears to have apportioned damages on the basis that it was able to apportion not the injury, but the risk to which the defendants had contributed in allegedly identifiable proportions. We will soon analyse the reasoning which led to this conclusion; and then consider the immediate legislative rejection of what the House of Lords had done (section 3 of the Compensation Act 2006); and subsequent reinterpretations as a matter of common law, in the *Trigger Litigation* and *IEG v Zurich Insurance plc*.

Apportionment before *Barker*

The *Holtby* case marks an important development but it is important to note that it does not deal with the same issue as *Fairchild*. The key difference is that it concerned a progressive disease. The harm could therefore be divided: each defendant had—provided scientific evidence could supply appropriate guidance—caused an identifiable injury which was less than the whole. This approach could in principle apply to facts like those in *Bonnington* itself.

Holtby v Brigham & Cowan (Hull) Ltd [2000] 3 All ER 423

The claimant was exposed to asbestos dust for several years in his work as a marine fitter. For about half of the relevant period, he worked for the defendant. He developed asbestosis. Asbestosis, unlike mesothelioma, is a progressive disease. It is made worse by each exposure. At first instance, Judge Altman held that the defendant was liable only for the extent that he had contributed to the disability. Rejecting an approach based simply on the length of exposure, he reduced the general damages by 25 per cent.

The Court of Appeal upheld the decision of Judge Altman. The court referred to the judgment of Mustill J in *Thompson v Smiths Shiprepairers* [1984] QB 405 (extracted in Chapter 7).

---

[8] In *Rahman v Arearose* [2001] QB 351, the Court of Appeal accepted that a psychiatric disorder was, on the facts, divisible damage. Though controversial, this is quite different. The Court of Appeal was persuaded on the basis of expert evidence that the various personality disorders from which the claimant suffered could be separated and attributed to different causes.

Here, there had been exposure over a number of years to dangerous noise levels leading to deafness. Since a substantial part of the *damage* could be shown to have been done before the time that the defendants were in breach of duty, Mustill J suggested that the right approach was to attempt an apportionment of damage accordingly. In *Holtby*, the judge had been right to err on the side of the claimant in making the apportionment, so that a reduction of 25 per cent could not be criticized. Clarke LJ dissented, on the basis that this placed too great a burden on the claimant. He pointed out that if this was the right approach it was odd that it had not been mentioned by any of the judges in the cases of *Bonnington* or *Nicholson* quoted earlier (at [34]).

However, *Holtby* has not been seriously doubted in subsequent decisions, and Smith LJ has suggested that if a case like *Bonnington* was argued again today, it could lead to an apportionment of damages between tortious and non-tortious causes (provided there is sufficient evidence to attempt a quantification).[9] This suggests an interpretation of *Bonnington* in which it is the progressiveness of the disease which made it possible to say that there had been a material contribution from the breach. By the same token, if scientific evidence can quantify this contribution, then damages will be apportioned accordingly: this would make it a *Holtby*-style case. But this has no application to *Fairchild*, which deals with a different problem. This should help to indicate the controversial nature of the decision in *Barker*.

Barker v Corus [2006] UKHL 20; [2006] 2 WLR 1027

Like *Fairchild*, in the appeals heard here, the claimants (or their husbands) had contracted mesothelioma through occupational exposure to asbestos dust over a number of years. Unlike *Fairchild*, in addition to periods of exposure on the part of employers including the defendant, in one case the deceased had also been self-employed for a period of time, and had been exposed to asbestos dust during this period of self-employment. Thus the question arose whether the *Fairchild* approach to proof of causation could apply where the disease had not necessarily been caused by a breach of duty, and where it might have been caused by the actions of the claimant himself. At first instance, Moses J had determined that this possibility was adequately dealt with by reducing damages on the basis of contributory negligence. He applied a reduction of 20 per cent.

The second issue to be resolved was the general issue of apportionment. The defendant argued that the damages awarded should have been reduced to reflect the limited extent to which the defendant could be proven to be responsible for the damage suffered. The trial judge, Moses J, held that there should be no apportionment of damages. The Court of Appeal upheld his decision on both issues.

Issue 1: Self-exposure

The House of Lords had no difficulty in agreeing with the Court of Appeal in relation to self-exposure. Where there was a period of self-employment, this did not defeat the *Fairchild* principle, since that was in any case based on *McGhee* where there was a potential non-tortious cause. In developing this point, the House also explicitly endorsed the 'single agent' rule, as a way of limiting the operation of the *Fairchild* principle. In single agent cases, there is no need to show that all of the exposures were tortious. Self-exposure which was also negligent (as here) would however be the basis for a reduction in damages pursuant to

9 Janet Smith, 'Causation—The Search for Principle' [2009] JPIL 101–13.

the contributory negligence legislation (Chapter 5). The difference is that the damages are reduced to reflect the claimant's share of responsibility; the defendant's liability is, other than this, for the full damage suffered, and not for their contribution to the overall risk.

Although this issue did not dominate the judgments of the House of Lords in *Barker*, it subsequently became very important. The House in *Barker* doubtless felt their judgment on this point was balanced by their approach on the second issue; now, however, that aspect of their judgment is not to be followed in cases to which section 3 of the Compensation Act applies.

Issue 2: Apportionment

This issue occupied far more of their Lordships' attention. Most of the majority judges (though not Baroness Hale who agreed in the outcome purely on grounds of fairness and policy—as to which views have of course differed) adopted a view of *Fairchild* which would make it possible to distinguish the existing case law on indivisible damage. That is, they said that in *Fairchild*, the House of Lords had *not* held that 'material contribution to risk' was treated as equivalent, within the exception, to 'material contribution to damage'. Lord Rodger, in dissent, argued persuasively that this is precisely what had been said in *Fairchild* and that this must be so, because their Lordships had all applied *McGhee*, which proceeded on this basis. Lord Rodger's judgment later appeared to be vindicated in *Sienkiewicz* and *Trigger*. Nevertheless, the outcome in *Barker* was recognized as still binding, outside the ambit of section 3 of the Compensation Act 2006, in *IEG v Zurich Insurance plc* [2015] UKSC 33.

Lord Hoffmann and Lord Scott took a novel approach. They suggested that since *exposure to risk* is itself the only harm which can be shown to have been caused by the defendants' breach of duty, risk of harm is the damage which they must compensate; and, further, that this was the basis of the decision in *Fairchild*.

Lord Hoffmann, *Barker v Corus*

[31] My Lords, the reasoning of Moses J and the Court of Appeal would be unanswerable if the House of Lords in *Fairchild v Glenhaven Funeral Services Ltd* had proceeded upon the fiction that a defendant who had created a material risk of mesothelioma was deemed to have caused or materially contributed to the contraction of the disease. The disease is undoubtedly an indivisible injury and the reasoning of Devlin LJ in *Dingle v Associated Newspapers Ltd* would have been applicable. But only Lord Hutton and Lord Rodger adopted this approach. The other members of the House made it clear that the creation of a material risk of mesothelioma was sufficient for liability . . .

Creating a risk as damage

[35] Consistency of approach would suggest that if the basis of liability is the wrongful creation of a risk or chance of causing the disease, the damage which the defendant should be regarded as having caused is the creation of such a risk or chance. If that is the right way to characterize the damage, then it does not matter that the disease as such would be indivisible damage. Chances are infinitely divisible and different people can be separately responsible to a greater or lesser degree for the chances of an event happening, in the way

that a person who buys a whole book of tickets in a raffle has a separate and larger chance of winning the prize than a person who has bought a single ticket.…

Fairness

…

[43] In my opinion, the attribution of liability according to the relative degree of contribution to the chance of the disease being contracted would smooth the roughness of the justice which a rule of joint and several liability creates. The defendant was a wrongdoer, it is true, and should not be allowed to escape liability altogether, but he should not be liable for more than the damage which he caused and, since this is a case in which science can deal only in probabilities, the law should accept that position and attribute liability according to probabilities. The justification for the joint and several liability rule is that if you caused harm, there is no reason why your liability should be reduced because someone else also caused the same harm. But when liability is exceptionally imposed because you may have caused harm, the same considerations do not apply and fairness suggests that if more than one person may have caused the harm, liability should be divided according to the probability that one or other caused the harm.

Quantification

[48] Although the *Fairchild* exception treats the risk of contracting mesothelioma as the damage, it applics only when the disease has actually been contracted. Mr Stuart-Smith, who appeared for Corus, was reluctant to characterise the claim as being for causing a risk of the disease because he did not want to suggest that someone could sue for being exposed to a risk which had not materialised. But in cases which fall within the *Fairchild* exception, that possibility is precluded by the terms of the exception. It applies only when the claimant has contracted the disease against which he should have been protected. And in cases outside the exception, as in *Gregg v Scott*, a risk of damage or loss of a chance is not damage upon which an action can be founded.

Lord Scott also considered the damage caused by the defendants in this case to be increase in the risk of mesothelioma. Baroness Hale took an approach which was based on 'fairness', and not on recasting the nature of the damage caused. This approach was quoted with approval by Lord Mance in *IEG v Zurich* (below).

Baroness Hale

126. But in the Fairchild situation we have yet another development. For the first time in our legal history, persons are made liable for damage even though they may not have caused it at all, simply because they have materially contributed to the risk of causing that damage. Mr Stuart-Smith does not quarrel with the principle in Fairchild. He simply argues that it does not follow from the imposition of liability in such a case that each should be liable for the whole. I agree with the majority of your Lordships that indeed it does not follow. There is in this situation no magic in the indivisibility of the harm. It is not being said that each has caused or materially contributed to *the harm*. It can only be said that each has materially contributed to the *risk of harm*. The harm may be indivisible but the material

contribution to the risk can be divided. There exists a sensible basis for doing so. Is it fair to do so?

127. In common with the majority of your Lordships, I think that it is fair to do so. On the one hand, the defendants are, by definition, in breach of their duties towards the claimants or the deceased. But then so are many employers, occupiers or other defendants who nevertheless escape liability altogether because it cannot be shown that their breach of duty caused the harm suffered by the claimant. For as long as we have rules of causation, some negligent (or otherwise duty-breaking) defendants will escape liability. The law of tort is not (generally) there to punish people for their behaviour. It is there to make them pay for the damage they have done. These Fairchild defendants may not have caused any harm at all. They are being made liable because it is thought fair that that they should make at least some contribution to redressing the harm that may have flowed from their wrongdoing. It seems to me most fair that the contribution they should make is in proportion to the contribution they have made to the risk of that harm occurring.

Lord Rodger (dissenting)

[89] As Mr Gore QC rightly emphasised on behalf of Mr Patterson, the real reason why the defendants want to get rid of liability in solidum is that quite a number of the potential defendants and their insurers in the field of mesothelioma claims are insolvent. So, if held liable in solidum, solvent defendants or, more particularly, their insurers will often find that they have to pay the whole of the claimant's damages without in fact being able to obtain a contribution from the other wrongdoers or their insurers, if any. So their only hope of minimising the amount they have to pay out by way of damages is to have liability to the claimant apportioned among the wrongdoers. Therefore they are asking for the introduction of apportionment because of this entirely contingent aspect of the situation regarding mesothelioma claims. If Fairchild-exception claims had first arisen in an area where the wrongdoers and their insurers were in good financial heart, matters could have been resolved satisfactorily for all concerned on the basis of liability in solidum and the use of the 1978 Act.

[90] Of course, it may seem hard if a defendant is held liable in solidum even though all that can be shown is that he made a material contribution to the risk that the victim would develop mesothelioma. But it is also hard—and settled law—that a defendant is held liable in solidum even though all that can be shown is that he made a material, say 5%, contribution to the claimant's indivisible injury. That is a form of rough justice which the law has not hitherto sought to smooth, preferring instead, as a matter of policy, to place the risk of the insolvency of a wrongdoer or his insurer on the other wrongdoers and their insurers. Now the House is deciding that, in this particular enclave of the law, the risk of the insolvency of a wrongdoer or his insurer is to bypass the other wrongdoers and their insurers and to be shouldered entirely by the innocent claimant. As a result, claimants will often end up with only a small proportion of the damages which would normally be payable for their loss. The desirability of the courts, rather than Parliament, throwing this lifeline to wrongdoers and their insurers at the expense of claimants is not obvious to me.

As already mentioned, the effect of this decision on claims for mesothelioma was immediately reversed by legislation, which sought to ensure that liability under Fairchild, like liability under McGhee, would be joint and several. Apart from this reversal, the section also provides that those defendants who are thereby exposed to an inequitable burden of liability because of insolvent liability insurers may be indemnified in a manner to be settled. The first step is to turn back the clock; but provision for greater fairness to liable parties can be developed. As the court in *Barker* will have been well aware from counsels' argument, the insurers had already responded to *Fairchild* through the introduction of a voluntary Code of Practice on apportionment of *Fairchild* liabilities between insurers according to the rough measure of time on cover in respect of tortious exposure.[10]

Compensation Act 2006

3 Mesothelioma: damages

(1) This section applies where:

    (a) a person ('the responsible person') has negligently or in breach of statutory duty caused or permitted another person ('the victim') to be exposed to asbestos,

    (b) the victim has contracted mesothelioma as a result of exposure to asbestos.

    (c) because of the nature of mesothelioma and the state of medical science, it is not possible to determine with certainty whether it was the exposure mentioned in paragraph (a) or another exposure which caused the victim to become ill, and

    (d) the responsible person is liable in tort, by virtue of the exposure mentioned in paragraph (a), in connection with damage caused to the victim by the disease (whether by reason of having materially increased a risk or for any other reason).

(2) The responsible person shall be liable—

    (a) in respect of the whole damage caused to the victim by the disease (irrespective of whether the victim was also exposed to asbestos—

        (i) other than by the responsible person, whether or not in circumstances in which another person has liability in tort, or,

        (ii) by the responsible person in circumstances in which he has no liability in tort), and

    (b) jointly and severally with other liable person.

(3) Subsection (2) does not prevent—

    (a) one responsible person from claiming a contribution from another, or,

    (b) a finding of contributory negligence.

(4) In determining the extent of contributions of different responsible persons in accordance with subsection (3)(a), a court shall have regard to the relative lengths of the periods of exposure for which each was responsible; but this subsection shall not apply—

    (a) if or to the extent that responsible persons agree to apportion responsibility amongst themselves on some other basis, or

    (b) if or to the extent that the court thinks that another basis for determining contributions is more appropriate in the circumstances of a particular case.

...

[10] ABI, *Guidelines for Apportioning and Handling Employers' Liability Mesothelioma Claims* (2003); R. Merkin, 'Insurance Claims and *Fairchild*' (2004) 120 LQR 233–41.

(7) The Treasury may make regulations about the provision of compensation to a responsible person where—

   (a) he claims, or would claim, a contribution from another responsible person in accordance with subsection (3)(a), but

   (b) he is unable or likely to be unable to obtain the contribution, because an insurer of the other responsible person is unable or likely to be unable to satisfy the claim for a contribution.

Regulations have been produced in respect of section 3(7), enabling a person who is liable in tort within the terms of section 3 (or their insurer) to recover a contribution from the Financial Services Compensation Scheme. This scheme is funded by levies on insurers.

Sienkiewicz v Greif (UK) Ltd; Willmore v Knowsley MBC [2011] UKSC 10; [2011] 2 AC 229

This was by no means the end of the asbestos litigation. The Supreme Court was required to consider the question of non-tortious exposures again in these joined appeals, which illustrate starkly the implications of our earlier observation that there is no safe level of exposure to asbestos. *Willmore v Knowsley BC* differs from all the cases of mesothelioma considered so far in that it was not a case of occupational exposure. The particular exposures which formed the basis of the claim were argued to have occurred while the deceased had been at a school operated by the defendant, and these were argued to have materially increased the risk of contracting the disease. There is a strong sense from the judgments of the Supreme Court that the judge's decision to accept the claimant's view of the evidence was generous (Baroness Hale described it as 'heroic'), but the findings of fact were not disturbed.

Sienkiewicz v Greif (UK) Ltd was an action brought on behalf of the deceased's estate by her daughter. Mrs Costello had been an office worker from 1966 until 1984 at factory premises of the defendant in Ellesmere Port. Although she chiefly spent her time in an office block, her duties took her all over the factory and she spent some time in areas which were contaminated with asbestos. The judge had found the defendants to be in breach of duty in exposing the deceased to asbestos dust throughout the years of her employment. However, he also found that like all inhabitants of Ellesmere Port, Mrs Costello had been exposed to a low level of asbestos in the general atmosphere. Since it is accepted that mesothelioma may be triggered by low-level exposures, though of course the risk increases with greater levels, there was thus a significant potential cause of mesothelioma which did not arise from the tort of an employer.

The defendant argued that in these circumstances, where there was only one employer,[11] it ought to be possible to show on the balance of probabilities whether the disease was or was not caused by the tortious exposure. Thus, there was no need to apply the special rule introduced by *Fairchild*, and the claimant should have to prove that the tort of the defendant had caused the deceased's mesothelioma on the normal 'balance of probabilities' test. In order

---

[11] As pointed out by Jane Stapleton, to approach the case as involving a 'single exposure' was probably somewhat misleading—the more so in the case of *Willmore*. At least some of the 'background' or environmental exposure may itself be tortious: J. Stapleton, 'Factual Causation, Mesothelioma and Statistical Validity' (2012) LQR 221.

to discharge this test, she must show that the occupational exposure had more than doubled her risk of contracting the disease. The judge accepted the defendants' argument, and carried out an assessment of the cumulative occupational and environmental exposures, concluding that it could not be shown in this case that the occupational exposure had more than doubled the risk. The claimant appealed, arguing both that the judge had been wrong in law, and that his assessment of the contribution to risk was incorrect. The 'doubling of risk' argument had not been set out in the original defence, and the claimant therefore had not obtained her own expert advice on the point.

In the Court of Appeal, Smith LJ said that she could not rule out that the House of Lords in *Fairchild* might have agreed with a proposition that in the case of a sole employer and a non-occupational exposure, the *Fairchild* exception was not required. However, she also argued that section 3 now prevented this route from being taken: Parliament allowed claimants to establish causation either by reason of 'material contribution to risk', or 'for any other reason' (section 3(1)(d)). She considered it to be clear from the statutory wording (extracted above) that proof of contribution to risk would now be sufficient proof of causation in any mesothelioma case in which conditions (a)–(c) of section 3(1) were satisfied, whether or not the House of Lords would have applied the test to the case in hand.

In the Supreme Court, the Justices rejected Smith LJ's reading of section 3. The change effected by the legislation came in section 3(2), and it ensured that liability, once established, was 'joint and several'. There was no intention to change the basis on which a causal link was established. The Supreme Court, therefore, set about assessing what *Fairchild* and *Barker* could be said to have established, where not all potential causes are tortious and most particularly, where the contribution of the tortious cause to the overall risk is relatively small. Two key issues emerged. First, does *Fairchild* apply to cases where there is only one tortious exposure?[12] Second, in such a case, can the same statistical evidence, which appears to be capable of being used to estimate the defendant's contribution to the risk of damage, also be used to establish whether the tortious exposure did, or did not, cause the damage?

Single Tortious Exposure

The Supreme Court determined that *Fairchild* applies to cases where only one source of the exposure is tortious, and where the contribution of that exposure is at a relatively low level. Members of the Court displayed varying degrees of contentment or unease with this result, but acknowledged that it follows logically from the reasoning in *Fairchild* and *Barker*. Perhaps the most willing to accept the implications was Lord Rodger.

Lord Rodger, *Sienkiewicz v Greif*

141 The response of English law to the problem posed by the rock of uncertainty in mesothelioma cases is…to be found in the combination of the common law, as laid down in *Fairchild* and *Barker* and section 3 of the 2006 Act. Defendants whose breaches of duty materially increase the risk that the victim will develop mesothelioma are liable jointly and severally for the damage which the victim suffers if he does in fact develop mesothelioma. This is the current version of the *Fairchild* exception, as it applies in cases of mesothelioma.

12 We noted earlier that this may not entirely capture the facts of these cases, but only one tort is argued before the court and it could be that only one proposed tortfeasor is within the claimant's knowledge.

142 Of course, the *Fairchild* exception was created only because of the present state of medical knowledge. If the day ever dawns when medical science can identify which fibre or fibres led to the malignant mutation and the source from which that fibre or those fibres came, then the problem which gave rise to the exception will have ceased to exist. At that point, by leading the appropriate medical evidence, claimants will be able to prove, on the balance of probability, that a particular defendant or particular defendants were responsible. So the *Fairchild* exception will no longer be needed. But, unless and until that time comes, the rock of uncertainty which prompted the creation of the *Fairchild* exception will remain.

Lord Brown accepted that this was the logical consequence of the law's development to date, but was far from content with the result.

Lord Brown, *Sienkiewicz v Greif*

185 In short, the die was inexorably cast in *Fairchild* —although, as already suggested, it is doubtful if that was then recognised and it is noteworthy too that, even when in *Barker* it came to be recognised, it was then thought palatable only assuming that compensation was going to be assessed on an aliquot basis. Parliament, however, then chose—although, of course, only in mesothelioma cases—to go the whole hog.

186 The result must surely be this. As I began by saying, mesothelioma cases are in a category all their own. Whether, however, this special treatment is justified may be doubted. True, as Lord Phillips PSC observes at the outset of his judgment, mesothelioma is indeed a hideous disease. (And it is perhaps also the case, as Lord Phillips PSC suggests at para 104, that mesothelioma, after all, may result from the cumulative effect of exposures to asbestos dust.) The unfortunate fact is, however, that the courts are faced with comparable rocks of uncertainty in a wide variety of other situations too and that to circumvent these rocks on a routine basis—let alone if to do so would open the way, as here, to compensation on a full liability basis—would turn our law upside down and dramatically increase the scope for what hitherto have been rejected as purely speculative compensation claims. Although, therefore, mesothelioma claims must now be considered from the defendant's standpoint a lost cause, there is to my mind a lesson to be learned from losing it: the law tampers with the "but for" test of causation at its peril.

Statistical Evidence

Lord Phillips pointed out what he considered to be a 'conundrum' arising from the defendants' arguments. If the state of medical knowledge makes it impossible to ascertain the cause of the claimant's mesothelioma, how is it nevertheless possible to make findings of fact based on statistical evidence, quantifying the defendant's particular 'contribution to the risk'? In other words, why cannot the same kind of evidence be used to estimate whether or not, on the balance of probabilities, a particular party's breach of duty has caused the cancer, in the usual way? If such evidence is accepted in relation to the contribution to risk, why does it not erode the 'rock of uncertainty'? If this is accepted, the rationale for *Fairchild* disappears altogether: there would be no impossibility of proof, because evidence of probability would exist. All of the Justices rejected these suggestions. Importantly, Lord Phillips made a distinction between 'material contribution' cases, and cases where 'but for' causation must be proved on the balance of probabilities, where in his view a 'doubling of risk' test may be applied.

Lord Phillips, *Sienkiewicz v Greif*

90 ... I see no scope for the application of the "doubles the risk" test in cases where two agents have operated cumulatively and simultaneously in causing the onset of a disease. In such a case the rule in *Bonnington* applies. Where the disease is indivisible, such as lung cancer, a defendant who has tortiously contributed to the cause of the disease will be liable in full. Where the disease is divisible, such as asbestosis, the tortfeasor will be liable in respect of the share of the disease for which he is responsible.

This clarifies that 'material contribution' is not *merely* applicable in cases of divisible disease; it applies also in cases of indivisible injury, though the effects of showing a 'material contribution' vary between divisible and indivisible injuries. It suggests that 'material contribution' is a test which is *appropriate to* certain sorts of case, and that it does not merely apply because of evidential difficulties. That in itself is an important recognition. We return to the point in the final part of this section.

Epidemiological Evidence

Lord Phillips debated the applicability of epidemiological evidence at some length, concluding that it was not sufficiently reliable in this particular instance to form the basis of conclusions as to causation. The other Justices were less convinced that the discussion needed to be had; but their observations are potentially significant for other 'toxic tort' cases. The key issues are outlined by Lord Dyson in the following discussion.

Lord Dyson, *Sienkiewicz v Greif*

216 Lord Rodger JSC draws a distinction between claimant A, who proves on the balance of probability that a defendant *probably* injured him, and claimant B, who proves on the balance of probability that a defendant *actually* injured him. He says that, as a matter of law, claimant B will succeed but claimant A will fail. A claimant who seeks to prove his case on the balance of probability in reliance entirely on statistical evidence will inevitably fail, since he is able to do no more than prove on the balance of probability that the defendant probably injured him.

217 I am grateful to Lord Rodger JSC for drawing attention to the article by Steve Gold, "Causation in Toxic Torts: Burdens of Proof, Standards of Persuasion, and Statistical Evidence" (1986) 96 Yale LJ 376. The article distinguishes between "fact probability" and "belief probability". The former is a more than 50% statistical probability of an event having occurred. An illustration of this is the 75% probability that the victim was run down by a blue cab in the example given by Brachtenbach J in *Herskovits v Group Health Cooperative of Puget Sound* (1983) 664 P 2d 474: see para 95 of Lord Phillips PSC's judgment. The latter is a more than 50% *belief* in the decision-maker that a knowable fact has been established. Mr Gold points out that, particularly in toxic tort cases, US courts have often "collapsed" the distinction between fact probability and belief probability and simply asked the question whether the fact that the claimant seeks to prove has been established as "more likely than not".

218 In my view, this is an important distinction and it is of particular relevance in relation to causation in toxic torts. It is often the basic impossibility of proving individual causation which distinguishes toxic tort cases from ordinary personal injury cases. As Mr Gold points out, epidemiology is based on the study of populations, not individuals. It seeks to establish associations between alleged causes and effects. With proper scientific interpretation, these correlations lend great weight to an inference of causation. However, in an individual case, epidemiology alone cannot *conclusively* prove causation. At best, it can establish only a certain probability that a randomly selected case of disease was one that would not have occurred absent exposure.

219 Ultimately, questions of burden and standard of proof are policy matters for any system of law. It is trite law that our system requires a civil claim to be proved by a claimant on the balance of probability. It is a matter of policy choice whether and, if so, in what circumstances the courts are willing to find causation proved on the balance of probability on the basis of epidemiological evidence alone. In the United States, some courts have been willing to find causation established on the balance of probability on the basis of epidemiological evidence alone. They have been criticised by Mr Gold for collapsing the distinction to which I have referred.

220 As I have said, the House of Lords produced in the *Fairchild* exception a particular policy response to the causation problems created by the lack of scientific knowledge about the aetiology of mesothelioma. This response has been confirmed by the 2006 Act. In these circumstances, I agree with Lord Phillips PSC and Lord Rodger JSC that there is no room for the application of a different test which would require a claimant to prove (whether on the basis of doubling of the risk or otherwise) that on the balance of probability the defendant caused or materially contributed to the mesothelioma.

What can we conclude from the discussions in *Sienkiewicz?* It seems clear that the law *selects* material contribution as sufficient causal link in cases where it is appropriate to do so, and not only because of a difficulty of proof. Equally, that 'material contribution' is not merely a form of 'but for' causation. This can apply in the case of an indivisible disease. In the case of a divisible disease, it appears to collapse into 'but for' cause, but this is either because there is not one harm to which the breach contributes, but a range of harms; or perhaps because the principles applied to assessment of damages would insist that the law takes into account what is known, namely that some elements of the injury would be suffered anyway.

So far as proof is concerned, where the relevant causal connection is 'material contribution', only this contribution needs to be proved. Lord Phillips proposed that this was the case in relation to 'cumulative concurrent causes.' 'Material contribution to *risk*' cases, making up a very small group including *McGhee* itself and mesothelioma claims, are for the same reason also outside the need to establish causation as a matter of probabilities. That means that causation also cannot be *disproved* as a matter of probabilities. The possibility of reaching an informed statistical estimate of the degree of contribution to risk cannot, logically, affect this position. Beyond that, the judges have expressed *caution* in relation to purely statistical or epidemiological evidence, and found it insufficient in this particular case. It is clear both for these specific and more general reasons that the possibility of making informed statistical estimates as to contribution to risk does not erode the rock of uncertainty on which *Fairchild*, in particular, is built.

Lower courts now have, of course, the task of determining other cases of occupational cancer where there are also background or non-tortious exposures, after *Sienkiewicz*. In this process, the question of when 'material contribution' is or is not the correct test has become crucial. We return to these issues in Section 2.6, when we consider material contribution beyond mesothelioma. Before that, we complete the saga (to date) of asbestos.

2.5 INSURANCE ISSUES AND FURTHER INTERPRETATION

In two consecutive cases, the Supreme Court has considered arguments raised by liability insurers about their liabilities to indemnify employers who are liable under *Fairchild*. In addition to their important consideration of principles of insurance law, these cases have also interpreted the nature of *Fairchild* liability and the status of *Barker v Corus* as a matter of common law.

Durham v BAI: The *Trigger* Litigation

The *Trigger* litigation brought to the surface the central role of insurance in the entire *Fairchild* saga. It has always been apparent that the defendants in the key cases were liability insurers, even if this has only intermittently been mentioned by the courts. Insurers have not only defended the claims and paid compensation where required, but have shaped the entire litigation by selecting cases in which to resist liability. *Sienkiewicz* and *Willmore*, for example, were particularly weak claims given the low levels of tortious exposure. The suspension of the usual approach to proof of causation in *Fairchild* would have been entirely fruitless had the liabilities not been insured. In the *Trigger* litigation, insurers turned from denying liability in tort, where their arguments had been lost, to denying insurance cover for those liabilities. With the exception of Lord Phillips, the Supreme Court was unanimous in rejecting this 'extraordinary' outcome.

It will not be possible to do full justice to the insurance issues in the context of a chapter concerned with causation in tort law.[13] The judgment of Lord Mance is a tour de force drawing upon and clarifying principles of interpretation of commercial contracts; overarching insurance law principles and policies; and the evolution of the *Fairchild* exception. It is worth noting that Lord Mance and the rest of the majority crafted their opinions on the basis of existing legal principles, including centrally the idea that the words of commercial contracts should be interpreted where possible to make 'commercial sense' (which is to say, to reflect the purpose of the contract), and not on general 'policy' grounds.

The dispute between the parties concerned the meaning of insurance policies which had been written to cover employers' liability to their employees. The various defendants argued that liabilities under *Fairchild* fell outside the wording of their policies, because they had undertaken to pay in respect of liability for injuries either 'sustained', or 'contracted', during the policy period. The Court of Appeal had opened a potential 'black hole' in cover[14] by determining that although 'contracted' was capable of meaning, in effect, 'caused', 'sustained' did

---

[13] On these insurance issues, readers may consult either the critique of the Court of Appeal's decision (duly reversed by the Supreme Court) by Merkin and Steele, 'Compensating Mesothelioma Victims' (2011) 127 LQR 329; or the more recent account, written after the Supreme Court decision, by the same authors: *Insurance and the Law of Obligations* (Oxford, 2013), chapter 13. On the more recent decision in *IEG v Zurich* [2015] UKSC 33, see R. Merkin, 'Insurance and Reinsurance in the Fairchild Enclave' (2016) 32 LS 302.

[14] The expression was used by the first instance judge, who reached the conclusion that the various policies did respond to *Fairchild* liabilities (a conclusion restored by the Supreme Court).

not naturally bear that meaning, so that policies containing 'sustained' wording responded only if the disease was actually suffered by the worker during the period of cover. Since employers often change their insurer; workers often change their employment and of course ultimately leave employment; and mesothelioma has a very long latency period during which no disease occurs with or without the knowledge of the sufferer, this would lead to many cases where no insurance cover responded to the injuries.

This appeared startling in itself, for a number of reasons. One reason is that none of the parties to the insurance contracts had thought there was any distinction between the two alternative forms of wording. Another is that diseases of long latency were hardly unknown before the recognition of mesothelioma, and it was assumed that employers who purchased insurance were covered in relation to their liability for these diseases. A further reason is that from 1972, when the Employers' Liability (Compulsory Insurance) Act 1969 came into force, employers were *required* to be insured against their liabilities to employees, and the policies in question had plainly been purchased on the understanding that they provided the mandated cover. Rix LJ carefully analysed the requirements of that Act and held—in an aspect of his judgment approved by the Supreme Court—that only policies written on a 'causation' basis would satisfy these demands. He therefore also concluded that employers buying policies with a 'sustained' wording were unknowingly in breach of their statutory obligations. Finally, the decision threatened to unravel what the House of Lords in *Fairchild*, and to some extent *Barker*, had sought to achieve.

A much bigger challenge arose in the Supreme Court. Lord Phillips raised the question of whether, if the true basis of *Fairchild* was actually liability for exposure to risk, either one of the wordings referred to above was capable of responding to the liabilities in question. In other words, Lord Phillips went far further than the Court of Appeal, and took a view which meant that very few *Fairchild* liabilities would be covered by available insurance policies at all: no 'injury' could be said to have been sustained or contracted in the policy period, because *Barker* tells us that what is taken to have been sustained is not causation of injury but causation of the risk of injury. Lord Phillips argued that the aim of the House of Lords in *Fairchild* had simply been to ensure that no party in breach escaped *liability* through the impossibility of causation—its aim was not, therefore, to secure compensation.[15]

Note: in the following extract, Lord Mance refers to the decision in Rothwell: *that decision is explored in the next section.*

Lord Mance, *Durham v BAI (Trigger Litigation)* [2012] 1 WLR 867

58 Lord Phillips PSC in his judgment addresses the basis of *Fairchild* in the light of *Barker*, the 2006 Act and *Sienkiewicz*. He accepts that, if *Fairchild* is now correctly to be understood as a special rule deeming employers who have exposed an employee to asbestos to have

---

[15] That view is criticized by Merkin and Steele, *Insurance and the Law of Obligations: Fairchild* is influenced by an intention to clear away the obstacles to compensation under the circumstances, and is not solely concerned with establishing 'liability' as a matter of principle. The House of Lords knew full well the claims were defended by insurers—not least because a very late offer to settle on the part of insurers (with a view to avoiding legal resolution of the issues) had led to the original appeal date being lost. Members of the House expressed 'regret' at this turn of events and the appeal was relisted. The decision itself was announced in advance of the reasons in recognition of the deteriorating condition of one of the claimants. The House could not have missed the insurance dimension, nor the significance of compensation.

caused any subsequently suffered mesothelioma, then the insurance policies should apply (para 109). But he concludes, at para 124, that *Fairchild* must be understood as creating liability not for the disease, but "for the creation of the risk of causing the disease". It follows in his view that employers and employees gain no assistance from the special rule in asserting that mesothelioma suffered by any person was caused or initiated in any particular policy period. On this basis, even though the insurances respond to injuries caused or initiated during their periods, the employers and employees fail for want of proof.

... **61** However, on further analysis, the distinction identified in paras 58–59 above proves more elusive. Even in *Barker* [2006] 2 AC 572 itself, Lord Walker described exposing the employee to the risk of mesothelioma as being "equated with causing his injury" and the result as "an explicit variation of the ordinary requirement as to causation" (para 104), and spoke of the rule as one "by which exposure to the risk of injury is equated with legal responsibility for that injury" (para 109). However, it is conceivable that he meant that the ordinary requirement of causation of the disease was entirely replaced by another liability-creating rule. It is in the later authority of *Sienkiewicz* that the difficulty of drawing any clear-cut distinction between creating a risk and causation of the disease becomes most apparent.

...

65 In reality, it is impossible, or at least inaccurate, to speak of the cause of action recognised in *Fairchild* and *Barker* as being simply "for the risk created by exposing" someone to asbestos. If it were simply for that risk, then the risk would be the injury; damages would be recoverable for every exposure, without proof by the claimant of any (other) injury at all. That is emphatically not the law: see Rothwell and the statements in *Barker* itself, cited above. The cause of action exists because the defendant has previously exposed the victim to asbestos, because that exposure *may* have led to the mesothelioma, not because it did, and because mesothelioma has been suffered by the victim. As to the exposure, all that can be said (leaving aside the remote possibility that mesothelioma may develop idiopathically) is that *some* exposure to asbestos by someone, something or some event led to the mesothelioma. In the present state of scientific knowledge and understanding, there is nothing that enables one to know or suggest that the risk to which the defendant exposed the victim actually materialised. What materialised was at most a risk of the same kind to which someone, who may or may not have been the defendant, or something or some event had exposed the victim. The actual development of mesothelioma is an essential element of the cause of action. In ordinary language, the cause of action is "for" or "in respect of" the mesothelioma, and in ordinary language a defendant who exposes a victim of mesothelioma to asbestos is, under the rule in *Fairchild* and *Barker*, held responsible "for" and "in respect of" both that exposure and the mesothelioma.

66 This legal responsibility may be described in various ways. For reasons already indicated, it is over-simple to describe it as being for the risk. Another way is to view a defendant responsible under the rule as an "insurer", but that too is hardly a natural description of a liability which is firmly based on traditional conceptions of tort liability as rooted in fault. A third way is to view it as responsibility for the mesothelioma, based on a "weak" or "broad" view of the "causal requirements" or "causal link" appropriate in the particular context to ground liability for the mesothelioma. This third way is entirely natural. It was adopted by Lords Reid and Wilberforce in *McGhee v National Coal Board* [1973] 1 WLR 1, by Lord Hoffmann, Baroness Hale and (possibly) Lord Walker in *Barker v Corus UK Ltd* [2006] 2 AC 572 and by Lord Hoffmann in his extra-judicial commentary. It seems to have received the perhaps instinctive endorsement of a number of members of this court, including myself, in *Sienkiewicz v Greif (UK) Ltd* [2011] 2 AC 229. Ultimately, there is no magic about concepts such as causation or causal requirements, wherever they appear. They have the meanings assigned to them and understood in ordinary usage in their context. A logician might disagree with a reference to causation or a causal link in a particular context, but that is not the test of meaning: see Lord Wilberforce's words in *McGhee*, at p 6 c–f (cited in para 56 above). The present appeals concern the meanings we assign to the concept of causation, first in the context of considering employers' liability to their employees and then in considering the scope of employers' insurance cover with respect to such liability.

Lord Mance concluded that liability under *Fairchild* was liability for causation of damage, applying the particular causal tests which the law had decided to adopt in light of the difficulties of proving causation in such cases. Having made that determination, he also concluded that on their proper construction, the insurance policies did indeed respond to the 'causation' of injury, whether they adopted the 'sustained' or 'contracted' wording. The law did not steer into a 'black hole' after all. Lord Clarke expressed the sense that any other outcome would be extraordinary:

Lord Clarke, *Durham v BAI*

88 I would only add this. It appears to me that, once it is held that, on these facts, the employers are liable to the employees, it would be remarkable if the insurers were not liable under the policies. Rather as in *AXA General Insurance Ltd v HM Advocate* [2011] 3 WLR 871, the whole purpose of the policies was to insure the employers against liability to their employees. That purpose would be frustrated if the insurers' submissions on this point were accepted. I agree with Lord Mance JSC, for the reasons he gives at paras 69–73, that these policies respond to these claims.

International Energy Group v Zurich Insurance plc UK [2015] UKSC 33; [2016] AC 509

The implication of the judgments of the Supreme Court in *Trigger* appeared to be that the full force of *Fairchild* was restored, without the exercise in proportionate recovery set out in *Barker*. *Fairchild* had determined, not that liability was for contribution to risk of injury; but that contribution to risk of injury was to be treated as a *sufficient causal link*: liability continued to be for the injury itself. But in *IEG v Zurich*, the Supreme Court unanimously held that as a question of common law, *Barker* continues to apply. What has changed since *Trigger* therefore is not the proportionality of recovery, but the rationale for that proportionality: it is an understandable response to the fact that a broad notion of 'causation' has been applied. Liability is imposed on an 'unconventional basis' ([30]), and there is no reason to think that a conventional approach to the 'measure of damages' should apply. The common law was directly relevant in *IEG* because section 3 of the Compensation Act 2006 does not apply in Guernsey, where the exposure took place.

Delivering the leading judgment in *IEG*, Lord Mance quoted at length from the judgment of Baroness Hale in *Barker*. Notably, Baroness Hale was concerned not with recognizing risk as a new form of injury, but with fashioning a response that was *fair*. It was in this way that the decision in *Trigger* could not be said to be inconsistent with *Barker*: *Barker* had not been impliedly overruled or departed from by the Supreme Court in *Trigger*.

Lord Mance, IEG v Zurich

27 In IEG's submission, *Barker* [2006] 2 AC 572 is fatally undermined by the Compensation Act 2006 and/or the decision in *"Trigger"* [2012] 1 WLR 867. IEG points out that section 16(3) of the 2006 Act provides that "section 3 shall be treated as having always had effect", and suggests that the Act was in section 3 declaring what the common law "has always been". I do not accept that. Section 16 is a section dealing with "Commencement", and the 2006 Act was clearly passed to change a common law rule expounded in *Barker*. It is true that the 2006 Act leads to a result which the common law *might* itself have accepted as appropriate: *"Trigger"*, para 70. But the common law did not do so, and the reasons why it did not are in my view both coherent and understandable. They are set out extensively in *Barker*, and I need not repeat them here. What the House did in *Barker* was to treat proportionality as a concomitant of the exceptional liability which derives from the special rule in *Fairchild* [2003] 1 AC 32 and which the House was, on that basis, prepared in *Barker* to extend to situations beyond those which *Fairchild* had held covered by it. The United Kingdom Parliament's reaction was its right, but does not alter the common law position apart from statute, or have any necessary effect in jurisdictions where the common law position has not been statutorily modified.

28 In *"Trigger"* [2012] 1 WLR 867 the court looked closely at *Barker*, and saw itself as applying what *Barker* established: see paras 63–66 and 72 of my judgment. At para 66 I noted that the speeches of "Lord Hoffmann, Baroness Hale and (possibly) Lord Walker in *Barker* "all viewed an employer's legal responsibility as "based on a 'weak' or 'broad' view of the 'causal requirements' or 'causal link' appropriate in the particular context to ground liability for the mesothelioma." To those references can be added that Lord Scott of Foscote, at para 50, and Lord Walker, at para 103, in *Barker* both expressly agreed with Lord Hoffmann's reasons for allowing the appeals on the issue of apportionment. Further, there was in *"Trigger"* no issue about or challenge to the correctness of *Barker*. In these circumstances, it would on the face of it be surprising to find that *"Trigger"* had consigned that decision to history.

29 IEG submits that, under *"Trigger"*, an employer shown to have significantly exposed a mesothelioma victim to asbestos dust is liable for having caused (in a weak or broad sense) the mesothelioma, and that anyone who is liable for causing a disease must answer for the whole loss resulting from that disease. In the Court of Appeal [2013] 3 All ER 395 that submission was accepted by Toulson LJ, at paras 30–31, and Aikens LJ, at paras 53–55. No doubt the submission is (subject to conventional limitations like remoteness and mitigation) generally correct in a conventional case where causation must exist in its ordinary sense of conduct which "on a balance of probability brought about or contributed to" the disease. But causation in a "weak" or "broad" sense is unconventional. *Barker*, as analysed in *"Trigger"*, accepted causation in this weak or broad sense and none the less held an employer's responsibility to be proportionate to that part for which that employer was responsible of the victim's total exposure to asbestos dust. *"Trigger"* cannot therefore be said to affect or undermine the reasoning or decision in *Barker*.

In interpreting insurance liabilities in *Trigger*, the 'injury caused' was clearly mesothelioma: the interpretation of *Barker* which says that the damage done is the risk of injury is no longer tenable. But the decision in *Barker* that liability is proportionate can be defended on other grounds; and as a matter of common law, that principle does not fall, as was widely thought (including by the third edition of this text), as a consequence of the decision in *Trigger*.

This having been clarified, the bulk of the judgments in *IEG v Zurich* concern the response of insurance law. Given that the liability of the employer was proportionate to the period of exposure which was attributable to them, what was the liability of an insurer who was on cover for only a proportion of that time? Should they have to cover the full liability of the assured employer? Or should their liability also reflect the period of time for which they were 'on cover'? This point divided the Supreme Court. The majority decided that the reasoning in *Trigger* made it inevitable that the insurer's liability was to indemnify its assured (the employer) in full: as Lord Hodge put it at [104], in that case 'the majority imported into the insurance contract the weak or broad concept of causation, which the House of Lords [in *Barker*] had adopted in imposing tortious liability on the employer'. However, in a case where the insurer had been on cover for less than the full period of exposure, this could lead to anomalies. These should be dealt with however by adapting principles of contribution between insurers in order to achieve an equitable result: though initially liable in full, the insurer could proceed against other insurers for a share of the liability. This was supported by the provisions of the Mesothelioma Act 2014, which provides for compensation where there is employer insolvency and no identifiable insurer. This compensation is unavailable where there is recovery from another employer, because it is assumed by the legislation that any such compensation will be made in full. Liability on a pro rata basis by an insurer would be inconsistent with this scheme (Lord Mance, at [81]). In a further extension of existing principles, given that the assured had for some periods not carried insurance at all, they should be treated as 'self-insurers', so that the liable insurer could also seek a contribution against them.

Lord Mance, *IEG v Zurich*

82 Finally, if Lord Sumption JSC be right and he has identified significant potential anomalies on the approach which has been advocated by counsel representing insurers before us and which in my opinion should be adopted, the reality is that the Fairchild enclave has necessitated adjustment from time to time of the legal and regulatory framework by the courts, the legislature and regulatory authorities. As Wikeley notes,[16] "further attempts to engineer improvements to the underlying compensation arrangements [are] almost inevitable": p 82. Lords Neuberger and Reed, in dissent, put the opposing view, albeit sympathetically:

In this final extract, Lord Mance recognizes that the process of innovation sparked by the decision in *Fairchild* is still in process, and that it is hard to predict what further anomalies will need to be dealt with. That, however, he does not see as a reason to return to orthodoxy: the courts should continue to seek just and practicable solutions, in association with statutory developments. Lords Neuberger and Reed, in dissent, put the opposing view, albeit sympathetically:

Lords Neuberger and Reed, *IEG v Zurich*

208 … Lord Sumption JSC's analysis appears to us to do significantly less violence (and we think it probably does no violence) to established legal principles, whereas Lord Mance JSC's analysis accords more with current practice and what is likely to be the view of the legislature.

We accept that the fact that we are in the Fairchild enclave is a reason for favouring what may be said to be the more practical solution. However, our preference is in favour of learning what Lord Mance JSC in *Sienkiewicz* [2011] 2 AC 229, para 189 referred to as "the lesson of caution that the history" of the decisions of the House of Lords and Supreme Court to which we have referred "may teach in relation to future invitations to depart from conventional principles", and agree with Lord Sumption JSC. But we can readily appreciate why the majority of the court has formed the opposite conclusion.

Perhaps surprisingly given the difficulties to which *Fairchild* has given rise, it has now been extended to cases of occupational lung cancer: *Heneghan v Manchester Dry Docks Limited* [2016] EWCA Civ 86. Lung cancer is different from mesothelioma in that it is often caused by factors other than exposure to asbestos dust: the influence of smoking, for example, is well recognized. Thus, cases of lung cancer are generally not 'single agent' cases, as *Fairchild* was. This point did not deter the Court of Appeal from applying *Fairchild* to such cases. Of course, outside mesothelioma cases, section 3 of the Compensation Act does not apply, and thus on the authority of *IEG v Zurich*, damages were proportionate to the contribution to risk.

Lord Dyson MR, *Heneghan v Manchester Dry Docks Ltd* [2016] EWCA Civ 86

46 Mr Allan seeks to invoke policy considerations of justice and to persuade the court to adopt a broader view of causation in this case. He says that such a view requires the application of the *Bonnington Castings* test. I do not agree. That test is to be applied where the court is satisfied on scientific evidence that the exposure for which the defendant is responsible has in fact contributed to the *injury*. This is readily demonstrated in the case of divisible injuries (such as silicosis and pneumoconiosis) whose severity is proportionate to the amount of exposure to the causative agent.

47 The response of the law to the problem posed in a case where the scientific evidence does not permit a finding that the exposure attributable to a particular defendant contributed to the injury is to apply the *Fairchild* exception. The factors identified in the *Fairchild* case for the application of this solution exist in the present case: (i) all the defendants concede their breach of duty; (ii) all increased the risk that the deceased would contract lung cancer; (iii) all exposed the deceased to the same agency that was implicated in causation (asbestos fibres); but (iv) medical science is unable to determine to which (if any) of the defendants there should be attributed the exposure which actually caused the cell changes which initiated the genetic changes culminating in the cancer.

48 In short, I can see no reason not to apply the *Fairchild* exception to the facts of the present case. There can be no objection in principle to extending it to situations which are not materially different from *Fairchild*'s case. Indeed, principle requires that in a situation which is truly analogous to that considered in that case, the *Fairchild* exception should be applied. Otherwise, the law in this area would be inconsistent and incoherent.

49 There is some support for this view in the Supreme Court decision in *International Energy Group Ltd v Zurich Insurance plc (Association of British Insurers intervening)* [2016] AC 509. Thus, Lord Neuberger PSC and Lord Reed JSC said, at para 191, that the *Fairchild* exception is "applicable to any disease which has the unusual features of mesothelioma". The

possibility of its application in cases concerning other injuries or diseases was also expressly contemplated by Lord Hodge JSC (para 109) and Lord Sumption JSC: para 127.

Conclusion

50 To summarise, Mr Allan concedes that causation cannot be established against any of the defendants on the conventional "but for" test. For the reasons that I have given, I do not accept his submission that it is possible to infer from the epidemiological evidence that all or any of the defendants made a material contribution to Mr Heneghan's contracting of lung cancer. All of the defendants did, however, materially contribute to the risk that he would contract lung cancer. The judge was, therefore, right to apply the *Fairchild* exception.

2.6 'MATERIAL CONTRIBUTION' AFTER THE *FAIRCHILD*

In the cases we have been discussing, more than one potential cause is in play. It appears from the judgments in *Sienkiewicz* that in some such cases the relevant causal link is 'material contribution to damage'; others require proof that the breach is a cause of the damage, on the balance of probabilities. According to Lord Phillips, where causes are *cumulative*, which is to say that they operate in combination, it will not be appropriate to demand proof that they caused the injury on *balance of probabilities*. The more significant impact of *Fairchild* on the surrounding law may lie in the application of the 'material contribution to damage' test.

A number of recent cases have explored the 'material contribution to damage' test in relation to 'cumulative causes'. *Sienkiewicz* supports the idea that proof on balance of probabilities is not required in such cases, and that this is not simply because such proof is impossible, but because the law selects an alternative approach to causation as more appropriate.

Bailey v Ministry of Defence [2008] EWCA Civ 883; [2009] 1 WLR 1052

This was a case of medical negligence, in which 'material contribution' to damage was adopted as the appropriate causal test. That in itself is significant, since *Wilsher* (Section 2.1) and *Hotson* and *Gregg* (Section 3) previously appeared to rule out variation of the 'but for' test in the medical context: this development is plainly supported by the subsequent case of *Williams v Bermuda Hospitals Board* (extracted later in this section).

The claimant had been admitted to a hospital managed by the defendants for surgery. She had become very weak due in part to negligent lack of post-operative care, but in part also to pancreatitis, which was not due to the defendants' negligence. She was then transferred to the renal ward at another hospital. She vomited after taking a drink and due to her weakened state (which had both tortious and non-tortious causes) she was unable to clear her airways, suffering a cardiac arrest and sustaining brain damage. The Court of Appeal found that the negligent lack of care had made a material contribution to the injury, so that the defendants were liable.

On the way to this conclusion, the Court distinguished the issues dealt with in *Wilsher* and *Hotson*, applying *Bonnington* instead. On one reading of *Bonnington* as we have said, material contribution to injury could be shown in the sense that any exposure will have worsened the injury: it was a progressive disease. On a slightly different reading of *Bonnington*, it was the interaction of different sources of dust which was taken to have caused the injury: it was a case of material contribution to causation of damage. The second reading of *Bonnington* is supported by the Supreme Court's decision in *Sienkiewicz*, and might extend to the facts of *Bailey*.

In the *Bailey* case itself, the weakness to which the breach contributed was no doubt progressive, but the weakness was not the injury. The injury was brain damage, which was brought about through weakness, to which a combination of factors including the defendant's breach materially contributed.[17] Brain damage is a single indivisible injury, but the weakness was regarded as the cumulative effect of different causes—like the dust-heavy air in *Bonnington*. It remains true that this case is different from *Wilsher* (there, it is shown on the balance of probabilities that the negligence probably played no part in causing the blindness), and it is different from *Hotson* (where again, the evidence is generally taken to have shown that probably the injury was independent of the medical negligence). Nor is it a *Fairchild* case. In *Bailey*, it can be shown that the negligence did more than contribute to the *risk*: it was one of two cumulative causes of the condition which led to the outcome. What cannot be said is that it contributed a *proportion* of the final injury (ascertainable or not), because the injury, like the injury in *Fairchild*, cannot be divided into proportions at all.[18]

Bailey was reasoned as a case where the negligence has played a material but unquantifiable part in the events which between them (cumulatively) brought about the injury. In this instance, the negligence is known to play a part in the weakness. That is not the case in *Fairchild*, where it remains the case that not all exposures will contribute to the effects, even if the interaction of a number of fibres creates the disease.

It has been suggested that since it is known that the negligence in *Bailey* contributed to the weakness, the judgment should simply have been expressed in terms of 'but for' cause.[19] One reason why it was, rather, expressed in terms of 'material contribution' is the unquantifiable role played by the breach in the final injury. The hypothetical question required by 'but for' is 'what would have happened without the breach?' In *Bonnington*, there was a progressive disease and therefore the answer is presumably, 'there would have been a less severe injury'.[20] In *Bailey*, it would appear that the hypothetical question cannot be answered. Although the breach contributed to the weakness, it is not known whether the claimant would have been sufficiently weak to suffer the injury (which is indivisible) without the contribution of the breach. It is also possible that the 'but for' test is in any event not the most appropriate test for a case of cumulative causes. To return to Jane Stapleton's recent analysis outlined in the first section of this chapter, the negligence in this instance is known to contribute causally, *even though* it is not known what would have happened without it. And to follow Stapleton's reasoning, which on this point is compatible with the comments of Lord Phillips in *Sienkiewicz*, this may be a case where the 'material contribution' analysis is *superior to* the 'but for' question in determining factual causation.

[17] See James Lee, 'Causation in Negligence: Another Fine Mess' (2008) 24 PN 194–8, cited with agreement by Foskett J in *B v Ministry of Defence* [2009] EWHC 1225 (QB), at [235].

[18] If the claimant had been forced to rely on *Fairchild* then she would have struggled to show this was a 'single agent' case.

[19] S. Green, 'Contributing to the Risk of Confusion? Causation in the Court of Appeal' (2009) 125 LQR 44–8; S. Bailey, 'What is a Material Contribution?' (2010) 30 LS 167.

[20] If, as suggested above, there is scope to interpret *Bonnington* as turning on the cumulative nature of the causes, this would make it closer to *Bailey*; but it would also take it further from *Holtby*. It would suggest that there would be no basis for apportioning damages in *Bonnington* after all.

Waller LJ, *Bailey v Ministry of Defence*
[2008] EWCA Civ 883; [2009] 1 WLR 1052

46. ...I would summarise the position in relation to cumulative cause cases as follows. If the evidence demonstrates on a balance of probabilities that the injury would have occurred as a result of the non-tortious cause or causes in any event, the claimant will have failed to establish that the tortious cause contributed. *Hotson* exemplifies such a situation. If the evidence demonstrates that 'but for' the contribution of the tortious cause the injury would probably not have occurred, the claimant will (obviously) have discharged the burden. In a case where medical science cannot establish the probability that 'but for' an act of negligence the injury would not have happened but can establish that the contribution of the negligent cause was more than negligible, the 'but for' test is modified, and the claimant will succeed.

47. The instant case involved cumulative causes acting so as to create a weakness and thus the judge in my view applied the right test, and was entitled to reach the conclusion he did.

This passage suggests that 'but for' is the dominant test, and that material contribution is used only where it is not possible to answer the 'but for' question. In *Williams v Bermuda Hospitals* however, *Bailey* was somewhat surprisingly reinterpreted as a conventional case: the outcome was correct, but the Court of Appeal was wrong to consider that there was a departure from the 'but for' test. One of the rival 'causes' (pancreatitis) was simply a pre-existing vulnerability of the claimant.

Lord Toulson JSC, *Williams v Bermuda Hospitals Board*

47. In the view of the Board, on those findings of primary fact Foskett J was right to hold the hospital responsible in law for the consequences of the aspiration. As to the parallel weakness of the claimant due to her pancreatitis, the case may be seen as an example of the well known principle that a tortfeasor takes his victim as he finds her. The Board does not share the view of the Court of Appeal that the case involved a departure from the "but-for" test. The judge concluded that the totality of the claimant's weakened condition caused the harm. If so, "but-for" causation was established. The fact that her vulnerability was heightened by her pancreatitis no more assisted the hospital's case than if she had an eggshell skull.

Does this resolve the problem of *Bailey*? It is suggested that it does not. If the pancreatitis is seen as a 'pre-existing condition', the only potential cause in operation is the additional weakness caused by the defendants' negligence. Applying a traditional 'but for' test to this weakness while treating the pancreatitis as a 'vulnerability' does not resolve the problems noted above: it still needs to be asked whether a material, but unquantifiable, contribution to the causal process is sufficient to satisfy the causation requirement. See also the discussion by J. Stapleton and S. Steel, 'Causes and Contributions' (2016) 132 LQR 363, arguing that it is right to call this a cause; but wrong to say that it satisfies the orthodox 'but for' test.

Williams v Bermuda Hospitals Board [2016] UKPC 4

Here, 'material contribution' once again operated in a medical context. Further, it operated in a situation where the contributing causes were not simultaneous, but successive.

The claimant went to the defendant's hospital suffering from acute appendicitis. There was a delay in his treatment, and although he had an appendectomy later that day, he suffered from complications causing injury to his heart and lungs. These complications were the result of sepsis, which had developed over approximately six hours. There had been a culpable delay of at least 140 minutes, during which the development of sepsis would have continued. Therefore, the negligence contributed to the sepsis and thus to the process which caused the final injury; but the contribution could not be quantified. It would appear that the Privy Council treated the injury in this case as *indivisible*, and not as varying according to the level of sepsis suffered.

Lord Toulson (giving the judgment of the Board), *Williams v Bermuda Hospitals Board*

41 In the present case the judge found that injury to the heart and lungs was caused by a single known agent, sepsis from the ruptured appendix. The sepsis developed incrementally over a period of approximately six hours, progressively causing myocardial ischaemia. (The greater the accumulation of sepsis, the greater the oxygen requirement.) The sepsis was not divided into separate components causing separate damage to the heart and lungs. Its development and effect on the heart and lungs was a single continuous process, during which the sufficiency of the supply of oxygen to the heart steadily reduced.

42 On the trial judge's findings, that process continued for a minimum period of two hours 20 minutes longer than it should have done. In the judgment of the Board, it is right to infer on the balance of probabilities that the hospital board's negligence materially contributed to the process, and therefore materially contributed to the injury to the heart and lungs.

How far does *Williams* assist with understanding 'material contribution'? It does demonstrate that a material contribution to the process by which an indivisible injury is brought about is capable of being accepted as a cause. Unfortunately, it does not offer any help with the critical question of whether this is an application of the 'but for' test, or a departure from it. Stapleton and Steel have argued that this result can be reached only by 'employing a causal concept that is broader than but-for causation':

J. Stapleton and S. Steel, 'Causes, Causes and Contributions' (2016) 132 LQR 363

Where, as it should, the law recognizes X is a cause of Y *simply* from the fact that X contributed to the process by which the indivisible injury, Y, occurred, it is accepting that factual causation can be established without the orthodox but-for test.

Summary

Is it possible to summarize the current position in relation to 'material contribution'? Plainly, *Fairchild* both adopted and built upon the 'material contribution' test in articulating its more specific 'material contribution to risk' principle. Since *Fairchild*, it has begun to be recognized that 'material contribution to damage' and 'but for causation' are two distinct approaches to showing a causal link. The first concentrates on causal 'contribution'; the second on the 'necessary' nature of the breach in the events that bring about damage. In

Sienkiewicz, Lord Phillips took the view that the two approaches may be appropriate to different kinds of case, and that 'material contribution' is an appropriate criterion in relation to cumulative concurrent causes. This implies that 'material contribution' is analytically preferable in such cases, and is not only applicable where there is insufficient evidence for the application of the 'but for' test. Further, it suggests that the relationship between different potential causes—and particularly the question of whether they operate cumulatively—is crucial to deciding which causal test to apply.

Lord Phillips went on to suggest that when the 'material contribution' relates to causation of a divisible disease, then the claimant will recover damages relating to the contribution that has been made. In these instances however, it may well be argued that 'material contribution' is in fact simply another name for 'but for' causation. [21] On the other hand, Lord Phillips also said that in the case of an indivisible disease, the defendant may nevertheless make a material contribution to the causal process, and the claimant will then recover in full. While most commentators have not shared this analysis, Jane Stapleton has developed the theory that 'contribution' is indeed an appropriate test for factual causation, and that the 'but for' test is merely one manifestation of the search for contributing causes. It was observed at an earlier stage that there was however a sting in the tail; and it is time to consider that now. It entails rejecting the final suggestion of Lord Phillips referred to above, namely that a claimant who shows that the breach made a material contribution to causation of an indivisible injury will necessarily recover in full.

Causing Events and Making a Difference?

Jane Stapleton does not accept that all claimants who succeed in showing that the defendant's breach made a material contribution to the causal process which led to their injury should recover damages. As we noted earlier, this is because it remains to be asked, on her analysis, whether this causal process made any difference to the harm caused by the claimant. That in turn is because the law only seeks to return tort victims to the position they would have been in, had the tort not been committed. What this approach does is to separate the causal question—which relates to processes in the world—from the question of whether the tort nevertheless resulted in any loss to the claimant. Previously, these have always been considered as one and the same question: did the breach cause the damage, *not* did the breach cause an adverse event, from which damage did or did not flow compared to another hypothetical version of events? This second question demands the use of hypotheticals, which appeared to be left behind by the idea of a 'material contribution'. If this approach merely deflects all of the questions of 'but for' to a further stage of analysis, concerned with 'damage', then it has done nothing to assist claimants, nor perhaps to advance the law's attempt to do justice, but has merely protected a conceptual approach to the meaning of 'causing' something. We have seen that many judges have little or no interest in protecting causal notions, and would most likely reject this distinction.

Stapleton argues however that the entire 'but for' question as it is traditionally encountered is not simply reintroduced in its familiar form at this second stage. Rather, she proposes that the law has 'a choice' in how it addresses this additional stage. This stage is referred to as the 'no better off' principle of compensatory damages—notice that trouble is taken to ensure that the language of causation is avoided in naming this question.

---

21 This is the general argument advanced by S. Bailey, 'What is a Material Contribution?' (2010) 30 LS 167.

J. Stapleton, 'Unnecessary Causes'

(2013) LQR 39, 58–9

VIII. The "No Better Off" Principle of Compensatory Tort Damages: Choice of Benchmark

At this point it might seem that the traditional but-for test has simply been re-introduced albeit at the stage when the legal analysis asks if the injury represented "damage". But this is not the case.

The question of whether the injury represents "damage" relative to what had been the victim's prospects "absent tortious conduct" is ambiguous in cases in which: the mechanism by which an indivisible injury occurred involved a step requiring a threshold concentration of some element; there were multiple wrongful contributions of that element; and the threshold had been oversubscribed. Here tort law has a choice whether the "no better off" principle mentioned earlier is that compensatory damages should not make a claimant better off relative to:

(i) where he would have been but for the individual defendant's tortious contribution; or

(ii) where he would have been but for all the tortious contributions.

The choice of benchmark will be critical to the outcome of the many medical negligence and toxic tort claims where: but for the defendant's individual contribution, the threshold would still have been reached and the injury would still have occurred; but in the absence of all wrongful contributions it would not have been reached and the injury would not have occurred.

Stapleton clearly considers the second benchmark to be preferable in a range of circumstances. While the idea of a 'contributing cause' may well match common usage and also helps to rationalize the recent cases on material contribution, this additional stage is likely to be problematic. How is the law to select its 'benchmark' for recoverability of damages, given that success or failure in the claim would turn on this newly recognized additional stage? Would courts welcome, or reject the opportunity to consider *other* tortious causes which are not the acts or omissions of the parties before the court, and how would they assess these contributions? Would the results appear just, and on what basis? The attempt to divide factual causation questions from questions of compensatory damages, and to allocate 'but for' to the second of these not the first, is an interesting one, and it is suggested that the resulting explanation of 'material contribution' is enlightening. The difficulties relating to the second stage however may discourage courts from embracing it.

3. LOSS OF A CHANCE

The conflict between a traditional 'all or nothing' approach, and an approach based on quantification of risk, arises again in relation to our final problem. Our question here is whether the tort of negligence could accommodate claims for a *lost chance of avoiding physical injury?* It already compensates in some circumstances for a lost chance of *financial gain.* So far, the answer in respect of personal injury has been 'no'.

In cases where the claimant is unable to establish the defendant's breach as a 'but for' cause of injury, it has sometimes been argued instead that the breach has diminished the claimant's chances of a better outcome. This argument treats a chance as itself a thing of value, so that loss of or perhaps diminution in such a chance should be regarded as sufficient damage to give rise to a claim in negligence. Claims for loss of chance are clearly accepted in certain cases of economic loss and of lost chance of economic gain (see for example *Kitchen v Royal Air Force Association* [1958] 1 WLR 563; *Allied Maples v Simmons and Simmons* [1995] 4 All ER 907; *Normans Bay v Coudert* [2003] EWCA Civ 215; [2004] All ER 458). In the last of these cases, members of the Court of Appeal expressed 'disquiet' about this apparent inconsistency. A possible principled basis on which to distinguish the cases of recoverable lost chance, from those in which the traditional all or nothing approach will apply, has been outlined by Helen Reece in an article extracted below. But even if this is accepted, cases arise which can be used to test the resistance to 'loss of chance' claims in a medical context. An example is *Wright v Cambridge Medical Group*, considered at the end of this section.

Hotson v East Berkshire Area Health Authority [1987] AC 750

In *Hotson*, the plaintiff fell 12 feet out of a tree. He was taken to hospital within a few hours. Medical staff failed to notice that he had suffered an acute traumatic fracture of the left femoral epiphysis, and he was sent home. For five days he suffered severe pain. He was then taken back to the hospital, and this time the injury was correctly identified. He was treated accordingly. He suffered an avascular necrosis. This resulted from a failure of the blood supply and led to a deformity in the hip, at the head of the femur. This would almost certainly be aggravated by osteoarthritis in the future. The plaintiff sued the defendant health authority for the initial failure to diagnose the injury which led to the avascular necrosis.

The difficulty with the plaintiff's claim was that he could not establish on the balance of probabilities that, with prompt treatment, the avascular necrosis would not have developed. The trial judge (Simon Brown J) assessed the available evidence and concluded that it was more likely than not that, even with prompt treatment, the injury would still have developed. The likelihood that he would have sustained the same injury was assessed at 75 per cent. However, the trial judge allowed the plaintiff's claim, subject to a discount of 75 per cent for the likelihood that the injury would still have been sustained but for the negligence. This amounted to a successful claim for loss of a 25 per cent chance of recovery. The Court of Appeal upheld this award. The health authority appealed to the House of Lords.

In the House of Lords, the traditional 'all or nothing' approach was restored. The reasoning of the House has been criticized for not dealing with the central issues, but the case has nevertheless become a 'fixed point' in the law, rather like *Wilsher*.

In the extract below, Lord Bridge leaves the issue of lost chance for another day.

Lord Bridge of Harwich, at 780

I would observe at the outset that the damages referable to the plaintiff's pain during the five days by which treatment was delayed in consequence of failure to diagnose the injury correctly, although sufficient to establish the authority's liability for the tort of negligence, have no relevance to their liability in respect of the avascular necrosis. There was no causal connection between the plaintiff's physical pain and the development of the necrosis. If the injury had been painless, the plaintiff would have to establish the necessary causal link between the necrosis and the authority's breach of duty in order to succeed. It makes no difference that the five days' pain gave him a cause of action in respect of an unrelated element of damage.

At 782–3

… The plaintiff's claim was for damages for physical injury and consequential loss alleged to have been caused by the authority's breach of their duty of care. In some cases, perhaps particularly medical negligence cases, causation may be so shrouded in mystery that the court can only measure statistical chances. But that was not so here. On the evidence there was a clear conflict as to what had caused the avascular necrosis. The authority's evidence was that the sole cause was the original traumatic injury to the hip. The plaintiff's evidence, at its highest, was that the delay in treatment was a material contributory cause. This was a conflict, like any other about some relevant past event, which the judge could not avoid resolving on a balance of probabilities. Unless the plaintiff proved on a balance of probabilities that the delayed treatment was at least a material contributory cause of the avascular necrosis he failed on the issue of causation and no question of quantification could arise. But the judge's findings of fact … are unmistakably to the effect that on a balance of probabilities the injury caused by the plaintiff's fall left insufficient blood vessels intact to keep the epiphysis alive. This amounts to a finding of fact that the fall was the sole cause of the avascular necrosis.

The upshot is that the appeal must be allowed on the narrow ground that the plaintiff failed to establish a cause of action in respect of the avascular necrosis and its consequences. Your Lordships were invited to approach the appeal more broadly and to decide whether, in a claim for damages for personal injury, it can ever be appropriate, where the cause of the injury is unascertainable and all the plaintiff can show is a statistical chance which is less than even that, but for the defendant's breach of duty, he would not have suffered the injury, to award him a proportionate fraction of the full damages appropriate to compensate for the injury as the measure of damages for the lost chance.

There is a superficially attractive analogy between the principle applied in such cases as *Chaplin v. Hicks* [1911] 2 K.B. 786 (award of damages for breach of contract assessed by reference to the lost chance of securing valuable employment if the contract had been performed) and *Kitchen v. Royal Air Force Association* [1958] 1 W.L.R. 563 (damages for solicitors' negligence assessed by reference to the lost chance of prosecuting a successful civil action) and the principle of awarding damages for the lost chance of avoiding personal injury or, in medical negligence cases, for the lost chance of a better medical result which might have been achieved by prompt diagnosis and correct treatment. I think there are formidable difficulties in the way of accepting the analogy. But I do not see this appeal as a suitable occasion for reaching a settled conclusion as to whether the analogy can ever be applied.

As I have said, there was in this case an inescapable issue of causation first to be resolved. But if the plaintiff had proved on a balance of probabilities that the authority's negligent failure to diagnose and treat his injury promptly had materially contributed to the development of avascular necrosis, I know of no principle of English law which would have entitled the authority to a discount from the full measure of damage to reflect the chance that, even given prompt treatment, avascular necrosis might well still have developed.…

In an influential article, Helen Reece argued that there is a key distinction between 'deterministic' cases, including *Hotson*, and 'quasi-indeterministic' cases, which are appropriately dealt with through a 'loss of chance' analysis. We will spend some time on this distinction because it might have provided the basis for distinguishing *Hotson* in the later case of *Gregg v Scott*, had there not been other complicating factors. In the closing part of the chapter, we will consider a rival account of the case based in 'material contribution' (continuing the discussion in the previous Section). Jane Stapleton's analysis attempts to revive the idea of discounted damages in such a case by taking issue with Lord Bridge's comments above,[22] treating the 'hypothetical' problem as relevant not to causation, but to questions of compensatory damages.

According to Reece, *deterministic* cases are appropriately dealt with on the usual all or nothing approach, where one assesses whether the damage itself was more probably than not caused by the defendant's breach. *Quasi-indeterministic* cases on the other hand are appropriately dealt with as loss of chance cases. Reece explains the meaning of 'determinism' and 'indeterminism' in this context as follows:

Helen Reece, 'Losses of Chances in the Law' (1996) 59 MLR 188, 194

... The intuitive notion of determinism ..., is that phenomena are deterministic when their past uniquely determines their future and that phenomena are indeterministic when they have a random component.

... An event will here be treated as indeterministic if and only if it could not have been predicted at any time in the past, it cannot be predicted in the present even given unlimited time, resources and evidence, and we cannot imagine how it would become possible in the future, even given the success of current research programmes. Such an event is indeterministic for all human purposes ... it is not humanly possible to predict the event. This type of event is referred to as a *quasi-indeterministic* event, ... to distinguish [it] from those processes which scientists believe to be truly indeterministic.

Why is this distinction of relevance in deciding whether to allow a claim for loss of chance? Because in the quasi-indeterministic case, it is not 'humanly possible' to answer the 'but for' question. This is not a question of lack of evidence; it is a question about the limits of knowability. Reece argues (at 204) that the reason for adopting a rule whereby the claimant must prove their case on the balance of probabilities is that the 'risk of non-persuasion' must fall on the person who wishes to disturb the status quo. But this does not apply to unknowable facts:

... the risk which it is reasonable to expect the plaintiff to bear is the risk of uncertainty in the evidence, not uncertainty in the world.

We should notice that despite the logical nature of the distinction outlined by Reece, this *consequence* is a matter of opinion. It returns us to the question of which risks, in terms of evidence, it is 'reasonable' to place on the claimant, or the defendant. For example, is it reasonable that the claimant should bear the risk of lack of evidence where the defendant's breach has removed the opportunity of obtaining that evidence? (An example is *Hotson* itself.)

Reece describes *Hotson* as a deterministic case, which could be appropriately dealt with on the balance of probabilities.

22 The remarks are described as 'untenable'.

At 195–6

... That *Hotson* was a deterministic case becomes clear when we look at the medical facts a little more closely. Avascular necrosis develops if and only if insufficient blood cells are left intact to keep the epiphysis alive. The trial judge found that it was likely (to a degree of 75%) that insufficient blood cells were left intact after the fall, so that necrosis would have been bound to develop; but that if, on the contrary, there were enough vessels left, then the delay would have made the onset of necrosis inevitable ...

Therefore, there was a time in the past when the cause of the necrosis could have been determined. If the blood vessels had been examined after the fall, then it would have been humanly possible to decide whether or not the plaintiff would develop necrosis even if he were treated. ...

If this is right, then Lord Mackay captured the essential feature of the evidence when he said:

Hotson v East Berkshire Area Health Authority
[1987] AC 750, at 915

It is not, in my opinion, correct to say that on arrival at the hospital he had a 25 per cent chance of recovery. If insufficient blood cells were left intact by the fall, he had no prospect of avoiding complete avascular necrosis, whereas if sufficient blood vessels were left intact ... if he had been given immediate treatment ... he would not have suffered the avascular necrosis.

The *Hotson* case therefore concerned a simple lack of evidence, and was not appropriately dealt with in terms of 'loss of chance'.

Jane Stapleton's recent analysis of 'unnecessary causes', which make a contribution to events, but do not necessarily make a difference,[23] treats *Hotson* very differently from the accounts above (including the account of the House of Lords itself). Rather than treating *Hotson* as a 'binary' case, where the negligent delay either made a difference to the injury suffered or it did not, Stapleton explains *Hotson* as a 'threshold' case, in which both the fall from the tree, and the delay in diagnosis, contributed to a process of physical change which culminated in the injury. This approach renders the negligence a material cause of the avascular necrosis. The question of whether the defendant's negligence 'made a difference' is deferred to the assessment of damages. It is most likely of course that courts will not entertain any attempt to argue for proportionate damages where the *injury* is indivisible. The point is however that this makes a link between loss of chance cases, and material contribution cases, discussed here in separate sections.

In the following case, the House of Lords again declined to embrace 'loss of chance' reasoning in a case of medical misdiagnosis.

Gregg v Scott [2005] UKHL 2; [2005] 2 AC 176

The claimant consulted his doctor about a lump under his left arm. The doctor ought to have referred the claimant to a hospital for further investigation. Instead, he reassured the claimant

23 J. Stapleton, 'Unnecessary Causes', discussed in the previous section.

that the lump was only a collection of fatty tissue. This was found by the trial judge to have been a breach of his duty of care. Had the claimant been referred for further investigation, it would have been found that a cancerous lymphoma was developing and he would have had treatment for his cancer at that stage. Because of the doctor's breach of duty, it was not until the claimant was admitted to hospital with acute chest pain some months later that the diagnosis was made and treatment commenced. Treatment was delayed by around nine months.

Defining the damage in this case is not entirely straightforward. But it appears that the appellant's claim was not for the pain and suffering associated with the spread of his cancer, nor for the need to undergo particular forms of treatment which might not have been necessary if the disease had been recognized promptly. The action was solely for the reduced chances of a successful recovery which resulted from the delay in treatment. As Lord Hope put it regretfully, all of the claimant's eggs were in one basket. Different interpretations of the statistical chances of recovery themselves were mentioned in the judgments. But it appears that the chance of making a full recovery (defined for these purposes as survival for 10 years) was diminished from around 42 per cent (at the time of the initial consultation), to around 25 per cent at the time of the trial. Survival was never a probability. (We should note however that at the time of the House of Lords' judgment, the claimant's prospects of recovery were increasing given his good response to treatment.)

The trial judge dismissed the claim, considering himself bound to this conclusion by the authority of *Hotson* (above). The Court of Appeal by a majority dismissed the appeal. In the House of Lords, a further appeal by Mr Gregg was dismissed by a majority, Lord Nicholls and Lord Hope dissenting.

Lord Nicholls of Birkenhead (dissenting)

[2] This is the type of case under consideration. A patient is suffering from cancer. His prospects are uncertain. He has a 45% chance of recovery. Unfortunately his doctor negligently misdiagnoses his condition as benign. So the necessary treatment is delayed for months. As a result the patient's prospects of recovery become nil or almost nil. Has the patient a claim for damages against the doctor? No, the House was told. The patient could recover damages if his initial prospects of recovery had been more than 50%. But because they were less than 50% he can recover nothing.

[3] This surely cannot be the state of the law today. It would be irrational and indefensible. The loss of a 45% prospect of recovery is just as much a real loss for a patient as the loss of a 55% prospect of recovery. In both cases the doctor was in breach of his duty to his patient. In both cases the patient was worse off. He lost something of importance and value. But, it is said, in one case the patient has a remedy, in the other he does not.

[4] This would make no sort of sense. It would mean that in the 45% case the doctor's duty would be hollow. The duty would be empty of content. For the reasons which follow I reject this suggested distinction. The common law does not compel courts to proceed in such an unreal fashion. I would hold that a patient has a right to a remedy as much where his prospects of recovery were less than 50-50 as where they exceeded 50-50 . . . .

Medical negligence

[20] . . . I turn to the primary question raised by this appeal: how should the loss suffered by a patient in Mr Gregg's position be identified? The Defendant says "loss" is confined to an

outcome which is shown, on balance of probability, to be worse than it otherwise would have been. Mr Gregg must prove that, on balance of probability, his medical condition after the negligence was worse than it would have been in the absence of the negligence. Mr Gregg says his "loss" includes proved diminution in the prospects of a favourable outcome. Dr Scott's negligence deprived him of a worthwhile chance that his medical condition would not have deteriorated as it did.

[21] Of primary relevance on this important issue is an evaluation of what, in practice, a patient suffering from a progressive illness loses when the treatment he needs is delayed because of a negligent diagnosis....

[24] Given this uncertainty of outcome, the appropriate characterisation of a patient's loss in this type of case must surely be that it comprises the loss of the chance of a favourable outcome, rather than the loss of the outcome itself. Justice so requires, because this matches medical reality. This recognises what in practice a patient had before the doctor's negligence occurred. It recognises what in practice the patient lost by reason of that negligence. The doctor's negligence diminished the patient's prospects of recovery. And this analysis of a patient's loss accords with the purpose of the legal duty of which the doctor was in breach. In short, the purpose of the duty is to promote the patient's prospects of recovery by exercising due skill and care in diagnosing and treating the patient's condition.

Comment

Lord Nicholls' primary argument is a good one. Given that in a case like this a patient will only ever have a 'prospect' of recovery, which can only be defined in terms of statistical chances, the whole purpose of a doctor's duty of care is to safeguard the patient's prospects. If loss of prospects is not recoverable, then the duty serves no purpose in respect of many medical conditions. The step proposed by Lord Nicholls can therefore be presented as a necessary one, designed to reflect the limitations of medical knowledge. But the other judgments expose complications associated with this solution.

Lord Hoffmann considered the cases of *Hotson*, *Wilsher*, and *Fairchild*, before continuing:

[79] What these cases show is that, as Helen Reece points out in an illuminating article ("Losses of Chances in the Law" (1996) 59 MLR 188) the law regards the world as in principle bound by laws of causality. Everything has a determinate cause, even if we do not know what it is. The blood-starved hip joint in *Hotson*, the blindness in *Wilsher*, the mesothelioma in *Fairchild*; each had its cause and it was for the plaintiff to prove that it was an act or omission for which the defendant was responsible. The narrow terms of the exception made to this principle in *Fairchild* only serves to emphasise the strength of the rule. The fact that proof is rendered difficult or impossible because no examination was made at the time, as in *Hotson*, or because medical science cannot provide the answer, as in *Wilsher*, makes no difference. There is no inherent uncertainty about what caused something to happen in the past or about whether something which happened in the past will cause something to happen in the future. Everything is determined by causality. What we lack is knowledge and the law deals with lack of knowledge by the concept of the burden of proof.

[80] Similarly in the present case, the progress of Mr Gregg's disease had a determinate cause. It may have been inherent in his genetic make-up at the time when he saw Mr Scott, as *Hotson's* fate was determined by what happened to his thigh when he fell out of the tree. Or it may, as Mance LJ suggests, have been affected by subsequent events and behaviour for

which Dr Scott was not responsible. Medical science does not enable us to say. But the outcome was not random; it was governed by laws of causality and, in the absence of a special rule as in Fairchild, inability to establish that delay in diagnosis caused the reduction in expectation in life cannot be remedied by treating the outcome as having been somehow indeterminate.

... [82] One striking exception to the assumption that everything is determined by impersonal laws of causality is the actions of human beings. The law treats human beings as having free will and the ability to choose between different courses of action, however strong may be the reasons for them to choose one course rather than another. This may provide part of the explanation for why in some cases damages are awarded for the loss of a chance of gaining an advantage or avoiding a disadvantage which depends upon the independent action of another person: see *Allied Maples Group Ltd v Simmons & Simmons* [1995] 4 All ER 907, [1995] 1 WLR 1602 and the cases there cited.

[83] But the true basis of these cases is a good deal more complex. The fact that one cannot prove as a matter of necessary causation that someone would have done something is no reason why one should not prove that he was more likely than not to have done it. So, for example, the law distinguishes between cases in which the outcome depends upon what the claimant himself (*McWilliams v Sir William Arrol & Co* [1962] 1 WLR 295) or someone for whom the defendant is responsible (*Bolitho v City and Hackney Health Authority* [1998] AC 232, [1997] 4 All ER 771) would have done, and cases in which it depends upon what some third party would have done. In the first class of cases the claimant must prove on a balance of probability that he or the defendant would have acted so as to produce a favourable outcome. In the latter class, he may recover for loss of the chance that the third party would have so acted. This apparently arbitrary distinction obviously rests on grounds of policy. In addition, most of the cases in which there has been recovery for loss of a chance have involved financial loss, where the chance can itself plausibly be characterised as an item of property, like a lottery ticket. It is however unnecessary to discuss these decisions because they obviously do not cover the present case ...

Control mechanisms

[86] The Appellant suggests that the expansion of liability could be held in reasonable bounds by confining it to cases in which the claimant had suffered an injury. In this case, the spread of the cancer before the eventual diagnosis was something which would not have happened if it had been promptly diagnosed and amounted to an injury caused by the Defendant. It is true that this is not the injury for which the Claimant is suing. His claim is for loss of the prospect of survival for more than 10 years. And the judge's finding was that he had not established that the spread of the cancer was causally connected with the reduction in his expectation of life. But the Appellant submits that his injury can be used as what Professor Jane Stapleton called a "hook" on which to hang a claim for damage which it did not actually cause: see (2003) 119 LQR 388, 423.

[87] An artificial limitation of this kind seems to me to be lacking in principle. It resembles the "control mechanisms" which disfigure the law of liability for psychiatric injury. And once one treats an "injury" as a condition for imposing liability for some other kind of damage, one is involved in definitional problems about what counts as an injury. Presumably the internal bleeding suffered by the boy Hotson was an injury which would have qualified him to sue for the loss of a chance of saving his hip joint. What about baby Wilsher? The doctor's negligence resulted in his having excessively oxygenated blood, which is potentially toxic: see [1987] QB 730, 764–766. Was this an injury? The boundaries of the concept would be a fertile source of litigation.

[88] Similar comments may be made about another proposed control mechanism, which is to confine the principle to cases in which inability to prove causation is a result of lack of medical knowledge of the causal mechanism (as in *Wilsher*) rather than lack of knowledge of the facts (as in *Hotson's* case). Again, the distinction is not based upon principle or even expediency. Proof of causation was just as difficult for Hotson as it was for Wilsher. It could be said that the need to prove causation was more unfair on Hotson, since the reason why he could not prove whether he had enough blood vessels after the fall was because the hospital had negligently failed to examine him. . . .

Comment

Lord Hoffmann is concerned to maintain the traditional 'all or nothing' approach. He rejects as 'arbitrary' and unprincipled attempts to define a small category of personal injury cases, including this one, in which 'loss of a chance' could be regarded as a loss appropriate for compensation. If no principled reason for distinguishing the cases can be found, he suggests, the introduction of claims for loss of chance will have such far-reaching implications that it ought not to be attempted by the common law, but left to Parliament. Lord Hoffmann does not entirely accurately reflect the arguments of Helen Reece whose article he cites in support of the 'all or nothing' approach (at [79]). Reece's article as we have seen proposed that there was a difference between 'deterministic' and 'quasi-indeterministic' cases, which was broadly compatible with the pattern of the case law and occasionally (as in *Hotson*, per Lord Mackay) apparent in legal reasoning. Lord Hoffmann presents her arguments as suggesting that law *always* takes a 'deterministic' approach. The only exception he mentions is the case of hypothetical acts of third parties.[24] In *Allied Maples v Simmons and Simmons* [1995] 4 All ER 907, for example, the defendants were solicitors, whose breach had removed the opportunity of negotiating a more favourable term in a contract. But it appears from Reece's article that she would include within the 'quasi-indeterministic' category some cases which do not involve hypothetical human actions.

Lord Hope of Craighead (dissenting)

The issue of damages

[95] The question which remains is whether the Appellant is entitled to damages. At first sight there can only be one answer to this question. A claimant who seeks damages for negligence in a case of personal injury must show on a balance of probabilities that the breach of duty caused or materially contributed to his injury. The judge held that the Appellant's condition deteriorated significantly during the period from April 1995 to January 1996. The medical experts were agreed that the lymphoma which had been developing in his left axilla spread into the pectoral muscle of the left side of his chest during this period, and that this is what precipitated the crisis in January 1996 (para 30). As both Latham and Mance LJJ said in the Court of Appeal, the delay in diagnosis caused the tumour to enlarge, invade neighbouring tissues and cause severe pain (paras 21 and 47). As Mance LJ put it, the enlarged tumour was a clear physical consequence of the doctor's negligence (para 86). On

---

[24] See further the discussion of *Wright v Cambridge Medical Group*, in the final part of this section.

the judge's findings a conventional view of the case would be that the delay in diagnosis resulted in a physical injury which entitled the Appellant to an award of damages for the consequences of that injury.

... [123] For the reasons which I have given at the outset of this opinion, ... I had hoped that it was not too late for the pain and suffering which the Appellant suffered due to the tumour's enlargement and the distress caused by his awareness that his condition had been misdiagnosed to be brought into account by way of an award of general damages. Unless this is done the Appellant will be left with no remedy at all for the consequences of the doctor's negligence. Very properly, as the facts that are needed are already there in the evidence and the action remains alive until this appeal and any further proceedings which may flow from it have been disposed of, the Respondent does not suggest that it would be either incompetent or unfair for the Claimant to seek such an award at this stage. The majority view that the appeal must be dismissed has deprived the Appellant of that opportunity.

Comment

Although Lord Hope joined Lord Nicholls in dissent, his reasons were different. He considered that the claimant would have had a straightforward claim for the pain, suffering and other immediate consequences of the spread of the tumour, including the need for any extra treatment if such were needed as a consequence of the breach. These effects he regards as sufficient damage to be the subject of a claim. It seems difficult to argue against this view, and it appeared to be accepted by Baroness Hale in the majority. However there is a conflict with the opinion of Lord Hoffmann. Lord Hoffmann included some difficult examples in his attempt to show that the immediate physical consequences of the breach should not be considered to give rise to a claim. For example, was the oxygenation of the blood in *Wisher* itself an injury? But it is hard to dismiss the pain and suffering associated with the larger tumour in *Gregg* and the claimant's knowledge of his likely death. These are not invented forms of injury, and it is suggested that at least in his narrower point (this damage in itself could have formed the basis of a claim), Lord Hope is correct. There are clear parallels with *Rothwell* (later in this Section), but there the condition was painless, and not causative of any reduced life expectancy.

The remaining issue is whether the diminution in survival prospects can be included as a head of damage in such a claim. Lord Hope suggests that it may be so included, subject to a reduction to reflect the fact that recovery was never a probability. This would be to allow 'loss of chance' via assessment of damages, rather than through redefinition of the damage suffered. It is similar to an argument which was rejected in the Court of Appeal and criticized by Lord Hoffmann in this case, namely that the physical changes can be regarded as a 'hook' on which to hang a claim for loss of chance:

Jane Stapleton, 'Cause-in-Fact and Scope of Liability for Consequences' (2003) 119 LQR 388, 423

... what is the minimum sufficient factor that can satisfy the orthodox form of past actionable damage in physical loss negligence claims? ... If C can come within whatever this requirement is held to be, C may well be able to use that factor as the 'hook' on to which to hang a lost chance as consequential on the actionable injury which is then recoverable under orthodox rules.

This is because the assessment of damages, far from ignoring chances and probabilities, habitually adjusts awards to reflect such chances and probabilities. Lord Hope derives support for his proposition from certain cases where some account of future prospects is made in assessment of damages (at [119]). But we have already seen that Lord Hoffmann distinguished these cases, suggesting that the estimated loss of prospects in such cases can be demonstrated on balance of probabilities to be the consequence of the defendant's breach (at [67]–[68]). This is precisely what remains to be proved in a case such as *Gregg v Scott*.

Baroness Hale of Richmond

[223] Until now, the gist of the action for personal injuries has been damage to the person. My negligence probably caused the loss of your leg: I pay you the full value of the loss of the leg (say £100,000). My negligence probably did not cause the loss of your leg. I do not pay you anything. Compare the loss of a chance approach: my negligence probably caused a reduction in the chance of your keeping that leg: I pay you the value of the loss of your leg, discounted by the chance that it would have happened anyway. If the chance of saving the leg was very good, say 90%, the claimant still gets only 90% of his damages, say £90,000. But if the chance of saving the leg was comparatively poor, say 20%, the claimant still gets £20,000. So the claimant ends up with less than full compensation even though his chances of a more favourable outcome were good. And the defendant ends up paying substantial sums even though the outcome is one for which by definition he cannot be shown to be responsible.

[224] Almost any claim for loss of an outcome could be reformulated as a claim for loss of a chance of that outcome. The implications of retaining them both as alternatives would be substantial. That is, the claimant still has the prospect of 100% recovery if he can show that it is more likely than not that the doctor's negligence caused the adverse outcome. But if he cannot show that, he also has the prospect of lesser recovery for loss of a chance. If (for the reasons given earlier) it would in practice always be tempting to conclude that the doctor's negligence had affected his chances to some extent, the claimant would almost always get something. It would be a "heads you lose everything, tails I win something" situation. But why should the Defendant not also be able to redefine the gist of the action if it suits him better?

[225] The Appellant in this case accepts that the proportionate recovery effect must cut both ways. If the claim is characterised as loss of a chance, those with a better than evens chance would still only get a proportion of the full value of their claim. But I do not think that he accepts that the same would apply in cases where the claim is characterised as loss of an outcome. In that case there is no basis for calculating the odds. If the two are alternatives available in every case, the defendant will almost always be liable for something. He will have lost the benefit of the 50% chance that causation cannot be proved. But if the two approaches cannot sensibly live together, the claimants who currently obtain full recovery on an adverse outcome basis might in future only achieve a proportionate recovery. This would surely be a case of two steps forward, three steps back for the great majority of straightforward personal injury cases. In either event, the expert evidence would have to be far more complex than it is at present. Negotiations and trials would be a great deal more difficult. Recovery would be much less predictable both for claimants and for defendants' liability insurers. There is no reason in principle why the change in approach should be limited

to medical negligence. Whether or not the policy choice is between retaining the present definition of personal injury in outcome terms and redefining it in loss of opportunity terms, introducing the latter would cause far more problems in the general run of personal injury claims than the policy benefits are worth . . . .

[227] . . . the Claimant would have been entitled to damages for any adverse outcomes which were caused by the doctor's negligence. But the possibilities there canvassed were not canvassed in evidence or argument before the Judge, nor have we been invited to remit the case for further findings. With some regret, therefore, I agree that this appeal should be dismissed.

Comment

Baroness Hale's judgment is dominated by policy concerns, and in particular by the prospects that a large proportion of personal injury actions would be transformed by the 'loss of chance' analysis into actions for a lost chance of avoiding personal injury. The alternative, of allowing claimants the freedom of choosing whether to make a claim for lost chance or for physical injury, would be unfair to defendants and, presumably, too expensive to be supported. Baroness Hale (at [192]) made clear that the prospect of major upheaval is what distinguishes the medical lost chance claim from the other key recent cases we have considered in this chapter.

Concluding Remarks: *Gregg v Scott*

As Baroness Hale noted, *Gregg v Scott* is different from previous cases where 'loss of chance' has been argued in one very significant respect. At the time of the House of Lords' judgments, it was still unclear whether the claimant was going to be a survivor. Although he had suffered significant pain, harm, and distress (none of which formed the basis of his claim), he had not lost his chance of survival. That chance had been diminished, rather than lost. In *Hotson*, the damage had been suffered, but causation was unclear. In the successful lost chance cases, such as *Allied Maples* or *Chaplin v Hicks*, it was clear that the claimant could not now be successful in negotiating a term in a contract, or in winning a beauty competition. Through the defendant's breach, the chance of success had gone. In *Gregg v Scott*, the chance is still in the future. It is a diminished chance case, rather than a lost chance case. This reason featured prominently in the majority judgments of Lord Phillips and Baroness Hale. It did not feature in the other majority judgment of Lord Hoffmann, who was more concerned to reiterate the traditional 'all or nothing' approach in general terms.

Issues concerning the nature of the required damage in a personal injury action arose in a very different form in an appeal heard soon afterwards by the House of Lords. This forms a part of the asbestos litigation, but is not concerned with mesothelioma.

Rothwell v Chemical and Insulating Company Limited [2007] UKHL 39; [2008] 1 AC 281

'Pleural plaques' are symptomless changes in the lungs, caused by exposure to asbestos. They are **not causally related** to the development of asbestos-related diseases such as lung cancer; but there is a **statistical** correlation between the development of the plaques, and the future development of such diseases. At first instance, the judge had held for the claimants. He argued that the plaques themselves did not constitute physical injury, but they were caused by the piercing of the lung by asbestos fibres. 'This *could* constitute injury; and the consequential losses (including the possibility of future disease) were recoverable. Indeed, employers and insurers had been paying compensation in respect of such plaques for the previous 20 years. The House of Lords, in agreement with the Court of Appeal, put an end to this practice. They concluded that there was no compensable physical harm in these cases.

Note: one of the claimants in this case also claimed to have suffered distinct damage in the form of 'anxiety neurosis'. This is a recognized psychiatric illness and is very different, in the eyes of the law, from pure anxiety. The parts of the judgment in this case relating to anxiety neurosis are extracted in Chapter 6, Section 1, 'Psychiatric damage'.

In our extracts from the House of Lords' judgment, members of the House make reference to the dissenting opinion, in the Court of Appeal, of Smith LJ. In this dissent, Smith LJ had argued quite convincingly that pleural plaques, though *usually* symptomless, were nevertheless a 'physical injury', and that when the other consequences of this injury were taken into account (particularly enhanced future risk) this injury could not be said to be trivial. That being so, they constituted actionable damage. This 'aggregation' argument was rejected by all members of the House of Lords. They argued that the crucial question is not whether the plaques amount to an 'injury', but whether they amount to 'damage'. Other factors such as anxiety and enhanced risk can increase the damages that ought to be awarded if there is an actionable harm; but they cannot turn a change which is not material damage into material damage. The curious result is that the damage in these cases was unrecoverable because it was too trivial (*de minimis non curat lex*); yet at the same time, awards have been made for the same condition, including amounts for future risk and anxiety, of a clearly non-trivial amount. The line taken by the House of Lords is that the *actionable damage itself* needs to be substantial.

Lord Hoffmann, *Rothwell*

18 Smith LJ said that pleural plaques amounted to "an injury". She gave two reasons: first, in rare cases plaques might (on account of the position in which they developed) cause symptoms. In such a case the symptoms are not the injury. It is the plaque. That shows that the plaque is an injury and it must be an injury whether it causes symptoms or not. Similarly, the plaque is a lesion to the pleura. A lesion to the body, for example, a disfiguring scar, would be a compensatable injury. That shows that a lesion is an injury.

19 It seems to me, with respect, that Smith LJ asked herself the wrong question. One is not concerned with whether the plaque is in some sense "injury" or (as she went on to decide) a "disease". The question is whether the claimant has suffered damage. That means: is he appreciably worse off on account of having plaques? The rare victim whose plaques are causing symptoms is worse off on that account. Likewise, the man with the disfiguring lesion is worse off because he is disfigured. In the usual case, however (including those of all the claimants in these proceedings) the plaques have no effect. They have not caused damage.

20 Smith LJ also found support for the aggregation theory in section 32A of the Supreme Court Act 1981.... She said, at para 133:

"In my view, the wording of section 32A is consistent only with the proposition that a claimant has only one cause of action for all personal injury consequences of a wrongful act or omission. The wording of the section is not consistent with the notion that the same exposure to asbestos can and does give rise to separate torts in respect of each consequence. Because he has only one cause of action, as soon as the claimant knows that he has one personal injury consequence, he must sue for all such possible consequences. Under section 32A, he is able to defer the assessment of that part of his damages which relates to future risks, instead of having to accept them now, imperfectly assessed, as he was required to do at common law. Whether he chooses a provisional or final award is a matter for him."

21 That seems to me undoubtedly correct. But she then went on to say:

"The important point is that, because he has only one cause of action, his damage must include the risks that other serious conditions might eventuate. Therefore, both the existing condition and the future risks must be brought into account when the judge is considering whether the damage is more than minimal."

22 It is the last "therefore" that seems to me, with respect, to precede a non sequitur. It is true that *if* he has a cause of action, his damage must include the risks that other serious conditions might eventuate. But that does not mean that such risks are taken into account in deciding whether he has a cause of action, that is to say, whether he has suffered (and not merely may suffer) more than minimal damage.

Lord Hope

50 I am not attracted by the other reasons of policy that led the majority in the Court of Appeal [2006] ICR 1458 to the conclusion that it was undesirable that the development of pleural plaques should give rise to a cause of action: para 67. I would hold however that there is no cause of action because the pleural plaques in themselves do not give rise to any harmful physical effects which can be said to constitute damage, and because of the absence of a direct causative link between them and the risks and the anxiety which, on their own, are not actionable. I would apply the same proposition for the purposes of the limitation rules. Time has not yet begun to run against any of the claimants who may have the misfortune of developing an asbestos-related disease in the future which is actionable.

Given our discussion of *Barker v Corus* and *Gregg v Scott*, earlier in this section, it is notable that members of the House of Lords declined to treat 'risk' as actionable damage for the purpose of this case. It is clear that the move made in *Barker*, to calculate damages on the basis of the increased risk imposed by the defendants rather than on the basis of the damage suffered, was a particular response to the issues arising in the *Fairchild* 'enclave' of cases. It has not been allowed to radiate out beyond the 'material contribution' cases. (In fact for somewhat similar reasons *Barker* has now been reinterpreted to omit this element.)

Further litigation flowed from the decision in *Pleural Plaques*. In Scotland, the effect of the case was reversed by legislation, providing that such plaques would constitute recoverable damage: Damages (Asbestos-related Conditions) (Scotland) Act 2009. This legislation was the subject of judicial review proceedings brought by a number of liability insurers, which once again required the attention of the Supreme Court. The application was based on a variety of grounds including inconsistency with the insurers' rights under the ECHR; the competence of the Scottish Parliament; and common law principles (an unreasonable, irrational, and arbitrary use of legislative authority). The argument that the principles of common law articulated in *Rothwell* were clear and simple, and in no way embodied judicial policy reasoning, played an important part in the insurers' challenge. Equally, the existence of an alternative possible approach as set out by Smith LJ in the Court of Appeal was important in leading the Outer House of the Court of Session to decline an initial application which sought to prevent the legislation from coming into force at all: *Axa General Insurance and Others, re Judicial Review of the Damages (Asbestos-related Conditions) (Scotland) Act 2009* [2009] CSOH 57.

The legislation has survived the challenge, the UK Supreme Court holding that the Scottish Parliament had legislated on the basis of a perception of social injustice, and its view could not be dismissed as unreasonable. Further, the means adopted were proportionate to the aim. The following short extract relates to the insurers' arguments under the Human Rights Act, that there had been interference with their 'possessions' (an appeal to Art 1, Protocol 1, ECHR). There are resonances with the subsequent opinion of the Supreme Court as to which risks are taken on by liability insurers, in the *Trigger Litigation* discussed in Section 2.5.

Lord Hope of Craighead, *AXA Insurers and Others*
[2011] UKSC 46

37 There are however two special features of this case which seem to me to show that the balance that was struck cannot be said to be disproportionate. The first is that the claims which the Act makes possible will only succeed if it is shown that the exposure to asbestos was caused by the employer's negligence. Indeed, the Act is conspicuously careful in its draftsmanship. Its effect is restricted to new claims and to claims that have been commenced but not yet determined. It preserves all the other defences that may be open on the law or the facts, other than the single question whether the pleural plaques themselves are actionable. It achieves what it has to achieve. But it does no more than that.

38 The second special feature is that the business in which insurers are engaged and in pursuance of which they wrote the policies that will give rise to the obligation to indemnify is a commercial venture which is inextricably associated with risk. Because they were long term policies there was inevitably a risk that circumstances, unseen at the date when they were written, might occur which would increase the burden of liability. Phrases such as "bodily injury or disease" are capable of expanding the meaning that they were originally thought to have as medical knowledge develops and circumstances change. Diseases that were previously unknown or rarely seen may become familiar and give rise to claims that had not at the outset been anticipated. The effects of asbestos provide ample evidence of this phenomenon, as people began to live long enough after exposure to it to contract mesothelioma and other harmful asbestos-related diseases.

39 The nature, number and value of claims were therefore always liable to develop in ways that were unpredictable. The premium income that was expected to meet the claims that were foreseen at the outset may have no relationship, in the long term, to the burden that in fact materialises. How best to provide for that eventuality is an art which takes the rough with the smooth and depends on the exercise of judgment and experience. So the fact that the effect of the Act will be to increase the burden on the insurers, even to the extent that was anticipated, does not seem to me to carry much weight.

4. CONCLUSIONS

i. Negligence, as we saw in Chapter 1, is a tort requiring damage. We set out the basic causal tests in Chapter 3. Causation, however, has been one of the most contested and difficult aspects of the tort of negligence, and cases involving multiple potential causes raise some of the most difficult questions in the entire law of tort. Here, we have addressed some of those issues, and it will be seen that they continue to test the courts at the highest level.

ii. We have seen in this chapter that courts sometimes recognize evidence of 'material contribution to damage' as sufficient evidence of a causal link. The nature of this 'material contribution' test, and its relationship to 'but-for' causation, have however been exceptionally difficult to identify. As things stand, there is some evidence that a claimant who can show that the defendant's negligence made a 'material contribution' to the *process* by which injury was caused will have satisfied the applicable causal tests. In the case of a divisible injury, there are grounds to think that this is no more than an application of the 'but-for' test, and in principle the damages should be proportionate to reflect the defendant's contribution. In the case of an indivisible injury however, the current state of the authorities suggests that liability will be for the full injury suffered. Further, this would appear to amount to a broader test than 'but-for', though courts have not stated this with clarity. It has been urged by Jane Stapleton that unnecessary contributing factors are indeed correctly called causes, and this is consistent with much of the case law. However, it has also been suggested by the same writer that damages might then be reduced to reflect the fact that injury may have been suffered in any event—a move which would appear to reintroduce the difficulties of 'but-for' causation, though leaving a greater element of choice.

iii. A more innovative move was made by the decision in *Fairchild*, recognizing evidence of material contribution to the *risk* of injury as sufficient proof of a causal link in certain defined circumstances of scientific uncertainty. Within the *Fairchild* 'enclave', damages at common law are recognized as proportionate to the contribution to risk, though since the insurance cases of *Trigger* and *IEG v Zurich*, this is perceived as a matter of broad fairness, rather than of redefinition of injury in terms of 'risk'. The latter possibility would have caused enormous difficulties for insured employers and in the case of *Trigger*, would have invalidated the very insurance policies which have been the clear source of compensation underlying the development in *Fairchild* itself. Where mesothelioma is concerned, section 3 of the Compensation Act 2006 ensures that liability is not proportionate, but full, within the range of application of the statute. *Fairchild* has however been applied to lung cancer, and thus the *Fairchild* enclave may be capable of expansion. So far, however, the courts have not been inclined to extend the treatment of risk as injury to other areas, and in particular have not recognized an action for 'lost chances' in the medical or industrial injury contexts. The approach taken in *Trigger* and *Zurich* makes plain that the proportionate nature of recovery in the *Fairchild* enclave of common law, like the rest of that enclave, is perceived to be a just and practical response, rather than a general development of legal principle. Legal development, however, is often unpredictable, and this chapter underlines the surprises it may hold.

FURTHER READING

Material Contribution

Bailey, S., 'What is a Material Contribution?' (2010) 30 LS 167.

Broadbent, A., 'Epidemiological Evidence in Proof of Specific Causation' (2011) 17 *Legal Theory* 237.

Green, S., 'Fairchild and the Single Agent Criterion' (2017) 133 Law Quarterly Review 25

Green, S., *Causation in Negligence* (Hart, 2014)

Hoffmann, L., 'Causation', in R. Goldberg (ed.), *Perspectives on Causation* (Hart Publishing, 2011)

Khoury, L., 'Causation and Risk in the Highest Courts of Canada, England and France' (2008) 124 LQR 103–31.

McIvor, C., 'The "Doubles the Risk" Test for Causation and Other Related Judicial Misconceptions about Epidemiology', in G. A. Pitel, J. W. Neyers and E. Chamberlain, *Tort Law: Challenging Orthodoxy* (Hart Publishing, 2013).

Merkin R., 'Insurance and Reinsurance in the *Fairchild* Enclave' (2016) 36 LS 302.

Merkin, R. and Steele, J., 'Compensating Mesothelioma Victims' (2011) 127 LQR 329.

Miller, C., 'Causation in Personal Injury: Legal or Epidemiological Common Sense?' (2006) 26 LS 544–69.

Morgan, J., 'Causation, Politics and Law: The English—and Scottish—Asbestos Saga', in R. Goldberg (ed.), *Perspectives on Causation* (Hart Publishing, 2011)

Morgan, J., 'Reinterpreting the reinterpretation of Fairchild' (2015) 74 CLJ 395

Stapleton, J., 'Choosing What We Mean By Causation in the Law' (2008) 73 Missouri Law Rev 433.

Stapleton, J., 'Factual Causation, Mesothelioma and Statistical Validity' (2012) 128 LQR 221.

Stapleton, J., 'Unnecessary Causes' (2013) 129 LQR 39.

Stapleton, J. and Steel, S., 'Causes and Contributions' (2016) 132 LQR 363

Stauch, M., 'Material Contribution as a Response to Causal Uncertainty—Time for a Rethink' (2009) CLJ 27–30.

Steel, S., 'Justifying Exceptions to Proof of Causation in Tort Law' (2015) 78 MLR 729

Steel, S., *Proof of Causation in Tort Law* (Cambridge University Press, 2015)

Wikeley, N., *Compensation for Industrial Disease* (Aldershot: Dartmouth, 1993).

Wright, R., 'Causation in Tort Law' (1985) 73 Cal L Rev 1735

Loss of a Chance

Fleming, J., 'Probabilistic Causation in Tort Law' (1989) Can Bar Rev 661.

Jansen, N., 'The Idea of a Lost Chance' (1999) 19 OJLS 271.

Lee, J., 'Inconsiderate Alterations in our Laws: Legislative Reversal of Supreme Court Decisions', in J. Lee (ed.), *From House of Lords to Supreme Court* (Hart Publishing, 2010).

Lunney, M., 'What Price a Chance?' (1995) 15 LS 1.

Neuberger of Abbotsbury, Lord, 'Loss of a Chance and Causation' (2008) 24 PN 206–14.

Stapleton, J., 'Cause-in-Fact and the Scope of Liability for Consequences' (2003) 119 LQR 388.

Stauch, M., 'Causation, Risk and Loss of Chance in Medical Negligence' (1997) 17 OJLS 205.

Steel, S., 'Rationalising Loss of a Chance in Tort', in S. Pitel, J. Neyers, and E. Chamberlain (eds), *Tort Law: Challenging Orthodoxy* (Hart Publishing, 2013).

5

DEFENCES TO NEGLIGENCE

CENTRAL ISSUES

i) This chapter introduces three defences to negligence. Each of these is also relevant to at least some other torts. One of them, illegality, is still more broadly relevant, applying across a broad range of civil claims. Additional defences are considered in relation to specific torts, in appropriate chapters.

ii) **Contributory negligence** is frequently encountered. Since 1945, if the claimant's own fault has contributed to the damage suffered then the court is required to reduce damages on the basis of relative 'responsibility'. Responsibility involves questions both of causal influence, and of fault.

iii) On some occasions, the claimant's role in the injury suffered is not adequately reflected by a reduction in damages. Instead, the action should fail altogether. This may be achieved by deciding that there is no duty of care; or that the chain of causation has been broken (Chapter 3). In addition, there are further defences which may achieve this outcome.

iv) The first of these is *volenti non fit injuria* or willing assumption of risk. This defence requires an agreement to waive the legal consequences of risk, or at least close and active participation in its creation. The defence is now rarely successful for reasons to be explored.

v) The **illegality** defence (also referred to as *ex turpi causa*) exists as a matter of public policy: a claim will fail if it arises directly out of the claimant's own 'illegal' act. Only in the last few decades has illegality become established as a defence to tort actions, and the criteria are still evolving. After a period of marked uncertainty, it has been determined that courts should seek to give effect to the policies which underlie the illegality bar and to the policies which underlie the criminal prohibitions themselves; and should not develop inflexible rules. Some difficulty remains in identifying how the general approach should be applied within the law of tort.

1. DEFENCES TO NEGLIGENCE AND DEFENCES TO OTHER TORTS

The defences considered here are all relevant to the tort of negligence, but each of them is also applicable to a range of other torts. Not all of them apply universally however. We saw in Chapter 2 that contributory negligence has been held not to be a defence to an action in deceit, nor to trespass to the person, on the basis that the pre-1945 version of the defence did not apply to these torts. At the same time, other torts are qualified by important defences quite distinct from those in negligence. Available defences are part of the balance struck in particular torts between tortfeasor, claimant, and other interests. For this reason, we will deal with specific defences in connection with specific torts, in later chapters.

2. CONTRIBUTORY NEGLIGENCE

Since 1945, contributory negligence has been a partial, rather than a complete defence. Where the court finds that 'fault' on the part both of the claimant and of the defendant has contributed to the damage suffered, then damages will be reduced to the extent that the court thinks just and equitable.

Law Reform (Contributory Negligence) Act 1945 ('the 1945 Act')

1. —(1) Where any person suffers damage as the result partly of his own fault and partly of the fault of any other person or persons, a claim in respect of that damage shall not be defeated by reason of the fault of the person suffering the damage, but the damages recoverable in respect thereof shall be reduced to such extent as the court thinks just and equitable having regard to the claimant's share in the responsibility for the damage ...

...

4. The following expressions have the meanings hereby respectively assigned to them, that is to say—

...

"damage" includes loss of life and personal injury; ... "fault" means negligence, breach of statutory duty or other act or omission which gives rise to a liability in tort or would, apart from this Act, give rise to the defence of contributory negligence;

Until this statutory reform, fault on the part of the plaintiff operated as a complete defence if it was found that the fault contributed to the damage:

Lord Blackburn, *Cayzer, Irvine & Co v Carron Ltd* **(1884)**
9 App Cas 873, at 881 (HL)

The rule of law is that if there is blame causing the accident on both sides, however small that blame may be on one side, the loss lies where it falls.

The statutory provisions mark a considerable improvement over the previous common law, in terms not only of fairness but also of simplicity, since the stalemate rule was subject to considerable variation over the years. For example, courts in England devised a 'last opportunity' rule, whereby a plaintiff whose fault had played some part in creating a hazard could still recover damages if the defendant had the last chance to avoid the harm.[1] This rule and the many intricate variations around it need not detain us,[2] because on the whole the move to apportionment on the basis of what the court 'thinks just and equitable' has had the effect of cutting through all this. This effect may however have been more far-reaching than intended, as we will see.

The statutory provisions impose an *obligation* on courts to give effect to fairness between the parties when considering relative responsibility for the injury: section 1(1) provides that the claim 'shall not' be defeated by reason of fault on the part of the person suffering the damage. This could be read as excluding any other defences that are justified by reference to the claimant's fault (as in illegality and in some instances *volenti*, discussed later). This interpretation has not been adopted; but there are signs that apportionment is thought by some to be a more appropriate response in the context of the modern law of tort.

Since fairness and justice are the guiding principles for reducing damages under section 1(1), we should note that fairness in *apportionment*, taking into account relative fault and responsibility for damage, might not produce fair *outcomes* once the bigger picture is considered. This is a particular issue in actions for personal injury, especially in those areas where liability insurance is compulsory (as is the case, for example, in respect of road traffic accidents and most injuries at work). The chances are that in these cases the claimant does not carry 'first party' personal insurance, which would cover the insured party's own loss. The portion of damages withheld because of contributory negligence frequently represents loss that the claimant must bear alone. For example, a cyclist who gets too close to a line of parked cars may well have damages reduced if a car driver carelessly opens a door into her path; and a pedestrian who does not take sufficient care in crossing the road may have damages reduced even if the car that hits her is travelling too fast. In each of these cases, since first party insurance is voluntary, it is likely that there will be an element of uncompensated loss that is not covered by insurance.

2.1 APPLYING THE STATUTORY PROVISIONS: SECTION 1(1)

Section 1(1) of the 1945 Act specifies that damages will be reduced where damage is suffered partly as a result of the claimant's fault, and partly as a result of the fault of another party. Clearly, both parties' 'fault' (the meaning of which we consider below) must be *a cause* of the damage suffered.

It is important to be clear that it is the *damage*, not the accident (if any) that must result partly from the fault of each party. Thus, a claimant who fails to wear a seatbelt will have damages reduced if his or her injuries are rendered more severe by that failure, even though failure to wear the belt does nothing to 'cause' the accident itself.

[1] *Davies v Mann* (1842) 152 ER 588.
[2] See G. Williams, *Joint Torts and Contributory Negligence* (Stevens & Sons, 1951), chapter 9.

Lord Denning MR, *Froom v Butcher*
[1976] QB 286, at 292

The question is not what was the cause of the accident. It is rather what was the cause of the damage. In most accidents on the road the bad driving, which causes the accident, also causes the ensuing damage. But in seat belt cases the cause of the accident is one thing. The cause of the damage is another. The *accident* is caused by the bad driving. The *damage* is caused in part by the bad driving of the defendant, and in part by the failure of the plaintiff to wear a seat belt. If the plaintiff was to blame in not wearing a seat belt, the damage is in part the result of his own fault. He must bear some share in the responsibility for the damage: and his damages fall to be reduced to such extent as the court thinks just and equitable.

'Fault' and intention

Section 1(1) refers to damage which results partly from the fault of the injured party, and partly from the fault of the defendant. The definition of 'fault' in section 4 (extracted above) is much broader than negligence or lack of care. It encompasses any act that may be tortious, or would give rise to a defence of contributory negligence at common law. What if it is not the defendant but the *claimant* who intentionally causes (self-)harm?

Reeves v Commissioner of Police of the Metropolis [2000] 1 AC 360

The police breached a duty of care owed to a prisoner, to keep him under watch in order to guard against a suicide attempt.

The House of Lords thought that this was a rare case where a duty is owed in order to protect a person against self-harm. It would be illogical then to accept that the deceased's act in killing himself could break the chain of causation (Chapter 3, Section 6). But could the intentional act of suicide amount to 'contributory negligence' within the meaning of the 1945 Act? The House of Lords held that it could.

Lord Hope emphasized that 'one should not be unduly inhibited by the use of the word "negligence" in the expression "contributory negligence"' (at 383). Section 1 could also apply where the claimant's fault takes the form of an intentional act.

Lord Hope, *Reeves v Commissioner of Police of the Metropolis*
[2000] 1 AC 360, at 382–3

It has been said that this definition of "fault" comprises two limbs ... The first limb, which is referable to the defendant's conduct, comprises various acts or omissions which give rise to a liability in tort. The second limb, which is referable to the plaintiff's conduct, deals with acts or omissions which would, but for the Act, have given rise to the defence of contributory negligence. The first is directed to the basis of the defendant's liability, while the second is concerned with his defence on the ground that the damage was the result partly of the plaintiff's own negligence ... the question whether the deceased was at fault in this case must be considered with reference to the words used to describe the second limb.

. . . It seems to me that the definition of 'fault' in section 4 is wide enough, when examined as a whole and in its context, to extend to a plaintiff's deliberate acts as well as to his negligent acts. This reading of the word would enable the court, in an appropriate case, to reduce the amount of damages to reflect the contribution which the plaintiff's own deliberate act of self-harm made to the loss.

Children

It is clearly possible for children to be contributorily negligent in appropriate circumstances. In *Young v Kent County Council* [2005] EWHC 1342, an action under the Occupiers' Liability Act 1984 (Chapter 12), a child of 12 was found to be contributorily negligent when he jumped on a skylight on the roof of a school. While the school ought to have taken more steps to keep children away from the roof, the claimant should have appreciated the risks associated with the skylight itself. Similarly, in *Honnor v Lewis* [2005] EWHC 747 (QB), damages were reduced by 20 per cent where a child of 11 stepped out into a road without checking for traffic. As explained in Chapter 3, children will be judged by a standard that is relevant to their age: very young children are unlikely to be found to have been contributorily negligent.

2.2 APPORTIONMENT

Apportionment of responsibility between the parties ought in principle to be the most difficult aspect of the contributory negligence defence. By section 1(1), this apportionment reflects relative 'responsibility' for the damage suffered. 'Responsibility' in this context is a question partly of causal influence, and partly of degree of fault. In practice, courts arrive at a reduction in a fairly rough and ready way. Apportionment has recently been considered in the Supreme Court.

Jackson v Murray
[2015] UKSC 5

The pursuer was thirteen when she stepped from behind a school minibus and was struck by the defender's car. The driver was travelling within the speed limit, but too fast: he did not make allowances for the possibility a child would attempt to cross, and did not keep a proper lookout. If he had taken due care, he would not have hit her. The trial judge assessed the child's contributory negligence at 90 per cent. On appeal, the court reduced this to 70 per cent. Unusually, there was an appeal to the Supreme Court on the question of apportionment. The reduction in damages for contributory negligence was reduced (by a majority) to 50 per cent. The Supreme Court needed to consider the basis on which an appellate court could interfere with the decision of a trial judge on the question of apportionment. It was concluded that there was a contradiction in the analysis of the trial judge which was not resolved in the first appeal; and that the appellate court could therefore legitimately intervene.

Lord Reed (for the majority), *Jackson v Murray*

Review of apportionment

27 It is not possible for a court to arrive at an apportionment which is demonstrably correct. The problem is not merely that the factors which the court is required to consider are incapable of precise measurement. More fundamentally, the blameworthiness of the pursuer and the defender are incommensurable. The defender has acted in breach of a duty (not necessarily a duty of care) which was owed to the pursuer; the pursuer, on the other hand, has acted with a want of regard for her own interests. The word "fault" in section 1(1), as applied to "the person suffering the damage" on the one hand, and the "other person or persons" on the other hand, is therefore being used in two different senses. The court is not comparing like with like.

28 It follows that the apportionment of responsibility is inevitably a somewhat rough and ready exercise (a feature reflected in the judicial preference for round figures), and that a variety of possible answers can legitimately be given. That is consistent with the requirement under section 1(1) to arrive at a result which the court considers "just and equitable". Since different judges may legitimately take different views of what would be just and equitable in particular circumstances, it follows that those differing views should be respected, within the limits of reasonable disagreement.

Lord Reed makes the point here that the process of apportionment required by the 1945 Act, is simply not *capable* of being 'exact'. He connects this to the preference for use of round figures: assessments of contributory negligence will take the form of multiples of ten and, sometimes, five. Turning to 'culpability', there is a difference in the type of 'fault' on the part of the claimant and on the part of the defendant. But in addition, there is a need to take account not only of fault, but also of 'causative potency'. These are, simply, different questions.[3] Ultimately, the Supreme Court felt able to assess the validity of the balance struck in this case by asking whether it was consistent in its own terms. As explained in the extract below, it could indeed be concluded that the court below had 'gone wrong'.

Lord Reed, *Jackson v Murray*

40 As the Extra Division recognised, it is necessary when applying section 1(1) of the 1945 Act to take account both of the blameworthiness of the parties and the causative potency of their acts. In relation to causation, the Extra Division based its view that "the attribution of causative potency to the driver must be greater than that to the pedestrian" on the fact that "a car is potentially a dangerous weapon". Like the Court of Appeal in *Eagle v Chambers*, I would take the potentially dangerous nature of a car being driven at speed into account when assessing blameworthiness; but the overall assessment of responsibility should not be affected by the heading under which that factor is taken into account. Even leaving out of account the potentially dangerous nature of a car being driven at speed, I would not have assessed the causative potency of the conduct of the defender as being any less than that

---

[3] For an argument that 'causative potency' should play no part in apportionment, see J Goudkamp and L Klar, 'Apportionment of Damages for Contributory Negligence: the Causal Potency Criterion' (2016) 15 *Alta L Rev* 1–14.

of the pursuer. This is not a case, such as *Ehrari v Curry* [2007] EWCA Civ 120; [2007] RTR 521 (where contributory negligence was assessed at 70%), in which a pedestrian steps directly into the path of a car which is travelling at a reasonable speed, and the driver fails to take avoiding action as promptly as he ought to have done. In such a case, the more direct and immediate cause of the damage can be said to be the conduct of the pedestrian, which interrupted a situation in which an accident would not otherwise have occurred. Nor is it a case, such as *Eagle v Chambers* (in which contributory negligence was assessed at 40%) or *McCluskey v Wallace* (where the contributory negligence of a child was assessed at 20%), in which a driver ploughs into a pedestrian who has been careless of her own safety but has been in his line of vision for long enough for him easily to have avoided her. In the present case, the causation of the injury depended upon the combination of the pursuer's attempting to cross the road when she did, and the defender's driving at an excessive speed and without keeping a proper look-out. If the pursuer had waited until the defender had passed, he would not have collided with her. Equally, if he had slowed to a reasonable speed in the circumstances and had kept a proper look-out, he would have avoided her.

41 Given the Extra Division's conclusion that the causative potency of the defender's conduct was greater than that of the pursuer's, their conclusion that "the major share of the responsibility must be attributed to the pursuer", to the extent of 70%, can only be explained on the basis that the pursuer was considered to be far more blameworthy than the defender. I find that difficult to understand, given the factors which their Lordships identified. As I have explained, they rightly considered that the pursuer did not take reasonable care for her own safety: either she did not look to her left within a reasonable time before stepping out, or she failed to make a reasonable judgment as to the risk posed by the defender's car. On the other hand, as the Extra Division recognised, regard has to be had to the circumstances of the pursuer. As they pointed out, she was only 13 at the time, and a 13 year old will not necessarily have the same level of judgment and self-control as an adult. As they also pointed out, she had to take account of the defender's car approaching at speed, in very poor light conditions, with its headlights on. As they recognised, the assessment of speed in those circumstances is far from easy, even for an adult, and even more so for a 13 year old. It is also necessary to bear in mind that the situation of a pedestrian attempting to cross a relatively major road with a 60 mph speed limit, after dusk and without street lighting, is not straightforward, even for an adult.

42 On the other hand, the Extra Division considered that the defender's behaviour was "culpable to a substantial degree". I would agree with that assessment. He had to observe the road ahead and keep a proper look-out, adjusting his speed in the event that a potential hazard presented itself. As the Extra Division noted, he was found to have been driving at an excessive speed and not to have modified his speed to take account of the potential danger presented by the minibus. The danger was obvious, because the minibus had its hazard lights on. Notwithstanding that danger, he continued driving at 50 mph. As the Lord Ordinary noted, the Highway Code advises drivers that "at 40 mph your vehicle will probably kill any pedestrians it hits" . . . . that level of danger points to a very considerable degree of blameworthiness on the part of a driver who fails to take reasonable care while driving at speed.

43 In these circumstances, I cannot discern in the reasoning of the Extra Division any satisfactory explanation of their conclusion that the major share of the responsibility must be attributed to the pursuer: a conclusion which, as I have explained, appears to depend on the view that the pursuer's conduct was far more blameworthy than that of the defender. As it appears to me, the defender's conduct played at least an equal role to that of the pursuer in causing the damage and was at least equally blameworthy.

44 The view that parties are equally responsible for the damage suffered by the pursuer is substantially different from the view that one party is much more responsible than the other. Such a wide difference of view exceeds the ambit of reasonable disagreement, and warrants the conclusion that the court below has gone wrong. I would accordingly allow the appeal and award 50% of the agreed damages to the pursuer.

Fixed Apportionment

The inexact nature of the apportionment exercise is very clearly illustrated by the existence of 'fixed tariffs' in some circumstances, most famously illustrated by *Froom v Butcher*:

Lord Denning MR, *Froom v Butcher*
[1976] QB 286, at 295–6

Whenever there is an accident, the negligent driver must bear by far the greater share of responsibility. It was his negligence which caused the accident. It also was a prime cause of the whole of the damage. But in so far as the damage might have been avoided or lessened by wearing a seat belt, the injured person must bear some share. But how much should this be? Is it proper to inquire whether the driver was grossly negligent or only slightly negligent? Or whether the failure to wear a seat belt was entirely inexcusable or almost forgivable? If such an inquiry could easily be undertaken, it might be as well to do it. In *Davies v. Swan Motor Co. (Swansea) Ltd.* [1949] 2 K.B. 291, 326, the court said that consideration should be given not only to the causative potency of a particular factor, but also its blameworthiness. But we live in a practical world. In most of these cases the liability of the driver is admitted, the failure to wear a seat belt is admitted, the only question is: what damages should be payable? This question should not be prolonged by an expensive inquiry into the degree of blameworthiness on either side, which would be hotly disputed. Suffice it to assess a share of responsibility which will be just and equitable in the great majority of cases.

The solution in *Froom* was to adopt a 'tariff' which would apply to the large majority of seat-belt cases, without having to reopen the particular question of degree of fault in each case. Where injuries would have been avoided altogether by wearing a seatbelt, there should be a reduction in damages of 25 per cent. In a case where injuries would have been less severe had a belt been worn, the reduction in damages would be 15 per cent.

In *Capps v Miller* [1989] 1 WLR 839, the plaintiff suffered severe brain damage when, through the 'atrocious driving' of the defendant, he was knocked off his moped. He was wearing a safety helmet, as was required by regulation,[4] but had not fastened it properly. Failure to wear a helmet was equated with failure to wear a seatbelt. But the Court of Appeal took the view that failure to fasten the helmet involved a lower degree of blameworthiness than failure to wear a helmet at all. Consequently, there should be a smaller reduction in damages than the lower figure in *Froom v Butcher*, and this was set at 10 per cent. The same lenient approach was not applied to a mother who had strapped her three-year-old daughter into a booster seat instead of an age-appropriate child seat in *Hughes v Williams* [2013] EWCA Civ 455: her contribution was assessed at 25 per cent. The greater controversy is in

---

[4] Motor Cycles (Protective Helmets) Regulations 1980.

applying the contributory negligence 'tariff' to a case concerned with the mother's share of *liability* to her daughter, an issue discussed in Chapter 7.

The approach to apportionment has become well settled in respect of seatbelts and motor-cycle helmets,[5] but what of cycle helmets? The wearing of cycle helmets is not mandatory, but the Highway Code informs cyclists that they 'should' wear a helmet which conforms to current regulations. *Froom v Butcher* applied a reduction for contributory negligence at a time before wearing a seatbelt became mandatory (although even at that time, it was mandatory for seatbelts to be fitted in the front seats of a vehicle). As Lord Denning put it:

Lord Denning MR, *Froom v Butcher*
[1976] QB 286, at 293

Everyone is free to wear it or not as he pleases. Free in this sense, that if he does not wear it he is free from any penalty by the magistrates. Free in the sense that everyone is free to run his head against a brick wall, if he pleases. He can do it if he likes without being punished by the law. But it is not a sensible thing to do. If he does it, it is his own fault; and he has only himself to thank for the consequences.

Much material has been put before us about the value of wearing a seatbelt. It shows quite plainly that everyone in the front seats of a car should wear a seatbelt.

A reminder that causation is a crucial element of contributory negligence and must be shown on the balance of probabilities is the case of *Stanton v Collinson* [2010] EWCA Civ 81. Here the claimant passenger had suffered very serious head injuries in a collision. The claimant was sharing the front passenger seat with another passenger, and neither was wearing a seatbelt. The judge however declined to make a deduction for contributory negligence. The crucial element in this case was the evidence before the court: this suggested that there would still have been a head injury had a seat belt been worn; and the judge concluded that the evidence did not establish that the severity of injury would have been 'significantly less' had that been the case. The Court of Appeal decided not to disturb this conclusion, but noted that the judgment reached was 'a fine one' ([24]). The judge, however, had heard the evidence first hand; and she was entitled to say in this particular case that 'medical evidence' was required to resolve the issues. As it was, the only expert evidence provided was from road accident engineers, expert in collisions, but not in the nature of brain injuries. The Court of Appeal realized that this might undermine the purpose of *Froom v Butcher*—namely, to reduce the time and costs which might be involved in assessing contributory negligence— and emphasized that this was a case involving grave injury in which the need for medical evidence was not disproportionate to the claim.

Cases Raising Diverse Issues

What happens in a more complex case where diverse issues of causation and relative blame have to be balanced? An important example is the case of *Reeves v Chief Commissioner of the Metropolis* [2000] 1 AC 360, which we extracted in Section 2.1.

[5] Though note the issue raised by *Stanton v Collinson*, later in this section.

Lord Hoffmann, at 372

In my view it would . . . have been right to apportion responsibility between the commissioner and Mr. Lynch in accordance with the Act of 1945. The judge and Morritt L.J. would have apportioned 100 per cent. to Mr. Lynch. But I think that this conclusion was heavily influenced by their view, expressed in connection with the question of causation, that Mr. Lynch, as a person of sound mind, bore full responsibility for taking his own life. This is of course a tenable moral view. . . . But whatever views one may have about suicide in general, a 100 per cent. apportionment of responsibility to Mr. Lynch gives no weight at all to the policy of the law in imposing a duty of care upon the police. It is another different way of saying that the police should not have owed Mr. Lynch a duty of care. The law of torts is not just a matter of simple morality but contains many strands of policy, not all of them consistent with each other, which reflect the complexity of life. An apportionment of responsibility "as the court thinks just and equitable" will sometimes require a balancing of different goals. It is at this point that I think that Buxton L.J.'s reference to the cases on the Factories Acts is very pertinent. The apportionment must recognise that a purpose of the duty accepted by the commissioner in this case is to demonstrate publicly that the police do have a responsibility for taking reasonable care to prevent prisoners from committing suicide. On the other hand, respect must be paid to the finding of fact that Mr. Lynch was "of sound mind." I confess to my unease about this finding, based on a seven-minute interview with a doctor of unstated qualifications, but there was no other evidence and the judge was entitled to come to the conclusion which he did. I therefore think it would be wrong to attribute no responsibility to Mr. Lynch and compensate the plaintiff as if the police had simply killed him. In these circumstances, I think that the right answer is that which was favoured by Lord Bingham of Cornhill C.J., namely to apportion responsibility equally.

This extract again emphasizes the rough and ready nature of apportionment. Causative influences cannot be accurately weighed against degrees of blameworthiness, and the policy reasons which justify a duty to prevent self-harm in this case cannot be scientifically measured against moral feelings concerning the wrongness (assuming sound mind) of self-harm. The court must seek a solution which appears to take into account all of the relevant factors.

Corr v IBC [2008] UKHL 13; (2008) 1 AC 884

Here, the defendant's negligence had caused an accident in which the claimant was physically injured. The accident led to depression which in turn led eventually to his suicide. Because the first instance judge had held against the claimant, there were no substantial findings of fact relevant to contributory negligence. In the House of Lords, there was a wide divergence of opinion over whether a reduction in damages for contributory negligence was justified either in principle, or on the evidence. Lord Bingham assessed contributory negligence at zero per cent.[6]

Lord Bingham, *Corr v IBC*

22 . . . I do not think that any blame should be attributed to the deceased for the consequences of a situation which was of his employer's making, not his.

---

[6] Arguably, it would be better to say that the claimant bore no causal responsibility, so that s 1(1) had no application: see the last part of this section, 'Causal Questions'.

Lord Walker agreed. In applying section 1(1) of the 1945 Act, 'the Court has to have regard both to blameworthiness and to what is sometimes called causal potency' (at [44]).

The other three judges approached the matter differently. In assessing whether the claimant's 'fault' as defined in section 4 of the 1945 Act was partially to blame for the accident, they interpreted fault in terms of personal choice: the guiding concept was autonomy rather than culpability. Lord Scott, applying this thinking, would have reduced damages by 20 per cent. He argued that the deceased might have been liable in tort if he had injured a third party when he threw himself from the building; thus his action satisfied the definition of 'fault' and there should be consistency between these two purposes. Although the remaining judges—Lords Mance and Neuberger—did not think there was sufficient evidence before the court to justify making a deduction in this case, they also seem to have approached the issue as one of 'autonomy' rather than 'culpability'.

Lord Mance, *Corr v IBC*

52 The different strands of policy which exist in this area, and the balancing of different goals which is necessary, may therefore make it appropriate not only to hold liable a defendant who causes an accident which leads to depression and suicide, but also to attribute an element of responsibility, small though it may be, to a person who commits suicide, so recognizing the element of choice which may be present even in the case of someone suffering an impairment due to an accident.

Similarly, Lord Neuberger thought that the critical question in any individual case would be 'the extent to which the deceased's personal autonomy has been overborne by the impairment to his mind attributable to the defendant' (at [69]).

Short of automatism, the law is reluctant to absolve individuals of responsibility for their actions on the basis that their actions were in some way caused by others. It may be questioned whether consistency really requires this thinking to be reflected in a reduction in damages here: contributory negligence is a matter of justice and fairness as between claimant and defendant, and explicitly requires consideration of *relative* fault. In other words, it can be argued that different issues may consistently be considered in different areas of the law.

Before the 1945 reform, the idea of legal or proximate cause was the means used to control the potentially savage implications of the complete defence. Recommending the reform, the Law Revision Committee made plain that it did not intend any change in this aspect of the law.[7]

Law Revision Committee 8th Report, *Contributory Negligence* (Cmd 6032, 1939), 16

While we recommend that the principle of apportioning the loss to the fault should be adopted at Common Law, we do not recommend any change in the method of ascertaining whose the fault may be, nor any abrogation from what has been somewhat inaptly called

[7] For fuller discussion see J. Steele, 'Law Reform (Contributory Negligence) Act 1945: Collisions of a Different Sort', in T. T. Arvind and J. Steele, *Tort Law and the Legislature* (Hart Publishing, 2013).

the 'last opportunity rule'. In truth there is no such rule – the question, as in all questions of liability for a tortious act, is, not who had the last opportunity of avoiding the last opportunity of causing the mischief, but whose act caused the wrong?'[8]

In practice, the existence of the proportionate defence has encouraged change in the approach to legal causation, and now it need only be shown that the damage was not too remote a consequence of the defendant's breach, so long as that damage fell within the scope of the relevant duty (Chapter 3).[9] The likelihood of this effect was realized very soon after the legislation.

Denning LJ, *Davies v Swan Motor Co (Swansea) Ltd*
[1949] 2 KB 291, 322

... the practical effect [of the 1945 Act] is wider than the legal effect.[10] Previously, in order to mitigate the harshness of the doctrine of contributory negligence, the courts in practice sought to select, from a number of competing causes, which was *the* cause – the effective or predominant cause – of the damage and to reject the rest. Now the courts have regard to all the causes and apportion the damages accordingly.

3. VOLENTI NON FIT INJURIA: WILLING ACCEPTANCE OF RISK

A defendant will escape liability for the consequences of negligence if the claimant has, expressly or impliedly, agreed to accept the legal risk associated with that negligence. *Volenti*—or acceptance of risk—is of very limited application to cases of negligence today, although there have been successful cases which we must seek to explain. But this has not always been the case. There was a time when courts were all too ready to find that plaintiffs had voluntarily accepted the risks in question, particularly where the plaintiff had suffered injury in the course of employment. As explained in the following passage, recognition of the narrow defence we have stated was a hard-won battle:

G. Williams, *Joint Torts and Contributory Negligence* (Stevens & Sons, 1951), 296–8

... In its heyday, the doctrine [of voluntary assumption of risk] was applied in almost every situation where the plaintiff knew of the risk and yet chose to undergo it rather than to give up on some enterprise on which he was engaged. At least, that was the attitude adopted

---

8 See also *The Boy Andrew v The St Rognvald* [1948] AC 140, where Lord Simon found one of the parties to be the sole cause, and did not apportion damages. This was a collision at sea, not covered by the 1945 Act, but governed by apportionment rules which had themselves inspired the legislation.

9 For discussion of broader effects see J. Goudkamp, 'Rethinking Contributory Negligence', in G. A. Pitel, J. W. Neyers, and E. Chamberlain (eds), *Tort Law: Challenging Orthodoxy* (Hart Publishing, 2013).

10 P. Atiyah, 'Common Law and Statute Law' (1985) 48 MLR 1, argues that the 'practical' effect referred to by Denning LJ is real but also, in fact, a further 'legal effect'. It is simply an unintended legal effect.

in the master-and-servant cases. The extreme limit of the doctrine was represented by *Woodley v Metropolitan District Rly* (1877) 10 QBD 685 at 696 (CA)]. The plaintiff, a workman in the employ of a contractor engaged by the defendants, had to work in a dark tunnel which he knew was rendered dangerous by passing trains. The jury found the company negligent in not stationing a person to warn the workmen of the approach of trains, and three of the five judges of the Court of Appeal (including one who was in the majority in the result reached) held that there was evidence of this. Yet three judges of the same court held that the plaintiff could not recover for his injuries, on the ground that he had voluntarily assumed the risk.

It may confidently be asserted that this appalling extension of the doctrine would not now be followed. A change in the judicial attitude took place towards the end of the last century—Beven associated it with the change of feeling represented by the passing of the Employers' Liability Act, 1880[11]—and the modern tendency has been to restrict the defence. A beginning was made in *Thomas v Quartermaine* (1887), when Bowen LJ let fall his celebrated dictum that 'the maxim is not *scienti non fit injuria* but *volenti*.'[12]

It is obvious why the broad version of the defence can be described as unjust and even, in some manifestations, 'appalling'. It rested on a wholly fictional idea of 'consent'. As Scott LJ explained in *Bowater v Rowley Regis* [1944] KB 476, at 479:

… a man cannot be said to be truly 'willing' unless he is in a position to choose freely, and freedom of choice predicates, not only full knowledge of the circumstances on which the exercise of choice is conditioned, so that he may be able to choose wisely, but the absence from his mind of any feeling of constraint so that nothing shall interfere with the freedom of his will.

Choices in respect of employment are scarcely likely to be made in the absence of any feelings of constraint. Ultimately, the pivotal case of *Smith v Baker & Sons* [1891] AC 325 made clear that a plaintiff who continues with an activity despite knowledge of certain risks associated with it is not thereby to be treated as having accepted those risks. This major turning point left the defence with little application to cases of negligence. As Lord Pearce put it in *ICI v Shatwell* [1965] AC 656, at 686:

One naturally approaches [the] defence with suspicion. For in the sphere of master and servant its role has been inglorious up to 1891, and, since that date, insignificant. In *SMITH V BAKER & SONS* it was laid down that the defence is not constituted by knowledge of the danger and acquiescence in it, but by an agreement to run the risk and to waive any rights to recompense for any injury in which that risk might result.

---

[11] This statute limited the scope of the 'doctrine of common employment'. By that doctrine, it was implied into any contract of employment that the employee consented to the risks associated with the work, including the risks posed by the negligence of fellow workers. The 1880 Act only excluded the operation of the doctrine in respect of negligence on the part of a superior worker with supervisory or managerial responsibilities. But this was a significant turning point and the remainder of the defence was abolished by the Law Reform (Personal Injuries) Act 1948, s 1. Indeed enhanced duties have long been recognized as associated with the employment relationship: Chapter 9.

[12] Knowledge (*scienti*) does not amount to consent (*volenti*).

3.1 THE RESTRICTED NATURE OF THE MODERN *VOLENTI* DEFENCE

The brief statement of the *volenti* defence in the quotation from Lord Pearce above contains all the elements set out at the start of this section. A similarly narrow view of the *volenti* defence was adopted by Lord Denning in *Nettleship v Weston* [1971] 2 QB 691.

> Knowledge of the risk of injury is not enough. Nor is a willingness to take the risk of injury. Nothing will suffice short of an agreement to waive any claim for negligence. The plaintiff must agree, expressly or impliedly, to waive any claim for any injury that may befall him due to the lack of reasonable care by the defendant.

It is important to note three limitations inherent in this statement.

Assumption of Legal Risk, Not Risk of Physical Consequences

There are many cases in which it is tempting to say that a claimant willingly *ran the risk of incurring harm*, but this is not sufficient for a defence of *volenti* to succeed. In the passage above, Lord Denning made clear that there is a difference between accepting *the risk of injury*, and accepting *the legal consequences of the injury*. The facts of *Nettleship v Weston* itself illustrate the contrast. The plaintiff had agreed to give driving lessons to the defendant, a neighbour. It is obvious to an instructor that a learner driver may lose control of her car *in circumstances in which a competent driver would not do so*—in other words, negligently.[13] But this is not enough to satisfy the narrow defence of *volenti*. This is because the instructor does not agree, merely by taking on the role of instructor in the event of full knowledge of the chance of negligence, to waive any right to *compensation* in the event that this should happen.

In this particular case, the plaintiff had checked that the defendant carried third party insurance, which would indemnify him in the event of injury. This was powerful specific evidence that he did not accept that the legal risk should fall on him. But Lord Denning's point was wider than this.

The *volenti* defence is now excluded from driver and passenger claims in any event:

Road Traffic Act 1988

149 Avoidance of certain agreements as to liability towards passengers

(1) This section applies where a person uses a motor vehicle in circumstances such that under section 143 of this Act there is required to be in force in relation to his use of it such a policy of insurance or such a security in respect of third-party risks as complies with the requirements of this Part of this Act.

(2) If any other person is carried in or upon the vehicle while the user is so using it, any antecedent agreement or understanding between them (whether intended to be legally binding or not) shall be of no effect so far as it purports or might be held—

---

[13] This is an application of the 'objective standard of care': Chapter 3.

(a) to negative or restrict any such liability of the user in respect of persons carried in or upon the vehicle as is required by section 145 of this Act to be covered by a policy of insurance, or

(b) to impose any conditions with respect to the enforcement of any such liability of the user.

(3) The fact that a person so carried has willingly accepted as his the risk of negligence on the part of the user shall not be treated as negativing any such liability of the user.

Need for Agreement

The need for agreement is the most severe of the three restrictions to the defence. In the passage from *Nettleship* quoted above, Lord Denning stated that a *volenti* defence will only succeed where there is an *agreement* to waive any claim for injury. A clear statement of this principle is to be found in the speech of Lord Bramwell in the leading case of *Smith v Baker & Sons* [1891] AC 325.

Lord Bramwell

In the course of the argument I said that the maxim *Volenti non fit injuria* did not apply to a case of negligence; that a person never was *volens* that he should be injured by negligence—at least, unless he specially agreed to it; I think so still.

According to Glanville Williams:

Consent, in modern law, means agreement, and it would be much better if the latter word replaced the former.

Despite these authorities, *volenti* has succeeded as a defence to negligence in one or two modern cases (including *Shatwell* itself) where there is no express 'agreement'. We will consider these cases below. In each case, the claimant is closely involved in creation of the risk.

Consent to the Negligence, Not Just the Risk

Quite apart from the requirements above, any consent must be *to the negligence itself*, and not to the general risk of injury. In *Wooldridge v Sumner* [1963] 2 QB 43, Diplock LJ thought that, for this reason alone, *volenti* would generally fail as a defence to negligence. Here, a spectator was injured when a sportsman lost control of his horse. But Diplock LJ's approach has been decisive in a number of cases where participants in sporting events have themselves been injured. In these cases, English courts have found it possible to dispose of *volenti* with ease. In *Smoldon v Whitworth and Nolan* (17 December 1996, Court of Appeal), an amateur rugby referee was found to have breached a duty of care owed to players (in this instance junior players or 'colts') when he failed to enforce a rule—designed for the safety of players—against collapsing scrums. Although rugby was 'a tough, highly physical game', the *volenti* defence could not succeed:

Lord Bingham of Cornhill CJ, Smoldon v Whitworth

The plaintiff had of course consented to the ordinary incidents of a game of rugby of the kind in which he was taking part. Given, however, that the rules were framed for the protection of him and other players in the same position, he cannot possibly be said to have consented to a breach of duty on the part of the official whose duty it was to apply the rules and ensure so far as possible that they were observed.

Volenti has been found inapplicable for similar reasons in other English cases concerning sports, such as *Wattleworth v Goodwood Road Racing Company Ltd and Others* [2004] EWHC 140. In *Watson v British Boxing Board of Control* [2001] QB 1134, the defendant Board—the sole organization responsible for regulating professional boxing in the UK—was liable in damages to the claimant, a professional boxer, who had incurred serious brain damage. The relevant breaches of duty concerned the prompt treatment of injuries and the provision of proper facilities to deal with head injuries during a fight. Although a boxer clearly consents to being hit by an opponent, it could not be said that the participant was *volens* in respect of these particular breaches of duty. The *volenti* defence in the context of sporting injuries has been justly described as 'otiose'.[14]

3.2 RECENT APPLICATIONS OF THE VOLENTI DEFENCE

Although we have been careful to set out the limits to the defence of *volenti*, we have also mentioned that there are some exceptional cases where that defence can still succeed in the context of a negligence action.

Passengers, Drivers, and Pilots: *Dann v Hamilton* and *Morris v Murray*

In *Dann v Hamilton* [1939] 1 KB 509, the plaintiff had accepted a lift with the defendant. She allowed him to drive her home, though she knew that he had been drinking over the course of the evening. When the plaintiff was injured, she was held not to have consented to the risk posed by the defendant's drunkenness.[15] Subsequently, *Dann v Hamilton* was mentioned with approval by Lord Denning in *Nettleship v Weston*, and by Diplock LJ in *Wooldridge v Summer*. As we have seen, the *volenti* defence is now excluded from road traffic actions between passenger and driver by section 149 of the Road Traffic Act 1988. Because of this, there have been few opportunities to consider whether accepting a lift from a person who is clearly incapable of driving safely could in principle be sufficient to give rise to the *volenti* defence.[16] *Morris v Murray* is in effect such a case. Since it involved a light aircraft rather than a road vehicle, it was not caught by the prohibition in the Road Traffic Act.

[14] D. McArdle and M. James, 'Are You Experienced? "Playing Cultures", Sporting Rules and Personal Injury Litigation after *Caldwell v Maguire*' (2005) Tort L Rev 193, at 210.

[15] Writing later in (1953) LQR 317, Lord Asquith (who decided *Dann v Hamilton* as Asquith J) explained that contributory negligence, then a complete defence, had not been pleaded: he thought that if it had been pleaded, the defence would probably have been successful. This is confirmed by *Owens v Brimmell* [1977] QB 859, where the Court of Appeal reduced damages payable to a plaintiff who had accepted a lift from a drunk driver.

[16] In *Pitts v Hunt* [1991] 1 QB 24, the plaintiff pillion passenger was closely involved in encouraging the wildly irresponsible driving of the deceased motorcyclist. Beldam LJ thought that the *volenti* defence would have succeeded if it had not been for s 149 of the Road Traffic Act 1988. Since the defence could not succeed, he did not give a full account of the reasons why this would be so.

Morris v Murray

[1991] 2 QB 6

The plaintiff and a friend (Murray) spent an afternoon drinking heavily. The two men decided to take a flight in a light aircraft, with Murray (who was found to have consumed the equivalent of 17 whiskies) at the controls. The plaintiff drove to the airfield and helped to start and refuel the aircraft. The plane crashed, killing Murray and seriously injuring the plaintiff. The *volenti* defence succeeded.

The Court of Appeal in *Morris v Murray* distinguished *Dann*, and argued that the case in hand was closer on its facts to *ICI v Shatwell* (below) than to *Dann v Hamilton*. But if this is so, the difference is not down to the immediacy of the danger. The method of working used in *Shatwell* was certainly dangerous, but the method had been used many times before and (unlike *Murray*) it was far from inevitable that any injury would follow. What other reason might there be for putting *Morris v Murray* with *ICI v Shatwell* into one category, and *Dann v Hamilton* into another?

ICI v Shatwell [1965] AC 656

Two brothers were employed by the appellants as shot-firers. They chose to operate a dangerous means of testing detonators, even though they knew that this method had been forbidden by their employers on safety grounds, and prohibited by regulation for the same reason. There was an explosion, and both brothers were injured. George, who according to Lord Reid bore a greater part of the responsibility for deciding to operate the dangerous and forbidden system, brought an action in negligence and for breach of statutory duty against his employers. He accepted that his damages must be reduced for contributory negligence, but he argued that his employers were vicariously liable for the tortious conduct of his brother, who was partly to blame for his injuries.

The House of Lords held by a majority that the defence of *volenti* should succeed. Lord Reid emphasized that there had been a *deliberate decision* to disobey instructions, rather than a merely careless collaboration between the men.

Lord Reid, at 672–3

If we adopt the inaccurate habit of using the word "negligence" to denote a deliberate act done with full knowledge of the risk it is not surprising that we sometimes get into difficulties. I think that most people would say, without stopping to think of the reason, that there is a world of difference between two fellow-servants collaborating carelessly so that the acts of both contribute to cause injury to one of them, and two fellow-servants combining to disobey an order deliberately though they know the risk involved. It seems reasonable that the injured man should recover some compensation in the former case but not in the latter. If the law treats both as merely cases of negligence it cannot draw a distinction. But in my view the law does and should draw a distinction. In the first case only the partial defence of contributory negligence is available. In the second *volenti non fit injuria* is a complete defence if the employer is not himself at fault and is only liable vicariously for the acts of the fellow-servant. If the plaintiff invited or freely aided and abetted his fellow-servant's disobedience, then he was *volens* in the fullest sense. He cannot complain of the resulting injury either against the fellow-servant or against the master on the ground of his vicarious responsibility for his fellow-servant's conduct.

Comparing Lord Reid's analysis with the facts of *Morris v Murray*, it could be said that in the latter case, although the manner in which the deceased was piloting the plane was 'careless', the decision to engage in a glaringly dangerous activity was entirely deliberate. This being so, the case may not fall within the doubts expressed by Diplock LJ in *Wooldridge v Summer* about the application of *volenti* to 'negligence simpliciter'.

But what of the need for an agreement? This element was not mentioned by Lord Reid, but it was considered by Lord Pearce. Lord Pearce was ready to infer such an agreement from deliberate conduct on the part of the plaintiff:

Lord Pearce, at 688

In the present case it seems clear that as between George and James there was a voluntary assumption of risk. George was clearly acting without any constraint or persuasion; he was in fact inaugurating the enterprise. On the facts it was an implied term (to the benefit of which the employers are vicariously entitled) that George would not sue James for any injury that he might suffer, if an accident occurred. Had an officious bystander raised the possibility, can one doubt that George would have ridiculed it?

An explanation of *ICI v Shatwell* and *Morris v Murray* can be arrived at by combining the insights of Lords Reid and Pearce. The cases show that *volenti* may succeed in the absence of *express* agreement, provided there is deliberate collusion in the creation of the risk. On the analysis adopted by Lord Pearce, this can be seen in terms of an implied agreement; it would be obvious to both parties that the plaintiff here accepted the risk, at the time of the collaboration.[17]

4. *EX TURPI CAUSA NON ORITUR ACTIO*: 'ILLEGALITY'

A claim in tort may be barred on the basis that it arises directly out of illegal conduct on the part of the claimant. The meaning of 'illegality' is explored in Section 4.1. *Ex turpi causa* has been described as not strictly a defence because it exists not to protect the defendant but to further the policy of the law itself. The balance it strikes is not a balance between the parties. For this reason, *ex turpi causa* may be raised by the court itself as a reason for dismissing a claim.[18] It is sometimes referred to simply as a 'public policy bar'.

---

[17] In the extract above, Lord Pearce refers to the 'officious bystander'. This is a shorthand reference to the test for implying terms into a contract, derived from the judgment of MacKinnon LJ in *Shirlaw v Southern Foundries Ltd* [1939] 2 KB 206: it is clear that both parties would have regarded the term as too obvious to merit discussion.

[18] For a recent example of this position being stated, see *Al Hassan-Daniel v Revenue and Customs Commissioners* [2010] EWCA Civ 1443, [9]: 'This is the basis of what we have called the criminality defence'

Illegality was the subject of extended consultation by the Law Commission: particularly relevant to tort are its *Consultation Paper on the Illegality Defence in Tort* (LCCP 160, 2001); *The Illegality Defence: A Consultative Report* (LCCP 189, 2009); and *The Illegality Defence* (Report No 320, 2010). These are referred to as the '2001 Paper'; the '2009 Paper'; and 'the 2010 Report'. Since then, illegality has been extensively considered in the highest court, with two decisions of the House of Lords and four of the Supreme Court. The general nature of the defence has been subject to significant disagreement and debate. Its application in the particular field of tort adds a further range of issues.

The underlying general question is whether the defence should operate on the basis of a confined set of clear rules or principles (informed, of course, by the policy that underpins the defence); or whether the courts should appeal more directly to policy in developing a discretionary approach. The Law Commission preferred an approach based on structured discretion. Subsequently, a series of cases in the Supreme Court disclosed considerable disagreement on precisely this point. In *Patel v Mirza* [2016] UKSC 42; [2016] 3 WLR 399, the conflict seems to have been settled in favour of discretion. *Patel* is not a tort case, but involves a claim in unjust enrichment. Nevertheless, it should now set the general approach to the illegality defence.

In the following sections, we consider general issues, before turning to the somewhat problematic application to tort law.

4.1 'ILLEGALITY'

First, what is meant by 'illegality'? The 'illegality' defence is sometimes captured in the Latin phrase *ex turpi causa non oritur actio*: no action arises from a bad cause. Historically, it has been stated in such a way as to extend not only to illegal but also to *immoral* conduct, perhaps reflecting its early association with enforceability of illegal or immoral contracts.[19] Recent decisions have confined the defence to acts which are criminal or 'quasi-criminal'; so that the language of 'illegality' remains appropriate.

It is clear however that not *every* breach of criminal law will suffice. For example, a driver is required by law to wear a seatbelt, and we have already seen that failure to do so may lead to reduction in damages on the basis of contributory negligence *(Froom v Butcher*, Section 2). It will not however lead to the claim being barred on grounds of illegality.

We can see, then, that not all misconduct attracting criminal sanctions is caught by the 'illegality' defence. But what of the question whether *only* criminal conduct is within the rule? In *Safeway Stores v Twigger* [2010] EWCA Civ 1472, the Court of Appeal applied the maxim *ex turpi causa* in a case where the relevant conduct (breach of competition law) was regarded as 'quasi-criminal', attracting a very substantial penalty in the nature of a fine. In *Les Laboratoires Servier v Apotex* [2014] UKSC 55; [2015] AC 430, the tort claimant had infringed the defendant's Canadian patent, while sincerely believing the patent to be invalid (as, indeed, the equivalent European patent held by the same party proved to be). The Supreme Court held that breach of a patent was a civil wrong only, and involved no criminality; thus, the illegality defence could not apply.

(though, since it is a point which the court itself will if necessary take, it is more correctly understood as a control on jurisdiction)'.

[19] Note the much-cited dictum of Lord Mansfield, *Holman v Johnson* (1775) 1 Cowp 341, Section 4.2.

Les Laboratoires Servier v Apotex

[2014] UKSC 55; [2015] AC 430

Lord Sumption

What is "turpitude"?

23 The paradigm case of an illegal act engaging the defence is a criminal offence. So much so, that much modern judicial analysis deals with the question as if nothing else was relevant. Yet in his famous statement of principle in *Holman v Johnson* 1 Cowp 341 Lord Mansfield CJ spoke not only of criminal acts but of "immoral or illegal" ones. What did he mean by this? I think that what he meant is clear from the characteristics of the rule as he described it, and as judges have always applied it. He meant acts which engage the interests of the state or, as we would put it today, the public interest. The illegality defence, where it arises, arises in the public interest, irrespective of the interests or rights of the parties. It is because the public has its own interest in conduct giving rise to the illegality defence that the judge may be bound to take the point of his own motion, contrary to the ordinary principle in adversarial litigation ...

...

28 ... In my opinion the question what constitutes "turpitude" for the purpose of the defence depends on the legal character of the acts relied on. It means criminal acts, and what I have called quasi-criminal acts. This is because only acts in these categories engage the public interest which is the foundation of the illegality defence. Torts (other than those of which dishonesty is an essential element), breaches of contract, statutory and other civil wrongs, offend against interests which are essentially private, not public. There is no reason in such a case for the law to withhold its ordinary remedies. The public interest is sufficiently served by the availability of a system of corrective justice to regulate their consequences as between the parties affected.

Clearly then, civil wrongs such as torts and breaches of contract are generally insufficient to amount to 'illegality' within the defence; but Lord Sumption suggests an exception for those torts—such as deceit—where dishonesty is an essential element.

4.2 UNDERLYING RATIONALES

Illegality has its basis in public policy. The following, much-cited passage refers to cases where there is an illegal or immoral contract, but it has been treated as applying to the illegality defence in all causes of action, including tort.

Lord Mansfield, *Holman v Johnson*

(1775) 1 Cowp 341, at 343

The objection, that a contract is immoral or illegal as between plaintiff and defendant, sounds at all times very ill in the mouth of the defendant. It is not for his sake, however, that the objection is ever allowed; but it is founded in general principles of policy, which the defendant has the advantage of, contrary to the real justice, as between him and the plaintiff, by accident, if I may say so. The principle of public policy is this: *ex dolo malo non oritur actio.* No court will lend its aid to a man who founds his cause of action upon an immoral or illegal act. If, from the plaintiff's own stating or otherwise, the cause of action appears to arise *ex turpi causa*, or the transgression of a positive law of this country, there the court says he has no right to be assisted. It is upon that ground that the court goes; not for the sake of the defendant, but because they will not lend their aid to such a plaintiff. So if the plaintiff and defendant were to change sides, and the defendant was to bring his action against the plaintiff, the latter would then have the advantage of it; for where both are equally in fault, *potior est conditio defendentis*.

The illegality defence is not about fairness between the parties, and is certainly not applied out of 'tenderness'[20] toward a defendant who (in a case of illegal contract or joint criminal enterprise) may also have acted illegally. The illegality defence is a rule of public policy and it prevents reliance upon the claimant's own illegal act in seeking a remedy. The same is true in cases of contract, trust, or tort.

Law Commission, *The Illegality Defence: A Consultative Report* (Consultation Paper No 189, TSO, 2009)

CONCLUSION ON THE POLICY RATIONALES

2.35 We provisionally recommend that the illegality defence should be allowed where its application can be firmly justified by the policies that underlie its existence. These include: (a) furthering the purpose of the rule which the illegal conduct has infringed; (b) consistency; (c) that the claimant should not profit from his or her own wrong; (d) deterrence; and (e) maintaining the integrity of the legal system.

The Law Commission recommended that in the field of tort, the courts should be relied upon to work towards principles which give effect to these underlying policies. In *Gray v Thames Trains* [2009] UKHL 33, Lord Hoffmann said that *ex turpi causa* 'expresses not so much a principle as a policy; and that 'that policy is not based upon a single justification but on a group of reasons, which vary in different situations' ([30]).

4.3 GENERAL APPROACH: RULES OR DISCRETION?

Tinsley v Milligan

Tinsley v Milligan [1994] 1 AC 340 was a claim relating to the acquisition of title to property, in which a narrow and rule-based approach to the illegality defence was established. A claim would fail only if the claimant had to rely upon his or her own illegality. It was never altogether clear how, or indeed whether, *Tinsley* ought to apply to tort cases. In *Patel v Mirza* [2016] UKSC 42; [2016] 3 WLR 399, *Tinsley* was overruled. But *Tinsley* has affected the illegality defence as a whole, and so it is important to outline broadly what was decided, and what approach now governs the area.

The plaintiff and defendant contributed to the purchase price of a house. The house was vested in the sole name of the plaintiff, but on the 'understanding' that the beneficial

[20] Schiemann LJ, *Sacco v Chief Constable of the South Wales Constabulary*, Court of Appeal, 15 May 1998.

interest in the property was jointly vested in both plaintiff and defendant. The purpose of this arrangement was an illegal one: to defraud the Department of Social Security. When the parties quarreled and the plaintiff moved out, the plaintiff gave the defendant notice to quit and asserted sole ownership. The defendant argued that the property was held on trust for both parties. The Court of Appeal accepted the defendant's argument: there was a 'resulting trust' which was not defeated by the parties' joint illegal purpose in registering the house in the plaintiff's sole name. If the illegality defence were to succeed, it would mean that the plaintiff, relying on her own illegal purpose, could obtain not only the legal title but the beneficial title also.

In the House of Lords, the Court of Appeal's reasoning was disapproved, although the majority agreed, for different reasons, with their conclusion. Lord Browne-Wilkinson explained that although a court will not *enforce* an illegal contract, this did not mean that such a contract had no effect at all in law or equity:

Lord Browne-Wilkinson, at 369

In particular it is now clearly established that at law ... property in goods or land can pass under, or pursuant to, such a contract. If so, the rights of the owner of the legal title ... will be enforced, provided that the plaintiff can establish such title without pleading or leading evidence of the illegality.

He went on to explain that the same applied to *equitable* interests in property, such as the beneficial ownership claimed by the defendant. On the facts of this particular case, the defendant had to bring evidence of the *arrangement* between the parties in order to make her claim. But crucially, she *did not have to depend on the **illegality** of that arrangement*. This was partly down to the 'presumption of resulting trust': the defendant only needed to show agreement to hold in equal shares, and contribution to the purchase price. A trust in her favour would then be presumed. On the contrary, it was the plaintiff who had to plead the illegality, in order to argue that *no* resulting trust should arise, since the presumption was against her. It has been pointed out that on this approach, whether the defence operates or not depended upon arbitrary factors unrelated to its policy rationale, and that it created a potential windfall to undeserving parties who were no less implicated in illegality than the claimant.

In *Les Laboratoires Servier v Apotex* [2014] UKSC 55; [2015] AC 430, Lord Sumption, at [20], criticizing the Law Commission's proposed discretionary approach, endorsed a remark of Lord Walker in the earlier case of *Stone & Rolls v Moore Stephens* [2009] AC 1391 that 'the present state of the law is as laid down by the majority of the House of Lords in *Tinsley v Milligan*'. However, in the same year in the following case (a tort claim), the Supreme Court seemed to take a very different view.

Hounga v Allen [2014] UKSC 47

The claimant had been brought to the UK illegally as a 14-year-old, to work for the defendant's family as a home help. She was aware of the illegality and participated in it—as is often the case with those who are 'trafficked'. She was told she would be able to attend school and would be paid: neither was true. She had very limited freedom of movement and was kept in a state of fear by threats that the authorities would be informed of her status should she leave.

A majority of the Supreme Court held that this satisfied the definition of trafficking. Claims arising from the employment contract necessarily failed because the contract was an illegal one and could not be enforced; instead, the only claim before the Supreme Court was for discrimination in the termination of the contract, under the Race Relations Act 1976. This was described as a tort. Therefore, the authorities on illegality as a defence to tort law applied.

All of the Justices agreed that this was not a case where the claimant should be denied a remedy on the basis of illegality. Lord Wilson suggested that a two-stage public policy balance needed to be struck. This approach is plainly at odds with the narrowness of the approach in *Tinsley* and commended by Lord Sumption in *Apotex*.

Lord Wilson JSC, *Hounga v Allen*
[2014] UKSC 47

Public policy

42 The defence of illegality rests on the foundation of public policy.... So it is necessary, first, to ask "What is the aspect of public policy which founds the defence?" and, second, to ask "But is there another aspect of public policy to which application of the defence would run counter?"

43 An answer to the first question is provided in the decision of the Canadian Supreme Court in *Hall v Hebert* [1993] 2 SCR 159.... At the outset of her judgment on behalf of the majority, McLachlin J, at p 169, announced her conclusion about the basis of the power to bar recovery in tort on the ground of illegality, which later she substantiated in convincing terms by reference to authority. Her conclusion was as follows:

"The basis of this power, as I see it, lies in [the] duty of the courts to preserve the integrity of the legal system, and is exercisable only where this concern is in issue. This concern is in issue where a damage[s] award in a civil suit would, in effect, allow a person to profit from illegal or wrongful conduct, or would permit an evasion or rebate of a penalty prescribed by the criminal law. The idea common to these instances is that the law refuses to give by its right hand what it takes away by its left hand."

44 Concern to preserve the integrity of the legal system is a helpful rationale of the aspect of policy which founds the defence even if the instance given by McLachlin J of where that concern is in issue may best be taken as an example of it rather than as the only conceivable instance of it. I therefore pose and answer the following questions: (a) Did the tribunal's award of compensation to Miss Hounga allow her to profit from her wrongful conduct in entering into the contract? No, it was an award of compensation for injury to feelings consequent on her dismissal, in particular the abusive nature of it. (b) Did the award permit evasion of a penalty prescribed by the criminal law? No, Miss Hounga has not been prosecuted for her entry into the contract and, even had a penalty been thus imposed on her, it would not represent evasion of it. (c) Did the award compromise the integrity of the legal system by appearing to encourage those in the situation of Miss Hounga to enter into illegal contracts of employment? No, the idea is fanciful. (d) Conversely, would application of the defence of illegality so as to defeat the award compromise the integrity of the legal system by appearing to encourage those in the situation of Mrs Allen to enter into illegal contracts of employment? Yes, possibly: it might engender a belief that they could even discriminate against such employees with impunity.

45 So the considerations of public policy which militate in favour of applying the defence so as to defeat Miss Hounga's complaint scarcely exist.

46 But what about the second question posed in para 42? It requires the court to consider whether Mrs Allen was guilty of "trafficking" in bringing Miss Hounga from Nigeria to the UK and into the home in Hanworth.

Arguing that it was a case of trafficking, Lord Wilson drew the following conclusion:

52 ... the decision of the Court of Appeal to uphold Mrs Allen's defence of illegality to her complaint runs strikingly counter to the prominent strain of current public policy against trafficking and in favour of the protection of its victims. The public policy in support of the application of that defence, to the extent that it exists at all, should give way to the public policy to which its application is an affront; and Miss Hounga's appeal should be allowed.

Although this was by no means the first case in which there had been direct appeal to public policy in determining application of the illegality defence, the weighing of one aspect of public policy (the criminal prohibition) against another (the policy objectives denied by refusing a claim), was novel. Arguably, it was an approach suggested by the particular facts of the case.

The underlying tension between narrow rules and flexible discretion was resolved in favour of discretion in the case of *Patel v Mirza*. The proposed way forward resembles that in *Hounga*, but is subtly different.

Patel v Mirza [2016] UKSC 42; [2016] 3 WLR 399

The claimant paid a large sum of money to the defendant, in return for which the defendant was to bet on the movement of shares on the basis of inside information. This was contrary to the prohibition on 'insider trading' in section 52 of the Criminal Justice Act 1993. In the end, no inside information was received and therefore the agreement was not carried out. The claimant sought the return of his money. In the Supreme Court, the claim was successful; but the Justices were divided in their reasons.

Lord Sumption argued that the sole justification for the defence of illegality was 'consistency' in the law. 'Consistency' was also recognized by the majority view of Lord Toulson as underlying the law. For Lord Sumption however, consistency required a limited range of rules and principles, without the need for the courts to make direct recourse to policy reasons. The majority of Justices endorsed a more flexible approach, in which courts should weigh relevant policy considerations and determine where the balance lay.

Lord Toulson, *Patel v Mirza*
[2016] UKSC 42; [2016] 3 WLR 399

120 The essential rationale of the illegality doctrine is that it would be contrary to the public interest to enforce a claim if to do so would be harmful to the integrity of the legal system (or, possibly, certain aspects of public morality, the boundaries of which have never been made entirely clear and which do not arise for consideration in this case). In assessing whether the public interest would be harmed in that way, it is necessary (a) to consider the underlying purpose of the prohibition which has been transgressed and whether that purpose will be enhanced by denial of the claim, (b) to consider any other relevant public policy on which the denial of the claim may have an impact and (c) to consider whether denial of the claim would be a proportionate response to the illegality, bearing in mind that punishment is a matter for the criminal courts. Within that framework, various factors may be relevant, but it would be a mistake to suggest that the court is free to decide a case in an undisciplined way. The public interest is best served by a principled and transparent assessment of the considerations identified, rather by than the application of a formal approach capable of producing results which may appear arbitrary, unjust or disproportionate.

The focus is directly on the purpose of the applicable criminal prohibition; which is then balanced against any other relevant public policy on which the denial of the claim might have an impact. Though different from *Hounga*, this approach could have been applied in that case to produce essentially the same outcome. In addition however, there is a direct reference to the 'proportionality' of denying the claim. In principle, the future development of illegality in tort cases will need to fit with this statement of general approach.

4.4 CATEGORIES OF ILLEGALITY IN TORT CASES

In its 2001 Paper, the Law Commission had addressed the tort cases in terms of three categories. The judgment of Lord Hoffmann in *Gray v Thames Trains* set out, in relation to tort, a 'narrow rule' based on 'consistency', which falls within Category 2; and a 'wide rule', which seems to include the cases that fall into Category 3. This lends support to a categorized approach in tort law, even if the emerging categories do not exactly match those below.

Law Commission, *The Illegality Defence in Tort* (Consultation Paper No 160, HMSO, 2001)

2.11 ... the range of cases in which the defence of illegality has featured is wide. It is not easy to state the principles governing this defence in tort other than in broad terms. One possible analysis is that a claim in tort will fail on any of three grounds:

1. where the claimant seeks, or is forced, to found the claim on his or her illegal act;

2. where the grant of relief to the claimant would enable him or her to benefit from his or her criminal conduct (or where what is sought is compensation for loss of liberty or an indemnity for the consequences of criminal behaviour); and

3. where, even though neither (1) nor (2) is applicable to the claim, the situation is nevertheless covered by a general residual principle that the court should not assist a claimant who has been guilty of illegal conduct of which the courts should take notice.

Category 1: The Claim is Founded on the Claimant's Illegal Act

This category was plainly derived from the decision in *Tinsley v Milligan*. *Clunis v Camden & Islington Health Authority* [1998] QB 978 illustrates that *Tinsley* was always a poor fit with tort cases, even before its overruling in *Patel v Mirza*. Here, the Court of Appeal attempted to apply the narrow rule in *Tinsley v Milligan* to a case of negligence. The plaintiff Clunis had attacked and killed a man. He was convicted of manslaughter on grounds of diminished responsibility. He claimed damages from the defendant health authority in respect of his consequent detention, on the basis that the defendant had not managed his case properly nor provided appropriate after-care given his violent history. According to the Court of Appeal:

> In our view the plaintiff's claim does not arise out of and depend upon proof of his commission of a criminal offence.

Clunis does not seem genuinely comparable to *Tinsley*. The plaintiff did not attack his victim in the hope of making a gain, and success in his tort claim would not result in any sense in perfecting an illegal intention. In its 2001 Paper, the Law Commission noted that it would be better to deal with such a case as an example of Category 2, and this is broadly what the House of Lords later did in the similar case of *Gray v Thames Trains* (below). Now that *Tinsley* has been overruled, it appears less likely that this will be a significant category in the law of tort.

Category 2: No Benefit from Illegal Act/No Indemnity for Consequences of Illegal Act/the 'Narrow Rule'

In contractual cases, a 'no benefit' rule prevents enforcement of a contract where the claimant stands to gain in consequence of his or her illegal act. A true example of this rule is *Beresford v Royal Insurance Co Ltd* [1938] AC 586, decided at a time when suicide was a crime. A life insurance contract was unenforceable where the assured had committed suicide, since otherwise his representative would benefit from his crime.[21] As the Law Commission noted in its 2001 Paper:

> 2.23 ... The tort cases are not strictly speaking cases of 'benefit', at least in the sense that the claimant is seeking a profit he or she hoped to make from his or her illegal activity. They are cases in which what is sought is an indemnity for losses or liabilities he or she has incurred as a result of his or her acts.

Most of the tort cases are thus better explained in terms of a 'no indemnity rule', rather than a 'no benefit' rule, though on one view *Moore Stephens v Stone & Rolls* is an exception.[22] A limited public policy bar based on 'no indemnity' has been justified in Canada on the basis of a threat to consistency or integrity within the law; and this is a close fit with the principle of 'consistency' which was identified as lying behind the illegality defence as a whole, in *Patel v Mirza*.

McLachlin J, *Hall v Hebert*
(1993) 101 DLR (4th) 129, at 179–80

[There] is a need in the law of tort for a principle which permits judges to deny recovery to a plaintiff on the ground that to do so would undermine the integrity of the justice system. The power is a limited one. Its use is justified where allowing the plaintiff's claim would introduce

---

21 Suicide is no longer a crime: note the successful actions in *Kirkham* and *Reeves* (discussed earlier).
22 It is also a case where the relevant breach of duty may be considered to be either contractual, or tortious.

inconsistency into the fabric of the law, either by permitting the plaintiff to profit from an illegal or wrongful act, or to evade a penalty prescribed by criminal law. Its use is not justified where the plaintiff's claim is merely for compensation for personal injuries sustained as a consequence of the negligence of the defendant.

McLachlin J would not extend the no-indemnity rule to claims for personal injury (some of which arise for consideration in Category 3 below). Through the decision of the House of Lords in *Gray v Thames Trains* and subsequent cases, the consistency principle has now been fully accepted as a matter of principle in English law, but it is clearly not the sole ground on which the illegality defence will operate.

In *Gray v Thames Trains* [2009] UKHL 33, the claimant had been caught up in a major rail crash, caused through the negligence of the defendants. He suffered minor physical injuries, and more significant psychiatric injury in the form of post-traumatic stress disorder (PTSD). Because of this condition, the claimant suffered reduced earnings. Matters were made much worse when, as a consequence of his PTSD, he obtained a knife and repeatedly stabbed a drunken pedestrian with whom he had had an argument. The pedestrian died as a consequence, and the claimant was detained in hospital pursuant to section 37 of the Mental Health Act 1983, indefinitely. Referring not only to *Hall v Hebert* but also to more recent developments in Canada and New South Wales, the Lords gave strong support to the 'consistency' or 'integrity' argument, which as a result is now a clearly accepted element in English law.[23] Indeed, this now stands as the most clearly reasoned area of application of the *ex turpi causa* defence in English tort law.

Lord Brown, *Gray v Thames Trains*

[93] ... the integrity of the justice system depends upon its consistency. The law cannot at one and the same time incarcerate someone for his criminality and compensate him civilly for the financial consequences. I shall refer to this henceforth as the consistency principle. It is the underlying rationale for the application of the *ex turpi causa non oritur actio* doctrine in the present context.

As Lord Hoffmann pointed out at [30], the claimant did not need to found his action upon the illegality of his acts (Category 1): 'in this kind of case, the question is whether recovery is excluded because the immediate cause of the damage was the act of manslaughter, which resulted in the sentence of the court'.

Other issues that remain less clear after *Gray* include the extent of this principle (could it deal with all of the issues in this case?), and the nature of any 'broader' principle. It appears that only Lord Hoffmann thought that any broader principle was required in this particular case. He thought it was required because certain of the losses claimed could not be said categorically to have been a consequence of the killing and detention. Lord Hoffmann expressed the justification for the broader rule as follows:

---

23 This was not previously the case: see the Law Commission's 2009 Paper at para 2.14.

Lord Hoffmann, Gray v Thames Trains

[51] I must therefore examine the wider version of the rule, which was applied by Flaux J ... It differs from the narrower version in at least two respects: first, it cannot, as it seems to me, be justified on the grounds of inconsistency in the same way as the narrower rule. Instead, the wide rule has to be justified on the ground that it is offensive to public notions of the fair distribution of resources that a claimant should be compensated (usually out of public funds) for the consequences of his own criminal conduct. Secondly, the wider rule may raise problems of causation which cannot arise in connection with the narrower rule. The sentence of the court is plainly a consequence of the criminality for which the claimant was responsible. But other forms of damage may give rise to questions about whether they can properly be said to have been caused by his criminal conduct.

Lord Hoffmann pointed out that this wider test could give rise to problems of causation which are not raised by the 'consistency' principle: was it the illegality which caused the injury, or not? These problems have become familiar and are explored in respect of the third category below. Lord Hoffmann's references to the older cases in this category have given them additional authority.

In summary, Gray v Thames Trains stated the existence of the 'consistency principle' as one justification for the illegality defence in English tort law. Beyond that, a number of cases where the illegality defence has been applied outside the 'consistency' principle and outside Category 1 were cited with approval by Lord Hoffmann, who seemed broadly to approve both the outcomes and the reasoning in those cases. We explore the 'wide rule' in relation to the third and final category.

Category 3: 'Residual'; the 'Wide Rule'

Most personal injury actions where illegality is relevant are likely to fall outside the above two categories. Aside from the general approval of Lord Hoffmann in Gray, where he referred to a 'wide rule' beyond the area justified by the 'consistency principle', the existence of a residual category received minimal attention from the House of Lords in the two cases explored above. This is likely to be the largest set of tort cases in which illegality is raised; but it is also the most lacking in clear underlying principles. Lord Hoffmann's remarks, some of which were quoted earlier, invoke two key ideas: causation, and an idea that a remedy would be 'offensive to public notions of the fair distribution of resources'. In general terms these two ideas can be identified in decisions of the courts both before and after Gray but Lord Hoffmann's judgment provided a focal point. Lord Hoffmann identified, in particular, a distinction between 'causing' the harm, and merely 'providing the occasion for it'.

Lord Hoffmann, Gray v Thames Trains

54 This distinction, between causing something and merely providing the occasion for someone else to cause something, is one with which we are very familiar in the law of torts. It is the same principle by which the law normally holds that even though damage would not have occurred but for a tortious act, the defendant is not liable if the immediate cause was the deliberate act of another individual. Examples of cases falling on one side of the line or the other are given in the judgment of Judge LJ in Cross v Kirby [2000] CA

Transcript No 321. It was Judge LJ, at para 103, who formulated the test of 'inextricably linked' which was afterwards adopted by Sir Murray Stuart-Smith LJ in *Vellino v Chief Constable of the Greater Manchester Police* [2002] 1 WLR 218. Other expressions which he approved, at paras 100 and 104, were 'an integral part or a necessarily direct consequence' of the unlawful act (Rougier J: see *Revill v Newbery* [1996] QB 567, 571) and 'arises directly ex turpi causa': Bingham LJ in *Saunders v Edwards* [1987] 1 WLR 1116, 1134. It might be better to avoid metaphors like 'inextricably linked' or 'integral part' and to treat the question as simply one of causation. Can one say that, although the damage would not have happened but for the tortious conduct of the defendant, it was caused by the criminal act of the claimant? (*Vellino*). Or is the position that although the damage would not have happened without the criminal act of the claimant, it was caused by the tortious act of the defendant? (*Revill v Newbery*).

Lord Hoffmann therefore sought to simplify the applicable principles, reducing them to more familiar and less *ad hoc* language.

The language of 'inextricable link' does continue however. In *Hounga v Allen* [2014] UKSC 47, the facts of which were outlined in Section 4.3, the Supreme Court held that the claimant's own involvement in illegality in entering the country was merely part of the 'context' of the defendant's illegal acts. Thus, the claim was not 'inextricably linked' with the claimant's own illegality. The operation of the 'wide rule' in personal injury cases after *Gray* is illustrated by two Court of Appeal decisions. In *Delaney v Pickett* [2011] EWCA Civ 1532, the claimant had been seriously injured while travelling as a passenger in a car driven by the defendant. Both claimant and defendant were found to be in possession of cannabis. Though the parties disputed it, and Ward LJ doubted it, the first instance judge held that the purpose of their journey was to supply drugs. Applying the test of causation within the 'wide rule', the claim was not barred as arising *ex turpi causa*: the possession of cannabis was incidental to the accident which caused the injury. Ward LJ referred to the approach taken in *Gray v Thames Trains*:

Ward LJ, *Delaney v Pickett*
[2011] EWCA Civ 1532

37 Therein lies the answer to the problem in this case. It is not a question of whether or not it is impossible to determine the appropriate standard of care. We are not concerned with the integrity of the legal system. We do not need to ask whether the claim would be an affront to the public conscience. There is no need for an analysis of the pleadings to establish whether or not the claimant is relying on his illegality to found his claim. It is not a question of the claimant profiting from his own wrongdoing. Here the crucial question is whether, on the one hand the criminal activity merely gave occasion for the tortious act of the first defendant to be committed or whether, even though the accident would never have happened had they not made the journey which at some point involved their obtaining and/or transporting drugs with the intention to supply or on the other hand whether the immediate cause of the claimant's damage was the negligent driving. The answer to that question is in my judgment quite clear. Viewed as a matter of causation, the damage suffered by the claimant was not caused by his or their criminal activity. It was caused by the tortious act of the first defendant in the negligent way in which he drove his motor car. In those circumstances the illegal acts are incidental and the claimant is entitled to recover his loss.

It is important to note that this was not sufficient to assist the claimant, for reasons explained at the end of this section.

McCracken v Smith was a further case involving a criminal joint enterprise. The claimant teenager was seriously injured while riding pillion on a stolen trials bike, which was driven negligently and at excessive speed, when it collided with a minibus. The minibus was also driven negligently. In the Court of Appeal, Richards LJ expressed the view that on the authority of *Joyce v O'Brien*, the claim against the driver of the stolen bike should be seen as barred for illegality: the claimant was party to a joint criminal enterprise, to ride the bike dangerously. However, this did not bar the claim against the driver of the minibus.

Richards LJ, *McCracken v Smith*
[2015] EWCA Civ 380; [2015] PIQR P19

51 …In my view the situation cannot be accommodated neatly within the binary approach of Lord Hoffmann in *Gray*. One cannot say that "although the damage would not have happened but for the tortious act of the defendant, it was caused by the criminal act of the claimant", but equally one cannot say that "although the damage would not have happened without the criminal act of the claimant, it was caused by the tortious act of the defendant". The accident had two causes, properly so called—the dangerous driving of the bike and the negligent driving of the minibus—and it would be wrong to treat one as the mere "occasion" and the other as the true "cause". Daniel's injury was the consequence of both, not just of his own criminal conduct and not just of Mr Bell's negligence.

52 I do not think that the fact that the criminal conduct was one of the two causes is a sufficient basis for the ex turpi causa defence to succeed…. for reasons I have explained, cases involving a claim by one party to a criminal joint enterprise against another party to that joint enterprise are materially different. In my judgment, the right approach is to give effect to both causes by allowing Daniel to claim in negligence against Mr Bell but, if negligence is established, by reducing any recoverable damages in accordance with the principles of contributory negligence so as to reflect Daniel's own fault and responsibility for the accident.

53 Lord Sumption has spelled out in *Les Laboratoires Servier* that the ex turpi causa defence is rooted in the public interest. The public interest is served by the approach I have indicated. It takes into account both the negligent driving for which Mr Bell is responsible and the dangerous driving for which Daniel is responsible. It enables damages to be recovered for the negligence of Mr Bell but not for Daniel's own criminal conduct. I see no reason why the court should instead apply a "rule of judicial abstention" (Lord Sumption in *Les Laboratoires Servier* at [23]) and withhold a remedy altogether.

'Proportionality'

The final point raised by Richards LJ in the extract above illustrates judicial recognition of a need to be proportionate, which is also present in *Patel v Mirza* (extracted above). Even in a case of serious criminal intent, it is not appropriate to treat the criminal as beyond the reach of tort law, so that *anything* may be done without legal consequence. *Revill v Newbery* [1996] QB 567 embraced the proposition that even the trespasser with criminal intent is not beyond the protection of the law. The plaintiff had intended to break into a shed on an allotment with a view to stealing from it. The defendant, who was sleeping in the shed with a shotgun because he planned to deter burglars, fired through a hole in the door and unintentionally injured the plaintiff. The plaintiff brought an action in negligence (and under the Occupiers' Liability Act 1984)[24] against the defendant. A defence of illegality was rejected by the Court of Appeal. Proportionality of effect is now an express element of the general approach to illegality, spelled out in *Patel v Mirza* (Section 4.3).

Insurance

The source of compensation for tort claimants may itself be affected by issues of illegality and *ex turpi causa*. Most personal injury damages, and almost all road traffic liabilities, are paid by liability insurers, and many would be unrecoverable in the absence of insurance. *Delaney v Pickett* raised a particular problem for the claimant. The defendant driver had liability cover in place; but this was 'avoided' by the insurer because of his failure to declare his drug use. This meant that the defendant was treated as uninsured and the claimant, having succeeded in his tort claim for the reasons already explored, was dependent on being compensated according to the terms of the MIB's Uninsured Drivers Agreement 2009. The Agreement entitles the MIB to refuse to satisfy a tort judgment where the claimant knew or ought to have known that the vehicle insured was being used 'in the course or furtherance of a crime'. The trial judge held that this criterion was fulfilled; and the Court of Appeal (Ward LJ dissenting) upheld his judgment on this point. Though the claimant was successful in tort because his illegal acts were peripheral or incidental, he failed to secure compensation, because a very different approach to the effect of his supposed knowledge was taken within the terms of the MIB Agreement. In this instance, insurers were able to use the claimant's 'incidental' unlawful conduct to bar his claim for compensation, even though in tort it was irrelevant.[25] Subsequently, in *Delaney v Secretary of State for Transport* [2015] EWCA Civ 172, it was held that the 'crime exception' in the relevant MIB agreement was in breach of the UK's obligations under a number of EC Directives, and that the breach was sufficiently serious to merit an award of damages to the claimant. For argument, prior to the latter decision, see Merkin and Steele, Further Reading.

5. CONCLUSIONS

i. There has been growing interest in the operation of tort law defences, with a number of new publications listed in Further Reading below. In relation to contributory negligence, key questions include how we should understand the unusually 'rough and ready' nature of the apportionment exercise required of the courts. Equally tricky is the combination of quite different factors—culpability and 'causal potency'—that must be weighed in reaching an apportionment. This raises the spectre of arbitrariness in apportionment, which is of particular significance where a claimant is seriously injured. The decision of the Supreme Court in *Jackson v Murray* illustrates that even so, judicial analysis of how responsibility is to be apportioned must be coherent, and there remains scope for appellate courts to question the apportionments that have been arrived at.

---

[24] Chapter 12.

[25] In *McCracken v Smith*, at first instance, the same result was achieved on the simpler basis that the claimant was aware that the bike was being driven uninsured, so that the MIB escaped liability; there was no appeal on this point.

ii. The frequent application of contributory negligence as a partial defence has led some to question whether total defences to negligence are too draconian, and perhaps outdated. This does not reflect the full picture of tort defences however. This is illustrated by the defence of illegality, which has been much litigated in recent years. The recent history of this defence illustrates the potential for tension between clear rules, and flexible judicial discretion, in the law of tort. It is clear that the courts are aware of the need to restrict the operation of the defence to cases where it genuinely serves public policy, and is not disproportionate in its impact on claimants. In tort law, and perhaps particularly in personal injury claims, this emphasis on proportionality is essential, since few tort claimants will be seeking to profit from their crimes; rather, the taint of illegality is more likely to be raised to prevent a compensatory remedy. Recent developments serve to restrict the defence to cases where its application is justified, and to avoid rules which may themselves result in arbitrary distinctions.

FURTHER READING

Baker, T., 'Liability Insurance at the Tort-Crime Boundary', in D. Engel and M. McCann, *Fault Lines: Tort Law as Cultural Practice* (Stanford University Press, 2009).

Deitrich, J., 'The Decline of Contributory Negligence and Apportionment: Choosing the Black and White of All or Nothing over Shades of Grey?' (2003) 11 TLJ 51.

Dyson, A., Goudkamp, J., and Wilmot-Smith, F. (eds), *Defences in Tort* (Hart Publishing, 2015).

Glofcheski, R., 'Plaintiff's Illegality as a Bar to the Recovery of Personal Injury Damages' (1999) 19 LS 6–23.

Goudkamp, J., *Tort Law Defences* (Hart Publishing, 2013).

Goudkamp, J., 'Apportionment of Damages for Contributory Negligence: A Fixed or Discretionary Approach?' (2015) 35 LS 621–47.

Goudkamp, J., and Nolan, D., 'Contributory Negligence in the Twenty-First Century: An Empirical Analysis of First Instance Decisions' (2016) 79 MLR 575–622.

Goudkamp, J., and Nolan, D., 'Contributory Negligence in the Court of Appeal: an Empirical Study' (2017) LS (forthcoming).

Jaffey, A. J. E., 'Volenti non fit injuria' [1985] CLJ 87.

Merkin, R., and Steele, J., *Insurance and the Law of Obligations* (Oxford, 2013), chapter 11.

Strauss, N., 'Ex Turpi Causa Oritur Actio?' (2016) 132 LQR 236.

Virgo, G., 'The Illegality Revolution', in S. Worthington, A. Robertson, and G. Virgo (eds), *Revolution and Evolution in Private Law* (Hart Publishing, 2018, forthcoming).

Williams, G., *Joint Torts and Contributory Negligence* (London: Stevens & Sons, 1951).

6

DUTY OF CARE: APPLICATIONS

CENTRAL ISSUES

i) The cases gathered in this chapter help to define the reach and scope of the tort of negligence. We explored the general nature of the duty of care in Chapter 3, and introduced the 'Caparo approach' to establishing whether a duty is owed. Here, we turn our attention to particular applications of the duty concept. These cases can be understood as determining the boundaries of the tort. We consider the cases on duty of care in terms of recognized categories. It will become clear, however, that some organizing ideas appear to reach across the categories.

ii) Our first set of cases relates to negligently inflicted psychiatric damage. For many years, attention in this category focused on claims by 'secondary victims', whose psychiatric injury is caused by witnessing (or otherwise experiencing) death, personal injury, or imperilment of others. In these cases, very restrictive rules have developed. But such cases are not typical of all claims for psychiatric damage, and a significant number of 'primary victim' cases are now decided without direct reference to the special control devices.

iii) We next turn our attention to cases of 'pure economic loss'. These cases

have long been recognized as posing particular difficulties. We will suggest that some order can be imposed on the case law here. There is not one general exclusionary rule applying to economic losses, but two specific exclusionary rules regarding 'relational economic losses' (where the claimant's interest in damaged property is merely contractual), and cases of mere defectiveness in a product. It is outside these categories that the difficulties arise. Particularly important, but also elusive, has been the **assumption of responsibility** criterion developed from the leading case of *Hedley Byrne v Heller* [1964] AC 465. This idea has made its way into other areas of the tort of negligence (including psychiatric damage claims and claims against public authorities), and has become a key organizing idea within negligence. Therefore, it is important to consider whether it has any substance, or is merely an empty label.

iv) The greatest volume of difficult case law surrounds the negligence liability of public authorities, which is also subject to considerable change. Restrictive rules for this area were adopted in the case of *X v Bedfordshire* [1995] 2 AC 633. These, however, were based on clearly articulated policy reasons and in this sense cannot be called 'arbitrary'. The influence of human rights and most particularly of Article 6 ECHR is clear to see in the development of this area, as English courts strove for a time to avoid being seen to confer 'immunities'. This led initially to expansion in liability, but growing familiarity with the Convention rights has led in turn to increased confidence in use of the *Caparo* test to deny a duty of care. The current trend is again toward restriction, but important new areas of liability have opened up. We also consider liability of public authorities under the Human Rights Act itself, since this provides important context to the restrictions on common law duties.

v) Our final group of cases is smaller, but like the psychiatric damage cases, it has caused the House of Lords to resort to unconventional reasoning. These are cases of 'wrongful birth' associated with failed sterilization operations. Like the psychiatric damage cases, the pattern of decisions in this category is hard to justify. In this instance, however, the problem is not one of inflexibility but of instability, as the House of Lords has reconsidered its reasons from case to case and produced conflicting decisions.

vi) Finally, we attempt an appraisal of the current state of play. We defend the use of policy reasoning in the *Caparo* approach, while also noting the existence of anomalous cases which have not been successfully explained either in terms of justice between the parties, or more broadly. Finally, we identify emerging organizing concepts which appear to span different categories of case law. These shared concepts may or may not have an easily identified core meaning. An interesting question is how far this matters, as they are capable of acquiring greater content through use.

1. PSYCHIATRIC DAMAGE

The case law in this section relates to negligently inflicted psychiatric damage. Such cases have been divided into claims by 'secondary victims', and claims by 'primary victims'. 'Secondary victims' are those who suffer psychiatric damage as a result of injury to, or death or imperilment of, another. In these cases, policy-based restrictions have applied to limit the recognized duties to take care. Not all of these restrictions apply to claims by primary victims. Indeed in some primary victim claims, none of the restrictions apply. 'Primary victims' include those who suffer psychiatric damage through stress at work, and those who are physically endangered. Other categories of primary victim claim are also emerging, for example where the defendant has assumed responsibility towards the claimant, or where there is a prior contractual relationship. Despite the restrictions applying to secondary victim claims, there seems to be expansion in the field of successful primary victim claims. However, the decision of the House of Lords in *Rothwell* indicates that the courts consider primary victim claims, too, to require a degree of control not found in physical injury claims.

1.1 THE NATURE OF 'PSYCHIATRIC DAMAGE'

It is clear that psychiatric damage is capable of being recoverable in the tort of negligence. However, a sharp distinction has been drawn between recognized psychiatric conditions (which may constitute 'damage'), and normal emotional distress of one sort or another.

Lord Bridge, *McLoughlin v O'Brian*
[1983] 1 AC 410, at 431

The common law gives no damages for the emotional distress which any normal person experiences when someone he loves is killed or injured. Anxiety and depression are normal human emotions. Yet an anxiety neurosis or a reactive depression may be recognisable psychiatric illnesses, with or without psychosomatic symptoms. So, the first hurdle which a plaintiff claiming damages of the kind in question must surmount is to establish that he is suffering, not merely grief, distress or any other normal emotion, but a positive psychiatric illness.

The Distinction between Physical and Psychiatric Harm: Injury or Means of Causation?

Is it possible to make a similarly clear distinction between psychiatric and *physical* disorders? Arguably, no clear distinction of this sort can be made.

Lord Wilberforce, *McLoughlin v O'Brian*
[1983] 1 AC 410, at 418

Whatever is unknown about the mind-body relationship (and the area of ignorance appears to expand with that of knowledge), it is now accepted by medical science that recognisable and severe physical damage to the human body and system may be caused by the impact, through the senses, of external events on the mind.

As long ago as 1901, in the case of *Dulieu v White*, Kennedy J speculated to similar effect:

Kennedy J, *Dulieu v White & Sons*
[1901] 2 KB 669, at 677

... For my own part, I would not like to assume it to be scientifically true that a nervous shock which causes serious bodily illness is not actually accompanied by physical injury, although it may be impossible, or at least difficult, to detect the injury at the time in the living subject. I should not be surprised if the surgeon or the physiologist told us that nervous shock is or may be in itself an injurious affection of the physical organism.

The difficulty of distinguishing between psychiatric and physical harm has long been recognized, but it is not always given the significance it deserves. The difficulty of this distinction helps to explain the case of *Page v Smith*, for example. In that case, the injury suffered by the claimant (chronic fatigue syndrome or 'ME') was genuinely difficult to categorize as physical or psychiatric. In many cases it is not the lack of any physical manifestation of harm to the claimant, but the lack of any physical mechanism of causation, which is perceived to cause the problems.[1]

1.2 CONTROL DEVICES

A number of control devices have been developed to limit recovery of psychiatric harm. These control devices create much of the difficulty of this area; but they also offer the key to understanding it.

'Shock'

Where the event that brings about the psychiatric harm is death, injury, or endangerment *of another*, a claimant will be owed a duty in respect of psychiatric harm *only* if the harm results from a sudden shocking event.[2] Such cases are referred to as 'secondary victim' cases. It is not altogether clear in which other cases (if any) shock is a requirement. It is possible that shock is required in cases where the claimant fears for his or her own safety (*Dulieu v White*; *Page v Smith*), though this was not the reason given for rejecting a claim based on *Page v Smith* in *Rothwell v Chemical and Insulating Co Ltd* [2007] UKHL 39, [2008] 1 AC 176 (discussed in Section 1.3). Shock is clearly not required where the claimant suffers psychiatric harm through being overworked, for example.

Traditionally, lawyers referred to psychiatric injuries as 'nervous shock'. That description of the injury has now fallen into disrepute because it fails to reflect any accepted medical description of the harm. But as we have just said, the requirement that the psychiatric damage must (at least in secondary victim cases) be *caused by* sudden shock continues.

Brennan J, *Jaensch v Coffey* (1984)
155 CLR 549, at 566–7

The notion of psychiatric illness induced by shock is a compound, not a simple, idea. Its elements are, on the one hand, psychiatric illness and, on the other, shock which causes it . . . I understand 'shock' in this context to mean the sudden sensory perception—that is, by seeing, hearing or touching—of a person, thing or event, which is so distressing that the perception of the phenomenon affronts or insults the plaintiff's mind and causes a recognisable psychiatric illness. A psychiatric illness induced by mere knowledge of a distressing fact is not compensable, perception by the plaintiff of the distressing phenomenon is essential.

The purpose of the 'sudden shock' requirement is largely to avoid claims by individuals who are considered too remote (in time and space) from the initial incident. However, it also rules out claims where, in the judgment of the court, an event is not sufficiently 'shocking' or sudden to cause foreseeable illness, even when witnessed first hand. This is to be judged on an 'objective' basis: *Shorter v Surrey and Sussex Healthcare NHS Trust* [2015] EWHC 614 (QB).

---

[1] In *Dulieu v White* itself there was a physiological response to shock: premature birth was brought about through shock and fear.

[2] This was clearly spelt out in *Alcock v Chief Constable of South Yorkshire Police* (Section 1.4).

For example, this has ruled out claims for a series of clinical events leading to the death of a relative (*Liverpool Women's Hospital v Ronayne* [2015] EWCA Civ 588); or for a dawning realization after seeing the aftermath of a fatal accident that a loved one was the victim of it (*Young v MacVean* [2015] CSIH 70). Patently, the requirement aims to close 'the floodgates of liability'.[3] In secondary victim claims, the division of cases where the psychiatric effects are caused by the mere fact of death of a loved one, or by a series of distressing events, can seem (on the facts) to be irrelevant in any principled terms. The 'sudden shock' requirement is a control device.

Reasonable Fortitude and Specific Foreseeability

There are three control devices working together in the applicable test for 'foreseeability'. According to the House of Lords in *Page v Smith*, and the Court of Appeal in *McLoughlin v Jones*, this special test applies in *secondary victim cases*. We need to ask whether the recent decision of the House of Lords in *Rothwell* extends its application to some primary victim claims.

In any case in negligence, foreseeability of harm is essential to establishing that a duty of care is owed, and that the harm is not too remote from the breach. But in cases of psychiatric harm to a secondary victim, the following distinctive question applies:

Would it be foreseeable that *a person of 'ordinary fortitude'* might suffer *psychiatric injury, in the circumstances as they occurred?*

In this deceptively simple question, there are three departures from the normal approach to foreseeability.

(a) The approach in the statement above constitutes **an exception to the egg-shell skull rule** (discussed in Chapter 3, Section 6.3). According to that rule, a defendant must generally 'take his (or her) victim as he finds him' (or her). In secondary victim cases involving psychiatric damage, it must be foreseeable that *a person of ordinary fortitude* would suffer psychiatric harm in the circumstances. If a secondary victim has a particular susceptibility to psychiatric harm (an 'egg-shell personality'), he or she may not be owed a duty. A duty will only be owed if a person of ordinary fortitude might foreseeably suffer harm in the same circumstances.[4]

(b) **Psychiatric injury** must be foreseeable, at least in secondary victim cases. As Denning LJ expressed it, again deceptively simply, 'the test for liability for shock is foreseeability of injury by shock' (*King v Phillips* [1953] 1 QB at 440).

(c) Foreseeability is also assessed in a different way. This third distinctive feature of foreseeability in secondary victim cases is not always noticed. In secondary victim cases, foreseeability of the psychiatric harm is judged with hindsight, on the basis of the events as they actually occurred. The ordinary approach in the tort of negligence is

---

[3] This expression is derived from the judgment of Cardozo CJ in the American case of *Ultramares v Touche* 174 NE 441 (1931), at 444. Cardozo used the metaphor of 'opening the floodgates' to refer to prospective liability 'in an indeterminate amount for an indeterminate time to an indeterminate class'. Strictly then, 'floodgates' refers to an *uncertain* liability, rather than *too much* liability.

[4] This criterion of 'ordinary fortitude', also referred to as 'customary phlegm', provides the opportunity for deeply evaluative judgments as to what is normal. There have been suspicions of male bias in this evaluation. What degree of fortitude is expected of an ordinary pregnant woman, for example? Or is no pregnant woman regarded as 'ordinary'? The issues do not only concern gender however: consider the facts of *McFarlane v EE Caledonia* (Section 1.4). What reaction to the violent deaths of one's colleagues is considered reasonable and ordinary?

to judge foreseeability at the time of the negligent act or omission. The special kind of foreseeability which is judged with hindsight, and which applies to secondary victim claims, can be referred to as **specific foreseeability**. The ordinary kind of foreseeability has been called **foreseeability in the practical sense** (Chapter 3). Foreseeability in the practical sense is generally regarded as a moral notion (what harm would the reasonable person have foreseen and guarded against?).

The third distinctive feature of foreseeability in secondary victim cases is identified as a control device by Brooke LJ in the following passage. He identifies reasonable fortitude (at [24]), and the judgment of foreseeability with hindsight (at [25]), as *separate* control devices, just as we have explained above.

Brooke LJ, *McLoughlin v Jones*
[2001] EWCA Civ 1743; [2002] QB 1312

24 It is now well established that English law has created special control and other mechanisms to determine the incidence of legal liability in [secondary victim cases]. One of these is that the law supposes the claimant to be a person of ordinary phlegm or fortitude. This requirement was justified by Lord Porter in *Bourhill v Young* [1943] AC 92, 117 in these terms:

"The driver of a car or vehicle, even though careless, is entitled to assume that the ordinary frequenter of the streets has sufficient fortitude to endure such incidents as may from time to time be expected to occur in them, including the noise of a collision and the sight of illness to others, and is not to be considered negligent towards one who does not possess the customary phlegm."

25 Another, mentioned by Lord Wright in *Bourhill v Young*, at p110, is that the court asks itself in such a case what the hypothetical reasonable man, viewing the position ex post facto, would say it was proper to foresee. Lord Lloyd of Berwick rationalised this test in *Page v Smith* [1996] AC 155, 188 by saying:

"This makes sense . . . where the plaintiff is a secondary victim. For if you do not know the outcome of the accident or event, it is impossible to say whether the defendant should have foreseen injury by shock. It is necessary to take account of what happened in order to apply the test of reasonable foreseeability at all."

26 Neither of these rules is apposite when the relationship between the parties is founded on contract, whether the breach of duty relied upon is a breach of a contractual term, or a breach of a duty of care arising out of the parties' contractual relationship which sounds in damages in tort. . . .

Brooke LJ made clear that neither foreseeability of harm to a person of reasonable fortitude, nor specific foreseeability based on hindsight, was applicable in *McLoughlin v Jones* itself, where there was a pre-existing contractual relationship between defendant and claimant, as solicitor and client (negligence on the part of the solicitor was said to have led to imprisonment of the claimant). This was a 'primary victim' claim.

There is real uncertainty concerning the scope of application of the 'specific foreseeability' control device following the decision of the House of Lords in *Rothwell v Chemical and*

Insulating Co [2007] UKHL 39. Lord Hoffmann appeared to construe all psychiatric damage cases, other than those arising in instances like *Page v Smith*, as requiring specific foreseeability. Yet the claimant (a former employee exposed to asbestos dust and now suffering anxiety neurosis) can hardly be seen as a secondary victim. It remains possible therefore that the 'specific foreseeability' control device is of application to all psychiatric damage cases, other than cases like *Page v Smith*, but that in the majority of 'primary victim' cases it has not been a major issue, because many of these cases turn in any event on the foreseeability of psychiatric harm to the particular claimant in the particular circumstances. If so then in future the landmark cases of *Alcock* and *Page v Smith* will come to represent isolated special cases where all control devices, and no control devices (respectively) apply. The rest of the field would be governed by specific foreseeability as a general control device. For the moment, however, we have not arrived at that sort of clarity.

Further 'Control Devices': The *Alcock* Criteria

Further control devices have been applied in secondary victim cases, introducing particular requirements described in terms of 'proximity'. These are clearly restricted to 'secondary victim' cases, and outside those cases they would generally make no sense, since they turn on the nature of the relationship with the endangered party and the shocking event. Often, there is no such person or event in a primary victim case. But as exemplified by *White v Chief Constable of South Yorkshire Police* (Section 1.4), there are cases which may be interpreted in different ways. It has been stated by the House of Lords that the additional control devices are 'arbitrary', so that they need not (and indeed cannot) be fully justified in terms of principle (*White v Chief Constable of South Yorkshire Police*). The existence of potentially arbitrary control devices poses the greatest challenge in this area. We will explain the *Alcock* criteria when we deal with secondary victim cases, later in this chapter. Problems in this area surround the applicability of control devices developed for other purposes (which is to say, for controlling claims by secondary victims).

1.3 'PRIMARY VICTIM' CLAIMS

Given the attention devoted to secondary victim cases, it may be surprising to note that there is a wide range of cases in which claimants have recovered damages for psychiatric harm, on the basis that they are 'primary' victims.

Primary Victim Cases where the Claimant is Physically Injured or Endangered

Physical Injury Accompanied by Psychiatric Harm

It is common for those suffering physical injury to recover damages not only in respect of their physical injuries but also for any mental effects (including psychiatric damage) associated with these injuries. Psychiatric injuries are no less real than the physical effects and in some circumstances they may be more long-lasting. Clearly, psychiatric harm and mental illness can also contribute to the financial consequences of an injury, including loss of earnings.

Physical Endangerment but the Only Harm Is Done Through the Psychiatric Route

It is also well recognized that endangerment *without* physical impact may itself lead to mental and physical effects. Where a claimant is physically endangered, illness or injury sustained as a result of fear or 'shock' is clearly potentially recoverable.

Dulieu v White [1901] 2 KB 669

The plaintiff (who was pregnant) was behind the bar of a public house when a horse-drawn van was negligently driven into the building. There was no physical contact with the plaintiff. The Court of Appeal accepted that as a consequence of the shock, she became seriously ill and gave birth prematurely. It was held that such an injury could be compensated, but Kennedy J expressed a limitation to his decision in the following terms:

> **Kennedy J, *Dulieu v White*, at 675**
>
> . . It is not, however, to be taken that in my view every nervous shock occasioned by negligence and producing physical injury to the sufferer gives a cause of action. There is, I am inclined to think, at least one limitation. The shock, where it operates through the mind, must be a shock which arises from a reasonable fear of immediate personal injury to oneself. A. has, I conceive, no legal duty not to shock B's nerves by the exhibition of negligence towards C., or towards the property of B. or C.

This is where Kennedy J drew the line in 1901. The line has been moved by later decisions, but in respect of secondary victims (Section 1.4) it is still accepted that a line must be drawn somewhere.

Page v Smith [1996] AC 155

This case involved a moderate-impact road accident in which the plaintiff was mildly physically endangered but suffered no immediate physical harm. After the accident, however, he suffered the exacerbation of a pre-existing condition, 'ME'. ME is very hard to categorize as either psychiatric or physical in its nature, but it had clearly been brought about 'by the psychiatric route'. By a majority, the House of Lords held that the plaintiff could in principle recover damages, subject to further consideration by the Court of Appeal of 'factual causation' (had the worsened condition truly been caused by the accident?).

The majority approach was to assess the foreseeability of *personal injury* (which included both physical and psychiatric harm) from the point of view of the defendant at the time of the negligence. In Chapter 3, we called this **foreseeability in the practical sense**. It is practical in that it focuses on what the defendant could reasonably have foreseen, at the time of the carelessness. This is the usual test applied to foreseeability in the tort of negligence; but it is not the approach applied to 'secondary' victim cases. Foreseeability in the practical sense does not require that the means by which damage actually came about should be foreseeable. This was important in *Page v Smith*, because the impact of the vehicles was not particularly forceful. Only in respect of a person with a *pre-existing disposition to illness* could it be foreseeable that *this* particular impact would lead to *psychiatric* harm. Therefore, if the test for foreseeability applicable to *secondary* victims was applied in this case, the claim would fail.

In the following passage, Lord Lloyd (for the majority) makes clear that the test of fore-seeability for 'secondary' victims is a special test which has no place in the case of primary victims.

Lord Lloyd of Berwick, *Page v Smith*
[1996] AC 155, at 188–9

My noble and learned friend, Lord Keith of Kinkel, has drawn attention to an observation of Lord Wright in *a* [1943] A.C. 92, 110, that in nervous shock cases the circumstances of the accident or event must be viewed ex post facto. There are similar observations by Lord Wilberforce and Lord Bridge in *McLoughlin v. O'Brian* [1983] 1 A.C. 410, 420 and 432. This makes sense, as Lord Keith points out, where the plaintiff is a secondary victim. For if you do not know the outcome of the accident or event, it is impossible to say whether the defendant should have foreseen injury by shock. It is necessary to take account of what happened in order to apply the test of reasonable foreseeability at all. But it makes no sense in the case of a primary victim. Liability for physical injury depends on what was reasonably foreseeable by the defendant before the event. It could not be right that a negligent defendant should escape liability for psychiatric injury just because, though serious physical injury was foreseeable, it did not in fact transpire. Such a result in the case of a primary victim is neither necessary, logical nor just. To introduce hindsight into the trial of an ordinary running-down action would do the law no service.

In fact, both Lord Browne-Wilkinson, and Lord Lloyd thought that in the case of a car accident such as this, both physical and psychiatric harm *were* foreseeable, judging this in the 'practical' way. Judged at the time of the careless driving, the defendant could have foreseen *either* physical harm, *or* psychiatric damage. But Lord Lloyd went on to explain that foreseeability of psychiatric injury was not essential in such a case, provided that *some* personal injury (of whatever kind) was foreseeable.

Lord Lloyd, at 190

… The test in every case ought to be whether the defendant can reasonably foresee that his conduct will expose the plaintiff to risk of personal injury. If so, then he comes under a duty of care to that plaintiff. If a working definition of "personal injury" is needed, it can be found in section 38(1) of the Limitation Act 1980: " 'Personal injuries' includes any disease and any impairment of a person's physical or mental condition …". There are numerous other statutory definitions to the same effect. In the case of a secondary victim, the question will usually turn on whether the foreseeable injury is psychiatric, for the reasons already explained. In the case of a primary victim the question will almost always turn on whether the foreseeable injury is physical. But it is the same test in both cases, with different applications. There is no justification for regarding physical and psychiatric injury as different "kinds" of injury. Once it is established that the defendant is under a duty of care to avoid causing personal injury to the plaintiff, it matters not whether the injury in fact sustained is physical, psychiatric or both.…

Lord Lloyd argues here that secondary victim cases are logically different from primary victim cases. In the case of a primary victim (of the sort represented by the plaintiff in this case), personal injury is foreseeable and a duty of care is easily established. That being the case, the *kind* of 'personal injury' suffered is irrelevant. In a secondary victim case, there is no likelihood of physical impact involving the claimant. Thus, the *only* way that damage can foreseeably be done is through the psychiatric route, and foreseeability of injury by this route must be established.

Page v Smith was severely criticized by Lord Goff in the course of his dissenting judgment in *White v Chief Constable of South Yorkshire Police* [1998] 3 WLR 1509 (extracted in Section 1.4), though it was defended by Lord Griffiths in the same case as a sensible development. In Lord Goff's view, the special meaning of foreseeability has historically been applied to primary victims as much as to secondary victims and ought to have applied in *Page v Smith* also. The case has also been subject to criticism focusing not on the generous approach to foreseeability in *Page v Smith*, but on its apparently restrictive approach to the definition of a *primary victim*. It is suggested however that Lord Lloyd did not intend to *limit* the category of primary victims to those who are endangered. This interpretation of his words was later adopted in *White v Chief Constable of South Yorkshire Police*. But it is equally likely that Lord Lloyd concentrated on primary victims who were physically endangered simply because that was the kind of primary victim case before him. His words on the matter are extracted below. Lord Lloyd referred to the three previous cases of psychiatric damage decided by the House of Lords[5] and continued:

Lord Lloyd of Berwick, *Page v Smith* [1995] 2 WLR 644

In all these cases the plaintiff was the secondary victim of the defendant's negligence. He or she was in the position of a spectator or bystander. In the present case, by contrast, the plaintiff was a participant. He was himself directly involved in the accident, and well within the range of foreseeable physical injury. He was the primary victim. This is thus the first occasion on which your Lordships have had to decide whether, in such a case, the foreseeability of physical injury is enough to enable the plaintiff to recover damages for nervous shock.

The factual distinction between primary and secondary victims of an accident is obvious and of long standing. It was recognized by Lord Russell of Killowen in *Bourhill v. Young* [1943] A.C. 92, when he pointed out that Mrs. Bourhill was not physically involved in the collision. In *Alcock's* case [1992] 1 A.C. 310 Lord Keith of Kinkel said, at p. 396, that in the type of case which was then before the House, injury by psychiatric illness "is a secondary sort of injury brought about by the infliction of physical injury, or the risk of physical injury, upon another person." In the same case, Lord Oliver of Aylmerton said, at p. 407, of cases in which damages are claimed for nervous shock:

"Broadly they divide into two categories, that is to say, those cases in which the injured plaintiff was involved, either mediately, or immediately, as a participant, and those in which the plaintiff was no more than the passive and unwilling witness of injury caused to others."

5   *Bourhill v Young; McLoughlin v O'Brian;* and *Alcock v Chief Constable of South Yorkshire Police.*

Later in the same speech, at pp. 410–411, he referred to those who are involved in an accident as the primary victims, and to those who are not directly involved, but who suffer from what they see or hear, as the secondary victims. This is, in my opinion, the most convenient and appropriate terminology.

Although Lord Lloyd clearly said that a party who is within the zone of physical danger is a primary victim, he did not say that *only* such a party is a primary victim. On the contrary, he referred to Lord Oliver's broader category of claimants who are 'involved as participants in events'.

Considerable difficulty surrounds the question of when a party who is *not* physically endangered will count as a primary victim. We will specify some categories of victim who are not physically endangered, but who are recognized to be 'primary' victims, immediately below. More recently, the House of Lords has restricted the categories of primary victim in cases where there *is* physical impact or endangerment of somebody. Most of the primary victim cases below involve no endangerment at all.

The following decision of the House of Lords is difficult to reconcile with *Page v Smith* and it has been taken by some judges, as well as by some commentators, to leave the authority of *Page v Smith* very vulnerable. An alternative is to see that case as dealing with a different set of circumstances from those in *Rothwell*, which is a 'fear of the future' rather than 'fear of impact' case.

Rothwell v Chemical and Insulating Co Ltd [2007] UKHL 39; [2008] 1 AC 281

The claimants had all developed 'pleural plaques' as a result of occupational exposure to asbestos dust, but these plaques were not considered by the House of Lords to amount to 'material physical injury'. Anxiety caused by the fear of future disease (a heightened risk of which is associated with the plaques) was also not recoverable damage. One of the claimants (Mr Grieves) had not only suffered anxiety, but also developed an anxiety neurosis concerning the prospect of future disease, and this would be capable of giving rise to liability if it could be established that a duty was owed. The House of Lords, like the Court of Appeal, decided that such a duty of care was *not* owed.

Lord Hoffmann, *Rothwell*

2 . . . The right to protection against psychiatric illness is limited and does not extend to an illness which would be suffered only by an unusually vulnerable person because of apprehension that he may suffer a tortious injury. The risk of disease is not actionable and neither is a psychiatric illness caused by contemplation of that risk.

The key means of distinguishing *Page v Smith* appears from this summary, namely that the earlier decision has no application to a case of fear of *future* injury. But it may also be noted that a reference to the claimant's status as an 'unusually vulnerable person' has been imported into this case, where the claimant appears to be a 'primary' victim. That control device does not generally exist in primary victim cases.

All members of the House of Lords in *Rothwell* distinguished *Page v Smith*, broadly on the same grounds though with some variation. For example:

Lord Hoffmann, *Rothwell*

32. ... I do not think it would be right to depart from *Page v Smith*. It does not appear to have caused any practical difficulties and is not, I think, likely to do so if confined to the kind of situation which the majority in that case had in mind. That was a foreseeable event (a collision) which, viewed in prospect, was such as might cause physical injury or psychiatric injury or both. Where such an event has in fact happened and caused psychiatric injury, the House decided that it is unnecessary to ask whether it was foreseeable that what actually happened would have that consequence. Either form of injury is recoverable.

33. In the present case, the foreseeable event was that the claimant would contract an asbestos-related disease. If that event occurred, it could no doubt cause psychiatric as well as physical injury. But the event has not occurred. The psychiatric illness has been caused by apprehension that the event may occur. The creation of such a risk is, as I have said, not in itself actionable. I think it would be an unwarranted extension of the principle in *Page v Smith* to apply it to psychiatric illness caused by apprehension of the possibility of an unfavourable event which had not actually happened.

There is room to debate elements of this particular formulation. For example, it treats the 'disease' as the 'event' and therefore separate from the damage, whereas it might be more natural to treat the onset of disease as damage; and it may be asked whether the initial exposure to asbestos might not be the relevant 'event' (which has, therefore, actually happened). Perhaps for this reason, some members of the House added to this sort of reasoning a reference to lack of 'directness' between the negligently caused exposure to risk, and the injury. This was used to distinguish the 'stress at work' cases, as well as *Page v Smith*.

Lord Hope, *Rothwell*

55. ... the causal chain between his inhalation of the asbestos dust and the psychiatric injury is stretched far beyond that which was envisaged in *Page v Smith* [1996] AC 155. That case was concerned with an immediate response to a sudden and alarming accident, for the consequences of which the plaintiff had no opportunity to prepare himself. In this case Mr Grieves inhaled asbestos dust for about eight years. It was not until the end of that period that he became worried. This was because of the risk that he or his wife or daughter might contract a disease in the future. And his depression did not occur until he was told twenty years later about the results of his chest X-ray. He believed then that his worst fears were being realized. But this was because of the information that he had now been given by his doctor, not because of anything that happened or was done to him by his employers while he was inhaling the asbestos. His exposure at work was not to stress, but to risk: Sarah Green, 'Risk Exposure and Negligence' [2006] 122 LQR 386, 389.

This too gives rise to potential problems. As we saw in Chapter 3, it is often difficult to establish that a result is 'because of' one operating cause to the exclusion of all others, and for the most part tort law does not even try to do this.

Lord Hoffmann's approach is different from the others in that he tells us more about the general question of the role of specific foreseeability, particularly through his discussion of 'stress at work' cases. Unlike Lord Hope, he did not treat such cases as being neatly distinguishable from cases of risk at work. In fact, he reasoned from the stress at work cases, to his conclusion.

Lord Hoffmann, *Rothwell*

25 [In *Barber v Somerset*] Hale LJ said that 'the threshold question is whether this kind of harm to this particular employee was reasonably foreseeable.' She rejected the general applicability of the test of whether psychiatric injury was foreseeable in a person of 'ordinary fortitude' because an employer's duty was owed to each individual employee and not an undifferentiated member of the public. An employer may know (or it may be that he should know) of a particular vulnerability in an employee. In that case, he has a duty to treat him with appropriate care. On the other hand, in the absence of some particular problem or vulnerability, the employer was entitled to assume (in a case of occupational stress) that the employee is 'up to the normal pressures of the job'. Applied to the broader question of psychiatric illness, that means that in the absence of contrary information, the employer is entitled to assume that his employees are persons of ordinary fortitude.

26 In the present case, the employer would be unlikely to have any specific knowledge of how a particular employee was likely to react to the risk of asbestos-related illness more than 30 years after he had left his employment. An assumption of ordinary fortitude is therefore inevitable.

Lord Hoffmann emphasized that 'stress at work' cases require a high degree of foreseeability of harm to the specific claimant. If there is no evidence to show that the claimant is particularly susceptible to psychiatric harm through stress, then the 'presumption of reasonable fortitude' applies. If foreseeability of physical injury is regarded as irrelevant for the purposes of the *Rothwell* case—which is done by distinguishing *Page v Smith*—then this case is just like a stress at work claim in which there is no evidence of vulnerability on the part of the claimant. Given that a person of ordinary fortitude would not suffer psychiatric harm, foreseeability is not established.

An important implication of all of the judgments of the House of Lords in *Rothwell* is that there is a control device applicable to psychiatric injury cases which do not fall within *Page v Smith*, namely the form of required foreseeability. Lord Hoffmann was most explicit about the nature of this restriction, which is (at least) the incorporation of the presumption of reasonable fortitude (rebuttable where the defendant ought to have known of the susceptibility). Because there has been no suggestion that this was a 'secondary victim' case, it would appear that at least this control device applies to primary victims who are not covered by *Page v Smith*. It is also possible that the full force of 'specific foreseeability'—foreseeability judged with hindsight in the light of the specific events—would be applied to such a case.

This brings us to an important question. If *Page v Smith* were to be departed from, which form of foreseeability would then apply to facts like those in that case? Presumably not 'practical' foreseeability in its simplest form—at the very least, a presumption of reasonable fortitude would need to apply on the authority of *Rothwell*. It is possible that *Page* itself might be decided in the same way even with this presumption in place, provided 'practical' foreseeability (foresight) was otherwise retained: applying foresight, any ordinary person might suffer psychiatric harm in a road traffic accident. But what of the other aspects of specific foreseeability, requiring a judgment based on hindsight in the light of the actual events? In *Page*, this would mean in light of the moderate nature of the collision and the absence of direct physical injury. Lord Lloyd expressly said in *Page* that this test was not satisfied on the facts of the case, as did the Court of Appeal. It seems by implication that Lord Hoffmann would include this requirement too for all cases falling outside *Page*, since he refers (at [30]) to foreseeability of psychiatric damage given '*the event that actually happened*'. Departing from *Page* without resolving questions of this type may itself lead to further unforeseen consequences. There is an argument then that departing from *Page* without securing broader clarification in the area is not a sensible way forward. There is nothing about the full set of judgments in *Rothwell* which suggests that such clarification is close.

'Stress at Work' Cases

Cases in this category do not typically involve the threat of physical impact. Damage is done 'by the psychiatric route', generally speaking without threat of injury of any other kind.[6] The claimant is not a 'secondary' victim but could be described as the primary beneficiary of a distinct duty to avoid psychiatric harm. The possibility of a negligence action in such cases was recognized only relatively recently, in the case extracted below, but the reasoning in that case has been applied and developed subsequently. Indeed, it can be said that since *Walker*, the entire shape of tort liability for psychiatric harm has altered. The previous focus on secondary victims has shifted. Until *Rothwell*, it seemed that it is not the *type of harm* that is the main problem here, so much as the 'secondary' status of some of the victims.

Walker v Northumberland County Council [1995] 1 All ER 737

The plaintiff was employed by the defendant as an area social services officer. He managed four teams of social services fieldworkers in an area with a high proportion of child care problems. In 1986 the plaintiff suffered a nervous breakdown and had three months away from work. Before his return, the plaintiff's superior agreed that assistance would be available to lessen the burden of his work. In the event, he had very limited assistance. Six months later he suffered a second breakdown and had to leave work permanently. Colman J held that an employer owed a duty to take reasonable steps to avoid exposing an employee to a health-endangering workload. The duty had not been breached at the time of the first breakdown, since this was unforeseeable in the light of information available to the employer. But it *had* been breached at the time of the second breakdown.

Colman J

There has been little judicial authority on the extent to which an employer owes to his employees a duty not to cause them psychiatric damage by the volume or character of the work which the employees are required to perform. It is clear law that an employer has a duty to provide his employee with a reasonably safe system of work and to take reasonable steps to protect him from risks which are reasonably foreseeable. Whereas the law on the extent of this duty has developed almost exclusively in cases involving physical injury to the employee as distinct from injury to his mental health, there is no logical reason why risk of psychiatric damage should be excluded from the scope of an employer's duty of care or from the co-extensive implied term in the contract of employment. That said, there can be no doubt that the circumstances in which claims based on such damage are likely to arise will often give rise to extremely difficult evidential problems of foreseeability and causation.

---

[6] Though note the variation in *White v Chief Constable*, Section 1.4.

This is particularly so in the environment of the professions, where the plaintiff may be ambitious and dedicated, determined to succeed in his career in which he knows the work to be demanding, and may have a measure of discretion as to how and when and for how long he works, but where the character or volume of the work given to him eventually drives him to breaking point. Given that the professional work is intrinsically demanding and stressful, at what point is the employer's duty to take protective steps engaged? What assumption is he entitled to make about the employee's resilience, mental toughness and stability of character, given that people of clinically normal personality may have a widely differing ability to absorb stress attributable to their work?

Colman J predicted that issues of foreseeability and causation would be particularly significant in the development of employers' liability, and this has proved to be correct. In *Hatton v Sutherland* [2002] EWCA Civ 76, the Court of Appeal accepted that a duty of care was owed in respect of psychiatric harm caused by stress at work, and set out guidance on the issues relating to breach of the duty. On the facts, there had been no breach of duty. One of the claimants appealed, and in *Barber v Somerset County Council* [2004] UKHL 13, the House of Lords upheld the appeal. The House of Lords unanimously approved the guidelines offered by the Court of Appeal though disagreeing with the conclusion reached in the particular case in hand. The following guidelines (extracted from the Court of Appeal) therefore carry significant authority.

Hale LJ, *Hatton v Sutherland*
[2002] EWCA Civ 76; [2002] 2 All ER 1

[43] From the above discussion, the following practical propositions emerge.

(1) There are no special control mechanisms applying to claims for psychiatric (or physical) illness or injury arising from the stress of doing the work the employee is required to do. . . . The ordinary principles of employer's liability apply. . . .

(2) The threshold question is whether this kind of harm to this particular employee was reasonably foreseeable: this has two components (a) an injury to health (as distinct from occupational stress) which (b) is attributable to stress at work (as distinct from other factors).

(3) Foreseeability depends upon what the employer knows (or ought reasonably to know) about the individual employee. Because of the nature of mental disorder, it is harder to foresee than physical injury, but may be easier to foresee in a known individual than in the population at large. An employer is usually entitled to assume that the employee can withstand the normal pressures of the job unless he knows of some particular problem or vulnerability.

(4) The test is the same whatever the employment: there are no occupations which should be regarded as intrinsically dangerous to mental health.

(5) Factors likely to be relevant in answering the threshold question include: (a) The nature and extent of the work done by the employee. Is the workload much more than is normal for the particular job? Is the work particularly intellectually or emotionally demanding for this employee? Are demands being made of this employee unreasonable when compared with the demands made of others in the same or comparable jobs? Or are there signs that others doing this job are suffering harmful levels of stress? Is there an abnormal level of sickness or absenteeism in the same job or the same department? (b) Signs from the employee of impending

harm to health. Has he a particular problem or vulnerability? Has he already suffered from illness attributable to stress at work? Have there recently been frequent or prolonged absences which are uncharacteristic of him? Is there reason to think that these are attributable to stress at work, for example because of complaints or warnings from him or others?

(6) The employer is generally entitled to take what he is told by his employee at face value, unless he has good reason to think to the contrary. He does not generally have to make searching inquiries of the employee or seek permission to make further inquiries of his medical advisers.

(7) To trigger a duty to take steps, the indications of impending harm to health arising from stress at work must be plain enough for any reasonable employer to realise that he should do something about it.

(8) The employer is only in breach of duty if he has failed to take the steps which are reasonable in the circumstances, bearing in mind the magnitude of the risk of harm occurring, the gravity of the harm which may occur, the costs and practicability of preventing it, and the justifications for running the risk.

(9) The size and scope of the employer's operation, its resources and the demands it faces are relevant in deciding what is reasonable; these include the interests of other employees and the need to treat them fairly, for example, in any redistribution of duties.

(10) An employer can only reasonably be expected to take steps which are likely to do some good: the court is likely to need expert evidence on this.

(11) An employer who offers a confidential advice service, with referral to appropriate counselling or treatment services, is unlikely to be found in breach of duty.

(12) If the only reasonable and effective step would have been to dismiss or demote the employee, the employer will not be in breach of duty in allowing a willing employee to continue in the job.

(13) In all cases, therefore, it is necessary to identify the steps which the employer both could and should have taken before finding him in breach of his duty of care.

(14) The claimant must show that that breach of duty has caused or materially contributed to the harm suffered. It is not enough to show that occupational stress has caused the harm.

(15) Where the harm suffered has more than one cause, the employer should only pay for that proportion of the harm suffered which is attributable to his wrongdoing, unless the harm is truly indivisible. It is for the defendant to raise the question of apportionment.

(16) The assessment of damages will take account of any pre-existing disorder or vulnerability and of the chance that the claimant would have succumbed to a stress-related disorder in any event . . .

Since *Walker*, claims for employment-related psychiatric illness have become common. There are many examples. In *Daw v Intel Corporation* [2007] EWCA Civ 70; [2007] 2 All ER 126, despite Hale LJ's point (11) above, it was emphasized by the Court of Appeal that providing a counseling service is not necessarily a route to avoiding liability. This was re-emphasized in another Court of Appeal decision. *Dickins v O2 Plc* [2008] EWCA Civ 1144. More significantly, the Court of Appeal in *Dickins* rejected the interpretation of Hale LJ's points (15) and (16) above which had been applied in the court below. There, the trial judge had reduced the claimant's damages to reflect her vulnerable personality and problematic relationship with her partner. The Court of Appeal said that this was the wrong approach. There were concurrent causes of the breakdown, but together they contributed to a single indivisible damage. Such damage should not be 'apportioned' as between tortious and non-tortious cause. Another way of putting this is that most such cases will result in damage which is 'truly indivisible' (Hale LJ's point (15)), despite the way that she expressed this point.

Beyond Employment Cases: Assumptions of Responsibility and Contractual Relationships

There are other cases where the claimant will be regarded as a primary victim in the absence of physical danger. In *Leach v Chief Constable of Gloucestershire Constabulary* [1999] 1 WLR 1421, the police asked the plaintiff, a volunteer worker on a youth homelessness project, to act as 'appropriate adult' during interviews of a suspect, West. This was in accordance with the Codes of Practice under section 66 of the Police and Criminal Evidence Act 1984, requiring such a person to be present if the suspect is mentally disordered. West proved to be a serial killer and the details of his murders were exceptionally harrowing. The plaintiff claimed that she was not warned of the circumstances of the case, was offered no counselling until after West committed suicide in custody, and was told (falsely) that she would not be required to give evidence in court. She brought an action against the police for damages, claiming that she had suffered post-traumatic stress disorder, psychological injury, and a stroke. A first instance judge held that no duty was owed. The Court of Appeal allowed her appeal in part. Although no duty should be recognized which would interfere with the conduct of police interviews, it was nevertheless possible that a duty to provide counselling may be owed, and there may also be a duty in respect of any false assurances given.

Brooke LJ emphasized that there is a wide range of cases where a duty of care is now recognized in respect of psychiatric illness, and that many of these are cases where there is no 'physical' imperilment at all. He stressed that some such cases are decided on the basis of an 'assumption of responsibility' (see further Section 2 of this chapter). In respect of the present claims, so far as they related to the *conduct of the interviews*, there was no such assumption of responsibility.

Brooke LJ

Most of the cases in the books are concerned with situations in which a plaintiff suffers psychiatric illness as a result of his own imperilment—as in *Page v. Smith*—or reasonable fear of danger to himself, or as a result of the physical injury or imperilment of a third party (or parties) which has been caused by the defendant....

There is, however, a less familiar line of cases in which, as in the present case, a defendant has neither imperilled nor caused physical injury to anyone. One example is *Walker v. Northumberland County Council*. There was, of course, no difficulty in identifying the existence of such a duty in the context of an employer–employee relationship.

Another example is *Attia v. British Gas Plc.*, where a plaintiff suffered reasonably foreseeable psychiatric illness as a result of the defendant causing damage to her property: she had to witness her house burning down as a result of the defendants' negligence. This court declined to strike the claim out, and allowed it to go to trial on the facts.

In addition to these two types of case which can be readily categorised, the Law Commission has identified a miscellaneous group of cases in which recovery may be available for a negligently inflicted psychiatric illness (assuming that the standard elements of the tort of negligence can be made out): see its report, Liability for Psychiatric Illness (1998) (Law Com.

No. 249), p. 29, para. 2.51. These include a case where a patient suffers a psychiatric illness because of negligent treatment by his/her psychiatrist (cf. *X (Minors) v. Bedfordshire County Council* [1995] 2 A.C. 633); where a prisoner foreseeably suffers a psychiatric illness as a result of ill-treatment by prison officers (cf. *Reg. v. Deputy Governor of Parkhurst Prison, Ex parte Hague* [1992] 1 AC 58, 165–166, *per* Lord Bridge of Harwich) and where recipients of distressing news suffer reasonably foreseeable psychiatric illness as a result of the news being broken in an insensitive manner: *A. B. v. Tameside & Glossop Health Authority* [1997] 8 Med.L.R. 91 and *Allin v. City & Hackney Health Authority* [1996] 7 Med.L.R. 167. These are useful illustrations, but there is not yet any English case of the types described in which it has not been comparatively easy to establish that the requisite duty of care exists, whether from a psychiatrist's duty to his patient, the prison service's assumption of responsibility for the care of prisoners, or, in the two medical cases I have mentioned, from the defendant health authorities' acceptance that they owed a relevant duty of care to their patient or former patients....

A case which appears to break new ground, but which was not mentioned by the Law Commission, is *Swinney v. Chief Constable of Northumbria Police Force* [1997] Q.B. 464. The plaintiffs, who were wife and husband, claimed that they were suffering from psychiatric illnesses because they had been threatened with violence and arson after some confidential information furnished by the first plaintiff to the police had been stolen from a police vehicle broken into by criminals. This court did not pay any particular attention to the fact that the claims were for damages for psychiatric illness. It allowed the action to proceed to trial on the facts because it was arguable that the police had assumed responsibility towards the first plaintiff and that there were no policy grounds on which the claim should be barred from proceeding. In evaluating all the public policy considerations that might apply, Peter Gibson L.J. said, at p. 486A, that it seemed to him plain that the position of a police informer required special consideration from the viewpoint of public policy; see also Hirst L.J., at p. 484A–C, and Ward L.J., at p. 487A–C.

Swinney's case illustrates vividly the way in which, after *Page v. Smith*, the courts in future are not going to have their way blocked by some supposed difference in kind between physical injury and psychiatric injury which may ipso facto bar cases of the latter type....

There is indeed a wide range of cases in which there is recognized to be a duty not to cause psychiatric damage to the claimant, contradicting any general perception that such damage by its very nature constitutes a 'problem'. In addition to the cases mentioned by Brooke LJ in the valuable summary above, we may add the recognized duty of a school to protect its pupils against bullying (*Bradford-Smart v West Sussex County Council* [2002] EWCA Civ 7); the duty of an employer not to expose employees to bullying by fellow employees (*Waters v Commissioner of Police for the Metropolis* [2000] 1 WLR 1607); the duty of a solicitor to conduct a client's defence with due care (*McLoughlin v Jones* [2002] 1 QB 1312, psychiatric injury after a period of imprisonment); and the duty of a prison to safeguard the well-being of a vulnerable prisoner.

1.4 SECONDARY VICTIMS

A secondary victim is one whose psychiatric injury flowed from the injury to, or death or endangerment of, another party. In some of the earliest case law to recognize a duty in respect of psychiatric harm, it was proposed that only if the plaintiff herself is injured or endangered can there be recovery (*Victorian Railways Commissioners v Coultas* (1888) 13

App Cas 222; *Dulieu v White* (Section 1.1); *Bell v Northern Railway of Ireland* (1890) 26 LR Ir 428). In later cases, it was accepted that some of those who were not endangered could recover for psychiatric harm, but only if their injury is the effect of 'shock' suffered in a relevant way. In *Hambrook v Stokes* [1925] 1 KB 141, a mother saw a lorry careering down a hill and round a bend, where she knew her three children to be. There was a collision, which was out of sight, and the plaintiff feared that her children were involved. The Court of Appeal held that in these circumstances, the mother was owed a duty so far as she suffered psychiatric injury as a consequence of what she saw and perceived directly.

McLoughlin v O'Brian [1983] 1 AC 410

The plaintiff's husband and three of her children were involved in a serious road accident caused by the negligence of the first defendant. The plaintiff was informed of the accident around two hours after the event and was driven to the hospital where her family had been taken. There she learned that her youngest daughter had been killed. In the midst of chaotic and harrowing scenes, she saw her husband and other children who were still being treated. She alleged that she had suffered severe shock resulting in psychiatric illness including depression and personality change. At first instance, her claim for psychiatric injury was dismissed on the basis that the injury was unforeseeable. The Court of Appeal accepted that her injury was foreseeable, but ruled that even so no duty was owed to a plaintiff who was not present at the scene of the accident and had not seen its consequences until two hours later.

There is agreement that compensation of secondary victims without the addition of control devices may lead to over-extensive liability.

Lord Wilberforce, at 420

... there remains, in my opinion, just because "shock" in its nature is capable of affecting so wide a range of people, a real need for the law to place some limitation upon the extent of admissible claims. It is necessary to consider three elements inherent in any claim: the class of persons whose claims should be recognised; the proximity of such persons to the accident; and the means by which the shock is caused. As regards the class of persons, the possible range is between the closest of family ties—of parent and child, or husband and wife—and the ordinary bystander. Existing law recognises the claims of the first: it denies that of the second, either on the basis that such persons must be assumed to be possessed of fortitude sufficient to enable them to endure the calamities of modern life, or that defendants cannot be expected to compensate the world at large. In my opinion, these positions are justifiable, and since the present case falls within the first class, it is strictly unnecessary to say more. I think, however, that it should follow that other cases involving less close relationships must be very carefully scrutinised. I cannot say that they should never be admitted. The closer the tie (not merely in relationship, but in care) the greater the claim for consideration. The claim, in any case, has to be judged in the light of the other factors, such as proximity to the scene in time and place, and the nature of the accident.

As regards proximity to the accident, it is obvious that this must be close in both time and space. It is, after all, the fact and consequence of the defendant's negligence that must be proved to have caused the "nervous shock." Experience has shown that to insist on direct and immediate sight or hearing would be impractical and unjust and that under what may be called the "aftermath" doctrine one who, from close proximity, comes very soon upon the scene should not be excluded. In my opinion, the result in *Benson v. Lee* [1972] V.R. 879 was correct and indeed inescapable. It was based soundly, upon

"direct perception of some of the events which go to make up the accident as an entire event, and this includes . . . the immediate aftermath . . . " (p. 880.)

. . . Lastly, as regards communication, there is no case in which the law has compensated shock brought about by communication by a third party. . . . The shock must come through sight or hearing of the event or of its immediate aftermath. Whether some equivalent of sight or hearing, e.g. through simultaneous television, would suffice may have to be considered.

My Lords, I believe that these indications, imperfectly sketched, and certainly to be applied with common sense to individual situations in their entirety, represent either the existing law, or the existing law with only such circumstantial extension as the common law process may legitimately make. They do not introduce a new principle. Nor do I see any reason why the law should retreat behind the lines already drawn. I find on this appeal that the appellant's case falls within the boundaries of the law so drawn. I would allow her appeal.

Lord Bridge, at 442–3

My Lords, I have no doubt that this is an area of the law of negligence where we should resist the temptation to try yet once more to freeze the law in a rigid posture which would deny justice to some who, in the application of the classic principles of negligence derived from *Donoghue v. Stevenson* [1932] A.C. 562, ought to succeed, in the interests of certainty, where the very subject matter is uncertain and continuously developing, or in the interests of saving defendants and their insurers from the burden of having sometimes to resist doubtful claims. I find myself in complete agreement with Tobriner J. in *Dillon v. Legg*, 29 A.L.R. 3d 1316, 1326 that the defendant's duty must depend on reasonable foreseeability and

"must necessarily be adjudicated only upon a case-by-case basis. We cannot now predetermine defendant's obligation in every situation by a fixed category; no immutable rule can establish the extent of that obligation for every circumstance of the future."

This judgment moved the line of recovery only slightly, so that it incorporates an extended understanding of the 'immediate aftermath'. More broadly, the speeches of Lords Wilberforce and Bridge contain the essential elements of the 'control devices' which were, later, authoritatively stated in *Alcock v Chief Constable of South Yorkshire Police* (extracted below). For a claimant who has no physical involvement in an accident to recover damages for psychiatric injury, it is clear that they must show **closeness** of more than one form: closeness to the victim in terms of relationship, and physical closeness in time and place, are essential elements. Also important is the 'means by which the shock is caused'. Although the judgments do not altogether rule out recovery for shock caused in some way other than through direct and unaided perception of the event, Lord Wilberforce states that any sufficient alternative would need to be 'equivalent to' such direct perception—for example, through watching simultaneous television broadcasts. Lord Bridge was willing to countenance a relaxation in this requirement in appropriate circumstances.

Beyond these common elements, there appears to be a major distinction in approach between the judgments of Lord Wilberforce, and Lord Bridge. Lord Wilberforce gives greater emphasis to policy considerations, and he recognizes that 'foreseeability' in the psychiatric damage cases is a 'limiting' device (though he gives the false impression that this is the same test that is applied throughout the tort of negligence). Lord Wilberforce also regards the requirements of 'closeness' in relationship and in time and space, and of directness of perception, as clearly set by the existing authorities. Lord Bridge on the other hand appears to suggest that the relevant questions are all questions of 'foreseeability', and he argues that the limiting rules should be supported by reasoned justifications. Lord Bridge maintained that this area of law could be developed cogently through incremental evolution. This latter approach was abandoned by the House of Lords, in *White v Chief Constable of South Yorkshire Police* (extracted later in this section).

Alcock v Chief Constable of South Yorkshire [1992] 1 AC 310

This case, like *White*, arose from the disaster at the Hillsborough Football Stadium on 15 April 1989, in which 96 people died and thousands of others were physically or mentally injured. The essence of the events is briefly outlined in the extract from Lord Keith's judgment, below. Over the intervening years, a fuller understanding of the horror of those events and the shortcomings of the official response to them has only gradually and painfully emerged, with an Independent Review reporting in September 2012.[7] The Review vindicated those close to the disaster who had been deeply unsatisfied with the official account of events. Following the Review, the result of an initial inquest into the disaster was quashed and a new inquest ordered. This inquest concluded on 26 April 2016, 27 years after the disaster, with a jury determination that the 96 people who died had been unlawfully killed. Contrary to what the police continued to argue, Liverpool fans did not contribute to the dangers through their behavior.[8] The civil litigation in *Alcock* and in *Hicks v Chief Constable of South Yorkshire* (Chapter 8, Section 2.2) can be seen as part of the families' efforts to uncover the truth. Seen in light of what is now accepted to be the truth, the role of tort in that process is disappointing. In these cases, as in *White v Chief Constable* (a claim brought by police officers), the chief concern of the House of Lords was with avoiding extensive liability and could be called protectionist.

The *Alcock* claims themselves were brought by relatives of some of the supporters who were killed, injured, or endangered through negligence in the policing of the crowd. The claim was for psychiatric harm to the relatives themselves. This case, restrictive as it was, remains the leading authority on the criteria of recovery by 'secondary victims'.

Lord Keith of Kinkel, at 392

My Lords, the litigation with which these appeals are concerned arose out of the disaster at Hillsborough Stadium, Sheffield, which occurred on 15 April 1989. On that day a football match was arranged to be played at the stadium between the Liverpool and the Nottingham Forest football clubs. It was a semi-final of the F.A. Cup. The South Yorkshire police force, which was responsible for crowd control at the match, allowed an excessively large number of intending spectators to enter the ground at the Leppings Lane end, an area reserved for Liverpool supporters. They crammed into pens 3 and 4, below the West Stand, and in

[7] *Hillsborough*, The Report of the Hillsborough Independent Panel, September 2012. This Report, and a great deal more, is freely available through the website of the Independent Panel: http://hillsborough.independent.gov.uk/.

[8] https://www.theguardian.com/uk-news/2016/apr/26/hillsborough-inquests-jury-says-96-victims-were-unlawfully-killed.

the resulting crush 95 people were killed and over 400 physically injured. Scenes from the ground were broadcast live on television from time to time during the course of the disaster, and recordings were broadcast later. The Chief Constable of South Yorkshire has admitted liability in negligence in respect of the deaths and physical injuries. Sixteen separate actions were brought against him by persons none of whom was present in the area where the disaster occurred, although four of them were elsewhere in the ground. All of them were connected in various ways with persons who were in that area, being related to such persons or, in one case, being a fiancée. In most cases the person with whom the plaintiff was concerned was killed, in other cases that person was injured, and in one case turned out to be uninjured. All the plaintiffs claimed damages for nervous shock resulting in psychiatric illness which they alleged was caused by the experiences inflicted on them by the disaster.

Lord Ackner, at 402–3

The three elements

Because "shock" in its nature is capable of affecting such a wide range of persons, Lord Wilberforce in *McLoughlin v. O'Brian* [1983] 1 A.C. 410, 422, concluded that there was a real need for the law to place some limitation upon the extent of admissible claims and in this context he considered that there were three elements inherent in any claim. It is common ground that such elements do exist and are required to be considered in connection with all these claims.. . .

The three elements are (1) the class of persons whose claims should be recognised; (2) the proximity of such persons to the accident—in time and space; (3) the means by which the shock has been caused.

I will deal with those three elements seriatim.

(1) The class of persons whose claim should be recognised

When dealing with the possible range of the class of persons who might sue, Lord Wilberforce in *McLoughlin v. O'Brian* [1983] 1 A.C. 410 contrasted the closest of family ties—parent and child and husband and wife—with that of the ordinary bystander. He said that while existing law recognises the claims of the first, it denied that of the second, either on the basis that such persons must be assumed to be possessed with fortitude sufficient to enable them to endure the calamities of modern life, or that defendants cannot be expected to compensate the world at large. He considered that these positions were justified, that other cases involving less close relationships must be very carefully considered, adding, at p. 422:

"The closer the tie (not merely in relationship, but in care) the greater the claim for consideration. The claim, in any case, has to be judged in the light of the other factors, such as proximity to the scene in time and place, and the nature of the accident."

I respectfully share the difficulty expressed by Atkin L.J. in *Hambrook v. Stokes Brothers* [1925] 1 K.B. 141, 158–159—how do you explain why the duty is confined to the case of parent or guardian and child and does not extend to other relations of life also involving intimate associations; and why does it not eventually extend to bystanders? As regards the latter category, while it may be very difficult to envisage a case of a stranger, who is not actively and foreseeably involved in a disaster or its aftermath, other than in the role of rescuer, suffering shock-induced psychiatric injury by the mere observation of apprehended or actual injury of a third person in circumstances that could be considered reasonably foreseeable, I see no reason in principle why he should not, if in the circumstances, a reasonably strong-nerved person would have been so shocked. In the course of argument your Lordships were given, by way of an example, that of a petrol tanker careering out of control into a school in session and bursting into flames. I would not be prepared to rule out a potential claim by a passer-by so shocked by the scene as to suffer psychiatric illness.

As regards claims by those in the close family relationships referred to by Lord Wilberforce, the justification for admitting such claims is the presumption, which I would accept as being rebuttable, that the love and affection normally associated with persons in those relationships is such that a defendant ought reasonably to contemplate that they may be so closely and directly affected by his conduct as to suffer shock resulting in psychiatric illness. While as a generalisation more remote relatives and, a fortiori, friends, can reasonably be expected not to suffer illness from the shock, there can well be relatives and friends whose relationship is so close and intimate that their love and affection for the victim is comparable to that of the normal parent, spouse or child of the victim and should for the purpose of this cause of action be so treated.

At 404–6

(2) The proximity of the plaintiff to the accident

It is accepted that the proximity to the accident must be close both in time and space. Direct and immediate sight or hearing of the accident is not required. It is reasonably foreseeable that injury by shock can be caused to a plaintiff, not only through the sight or hearing of the event, but of its immediate aftermath.

Only two of the plaintiffs before us were at the ground. However, it is clear from *McLoughlin v. O'Brian* [1983] 1 A.C. 410 that there may be liability where subsequent identification can be regarded as part of the "immediate aftermath" of the accident. Mr. Alcock identified his brother-in-law in a bad condition in the mortuary at about midnight, that is some eight hours after the accident. This was the earliest of the identification cases. Even if this identification could be described as part of the "aftermath," it could not in my judgment be described as part of the *immediate* aftermath. *McLoughlin's* case was described by Lord Wilberforce as being upon the margin of what the process of logical progression from case to case would allow. Mrs. McLoughlin had arrived at the hospital within an hour or so after the accident. Accordingly in the post-accident identification cases before your Lordships there was not sufficient proximity in time and space to the accident.

(3) The means by which the shock is caused

Lord Wilberforce concluded that the shock must come through sight or hearing of the event or its immediate aftermath but specifically left for later consideration whether some equivalent of sight or hearing, e.g. through simultaneous television, would suffice: see p. 423. Of course it is common ground that it was clearly foreseeable by the defendant that the scenes at Hillsborough would be broadcast live and that amongst those who would be watching would be parents and spouses and other relatives and friends of those in the pens behind the goal at the Leppings Lane end. However he would also know of the code of ethics which the television authorities televising this event could be expected to follow, namely that they would not show pictures of suffering by recognisable individuals. Had they done so, Mr. Hytner accepted that this would have been a "novus actus" breaking the chain of causation between the defendant's alleged breach of duty and the psychiatric illness. As the defendant was reasonably entitled to expect to be the case, there were no such pictures. Although the television pictures certainly gave rise to feelings of the deepest anxiety and distress, in the circumstances of this case the simultaneous television broadcasts of what occurred cannot be equated with the "sight or hearing of the event or its immediate aftermath." Accordingly shocks sustained by reason of these broadcasts cannot found a claim. I agree, however, with Nolan L.J. that simultaneous broadcasts of a disaster cannot in all cases be ruled out as providing the equivalent of the actual sight or hearing of the event or its immediate aftermath. Nolan L.J. gave, ante, pp. 386G–387A, an example of a situation where it was reasonable to anticipate that the television cameras, whilst filming and transmitting pictures of a special event of children travelling in a balloon, in which there was media interest, particularly amongst the parents, showed the balloon suddenly bursting into flames. Many other such situations could be imagined where the impact of the simultaneous television pictures would be as great, if not greater, than the actual sight of the accident.

Conclusion

Only one of the plaintiffs, who succeeded before Hidden J., namely Brian Harrison, was at the ground. His relatives who died were his two brothers. The quality of brotherly love is well known to differ widely—from Cain and Abel to David and Jonathan. I assume that Mr. Harrison's relationship with his brothers was not an abnormal one. His claim was not presented upon the basis that there was such a close and intimate relationship between them, as gave rise to that very special bond of affection which would make his shock-induced psychiatric illness reasonably foreseeable by the defendant. Accordingly, the judge did not carry out the requisite close scrutiny of their relationship. Thus there was no evidence to establish the necessary proximity which would make his claim reasonably foreseeable and, subject to the other factors, to which I have referred, a valid one. The other plaintiff who was present at the ground, Robert Alcock, lost a brother-in-law. He was not, in my judgment, reasonably foreseeable as a potential sufferer from shock-induced psychiatric illness, in default of very special facts and none was established. Accordingly their claims must fail, as must those of the other plaintiffs who only learned of the disaster by watching simultaneous television. I, too, would therefore dismiss these appeals.

Lord Oliver of Aylmerton added some very important comments regarding the distinction between 'primary' and 'secondary' victims; and the nature of 'proximity'.

Lord Oliver, at 407–8

It is customary to classify cases in which damages are claimed for injury occasioned in this way under a single generic label as cases of "liability for nervous shock." . . . Broadly . . . [the cases] divide into two categories, that is to say, those cases in which the injured plaintiff was involved, either mediately or immediately, as a participant, and those in which the plaintiff was no more than the passive and unwilling witness of injury caused to others. . . .

Lord Oliver considered case law including *Dulieu v White* (Section 1.1) and *Schneider v Eisovitch* [1960] 2 QB 430, where the plaintiff had been directly involved in the same accident in which her husband had died. These were 'primary victim' cases.

At 408

Into the same category, as it seems to me, fall the so called "rescue cases." It is well established that the defendant owes a duty of care not only to those who are directly threatened or injured by his careless acts but also to those who, as a result, are induced to go to their rescue and suffer injury in so doing. The fact that the injury suffered is psychiatric and is caused by the impact on the mind of becoming involved in personal danger or in scenes of horror and destruction makes no difference.

"Danger invites rescue. The cry of distress is the summons to relief…the act, whether impulsive or deliberate, is the child of the occasion:" *Wagner v. International Railway Co.* (1921) 232 N.Y. 176, 180–181, *per* Cardozo J.

So in *Chadwick v. British Railways Board* [1967] 1 W.L.R. 912, the plaintiff recovered damages for the psychiatric illness caused to her deceased husband through the traumatic effects of his gallantry and self-sacrifice in rescuing and comforting victims of the Lewisham railway disaster.

These are all cases where the plaintiff has, to a greater or lesser degree, been personally involved in the incident out of which the action arises, either through the direct threat of bodily injury to himself or in coming to the aid of others injured or threatened. Into the same category, I believe, fall those cases such as *Dooley v. Cammell Laird & Co. Ltd.* [1951] 1 Lloyd's Rep. 271, *Galt v. British Railways Board* (1983) 133 N.L.J. 870, and *Wigg v. British Railways Board*, The Times, 4 February 1986, where the negligent act of the defendant has put the plaintiff in the position of being, or of thinking that he is about to be or has been, the involuntary cause of another's death or injury and the illness complained of stems from the shock to the plaintiff of the consciousness of this supposed fact. The fact that the defendant's negligent conduct has foreseeably put the plaintiff in the position of being an unwilling participant in the event establishes of itself a sufficiently proximate relationship between them and the principal question is whether, in the circumstances, injury of that type to that plaintiff was or was not reasonably foreseeable.

In those cases in which, as in the instant appeals, the injury complained of is attributable to the grief and distress of witnessing the misfortune of another person in an event by which the plaintiff is not personally threatened or in which he is not directly involved as an actor, the analysis becomes more complex.

The 'Alcock Criteria'

To be successful, a 'secondary victim' must satisfy each of the following criteria.

Category of Relationship

The plaintiff must be in a close and loving relationship with the primary victim. In certain cases (spouse, parent, or child…), the law will presume such a close and loving relationship, though the defendant may rebut this presumption by bringing evidence that the relationship was not close and loving. In other cases, no close ties of affection are presumed, and therefore the plaintiff must prove that they existed. This applies even to siblings.

Physical Proximity

The plaintiff must be close to the accident in time and space. Although the 'immediate aftermath' will suffice, identification of a body some eight hours later was held in this case not to be close enough.

Immediate Perception and 'Shock'

The injury must have been caused by a 'shocking event' and there must be either direct sight or hearing of the event, or something equivalent to this. In *Alcock*, some of the plaintiffs saw the events unfold on television. However, it was held that because the broadcasts did not show the suffering of individuals, they were not sufficient to give rise to the sort of 'shock' that would be equivalent to witnessing an event. It was again left open whether broadcasts could ever be equivalent to direct perception, but it was pointed out that a broadcast which showed individual suffering would be in breach of the Broadcasting Code of Ethics and might well amount to a *novus actus interveniens* (see Chapter 3, Section 6, Remoteness).

It was left open whether there might be circumstances so horrific that even a bystander without close relationship to the primary victims (but fulfilling the other requirements) might be able to recover. We will consider where we stand with this potential exception to the first requirement, in relation to 'Bystanders', below.

Arbitrary or Principled?

There are substantial differences in approach between the judgments extracted, despite their agreement on the outcome of the case. Lord Ackner continued to seek sound reasons of principle for the limitations placed on recovery by 'non-participating' plaintiffs. Specifically, he explains the need for a close and loving relationship (the first criterion above) in terms of foreseeability. If there is a particularly close and loving relationship, he explains, then the defendant ought to foresee that psychiatric harm to that plaintiff is likely to follow. But this is a long way from the usual, 'practical' form of foreseeability. The defendant would never be aware of the precise relationship between the primary victim, and any friends or relatives who may be within sight and hearing of events. Indeed the defendant would not be likely to know who was present, let alone the details of their relationships (see S. Hedley, 'Morbid Musings of the Reasonable Chief Constable' [1992] CLJ 16). The truth is, foreseeability here is itself a 'control device', as we have recognized throughout this chapter, and as was recognized in *Page v Smith*. Lord Oliver on the other hand appealed not to foreseeability but to 'proximity'. Although he thought that proximity did not operate as a precise test, he suggested that it captured the real issues of policy that arose—where, in other words, to draw the line.

Bystanders

This category provides a particular challenge for a 'foreseeability' approach. Even the restrictive form of foreseeability would allow that, in an extreme case, a mere bystander may be able to recover. Some incidents are so shocking that even a person of reasonable fortitude having no relationship with the immediate victims would foreseeably suffer harm if they witnessed the incident closely and directly. If on the other hand the true justification for the control devices lies in avoiding claims by remote parties, then the courts might be reluctant to recognize a duty to bystanders even in the case of an extremely shocking event.

In *McFarlane v EE Caledonia* [1994] 2 All ER 1, the Court of Appeal tended to the latter course. The Court could not reconcile the existence of control devices in *Alcock* (above), with the possibility that a mere bystander may exceptionally be owed a duty on the grounds of specific foreseeability. The Court of Appeal preferred not to undermine the control devices.

The plaintiff was at sea on board a vessel within sight of a major disaster in which flames engulfed the Piper Alpha oil rig, in which 164 men were killed. This was an unusually 'horrific' event and so the Court of Appeal decision comes close to a rejection of the dicta in *Alcock* concerning recovery of damages by bystanders. In a comprehensive rejection of the plaintiff's claims, the Court of Appeal found that he was not in danger; was not reasonably in fear for his own safety; and could not be counted as a rescuer because although the vessel went to offer assistance, he personally played no useful role. He was also not a person of reasonable fortitude, although after *Page v Smith* this would not be relevant if he was physically endangered. In *Hegarty v EE Caledonia* [1997] 2 Lloyd's Rep 259, another plaintiff who had been on the same support vessel at the same incident also failed to recover damages. This plaintiff was considered to be of reasonable fortitude, but it was judged that he had not been in physical danger and it was concluded that his fear for his own safety could not therefore have been 'reasonable'. We can take it that 'reasonable fear' is interpreted narrowly, since it was not satisfied by a claimant who turned and ran from a fireball which landed just short of the bow of the vessel he was on.

Summary

Despite Lord Ackner's attempts to provide a principled basis for the *Alcock* criteria, the end result does not pass the most basic test, of offering satisfactory reasons why the disappointed party should have lost. For a brother to be required to provide *evidence* of close ties of love and affection is unseemly. To have Cain and Abel cited in evidence against presuming such close ties will have added insult to the injury. Jane Stapleton has justly described the law as stated in the *Alcock* case in the following terms:

J. Stapleton, 'In Restraint of Tort' in P. Birks (ed.), *The Frontiers of Liability*, vol 2 (Oxford University Press, 1994), 95

That at present claims can turn on the requirement of 'close ties of love and affection' is guaranteed to produce outrage. Is it not a disreputable sight to see brothers of Hillsborough victims turned away because they had *no more* than brotherly love towards the victim? In future cases will it not be a grotesque sight to see relatives scrabbling to prove their especial love for the deceased in order to win money damages and for the defendant to have to attack that argument?

Employees and Rescuers Who Witness Injury to Others: Primary or Secondary Victims?

White v Chief Constable of South Yorkshire Police [1999] 2 AC 455 (on appeal from *Frost v Chief Constable of South Yorkshire Police* [1998] QB 254)

This case also arose from the Hillsborough football stadium disaster. A number of police officers brought claims for psychiatric injury suffered as a result of involvement in the event and its aftermath. Liability was admitted in respect of those officers who were most actively involved in the immediate area of the ground where the deaths and injuries occurred. Five plaintiffs were chosen as representative of the roles played by the other plaintiffs. Four were on duty at the stadium; the fifth was responsible for stripping bodies and completing casualty forms in hospital. Waller J dismissed the claims, although he accepted that the Chief Constable owed a duty to his officers analogous to an employer's duty to employees (see *Walker v Northumberland*, earlier in the present chapter). The Court of Appeal allowed appeals by the four officers who had been on duty at the stadium, on the ground that the Chief Constable's duty of care to a police officer in relation to psychiatric injury suffered in the course of employment arose irrespective of whether the employee would otherwise have been classified as a primary or a secondary victim. Likewise, a tortfeasor owed a rescuer a duty of care irrespective of whether the rescuer was physically endangered.

In the House of Lords, the defendant's appeal was allowed. The House of Lords ruled (by a majority on each point):

1. That the employer's duty to employees did not extend to avoiding psychiatric harm where the employee would (without the contract of employment) be a secondary victim. The '*Alcock* criteria' applied. They were of course unable to show close ties of love and affection with the victims, and therefore failed to satisfy the criteria.

2. That a rescuer who had not been exposed to the risk of physical injury was not a 'primary victim' and also had to satisfy the *Alcock* criteria.

Lord Hoffmann, at 505–7

... Should the employment relationship be a reason for allowing an employee to recover damages for psychiatric injury in circumstances in which he would otherwise be a secondary victim and not satisfy the *Alcock* control mechanisms? I think, my Lords, that the question vividly illustrates the dangers inherent in applying the traditional incrementalism of the common law to this part of the law of torts. If one starts from the employer's liability in respect of physical injury, it seems an easy step, even rather forward-looking, to extend liability on the same grounds to psychiatric injury. It makes the law seem more attuned to advanced medical thinking by eliminating (or not introducing) a distinction which rests upon uneasy empirical foundations. It is important, however, to have regard, not only to how the proposed extension of liability can be aligned with cases in which liability exists, but also to the situations in which damages are not recoverable. If one then steps back and looks at the rules of liability for psychiatric injury as a whole, in their relationship with each other, the smoothing of the fabric at one point has produced an ugly ruck at another. In their application to other secondary victims, the *Alcock* control mechanisms stand obstinately in the way of rationalisation and the effect is to produce striking anomalies. Why should the policemen, simply by virtue of the employment analogy and irrespective of what they actually did, be treated different from first aid workers or ambulance men?

... In principle ..., I do not think it would be fair to give police officers the right to a larger claim merely because the disaster was caused by the negligence of other policemen. In the circumstances in which the injuries were caused, I do not think that this is a relevant distinction and if it were to be given effect, the law would not be treating like cases alike.

At 508

The second way in which the plaintiffs put their case is that they were not "bystanders or spectators" but participants in the sense that they actually did things to help. They submit that there is an analogy between their position and that of a "rescuer," who, on the basis of the decision of Waller J. in *Chadwick v. British Railways Board* [1967] 1 W.L.R. 912, is said to be treated as a primary victim, exempt from the control mechanisms.

In *Chadwick's* case, the plaintiff suffered psychiatric injury as a result of his experiences in assisting the victims of a railway accident. He spent 12 hours crawling in the wreckage, helping people to extricate themselves and giving pain killing injections to the injured. Waller J. said, at p. 921, that it was foreseeable that "somebody might try to rescue passengers and suffer injury in the process." The defendants therefore owed a duty of care to the plaintiff. He went on to say that it did not matter that the injury suffered was psychiatric rather than physical but in any event "shock was foreseeable and . . . rescue was foreseeable." Thus the judge's reasoning is based purely upon the foreseeability of psychiatric injury in the same way as in other cases of that time.

At 509–11

There does not seem to me to be any logical reason why the normal treatment of rescuers on the issues of foreseeability and causation should lead to the conclusion that, for the purpose of liability for psychiatric injury, they should be given special treatment as primary victims when they were not within the range of foreseeable physical injury and their psychiatric injury was caused by witnessing or participating in the aftermath of accidents which caused death or injury to others. It would of course be possible to create such a rule by an ex post facto rationalisation of *Chadwick v. British Railways Board* [1967] 1 W.L.R. 912. In both *McLoughlin v. O'Brian* [1983] 1 A.C. 410 and . . . *Alcock v. Chief Constable of South Yorkshire* [1992] 1 A.C. 310, members of the House referred to *Chadwick's* case [1967] 1 W.L.R. 912 with approval. But I do not think that too much should be read into these remarks. In neither case was it argued that the plaintiffs were entitled to succeed as rescuers and anything said about the duty to rescuers was therefore necessarily obiter. If one is looking for an ex post facto rationalisation of *Chadwick's* case, I think that the most satisfactory is that offered in the Court of Appeal in *McLoughlin v. O'Brian* [1981] Q.B. 599, 622 by my noble and learned friend, Lord Griffiths, who had been the successful counsel for Mr. Chadwick. He said:

"Mr. Chadwick might have been injured by a wrecked carriage collapsing on him as he worked among the injured. A duty of care is owed to a rescuer in such circumstances . . ."

If Mr. Chadwick was, as Lord Griffiths said, within the range of foreseeable physical injury, then the case is no more than an illustration of the principle applied by the House in *Page v. Smith*, namely that such a person can recover even if the injury he actually suffers is not physical but psychiatric. And in addition (unlike *Page v. Smith*) Waller J. made a finding that psychiatric injury was also foreseeable.

Should then your Lordships take the incremental step of extending liability for psychiatric injury to "rescuers" (a class which would now require definition) who give assistance at or after some disaster without coming within the range of foreseeable physical injury? It may be said that this would encourage people to offer assistance. The category of secondary victims would be confined to "spectators and bystanders" who take no part in dealing with the incident or its aftermath. On the authorities, as it seems to me, your Lordships are free to take such a step.

In my opinion there are two reasons why your Lordships should not do so. The less important reason is the definitional problem to which I have alluded. The concept of a rescuer as someone who puts himself in danger of physical injury is easy to understand. But once this notion is extended to include others who give assistance, the line between them and bystanders becomes difficult to draw with any precision. For example, one of the plaintiffs in the *Alcock* case [1992], a Mr. O'Dell, went to look for his nephew. "He searched among the bodies . . . and assisted those who staggered out from the terraces:", p. 354. He did not contend that his case was different from those of the other relatives and it was also dismissed. Should he have put himself forward as a rescuer?

But the more important reason for not extending the law is that in my opinion the result would be quite unacceptable. I have used this word on a number of occasions and the time has come to explain what I mean. I do not mean that the burden of claims would be too great for the insurance market or the public funds, the two main sources for the payment of damages in tort. The Law Commission may have had this in mind when they said that removal of all the control mechanism would lead to an "unacceptable" increase in claims, since they described it as a "floodgates" argument. These are questions on which it is difficult to offer any concrete evidence and I am simply not in a position to form a view one way or the other. I am therefore willing to accept that, viewed against the total sums paid as damages for personal injury, the increase resulting from an extension of liability to helpers would be modest. But I think that such an extension would be unacceptable to the ordinary person because (though he might not put it this way) it would offend against his notions of distributive justice. He would think it unfair between one class of claimants and another, at best not treating like cases alike and, at worst, favouring the less deserving against the more deserving. He would think it wrong that policemen, even as part of a general class of persons who rendered assistance, should have the right to compensation for psychiatric injury out of public funds while the bereaved relatives are sent away with nothing.

. . . It may be said that the common law should not pay attention to these feelings about the relative merits of different classes of claimants. It should stick to principle and not concern itself with distributive justice. An extension of liability to rescuers and helpers would be a modest incremental development in the common law tradition and, as between these plaintiffs and these defendants, produce a just result. My Lords, I disagree. It seems to me that in this area of the law, the search for principle was called off in *Alcock v. Chief Constable of South Yorkshire Police* [1992] 1 A.C. 310. No one can pretend that the existing law, which your Lordships have to accept, is founded upon principle. I agree with Jane Stapleton's remark that "once the law has taken a wrong turning or otherwise fallen into an unsatisfactory internal state in relation to a particular cause of action, incrementalism cannot provide the answer." see *The Frontiers of Liability*, vol. 2, p. 87.

Consequently your Lordships are now engaged, not in the bold development of principle, but in a practical attempt, under adverse conditions, to preserve the general perception of the law as a system of rules which is fair between one citizen and another.

Lord Hoffmann's judgment contains some unusually open statements concerning the arbitrary nature of the law on psychiatric harm and indeed on the distributive failings of the law of tort in general. If (he argues) we recognize that very few of those in need of compensation are able to establish claims in tort, it becomes clear that abolishing some or even all recovery for psychiatric injury would 'add little to the existing stock of anomaly' to be found in the law of tort (at 504). Lord Hoffmann said, loud and clear, that there was no longer scope for incremental development in this area, as a result of *Alcock*. Lord Steyn said the same thing:

Lord Steyn, at 500

The only sensible strategy for the courts is to say thus far and no further... In reality there are no refined analytical tools which will enable the courts to draw lines by way of compromise solution in a way that is coherent and morally defensible.

These comments amount to an abandonment of the traditional common law method, and of incremental development under *Caparo*, in respect of this category of case.

Rescuers after *White*

According to Lord Hoffmann, the majority in this case merely declined to *extend* the boundaries of liability to rescuers who were not themselves primary victims, because they were not physically endangered. The definition of a primary victim as one who is physically endangered was said to be drawn from *Page v Smith*. But as Lord Goff pointed out in his dissent, and as we said clearly above, it is most unlikely that Lord Lloyd in *Page v Smith* was seeking to set out an *exclusive* test for primary victims. The majority was introducing a new control device.

Lord Goff, at 486 (dissenting)

A new control mechanism?

As I have already recorded, it was submitted by Mr. Collender on behalf of the appellants, relying on certain passages in the opinion of Lord Lloyd in *Page v. Smith* [1996] A.C. 155, 184A–B, 187E–F, that it was a prerequisite of the right of recovery by primary victims in respect of psychiatric injury suffered by them that they should have been within the range of foreseeable physical injury. I have already expressed the opinion that no such conclusion can be drawn from Lord Lloyd's opinion in *Page v. Smith*. I understand however that, even if my view on that point is accepted as correct, some of your Lordships nevertheless consider that a new control mechanism to the same effect should now be introduced and imposed by this House as a matter of policy.

I am compelled to say that I am unable to accept this suggestion because in my opinion (1) the proposal is contrary to well established authority; (2) the proposed control mechanism would erect an artificial barrier against recovery in respect of foreseeable psychiatric injury and as such is undesirable; and (3) the underlying concern is misconceived.

Lord Goff considered reasons (1) and (2) in the light of the case law before continuing:

...

(3) The underlying concern is misconceived

I sense that the underlying concern, which has prompted a desire to introduce this new control mechanism, is that it is thought that, without it, the policemen who are plaintiffs in the present case would be "better off" than the relatives in the *Alcock* case who failed in their claims, and that such a result would be undesirable. To this, there are at least three answers. First, the control mechanisms which excluded recovery by the relatives in the *Alcock* case would, in my opinion, have been equally applicable to the policemen in the present case if on the facts they had (like the relatives) been no more than witnesses of the consequences of the tragedy. Second, the question whether any of the relatives might be able to recover because he fell within the broad category of rescuer is still undecided; and, strangely, the control mechanism now proposed to exclude the claims of relatives if advanced on the basis that they were rescuers. Third, however, it is in any event misleading to think in terms of one class of plaintiffs being "better off" than another. Tort liability is concerned not only with compensating plaintiffs, but with awarding such compensation against a defendant who is responsible in law for the plaintiff's injury. It may well be that one plaintiff will succeed on the basis that he can establish such responsibility, whereas another plaintiff who has suffered the same injury will not succeed because he is unable to do so. In such a case, the first plaintiff will be "better off" than the second, but it does not follow that the result is unjust or that an artificial barrier should be erected to prevent those in the position of the first plaintiff from succeeding in their claims. The true requirement is that the claim of each plaintiff should be judged by reference to the same legal principles.

For all these reasons I am unable to accept the need for, or indeed the desirability of, the new control mechanism now proposed.

In later sections of this chapter, the general conclusion is that decisions in most 'problem' areas are becoming more convincing. That is not the case with *White*. Existing doctrinal confusion was described as beyond remedy; and then extended to rescuers.

Unwilling Participants Other than Rescuers

In the extract, Lord Hoffmann expressly left open the possibility that claims may be brought by other unwilling participants, particularly those who reasonably believe that they are responsible for death or serious injury to others. This category of case was described by Lord Oliver in *Alcock* in terms of harm to a 'participant'. He treated such participants as primary victims. Lord Oliver's comments were based partly on previous cases such as *Dooley v Cammell Laird & Co Ltd* [1951] 1 Lloyd's Rep 271 (a crane operator whose crane, due to a fault, dropped its load towards fellow workers was owed a duty of care in respect of psychiatric damage).

The current restrictive approach both to rescuers and to 'unwilling participants' is illustrated by *Monk v Harrington* [2008] EWHC Civ 1879 (QB); [2009] PIQR P3. The claimant witnessed the aftermath of an accident at work during the construction of the new Wembley Stadium, in which a platform fell 60 feet, killing a worker below and injuring another. The claimant was foreman at the site and went quickly to the scene in order to assist, crawling under the platform in order to offer first aid. Although he was classified as a rescuer, he was not physically endangered nor (the court held) reasonably in fear for his own safety, and he therefore could not count as a primary victim. Because the claimant had also played a role in supervising the erection of the platforms, he argued that belief in his own responsibility played a part in causing his psychiatric illness. This took the form, in part, of an obsessive concern with safety which ultimately led to his being unable to return to work elsewhere. The court rejected this part of his claim also. This was an unreasonable belief on his part, for which the defendants could not be responsible. Determination of the case turned on an evaluation of the claimant's evidence given the clear and restrictive legal principles set out in *White*. But the case makes it legitimate to wonder whether it is really appropriate to force claimants whose mental harm is not denied to claim that they were fearful for their own safety, rather than appalled by witnessing at close proximity fatal injuries to a fellow human being.

Conclusions

Where secondary victims are concerned, the law has always imposed certain restrictions. It has proved difficult to provide a proper justification which would allow the courts to distinguish between successful and unsuccessful cases. Justifications have ranged from foreseeability, through floodgates, to proximity. We have pointed out that foreseeability itself is applied in a particular form in respect of psychiatric injury. In *White*, the various control devices set out in the case of *Alcock v Chief Constable of South Yorkshire Police* were first declared to be arbitrary, and then extended to categories (employees and rescuers) who had not previously been subject to them, in order to avoid apparent inconsistency between classes of claimant.

Meanwhile, however, duty techniques such as 'voluntary assumption of responsibility' in combination with the test for *breach* of duty have been applied by the Court of Appeal in order to distinguish between recoverable and unrecoverable psychiatric damage in a wide range of cases where there was no endangered party at all. This might suggest that there is nothing intrinsically problematic about psychiatric damage. Rather, there is a problem where the person suffering the eventual illness is not the immediate victim of a physical impact, nor close to the event. *White* suggests that incremental change is now impossible, and *Rothwell* makes it unlikely that change would take the form of increasing liability.

Legislative Change?

In conclusion to its *Report on Liability for Psychiatric Illness* (Law Com Report No 249, 1998), the Law Commission proposed legislation in this area. The proposals would abolish some of the existing control devices and make adjustments to the requirement for close ties of love and affection. Somewhat similar recommendations have subsequently been made by the Scottish Law Commission.[9]

In the proposed new duty of care (Clause 1), there is no requirement that the damage should be shock-induced, and no requirement that the claimant should have directly witnessed an event or been in close physical proximity to it. These changes would mark a considerable relaxation of the controls applied. The prospect of 'indeterminate claims' is met by retaining a requirement that there be close ties of love and affection between claimant and immediate victim, and by retaining a foreseeability requirement. There is no definition of the *kind* of foreseeability required, except that it must be foreseeability of psychiatric harm. It is not clear whether foreseeability will be judged in the light of the accident in question, or in the more usual way from the point of view of the defendant without hindsight. It seems likely that the former, 'specific' form of foreseeability traditionally applied to psychiatric damage cases is intended. This 'control device' would therefore continue to apply.

---

[9] Scot Law Comm No 196 (2004).

More 'modest changes were proposed for the 'relationship' criterion. In particular, Clause 3 expands the list of relationships in which close ties of love and affection are assumed, to include siblings and cohabitants. The latter category is further defined and includes same-sex relationships. Claimants who fall into the listed categories would be *conclusively* taken to have a close enough tie of love and affection, avoiding the prospect of intrusive evidence being gathered by defendants who are eager to avoid liability.

In summary, in abolishing the other control devices, but retaining closeness of relationship, the Law Commission accepted the possibility of indeterminacy in claimants as a valid policy concern, but has not accepted the argument that illness *flowing from bereavement* needs to be excluded from compensation, where the family relationship is sufficiently close.

In Clause 2, the Law Commission sets out a new duty where the defendant foreseeably causes injury to another by harming or endangering himself. This was ruled out as a matter of public policy in the case of *Greatorex v Greatorex* [2000] 1 WLR 1970 (a first instance decision), partly because it would inhibit the defendant's freedom of action, and partly because it may cause family strife where claimant and defendant are related.

The Law Commission did not include any provisions relating to employees or rescuers, believing that there was no particular reason to interfere with the then developing common law on these issues. This has proved to be incorrect. In Clause 4, the Law Commission only proposed to abolish the common law duty so far as it depended on close ties of love and affection to the immediate victim. It was not thought at the time of drafting the Bill (before the House of Lords' decision in *White*) that this requirement had any application to rescuers or employees. Similarly, it never applied (by definition) to mere bystanders, so that the Bill would not resolve the question of whether they can seek compensation. But the larger question is whether any broadening of liability is likely to be taken forward, given the political climate currently surrounding tort liability.

2. PURE ECONOMIC LOSSES

This section relates to the recovery of 'pure economic losses'. Economic losses suffered by the claimant will be regarded as 'pure' if they do not flow from any personal injury to the claimant nor from any physical damage to his or her property.

Like psychiatric injury, pure economic loss is often described as a problematic form of damage. The problems in question are, however, rather different. Although 'floodgates' arguments are sometimes encountered in this area (for example in cases of 'relational' economic loss, Category A, Section 2.1), there are other reasons why *a duty to take care not to cause foreseeable economic loss to the claimant is not always appropriate.*

Hale LJ, *McLoughlin v Jones*
[2002] QB 1312

58 Psychiatric injury is different in kind from economic loss. The law has traditionally regarded both with some scepticism. It has restricted the scope of any duty to avoid causing purely economic loss: this is obviously right. The object of a great deal of economic activity is to succeed while others fail. Much economic loss is intentionally, let alone negligently, caused. Only, therefore, where unlawful means are used or the defendant has assumed some responsibility towards another to avoid such loss should there be liability. The considerations in relation to psychiatric injury are rather different: hardly anyone sets out to cause such injury to competitors or anyone else (if they do, the tort of intentionally inflicting harm under the principle in *Wilkinson v Downton* [1897] 2 QB 57 is committed). The law's scepticism has rather to do with the infinite scope of adverse psychiatric reactions and the other difficulties identified by Lord Steyn in the *Frost* case....

Hale LJ reminds us here of the limited scope of liability in 'the economic torts' (considered in Chapter 2). It is not always appropriate to impose liability for *deliberate* infliction of economic loss, in the absence of unlawful means. By definition, it cannot always be appropriate to impose a duty of care to avoid causing foreseeable economic loss through negligence. Even proximity is unlikely to supply the necessary additional factors. This is very different from the argument that 'over-extensive' liability may follow, which Hale LJ perceives to be the main concern in cases of psychiatric harm. Rather, it is an argument that cases of economic loss do not always require a remedy.

Even so, the issues arising are not entirely concerned with the nature of the injury. Cases involving economic loss frequently share certain other features. The damage is often caused 'indirectly'; the relationship between claimant and defendant is sometimes remote; and the number of potential parties is sometimes large. In these respects, economic loss claims do indeed bear comparison with claims by 'secondary victims' considered in Section 1.4 of the present chapter. Courts also have regard to a broader legal policy context including the availability of other protection for the claimant and the possibility for conflict with the law of contract.[10] Factors of this sort are considered in determining whether a duty to take care is owed.

It is important to note that such concerns are not *only* relevant to cases of pure economic loss. The House of Lords has made clear that if similar considerations are relevant to a case involving *physical damage to property*, then a restricted approach to the duty of care may be taken in that case also: *Marc Rich v Bishop Rock Marine (The Nicholas H)* [1996] AC 211;[11] *D. Pride and Partners v Institute for Animal Health and Others* [2009] EWHC 296. Equally, approaches forged in cases of economic loss (particularly the 'assumption of responsibility') are also being applied in other areas of negligence, where the circumstances require.

Categories of Economic Loss Case

In Chapter 3, Section 3, we outlined the *Caparo* approach to establishing a duty of care in negligence. The hallmarks of the *Caparo* approach included the reinstatement of 'proximity' as a separate criterion which would *restrict* the operation of foreseeability; and the adoption of an 'incremental' technique in which courts will turn to established categories of case rather than to broad universal principles in order to reach their decisions. In a major article

---

[10] Peter Benson, "The Basis for Excluding Economic Loss in Tort Law', in D. Owen (ed.), *Philosophical Foundations of Tort Law* (Oxford University Press, 1997), offers a holistic explanation of the shape of recovery (and non-recovery) of pure economic losses, through analysis of the contractual context of many such losses and the relationship with concepts of ownership.

[11] The contractual allocation of risks between claimant cargo owner and the ship owner (who was not a party to the tort action) would be disturbed if the defendant ship surveyors were liable for damage to the

published soon after the decision in *Caparo*, Jane Stapleton criticized the new approach as likely to further entrench 'pockets' of liability.

Jane Stapleton, 'Duty of Care and Economic Loss: A Wider Agenda' (1991) 107 LQR 249, at 284

The central flaw in the House of Lords' approach to economic loss is the assumption—most explicit in *Caparo*—that difficult issues of duty should be analysed within and by analogy to pockets of 'relevant' case law. With respect, this can become a process akin to the tail wagging the dog, because the selection of the 'relevant' pocket can, at the outset, preclude consideration of factors or 'policies' which would provide a more coherent overall approach.

Stapleton's key point was that by dividing the case law into categories, artificial barriers would be set up and too much attention would be paid to irrelevant considerations (such as whether the damage was caused by an act or a statement), distracting attention from the more important policy issues that ought to drive decision-making in this area. Some of these, she argued, could be seen as relevant to all categories of economic loss.

Stapleton was correct to argue that the apparent distinction between 'losses caused by words' and 'losses caused by acts' is not a reliable way to divide the case law. It is now clear that *Hedley Byrne v Heller* extends beyond losses caused by statements. Certainly, it extends to professional services more broadly. This is in itself a good enough reason for abandoning the acts/words distinction. But it would also be beneficial to go further, and to recognize that there is no *general* exclusionary rule applying to economic losses caused by acts, nor to economic losses generally. (For support of this view see further B. Feldthusen, 'Pure Economic Loss in the High Court of Australia: Reinventing the Square Wheel?' (2000) 8 Tort L Rev 33.) Rather than a *general* exclusionary rule, in English law there are two specific areas where exclusionary rules apply. Even here, the exclusionary rules are not applied *because* the loss is purely economic, but for more specific reasons. These are categories A and B below.

The following categories are used to explain the law in this section.

A. Economic loss caused by **damage to property of another party**. This sort of loss can also be referred to as **'relational' economic loss**. It is not recoverable in English law, with one exception (*The Greystoke Castle*, discussed in Section 2.1), and a significant qualification (*Shell UK Ltd v Total UK Ltd*, discussed in Section 2.2). One reason against liability is the prospect of actions by an indeterminate number of claimants (*Spartan Steel*). If physical harm is done to the property (or person) of one party, this may have a 'ripple effect' on the *financial* interests of many others. But this reason for the exclusionary rule is not always valid. Supplementary reasons include reluctance to interfere with contractual allocations of risk, and desire to encourage other means of protecting the claimant's interests (*Spartan Steel*; *The Aliakmon*). This general rule against liability has no application in Australia, and Canada recognizes a number of exceptions to it.

cargo. This was a reason for finding that there was no duty of care under *Caparo*: it would not be 'fair, just and reasonable' to impose such a duty.

B. **Economic loss caused by acquiring a product that turns out to be defective.** This sort of loss is also not recoverable in English law. In *Murphy v Brentwood*, it was explained that such cases are simply not covered by *Donoghue v Stevenson*. Cases of this kind involve no injury to the person or to property other than the defective product itself. To recognize a duty here would make significant inroads into the rules of contract, because these cases involve a 'bad bargain' rather than harm to separate property. This approach is most controversial when it is applied to realty (specifically buildings) rather than to chattels, and in these cases, *Murphy v Brentwood* has been rejected in a number of common law jurisdictions. *Murphy* cannot be said to state a truly *arbitrary* rule (it is clear why it sets the boundaries where they are set), but is it overly restrictive given the policy context?

C. **Economic loss caused by reliance on negligent statements.** This kind of case was the subject of the key decision in *Hedley Byrne v Heller*. *Hedley Byrne* set out specific criteria for recognizing a duty of care where the claimant has relied upon a statement made by the defendant. There is much debate surrounding the exact criteria set out in *Hedley Byrne* and concerning its rationale and limits. But criteria drawn from *Hedley Byrne* are extensively in use in the English case law, even if they no longer capture the same concepts that were intended in that case. The relationship between the *Hedley Byrne* criteria, and the 'three-stage test' under *Caparo v Dickman*, continues to cause problems.

D. **'Extended'** *Hedley Byrne* **liability.** *Hedley Byrne* liability has been recognized as extending beyond its particular context, in which statements were delivered by one party directly to another party. First, *Hedley Byrne* liability has been extended to cases that involve more than one party, including some where the claimant does not rely on the statement at all. Second, liability on the basis of *Hedley Byrne* has been found outside the area of negligent statements, including cases of professional services more generally. In fact, these cases form the historical background to *Hedley Byrne*, and if anything it was the application in that case to mere statements (outside an existing relationship) that constituted the 'extension'. There seems to have been further movement at the margins of this category, suggesting that the existing boundaries are provisional. The problem here is certainly not rigidity of categories, but the elusive nature of the relevant criteria. Chief among these criteria is the idea of an 'assumption of responsibility'. The relationship between this criterion, and the broader idea of 'proximity', has been as hard to define as the meaning of the terms themselves.

The English solution has generally been to maintain the specific exclusionary rules in categories A and B against challenge. These exclusionary rules are based on policy reasons as we will explain. In other cases, there is an attempt to develop some general principles to explain the division between recoverable and unrecoverable losses.

Are 'Categories' Appropriate?

It will be obvious that we are taking a 'categorized' approach to the case law on economic loss. The virtues of categorization are hotly contested. Feldthusen (above), writing from a Canadian perspective, has suggested that a categorized approach is likely to shorten the length of judgments and enhance certainty. Feldthusen's proposed list of categories is longer and more complete than the one adopted in this section, which reflects the development of

English law.[12] Categorization has been particularly criticized by certain Australian writers (P. Cane, 'The Blight of Economic Loss: Is There Life After *Perre v Apand*?' (2000) 8 TLJ 1; J. Stapleton, 'Comparative Economic Loss: Lessons From Case-Law-Focused "Middle Theory"' 50 UCLA L Rev 531), who would prefer the courts to develop more satisfying criteria based on identifiable and generalized policy goals. For our more modest purpose, namely explanation of the English case law, a degree of categorization will certainly be helpful. No grand claims are being made for our categories, and there is room for overlap and for conflict between them.[13]

We now turn to the case law, organized in accordance with the four categories A–D above.

2.1 RELATIONAL ECONOMIC LOSS (CATEGORY A)

In a typical case of 'relational' economic loss, A causes damage to the property of B, causing C to lose money. C may lose money for a number of different reasons when the property of B is damaged. One such reason is that there may be a *contractual* link between C and the damaged property.

Cattle v The Stockton Waterworks Co (1875) LR 10 QB 453

The plaintiff was engaged by K (a landowner) to carry out work on K's land. Due to a leak in the defendants' pipes, the work had to be delayed, causing the plaintiff to lose money under the terms of the contract. Blackburn, Mellor, and Lush JJ held that the plaintiff could not maintain an action against the defendant water company in these circumstances, even if K could have done so. (Any such action might have been in negligence, or under the rule in *Rylands v Fletcher* (1868) LR 3 H 330: see Chapter 11.) Even at this early stage, the reason offered is one of proximity; but behind proximity lies a reluctance to open the floodgates to an indeterminate number of claims. Because of these considerations, there would be no recovery even in a case, such as this one, where no threat of excessive liability arose on the facts. This case still encapsulates the English approach to relational economic loss.

Blackburn J, at 457–8

In the present case the objection is technical and against the merits, and we should be glad to avoid giving it effect. But if we did so, we should establish an authority for saying that, in such a case as that of *Fletcher v. Rylands* ... the defendant would be liable, not only to an action by the owner of the drowned mine, and by such of his workmen as had their tools or clothes destroyed, but also to an action by every workman and person employed in the mine, who in consequence of its stoppage made less wages than he would otherwise have done. And many similar cases to which this would apply might be suggested. It may be said that it is just that all such persons should have compensation for such a loss, and that, if the law does not give them redress, it is imperfect. Perhaps it may be so. But, as was pointed out by Coleridge, J., in *Lumley v. Gye* [22 LJ QB 479], Courts of justice should not

---

12 See P. Giliker, 'Revisiting Pure Economic Loss: Lessons to be Learnt From the Supreme Court of Canada?' (2005) LS 49, arguing that English law could learn from a more complete categorizing approach.

13 For example, the case of *Junior Books v Veitchi* [1983] 1 AC 520, which has rarely if ever been followed, could be explained as a case under category C or D—special relationship and reliance. Instead, it is regarded as incorrect because of the strength of the general rule against recovery in category B cases.

"allow themselves, in the pursuit of perfectly complete remedies for all wrongful acts, to transgress the bounds, which our law, in a wise consciousness as I conceive of its limited powers, has imposed on itself, of redressing only the proximate and direct consequences of wrongful acts." In this we quite agree. No authority in favour of the plaintiff's right to sue was cited, and, as far as our knowledge goes, there was none that could have been cited.

The rule against recovery of relational economic loss clearly illustrates the fear of a potential 'ripple effect' if liability is imposed. The effect of damage to one party may be multiplied as others suffer economic losses, giving rise to 'indeterminate liability'.

A good example is *Weller v Foot and Mouth Disease Research Institute* [1966] 1 QB 569. The plaintiffs (who were cattle auctioneers) claimed that the defendant research institute had imported an African virus and allowed it to escape, causing the disease to spread to cattle and giving rise to financial harm to the plaintiffs since cattle markets had to be closed. Widgery J held that no duty was owed to the auctioneers. The then recent authority of *Hedley Byrne* (Section 2.3) made no difference to the general rule on relational economic loss. (We should note that the auctioneers in this case did not even have a contractual interest in the cattle whose health was foreseeably affected by the virus. Theirs was a very general economic interest.) Slightly different issues arising from a much more recent outbreak of foot and mouth disease were considered in *D. Pride and Partners v Animal Health Institute* [2009] EWHC 296. Here, the defendants had settled claims brought by the owners of cattle which had to be culled because they were infected or were at risk of being infected. But no duty was held to be owed to farmers whose animals passed the point of maturity at which they would most profitably have been slaughtered, or whose animals suffered 'welfare problems'. Here, the exclusionary rule was applied to 'relational' harm that had been held to be arguably physical.

Spartan Steel & Alloys v Martin & Co [1973] QB 27

Through negligence in digging up a road, the defendant contractors inadvertently severed a power supply. The plaintiffs' factory was engaged in smelting. Loss of power supply for a period of 14 hours or more caused a number of forms of damage to the plaintiff which are set out in Lord Denning's judgment.

Lord Denning MR, at 34

At the time when the power was shut off, there was an arc furnace in which metal was being melted in order to be converted into ingots. Electric power was needed throughout in order to maintain the temperature and melt the metal. When the power failed, there was a danger that the metal might solidify in the furnace and do damage to the lining of the furnace. So the plaintiffs used oxygen to melt the material and poured it from a tap out of the furnace. But this meant that the melted material was of much less value. The physical damage was assessed at £368.

In addition, if that particular melt had been properly completed, the plaintiffs would have made a profit on it of £400.

Furthermore, during those 14 hours, when the power was cut off, the plaintiffs would have been able to put four more melts through the furnace: and, by being unable to do so, they lost a profit of £1,767.

Lord Denning considered the case law on relational economic loss and continued:

At 37–9

... I turn to the relationship in the present case. It is of common occurrence. The parties concerned are: the electricity board who are under a statutory duty to maintain supplies of electricity in their district; the inhabitants of the district, including this factory, who are entitled by statute to a continuous supply of electricity for their use; and the contractors who dig up the road. Similar relationships occur with other statutory bodies, such as gas and water undertakings. The cable may be damaged by the negligence of the statutory undertaker, or by the negligence of the contractor, or by accident without any negligence by anyone; and the power may have to be cut off whilst the cable is repaired. Or the power may be cut off owing to a short-circuit in the power house: and so forth. If the cutting off of the supply causes economic loss to the consumers, should it as [a] matter of policy be recoverable? And against whom?

Lord Denning offered a number of reasons why pure economic loss should not, as a matter of policy, be recoverable in such a situation, including the following:

The second consideration is the nature of the hazard, namely, the cutting of the supply of electricity. This is a hazard which we all run. It may be due to a short circuit, to a flash of lightning, to a tree falling on the wires, to an accidental cutting of the cable, or even to the negligence of someone or other. And when it does happen, it affects a multitude of persons: not as a rule by way of physical damage to them or their property, but by putting them to inconvenience, and sometimes to economic loss. The supply is usually restored in a few hours, so the economic loss is not very large. Such a hazard is regarded by most people as a thing they must put up with—without seeking compensation from anyone. Some there are who install a stand-by system. Others seek refuge by taking out an insurance policy against breakdown in the supply. But most people are content to take the risk on themselves....

The third consideration is this: if claims for economic loss were permitted for this particular hazard, there would be no end of claims. Some might be genuine, but many might be inflated, or even false.... Rather than expose claimants to such temptation and defendants to such hard labour—on comparatively small claims—it is better to disallow economic loss altogether, at any rate when it stands alone, independent of any physical damage.

The fourth consideration is that, in such a hazard as this, the risk of economic loss should be suffered by the whole community who suffer the losses—usually many but comparatively small losses—rather than on the one pair of shoulders, that is, on the contractor on whom the total of them, all added together, might be very heavy....

These considerations lead me to the conclusion that the plaintiffs should recover for the physical damage to the one melt (£368), and the loss of profit on that melt consequent thereon (£400): but not for the loss of profit on the four melts (£1,767), because that was economic loss independent of the physical damage. I would, therefore, allow the appeal and reduce the damages to £768.

In this case, it was found that even where a plaintiff is clearly owed a duty in respect of physical damage to property, any 'pure' economic losses suffered in addition to physical damage are unrecoverable as either too remote, or outside the scope of the duty of care. These 'pure' economic losses are not consequent on damage to the plaintiff's property, but on damage to some other property (in this case, the cable) in which the plaintiff has no proprietary interest. Thus, these losses are an example of 'relational' economic loss. It will be seen that in this case, there were also *recoverable* economic losses, which were judged not to be 'purely' economic, but to be **consequential upon** the damage to the metal in the melt. Into this category fell the lost profits on the *damaged* metal.

It is clear that Lord Denning considered it best that *relational* economic losses should be covered by a general exclusionary rule. On the particular facts of *Spartan Steel*, one of the more persuasive of the reasons he offers is his fourth: it is better that a series of small losses should be spread across the community, rather than being concentrated on the shoulders of one party. But this reason does not apply to all cases of relational economic loss. It would not apply to *Cattle*, for example. Neither would it apply to *The Aliakmon* (below). Therefore, we should also note his second reason. Losing one's power supply is a fairly normal occurrence and most people take steps to deal with the risk that it will happen. They might do so through insurance, or through having an emergency generator. This is arguably the strongest reason in support of the category A exclusionary rule, because in order to encourage people (at least in a commercial setting) to take precautions before the event, it is best to have a clear rule: see further the discussion of the Canadian case law, later in this section.

In *Candlewood v Mitsui* (*The Mineral Transporter*) [1986] AC 1, the Privy Council confirmed that the general exclusionary rule for relational losses survived the new approach to the duty of care set out in *Anns v Merton* [1978] AC 728 (discussed in Chapter 3, Section 3). The Privy Council argued that the well-understood policy reasons behind the exclusionary rule were sufficient reason for its retention under the second limb of the *Anns* test, amounting to policy concerns that would justify negativing the duty of care.[14]

A long-standing exception to the rule is the case of *Morrison Steamship v Greystoke Castle* [1947] AC 265. A ship was damaged in a collision and had to put into port, discharging and reloading her cargo. The cargo owners became liable to the ship owners for 'general average contribution'. This refers to a means of pooling risk among cargo owners, by which they would have to pay a percentage of the costs of loading and reloading. It was held by the House of Lords that the cargo owners could claim against the defendant, whose negligence was partly to blame for the collision, even though their own property was not damaged. The House of Lords did not indicate that *Cattle v Stockton Waterworks* was in any way relevant to this case, citing only maritime authorities. In the course of their judgments, the House of Lords expressed the view that the plaintiff cargo owners were engaged in a 'common adventure' (Lord Roche) or 'joint adventure' (Lord Porter) with the ship owners. This idea has not been developed into a broader exception in English law, where it is regarded as confined to this special area of maritime law and the particular collusion of interests between the 'ship' and the 'cargo' (for further discussion see *The Nicholas H* [1996] AC 211, at 226–7, per Lord Lloyd of Berwick). But the idea of 'joint

---

[14] *Candlewood v Mitsui* was an appeal from the Supreme Court of New South Wales. The exclusionary rule stated by the Privy Council has however been rejected in Australia: see the discussion of *Perre v Apand*, later in this section.

venture' has been used as the basis of a duty of care for relational economic loss in Canada (*Norsk Pacific*, later in this section).

Leigh and Sillivan v Aliakmon Shipping Co Ltd [1986] AC 785 ('*The Aliakmon*')

In this case, the House of Lords refused to recognize a *limited* exception to the rule against recovery for relational economic loss. There was no prospect of indeterminate liability, and the case demonstrates a robust defence of the exclusionary rule in respect of relational economic loss.

Goods were damaged during shipment, through the negligence of charterers. Due to an unusual series of negotiations, the final contractual arrangements were not of a standard type. The end result was that the *risk of damage* had already passed to the plaintiffs on shipment, but *property* in the goods did not pass to the plaintiff until the goods were discharged and warehoused. The plaintiffs did not acquire any rights of suit in respect of damage done during shipment, their interest in the goods at that time being merely contractual. The sellers meanwhile had suffered no loss, so that they could not bring an action on their own account. This was an instance of property damage in respect of which neither buyer nor seller could bring an action, much to the benefit of the negligent party. On the other hand, the plaintiff buyers could argue that they were *prospectively* the legal owners of the damaged goods, a feature of their case that a sympathetic court might use to distinguish them from the unsuccessful plaintiffs in previous cases such as *Cattle v Stockton Waterworks*.

In the Court of Appeal, Robert Goff LJ suggested that this could be treated as a case of 'transferred loss'. Such cases, he argued, were in a special category to which the policy arguments against recovering relational losses did not apply. The concept is explained in the following extract.

Robert Goff LJ
[1985] QB 350, at 399 (CA)

In my judgment, there is no good reason in principle or in policy, why the c. and f. buyer should not have . . . a direct cause of action. . . . I am particularly influenced by the fact that the loss in question is of a character which will ordinarily fall on the goods owner who will have a good claim against the shipowner, but in a case such as the present the loss may, in practical terms, fall on the buyer. It seems to me that the policy reasons pointing towards a direct right of action by the buyer against the shipowner in a case of this kind outweigh the policy reasons which generally preclude recovery for purely economic loss. There is here no question of any wide or indeterminate liability being imposed on wrongdoers; on the contrary, the shipowner is simply held liable to the buyer in damages for loss for which he would ordinarily be liable to the goods owner. There is a recognisable principle underlying the imposition of liability, which can be called the principle of transferred loss. Furthermore, that principle can be formulated. For the purposes of the present case, I would formulate it in the following deliberately narrow terms, while recognising that it may require modification in the light of experience. Where A owes a duty of care in tort not to cause physical damage to B's property, and commits a breach of that duty in circumstances in which the loss of or physical damage to the property will ordinarily fall on B but (as is reasonably foreseeable by A) such loss or damage, by reason of a contractual relationship between B and C, falls upon C, then C will be entitled, subject to the terms of any contract restricting A's liability to B, to bring an action in tort against A in respect of such loss or damage to the extent that it falls on him, C.

This suggested innovation was not accepted by other members of the Court of Appeal, and it was also rejected on appeal by the House of Lords. Lord Brandon said that he would, even if he felt there to be a pressing need for such a remedy, be too 'faint-hearted' to introduce it given that it was clearly, in his view, against the established authorities. He also emphasized the importance of certainty, which was protected by the existence of the general rule. But he clearly felt that there was no need for such an innovation. If the buyers had been well advised, they would have negotiated a different form of contract, which would have provided them with a remedy in the event of loss. The exception proposed by Robert Goff LJ could not be said to create any excessive liability to defendants, since it would apply only to cases where the same loss which was foreseeably caused by damage to goods is transferred through the contractual structure, from the property owner, to a third party. Lord Brandon's reluctance to allow such a claim stems from a wish to protect the general rule for reasons unconnected with the specific parties.[15]

In more recent years, the House of Lords has been far from 'faint-hearted' in this context (see category D, Section 2.4). In the House of Lords, Lord Goff later used a very similar argument to his proposed 'transferred loss' idea, in a case where intended beneficiaries sued a solicitor for depriving them of legacies under a will: *White v Jones* [1995] 2 AC 207. Clearly, *White v Jones* was not a case of 'relational' economic loss because there was no property damage, but given that the case did not involve reliance by the beneficiaries upon the solicitor and was not even a statements case, neither did it fit easily within the *Hedley Byrne* category of recoverable economic losses. Here, there is a jangling inconsistency between different categories of case law, though whether blame should fall on the exclusionary rule in *The Aliakmon*, or on the creative interpretation of the law in *White v Jones*, is a matter for debate. Alternatively, the problem in these cases may be said to lie with rigidity in the rules of contract law.

Some assistance in assessing the exclusionary rule can be gained from looking to other common law jurisdictions and their treatment of 'relational' economic loss. Of particular interest is the approach taken in Canada.

Canadian National Railway Co v Norsk Pacific Steamship Co (1992) 91 DLR (4th) 289 (Supreme Court of Canada)

The defendants damaged a railway bridge over the Fraser river. The bridge was owned by Public Works Canada and the plaintiff railway company was its principal user, accounting for 85–6 per cent of the traffic. The plaintiff suffered economic loss in rerouting its traffic while the bridge was being repaired, and brought the present action against the defendants to recover that loss. By a majority, the Supreme Court held in the plaintiff's favour.

---

[15] Subsequently, the position was reversed by legislation, giving a remedy to the buyers: Carriage of Goods by Sea Act 1992, s 2(1).

We first extract the judgment of McLachlin J, for the majority. (Stevenson J delivered a separate and different judgment for the plaintiffs. L'Heureux-Dubé and Cory JJ agreed with McLachlin J.)

McLachlin J

49 In summary, it is my view that the authorities suggest that pure economic loss is prima facie recoverable where, in addition to negligence and foreseeable loss, there is sufficient proximity between the negligent act and the loss. Proximity is the controlling concept which avoids the spectre of unlimited liability. …

65 The plaintiff, CN, suffered economic loss as a result of being deprived of its contractual right to use the bridge damaged by the defendants' negligence. Applying the *Kamloops* approach, its right to recover depends on: (1) whether it can establish sufficient proximity or "closeness," and (2) whether extension of recovery to this type of loss is desirable from a practical point of view.

66 The first question is whether the evidence in this case establishes the proximity necessary to found liability. The case does not fall within any of the categories where proximity and liability have been hitherto found to exist. So we must consider the matter afresh.…

68 In addition to focusing upon the relationship between the appellant Norsk and CN—a significant indicator of proximity in and of itself—the trial judge based his conclusion that there was sufficient proximity on a number of factors related to CN's connection with the property damaged, the bridge, including the fact that CN's property was in close proximity to the bridge, that CN's property could not be enjoyed without the link of the bridge, which was an integral part of its railway system, and that CN supplied materials, inspection and consulting services for the bridge, was its preponderant user, and was recognized in the periodic negotiations surrounding the closing of the bridge.

69 MacGuigan J. A. summarized the trial judge's findings on proximity as follows, at p. 167 [F.C.]:

> In effect, the Trial Judge found that the CNR was so closely assimilated to the position of PWC that it was very much within the reasonable ambit of risk of the appellants at the time of the accident. That, it seems to me, is sufficient proximity: In Deane J.'s language, it is both physical and circumstantial closeness.

70 Such a characterization brings the situation into the "joint" or "common venture" category under which recovery for purely economic loss has heretofore been recognized in maritime law cases from the United Kingdom (*Greystoke Castle*) and the United States (*Amoco Transport*). The reasoning, as I apprehend it, is that where the plaintiff's operations are so closely allied to the operations of the party suffering physical damage and to its property (which—as damaged—causes the plaintiff's loss) that it can be considered a joint venturer with the owner of the property, the plaintiff can recover its economic loss even though the plaintiff has suffered no physical damage to its own property. To deny recovery in such circumstances would be to deny it to a person who for practical purposes is in the same position as if he or she owned the property physically damaged.

71 The second question is whether extension of recovery to this type of loss is desirable from a practical point of view. Recovery serves the purpose of permitting a plaintiff whose position for practical purposes, vis-à-vis the tortfeasor, is indistinguishable from that of the owner of the damaged property to recover what the actual owner could have recovered. This

is fair and avoids an anomalous result. Nor does the recovery of economic loss in this case open the floodgates to unlimited liability. The category is a limited one. It has been applied in England and the United States without apparent difficulty. It does not embrace casual users of the property or those secondarily and incidentally affected by the damage done to the property. Potential tortfeasors can gauge in advance the scope of their liability. Businesses are not precluded from self-insurance or from contracting for indemnity, nor are they "penalized" for not so doing. Finally, frivolous claims are not encouraged.

72 I conclude that here, as in *Kamloops*, the necessary duty and proximity are established; that valid purposes are served by permitting recovery; and that recovery will not open the floodgates to unlimited liability. In such circumstances, recovery should be permitted.

In a very full dissenting judgment, La Forest J objected that McLachlin J had not given appropriate emphasis to the specific exclusionary rule relating to relational economic loss. Instead, she had considered and rejected a *general* rule against recoverability of economic loss, and explained the *general* approach to identifying recoverable cases, in terms of proximity. There is, he argued, no such general rule.

La Forest J defined the case from the outset as raising the question of whether the exclusionary rule on *relational* economic loss was justified, and whether there were sound reasons to depart from it in this kind of case. The dominant consideration in a commercial setting such as this, he argued, was that the rules should 'place some incentive on both parties to act in an economically rational manner' (at 336). He made the following remarks in his conclusions:

At 355

    ... In making arrangements for allocating risks in essentially maritime matters, those engaged in navigating and shipping should, so far as possible, be governed by a uniform rule, so that they can plan their affairs ahead of time, whether by contract or insurance against possible contingencies.

    In my view, to justify recovery in cases of this nature, the plaintiff would, at the very least, have to respond effectively not only to the concern about indeterminacy but also show that no adequate means of protection was available....

La Forest J stated that the rule should be departed from only on compelling grounds and that this was not even a borderline case. It was not truly a joint venture, and was certainly not a case of transferred loss. The plaintiff was well aware of the risk of bridges being damaged, and ought to have taken steps to protect itself against losses in case this should occur. Finally, this sort of case did not raise issues of 'social justice', and practicality was the most important concern.

On the face of it, most of the disagreements between La Forest and McLachlin JJ relate to the substance of the policy considerations. But there is also a difference in the structure of their reasoning. With the majority approaching this case through a general analysis in terms of proximity, had the Supreme Court rejected the rule against liability for relational economic losses in particular?

If so, then the rejection was short-lived. In the case of *Bow Valley Husky v Saint John Shipbuilding Ltd* [1997] 3 SCR 1210, McLachlin J managed to 'meld' her own approach with that of La Forest J in a judgment with which the latter agreed. This judgment resembled La

Forest's approach in that it stated the *specific* exclusionary rule relating to relational economic loss at the outset. It then outlined three very limited exceptions to that rule, and stated that any further exceptions should be justified on policy grounds. On the facts of that case, there was no joint venture, and no compelling reason for departing from the exclusionary rule.

It is clear therefore that Canadian law recognizes a policy-based rule against recovery of relational economic loss in particular. Although Canadian law is more receptive to exceptions to this rule than English law has been, the intention is to recognize only clear *categories* of exception, rejecting an excessively 'case by case' approach as unworkable.

In Australia, relational economic loss was accepted as capable of giving rise to a duty of care in the case of *Caltex Oil v The Dredge 'Willemstad'* (1976) 136 CLR 529. There, the defendant had damaged a pipeline carrying oil, and was held to owe a duty of care to the plaintiff who depended upon the supply of oil through the pipeline. *Caltex Oil* was rejected by the Privy Council in *Candlewood v Mitsui* (above), but it is clearly *Caltex* and not *Candlewood v Mitsui* that is taken to represent Australian law on relational economic loss.

In *Perre v Apand* (1999) 198 CLR 180, the High Court set out a diversity of approaches to the case in hand but it was common ground that many factors will be relevant to establishing a duty of care where economic loss is concerned. Particularly relevant factors would be knowledge on the part of the defendant; the existence of an ascertainable class of plaintiffs; and 'vulnerability' to loss. The idea of 'vulnerability' focuses upon other reasonable avenues of protection that may be open to the plaintiff. Also relevant would be the likely impact of any finding of liability. The relevant factors appear to be intended for application to *all* cases of economic loss, and not specifically to cases of relational economic loss. In *Perre v Apand*, the High Court also reaffirmed its earlier rejection of 'proximity' as providing a test for the existence of a duty of care (*Hill v Van Erp* (1999) 188 CLR 159; S. Yeo, 'Rethinking Proximity: A Paper Tiger?' (1997) Tort L Rev 174–80; see later a definitive statement in *Sullivan v Moody* (2001) 207 CLR 562, at 578–9).

The High Court of Australia has now rejected *Anns v Merton, Caparo v Dickman*, proximity, and any exclusionary rule, as the basis for approaching cases of liability for economic loss, and replaced all these with a 'multi-factoral' approach. However, it was accepted by the High Court in *Perre v Apand* that 'incremental' (gradual) development is therefore essential in order to provide some guidance on likely future outcomes. It seems inevitable that categorization will be an *effect* of the multi-factoral approach. In the meantime, courts will need to 'hug the coast' of established principle, 'avoiding the open sea of system or science' (McHugh J at para 93, referring to Lord Wright, 'The Study of Law' (1938) 54 LQR 185, 186) in order to develop the law on a case-by-case basis.

Our review has suggested that it is possible to defend the exclusion of liability for relational losses, as requiring few judicial resources in most cases and giving rise to no less workable rules than the exclusionary rule with predictable exceptions (the Canadian approach). Against this background, two more recent decisions of the Court of Appeal merit discussion.

Shell UK Ltd v Total UK Ltd [2010] EWCA Civ 180; [2011] QB 86

The result in this case is perhaps surprising given the solidity of the relational category over many years and the high authority of cases which have maintained the exclusionary rule. Fuel pipelines were damaged in an enormous explosion. Those pipelines were held on trust for Shell, among others. Was the negligent party liable to compensate Shell for the economic loss it suffered as a result of this damage? Shell was not the legal owner; but the Court of Appeal concluded that it could claim nevertheless. The key move was to treat the beneficial owner in the same way as the legal owner, *provided that* the legal owner was also joined in the proceedings.

The decision has been subject to criticism as producing a 'strange hybrid of tort and trust law', which is apparent in the proviso that the legal owner must also be a party (PG Turner, 'Consequential Economic Loss and the Trust Beneficiary' (2010) CLJ 445). One alternative route (though not the only one) would have been to allow the trustee (the legal owner) to recover a sum representing the beneficial owner's losses, and to account to the beneficial owner accordingly.[16] This would extend a principle that operates in the law of contract,[17] into the law of tort. Contentiously, the Court of Appeal rejected as 'legalistic' any sharp distinction between legal and equitable ownership, a move which has attracted further criticism.[18] The important point for our purposes is that the decision makes an inroad into the principle set out in *The Aliakmon*, and does so on the basis that a legalistic approach is to be rejected. The Court drew an analogy with the case of *White v Jones*, explored in Category D, in which Lord Goff developed the views he had expressed in *The Aliakmon* but which were not taken up by other judges in that case. This illustrates the significance of countercurrents in the law: what Lord Goff failed to do in *The Aliakmon* but later put into effect in another category has begun to have an influence in a case within the area of application of *The Aliakmon* itself.

Waller LJ, *Shell UK v Total UK* (judgment of the Court)

143 We must confess to being somewhat influenced...by what Lord Goff of Chieveley in *White v Jones*... called 'the impulse to do practical justice'. It should not be legally relevant that the co-owners of the relevant pipelines, for reasons that seemed good to them, decided to vest the legal title to the pipelines in their service companies and enjoy the beneficial ownership rather than the formal legal title. Differing views about the wisdom of the exclusionary rule are widely held but however much one may think that, in general, there should be no duty to mere contracting parties who suffer economic loss as result of damage to a third party's property, it would be a triumph of form over substance to deny a remedy to the beneficial owner of that property when the legal owner is a bare trustee for that beneficial owner.

It has been argued that from the point of view of tort law, the result is satisfactory and that the policy issues which underpin *The Aliakmon* itself, being concerned with protection of existing contractual allocations of risk, simply do not exist in this case.[19] However, it is plain that the authority of *The Aliakmon* would have been directly challenged before the Supreme Court, had a settlement in the case not been reached a matter of weeks before it was due to be heard.[20] The case almost launched a full-scale assault on the existence of our first category, and in that sense it is the 'one that got away'.

---

[16] This and other possibilities are explored by K. Low, 'Equitable Title and Economic Loss' (2010) 126 LQR 507.

[17] *The Albazero* [1977] AC 774.

[18] J. Edelman, 'Two Fundamental Questions for the Law of Trusts' (2013) 129 LQR 66.

[19] K. Barker, 'Relational Economic Loss and Indeterminacy: The Search for Rational Limits', in S. Degeling, J. Edelman and J. Goudkamp (eds), *Torts in Commercial Law* (Thomson Reuters, 2011)

[20] Edelman, n 18.

Network Rail Infrastructure Ltd v Conarken Group Ltd [2011] EWCA Civ 644

This case also illustrates that the categories of economic loss are, in any principled or policy-based sense, porous. But by contrast to *Shell*, this case shows how policy issues akin to those that explain the 'relational' exclusion may be extended *outside* the boundaries of the category. In this instance, ordinary principles of negligence law were nevertheless applied to allow recovery; and the virtues of simplicity were underlined.

The question in *Network Rail* was economically significant. Damage to rail track and (for example) bridges by drivers is not uncommon and the financial consequences attached to the resulting disruption can be severe. The question here is whether those consequences lie with negligent drivers, or rather with their employers (for example in the case of most heavy goods vehicles) and insurers; or with the claimants in this case.

The claimant company owns the railway infrastructure and enters into contracts with various companies which operate train services on the its track. When track is damaged, and services are unable to operate, train operators are subject to penalties from the franchising authority. Network Rail is contractually bound to compensate the train operators in respect of these penalties, and certain other losses, according to a formula set out in the contracts. The question arising in this case was whether Network Rail is itself able to seek compensation to cover these compensatory payments. The contractual payments made are losses to Network Rail which are consequential on damage to its property, caused by negligence (in this instance, negligence on the part of motorists). The train operators themselves would have been unable to claim in tort had the contractual compensation not been payable, and the existence of the contract would therefore impose an additional liability on negligent parties (or their insurers), if the losses were recoverable. Those drivers were of course not privy to those contracts.

Despite these features, the court categorized the loss as 'consequential' rather than pure economic loss, and found it to be recoverable: applying ordinary *Wagon Mound* principles, loss of revenue is a foreseeable type of loss when damaging what is clearly commercial property (for example, power lines).[21] 'This is a form of 'taking your victim as you find him', which has been extended to the claimant's financial position since *Lagden v O'Connor* (Chapter 3). It was necessary that the agreement embodied a reasonable and genuine attempt at compensating for losses (even though, as we have said, those losses themselves would be unrecoverable); but close analysis of its terms was discouraged.

Jackson LJ, *Network Rail Infrastructure v Conarken Group*

153. Absent some exceptional circumstance or obviously unreasonable feature in the claimant's business arrangements, in my view it is not appropriate for the court to explore in detail the build-up of any loss of revenue following damage to revenue generating property. It is sufficient for the claimant to prove that the loss of revenue has occurred.

154. The law of tort should, so far as possible, be clear and simple. This court should not superimpose a requirement for expensive legal inquiry upon categories of case where there is an established entitlement to recover economic loss.

---

[21] The consequential losses in this case far outstripped the repair costs associated with the physical damage. Compulsory liability insurance under the Road Traffic Act extends to property damage with required coverage of £1 million.

While the Court in *Shell UK* recognized an important exception to the 'relational' category, the Court in this case declined to expand the area of non-recovery. Both cases recognized limits to the relational category, which has hitherto embodied the strongest exclusionary rule. Despite the reluctance of the Court in *Shell* to allow 'form' to triumph over 'substance', in this second case categorization—and simplicity in determining who bore the relevant risks—seems to have been prioritized (or perhaps, simply found convenient).

2.2 ECONOMIC LOSSES CAUSED BY ACQUIRING DEFECTIVE PRODUCTS OR PREMISES (CATEGORY B)

In *Anns v Merton LBC*, as we saw in Chapter 3, the House of Lords held that a local authority may owe a duty of care in negligence in exercise of its powers of inspection under the Public Health Act 1936. The judgment was dominated by the interplay between statutory powers and common law duties (as to which, see the discussion in the next section of this chapter). Relatively little attention was paid to the definition of the *loss* suffered by the disappointed purchasers. Lord Wilberforce clearly thought that the loss was not purely economic:

Lord Wilberforce, *Anns v Merton LBC*
[1978] AC 728, at 759

… The damages recoverable include all those which foreseeably arise from the breach of the duty of care which, as regards the council, I have held to be a duty to take reasonable care to secure compliance with the byelaws. Subject always to adequate proof of causation, these damages may include damages for personal injury and damage to property. In my opinion they may also include damage to the dwelling house itself; for the whole purpose of the byelaws in requiring foundations to be of a certain standard is to prevent damage arising from weakness of the foundations which is certain to endanger the health or safety of occupants.

To allow recovery for such damage to the house follows, in my opinion, from normal principle. If classification is required, the relevant damage is in my opinion material, physical damage, and what is recoverable is the amount of expenditure necessary to restore the dwelling to a condition in which it is no longer a danger to the health or safety of persons occupying and possibly (depending on the circumstances) expenses arising from necessary displacement.

As a matter of 'classification', Lord Wilberforce was mistaken. The damage suffered was economic loss. No separate 'damage' had been done to property of the plaintiffs, other than the building itself, by the defendants' alleged breach of duty. Eleven years later in the case next extracted, the House of Lords seized upon this error. But did this case set the law on another wrong turning by exaggerating the importance of the type of loss?

D and F Estates v Church Commissioners [1989] AC 177

The defendants were employed in the construction of a block of flats. The plasterwork was carried out by subcontractors who were not parties to the action. The plaintiffs were lessees of a flat in the block. In the fullness of time, it was discovered that some of the plaster was loose. Some of it fell down. The plaintiffs brought an action in negligence claiming the cost of stripping and replacing the plaster, and a number of other items including loss of rent, cleaning of carpets, and damage to possessions in the flat. The judge at first instance held that the plaster had been incorrectly applied and that the defendants were in breach of duty. An appeal by the defendants was successful, and the House of Lords dismissed a further appeal by the plaintiffs. The damage amounted to irrecoverable economic loss falling outside the ambit of *Donoghue v Stevenson*.

What were the reasons for suggesting that this kind of economic loss can give rise to no liability in the tort of negligence? The logic in *D and F Estates* (and also in *Murphy v Brentwood*, below) is that a builder is like the manufacturer of any other product. The builder may owe duties in contract or in tort. Contract duties are generally owed only to those who are parties to the contract (see our discussion of *Donoghue v Stevenson*, Chapter 3, Section 1). (This latter point, concerning contract, must now be qualified for reasons discussed briefly in respect of Category D cases, Section 2.4). First and subsequent purchasers who wished to benefit from contractual terms should negotiate to secure such protection. Tort duties on the other hand may be owed to ultimate consumers of a product even though these consumers do not contract with the manufacturer, as we saw in respect of *Donoghue* itself.

According to the House of Lords in *D and F Estates*, and later in *Murphy*, tort duties within *Donoghue v Stevenson* are only owed in respect of *damage done* by the item that is manufactured by the defendant. To go further than this, and to hold that the defendant is liable for repair costs or loss of investment in the property itself, would be (as Lord Bridge put it) 'to impose upon [the contractor] for the benefit of those with whom he had no contractual relationship the obligation of one who warranted the quality of the plaster as regards materials, workmanship and fitness for purpose' (at 207). A warranty, it is argued, will be available *free of charge*, and *for the benefit of non-contracting parties*, if a duty of care in tort is recognized in respect of losses of this nature. This justification is specific to losses arising from defects in quality. Although the cases concerning defective premises have been controversial, the same analysis has been applied to defective products, where recovery in tort is limited to damage done to separate property or to the person.[22]

Where did this leave *Anns*?

D and F Estates was not the appropriate case in which to depart from *Anns*. There was no question of damage to the structure itself. Did the decision in *D and F Estates* nevertheless make the later departure in *Murphy v Brentwood* inevitable?

Lord Bridge attempted to point out a way in which *Anns* itself could be salvaged. This was the '*complex structure theory*'. Lord Bridge's comments were offered as a means of bringing *Anns v Merton* within the ambit of *Donoghue v Stevenson* liability, by suggesting that in the case of a complex structure (or even chattel) such as a house, a defect in one part of the property could be seen as causing damage to a 'separate' piece of property. The larger structure would then be treated as a separate item. For example, a defect in foundations could conceivably, on this approach, be said to cause damage to other property if it leads to cracks in walls and floors. But this could not be extended to the defective plaster. This 'theory' (which was really only a suggestion) was considered and rejected by the House of Lords in *Murphy*. *Anns* was beyond salvation by these means. However, the rejection of this theory came with qualifications, leaving some uncertainty in the law.

22 See for example *Muirhead v Industrial Tank Specialities* [1985] 3 All ER 705.

Murphy v Brentwood DC [1991] 1 AC 398

Two houses, constructed on landfill, required a concrete raft foundation. The plans for the raft were submitted to Brentwood District Council for approval, pursuant to its duty under section 64 of the Public Health Act 1936. Having no suitably qualified staff of its own, Brentwood District Council referred the plans to qualified structural engineers. Their report was favourable, and the plans were duly passed. As it turned out, there were errors in the design of the foundations which were not spotted by the engineers consulted by the council, and as a result the foundations as constructed were faulty.

The foundations cracked and there was damage to the walls and pipes of the house. The plaintiff could not raise the entire repair costs (£45,000) from his insurer. Instead he sold the house for £35,000 less than its market value if sound. (Incidentally, he recovered from his insurer the sum of £35,000 in respect of a claim for subsidence damage.) A first instance judge awarded the plaintiff £38,777 in respect of diminution in the value of the house, and expenses incurred as a result of damage to it. The Court of Appeal dismissed an appeal by the council.

On appeal to the House of Lords, a specially constituted panel of seven judges invoked the practice statement of 26 July 1966 (*Practice Statement (Judicial Precedent)* [1966] 1 WLR 1234), and departed from its previous decision in *Anns v Merton*. This is equivalent to overruling the earlier decision (see J. W. Harris, 'And *Murphy* Makes It Eight—Overruling Comes to Negligence' (1991) 11 OJLS 416–30).

Lord Keith of Kinkel, at 468

It being recognised that the nature of the loss held to be recoverable in *Anns* was pure economic loss, the next point for examination is whether the avoidance of loss of that nature fell within the scope of any duty of care owed to the plaintiffs by the local authority. On the basis of the law as it stood at the time of the decision the answer to that question must be in the negative. The right to recover for pure economic loss, not flowing from physical injury, did not then extend beyond the situation where the loss had been sustained through reliance on negligent mis-statements, as in *Hedley Byrne*. There is room for the view that an exception is to be found in *Morrison Steamship Co. Ltd. v. Greystoke Castle (Cargo Owners)* [1947] A.C. 265. That case, which was decided by a narrow majority, may, however, be regarded as turning on specialties of maritime law concerned in the relationship of joint adventurers at sea. Further, though the purposes of the Act of 1936 as regards securing compliance with building byelaws covered the avoidance of injury to the safety or health of inhabitants of houses and of members of the public generally, these purposes did not cover the avoidance of pure economic loss to owners of buildings: see *Governors of the Peabody Donation Fund v. Sir Lindsay Parkinson & Co. Ltd.* [1985] A.C. 210, 241. Upon analysis, the nature of the duty held by *Anns* to be incumbent upon the local authority went very much further than a duty to take reasonable care to prevent injury to safety or health. The duty held to exist may be formulated as one to take reasonable care to avoid putting a future inhabitant owner of a house in a position in which he is threatened, by reason of a defect in the house, with avoidable physical injury to person or health and is obliged, in order to continue to occupy the house without suffering such injury, to expend money for the purpose of rectifying the defect.

The existence of a duty of that nature should not, in my opinion, be affirmed without a careful examination of the implications of such affirmation. To start with, if such a duty is incumbent upon the local authority, a similar duty must necessarily be incumbent also upon the builder of the house. If the builder of the house is to be so subject, there can be no grounds in logic or in principle for not extending liability upon like grounds to the manufacturer of a chattel. That would open up an exceedingly wide field of claims, involving the introduction of something in the nature of a transmissible warranty of quality. The purchaser of an article who discovered that it suffered from a dangerous defect before that defect had caused any damage would be entitled to recover from the manufacturer the cost of rectifying the defect, and presumably, if the article was not capable of economic repair, the amount of loss sustained through discarding it. Then it would be open to question whether there should not also be a right to recovery where the defect renders the article not dangerous but merely useless. The economic loss in either case would be the same. There would also be a problem where the defect causes the destruction of the article itself, without causing any personal injury or damage to other property. A similar problem could arise, if the *Anns* principle is to be treated as confined to real property, where a building collapses when unoccupied.

At 471

In my opinion it is clear that *Anns* did not proceed upon any basis of established principle, but introduced a new species of liability governed by a principle indeterminate in character but having the potentiality of covering a wide range of situations, involving chattels as well as real property, in which it had never hitherto been thought that the law of negligence had any proper place.

Lord Bridge of Harwich, at 476–9

The complex structure theory

In my speech in *D. & F. Estates* [1989] A.C. 177, 206G–207H I mooted the possibility that in complex structures or complex chattels one part of a structure or chattel might, when it caused damage to another part of the same structure or chattel, be regarded in the law of tort as having caused damage to "other property" for the purpose of the application of *Donoghue v. Stevenson* principles. I expressed no opinion as to the validity of this theory, but put it forward for consideration as a possible ground on which the facts considered in *Anns* [1978] A.C. 728 might be distinguishable from the facts which had to be considered in *D. & F. Estates* itself. I shall call this for convenience "the complex structure theory" . . . The reality is that the structural elements in any building form a single indivisible unit of which the different parts are essentially interdependent. To the extent that there is any defect in one part of the structure it must to a greater or lesser degree necessarily affect all other parts of the structure. Therefore any defect in the structure is a defect in the quality of the whole and it is quite artificial, in order to impose a legal liability which the law would not otherwise impose, to treat a defect in an integral structure, so far as it weakens the structure, as a dangerous defect liable to cause damage to "other property."

A critical distinction must be drawn here between some part of a complex structure which is said to be a "danger" only because it does not perform its proper function in sustaining the other parts and some distinct item incorporated in the structure which positively malfunctions so as to inflict positive damage on the structure in which it is incorporated. Thus, if a defective central heating boiler explodes and damages a house or a defective electrical installation malfunctions and sets the house on fire, I see no reason to doubt that the owner of the house, if he can prove that the damage was due to the negligence of the boiler manufacturer in the one case or the electrical contractor on the other, can recover damages in tort on *Donoghue v. Stevenson* [1932] A.C. 562 principles. But the position in law is entirely different where, by reason of the inadequacy of the foundations of the building to support the weight of the super-structure, differential settlement and consequent cracking occurs. Here, once the first cracks appear, the structure as a whole is seen to be defective and the nature of the defect is known. Even if, contrary to my view, the initial damage could be regarded as damage to other property caused by a latent defect, once the defect is known the situation of the building owner is analogous to that of the car owner who discovers that the car has faulty brakes. He may have a house which, until repairs are effected, is unfit for habitation, but, subject to the reservation I have expressed with respect to ruinous buildings at or near the boundary of the owner's property, the building no longer represents a source of danger and as it deteriorates will only damage itself.

For these reasons the complex structure theory offers no escape from the conclusion that damage to a house itself which is attributable to a defect in the structure of the house is not recoverable in tort on *Donoghue v. Stevenson* principles, but represents purely economic loss which is only recoverable in contract or in tort by reason of some special relationship of proximity which imposes on the tortfeasor a duty of care to protect against economic loss.

Lord Oliver of Aylmerton, at 485–7

The fact is that the categorisation of the damage in *Anns* as "material, physical damage," whilst, at first sight, lending to the decision some colour of consistency with the principle of *Donoghue v. Stevenson* [1932] A.C. 562, has served to obscure not only the true nature of the claim but, as a result, the nature and scope of the duty upon the breach of which the plaintiffs in that case were compelled to rely.

It does not, of course, at all follow as a matter of necessity from the mere fact that the only damage suffered by a plaintiff in an action for the tort of negligence is pecuniary or "economic" that his claim is bound to fail. It is true that, in an uninterrupted line of cases since 1875, it has consistently been held that a third party cannot successfully sue in tort for the interference with his economic expectations or advantage resulting from injury to the person or property of another person with whom he has or is likely to have a contractual relationship: see *Cattle v. Stockton Waterworks Co.* (1875) L.R. 10 Q.B. 453; *Simpson & Co. v. Thomson* (1877) 3 App. Cas. 279; *Société Anonyme de Remorquage à Hélice v. Bennetts* [1911] 1 K.B. 243. That principle was applied more recently by Widgery J. in *Weller & Co. v. Foot and Mouth Disease Research Institute* [1966] 1 Q.B. 569 and received its most recent reiteration in the decision of this House in *Leigh and Sillivan Ltd. v. Aliakmon Shipping Co. Ltd.* [1986] A.C. 785. But it is far from clear from these decisions that the reason for the plaintiff's failure was simply that the only loss sustained was "economic." Rather they seem to have been based either upon the remoteness of the damage as a matter of direct causation or, more probably, upon the "floodgates" argument of the impossibility of containing liability within any acceptable bounds if the law were to permit such claims to succeed. The decision of this House in *Morrison Steamship Co. Ltd. v. Greystoke Castle (Cargo Owners)* [1947] A.C. 265 demonstrates that the mere fact that the primary damage suffered by a plaintiff is pecuniary is no necessary bar to an action in negligence given the proper circumstances—in that case, what was said to be the "joint venture" interest of shipowners and the owners of cargo carried on board—and if the matter remained in doubt that doubt was conclusively resolved by the decision of this House in *Hedley Byrne & Co. Ltd. v. Heller & Partners Ltd.* [1964] A.C. 465 where Lord Devlin, at p. 517, convincingly demonstrated the illogicality of a distinction between financial loss caused directly and financial loss resulting from physical injury to personal property.

The critical question, as was pointed out in the analysis of Brennan J. in his judgment in *Council of the Shire of Sutherland v. Heyman*, 157 C.L.R. 424, is not the nature of the damage in itself, whether physical or pecuniary, but whether the scope of the duty of care in the circumstances of the case is such as to embrace damage of the kind which the plaintiff claims to have sustained: see *Caparo Industries Plc. v. Dickman* [1990] 2 A.C. 605. The essential question which has to be asked in every case, given that damage which is the essential ingredient of the action has occurred, is whether the relationship between the plaintiff and the defendant is such—or, to use the favoured expression, whether it is of sufficient "proximity"—that it imposes upon the latter a duty to take care to avoid or prevent that loss which has in fact been sustained. That the requisite degree of proximity may be established in circumstances in which the plaintiff's injury results from his reliance upon a statement or advice upon which he was entitled to rely and upon which it was contemplated that he would be likely to rely is clear from *Hedley Byrne* and subsequent cases, but *Anns* [1978] A.C. 728 was not such a case and neither is the instant case. It is not, however, necessarily to be assumed that the reliance cases form the only possible category of cases in which a duty to take reasonable care to avoid or prevent pecuniary loss can arise. *Morrison Steamship Co. Ltd. v. Greystoke Castle (Cargo Owners)*, for instance, clearly was not a reliance case. Nor indeed was *Ross v. Caunters* [1980] Ch. 297 so far as the disappointed beneficiary was concerned. . . .

Lord Oliver referred to the decision in *Spartan Steel v Martin* and the attempt to draw the line between recoverable and unrecoverable losses, and continued:

I frankly doubt whether, in searching for such limits, the categorisation of the damage as "material," "physical," "pecuniary" or "economic" provides a particularly useful contribution. Where it does, I think, serve a useful purpose is in identifying those cases in which it is necessary to search for and find something more than the mere reasonable foreseeability of damage which has occurred as providing the degree of "proximity" necessary to support the action. In his classical exposition in *Donoghue v. Stevenson* [1932] A.C. 562, 580–581, Lord Atkin was expressing himself in the context of the infliction of direct physical injury resulting from a carelessly created latent defect in a manufactured product. In his analysis of the duty in those circumstances he clearly equated "proximity" with the reasonable foresight of damage. In the straightforward case of the direct infliction of physical injury by the act of the plaintiff there is, indeed, no need to look beyond the foreseeability by the defendant of the result in order to establish that he is in a "proximate" relationship with the plaintiff. But, as was pointed out by Lord Diplock in *Dorset Yacht Co. Ltd. v. Home Office* [1970] A.C. 1004, 1060, Lord Atkin's test, though a useful guide to characteristics which will be found to exist in conduct and relationships giving rise to a legal duty of care, is manifestly false if misused as a universal; and Lord Reid, in the course of his speech in the same case, recognised that the statement of principle enshrined in that test necessarily required qualification in cases where the only loss caused by the defendant's conduct was economic. The infliction of physical injury to the person or property of another universally requires to be justified. The causing of economic loss does not. If it is to be categorised as wrongful it is necessary to find some factor beyond the mere occurrence of the loss and the fact that its occurrence could be foreseen. Thus the categorisation of damage as economic serves at least the useful purpose of indicating that something more is required and it is one of the unfortunate features of *Anns* that it resulted initially in this essential distinction being lost sight of.

On the whole, the judgments in *Murphy* do not set out (and certainly do not seek to justify) a *general* exclusionary rule for recovery of economic losses. Lord Keith's judgment comes the closest in stating that, at the time of the decision in *Anns*, liability for pure economic losses did not extend beyond the ambit of *Hedley Byrne* liability (Category C). Even so, Lord Keith went on to state a *specific* justification for the exclusion of liability in 'defective product' cases, such as this one. Lord Oliver referred to several different categories of economic loss case and explained that the *Hedley Byrne* category was not necessarily the only one in which such losses might be recoverable. Indeed, he pointed out that the only clear exclusionary rule related to 'relational economic loss' (which we have already considered), and doubted whether definition of the loss as 'pecuniary' or 'economic' was of particularly great assistance, except in identifying those cases where 'something more' is required, over and above mere foreseeability. As we noted in the introduction to this section, cases of pure economic loss are by no means the only cases in which 'something more' is required.

Complex Structures and the Separate Damage Requirement

Their Lordships were united in dismissing the complex structure theory as a means of saving *Anns*. It was not possible in this case to treat the foundations as a separate structure from the house. On the other hand, their Lordships thought that in cases where some entirely independent component went wrong, it might be possible to bring the case within the ambit of *Donoghue v Stevenson*. There were variations in the approach to when this might be the case. Lord Bridge distinguished between foundations (an integral part of the larger structure), and a central heating boiler (a 'distinct item'). Lord Keith argued that components could not realistically be seen as separate property if the entire house was provided by a single contractor. Lord Jauncey (at 497) also clearly stated that certain 'integral' components could be treated as 'separate property' only if they were installed by a separate contractor. He seems to have thought however that these 'integral components' could be distinguished from the examples of the central heating boiler or electrical installations, which he described as 'ancillary equipment'. This illustrates that the potential exists for quite complex argument about the application of *Murphy*.[23]

On the other hand in *Bellefield Computers v Turner* [2000] BLR 97, it proved that the *Murphy* approach was too clear to be evaded despite reservations on the part of the Court of Appeal. A fire broke out in the claimants' premises, damaging the premises themselves and some of their contents. On the assumed facts, the builders had not complied with building regulations in respect of a fire wall which would, if properly constructed, have prevented the fire from spreading. There was no claim for damage to the wall itself. The Court of Appeal concluded reluctantly that any claim for damage to the building itself was ruled out by the decision in *Murphy v Brentwood*, although the court clearly thought it artificial to describe the loss as 'purely economic' where there had in fact been fire damage to the premises. It was concluded that *Murphy* left no room for manoeuvre in a case, such as this, where the 'fire wall' was provided at the same time, and by the same contractors, as the rest of the building. Schiemann LJ described the conclusion as 'odd' and perceived it

[23] In *Jacobs v Morton* 1994 72 BLR 92, a concrete raft was added to foundations as part of repair work. In all the circumstances, the raft (added later, by a different contractor) was separate property. If it was defective, a duty may be owed in respect of damage to the house as a whole.

as arising from a policy decision to impose control devices over the liability to subsequent purchasers of a building.

Latency of Defect

It is clear from their Lordships' judgments in *Murphy* that even in the case of defects that cause actual damage to a separate structure or indeed to the person, there will be liability only if the damage is caused by a defect that remains 'latent'. Once the defect becomes known, then the defect 'no longer poses a danger'. (Lord Bridge conceded that a danger may remain if the property is close to the boundary of a neighbour's land, and suggested that the occupier may perhaps be able to recover for the costs of avoiding such dangers.) This was sound enough reasoning in respect of defective plaster (*D and F Estates*) but is an over-simplification when applied to more fundamental defects. A defect will 'no longer pose a danger' *only* if the owner or occupier of the premises is reasonably able to do something to prevent the danger. This may depend upon financing costly repairs, or it may mean moving house or premises (itself a costly undertaking). The truth is that knowledge of the defect does not per se remove the danger associated with it. Rather, the law chooses to treat defects that are 'patent' as the responsibility of the occupier, together with associated costs. In *Targett v Torfaen BC* (1992) HLR 164, the Court of Appeal took the view that the bar on recovery where damage is done by a patent defect did not apply where a weekly tenant was injured when a handrail on a staircase gave way. He knew of the defect, but could not reasonably have done anything about it. There has not, however, been a general reopening of this issue subsequent to *Targett*.[24]

The Wider Picture: The Role of Policy

In *Murphy v Brentwood*, their Lordships unanimously rejected the idea that policy and justice required a remedy at common law. Relatively little space was devoted to the policy arguments, and the judgments were chiefly presented as confirming a definitional error into which *Anns* had fallen. The majority of commentators have thought that this was a misleading presentation of their Lordships' decision in *Murphy*.

Sir Robin Cooke
(1991) 107 LQR 46, at 57

... the majority speeches in *Donoghue v Stevenson* were patently not meant to close the categories of liability in negligence, so the decision in that great case could certainly not be said to require the decisions now reached in *D and F Estates*, *Murphy*, and *Thomas Bates*. Analytically it was open to the House of Lords in those recent cases to decline to take further the ideas which won the day in *Donoghue v Stevenson*. But, analytically, it was just as open to the House as constituted in the *Anns* and *Dorset Yacht* cases to take the more expansive approach. (I avoid the word "liberal" in this context as being emotive.) The choice was a policy one.

[24] Though in *Nitrigin Eireann Teoranta v Inco Alloys Ltd* [1992] 1 WLR 498, May J was reluctant to categorize a defect as 'patent' even though there had been awareness of cracks in the product (a factory pipe); he reasoned that since the plaintiff had taken reasonable steps to investigate the cause of the cracks, the true defect remained 'latent' and a claim was not ruled out by *Murphy*.

In *Invercargill City Council v Hamlin* [1996] AC 624, an appeal from the Court of Appeal of New Zealand,[25] it was found by the Privy Council to be appropriate for New Zealand law to continue to develop in a direction influenced both by *Anns* and by the prior New Zealand decision in *Bowen v Paramount Builders* [1977] 1 NZLR 394, even though this was inconsistent with *Murphy*. The New Zealand approach was partly determined by the New Zealand courts' reading of social conditions in that jurisdiction and therefore involved no error of law.

Invercargill CC v Hamlin
[1996] AC 624

Lord Lloyd of Berwick (giving the judgment of the Board), at 642–3

In truth, the explanation for divergent views in different common law jurisdictions (or within different jurisdictions of the United States of America) is not far to seek. The decision whether to hold a local authority liable for the negligence of a building inspector is bound to be based at least in part on policy considerations ... .

In a succession of cases in New Zealand over the last 20 years it has been decided that community standards and expectations demand the imposition of a duty of care on local authorities and builders alike to ensure compliance with local byelaws. New Zealand judges are in a much better position to decide on such matters than the Board. Whether circumstances are in fact so very different in England and New Zealand may not matter greatly. What matters is the perception. Both Richardson and McKay JJ. [1994] 3 N.Z.L.R. 513, 528, 546 in their judgments in the court below stress that to change New Zealand law so as to make it comply with *Murphy's* case [1991] 1 A.C. 398 would have "significant community implications" and would require a "major attitudinal shift." It would be rash for the Board to ignore those views.

After a period of some doubt in respect of commercial property, the Supreme Court of New Zealand has recently held that councils owe a duty to all owners of buildings in relation to their functions under the Building Act 1991, developing the decision in *Hamlin: Body Corporate No. 207624 v North Shore City Council* [2012] NZSC 83.

Murphy v Brentwood: Relevant Policy Factors

What then were the policy arguments which influenced the House of Lords in *Murphy*? First, their Lordships noted that *Anns* had instigated an entirely novel form of liability (or rather, it had confirmed a novel form of liability introduced when the Court of Appeal decided *Dutton v Bognor Regis* [1972] 1 QB 373 six years previously). The introduction of novel forms of liability was best left to Parliament.

Second, in respect of local authorities in particular, it was noted that the majority of English cases on defective premises were fought between insurance companies—*Murphy* itself included. It was not obvious that drawing on the insurance policies of local authorities (thereby tending to increase their insurance premiums) was preferable to leaving

---

[25] At the time of the *Invercargill* litigation, the Judicial Board of the Privy Council was the final appellate authority for New Zealand. This is no longer the case since the creation of a New Zealand Supreme Court.

the job to first party insurance (by which the homeowner takes out insurance to cover defects in their home). This is, in part, an argument that the consumer is already adequately protected by alternative means, which is one of the main policy reasons isolated by Jane Stapleton in her influential article 'Duty of Care and Economic Loss' (1991) 107 LQR 249. It is also similar to the Australian focus on 'vulnerability': *Perre v Apand*, earlier in this section. This point can be amplified into an argument that purchasers can in some circumstances seek alternative protection, in which case they are not to be regarded as vulnerable. The first purchaser of a property, for example, may be able to negotiate contractual terms which could include a 'transmissible' warranty—that is to say, a warranty that may operate for the benefit of subsequent purchasers. The advantage to the first purchaser is that this may increase the market value of their premises, or simply assist future sales. In *Woolcock Street Investments Pty Ltd v CDG Pty Ltd* [2004] HCA 16, the High Court of Australia relied on the possibility of such a 'transmissible warranty' as one reason why a subsequent purchaser of property may *not* be regarded as 'vulnerable' in the relevant sense.[26] An alternative route is for the purchaser to seek independent appraisal of the state of the premises, and it is recognized that a surveyor offering such an appraisal may owe duties to take care both in contract and, in an appropriate case, in tort (*Smith v Eric Bush*, Section 2.3). It should be noted however that some defects may remain genuinely hidden from a competent surveyor.

The third policy reason is that there is a consumer protection statute in this area which was ignored by the House of Lords in *Anns*. The Defective Premises Act (DPA) 1972 would not have provided a remedy to the plaintiffs in *Murphy* or *Anns*, because the local authorities in those cases would not be covered in the wording of section 1: 'a person taking on work for or in connection with the provision of a dwelling'. The point is rather that the common law should not provide *more* extensive liabilities than the legislature had adopted after lengthy consideration by the Law Commission. The DPA 1972 does apply to the benefit of subsequent purchasers, and its protection cannot be excluded or limited via contract. On the other hand, it only applies to 'dwellings'; and (crucially) an action can only be brought within six years of completion of the work (section 1(5)).

In summary, although purchasers of defective premises are not owed a tort duty in respect of mere defects, they are not left without any means of protection. They may be able to avoid or recover their losses in the following ways:

1. Through first party insurance, as in the case of *Murphy v Brentwood* itself.

2. Through obtaining advice at the time of purchase. If the advice should prove to be negligent, there may be an action in contract or in tort: *Smith v Eric Bush* [1990] 1 AC 831. The relationship between this case and *Murphy v Brentwood* is considered below.

3. In the case of dwellings, a builder, architect, or other party involved in the 'provision' of the dwelling may be liable under the DPA 1972. This, however, is subject to a limitation period of six years from the time that the work is completed. By contrast, the six-year limitation period in negligence begins to run at the time that the damage occurs, which may be significantly later. In cases of latent damage, a special three-year time period may begin to run later than this, at the time when the claimant could have discovered the damage (Limitation Act 1980, section 14A). There is an overriding

---

[26] Although the case concerned commercial, rather than domestic, property, the High Court was careful to explain that this was not the decisive factor.

limitation period for such cases of 15 years from the time of the negligence (Limitation Act 1980, section 14B): see further Chapter 7.

4. If the builder of the premises is a member of the National House Building Council (NHBC), purchasers (including subsequent purchasers) of the building will benefit from the terms of the NHBC's 'Buildmark' warranty. This is a voluntary guarantee and insurance scheme operated by the NHBC and which offers significant protection to purchasers of property in respect of which the scheme operates. Further details are available on the NHBC website: http://www.nhbc.co.uk/.

Effectively, both section 1 of the DPA 1972 and the NHBC scheme provide 'transmissible warranties' in respect of properties to which they apply, during the period for which they are effective.

The Surveyor's Liability: Reconcilable Contradiction?

Among the alternative forms of liability just listed, the only one that operates through the common law is the potential liability of valuers and surveyors who negligently advise on the state of premises.

Where a surveyor is instructed directly by the purchaser of premises, it is clear that the surveyor will owe a duty to take reasonable care in the inspection and report, both in contract and in tort. There is no real controversy surrounding this duty even though the most likely form of damage to flow from breach of such a duty is economic. Why, it is sometimes asked, should a surveyor be liable for failing to spot a defect, when a builder is not liable to a subsequent purchaser for the defective act of building in the first place, unless some separate damage is done? The answer lies in the relationship between the parties, whether this is expressed in terms of assumption of responsibility, of direct and specific reliance, or in some other way. The surveyor offers targeted advice to a particular client and in respect of a specific transaction. We continue this discussion in relation to category C.

Summary of Categories A and B

In categories A and B, we have found that English law is at least substantially clear and predictable, even if not generous to claimants. Furthermore, we have found that some reasonably clear policy reasons are available which would explain the existence of rules against recovery for economic losses of these types. In each case, it is not particularly the nature of the loss as 'purely economic', but other identifiable considerations, which explained the rule against recovery. In the case of relational economic loss, the general reason is the 'ripple effect'; but *The Aliakmon* confirms that the no-liability rule will be maintained even where the ripple effect does not exist. Alternative protection could have been obtained by the plaintiff, *via* contractual negotiation. In the case of economic losses caused by defectiveness in a product or premises, the policy reasons are concerned with the maintenance of contractual rules and avoidance of new legal categories whose recognition may lead to awkward problems of definition. There is, again, an argument that claimants have alternative protection available to them. In neither category A nor category B is the non-availability of recovery for pure economic losses said to follow logically from the nature of the loss.

However, there are counter-currents in the law which affect these categories and create pressure for change or even departure from the settled areas of non-recovery. We particularly noted *Shell (UK) v Total (UK)* in relation to category A, and the influence of the categories to which we turn next. Generally, our difficulties lie in reconciling these areas of no liability, with the recognized and emerging categories of recoverable economic loss instigated by *Hedley Byrne v Heller* [1964] AC 465. A particular difficulty is that the cases can be approached in more than one way. For example, a builder may be thought to be assuming responsibility to a direct client in the same way that a surveyor does. We must return to these challenges at the end of our analysis of economic losses and the duty of care.[27]

2.3 ECONOMIC LOSS CAUSED BY RELIANCE ON NEGLIGENT STATEMENTS (CATEGORY C)

The Decision in *Hedley Byrne* and its Legacy

According to McHugh J of the High Court of Australia, 'Since the decision in *Hedley Byrne & Co Ltd v Heller & Partners Ltd*, confusion bordering on chaos has reigned in the law of negligence' (*Woolcock Street Investments v CDG Pty Ltd* [2004] HCA 16, para 45). There is some truth in this. *Hedley Byrne* is a difficult case to interpret even in its own terms, but to establish its relationship with other categories of economic loss is an even harder task. This is important because English judges have to a large extent adopted and adapted language employed in *Hedley Byrne* in order to identify cases of recoverable loss—and not just economic loss—in other contexts.

Hedley Byrne v Heller & Partners [1964] AC 465

The appellants were advertising agents, who planned to place orders for a company and who therefore asked their bankers to enquire into the financial stability of the company. Their bankers approached the company's bankers, the respondents, with inquiries. The respondents gave favourable responses to the inquiries, but stipulated that these statements were made 'without responsibility'. No fee was charged. The appellants relied upon the favourable references in placing orders, and suffered a loss. They brought an action against the company's bankers, in respect of alleged negligence.

The majority of the House of Lords concluded that in principle, a negligent (but honest) misrepresentation may give rise to a cause of action even in the absence of a contract or fiduciary relationship. However, since in this case there was an express disclaimer of responsibility, no such duty would be implied. Lords Morris and Hodson doubted whether, in circumstances such as these, there could be any duty to take care, even in the absence of the disclaimer. Arguably, they thought, the only duty would be to give an honest answer.

The majority of the discussion in *Hedley Byrne* related to the special status of statements, as opposed to acts. The fact that the loss was 'purely economic' seems to have been treated as of little importance. Perhaps this is because in this particular context, no form of loss other than economic loss was involved or could have been anticipated. That being so, the *economic* losses are in no sense 'secondary' or 'remote' consequences of any carelessness.

Here we extract three of the judgments. These have continued to influence the law on recovery of economic losses. But the most influential of the three is the judgment of Lord Devlin.

27 See particularly our later discussion of *Robinson v PE Jones (Contractors) Ltd* [2011] EWCA Civ 9.

Lord Reid, at 482–4

The appellants' first argument was based on *Donoghue v. Stevenson*. That is a very important decision, but I do not think that it has any direct bearing on this case. That decision may encourage us to develop existing lines of authority, but it cannot entitle us to disregard them. Apart altogether from authority, I would think that the law must treat negligent words differently from negligent acts. The law ought so far as possible to reflect the standards of the reasonable man, and that is what *Donoghue v. Stevenson* sets out to do. The most obvious difference between negligent words and negligent acts is this. Quite careful people often express definite opinions on social or informal occasions even when they see that others are likely to be influenced by them; and they often do that without taking that care which they would take if asked for their opinion professionally or in a business connection. The appellant agrees that there can be no duty of care on such occasions.... But it is at least unusual casually to put into circulation negligently made articles which are dangerous. A man might give a friend a negligently-prepared bottle of homemade wine and his friend's guests might drink it with dire results. But it is by no means clear that those guests would have no action against the negligent manufacturer.

Another obvious difference is that a negligently made article will only cause one accident, and so it is not very difficult to find the necessary degree of proximity or neighbourhood between the negligent manufacturer and the person injured. But words can be broadcast with or without the consent or the foresight of the speaker or writer. It would be one thing to say that the speaker owes a duty to a limited class, but it would be going very far to say that he owes a duty to every ultimate "consumer" who acts on those words to his detriment.... ..

So it seems to me that there is good sense behind our present law that in general an innocent but negligent misrepresentation gives no cause of action. There must be something more than the mere misstatement. I therefore turn to the authorities to see what more is required. The most natural requirement would be that expressly or by implication from the circumstances the speaker or writer has undertaken some responsibility, and that appears to me not to conflict with any authority which is binding on this House. Where there is a contract there is no difficulty as regards the contracting parties: the question is whether there is a warranty. The refusal of English law to recognise any jus quaesitum tertii causes some difficulties, but they are not relevant, here. Then there are cases where a person does not merely make a statement but performs a gratuitous service. I do not intend to examine the cases about that, but at least they show that in some cases that person owes a duty of care apart from any contract, and to that extent they pave the way to holding that there can be a duty of care in making a statement of fact or opinion which is independent of contract.

Much of the difficulty in this field has been caused by *Derry v. Peek* ((1889) 14 App. Cas. 337). The action was brought against the directors of a company in respect of false statements in a prospectus. It was an action of deceit based on fraud and nothing else. But it was held that the directors had believed that their statements were true although they had no reasonable grounds for their belief. The Court of Appeal held that this amounted to fraud in law, but naturally enough this House held that there can be no fraud without dishonesty and that credulity is not dishonesty. The question was never really considered whether the facts had imposed on the directors a duty to exercise care. It must be implied that on the facts of that case there was no such duty. But that was immediately remedied by the Directors' Liability Act, 1890, which provided that a director is liable for untrue statements in a prospectus unless he proves that he had reasonable ground to believe and did believe that they were true.

It must now be taken that *Derry v. Peek* did not establish any universal rule that in the absence of contract an innocent but negligent misrepresentation cannot give rise to an action. It is true Lord Bramwell said (p.347): "To found an action for damages there must be a contract and breach, or fraud." And for the next 20 years it was generally assumed that *Derry v. Peek* decided that. But it was shown in this House in *Nocton v. Lord Ashburton* [1914] A.C. 932) that that is much too widely stated. We cannot, therefore, now accept as accurate the numerous statements to that effect in cases between 1889 and 1914, and we must now determine the extent of the exceptions to that rule.

In *Nocton v. Lord Ashburton* a solicitor was sued for fraud. Fraud was not proved but he was held liable for negligence. Viscount Haldane L.C. dealt with *Derry v. Peek* (14 App.Cas. 337) and pointed out that while the relationship of the parties in that case was not enough, the case did not decide "that where a different sort of relationship ought to be inferred from the circumstances the case is to be concluded by asking whether an action for deceit will lie... There are other obligations besides that of honesty the breach of which may give a right to damages. These obligations depend on principles which the judges have worked out in the fashion that is characteristic of a system where much of the law has always been judge-made and unwritten." It hardly needed *Donoghue v. Stevenson* to show that that process can still operate. Then Lord Haldane quoted a passage from the speech of Lord Herschell in *Derry v. Peek* where he excluded from the principle of that case "those cases where a person within whose special province it lay to know a particular fact has given an erroneous answer to an inquiry made with regard to it by a person desirous of ascertaining the fact for the purpose of determining his course."

At 485–6

... A reasonable man, knowing that he was being trusted or that his skill and judgment were being relied on, would, I think, have three courses open to him. He could keep silent or decline to give the information or advice sought; or he could give an answer with a clear qualification that he accepted no responsibility for it or that it was given without that reflection or inquiry which a careful answer would require; or he could simply answer without any such qualification. If he chooses to adopt the last course he must, I think, be held to have accepted some responsibility for his answer being given carefully, or to have accepted a relationship with the inquirer which requires him to exercise such care as the circumstances require.

At 493

I am...of opinion that it is clear that the respondents never undertook any duty to exercise care in giving their replies. The appellants cannot succeed unless there was such a duty and therefore this appeal must fail.

Lord Morris of Borth-y-Gest, at 502–3

My Lords, I consider that it follows and that it should now be regarded as settled that if someone possessed of a special skill undertakes, quite irrespective of contract, to apply that skill for the assistance of another person who relies upon such skill, a duty of care will arise. The fact that the service is to be given by means of or by the instrumentality of words can make no difference. Furthermore, if in a sphere in which a person is so placed that others could reasonably rely upon his judgment or his skill or upon his ability to make careful inquiry, a person takes it upon himself to give information or advice to, or allows his information or advice to be passed on to, another person who, as he knows or should know, will place reliance upon it, then a duty of care will arise.

Lord Devlin, at 524–5

What Lord Atkin called [in *Donoghue v Stevenson*] a "general conception of relations giving rise to a duty of care" is now often referred to as the principle of proximity. You must take reasonable care to avoid acts or omissions which you can reasonably foresee would be likely to injure your neighbour. In the eyes of the law your neighbour is a person who is so closely and directly affected by your act that you ought reasonably to have him in contemplation as being so affected when you are directing your mind to the acts or omissions which are called in question.

… In my opinion, the appellants in their argument tried to press *Donoghue v. Stevenson* too hard. They asked whether the principle of proximity should not apply as well to words as to deeds. I think it should, but as it is only a general conception it does not get them very far.…

At 529–31

I have had the advantage of reading all the opinions prepared by your Lordships and of studying the terms which your Lordships have framed by way of definition of the sort of relationship which gives rise to a responsibility towards those who act upon information or advice and so creates a duty of care towards them. I do not understand any of your Lordships to hold that it is a responsibility imposed by law upon certain types of persons or in certain sorts of situations. It is a responsibility that is voluntarily accepted or undertaken, either generally where a general relationship, such as that of solicitor and client or banker and customer, is created, or specifically in relation to a particular transaction. In the present case the appellants were not, as in *Woods v. Martins Bank Ltd.* ([1959] 1 Q.B. 55) the customers or potential customers of the bank. Responsibility can attach only to the single act, that is, the giving of the reference, and only if the doing of that act implied a voluntary undertaking to assume responsibility. This is a point of great importance because it is, as I understand it, the foundation for the ground on which in the end the House dismisses the appeal. I do not think it possible to formulate with exactitude all the conditions under which the law will in a specific case imply a voluntary undertaking any more than it is possible to formulate those in which the law will imply a contract. But in so far as your Lordships describe the circumstances in which an implication will ordinarily be drawn, I am prepared to adopt any one of your Lordships' statements as showing the general rule: and I pay the same respect to the statement by Denning L.J. in his dissenting judgment in *Candler v. Crane, Christmas & Co* about the circumstances in which he says a duty to use care in making a statement exists.

I do not go further than this for two reasons. The first is that I have found in the speech of Lord Shaw in *Nocton v. Lord Ashburton* and in the idea of a relationship that is equivalent to contract all that is necessary to cover the situation that arises in this case. Mr. Gardiner does not claim to succeed unless he can establish that the reference was intended by the respondents to be communicated by the National Provincial Bank to some unnamed customer of theirs, whose identity was immaterial to the respondents, for that customer's use. All that was lacking was formal consideration. The case is well within the authorities I have already cited and of which *Wilkinson v. Coverdale* (1 Esp. 75) is the most apposite example.

I shall therefore content myself with the proposition that wherever there is a relationship equivalent to contract, there is a duty of care. Such a relationship may be either general or particular. Examples of a general relationship are those of solicitor and client and of banker and customer. For the former *Nocton v. Lord Ashburton* has long stood as the authority and for the latter there is the decision of Salmon J. in *Woods v. Martins Bank Ltd* ([1959] 1 Q.B. 55) which I respectfully approve. There may well be others yet to be established. Where there is a general relationship of this sort, it is unnecessary to do more than prove its existence and the duty follows. Where, as in the present case, what is relied on is a particular relationship created ad hoc, it will be necessary to examine the particular facts to see whether there is an express or implied undertaking of responsibility.

> I regard this proposition as an application of the general conception of proximity. Cases may arise in the future in which a new and wider proposition, quite independent of any notion of contract, will be needed. There may, for example, be cases in which a statement is not supplied for the use of any particular person, any more than in *Donoghue v. Stevenson* the ginger beer was supplied for consumption by any particular person; and it will then be necessary to return to the general conception of proximity and to see whether there can be evolved from it, as was done in *Donoghue v. Stevenson*, a specific proposition to fit the case. When that has to be done, the speeches of your Lordships today as well as the judgment of Denning L.J. to which I have referred—and also, I may add, the proposition in the American Restatement of the Law of Torts, Vol. III, p. 122, para. 552, and the cases which exemplify it—will afford good guidance as to what ought to be said. I prefer to see what shape such cases take before committing myself to any formulation, for I bear in mind Lord Atkin's warning, which I have quoted, against placing unnecessary restrictions on the adaptability of English law. I have, I hope, made it clear that I take quite literally the dictum of Lord Macmillan, so often quoted from the same case, that "the categories of negligence are never closed." English law is wide enough to embrace any new category or proposition that exemplifies the principle of proximity.

Although there was clearly a difference of view between Lords Reid and Morris on the important question of whether there would, in the absence of the disclaimer, be a duty to take care in this case, the greater difference in method is between these two judgments, and that of Lord Devlin. Lords Reid and Morris attempted to set out in quite general terms the circumstances in which there will be a duty to take care in respect of statements. In the extract above, Lord Reid seeks to identify the components of a 'special relationship' that will be sufficient to establish that the duty of care arises. This he says will be established if it is plain that the recipient of a statement is trusting the defendant to take care; if it is reasonable to trust the statement-maker in this way; and if the information or advice was given where the statement-maker ought to have known that the inquirer was relying on him. Lord Morris on the other hand adds the requirement of 'special skill'. The reason why Lord Morris doubted whether this was a case where a duty of care should arise, even in the absence of the disclaimer, is that there was no reasonable expectation that the defendant would go to any great lengths to ensure that their opinion was soundly based. One could say that this was not a statement on which it was reasonable to rely; alternatively, that there is no greater duty in this case than one of honesty.

Lord Devlin and the 'Voluntary Undertaking of Responsibility'

Lord Devlin, by contrast with Lords Reid and Morris, did not seek to establish *general* rules for application to all future cases of negligent misstatement. In disposing of this particular case, he emphasized the closeness to contract of the relationship between the parties. The only difference between this case and a formal contract, he argued, is that in this case there is no consideration since no fee was payable for the bankers' statement. In such circumstances, he argued, it is clear that there would have been an 'undertaking of responsibility' on the part of the defendant, if it had not been for the disclaimer of responsibility. He stressed that a *voluntary* undertaking of responsibility in the making of the statement was also required by each of the other judges, despite the broader statements highlighted above; and that this was evidenced by the fact that all of the other judges gave decisive weight to the disclaimer of responsibility, which was thought to exclude the possibility that any duty of care might arise.

Lord Devlin made clear that he thought the 'voluntary undertaking of responsibility' was an application of the broader conception of 'proximity'. In the passages extracted above, he made plain that there is no sense in asking courts simply to 'decide whether there is proximity' in a given case. Proximity is only a *general conception*, whose meaning will vary from one category of case law to another. Lord Devlin proposes that the particular facet of 'proximity' which is decisive in this particular case is 'nearness to contract'.

Although Lord Devlin argues that nearness to contract is a sufficient idea to dispose of this case, he concedes that there will be future cases in which this idea is not applicable. Unlike Lords Reid and Morris, he prefers not to predict the likely criteria that will need to be met in order to determine whether there is indeed proximity in such a case. Therefore it is a mistake to suggest that Lord Devlin thought that 'nearness to contract' was *essential* (or a duty to take care in the giving of statements. He merely said that it sufficed. He suggested that the criteria set out by the other judges in *Hedley Byrne* itself will be helpful in future cases, but he considered it unwise to attempt a broad general statement in advance of seeing the particular circumstances that might arise. Apart from the other judgments in *Hedley Byrne*, he also commended as likely to provide helpful guidance the *dissenting* judgment of Denning LJ in *Candler v Crane Christmas* [1951] 2 KB 164. (The majority decision in that case was overruled by the House of Lords in *Hedley Byrne*.)

Denning LJ would have recognized that a duty was owed by accountants where they were instructed to draw up accounts specifically for the purpose of inducing the plaintiff to invest money in a company. The majority of the Court of Appeal held that there could be no such duty in the absence of a contractual or fiduciary relationship between the parties. The following passage was approved by Lord Devlin in *Hedley Byrne*:

Denning LJ, *Candler v Crane Christmas*, at 181

... there are some cases—of which the present is one—where the accountants know all the time, even before they present their accounts, that their employer requires the accounts to show to a third person so as to induce him to act on them, and then they themselves, or their employers, present the accounts to him for the purpose. In such cases I am of opinion that the accountants owe a duty of care to the third person.

The test of proximity in these cases is: Did the accountants know that the accounts were required for submission to the plaintiff and use by him?

Lord Devlin's endorsement of the approach of Denning LJ in *Candler* is important, because that approach is consistent with the decision of a later House of Lords in the case of *Caparo v Dickman*. It has often been said that the approach in *Caparo* is in conflict with the approach in *Hedley Byrne*. Indeed this perceived conflict has led to tension in recent case law. Since the expression 'assumption of responsibility'—adapted from Lord Devlin's words in *Hedley Byrne*—has come increasingly into vogue (Section 2.4), it is possible that part of the perceived conflict between *Hedley Byrne* and *Caparo* results from reading Lord Devlin as laying down *criteria* (which, in fact, he sought to avoid), rather than simply *explaining* which elements of the case had led him to conclude that there was sufficient proximity between the parties. The latter makes his approach entirely compatible with the 'case by case' approach heralded by *Caparo v Dickman*. Indeed, Lord Devlin's judgment was quoted at length, and with approval, by Lord Oliver in *Caparo*. Lord Devlin's reading of proximity in the passage extracted may have inspired Lord Oliver's idea that proximity is no more than a 'general conception'.

Shortly before *Caparo*, doubt was cast on the continued relevance of 'assumption of responsibility' by the next case.

Smith v Eric S Bush; Harris v Wyre Forest District Council [1990] 1 AC 831

This case concerned a purchase of relatively low value domestic property. The claimants had paid for a valuation of the property which was arranged by their mortgage company. They had no direct contractual relationship with the surveyor, and the report stated that only the mortgage company should rely upon the report. It was clear however that the report would be supplied to the purchasers. They did not secure a further survey of the property (having, after all, paid for the one secured by their lender). The House of Lords held that the surveyor owed a duty in tort directly to the purchasers, despite the contractual structure. Here we are most concerned with what this case said about the *approach* to be taken where economic losses have been caused by negligent statements.

Lord Templeman considered that the relationship between the parties fitted Lord Devlin's criterion of being 'akin to contract' (a conclusion expressly doubted by Lord Jauncey):

Lord Templeman, at 846

In the present appeals, the relationship between the valuer and the purchaser is "akin to contract." The valuer knows that the consideration which he receives derives from the purchaser and is passed on by the mortgagee, and the valuer also knows that the valuation will determine whether or not the purchaser buys the house.

He also considered that, even though there was a disclaimer in the valuation report, the valuer could still be said to have assumed responsibility to the purchaser.

At 847

... in my opinion the valuer assumes responsibility to both mortgagee and purchaser by agreeing to carry out a valuation for mortgage purposes knowing that the valuation fee has been paid by the purchaser and knowing that the valuation will probably be relied upon by the purchaser in order to decide whether or not to enter into a contract to purchase the house. The valuer can escape the responsibility to exercise reasonable skill and care by an express exclusion clause, provided the exclusion clause does not fall foul of the Unfair Contract Terms Act 1977.

Since the decision in *Hedley Byrne*, the law on exclusion of liability had been altered by the Unfair Contract Terms Act 1977. An attempted exclusion of liability would be effective only if it was judged to be 'reasonable'. In the case of *Smith v Eric Bush*, the valuation had included a specific disclaimer of responsibility to any party other than the mortgagee building society which had commissioned the valuation (though at the purchaser's expense). Lord Templeman treated the disclaimer as relevant only to the question of whether liability had been validly excluded, *not* to the question of whether responsibility had been 'assumed' in the first place. In his view, the exclusion of liability was not, in these circumstances, reasonable:

At 854

The public are exhorted to purchase their homes and cannot find houses to rent. A typical London suburban house, constructed in the 1930s for less than £1,000 is now bought for more than £150,000 with money largely borrowed at high rates of interest and repayable over a period of a quarter of a century. In these circumstances it is not fair and reasonable for building societies and valuers to agree together to impose on purchasers the risk of loss arising as a result of incompetence or carelessness on the part of valuers... different considerations may apply where homes are not concerned.

Lord Griffiths by contrast cast doubt on the usefulness of the 'voluntary assumption of responsibility' idea. Understandably, he thought that he could not hold that there was a duty of care on the basis of a 'voluntary assumption' when the defendants had done all in their power to *disclaim* responsibility. Unlike Lord Templeman, who approached the disclaimer in terms of an attempted 'exclusion of liability', he treated the disclaimer as important to the very question of whether a duty of care could be said to arise. A judgment in favour of the plaintiff in this case could only be compatible with *Hedley Byrne* if the criterion of 'assumption of responsibility' was very considerably watered down.

Lord Griffiths, at 862

Mr Ashworth... submitted, on the authority of *Hedley Byrne & Co. Ltd. v. Heller & Partners Ltd.* [1964] A.C. 465 that it was essential to found liability for a negligent misstatement that there had been "a voluntary assumption of responsibility" on the part of the person giving the advice. I do not accept this submission and I do not think that voluntary assumption of responsibility is a helpful or realistic test for liability. It is true that reference is made in a number of the speeches in *Hedley Byrne* to the assumption of responsibility as a test of liability but it must be remembered that those speeches were made in the context of a case in which the central issue was whether a duty of care could arise when there had been an express disclaimer of responsibility for the accuracy of the advice. Obviously, if an adviser expressly assumes responsibility for his advice, a duty of care will arise, but such is extremely unlikely in the ordinary course of events. The House of Lords approved a duty of care being imposed on the facts in *Cann v. Willson* (1888) 39 Ch.D. 39 and in *Candler v. Crane, Christmas & Co.* [1951] 2 K.B. 164. But if the surveyor in *Cann v. Willson* or the accountant in *Candler v. Crane, Christmas & Co.* had actually been asked if he was voluntarily assuming responsibility for his advice to the mortgagee or the purchaser of the shares, I have little doubt he would have replied, "Certainly not. My responsibility is limited to the person who employs me." The phrase "assumption of responsibility" can only have any real meaning if it is understood as referring to the circumstances in which the law will deem the maker of the statement to have assumed responsibility to the person who acts upon the advice.

Later in his judgment, Lord Griffiths set out an alternative formulation by which to judge whether a duty of care should be recognized as arising in such a case, avoiding the terminology of 'assumption of responsibility'.

At 864–5

I have already given my view that the voluntary assumption of responsibility is unlikely to be a helpful or realistic test in most cases. I therefore return to the question in what circumstances should the law deem those who give advice to have assumed responsibility to the person who acts upon the advice or, in other words, in what circumstances should a duty of care be owed by the adviser to those who act upon his advice? I would answer—only if it is foreseeable that if the advice is negligent the recipient is likely to suffer damage, that there is a sufficiently proximate relationship between the parties and that it is just and reasonable to impose the liability. In the case of a surveyor valuing a small house for a building society or local authority, the application of these three criteria leads to the conclusion that he owes a duty of care to the purchaser. If the valuation is negligent and is relied upon damage in the form of economic loss to the purchaser is obviously foreseeable. The necessary proximity arises from the surveyor's knowledge that the overwhelming probability is that the purchaser will rely upon his valuation, the evidence was that surveyors knew that approximately 90 per cent. of purchasers did so, and the fact that the surveyor only obtains the work because the purchaser is willing to pay his fee. It is just and reasonable that the duty should be imposed for the advice is given in a professional as opposed to a social context and liability for breach of the duty will be limited both as to its extent and amount. The extent of the liability is limited to the purchaser of the house—I would not extend it to subsequent purchasers. The amount of the liability cannot be very great because it relates to a modest house. There is no question here of creating a liability of indeterminate amount to an indeterminate class. I would certainly wish to stress that in cases where the advice has not been given for the specific purpose of the recipient acting upon it, it should only be in cases when the adviser knows that there is a high degree of probability that some other identifiable person will act upon the advice that a duty of care should be imposed. It would impose an intolerable burden upon those who give advice in a professional or commercial context if they were to owe a duty not only to those to whom they give the advice but to any other person who might choose to act upon it.

As we saw earlier, the search for a 'voluntary assumption of responsibility' was intended by Lord Devlin to be a way to judge whether proximity was present in a case like *Hedley Byrne*. Doubting the relevance of 'voluntary assumption' on the facts of *Smith v Eric Bush*, Lord Griffiths suggests an alternative approach which appears to take us straight back to that general conception—proximity—together with foreseeability and the question of what is 'fair, just and reasonable'. Together, these became the components of the 'three-stage test' in *Caparo v Dickman* (Chapter 3, Section 3). However, it should be noted that the reasons why Lord Griffiths ultimately thought that the relationship in this case was 'proximate' are compatible with Lord Devlin's analysis of *Candler v Crane Christmas*. The surveyors knew at all times for whose benefit, and for what purpose, they were producing the valuation. This was perhaps a case in which an alternative approach to justifying the duty of care was simply more appropriate. Lord Griffiths' attempt to make the assumption of responsibility fit the facts amounted to a complete distortion of the concept, and has caused considerable subsequent confusion (see the discussion of category D in Section 2.4).

The decision in *Smith v Bush* is sensitive to its facts. In *Scullion v Bank of Scotland* [2011] EWCA Civ 2011; [2011] 1 WLR 3212, the purchaser of a 'buy to let' property was held *not to* be owed a duty of care by a valuer instructed by his mortgagee company. Many of the considerations which were central to *Smith v Bush* did not apply here. In particular, the Court of Appeal felt the facts were such that it could *not* be said that it would have been plain to the valuer that the purchaser would rely upon its report. It was significant, for example, that a report produced for a buy to let purchaser would have been different, with a particular emphasis on rental value rather than capital value.

Caparo Industries plc v Dickman plc [1990] 2 AC 605

The facts of this case were outlined in Chapter 3, Section 3, where we also noted the general approach to the duty of care which it set out.

Once again, the idea of 'voluntary assumption of responsibility' was not found helpful by the House of Lords, who concentrated instead on various features of the case which showed that there was, on the facts, insufficient proximity between the parties. In particular, the defendant auditors had produced only general audited accounts, and had not envisaged that they would be relied upon by the claimants in making decisions concerning a takeover of the company. The purpose of the accounts was not to advise in respect of such transactions. Even though the claimants were existing shareholders of the company, they could not reasonably rely on published annual accounts in making such decisions. The Court of Appeal, whose decision was reversed by the House of Lords, had held that a duty of care was owed *to existing shareholders* (including the plaintiffs) in respect of the accuracy of the accounts. The House of Lords added that this was not specific enough. One must also take into account the *purpose* for which it is reasonable to rely upon the accounts, and the purpose for which the defendants know that the statement will be relied upon. The only duty of accuracy owed to shareholders related to the governance of the company.

In commenting on the cases in which a duty of care is recognized to arise (at least potentially) in respect of statements (*Cann v Wilson, Candler v Crane Christmas, Hedley Byrne v Heller, Smith v Eric Bush*), Lord Bridge said:

Lord Bridge, at 620–1

The salient feature of all these cases is that the defendant giving advice or information was fully aware of the nature of the transaction which the plaintiff had in contemplation, knew that the advice or information would be communicated to him directly or indirectly and knew that it was very likely that the plaintiff would rely on that advice or information in deciding whether or not to engage in the transaction in contemplation. In these circumstances the defendant could clearly be expected, subject always to the effect of any disclaimer of responsibility, specifically to anticipate that the plaintiff would rely on the advice or information given by the defendant for the very purpose for which he did in the event rely on it. So also the plaintiff, subject again to the effect of any disclaimer, would in that situation reasonably suppose that he was entitled to rely on the advice or information communicated to him for the very purpose for which he required it. The situation is entirely different where a statement is put into more or less general circulation and may foreseeably be relied on by strangers to the maker of the statement for any one of a variety of different purposes which the maker of the statement has no specific reason to anticipate. To hold the maker of the statement to be under a duty of care in respect of the accuracy of the statement to all and sundry for any purpose for which they may choose to rely on it is not only to subject him, in the classic words of Cardozo C.J. to "liability in an indeterminate amount for an indeterminate time to an indeterminate class:" see *Ultramares Corporation v. Touche* (1931) 174 N.E. 441, 444; it is also to confer on the world at large a quite unwarranted entitlement to appropriate for their own purposes the benefit of the expert knowledge or professional expertise attributed to the maker of the statement. Hence, looking only at the circumstances of these decided cases where a duty of care in respect of negligent statements has been held to exist, I should expect to find that the "limit or control mechanism....imposed upon the liability of a wrongdoer towards those who have suffered economic damage in consequence of his negligence" rested in the necessity to prove, in this category of the tort of negligence, as an essential ingredient of the "proximity" between the plaintiff and the defendant, that the defendant knew that his statement would be communicated to the plaintiff, either as an individual or as a member of an identifiable class, specifically in connection with a particular transaction or transactions of a particular kind (e.g. in a prospectus inviting investment) and that the plaintiff would be very likely to rely on it for the purpose of deciding whether or not to enter upon that transaction or upon a transaction of that kind.

I find this expectation fully supported by the dissenting judgment of Denning L.J. in *Candler v. Crane, Christmas & Co.* [1951] 2 K.B. 164, 179, 180–181, 182–184 ...

According to the logic of Lord Bridge's approach, there will be cases in which auditors do owe a duty of care to particular claimants in the preparation of accounts, provided it is clear at the time of preparing the accounts that they may be relied upon for the particular purpose and by the claimant. This was accepted in *Morgan Crucible v Hill Samuel Bank Ltd* [1991] 1 All ER 148, where the directors and financial advisers of a company had made representations about that company's accounts after a takeover bid had been made by the plaintiffs. The Court of Appeal thought it arguable that *Caparo* could be distinguished, since the representations were made after the bid emerged, and with the intention that they should be relied upon. Similarly, in *Law Society v KPMG Peat Marwick* [2000] 4 All ER 540, the Court of Appeal held that the criteria set out in *Caparo* were fulfilled. Here the defendants prepared the accounts of a firm of solicitors, which subsequently proved to have defrauded its clients. This led to claims against the Law Society's compensation fund. The accountants knew that the purpose of the accounts was to enable the Law Society to ensure that there were no irregularities, and that they would be both communicated to the Law Society and relied upon. Therefore, a duty was owed.

Buxton LJ has suggested that despite its origins, *Hedley Byrne* has gradually been brought back into the fold of general negligence law through the decisions in the next section, and particularly *Henderson v Merrett*: R. Buxton, 'How the Common Law gets Made: Hedley Byrne and other Cautionary Tales' (2009) 125 LQR 60–78. Terms derived from *Hedley Byrne* are used to resolve many of the most difficult duty of care issues today, although their use is in many cases deployed to identify an *exceptional* case in which the generally restrictive principles applicable to a variety of areas (such as public authority liability, or omissions liability) will not foreclose a duty. Yet immediately after *Caparo*, 'assumption of responsibility' appeared to have been fatally weakened as a justification for the duty of care in cases of economic loss. Certainly, it seemed clear that the duty of care is to be understood as 'imposed by law' rather than voluntarily assumed, and the strongest interpretation of the concept, as applied by Lord Devlin in *Hedley Byrne*, was therefore not available. The next section concerns the resuscitation of that concept, and its consequences.

2.4 'EXTENDED' *HEDLEY BYRNE* LIABILITY (CATEGORY D)

Hedley Byrne principles are no longer restricted to cases of negligent statement. In three House of Lords decisions delivered between July 1994 and February 1995, Lord Goff almost single-handedly propelled the concept of 'assumption of responsibility' back to a prominent place. The second of the cases in this sequence of three, *Henderson v Merrett* [1995] 2 AC 145, was described by Lord Mustill in his dissenting opinion in *White v Jones* [1995] 2 AC 207 as having 'brought back to prominence' both *Hedley Byrne* itself and *Nocton v Lord Ashburton*, and as the case that 'gave them new life as a growing point for the tort of negligence'. It will be seen that Lord Mustill, in this comment, emphasizes the importance of *Hedley Byrne* in very general terms. He does not describe it as important only in respect of the recovery of economic losses, nor solely in respect of statements. This has proved to be prophetic.[28] These cases also 'extended' the liability in *Hedley Byrne* to circumstances outside the reliance by one party (the claimant) on a statement given directly to him or her by the defendant.

Spring v Guardian Assurance [1995] 2 AC 296

The plaintiff had been a company representative for the first defendants. He later sought a position with a different company. Under the rules of the relevant regulatory body ('Lautro'), the prospective employer was under a duty to obtain a reference, and the first defendants were under a duty to supply a reference. The reference was unfavourable, and the plaintiff was not appointed. At first instance, the judge held that the reference was negligently prepared, and that this amounted to a breach of a duty of care owed by the first defendant to the plaintiff.

Part of the special controversy of this case lies in the fact that the same facts might give rise to an action in defamation, since it is natural to define the harm caused by a negligent reference in terms of damage to reputation (Chapter 13). If approached as a defamation case, it is clear that the reference would be protected by the defence of 'qualified privilege'. This defence exists in order to protect free expression on a privileged occasion (*Horrocks v Lowe* [1975] AC 135). Assuming the statement to be made on a privileged occasion, a defendant will lose the protection of qualified privilege only if the statement is made with 'malice'. Although malice is not always easy to define, it is clear that mere lack of care is insufficient. To recognize a duty of care in negligence would appear to circumvent this important public policy defence.

The judgments in the House of Lords varied in approach. Lord Keith, who dissented, thought it significant that the plaintiff had not relied upon the statement. In his view, this took the case outside the ambit of *Hedley Byrne*. He was also concerned not to circumvent the existing limitations on the action in defamation through recognizing a duty of care. For the majority, Lord Woolf approached the question of whether a duty of care was owed through a direct application of the three *Caparo* criteria of **foreseeability; proximity;** and what was **'fair, just and reasonable'**. He conceded that this was not determinative since *Caparo* also required that a court consider whether the case was sufficiently analogous to existing categories where a duty is owed. Since *Hedley Byrne* concerned an allegedly negligent *positive* reference, Lord Woolf reasoned that it was not too large a step to recognize a duty in respect of a negligent *negative* reference. Of course, one significant difference not

[28] See the discussion of cases such as *Phelps v Hillingdon* [2001] 2 AC 619 in Section 3.5.

noted by Lord Woolf is that the person who suffers loss as a result of the *negative reference* is not the person to whom the statement was directed, nor the person who relied upon it. As we have already noted, Lord Keith thought that this took the case outside the ambit of *Hedley Byrne* liability. But Lord Woolf applied looser criteria, drawn directly from *Caparo*.

Applying the *Caparo* criteria, Lord Woolf concluded that loss to the plaintiff was clearly a foreseeable result of an adverse reference. Lord Woolf dealt very briefly with the 'proximity' criterion, saying (at 342) that '[t]he relationship between the plaintiff and the defendants could hardly have been closer'. This tends to prove Lord Devlin's point when he said, in *Hedley Byrne*, that 'proximity' is not the sort of criterion that judges can sensibly be invited to apply directly. The public policy considerations that surrounded the qualified privilege defence were dealt with by Lord Woolf under the third of the *Caparo* criteria. He weighed up the public interest (protected by qualified privilege) in 'full and frank' expression in this context, with the competing public interest (as he saw it) that references should not be based upon negligent investigation. He concluded that public policy did not preclude the recognition of a duty to take care in the giving of references.

Alone among the majority, Lord Goff reached his decision through a specific application of principles drawn from *Hedley Byrne v Heller*, rather than through interpretation of the *Caparo* three-stage test. As he made clear, counsel had not considered this line to be worth arguing. He proposed that the basis of *Hedley Byrne* liability was indeed an assumption of responsibility, coupled with reliance on that assumption. In this case, he thought that there was reliance in the general sense that the 'employee' (whose exact employment status was not relevant) relied upon an 'employer' to take due care in the protection of his interests. This amounts to general reliance on the defendant 'to take due care', but *not* reliance upon the truth of the statement.

Arguably, Lord Goff thereby misapplied the idea of reliance to be found in *Hedley Byrne*, which clearly did concern reliance upon the truth of a statement. But alternatively, he might be said to have merely resurrected the broader basis of *Hedley Byrne* liability in relationships of responsibility and reliance, such as professional services between a solicitor and a client, rather than in the giving of statements more narrowly. Although the careless act in *Spring* is the making of a statement, Lord Goff's judgment opened the door for *Hedley Byrne* to be released from its perceived restriction to statements. For example, discussing a relationship in which a *Hedley Byrne* 'assumption of responsibility' is recognized to apply—the relationship between solicitor and client—Lord Goff explained:

Lord Goff, at 319

I can see no reason why a solicitor should not be under a duty to his client to exercise due care and skill when making statements to third parties, so that if he fails in that duty and his client suffers damage in consequence, he may be liable to his client in damages.

In general terms, Lord Goff approached *Hedley Byrne* in the following way:

Lord Goff, at 318

... All the members of the appellate Committee in [*Hedley Byrne*] spoke in terms of the principle resting upon an assumption of responsibility by the defendant towards the plaintiff, coupled with reliance by the plaintiff on the exercise by the defendant of due care and skill ...

Accordingly, where the plaintiff entrusts the defendant with the conduct of his affairs, in general or in particular, the defendant may be held to have assumed responsibility to the plaintiff, and the plaintiff to have relied on the defendant to exercise due skill and care, in respect of such conduct.

The main mystery here is in the meaning that Lord Goff attached to the key criterion of 'assumption of responsibility'. Since Lord Goff has dropped the word 'voluntary', and since he speaks of the defendant as being 'held to have assumed responsibility to the plaintiff', we can take it that his test is objective, and does not reflect an intention on the part of the defendant to assume potential liability. If so, then arguably this formulation has lost its foundation as expressed by Lord Devlin. The latter, it will be recalled, suggested that the relevant duty is not 'imposed by law', but is voluntarily undertaken by the defendant. Instead, there is a reference to the plaintiff 'entrusting the defendant with his affairs'. But the criterion is not wholly empty. In this particular case, Lord Goff's formulation appears to place emphasis on relationships of trust and reliance, an element which was expressly developed by Lord Browne-Wilkinson in the subsequent cases of *Henderson v Merrett*, and *White v Jones*.

An important subsidiary mystery lies in the relationship between the duty under *Hedley Byrne*, and the policy issue in respect of qualified privilege which was outlined above. Lord Goff stated that the policy issues were irrelevant where there was a sufficient relationship under *Hedley Byrne*, but he did not explain why this was so:

At 324

Since, for the reasons I have given, it is my opinion that in cases such as the present the duty of care arises by reason of an assumption of responsibility by the employer to the employee in respect of the relevant reference, I can see no good reason why the duty to exercise due skill and care which rests upon the employer should be negatived because, if the plaintiff were instead to bring an action for damage to his reputation, he would be met by the defence of qualified privilege which could only be defeated by proof of malice. It is not to be forgotten that the *Hedley Byrne* duty arises where there is a relationship which is, broadly speaking, either contractual or equivalent to contract. In these circumstances, I cannot see that principles of the law of defamation are of any relevance.

In the next case extracted, Lord Goff clearly proposed that the presence of an 'assumption of responsibility' made it unnecessary to consider policy factors in accordance with the third stage of the *Caparo* test. This conclusion surely requires the idea of 'assumption of responsibility' to have some real meaning, even if it falls short of the strongest, 'voluntary' meaning which was present in *Hedley Byrne* itself, since it seems to be proposed that it *compels* a finding of responsibility, if established to be present.

Henderson v Merrett [1995] 2 AC 145

The facts of *Henderson* were complex, but the solution favoured by the House of Lords was reasonably simple. The case arose out of losses suffered by investors (referred to as 'Names') in the Lloyds Insurance market in London during the 1980s. The plaintiffs brought these actions against underwriting and managing agents for negligent conduct of their affairs which, they argued, exposed them to unreasonable risk of losses. The role of the various agents is explained in the following extract from the judgment of Lord Goff:

Every person who wishes to become a Name at Lloyd's and who is not himself or herself an underwriting agent must appoint an underwriting agent to act on his or her behalf, pursuant to an underwriting agency agreement. Underwriting agents may act in one of three different capacities. (1) They may be members' agents, who (broadly speaking) advise Names on their choice of syndicates, place Names on the syndicates chosen by them, and give general advice to them. (2) They may be managing agents, who underwrite contracts of insurance at Lloyd's on behalf of the Names who are members of the syndicates under their management, and who reinsure contracts of insurance and pay claims. (3) They may be combined agents, who perform both the role of members' agents, and the role of managing agents in respect of the syndicates under their management.

The agency agreements were contractual. In some cases, there was a direct contract between the Names and the managing agents. In these cases, the plaintiffs were referred to as 'direct Names'. In other cases, the Names entered into a contract with the underwriting agent, who entered into a 'sub-Agency' agreement with the managing agent. In these cases, the plaintiffs were referred to as 'indirect Names'. The plaintiffs argued that the defendant managing agents were liable in tort to both the 'direct' and 'indirect' Names. The reason for pursuing actions in tort as well as in contract is partly that in some instances as we have seen there was no contract between the Name and the managing agent; and partly because in the case of the direct Names the plaintiffs could claim the benefit of a more generous 'limitation period' in tort. As we noted in respect of defective premises, the limitation period in negligence begins to run only when some damage has been caused, since this is when the 'cause of action' accrues. In contract, the relevant period runs from the breach.

Giving the leading judgment in a unanimous House of Lords, Lord Goff decided that the *direct Names* could choose to sue the managing agents either in contract, or in tort. Furthermore, the *indirect Names* could sue the managing agents in tort despite the existence of a contractual chain. Building on his own judgment in *Spring v Guardian Assurance*, Lord Goff again emphasized the concept of assumption of responsibility drawn from *Hedley Byrne*; noted that *Hedley Byrne* was founded on earlier case law in which there was concurrent liability in contract and in tort which was not solely for negligent statements but extended to professional services more generally; and defended the idea that there was a role for tort law even in circumstances where the parties had entered into contractual arrangements. Such arrangements did not exclude the possibility of a tort action. However, he also emphasized that the action in tort would be subject to limitations derived from the terms of the relevant contracts.

Lord Goff, at 180–1

We can see that [the decision in *Hedley Byrne*] rests upon a relationship between the parties, which may be general or specific to the particular transaction, and which may or may not be contractual in nature. All of their Lordships spoke in terms of one party having assumed or undertaken a responsibility towards the other . . . though *Hedley Byrne* was concerned with the provision of information and advice, the example given by Lord Devlin of the relationship between solicitor and client, and his and Lord Morris's statements of principle, show that the principle extends beyond the provision of information and advice to include the performance of other services. It follows, of course, that although, in the case of the provision of information and advice, reliance upon it by the other party will be necessary to establish a cause of action (because otherwise the negligence will have no causative effect), nevertheless there may be other circumstances in which there will be the necessary reliance to give rise to the application of the principle. In particular, as cases concerned with solicitor and client demonstrate, where the plaintiff entrusts the defendant with the conduct of his affairs, in general or in particular, he may be held to have relied on the defendant to exercise due skill and care in such conduct.

In subsequent cases concerned with liability under the *Hedley Byrne* principle in respect of negligent misstatements, the question has frequently arisen whether the plaintiff falls within the category of persons to whom the maker of the statement owes a duty of care. In seeking to contain that category of persons within reasonable bounds, there has been some tendency on the part of the courts to criticise the concept of "assumption of responsibility" as being "unlikely to be a helpful or realistic test in most cases" (see *Smith v. Eric S. Bush* [1990] 1 A.C. 831, 864–865, *per* Lord Griffiths; and see also *Caparo Industries Plc. v. Dickman* [1990] 2 A.C. 605, 628, *per* Lord Roskill). However, at least in cases such as the present, in which the same problem does not arise, there seems to be no reason why recourse should not be had to the concept, which appears after all to have been adopted, in one form or another, by all of their Lordships in *Hedley Byrne* [1964] A.C. 465 (see, e.g., Lord Reid, at pp. 483, 486 and 487, Lord Morris (with whom Lord Hodson agreed), at p. 494; Lord Devlin, at pp. 529 and 531; and Lord Pearce at p. 538). Furthermore, especially in a context concerned with a liability which may arise under a contract or in a situation "equivalent to contract," it must be expected that an objective test will be applied when asking the question whether, in a particular case, responsibility should be held to have been assumed by the defendant to the plaintiff: see *Caparo Industries Plc. v. Dickman* [1990] 2 A.C. 605, 637, *per* Lord Oliver of Aylmerton. In addition, the concept provides its own explanation why there is no problem in cases of this kind about liability for pure economic loss; for if a person assumes responsibility to another in respect of certain services, there is no reason why he should not be liable in damages for that other in respect of economic loss which flows from the negligent performance of those services. It follows that, once the case is identified as falling within the *Hedley Byrne* principle, there should be no need to embark upon any further enquiry whether it is "fair, just and reasonable" to impose liability for economic loss—a point which is, I consider, of some importance in the present case.

In respect of the question of 'concurrency' (liability in both contract and tort on the same facts), Lord Goff examined the case of *Hedley Byrne* and considered whether the principle of 'assumption of responsibility' should be thought to apply only in the *absence* of a contract. Like Oliver J in the earlier case of *Midland Bank Trust Co v Hett, Stubbs and Kemp* [1979] Ch 384, Lord Goff considered that the *Hedley Byrne* principle of 'assumption of responsibility' could give rise to a claim in tort in contractual situations. He also considered that, if his reading of *Hedley Byrne* was incorrect in this respect, it was time to develop tort liability based on assumptions of responsibility to cases where there is indeed a contractual relationship between the parties (at 192). The practical result of this was that a plaintiff who had available remedies in both contract and tort could 'choose that remedy which appears to him to be the most advantageous' (at 194).

White v Jones [1995] 2 AC 207

In terms of its treatment of the legal principles, *White v Jones* is perhaps the most controversial of this sequence of three cases. The solution adopted was intended to be confined to the facts of this and other cases relating to negligence in respect of wills; but we have seen that much more recently, it has inspired an exception to the exclusion of 'relational' losses, on behalf of beneficial owners.[29] The decision was also applied in the different but analogous situation of advice in respect of pension rights, where the defendant adviser is aware that the client intends to make provision for his or her dependents: *Gorham v British Telecommunications plc* [2000] 1 WLR 2129, Court of Appeal.

In *White v Jones*, a testator executed a new will after a family quarrel, disinheriting his two daughters, the plaintiffs. After a reconciliation, he contacted his solicitors with instructions to draw up a new will, restoring the legacies to the plaintiffs. Little progress was made, and the testator died before the new will was completed. In the earlier case of *Ross v Caunters* [1980] Ch 297, a solicitor was held to owe a duty of care to intended beneficiaries in respect of the proper execution of a will. In that earlier case, it was held that a duty was owed through application of the principle in *Donoghue v Stevenson*. In *White v Jones*, the House of Lords accepted that the simple approach in *Ross v Caunters* could not be maintained in view of the many conceptual problems involved in the case. However, it was also noted that no significant dissatisfaction had ever been expressed with the practical impact of that decision.

Lord Goff frankly acknowledged that there was no true assumption of responsibility on the part of the defendant, towards the plaintiffs. In his judgment, this case concerned a wrong which required a remedy, and the best way of providing this remedy was to 'deem' that the assumption of responsibility which existed between the defendant solicitor and his client also *extended to* the intended beneficiaries who were the plaintiffs in the case. Although this was not truly a case of 'transferred loss' (see our discussion of *The Aliakmon*, Section 2.1), it was analogous to such a case. The reasons why it was not such a case are set out in the extract below. Part of the controversy was whether this case would have been more appropriately resolved through a contractual remedy.

Lord Goff, at 265–9

. . . Here there is a lacuna in the law, in the sense that practical justice requires that the disappointed beneficiary should have a remedy against the testator's solicitor in circumstances in which neither the testator nor his estate has in law suffered a loss. Professor Lorenz (*Essays in Memory of Professor F. H. Lawson*, p. 90) has said that "this is a situation which comes very close to the cases of 'transferred loss,' the only difference being that the damage due to the solicitor's negligence could never have been caused to the testator or to his executor." In the case of the testator, he suffers no loss because (in contrast to a gift by an inter vivos settlor) a gift under a will cannot take effect until after the testator's death, and it follows that there can be no depletion of the testator's assets in his lifetime if the relevant asset is, through the solicitors' negligence, directed to a person other than the intended beneficiary. The situation is therefore not one in which events have subsequently occurred which have resulted in the loss falling on another. It is one in which the relevant loss could never fall on the testator to whom the solicitor owed a duty, but only on another; and the loss which is suffered by that other, i.e. an expectation loss, is of a character which in any event could never have been suffered by the testator. Strictly speaking, therefore, this is not a case of transferred loss.

Even so, the analogy is very close. In practical terms, part or all of the testator's estate has been lost because it has been dispatched to a destination unintended by the testator. Moreover, had a gift been similarly misdirected during the testator's lifetime, he would either have been able to recover it from the recipient or, if not, he could have recovered the full amount from the negligent solicitor as damages. In a case such as the present, no such remedies are available to the testator or his estate. The will cannot normally be rectified: the testator has of course no remedy; and his estate has suffered no loss, because it has been distributed under the terms of a valid will. In these circumstances, there can be no injustice if the intended beneficiary has a remedy against the solicitor for the full amount which he should have received under the will, this being no greater than the damage for which the solicitor could have been liable to the donor if the loss had occurred in his lifetime.

A contractual approach

It may be suggested that, in cases such as the present, the simplest course would be to solve the problem by making available to the disappointed beneficiary, by some means or another, the benefit of the contractual rights (such as they are) of the testator or his estate against the negligent solicitor, as is for example done under the German principle of Vertrag mit Schutzwirkung fur Dritte. Indeed that course has been urged upon us by Professor Markesinis, 103 L.Q.R. 354, 396–397, echoing a view expressed by Professor Fleming in (1986) 4 O.J.L.S. 235, 241. Attractive though this solution is, there is unfortunately a serious difficulty in its way. The doctrine of consideration still forms part of our law of contract, as does the doctrine of privity of contract which is considered to exclude the recognition of a jus quaesitum tertio. To proceed as Professor Markesinis has suggested may be acceptable in German law, but in this country could be open to criticism as an illegitimate circumvention of these long established doctrines; and this criticism could be reinforced by reference to the fact that, in the case of carriage of goods by sea, a contractual solution to a particular problem of transferred loss, and to other cognate problems, was provided only by recourse to Parliament. Furthermore, I myself do not consider that the present case provides a suitable occasion for reconsideration of doctrines so fundamental as these.

Lord Goff considered potential contractual routes to a remedy in this case, none of which would suffice to fill the 'lacuna':

The tortious solution

I therefore return to the law of tort for a solution to the problem. For the reasons I have already given, an ordinary action in tortious negligence on the lines proposed by Sir Robert Megarry V.-C. in *Ross v. Caunters* [1980] Ch. 297 must, with the greatest respect, be regarded as inappropriate, because it does not meet any of the conceptual problems which have been raised. Furthermore, for the reasons I have previously given, the *Hedley Byrne* [1964] A.C. 465 principle cannot, in the absence of special circumstances, give rise on ordinary principles to an assumption of responsibility by the testator's solicitor towards an intended beneficiary. Even so it seems to me that it is open to your Lordships' House, as in the *Lenesta Sludge* case [1994] 1 A.C. 85, to fashion a remedy to fill a lacuna in the law and so prevent the injustice which would otherwise occur on the facts of cases such as the present. In the *Lenesta Sludge* case [1994] 1 A.C. 85, as I have said, the House made available a remedy as a matter of law to solve the problem of transferred loss in the case before them. The present case is, if anything, a fortiori, since the nature of the transaction was such that, if the solicitors were negligent and their negligence did not come to light until after the death of the testator, there would be no remedy for the ensuing loss unless the intended beneficiary could claim. In my opinion, therefore, your Lordships' House should in cases such as these extend to the intended beneficiary a remedy under the *Hedley Byrne* principle by holding that the assumption of responsibility by the solicitor towards his client should be held in law to extend to the intended beneficiary who (as the solicitor can reasonably foresee) may, as a result of the solicitor's negligence, be deprived of his intended legacy in circumstances in which neither the testator nor his estate will have a remedy against the solicitor. Such liability will not of course arise in cases in which the defect in the will comes to light before the death of the testator, and the testator either leaves the will as it is or otherwise continues to exclude the previously intended beneficiary from the relevant benefit. I only wish to add that, with the benefit of experience during the 15 years in which *Ross v. Caunters* has been regularly applied, we can say with some confidence that a direct remedy by the intended beneficiary against the solicitor appears to create no problems in practice. That is therefore the solution which I would recommend to your Lordships.

As I see it, not only does this conclusion produce practical justice as far as all parties are concerned, but it also has the following beneficial consequences.

1. There is no unacceptable circumvention of established principles of the law of contract.

2. No problem arises by reason of the loss being of a purely economic character.

3. Such assumption of responsibility will of course be subject to any term of the contract between the solicitor and the testator which may exclude or restrict the solicitor's liability to the testator under the principle in *Hedley Byrne*. It is true that such a term would be most unlikely to exist in practice; but as a matter of principle it is right that this largely theoretical question should be addressed.

4. Since the *Hedley Byrne* principle is founded upon an assumption of responsibility, the solicitor may be liable for negligent omissions as well as negligent acts of commission: see the *Midland Bank Trust Co.* case [1979] Ch. 384, 416, *per* Oliver J. and *Henderson v. Merrett Syndicates Ltd.* [1995] 2 A.C. 145, 182, *per* Lord Goff of Chieveley. This conclusion provides justification for the decision of the Court of Appeal to reverse the decision of Turner J. in the present case, although this point was not in fact raised below or before your Lordships.

5. I do not consider that damages for loss of an expectation are excluded in cases of negligence arising under the principle in the *Hedley Byrne* case [1964] A.C. 465, simply because the cause of action is classified as tortious. Such damages may in principle be recoverable in cases of contractual negligence; and I cannot see that, for present purposes, any relevant distinction can be drawn between the two forms of action. In particular, an expectation loss may well occur in cases where a professional man, such as a solicitor, has assumed responsibility for the affairs of another; and I for my part can see no reason in principle why the professional man should not, in an appropriate case, be liable for such loss under the *Hedley Byrne* principle.

In the result, all the conceptual problems, including those which so troubled Lush and Murphy JJ. in *Seale v. Perry* [1982] V.R. 193, can be seen to fade innocuously away. Let

The emphasise that I can see no injustice in imposing liability upon a negligent solicitor in a case such as the present where, in the absence of a remedy in this form, neither the testator's estate nor the disappointed beneficiary will have a claim for the loss caused by his negligence. This is the injustice which, in my opinion, the judges of this country should address by recognising that cases such as these call for an appropriate remedy, and that the common law is not so sterile as to be incapable of supplying that remedy when it is required.

Lord Goff pointed out that the route to a contractual remedy is blocked by the doctrine of privity. English law did not recognize a right on behalf a stranger to a contract to sue on the terms of the contract. He considered some important cases which qualified the doctrine of privity, including *The Albazero* [1977] AC 774 and *Linden Gardens v Lenesta Sludge* [1994] 1 AC 85. However, these cases were inapplicable for two reasons. First, the cases did not give a remedy directly to the third party, but only allowed a *contracting* party to sue for damages that they had suffered.[30] The cases did not allow the third party (who had suffered the loss) to *compel* the contracting party to sue. Here, the executors, as representatives of the contracting party (the testator), may have been unwilling to commit resources to bringing an action on behalf of the disappointed beneficiaries, to the possible detriment of the estate. Second, the previous case law only allowed actions in contract on behalf of third parties where the loss suffered by the third parties was *the same loss* that the contracting party would have suffered, had that loss not been 'transferred' in one way or another. In *Linden Gardens*, for example, there had been an assignment of contractual rights. In *White v Jones*, as Lord Goff pointed out, the loss of expectation on the part of the beneficiaries was not the sort of loss that the testator could ever have suffered.

Subsequently, there has been significant legislative qualification of the doctrine of privity of contract. The Contracts (Rights of Third Parties) Act 1999 provides that:

1.—(1)...a person who is not a party to a contract (a 'third party') may in his own right enforce a term of the contract if—

    (a) the contract expressly provides that he may, or

    (b) ...the term purports to confer a benefit on him

The Law Commission, in its Report *Privity of Contract: Contracts for the Benefit of Third Parties* (Law Com No 242, 1996), stressed that this reform was intended to be 'a relatively conservative and moderate measure' (para 5.10), which should not prevent the courts from instigating more radical change if they thought it appropriate. The Law Commission (referring to Kit Barker's analysis in 'Are We Up To Expectations? Solicitors, Beneficiaries and the 'Tort/Contract Divide'' (1994) 14 OJLS 137, 142) explained that:

7.25 It is our view...that the negligent will-drafting situation ought to lie, and does lie, just outside our proposed reform. It is an example of the rare case where the third party, albeit expressly designated "as a beneficiary" in the contract, has no presumed right of enforcement. Indeed it is arguable that, by merely adjusting the wording of the second

---

[30] As we saw in relation to category A, some writers have preferred this sort of route to resolving the problem in *Shell UK v Total UK*.

limb to include promises that are "of benefit to" expressly designated third parties, rather than those that "confer benefits on" third parties, we would have brought the negligent will-drafting situation within our reform. But we believe that these words draw the crucial distinction between the situation where it is natural to presume that the contracting parties intended to confer legal rights on the third party and the situation where that presumption is forced and artificial.

The Law Commission would support the extension of tort law to fit a case such as this.

As we have seen, Lord Goff's solution was intended to be contained in its scope. It was an attempt to resolve what he considered to be an obvious injustice, and the extension of the assumption of responsibility was overtly fictional. Lord Browne-Wilkinson, on the other hand, decided the case not on the basis of a fiction, but by an extended understanding of the concept of 'voluntary assumption of responsibility' itself. Again, he argued that the duty of care in *Hedley Byrne* cases is but one example of a fiduciary duty. In the case of fiduciary duties, he argued, it was not necessary to show that the plaintiff had consciously relied upon the defendant. In fact, it was not necessary to show that the plaintiff had any knowledge of the defendant's role in respect of his or her interests at all. Rather, it is sufficient for the fiduciary to know that the 'economic welfare' of the plaintiff depends upon his exercise of due care. The difference between Lord Goff's understanding of 'assumption of responsibility' (rooted in 'closeness to contract'), and Lord Browne-Wilkinson's understanding (based in 'fiduciary relationships') becomes clear. On the latter interpretation, the plaintiffs here are owed a fiduciary duty, since this can arise without any knowledge on their part. There is a true 'assumption of responsibility'. On Lord Goff's analysis, the assumption was merely 'deemed' to extend to the plaintiffs, in order to deal with a particular, perceived injustice.

The three cases extracted above sought to articulate principles which cross the boundaries between acts and statements, acts and omissions, and contract and tort. Importantly, one of the boundaries that is broken down is the boundary between economic and other forms of loss. The nature of the loss as purely 'economic' received little emphasis in these cases. Whether or not there is a 'statement' is barely mentioned. Subsequently, the verbal formula 'assumption of responsibility' has been increasingly used in a wide range of different situations, including cases of psychiatric harm and educational failure. It is not confined to economic loss. On the other hand, the meaning of that term has remained elusive.

2.5 DEVELOPMENTS IN CATEGORIES C AND D: THE ROLE OF 'VOLUNTARY ASSUMPTION OF RESPONSIBILITY' CONSIDERED

Since *White v Jones*, the House of Lords has had two major opportunities to reconsider the proper approach to cases of economic loss outside categories A and B.[31] The Court of Appeal, meanwhile, has struggled to divine from the existing case law what approach ought to be taken to such cases. It is suggested that the House of Lords in *CEC v Barclays Bank* offered some important clarification.

---

31 We do not here include *Phelps v Hillingdon* or *McFarlane v Tayside* (and its follow-up *Rees v Darlington*). These cases said little about assumption of responsibility and the former is now interpreted as a case of personal injury. These cases are discussed in subsequent sections of this chapter.

Williams v Natural Life Health Foods [1998] 1 WLR 830

The second defendant M, an individual, formed a limited company (the first defendant). He was the managing director and principal shareholder in the company. The plaintiffs negotiated a franchise with the company, dealing directly with M. The franchise was much less successful than expected, and the plaintiffs traded at a loss before eventually going out of business. They argued that they had been negligently advised. When the company was wound up, the plaintiffs joined M as a party to the action. Ordinarily, the director of a limited company has no personal liability in respect of the company's debts. The plaintiffs argued that M had *assumed personal responsibility* to them, so that he owed a duty in tort. The judgment should be understood as directed to this rather special argument. As Lord Steyn put it:

Lord Steyn, at 835

What matters is not that the liability of the shareholders is limited but that a company is a separate entity, distinct from its directors, servants or other agents. The trader who incorporates a company to which he transfers his business creates a legal person on whose behalf he may afterwards act as director.

Giving the sole judgment in the case, Lord Steyn made clear that the guiding principles to be applied were to be drawn from the judgments of Lord Goff (rather than of Lord Browne-Wilkinson) in the cases of *Henderson v Merrett* and *White v Jones*. Not only must there be an assumption of responsibility on the part of the defendant (in the case of M, an assumption of 'personal' responsibility), but the plaintiffs must have *reasonably relied upon* that assumption. *White v Jones* itself did not fit this description particularly well since there was no reliance, and *Smith v Eric Bush* also did not fit it well for the reasons we explored earlier. Lord Steyn explained both cases on the basis that, '[c]oherence must sometimes yield to practical justice' (at 837). Academic criticisms of the principle of assumption of responsibility, he argued, were overstated so far as they were based on these two exceptional cases. In this particular case:

Lord Steyn, at 835

... it is important to make clear that a director of a contracting company may only be made liable where it is established by evidence that he assumed personal liability and that there was the necessary reliance. There is nothing fictional about this species of liability in tort.

This being the case, it was necessary to show evidence of specific words or conduct which crossed an important line.

Lord Steyn, at 838

In the present case there were no personal dealings between Mr Mistlin and the plaintiffs. There were no exchanges or conduct which crossed the line which could have conveyed to the plaintiffs that Mr Mistlin was willing to assume personal responsibility to the plaintiffs... I am also satisfied that there was not even evidence that the plaintiffs believed that

Mr Mistlin was undertaking personal responsibility to them. Certainly, there was nothing in the circumstances to show that the plaintiffs could reasonably have looked to Mr Mistlin for indemnification of any loss.

If this seems a very strong test for assumption of responsibility, this can be explained by the particular need to show an assumption of *personal* responsibility sufficient to bypass the corporate structure within which the parties were working.

Customs and Excise Commissioners v Barclays Bank [2004] 1 WLR 2027 (Colman J); [2005] 1 WLR 2082 (CA); [2006] 3 WLR 1 (HL)

The decision of the House of Lords in this case sheds significant light on the role of voluntary assumption of responsibility, and on the appropriate general method in deciding economic loss cases outside the exclusionary rules in categories A and B.

The Customs and Excise Commissioners obtained 'freezing orders', and served them on the defendant bank. The purpose of these orders was to prevent two companies from removing funds from their bank accounts, so that the claimants could recover outstanding VAT from those accounts. The defendant bank, which held the relevant accounts, failed to take action to prevent funds from being moved out of the accounts. It was alleged that this failure was negligent. The Customs and Excise Commissioners could not recover the full sums owing. They sought to recover the shortfall (amounting to several million pounds) from the defendant bank on the basis that it had breached a duty of care owed to them, to abide by the orders. On a preliminary issue, Colman J held that no duty of care was owed by the bank ([2004] 1 WLR 2027). His decision was reversed by the Court of Appeal.

The first instance judgment of Colman J was particularly cogent. In respect of the 'assumption of responsibility', he made clear that this was not *always* a prerequisite of the duty of care in cases of economic loss. Colman J accepted that the assumption of responsibility was based on an 'objective' test, not on voluntary acceptance of legal responsibility in the fullest sense. But he was clear that the 'assumption of responsibility' is not an entirely empty phrase.

Colman J [2004] EWHC 122 (Comm)

51 In my judgment, [the] authorities do not support the proposition that in every case where there has been negligent provision of a service which is said to have caused the claimant pure economic loss there has to be a relationship akin to contract before a duty of care can be imposed. If, objectively analysed, the relationship is too oblique or indirect to bear that analogy there can be an assumption of responsibility only in the artificial sense that a responsibility is imposed as a matter of law. However, when one comes to the void at which Lord Oliver arrived in *Caparo Industries plc v Dickman* [1990] 2 AC 605, 637G, the methodology appropriate to a relationship akin to contract has to be replaced and in those circumstances it is the threefold test which provides a broad analytical guideline towards the existence of a duty of care. However, there may be novel factual situations where it is appropriate to supplement application of the threefold test by reference to other comparable situations in which the courts have imposed or, as the case may be, declined to impose a duty of care. This supplementation has been explained by Phillips LJ in *Reeman v Department of Transport* [1997] 2 Lloyd's Rep 648, 677:

"When confronted with a novel situation the court does not . . . consider these matters [foreseeability, proximity, and fairness] in isolation. It does so by comparison with established categories of negligence to see whether the facts amount to no more than a small extension of a situation already covered by authority, or whether a finding of the existence of a duty of care would effect a significant extension to the law of negligence. Only in exceptional cases will the court accept that the interests of justice justify such an extension of the law."

Colman J argued that if there is a relationship 'akin to contract' in the sense explained in *Henderson v Merrett*, there is no reason to consider the three-stage test under *Caparo v Dickman*. If however there is no relationship akin to contract (if the relationship is 'too oblique'), then in terms of *Hedley Byrne* we arrive at a 'void'. This is the void that the *Caparo* three-stage test was designed to fill. The three-stage test cannot however be applied without reference to analogous cases, otherwise proximity in particular has no clear meaning.

In this case, there was no relationship akin to contract. Colman J saw this as a case where the relationship between the parties was akin to that between adversaries in civil litigation.[32] The bank had not *chosen* to enter any relationship at all with the claimants, but had been served with an order, carrying potential legal implications should they fail to act. In *Connolly-Martin v Davis* [1999] PNLR 826; *Welsh v CC of Merseyside Police* [1993] 1 All ER 692; and *Elguzouli-Daf v Commissioner of Police for the Metropolis* [1995] QB 335, it had been said that parties to litigation could only owe one another duties to take care if there was some special feature of conduct to suggest an assumption of responsibility. Colman J regarded this as requiring an assumption of responsibility in the strong sense exemplified by *Williams* (above). Without this, there could not be said to be 'proximity'; and Colman J also doubted whether the imposition of the duty could be 'fair, just and reasonable'.

It is suggested that this element of Colman J's reasoning is particularly useful. It amounts to an argument that an assumption of responsibility *either* may be deduced from the general nature of the relationship (as in *Henderson v Merrett*), *or*—if the general nature of the relationship is not compatible with such a deduction—may be deduced from specific words, conduct, or circumstances which (applying *Williams*) override the general features of the relationship. This is consistent with the subsequent decision of the House of Lords.

The only special element of the defendants' conduct which could be said to show that they had assumed responsibility was the writing of a letter, acknowledging the freezing order. This, however, was received by the claimants only after the funds had been released. So even if this letter could amount to conduct which established that responsibility was assumed, it was too late. The House of Lords for its part declined to attach any importance at all to the letter:

Lord Bingham (HL)

3. . . . Had the letters reached the Commissioners before release of the funds, the judge would have attached significance to them. . . . But in my respectful opinion they were of no significance. The Bank was bound to comply with the order of the court irrespective

[32] The House of Lords did not go quite so far, but did decide that the relationship was 'adverse'. See also the more recent House of Lords decision in *Jain v Trent Strategic Health Authority* [2009] UKHL 4; [2009] 2 WLR 248, a case of economic loss where the issues arising are better discussed in connection with public authority liability generally. *Jain* is discussed in the following section.

of any confirmation on its part. The letters did not affect the factual or the legal position. Their purpose was to pave the way to reimbursement of the costs of compliance incurred by the Bank.

In support of Colman J's conclusion that no duty is owed, there were strongly involuntary elements in the relationship between the parties. The defendants had done nothing other than accept deposits from clients that might, in the future, attract freezing orders. It is a very long stretch to fit this relationship into any meaningful interpretation of *Hedley Byrne*.

CEC v Barclays Bank [2006] UKHL 28; [2006] 3 WLR 1 (HL)

The House of Lords restored Colman J's decision that no duty of care was owed.

There were five separate and subtly different judgments in the *Barclays Bank* case (though no dissents). What follows may be seen as a guide to reading the full report. In terms of method for deciding economic loss cases, the key conclusions can be summarized as follows:

1. The first stage in deciding a novel case of economic loss is to ask whether there is a voluntary assumption of responsibility.

2. If an assumption of responsibility is established, this may be sufficient.

In other words, there may be no need to consider policy issues.

Lord Bingham

4 . . . there are cases in which one party can accurately be said to have assumed responsibility for what is said or done to another, the paradigm situation being a relationship having all the indicia of contract save consideration. *Hedley Byrne* would, but for the express disclaimer, have been such a case. *White v Jones* and *Henderson v Merrett Syndicates Ltd,* although the relationship was more remote, can be seen as analogous. Thus, like Colman J (whose methodology was commended by Paul Mitchell and Charles Mitchell, "Negligence Liability for Pure Economic Loss" (2005) 121 LQR 194, 199), I think it is correct to regard an assumption of responsibility as a sufficient but not a necessary condition of liability, a first test which, if answered positively, may obviate the need for further inquiry. If answered negatively, further consideration is called for.

This is consistent with the approach of Colman J.

3. At least two of the judges seem to have treated assumption of responsibility as an aspect of proximity.

Lord Hoffmann was particularly clear on this point.

Lord Hoffmann

35 . . . In . . . cases in which the loss has been caused by the claimant's reliance on information provided by the defendant, it is critical to decide whether the defendant (rather than someone else) assumed responsibility for the accuracy of the information to the claimant (rather than to someone else) or for its use by the claimant for one purpose (rather than another). The answer does not depend upon what the defendant intended but, as in the case of contractual liability, upon what would reasonably be inferred from his conduct against the background of all the circumstances of the case. The purpose of the inquiry is to establish whether there was, in relation to the loss in question, the necessary relationship (or "proximity") between the parties and, as Lord Goff of Chieveley pointed out in *Henderson v Merrett Syndicates Ltd* at 181, the existence of that relationship and the foreseeability of economic loss will make it unnecessary to undertake any further inquiry into whether it would be fair, just and reasonable to impose liability. In truth, the case is one in which, but for the alleged absence of the necessary relationship, there would be no dispute that a duty to take care existed and the relationship is what makes it fair, just and reasonable to impose the duty.

It is suggested that Lord Walker also treated assumption of responsibility as an aspect of proximity, although his reasoning was less explicit (at [74]).

We have already argued that this is the right approach. But if 'assumption of responsibility' is an aspect of proximity, then it forms part of the three-stage test. And if this is the case, how can an assumption of responsibility be 'sufficient', without regard to policy concerns? Proximity supplies only one of the three necessary elements of the three-stage test. In the extract above, Lord Hoffmann hints that where there is an assumption of responsibility, it is the *nature of the relationship* which *makes* the duty fair, just, and reasonable. The proposed 'sufficiency' of assumption of responsibility is important, particularly given the use of the concept *beyond* the area of economic loss.

4. No assumption of responsibility could be established.

In this case, there was an *adverse* relationship between the parties. A degree of voluntariness is essential to any 'assumption of responsibility', even if the test for its existence is objective. Here, the defendants did not choose their relationship with the claimant. On the contrary they were exposed, through the freezing order, to the risk of proceedings for contempt of court. On any established test, there was no assumption of responsibility.

Lord Bingham

14 I do not think that the notion of assumption of responsibility, even on an objective approach, can aptly be applied to the situation which arose between the commissioners and the bank on notification to it of the orders. Of course it was bound by law to comply. But it had no choice. It did not assume any responsibility towards the commissioners as the giver of references in *Hedley Byrne* (but for the disclaimer) and *Spring*, the valuers in *Smith v Eric S Bush*, the solicitors in *White v Jones* and the agents in *Henderson v Merrett Syndicates Ltd* may plausibly be said to have done towards the recipient or subject of the references, the purchasers, the beneficiaries and the Lloyd's Names. Save for the notification of the orders (and treating as irrelevant the letters written by the bank: see para 3 above) nothing crossed the line between the commissioners and the bank: see *Williams v Natural Life Health Foods Ltd* [1998] 1 WLR 830, 835. Nor do I think that the commissioners can be said in any meaningful sense to have relied on the bank. The commissioners, having obtained their orders and notified them to the bank, were no doubt confident that the bank would act promptly and effectively to comply. But reliance in the law is usually taken to mean that if A had not relied on B he would have acted differently. Here the commissioners could not have acted differently, since they had availed themselves of the only remedy which the law provided. Mr Sales suggested, although only as a fall-back argument, that the relationship between the commissioners and the bank was, in Lord Shaw's words (in *Nocton v Lord Ashburton* [1914] AC 932, 972) adopted by Lord Devlin in *Hedley Byrne* [1964] AC 465, 529, "equivalent to contract". But the essence of any contract is voluntariness, and the bank's position was wholly involuntary.

This conclusion seems incontrovertible. But it also shows that the House of Lords regards the assumption of responsibility as having *some* meaning. No matter how elastic, it could not stretch to cover this case. In the very different context of provision of equipment or other benefits which are required in accordance with statutory duties, the same sort of thinking has also been adopted: if provision is required by statute, the duty to provide cannot be assumed voluntarily—it is simply imposed: *Rowley v Secretary for Work and Pensions* [2007] EWCA Civ 598; [2007] 1 WLR 2861 (Child Support payments); *Sandford v London Borough of Waltham Forest* [2008] EWHC 1106 (QB) (equipment assessed under statute as being required).

5. If there is no assumption of responsibility (as here), this is not the end of the matter.

The three-stage test from *Caparo* may still lead to the conclusion that a duty is owed. On our preferred account, if there is no assumption of responsibility, the three-stage test is still to be applied. In such a case, proximity must be present but (in the absence of an assumption of responsibility) will not be sufficient. It is suggested that this explains the otherwise obscure reference to proximity in the following paragraph:

Lord Bingham

15 It is common ground that the foreseeability element of the threefold test is satisfied here. The bank obviously appreciated that, since risk of dissipation has to be shown to obtain a freezing injunction, the commissioners were liable to suffer loss if the injunction were not given effect. It was not contended otherwise. The concept of proximity in the context of pure economic loss is notoriously elusive. But it seems to me that the parties were proximate only in the sense that one served a court order on the other and that other appreciated the risk of loss to the first party if it was not obeyed. I think it is the third, policy, ingredient of the threefold test which must be determinative.

Lord Bingham says there is 'proximity' here, but only in a form that does not provide a particularly compelling reason for finding that the defendants owed a duty of care. This is why the policy ingredient would be decisive.

Again, this approach (accepting that the three-stage test may be satisfied where there is *no* assumption of responsibility) shows that it is wrong to assume that both tests must arrive at the same result, or that there must always be an assumption of responsibility in a successful economic loss case. *Smith v Eric Bush* can finally be reconciled with the other case law under *Hedley Byrne*. It is simply a case where there was no assumption of responsibility; but the three requirements of foreseeability, proximity, and 'policy' were satisfied in the claimants' favour. *Barclays Bank* however is *not* such a case, because the policy arguments were determined against the claimant.

6. Policy issues were decisive against a duty of care in this case.

A common theme of the judgments in the House of Lords is that in the absence of an assumption of responsibility, and given that there was foreseeability and arguable proximity, policy issues would be key to the outcome. On analysis of the policy issues, it was not 'fair, just and reasonable' to recognize a duty of care on the present facts. Lord Walker found the issues to be more finely balanced than the others, but noted that if freezing orders give rise to duties of care for banks, then other actors who are subject to such orders may also find themselves owing duties of care to the tax authorities. For him, this was the decisive consideration against a duty of care. Lord Bingham usefully encapsulated his own approach to the policy issues as follows:

Lord Bingham

23   Lastly, it seems to me in the final analysis unjust and unreasonable that the bank should, on being notified of an order which it had no opportunity to resist, become exposed to a liability which was in this case for a few million pounds only, but might in another case be for very much more. For this exposure it had not been in any way rewarded, its only protection being the commissioners' undertaking to make good (if ordered to do so) any loss which the order might cause it, protection scarcely consistent with a duty of care owed to the commissioners but in any event valueless in a situation such as this.

These considerations are broadly present in the other judgments too.

It was also astutely pointed out (for example by Lord Rodger) that the Commissioners did not *rely on the defendants* to comply with the order. The Commissioners relied on the courts to enforce the order, not on the defendants to comply with it.

Lord Rodger's point about reliance brings us to another distinctive feature of this case.

7.   Lord Hoffmann's short cut: no common law duty of care could be said to arise *out of the freezing order itself.*

Lord Hoffmann drew a parallel between this case, and the cases of *Stovin v Wise* [1996] AC 923 and *Gorringe v Calderdale* [2004] 1 WLR 1057 (extracted in Section 3.5 of this chapter). The *only* reason for saying that the defendant bank owed a duty to the claimant, other than foreseeability, is that it had been served with a freezing order. But the order was enforceable through an action for contempt of court, should the bank or its employees 'flout' the order with the required degree of intention. There was no valid way of getting from this order, with its criminal sanctions, to the proposition that a duty was owed *to take care* to comply with the order. Quite the reverse.

Lord Hoffmann

39   There is, in my opinion, a compelling analogy with the general principle that, for the reasons which I discussed in *Stovin v Wise* [1996] AC 923, 943–944, the law of negligence does not impose liability for mere omissions. It is true that the complaint is that the bank did something: it paid away the money. But the payment is alleged to be the breach of the duty and not the conduct which generated the duty. The duty was generated ab extra, by service of the order. The question of whether the order can have generated a duty of care is comparable with the question of whether a statutory duty can generate a common law duty of care. The answer is that it cannot: see *Gorringe v Calderdale Metropolitan Borough Council* [2004] 1 WLR 1057. The statute either creates a statutory duty or it does not. (That is not to say, as I have already mentioned, that conduct undertaken pursuant to a statutory duty cannot generate a duty of care in the same way as the same conduct undertaken voluntarily.) But you cannot derive a common law duty of care directly from a statutory duty. Likewise, as it seems to me, you cannot derive one from an order of court. The order carries its own remedies and its reach does not extend any further.

Summary: *CEC v Barclays Bank*

Their Lordships were unanimous that there was no voluntary assumption of responsibility where the defendant was served with an order compelling it to safeguard certain funds. That being so, all agreed that 'voluntary assumption of responsibility' has some meaning. Some referred to the assumption of responsibility as a particularly important form of proximity. But all were agreed that absence of such an assumption was not the end of the matter. The three-stage test was still to be applied, and policy would be determinative in this case. Lord Hoffmann found a short cut on the policy issues, reasoning that an order of this sort cannot be the basis for a duty to take care in negligence.

Although Lord Mance observed that there is no 'common denominator' to the various tests for a duty of care in economic loss cases, *Barclays Bank* has improved understanding of the relationship between the various tests. In *Playboy Club London Ltd v Banca Nazionale Del Lavoro SpA* [2016] EWCA Civ 457, the Court of Appeal noted that the various tests could be used as a check on one another and would generally lead to the same answer. Here, a bank had offered a reference for a customer without limiting its liability. Therefore the case is close to *Hedley Byrne v Heller*. However, the claimant (who relied on the reference) did not reveal its identity, and the reference was believed to be for the benefit of its agent. Under these circumstances, there could be no assumption of responsibility: the defendant did not even know of the claimant's existence. Further, because the claimant had concealed its existence, it could not be 'fair, just and reasonable' for liability to be imposed. Neither test was satisfied.

In the light of *Barclays Bank*, we can attempt the following position statement:

1. There is no general exclusionary rule applying to economic loss. Rather, there are two specific exclusionary rules, applying to categories A and B.

2. Outside the scope of the exclusionary rules, additional criteria will apply, in addition to foreseeability or 'neighbourhood'. On the other hand, these criteria also apply to other 'novel' cases in negligence. There are many examples in other sections of this chapter.

3. The 'voluntary assumption of responsibility' is not a mere label, though there remains a strong suspicion that it is given more or less content depending on the circumstances of the case. If it is present, then it may suffice without separate consideration of policy issues.

4. Though sufficient, the assumption of responsibility is not always necessary.[33] If there is no voluntary assumption of responsibility, the three-stage test may nevertheless be satisfied. But in such cases, policy considerations will be especially important. The

---

[33] It may be necessary in a case with strong countervailing policy considerations; in these circumstances, it may be a means of overcoming those policy considerations in a particular case: see, for example, discussion in Section 3.4 in the present chapter.

'fair, just and reasonable' criterion can be frankly and openly reassessed in terms of 'policy': Lord Bingham, *CEC v Barclays Bank*, at [4].

5. Even if a duty is owed, it is important to consider the 'scope' of the duty. Does the claimant's loss fall within its scope? This question applies whether the duty is derived from *Hedley Byrne*, or directly from *Caparo*.

Tension between Categories

The fact remains that the ideas used by Lord Goff to revive the idea of 'assumption of responsibility' could also have been invoked when deciding cases of relational damage and defective property. Now that the 'assumption of responsibility' is advancing into other areas of negligence, it is plainly more difficult to maintain a bright line against their use in categories A and B. *White v Jones* was built upon Lord Goff's preferred response to *The Aliakmon*, which was rejected by the House of Lords in that case, yet was used as inspiration in a recent case which could have undermined *The Aliakmon* itself. What of the interface between liability based on assumption of responsibility, and category B cases, under *Murphy*? Now that it is plain that 'assumption of responsibility' is not solely applicable to statements, and that it may operate even in the presence of a contract, are builders excluded from its reach; or is it necessary to ask in each case of defective workmanship *what the nature of the parties' relationship was?*

In *Robinson v PE Jones (Contractors) Ltd* [2011] EWCA Civ 9, the Court of Appeal preferred to rely upon *Murphy v Brentwood*. The claimant was not a subsequent purchaser of property, but had directly contracted with the builder while the property was under construction. Some 12 years after completion, a surveyor advised that the flues had not been properly constructed. Like *D & F Estates*, this was not a case where any personal injury was threatened. On the other hand, the relationship between the parties was plainly not only direct, but also contractual. Why should it not be considered as akin to *Henderson v Merrett*? It is the contractual relationship itself which explains the decision of the Court of Appeal, that no duty of care in tort was owed in relation to the economic losses suffered as a result of the defect. Clauses 8 and 10 of the building conditions *excluded* concurrent liability in tort; but Jackson LJ (with whom the other judges agreed) would have come to the same conclusion in any event given the nature of the contract.

Jackson LJ, *Robinson v PE Jones (Contractors) Ltd*
[2011] EWCA Civ 9; [2012] QB 44

83 In the present case I see nothing to suggest that the defendant 'assumed responsibility' to the claimant in the Hedley Byrne sense. The parties entered into a normal contract whereby the defendant would complete the construction of a house for the claimant to an agreed specification and the claimant would pay the purchase price. The defendant's warranties of quality were set out and the claimant's remedies in the event of breach of warranty were also set out. The parties were not in a professional relationship whereby, for example, the claimant was paying the defendant to give advice or to prepare reports or plans upon which the claimant would act.

...

87 Let me now draw the threads together. The rights and remedies of the parties to this case were set out in a written contract, the terms of which are clear and simple. That

contract provided the claimant with extensive (but not total) protection against defects. The contract represents a perfectly sensible allocation of risk between the parties. At the time of contracting, both parties were represented by solicitors and they must have known where they stood.

88 It is a matter of great misfortune that a latent defect in the claimant's house emerged 12 and a half years after completion and that this defect was outside the scope of the NHBC agreement. That, however, is a consequence of the contractual allocation of risk between the parties. In my judgment it is not possible for the claimant to invoke the law of tort in order to impose liabilities upon the defendant which are inconsistent with the contract.

General Conclusions on Economic Loss

The restrictions on recovery for economic losses are not arbitrary in the sense we identified in the last section. In categories A and B, the reasons for restricting liability are based in legal policy. In the case of the remaining categories, there has been an attempt to articulate guiding 'principles'. Here however it has been found that the possible range of cases is too diverse to state applicable principles in any simple way. Outside categories A and B, English law has committed itself to a certain amount of uncertainty associated with open categories and variable concepts. The end result could certainly be described as unpredictable and hard to interpret. One commentator has suggested that the guiding principles are mere 'veils' for hidden or partly revealed policy concerns (Kit Barker, 'Unreliable Assumptions in the Modern Law of Negligence' (1993) 109 LQR 461). Perhaps, with cases such as *Barclays Bank*, the policy concerns are becoming more express. Certainly there is little coyness about policy reasoning in this case, nor in many other key cases dealing with the duty of care in the past few years. The difficulty is in getting beyond a highly specific case-by-case analysis; and with finding coherent rationalization of the different approaches that may be taken to any given case.

3. PUBLIC AUTHORITIES

3.1 THE GENERAL ISSUES

In principle, the nature of the potential defendant—whether that defendant is a public authority or private party, corporation, or individual—makes no difference to the availability of an action in the tort of negligence. Historically however, the Crown (though not other public authorities) was accorded a general immunity against liability at common law. This immunity was removed by the Crown Proceedings Act 1947, although the statute preserved an immunity in respect of the armed forces.[34] Far from being generally protected from actions in tort, public authorities and their individual officers are particularly vulnerable to certain tort actions,[35] and are especially exposed to an award of exemplary damages,[36]

[34] Crown Proceedings Act 1947, s 10. This immunity was prospectively repealed in 1987.
[35] Actions for misfeasance in a public office are only available against those holding public office (and their employers). The action is discussed in Chapter 2. Malicious prosecution and false imprisonment are of general application but they are inclined to be used against public authorities.
[36] See the discussion in Chapter 8.

as well as the usual actions in negligence, nuisance, trespass, and so on.[37] Outside tort law, damages may also be sought against a public authority under the Human Rights Act 1998 (HRA).[38] The availability of this action inevitably casts new light on how courts have chosen to set limits to negligence liability in this context.

In this part of the chapter, there are three key themes. First is the application of the tort of negligence in the presence of various statutory powers and duties. It is this which has given the area much of its technical complexity. Second is the invocation of policy reasoning to restrict the availability of negligence actions against public authorities in many contexts, and the inevitable comparison with the action for damages under the HRA. Third is the influence of this parallel source of remedy. That influence is still slowly taking shape.

3.2 THE VARIETY OF POWERS AND DUTIES

In approaching this area of law, it is important to keep in mind that the following powers and duties are distinct. The coexistence of these powers and duties gives the area much of its complexity.

1. **The duty of care at common law.** The duty of care arises at common law. Any party, including a public authority, may owe such a duty to another if the applicable criteria (derived from *Donoghue v Stevenson* and *Caparo v Dickman*) are fulfilled. This seems a simple or even obvious statement in isolation, but it becomes hard to remember in the hurly-burly of the case law (below). Remembering that common law duties arise at common law and nowhere else,[39] no matter what other powers and duties are in issue, is the key to understanding the case law in this field.

2. **Statutory duties.** Legislation often imposes duties. From the point of view of the law of tort, statutory duties can be divided into two types:

    i. Duties which are clear, precise, designed to benefit a particular group including the claimant, and intended to be actionable at common law. Such duties are actionable through the distinct tort of breach of statutory duty (Chapter 16). A leading example is the duty in *Groves v Wimborne* [1898] 2 QB 402: factory legislation required that certain machinery be fenced. This was for the benefit of workers. When a worker lost his forearm because machinery was unfenced, he was able to claim in tort. Recent legislative change in the law means that in future, this sort of claim will no longer be actionable unless there is proof of negligence—a major change to a long-standing principle.[40]

    ii. The more usual type of statutory duty is one which is *not* actionable at common law. A very *general* statutory duty, or one not designed to benefit a particular group of people including the claimant, or one that Parliament did not intend

---

[37] See C. Harlow, *State Liability* (Oxford University Press, 2004), chapter 1, relating this to Dicey's constitutional theory. The Law Commission's Consultation Paper, *Administrative Redress: Public Bodies and the Citizen* (LCCP 187, 2008), caused some consternation amongst private lawyers when it floated the idea of removing 'truly public' activities from the law of tort, and introducing an alternative scheme of compensation for these cases based on more serious fault. The Consultation has however now been withdrawn.

[38] Sections 7 and 8 (see the discussion in Chapter 1).

[39] As explained in point (2)(a), some statutory duties are actionable at common law. But this means that the common law provides a remedy. The duty is not a duty at common law.

[40] Enterprise and Regulatory Reform Act 2013, s 69.

to be actionable, will not be enforceable through the action for breach of statutory duty. Many duties where there is a criminal or other sanction set out in the statute will not fall into this category, though this is not conclusive.[41] An example of a duty not actionable at common law arises in *O'Rourke v Camden* [1998] AC 188. The duty to offer accommodation to those who are homeless was not narrow and defined and was not for the benefit of a prescribed class of people. It was a social welfare duty. A person who was not housed when he presented himself as homeless could not seek damages in tort, and must instead seek judicial review.

3. **Statutory powers.** Unlike a duty, a power confers permission: it specifies that the recipient of the power *may* do something, not that they *must*. Formally, statutory powers allow the recipient to decide what to do, and whether to do it. They generally confer discretion. Public law provides remedies if discretion is *improperly exercised*, or if there is *an improper failure to exercise a power*. Generally speaking, *damages are not readily available in an action at public law.*

4. **Duties to respect Convention rights.** Under the HRA, section 6, all 'public authorities' are under a duty to act compatibly with Convention rights (those rights of the European Convention on Human Rights (ECHR) which are listed in the Appendix to the HRA: see Chapter 1). An action against a public authority for failure to do so is created by the HRA, sections 7–8. These duties are separate from common law duties, though they may arise on similar facts and be argued alongside a claim in tort. Common law duties are unlikely to be adapted to resemble the duties to protect Convention rights, or to fill gaps where the Act does not apply: *Van Colle v Chief Constable of the Hertfordshire Police* [2008] UKHL 50; [2009] 1 AC 225; *Mitchell v Glasgow City Council* [2009] UKHL 11; [2009] 2 WLR 481. The starting point is that common law and the HRA, sections 7–8 provide two different routes to two different remedies.[42] But the European Court of Human Rights has interpreted positive duties to protect the Convention rights in such a way as to create a 'tort-like' form of liability against States which is, through the HRA, also available against public authorities in domestic courts.

The Role of These Powers and Duties in a Negligence Action

1. **Duties of care at common law.** A claim in the tort of negligence cannot succeed unless a duty of care at common law is owed to the claimant. A public body, like anyone else, will be liable in negligence only if the *Caparo* criteria are satisfied, and a duty of care is held to exist.

2. **Statutory duties.** We noted above that the action for breach of statutory duty will be available only if the duty in question is a type (a) statutory duty. The majority of statutory duties are not actionable in this way.[43]

Supposing there is a statutory duty which is *not* actionable at common law, does the existence of the statutory duty in any sense *exclude* the existence of a duty to take care at common

---

41 See *Groves v Wimborne* itself: Chapter 16.
42 This 'starting point' has only gradually been recognized. Some cases decided soon after the enactment of the HRA proceeded on the basis that common law would simply need to change to fill gaps in the remedies provided.
43 The applicable principles are discussed in Chapter 16.

law? It does not; but the common law duty must at least be compatible with the statute and not, for example, 'cut across' the legislative scheme.

3. **Statutory powers.** Some of the most difficult issues in all of negligence law have surrounded statutory powers. Can there be a duty of care at common law in respect of a *negligent exercise, or negligent failure to exercise,* a statutory power?

It is now apparent that the answer to this question is much simpler than first appeared. The key is to remember that statutory power, and common law duty, are separate and distinct. If a common law duty is to arise, it will arise through application of the criteria developed in *Donoghue, Hedley Byrne,* and *Caparo,* and nothing more complicated than that really needs to be said.[44]

4. **Duties to respect Convention rights.** Increasingly, as we have already said, duties to respect Convention rights (including positive duties to act) are also seen to be separate from common law duties. Some such positive duties are imposed upon public authorities such as the police and health authorities. These are a significant source of remedies in their own right. Their existence does not necessarily imply that common law ought to change to achieve the same outcome; but it may nevertheless lead to more questions about the soundness of the arguments through which restrictive tort rules are justified.

3.3 LEADING CASES FROM *GEDDIS* TO *X v BEDFORDSHIRE*

Geddis v Proprietor of the Bann Reservoir (1878) 3 App Cas 430 (HL) (on appeal from the Exchequer Chamber in Ireland)

The defendants were incorporated by Act of Parliament for the purpose of securing a regular supply of water to mills on the banks of the River Bann. The relevant statute conferred power to collect several small streams into a reservoir, and to send down waters through a smaller stream, the Muddock. The defendants did not properly regulate the flow of water or scour the stream; and they were liable for the flooding of the plaintiffs' land which resulted.

Geddis shows that activities undertaken in the exercise of a statutory power are not beyond the reach of private law, *if* those powers are carelessly exercised. The most influential judicial statement in *Geddis* is the remark of Lord Blackburn which is italicized below. It is important to read this highlighted passage within its context.

Lord Blackburn, *Geddis v Proprietors of the Bann Reservoir,* at 455–6

It is agreed on all sides that the Act requires the promoters, the Defendants, to pour into the channel of the River *Muddock* as much water as, on the average, used formerly to go.... And they have a permissive power, for the benefit of the millowners on the *Bann,* to send down more water, both greater in quantity and in a different way from what would have gone in the ordinary natural state of things down the *Muddock* if the Act had not been

[44] Much more complex things *were* said in *Anns v Merton,* but *Anns* is no longer considered correct on this point.

passed. Now, certainly the result has been that the channel of the *Muddock* as it exists at present is not able to carry off the water they have put into it, and if they have no power to cleanse the channel of the *Muddock*, or to alter it, which was the view taken by the majority of the learned Judges of the Court of Exchequer Chamber below, then they are not liable to damages for doing that which the Act of Parliament authorizes, namely, pouring part of the water of the reservoir into the *Muddock* that it may go to the Bann. *For take it, without citing cases, that it is now thoroughly well established that no action will lie for doing that which the legislature has authorized, if it be done without negligence, although it does occasion damage to anyone; but an action does lie for doing that which the legislature has authorized, if it be done negligently. And I think that if by a reasonable exercise of the powers, either given by statute to the promoters, or which they have at common law, the damage could be prevented it is, within this rule, "negligence" not to make such reasonable exercise of their powers.* I do not think that it will be found that any of the cases (I do not cite them) are in conflict with that view of the law.

Now, upon that view of the law, if in this case the learned Judges in the Exchequer Chamber are right in holding that the Defendants have no power to interfere with the channel of the *Muddock* at all, of course no action will lie against them. But if on the other hand Baron *Fitzgerald* and Chief Baron *Palles* are right in the view which they took, that they have power to do so, I think that the conclusion becomes irresistible that they ought to adopt a reasonable exercise of that power by cleansing, scouring, widening, and deepening, the natural channel of the *Muddock*, so as to make it capable of receiving the waters which they pour down it, and that not to do so before they poured down the water, was a neglect to make a reasonable use of the powers given to them by the statute.

[Emphasis added]

Lord Blackburn's reference to 'negligence' is not a reference to the *tort* of negligence. Rather, it is a reference to the limited scope of 'statutory authority' as a defence. This defence does not assist a defendant who has acted *without due care*. (Statutory authority is analysed as a defence to private nuisance, in Chapter 10, and to the action in *Rylands v Fletcher*, in Chapter 11.)

The last paragraph extracted seems to suggests that there is greater scope for liability where there is a power to do something, than where there is not. This may seem puzzling. A power after all confers a choice over what to do. How can the existence of a *choice* be the basis for liability? The point being made by Lord Blackburn here is that the defendants could not be made liable for *failing* to do something (adjust the nature of the River *Muddock*) if they were not *entitled* to do it. In this context then, the crucial question was whether the defendants even had power to do that which they failed to do. It is important to note that this is not a case of a *pure* omission (like *Gorringe v Calderdale*, Section 3.5). It is a case where the *activities* of the defendants caused the flooding, because they failed to take steps, which they were authorized to take, to ameliorate the effects of their own actions.

East Suffolk Rivers Catchment Board v Kent [1941] 1 AC 74

Owing to a very high tide, a sea wall was breached, and the respondent's farmland was flooded. The appellants, in the exercise of their statutory powers under the Land Drainage Act 1930, entered the respondents' land and began repair work. They carried out the work so inefficiently that the respondents' land remained flooded for 178 days. It appears that the work could have been done, if it had been done with reasonable skill, within 14 days. The respondents claimed damages for the excess time during which their land remained flooded.

A majority of the House of Lords held that the appellants were not liable. They were under no obligation to repair the wall, nor to complete the work after they had begun it. Further, their lack of reasonable skill *had not caused the damage suffered*, which was the result of natural forces. This conclusion was disapproved in *Anns v Merton*, but has returned to haunt the law, particularly in respect of duties owed by emergency services' (below).

This case was decided a few years later *after* the decision in *Donoghue v Stevenson*, which first recognized a unified tort of negligence. So its legal context is very different from the context of *Geddis*. Lord Atkin, the key figure in the recognition of the unified tort of negligence in *Donoghue*, dissented in *East Suffolk*. Only Lord Atkin adequately recognized the independence of the duty of care in negligence from the statutory powers and duties; and indeed only Lord Atkin mentioned *Donoghue v Stevenson* at all in explaining the potential source of a duty to take care in this case. Viscount Simon, in the majority, did refer to the tort of negligence as connoting 'the complex notion of duty, breach and damage'. However, he mentioned this only to argue that no damage had been caused by the defendant's lack of skill.

Of the majority judgments, Lord Romer's is the most often cited. He distinguished *Geddis*—and particularly the words of Lord Blackburn quoted earlier—on the basis that *Geddis* was a case where the damage was *caused by* the acts of the defendants. In this case, the defendants had merely permitted the damage to continue.

Lord Romer, at 102

[*Geddis* and *Shepphard v Glossop Corporation* [1921] 3 KB 132[45]] seem to lay down a principle which in my opinion is a thoroughly sound one. It is this: Where a statutory authority is entrusted with a mere power it cannot be made liable for any damage sustained by a member of the public by reason of a failure to exercise that power. If in the exercise of their discretion they embark upon an execution of the power, the only duty they owe to any member of the public is not thereby to add to the damages that he would have suffered had they done nothing. So long as they exercise their discretion honestly, it is for them to determine the method by which and the time within which and the time during which the power shall be exercised; and they cannot be made liable, except to the extent that I have just mentioned, for any damage that would have been avoided had they exercised their discretion in a more reasonable way.

Lord Atkin (dissenting) approached the matter in a very different way. He began by stating the sources of duty in such cases. Amidst the chaos that has followed, the following passages from Lord Atkin's judgment stand out for their clarity of approach:

Lord Atkin, at 88–9 (dissenting)

My Lords, two material points emerged on the argument of this appeal: (1) Was there a duty owed to the plaintiffs and, if so, what was its nature? (2) If there was a duty owed to the plaintiffs to conduct the work with reasonable dispatch, was there any damage caused to the plaintiffs by the breach of the duty? On the first point I cannot help thinking that the

---

[45] In this case, decided before *Donoghue v Stevenson* by a Court of Appeal including Lord Atkin (then Atkin LJ), a corporation which had a *statutory power to provide lighting* was held to owe no *duty* to provide lighting that would be enforceable by an individual in a claim for damages.

argument did not sufficiently distinguish between two kinds of duties: (1) A statutory duty to do or abstain from doing something. (2) A common law duty to conduct yourself with reasonable care so as not to injure persons liable to be affected by your conduct.

(1) The duty imposed by statute is primarily a duty owed to the State. Occasionally penalties are imposed by the statute for breach; and, speaking generally, in the absence of special sanctions imposed by the statute the breach of duty amounts to a common law misdemeanour. The duty is not necessarily a duty owed to a private citizen. The duty may, however, be imposed for the protection of particular citizens or class of citizens, in which case a person of the protected class can sue for injury to him due to the breach. The cases as to breach of the Factory or Coal Mines Act are instances. As a rule the statutory duty involves the notion of taking care not to injure and in such cases actions for breach of statutory duty come within the category of negligence: see *Lochgelly Iron and Coal Co. v. M'Mullan.*

(2) But apart from the existence of a public duty to the public, every person whether discharging a public duty or not is under a common law obligation to some persons in some circumstances to conduct himself with reasonable care so as not to injure those persons likely to be affected by his want of care. This duty exists whether a person is performing a public duty, or merely exercising a power which he possesses either under statutory authority or in pursuance of his ordinary rights as a citizen. To whom the obligation is owed is, as I see it, the principal question in the present case.

The second kind of duty referred to by Lord Atkin in the passage above is, of course, the duty of care in negligence.

At 90–1

I treat it . . . as established that a public authority whether doing an act which it is its duty to do, or doing an act which it is merely empowered to do, must in doing the act do it without negligence, or as it is put in some of the cases must not do it carelessly or improperly. . . .

I thus come to the crucial point in this case to whom is such a duty owed, or who can complain of the failure to use reasonable dispatch. Now it must be conceded that instances will occur of the performance of powers where it might be difficult for a member of the public generally to complain of unreasonable delay. For instance delay in the work of relaying the surface of a highway may not be actionable at the suit of members of the public who are put to expense and inconvenience by having to make a detour. Even in this case I think something might be said for a householder or shopkeeper on the route under repair who is for an unreasonably long time deprived of access to his premises for himself and his customers. *But we have to deal here with relations between the plaintiffs and the Board which I suggest are much closer than the general relations of members of the public to a public authority. The Board were engaging themselves in repairing the plaintiffs' wall with the object of preventing the further flooding of the land of the plaintiffs and, I think, also one other occupier, and they were operating upon the plaintiffs' land.* Subject to what I have to say upon the causation of damage which I wish for the present purpose to assume, they would know that the longer the work was delayed the longer would the waters ebb and flow over the land with the possibility of damage therefrom. I consider that these relations give rise to a duty owed to the plaintiffs to use reasonable care, including dispatch in doing the work.

[Emphasis added]

The italicized passage in this extract approaches the matter through the concept of *proximity*, which was an aspect of 'neighbourhood' as it was explained in *Donoghue v Stevenson*. Now, we recognize a more complex set of criteria for establishing a duty of care, in accordance with *Caparo v Dickman*. But Lord Atkin's method remains sound: the duty, if it arises, arises through the proximity of the parties, subject to questions of fairness, justice, and reasonableness, and it arises at common law. It is irrelevant that the statute conferred a mere power.

Lord Atkin *also* went on to conclude that the breach of duty might indeed have caused the damage in this case, and that this question should be addressed at trial (at 93).

Anns v Merton [1977] 2 WLR 1024

This is our third visit to this case. We have already seen that *Anns* has been departed from as to its *ratio*, because it incorrectly stated the form of damage suffered by the plaintiff;[46] and that the expansive two-stage test for a duty of care adopted in *Anns* has been superseded by the more cautious (but equally open-textured) *Caparo* test. Here we consider a different aspect of Lord Wilberforce's judgment, concerning the statutory context of the defendant's act (or failure to act). This aspect of his judgment fared rather better than the rest, but this final element of *Anns* has now been demolished by *Gorringe v Calderdale* [2004] 1 WLR 1057. We must still consider *Anns*, because it provides a vital link between *East Suffolk* and *Geddis*, and the law as it stands now.

Anns: The Issues

We outlined the facts of *Anns* in Chapter 3.

Even leaving aside the 'type of damage', one would have thought the obstacles to the claim were formidable. In particular:

(a) The statute conferred a power not a duty.

(b) On one hypothesis, the local authority had merely failed to inspect.

(c) Applying the majority approach in *East Suffolk*, this is a case of mere failure to avoid harm. The harm was not caused by natural forces, but it was caused by a builder, and the local authority had merely failed to notice and prevent the defect.

Despite these features, the House of Lords held that a claim in negligence was arguable, *whether there had been an inspection or not.*

Lord Wilberforce, *Anns v Merton*,
at 1035–6

… It is said that there is an absolute distinction in the law between statutory duty and statutory power—the former giving rise to possible liability, the latter not, or at least not doing so unless the exercise of the power involves some positive act creating some fresh or additional damage.

[46] *Murphy v Brentwood*, Section 2.

My Lords, I do not believe that any such absolute rule exists: or perhaps, more accurately, that such rules as exist in relation to powers and duties existing under particular statutes, provide sufficient definition of the rights of individuals affected by their exercise, or indeed their non-exercise, unless they take account of the possibility that, parallel with public law duties there may coexist those duties which persons—private or public—are under at common law to avoid causing damage to others in sufficient proximity to them. This is, I think, the key to understanding of the main authority relied upon by the appellants—*East Suffolk Rivers Catchment Board v. Kent* [1941] AC 74.

At 1037–8

... the law, as stated in some of the speeches in *East Suffolk Rivers Catchment Board v. Kent* [1941] AC 74, but not in those of Lord Atkin or Lord Thankerton, requires at the present time to be understood and applied with the recognition that, quite apart from such consequences as may flow from an examination of the duties laid down by the particular statute, there may be room, once one is outside the area of legitimate discretion or policy, for a duty of care at common law. It is irrelevant to the existence of this duty of care whether what is created by the statute is a duty or a power: the duty of care may exist in either case. The difference between the two lies in this, that, in the case of a power, liability cannot exist unless the act complained of lies outside the ambit of the power. In *Dorset Yacht Co. Ltd. v. Home Office* [1970] AC 1004 the officers may (on the assumed facts) have acted outside any discretion delegated to them and having disregarded their instructions as to the precautions which they should take to prevent the trainees from escaping: (see *per* Lord Diplock, at p. 1069). So in the present case, the allegations made are consistent with the council or its inspector having acted outside any delegated discretion either as to the making of an inspection, or as to the manner in which an inspection was made. Whether they did so must be determined at the trial. In the event of a positive determination, and only so, can a duty of care arise. ...

Apart from anything else, Lord Wilberforce's approach is difficult to apply in practice. The first step, where there is a statutory power, is to show that the act or omission complained of 'lay outside the ambit of the power'. If it is within the ambit of the power, there is no room for the negligence action. The difficulty is that whether the act or omission is within the ambit of a power is a question of public law. Under the *Anns* approach, we therefore have to deal with public law concepts, in a private law action.

Lord Wilberforce seems to have used these public law concepts in order to explain how a *duty* can be derived from a *power* (see the first extract above, from p. 1035). But this is not true to the dissenting judgment of Lord Atkin in *East Suffolk* (which Lord Wilberforce was trying to apply). There, Lord Atkin emphasized the *independence* of the duty of care in negligence, from statutory powers and duties. He determined whether a duty of care arose at common law by applying the neighbourhood test. The duty of care, if it arises at all, arises in its own right, out of foreseeability, proximity, and so on: in short, it arises out of the neighbour principle (now qualified by *Caparo*).

This question about statutory powers has returned to exercise the House of Lords on a number of occasions. In the next case extracted, the House of Lords made a serious attempt to resolve the issue. In *some* respects, the solution proved short-lived. But this case is the source of much of the current law on child abuse and education claims in negligence.

X v Bedfordshire County Council; M v Newham LBC & Others [1995] 2 AC 633

The House of Lords dealt with five appeals, all involving claims in negligence and some involving claims for breach of statutory duty. The first two appeals concerned (respectively) an allegation that a local authority had failed to take children into care despite evidence of neglect and abuse by their parents (*X v Bedfordshire* itself), and that a local authority had carelessly taken a child away from her mother on a mistaken suspicion that the mother's partner was abusing the child (*M v Newham*). These are referred to as the 'child abuse cases'. In the remaining three appeals (*E v Dorset; Christmas v Hampshire*; and *Keating v Bromley*), local authorities had failed to diagnose learning difficulties on the part of the claimants, or failed to make adequate provision for schooling. These are referred to as the 'education cases'.

General: Three Types of Claim

Lord Browne-Wilkinson broke down the claims in the five cases into three types. Not all types of claim were present in every case; but in most cases, they were.

1. Claims for breach of statutory duty. The relevant statutes in the abuse cases were the Children and Young Persons Act 1969; the Child Care Act 1980; and the Children Act 1989 (*Bedfordshire* only). In the education cases, the relevant statutes were the Education Acts 1944 and 1981. In no case was a claim for breach of statutory duty successful. The statutory duties were not of the appropriate sort. They were social welfare duties for the benefit of the public as a whole, and they were not actionable by individuals at common law.

2. Claims for negligent breach of a direct duty of care on the part of the defendant local authority, in the exercise of their statutory functions. With one exception, these claims failed too, and were struck out. In general, the duties argued for would be inconsistent with the purposes of the statutes.

3. Claims that the local authority was vicariously liable for the breach of a duty of care by an individual employee. Here there was a difference in fortunes between the two types of case.

 (a) Applying the criteria in *Caparo v Dickman*, the abuse cases were struck out. It would not be fair, just, and reasonable to impose a duty of care on the professional social workers and psychologists who made judgments as to the child's welfare. This conclusion would now be different following *D v East Berkshire*.

 (b) Applying the same criteria, the education cases had a chance of success, and would not be struck out. This is because the relationship between professional and child in these cases was arguably similar to a 'normal professional relationship' carrying no potential conflict of interest. In the case of a headmaster, there was also a voluntary assumption of responsibility towards a pupil at the school (applying *Henderson v Merrett*, Section 6.2). Later education cases have succeeded on their merits.

Lord Browne-Wilkinson rightly rejected a fourth argument, that there could be an action for 'negligent breach of a statutory duty', distinct from the claim in the tort of negligence *and* from the action at private law for breach of statutory duty. No such action exists (at 732). This is consistent with our analysis so far, and with Lord Atkin's judgment in *East Suffolk*. It is not contradicted by Lord Blackburn's remarks in *Geddis*, provided these are read in context, as we read them above.

The Abuse Cases

The following reasoning explains the rejection of the **direct duty of care in the abuse cases.**

Lord Browne-Wilkinson, at 749

I turn then to consider whether, in accordance with the ordinary principles laid down in the *Caparo* case [1990] 2 A.C. 605, the local authority in the *Bedfordshire* case owed a direct duty of care to the plaintiffs. The local authority accepts that they could foresee damage to the plaintiffs if they carried out their statutory duties negligently and that the relationship between the authority and the plaintiffs is sufficiently proximate. The third requirement laid down in *Caparo* is that it must be just and reasonable to impose a common law duty of care in all the circumstances.... Is it, then, just and reasonable to superimpose a common law duty of care on the local authority in relation to the performance of its statutory duties to protect children? In my judgment it is not. Sir Thomas Bingham M.R. took the view, with which I agree, that the public policy consideration which has first claim on the loyalty of the law is that wrongs should be remedied and that very potent counter considerations are required to override that policy ante, p. 663C–D. However, in my judgment there are such considerations in this case.

First, in my judgment a common law duty of care would cut across the whole statutory system set up for the protection of children at risk. As a result of the ministerial directions contained in "Working Together" the protection of such children is not the exclusive territory of the local authority's social services. The system is inter-disciplinary, involving the participation of the police, educational bodies, doctors and others. At all stages the system involves joint discussions, joint recommendations and joint decisions. The key organisation is the Child Protection Conference, a multi-disciplinary body which decides whether to place the child on the Child Protection Register.... To impose such liability on all the participant bodies would lead to almost impossible problems of disentangling as between the respective bodies the liability, both primary and by way of contribution, of each for reaching a decision found to be negligent.

Second, the task of the local authority and its servants in dealing with children at risk is extraordinarily delicate. Legislation requires the local authority to have regard not only to the physical wellbeing of the child but also to the advantages of not disrupting the child's family environment: see, for example, section 17 of the Act of 1989. In one of the child abuse cases, the local authority is blamed for removing the child precipitately; in the other, for failing to remove the children from their mother. As the Report of the Inquiry into Child Abuse in Cleveland 1987 (Cm. 412) said, at p. 244:

"It is a delicate and difficult line to tread between taking action too soon and not taking it soon enough. Social services whilst putting the needs of the child first must respect the rights of the parents; they also must work if possible with the parents for the benefit of the children. These parents themselves are often in need of help. Inevitably a degree of conflict develops between those objectives."

Next, if a liability in damages were to be imposed, it might well be that local authorities would adopt a more cautious and defensive approach to their duties. For example, as the

Cleveland Report makes clear, on occasions the speedy decision to remove the child is sometimes vital. If the authority is to be made liable in damages for a negligent decision to remove a child (such negligence lying in the failure properly first to investigate the allegations) there would be a substantial temptation to postpone making such a decision until further inquiries have been made in the hope of getting more concrete facts. Not only would the child in fact being abused be prejudiced by such delay: the increased workload inherent in making such investigations would reduce the time available to deal with other cases and other children.

The relationship between the social worker and the child's parents is frequently one of conflict, the parent wishing to retain care of the child, the social worker having to consider whether to remove it. This is fertile ground in which to breed ill feeling and litigation, often hopeless, the cost of which both in terms of money and human resources will be diverted from the performance of the social service for which they were provided. The spectre of vexatious and costly litigation is often urged as a reason for not imposing a legal duty. But the circumstances surrounding cases of child abuse make the risk a very high one which cannot be ignored.

If there were no other remedy for maladministration of the statutory system for the protection of children, it would provide substantial argument for imposing a duty of care. But the statutory complaints procedures contained in section 76 of the Act of 1980 and the much fuller procedures now available under the Act of 1989 provide a means to have grievances investigated, though not to recover compensation. Further, it was submitted (and not controverted) that the local authorities Ombudsman would have power to investigate cases such as these.

Finally, your Lordships' decision in the *Caparo* case [1990] 2 A.C. 605 lays down that, in deciding whether to develop novel categories of negligence the court should proceed incrementally and by analogy with decided categories. We were not referred to any category of case in which a duty of care has been held to exist which is in any way analogous to the present cases. Here, for the first time, the plaintiffs are seeking to erect a common law duty of care in relation to the administration of a statutory social welfare scheme. Such a scheme is designed to protect weaker members of society (children) from harm done to them by others. The scheme involves the administrators in exercising discretions and powers which could not exist in the private sector and which in many cases bring them into conflict with those who, under the general law, are responsible for the child's welfare. To my mind, the nearest analogies are the cases where a common law duty of care has been sought to be imposed upon the police (in seeking to protect vulnerable members of society from wrongs done to them by others) or statutory regulators of financial dealings who are seeking to protect investors from dishonesty. In neither of those cases has it been thought appropriate to superimpose on the statutory regime a common law duty of care giving rise to a claim in damages for failure to protect the weak against the wrongdoer: see *Hill v. Chief Constable of West Yorkshire* [1989] A.C. 53 and *Yuen Kun Yeu v. Attorney-General of Hong Kong* [1988] A.C. 175.

The policy arguments in the above passage remain influential, although the European Court of Human Rights in *Z v UK* (Section 3.6) clearly disagreed with the argument that alternative remedies were adequate.

Lord Browne-Wilkinson also rejected claims that the local authority should be *vicariously* liable. The following remarks relate to the rejection of the vicarious liability claims in the abuse cases. Vicarious liability is explored in Chapter 9.

At 752–3

The claim based on vicarious liability is attractive and simple. The normal duty of a doctor to exercise reasonable skill and care is well established as a common law duty of care. In my judgment, the same duty applies to any other person possessed of special skills, such as a social worker. It is said, rightly, that in general such professional duty of care is owed irrespective of contract and can arise even where the professional assumes to act for the plaintiff pursuant to a contract with a third party: *Henderson v. Merrett Syndicates Ltd.* [1995] 2 A.C. 145; *White v. Jones* [1995] 2 A.C. 207. Therefore, it is said, it is nothing to the point that the social workers and psychiatrist only came into contact with the plaintiffs pursuant to contracts or arrangements made between the professionals and the local authority for the purpose of the discharge by the local authority of its statutory duties. Once brought into contact with the plaintiffs, the professionals owed a duty properly to exercise their professional skills in dealing with their "patients," the plaintiffs. This duty involved the exercise of professional skills in investigating the circumstances of the plaintiffs and (in the *Newham* case) conducting the interview with the child. Moreover, since the professionals could foresee that negligent advice would damage the plaintiffs, they are liable to the plaintiffs for tendering such advice to the local authority.

Like the majority in the Court of Appeal, I cannot accept these arguments. The social workers and the psychiatrists were retained by the local authority to advise the local authority, not the plaintiffs. The subject matter of the advice and activities of the professionals is the child. Moreover the tendering of any advice will in many cases involve interviewing and, in the case of doctors, examining the child. But the fact that the carrying out of the retainer involves contact with and relationship with the child cannot alter the extent of the duty owed by the professionals under the retainer from the local authority. The Court of Appeal drew a correct analogy with the doctor instructed by an insurance company to examine an applicant for life insurance. The doctor does not, by examining the applicant, come under any general duty of medical care to the applicant. He is under a duty not to damage the applicant in the course of the examination: but beyond that his duties are owed to the insurance company and not to the applicant.

...

In my judgment in the present cases, the social workers and the psychiatrist did not, by accepting the instructions of the local authority, assume any general professional duty of care to the plaintiff children. The professionals were employed or retained to advise the local authority in relation to the well being of the plaintiffs but not to advise or treat the plaintiffs.

The child is merely the 'subject of the report' prepared. The only *duty* is owed to the local authority, as employer. This part of the reasoning did not survive enactment[47] of the HRA (see our discussion of *D v East Berkshire*, later). But the policy reasons listed remain influential in denying that a duty is owed to *parents* who are wrongly suspected of child abuse; and to others in rather different contexts where conflicts of interest may arise (*Jain v Trent Strategic Health Authority* [2009] UKHL 4; [2009] 2 WLR 248).

[47] Some significant changes in the common law were made after the HRA was enacted, but before it came into force, because of the perceived implications of the legislation. (Not all of those perceptions have proved to be well-founded.)

The Education Cases

Although the claims for direct duties were also found untenable in the education cases generally, in the *Dorset* case there was thought to be one potential route to establishing such a duty. The duty might arise by analogy with *Hedley Byrne v Heller* and *Henderson v Merrett*, irrespective of the kind of damage (economic loss or not) that followed (at 762–3).[48]

The other critical difference between the abuse cases, and the education cases, was that the **vicarious liability** claims in respect of education were not doomed to fail. The following extract relates specifically to the *Dorset* case, but it is indicative of the general approach.

Lord Browne-Wilkinson, at 763
Common law duty of care—vicarious

The claim is that the educational psychologists and other members of the staff of the defendant authority owed a duty to use reasonable professional skill and care in the assessment and determination of the plaintiff's educational needs. It is further alleged that the plaintiff's parents relied on the advice of such professionals. The defendant authority is vicariously liable for any breach of such duties by their employees.

Again, I can see no ground for striking out this claim at least in relation to the educational psychologists. Psychologists hold themselves out as having special skills and they are, in my judgment, like any other professional bound both to possess such skills and to exercise them carefully. Of course, the test in *Bolam v. Friern Hospital Management Committee* [1957] 1 W.L.R. 582 will apply to them, i.e. they are only bound to exercise the ordinary skill of a competent psychologist and if they can show that they acted in accordance with the accepted views of some reputable psychologist at the relevant time they will have discharged the duty of care, even if other psychologists would have adopted a different view. In the context of advice on the treatment of dyslexia, a subject on which views have changed over the years, this may be an important factor. But that said, I can see no ground on which, at this stage, the existence of a professional duty of care can be ruled out. The position of other members of the defendant's staff is not as clear, but I would not at this stage strike out the claims relating to them.

The position of the psychologists in the education cases is quite different from that of the doctor and social worker in the child abuse cases. There is no potential conflict of duty between the professional's duties to the plaintiff and his duty to the educational authority. Nor is there any obvious conflict between the professional being under a duty of care to the plaintiff and the discharge by the authority of its statutory duties. If, at trial, it emerges that there are such conflicts, then the trial judge may have to limit or exclude any duty of care owed by the professional to the plaintiff. But at this stage no obvious conflict has been demonstrated....

In respect of the *Hampshire* case, an additional factor was that the claimant was a child at a school run by the defendant local authority, and claimed partly in respect of breaches of duty on the part of the headmaster. Lord Browne-Wilkinson pointed out that the relationship between headmaster and pupil was closely analogous to the relationships giving rise to a duty of care in cases of economic loss. Arguably, there was a **voluntary assumption of responsibility** towards the child.

[48] The type of damage suffered in the education cases was not settled in *X v Bedfordshire*. See further the discussion of *Phelps v Hillingdon*, later in this chapter.

The House of Lords therefore permitted the education cases to proceed to trial on the basis that not only a local education authority *but also its individual teachers* potentially owe a duty of care to their pupils.

3.4 AFTER X V BEDFORDSHIRE

Welfare Cases

The Influence of Osman v UK

In *Osman v UK* [2000] EHRR 245, the European Court of Human Rights concluded that English law conferred an 'immunity' on the police in respect of certain actions in negligence. This immunity was contrary to Article 6 of the ECHR, which states that everyone is entitled to a hearing by a tribunal in respect of their civil rights. This aspect of *Osman v UK* has since been recognized as mistaken by the European Court of Human Rights itself, in Z v UK (2002) 34 EHRR 3. But before Z v UK *Osman* had a real (though not precisely quantifiable) influence on UK negligence cases. Courts undoubtedly showed a new reluctance to strike out actions on policy grounds. More recently, the HRA and the introduction of domestic law remedies for violations of Convention rights exert a new influence. Attention has focused on the substantive Convention rights, and the right to compensation, rather than the right of access to a court under Art 6.

Barrett v Enfield [2001] 2 AC 550

The first significant test of *X v Bedfordshire* after the decision in *Osman v UK* arose from distinctly different facts. *Barrett v Enfield* was not a case of suspected child abuse, nor did it concern a decision about whether to take a child into care. Rather, the claimant brought an action in negligence in respect of the conduct of his care. The claim was for personal injuries. The House of Lords declined to strike out the claim, concluding that the case should be heard on its merits.

There are three important points to make about *Barrett*.

1. Less Enthusiasm for Striking Out

Lord Browne-Wilkinson, in this case, was critical of the decision in *Osman v UK*, but also thought that if this case was struck out, a claim would be initiated before the European Court of Human Rights for a violation of Article 6.

Lord Browne-Wilkinson, at 560

In view of the decision in the *Osman* case it is now difficult to foretell what would be the result in the present case if we were to uphold the striking out order. It seems to me that it is at least probable that the matter would then be taken to Strasbourg. That court, applying its decision in the *Osman* case if it considers it to be correct, would say that we had deprived the plaintiff of his right to have the balance struck between the hardship suffered by him and the damage to be done to the public interest in the present case if an order were to be made against the defendant council. In the present very unsatisfactory state of affairs, and bearing in mind that under the Human Rights Act 1998 article 6 will shortly become part of English law, in such cases as these it is difficult to say that it is a clear and obvious case calling for striking out; see also *Markesinis & Deakin, Tort Law*, 4th ed (1999), pp 145 et seq.

On the other hand, elsewhere in his judgment Lord Browne-Wilkinson called for caution in striking out on entirely different grounds, namely that it is difficult to judge the policy issues unless one has a full grasp of the facts (at 557–8). The other judges in *Barrett* also called for caution in striking out, without relying on *Osman v UK*.

2. Less Broad Brush Policy Reasoning and More Confidence in the Negligence Action

This second point is related to the first. The policy arguments which proved fatal to the child abuse claims in *X v Bedfordshire* were not thought to apply with the same force to the claims in this case. The potential conflicts identified in *X v Bedfordshire* would not necessarily apply here, and there was much less confidence in the availability of other suitable remedies. Lord Slynn referred to the dissenting judgment of Lord Bingham MR in *X v Bedfordshire* (in the Court of Appeal), suggesting greater confidence that tort law may have a positive role in responding to malpractice in the social welfare sphere, as elsewhere.

3. A Simpler Approach to 'Justiciability'

As we have seen, the approach adopted in *Anns v Merton* threatened to make negligence cases turn on an interpretation of public law concepts. In *X v Bedfordshire*, Lord Browne-Wilkinson expressed the view that it was best to keep public law concepts away from the negligence enquiry, but he nevertheless appeared to say that both policy and discretion were protected spheres. In *Barrett*, Lord Slynn and Lord Hutton advocated a more straightforward approach which would keep questions of public law out of negligence cases. At the same time, their approach would permit broader enquiry into local authority decision-making.

Lord Slynn, at 571

Where a statutory power is given to a local authority and damage is caused by what it does pursuant to that power, the ultimate question is whether the particular issue is justiciable or whether the court should accept that it has no role to play. The two tests (discretion and policy/operational) to which I have referred are guides in deciding that question. The greater the element of policy involved, the wider the area of discretion accorded, the more likely it is that the matter is not justiciable so that no action in negligence can be brought.... A claim of negligence in the taking of a decision to exercise a statutory discretion is likely to be barred, unless it is wholly unreasonable so as not to be a real exercise of the discretion, or if it involves the making of a policy decision involving the balancing of different public interests; acts done pursuant to the lawful exercise of the discretion can, however, in my view be subject to a duty of care, even if some element of discretion is involved. Thus, accepting that a decision to take a child into care pursuant to a statutory power is not justiciable, it does not in my view follow that, having taken a child into care, an authority cannot be liable for what it or its employees do in relation to the child without it being shown that they have acted in excess of power. It may amount to an excess of power, but that is not in my opinion the test to be adopted: the test is whether the conditions in the *Caparo* case [1990] 2 AC 605 have been satisfied.

D. Fairgrieve and P. Craig, *'Barrett*, Negligence and Discretionary Powers'* (1999) PL 626–50, at 633

A public law hurdle will therefore only be of relevance where the allegation of negligence raised by the plaintiff is felt to raise matters which are not justiciable. Where this was not so then the courts would consider any issue regarding the way in which discretion was exercised within the ordinary framework of the negligence action. Assuming that the courts decide that a duty of care is owed, this will then mean that the way in which the discretion was exercised will, as Lord Hutton stated, be of relevance in deciding whether there was a breach of the duty of care.

Exploring the various policy factors debated in both *X v Bedfordshire* and *Barrett v Enfield*, Fairgrieve and Craig also explain the broader concerns:

Fairgrieve and Craig, at 636–7

Underlying many of these policy factors are complex questions striking at the heart of the role of the State. Is it desirable for financially stretched public authorities to pay compensation to publicly funded complainants for poor services? Is potential liability likely to improve services in the long-term or to be counter-productive? Should causally peripheral public bodies with perceived deep pockets underwrite losses caused by primary wrongdoers? Should the overriding concern of the law be that 'wrongs should be remedied'? Members of the judiciary hold very different views on this, and the debate is not restricted to the legal world. Barrett undoubtedly represents a shift in favour of compensation-seekers.

Z v UK and After

The plaintiffs in *X v Bedfordshire* (their claims in negligence having been struck out) brought an action against the UK alleging violations of Article 6 (right of access to a court), Article 3 (freedom from inhuman and degrading treatment), Article 8 (respect for private and family life), and Article 13 (right to compensation in the event of a violation of one of the substantive rights). The Court admitted that its interpretation in *Osman v UK* had been in error. There had been no violation of Article 6. However, there *had* been violations of Article 3 and Article 13 in this case. The absence of protection for the interests of the children in this case, *and also the lack of a remedy in the form of compensation*, had violated their Convention rights.

Given the finding that Article 6 had not been violated, there was no necessity that the law of tort should provide a remedy in such a case. The HRA as we have seen provides a remedy against public authorities who do not act consistently with Convention rights, under section 8. This is an alternative to the law of tort. But, in the formative years of litigation over child welfare and education after *X v Bedfordshire*, the courts thought they should adjust *the law of tort* to provide remedies, rather than leaving claimants to an action under section 7. Courts are themselves public authorities under section 6, and by section 2(1) they must have regard to the 'Strasbourg jurisprudence' when interpreting the applicable law. In *D v East Berkshire*, it was further pointed out that an action against the local authority for damages under section 8 would not be available where the actions in question occurred before October 2000, when the HRA came into force; and that in cases of child abuse it was quite typical for actions to be brought many years after the event.[49] The only route to a remedy was through adaptation of common law.

D v East Berkshire Community Health NHS Trust and Another [2004] 2 WLR 58 (CA)

Actions were brought by parents and in one case a child for psychiatric injury suffered as a result of mistaken, and allegedly negligent allegations of child abuse by the parents against the children. The parents' claims were dismissed; but the child's appeal was allowed.

The House of Lords heard an appeal from this decision; but that appeal related only to the unsuccessful claims brought by parents, and the appeal failed. The historic decision of the Court of Appeal in this case *not to follow the decision of the House of Lords in X v Bedfordshire* was not criticized by the House of Lords. More recent developments in interpretation of the HRA suggest however that this sort of move is unlikely to be made again. In *CN v Poole BC* [2016] EWHC 569 (QB), the defendant argued that the Court of Appeal's decision in *D v East Berkshire* should no longer be followed. It was held that the later cases of *Mitchell v Glasgow* [2009] UKHL 11 and *Michael v Chief Constable of South Wales* [2015] UKSC 2 did not impliedly overrule the decision, which therefore remained binding; but an appeal from this decision is pending.

D v East Berkshire Health Authority [2005] UKHL 23; [2005] 2 AC 373

The question on appeal before the House of Lords concerned the rejected claims on behalf of the parents. The decision of the Court of Appeal to depart from *X v Bedfordshire* was not criticized by their Lordships. Lord Bingham (dissenting) would have gone further than the Court of Appeal, allowing the claims of the parents to proceed to trial. But the majority held that no duty was owed to the parents, and the actions must be struck out.

Lord Bingham of Cornhill (dissenting)

3 The courts below have concluded that . . . no duty of care can be owed by the doctor or the social worker to the parent, that accordingly no claim may lie and that these claims brought by the parents must be dismissed with no evidence called and no detailed examination of the facts. . . . I understand that a majority of my noble and learned friends agree with this conclusion, for which there is considerable authority in the United Kingdom and abroad. But the law in this area has evolved very markedly over the last decade. What appeared to be hard-edged rules precluding the possibility of any claim by parent or child have been eroded or restricted. And a series of decisions of the European Court of Human Rights has shown that application of an exclusionary rule in this sensitive area may lead to serious breaches of Convention rights for which domestic law affords no remedy and for which, at any rate arguably, the law of tort should afford a remedy if facts of sufficient gravity are shown.

. . .

[49] See further the discussion in Chapter 7.

In the present cases, where the parents had sought medical advice from their accusers and proximity therefore was particularly strong (at [83]), it was not appropriate to strike out the claims.

Lord Bingham (dissenting)

[50] ...the question does arise whether the law of tort should evolve, analogically and incrementally, so as to fashion appropriate remedies to contemporary problems or whether it should remain essentially static, making only such changes as are forced upon it, leaving difficult and, in human terms, very important problems to be swept up by the Convention. I prefer evolution.

The majority of the House of Lords took a more traditional approach. Lords Nicholls, Brown, and Rodger delivered judgments explaining why the claims by the parents should be struck out. Lord Steyn agreed with all three of these.

Lord Nicholls of Birkenhead

[85] In my view the Court of Appeal reached the right conclusion on the issue arising in the present cases. Ultimately the factor which persuades me that, at common law, interference with family life does not justify according a suspected parent a higher level of protection than other suspected perpetrators is the factor conveniently labelled "conflict of interest". A doctor is obliged to act in the best interests of his patient. In these cases the child is his patient. The doctor is charged with the protection of the child, not with the protection of the parent. The best interests of a child and his parent normally march hand-in-hand. But when considering whether something does not feel "quite right", a doctor must be able to act single-mindedly in the interests of the child. He ought not to have at the back of his mind an awareness that if his doubts about intentional injury or sexual abuse prove unfounded he may be exposed to claims by a distressed parent.

... [88] The claimants sought to meet this "conflict of interest" point by noting that the suggested duty owed to parents has the same content as the duty owed to the child: to exercise due skill and care in investigating the possibility of abuse. This response is not adequate. The time when the presence or absence of a conflict of interest matters is when the doctor is carrying out his investigation. At that time the doctor does not know whether there has been abuse by the parent. But he knows that when he is considering this possibility the interests of parent and child are diametrically opposed. The interests of the child are that the doctor should report any suspicions he may have and that he should carry out further investigation in consultation with other child care professionals. The interests of the parent do not favour either of these steps. This difference of interest in the outcome is an unsatisfactory basis for imposing a duty of care on a doctor in favour of a parent.

... [92] A wider approach has also been canvassed. The suggestion has been made that, in effect, the common law should jettison the concept of duty of care as a universal prerequisite to liability in negligence. Instead the standard of care should be "modulated" to accommodate the complexities arising in fields such as social workers dealing with children at risk of abuse: *Tort Liability of Public Authorities in Comparative Perspective*, ed Fairgrieve, Andenas and Bell (2002), p 485. The contours of liability should be traced in other ways.

[93] For some years it has been all too evident that identifying the parameters of an expanding law of negligence is proving difficult, especially in fields involving the discharge of

statutory functions by public authorities. So this radical suggestion is not without attraction. This approach would be analogous to that adopted when considering breaches of human rights under the European Convention. Sometimes in human rights cases the identity of the defendant, whether the state in claims under the Convention or a public authority in claims under the Human Rights Act 1998, makes it appropriate for an international or domestic court to look backwards over everything which happened. In deciding whether overall the end result was acceptable the court makes a value judgment based on more flexible notions than the common law standard of reasonableness and does so freed from the legal rigidity of a duty of care.

[94] This approach, as I say, is not without attraction. It is peculiarly appropriate in the field of human rights. But I have reservations about attempts to transplant this approach wholesale into the domestic law of negligence in cases where, as here, no claim is made for breach of a Convention right. Apart from anything else, such an attempt would be likely to lead to a lengthy and unnecessary period of uncertainty in an important area of the law. It would lead to uncertainty because there are types of cases where a person's acts or omissions do not render him liable in negligence for another's loss even though this loss may be foreseeable.... Abandonment of the concept of a duty of care in English law, unless replaced by a control mechanism which recognises this limitation, is unlikely to clarify the law. That control mechanism has yet to be identified. And introducing this protracted period of uncertainty is unnecessary, because claims may now be brought directly against public authorities in respect of breaches of Convention rights.

Did Lord Bingham's dissent (extracted earlier) amount to an argument for abandonment of the duty of care as a control mechanism? It is suggested that it did not. Lord Bingham argued that the absence of a duty should not be too readily assumed in the absence of knowledge of the relevant facts. Policy reasons should not be applied in too broad and general a fashion. The existence of a duty of care involved a sensitive enquiry and should be dealt with in the light of the particular facts of the case. Lord Bingham further argued that in circumstances where a duty of care was owed—applying the normal *Caparo* test—public authorities and their employees should be protected by demanding that a high level of fault should be shown, before the breach could be actionable.

This form of 'evolution' (as Lord Bingham put it) would be adventurous indeed for the English tort of negligence. The approach of the majority uses generic policy arguments to block claims by parents even in the case of the most outrageous accusations, in order to protect those who make genuinely difficult decisions. Lord Nicholls' comparison with those who are accused of other serious crimes has substance, although it could also be argued that the parents accused in these cases did not enjoy the same procedural rights that are engaged in the usual criminal process.

Breach of Duty

Where decisions of social workers and medical professionals are concerned, the relevant test to apply in addressing breach is clearly the *Bolam* test (see Chapter 3). This poses a formidable hurdle for claimants who have managed to establish that a duty is owed, though it is capable of being passed. For example, in *Pierce v Doncaster* [2008] EWCA Civ 1416, the judge concluded that no reasonable authority assessing the case could have permitted the claimant to be returned to his mother. On the other hand, this case illustrates a further potential problem with cases of abuse: many of them are brought many years after the event. In *Pierce v Doncaster* itself, the judge would need to consider whether he should exercise his discretion in favour of the claimant, to allow the action to proceed even though it was outside the statutory 'limitation period' (see Chapter 7).

Education Cases

It will be recalled that in *X v Bedfordshire*, Lord Browne-Wilkinson did not strike out all of the 'education claims'. He said that the individual professionals involved may owe duties of care to the children and, if these were breached, the local authorities could be vicariously liable. Equally, there was one claim based on breach of a direct duty of care which was not struck out. This was a claim based on the proposition that the local authority was offering a 'psychology service' to the public, and that it therefore owed duties of care to members of the public who made use of the service, along the lines of the duty of care for professional services recognized in *Henderson v Merrett*.

In *Barrett v Enfield* (at 557–8), Lord Browne-Wilkinson suggested (rather unusually) that he had been wrong not to strike out the single surviving 'direct duty' claim in *X v Bedfordshire*. This, he thought, had exposed local education authorities to a proliferation of claims. It also illustrated the dangers of striking out, because it showed that appeal courts who are asked to determine questions on a striking out action are in danger of making too many assumptions about the nature of the facts. His mistake was, he now thought, to assume that the 'psychology service' was offered to the public in the same way as any other professional service. In fact, he now understood that the point of the psychology service was not to inform the individuals who were referred to it, but to advise schools and education authorities on the appropriate provision for those individuals. This, he argued, was quite different, and he now thought that recognition of a duty of care would be inappropriate in such circumstances. This point fell to be decided by the House of Lords in the next case, not on assumed facts but in an action on its merits.[50] The claimant succeeded not just in taking her claim to trial, but also in winning damages.

Phelps v Hillingdon [2001] 2 AC 619

In the first of four appeals heard together by the House of Lords, the claimant was referred by her school, at the age of 12, to the defendant local education authority's school psychology service. An educational psychologist employed by the authority reported no specific weaknesses on the part of the claimant. Shortly before leaving school, the claimant was diagnosed as dyslexic. She brought an action against the local authority, and was awarded damages.

The House of Lords agreed that the individual educational psychologist owed a duty to the claimant, which had been breached, causing recoverable damage. The local authority was vicariously liable.[51]

[50] *Phelps v Hillingdon* itself was not a striking out action. But the House of Lords heard that appeal together with three other appeals, which were striking out actions.

[51] The other appeals were all determined in favour of the claimants, and their claims were allowed to proceed to trial. They principally concerned failure to provide for recognized special needs (and failure to recognize specific special needs).

Lord Slynn, *Phelps v Hillingdon*

The common law

... This House decided in *Barrett v Enfield London BC*...that the fact that acts which are claimed to be negligent are carried out within the ambit of a statutory discretion is not in itself a reason why it should be held that no claim for negligence can be brought in respect of them. It is only where what is done has involved the weighing of competing public interests or has been dictated by considerations on which Parliament could not have intended that the courts would substitute their views for the views of ministers or officials that the courts will hold that the issue is non-justiciable on the ground that the decision was made in the exercise of a statutory discretion. In Pamela's case there is no such ground for holding that her claim is non-justiciable and therefore the question to be determined is whether the damage relied on is foreseeable and proximate and whether it is just and reasonable to recognise a duty of care (*Caparo Industries plc v Dickman*). If a duty of care would exist where advice was given other than pursuant to the exercise of statutory powers, such duty of care is not excluded because the advice is given pursuant to the exercise of statutory powers. This is particularly important where other remedies laid down by the statute (eg an appeals review procedure) do not in themselves provide sufficient redress for loss which has already been caused.

Where, as in Pamela's case, a person is employed by a local education authority to carry out professional services as part of the fulfilment of the authority's statutory duty, it has to be asked whether there is any overriding reason in principle why (a) that person should not owe a duty of care (the first question) and (b) why, if the duty of care is broken by that person, the authority as employer or principal should not be vicariously liable (the second question).

I accept that, as was said in *X (minors) v Bedfordshire CC*, there may be cases where to recognise such a vicarious liability on the part of the authority may so interfere with the performance of the local education authority's duties that it would be wrong to recognise any liability on the part of the authority. It must, however, be for the local authority to establish that: it is not to be presumed and I anticipate that the circumstances where it could be established would be exceptional.

As to the first question, it is long and well-established, now elementary, that persons exercising a particular skill or profession may owe a duty of care in the performance to people who it can be foreseen will be injured if due skill and care are not exercised, and if injury or damage can be shown to have been caused by the lack of care. Such duty does not depend on the existence of any contractual relationship between the person causing and the person suffering the damage. A doctor, an accountant and an engineer are plainly such a person. So in my view is an educational psychologist or psychiatrist or a teacher including a teacher in a specialised area, such as a teacher concerned with children having special educational needs. 'So may be an education officer performing the functions of a local education authority in regard to children with special educational needs ... .

I fully agree with what was said by Lord Browne-Wilkinson in *X (minors) v Bedfordshire CC*...at 766 that a head teacher owes 'a duty of care to exercise the reasonable skills of a headmaster in relation to such [sc a child's] educational needs' and a special advisory teacher brought in to advise on the educational needs of a specific pupil, particularly if he knows that his advice will be communicated to the pupil's parents, 'owes a duty to the child to exercise the skill and care of a reasonable advisory teacher'. A similar duty on specific facts may arise for others engaged in the educational process, eg an educational psychologist being part of the local authority's team to provide the necessary services. The fact that the educational psychologist owes a duty to the authority to exercise skill and care in the performance of his contract of employment does not mean that no duty of care can be or is owed to the child. Nor does the fact that the educational psychologist is called in pursuance of the performance of the local authority's statutory duties mean that no duty of care is owed by him, if in exercising his profession he would otherwise have a duty of care.

Lord Slynn repeated the simpler approach to policy and discretion, that was adopted in *Barrett v Enfield*: so long as the issue is suitable for adjudication (it is 'justiciable'), the court will apply the *Caparo* test. The statutory context will of course be *relevant* to an application of this test. But the existence of statutory powers (or of statutory duties which are themselves unenforceable at private law) is in no sense a 'defence' to a negligence action; nor does it justify immunity from the duty of care.

What is the Damage?

It is not entirely clear whether Lord Slynn regarded the claim as principally for personal injury in the form of psychological harm, or for economic losses flowing from the failure to diagnose. Indeed he does not seem to have differentiated particularly between these forms of damage. One reason why he did not do so is that he thought the *Caparo* criteria would apply in the same way in either event. But the relevant damage may be important for certain purposes, not least for determining the relevant *limitation period*. The identification of 'damage' was raised in one of the other appeals decided together with *Phelps* by the House of Lords: *Anderton v Clwyd*. It had been argued by the Court of Appeal in this case that even if dyslexia could be treated as 'impairment of a person's physical and mental condition' (the definition of 'personal injuries' adopted in section 35(5) of the Supreme Court Act 1981),[52] that impairment had not been *caused by the defendants*. The defendants had not caused the dyslexia, but had failed to benefit the claimant by offering the best educational options. This argument was rejected by the House of Lords:

Lord Slynn, at 664

... Having regard to the purpose of the provision it would in any event, in my view, be wrong to adopt an overly legalistic view of what are 'personal injuries to a person'. For the reasons given in my decision in the *Phelps* case, psychological damage and a failure to diagnose a congenital condition and to take appropriate action as a result of which a child's level of achievement is reduced (which leads to loss of employment and wages) may constitute damage for the purpose of a claim. . . . Garland J was right . . . that a failure to mitigate the adverse consequences of a congenital defect is capable of being 'personal injuries to a person' within the meaning of the rules.

Although the reasoning on this point is less than clear, it was adopted by a later House of Lords in *Adams v Bracknell Forest BC* [2005] 1 AC 76. In this case, which was concerned

[52] Now Senior Courts Act 1981. The same wording is used in the Limitation Act 1980, s 38.

with the important practical question of *when the limitation period begins to run* in a case of failure to diagnose dyslexia, the House of Lords concluded that it was sensible to treat the damage in a case of this sort *as* personal injury. However, this was not an appropriate case in which to exercise the discretion which is available to a court in certain personal injury cases to, in effect, override the applicable time limit. This serves as a reminder that the test for duty of care is not the only mechanism for controlling claims.

Limitation periods in general, and *Adams v Bracknell* in particular, are further discussed in Chapter 7.

Conflict of Interest: Generalization

Concepts and policy reasons developed in the specific areas of child welfare and educational negligence have become generalized, as new types of claim against public authorities emerge.

Jain v Trent Strategic Health Authority [2009] UKHL 4; [2009] 2 WLR 248

The defendant authority had made an application for an order cancelling the claimants' nursing home registration, believing conditions in the home to be unacceptable due to building works, and without giving the defendants the opportunity to rebut the claims. In a challenge before a Registered Homes Tribunal, this belief was found to have been unfounded, but it was too late to avoid the destruction of the claimants' business. They were therefore caused considerable economic loss.

The House of Lords held that no duty was owed to the claimants at common law. The crucial factor in this was the potential for conflict of interest where the defendants were seeking to protect the interests of elderly people such as the residents of the claimants' home. This reason is of course derived from *D v East Berkshire*, and *X v Bedfordshire* before it, and these as well as a number of other cases were referred to by the House.

Lord Scott, *Jain v Trent Strategic Health Authority* [2009] UKHL 4; [2009] 2 WLR 248

28 This line of authority demonstrates, in my opinion, that where action is taken by a State authority under statutory powers designed for the benefit or protection of a particular class of persons, a tortious duty of care will not be held to be owed by the State authority to others whose interests may be adversely affected by an exercise of the statutory power. The reason is that the imposition of such a duty would or might inhibit the exercise of the statutory powers and be potentially adverse to the interests of the class of persons the powers were designed to benefit or protect, thereby putting at risk the achievement of their statutory purpose.

This reasoning was reinforced by the fact that the claimant and defendant were effectively adversaries engaged in litigation. *CEC v Barclays Bank* (Section 2) had re-emphasized the absence of duty between parties in such 'adverse' relationships, which was also regarded as incompatible with a duty of care, at least in the absence of an assumption of responsibility, in *Elguzouli-Daf v Commissioner of Police of the Metropolis* [1995] QB 335 (no action against the Crown Prosecution Service by a suspect in relation to the handling of the prosecution).

Equally important was the approach taken in *Jain* to Convention rights. It was thought at least possible—and it would appear by Lord Scott almost certain—that there had been a violation of Article 6 (fair trial), and Article 1 Protocol 1 (protection of property) ECHR. Lord Scott said he found it 'very difficult' to see how there could be compliance with the Convention.

Lord Scott, *Jain v Trent Strategic Health Authority*

18. My Lords, the considerations to which I have referred lead me to suppose that, if the application and order of which Mr and Mrs Jain complain had post-dated 2 October 2000, they would have been entitled to compensation under domestic law. How could it be compatible with their Convention rights to deprive them by judicial order of the benefit of registration of their Ash Lea Court nursing home without according them the opportunity of showing the application to be insubstantial and based on insufficient grounds and without there being any circumstances of urgency arguably sufficient to justify depriving them of that opportunity?

Other judges preferred not to express a conclusion in respect of compatibility with Convention rights, not having heard argument on the point. But in any event, all members of the House agreed that this was irrelevant to the common law. In this particular instance, since the HRA was not in force at the time of the events complained of, the only potential remedy available to the claimants lay in Strasbourg, requiring a costly action before the European Court of Human Rights. The rejection of Lord Bingham's plea for evolution, not leaving the Convention to mop up important issues, appeared complete.

Lord Scott, *Jain v Trent Strategic Health Authority*

39. It is, moreover, the case that, post-2 October 2000, article 6 and article 1 of the First Protocol have become part of our domestic law and that breaches of these articles can be met by damages remedies under domestic law. As Lord Brown of Eaton-under-Heywood observed in *Van Colle v Chief Constable of the Hertfordshire Police* [2008] UKHL 50; [2008] 3 WLR 593 at 633/ (para. 136)

"... it is quite simply unnecessary now to develop the common law to provide a parallel cause of action..."

Policy reasons familiar from *X v Bedfordshire* were also deployed in denying a duty of care in *Rowley v Secretary of State for Work and Pensions* [2007] EWCA Civ 598; [2007] 1 WLR 1861. Such a duty would be inconsistent with the statutory scheme which bestowed powers upon the Child Support Agency, and offered sufficient remedies. These remedies were not as generous as those which might be available in the event of a successful claim at common law, but as we will see in Chapter 10 (where we discuss the important case of *Marcic v Thames Water Utilities* [2003] UKHL 66; [2004] 2 AC 42), this has been no obstacle to denial of cross-cutting duties at common law in a statutory context. The constant message is that common law remedies should not be awarded which would contradict the balance arrived at by a statutory scheme.

3.5 OMISSIONS

Omissions and Powers

Shortly after the decision in *X v Bedfordshire*, the House of Lords decided the case of *Stovin v Wise* [1996] AC 923. This decision initially seemed puzzling and hard to place. The subsequent decision in *Gorringe v Calderdale* [2004] UKHL 15 helped to explain the ambit of *Stovin*. *Stovin v Wise* and *Gorringe v Calderdale* are cases of pure omission, or of *doing nothing at all*, where the grounds for suggesting that a duty exists is the existence of a statutory power. These cases state that the existence of a statutory power, or of a very general and unenforceable statutory duty, cannot be the sole basis for holding that there is a duty to take positive action. There needs to be some independent reason for holding that there is a positive duty to act *at common law*. The outcome is (simply) that existence of a power or a purely 'public law' style duty does not provide a short cut to finding a duty at common law. The usual principles on positive duties at common law will apply.

Stovin v Wise [1996] AC 923

The plaintiff was riding his motorcycle, when the defendant pulled out at a junction and collided with him. The plaintiff was seriously injured. When the plaintiff commenced an action against the defendant, the defendant (or rather, the defendant's insurer) joined the local authority as co-defendant, arguing that the junction was known to be dangerous because visibility was impaired by the existence of a bank on adjoining land. Accidents had occurred there on at least three previous occasions. The council had looked into the matter, and agreed a surveyor's recommendation that the bank be removed if the landowner agreed. A letter was written to the landowner, but there was no reply and no action was taken to follow it up. The trial judge held that the council, as highway authority, had not breached any statutory duties, but it was in breach of a common law duty of care. He judged the council to be 30 per cent to blame for the damage. The Court of Appeal dismissed an appeal by the council.

The House of Lords held that the local authority owed no duty (either in public law or in negligence) to take positive steps to remove the bank. On the way to this conclusion, their reasoning was complex and in many respects confusing. The issues have subsequently been better explained in *Gorringe v Calderdale* (later in this section).

Lord Hoffmann delivered the leading judgment for the majority. He pointed out (at 943) that this was a case of an *omission to act*. Equally, in this case the *only* reason why the local authority might be thought to be under a duty to act at all was that it had certain powers and duties conferred or imposed upon it by statute. Indeed, the dissenting judgment of Lord Nicholls (with whom, notably, Lord Slynn agreed)[53] argued that a duty to act was *justified by* the existence of a power.

Lord Nicholls, at 931 (dissenting)

Omissions and proximity

The council was more than a bystander. The council had a statutory power to remove this source of danger, although it was not under a statutory duty to do so. Before 1978 the accepted law was that the council could be under no common law liability for failing to act. A simple

---

[53]   This is notable because of Lord Slynn's important role in *Barrett* and *Phelps*.

failure to exercise a statutory power did not give rise to a common law claim for damages: see *East Suffolk Rivers Catchment Board v. Kent*. The decision in *Anns v. Merton London Borough Council* ... liberated the law from this unacceptable yoke. This was the great contribution the Anns case made to the development of the common law.

The true *ratio of Stovin* is its rejection of the proposition above. *The existence of a statutory power does not itself give rise to a common law duty to act.* The last remaining 'great contribution of *Anns*' is therefore rejected by the majority in *Stovin* and, subsequently, by *Gorringe*.

Lord Hoffmann clearly considered that the local authority while not a 'mere bystander' was nevertheless a 'peripheral party'—a party who has failed to benefit others. He emphasized that *positive reasons*, beyond foreseeability of harm, must be shown to justify the imposition of a duty of care. This applies to both acts and omissions.

Lord Hoffmann, at 949

... The trend of authorities has been to discourage the assumption that anyone who suffers loss is prima facie entitled to compensation from a person (preferably insured or a public authority) whose act or omission can be said to have caused it. The default position is that he is not.

This approach is (to adopt the language of Fairgrieve and Craig in their comment on *Barrett*, earlier in Section 3), very much against the 'compensation-seekers'. But on this occasion it is against compensation-seekers in the particular context of *failure to confer a benefit*.

Despite the conclusion in *Stovin* that the existence of a statutory power does not *in itself* give rise to a duty to act, the possibility was conceded that in some circumstances—primarily in cases of general or specific *reliance*—a positive duty to act may exist.[54] This is very important. The duty in such cases arises from proximity and reliance, subject to policy considerations. It does not arise from the statutory power.

Certain other features of Lord Hoffmann's majority judgment in *Stovin* sowed some confusion, but were clarified in the subsequent case of *Gorringe* (below).

Lord Hoffmann, at 952–3

In the case of a mere statutory power, ... the legislature has chosen to confer a discretion rather than create a duty. Of course there may be cases in which Parliament has chosen to confer a power because the subject matter did not permit a duty to be stated with sufficient precision. It may nevertheless have contemplated that in circumstances in which it would be irrational not to exercise the power, a person who suffered loss because it had not been exercised, or not properly exercised, would be entitled to compensation. I therefore do not say that a statutory "may" can never give rise to a common law duty of care. I prefer to leave open the question of whether the *Anns* case was wrong to create any exception to Lord Romer's statement of principle in the *East Suffolk* case and I shall go on to consider the circumstances (such as "general reliance") in which it has been suggested

---

54 An example of general reliance has appeared to exist in New Zealand in respect of local authority supervision of the safety of buildings. Lord Hoffmann referred with approval to *Invercargill v Hamlin* (earlier). *Specific* reliance exists where the particular claimant relies on conduct of the defendant in particular circumstances.

that such a duty might arise. But the fact that Parliament has conferred a discretion must be some indication that the policy of the act conferring the power was not to create a right to compensation. The need to have regard to the policy of the statute therefore means that exceptions will be rare.

In summary, therefore, I think that the minimum preconditions for basing a duty of care upon the existence of a statutory power, if it can be done at all, are, first, that it would in the circumstances have been irrational not to have exercised the power, so that there was in effect a public law duty to act, and secondly, that there are exceptional grounds for holding that the policy of the statute requires compensation to be paid to persons who suffer loss because the power was not exercised.

The difficulties are that Lord Hoffmann appears to accept Lord Romer's general statement in *East Suffolk v Kent* (disapproved in *Anns*, and also not consistent with later cases such as *Barrett* and *Phelps*); and that he appears to argue that any common law duty in this context would grow out of the statutory powers, whereas we have said that they are independent of such powers.

Gorringe v Calderdale [2004] UKHL 15; [2004] 1 WLR 1057

The claimant was driving too fast towards the brow of a hill. Having got to the top, she caught sight of a bus coming up the other side. It was not in her lane but she panicked, crashed, and was injured. She brought an action against the local authority on the basis that it should have repainted the word 'slow' on the road towards the top of the hill.

Here, the local authority was under a relevant statutory *duty*, but this was expressed in such broad and general terms that it could not form the basis of an action at private law. This duty was therefore treated in the same way as the statutory *power* in *Stovin v Wise*. Lord Hoffmann explained:

(a) that the approach in *Stovin v Wise* was limited to cases of pure omission ('doing nothing at all') in which the *only* basis for suggesting there is a duty to act is the existence of a statutory power (or, now, broad public law duty); and

(b) that there probably would be no exceptional cases meeting his criteria of actionability after all. This being the case, there was no need to discuss the concept of 'irrationality' at public law in *Stovin v Wise*. It was probably a mistake to have made any remarks on this subject.

Lord Hoffmann

31 . . . The majority [in *Stovin*] rejected the argument that the existence of the statutory power to make improvements to the highway could in itself give rise to a common law duty to take reasonable care to exercise the power or even not to be irrational in failing to do so. It went no further than to leave open the possibility that there might somewhere be a statutory power or public duty which generated a common law duty and indulged in some speculation (which may have been ill-advised) about what that duty might be.

32 Speaking for myself, I find it difficult to imagine a case in which a common law duty can be founded simply upon the failure (however irrational) to provide some benefit which a public authority has power (or a public law duty) to provide. For example, the majority reasoning in *Stovin v Wise* was applied in *Capital & Counties plc v Hampshire County Council* [1997] QB 1004 to fire authorities, which have a general public law duty to make provision for efficient fire-fighting services: see section 1 of the Fire Services Act 1947. The Court of Appeal held, in my view correctly, that this did not create a common law duty.

Emphasizing that the outcomes in these cases do not conflict directly with other developments (in cases such as *Barrett* and *Phelps*), he added:

38 My Lords, I must make it clear that this appeal is concerned only with an attempt to impose upon a local authority a common law duty to act based solely on the existence of a broad public law duty. We are not concerned with cases in which public authorities have actually done acts or entered into relationships or undertaken responsibilities which give rise to a common law duty of care. In such cases the fact that the public authority acted pursuant to a statutory power or public duty does not necessarily negative the existence of a duty. A hospital trust provides medical treatment pursuant to the public law duty in the 1977 Act, but the existence of its common law duty is based simply upon its acceptance of a professional relationship with the patient no different from that which would be accepted by a doctor in private practice. The duty rests upon a solid, orthodox common law foundation and the question is not whether it is created by the statute but whether the terms of the statute (for example, in requiring a particular thing to be done or conferring a discretion) are sufficient to exclude it. The law in this respect has been well established since *Geddis v Proprietors of Bann Reservoir* (1878) 3 App Cas 430.

Lord Steyn agreed in the result, but added some distinct comments. These underline the independence of common law duties from statutory powers and duties. These comments are particularly helpful in explaining the limited ambit of *Stovin* and *Gorringe*, and placing them in the context of other developments.

Lord Steyn, *Gorringe v Calderdale*
[2004] 1 WLR 1057

2 There are . . . a few remarks that I would wish to make about negligence and statutory duties and powers. This is a subject of great complexity and very much an evolving area of the law. No single decision is capable of providing a comprehensive analysis. It is a subject on which an intense focus on the particular facts and on the particular statutory background, seen in the context of the contours of our social welfare state, is necessary. On the one hand the courts must not contribute to the creation of a society bent on litigation, which is premised on the illusion that for every misfortune there is a remedy. On the other hand, there are cases where the courts must recognise on principled grounds the compelling demands of corrective justice or what has been called "the rule of public policy which has first claim on the loyalty of the law: that wrongs should be remedied": *M (A Minor) v Newham London Borough Council* and *X (Minors) v Bedfordshire County Council* [1995] 2 AC 633, 663, per Sir Thomas Bingham MR. Sometimes cases may not obviously fall in one category or the other. Truly difficult cases arise.

3 In recent years four House of Lords decisions have been milestones in the evolution of this branch of the law and have helped to clarify the correct approach, without answering all the questions: *X (Minors) v Bedfordshire County Council, Stovin v Wise, Barrett v Enfield London Borough Council* and *Phelps v Hillingdon London Borough Council*. There are two comments on these decisions which I would make. First, except on a very careful study of these decisions, there is a principled distinction which is not always in the forefront of discussions. It is this: in a case founded on breach of statutory duty the central question is whether from the provisions and structure of the statute an intention can be gathered *to create a private law remedy?* In contradistinction in a case framed in negligence, against the background of a statutory duty or power, a basic question is whether the statute *excludes* a private law remedy? An assimilation of the two inquiries will sometimes produce wrong results.

4 The second point relates to observations of Lord Hoffmann in his landmark majority judgment in *Stovin v Wise*, to which Lord Hoffmann has made reference in his opinion.....

"In summary, therefore, I think that the minimum preconditions for basing a duty of care upon the existence of a statutory power, if it can be done at all, are, first, that it would in the circumstances have been irrational not to have exercised the power, so that there was in effect a public law duty to act, and secondly, that there are exceptional grounds for holding that the policy of the statute requires compensation to be paid to persons who suffer loss because the power was not exercised."

Since *Stovin v Wise* these observations have been qualified in *Barrett's* and *Phelps's* cases. I say that not because of the context of the actual decisions in those cases—in *Barrett's* case a council's duty to a child in care and in *Phelps's* case a duty of care in the educational field. Rather it is demonstrated by the legal analysis which prevailed in those decisions.

5 These qualifications of *Stovin v Wise* have been widely welcomed by academic lawyers. A notably careful and balanced analysis is that of Professor Paul Craig, *Administrative Law*, 5th ed (2003), pp 888–904. He stated, at p 898:

"There are many instances where a public body exercises discretion, but where the choices thus made are suited to judicial resolution. The mere presence of some species of discretion does not entail the conclusion that the matter is thereby non-justiciable. In the United States, it was once argued that the very existence of discretion rendered the decision immune from negligence. As one court scathingly said of such an argument, there can be discretion even in the hammering of a nail. Discretionary judgments made by public bodies, which the courts feel able to assess, should not therefore preclude the existence of negligence liability. This does not mean that the presence of such discretion will be irrelevant to the determination of liability. It will be of relevance in deciding whether there has been a breach of the duty of care. It is for this reason that the decisions in *Barrett* and *Phelps* are to be welcomed. Their Lordships recognised that justiciable discretionary choices would be taken into account in deciding whether the defendant had acted in breach of the duty of care. There may also be cases where some allegations of negligence are thought to be non-justiciable, while others may be felt suited to judicial resolution in accordance with the normal rules on breach."

Although the *result* in *Stovin v Wise* has been endorsed by the House of Lords in *Gorringe*, its narrow ambit has been clarified. Besides the specific conclusion that the local authority owed no duty to take positive steps to remove the hazard in *Stovin*, or to provide a warning in *Gorringe*, the cases hold that existence of a power or public law duty does not give rise to a duty to act at private law; and that there was no reason (for example, of general or specific reliance) to recognize a duty in such cases.

This means the cases should have no application in circumstances where positive steps are taken, such as *East Suffolk* itself. There is a lingering difficulty in that *East Suffolk* seems to have been applied in certain 'emergency cases', and one of these was referred to by Lord Hoffmann with approval in *Gorringe* (above). In this case, *Capital and Counties plc v Hampshire County Council* [1997] 1 QB 1004, the Court of Appeal held that a fire officer service attending a fire was not in a sufficient relationship of proximity with the owner of the premises to come under a duty of care. Their duties were owed to the public at large, even if they were in attendance. This conclusion was supported by the authority of *Alexandrou v Oxford* [1993] 4 All ER 328, in which it was held that no duty was owed by police officers to the owner or occupier of premises which they attended in response to a burglar alarm, on the basis of lack of proximity. Yet there *was* liability in a case where the fire brigade had not only attended and fought the fire, but also turned off the sprinkler system which was the plaintiffs' own defence against the spread of fire. The Court of Appeal clearly reasoned in terms of *East Suffolk*.

Compounding the problems, subsequently in *Kent v Griffiths* [2000] 2 WLR 1158, a different Court of Appeal thought there could be liability where an ambulance had failed to attend quickly, and no convincing reason or explanation was ever given. The consequence was that the claimant suffered very severe injury, which could have been avoided.[55] The court tried to distinguish between the ambulance service, as an element of a health service, and a fire service, but this distinction is not particularly convincing. *Kent v Griffiths* may illustrate the impact that a finding of fact can have upon a court: the action had proceeded to trial, and the judge had found that the ambulance crew had even attempted to falsify the records. Lord Woolf echoed the idea in *Barrett* that striking out should be exercised with restraint, and that the test for breach of duty will itself restrict the number of successful claims. This approach, as we have seen, has not generally found favour in recent years; although the decision of the Supreme Court in *Smith v Ministry of Defence*, explored below, suggests some renewed scope.

Compatible Private and Public Duties

The theme of *Stovin* and *Gorringe* is that the existence of a statutory power or broad statutory duty does not *provide a justification for* a positive duty to act at common law. If that duty is to arise, it must arise through the criteria of the *Caparo* test, in the more demanding form required by omissions liability. We have also noted that even outside the realm of *Stovin* and *Gorringe*, common law courts will often be reluctant to recognize a duty of care in negligence where it may conflict with or 'cut across' a 'statutory scheme'. In fact, as we will see in Chapter 10, this issue is not restricted to negligence, but arises also in relation to nuisance. There appear to be cases where the courts should 'stay off the field', which is occupied by public law. However, there have nevertheless been recent cases where duties—or the potential for duties—have been recognized even in a statutory context. Observing these exceptional cases is a good way of addressing the restrictions themselves.

Connor v Surrey County Council [2010] EWCA Civ 286; [2011] QB 328

This case concerned a *recognized* duty of care, namely that owed by an employer to an employee. That distinguishes it from cases where only the defendant's statutory duties could create proximity between the parties. Here, that proximity arose through the relationship of employer and employee.

The claimant was a head teacher who had been hounded into a mental breakdown through the concerted actions of a group within the school's Board of Governors. Powers to remove a dysfunctional Board of Governors and replace it with an interim executive board were available under the School Standards and Framework Act 1998. It is clear that employers owe a duty in respect of their employees' mental health, subject to the foreseeability of the harm (Section 1 of this chapter). In this case, however, the proposed *breach* of this recognized duty lay in the failure to exercise a statutory power *in order to protect* the claimant employee. The question raised was therefore whether a failure to exercise a power can amount to a breach of duty. There was no attempt to create a duty from a statutory power: the duty plainly existed at common law. All three members of the Court of Appeal agreed that such a claim could succeed. Despite some variety in their reasoning, the key was *compatibility* between the behaviour required to fulfil the duty of care in negligence, and the duties owed under the statute. Here, the public and private law duties did not pull against one another. In the words of Laws LJ, it was not a case where private law should 'stay off the field' ([106]). Sedley LJ made the important point that a possible conflict between statutory and private law duties is not uniquely confined to public authorities, agreeing that here the two were mutually reinforcing.

Sedley LJ, *Connor v Surrey CC*

117 This was a claim at common law for damages for negligence, built upon the duty of care which every contract and relationship of employment contains. The negligence alleged here was, in brief, that the claimant's authority as a headteacher and eventually her health and well being were unnecessarily and foreseeably put in jeopardy by the inaction of her employer in the face of a campaign to undermine her professional standing.

118 It is upon the adverb "unnecessarily" that this appeal turns. The council point out, rightly, that in addition to their contractual obligations as the employer of teachers in their schools, they have a series of public law functions to fulfil, and some of the latter may well be in tension with the former. This, Mr Edward Faulks QC submits, is what has happened here, and it exonerates the council from blame for the impact on Ms Connor ("the claimant") of what were undoubtedly distressing events.

119 It is equally true of many private employers that they have obligations – to shareholders, to the public, to regulators and so forth – which may pull against their obligations to their own staff. No employer, for example, can responsibly fail to investigate an allegation of fraud, even though it will plainly cause the employee concerned much stress. But it can be fairly said that the public law duties resting on a local education authority are larger and in many ways less manageable. Their performance, too, is controlled by an elected body which may act according to a political agenda. All of this is capable of producing legitimately different outcomes

where negligence is alleged in the public sphere of employment; but it does not alter the essential common law duty resting on an employer.

120 Surrey County Council found themselves faced with the unenviable task of responding in an equitable fashion to an inequitable campaign designed to capture a secular state school for a particular faith which happened to be that of a majority of the families whose children attended the school. Had this been a purely theological issue, the council's proper response would have been simple and straightforward; it was because there was a strong ethnic component that the issue became complicated.

121 Where, on the deputy judge's entirely justified findings, the council nevertheless went wrong was in temporising and compromising with this move instead of protecting the head, the staff and the school from it. What is critical in this case is that doing so would have been consonant both with their public law functions and with their private law obligations. We are not, in other words, considering a situation in which private law demanded one thing and public law demanded its opposite.

Protection from Others: Assumption of Responsibility

In *Mitchell v Glasgow City Council* [2009] UKHL 11; [2009] 1 AC 874, Lords Hope and Brown set out a range of cases where a defendant (in this instance a public authority) may owe a duty of care to an individual, to protect them from harm done by a third party. These are situations where:

(i)   the defendant created the risk or danger that the third party may cause harm;[56]

(ii)   the third party is under the control or supervision of the defendant, as in *Dorset Yacht v Home Office* ([1970] AC 1004); or

(iii)   the defendant assumed responsibility towards the claimant.

We saw in relation to pure economic losses, in the previous section, that an assumption of responsibility is sometimes treated as justifying a duty of care where none would otherwise exist. We also explained that the notion of duty arising from an 'assumption of responsibility' has come to be deployed outside the field of economic losses; and that it has been narrowly or broadly defined in different circumstances.

In the particular context of statutory powers and duties, it has been made clear that the exercise of a statutory power or duty in relation to the claimant cannot itself amount to an 'assumption of responsibility'. To be effective, an assumption of responsibility must be both *specific*, and to some degree *voluntary*.

Mitchell v Glasgow itself illustrates the point. The deceased was a tenant of the defendant council, and had been attacked by a fellow tenant and neighbour. The attacker had attended a meeting with the council where he had been told that he risked eviction following earlier threats to the deceased. He had previously attacked the home of the deceased with an iron bar, albeit some years previously, and had been threatening and abusive. The deceased had been given no warning of the meeting. The House of Lords held that no relevant duty of care had been owed to the deceased. There would generally be no duty to warn. Policy issues— particularly a desire not to prevent the authority from pursuing its essential social welfare

---

[56] An example of 'creating a danger' more generally is *Yetkin v Mahmood* [2010] EWCA Civ 776, where a highway authority had planted shrubs in a central reservation, obscuring pedestrians' view of the road.

functions—were to the fore, and such a duty was considered likely to be onerous. It was surmised that it would add complexity to an already sensitive process.[57] It was recognized that the usual approach may be overridden in the circumstances set out above. However, they were not present in this case. As Lord Rodger put it (at [63]), 'The pursuers point to no undertaking or other circumstance which would show that, exceptionally, the Council had made themselves responsible for protecting Mr Mitchell'.

This restrictive approach to finding an assumption of responsibility was followed by the Court of Appeal in *X & Y v Hounslow LBC* [2009] EWCA Civ 286. Here, the claimants were vulnerable adults and were subjected to abuse in their own flat by young people who were known to be entering their home. The Court of Appeal emphasized that a specific assumption of responsibility, by words or deeds, would need to be shown, if a duty to protect from others was to be established. Indeed, the court went so far as to suggest that a specific individual would need to have both assumed responsibility, and breached the duty, for the claim to be actionable. It is suggested that this is, to say the least, an unusual requirement where the defendant is an organization.

In *Michael v Chief Constable of South Wales and Another* [2015] UKSC 2, a general rule against omissions liability was treated as the key reason for denying a duty of care on the part of the police when failing to respond sufficiently quickly to an emergency call. We explore the significance of this in the next section. In Chapter 1, it was pointed out that in a range of circumstances, positive duties to act may also be imposed upon public authorities under the HRA, bringing into domestic law the positive duties imposed on States under the ECHR. The existence of these duties in parallel with the restrictive duties at common law is one element in the following discussion.

3.6 NEGLIGENCE AND THE DEVELOPMENT OF CONVENTION RIGHTS

Even before the advent of the HRA, the UK's obligations under the ECHR had made themselves felt in respect of liability in the tort of negligence, against State defendants, and most particularly the police. At that stage, when the Convention rights were not directly part of English law, it was largely Article 6 which was in issue, as it was argued (initially successfully) that the courts' invocation of policy reasons for restricting liability offended claimants' right to have their civil claim heard. That argument has largely been defeated now, although its after-effects are still to be seen. More recently, with direct liability on the part of public authorities under the HRA for failure to act compatibly with the rights (and sometimes, for failure to secure the rights), attention has moved to other Articles of the Convention. Claims under the HRA now often run parallel to negligence claims. Other issues relating to Convention rights have already been raised in this chapter (see the discussion of *D v East Berkshire*, above), and more are to be found in Chapters 2 (especially in respect of Article 5, Liberty); 10 (Article 1, First Protocol—property); and Chapters 13 and 14 (Articles 8 and 10, Privacy and expression). The approach to assessment of damages for breach of Convention rights under the HRA is explored in Chapter 8.

For present purposes, we begin by exploring the influence of Article 6, which has led the courts to avoid 'immunities' and, for a time, caused caution in striking out on policy

---

[57] For discussion of this '*in terrorem*' stance (seeking to avoid an assumed adverse impact on provision of public services), see R. Mullender, 'Negligence, Human Rights, and Public Bodies' (2009) 125 LQR 384.

grounds. We have already seen that such caution is no longer evident, but the history of Article 6 has nevertheless affected the current pattern of liabilities imposed upon public authorities. We will then turn our attention to the present role of substantive Convention rights, and most particularly Article 2 (Right to Life). The existence of positive duties to protect such rights arguably creates new pressures on the law of tort, as remedies for breach of the positive duty become more familiar in domestic courts. How far can policy arguments against private law duties in the same circumstances be maintained?

European Convention on Human Rights

Article 6 Right to a fair trial

1 In the determination of his civil rights and obligations or of any criminal charge against him, everyone is entitled to a fair and public hearing within a reasonable time by an independent and impartial tribunal established by law. . . .

Hill v Chief Constable of South Yorkshire Police [1989] 1 AC 53

The plaintiff's daughter was the final victim of a serial killer, Peter Sutcliffe, who had been preying on young single women in the area. The plaintiff argued that the police owed a duty to her daughter to conduct their investigation into the murders with reasonable care, that they had breached this duty, and that this had led to the death of her daughter. The House of Lords agreed with the first instance judge and with the Court of Appeal that no duty of care was owed, and the action was struck out.

After reviewing the applicable authorities including *Anns v Merton* and *Dorset Yacht v Home Office*, Lord Keith outlined two separate reasons why no duty of care could be established in this case. Either reason would be sufficient in its own right.

The first reason relates to lack of proximity between the parties. The second reason relates to *policy concerns. Hill* was decided by applying the two-stage test for the existence of a duty of care, under *Anns v Merton*. These reasons correspond with the two stages of *Anns*.

Lord Keith, at 62–3

In the instant case the identity of the wanted criminal was at the material time unknown and it is not averred that any full or clear description of him was ever available. The alleged negligence of the police consists in a failure to discover his identity. But if there is no general duty of care owed to individual members of the public by the responsible authorities to prevent the escape of a known criminal or to recapture him, there cannot reasonably be imposed upon any police force a duty of care similarly owed to identify and apprehend an unknown one. Miss Hill cannot for this purpose be regarded as a person at special risk simply because she was young and female. Where the class of potential victims of a particular habitual criminal is a large one the precise size of it cannot in principle affect the issue. All householders are potential victims of an habitual burglar, and all females those of an habitual rapist. The conclusion must be that although there existed reasonable foreseeability of likely harm to such as Miss Hill if Sutcliffe were not identified and apprehended, there is absent from the case any such ingredient or characteristic as led to the liability of the Home Office in the *Dorset Yacht* case. Nor is there present any additional characteristic such as might make up the deficiency. The circumstances of the case are therefore not capable of establishing a duty of care owed towards Miss Hill by the West Yorkshire Police.

That is sufficient for the disposal of the appeal. But in my opinion there is another reason why an action for damages in negligence should not lie against the police in circumstances such as those of the present case, and that is public policy. In *Yuen Kun Yeu v. Attorney-General of Hong Kong* [1988] A.C. 175, 193, I expressed the view that the category of cases where the second stage of Lord Wilberforce's two stage test in *Anns v. Merton London Borough Council* [1978] A.C. 728, 751–752 might fall to be applied was a limited one, one example of that category being *Rondel v. Worsley* [1969] 1 A.C. 191. Application of that second stage is, however, capable of constituting a separate and independent ground for holding that the existence of liability in negligence should not be entertained. Potential existence of such liability may in many instances be in the general public interest, as tending towards the observance of a higher standard of care in the carrying on of various different types of activity. I do not, however, consider that this can be said of police activities. The general sense of public duty which motivates police forces is unlikely to be appreciably reinforced by the imposition of such liability so far as concerns their function in the investigation and suppression of crime. From time to time they make mistakes in the exercise of that function, but it is not to be doubted that they apply their best endeavours to the performance of it. In some instances the imposition of liability may lead to the exercise of a function being carried on in a detrimentally defensive frame of mind. The possibility of this happening in relation to the investigative operations of the police cannot be excluded. Further it would be reasonable to expect that if potential liability were to be imposed it would be not uncommon for actions to be raised against police forces on the ground that they had failed to catch some criminal as soon as they might have done, with the result that he went on to commit further crimes. While some such actions might involve allegations of a simple and straightforward type of failure—for example that a police officer negligently tripped and fell while pursuing a burglar—others would be likely to enter deeply into the general nature of a police investigation, as indeed the present action would seek to do. The manner of conduct of such an investigation must necessarily involve a variety of decisions to be made on matters of policy and discretion, for example as to which particular line of inquiry is most advantageously to be pursued and what is the most advantageous way to deploy the available resources. Many such decisions would not be regarded by the courts as appropriate to be called in question, yet elaborate investigation of the facts might be necessary to ascertain whether or not this was so. A great deal of police time, trouble and expense might be expected to have to be put into the preparation of the defence to the action and the attendance of witnesses at the trial. The result would be a significant diversion of police manpower and attention from their most important function, that of the suppression of crime. Closed investigations would require to be reopened and retraversed, not with the object of bringing any criminal to justice but to ascertain whether or not they had been competently conducted. I therefore consider that Glidewell L.J., in his judgment in the Court of Appeal [1988] Q.B. 60, 76 in the present case, was right to take the view that the police were immune from an action of this kind on grounds similar to those which in *Rondel v. Worsley* [1969] 1 A.C. 191 were held to render a barrister immune from actions for negligence in his conduct of proceedings in court.

At the end of this catalogue of policy reasons, Lord Keith refers to the police as 'immune' from such an action. This was perhaps not the best terminology to use to summarize the preceding discussion. But the effect was reinforced by comparison with the barristers' immunity recognized in *Rondel v Worsley* [1969] 1 AC 191. That immunity was abolished in *Arthur JS Hall v Simons* [2002] 1 AC 615. The policy considerations had changed, as had the tort of negligence and the organization of the legal profession.[58] Having decided that policy arguments now weighed *against* the immunity, the House of Lords did not consider whether the immunity would be in violation of Article 6 of the ECHR. But it is probable that the barristers' immunity was considered to be under threat, given the European Court of Human Rights' decision in *Osman v UK*. In order to understand *Osman v UK*, it is necessary to examine the way that *Hill* was interpreted by the Court of Appeal in *Osman v Ferguson*, which led to the action against the UK.

Osman v Ferguson [1993] 4 All ER 344 (CA)

A school teacher (P) became obsessed with a 15-year-old pupil (O). Because of his conduct (including criminal damage, painting graffiti about O, and changing his name to Osman), he was dismissed from his job. He continued to harass O and his family. The police were aware of these events, and P had told police that he might 'do something criminally insane'. After further acts of aggression, of which the police were aware, P eventually followed O home, and shot him (causing serious injury) and his father (who was killed). P was convicted of manslaughter. O and his mother (for her husband's estate) brought an action in negligence against the police, for failing to arrest and charge P on the basis of what was known, therefore failing to prevent the shooting.

The Court of Appeal accepted that this case was different from *Hill*, in that it was arguable that there was *proximity* and indeed *a special relationship* between the parties.

McCowan J

Returning to the facts of the present case and again on the assumption that they are proved, it seems to me that it can well be said on behalf of the plaintiffs that the second plaintiff and his family were exposed to a risk from Paget-Lewis over and above that of the public at large. In my judgment the plaintiffs have therefore an arguable case that as between the second plaintiff and his family, on the one hand, and the investigating officers, on the other, there existed a very close degree of proximity amounting to a special relationship . . . .

The claim was struck out, however, because the policy arguments set out in *Hill* were thought to determine this case. The difficulty is that the judgments in *Hill* seem to have been interpreted as though they laid down a binding rule, that no action against the police could succeed in respect of 'investigation and suppression of crime'. The *Caparo* criteria were not considered afresh in relation to the facts of the case in hand. Rather, the conclusion in one case was seen as binding in another.

. . . Mr Hendy submitted that the present was a case depending on the decision of one or more difficult points of law and that we should therefore refuse to entertain the claim to strike out. I cannot agree. I consider this a plain and obvious case falling squarely within a House of Lords decision. I would therefore allow the appeal.

It is understandable that the European Court of Human Rights interpreted this *particular* case as disclosing an 'immunity'—not least because that word was used in *Hill* itself, and a

[58] We deal with the gradual erosion of immunities in the next section.

parallel was drawn with the true immunity, now discontinued, afforded to barristers in the conduct of a case.

Osman v UK
[1999] 1 FLR 193

(134) ... The applicants maintained that although they had established all the constituent elements of the duty of care, the Court of Appeal was constrained by precedent to apply the doctrine of police immunity developed by the House of Lords in the *Hill* case (see para (90) above) to strike out their statement of claim. In their view the doctrine of police immunity was not one of the essential elements of the duty of care as was claimed by the Government, but a separate and distinct ground for defeating a negligence action in order to ensure, inter alia, that police manpower was not diverted from their ordinary functions or to avoid overly cautious or defensive policing.

(135) The Commission agreed with the applicants that Art 6(1) was applicable. It considered that the applicants' claim against the police was arguably based on an existing right in domestic law, namely the general tort of negligence. The House of Lords in the *Hill* case modified that right for reasons of public policy in order to provide an immunity for the police from civil suit for their acts and omissions in the context of the investigation and suppression of crime. In the instant case, that immunity acted as a bar to the applicants' civil action by preventing them from having an adjudication by a court on the merits of their case against the police.

...

(139) ... the Court considers that the applicants must be taken to have had a right, derived from the law of negligence, to seek an adjudication on the admissibility and merits of an arguable claim that they were in a relationship of proximity to the police, that the harm caused was foreseeable and that in the circumstances it was fair, just and reasonable not to apply the exclusionary rule outlined in the *Hill* case. In the view of the Court the assertion of that right by the applicants is in itself sufficient to ensure the applicability of Art 6(1) of the Convention.

(140) For the above reasons, the Court concludes that Art 6(1) is applicable. It remains to be determined whether the restriction which was imposed on the exercise of the applicants' right under that provision was lawful.

The denial of the opportunity for adjudication was sufficient to *engage* Article 6(1). It did not mean in itself that Article 6 had been violated. This is because the general policy objective of *Hill* was legitimate. In finding that there was a violation of Article 6, the court had regard to the *proportionality* of the protection accorded to this policy objective, bearing in mind the gravity of the harm foreseeably suffered by the plaintiff,[59] *and* the way in which the immunity was interpreted in *Osman v Ferguson* itself:

[59] The relationship between Art 2 and Art 6 is interesting in this regard. There was no violation of Art 2, because there was no precise moment at which the police *should* clearly have acted. They could not be criticized, for example, for applying the presumption of innocence. But the gravity of the harm suffered (death and serious injury) was relevant to the way that the policy objectives behind the 'immunity' in tort law were fulfilled.

Osman v UK
[1999] 1 FLR 193

(149) The reasons which led the House of Lords in the *Hill* case to lay down an exclusionary rule to protect the police from negligence actions in the context at issue are based on the view that the interests of the community as a whole are best served by a police service whose efficiency and effectiveness in the battle against crime are not jeopardised by the constant risk of exposure to tortious liability for policy and operational decisions.

(150) Although the aim of such a rule may be accepted as legitimate in terms of the Convention, as being directed to the maintenance of the effectiveness of the police service and hence to the prevention of disorder or crime, the Court must nevertheless, in turning to the issue of proportionality, have particular regard to its scope and especially its application in the case at issue. While the Government have contended that the exclusionary rule of liability is not of an absolute nature (see para (144) above) and that its application may yield to other public policy considerations, it would appear to the Court that in the instant case the Court of Appeal proceeded on the basis that the rule provided a watertight defence to the police and that it was impossible to prise open an immunity which the police enjoy from civil suit in respect of their acts and omissions in the investigation and suppression of crime.

(151) The Court would observe that the application of the rule in this manner without further inquiry into the existence of competing public interest considerations only serves to confer a blanket immunity on the police for their acts and omissions during the investigation and suppression of crime and amounts to an unjustifiable restriction on an applicant's right to have a determination on the merits of his or her claim against the police in deserving cases.

Osman v UK has been criticized for its interpretation of the role of policy in the tort of negligence.[60] It is indeed incorrect to say that 'policy' is an additional factor, in addition to the *Caparo* criteria. It is a core part of those criteria. But *Hill* was decided in accordance with *Anns*, and the division of that test into two stages may understandably give the false impression that policy is an additional criterion. Lord Hoffmann, writing extra-judicially, was particularly trenchant about *Osman v UK*. His broader remarks have some continuing force despite the discrediting of *Osman* itself:

Rt Hon Lord Hoffmann, 'Human Rights and the House of Lords'
(1999) 62 MLR 159, at 164, 165–6

I am bound to say that this decision [*Osman v UK*] fills me with apprehension. Under the cover of an Article which says that everyone is entitled to have his civil rights and obligations determined by a tribunal, the European Court of Human Rights is taking upon itself to decide what the content of those civil rights should be. In so doing, it is challenging the autonomy of the courts and indeed the Parliament[61] of the United Kingdom to deal with what are essentially social welfare questions involving budgetary limits and efficient public administration . . . .

---

60 *See* C. Gearty, 'Unravelling *Osman*' (2001) 64 MLR 159.

61 Note that subsequently, in *Roche v UK* (see later), the European Court of Human Rights has accepted (albeit only by a majority) that a statutory immunity from civil action does not violate Art 6.

Of course it is true that the Strasbourg court acknowledges the fact that often there is no right answer by allowing what it calls a 'margin of appreciation' to the legislature or courts of a member State. Within limits, they are allowed to differ. And, as I have said, I accept that there is an irreducible minimum of human rights which must be universally true. But most of the jurisprudence which comes out of Strasbourg is not about the irreducible minimum.... The *Osman* case, dealing with the substantive civil law right to financial compensation for not receiving the benefit of a social service, is as far as one can imagine from basic human rights.... .

Notice that here Lord Hoffmann argues that the right to compensation for not receiving the benefit of a social service (protection from crime) is a matter *not* of human rights, but of 'social welfare', involving budgetary constraints. His opinion of the European Court of Human Rights did not appear to mellow once *Z v UK* altered the approach to negligence.[62]

On the other hand, certain criticisms of *Osman v Ferguson* itself are well made. The Court of Appeal in that decision did indeed seem to interpret the immunity in *Hill* as if it were a general rule to be applied in all cases of 'investigation and suppression of crime', without regard to the precise facts of the case. Subsequent cases such as *Barrett v Enfield* (and *Brooks v Commissioner of the Metropolis*, below) have adopted a much more nuanced approach to the policy issues and courts will not so readily translate—let alone 'apply'—policy arguments developed in one case, in order to dispose of a quite different case.

Z v UK [2001] 2 FLR 612

The losing plaintiffs in *X v Bedfordshire* commenced proceedings against the UK, alleging violations of Articles 3, 6, 8, and 13 of the Convention. Importantly, the European Court of Human Rights accepted that it had been mistaken in the earlier case of *Osman v UK* as to the role of policy in the tort of negligence. The Court concluded that no 'immunity' was applied in *X v Bedfordshire* itself. There was therefore no violation of Article 6. This conclusion was assisted by consideration of *Barrett v Enfield* and other later cases. In the rush to note that *Osman* has been discredited on the 'immunity' point, it is easy to overlook that this has happened partly because courts have become careful not to be seen to apply 'blanket' policy reasoning; and to treat 'policy' as part and parcel of the general *Caparo* test.

In the following passage, the Court considers the policy reasoning in *X v Bedfordshire*.

European Court of Human Rights, *Z v UK*

1. Nor is the Court persuaded by the suggestion that, irrespective of the position in domestic law, the decision disclosed an immunity in fact or practical effect due to its allegedly sweeping or blanket nature. That decision concerned only one aspect of the exercise of local authorities' powers and duties and cannot be regarded as an arbitrary removal of the courts'

---

[62] 'The Universality of Human Rights' (2009) 125 LQR 416–32.

jurisdiction to determine a whole range of civil claims (see Fayed v. the United Kingdom judgment of 21 September 1994, Series A no. 294, pp. 49–50, § 65). As it has recalled above in paragraph 87 it is a principle of Convention case-law that Article 6 does not in itself guarantee any particular content for civil rights and obligations in national law, although other Articles such as those protecting the right to respect for family life (Article 8) and the right to property (Article 1 of Protocol No. 1) may do so. It is not enough to bring Article 6 § 1 into play that the non-existence of a cause of action under domestic law may be described as having the same effect as an immunity, in the sense of not enabling the applicant to sue for a given category of harm.

2. Furthermore, it cannot be said that the House of Lords came to its conclusion without a careful balancing of the policy reasons for and against the imposition of liability on the local authority in the circumstances of the applicants' case. Lord Browne-Wilkinson in his leading judgment in the House of Lords acknowledged that the public policy principle that wrongs should be remedied required very potent counter considerations to be overridden (see paragraph 46 above). He weighed that principle against the other public policy concerns in reaching the conclusion that it was not fair, just or reasonable to impose a duty of care on the local authority in the applicants' case. It may be noted that in subsequent cases the domestic courts have further defined this area of law concerning the liability of local authorities in child care matters, holding that a duty of care may arise in other factual situations, where, for example, a child has suffered harm once in local authority care or a foster family has suffered harm as a result of the placement in their home by the local authority of an adolescent with a history of abusing younger children (see W and Others v. Essex County Council and Barrett v. Enfield LBC . . .).

3. The applicants, and the Commission in its report, relied on the Osman case (cited above) as indicating that the exclusion of liability in negligence, in that case concerning the acts or omissions of the police in the investigation and prevention of crime, acted as a restriction on access to court. The Court considers that its reasoning in the Osman judgment was based on an understanding of the law of negligence (see, in particular, paragraphs 138 and 139 of the Osman judgment) which has to be reviewed in the light of the clarifications subsequently made by the domestic courts and notably the House of Lords. The Court is satisfied that the law of negligence as developed in the domestic courts since the case of Caparo, and as recently analysed in the case of Barrett v. Enfield LBC, includes the fair, just and reasonable criterion as an intrinsic element of the duty of care and that the ruling of law concerning that element in this case does not disclose the operation of an immunity. In the present case, the Court is led to the conclusion that the inability of the applicants to sue the local authority flowed not from an immunity but from the applicable principles governing the substantive right of action in domestic law. There was no restriction on access to court of the kind contemplated in the Ashingdane judgment . . . .

The Court held that there were violations of Articles 3 and 13 in this case. We have already explored the impact of this in domestic law, via the HRA, when we considered D v East Berkshire (earlier).

Brooks v Commissioner of Police for the Metropolis [2005] 1 WLR 1495

In this case the House of Lords considered whether Hill v Chief Constable can be followed, without falling foul of Article 6. The essential facts and background to the case are encapsulated in the first paragraph of Lord Bingham's judgment.[63] In paragraph two, Lord Bingham also sets out the three specific duties argued for by the claimant.

Lord Bingham, *Brooks v Commissioner of Police for the Metropolis*
[2005] UKHL 24; [2005] 1 WLR 1495

1 My Lords, Duwayne Brooks, the respondent, was present when his friend Stephen Lawrence was abused and murdered in the most notorious racist killing which our country has ever known. He also was abused and attacked. However well this crime had been investigated by the police and however sensitively he had himself been treated by the police, the respondent would inevitably have been deeply traumatised by his experience on the night of the murder and in the days and weeks which followed. But unfortunately, as established by the public inquiry into the killing (The Stephen Lawrence Inquiry: Report of an Inquiry by Sir William Macpherson of Cluny (1999)) (Cm 4262–I), the investigation was very badly conducted and the respondent himself was not treated as he should have been. He issued proceedings against the Metropolitan Police Commissioner and a number of other parties, all but one of whom were police officers.

2 ...the only issue before the House is whether, assuming the facts pleaded by the respondent to be true, the Commissioner and the officers for whom he is responsible arguably owed the respondent a common law duty sounding in damages to (1) take reasonable steps to assess whether the respondent was a victim of crime and then to accord him reasonably appropriate protection, support, assistance and treatment if he was so assessed; (2) take reasonable steps to afford the respondent the protection, assistance and support commonly afforded to a key eye-witness to a serious crime of violence; (3) afford reasonable weight to the account that the respondent gave and to act upon it accordingly.

Lord Steyn

27 Since the decision in *Hill's* case there have been developments which affect the reasoning of that decision in part. In *Hill's* case the House relied on the barrister's immunity enunciated in *Rondel v Worsley* [1969] 1 AC 191. That immunity no longer exists: *Arthur J S Hall & Co v Simons* [2002] 1 AC 615. More fundamentally since the decision of the European Court of Human Rights in *Z v United Kingdom* (2001) 34 EHRR 97, 138, para 100, it would be best for the principle in *Hill's* case to be reformulated in terms of the absence of a duty of care rather than a blanket immunity.

28 With hindsight not every observation in *Hill's* case [1989] AC 53 can now be supported. Lord Keith of Kinkel observed, at p 63, that

"From time to time [the police] make mistakes in the exercise of that function, but it is not to be doubted that they apply their best endeavours to the performance of it".

Nowadays, a more sceptical approach to the carrying out of all public functions is necessary.

29 Counsel for the Commissioner concedes that cases of assumption of responsibility under the extended *Hedley Byrne* doctrine (*Hedley Byrne & Co Ltd v Heller & Partner Ltd* [1964] AC 465) fall outside the principle in *Hill's* case. In such cases there is no need to

---

[63] A longer exploration of the mistreatment of the claimant by investigating officers is to be found in the judgment of Lord Steyn.

embark on an inquiry whether it is "fair, just and reasonable" to impose liability for economic loss: *Williams v Natural Life Health Foods Ltd* [1998] 1 WLR 830.

30 But the core principle of *Hill's* case has remained unchallenged in our domestic jurisprudence and in European jurisprudence for many years. If a case such as the Yorkshire Ripper case, which was before the House in *Hill's* case, arose for decision today I have no doubt that it would be decided in the same way. It is, of course, desirable that police officers should treat victims and witnesses properly and with respect: compare the Police (Conduct) Regulations 2004 (SI 2004/645). But to convert that ethical value into general legal duties of care on the police towards victims and witnesses would be going too far. The prime function of the police is the preservation of the Queen's peace. The police must concentrate on preventing the commission of crime; protecting life and property; and apprehending criminals and preserving evidence: see section 29 of the Police Act 1996, read with Schedule 4 as substituted by section 83 of the Police Reform Act 2002; section 17 of the Police (Scotland) Act 1967; *Halsbury's Laws of England*, 4th ed reissue (1999), vol 36(1), para 524; *The Laws of Scotland, Stair Memorial Encyclopaedia*, vol 16, (1995), para 1784; *Moylan, Scotland Yard and the Metropolitan Police*, (1929), p 34. A retreat from the principle in *Hill's* case would have detrimental effects for law enforcement. Whilst focusing on investigating crime, and the arrest of suspects, police officers would in practice be required to ensure that in every contact with a potential witness or a potential victim time and resources were deployed to avoid the risk of causing harm or offence. Such legal duties would tend to inhibit a robust approach in assessing a person as a possible suspect, witness or victim. By placing general duties of care on the police to victims and witnesses the police's ability to perform their public functions in the interests of the community, fearlessly and with despatch, would be impeded. It would, as was recognised in *Hill's* case, be bound to lead to an unduly defensive approach in combating crime.

On a cynical day, one might say that the only difference between this approach, and *Hill* itself, is the emphasis on the possibility of 'extreme cases' (indicating that this is not a case of 'blanket' policy thinking), and the change in language from 'immunity', to 'no duty'. But Lord Steyn also makes the fundamentally important point that it is not always appropriate for individuals' claims in tort to succeed, without regard to the impact on broader interests. The HRA, like the European Convention on Human Rights itself, in no way requires that individual interests should always prevail over community interests. This interpretation of the Convention rights is further illustrated in Chapter 13, in respect of defamation and Chapter 2, in connection with false imprisonment.

So far as the law of tort is concerned, the question that arises after *Brooks* is whether there is any scope for a duty on the part of the police to prevent harm being caused to a claimant. If not, then the denial of duty looks very much like immunity by a different name. Now that the HRA is in force, a subsidiary question is under what circumstances a similar duty arises under that Act. This brings us to a particularly significant issue in the current development of the law.

Positive Duties to Protect Convention Rights

Following *Osman v UK*, a positive duty under Article 2 will be owed by states—and, under the HRA, by a relevant public authority—when that public authority knows or ought reasonably to know that there is an imminent threat to the life of the victim. This positive duty to protect life is not expressly set out in Article 2 itself, but has become well established. There is more than one positive duty under Article 2, as Lord Dyson explains.

Lord Dyson, *Rabone v Pennine Care NHS Trust*
[2012] UKSC 2

12 ... I need to set the scene by making a few introductory comments about article 2 of the Convention which provides: "Everyone's right to life shall be protected by law." These few words have been interpreted by the European Court of Human Rights ("the ECtHR" or "Strasbourg") as imposing three distinct duties on the state: (i) a negative duty to refrain from taking life save in the exceptional circumstances described in article 2.2; (ii) a positive duty to conduct a proper and open investigation into deaths for which the state might be responsible; and (iii) a positive duty to protect life in certain circumstances. This latter positive duty contains two distinct elements. The first is a general duty on the state "to put in place a legislative and administrative framework designed to provide effective deterrence against threats to the right to life": see *Öneryıldız v Turkey* (2004) 41 EHRR 325, para 89 applying, mutatis mutandis, what the court said in *Osman v United Kingdom* (1998) 29 EHRR 245, para 115. The second is what has been called the "operational duty" which was also articulated by the court in the Osman case. This was a case about the alleged failure of the police to protect the Osman family who had been subjected to threats and harassment from a third party, culminating in the murder of Mr Osman and the wounding of his son. The court said that in "well-defined circumstances" the state should take "appropriate steps" to safeguard the lives of those within its jurisdiction including a positive obligation to take "preventative operational measures" to protect an individual whose life is at risk from the criminal acts of another: para 115. At para 116, the court went on to say that the positive obligation must be interpreted "in a way which does not impose an impossible or disproportionate burden on the authorities". In a case such as Osman, therefore, there will be a breach of the positive obligation where:

"the authorities knew or ought to have known at the time of the existence of a real and immediate risk to the life of an identified individual or individuals from the criminal acts of a third party and that they failed to take measures within the scope of their powers which, judged reasonably, might have been expected to avoid that risk." (See para 116.)

In *Mitchell v Glasgow City Council* [2009] UKHL 11, as we have seen, there was considered to have been no reason for the defendants to apprehend an imminent threat to the life of the claimant, and there was no actionable failure to respect the Article 2 rights of the deceased. A similar result was found in the following case, decided by the House of Lords shortly before *Mitchell*. But, as we will see, the range of circumstances in which the operational duty to protect life will be recognized both by Strasbourg, and by our domestic courts, has subsequently appeared to expand. The landscape has changed markedly in a short time where positive duties to protect Convention rights are concerned.

Van Colle v Chief Constable of the Hertfordshire Police and *Smith v Chief Constable of the Sussex Police* [2008] UKHL 50; [2009] 1 AC 225

In these joined appeals, the House of Lords considered two different sources of duty—common law and the HRA—in connection with failures to prevent attacks on the claimants. The *Van Colle* claim was argued only under the HRA, on the basis of a failure to secure the Article 2 right to life. This claim failed, because there were insufficient grounds to apprehend an imminent threat to the life of the subject. The proposed involvement of the defendants in creating the danger to the deceased, in that he was due to appear as a witness in a criminal trial and was murdered by the accused, did not in any sense lower the threshold for application of the *Osman* test, which was invariable. In *Van Colle v UK* (2013) 56 EHRR 23, the European Court of Human Rights came to the same conclusion: the risk factors were lower than in *Osman* itself.

The *Smith* case by contrast was argued only in negligence at common law. Here, the claimant had been attacked and seriously injured by his former partner. He had clearly apprehended the threat that this former partner posed to him and had disclosed this to police. The claim therefore was that they had ample reason to arrest his attacker, and owed a duty to the claimant to do so. This is a similar case to *Osman v Ferguson*.[64] Its resolution should clearly indicate whether intervening developments have altered the blanket nature of the *Hill* policy concerns.

If the policy arguments set out in *Hill* and more selectively adopted in *Brooks* allowed for any exceptions on the basis of proximity or clear identification of the likelihood of attack by an identified assailant,[65] one would have thought that *Smith* was that case. Equally, if common law duties were still expanding under the influence of the Convention rights, then this case (where there surely might have been reasonable grounds to apprehend an attack) should stand a chance of success. The House, however, held that no duty of care arose.

Lord Bingham, in dissent, would have recognized a duty on the police in this case. His view on the separation of common law and Convention rights is far less stark than the majority view.

Lord Bingham (dissenting)

58. ... It seems to me clear, on the one hand, that the existence of a Convention right cannot call for instant manufacture of a corresponding common law right where none exists: see *Wainwright v Home Office* [2003] UKHL 53, [2004] 2 AC 406. On the other hand, one would ordinarily be surprised if conduct which violated a fundamental right or freedom of the individual did not find a reflection in a body of law ordinarily as sensitive to human needs as the common law, and it is demonstrable that the common law in some areas has evolved in a direction signalled by the Convention: see the judgment of the Court of Appeal in *D v East Berkshire Community NHS Trust* [2003] EWCA Civ 1151, [2004] QB 558, paras 55–88. There are likely to be persisting differences between the two regimes, in relation (for example) to limitation periods and, probably, compensation. But I agree with Pill LJ in the present case (para 53) that "there is a strong case for developing the common law action for negligence in the light of Convention rights" and also with Rimer LJ (para 45) that "where a common law duty covers the same ground as a Convention right, it should, so far as practicable, develop in harmony with it". Since there is no reliance on the Convention in this case I do not think it profitable to consider whether, had he chosen to do so in time, Mr Smith could have established a breach of article 2 on the facts of this case.

Lord Bingham proposed a 'liability principle' which reflects the content of the Convention right to life. He was prepared to say there was an 'assumption of responsibility', if that was thought necessary.

[64] Lord Brown made the point that this was an exceptional case—but that, at the time of *Osman v Ferguson*, he thought that was an exceptional case too.
[65] It seems clear that there is a recognized exception in the case of a voluntary assumption of responsibility, just as in omissions liability generally.

Lord Bingham (dissenting)

44. Differing with regret from my noble and learned friends, I consider that the Court of Appeal were right, although I would go further: if the pleaded facts are established, the Chief Constable did owe Mr Smith a duty of care. The question whether there was a breach of that duty cannot be addressed until the defence is heard. I would hold that if a member of the public (A) furnishes a police officer (B) with apparently credible evidence that a third party whose identity and whereabouts are known presents a specific and imminent threat to his life or physical safety, B owes A a duty to take reasonable steps to assess such threat and, if appropriate, take reasonable steps to prevent it being executed. I shall for convenience of reference call this 'the liability principle'.

This principle was not accepted by the other members of the House. Lord Hope concluded that the policy goals served by *Hill* and *Brooks* could not be secured if duty depended on a case-by-case analysis. There needed to be a clear and general denial of duty. This would appear to be the very sort of 'immunity' based on policy considerations, rather than proximity, which was applied in *Osman v Ferguson*. It stands in contrast to Lord Hope's own judgment in relation to service personnel in the later case of *Smith v Ministry of Defence* (extracted later in this section).

Lord Hope

75. The phrase "the interests of the whole community" was echoed in the last sentence of the passage which I have quoted from Lord Steyn's opinion in *Brooks*. There is an echo too in *Brooks* of the warning against yielding to arguments based on civil liberties: see the first sentence of that quotation where he warns against a retreat from the core principle. The point that he was making in *Brooks*, in support of the core principle in *Hill*, was that the principle had been enunciated in the interests of the whole community. Replacing it with a legal principle which focuses on the facts of each case would amount, in Lord Steyn's words, to a retreat from the core principle. We must be careful not to allow ourselves to be persuaded by the shortcomings of the police in individual cases to undermine that principle. That was the very thing that he was warning against, because of the risks that this would give rise to. As Ward LJ said in *Swinney v Chief Constable of Northumbria Police Force* [1997] QB 464, 487, the greater public good outweighs any individual hardship. A principle of public policy that applies generally may be seen to operate harshly in some cases, when they are judged by ordinary delictual principles. Those are indeed the cases where, as Lord Steyn put it, the interests of the wider community must prevail over those of the individual.

Lord Brown emphatically proposed that there was no need for common law to develop in such cases. He argued, like Lord Hope, that such claims were much better ruled out 'on a class basis', since cases far less meritorious than the one before the House would be brought if the doors were opened to this claim. He also, like Lord Hope, emphasized that on occasion, individuals will lose out in their civil claims in order to benefit the public. *Caparo* itself was an instance of this. Lord Bingham's view was that the content of basic human rights guarantees should be reflected in domestic law, and that such rights are rather different from the kind of interest that the claimants in *Caparo* sought to protect. By contrast, the existence of a remedy under the HRA is a vital link in Lord Brown's argument: given the existence of liabilities under the HRA, development of the common law is 'simply unnecessary'. The question is, which view will prevail over time? Will policy reasons for restraining the tort of negligence continue to be invoked, even as claims in respect of positive duties under Article 2 become increasingly familiar? The following case makes an important contribution to the developments described here.

Michael v Chief Constable of South Wales Police [2015] UKSC 2

The victim was murdered by her former partner. She had made an emergency call to the police on her mobile phone, saying that the former partner had found her at her home with another man and had left to take him home, but that she said he would kill her, and hit her. She also mentioned that he had said he would kill her, but this was not logged by the operator. The call, which was passed from one police force to another, was initially categorized as a high priority requiring attendance within five minutes; but was downgraded to a lower priority level, requiring a response within sixty minutes. Fifteen minutes after the initial call, the victim called the police again and was heard to scream, and was found to have been stabbed to death. The claim was brought both in negligence, and under the HRA 1998.

The majority found that no duty of care was owed in negligence. This might be seen as merely a further illustration of the principles developed from *Hill* to *Van Colle*. However, the majority judgment of Lord Toulson is notable for its reliance not on policy discussion particular to the police force or public authorities; but on general principles of negligence. Thus, the key issue where the duty of care was concerned was that it was a case of *omissions liability*; the question therefore was not whether the police should benefit from particular protection; but whether an exceptional liability should be imposed upon them.

Lord Toulson JSC, *Michael v Chief Constable of South Wales Police and Another* [2015] UKSC 2

Issues 1 and 2: did the police owe a duty of care to Ms Michael on receiving her 999 call?

97 English law does not as a general rule impose liability on a defendant (D) for injury or damage to the person or property of a claimant (C) caused by the conduct of a third party (T): *Smith v Littlewoods Organisation Ltd* [1987] AC 241, 270 (a Scottish appeal in which a large number of English and Scottish cases were reviewed). The fundamental reason, as Lord Goff explained, is that the common law does not generally impose liability for pure omissions. It is one thing to require a person who embarks on action which may harm others to exercise care. It is another matter to hold a person liable in damages for failing to prevent harm caused by someone else.

98 The rule is not absolute. Apart from statutory exceptions, there are two well recognised types of situation in which the common law may impose liability for a careless omission.

99 The first is where D was in a position of control over T and should have foreseen the likelihood of T causing damage to somebody in close proximity if D failed to take reasonable care in the exercise of that control. The *Dorset Yacht case* [1970] AC 1004 is the classic example, and in that case Lord Diplock set close limits to the scope of the liability. As Tipping J explained in *Couch v Attorney General* [2008] 3 NZLR 725, this type of case requires careful analysis of two special relationships, the relationship between D and T and the relationship between D and C. I would not wish to comment on Tipping J's formulation of the criteria for establishing the necessary special relationship between D and C without further argument. It

is unnecessary to do so in this case, since Ms Michael's murderer was not under the control of the police, and therefore there is no question of liability under this exception.

100 The second general exception applies where D assumes a positive responsibility to safeguard C under the Hedley Byrne principle, as explained by Lord Goff in *Spring v Guardian Assurance plc* [1995] 2 AC 296 . It is not a new principle. It embraces the relationships in which a duty to take positive action typically arises: contract, fiduciary relationships, employer and employee, school and pupil, health professional and patient. The list is not exhaustive. This principle is the basis for the claimants' main submission, to which I will come (issue 3). There has sometimes been a tendency for courts to use the expression "assumption of responsibility" when in truth the responsibility has been imposed by the court rather than assumed by D. It should not be expanded artificially.

101 These general principles have been worked out for the most part in cases involving private litigants, but they are equally applicable where D is a public body. *Mitchell v Glasgow City Council* [2009] AC 874 is a good example. The victim and T were secure tenants of D and were next door neighbours. On a number of occasions T directed abuse and threats to kill at the victim, which he reported to D. D summoned T to a meeting and threatened him with eviction, without informing the victim. Soon afterwards T attacked the victim, causing fatal injuries. The victim's widow and daughter sued D, alleging negligence in failing to warn him of the meeting with T. The House of Lords held that D was not under a duty to do so, applying the principle in *Smith v Littlewoods Organisation Ltd* [1987] AC 241. It rejected the pursuers' arguments that D's relationship with its tenant T was analogous to the relationship of D and T in the *Dorset Yacht case* [1970] AC 1004 or that D assumed a responsibility to protect the victim from T. Mere foreseeability was not enough.

In the above extract, Lord Toulson expressly moves from cases involving private parties, to cases involving public authorities. In making this move, policy is relevant in the sense that there ought to be a compelling reason to override the general rule against omissions liability in this particular instance.

Lord Toulson, *Michael v Chief Constable of South Wales*

113 . . . it is a feature of our system of government that many areas of life are subject to forms of state controlled licensing, regulation, inspection, intervention and assistance aimed at protecting the general public from physical or economic harm caused by the activities of other members of society (or sometimes from natural disasters). Licensing of firearms, regulation of financial services, inspections of restaurants, factories and children's nurseries, and enforcement of building regulations are random examples. To compile a comprehensive list would be virtually impossible, because the systems designed to protect the public from harm of one kind or another are so extensive.

114 It does not follow from the setting up of a protective system from public resources that if it fails to achieve its purpose, through organisational defects or fault on the part of an individual, the public at large should bear the additional burden of compensating a victim for harm caused by the actions of a third party for whose behaviour the state is not responsible. To impose such a burden would be contrary to the ordinary principles of the common law.

115 The refusal of the courts to impose a private law duty on the police to exercise reasonable care to safeguard victims or potential victims of crime, except in cases where there has been a representation and reliance, does not involve giving special treatment to the police. It is consistent with the way in which the common law has been applied to other authorities vested with powers or duties as a matter of public law for the protection of the public. Examples at the highest level include *Yuen Kun Yeu v Attorney General of Hong Kong* [1988] AC 175 and *Davis v Radcliffe* [1990] 1 WLR 821 (no duty of care owed by financial regulators towards investors), *Murphy v Brentwood District Council* [1991] 1 AC 398 (no duty of care owed to the owner of a house with defective foundations by the local authority which passed the plans), *Stovin v Wise* [1996] AC 923 and *Gorringe v Calderdale Metropolitan Borough Council* [2004] 1 WLR 1057 (no duty of care owed by a highway authority to take action to prevent accidents from known hazards).

116 The question is therefore not whether the police should have a special immunity, but whether an exception should be made to the ordinary application of common law principles which would cover the facts of the present case.

117 Ms Monaghan has advanced essentially two arguments in support of the interveners' liability principle. The first is that the nature and scale of the problem of domestic violence is such that the courts ought to introduce such a principle to provide protection for victims and a spur to the police to respond to the problem more effectively. The second is that the common law should be extended in harmony with the obligations of the police under articles 2 and 3 of the Convention.

Lord Toulson and the majority rejected both of the arguments referred to in the final paragraph above. Yet this might have seemed a strong case for an assumption of responsibility: the victim had, after all, spoken directly to an operator. The treatment was brief, and it seems that the argument for an assumption was rejected because no *assurances* were given about the speed of response, nor instructions given. This appears a rather narrow reading of the 'assumption of responsibility':

Lord Toulson, *Michael v Chief Constable of South Wales*

138 Mr Bowen submitted that what was said by the Gwent call handler who received Ms Michael's 999 call was arguably sufficient to give rise to an assumption of responsibility on the Hedley Byrne principle as amplified in *Spring v Guardian Assurance plc* [1995] 2 AC 296. I agree with the Court of Appeal that the argument is not tenable. The only assurance which the call handler gave to Ms Michael was that she would pass on the call to the South Wales Police. She gave no promise how quickly they would respond. She told Ms Michael that they would want to call her back and asked her to keep her phone free, but this did not amount to advising or instructing her to remain in her house, as was suggested. Ms Michael's call was made on her mobile phone. Nor did the call handler's inquiry whether Ms Michael could lock the house amount to advising or instructing her to remain there. The case is very different from *Kent v Griffiths* [2001] QB 36 where the call handler gave misleading assurances that an ambulance would be arriving shortly.

In dissent, Lord Kerr disagreed with the starting point of Lord Toulson's analysis, namely that the authorities indicate a general rule that there is no liability for omissions. For Lord Kerr, the critical feature of the case which was overlooked by Lord Toulson was the proximity of relationship between the victim, and the defendant. Lord Kerr also explored the policy reasons behind cases such as *Hill* and *Brooks*, and argued that they were not compelling.

Lord Kerr's approach recognizably derives from *Caparo v Dickman*. Lord Toulson by contrast avoided reliance on *Caparo*, arguing instead as we have seen from the position in respect of omissions liability particularly.

In the remainder of this section, we will explore expansion in the positive duties under Articles 2 and 3 ECHR that are recognized by English courts. Before leaving *Michael*, we extract Lord Toulson's reasons for rejecting the second argument, that common law should develop in harmony with the positive duties under Articles 2 and 3. Lord Toulson conceded that tort law had developed significantly in response to HRA through the development of privacy actions (Chapter 14), but continued as follows:

Lord Toulson, *Michael v Chief Constable of South Wales*

125 The circumstances of the present case are different. The suggested development of the law of negligence is not necessary to comply with articles 2 and 3. On orthodox common law principles I cannot see a legal basis for fashioning a duty of care limited in scope to that of articles 2 and 3, or for gold plating the claimant's Convention rights by providing compensation on a different basis from the claim under the Human Rights Act 1998. Nor do I see a principled legal basis for introducing a wider duty in negligence than would arise either under orthodox common law principles or under the Convention.

126 The same argument, that the common law should be developed in harmony with the obligations of public bodies including the police under the Human Rights Act 1998 and articles 2 and 3 of the Convention, was advanced in the *Smith* case [2009] AC 225 as a ground for holding that the police owed a duty of care to the deceased after he reported receiving threats. Reliance was similarly placed on the approach of the Court of Appeal in *D v East Berkshire Community NHS Trust* [2004] QB 558 (as noted by Lord Phillips MR, who had delivered the judgment of the Court of Appeal in that case). Counsel for Mr Smith relied particularly on the analysis of the effect of the Human Rights Act 1998 in *D v East Berkshire Community NHS Trust*, at paras 55–87: see the reported argument [2009] AC 225, 240. The argument by analogy with that case which presently commends itself to Baroness Hale DPSC is therefore not a new argument, but one which failed to persuade the majority in the Smith case.

127 The argument was rejected by the House of Lords for reasons given by Lord Hope (paras 81–82), Lord Phillips (paras 98–99) and most fully by Lord Brown: paras 136–139. Lord Brown did not consider that the possibility of a Human Rights Act claim was a good reason for creating a parallel common law claim, still less for creating a wider duty of care. He observed that Convention claims had different objectives from civil actions, as Lord Bingham pointed out in *R (Greenfield) v Secretary of State for the Home Department* [2005] 1 WLR 673. Whereas civil actions are designed essentially to compensate claimants for losses, Convention claims are intended to uphold minimum human rights standards and to vindicate those rights. The difference in purpose has led to different time limits and different approaches to damages and causation. Lord Brown recognised that the violation of a fundamental right is a very serious thing, but he saw no sound reason for matching the Convention claim with a common law claim. To do so would in his view neither add to the vindication of the right, nor be likely to deter the police from the action or inaction which risked violating it in the first place.

Lord Toulson suggests here that the functions of HRA claims and tort claims are very different; and that there is no reason for tort to develop in order to provide remedies that are often more generous than those under HRA ('gold-plating'). In discussing the decision in *Michael*, Nick McBride has suggested that whether this is persuasive depends on one's approach both to the functions of the law of tort (which many recognize as capable of protecting rights); and to what is required to protect rights effectively. Does common law appear to fall short of the more 'ambitious' rights recognized through the Human Rights Act, and if so is this a defect that needs correcting? If the Human Rights Act were to be repealed, would common law once again expand to create remedies for similar wrongs? The 'uniform' approach mentioned here by McBride refers to an approach which treats public bodies, like the police, as owing the same duties as any other defendant.

Nick McBride, '*Michael* and the Future of Tort Law' (2016) PN 14

If the ambitious view of what positive human rights we have against the state is correct, then it does indeed follow that the common law of negligence - as set out in *Michael* - is backward in adopting a uniform approach to determining when a public body owes us a duty of care to save us from harm. If, on the other hand, the personalist view is correct, then it is cases like *Osman* that have taken a wrong turn and that need to be hauled back so that a public body only comes under a positive obligation under the ECHR (and, by extension, the HRA) where it knows someone is in serious danger of suffering serious harm, and even then the only duty it will come under is a duty to try to save that person from harm, not a duty to take care that it does so. And if the contractual view is correct, nothing need change - while the decision in *Michael* was correct to have adopted a uniform approach to determining what rights we have against the state under the common law of negligence, so long as the UK government binds itself to the mast of the ECHR by keeping the HRA in force, it must follow the ECHR ship wherever the decisions of the ECtHR take it.

For the time being, the difference between negligence duties, and the more ambitious duties under the HRA, is well illustrated by *Michael*, since a claim under the HRA was said to depend upon determination of the facts of the case, so that it should go to trial. Also significant is *DSD v Commissioner of Police of the Metropolis* [2015] EWCA Civ 646. This case involved three appeals. In the first two, the claimants were subjected to serious sexual assaults by a taxi driver, who was a serial rapist attacking over 100 women. They brought actions against the defendant for failure to conduct effective investigations, and were awarded compensation on the basis that the investigations were so significantly flawed that they constituted violations of a duty to investigate inherent in Article 3 ECHR, which protects against inhuman and degrading treatment by the state. The contrast with *Hill* could not be more marked, since negligent investigation of a serial murderer was the very subject matter of the rejected duty in that case. At the time of going to press, an appeal in *DSD* is pending.

Positive Convention Duties: Developments

Before *Michael*, the courts had themselves been extending the ambit of positive operational duties under the ECHR, creating tort-like liability. In *Savage v South Essex Partnership Trust* [2008] UKHL 74; [2009] 2 WLR 115, the House of Lords recognized that although negligence in the course of hospital treatment will not generally breach the positive duty to protect life under Article 2,[66] the situation is different in the case of a 'detained' patient—that is, a patient who is not voluntarily in hospital. The deceased here was to be treated as akin to a prisoner in custody. Where prisoners are concerned, the European Court of Human Rights had recognized positive 'operational' duties, for example to protect from the risk of suicide: *Keenan v UK* (2001) 33 EHRR 913. The vulnerability and lack of freedom of a detained patient were significant.

The later case of *Rabone v Pennine Care NHS Trust* [2012] UKSC 2; [2012] 2 AC 72 moved this line of cases forward significantly. The Supreme Court extended the positive duty under Article 2 further than in *Savage* and, perhaps more importantly, further than it had been pressed by the European Court of Human Rights itself. The patient in this case was not formally detained, but she was known to be at risk of suicide. The Court found that she was owed the positive operational duty under Article 2.

Lord Dyson, *Rabone v Pennine Care NHS Trust* [2012] UKSC 2

33 ... the ECtHR has not considered whether an operational duty exists to protect against the risk of suicide by informal psychiatric patients. But the Strasbourg jurisprudence shows that there is such a duty to protect persons from a real and immediate risk of suicide at least where they are under the control of the state. By contrast, the ECtHR has stated that in the generality of cases involving medical negligence, there is no operational duty under article 2.

34 So on which side of the line does an informal psychiatric patient such as Melanie fall? I am in no doubt that the trust owed the operational duty to her to take reasonable steps to protect her from the real and immediate risk of suicide. Whether there was a real and immediate risk of suicide on 19 April 2005 (and if so whether there was a breach of duty) is the second issue that arises on this appeal. But if there was a real and immediate risk of suicide at that time, of which the trust was aware or ought to have been aware, then in my view the trust was under a duty to take reasonable steps to protect Melanie from it. She had been admitted to hospital because she was a real suicide risk. By reason of her mental state, she was extremely vulnerable. The trust assumed responsibility for her. She was under its control. Although she was not a detained patient, it is clear that, if she had insisted on leaving the hospital, the authorities could and should have exercised their powers under the MHA to prevent her from doing so. In fact, however, the judge found that, if the trust had refused to allow her to leave, she would not have insisted on leaving. This demonstrates the control that the trust was exercising over Melanie. In reality, the difference between her position and that of a hypothetical detained psychiatric patient, who (apart from the fact of being detained) was in circumstances similar to those of Melanie, would have been one of form, not substance. Her position was far closer to that of such a hypothetical patient than to that of a patient undergoing treatment in a public hospital for a physical illness. These factors, taken together, lead me to conclude that the ECtHR would hold that the operational duty existed in this case.

The boundary between cases governed exclusively by negligence, and cases where an operational duty to protect life is found to exist, is thus more difficult to place. This point was made by Lord Mance, who concurred in the result but appears to have been markedly less comfortable than Lord Dyson with the path taken. There is a distinct shadow of the Article

6 issue, and a resistance to Strasbourg intrusion into an area governed by private law,[67] in the following comments, which capture the particular significance—for tort law—of the development of positive duties under Article 2.

Lord Mance, *Rabone v Pennine Care NHS Trust* [2012] UKSC 2

118 An extending series of cases exemplifies the specific operational duty.... Although the European Court of Human Rights described the incidence of this duty as "well-defined" in the *Osman* case, the subsequent case law suggests that this was over-optimistic.... But it is at least clear ... that various factors, such as control, assumption of responsibility and the nature (as well as the reality or immediacy) of the risk, may lead to the duty arising. Taking those factors into account in the present case, I agree with Lord Dyson JSC that, for reasons he gives in para 34, the operational duty existed in relation to Melanie. It was a duty to protect her from any real or immediate risk that she would commit suicide, of which state authorities knew or ought to have known. In that context (although the contrary was submitted to us) simple negligence in failing to identify or to guard appropriately against such a risk appears sufficient to establish breach of the duty.

119 A line has been sought to be drawn between this series of cases and cases of "casual acts of negligence" by medical authorities in relation to persons submitting themselves voluntarily to medical care. Such persons are entitled to the benefit of the general substantive duty referred to in para 113 above, but the state does not answer directly for ordinary acts of negligence by public health authorities, however clear it was that the particular medical emergency, procedure or treatment in the context of which the negligence occurred involved a real or immediate risk to the patient's life.

120 It follows that, in the event of a breach of the operational duty, the range of persons entitled as victims to bring claims against the state, and the nature and scale of compensation or just satisfaction which they may receive, will depend upon legal principles established by the European Court of Human Rights. In contrast, in the event of ordinary negligence by a public health authority, the range of victim and the nature and scale of compensation are defined by the domestic law of tort.

121 In this way, the European Court of Human Rights has, under the operational duty, began to develop its own Convention rules of, in effect, tortious responsibility, when in other areas it is left to national systems (as part of their general systematic duty "to establish a framework of laws, precautions and means of enforcement which will, to the greatest extent reasonably practicable, protect life") to develop an appropriate law of tort in the light of particular legal traditions and needs. The court might have left it to national systems in all areas to address any real or immediate risk to life which is or ought to be within their knowledge. It could have left it to national systems, in the event of any failure by state authorities to address such a risk, to recognise a range of victims and to provide compensation consistent with their ordinary law of tort. The court could still have reviewed the appropriateness of the protection and of the recourse available under national tort law. But that is not how the Convention has been interpreted. Hence, the difficult line to be drawn between direct Convention rights and national tort law in cases such as the present.

---

[67] For discussion of judicial sensitivity to this issue, see J. Steele, '(Dis)owning the Convention in the Law of Tort', in J. Lee (ed.), *From House of Lords to Supreme Court* (Hart Publishing, 2010).

It is highly significant that the Supreme Court was willing to lead the way into an area not yet considered in Strasbourg.[68] The need for the HRA claim arose because damages may be awarded to a wider range of claimants under the HRA than in the law of tort, as the crucial question is whether they will meet the definition of a 'victim' under the ECHR. Thus, the fact that these particular claimants had already settled a negligence claim was no barrier to their claim under the HRA: they had recovered nothing on their own account for 'bereavement'. These issues are dealt with in Chapter 8, in relation to HRA remedies; but the idea that the Supreme Court should develop the law in this significant way in order to supply a further head of damages to parties that would otherwise have been compensated has been strongly criticized as undermining the very notion of human rights: A. Tettenborn, 'Wrongful Death, Human Rights, and the Fatal Accidents Act' (2012) 128 LQR 327.

Smith v Ministry of Defence [2013] UKSC 41; [2014] 1 AC 52

This case is of equal significance in extending positive operational duties in domestic courts. Here we deal with the HRA aspects of the decision. We pick up the negligence issues in the following section, where we deal more generally with the decline of immunities. The majority and dissenting judges differed partly on the question of whether one should start with the common law position (the view of the dissenters), or with the positive duty to protect life under the Convention (the approach of the majority).

The claims in *Smith* were brought by the relatives of service men and women who had been killed on active service overseas, but not on the field of battle. It is established that 'combat immunity' prevents negligence claims arising out of actions on the field of battle, although the boundaries of this immunity—and its precise rationale—are somewhat uncertain. The claims in the cases heard together in *Smith* focused on decisions made away from the field of battle, which would affect the safety of personnel on active service, particularly decisions relating to equipment and training. Claims were made in negligence at common law; and in respect of Article 2, under the HRA. The Article 2 claims related to equipment and particularly the use of 'Snatch Land Rovers' rather than heavier armoured vehicles for patrols, and the use of patrols themselves. The claimants argued that the lives of service men and women were left vulnerable to the actions of the enemy through these decisions.

The Supreme Court first had to decide a question of territorial jurisdiction: did the Convention extend to these claims at all, since the service men and women in question were overseas? That raised the question of how to interpret Article 1 ECHR. Unanimously, the Justices decided that the deceased service personnel were within the jurisdiction of the UK at the time of their deaths. Following the decision of the European Court of Human Rights in *Al-Skeini v UK*, and contrary to the approach taken in earlier case law by the same Court, the question is in each case whether the state was exercising jurisdiction extra-territorially. There is no single answer to the question of jurisdiction. This was a reversal of the Supreme Court's conclusion only two years previously in *R (Smith) v Oxfordshire Assistant Deputy Coroner* [2010] UKSC 29, also concerning the death of a service woman overseas. It shows how rapidly the jurisprudence of the Convention is developing, and illustrates both its capacity to change direction, and the need for domestic law to follow.

So far as the positive duty under Article 2 is concerned, the judges were not unanimous. Lord Hope for the majority was undeterred by the fact that the Strasbourg Court

---

[68] Strasbourg followed the lead and recognized a positive operational duty towards a voluntary patient in *Reynolds v UK* (2012) 55 EHRR 35.

had not yet considered the question of whether Article 2 extends to protection of the lives of military personnel from enemy action. The distance between this case and instances where the State itself has posed risks to its service personnel through training exercises, was noted; and Lord Hope also underlined 'the Strasbourg court's concern not to impose a disproportionate and unrealistic obligation on the state' ([74]). He also accepted that decisions which are 'essentially political' should not be reopened in the name of Convention rights. But he did not use these concerns in order to conclude that no duties arose under Article 2. Rather, there *may* be cases where the positive duty under Article 2 is applicable; and trial of the facts was necessary before it could be concluded whether this was the case.

Lord Hope, *Smith v Ministry of Defence* [2013] UKSC 41

76 The guidance which I would draw from the court's jurisprudence in this area is that the court must avoid imposing positive obligations on the state in connection with the planning for and conduct of military operations in situations of armed conflict which are unrealistic or disproportionate. But it must give effect to those obligations where it would be reasonable to expect the individual to be afforded the protection of the article. It will be easy to find that allegations are beyond the reach of article 2 if the decisions that were or ought to have been taken about training, procurement or the conduct of operations were at a high level of command and closely linked to the exercise of political judgment and issues of policy. So too if they relate to things done or not done when those who might be thought to be responsible for avoiding the risk of death or injury to others were actively engaged in direct contact with the enemy. But finding whether there is room for claims to be brought in the middle ground, so that the wide margin of appreciation which must be given to the authorities or to those actively engaged in armed conflict is fully recognised without depriving the article of content, is much more difficult. No hard and fast rules can be laid down. It will require the exercise of judgment. This can only be done in the light of the facts of each case....

80 I agree with Owen J that the procurement issues may give rise to questions that are essentially political in nature but that it is not possible to decide whether this is the case without hearing evidence. He said that there was no sound basis for the allegations that relate to operational decisions made by commanders, and for this reason took a different view as to whether they were within the reach of article 2. But it seems to me that these allegations cannot easily be divorced from the allegations about procurement, and that here too the question as to which side of the line they lie is more appropriate for determination after hearing evidence. Much will depend on where, when and by whom the operational decisions were taken and the choices that were open to them, given the rules and other instructions as to the use of equipment under which at each level of command they were required to operate.

81 I would therefore dismiss the MOD's appeal against Owen J's decision, while the Court of Appeal found it unnecessary to consider, that none of these claims should be struck out. The claimants are, however, on notice that the trial judge will be expected to follow the guidance set out in this judgment as to the very wide measure of discretion which must be accorded to those who were responsible on the ground for the planning and conduct of the operations during which these soldiers lost their lives and also to the way issues as to

procurement too should be approached. It is far from clear that they will be able to show that the implied positive obligation under article 2.1 of the Convention to take preventative operational measures was breached in either case.

Lords Mance and Carnwath, dissenting, preferred to approach the issues by considering domestic tort law—and the limitations to duty—first. In different ways, they each suggested that the position under the Convention was uncertain at best and that the sound reasons which they thought would exclude a duty in the law of tort should, since the claim under Article 2 had no precedent, take priority.

Lord Carnwath

156...I consider that our primary responsibility should be for the coherent and principled development of the common law, which is within our own control. We cannot determine the limits of article 2. Indeed, the multiplicity of views expressed by the nine members of this court, when this issue was previously considered in Catherine Smith, shows how difficult and unproductive it can be, even at this level, to attempt to predict how Strasbourg will ultimately draw the lines. The trial judge will be in no stronger position. With respect to Lord Hope DPSC (para 79), if the problem is a lack of directly relevant guidance from Strasbourg, it is hard to see how, simply by hearing further evidence or finding further facts, he or she will be better able to fill that gap, still less to do so "with complete confidence".

Common law—the nature of the issues

157 It is important to recognise that we are being asked to authorise an extension of the law of negligence (as indeed of article 2), into a new field. We have not been referred to any authority in the higher courts, in this country or any comparable jurisdiction, in which the state has been held liable for injuries sustained by its own soldiers in the course of active hostilities. Further we are concerned only with duties at common law, rather than under statute. As the Court of Appeal recognised..., statutory regulations governing the responsibilities of the ministry as employers do not apply outside the United Kingdom.

Lord Mance also made the point that there was something unattractive about the existence of an Article 2 claim which was nevertheless restricted to the 'middle ground' described by Lord Hope. Richard Mullender (Further Reading) has pointed out that Lord Hope's judgment, extracted above, will be hard for lower courts to interpret. Lord Mance took the view that it would be wrong to leave such decisions to trial.

Particularly notable are the different approaches taken to the capacity of domestic courts to take on the role of developing Convention rights. Lord Carnwath made plain his view that the inability of domestic courts to determine the extent of those rights should lead to caution in extending them to areas where Strasbourg itself has not yet ventured. This raises the general issue, of how far domestic courts will embrace rights with a direct impact on matters previously dealt with as aspects of domestic private law, and where interpretive authority now lies elsewhere.[69]

[69] For strong view on this, see Lord Hoffmann, and Andrew Tettenborn, Further Reading.

4. IMMUNITIES

4.1 IMMUNITIES AND ARTICLE 6

In the preceding section, we considered the role played by Article 6 in leading courts to avoid ruling out duties of care in any general or 'blanket' sense and, in particular, to avoid use of the term 'immunity'. In *Matthews v Ministry of Defence* [2003] 1 AC 163, the House of Lords considered the validity, in respect of the Convention, of an immunity conferred by statute. Proceedings against the Crown were made possible by the Crown Proceedings Act 1947; but section 10 of this statute preserved an exception for the armed forces in relation to injury or death in service, subject to certain conditions. The legislation selected an alternative route to supporting injured service personnel, in place of tort actions. This immunity itself was repealed by the Crown Proceedings (Armed Forces) Act 1987; but with a provision allowing the Secretary of State to revive section 10 in circumstances of 'imminent national danger or great emergency'; or 'for the purpose of any warlike operations'. The House of Lords concluded that such an immunity, being substantive rather than procedural, did not violate Article 6. There was some doubt whether this stance would be accepted by the European Court of Human Rights. But in *Roche v UK* (2005), the court considered the same statutory immunity against actions in tort, and held that Article 6 is violated only when a *procedural* immunity is created.

4.2 IMMUNITIES AND COMMON LAW

The question remains whether common law immunities, not conferred by statute, retain a place in the modern tort of negligence. The general trend of recent years has been for immunities recognized at common law, rather than created by statute, to be analysed critically; and in important instances, they have been overturned or restricted. The House of Lords, and subsequently the Supreme Court, have been inclined to ask whether the policy concerns which justify immunity from negligence proceedings are sufficiently compelling.

Immunities connected with legal proceedings offer an illustration. The immunity of **advocates** was recognized in *Rondel v Worsley* [1969] 1 AC 191, but abolished in *Arthur JS Hall v Simons* [2002] 1 AC 615, the House of Lords declaring that the underlying policy considerations had changed, as had the tort of negligence itself and the organization of the legal profession. More recently, in *Jones v Kaney* [2011] UKSC 13; [2011] 2 AC 398, the immunity of **expert witnesses** to negligence liability was also ended.[70] A majority of the Supreme Court reasoned that expert witnesses who are paid by a client should be treated as analogous to other professionals providing services, so that a duty was appropriate. The decision does not alter the immunity enjoyed by witnesses of 'fact' (for example, eyewitnesses), who do not work for a particular party to litigation. The majority took the view that relevant safeguards were provided through the law's general approach to the existence and breach of a duty of care; and that expert witnesses could in any event be expected to insure against liability. The dissenting judges, Baroness Hale and Lord Hope, were less comfortable with making such a change in the established principles of liability on the basis of suppositions and

[70] Participants in legal proceedings continue to be enjoy protection from defamation actions.

presumptions about its likely impact, and would have preferred such a change in established principles to be considered by the Law Commission, on the basis of empirical evidence and broad consultation. Lord Phillips' judgment, extracted below, illustrates the way that the Supreme Court is now inclined to question immunities, retaining them only where there are clear reasons to do so.

Lord Phillips, Jones v Kaney
Is the immunity justified?

51 In the *Darker* case [2001] 1 AC 435, 456–457, Lord Clyde remarked:

"since the immunity may cut across the rights of others to a legal remedy and so runs counter to the policy that no wrong should be without a remedy, it should be only allowed with reluctance, and should not readily be extended. It should only be allowed where it is necessary to do so."

With this principle in mind, I would adopt the approach advocated by Lord Reid in *Rondel v Worsley* [1969] 1 AC 191, 228, when considering the immunity from suit enjoyed by advocates: "the issue appears to me to be whether the abolition of the rule would probably be attended by such disadvantage to the public interest as to make its retention clearly justifiable." It would not be right to start with a presumption that because the immunity exists it should be maintained unless it is shown to be unjustified. The onus lies fairly and squarely on the defendant to justify the immunity behind which she seeks to shelter.

In reality, only the highest court will be able to go through this process of disposing of an established immunity; but it seems generally clear that immunities are to be treated as exceptional and always need to be justified. The decision of the Court of Appeal in *Smart v Forensic Science Services* [2013] EWCA Civ 783 illustrates that there is some role for this approach in lower courts. The Court concluded that a claim in negligence could be brought in respect of incorrect forensic evidence which had been used in the course of prosecution of the claimant for a criminal offence, namely possessing live ammunition. Since this is a strict liability offence, the claimant had no choice but to plead guilty in light of the forensic report, which stated that ammunition taken from his home was live. The report proved to be incorrect. As the Court pointed out, in terms of the effect on the claimant this was equivalent to planting evidence in his home. Since a claim in deceit was to be pursued, exploring whether there was intention, there was no legitimate reason why a claim in negligence should not also proceed: the evidence would in any case need to be reviewed. There was no space for an immunity in negligence to operate, when the issues were to be before a court in any event.

4.3 COMBAT IMMUNITY

One possible justification for an immunity is that it sets out an area of 'non-justiciability', where courts have no jurisdiction to question the decisions and actions taken by participants. This is not so much a generalized policy judgment, as a question of the court's jurisdiction. A form of immunity which has been understood in these terms is 'combat immunity'. While the specific statutory immunity of the armed forces against claims on the part of injured servicemen has been repealed, 'combat immunity' at common law remains well established even if its scope, boundaries, and justification remain uncertain. The existence of the immunity was recognized in the Australian case of *Shaw Savill & Albion v Commonwealth* (1940) 66 CLR 344; and much more recently in the UK courts in *Mulcahy v Ministry of Defence* [1996] QB 732.

We outlined the nature of the claims in *Smith v Ministry of Defence* in the previous section, where we dealt with the way that the Supreme Court handled positive duties under Article 2. The case was also argued in negligence, and raised the question of the scope of combat immunity. The majority interpreted the scope of the immunity relatively narrowly, but its discussion was consistent with a basis in 'justiciability' rather than in, for example, the difficulties facing decision-makers in the heat of battle.

Lord Hope

90 . . . In *Bici v Ministry of Defence* [2004] EWHC 786 (QB) at [90], Elias J noted that combat immunity was exceptionally a defence to the government, and to individuals too, who take action in the course of actual or imminent armed conflict and cause damage to property or death or injury to fellow soldiers or civilians. It was an exception to the principle that was established in *Entick v Carrington* (1765) 19 State Tr. 1029 that the executive cannot simply rely on the interests of the state as a justification for the commission of wrongs. In his opinion the scope of the immunity should be construed narrowly. That approach seems to me to be amply justified by the authorities.

Some of the claims, on this basis, did not fall within combat immunity because they referred to decisions taken 'far from the theatre of war', even if the deaths themselves were suffered in the course of active engagement. But some of the claims were 'less obviously' directed to decisions taken at such a remove. They might raise issues for example about what patrols should have been undertaken, and with which vehicles, in the context of war-like engagement, even if not strictly in the course of combat. Strikingly, the lower courts which would now hear the claims would need to determine not just whether there was a breach of Article 2 (above), but also whether the facts disclosed a proper case for the application of combat immunity ([96]).

Perhaps curiously, having dismissed the argument that the claims in these cases necessarily fell into the area of the immunity, the majority did little to consider whether—applying the general *Caparo* criteria—there were nevertheless reasons for rejecting the duties proposed by the claimants. The minority Justices, Lords Mance and Carnwath, approached matters very differently, and particularly highlighted these policy issues. Lord Mance thought that the immunity itself was simply a particular instance of a case where it was not 'fair, just and reasonable' to impose a duty on policy grounds; and reasoned by analogy with the restrictive approach taken to claims against the police in relation to the investigation and suppression of crime, concluding that no duty was owed.

Lord Mance, *Smith v Ministry of Defence* [2013] UKSC 41

150 Still more fundamentally, the approach taken by the majority will in my view make extensive litigation almost inevitable after, as well as quite possibly during and even before, any active service operations undertaken by the British army. It is likely to lead to the judicialisation of war, in sharp context with Starke J's dictum in the *Shaw Savill* case (1940) 66

CLR 344, 350 that "war cannot be controlled or conducted by judicial tribunals". No doubt it would be highly desirable if all disputes with international legal implications were to be submitted to international judicial resolution, with those involved abiding by the outcome; and if wars were no more. But, in the present imperfect world, there is no precedent for claims to impose civil liability for damages on states whose armed forces are killed or injured in armed combat as a result of alleged failures of decision-making either in the course of, or in procuring equipment or providing training for, such combat. All the claims made in these appeals fall in my view within one or other of these areas where the common law should not tread.

While the restriction of a combat 'immunity' in this case may be in harmony with other developments in the tort of negligence, the decision that duties at common law and under the HRA are arguable despite policy concerns indicates that the Supreme Court has at least changed gear, if it has not changed course, since the days when the House of Lords decided *Mitchell* and *Van Colle.*

5.   FAILED STERILIZATIONS

In the cases explored in this final section, the claimants decided they did not want any children (or any more children). They underwent sterilization procedures, but these procedures were negligently performed, or the claimants were negligently advised that they had succeeded and they need not use contraception. The female claimants conceived. Could they recover damages from the negligent parties in respect of the pregnancy, the birth, and (most controversially) the upbringing of the children?

Courts in many jurisdictions have found it genuinely difficult to decide these cases; and to express their decisions in terms of existing criteria. On some occasions, they have chosen to step outside the usual terminology. Divergent results have been reached in the UK, where the costs of raising a child have been denied, and Australia, where the costs of raising a child have been awarded. But even within those jurisdictions, variations in the factual context in subsequent cases have caused the courts to create novel liabilities nevertheless (in the UK); or to draw the line against certain types of claim (Australia). This gives us a valuable opportunity to compare not only the merits of the decisions, but also the kinds of reasoning applied.

McFarlane v Tayside [2000] 2 AC 59

The pursuers, a married couple, already had four children. They did not want a fifth, and decided that the husband would undergo a vasectomy. The pursuers were told that the husband's sperm count was negative and that they could dispense with contraceptive measures. It was claimed that this advice, rather than the operation itself, was negligent. The pursuers acted on the advice, but the wife became pregnant and delivered a healthy child. The pursuers claimed damages associated with the pregnancy and birth, and also claimed the costs of rearing an unwanted (though now of course much loved) but healthy child.

On appeal, the majority of the House of Lords held that the mother would, if negligence was established, be entitled to damages in respect of the pain, suffering, and inconvenience of pregnancy and childbirth, and for the immediate medical and other expenses, and loss of earnings, associated with the birth. However, it was decided (unanimously) that the costs of raising the child were not recoverable.

Lord Slynn of Hadley, at 76

The doctor undertakes a duty of care in regard to the prevention of pregnancy: it does not follow that the duty includes also avoiding the costs of rearing the child if born and accepted into the family. Whereas I have no doubt that there should be compensation for the physical effects of the pregnancy and birth, including of course solatium for consequential suffering by the mother immediately following the birth, I consider that it is not fair, just or reasonable to impose on the doctor or his employer liability for the consequential responsibilities, imposed on or accepted by the parents to bring up a child. The doctor does not assume responsibility for those economic losses. If a client wants to be able to recover such costs he or she must do so by an appropriate contract.

...

The question remains whether as a matter of legal principle the damages should include, for a child by then loved, loving and fully integrated into the family the cost of shoes at 14 and a dress at 17 and everything that can reasonably be described as necessary for the upbringing of the child until the end of school, university, independence, maturity?

By contrast with Lord Slynn, who applied an existing 'label' in order to justify his decision, Lord Steyn decided that the ordinary principles of tort law, which he captured in terms of 'corrective justice', did not adequately dispose of the case. While he *could* explain that a duty in this case was not 'fair, just, and reasonable' under *Caparo*, he thought that his reasons were best explained as *distributive*. On this occasion, he proposed, there was a reason of distributive justice for rejecting the claims. People generally would consider it unfair that parents who are fortunate to enjoy the benefit of a loved and healthy child (albeit one they had already decided not to have) should be handsomely compensated for the upkeep of that child. Expressing this, he thought, was better than resorting to a 'formalistic proposition' derived from the terms of an existing legal test.

Lord Steyn, at 82–3

It is possible to view the case simply from the perspective of corrective justice. It requires somebody who has harmed another without justification to indemnify the other. On this approach the parents' claim for the cost of bringing up Catherine must succeed. But one may also approach the case from the vantage point of distributive justice. It requires a focus on the just distribution of burdens and losses among members of a society. If the matter is approached in this way, it may become relevant to ask commuters on the Underground the following question: "Should the parents of an unwanted but healthy child be able to sue the doctor or hospital for compensation equivalent to the cost of bringing up the child for the years of his or her minority, i.e. until about 18 years?" My Lords, I am firmly of the view that an overwhelming number of ordinary men and women would answer the question with an emphatic "No." And the reason for such a response would be an inarticulate premise as to what is morally acceptable and what is not. Like Ognall J. in *Jones* v. *Berkshire Area Health Authority*, 2 July 1986, they will have in mind that many couples cannot have children and others have the sorrow and burden of looking after a disabled child. The realisation that compensation for financial loss in respect of the upbringing of a child would necessarily have to discriminate between rich and poor would, surely appear unseemly to them. It would also worry them that parents may be put in a position of arguing in court that the unwanted child, which they accepted and care for, is more trouble than it is worth. Instinctively, the traveller on the Underground would consider that the law of tort has no business to provide legal remedies consequent upon the birth of a healthy child, which all of us regard as a valuable and good thing.

My Lords, to explain decisions denying a remedy for the cost of bringing up an unwanted child by saying that there is no loss, no foreseeable loss, no causative link or no ground for reasonable restitution is to resort to unrealistic and formalistic propositions which mask the real reasons for the decisions. And judges ought to strive to give the real reasons for their decision. It is my firm conviction that where courts of law have denied a remedy for the cost of bringing up an unwanted child the real reasons have been grounds of distributive justice. That is of course, a moral theory. It may be objected that the House must act like a court of law and not like a court of morals. That would only be partly right. The court must apply positive law. But judges' sense of the moral answer to a question, or the justice of the case, has been one of the great shaping forces of the common law. What may count in a situation of difficulty and uncertainty is not the subjective view of the judge but what he reasonably believes that the ordinary citizen would regard as right.... The truth is that tort law is a mosaic in which the principles of corrective justice and distributive justice are interwoven. And in situations of uncertainty and difficulty a choice sometimes has to be made between the two approaches.

In my view it is legitimate in the present case to take into account considerations of distributive justice. That does not mean that I would decide the case on grounds of public policy. On the contrary, I would avoid those quicksands. Relying on principles of distributive justice I am persuaded that our tort law does not permit parents of a healthy unwanted child to claim the costs of bringing up the child from a health authority or a doctor. If it were necessary to do so, I would say that the claim does not satisfy the requirement of being fair, just and reasonable.

Lord Steyn's hypothetical opinion poll on the London Underground[71] was criticized by Laura Hoyano (in an article which seems to have influenced the High Court of Australia in *Cattanach v Melchior*, later in this section).

Laura Hoyano, 'Misconceptions about Wrongful Conception' [2002] 65 MLR 883, at 904

... Distributive justice has become just another label, without pretending to intellectual rigour. The transmogrification of the man on the Clapham omnibus is not limited to a change of public transport, as he is no longer just a convenient measure for the standard of care expected of non-experts, but also the gatekeeper for negligence law itself.... Appeals to commuters on the London underground to decide duty of care issues allow the courts to avoid confronting the sharp edges of competence, cheapest cost avoidance of the risk, insurability against

[71] Lord Steyn's reference to the passenger on the London Underground is an updated and now suitably gender neutral version of the 'man on the Clapham omnibus', who has traditionally set the standard for judgments as to reasonableness, but not necessarily morality.

loss, other modes of loss-spreading—and whether carving out *ad hoc* exceptions to well-established legal principles is a matter for parliamentary rather than judicial action. . . .

. . . A principled approach can enhance the flexibility which gives the common law its vitality, if the courts directly confront policy factors, both intrinsic and extrinsic to the relationship of the particular parties. . . .

The 'wrongful conception' cases demonstrate that distributive justice can be just as unruly a horse as public policy for the courts to ride. The London Underground is not the BBC's *Moral Maze*. Since we are apparently stuck on the Circle Line, however, we can only hope that the House of Lords, having now granted leave to appeal in *Rees*, will clarify what they really meant in *McFarlane*.

In the later case of *Rees v Darlington*, to which we turn next, Lord Steyn conceded that reading the judgments in *McFarlane* is a 'gruesome task'. The most that was said to meet Laura Hoyano's wish at the end of the extract above (to explain what the grounds of the decision actually were) is forthcoming in the following short passage. Lord Steyn contends that all the different judgments were based not on 'public policy' in the full sense, but on legal policy:

Lord Steyn, *Rees v Darlington*, at 322

29 . . . The House [in *McFarlane*] did not rest its decision on public policy in a conventional sense: Lord Slynn of Hadley, at p 76D; my judgment, at p 83D–E; Lord Hope of Craighead, at p 95A; Lord Clyde, at p 100A–C; and Lord Millett, at p 108A–C. Instead the Law Lords relied on legal policy. In considering this question the House was bound, in the circumstances of the case, to consider what in their view the ordinary citizen would regard as morally acceptable. Invoking the moral theory of distributive justice, and the requirements of being just, fair and reasonable, culled from case law, are in context simply routes to establishing the legal policy.

Lord Steyn's use of the hypothetical commuter in this instance has been defended by Peter Cane, who agrees that where settled principles do not appropriately determine a case, it would be wrong either to decide regardless of issues of morality and distributive justice; or to hide the real reasons behind some distorted version of established principles: see P. Cane, 'Taking Disagreement Seriously: Courts, Legislatures and the Reform of Tort Law' (2005) 25 OJLS 393.

To return to *McFarlane*, Lord Hope thought that the parents of the child derived benefits from the presence of that child within the family, as well as costs. Since those benefits were 'incalculable', they could not be set against the costs. Yet the benefits could not be left out of account, or too much compensation would be paid. Therefore, the economic losses were not recoverable. Lord Clyde, controversially, argued that the amount of damages recoverable as a consequence of a wrong ought to be limited to those that are 'reasonable', and indeed proportionate: 'The restitution which the law requires is a reasonable restitution' (at 105).

Lord Millett on the other hand expressly rejected the argument that the potential liability was disproportionate to the wrong in this case (at 109). He conceded that the parents of a healthy child could decide for themselves that the burden of a healthy child outweighed the benefits (clearly, since otherwise parents would simply continue to have as many children as possible). But society, and the law, could not treat a healthy child as a loss. Lord Millett would also not have allowed any damages in respect of the pregnancy or birth. Yet surely *these* cannot be described as a 'blessing', mixed or otherwise?[72] In New Zealand, where actions for damages for 'personal injury' caused by accident and with causes falling into a range of other categories[73] have been removed from the law of tort and dealt with through a statutory compensation scheme, it is clear that pregnancy is capable of being a personal injury.[74] Lord Millett would however have awarded the parents jointly a sum of (around) £5,000, to reflect a different loss: deprivation of the right to limit the size of their family (at 114).

The House of Lords did not express a view on the correct position where either the mother (or presumably the father), or the child, or conceivably both (or all three), is not healthy, and where this too increases the burden and the costs of upbringing. Such issues were raised in subsequent cases.

In *Parkinson v St James and Seacroft University NHS Trust* [2002] QB 266, the mother was healthy but the child was disabled. The court decided that the additional costs of rearing the child associated with its disability could be the subject of damages. Unfortunately, the status of *Parkinson* is wholly unclear since *Rees v Darlington* (below). It would appear that the three dissenting judges in *Rees* approved it,[75] and three of the four majority judges disapproved it.[76] *Parkinson* was followed in *Farraj v King's Healthcare NHS Trust* [2008] EWHC 2468 (QB), a first instance decision where *Parkinson* was binding upon the court. A pre-natal DNA test had been carried out with the intention of determining whether the child would suffer from a blood disorder. Through negligence of the defendants, the parents were falsely led to believe that the disorder could be excluded. In line with *Parkinson*, they could be compensated for the costs of upbringing associated with the child's disability.[77]

Rees v Darlington Memorial Hospital NHS Trust [2004] 1 AC 309

The claimant suffered from severe visual impairment. Because of this, she particularly did not want the burden of raising a child. She underwent a sterilization operation which was negligently performed at a hospital managed by the defendants. She gave birth to a healthy child, whose father wanted no part in its upbringing.

---

[72] Lord Millett's treatment of the claim in respect of pain and suffering is broadly explored by C. Witting, 'Physical Damage in Negligence' [2002] CLJ 189–208.

[73] Including treatment injuries.

[74] For discussion see S. Todd, 'Accidental Conception and Accident Compensation' (2012) PN 196. The article explores the decision of the New Zealand Supreme Court in *Allenby v H* [2012] NZSC 33, holding that there was cover under the statutory scheme for conception following a failed sterilization. The decision means that claims at common law are barred in relation to the pregnancy itself; but not, the article argues, for upbringing costs.

[75] Importantly perhaps, two of these three (Lords Steyn and Hope) were in the majority in *McFarlane*, suggesting that the decision of the Court of Appeal in *Parkinson* is consistent with *McFarlane* (and reinforcing the suspicion that *Rees v Darlington* is not).

[76] Lord Scott particularly pointed out that the disability of the child in *Parkinson* was in no way related to the negligence of the defendant.

[77] On appeal, in *Farraj v King's Healthcare NHS Trust* [2009] EWCA Civ 1203; [2010] 1 WLR 2139, the Court of Appeal held that the defendants had not breached a duty of care, since they had contracted out the relevant procedure and owed no 'non-delegable duty' (Chapter 9). The appeal did not raise the issues discussed here.

The House of Lords decided that no duty was owed in respect of the upbringing of a healthy baby, notwithstanding the particular burden this would place upon someone in the position of the claimant. The additional costs of upbringing relating to the mother's visual disability were equally not recoverable. However, the majority decided that a wrong had been committed towards the mother, and that she should be awarded a 'conventional sum' of £15,000 as a measure of recognition of that wrong. She had been denied 'the opportunity to live her life in the way that she wished and planned'. This is, in effect, protection of 'autonomy'.

Lord Bingham, at 316–17

The policy considerations underpinning the judgments of the House were, as I read them, an unwillingness to regard a child (even if unwanted) as a financial liability and nothing else, a recognition that the rewards which parenthood (even if involuntary) may or may not bring cannot be quantified and a sense that to award potentially very large sums of damages to the parents of a normal and healthy child against a National Health Service always in need of funds to meet pressing demands would rightly offend the community's sense of how public resources should be allocated. Kirby J was surely right to suggest in *Cattanach v Melchior* [2003] HCA 38, para 178, that:

"Concern to protect the viability of the National Health Service at a time of multiple demands upon it might indeed help to explain the invocation in the House of Lords in *McFarlane* of the notion of 'distributive justice'."

It is indeed hard to think that, if the House had adopted the first solution discussed above, its decision would have long survived the first award to well-to-do parents of the estimated cost of providing private education, presents, clothing and foreign holidays for an unwanted child (even if at no more expensive a level than the parents had provided for earlier, wanted, children) against a National Health Service found to be responsible, by its negligence, for the birth of the child. In favouring the third solution, holding the damages claimed to be irrecoverable, the House allied itself with the great majority of state courts in the United States and relied on arguments now strongly supported by the dissenting judgments of Gleeson CJ, Hayne and Heydon JJ in *Melchior*.

7 I am of the clear opinion, for reasons more fully given by my noble and learned friends, that it would be wholly contrary to the practice of the House to disturb its unanimous decision in *McFarlane* given as recently as four years ago, even if a differently constituted committee were to conclude that a different solution should have been adopted. It would reflect no credit on the administration of the law if a line of English authority were to be disapproved in 1999 and reinstated in 2003 with no reason for the change beyond a change in the balance of judicial opinion. I am not in any event persuaded that the arguments which the House rejected in 1999 should now be accepted, or that the policy considerations which (as I think) drove the decision have lost their potency. Subject to one gloss, therefore, which I regard as important, I would affirm and adhere to the decision in *McFarlane*.

8 My concern is this. Even accepting that an unwanted child cannot be regarded as a financial liability and nothing else and that any attempt to weigh the costs of bringing up a child against the intangible rewards of parenthood is unacceptably speculative, the fact remains that the parent of a child born following a negligently performed vasectomy or sterilisation, or negligent advice on the effect of such a procedure, is the victim of a legal wrong. The members of the House who gave judgment in *McFarlane* recognised this by holding, in each case, that some award should be made to Mrs McFarlane (although Lord Millett based this on a ground which differed from that of the other members and he would have made a joint award to Mr and Mrs McFarlane). I can accept and support a rule of legal policy which precludes recovery of the full cost of bringing up a child in the situation postulated, but I question the fairness of a rule which denies the victim of a legal wrong any recompense at all beyond an award immediately related to the unwanted pregnancy and birth. The spectre of well-to-do parents plundering the National Health Service should not blind one to other realities: that of the single mother with young children, struggling to make ends meet and counting the days until her children are of an age to enable her to work more hours and so enable the family to live a less straitened existence; the mother whose burning ambition is to put domestic chores so far as possible behind her and embark on a new career or resume an old one. Examples can be multiplied. To speak of losing the freedom to limit the size of one's family is to mask the real loss suffered in a situation of this kind. This is that a parent, particularly (even today) the mother, has been denied, through the negligence of another, the opportunity to live her life in the way that she wished and planned. I do not think that an award immediately relating to the unwanted pregnancy and birth gives adequate recognition of or does justice to that loss. I would accordingly support the suggestion favoured by Lord Millett in *McFarlane*, at p 114, that in all cases such as these there be a conventional award to mark the injury and loss, although I would favour a greater figure than the £5,000 he suggested (I have in mind a conventional figure of £15,000) and I would add this to the award for the pregnancy and birth. This solution is in my opinion consistent with the ruling and rationale of *McFarlane*. The conventional award would not be, and would not be intended to be, compensatory. It would not be the product of calculation. But it would not be a nominal, let alone a derisory, award. It would afford some measure of recognition of the wrong done. And it would afford a more ample measure of justice than the pure *McFarlane* rule.

The minority judges noted that this conventional award was more than a 'gloss'. It was inconsistent with *McFarlane* itself, where such an award had been proposed by Lord Millett alone.

Lord Steyn

45 No United Kingdom authority is cited for the proposition that judges have the power to create a remedy of awarding a conventional sum in cases such as the present. There is none. It is also noteworthy that in none of the decisions from many foreign jurisdictions, with varying results, is there any support for such a solution. This underlines the heterodox nature of the solution adopted.

46 Like Lord Hope I regard the idea of a conventional award in the present case as contrary to principle. It is a novel procedure for judges to create such a remedy. There are limits to permissible creativity for judges. In my view the majority have strayed into forbidden territory. It is also a backdoor evasion of the legal policy enunciated in *McFarlane*. If such a rule is to be created it must be done by Parliament. The fact is, however, that it would be a hugely controversial legislative measure. It may well be that the Law Commissions and Parliament ought in any event, to consider the impact of the creation of a power to make a conventional award in the cases under consideration for the coherence of the tort system.

47 I cannot support the proposal for creating such a new rule.

Given his unconventional reasoning in *McFarlane*, is it surprising to see Lord Steyn, in particular, criticizing judicial creativity? There are two reasons why the dissenting judges may make some claim to consistency.

First, there was no 'conventional award' in *McFarlane*, and yet it could be said that in that case too the parents had been denied their right to live as they wanted, through the negligence of the defendant. It was not solely because of the claimant's disability, in *Rees*, that the defendants' negligence interfered with her autonomy, although this made the impact greater. The decision of the healthy mother of four children to avoid another pregnancy is equally a decision as to how to lead her life. That being so, Lord Bingham here does to some extent undermine his own argument that it is too soon to depart from *McFarlane*.

Second, the idea of a 'conventional award' in recognition of a wrong assumes that a wrong can be specified. Since the majority *also* held that no duty of care was owed in respect of the cost of upbringing, it would appear that there was no recognized legal wrong to which this award could relate. The award requires creation of a new wrong, not just a controversial new remedy for an existing wrong (breach of a duty of care). Duties of care are owed to individuals in respect of particular damage. The majority did not go so far as to spell out what *duty* was being recognized. Was it a duty to take care not to interfere with the claimant's ability to plan her life? This would indeed be novel;[78] but it might also be asked why the costs of upbringing should not then be recoverable.

In *Cattanach v Melchior* [2003] HCA 38, the High Court of Australia decided a factually similar case. The plaintiff had undergone a sterilization operation which was negligently performed. She claimed damages for the costs of rearing a healthy child. A majority of the High Court of Australia held that damages could be recovered in such a case. As Peter Cane has pointed out,[79] Kirby J is regarded as the least 'legalistic' and the most 'policy-oriented' of recent Australian High Court judges (and is a supporter of the *Caparo* test which he considers to provide a useful way of structuring policy discussion).[80] Even so, he decided with the majority not to follow *McFarlane v Tayside*, which is seen as representing a departure from ordinary legal principles. (*Cattanach v Melchior* was decided before *Rees v Darlington* which, as we have seen, represented an even larger departure from normal tort principles.)

Cattanach could be seen as a rather narrow decision since much was already conceded between the parties. In particular, it was conceded that a duty of care was owed, which was the very issue on which the pursuers lost in the case of *McFarlane v Tayside*. As this was so, it would have been a larger departure from ordinary tort principles to determine that the consequential losses were unrecoverable, if the existence (and breach) of the duty was assumed.[81] But Peter Cane convincingly argues that there is much more to the decision

---

78 See *Chester v Afshar* (Chapters 2 and 4); and D. Nolan, 'New Forms of Damage in Negligence' (2007) 70 MLR 59–88.

79 P. Cane, 'The Doctor, the Stork and the Court: A Modern Morality Play' (2004) 120 LQR 23.

80 As we have noted before, the *Caparo* test is generally rejected in Australia.

81 Contrast the subsequent decision of the High Court of Australia in *Harriton v Stephens* [2006] HCA 15. A doctor owed no duty of care to a severely disabled child to warn her mother of the real risk of profound disability given her exposure to the rubella virus in early pregnancy. It was agreed that with competent legal advice, the pregnancy would have been terminated. The majority regarded this as a 'wrongful life' claim rather than a 'wrongful birth' claim as in *Cattanach*; and such claims are not admitted. Kirby J, in dissent, rejected these labels, and treated it as a claim for suffering, not for life. It has been argued by D. Morgan and B. White, 'Everyday Life and the Edges of Existence: Wrongs with no

than this. The decision was widely criticized in the Australian media and this was partly because it seemed to fly in the face of legislative reform of tort law in Australia. These reforms have been aimed at controlling both liability and quantum of damage.[82] Peter Cane argues that the High Court was deliberately reasserting the independence of tort law in this case.

Peter Cane, 'The Doctor, the Stork and the Court: A Modern Morality Play' [2004] 120 LQR 23–6

… it is tempting to interpret both the outcome and the majority reasoning in *Cattanach v Melchior* as an attempt by the court to re-assert its role as a forum of legal principle, above the political fray, immune to the siren call of "community values" and contestable moral opinions. Kirby J. captured the mood in a particularly vivid way (at [137]). Referring to the Ipp Review and its legislative aftermath, he argued that Parliaments cannot be trusted to set limits to tort liability. Their interventions, he said, "can be arbitrary and dogmatic"; and they "sometimes respond to the 'echo chamber inhabited by journalists and public moralists'" (quoting Sedley L.J. in *Vellino v Chief Constable of the Greater Manchester Police* [2002] 1 W.L.R. 218 at [60]).[83] "Judges, on the other hand", express and refine the common law "in ways that are logically reasoned and shown to be a consistent development of past decisional law". The understated comment of the leader writer of Melbourne's Age newspaper ("Babies, bungles and compensation" July 18, 2003) offers a different perspective: "The Australian Medical Association…has described the ruling as a 'horror story'. This is an overreaction, but the case does illustrate [that]…[n]ot all issues are best dealt with in a courtroom, and this may well be one of them".

Lord Reid was famous (amongst other things) for having called the view, that judges do not make law, a "fairy tale". The same might be said of the view of the majority in *Cattanach* that "legal principle" can tell us whether Dr Cattanach should have been held responsible for the cost of rearing Jordan Melchior.

Quite possibly, the stress suffered by the established techniques when some members of the House of Lords sought to apply (or disapply) them in *McFarlane v Tayside* tells us little about the inherent shortcomings of those techniques, although it does tell us that there are limits to the fact situations in which they are useful. It is also instructive to note that there was a significant public reaction to the outcome in *Cattanach v Melchior*. Perhaps Lord Steyn was not so wrong to consult (at least hypothetically) the commuter on the London Underground. There is evidence that the person on the Bourke Street tram or the Bondi bus might have agreed with the proposition he derived from that imaginary poll.[84]

Name or the Wrong Name?' (2010) 1 PN 39 that since the common law has gradually come to recognize autonomy as capable of overriding sanctity of life itself as a value, such claims should not necessarily be impossible.

[82] *Review of the Law of Negligence*, Commonwealth of Australia, 2003, chaired by Ipp JA.
[83] *Vellino* is discussed in Chapter 5.
[84] Persons on the 'Bourke Street tram' and on the 'Bondi bus' have been referred to as cousins of the man on the Clapham omnibus in Melbourne and Sydney respectively.

6. GENERAL ASSESSMENT: THE DUTY OF CARE TODAY

When we introduced the duty concept in Chapter 3, we ended with a challenge. Are questions of duty currently being resolved in a properly reasoned manner? A first stage in answering this question is to ask whether the outcomes of cases are *predictable*. It has to be admitted that, often, they are not. On the other hand, this may indicate only that the issues arising in negligence are both complex and debatable. Perhaps predictability is too much to hope for, as the most settled categories can become unsettled by new arguments. An example of this is the decision of the Court of Appeal in *Shell (UK) v Total (UK)*. A second aspect of the question is whether decisions can be understood in rational terms once they have been reached. As to this, there have been doubts, and even anomalies, in some areas. An example is the law of psychiatric harm, where the decision in *White v Chief Constable* is a confessed obstacle to achieving a rational and consistent approach.

But this kind of criticism can be overstated—or at least over-generalized. In some instances, the *Caparo* criteria have offered quite a successful means of focusing attention on the most relevant issues. Indeed in two of the most notoriously difficult areas of application for the tort of negligence—economic loss and public authority liability—it can be argued that courts have applied *Caparo* criteria with increasing success in recent years, and edged their way towards a more consistent method of deciding such cases. The *Caparo* approach is also politically expedient in certain respects. As we explained in Chapter 3, *Caparo* requires *positive reasons* for a duty of care to be imposed in a novel situation. That being so, *Caparo* can deal with (and even in some respects has allowed the courts to anticipate) the emergent concern with 'compensation culture': the idea that responsibility for harm (even if it is carelessly caused, or carelessly not prevented) should not be too easily passed to others. If tort is becoming more open to public criticism, then the *Caparo* test provides tools for adjusting the balance between claimants, defendants, and broader interests.

If we take the recent developments discussed in this chapter together, the overwhelming impression is that the 'state of the art' in duty questions has become well attuned to *controlling* liability. Does it also now assist in identifying cases where a duty should be recognized? The culture of negligence—and perhaps of tort liability generally—has been one of restraint. The dominance of duty as the means of controlling claims (to the exclusion of breach, for example), is partly to be explained in this way. To leave the determination of liability questions to the results of a case-specific and factual enquiry by contrast would be to invite litigation, in which courts may respond with sympathy to a meritorious claimant.

The House of Lords in its final few years was keen to remove the temptation for case-by-case expansion of the tort of negligence. Yet despite this, two of the most significant recent decisions in this area from its successor, the Supreme Court, have moved forward the boundaries of liability. These are *Smith v Ministry of Defence*, considered in the present chapter, and *Woodland v Essex County Council* [2013] UKSC 66; [2013] 3 WLR 1227, discussed in Chapter 9. Not only were novel duties accepted in principle in these cases, but the majority of the Supreme Court in *Smith* seemed to avoid both the usual preference for dealing with policy questions at the duty stage; and the general caution of domestic courts in pressing forward liabilities in policy-sensitive areas. The court also pressed forward positive duties to protect Convention rights where the Strasbourg court has yet to venture. It is too soon to say whether a new chapter in development of the tort of negligence is therefore now opening; and the more recent decision in *Michael* appears to pull the other way; but these decisions illustrate the capacity of the law of tort to change, and to deliver surprises.

7. CONCLUSIONS

i.   On the whole, the issues explored in this chapter illustrate that the duty concept, which first emerged as a unifying device in *Donoghue v Stevenson*, now plays a significant role as a control device, setting the boundaries of the tort of negligence. This is particularly notable in relation to psychiatric damage, and especially the duties owed to secondary victims. Here, it is hard to deny that some of the control devices are arbitrary in the sense that no principled reason can be offered for the distinctions that are made by the law. In *White v Chief Constable*, this was expressly noted by the House of Lords, in declining to move the law forward incrementally.

ii. Nevertheless, the general story is one of incremental development. There are some clear areas of no liability defined through use of the duty concept: one of these is the non-recoverability of purely economic loss consequent on the purchase of defective property. Beyond these clear areas of no liability however, the courts have developed concepts which are capable of being used across categories of case. With the assistance of the House of Lords in *CEC v Barclays Bank*, potentially conflicting approaches to duty—under *Caparo v Dickman*, and *Hedley Byrne*—have been reconciled as alternatives with largely compatible answers.

iii. A newer challenge applying to public authority defendants is the relationship between duty of care issues, and the expansion of tort-like positive duties under the ECHR, given their new status in domestic courts since the enactment of the HRA 1998. As these tort-like duties expand, a challenge is created for corresponding areas of 'no liability' at common law. Whether the judgment against liability in such cases is based in policy, or in application of general principle, why is it that common law is so much more reluctant than the European Convention to impose positive duties to avoid harm to citizens? Can this distinction be justified? With discussion of a potential repeal of the HRA, would domestic courts be content to see these duties disappear? Or would common law need to expand to fill the gap? This is one of the key developing tensions for the tort of negligence.

FURTHER READING

Psychiatric Harm

Bailey, S., and Nolan, D., 'The *Page v Smith* Saga: a Tale of Inauspicious Origins and Unintended Consequences' (2010) 69 CLJ 495.

Case, P., 'Secondary Iatrogenic Harm: Claims for Psychiatric Damage Following a Death Caused by Medical Error' (2004) 67 MLR 561.

Handford, P., 'Psychiatric Injury: The New Era' (2003) 11 Tort L Rev 13.

Handford, P., 'Psychiatric Injury in Breach of a Relationship' (2007) 27 LS 26–50.

Hedley, S., 'Morbid Musings of the Reasonable Chief Constable' [1992] CLJ 16.

Hilson, C., 'Liability for Psychiatric Injury: Primary and Secondary Victims Revisited' (2002) 18 PN 167–76.

Jones, M., 'Liability for Psychiatric Illness—More Principle, Less Subtlety?' [1995] 4 Web JCLI.

Lee, J., 'The Fertile Imagination of the Common Law' (2009) 17 Torts Law Journal 130–43.

Mullaney N. J., and Handford P. R., *Tort Liability for Psychiatric Damage* (2nd edn, Lawbook Co., 2005).

Nolan, D., 'Reforming Liability for Psychiatric Injury in Scotland: A Recipe for Uncertainty?' (2005) 68 MLR 983.

Stapleton, J., 'In Restraint of Tort', in P. Birks (ed.), *The Frontiers of Liability*, vol 2 (Oxford: Oxford University Press, 1994).

Teff, H., 'Liability for Negligently Inflicted Psychiatric Harm: Justifications and Boundaries' [1998] 57 CLJ 91.

Teff, H., 'Liability for Psychiatric Illness: Advancing Cautiously' (1998) 61 MLR 849.

Teff, H., *Causing Psychiatric and Emotional Harm: Reshaping the Boundaries of Legal Liability* (Oxford: Hart Publishing, 2008).

Trindade, F., 'Nervous Shock and Negligent Conduct' (1996) 112 LQR 22.

Pure Economic Loss

Barker, K., 'Unreliable Assumptions in the Modern Law of Negligence' (1993) 109 LQR 461.

Barker, K., 'Are We Up To Expectations? Solicitors, Beneficiaries, and the Tort/Contract Divide' (1994) 14 OJLS 137.

Barker, K., 'Economic Loss and the Duty of Care: A Study in the Exercise of Legal Justification', in C. E. F. Rickett (ed.), *Justifying Private Law Remedies* (Oxford: Hart Publishing, 2008).

Benson, P., 'The Basis for Excluding Economic Loss in Tort Law', in D. Owen (ed.), *Philosophical Foundations of Tort Law* (Oxford: Clarendon Press, 1995).

Burrows, A., 'Solving the Problem of Concurrent Liability' (1995) CLP 103.

Buxton, R., 'How the Common Law gets Made: *Hedley Byrne* and other Cautionary Tales' (2009) 125 LQR 60–78.

Cane, P., *Tort Law and Economic Interests* (2nd edn, Oxford: Clarendon Press, 1995).

Cane, P., 'The Blight of Economic Loss: Is There Life After *Perre v Apand*?' (2000) 8 TLJ 246.

Cooke, R., 'An Impossible Distinction' (1991) 107 LQR 46.

Duncan Wallace, I., '*Anns* Beyond Repair' (1991) 107 LQR 228.

Feldthusen, B., *Economic Negligence: The Recovery of Pure Economic Loss* (Toronto: Carswell, 2000).

Feldthusen, B., 'Pure Economic Loss in the High Court of Australia: Reinventing the Square Wheel?' (2000) 8 Tort L Rev 33.

Mitchell, P., and Mitchell, C., 'Negligence Liability for Pure Economic Loss' (2005) 121 LQR 194.

O'Dair, R., '*Murphy v Brentwood*: A House With Firm Foundations?' (1991) MLR 561.

Spencer, J. R., 'Defective Premises Act 1972—Defective Law and Defective Law Reform' [1974] 33 CLJ 307.

Stapleton, J., 'Duty of Care and Economic Loss: A Wider Agenda' (1991) 107 LQR 249.

Stapleton, J., 'Comparative Economic Loss: Lessons From Case-Law-Focused Middle Theory' (2002) 50 UCLA L Rev 531.

Stapleton, J., 'The Golden Thread at the Heart of Tort Law: Protection of the Vulnerable' (2003) 24 Aust Bar Rev 135.

Whittaker, S., 'The Application of the "Broad Principle" of *Hedley Byrne* as between Parties to a Contract' (1997) 17 LS 169.

Witting, C., 'Distinguishing Between Property Damage and Economic Loss: A Personality Thesis' (2001) 21 LS 481.

Witting, C., 'Duty of Care: An Analytical Approach' (2005) 25 OJLS 33.

Yap, Po Jen, 'Pure Economic Loss and Defects in the Law of Negligence' (2009) 17 Tort L Rev 80–99.

Yeo, S., 'Rethinking Proximity: A Paper Tiger?' (1997) Tort L Rev 174–80.

Public Authorities

Arden, M., 'Human Rights and Civil Wrongs: Tort Law Under the Spotlight' (2010) PL 140–59.

Bailey, S., 'Public Authority Liability in Negligence: the Continued Search for Coherence' (2006) 26 LS 155.

Bowman, M. J., and Bailey, S., 'Negligence in Public Law—A Positive Obligation to Rescue' [1994] PL 277.

Carnwath, R., 'Welfare Services—Liabilities in Tort After the Human Rights Act' [2001] PL 210.

Carnwath, R., 'Postscript' [2001] PL 475.

Craig, P., 'Compensation and Public Law' (1980) 96 LQR 413.

Craig, P., and Fairgrieve, D., '*Barrett*, Negligence and Discretionary Powers' [1999] PL 626.

Fairgrieve, D., 'The Human Rights Act 1998, Damages, and Tort Law' [2001] PL 695.

Fairgrieve, D., *State Liability in Tort: A Comparative Study* (Oxford: Oxford University Press, 2003).

Goudkamp, J., 'A Revolution in Duty of Care?' (2015) 131 LQR 519.

Harlow, C., *State Liability—Tort Law and Beyond* (Oxford: Clarendon Press, 2004).

Hickman, T., 'Negligence and A.6, The Great Escape?' [2002] CLJ 14.

Hoffmann, Lord, 'The Universality of Human Rights' (2009) 125 LQR 416–32.

Mullender, R., 'Military Operations, Fairness and the British State' (2014) 130 LQR 28

Nolan, D., 'The Liability of Public Authorities for Failing to Confer Benefits' (2011) 127 LQR 260.

Tettenborn, A., 'Wrongful Death, Human Rights, and the Fatal Accidents Act' (2012) 128 LQR 327.

Tofaris, S., and Steel, S., 'Negligence Liability for Omissions and the Police' (2016) 75 CLJ 128.

Immunities

Hughes, K., 'The Abolition of Expert Witness Immunity' (2011) 70 CLJ 516

Mullender, R., 'Military Operations, Fairness and the British State' (2014) 130 LQR 28.

Failed Sterilizations

Hoyano, L., 'Misconceptions About Wrongful Conception' (2002) 65 MLR 883.

Priaulx, N., 'Joy to the World: A (Healthy) Child is Born! Reconceptualizing "Harm" in Wrongful Conception' (2004) 13 S & LS 5.

Priaulx, N., *The Harm Paradox: Tort Law and the Unwanted Child in an Era of Choice* (London: Routledge, 2007).

Stewart, A., 'Damages for the Birth of a Child' (1995) 40 JLSS 298.

Todd, S., 'Wrongful Conception, Wrongful Birth and Wrongful Life' (2005) 27 Sydney Law Review 525.

Todd, S., 'Accidental Conception and Accident Compensation' (2012) 28 PN 196.

PART IV

GENERAL MATTERS

The next three chapters introduce a range of matters which will decisively affect the remedy that can be obtained by a successful claimant. Vicarious liability (Chapter 9) and principles of contribution (Chapter 7) affect the range of parties who may bear, or share in, the burden of liability. Principles applying to assessment of damages (Chapter 8) determine what that burden is.

The issues considered here are not confined to negligence. They apply to all actions in tort, even if in some respects the issues raised are different. That is why these chapters occupy a separate section of their own, while the rest of the text is divided according to causes of action. The issues explored in these chapters are, however, particularly significant for negligence. As a damage-based tort, the components of negligence cannot really be understood without reference to the recoverable damage for which the defendant may be liable. The question of who will ultimately bear the liability (for example, an employer of the tortfeasor, or two or more parties through the principles of contribution) also sheds additional light on the tests of liability, and especially fairness, which operate within negligence.

These matters are of such great practical and theoretical importance to all torts that they deserve to be at the heart of the book. But it is also important that they are not separated too far from the chapters concerned with the essential components of liability in negligence. Rightly or wrongly, most undergraduate courses focus to a large extent on negligence. The truth is that only a very partial understanding of that tort can be gleaned without consideration of the issues, including remedies and the sharing of liability, introduced in this Part.

7

LIMITATION AND CONTRIBUTION

CENTRAL ISSUES

i) A claim may eventually become 'time-barred' if no proceedings are commenced. Statutory rules of 'limitation' govern the time-barring of claims, and are justified by reasons of both practicality and fairness. The current rules of limitation applying to tort are mainly to be found in the Limitation Act 1980.

ii) A liable party may seek a 'contribution' to damages from other parties who could be sued in respect of the same damage. In principle, contribution proceedings are not the business of the tort claimant and rules of contribution generally play no role in the claim itself. The rules of contribution are set out in the Civil Liability (Contribution) Act 1978.

1. LIMITATION OF ACTIONS

1.1 WHAT ARE LIMITATION RULES AND WHY DO WE HAVE THEM?

'Limitation' is generally referred to as a 'defence' to an action. It is for the defendant to establish that the relevant period has expired and that the action is 'time-barred'. However, strictly speaking the claim itself is not extinguished by the expiry of the relevant period (with the exception of the action in conversion).[1] Instead, the *remedy* becomes unavailable.

Ronex Properties v John Laing [1983] QB 398

The defendants applied to have the claim against them struck out as disclosing no cause of action, because the applicable time period for bringing the action had expired. The Court of Appeal refused to strike out on this ground (although it would have considered striking out on different grounds, if evidence and argument had been presented).

---

[1] By Limitation Act 1980, s 3, *title to goods is extinguished* if a claim in conversion is not brought within the relevant limitation period.

Donaldson LJ

Authority apart, I would have thought that it was absurd to contend that a writ or third party notice could be struck out as disclosing no cause of action, merely because the defendant may have a defence under the Limitation Acts . . . it is trite law that the English Limitation Acts bar the remedy and not the right; and, furthermore, that they do not even have this effect unless and until pleaded . . . .

Why have Limitation Rules?

The need for some rules of limitation is not seriously in doubt.[2] Rather, it is the complexity of the current rules, and the existence of potential anomalies in their application, which give rise to most criticism.

A. McGee and G. P. Scanlan, 'Judicial Attitudes to Limitation' (2005) 24 CJQ 460–80

. . . despite the present unsatisfactory state of the law of limitation, the rationale behind a coherent and practical law of limitation is both clear and simple. Potential defendants should not have to live with the risk of legal action indefinitely if for any reason a potential claimant does not pursue his remedy, furthermore, old or stale claims are difficult to try when memories are clouded, and where evidence has probably been lost. Parties should be certain that, in conducting their business and professional affairs, or indeed their everyday activities, they are able to predict when they can regard a potential action in which they could be defendants as stale and expired. The expiration of stale claims is also in the interests of the state, since the state has a legitimate interest in the quality of the justice it achieves for its citizens.

Prompt litigation increases the chances of a measured and just result. It also ensures that public money is not wasted in hearing claims which cannot be dealt with properly. The interests of claimants are also served by a rational law of limitation. The Committee on Limitation of Actions in Cases of Personal Injury in its Report recognized the value of limitation periods in prompting claimants to act swiftly in pursuit of their rights. The authors noted that: "We apprehend that the law is designed to encourage plaintiffs [claimants] not to go to sleep on their rights, but to institute proceedings as soon as it is reasonably practicable for them to do so."

1.2 THE GENERAL POSITION UNDER THE LIMITATION ACT 1980

The present rules on limitation are largely set out in the Limitation Act 1980. The following section states the general approach in cases of tort. It is important to note that there are some large and very important exceptions to this general rule, explored below. Equally, some

[2] Exceptionally, Keith Patten argues against such rules in cases of personal injury in 'Limitation Periods in Personal Injury Claims—Justice Obstructed' (2006) CJQ 349–66. P. J. Davies, 'Limitations on the Law of Limitation' (1982) 98 LQR 249, argues that all fixed periods should be abolished, to be replaced by an entirely discretionary system.

individual actions—such as actions in defamation, and actions under the Human Rights Act 1998 (HRA)—have their own statutory limitation periods.[3]

Limitation Act 1980

2 Time limit for actions founded on tort

An action founded on tort shall not be brought after the expiration of six years from the date on which the cause of action accrued.

Generally speaking, a cause of action in tort accrues when the relevant invasion of a protected right or interest (which may or may not be the result of wrongful conduct) has occurred. This is when the tort is actionable. It is not necessarily the date of the defendant's tortious act or omission. In the case of torts of damage (including negligence), the cause of action accrues when the relevant *damage* occurs. These torts are *actionable* when there is damage which is not 'insignificant' (*Cartledge v Jopling*, below). That is also when the limitation period starts to run.

As a result, in cases where there are potential claims in *both* tort *and* contract, the tort action is often more long-lived than the action in contract. An action in contract starts to run when the contract is breached, and expires six years later.[4] Time will not begin to run in respect of a claim in the tort of negligence until the damage is done. An illustrative case where this led the claimants to choose to sue in tort—and where the House of Lords allowed them to make this choice—is *Henderson v Merrett* [1995] 2 AC 145 (Chapter 6, Section 2). Nevertheless, this will not always mean the date at which the claimant actually suffered financial loss. For example in *Axa Insurance Ltd v Akther & Darby* [2009] EWCA Civ 1166, a claim in respect of failure to vet claims under a legal expenses insurance scheme was held to have accrued when insurance policies were issued: it was at this point that the claimants had incurred 'damage', since a proper valuation of the policies at that point would take into account the vetting failure.

In other respects also, identifying the time *when damage occurred* is not as straightforward as it might sound. We will consider two areas where the interpretation of section 2 and its statutory predecessors has led to recognized injustice, so that further legislation has been required. The first relates to personal injury generally; the second relates to other instances of negligence specifically.

1.3 PERSONAL INJURY CASES

Cartledge v Jopling [1963] 758

The applicable limitation periods were set out in section 2(1) of the Limitation Act 1939. That provision was expressed in similar terms to the present section 2 (above), but was subject to fewer exceptions and qualifications.[5] This case shows the pressing need for the reforms that

---

[3] Defamation Act 1996, s 5, and HRA, s 7(5), specify periods of one year; in each case, there is a statutory discretion to override the time limit.

[4] Limitation Act 1980, s 5.

[5] There were exceptions for cases of disability (e.g. where the plaintiff was a minor), fraud, and mistake.

are now encapsulated in sections 11, 14, and 33 of the Limitation Act 1980. Later we will see the problems of interpretation to which section 14, in particular, has led.

The plaintiffs were steel dressers working in a factory. Through exposure to dust, they contracted a lung disease, pneumoconiosis. This is a 'progressive' disease. The workmen commenced actions in negligence and breach of statutory duty, on 1 October 1956. It was established that there had been no breaches of duty after (at the latest) September 1950. Thus, the claim would be out of time unless the cause of action 'accrued' later than the breaches themselves.

Available evidence suggested the plaintiffs had suffered substantial injury without becoming aware of it. They argued that, as a matter of principle, their action could not become time-barred *before they had any relevant knowledge* of the injury suffered. The House of Lords felt compelled to reject their argument. As a matter of statutory interpretation, unless discovery of the injury was prevented by fraud or mistake within section 26 of the Limitation Act 1939, time would begin to run when the injury occurred, and not when the injured party was able to discover it. The House was under no illusions as to the injustice of this, and strongly supported the need for legislative reform.

Lord Reid, at 771–3

… It is now too late for the courts to question or modify the rule that a cause of action accrues as soon as a wrongful act has caused personal injury beyond what can be regarded as negligible, even when that injury is unknown to and cannot be discovered by the sufferer, and that further injury arising from the same act at a later date does not give rise to a further cause of action. It appears to me to be unreasonable and unjustifiable in principle that a cause of action should be held to accrue before it is possible to discover any injury and, therefore, before it is possible to raise any action. If this were a matter governed by the common law I would hold that a cause of action ought not to be held to accrue until either the injured person has discovered the injury or it would be possible for him to discover it if he took such steps as were reasonable in the circumstances. The common law ought never to produce a wholly unreasonable result, nor ought existing authorities to be read so literally as to produce such a result in circumstances never contemplated when they were decided.

But the present question depends on statute, the Limitation Act, 1939, and section 26 of that Act appears to me to make it impossible to reach the result which I have indicated. That section makes special provisions where fraud or mistake is involved: it provides that time shall not begin to run until the fraud has been or could with reasonable diligence have been discovered. Fraud here has been given a wide interpretation, but obviously it could not be extended to cover this case. The necessary implication from that section is that, where fraud or mistake is not involved, time begins to run whether or not the damage could be discovered. So the mischief in the present case can only be prevented by further legislation.

Legislation remedied the problem, initially through the Limitation Act 1963. The current position is to be found in sections 11, 14, and 33 of the Limitation Act 1980.

11 Special time limit for actions in respect of personal injuries

(1) This section applies to any action for damages for negligence, nuisance or breach of duty (whether the duty exists by virtue of a contract or of provision made by or under a statute or independently of any contract or any such provision) where the damages claimed by the

plaintiff for the negligence, nuisance or breach of duty consist of or include damages in respect of personal injuries to the plaintiff or any other person.

[(1A)   This section does not apply to any action brought for damages under section 3 of the Protection from Harassment Act 1997.]

(2) None of the time limits given in the preceding provisions of this Act shall apply to an action to which this section applies.

(3) An action to which this section applies shall not be brought after the expiration of the period applicable in accordance with subsection (4) or (5) below.

(4) Except where subsection (5) below applies, the period applicable is three years from—

    (a) the date on which the cause of action accrued; or

    (b) the date of knowledge (if later) of the person injured.

(5) If the person injured dies before the expiration of the period mentioned in subsection (4) above, the period applicable as respects the cause of action surviving for the benefit of his estate by virtue of section 1 of the Law Reform (Miscellaneous Provisions) Act 1934 shall be three years from—

    (a) the date of death; or

    (b) the date of the personal representative's knowledge;

    whichever is the later.

Compared with the general statement about civil claims in section 2, section 11 sets out a *shorter* time period of three years for most actions in personal injury. However, this is capable of running from a later date, namely *the date of knowledge of the injured party* (or, if that party has died, from the date of knowledge of their personal representative).

Clearly, the section relates only to claims in respect of personal injury. By section 38 of the Limitation Act 1980:

"personal injuries" includes any disease and any impairment of a person's physical or mental condition ... In terms of limitation periods, there is no distinction between *physical* or *mental* injuries: see further *Adams v Bracknell* [2005] AC 76, below.

But to what range of *torts* does section 11 apply? The statutory wording (set out above) refers to 'negligence, nuisance or breach of duty'. In Chapter 2, we noted the interpretation of this section in *Stubbings v Webb* [1993] AC 498, in which the House of Lords held that actions in *trespass to the person* involve no 'breach of duty', and therefore come outside the reach of section 11, even if they involve personal injury.[6] As we also noted, this has now been remedied by *A v Hoare* [2008] UKHL 6, in which the House of Lords departed from *Stubbings v Webb*. Trespass to the person which causes personal injury (including mental harm) will now be subject to the same limitation period as negligence causing personal injury. The limitation period begins not with the injury but with the 'date of knowledge'. As we will see, there is also the possibility of a further extension within the discretion of the court.

[6] Trespass to the person does not *necessarily* involve personal injury, since trespass is actionable per se.

'What is the Date of Knowledge?'

14 Definition of date of knowledge for purposes of sections 11 and 12[7]

(1) … In sections 11 and 12 of this Act references to a person's date of knowledge are references to the date on which he first had knowledge of the following facts—

that the injury in question was significant; and

(a) that the injury was attributable in whole or in part to the act or omission which is alleged to constitute negligence, nuisance or breach of duty; and

(b) the identity of the defendant; and

(c) if it is alleged that the act or omission was that of a person other than the defendant, the identity of that person and the additional facts supporting the bringing of an action against the defendant;

(d) and knowledge that any acts or omissions did or did not, as a matter of law, involve negligence, nuisance or breach of duty is irrelevant.

…

(2) For the purposes of this section an injury is significant if the person whose date of knowledge is in question would reasonably have considered it sufficiently serious to justify his instituting proceedings for damages against a defendant who did not dispute liability and was able to satisfy a judgment.

(3) For the purposes of this section a person's knowledge includes knowledge which he might reasonably have been expected to acquire—

(a) from facts observable or ascertainable by him; or

(b) from facts ascertainable by him with the help of medical or other appropriate expert advice which it is reasonable for him to seek;

but a person shall not be fixed under this subsection with knowledge of a fact ascertainable only with the help of expert advice so long as he has taken all reasonable steps to obtain (and, where appropriate, to act on) that advice.

This section is of fundamental importance. Its interpretation, however, has created continuing difficulties, stemming from the need for limitation rules to reflect what a claimant knew or could be expected to have known about their injury and its causes, rather than being based simply on issues of factual causation of injury. Here we explore some key recent cases where courts have grappled with those difficulties. The last case in particular shows that the difficulties are by no means fully resolved.

A first problem is posed by subsection (3), which refers to knowledge which the claimant 'might reasonably have been expected to acquire'. Clearly, this necessitates a judgment as to 'reasonableness'. But should reasonableness be assessed *objectively* (by reference to *the reasonable person*), or *subjectively* (taking into account characteristics of the particular claimant)? The answer given in the following case is that the test is *objective*; but that it reflects the circumstances in which the claimant is placed.

7 Section 12 relates to claims under the Fatal Accidents Act 1976. These are claims for bereavement and loss of dependency by the dependents of a deceased victim of tort: see further Chapter 8.

Adams v Bracknell Forest BC [2005] 1 AC 76

The claimant, an adult, argued that the defendant education authority had negligently failed to diagnose his dyslexia as a child, and that his untreated condition had led to psychological ill-effects. The House of Lords determined, following *Phelps v Hillingdon* [2005] 1 AC 76, that the claim was one for *personal injuries*, so that it came within the scope of sections 11, 14, and 33.

Under section 11, the claim would be time-barred unless the claimant could show that the 'date of knowledge' (defined, as we have said, by section 14) was substantially delayed. The claimant argued that he could not have been reasonably expected to realize that the problems he experienced in adulthood were related to his undiagnosed dyslexia. This was accepted. However, he further argued that he had no grounds for acting sooner in order to *seek expert advice* in respect of his problems, which would have revealed the connection. Eventually, he told his life story to an educational psychologist whom he met at a party, and she persuaded him to consult a solicitor. Resolution of the limitation question therefore turned on interpretation of section 14(3)(b) above, setting out the circumstances under which a claimant may reasonably be expected to seek expert advice.

Lord Hoffmann argued that the test for reasonableness in section 14(3) is generally 'objective'. He accepted that the test should reflect the likely characteristics *of a person who had suffered the injury in question*. But even allowing for this, Lord Hoffmann was not persuaded that a reasonable person suffering from undiagnosed dyslexia and its mental effects could fail, over many years, to disclose to his medical adviser the essential facts which would lead to relevant advice under section 14(3)(b) above. In effect, it might be said that there is an 'obligation of curiosity' upon the injured party.[8]

Lord Hoffmann, *Adams v Bracknell*

47 It is true that the plaintiff must be assumed to be a person who has suffered the injury in question and not some other person. But … I do not see how his particular character or intelligence can be relevant. In my opinion, section 14(3) requires one to assume that a person who is aware that he has suffered a personal injury, serious enough to be something about which he would go and see a solicitor if he knew he had a claim, will be sufficiently curious about the causes of the injury to seek whatever expert advice is appropriate.

Constructive knowledge in this case

48 The judge held that Mr Adams acted reasonably in making no inquiry into the reasons for his literacy problems. I do not think that he based this finding upon matters of character or intelligence which were peculiar to Mr Adams. If the judge had been relying upon his personal characteristics, he might have been hard put to explain why someone who was willing to confide in a lady he met at a dancing party was unable to confide in his doctor. But the judge appears to have thought that extreme reticence about his problems was the standard behaviour which ought to be expected from anyone suffering from untreated dyslexia and that the conversation with Ms Harding was an aberration.

49 In principle, I think that the judge was right in applying the standard of reasonable behaviour to a person assumed to be suffering from untreated dyslexia. If the injury itself would reasonably inhibit him from seeking advice, then that is a factor which must be taken into account. My difficulty is with the basis for the finding that such a person could not reasonably be expected to reveal the source of his difficulties to his medical adviser. In the absence of some special inhibiting factor, I should have thought that Mr Adams could reasonably have been expected to seek expert advice years ago. The congeries of symptoms which he described to Dr Gardner, which he said had been making his life miserable for years, which the knew to be rooted in his inability to read and write and about which he had sought medical advice, would have made it almost irrational not to disclose what he felt to be the root cause. If he had done so, he would no doubt have been referred to someone with expertise in dyslexia and would have discovered that it was something which might have been treated earlier.

The existence of an 'obligation of curiosity' giving rise to general rules was doubted by the Court of Appeal in *Whiston v London SHA* [2010] EWCA Civ 195, Dyson LJ suggesting that the remarks in para [47] quoted above did not form part of the *ratio* of *Adams*; nor were they fully reflected in the language of section 14(3). The court should simply consider 'what is reasonably to have been expected of the claimant in all the circumstances of the case' ([59]). A claimant is not fixed in all cases—as the defendant had argued—with knowledge of 'such facts as he would have ascertained if he had made appropriate inquiries'. In *Whiston* itself, the claimant had suffered a deterioration of a condition which he had suffered all his life, rather than a sudden event; and this affected the time at which a reasonable person in his position would have sought advice. In *Johnson v Ministry of Defence* [2012] EWCA Civ 1505, a case concerning the gradual onset of deafness, Smith LJ thought that Lord Hoffmann's remarks about 'curiosity' were not intended to be insensitive to circumstances:

Smith LJ, *Johnson v Ministry of Defence*

[24] … It seems to me that what Lord Hoffmann must have meant was that there would be an assumption that a person who had suffered a significant injury would be sufficiently curious to seek advice unless there were reasons why a reasonable person in his position would not have done.…

[25] … there are good policy reasons for this objective and more demanding standard. If a claimant is entitled to bring an action *as of right*, many years, possibly decades, after the relevant events, there may be real unfairness to defendants. So the *right* to bring a long delayed action must be circumscribed.…

In *Adams v Bracknell*, the primary limitation period having passed, this left the question of discretion under section 33. The existence of this discretion was one of the factors justifying a 'tightening up' in the determination of the 'primary' limitation period, as defined in sections 11 and 14. Before we turn to section 33 in its own right however, we should consider further important developments in the interpretation of section 14.

Sexual Assault Cases

In *KR v Bryn Alyn* [2003] 1 QB 1441 the Court of Appeal adopted a broadly subjective approach to section 14(2) of the Limitation Act 1980, which defines 'serious damage'.[9] Given the wording of the subsection, the court thought that it had to decide whether it would reasonably have occurred to the claimant, given his life history, to bring a civil action for damages within three years of his majority. Each case had to be considered individually taking account of all the circumstances. This approach has been disapproved by the House of Lords in *A v Hoare*, extracted below. While section 14(3) might involve some subjective as well as objective elements (what should C reasonably have done?), section 14(2) is an entirely objective provision. It was concerned with the objective seriousness of the injury suffered.

A v Hoare [2008] UKHL 6; [2008] 1 AC 844

We have seen, in Chapter 2, that *A v Hoare* released the law of trespass in personal injury cases from the inflexible limitation period imposed upon it by the House of Lords in *Stubbings v Webb* [1993] AC 498. It ensured that claimants who alleged that they are the victims of abuse no longer have to frame their claims in negligence to avoid the limitation problem. The importance of this was encapsulated by Baroness Hale:

Baroness Hale, *A v Hoare*

54 My Lords, until the 1970s many people were reluctant to believe that child sexual abuse took place at all. Now we know only too well that it does. But it remains hard to protect children from it. This is because the perpetrators are so often people in authority over the victims, sometimes people whom the victims love and trust. These perpetrators have many ways, some subtle and some not so subtle, of making their victims keep quiet about what they have suffered. The abuse itself is the reason why so many victims do not come forward until years after the event. This presents a challenge to a legal system which resists stale claims. Six years, let alone three, from reaching the age of majority is not long enough, especially since the age of majority was reduced from 21 to 18.

55 Fortunately, by the time the problem was recognised, some flexibility had been introduced in personal injury cases, albeit to meet the rather different problem of the insidious and unremarked onset of industrial disease. Then along came *Stubbings v Webb* [1993] AC 498, holding that this flexibility did not apply to cases of deliberate assault. For the reasons given by my noble and learned friend, Lord Hoffmann, I agree that *Stubbings* was wrongly decided and have nothing to add on that point.

However, when it came to the details of the relevant limitation periods, the House took a restrictive approach to the meaning of section 14(2) Limitation Act 1980. Our next extract focuses on the section 14 issues; later we will turn to the more generous interpretation of the discretion conferred by section 33.

---

[9] Section 14(2) is extracted above. In order to avoid the problem in *Stubbings v Webb*, which was then still binding on the court, this case was treated as raising a claim in negligence.

Lord Hoffmann, A v Hoare

33 The question which has arisen is whether the definition of significance in section 14(2) allows any (and if so, how much) account to be taken of personal characteristics of the claimant, either pre-existing or consequent upon the injury which he has suffered. This question was first considered in *McCafferty v Metropolitan Police District Receiver* [1977] 1 WLR 1073, 1081, soon after the 1975 Act had come into force. After reading the then equivalent of subsection 14(2), Geoffrey Lane LJ said: "the test is partly a subjective test, namely: 'would this plaintiff have considered the injury sufficiently serious?' and partly an objective test, namely: 'would he have been reasonable if he did not regard it as sufficiently serious?' ..."

34 I respectfully think that the notion of the test being partly objective and partly subjective is somewhat confusing. Section 14(2) is a test for what counts as a significant injury. The material to which that test applies is generally "subjective" in the sense that it is applied to what the claimant knows of his injury rather than the injury as it actually was. Even then, his knowledge may have to be supplemented with imputed "objective" knowledge under section 14(3). But the test itself is an entirely impersonal standard: not whether the claimant himself would have considered the injury sufficiently serious to justify proceedings but whether he would "reasonably" have done so ...

35 It follows that I cannot accept that one must consider whether someone "with [the] plaintiff's intelligence" would have been reasonable if he did not regard the injury as sufficiently serious. That seems to me to destroy the effect of the word "reasonably". Judges should not have to grapple with the notion of the reasonable unintelligent person. Once you have ascertained what the claimant knew and what he should be treated as having known, the actual claimant drops out of the picture. Section 14(2) is, after all, simply a standard of the seriousness of the injury and nothing more. Standards are in their nature impersonal and do not vary with the person to whom they are applied.

36 In *KR v Bryn Alyn Community (Holdings) Ltd* [2003] QB 1441, 1459, the Court of Appeal ventured even further into subjectivity. That too was a case of claims by victims of sexual abuse. In giving the judgment of the Court, Auld LJ said that victims of such abuse may regard such conduct by persons in authority as normal. It might be unreal to expect people with such psychological injuries to commence proceedings. Therefore, he said, at para 42:

"However artificial it may seem to pose the question in this context, section 14 requires the court, on a case by case basis, to ask whether such an already damaged child would reasonably turn his mind to litigation as a solution to his problems?"

37 This approach treats the statute as if it had said that time should run from the date on which it would have been reasonable to expect the claimant to institute proceedings. If it had said that, the question posed in *Bryn Alyn* would have been correct. But section 14 makes time run from when the claimant has knowledge of certain facts, not from when he could have been expected to take certain steps. Section 14(2) does no more than define one of those facts by reference to a standard of seriousness.

...

39 The difference between section 14(2) and 14(3) emerges very clearly if one considers the relevance in each case of the claimant's injury. Because section 14(3) turns on what the claimant ought reasonably to have done, one must take into account the injury which the claimant has suffered. You do not assume that a person who has been blinded could reasonably have acquired knowledge by seeing things. In section 14(2), on the other hand, the

test is external to the claimant and involves no inquiry into what he ought reasonably to have done. It is applied to what the claimant knew or was deemed to have known but the standard itself is impersonal. The effect of the claimant's injuries upon what he could reasonably have been expected to do is therefore irrelevant.

Section 14 having been restricted in this way, the House turned its attention to the discretion in section 33, to which we return later.

AB v Ministry of Defence [2012] UKSC 9

The claims in *AB v Ministry of Defence* related to injuries alleged to have been caused by nuclear testing in the 1950s. At first instance, Foskett J held that the claims were not statute-barred: not until a scientific study published in 2007 would evidence be available to make it reasonable to link their illnesses with the testing. And yet, the majority of claimants had already initiated their claims by 2004, well ahead of this date. The Court of Appeal reversed the judge's decision in relation to limitation; and there was a further appeal to the Supreme Court. Here, a bare majority of Justices decided that the claims were indeed outside the limitation period. Since they also thought the actions to be without chance of success, they did not exercise their discretion to disapply the period under section 33.

The particular difficulty in *AB v Ministry of Defence* was that (in the view of the Justices) there was—even at the time of the Supreme Court's decision—no convincing evidence that the various medical conditions suffered by the claimants were in fact caused by breach of duty on the part of the defendants. Could it be that the limitation period had not yet begun to run, even though actions had long since been commenced? At the same time, many of the claimants had for several years sincerely believed that the nuclear tests were the cause of their injuries. Could such a *belief* be sufficient reason for the time period to begin to run? The statutory language, extracted earlier in this section, relates to *knowledge*, which might well be thought to imply the existence of a fact. This was the view taken by Lord Phillips, in the minority. 'Belief'—or even 'reasonable belief'[10]—is not what the statute requires. Lord Phillips proposed that the only appropriate basis for striking out would be, not limitation, but the lack of prospect of success. This had not been pleaded by the defendants.[11] The interpretation adopted by the minority does, on one view, have the awkward implication that a claim based on insufficient evidence can never become time-barred.

The majority reached the opposite conclusion: the claim was indeed time-barred. Their decision was influenced by an understandable preference that a claim they considered to be hopeless should not be allowed to proceed. But unfortunately, some of the majority judgments appear to interpret a provision referring to 'knowledge' as satisfied where a claimant has formed a strong 'belief'. It is also uncommonly difficult in this case to pinpoint a core argument to unite the views of the majority judges. Lord Wilson appeared to require a particularly high 'degree of confidence' for a 'belief' to amount to 'knowledge' (para [12]). This seems to fly in the face of the objectivism set out in *Adams v Bracknell* and later cases: time begins to run when the reasonable person would have become aware

[10] In this context, any such belief could only be reasonable in the sense that it is not unreasonable. It cannot be that the reasonable person would *objectively* believe there to be a link, since the court at the same time plainly thought there was no evidence to support such a conclusion. Part of the confusion in this case may stem from different senses of what is 'reasonable'.

[11] Lord Brown would have preferred to strike out on this ground nonetheless.

of the defined issues (*Adams*); yet here, a sincere and strong belief which the reasonable person would not have formed can also start the clock ticking. Lord Walker's approach is no easier to pin down:

Lord Walker

50 *Adams* marks a very important shift towards a more objective approach to the claimant's state of knowledge. This goes a long way to blunt or blur the clear distinction, in ordinary discourse, between knowledge and belief. As Simon Brown LJ said in *O'Driscoll v Dudley Health Authority* [1998] Lloyd's Rep Med 210, 221, "knowledge and belief inevitably shade into one another". Lord Donaldson MR's well known statement that "reasonable belief will normally suffice" is reinforced, but weight must be given to the belief being "reasonable"—or, as Lord Wilson JSC suggests, "reasoned".

Adams v Bracknell and its emphasis on an objective test is being used here to support a quite contrary argument, based on a very strong form of subjectivism: believe something enough, and time will begin to run. Lord Brown for his part proposed a significant general principle, namely that 'it is a legal impossibility for a claimant to lack knowledge of attributability for the purpose of s 14(1) at a time after the date of issue of his claim.'

A possible explanation for the 'legal impossibility' referred to may be found in the judgment of Lord Mance. He proposed that the statutory language simply *assumes* that the facts pleaded by the claimant do exist for the purposes of the limitation enquiry. In order to succeed, the defendant needed to show that there had been 'knowledge' (actual or constructive) of those *presumed facts* to the required standard. Adopting this approach, the difference between 'belief' and 'knowledge' would simply cease to be pertinent; and the logical difficulties are avoided. In the present case, assuming the facts asserted by the claimants to be correct, they plainly had sufficient 'knowledge' of them.

Lord Mance, *AB v Ministry of Defence*

86 As matters stand, the claimants clearly have no case on causation. But that is no answer in my opinion to their limitation problems. They have chosen to bring proceedings on the basis of certain facts. Whether the facts by reference to which their case falls to be assessed for limitation purposes are those pleaded (a straightforward allegation of causation) or those later asserted (an increase in the risk of injury being caused or, now, an admission that the claimants cannot presently establish causation, coupled with a submission that the proceedings should continue in the hope that causation will in future prove possible to establish), the limitation question is not whether those facts give rise to a good claim in law. It is when the claimants first had knowledge of those facts. This they did, in each of the nine cases before the court, more than three years prior to the issue of the proceedings (or, in the case of Mr Ogden, more than three years prior to his death).

Section 33: Discretion to Exclude the Time Limit

As already explained, section 11 and section 14 set out the 'primary' limitation period in respect of personal injuries and death. One justification for a fairly tightly defined approach to this primary limitation period is the existence of a discretion to set aside that period, in section 33.

33 Discretionary exclusion of time limit for actions in respect of personal injuries or death

(1) If it appears to the court that it would be equitable to allow an action to proceed having regard to the degree to which—

(a) the provisions of section 11 [or 11A] or 12 of this Act prejudice the plaintiff or any person whom he represents; and

(b) any decision of the court under this subsection would prejudice the defendant or any person whom he represents;

the court may direct that those provisions shall not apply to the action, or shall not apply to any specified cause of action to which the action relates.

(2) In acting under this section the court shall have regard to all the circumstances of the case and in particular to—

(a) the length of, and the reasons for, the delay on the part of the plaintiff;

(b) the extent to which, having regard to the delay, the evidence adduced or likely to be adduced by the plaintiff or the defendant is or is likely to be less cogent than if the action had been brought within the time allowed by section 11, [by section 11A] or (as the case may be) by section 12;

(c) the conduct of the defendant after the cause of action arose, including the extent (if any) to which he responded to requests reasonably made by the plaintiff for information or inspection for the purpose of ascertaining facts which were or might be relevant to the plaintiff's cause of action against the defendant;

(d) the duration of any disability of the plaintiff arising after the date of the accrual of the cause of action;

(e) the extent to which the plaintiff acted promptly and reasonably once he knew whether or not the act or omission of the defendant, to which the injury was attributable, might be capable at that time of giving rise to an action for damages;

(f) the steps, if any, taken by the plaintiff to obtain medical, legal or other expert advice and the nature of any such advice he may have received.

In *A v Hoare*, the House of Lords underlined that section 33 provides an unfettered discretion which should not, as some cases had previously suggested, be taken to be weighted against the claimant. The result was that the House of Lords broadened the potential application of discretion in favour of claimants, while tightening the approach to the primary limitation period, which would give claimants a *right* to proceed irrespective of the merits of the issue.

Lord Hoffmann, A v Hoare

49 That brings me, finally, to the approach of the judge and the Court of Appeal to the exercise of the discretion. In *Bryn Alyn* [2003] QB 1441, para 76, the Court of Appeal said that the judge in that case had gone wrong in giving undue weight to his conclusion that "the claimants' reasons for delay were a product of the alleged abuse … and that, accordingly, it would be unjust to deprive them of a remedy". These matters, said the Court of Appeal, were more appropriately considered under section 14. I am of precisely the opposite opinion, and if your Lordships share my view, the approach to the discretion will have to change.

In *Horton v Sadler* [2007] 1 AC 307 the House rejected a submission that section 33 should be confined to a "residual class of cases", as was anticipated by the 20th Report of the Law Reform Committee (Cmnd 5630) (1974), at para 56. It reaffirmed the decision of the Court of Appeal in *Firman v Ellis* [1978] QB 886, holding that the discretion is unfettered. The judge is expressly enjoined by subsection (3)(a) to have regard to the reasons for delay and in my opinion this requires him to give due weight to evidence, such as there was in this case, that the claimant was for practical purposes disabled from commencing proceedings by the psychological injuries which he had suffered.

These comments should be read in the light of the new acceptance in *A v Hoare* that trespass to the person falls within the same limitation rules as negligence. As the House of Lords pointed out, the issues arising in a negligence claim brought against an organization, on the basis that there had been systemic negligence in respect of the abuse of children in its care, are typically diverse and complex. Many documents and witness statements would be needed if such an allegation were to be properly investigated. If instead the action was one for trespass to the person, the investigation could be expected to be much narrower and more straightforward, raising fewer questions and requiring fewer witnesses. All this is relevant to the exercise of the section 33 discretion. Equally, issues about the particular claimant, which were irrelevant to section 14(2), are relevant to section 33. Some cautionary notes were sounded by Lord Brown, who underlined that the change in emphasis from section 14(2) to section 33 did not mean that section 33 would be used to replicate the extension of the limitation period 'as of right' as had been the effect of the previous interpretation of section 14(2). There was no disagreement with this view. Equally, issues about the particular claimant, which are irrelevant now to section 14(2), are relevant to section 33.

The effect of *A v Hoare* was to release a spate of trespass actions in respect of historic abuse. A number of appeals in such cases were heard together by the Court of Appeal, which sought to clarify the implications of *A v Hoare*.

B v Nugent Care Society [2009] EWCA Civ 827

The Court of Appeal confirmed that the impact of *A v Hoare* was to ensure that the date of knowledge in cases of sexual abuse (and perhaps in numerous other cases) 'is now much earlier than it was previously thought to be'. This was due to the new 'objective' interpretation of section 14(2), as set out above. The court also stressed that in releasing the trespass action from the inflexible limitation period imposed by *A v Hoare*, the difficulties in persuading a court to exercise its discretion and permit an action to be brought outside the period should not be overstated. In the majority of the cases considered, the claims were allowed to proceed.

Cases still Governed by *Cartledge v Jopling*

The interpretation in *Cartledge v Jopling*, as we have seen, no longer applies to most personal injury claims, since legislation provides that the relevant limitation period begins with the claimant's date of knowledge. On the other hand, section 11 (and therefore section 14 and section 33) does not apply to actions which **were already time-barred** before the first 'date of knowledge' provision took effect, in 1963. For these claims, the approach in *Cartledge v Jopling* still applies. An illustration is *McDonnell v Congregation of Christian Brothers Trustees and Others* [2003] UKHL 63; [2004] 1 AC 1101, where the claim had expired six months before section 1 of the Limitation Act 1963 came into force. This section was clearly intended to remove the injustice reflected in *Cartledge v Jopling*, and it provided for a new limitation period running, in an appropriate case, *from the date of knowledge*. But because the claim had become statute-barred, it was not *revived* by later legislation.

1.4 OTHER CASES IN NEGLIGENCE

As we have seen, the effects of *Cartledge* were removed for most cases of personal injury by the Limitation Act 1963 and subsequent legislation. But the *Cartledge* approach was still applicable outside the realms of personal injury.

Pirelli General Cable Works v Oscar Faber & Partners [1983] 2 AC 1

A factory chimney was constructed in 1969 and the defendants provided advice as to the appropriate lining for it. The lining turned out to be unsuitable. Evidence suggested that the chimney cracked no later than 1970. The cracks were not discovered however until 1977. This was outside the general limitation period of six years from the 'damage' (if the damage was, indeed, the cracking in the chimney). The plaintiff could not, with reason-able diligence, have discovered the defect, but the House of Lords held that the general six-year limitation period must be applied. Parliament had chosen, in 1963, to alter the effect of *Cartledge v Jopling* but had done so only for a range of **personal injury** cases; by implication, there was no intention to alter the effect of *Cartledge* where other types of damage were concerned.

By the Latent Damage Act 1986, two new sections (14A and 14B) were inserted into the Limitation Act 1980 in order to reverse the effect of *Pirelli*. Section 14A provided a 'date of knowledge' alternative to the usual starting date for **claims in negligence** which did not come within section 11. This section is identical to section 14 in the way that it defines 'knowledge'. However, claims to which these sections apply are subject to a long-stop of **15 years** from the date of breach (section 14B).

Nowadays, these sections are unlikely to be needed for a case like *Pirelli*. The claim in *Pirelli* was regarded as a claim for 'damage' to the factory chimney, in the form of cracking. Such a claim was actionable on the authority of *Anns v Merton* [1978] AC 728. As we saw in Chapter 6, *Anns v Merton* has been overruled by *Murphy v Brentwood* [1991] 1 AC 398, and the House of Lords has defined the relevant loss as *pure economic loss flowing from the acquisition of a defective product*. It is not to be seen as 'damage to property' at all. In *Murphy* itself, a claim for this sort of economic loss was held to be not actionable.

Therefore, the sort of claim for which sections 14A and 14B were principally designed may not now be actionable. Sections 14A and 14B are not, however, without application, because they are not limited to cases of 'latent damage'. They extend to any claim in neg-ligence, other than a claim for personal injuries, where the claimant's date of knowledge is (reasonably) delayed. For example, they have been applied in cases of professional neg-ligence, where a claimant has been slow to take advice about whether they have an action, despite their loss being apparent to them: for one example, see *Jacobs v Sesame* [2014] EWCA Civ 1410.

2. CONTRIBUTION BETWEEN LIABLE PARTIES

If more than one party is potentially liable for 'the same damage', then the claimant need not bring actions against each such party but may choose to proceed against any one, and recover in full. 'Contribution proceedings' may then be pursued by the liable party, in order to recover a portion of the damages payable.

'Contribution' between liable parties is clearly not in any sense a 'defence' to an action by the claimant since it is generally irrelevant to the tort claim. It is therefore an entirely separate issue from the defence of 'contributory negligence' (which we discussed in Chapter 5). It requires *apportionment* of damages on the basis of relative responsibility; while contributory negligence requires a reduction in damages to reflect fault (in a broad sense) on both sides. The collisions were separate. Both drivers were at fault; but so too was the distinction is exemplified by the decision of the House of Lords in *Fitzgerald v Lane* [1989] AC 328. A pedestrian was struck by two cars while crossing a road. The collisions were separate. Both drivers were at fault; but so too was the pedestrian. The House of Lords concluded that the correct approach was not to determine the relative responsibility of all three parties, and divide the damage accordingly. Rather, the pedestrian claimant's own responsibility for the harm suffered should be determined first, and this established the relevant amount of the deduction from damages. The defendants' liability was then shared in order to achieve a 'just and equitable result' between them.

In a case of indivisible damage, the principle is that the claimant may recover in full against any wrongdoer who has 'caused' that damage. The liable party may then seek contribution. It is not for the *claimant* to seek out every person contributing to the harm.[12] That being so, the risk that any particular liable party will turn out to be insolvent (and/or uninsured) remains with liable parties (and with their insurers), rather than with claimants. This is the principle of **joint and several liability**.

2.1 THE STARTING POINT: WHEN A LIABLE PARTY MAY SEEK CONTRIBUTION

Civil Liability (Contribution) Act 1978

1 Entitlement to Contribution

(1) Subject to the following provisions of this section, any person liable in respect of any damage suffered by another person may recover contribution from any other person liable in respect of the same damage (whether jointly with him or otherwise).

For the application of this statute, neither party needs to be liable *in tort*. For example, one or both parties might be liable in contract, for breach of a statutory duty to which the provisions of the statute extend, or for breach of trust. Certainly, if both *are* liable in tort, they need not be liable in the *same* tort, nor for the same amount. The important thing is that they should both be liable 'for the same damage'.

[12] As we saw in Chapter 4, *Barker v Corus* [2006] UKHL 20 created an important exception to this principle.

The above provision applies not only where there is judgment against the defendant, but also where the defendant has *settled* a claim:

Section 1

(4) A person who has made or agreed to make any payment in bona fide settlement or compromise of any claim made against him in respect of any damage (including a payment into court which has been accepted) shall be entitled to recover contribution in accordance with this section without regard to whether or not he himself is or ever was liable in respect of the damage, provided, however, that he would have been liable assuming that the factual basis of the claim against him could be established.

As a result of this section, a party seeking contribution after settling a claim need not 'prove' the case against him or herself, but needs to show that the claim was settled in good faith, for a sound reason of law.

2.2 'THE SAME DAMAGE'

Section 1(1) of the Civil Liability (Contribution) Act 1978 specifies that a liable party can seek contribution from anyone who is liable 'in respect of the same damage'. Contribution proceedings are *not* available where different parties are liable in respect of *different* damage. We need to remind ourselves of the basic principles governing recovery of damages from joint, concurrent, and consecutive tortfeasors, in order to identify clearly when tortfeasors will be considered to have contributed to 'the same damage'. The first step in understanding the contribution legislation therefore requires a grasp of some essential principles of causation.

One type of case to which the contribution legislation applies is the case of **joint liability**. Here, there is only one wrongful act, although several parties may be responsible for it. One form of joint liability is 'vicarious liability' (explored in Chapter 9). Where an employee commits a tort in the course of employment, the employer is held to be 'vicariously liable' in respect of that tort. There is no need to show any breach of duty or other wrongful conduct on the part of the employer at all. Here, there is only one tort (the employee's), but two parties are potentially liable in respect of it. Another example of joint liability is the case where two (or more) parties set out **with a common design** and act to cause harm. It is the collective action in concert which leads to damage; and thus both parties commit the *same* wrong, between them. The claimant can choose to proceed against either wrongdoer. The party found liable may seek contribution from the other. In *Fish & Fish Ltd v Sea Shepherd UK* [2015] UKSC 10; [2015] AC 1229, the Supreme Court ruled that a UK charity was not a joint tortfeasor, because its acts in furtherance of a common design (an attack on a bluefin tuna farm) were 'de minimis'. The charity had clearly appreciated that a conservation society which it supported would commit tortious acts as part of its campaign, particularly in the light of the society's statement that it would destroy illegal nets; thus, if the charity's role had been more than de minimis, even if relatively trivial, its liability as an 'accessory' would have been in full; and it would have been forced to seek contribution against the principal tortfeasor.

Lord Neuberger, *Fish & Fish v Sea Shepherd*

57 … the assistance provided by the defendant must be substantial, in the sense of not being de minimis or trivial. However, the defendant should not escape liability simply because his assistance was (i) relatively minor in terms of its contribution to, or influence over, the tortious act when compared with the actions of the primary tortfeasor, or (ii) indirect so far as any consequential damage to the claimant is concerned. Nor does a claimant need to establish that the tort would not have been committed, or even that it would not have been committed in the precise way that it was, without the assistance of the defendant. I agree with Lord Sumption JSC that, once the assistance is shown to be more than trivial, the proper way of reflecting the defendant's relatively unimportant contribution to the tort is through the court's power to apportion liability, and then order contribution, as between the defendant and the primary tortfeasor.

Section 1(1) is explicitly not confined to 'joint liability'. It applies in *any* case where two or more wrongdoers contribute to the same damage, even if they do so through separate actions amounting to separate torts (or other wrongs). If two or more separate wrongs are committed by parties acting without any 'common design', each party will be liable in full (and the contribution legislation will apply) *if and only if* each wrong contributes to damage which is considered to be **indivisible**. This is referred to as a case of **concurrent torts** (or wrongs).

'Indivisible Damage'

In cases where the wrong is not 'joint' (which is to say, where there are separate contributing wrongs), we therefore need to consider the meaning of 'indivisible damage'. The leading statement on this subject is to be found in the judgment of Devlin LJ in *Dingle v Associated Newspapers* [1961] 2 QB 162, at 188–9. This was a case in defamation. A libel was published by several different newspapers and the question was whether one of those newspapers was liable in full for the effect of the libel. The following statement of 'elementary principles' applicable to cases of *personal injury* was set out by Devlin LJ in order to assist consideration of the best approach in a case of damage to *reputation*.

Devlin LJ, *Dingle v Associated Newspapers and Others*
[1961] 2 QB 162 at 188–9

… Where injury has been done to the plaintiff and the injury is indivisible, any tortfeasor whose act has been a proximate cause of the injury must compensate for the whole of it. As between the plaintiff and the defendant it is immaterial that there are others whose acts also have been a cause of the injury and it does not matter whether those others have or have not a good defence. These factors would be relevant in a claim between tortfeasors for contribution, but the plaintiff is not concerned with that; he can obtain judgment for total compensation from anyone whose act has been a cause of his injury. If there are more than one of such persons, it is immaterial to the plaintiff whether they are joint tortfeasors or not. If four men, acting severally and not in concert, strike the plaintiff one after another and as a result of his injuries he suffers shock and is detained in hospital and loses a month's wages, each wrongdoer is liable to compensate for the whole loss of earnings. If there were four distinct physical injuries, each man would be liable only for the consequences peculiar to the injury he inflicted, but in the example I have given the loss of earnings is one injury caused in part by all four defendants. It is essential for this purpose that the loss should be one and indivisible; whether it is so or not is a matter of fact and not a matter of law. If, for example, a ship is damaged in two separate collisions by two wrongdoers and consequently is in dry dock for a month for repairs and claims for loss of earnings, it is usually possible to say how many days' detention is attributable to the damage done by each collision and divide the loss of earnings accordingly.

These are elementary principles and readily recognisable as such in the law of damage for physical injury ... [Emphasis added]

Devlin LJ went on to conclude that the same principle must apply in a case of libel, where the injury to reputation is indivisible.

The same principle must apply to general damage for loss of reputation. If a man reads four newspapers at breakfast and reads substantially the same libel in each, liability does not depend on which paper he opens first. Perhaps one newspaper influences him more than another, but unless he can say he disregarded one altogether, then each is a substantial cause of the damage done to the plaintiff in his eyes. . . .

Returning to Devlin LJ's general statement in respect of personal injury, we should note the following points:

1. The principle that each tortfeasor is potentially liable for the full damage depends, as Devlin LJ expressed it, on showing that each tortfeasor has caused the harm in question ('a tortfeasor whose act has been a proximate cause of the injury . . .'). This means that each tort must satisfy the tests for causation that we set out in Chapter 3 and further explored (noting relevant complexities) in Chapter 4.

2. If the various torts of different tortfeasors lead to more than one *injury*—or, to put it another way, if the harm is treated as *divisible*—each tortfeasor is liable *only* for the injury that is caused by his or her tort. There is then no scope for contribution proceedings between tortfeasors, because the other parties will not be held to have caused 'the same damage'. The liability of each tortfeasor does not extend to damage to which others have also contributed. The risk of insolvency and the burden of proving each tort lie upon the claimant.

3. In the case where four men in turn hit the claimant and he suffers a single consequential injury (for example in the form of psychiatric harm leading to loss of earnings), then the damage will be treated as indivisible and any of the four may be liable for the whole damage. It is important to notice that it is not the physical harm that, in the example given by Devlin LJ, is said to be indivisible, but the psychiatric consequences of the four incidents. If there are four separate physical injuries, then clearly the damage is divisible. Each assailant will be liable only for the part of the damage that he or she causes; there is no scope for *contribution*. The following case shows that what appears to be a single injury may also be judged to be 'divisible'. A disease or injury which is *made worse* by each tort may be treated as divisible; each tortfeasor is liable only for the *additional harm* that they cause. *Thompson v Smiths Shiprepairers* [1984] QB 405.

The plaintiffs suffered hearing impairment through exposure to excessive noise in ship-repair and shipbuilding yards. Mustill J awarded damages which reflected not the full impairment of hearing suffered, but only the part of that impairment of hearing which could be said to flow from a *breach of duty*.

The plaintiffs' hearing loss in these cases had been progressive. Mustill J held that at the beginning of the process of impairment, there was no breach of duty because it was not generally recognized that the levels of noise were harmful. Only later, when the possibility of harm was recognized, was the exposure in breach of duty. Although the end result—hearing loss to a particular level—appeared to be a single *injury*, it was not 'indivisible'.

Mustill J relied upon expert evidence in order to calculate the *amount* of impairment likely to have been caused during the period of breach, in order to determine the appropriate level of compensation. The damages only compensated for a part of the loss suffered, reflecting the fact that at the time of breach, the claimant's hearing was already impaired.

Mustill J

This condition is not the direct product of a group of acts, not necessarily simultaneous, but all converging to bring about one occurrence of damage. Rather, it is the culmination of a progression, the individual stages of which were each brought about by the separate acts of the persons sued, or (as the case may be) the separate non-faulty and faulty acts of the only defendant. In my judgment, the principle stated by Devlin L.J. does not apply to this kind of case. Moreover, even if it could be regarded as apposite where the successive deteriorations and their respective causes cannot on the evidence be distinguished, it does not in my opinion demand the conclusion that where the court knows that the initial stage of the damage was caused by A (and not B) and that the later stage was caused by B (and not A), it is obliged in law to proceed (contrary to the true facts) on the assumption that the faults of each had caused the whole damage. So also in the case where it is known that when the faulty acts of the employer began, the plaintiffs' hearing had already suffered damage.

Rahman v Arearose [2001] QB 351

The plaintiff was assaulted at work while employed by the first defendants, and sustained damage to his eye. He then underwent an operation at the second defendant's hospital. This operation was negligently performed, and led to the loss of the eye. Apart from this physical impairment, the plaintiff suffered a number of consequential psychological difficulties, attributed by experts variously to the initial assault, and to the loss of the eye. Here we consider the *psychological* harm.

The Court of Appeal concluded that this case differed from Devlin LJ's example of four separate assaults causing one sort of psychological harm. Here, the psychological impairment took several different forms (post-traumatic stress disorder; phobia; personality change; depressive disorder of psychotic intensity), and these various forms *could* be attributed, according to the experts, to one or other of the torts committed—even if this could be done only with some lack of certainty. Hence, this was *not* a case of joint or concurrent torts contributing to 'the same damage'.

Laws LJ

23 ... on the evidence the respective torts committed by the defendants were the causes of distinct aspects of the claimant's overall psychiatric condition, and it is positively established that neither caused the whole of it. So much is demonstrated by the document which sets out the conclusions of the three experts. It is true that this agreed evidence does not purport to distribute causative responsibility for the various aspects of the claimant's psychopathology between the defendants with any such degree of precision as would allow for an exact quantification by the trial court; no doubt any attempt to do so would be highly artificial. But the lack of it cannot drive the case into the regime of the 1978 Act to which, in principle, it does not belong. This view of the matter is by no means displaced by consideration of the oral testimony of the doctors, to which Mr Livesey invited our attention. The fact-finding court's duty is to arrive at a just conclusion on the evidence as to the respective damage caused by each defendant, and even if it can only do it on a broad-brush basis which then has to be translated into percentages.

This is a very different case from *Thompson* because different 'aspects' of the psychiatric harm were identified by the experts as continuing to affect the plaintiff. Examining the plaintiff in *Rahman*, medical experts identified a number of different continuing harms. In *Thompson*, the plaintiff was suffering from one harm, impaired hearing. But different levels of impairment were attributed, in the main action and without the need for contribution proceedings, to different periods. In either of these ways, it may be concluded that the different tortfeasors have not contributed to 'the same damage'.

Whether the expert reports *should* have been accepted in *Rahman* is a different matter:

Tony Weir, 'The Maddening Effect of Consecutive Torts' [2001] CLJ 237, at 238

That left the ... question of what damage each was liable for. Here the Court accepted an absurd report confected jointly by the experts for the three parties, who tentatively divided up the victim's present condition in terms of the two causes. They should not have been asked to do this, and their answer should have been ignored, for there is no scientific basis for any such attribution of causality; the claimant is not half-mad because of what the first defendant did and half-mad because of what the second defendant did, he is as mad as he is because of what both of them did. His mania is aetiologically indiscerptible, as when grief and shock combine to wreck the life of a parent who witnesses the death of her children. Suppose that the claimant was so maddened that he committed suicide: would his death be divided up by those responsible for triggering the injuries?

The approach in *Rahman v Arearose* was considered doubtful by a later Court of Appeal in *Dickins v O2 Plc* [2008] EWCA Civ 1144. The court ruled in this case that psychiatric damage with a number of sources was to be seen as an indivisible injury. This was not a case concerned with contribution but with factual causation: it was proposed that the defendant's breach of duty made a material contribution to an indivisible injury and that the defendant was therefore liable in full.

'Damage' not 'Damages'

In *Royal Brompton NHS Trust v Hammond* [2002] 1 WLR 1397, Lord Bingham emphasized that 'the same damage' in section 1(1) (see Section 2.1 of the present chapter) does not mean 'the same *damages*'. 'Damage' is equivalent to 'loss' or 'harm', not to amount payable. That being so, it is not necessary that the two (or more) liable parties would, if successfully sued, be liable for identical amounts. For example, one party may have acted in such a way that he or she is susceptible to a claim for aggravated or punitive damages, while the other is not. Or, the parties may be liable on the basis of different causes of action, in which different rules on the extent of recoverable damage apply. These differences may be relevant to the apportionment stage; but they will not affect the prior question of whether the parties are potentially liable in respect of the same damage.

On the other hand, the different nature of the two liable parties' wrongs may make a significant difference to the sum that is treated as 'the same damage' to be apportioned. In *Nationwide Building Society v Dunlop Haywards (DHL) Ltd* [2009] EWHC 254 (Comm), the first defendant was liable in deceit (for a major mortgage fraud), while the second defendants were liable only in negligence (for failing, as the first defendants' solicitors, to spot the fraud). As explained in Chapter 2, damages in deceit are calculated differently from damages in negligence. Some damage which would be considered too remote in a negligence claim is awarded in deceit; and contributory negligence is not an available defence in an action for deceit. That being so, it was concluded in this case that the 'same damage' which had to be apportioned in the contribution proceedings would be the 'overlapping' liability of the two defendants. This may appear at first to be hard to tally with the statement of Lord Bingham above, but the purpose of the remoteness or attribution rules is precisely to identify what damage is to be treated as occasioned by any particular tort. If different damage has been done by the different torts, then the 'same damage' can indeed only be the overlapping amount. As we will see, the proportion that a fraudulent party is liable to pay is likely to be far higher than the amount payable by a merely negligent tortfeasor. In this instance the first defendants were liable for 80 per cent of the 'overlapping' damage; they were also liable in full for the parts of the damage not attributable to negligence.

2.3 APPORTIONMENT
Civil Liability (Contribution) Act 1978

2 Assessment of contribution

2.—(1) … in any proceedings for contribution under section 1 above the amount of the contribution recoverable from any person shall be such as may be found by the court to be just and equitable having regard to the extent of that person's responsibility for the damage in question.

(2) … the court shall have power in any such proceedings to exempt any person from liability to make contribution, or to direct that the contribution to be recovered from any person shall amount to a complete indemnity.

Section 7(3) of the Act expressly preserves contractual indemnities and exclusions of contribution, and section 2(3)(a) effectively gives priority to contractual and statutory allocations of responsibility. Subject to these caveats, the guiding principle is that apportionment between liable parties should be on the basis of what is 'just and equitable', having regard to 'responsibility for the damage'.

We saw in Chapter 5 that very similar language is used in the Law Reform (Contributory Negligence) Act 1945, which sets out the approach to be taken where damages fall to be reduced for contributory negligence. However, there are significant differences in the way that these two provisions operate. In particular, it is well established that the idea of 'responsibility for damage' incorporates issues of causation, and of relative culpability. However, in respect of contribution under the 1978 Act, 'responsibility' (incorporating causation and culpability) is only a matter to which courts must 'have regard'. *The guiding aim is not to reflect relative responsibility, but to achieve a 'just and equitable' distribution.*

The Role of Culpability

Culpability may be a particularly significant consideration where one party has acted with wrongful and perhaps criminal intent, while the other has merely been careless or even acted with no degree of culpability at all. Clearly, these may be circumstances in which the court might lean towards a conclusion that the more 'culpable' party should take a greater share of liability, or indemnify the innocent liable party in full. A similar result—liability being allocated 100 per cent to one of two parties—was reached in *Dawson v Bell* [2016] EWCA Civ 96. The claimant in the contribution proceedings had misappropriated funds from a company in which he and the defendant were directors and shareholders. Even assuming that the defendant knew of this and in breach of her duty to the company, did nothing, it would not be 'just and equitable' to order the defendant to make a contribution given the extent of her responsibility, and given that the funds were misappropriated for the claimant's exclusive benefit.

Special considerations apply however where one of the defendants is liable 'vicariously' for the torts of another (typically an employee, or a partner under section 10 of the Partnership Act 1890).[13] In these circumstances, the employer is liable independently of any fault on his or her own part; and the employer does not need to have done anything to 'cause' the harm. Should the 'responsibility' of a vicariously liable employer be judged at zero whenever the other potentially liable parties are wrongdoers in their own right? The House of Lords has decided that this is *not* the right approach. In *Dubai Aluminium v Salaam* [2003] 2 AC 366, the 'responsibility' of a vicariously liable party was judged not in terms of their own innocence, but in terms of the tort of the tortfeasor (a wrongdoing partner). The employer 'stands in the shoes' of the party for whose torts they are liable; and if that party was fraudulent, the vicariously liable party takes a share of the liability accordingly.

Factors not Causative of the Damage

The House of Lords in *Dubai Aluminium* accepted a reason, unrelated to causative responsibility, for ordering the other fraudulent parties to indemnify the innocent partners completely. This reason was not based on 'responsibility' (to which, according to section 2(1), the

---

[13] The nature of the liability under this section is debatable; we will simply call it 'vicarious liability' in common with Lords Nicholls and Millett. For debate see C. Mitchell, 'Partners in Wrongdoing' (2003) 119 LQR 364.

court must 'have regard'). It was based on the fact that S and T still held undisgorged profits of their wrongdoing, whereas the co-partners did not. This factor justified a total indemnity, despite being irrelevant to 'responsibility' for the damage. The guiding aim is to distribute liability in a manner that is 'just and equitable'; 'responsibility' (incorporating both culpability and causation) is one factor to which the court must 'have regard', but is not the *only* factor.

Lord Nicholls, *Dubai Aluminium v Salaam*

Contribution and proceeds of wrongdoing

50 The other major factor which weighed with the judge when deciding to direct that the Amhurst firm should be entitled to an indemnity was that Mr Salaam and Mr Al Tajir had still not disgorged their full receipts from the fraud. The judge considered it would not be just and equitable to require one party to contribute in a way which would leave another party in possession of his spoils: see [1999] 1 Lloyd's Rep 415, 475.

51 Mr Salaam and Mr Al Tajir submitted that this approach is impermissible. Under section 2(1) of the Contribution Act the court is required to assess the amount of contribution recoverable from a person which is just and equitable "having regard to the extent of that person's responsibility for the damage". "Responsibility" includes both blameworthiness and causative potency. However elastically interpreted, "responsibility" does not embrace receipts.

52 I cannot accept this submission. It is based on a misconception of the essential nature of contribution proceedings. The object of contribution proceedings under the Contribution Act is to ensure that each party responsible for the damage makes an appropriate contribution to the cost of compensating the plaintiff, regardless of where that cost has fallen in the first instance. The burden of liability is being redistributed. But, of necessity, the extent to which it is just and equitable to redistribute this financial burden cannot be decided without seeing where the burden already lies. The court needs to have regard to the known or likely financial consequences of orders already made and to the likely financial consequences of any contribution order the court may make. For example, if one of three defendants equally responsible is insolvent, the court will have regard to this fact when directing contribution between the two solvent defendants. The court will do so, even though insolvency has nothing to do with responsibility....

53 In the present case a just and equitable distribution of the financial burden requires the court to take into account the net contributions each party made to the cost of compensating Dubai Aluminium. Regard should be had to the amounts payable by each party under the compromises and to the amounts of Dubai Aluminium's money each still has in hand. As Mr Sumption submitted, a contribution order will not properly reflect the parties' relative responsibilities if, for instance, two parties are equally responsible and are ordered to contribute equally, but the proceeds have all ended up in the hands of one of them so that he is left with a large undisgorged balance whereas the other is out of pocket.

54 Rix J considered this was obvious. So did Ferris J, in *K v P* [1993] Ch 140, 149. I agree with them.

In *Re-source America v Platt Site Services* [2004] EWCA Civ 665, even the manner in which a defendant runs its defence—and any unreasonable attempt to deny responsibility or evade detection—was regarded as a relevant factor in determining contribution. This is not the same as the position in contributory negligence, where it is settled that only fault that *contributes* to the harm is relevant.

In *West London Pipeline v Total UK Ltd* [2008] EWHC 1296 (Comm) (an aspect of the Buncefield litigation discussed in Chapters 9 and 10), the claimants argued that insurance cover on the part of another potential party to the litigation should be a relevant factor for contribution proceedings. This was rejected:

David Steel J, *West London Pipeline and Storage Ltd v Total UK Ltd* [14]

The judge considered the authorities above concerning non-causative factors relevant to apportionment and continued:

9 … the circumstances in which non-causative factors can properly be taken into account will be exceptional (and of limited impact). Certainly, in my Judgement, there needs to be a close connection between the non-causative factors which it is just and equitable to take into account and the causative activity (or lack of it) which has given rise to the liability.

10 I do not regard it as arguable that the existence or scope of any insurance cover can be material to the issue of apportionment. There is nothing exceptional in there being some form of insurance cover. It has no connection whatsoever with the alleged causative conduct. In this regard I should note that it is expressly disclaimed by TAV that it proposes to rely upon the fact of it being an economically small business in assessing blameworthiness.

Ability to pay, therefore, appears to be an irrelevant factor, and it is exceptional for non-causative factors to play a part. Generally speaking, they should be related to the conduct which creates that party's tortious liability.

2.4 TIME LIMIT FOR CONTRIBUTION CLAIMS

Contribution proceedings attract their own limitation period, set by section 10 of the Limitation Act 1980 at two years.

3. CONCLUSIONS

i   The rules of limitation and contribution discussed in this chapter exist for reasons of fairness and practicality, and have a significant impact on civil litigation, including litigation in tort. Principles of limitation have been adjusted over the years to reflect the difficulties claimants may have in realizing that their potential claim exists; but these adjustments continue to be balanced against the need to ensure that claims are brought as expeditiously as reasonably possible and so that courts and defendants are protected against open-ended potential litigation. In personal injury claims in particular, the court's discretion to permit claims outside the statutory limitation period is of continued significance.

ii Rules of contribution are of great significance in a system in which liability is joint and several. A tortfeasor whose blameworthy behaviour or contribution to causation

[14] Noted by N. Dunleavy, 'Principles of Apportionment in Contribution Cases' (2009) 125 LQR 239–44.

is relatively trivial can be held liable in full, and must seek contribution against the principal tortfeasor. The principles of apportionment set out in section 2(1) of the Contribution Act 1978 bear some resemblance to the principles guiding apportionment in contributory negligence, but in important respects the two regimes are very different. In contribution proceedings, it is possible that a court will find it just and equitable to order either 0 per cent contribution or 100 per cent contribution, which are not available options in contributory negligence; and factors other than those relating to the causation of damage are considered relevant. The overriding goal is not to determine relative responsibility, as in contributory negligence, but to achieve a 'just and equitable' distribution.

FURTHER READING

Limitation of Actions

Davies, P. J., 'Limitations on the Law of Limitation' (1982) 98 LQR 249.

James, R., 'The Law Commission Report on the Limitation of Actions' (2003) 22 CJQ 41.

Law Commission, *Limitation of Actions* (LCCP 151, HMSO, 1998).

Law Commission, *Limitation of Actions* (Report No 270, HC 23, HMSO, 2001).

McGee, A., *Limitation of Actions*, 6th edn (London: Sweet & Maxwell, 2010)

McGee, A., and Scanlan, G. P., 'Constructive Knowledge Within the Limitation Act' (2003) CJQ 248–64.

Mosher, J., 'Challenging Limitation Periods: Civil Claims by Adult Survivors of Incest' (1994) 44 UTLJ 169.

Patten, K., 'Limitation Periods in Personal Injury Claims—Justice Obstructed' (2006) CJQ 349.

Contribution Between Liable Parties

Davies, P.S., 'Accessory Liability in Tort' (2016) 132 LQR 15.

Dugdale, T., 'Civil Liability (Contribution) Act 1978' (1979) 42 MLR 182.

McCaul, C., 'Holtby and the End Game' (2006) JPIL 6–11.

Mitchell, C., *The Law of Contribution and Reimbursement* (Oxford: Oxford University Press, 2003).

Tettenborn, A., 'Contribution between Wrongdoers' (2005) 155 NLJ 1722.

DAMAGES, COMPENSATION, AND RESPONSIBILITY

CENTRAL ISSUES

i) This chapter is concerned not with rules of liability, but with remedies, and specifically with monetary remedies. The chapter is at the heart of the book because this is where it belongs. The previous part of the book dealt with principles of liability in negligence but, as we explained, no consideration of these principles makes sense without asking what liability is being debated. However, in this chapter we also discuss remedial issues in connection with a wide range of torts. The discussion therefore connects with the analysis in a number of different chapters.

ii) We begin by outlining the heads of loss for which damages in tort may be awarded. The heads of damage illustrate the general goal of tort compensation, which is to restore claimants to their pre-tort position. We will see

that there are some serious conceptual difficulties involved with this. We will also outline the potential for non-compensatory awards; and explore the challenge to tort law represented by the growth of damages under the Human Rights Act 1998.

iii) Also considered in this chapter are recent developments in respect of the assessment and delivery of damages, the funding of litigation, and the relationship between tort damages and welfare support. Despite their apparent technicality, these developments raise important issues about the nature of tort law, and its broader economic role. Following an extensive review of litigation funding in 2009–10, there have been very significant changes to the way in which civil litigation as a whole is funded.

1. COMPENSATORY DAMAGES

Compensatory damages are not the only remedy available in tort. In particular:

- Some monetary awards are not compensatory. We address these later in the chapter.

- Some remedies are available which do *not* take the form of a monetary award. These are not considered in this chapter, though we will make reference to discussion in other parts of the book. Injunctive remedies, in particular, are discussed in relevant substantive chapters particularly Chapter 10 (Nuisance) and Chapters 13 (Defamation) and 14 (Privacy).

Assessment of damages in cases of conversion raise particular issues which are most easily dealt with in Chapter 17.

1.1 THE BASIC APPROACH: *RESTITUTIO IN INTEGRUM*

The guiding principle for an award of compensatory damages is that the award should repair in full the damage done by the tort. The goal is '*restitutio in integrum*', or 100 per cent compensation.

This guiding principle is common to all torts. Where actions in respect of *personal injuries* are concerned, there is a fundamental problem with this principle. Where non-pecuniary losses are concerned, full compensation is strictly not possible, since damages cannot achieve equality between the circumstances of the claimant before and after the injury.

More generally, in respect of all heads of compensatory damages, it is important to remember that *only* losses that are caused by the tort will be compensated. Rules of causation and remoteness must be applied. In negligence actions at least, only damage which is 'within the scope of the duty' will be compensated (*South Australia Asset Management Company v York Montague Ltd* [1997] AC 191). Any other damage is treated as not attributable to the tort of the defendant.

Also of general importance is the impact of contributory negligence (Chapter 5) in reducing damages. If a reduction for contributory negligence is found to be appropriate, then the reduction will operate in respect of pecuniary and non-pecuniary awards, and in respect of compensatory and non-compensatory aspects of the award, whether delivered in a lump sum, or through periodical payments. In the case of a serious injury, this clearly affects the adequacy of compensation, particularly where future income and expenses are concerned.

1.2 PECUNIARY LOSSES IN PERSONAL INJURY CLAIMS: INTRODUCTION

In personal injury claims, 'pecuniary' losses fall under two general heads:

- lost earnings; and
- expenses.

Both sorts of pecuniary loss may be divided into two further categories:

- lost earnings and expenses *before* trial; and
- future loss of earnings and expenses.

Most of the problematic issues examined in this chapter relate to future losses.

1.3 LOST EARNINGS AND EXPENSES BEFORE TRIAL

The claimant should be compensated in full for any wages or other earnings lost as a result of the tort whilst awaiting trial, as well as for any expenses reasonably incurred. These may include travel expenses to and from hospital, as well as care costs incurred. Although there is a general principle that only reasonable expenses may be recovered (and that a claimant must 'mitigate his or her loss' by acting reasonably), the claimant is nevertheless not obliged to make use of free care and treatment through the National Health Service. The cost of *private care* may be recovered:

Law Reform (Personal Injuries) Act 1948

2 Measure of damages

(4) In an action for damages for personal injuries (including any such action arising out of a contract), there shall be disregarded, in determining the reasonableness of any expenses, the possibility of avoiding those expenses or part of them by taking advantage of facilities available under the National Health Service Act, 1977, or the National Health Service (Scotland) Act, 1978, or of any corresponding facilities in Northern Ireland.

1.4 FUTURE LOST EARNINGS

Calculation of future losses poses far more difficulty. 'Calculation', in fact, may not be the right description.

In the case of a serious long-term injury, lost earnings will typically represent one of the largest elements in the claim. Estimation of future lost earnings is necessarily imprecise. There are two large areas of uncertainty:

1. Uncertainty over what *will* happen to the claimant, in the light of the injury. How long will the claimant live? What work, if any, will the claimant be able to secure? Will the condition improve, or deteriorate?

2. Uncertainty over what *would have* happened to the claimant, had it not been for the injury. Would the claimant have secured promotion? Have worked to pensionable age? Or left the job market early (whether through ill-health or for other reasons) in any event?

While some forms of delayed, staged, or periodic payments could deal with the first sort of uncertainty, no amount of delay in determining or delivering damages will deal with the second sort of uncertainty, because it concerns hypothetical events.

Multiplier and Multiplicand

The first step in 'calculating' an award for future lost earnings is to identify two figures, referred to as the multiplier and the multiplicand. These are multiplied, and certain additions and deductions are then applied. Broadly the same technique is used in assessing future expenses (including care costs), but the figures adopted will be different.

The Multiplicand

The multiplicand (or figure 'to be multiplied') represents the claimant's net annual loss, taking into account earnings at the time of the accident, and likely promotion prospects lost as a result of the accident. If the claimant is not totally incapacitated or unable to work, this figure should take account of residual earning capacity. The figure used is not gross but net: there are deductions for income tax, social security contributions, and other expenditure which would have been incurred as a condition of earnings. Particularly where a young person with identifiable prospects is injured, there may be 'staged' increases in the multiplicand to reflect promotion prospects.

The following case is a useful illustration of the approach to younger claimants, and shows the kind of 'informed guesswork' that operates, as well as indicating some policy issues.

An Illustration: *Dixon v John Were* [2004] EWHC 2273 (QB)

The claimant was seriously injured in a road traffic accident at the age of 20, when he was a university student.[1] He suffered brain damage and a consequent personality disorder which made him unemployable. Given his previous 'attractive personality and very considerable charm,' together with 'his background, the fact of his degree and, to some extent, his contacts' (and even though his predicted grade on graduation was a lower second), it was considered likely that he would have secured a good job at above average national earnings for a professional male.[2] This having been decided, the multiplicand was then increased in line with the percentage chance of promotions, in a staged increase. There was also allowance in the multiplicand for additional 'benefits' such as a company car and private health insurance, which it was found would most probably have been acquired as part of the employment 'package'. However, the judge rejected an argument that the multiplicand should be further increased to reflect the percentage chance of even higher earnings. Such a possibility was merely speculative, in this case. Had there been a stronger possibility of such a promotion, a 'percentage increase' might have been allowed, on the authority of *Herring v MOD* [2003] EWCA Civ 528.

A more exceptional case is *Gary Smith v Ben Collett* [2009] EWCA Civ 583, where the Court of Appeal dismissed an appeal in respect of an award of £3,854,328 for lost future earnings (and £4,577,323 in all) to a claimant who was 18 years old at the time of the tort. This was a sporting injury caused by a high tackle while the claimant was playing for Manchester United Reserves against Middlesbrough Reserves. Given almost unanimous expert evidence that he would have developed into a very successful top-flight footballer without the incident, the award reflected the amount that the judge thought would be earned by such a footballer, less a 15 per cent discount to reflect risks and contingencies.

---

[1] His damages were reduced by 27.5 per cent to reflect his contributory negligence. The driver (defendant) and all of the passengers (two of whom were killed in the accident) had been drinking heavily.

[2] Gross J at para [29]. This illustrates an important point. The court must consider what the claimant *has lost*, even if this means that two equally deserving claimants of the same age and with the same injuries will receive very different awards. Their life prospects without the accident will be reflected in the award and in a sense, social injustice (as well as pure luck) are maintained. This is because tort damages aim to be primarily corrective, and do not aim to be distributive, even if the effect of tort law is on some level to distribute the risks of accidents.

The Multiplier

The court must also make an informed estimate of the number of years for which the claimant has lost earnings. This figure represents the 'multiplier' (though it will also be varied to deal with matters such as investment return, as explained later). A first step in arriving at a multiplier is to identify the number of years between the accident and the retirement age for the type of employment the claimant would have had but for the accident. However, the court will reduce this figure to reflect the chance that the claimant would not have worked until retirement age, even without the accident. The claimant might have left employment, changed employment, died before retirement, or been incapacitated for some other reason.

Two sorts of reasons why the multiplier might be reduced ought to be distinguished. First, there may be particular evidence relating to the claimant which suggests that their earning life would, even without the accident, have been shortened. For example, they may demonstrably have no desire to work, or they may have a predisposition to develop a particular disease or disability at some stage in the future. It is clear that a court should take account of any such evidence in making deductions from the multiplier.

Second, courts might also take into account the general possibility, not connected to particular features of the claimant, that a working life will be shortened. In judicial language, these general factors are referred to as the vicissitudes of life. Historically, it is accepted that some reduction in the multiplier should be applied on account of life's contingencies or 'vicissitudes'. But how much?

The answer to this last question has been transformed through reference to the Ogden Tables.

The Ogden Tables and their Influence

The 'Actuarial tables with explanatory notes for use in personal injury and fatal accident cases' ('the Ogden Tables') were prepared by an inter-professional working party chaired by Sir Michael Ogden QC and their first edition was published in 1984. The most recent version, 'Ogden 7', was published in 2011 and comprises 28 different tables and explanatory notes.[3] Since the sixth edition, in 2007, these tables have incorporated data from labour force surveys, allowing calculation of expected periods in employment until retirement age according to gender; employment status; educational attainment; and disability. Clearly, these ought to have a significant effect on predicting the multiplier (likely years in employment if the tort had not been committed).

When the Tables first appeared, judges were reluctant to adopt multipliers by reference to them, preferring to trust to their own experience and to specific evidence related to the individual claimant, rather than to the actuarial experience represented in the tables. In the following case, the House of Lords guided lower courts to give the tables a more central role. But as we will see, the newer, expanded tables seem to be encountering a degree of resistance once more.

In *Wells v Wells* [1999] AC 345, Lord Lloyd criticized the habit of deducting too many years from the multiplier, and argued for greater use of the tables.

---

[3] The Ogden Tables are published by The Stationery Office and available online: https://www.gov.uk/government/publications/ogden-tables-actuarial-compensation-tables-for-injury-and-death.

Lord Lloyd, *Wells v Wells*, at 379

I do not suggest that the judge should now be a slave to the tables. There may well be special factors in particular cases. But the tables should now be regarded as the starting-point, rather than a check. A judge should be slow to depart from the relevant actuarial multiplier on impressionistic grounds, or by reference to "a spread of multipliers in comparable cases" especially when the multipliers were fixed before actuarial tables were widely used.. . .

The result of greater reliance on the tables ought to be that smaller deductions from the multiplier are made on account of the general 'vicissitudes of life'; and that courts have a basis in evidence on which to determine any deduction. It should also mean that settlements are easier to reach. We explore the degree of acceptance of the new tables in respect of 'disadvantage in the job market', later.

Rate of Return and the Multiplier

If damages are awarded as a single lump sum payment (as they always are at common law),[4] it is assumed the lump sum will be invested, and earn interest. The lump sum should be reduced to take account of the fact that it will yield a return in this way. On the other hand, claimants who are dependent on damages—and particularly those with long-term serious injuries who have no opportunity of making up their losses—should not be expected to invest their lump sums in such a way that they are exposed to significant risk. So courts will reduce the multiplier in order to reflect the fact that the sum will earn interest. But what rate of interest should be assumed?

Historically, the courts assumed a high rate of return on investment and discounted the multiplier by 4–5 per cent: see *Mallett v McMonagle* [1970] AC 166, and *Cookson v Knowles* [1979] AC 556. In *Wells v Wells* [1999] 1 AC 345, the House of Lords took a different and much more protective approach to claimants. Claimants could be assumed to invest their lump sums in index-linked government stock (ILGS), which offers a 'risk-free environment' and (naturally) a much lower rate of return than investment in equities. The House of Lords followed the recommendations of the Law Commission, and of Sir Michael Ogden.[5]

Sir Michael Ogden, *The Ogden Tables* (1st edn, TSO, 1984), 8

Investment policy, however prudent, involves risks and it is not difficult to draw up a list of blue chip equities or reliable unit trusts which have performed poorly and, in some cases, disastrously. Index-linked government stocks eliminate the risks. Whereas, in the past, a plaintiff has had to speculate in the form of prudent investment by buying equities, or a 'basket' of equities and gilts or a selection of unit trusts, he need speculate no longer if he buys index-linked government stock. If the loss is, say, £5,000 per annum, he can be awarded damages which, if invested in such stocks, will provide him with almost exactly that sum in real terms.

[4] For new possibilities created by statute, see Section 4 of this chapter.
[5] Cited by Lord Lloyd at 369.

Lord Lloyd, *Wells v Wells*, at 373–4

My conclusion is that the judges in these three cases were right to assume for the purpose of their calculations that the plaintiffs would invest their damages in I.L.G.S. for the following reasons.

(1) Investment in I.L.G.S. is the most accurate way of calculating the present value of the loss which the plaintiffs will actually suffer in real terms.

(2) Although this will result in a heavier burden on these defendants, and, if the principle is applied across the board, on the insurance industry in general, I can see nothing unjust. It is true that insurance premiums may have been fixed on the basis of the 4 to 5 per cent. discount rate indicated in *Cookson v. Knowles* [1979] A.C. 556 and the earlier authorities. But this was only because there was then no better way of allowing for future inflation. The objective was always the same. No doubt insurance premiums will have to increase in order to take account of the new lower rate of discount. Whether this is something which the country can afford is not a subject on which your Lordships were addressed. So we are not in a position to form any view as to the wider consequences.

(3) The search for a prudent investment will always depend on the circumstances of the particular investor. Some are able to take a measure of risk, others are not. For a plaintiff who is not in a position to take risks, and who wishes to protect himself against inflation in the short term of up to 10 years, it is clearly prudent to invest in I.L.G.S. It cannot therefore be assumed that he will invest in equities and gilts. Still less is it his duty to invest in equities and gilts in order to mitigate his loss.

(4) Logically the same applies to a plaintiff investing for the long term. In any event it is desirable to have a single rate applying across the board, in order to facilitate settlements and to save the expense of expert evidence at the trial. I take this view even though it is open to the Lord Chancellor under section 1(3) of the Act of 1996 to prescribe different rates of return for different classes of case. Mr. Leighton Williams conceded that it is not desirable in practice to distinguish between different classes of plaintiff when assessing the multiplier.

(5) How the plaintiff, or the majority of plaintiffs, in fact invest their money is irrelevant. The research carried out by the Law Commission suggests that the majority of plaintiffs do not in fact invest in equities and gilts but rather in a building society or a bank deposit.

(6) There was no agreement between the parties as to how much greater, if at all, the return on equities is likely to be in the short or long term. But it is at least clear that an investment in I.L.G.S. will save up to 1 per cent. per annum by obviating the need for continuing investment advice.

The end result was to recommend that a lower discount, of 3 per cent, would now be applied to the multiplier to account for investment of the capital sum. Lord Steyn explained the wider importance of this technical issue:

Lord Steyn, *Wells v Wells*
[1999] AC 345, at 382

The importance of the issue is shown by a comparison of the awards of the three trial judges, who relied on index-linked government securities to fix the discount rate, and the figures substituted by the Court of Appeal, who used the conventional rate… . the use of a

3 per cent. discount rate instead of 4.5 per cent. would increase the awards by very roughly the following sums: Margaret Wells (a 58-year-old nurse), £108,000; Page (a 28-year-old steelworker), £186,000; Thomas (aged six years), £300,000. These figures show the impact of the reduction of the discount rate in cases where damages are calculated over many years. But, since a judicial decision ought to take into account general as well as particular consequences, it is important to realise that the proposed modification of the discount rate would lead to an enormous general increase in the size of awards for future losses. Nobody has ventured a prediction of the likely cost. The sums involved would undoubtedly be huge. The implications of a modification of the conventional rate for the insurance industry would be considerable. Inevitably, it would be reflected in increased premiums. The one certain thing is that if the right decision is to make the suggested modification of the discount rate the public would by and large have to pay for the increase in awards.

Here, Lord Steyn specifically makes the point that awards in tort are ultimately paid for by the public at large.

Subsequent Developments in the Discount Rate
In our earlier extract from *Wells*, Lord Lloyd referred to section 1 of the Damages Act 1996.

Damages Act 1996

1 Assumed rate of return on investment of damages

(1) In determining the return to be expected from the investment of a sum awarded as damages for future pecuniary loss in an action for personal injury the court shall, subject to and in accordance with rules of court made for the purposes of this section, take into account such rate of return (if any) as may from time to time be prescribed by an order made by the Lord Chancellor.

(2) Subsection (1) above shall not however prevent the court taking a different rate of return into account if any party to the proceedings shows that it is more appropriate in the case in question.

In June 2001, the Lord Chancellor exercised his power under this section and specified a discount rate: Damages (Personal Injury) Order 2001 (SI 2001/2301). He largely accepted the approach of the House of Lords in *Wells v Wells* and indeed, in light of changed economic circumstances, adopted a *lower* discount, of 2.5 per cent. Subsequently, attempts to use section 1(2) above to argue that a lower discount rate should apply in particular cases have been brushed aside by the courts as inconsistent with the Lord Chancellor's approach.

In *Warriner v Warriner* [2003] 3 All ER 447, Dyson LJ explained this narrow approach to section 1(2):

33. We are told that this is the first time that this court has had to consider the 1996 Act, and that guidance is needed as to the meaning of 'more appropriate in the case in question' in section 1(2). The phrase 'more appropriate', if considered in isolation, is open-textured. It prompts the question: by what criteria is the court to judge whether a different rate of return is more appropriate in the case in question? But the phrase must be interpreted in its proper context which is that the Lord Chancellor has prescribed a rate pursuant to section 1(1) and has given very detailed reasons explaining what factors he took into account in arriving at the rate that he has prescribed. I would hold that in deciding whether a different rate is more appropriate in the case in question, the court must have regard to those reasons. If the case in question falls into a category that the Lord Chancellor did not take into account and/or there are special features of the case which (a) are material to the choice of rate of return and (b) are shown from an examination of the Lord Chancellor's reasons not to have been taken into account, then a different rate of return may be 'more appropriate'.

Subsequently, in *Cooke v United Bristol Healthcare Trust* [2004] 1 WLR 251, it was argued for the claimants that the costs of care are inclined to rise at a faster rate than inflation, and that the discount method adopted in *Wells v Wells* would therefore leave claimants whose damages include a significant component for future care under-compensated. The claimants wished to bring expert evidence of the likely costs of care over time, and sought a lower discount than the 2.5 per cent adopted by the Lord Chancellor. The Court of Appeal rejected the claimants' applications to bring expert evidence to this effect, and said (rather dramatically) that they amounted to an 'illegitimate assault' on the Lord Chancellor's discount rate (at [30]). Laws LJ conceded that through application of a general discount rate, the 100 per cent compensation principle would only be achieved in a 'rough and ready way', but thought that this was the premise of the Lord Chancellor's decision to set a standard discount.

Subsequently, the general economic position has made it even more apparent that the discount rate set in 2001 does not reflect the likely return on investments nor the likely rise over time in costs of care. The severe impact on the most seriously injured claimants is illustrated by the case of *Harries v Stevenson* [2012] EWHC 3447 (QB). The claimant in this case had suffered catastrophic brain damage when he was an infant, and claimed damages from his doctor on the basis of negligent failure to diagnose. The claimant argued that applying the Lord Chancellor's discount rate of 2.5 per cent, and in light of the actual likely return on investments, he would be undercompensated by an amount in excess of £2 million. The judge concluded however that the argument for a different, lower discount rate was an 'assault upon' the Lord Chancellor's rate, and the argument was rejected. Yet if the approach taken by the Lord Chancellor when setting the discount rate in 2001 were to be applied today, the discount rate ought to be -1 per cent or, in other words, an uplift, rather than a discount.

The underlying difficulty is affordability. The same economic conditions which have reduced the rate of return on investment have made unattractive the idea of increased awards of damages the costs of which will fall upon public services or, via insurance, consumers and businesses. It is presumably for this reason that consideration of a revised discount rate was delayed.[6] The review culminated in a controversial announcement on 27 February 2017, that the rate would indeed be cut to -0.75%.[7] Notably, a second consultation is also under way,

[6] Ministry of Justice, *Damages Act 1996: The Discount Rate—How Should it be Set?* (CP 12/2012). The Consultation provoked diametrically opposed views from claimant and defendant representatives, the latter pressing the idea that claimants do not and should not 'play safe' with their investments. Research published in October 2013 delves into the question of the likely effect on claimants of risk in relation to the adequacy of their damages, and of a change in the discount rate: Ipsos MORI Social Research Institute, *Personal Injury Discount Rate Research* (Ministry of Justice Analytical Series, 2013).

[7] https://www.gov.uk/government/news/new-discount-rate-for-personal-injury-claims-announced. As expected, insurers have been vocal in their condemnation of the rate cut and the likely increased costs to motorists and to the NHS. See for example the ABI's news release: https://www.abi.org.uk/News/News-releases/2017/02/BI-RESPONDS-TO-CHANGES-IN-PERSONAL-INJURY-DISCOUNT-RATE. The new rate came into force on 20 March 2017. In what is said to be the first case applying the rate, solicitors acting for a claimant suffering severe brain injuries at birth report an increase in damages of £5.5 million: https://

asking whether the legal principles behind the discount rate should be changed.[8] One way of avoiding the entire issue of a future-proof lump sum is to make an order for periodic payments, since the problem is caused by the need to calculate a lump sum. But such an order is not always suitable. In *Harries v Stevenson* it was argued that the defendant, through the Medical Defence Union, would be unable to provide adequate security to assure payments.

Notable is the decision of the Privy Council in *Simon v Helmot* [2012] UKPC 5. This was an appeal from Guernsey, where section 2 of the Damages Act 1996, and therefore the Lord Chancellor's discount rate, do not apply. The Privy Council unanimously accepted the decision by the Guernsey Court of Appeal to apply two different discount rates to distinct aspects of the damages claimed—the approach rejected by the Court of Appeal in *Cooke*. One of these was in fact a 'negative'—not a discount, but an uplift—and was applied to earnings-related losses. Members of the Privy Council repeatedly commented that the guiding principle was attainment of full compensation, based on the best available evidence. This was not a goal achieved by retention of the discount rate of 2.5 per cent. If it is felt that full compensation is in some respects unattainable in the present climate, this is a challenge to the theory of tort damages. This is more or less admitted by the most recent consultation paper from the Ministry of Justice: the question in relation to the discount rate is whether the current approach 'produces a rate that is as "right" as it ought reasonably to be.'

Disadvantage in the Job Market

The traditional method of assessing lost earnings does not deal comfortably with certain unpredictable factors. In particular, a claimant with a long-term injury may be in gainful employment at the date of the trial, but what if they lose that employment at some time in the future? Will their impairment (assuming it to be long-term) lead them to struggle to find further work at a similar rate of pay? It is usual to make a modest addition to damages, called a *Smith v Manchester* award,[9] to reflect the claimant's future 'disadvantage in the job market'.

The publication of 'Ogden 6' in 2007 offers courts some assistance on this issue, since the new Tables (maintained and updated in 2011) indicate an appropriate multiplier in the context of 'non-mortality risks' (which affect a person's prospects of employment). The key variables include educational qualifications, employment or unemployment at the time of trial, and disability. To date, however, many courts have been prepared to add extra discounts because they believe that the multipliers suggested by the Tables would, if applied, be too generous to the individual claimant; in others they have been prepared to give an award not based on a multiplier at all, along the lines of *Smith v Manchester*.[10] Examples are *Peters v East Midlands SHA* [2008] EWHC 778 (QB), where the multiplier was reduced on the basis that the claimant's family background would have been inclined to instil a culture of dependency on benefits; and *Conner v Bradman* [2007] EWHC 2789, where the judge considered that the claimant was not sufficiently seriously disabled to justify applying to his case the figures presented by the Tables for the 'disabled' category. More recent cases

---

[8] Ministry of Justice, *Damages Act 1996: The Discount Rate—Review of the Legal Framework* (CP 3/2013).

www.forbessolicitors.co.uk/news/display/38628/15/accrington-solicitor-acts-in-legal-first. This is, of course, exactly the kind of case where it was felt action was needed to protect claimants in need of long-term care.

[9] By reference to *Smith v Manchester Corporation* (1974) 17 KIR 1 (CA).

[10] C. Melton, 'Ogden Six—Adjustments to Working Life Multipliers' (2009) JPIL 66–83.

illustrate a similar propensity. In *Billett v Ministry of Defence* [2015] EWCA Civ 773, the Court of Appeal considered the new Tables, and neither endorsed, nor criticized them. In *Billett* itself, the Court preferred to make a *Smith v Manchester* award, awarding £45,000 for loss of future earning capacity on a 'broad brush' basis. Had the Tables been applied, the view of the Court was that as the claimant only 'scraped into' Table B, barely meeting the definition of 'disabled', the correct approach would have been to select a reduction factor closer to Table A. The result would have been an award of around two years' loss of earnings, which was the same as the *Smith v Manchester* route.

The general impression is that the new statistics are not (or at least not yet) trusted as a means of determining answers in individual cases, leaving heavy emphasis on 'judgment' in light of individual circumstances, although there are exceptions (*Higgs v Pickles* [2011] PIQR P15). This situation is reviewed and criticized by W. Latimer-Sayer and V. Wass, 'Ogden Reduction Factor Adjustments since *Connor v Bradman*: Part 1' (2012) JPIL 219.

Hypothetical Future Benefits: Balance of Probabilities or Probabilistic Causation?

'One hundred per cent compensation' requires an award for lost future benefits in some circumstances. An important example is *loss of pension rights*. How will the court decide whether the claimant would have remained in employment long enough to have achieved those rights, if the tort had not occurred? This question raises a fundamental issue, related to prediction of future hypothetical events. Should loss of pension rights, for example, be addressed simply *on the balance of probabilities*? If so, the value of a full pension will be awarded if the claimant showed they would probably have stayed in employment for long enough. Or, should the court assess the *degree of likelihood of attaining such rights*, and assess damages accordingly? This would lead to partial compensation, proportionate to the assessed chances.

Brown v Ministry of Defence [2006] EWCA Civ 546 (CA)

Eight weeks into her service with the army, at the age of 24, the claimant B suffered a serious fracture of her ankle. She could no longer pursue her dream of an army career, and retrained as a physiotherapist. The defendants admitted liability, but challenged the substantial damages claimed. The sums claimed included compensation for loss of pension rights (£148,856.31) calculated on the assumption that B would have remained in the army for the required period of 22 years; and compensation for disadvantage in the labour market (£107,028). The sum for lost pension rights was very considerable because, had B remained in the army for 22 years, she would have become entitled to the pension at age 46, rather than at the age of 60 which would be the rule in most employment. The judge accepted B's argument that she would 'probably' have remained in the army for the required period, applying a 'balance of probabilities' test—informed by her personal commitment to such a career—as he thought was compatible with the approach in *Herring v MOD* [2003] EWCA Civ 528.

The Court of Appeal found that this approach was wrong, and that he had misunderstood the impact of *Herring v MOD*. He had also overlooked a principle, referred to by the House of Lords in both *Mallet v McMonagle* [1970] AC 166, 176 and *Davies v Taylor* [1974] AC 297, that in respect of hypothetical future events (as opposed to past events), it was appropriate to make decisions to reflect the *probability* of those events occurring, and to assess damages accordingly. He should therefore have made a *proportionate* award. *Davies v Taylor* was a dependency claim.

Lord Reid, *Davies v Taylor*
[1974] AC 207, at 212–13

The peculiarity in the present case is that the appellant had left her husband some five weeks before his death and there was no immediate prospect of her returning to him. He wanted her to come back but she was unwilling to come. But she says that there was a prospect or chance or probability that she might have returned to him later and it is only in that event that she would have benefited from his survival. To my mind the issue and the sole issue is whether that chance or probability was substantial. If it was it must be evaluated. If it was a mere possibility it must be ignored. . . .

When the question is whether a certain thing is or is not true—whether a certain event did or did not happen—then the court must decide one way or the other. There is no question of chance or probability. Either it did or it did not happen. But the standard of civil proof is a balance of probabilities. If the evidence shows a balance in favour of it having happened then it is proved that it did in fact happen.

But here we are and could not be seeking a decision either that the wife would or that she would not have returned to her husband. You can prove that a past event happened, but you cannot prove that a future event will happen and I do not think that the law is so foolish as to suppose that you can. All that you can do is to evaluate the chance. Sometimes it is virtually 100 per cent.: sometimes virtually nil. But often it is somewhere in between. And if it is somewhere in between I do not see much difference between a probability of 51 per cent. and a probability of 49 per cent.

Gregg v Scott [2005] 2 AC 176, as we have seen in Chapter 4, rejected a 'proportionate' approach to recovery of damages for lost chance of a cure where there was a negligent failure to diagnose cancer. *Davies v Taylor*, like *Brown*, is not a case like *Gregg v Scott*, since it involves the question of hypothetical future actions of individuals.

Lost Life Expectancy

Where the effect of a tort is to shorten the claimant's life expectancy, difficult issues arise. In this section, we are concerned with *pecuniary* losses. Therefore, we leave aside for the time being questions relating to the award of *non-pecuniary* damages where life expectancy is shortened.

Where a claimant is likely to die earlier because of their injuries, the relevant multiplier for the cost of *expenses* will be lower, since costs will not be incurred beyond the time of their death. But what of the multiplier for *lost earnings*? Should the injured party be able to claim for lost earnings in the years they *would have been earning* but for the tort, which now fall after the expected date of their death? The answer to this depends on the *purpose* of an award for lost earnings. If the purpose of this award is income replacement for the benefit of the claimant, then income that would have been earned during the 'lost years' should not be recoverable, even if it was 'caused by' the tort. The claimant will not now 'need' that income. This, however, would mean that the tort is allowed to reduce the *estate* of the injured party.

There will be less money flowing into the estate for the benefit of those inheriting it after his or her death. Is it the claimant, or the claimant's estate, that should be returned to the pre-tort position?

Pickett v British Rail Engineering Ltd [1980] AC 136

At the age of 51, the plaintiff contracted mesothelioma through his employer's breach of duty. His expectation of life was reduced to one year. He would otherwise have expected to work to age 65. Thus, compensation for earnings which would have been made during the 'lost years' was the major component of the damages claimed. Future expenses and lost earnings during the remaining year of life were relatively small, although there was an award of general damages (for non-pecuniary losses) of £7,000.

The House of Lords held that the claimant could recover for earnings that would have been made during the lost years. However, an amount must be deducted from this sum to represent the claimant's own living expenses during those years. Leaving aside the interpretation of earlier case law, Lord Scarman encapsulated the difficulties that remained with this solution:

Lord Scarman, at 169–71

Principle would appear ... to suggest that a plaintiff ought to be entitled to damages for the loss of earnings he could have reasonably expected to have earned during the "lost years." But it has been submitted by the defendant that such a rule, if it be thought socially desirable, requires to be implemented by legislation. It is argued that a judicial graft would entail objectionable consequences—consequences which legislation alone can obviate. There is force in this submission. The major objections are these. First, the plaintiff may have no dependants. Secondly, even if he has dependants, he may have chosen to make a will depriving them of support from his estate. In either event, there would be a windfall for strangers at the expense of the defendant. Thirdly, the plaintiff may be so young (in *Oliver v. Ashman* [1962] 2 Q.B. 210 he was a boy aged 20 months at the time of the accident) that it is absurd that he should be compensated for future loss of earnings. Fourthly—a point which has weighed with my noble and learned friend, Lord Russell of Killowen—if damages are recoverable for the loss of the prospect of earnings during the lost years, must it not follow that they are also recoverable for loss of other reasonable expectations, e.g. a life interest or an inheritance? Fifthly, what does compensation mean when it is assessed in respect of a period after death? Sixthly, as my noble and learned friend Lord Wilberforce has pointed out, there is a risk of double recovery in some cases, i.e. of both the estate and the dependants recovering damages for the expected earnings of the lost years.

Lord Scarman countered most of these objections but continued:

...

There is, it has to be confessed, no completely satisfying answer to the fifth objection. But it does not, I suggest, make it unjust that such damages should be awarded. The plaintiff has lost the earnings and the opportunity, which, while he was living, he valued, of employing them as he would have thought best. Whether a man's ambition be to build up a fortune, to provide for his family, or to spend his money upon good causes or merely a pleasurable existence, loss of the means to do so is a genuine financial loss. The logical and philosophical difficulties of compensating a man for a loss arising after his death emerge only if one treats the loss as a non-pecuniary loss—which to some extent it is. But it is also a pecuniary loss—the money would have been his to deal with as he chose, had he lived. The sixth objection appears to me unavoidable, though further argument and analysis in a case in which the point arose for decision might lead to a judicial solution which was satisfactory. But I suspect that the point will need legislation. However, if one must choose between a law which in some cases will deprive dependants of their dependency through the chances of life and litigation and a law which, in avoiding such a deprival, will entail in some cases both the estate and the dependants recovering damages in respect of the lost years, I find the latter to be the lesser evil.

These damages are justified chiefly on the basis that they maintain the value of the claimant's estate. Thus they raise issues of overlap with the provisions on dependency damages under the Fatal Accidents Act 1976, and with the survival of claims after the death of the injured party under the Law Reform (Miscellaneous Provisions) Act 1934. Indeed this is broadly the sixth point referred to by Lord Scarman, and he was correct to suggest that it would need legislative solution. The risk of double recovery was removed by an amendment to the Law Reform (Miscellaneous Provisions) Act 1934, which now holds that the claim for earnings in 'the lost years' no longer survives the claimant's death. We extract this statute in Section 2 of this chapter.

Not long after *Pickett*, in *Croke v Wiseman* [1982] 1 WLR 71, the Court of Appeal decided no award for earnings in 'the lost years' was appropriate for a 7-year-old with very severe injuries. The court reasoned that the award for 'the lost years' is made for the benefit of dependants, and in the presence of such severe injuries, it is clear the claimant will not have dependants. Yet the House of Lords had appeared to counter any such suggestions quite explicitly in the course of its decision in *Pickett*, and soon before *Croke v Wiseman* it had awarded damages for the 'lost years' to two claimants without requiring any evidence that they had any prospective dependants: the claimants were 15 and 22 years old (*Gammell v Wilson* [1982] AC 27).[11] Much more recently, in *Iqbal v Whipps Cross University Hospital NHS Trust* [2007] EWCA Civ 1190; [2008] PIQR P9, these matters came to a head as the Court of Appeal decided the case of a child who had been injured at birth and whose claim included an amount for 'the lost years'. It might have been possible to reason that *Croke v Wiseman* was reconcilable with *Pickett*, but only by accepting that each case must turn on its own facts, so that only claimants who were likely to have dependants would be able to claim for 'the lost years'. This was not the interpretation of *Pickett* adopted by the Court of Appeal. Rather, the court decided that *Croke v Wiseman* was inconsistent with *Pickett*. But they went on to reason that they were unable to depart from a decision of the Court of Appeal which was binding upon them. Only the House of Lords authority and which was subsequent to the House of Lords (or now, the Supreme Court) would be able to correct the error. For now, therefore, claimants injured as children will be unable to claim for the lost years, but the Court of Appeal has made clear that in its view the effect of *Pickett* was intended to be that all claimants

---

11 The House of Lords in this case ruled that a claim for these damages survived the death of the victim for the benefit of the estate, giving rise to the risk of double recovery where there is also an independent action by a dependant for their own loss, under the Fatal Accidents Act 1976. As explained in connection with fatal accidents, below, this possibility was reversed by statute.

could do so as long as a prediction of likely future earning and life expectancy is possible. With enhanced actuarial tools, this will more often seem attainable. On the other hand, any appeal of this issue to the Supreme Court will raise the possibility that *Pickett* itself would be considered incorrect.

1.5 EXPENSES

The cases considered here concern some of the most serious injuries, where care costs can outstrip lost earnings.

In the case of long-term injury, calculation of care costs will involve its own multiplier, relating not to working years, but to the *life expectancy* of the claimant. Since a claimant with a lower life expectancy will benefit from a lower 'multiplier' under the expenses head, the result is that the defendant will generally pay less under the heading of pecuniary losses if the accident actually *shortens* the life expectancy of the victim. This shows us a different side of the '100 per cent compensation' principle—if the damages are not 'needed', then they are not awarded.

Voluntary Provision of Care

Many injured people are cared for by relatives or friends, who make no charge for the care provided. To the extent that these carers incur pecuniary losses, particularly by giving up paid employment, it is clear that the award of damages may contain an amount to compensate for this. However, this amount is part of the claim made by the injured party. The care-giver has no claim against the tortfeasor in his or her own right. Although the House of Lords in *Hunt v Severs* (below) concluded that this amount is to be 'held on trust' by the injured party for the care-giver, the volunteer is still dependent on the injured party to bring the action at all.[12]

In *Donnelly v Joyce* [1974] QB 454, the plaintiff was a 6-year-old boy, whose mother gave up her part-time work in order to care for him. The Court of Appeal held that the plaintiff could claim for the cost of the services provided, as an element of his own claim. Rather awkwardly, the cost of services to him was valued in terms of the mother's lost earnings. This tends to show that the Court of Appeal's decision, though no doubt fair and just, was based on a fiction. This fiction is encapsulated in the following passage:

Megaw LJ, *Donnelly v Joyce*
[1974] QB 454, at 461–2

Mr. Hamilton's first proposition is that a plaintiff cannot succeed in a claim in relation to someone else's loss unless the plaintiff is under a legal liability to reimburse that other person. The plaintiff, he says, was not under a legal liability to reimburse his mother. A moral obligation is not enough. Mr. Hamilton's second proposition is that if, contrary to his submission, the existence of a moral, as distinct from a legal, obligation to reimburse the benefactor is sufficient, nevertheless there is no moral obligation on the part of a child of six years of age to repay its parents for money spent by them, as in this case.

---

[12] See J. Herring, 'Where are the Carers in Health Care Law and Ethics?' (2007) 27 LS 51–73.

We do not agree with the proposition, inherent in Mr. Hamilton's submission, that the plaintiff's claim, in circumstances such as the present, is properly to be regarded as being, to use his phrase, "in relation to someone else's loss," merely because someone else has provided to, or for the benefit of, the plaintiff—the injured person—the money, or the services to be valued as money, to provide for needs of the plaintiff directly caused by the defendant's wrongdoing. The loss is the plaintiff's loss. The question from what source the plaintiff's needs have been met, the question who has paid the money or given the services, the question whether or not the plaintiff is or is not under a legal or moral liability to repay, are, so far as the defendant and his liability are concerned, all irrelevant. The plaintiff's loss, to take this present case, is not the expenditure of money to buy the special boots or to pay for the nursing attention. His loss is the existence of the need for those special boots or for those nursing services, the value of which for purposes of damages—for the purpose of the ascertainment of the amount of his loss—is the proper and reasonable cost of supplying those needs. That, in our judgment, is the key to the problem. So far as the defendant is concerned, the loss is not someone else's loss. It is the plaintiff's loss.

The problem with this was exposed in *Hunt v Severs* [1994] 2 AC 350. Referring to the above passage in *Donnelly v Joyce*, Lord Bridge said:

Lord Bridge, *Hunt v Severs*, at 361

With respect, I do not find this reasoning convincing. I accept that the basis of a plaintiff's claim for damages may consist in his need for services but I cannot accept that the question from what source that need has been met is irrelevant. If an injured plaintiff is treated in hospital as a private patient he is entitled to recover the cost of that treatment. But if he receives free treatment under the National Health Service, his need has been met without cost to him and he cannot claim the cost of the treatment from the tortfeasor. So it cannot, I think, be right to say that in all cases the plaintiff's loss is "for the purpose of damages ... the proper and reasonable cost of supplying [his] needs."

This passage is correct in its criticism of the reasoning in *Donnelly*. But the conclusion reached in *Hunt v Severs* has itself been widely criticized, and rightly so.

Hunt v Severs [1994] 2 AC 350

The unusual but by no means unique feature of this case was that the defendant was both the tortfeasor, and the care-giver. Through the defendant's negligence, the plaintiff was very severely injured when riding as a pillion passenger on his motorcycle. The defendant later married the plaintiff and provided her with nursing care. Rejecting as a fiction the idea in *Donnelly v Joyce* that the loss represented by the nursing expenses is really the plaintiff's loss, the House of Lords preferred to say that such sums are paid for the benefit of those providing the gratuitous services, and not for the benefit of the plaintiff at all. Unfortunately, the House of Lords went on to hold that *because* the loss is really that of the carer rather than of the plaintiff, *therefore* there could be no claim for such amounts *where the defendant is also the care-giver*; because this would require the defendant to bear the cost of the care twice—once by offering the services, and then again by paying for them:

Lord Bridge, *Hunt v Severs*
[1994] 2 AC 350, at 363

By concentrating on the plaintiff's need and the plaintiff's loss as the basis of an award in respect of voluntary care received by the plaintiff, the reasoning in *Donnelly v. Joyce* diverts attention from the award's central objective of compensating the voluntary carer. Once this is recognised it becomes evident that there can be no ground in public policy or otherwise for requiring the tortfeasor to pay to the plaintiff, in respect of the services which he himself has rendered, a sum of money which the plaintiff must then repay to him. If the present case had been brought in Scotland and the claim in respect of the tortfeasor's services made in reliance on section 8 of the Administration of Justice Act 1982, it would have been immediately obvious that such a claim was not sustainable.

The case for the plaintiff was argued in the Court of Appeal without reference to the circumstance that the defendant's liability was covered by insurance. But before your Lordships Mr. McGregor, recognising the difficulty of formulating any principle of public policy which could justify recovery against the tortfeasor who has to pay out of his own pocket, advanced the bold proposition that such a policy could be founded on the liability of insurers to meet the claim. Exploration of the implications of this proposition in argument revealed the many difficulties which it encounters. But I do not think it necessary to examine these in detail. The short answer, in my judgment, to Mr. McGregor's contention is that its acceptance would represent a novel and radical departure in the law of a kind which only the legislature may properly effect. At common law the circumstance that a defendant is contractually indemnified by a third party against a particular legal liability can have no relevance whatever to the measure of that liability.

This reasoning is very selective about which consequences of an award of damages may be considered. The very point of the claim for care offered by the defendant was that he could then be reimbursed by his liability insurer. To hold that it would be *unfair* to such a defendant to require him to pay 'twice' is misplaced.

Lord Bridge's point in the final paragraph is, essentially, that courts should not distinguish between individual cases depending on whether the *particular* defendant is or is not insured. The existence of an insurance policy should not be a decisive factor. But this misses the point that claims of this sort simply would not be brought unless liability insurance was in place. What benefit could there otherwise be in bringing the claim?[13]

The Law Commission in its Consultation Paper on *Damages for Personal Injury: Medical, Nursing and Other Expenses* (LCCP 144, 1996) took the view that legislation should reverse the effect of *Hunt v Severs*, but at the same time accepted the House of Lords' decision to ignore the insurance position of the defendant:

3.65 … Although the existence of insurance was a vital part of the factual picture, and indeed litigation would scarcely have made sense if the defendant had not been insured against such liability, we do not consider that the existence of insurance should be permitted to affect liability. We believe that the question of the defendant's liability must necessarily precede the one of the defendant's insurer's liability.

---

[13] See L. Hoyano, 'The Dutiful Tortfeasor in the House of Lords' [1995] Tort L Rev 63.

This argument might have been acceptable (though not especially persuasive), had the House of Lords in *Hunt v Severs* not made an exception to general principle precisely in order to avoid unfairness to the defendant. Decisions as to 'fairness' in particular should not be made without reference to the consequences of the decision for the parties concerned, even if some of the more formal ideas of justice applied to the law of tort do proceed on this basis.

Local Authority Care

Earlier in this chapter, we explained that claimants need not use NHS medical services, but are entitled to choose private medical care, and to claim an amount in respect of this care from the defendant: Law Reform (Personal Injuries Act) 1948, section 2. No equivalent provision exists in respect of care provided by a local authority. Given that local authorities are in many cases under a statutory obligation to provide such care, or indeed to provide direct financial assistance, the question arises of whether the claimant is obliged to depend upon this care, and whether he or she may claim for the costs of future *private* provision.

In *Sowden v Lodge; Crookdale v Drury* [2005] 1 WLR 2129, the Court of Appeal explained that if claimants generally were permitted to claim for private care for the rest of their lives, claims would tend to be 'astronomically high' (at [90]). The solution must depend on what was reasonable on the facts of the individual case. One alternative was for defendants to set out whether the claimant's reasonable needs may be met by local authority care, allowing for potential 'top-ups'.

Scott-Baker LJ, *Sowden v Lodge*

[102] … private care awards are liable to be astronomically high where awarded on a full life basis while care provided by the local authority may fall short of a claimant's reasonable needs. It is against this background that the principle of 'top up' has emerged. For my part I can see nothing wrong with 'top up' in an appropriate case.

In *Peters v East Midlands Strategic Health Authority* [2009] EWCA Civ 145, a later Court of Appeal reached a conclusion which appears to be inconsistent with *Sowden*. It distinguished *Sowden* on the basis that the court had not there been asked to consider whether a claimant was entitled as of right to select private care even if there was a statutory right to provision by the local authority—the key point considered in *Peters*.

Dyson LJ, *Peters v East Midlands Strategic Health Authority* (giving the judgment of the court)

53. … We can see no reason in policy or principle which requires us to hold that a claimant who wishes to opt for self-funding and damages in preference to reliance on the statutory obligations of a public authority should not be entitled to do so as a matter of right. The claimant has suffered loss which has been caused by the wrongdoing of the defendants. She is entitled to have that loss made good, so far as this is possible, by the provision of accommodation and care. There is no dispute as to what that should be and the Council currently arranges for its provision at The Spinnies. The only issue is whether the defendant wrongdoers or the Council and the PCT should pay for it in the future.

The court reasoned that just as a claimant who is the victim of two torts may choose which tortfeasor to proceed against and then leave the tortfeasors to battle over contribution (Chapter 7), so a claimant who has a choice of routes as between a tortfeasor and another party with an obligation to meet her needs may likewise decide which party to claim against. In this case, the claimant's choice was between claiming damages and purchasing care; and obtaining free care from her local authority. The court held that she was entitled as of right to 'prefer self-funding and damages rather than provision at public expense' (at [89]). It does seem worth pointing out, given this way of phrasing the choice, that payment by the tortfeasor also amounts to payment 'at public expense' in this particular case, since the first defendant was a local health authority. The point made in *Sowden* was that life-time private care costs are likely to be very much more costly than the local authority alternative, while accepting that there may sometimes be a need for more (or better?) care than the local authority can provide. *Peters* seems to replace this fact-sensitive approach with a statement of general principle, that a claimant may choose which way to go, and that the principle of mitigation of loss simply has no application in this context.

1.6 DEDUCTIONS

The principle of 100 per cent compensation cuts both ways. The common law does not allow recovery, under the head of compensatory damages, of more than has been lost. Therefore, deductions from the damages award will be made to reflect benefits received. However, certain benefits are not deducted in this way. These are payments from first party insurance policies where premiums were paid by the claimant; and 'benevolent' payments from third parties.

In principle, any deductions to reflect benefits received will be made *only* on a 'like for like' basis. If there is a benefit in the nature of *income*, then it will be deducted only from the amount awarded for *loss of earnings*. This being so, in a case where there is no pecuniary loss and the award is entirely made up of damages for non-pecuniary losses, there will be no deduction on account of financial benefits. No 'double recovery' arises in such a case.

Deductions in Respect of 'Lost Earnings'

Some examples of the principle against double recovery in respect of lost earnings are as follows:

- In *Hussain v New Taplow Mills* (1988) AC 514, a deduction from lost earnings was made in respect of *statutory sick pay*.

- In general, a contributory pension will *not* be set off against the award of damages for lost earnings (*Parry v Cleaver* [1969] 1 All ER 555), *even if* the defendant (generally an employer) also contributed to the pension (*Smoker v London Fire and Defence Civil Authority* [1991] 2 AC 502). However, a disablement pension will be set off against the part of the award which compensates for loss of pension, rather than earnings (*Longden v British Coal Corporation* [1997] 3 WLR 1336).

- By section 5 of the Administration of Justice Act 1982, a claimant who is maintained at public expense will be susceptible to a deduction from damages *if and to the extent that this leads to reduced living expenses*. For example, they may no longer have to pay rent, or 'board and lodgings'.

The 'Thrift or Gift' Exceptions

Two established exceptions to the rule that benefits should be deducted from relevant heads of damage relate to:

1. insurance ('thrift'); and
2. benevolence ('gift').

The general thinking is that it is not appropriate for the defendant to gain the benefit of the claimant's thrift and prudence, or of the good motives of third parties.

The Insurance Exception

Lord Reid, *Parry v Cleaver*
[1970] AC 1 14

As regards moneys coming to the plaintiff under a contract of insurance, I think that the real and substantial reason for disregarding them is that the plaintiff has bought them and that it would be unjust and unreasonable to hold that the money which he prudently spent on premiums and the benefit from it should enure to the benefit of the tortfeasor.

The Benevolence Exception

Lord Reid, *Parry v Cleaver*, at 14

It would be revolting to the ordinary man's sense of justice, and therefore contrary to public policy, that the sufferer should have his damages reduced so that he would gain nothing from the benevolence of his friends or relations or of the public at large.

This thinking has not been broadened and indeed if the reasoning adopted in recent cases were to be extended, it would challenge the exceptions themselves.

Hodgson v Trapp [1989] AC 807

The plaintiff sustained injuries in a road traffic accident for which the defendants admitted liability. As a result, she was wholly and permanently dependent on the care of others. The defendants argued that her award should be reduced to take account of statutory care and mobility allowances received. These social security benefits relate to elements of the claimant's *care*.

The plaintiff argued that the allowances should be disregarded, since social welfare benefits of this nature were akin to 'benevolent' payments made out of altruistic motives. The House of Lords rejected the 'benevolence' interpretation, and held that the allowances were deductible.

Note: the effect of Hodgson v Trapp has been modified by the Social Security (Recovery of Benefits) Act 1997. Now, relevant benefits listed in the Act are deducted for a maximum of five years, and the amount deducted is repaid to the state by the party paying compensation. Hodgson v Trapp is still an important authority because common law continues to govern any benefits not listed within the statutory provisions.

In the following short extract, Lord Bridge elaborates on the general reasons for deductions of this nature. The deductions are of course compatible with the 100 per cent principle, but importantly, he also calls attention to the broader economic context of tort damages.

Lord Bridge, at 823

In the end the issue in these cases is not so much one of statutory construction as of public policy. If we have regard to the realities, awards of damages for personal injuries are met from the insurance premiums payable by motorists, employers, occupiers of property, professional men and others. Statutory benefits payable to those in need by reason of impecuniosity or disability are met by the taxpayer. In this context to ask whether the taxpayer, as the "benevolent donor," intends to benefit "the wrongdoer" as represented by the insurer who meets the claim at the expense of the appropriate class of policy holders, seems to me entirely artificial. There could hardly be a clearer case than that of the attendance allowance payable under section 35 of the Act of 1975[14] where the statutory benefit and the special damages claimed for cost of care are designed to meet the identical expenses. To allow double recovery in such a case at the expense of both taxpayers and insurers seems to me incapable of justification on any rational ground. It could only add to the enormous disparity, to which the advocates of a "no-fault" system of compensation constantly draw attention, between the position of those who are able to establish a third party's fault as the cause of their injury and the position of those who are not.

Lord Bridge's comments here are thought-provoking. In particular:

(a) By extension to the general justification of the 'thrift' exception, why should the defendant in this sort of case be entitled to pay less simply because the state has stepped in with some support? Lord Bridge's answer is that most of us pay or contribute to insurance premiums, so that ultimately, it is the ordinary person who would have to pay twice if there was no deduction from damages in these cases—once through insurance, and once through tax.

(b) Since (as Lord Bridge observes) most damages are paid by insurance companies, is it still appropriate to make awards which are recognized to exceed 100 per cent compensation,[15] in order to avoid benefiting tortfeasors? Those tortfeasors are not very likely to have to pay damages themselves.

Like *Hodgson v Trapp*, the more recent case of *Gaca v Pirelli* [2004] 1 WLR 2683 also declined to extend the recognized thrift or gift exceptions. The Court of Appeal held that payments which essentially amounted to part of the employment package offered to

---

14 Social Security Act 1975.
15 Because the claimant has not in fact 'lost' all the sums repaid as a consequence of the tort.

the claimant, and which were made through insurance *funded by the tortfeasor*, did not fall within the 'gift' or 'benevolence' exception. Nor did they fall within the insurance exception. The claimant had not paid the premiums himself, so that it was the *tortfeasor's* thrift and prudence, not the claimant's, which enabled the insurance payments to be made.

1.7 NON-PECUNIARY LOSSES IN PERSONAL INJURY CASES

'Non-pecuniary losses' suffered in a personal injury case may be divided into two main categories:

1. pain and suffering;
2. loss of amenity.

In practice, a single award for 'general damages' will be made covering both of these forms of loss, without itemization between them. Both come close to being purely 'conventional' sums, within a range set out in guidelines from the Judicial Studies Board. In *principle*, the two forms of non-pecuniary loss are rather different. Pain and suffering is supposedly assessed subjectively (how much has the claimant suffered?); 'loss of amenity' is partly objective, so that the award is made *for the fact of loss*, rather than for the experience of loss. The true test of this comes in cases where the claimant is so severely injured that she or he has no awareness of their loss, still less of the award of damages which is supposed to 'make it good'.

West v Shephard [1964] AC 326

The plaintiff sustained very severe injuries in a road traffic accident caused through the negligence of an employee of the defendant. She may or may not have been able to appreciate the condition she was in. Given that she suffered severe mental impairment and was unable to understand very much if anything that was said to her, she would have no awareness of the award of damages itself. In the face of a strong dissent by Lord Reid, the House of Lords held that substantial damages might be awarded for loss of amenity to a plaintiff who is unable to appreciate the award—and, indeed, even to a plaintiff who is unconscious.

The result in *West v Shephard* was confirmed by the House of Lords in *Lim Poh Choo v Camden and Islington Area Health Authority* [1980] AC 174. The claimant here suffered a cardiac arrest when undergoing minor surgery and was left with very severe injuries. She was barely sentient and then only intermittently so. The House of Lords upheld an award of £20,000 for pain, suffering, and loss of amenity, as part of a much larger award including substantial sums for lost earnings and future care costs.

Some fierce arguments have been conducted over non-pecuniary losses, and the decision in *West v Shephard* serves to fuel these arguments. While the '100 per cent principle' clearly requires the court to attempt to quantify pain, suffering, and loss of amenity, it has been argued that these heads of damages are entirely wasteful in a case like *West v Shephard*, and not necessarily justified even in a more typical case. While general damages will usually amount to a small proportion of the damages awarded to a seriously injured claimant, in a small claim general damages may even be the major component of the award. Are tort damages being appropriately targeted?

Increasing General Damages

In its Report on *Damages for Non-Pecuniary Loss* (Report No 257, 1999), the Law Commission proposed that the level of awards for loss of amenity and pain and suffering should be increased considerably. Awards of £3,000 should be increased by 50–100 per cent, and smaller claims over £2,000 should be subject to a tapered increase. Their thinking on this was heavily based on certain empirical studies, and on responses to the Commission's Consultation Paper. One of the empirical studies was commissioned by the Law Commission itself and carried out by the Office of National Statistics. It sought public opinion on whether damages awards for pain, suffering, and loss of amenity should be increased, and sought to improve the validity of the responses by spelling out to respondents the likely consequence for insurance premiums.

In *Heil v Rankin* [2001] QB 272, the Court of Appeal considered the Law Commission Report, but declined to follow its recommendations. The court did take the important step of recommending a significant increase in the damages to be awarded for pain, suffering, and loss of amenity,[16] but did so only for the more serious cases, defined as awards of over £10,000. These increases should be tapered to a maximum of one-third for 'the most catastrophic' injuries. To the relief of the insurance industry, there would be no increase at all for awards of less than £10,000, which make up the majority of tort claims. The Court of Appeal evidently considered the award of general damages to have a serious role to play in compensation awards. But it doubted the frame of reference employed in the Law Commission Report and pointed out, for example, that the research did not explicitly build in the impact on NHS funding. It is of interest that the Court of Appeal mentioned this element of the broader picture.

Heil v Rankin (as well as the Law Commission Report which preceded it) has offered an opportunity for some deeper criticism of the role of non-pecuniary damages.

Richard Lewis, 'Increasing the Price of Pain' (2001) 64 MLR 100, at 107

... let us consider questions which people might have been asked if a wider perspective on tort had been taken. These questions explicitly deal with relative priorities for expenditure. The likely responses to these questions are no less predictable than those asking whether victims should get more money, but they carry very different implications for the future of damages for non-pecuniary loss. The first question begins by explaining that more than two-thirds of accident victims who are so seriously injured that they are unable to work for more than six months are unable to claim any damages at all and, instead, must rely on social security benefits. The remaining third are able to claim not only for their full financial loss but also for their pain and suffering. The question then to ask is: 'When allocating further resources to accident victims, should more money be spent on those already able to claim damages by giving them more for their pain and suffering?'

Similarly, a second question, although taking a narrower focus, could still attack the priority now given to PSLA.[17] It asks people to place in order of importance the losses which they might choose to insure themselves against if they were to take out a policy against being involved in an accident causing personal injury. Which would they regard as the most

---

[16] It should be pointed out that this was an *additional* increase above the level of the Retail Price Index.
[17] Pain, suffering, and loss of amenity.

important loss to insure against: an interruption in earnings; the cost of medical and other care; or PSLA? ... It is clear that those who are knowledgeable about the risks of accident or illness, and seek policies to protect themselves against such eventualities, do not wish to pay much higher premiums for a type of loss for which money cannot easily provide a substitute. If it were left to market forces there would be no cover for PSLA ....

The second of the 'alternative questions' proposed by Lewis recalls a hypothetical scenario used by P. S. Atiyah in his essay, 'Personal Injuries in the Twenty First Century: Thinking the Unthinkable', in P. B. H. Birks (ed.), *Wrongs and Remedies in the Twenty-First Century* (Oxford University Press, 1996). Atiyah proposed that, if an insurance salesman were to try to sell the tort system door to door, he would have very few takers for the 'policy' it offers, given its costs. Its coverage is far too patchy, leaving the majority of accident victims uncompensated chiefly because of its dependence on showing fault, and providing very expensive benefits only to a lucky few. Atiyah's argument is that it is wrong to force people to pay for a level of 'insurance cover' that they would not buy if left to their own devices—*particularly* if that cover is so full of holes that there is only a 33 per cent chance of recovering under the policy. On this view, the costs of tort law are accepted by the general public only because they are hidden. The appearance (that tort attaches costs to those who wrongfully cause injury) is deceptive.

From April 2013, general damages have been strategically increased by 10 per cent across the board. This is not because they are considered too low. Rather, the increase is part of a package of measures designed to provide a new approach to litigation funding, and recommended by Lord Justice Jackson following his extensive review of litigation costs and funding.[18] A number of other key recommendations of that review have been enacted in the Legal Aid, Sentencing and Punishment of Offenders Act 2012, which came into force in April 2013. But the statute did not itself provide for the increase in damages. In *Simmons v Castle* [2012] EWCA Civ 1039, the Court of Appeal *announced* that general damages in almost[19] all civil claims for pain and suffering, loss of amenity, physical inconvenience and discomfort, social discredit, and mental distress, would be 10 per cent higher than previously, with effect from 1 April 2013. The division of roles between courts and legislature here is unusual, and as the Court of Appeal pointed out, it reflects the close involvement of the judiciary in designing the new costs regime.

Lord Judge CJ (giving judgment of the court), *Simmons v Castle* **[2012] EWCA Civ 1039**

15 ... the increase we are laying down arises from a different set of facts from those in Heil v Rankin. It is attributable to the forthcoming change in the civil costs regime initiated by Sir Rupert Jackson's reforms, as accepted by the executive and enacted by the legislature. As already explained, the increase was recommended by Sir Rupert as an integral part of his proposed reforms, which were unconditionally endorsed and supported as such by the judiciary publicly, and it was plainly on the basis that the 10 per cent increase would be formally adopted by the judiciary that the 2012 Act was introduced and enacted.

[18] *Review of Civil Litigation Costs: Final Report* (TSO, 2010).

[19] Excluded are claimants who are able to recover a 'success fee' pursuant to s 44(6) LASPO 2012. The uplift is designed to replace the recoverable success fee.

16 This is, no doubt, an unusual basis on which to rest a judgment or to adjust guidelines. However the recommendation to adjust the level of damages arises from a report prepared by a judge, which was initiated by the judiciary (as it was Lord Clarke of Stone-cum-Ebony, who, as Master of the Rolls, initiated Sir Rupert's report) and which contains policy recommendations, which is itself unusual (and, we would add, can only be justified in relation to a topic as closely concerned with the administration of, and access to, justice, as legal costs). With the exception of the 10 per cent increase in general damages, the great bulk of those policy recommendations have been adopted in full by the legislature in an Act sponsored by the executive, on the clear understanding that the judges would implement the 10 per cent increase. It would therefore be little short of a breach of faith for the judiciary not to give effect to the 10 per cent increase in damages recommended by Sir Rupert.

The reforms as a whole are explored in Section 7.

2. DEATH AND DAMAGES: WHERE THE INJURED PARTY DIES

At common law, causes of action were treated as personal. Where death was concerned, this had two important consequences. First, the death of either party extinguished a civil claim. Second, death could not give rise to a right of action for the benefit of others. In both respects, the position has been reformed by statute.

In this section, we consider the relevant issues in three stages:

1. In what circumstances does a civil claim survive the death of the victim of the tort? The answer to this question is governed by the Law Reform (Miscellaneous Provisions) Act 1934.

2. In what circumstances does causing death create a right of action? And who benefits from such an action? The answers to these questions are governed by the Fatal Accidents Act 1976.

3. How has the development of domestic remedies for failure to protect life under Article 2 ECHR affected the picture? These remedies, though not modelled on tort, are provided by the HRA for effectively 'tort-like' failures on the part of public authorities. They are available to a wider range of claimants than the tortious remedies above.

2.1 CLAIMS SURVIVING DEATH

1 Effect of death on certain causes of action[20]

(1) Subject to the provisions of this section, on the death of any person after the commencement of this Act all causes of action subsisting against or vested in him shall survive against, or, as the case may be, for the benefit of, his estate. Provided that this subsection shall not

---

[20] Sections 1A and 1(2)(a) were inserted and substituted (respectively) by the Administration of Justice Act 1982.

2.2 CLAIMS FOR THE DEATH OF ANOTHER

By the Fatal Accidents Act 1976, two distinct actions are defined in respect of the death of another.[22]

- Section 1 defines a cause of action on the part of 'dependants' of the deceased (a category defined in the section), for **loss of dependency**. Loss of dependency is essentially pecuniary in nature.

- Section 1A defines a cause of action for **bereavement**. Bereavement is non-pecuniary in nature, and the damages available are set at a conventional sum of (for the time being) £11,800. Only those people listed in section 1A have the benefit of a claim for bereavement.

The parties with a cause of action for loss of dependency under section 1 will not necessarily have a cause of action for bereavement under section 1A, and vice versa. They are separately defined.

Section 1: Dependency Damages

Fatal Accidents Act 1976

1 Right of action for wrongful act causing death[23]

(1) If death is caused by any wrongful act, neglect or default which is such as would (if death had not ensued) have entitled the person injured to maintain an action and recover damages in respect thereof, the person who would have been liable if death had not ensued shall be liable to an action for damages, notwithstanding the death of the person injured.

(2) Subject to section 1A(2) below, every such action shall be for the benefit of the dependants of the person ("the deceased") whose death has been so caused.

(3) In this Act "dependant" means—

(a) the wife or husband or former wife or husband of the deceased;[(aa)the civil partner or former civil partner of the deceased;][24]

(b) any person who—

(i) was living with the deceased in the same household immediately before the date of the death; and

(ii) had been living with the deceased in the same household for at least two years before that date; and

(iii) was living during the whole of that period as the husband or wife of the deceased;

(c) any parent or other ascendant of the deceased;

(d) any person who was treated by the deceased as his parent;

---

[22] For a history of the first Fatal Accidents Act, see D. Nolan, 'The Fatal Accidents Act 1846', in T. T. Arvind and J. Steele (eds) *Tort Law and the Legislature* (Hart Publishing, 2013).

[23] This section was substituted by the Administration of Justice Act 1982, s 3, and amended by the Civil Partnership Act 2004.

[24] This subsection and ss 1(2)(fa) and 1(4A) were inserted by the Civil Partnership Act 2004.

(e)   any child or other descendant of the deceased;

(f)   any person (not being a child of the deceased) who, in the case of any marriage to which the deceased was at any time a party, was treated by the deceased as a child of the family in relation to that marriage;

[(fa) any person (not being a child of the deceased) who, in the case of any civil partnership in which the deceased was at any time a civil partner, was treated by the deceased as a child of the family in relation to that civil partnership]

(g)   any person who is, or is the issue of, a brother, sister, uncle or aunt of the deceased.

(4) The reference to the former wife or husband of the deceased in subsection (3)(a) above includes a reference to a person whose marriage to the deceased has been annulled or declared void as well as a person whose marriage to the deceased has been dissolved.

[(4A) The reference to the former civil partner of the deceased in subsection (3)(aa) above includes a reference to a person whose civil partnership with the deceased has been annulled as well as a person whose civil partnership with the deceased has been dissolved.]

(5) In deducing any relationship for the purposes of subsection (3) above—

(a)   any relationship by affinity shall be treated as a relationship by consanguinity, any relationship of the half blood as a relationship of the whole blood, and the stepchild of any person as his child, and

(b)   an illegitimate person shall be treated as the legitimate child of his mother and reputed father.

(6) Any reference in this Act to injury includes any disease and any impairment of a person's physical or mental condition.

Section 1(3)(b) has recently survived a challenge on the basis that it is incompatible with the HRA. The claimant in *Swift v Secretary of State for Justice* [2013] EWCA Civ 193 was living with the deceased when the latter was killed in an accident at work, but they had not been cohabiting for two years as required by section 1(3)(b)(ii). Their son, who was born after the death of his father, was able to claim as a dependent; but his mother could not. She argued that this violated her rights under Article 14 ECHR (non-discrimination), together with Article 8 ECHR (protection of private and family life). Though accepting that the subsection might give rise to 'some results which many would regard as unjust', the Court of Appeal concluded that there was no such violation: the legislation raised 'difficult issues of social and economic policy', and it was legitimate for the legislature to require a degree of permanence in relationships to which the legislation would apply. Nor was the qualifying period of two years either disproportionate or arbitrary. In the words of Lord Dyson, 'the requirement of habitation for two years is a simple way of demonstrating a real relationship of constancy and permanence' ([37]). Parliament 'was entitled to prefer a bright-line distinction to an approach which depended on fact-sensitive decisions in each case' ([39]) and, indeed, the alternative would itself have undesirable features:

Lord Dyson MR, *Swift v Secretary of State for Justice*

40 In summary, the two-year requirement provides greater certainty as to the scope of the 1976 Act; it ensures that the court has some evidence of past experience and the nature of the relationship to inform its assessment of damages under section 3(1) of the Act; and

it reduces the need to conduct an intrusive and intimate inquiry into the nature and quality of the relationship, in order to establish whether it satisfies some objective standard of permanence and constancy.

Fatal Accidents Act 1976

1A Bereavement[25]

(1) An action under this Act may consist of or include a claim for damages for bereavement.

(2) A claim for damages for bereavement shall only be for the benefit—

(a) of the wife or husband [or civil partner] of the deceased; and

(b) where the deceased was a minor who was never married [or a civil partner]—

   (i) of his parents, if he was legitimate; and

   (ii) of his mother, if he was illegitimate.

(3) Subject to subsection (5) below, the sum to be awarded as damages under this section shall be [£12,980].

(4) Where there is a claim for damages under this section for the benefit of both the parents of the deceased, the sum awarded shall be divided equally between them (subject to any deduction falling to be made in respect of costs not recovered from the defendant).

(5) The Lord Chancellor may by order made by statutory instrument, subject to annulment in pursuance of a resolution of either House of Parliament, amend this section by varying the sum for the time being specified in subsection (3) above.

It will be apparent that a limited range of people is entitled to bereavement damages. If an unmarried adult, without a civil partner, is killed, and has no children, then there is often no person who can claim bereavement damages. Not even the parent of an adult, or a cohabitant unless they have lived with the deceased for over two years, may claim such damages. This is one reason for the importance of actions under the HRA in relation to Article 2.

Bereavement damages may be considered rather low (though they are higher than some recent awards under the HRA). They represent a conventional sum, which may be described as compensatory only in a limited sense. The sum is varied periodically by Order, most recently (at the time of writing) in 2013, increasing bereavement damages by 10 per cent in line with other increases in general damages.[26]

Issues Arising in Respect of Dependency Damages

Relationship between the Section 1 Claim, and a Claim by the Deceased

The action arising under section 1 is an action on the part of dependants in their own right, but by section 1(1) the action will exist only if the deceased, had he or she been injured rather than killed, could have brought an action. A number of issues flow from this.

[25] Amended by the Civil Partnership Act 2004.
[26] SI 2013 No 510, The Damages for Bereavement (Variation of Sum) (England and Wales) Order 2013, increasing bereavement damages from £11,800 to £12,980).

1. If the claim of the deceased was *time-barred* under the applicable Limitation Act at the time of their death, then the dependants have no action. However, provided the claim is not time-barred at the date of death, the dependants have three years from the death in which to bring a claim (Limitation Act 1980, section 12(2)).

2. It is expressly provided by section 5 of the Fatal Accidents Act 1976 that if damages payable to the deceased would in the circumstances have been reduced by reason of contributory negligence, any damages payable under the Act will also fall to be reduced in the same way.

3. Particular problems arise where more than one tortfeasor is potentially liable for the harm suffered, and the deceased person has settled their claim against one of those parties.

Jameson v CEGB [2000] 1 AC 455

A few days before his death from malignant mesothelioma, J agreed to accept a payment of £80,000 from his former employer B, in 'full and final settlement and satisfaction of all the causes of action in respect of which the plaintiff claimed in the statement of claim'.

The full value of the claim was much greater than £80,000. After J's death, his widow commenced proceedings under the Fatal Accidents Act 1976, section 1 against another former employer, the defendant in this action.

The two employers, the defendant and B, were 'concurrent tortfeasors'. They had committed separate torts, but were each potentially liable in full for the same indivisible damage to which they were to be treated as having made a material contribution.[27] By section 4 of the Fatal Accidents Act 1976, the plaintiff if she had succeeded in her action would not have had to account for the benefit that she gained, via her husband's estate, from his settlement of the claim against B:

4 Assessment of damages; disregard of benefits

In assessing damages in respect of a person's death in an action under this Act, benefits which have accrued or will or may accrue to any person from his estate or otherwise as a result of his death shall be disregarded.

There was a chance of over-compensation.

Furthermore, because the two employers were potentially liable *in respect of the same damage*, the provisions of the Civil Liability (Contribution) Act 1978 would apply.[28] The defendant, if found liable to the claimant, could claim contribution from B, who had already settled the claim (admittedly below its full value) against the deceased.[29]

---

27. See Chapter 7.
28. Section 1(1) of the Civil Liability (Contribution) Act 1978, explained in Chapter 7.
29. It is not clear what a court would do if a widow succeeded in such an action, so that contribution between the two tortfeasors fell to be decided. As we explained in Chapter 7, the factors which can be considered by a court in making the apportionment are not limited to those which are causative of the harm suffered. In principle, the fact that B had already paid a sum to the deceased could therefore be taken into account; what is less clear is *how* this factor ought to be treated in proceedings between tortfeasors in a case where there is an element of double compensation. Which party should bear the cost of the double compensation element? This problem is not insurmountable, since the court could decide to share the double compensation element (which is after all a creation of statute) equitably between the tortfeasors.

The House of Lords decided that the widow could not satisfy the terms of section 1(1) of the Fatal Accidents Act 1976, requiring that the deceased would have had a claim against the defendant had he not died. He would not have had such a claim, because he had settled his claim in full against B. His hypothetical claim against the defendant was thus precluded. This was *not* however because the terms of the settlement with B in any sense 'bound' the deceased not to pursue another tortfeasor—such as the defendant—in separate proceedings. The agreement made no mention of any other tortfeasor. Rather, it was because the deceased's claim for damages was *treated* as having been satisfied in full, even though the full *value* of the claim had clearly not been received.

Lord Hope, *Jameson v CEGB*, at 473

... The causes of action [against concurrent tortfeasors] are indeed separate. And it is clear that an agreement reached between the plaintiff and one concurrent tortfeasor cannot extinguish the plaintiff's claim against the other concurrent tortfeasor if his claim for damages has still not been satisfied. The critical question ... is whether the claim has in fact been satisfied. I think that the answer to it will be found by examining the terms of the agreement and comparing it with what has been claimed. The significance of the agreement is to be found in the effect which the parties intended to give to it. The fact that it has been entered into by way of a compromise in order to conclude a settlement forms part of the background. But the extent of the element of compromise will vary from case to case. The scope for litigation may have been reduced by agreement, for example on the question of liability. There may be little room for dispute as to the amount which a judge would award as damages. So one cannot assume that the figure which the parties are willing to accept is simply their assessment of the risks of litigation. The essential point is that the meaning which is to be given to the agreement will determine its effect.

A later House of Lords in *Heaton v Axa Equity and Law* [2002] UKHL 15; [2002] 2 WLR 1081 (which did not concern a claim under the Fatal Accidents Act) emphasized that *Jameson* laid down no *general* rule. It is not the case that a settlement against one tortfeasor necessarily precludes an action against another concurrent tortfeasor. The question in each case will be whether the claim has been satisfied in full by the settlement. In *Jameson*, it was the deceased's 'loss' which was treated as having been extinguished by the terms and intention of the agreement. In *Heaton*, Lord Bingham proposed that the proposition that '[a] sum accepted in settlement of such a claim may also fix the full measure of a claimant's loss', 'may perhaps have been stated a little too absolutely' in *Jameson*' (Lord Bingham, *Heaton v Axa*, at [8]).[30]

In fact, the reasoning in *Jameson* is none too convincing. It does not seem natural to argue that a settlement at a clear undervalue is intended by both parties to 'extinguish the loss', where there is another party against whom to proceed. After *Heaton*, the way is open for courts to interpret settlements in a less 'absolute' fashion.

Suicide

It is clear that an action for dependency damages may be available even if the deceased committed suicide, provided the usual criteria for liability (including remoteness of damage) are

[30] Lord Hope, who gave the leading judgment in *Jameson*, agreed with Lord Bingham in *Heaton v Axa*.

satisfied: *Reeves v Commissioner of Police for the Metropolis* [2000] 1 AC 360 (Chapter 3). In *Corr v IBC* [2006] EWCA Civ 331; (2006) 2 All ER 929, the deceased had been injured through an accident at work and eventually committed suicide in response to depression. Death was within the 'compensable damage' flowing from the injury. On the other hand, three members of the House thought that a deduction for contributory negligence would be appropriate: Chapter 5.

Who May Claim

Those individuals who may claim dependency damages are listed in section 1. Such a claim is generally brought on behalf of dependants by the executor or administrator of the estate, but the dependants may bring an action in their own right if the executor or administrator declines to do so, or fails to do so within six months of the death.

Damages Payable to Dependants

The Act is fairly general in its outline of the damages that will be recoverable:

3 Assessment of damages

(2) In the action such damages, other than damages for bereavement, may be awarded as are proportioned to the injury resulting from the death to the dependants respectively.

    …

The general principle is that damages should reflect *what each dependant has actually lost through the death of the deceased*. This process is highly fact-sensitive. The simplest approach is to calculate what income has been lost through the death, chiefly in the form of lost income but with deduction for the living expenses and other outlay that the deceased would have incurred, and then to share this between the dependants appropriately. This may involve complex calculation, since the court must arrive at a multiplier and multiplicand in respect of the deceased (what would have happened to the deceased but for the accident?), and must then assess the expectations of the various claimants. Would a spouse or partner, for example, have survived long enough to have the benefit of the deceased's pension? And at what age would a child cease to be maintained by a parent?

In *Haxton v Phillips* [2014] EWCA Civ 4, a widow whose husband had died of mesothelioma was herself diagnosed with the same disease, which was found to be due to breaches of duty by the same defendant: she had contracted the disease through exposure to dust on her husband's overalls. Strikingly, the defendants argued that she could not claim loss of dependency because, through their breach of duty, her life expectancy had been radically curtailed. This would be the effect of the statutory language, if claiming under the statute. However, the Court of Appeal rejected this argument: the loss of a statutory claim for dependency could form part of the widow's *common law* claim in respect to the breach of duty to her, even though the statutory claim in its own right would now fail.

Where deductions are concerned, the law is more generous to those claiming dependency damages, than it is to those claiming in respect of injuries to themselves. By section 4 of the Fatal Accidents Act (extracted above in respect of *Jameson*), no account is to be taken of benefits accruing to the dependant as a consequence of the death. Case law on this point has seemed inconsistent.

In *Auty v National Coal Board* (1985) 1 WLR 784 (CA), the claimant received widow's benefits from her husband's pension fund on his death. Subsequently, in an action under the Fatal Accidents Act, she was clearly able to claim in respect of sums her husband would have *earned* but for his death. There would be no deduction from this sum for the widow's benefits received: they came within section 4. However, she could not *also* claim, on the basis of lost dependency, for a widow's pension that she would have received if her husband had lived until retirement age, and then predeceased her. She was entitled to receive widow's benefits only once—*either* on the event of her husband's death in service (as was the case), *or* in the event of his death in retirement. The court reasoned that there was no 'loss of dependency' arising from the death in respect of the widow's benefits, because she had herself received the alternative payment at an earlier stage. There was no 'injury' within section 3.

In *Harland and Wolff Plc v McIntyre* [2006] EWCA Civ 287, the claimant's husband died of mesothelioma through exposure to asbestos in breach of duty on the part of the appellants. When he became aware of his fatal cancer, he decided to return home and his employment was therefore terminated on grounds of ill health. At this stage he received a payment from the company's Provident Fund. Had he remained in employment, he would have received a payment from the same fund on his retirement. The Court of Appeal held that his widow could claim for loss of dependency in the form of the lost benefits on retirement, and that she did not have to account for the benefits received by the deceased on termination of employment. These fell to be disregarded, in accordance with section 4. *Auty* was distinguished because it was treated as being concerned with the widow's *own* benefits under the relevant scheme, and not (as here) with benefits paid to the deceased and accruing to the widow through his estate. There is no denying that in *Harland and Wolff*, the widow is allowed to receive substantially the same benefits twice over. But double counting is in some circumstances an inevitable result of section 4.

More recently in *Arnup v White* [2008] EWCA Civ 447; [2008] ICR 1064, the Court of Appeal resoundingly accepted this claimant-friendly interpretation of the intention behind section 4. Applying the section, payments made under an employer's death-in-service and life insurance schemes were disregarded.[31] If they were to be treated as benefits 'accruing as a result of the death of the employee' then they were within section 4 and should not be deducted. But the Court of Appeal went much further in its interpretation of the Act, holding that if (in the alternative) the benefits did not result from the death, there was no reason at all to deduct them from a Fatal Accidents Act award. Either way, they should not be deducted.

Auty was not mentioned. But it will be recalled that in that case, the widow had sought to recover for loss of her own future pension rights (a post-retirement widow's pension), when she had already qualified for a widow's pension on her husband's death. There was no loss of her own rights as a consequence of the tort, and that is why this element of the claim could not succeed. *Auty* now seems to be of relatively narrow application, given the approach in *Arnup*.

---

31 The judge at first instance had instead applied common law principles on deductions.

2.3 DEATH AND DAMAGES UNDER THE HRA 1998

The availability of a civil action for damages under the HRA brings with it a new potential route to liability on the part of 'public authorities' (though not other parties), in cases involving death. In Chapter 6, Section 3.6, we visited the cases of *Savage* and *Rabone*, and explained the nature of the positive operational duty to protect life which arises under Article 2 ECHR ('right to life'). Though HRA damages are not calculated on the same basis as tort damages, damages awarded under Article 2 invite comparison with bereavement damages in domestic law. Most importantly for the present section, the range of individuals who can bring proceedings in relation to violation of Article 2 is much broader than the category of potential claimants of bereavement damages under the Fatal Accidents Act 1976. A potential claimant need show only that he or she is a 'victim' of a violation of a relevant Convention right, and the category of victim is interpreted in accordance with Strasbourg principles. In *Savage* and *Rabone*, parents of adult victims were able to recover damages to 'mark' the violation, which would not be possible under domestic legislation. In *Morgan v Ministry of Justice* [2010] EWHC 2248 (QB), a fiancée was accepted to be a victim; in the absence of an engagement, the facts would have been scrutinized in order to determine whether or not 'victim' status was established. This is the route not taken by domestic law on bereavement (*Swift*, Section 2.2 of this chapter).

In terms of quantum, how closely do damages for violation of Article 2 resemble bereavement damages? They have, to date, been slightly lower than bereavement damages. In *Savage v South Essex Partnership NHS Foundation Trust* [2010] PIQR P14, Mackay J awarded £10,000, noting that this was in effect a 'symbolic acknowledgement' in relation to the death and the violation of the right. In *Rabone v Pennine Care NHS Trust* [2012] UKSC 2, the Supreme Court approved the Court of Appeal's award of £5,000 to each of two bereaved parents, though noting that no appeal had been made on quantum. Lord Dyson suggested that the award was too low. Unlike tort damages, it appears that quantum may be sensitive to the closeness of family ties, and the gravity of the breach of Article 2. This is consistent with a more general point, that HRA damages reflect all aspects of the case, including the nature of the breach. While performing some of the same functions as bereavement damages, and being reasonably close to those damages in their size to date, they are therefore more flexible and—unlike bereavement damages—sensitive to many factors and to the experience of awards in Strasbourg. It is relevant, for example, that the violation in these cases was one of failure to safeguard, rather than direct infliction of harm. There is more general discussion of HRA damages in Section 5 of this chapter.

3. DELIVERY OF COMPENSATORY DAMAGES: LUMP SUM OR PERIODICAL PAYMENTS

At common law, damages are paid solely by means of a single lump sum. The award is final, and should it prove to be insufficient (because the claimant's condition deteriorates, or they live far longer than expected), or excessive (because they recover quickly, or because they die earlier than expected), then it is simply too late to make any adjustment. An important but limited statutory exception to this was created by the Administration of Justice Act 1982, which inserted the following provision into what is now the Senior Courts Act 1981.

Senior Courts Act 1981

32A Orders for provisional damages for personal injuries

(1) This section applies to an action for damages for personal injuries in which there is proved or admitted to be a chance that at some definite or indefinite time in the future the injured person will, as a result of the act or omission which gave rise to the cause of action, develop some serious disease or suffer some serious deterioration in his physical or mental condition.

(2) Subject to subsection (4) below, as regards any action for damages to which this section applies in which a judgment is given in the High Court, provision may be made by rules of court for enabling the court, in such circumstances as may be prescribed, to award the injured person—

    (a) damages assessed on the assumption that the injured person will not develop the disease or suffer the deterioration in his condition; and

    (b) further damages at a future date if he develops the disease or suffers the deterioration.

…

Clearly, this section permits variation in respect of *an identified contingency* of a particular type. That is, it must be established or accepted that the claimant may at some time in the future suffer a serious disease, or experience a significant deterioration in their condition, as a result of the tort. In these circumstances, provisional damages are wholly appropriate. If damages were awarded on the basis of the percentage chance of developing the serious disease or condition, it would be perfectly clear that these damages would turn out to be *either* wholly excessive (the disease or condition does not develop), *or* wholly inadequate (it *does* develop, and only proportionate damages have been awarded).

In this section we consider a more far-reaching development in the law, which has extended the ability of the court to make an order for **periodical payments** in place of a lump sum, or in respect of certain elements of the award. This has only grown in importance as problems with calculating the 'discount rate' applicable to lump sums have intensified with economic conditions.

The following provision of the Damages Act 1996 (substituted by section 100 of the Courts Act 2003 and SI 2005/841) took effect in April 2005. It *requires* courts to consider whether to make an order for periodical payments of damages, rather than a lump sum; and it *permits* the court to make such an order, whether or not the parties have agreed that this would be preferable.

Damages Act 1996

2 Periodical payments

A court awarding damages for future pecuniary loss in respect of personal injury—

    (a) may order that the damages are wholly or partly to take the form of periodical payments, and

    (b) shall consider whether to make that order.

Formerly, section 2 allowed a court to make an order for periodical payments *only* with the consent of both the parties.[32]

3.1 POTENTIAL ADVANTAGES OF PERIODICAL PAYMENTS

In *Wells v Wells* (extracted earlier), Lord Steyn strongly criticized the almost universal award of damages through lump sums, and supported the greater use of orders for periodical payments.

Lord Steyn, *Wells v Wells* [1999] 1 AC 345, at 384

Leaving to one side the policy arguments for and against the 100 per cent. principle, there is a major structural flaw in the present system. It is the inflexibility of the lump sum system which requires an assessment of damages once and for all of future pecuniary losses. In the case of the great majority of relatively minor injuries the plaintiff will have recovered before his damages are assessed and the lump sum system works satisfactorily. But the lump sum system causes acute problems in cases of serious injuries with consequences enduring after the assessment of damages. In such cases the judge must often resort to guesswork about the future. Inevitably, judges will strain to ensure that a seriously injured plaintiff is properly cared for whatever the future may have in store for him. It is a wasteful system since the courts are sometimes compelled to award large sums that turn out not to be needed. It is true, of course, that there is statutory provision for periodic payments: see section 2 of the Damages Act 1996. But the court only has this power if both parties agree. Such agreement is never, or virtually never, forthcoming. The present power to order periodic payments is a dead letter. The solution is relatively straightforward. The court ought to be given the power of its own motion to make an award for periodic payments rather than a lump sum in appropriate cases. Such a power is perfectly consistent with the principle of full compensation for pecuniary loss. Except perhaps for the distaste of personal injury lawyers for change to a familiar system, I can think of no substantial argument to the contrary. But the judges cannot make the change. Only Parliament can solve the problem.

Periodical payments have the following advantages over lump sums.

1. They are less wasteful. This is because they do not (in their present form) require a calculation of the claimant's life expectancy, which may turn out to be incorrect. So those parts of the award which relate to care costs, for example, may be seriously over-estimated in a lump sum award. Periodical payments, on the other hand, will simply cease when the claimant dies, so that there is no wasteful expenditure on costs that will never be incurred.

2. They provide the claimant with security, since there is no need to seek investment advice and manage a capital sum to produce income. The award cannot be frittered away. Clearly, the order will provide security *only* if the payments are made from a reliable source, and courts must consider this when making an order:

[32] R. Wilde, 'Periodical Payments—A Journey Into the Unknown' (2005) 4 JPIL 320; R. Lewis, 'The Politics and Economics of Tort Law: Judicially Imposed Periodical Payments' (2006) 69 MLR 418.

Damages Act 1996

2(3) A court may not make an order for periodical payments unless satisfied that the continuity of payment under the order is reasonably secure.

NHS Litigation Authorities have been the most significant users of periodical payment orders, although insurers—and particularly motor insurers, including the MIB—are reported to be catching up.[33]

3. Periodical payments are in one important respect cheaper for defendants to provide. The interest on lump sums invested by claimants is subject to tax. In order to achieve 100 per cent compensation, the lump sum award is therefore increased to take account of this future and continuing tax on interest. Periodical payments are tax-free in the hands of the claimant. Thus, the increase in respect of tax will not apply to periodical payments. This is, in fact, of no benefit to the claimant, and it means lower revenue to the Exchequer. But it results in lower costs to tortfeasors or their insurers.

4. The order for periodical payments must aim to ensure that they are increased over time to ensure that the claimant is not left under-compensated in future years. However, periodical payments are not inherently sensitive to changes in needs or circumstances. By the statutory instrument extracted below, a court may provide at the time of making an order for periodical payments that it may be varied. This, like the order itself, does not require the consent of the parties. However, like the equivalent provision in respect of provisional damages in lump sums (Senior Courts Act 1981, section 32A), this will have effect *only* in circumstances where there is some identified contingency relating to the claimant's condition. Unlike that section, the contingency may take the form of *improvement* in the claimant's condition, as well as deterioration. There is scope for the periodical payments to be reduced.

Damages (Variation of Periodical Payments) Order 2005 (SI 2005/841)

2. If there is proved or admitted to be a chance that at some definite or indefinite time in the future the claimant will—

(a) as a result of the act or omission which gave rise to the cause of action, develop some serious disease or suffer some serious deterioration, or

(b) enjoy some significant improvement, in his physical or mental condition, where that condition had been adversely affected as a result of that act or omission,

the court may, on the application of a party, with the agreement of all the parties, or of its own initiative, provide in an order for periodical payments that it may be varied.

There are, however, problems of uncertainty that periodical payments cannot resolve. Obviously, no system for delivering damages could resolve the problem of uncertainty over *hypothetical matters*, or what *would have happened to the claimant if he or she had not*

[33] C. Malla, 'PPOs in Catastrophic Injury Claims' (2013) JPIL 169, 172, reporting the findings of a Study published in 2011, by the International Underwriting Association.

suffered the accident. This aspect of the calculation of 'what has been lost' will remain as uncertain under periodical payments as it does under a lump sum award.

3.2 POTENTIAL PROBLEMS OF PERIODICAL PAYMENTS

1. It is not obvious that the periodical payments will be cheaper overall. Their delivery will be more expensive, even if the total amount payable is less, since a fund will require long-term administration.

2. Although the payments are secure, the claimant loses the opportunity to invest a capital sum in such a way as to gain an above inflation rate of return. It could be argued that this flexibility is essential in order to protect against higher than inflation rates of increase in certain expenses, because of wage inflation.

3. There is a certain *loss* of flexibility in the hands of the claimant. Although there is provision for foreseen contingencies (in the nature of deterioration and improvement) there is no way of dealing with *unforeseen* circumstances. The claimant with a capital sum can, in principle, draw it down more quickly in certain circumstances. The recipient of periodical payments has no such options.

4. Periodical payments impose a continuing relationship on the claimant and defendant (or defendant's insurer). This may be unwelcome to either side. In *Wallace v Follett* [2013] EWCA Civ 146, the Court of Appeal intervened to set quite detailed terms of a periodical payment in relation to future medical examination (in order to update life expectancy), also requiring periodic letters to confirm the claimant's continued survival.

5. Periodical payments may not be sufficient to cover pecuniary losses in a case where there is a reduction in the award for contributory negligence. Nor is there the opportunity to attempt a high risk, high yield solution, as with a lump sum.

Despite this mixed picture, there is increasing interest in periodical payments as a solution to the mounting problems of assessing a lump sum that is properly adjusted to future economic circumstances. This is reflected in our earlier discussion of the 'discount rate'. The attractiveness of periodical payments has also been enhanced by decisions of the courts which require their value to be carefully protected. These developments are discussed in the next section.

3.3 PROTECTING THE VALUE OF PERIODICAL PAYMENTS

Where lump sums are concerned, no increase to the award is applied to allow for inflation. Money is assumed to 'hold its value' over time, and the capital sum is expected to grow in value so as to outstrip inflation. Rather, a *discount* to the multiplier is applied to account for investment opportunity. We noted that this discount is now more modest than it has been in the past; but that it is arguably too high for the economic conditions; and that it also creates a potential problem in respect of *expenses*, since no account is taken of the faster than inflation growth in wages, and thus in care costs (*Cooke v Bristol Healthcare Trust*).

In the case of periodical payments, no investment by the claimant is possible. Such payments must instead be 'index linked' to protect them from inflation. But the problem of care costs arises again, because index linking to general inflation may leave the recipient of these payments over-exposed to above inflation rises in the costs of care.

Damages Act 1996

Section 2[34]

(8) An order for periodical payments shall be treated as providing for the amount of payments to vary by reference to the retail prices index (within the meaning of section 833(2) of the Income and Corporation Taxes Act 1988) at such times, and in such a manner, as may be determined by or in accordance with Civil Procedure Rules.

(9) But an order for periodical payments may include provision—

(a) disapplying subsection (8), or

(b) modifying the effect of subsection (8).

Tarlochan Singh Flora v Wakom (Heathrow) Ltd [2006] EWCA Civ 1103

The claimant was seriously injured at work. Liability was admitted. Only the form of the order for compensation, and the amount of compensation, were in issue.

The defendant argued that a court should *ordinarily* make the order identified in section 2(8) above, and that subsection (9) should only be triggered in exceptional circumstances. This would provide some symmetry between the approach to be taken in protecting the value of periodical payments and the approach to be taken in protecting the value of lump sums, through adjustments to the multiplier. The claimant argued to the contrary that the statutory language did not suggest a *presumption* that the approach in section 2(8) should be adopted, and that the court was free to substitute another approach whenever it thought this would be more appropriate. In addition, the claimant would be considerably under-compensated if his periodical payments were linked only to the retail price index (RPI). Rather, he should be able to argue at trial that linking to a wage-related index such as the Average Earnings Index (AEI) was a more appropriate mechanism for achieving 100 per cent compensation—and that 100 per cent compensation remained the aim of compensation whether it was delivered through periodical payments, or through a lump sum. The Court of Appeal accepted the claimant's argument, and rejected the analogy with the calculation of lump sums.

Brooke LJ

27 ... an award of a lump sum is entirely different in character from an award of periodical payments as a mechanism for compensating for such loss. When setting the appropriate discount rate in the context of a lump sum award the House of Lords or the Lord Chancellor had to guess the future and to hope that prudent investment policy would enable a seriously injured claimant to benefit fully from the award for the whole period for which it was designed to provide him/her with appropriate compensation.

---

34 The following subsections were added by the Courts Act 2003.

28 A periodical payments order is quite different. This risk is taken away from the claimant. The award will provide him or her year by year with appropriate compensation, and the use of an appropriate index will protect him/her from the effects of future inflation. If he or she dies early the defendants will benefit because payments will then cease. It is unnecessary in the context of this statutory scheme to make the kind of guesses that were needed in setting the discount rate. The fact that these two quite different mechanisms now sit side by side in the same Act of Parliament does not in my judgment mean that the problems that infected the operation of the one should be allowed to infect the operation of the other. There is nothing in the statute to indicate that in implementing s 2 of the 1996 Act (as substituted) Parliament intended the courts to depart from what Lord Steyn described in *Wells v Wells* … as the '100% principle', namely that a victim of a tort was entitled to be compensated as nearly as possible in full for all pecuniary losses …

In response to an argument that courts would as a consequence be besieged by an army of expert witnesses in the nature of accountants, actuaries, and economists (the very problem that a single discount rate was designed to prevent: *Cooke v Bristol Healthcare Trust*), Brooke LJ explained that this would be a temporary phenomenon:

33 … if the experience of the past is any useful guide, it is likely that there will be a number of trials at which the expert evidence on each side can be thoroughly tested. A group of appeals will then be brought to this court to enable it to give definitive guidance in the light of the findings of fact made by a number of trial judges. The armies of experts will then be able to strike their tents and return to the offices or academic groves from which they came.

Thameside and Glossop Acute Services NHS Trust v Thompstone [2008] EWCA Civ 5

Here, the Court of Appeal went further than it had in *Flora*, which was a decision about what the claimant could *argue*, and actually allowed the use of a different index from the RPI when making an order for periodical payments. This is consistent with the comments of Brooke LJ extracted above. The preferred index was the Annual Survey of Hours and Earnings (ASHE), an annual earnings survey, which was considered to be much more closely linked to rising care costs than the RPI. Perhaps bravely, the defendants had included among their arguments a proposal that a principle of 'distributive justice' could be seen at work in recent tort cases, and that this included a need to constrain the potentially enormous sums that might be needed to compensate a claimant with future care costs. The Court of Appeal rejected this argument. Though the social cost of compensation has indeed been recognized in a range of cases, this recognition could not be allowed to interfere with the '100 per cent principle' once liability for personal injury had been established.

Waller LJ, *Thameside and Glossop v Thompstone*

47. [The defendant's] difficulty is that 'distributive justice' is not a principle of English law recently adopted so as to allow free rein to ignore basic principles long established. It may come into play when considering whether it is fair, just and reasonable to hold that a duty of care is owed (as in *Frost and Rees*) or in considering a public policy question such as damages for the birth of a healthy child (as in *McFarlane*). It is perhaps also understandable how it plays

some part in considering the essentially judgemental question of whether the level of general damages should be increased (as in *Heil*), but this is all a far cry from seeking to influence the calculation of actual financial loss where the 100% recovery principle is fundamental. Once liability is established and once financial loss is being assessed, it is 'corrective justice' and not distributive justice with which the court should be concerned.

4. NON-COMPENSATORY DAMAGES

Not all pecuniary awards in tort are compensatory in nature. Here, we address some of those that are not.[35]

4.1 EXEMPLARY DAMAGES

Exemplary (or 'punitive') damages go beyond what is required to make good the claimant's loss. These damages are inherently controversial, and there is considerable doubt whether they play an appropriate part in the law of tort. Generally speaking, the argument against exemplary damages is that they are *punitive*, and that punishment should be left to criminal law, where standards of proof and rules of admissible evidence are different.[36]

What are Exemplary Damages?

An important first step is to distinguish between exemplary damages and aggravated damages.[36] Exemplary damages have come the closest to extinction; and although the immediate effect of *Kuddus v Chief Constable of Leicestershire* [2002] 2 AC 122 was expansion in their availability, even though the House of Lords expressed a willingness to restrict or even (in the case of Lord Scott) to abolish exemplary damages without waiting for Parliament to take action.

Aggravated damages are compensatory by nature. The principle behind aggravated damages is that the injury caused to the claimant is made worse by the 'aggravating' behaviour of the defendant. This contributes to mental torment or hurt suffered by the claimant, and this requires compensation (even if it would not give rise to a cause of action in its own right, in a tort requiring damage such as negligence or misfeasance in a public office). Aggravated damages are clearly regarded as an appropriate aspect of defamation awards, for example, if the behaviour of the defendant is particularly aggressive or the defendant unreasonably maintains the truth of defamatory allegations.[37] It is for this reason they are not available to corporate claimants: see the discussion below.

The following extract clearly indicates both the compensatory nature of aggravated damages, and the separateness of such damages from a 'basic' compensatory award. The case

[35] We should also note the existence of 'conventional awards', such as the award for bereavement. These are compensatory in a limited sense, because they relate to the claimant's loss. But they do not seek to *make good* the claimant's loss.

[36] For discussion of aggravated damages see J. Murphy, 'The Nature and Domain of Aggravated Damages' (2010) CLJ 353. A defence of exemplary damages against certain sorts of attack can be found in J. Edelman, 'In Defence of Exemplary Damages', in C. Rickett (ed.), *Justifying Private Law Remedies* (Hart Publishing, 2008).

[37] See for example the discussion of *Sutcliffe v Pressdram* in Chapter 13.

was an extreme one, and is considered again under exemplary damages, later. The claimants had been imprisoned and sexually enslaved for the profit of the defendants. The judge found no precedents which were directly to the point. Relatively few cases of sexual assault have resulted in civil claims against individuals,[38] and it would appear this may be the first in this jurisdiction to result from forced prostitution.[39] 'Basic' compensatory damages were also assessed and the final individual awards, incorporating basic, aggravated, and exemplary damages, ranged from £132,000 to £175,000. The 'aggravated' part of the award was around £30,000 in each case. We will explore the exemplary award below. It was important that no two aspects of damages were allowed to replicate one another, as this would lead to 'double recovery', even though the amounts arrived at have a very imprecise quality.

Treacy J, *AT & Others v Dulghieru* [2009] EWHC 225 (QB)

56 These Claimants seek additional compensation in the form of an award of aggravated damages. It is important to be aware of the risk of double recovery. These Claimants must not be compensated twice over for the same injury.

57 In my award of general damages, I have included an element to cover the psychiatric harm suffered. That however, is to be distinguished from the injury to feelings, humiliation, loss of pride and dignity and feelings of anger or resentment caused by the actions of the Defendants.

58 .... I consider it appropriate in this case to make an award of aggravated damages. I have also considered the observations of Smith LJ in *Choudhary v Martins* [2008] 1 WLR 617, where at paragraph 18 she observed that it was positively helpful if the judge separated the award for psychiatric injury from that for injury to feelings. This, she said, was a helpful process as long as the judge takes care to avoid the risk of double recovery.

59 In this case I find that the behaviour of the Defendants amounted to insulting and arrogant treatment of these Claimants, trampling, as it did, upon their rights as autonomous human beings and subjecting them to repeated episodes of degrading non consensual sexual activity over a significant period of time.

Consistently with this account of the nature of aggravated damages, in *Eaton Mansions (Westminster) Ltd v Stinger Compania de Inversion SA* [2013] EWCA Civ 1308, the Court of Appeal ruled that aggravated damages are not recoverable by a limited company. The case of *Messenger Newspapers Group Ltd v National Graphical Association* [1984] IRLR 397, concerned with industrial action, was therefore wrongly decided. The judge in that case had noted 'aggravated conduct' on the part of the defendant. This however was more appropriately a matter of relevance to *exemplary* damages. Aggravated damages reflect *aggravated harm* to the claimant, not aggravated *conduct* per se.

[38] An exception is *A v Hoare* where the reasons making the claim viable were exceptional: the defendant had bought a winning lottery ticket while on day release. There are of course many recent cases where claims for sexual abuse are brought against *organizations* on the basis of vicarious liability or systemic negligence: see the discussion of *Lister v Hesley Hall* (Chapter 9) and *A v Hoare* (Chapter 7), and associated cases.

[39] For comprehensive argument around the possibilities offered by civil liability in this context, see T. Keren-Paz, *Sex-Trafficking: A Private Law Response* (Routledge, 2013).

Exemplary damages by contrast are not intended to compensate the claimant. They are available if the defendant's behaviour is such as to give rise to the need for something *more than* a compensatory award. Thus they punish, or express strong disapproval of, the defendant's wrongdoing or invasion of the claimant's rights, even if that wrongdoing adds no extra element to the injury suffered by the claimant.[40] They have a role in 'vindicating the strength of the law'.[41] This, anyway, is the classic understanding of exemplary damages.

The availability of exemplary damages is limited. In the leading case of *Rookes v Barnard* [1964] AC 1129, Lord Devlin set out the three categories of case in which exemplary damages are available:

1. cases involving 'oppressive, arbitrary or unconstitutional actions by servants of the government';

2. cases where 'the defendant's conduct has been calculated by him to make a profit for himself which may well exceed the payment to the plaintiff';

3. cases where the award of such damages is expressly authorized by statute.

The general thrust of Lord Devlin's judgment was that exemplary damages were anomalous and should be carefully confined to these three categories of case. On the other hand, he also expressed the view that in the first two categories of case, exemplary damages could serve a valuable purpose.

In *Cassell v Broome* [1972] AC 1207, the House of Lords confirmed that these were the three categories in which exemplary damages are available, and agreed that the categories were not to be extended. Much debate, in *Cassell v Broome* and since, has surrounded the question of whether Lord Devlin intended a further restriction to the availability of exemplary damages, confining them to causes of action in which such damages had been available *before* 1964. This is the so-called 'cause of action condition'. The general consensus is that the House of Lords in *Cassell v Broome* (or at least, some members of the House) thought that Lord Devlin *did* intend to apply this additional restriction. And even if he did not, such a condition was introduced by *Cassell v Broome*.

Kuddus v Chief Constable of Leicestershire [2002] 2 AC 122

The claimant sought exemplary damages against the defendant in an action for misfeasance in a public office (Chapter 2). Exemplary damages had not been awarded before 1964 in this tort, largely because the tort was virtually unrecognized at the time. Lord Nicholls explained that the cause of action condition 'represents in practice an arbitrary and irrational restriction on the availability of exemplary damages' (at [55]). The restriction would no longer be applied. This decision does not mean that the House of Lords wishes to see expansion of exemplary damages. It means rather that the House would prefer to see restrictions on exemplary damages which (unlike the cause of action condition) are consistent and rational.

In every other respect, *Kuddus* is an extremely inconclusive decision. Since only the cause of action condition was directly in issue, other judicial remarks in the case were non-binding. The following summary of the position after *Kuddus* may be found useful:

---

[40] It is this which leads to much of the overlap between aggravated and exemplary damages. Some authors are sceptical that high-handed behaviour which deserves additional sanctions could fail to add to the claimant's injury.

[41] Lord Devlin, *Rookes v Barnard* [1964] AC 1129, at 1226.

1. there is no 'cause of action condition' in respect of exemplary damages. If criteria for availability are met, it makes no difference which cause of action is argued;

2. exemplary damages continue to be available in the three categories of case referred to by Lord Devlin;

3. some members of the House of Lords might have preferred exemplary damages for torts to be abolished at common law (particularly Lord Scott at [111], and possibly Lord Mackay);[42]

4. some members of the House of Lords would probably prefer to retain exemplary damages, but with variation in the categories they would support (for example Lord Nicholls seemed to prefer a general criterion of 'outrageous conduct' and did not see why category 1 should be confined to agents of the state), and perhaps with particular emphasis on protection of civil liberties (Lord Hutton), though this may be harder to support given that exemplary damages are not available in relation to violations of Convention rights;

5. most members of the House of Lords would not wait for legislation, and would consider departing from *Rookes v Barnard* in order to abolish exemplary damages for torts altogether, or to change the applicable categories, since statutory change is plainly unforthcoming (only Lord Slynn seemed reluctant to question the older decisions).[43] The House would have been receptive to hearing argument on these points, and regretted that such argument was not put before them in this case (Lord Scott at [106]).

Kuddus v Chief Constable of Leicestershire [2002] 2 AC 122

Lord Nicholls

63 ... The availability of exemplary damages has played a significant role in buttressing civil liberties, in claims for false imprisonment and wrongful arrest. From time to time cases do arise where awards of compensatory damages are perceived as inadequate to achieve a just result between the parties. The nature of the defendant's conduct calls for a further response from the courts. On occasion conscious wrongdoing by a defendant is so outrageous, his disregard of the plaintiff's rights so contumelious, that something more is needed to show that the law will not tolerate such behaviour. Without an award of exemplary damages, justice will not have been done. Exemplary damages, as a remedy of last resort, fill what otherwise would be a regrettable lacuna.

...

65 If exemplary damages are to continue as a remedial tool, as recommended by the Law Commission after extensive consultation, the difficult question which arises concerns the circumstances in which this tool should be available for use. Stated in its broadest form, the relevant principle is tolerably clear: the availability of exemplary damages should be co-extensive with its rationale. As already indicated, the underlying rationale lies in the sense

---

[42] Obviously, such damages would still be available where legislation so provided.

[43] The House of Lords has the power to depart from its previous decisions under the Practice Direction of 1966. The House did not have this power in 1964; but it is doubtful whether any previous decision of the House of Lords required the retention of exemplary damages at that date.

of outrage which a defendant's conduct sometimes evokes, a sense not always assuaged fully by a compensatory award of damages, even when the damages are increased to reflect emotional distress.

66 In *Rookes v Barnard* [1964] AC 1129, 1226, Lord Devlin drew a distinction between oppressive acts by government officials and similar acts by companies or individuals. He considered that exemplary damages should not be available in the case of non-governmental oppression or bullying. Whatever may have been the position 40 years ago, I am respectfully inclined to doubt the soundness of this distinction today. So do some individuals. I am not sure it would be right to draw a hard-and-fast line which would always exclude such companies and persons from the reach of exemplary damages. Indeed, the validity of the dividing line drawn by Lord Devlin when formulating his first category is somewhat undermined by his second category, where the defendants are not confined to, and normally would not be, government officials or the like.

67 Nor, I may add, am I wholly persuaded by Lord Devlin's formulation of his second category (wrongful conduct expected to yield a benefit in excess of any compensatory award likely to be made). The law of unjust enrichment has developed apace in recent years. In so far as there may be a need to go further, the key here would seem to be the same as that already discussed: outrageous conduct on the part of the defendant. There is no obvious reason why, if exemplary damages are to be available, the profit motive should suffice but a malicious motive should not.

68 ... For the purposes of the present appeal it is sufficient, first, to express the view that the House should now depart from its decision in *Broome v Cassell & Co Ltd* [1972] AC 1027, in so far as that decision confirmed the continuing existence of what has subsequently been described as the "cause of action" condition and, secondly, to note that the essence of the conduct constituting the court's discretionary jurisdiction to award exemplary damages is conduct which was an outrageous disregard of the plaintiff's rights....

Lord Scott

120 Your Lordships are, it seems to me, caught on the horns of a dilemma. On the one hand, the cause of action test is not based on principle and has serious practical difficulties. On the other hand, the removal of the cause of action test would expand the cases in which exemplary damages could be claimed. Claims could be made in cases of negligence and cases of deceit provided only that the conduct complained of fell within one or other of the two Devlin categories (*Rookes v Barnard* [1964] AC 1129, 1226). Claims could probably also be made, subject to the same proviso, in actions based upon breach of statutory duty whether or not the statute had expressly authorised such claims.

121 My Lords, I view the prospect of any increase in the cases in which exemplary damages can be claimed with regret. I have explained already why I regard the remedy as no longer serving any useful function in our jurisprudence. Victims of tortious conduct should receive due compensation for their injuries, not windfalls at public expense.

No great enthusiasm was displayed in the judgments of Lords Nicholls and Scott for Lord Devlin's second category of case, namely cases where the defendant *seeks to make a profit* at the expense of the claimant. Here, it seems clear that compensatory damages will not be enough to deter the wrongdoing, because the defendant has already taken account of the likely damages in deciding to go ahead and commit the wrong. Both Lord Nicholls, and Lord Scott, hint that there is no longer any need to deal with these cases through exemplary damages, because the law of 'unjust enrichment' (Lord Nicholls) or 'restitution' (Lord Scott) has moved on and remedies will accordingly be available which will deter the wrong. This seems to amount to an argument that a remedy more appropriate to the law of civil obligations has now been fashioned. Exemplary damages can be put aside while keeping the deterrent effect. But it is possible that in some cases, there is a need to express disapproval of an intention to make a gain through gross violation of the claimant's rights, irrespective of the success of the venture (see the discussion of *AT v Dulghieru*, later). It may be the very mismatch between claimants' fundamental rights, and defendants' callous, indeed malevolent profit motive, which makes exemplary damages rather than unjust enrichment appear the better analysis in this case.

There was disagreement, particularly between Lords Hutton and Scott, on the important question of *whether exemplary damages can appropriately be awarded against a vicariously liable party*. Although the House of Lords was not called upon to decide this issue, in this case the defendant's liability was 'vicarious': the chief constable had not himself committed a tort, but was potentially liable for misfeasance in a public office on the part of one of his officers.[44]

In *Muuse v Secretary of State for the Home Department* [2010] EWCA Civ 453, the Court of Appeal upheld an award of exemplary damages in a case of false imprisonment where the actions of officers were unconstitutional, arbitrary, and outrageous: there was no need to add 'malice' or similar states of mind to the established *Rookes* criteria.[45] But in *R (Lumba) v Secretary of State for the Home Department* [2011] UKSC 12; [2012] 1 AC 245, a claim for exemplary damages was rejected despite evidence not only that an illegal detention policy had been adopted, but that officials had been encouraged to lie about the basis on which their decisions were reached.

Lord Dyson, *R (Lumba) v Secretary of State for the Home Department*

166 Whether the high threshold for the award of exemplary damages has been crossed in any particular case is ultimately a matter of judgment. Opinions can reasonably differ on whether a defendant's conduct has been so outrageous and so unconstitutional, oppressive or arbitrary as to justify the imposition of the penalty of exemplary damages. An appellate court should not interfere with the judgment of the court below unless that judgment is plainly wrong. On the material that was before him, Davis J was entitled to reach the conclusion that he reached. In my view, the Court of Appeal were also entitled to reach the conclusion that they reached on the more extensive material that was before them. Both the judge and the Court of Appeal applied the correct test. In particular, the Court of Appeal were right to place some weight on the fact that the Secretary of State had the statutory power to detain the appellants pending deportation and that, although she in fact exercised that power unlawfully, she could have done so lawfully. They were also right to say that, if her conduct is properly to be described as unconstitutional, oppressive or arbitrary, it was at the less serious end of the scale. It is material that there is no suggestion that officials acted for ulterior motives or out of malice towards the appellants. Nevertheless, there was a

---

[44] The operation of vicarious liability, and the underlying arguments of policy and justice for such liability, are investigated in Chapter 9. It has been said that vicarious liability should be the usual route in an action for misfeasance, thus protecting individuals from potentially oppressive actions from aggrieved parties: *Adams v Law Society of England and Wales* [2012] EWHC 980 (QB).

[45] The constitutional role of tort remedies in such a case is emphasized by J. Varuhas, 'Exemplary Damages: "Public Law" Functions, Mens Rea and Quantum' (2011) 70 CLJ 284.

deliberate decision taken at the highest level to conceal the policy that was being applied and to apply a policy which, to put it at its lowest, the Secretary of State and her senior officials knew was vulnerable to legal challenge. For political reasons, it was convenient to take a risk as to the lawfulness of the policy that was being applied and blame the courts if the policy was declared to be unlawful.

It would appear that the kind of action sufficient to amount to 'oppressive and unconstitutional' behaviour for this purpose is a matter of degree, and that the threshold is 'high', Lord Dyson added that because the goal of exemplary damages is not compensatory, a single award of such damages should be made, to be shared between all claimants. It was therefore considered inappropriate to make an award of exemplary damages where there is a large number of potential claimants and they are not all before the court ([167]). It is suggested that there is something odd about this argument: it makes it much more likely that a defendant who has acted in such a way that exemplary damages are justified, but who has committed wrongs against a large number of people, will escape being subject to such damages.

Exemplary Damages and Vicarious Liability

According to Lord Scott in *Kuddus*, the present position in which awards of exemplary damages can clearly be made against vicariously liable parties has arisen without careful consideration and cannot be justified: the reasons underlying vicarious liability are largely compensatory, and no reason of fairness can be found for attaching a *punitive* award to a party who is not personally responsible for the wrongdoing. Lord Hutton questioned this approach, citing with approval the arguments of Patrick Atiyah in *Vicarious Liability in the Law of Torts* (Butterworths, 1967): an award of exemplary damages against vicariously liable parties will encourage superior officers to exert control over the actions of their agents.

In *Rowlands v Chief Constable of Merseyside Police* [2006] EWCA Civ 1773; [2007] 1 WLR 1065, the Court of Appeal considered this question. The claimant had called the police to attend to a neighbourhood noise problem. There was an altercation between the claimant and the police officers, and the officers arrested the claimant in front of her children, handcuffed her, and took her to the police station. She was charged with an offence and was tried and acquitted seven months later. Hearing her claim for false imprisonment and malicious prosecution, a judge awarded compensatory damages but thought it was not a proper case for aggravated or exemplary damages. The Court of Appeal disagreed, and awarded both.

Moore-Bick LJ, *Rowlands v Chief Constable of Merseyside Police*

47 … There undoubtedly are strong arguments of principle in favour of limiting the application of an avowedly punitive award to those who are personally at fault, who, in all but a tiny minority of cases brought against the police, could confidently be expected not to include the chief constable. However, since the power to award exemplary damages rests on policy rather than principle, it seems to me that the question whether awards can be made against persons whose liability is vicarious only must also be answered by resort to considerations of policy rather than strict principle. While the common law continues to recognise a power to award exemplary damages in respect of wrongdoing by servants of the government of a kind that has a direct effect on civil liberties, which for my own part I think it should, I think that it is desirable as a matter of policy that the courts should be able to make punitive awards against those who are vicariously liable for the conduct of their subordinates without being

constrained by the financial means of those who committed the wrongful acts in question. Only by this means can awards of an adequate amount be made against those who bear public responsibility for the conduct of the officers concerned.

As the Court of Appeal pointed out, the liability of a Chief Constable generally will be vicarious only; and there is a clear purpose in holding those who 'bear public responsibility' accountable in cases which merit exemplary damages. These will be much the same reasons as those behind the vicarious liability of superiors for torts with a strong mental element, such as malicious prosecution and misfeasance in a public office.

Exemplary Damages and Insurance

Generally speaking, it is against the policy of the law to allow enforcement of a contract of insurance indemnifying the insured for the consequences of his or her *criminal* acts.[46] But assuming the tortious act is also criminal, what of the vicariously liable party? In *Lancashire County Council v Mutual Municipal Insurance* [1997] QB 897, the plaintiff was liable vicariously for an amount including exemplary damages in respect of wrongful arrest and false imprisonment on the part of police officers. The Court of Appeal held that the defendant insurers were liable to reimburse the plaintiff for these amounts under a policy of liability insurance. Two strands to the reasoning are of concern to us. First, where the wrongdoing is *criminal* in nature, then a *vicariously* liable party may still enforce the insurance contract in respect of exemplary damages. The wrongdoer would not be able to do so. Second, where the tortfeasor's wrongdoing does *not* amount to a criminal offence, the Court of Appeal reasoned that both personally responsible parties, *and* vicariously liable parties, should be able to insure against liability for exemplary damages. Against the argument that such damages thereby fail to *punish*, it may be argued that their role is primarily to demonstrate the wrongfulness of conduct, rather than to punish it. In this sense, they are closer to vindicatory damages than is generally assumed.

The Quantum of Exemplary Damages

Another awkward feature of exemplary damages is that there is no clear measure by which they may be 'calculated'. Given that actions for false imprisonment and malicious prosecution—which for obvious reasons may often raise claims derived from Lord Devlin's first category—are still in many instances tried by jury, the scope for high awards could be considerable. In *Thompson v Commissioner of Police for the Metropolis* [1998] QB 498, the Court of Appeal moved decisively to limit the amounts awarded in respect of exemplary damages, clarifying that the maximum figure to mark disapproval of 'oppressive or arbitrary conduct' should be £50,000. In one of the two cases heard by the Court of Appeal, exemplary damages of £200,000 had been awarded by a jury. The Court of Appeal reduced this award to £15,000.[47] In *Rowlands* (above), the amount awarded was £7,500. The Court of Appeal reasoned that far less violence had been exercised against the claimant than in

---

[46] Indeed in *Gray v Barr* [1971] 2 QB 554, indemnity was denied to a man liable in damages for killing another, even though he had been acquitted of murder and manslaughter. More generally, see our discussion of *ex turpi causa* in Chapter 5; and R. Merkin and J. Steele, *Insurance and the Law of Obligations* (Oxford University Press, 2013), Chapter 11.

[47] This case is closely comparable to other Court of Appeal decisions in the same period, which limited damages in defamation actions by offering 'guidance' to juries. We consider these cases in Chapter 13: see in particular *John v MGN* [1997] QB 586, referred to by the Court of Appeal in *Thompson*.

Thompson; but also thought the damages should recognize the fact that evidence had subsequently been given in criminal proceedings by the officers (malicious prosecution).

4.2 VINDICATORY DAMAGES?

There has been growing interest in recent years in the possibility of an additional function of damages, distinct from both compensation and punishment, and different also from the goal of avoiding or preventing wrongful gain. That is, that damages may be awarded in order to vindicate rights.

Arguably, the above statement makes little sense, since all damages awards 'vindicate rights'. To make sense, we need to ask a new question. Does vindication of rights operate as a distinct goal which would permit an award of damages either *in addition to* compensatory, exemplary, and perhaps gain-based awards; or in circumstances where none of those are appropriate? Although this notion has gathered some academic support, the Supreme Court in *R(Lumba) v Secretary of State for the Home Department* [2011] UKSC 12; [2012] 1 AC 245 emphatically rejected the idea: English courts do not recognize an additional head of 'vindicatory' damages at common law, akin to the idea of 'constitutional damages' in certain other jurisdictions.

Previously, the Privy Council in a number of appeals from the Commonwealth had awarded damages in vindication of *constitutional rights* which clearly *were* additional to the compensatory (including aggravated) damages measure. This was initiated in the cases of *Merson v Cartwright* [2004] UKPC 38 and *Ramanoop v Attorney-General* [2005] UKPC 15; (2006) 1 AC 328.[48] A similar approach was taken in *Takitota v Attorney General, Director of Immigration, Minister of National Security* [2009] UKPC 11. This was a case on appeal from the Bahamas, where the claimant, who had lost his papers and passport, had been unlawfully detained, for most of the time in inhumane and deeply degrading conditions, for eight years. The Privy Council thought the compensatory award could not be accepted as it stood since the court had not expressly explained whether it included a sum for aggravated damages, which were clearly appropriate here. This award could legitimately have been larger, therefore. In addition, it upheld an award of $100,000 for breach of constitutional rights, which are recognized to be 'vindicatory' in nature following earlier Privy Council decisions.

It is significant that there would not, however, be separate awards of vindicatory and exemplary damages, because the English courts have subsequently made clear that they see these as closely analogous awards. How do these developments compare with UK law? We will first compare these vindicatory damages for violation of Convention rights with damages under the HRA; and then turn to the discussion, then rejection of vindicatory damages at common law.

Vindicatory Damages under the Human Rights Act 1998?

As explored in Chapter 1, the UK now has a new set of rights incorporated into domestic law, namely the Convention rights derived from the ECHR and annexed to the HRA. Remedies against public authorities are available in respect of violation of these rights, under section 8 (extracted in Chapter 1). However, the differences from the approach in *Merson, Ramanoop*, and *Takitoka* are very marked. When awarded, the quantum of damages will generally be

[48] See D. Pearce and R. Halson, 'Damages for Breach of Contract: Compensation, Restitution and Vindication' (2008) 28 OJLS 73–98, for discussion of these cases in the context of contractual remedies and the goal of vindication.

more modest than in tort. This is thought to reflect the primary function of such actions; but it also reflects the fact that remedies as well as rights under the HRA have been deliberately modelled on the Convention itself as interpreted by the European Court of Human Rights in Strasbourg: this is known as the 'mirror' principle.[49] It is clear that the assessment of constitutional damages by the Privy Council is not considered relevant.

Lord Bingham, *R (Greenfield) v Secretary of State for the Home Department*
[2005] UKHL 14; [2005] 1 WLR 673

19 None of the three English cases cited involved a violation of Art.6, and to that extent they have only a limited bearing on the present problem. But there are in my opinion broader reasons why this approach should not be followed. First, the 1998 Act is not a tort statute. Its objects are different and broader. Even in a case where a finding of violation is not judged to afford the applicant just satisfaction, such a finding will be an important part of his remedy and an important vindication of the right he has asserted. Damages need not ordinarily be awarded to encourage high standards of compliance by member states, since they are already bound in international law to perform their duties under the Convention in good faith, although it may be different if there is felt to be a need to encourage compliance by individual officials or classes of official. Secondly, the purpose of incorporating the Convention in domestic law through the 1998 Act was not to give victims better remedies at home than they could recover in Strasbourg but to give them the same remedies without the delay and expense of resort to Strasbourg. This intention was clearly expressed in the White Paper "Rights Brought Home: The Human Rights Bill" (Cm 3782, October 1, 1997), para.2.6:

> "The Bill provides that, in considering an award of damages on Convention grounds, the courts are to take into account the principles applied by the European Court of Human Rights in awarding compensation, so that people will be able to receive compensation from a domestic court equivalent to what they would have received in Strasbourg."

Thirdly, s.8(4) requires a domestic court to take into account the principles applied by the European Court under Art.41 not only in determining whether to award damages but also in determining the amount of an award. There could be no clearer indication that courts in this country should look to Strasbourg and not to domestic precedents. The appellant contended that the levels of Strasbourg awards are not "principles" applied by the Court, but this is a legalistic distinction which is contradicted by the White Paper and the language of s.8 and has no place in a decision on the quantum of an award, to which principle has little application. The Court routinely describes its awards as equitable, which I take to mean that they are not precisely calculated but are judged by the Court to be fair in the individual case. Judges in England and Wales must also make a similar judgment in the case before them. They are not inflexibly bound by Strasbourg awards in what may be different cases. But they should not aim to be significantly more or less generous than the Court might be expected to be, in a case where it was willing to make an award at all.

This passage makes a sharp distinction between domestic law, and the Strasbourg jurisprudence. Some of the remarks need to be read subject to the more recent decision of the

[49] The process of reasoning is explored and criticized by the present author in J. Steele, 'Damages in Tort and under the Human Rights Act: Remedial or Functional Separation?' (2008) 67 CLJ 606–34. For an argument that damages under the Act ought to be modelled on tort, see J. Varuhas, 'A Tort-based Approach to Damages under the Human Rights Act 1998' (2009) 72 MLR 750–82.

Supreme Court in *R(Faulkner) v Secretary of State for the Home Department* [2013] UKSC 23, which is extracted in Section 5 of this chapter. In *Greenfield*, the House of Lords emphasized that the finding of a violation will itself be an important part of the vindication of the claimant's right. Slightly more problematic, logically speaking, is the modelling of the domestic remedy closely on the Strasbourg remedy under Article 41. This Article provides that there should be 'just satisfaction' (against the state) where a sufficient domestic remedy is lacking. Here, the House of Lords tied the domestic remedy closely to the international remedy for failing to provide a sufficient remedy in domestic law. It is quite unlike the Privy Council's approach to constitutional damages in the cases mentioned earlier. The idea that a declaration of violation may sufficiently vindicate a Convention right appears to have influenced the Supreme Court in its rejection of 'purely' vindicatory damages in *Lumba*. We return to the assessment of damages under the HRA in the following section. But first, we should review the position in respect of vindicatory damages at common law.

Vindicatory Damages in Tort?

Earlier editions of this book asked whether vindicatory damages might be emerging in the law of tort. It was conceded that vindicatory damages had not so far been awarded as a separate head of damages.[50] Some consideration was given to the issue in *Ashley v Chief Constable of Sussex* [2008] UKHL 25 (extracted in Chapter 2). Here, the Chief Constable had admitted liability to compensate the claimants in full in negligence, but resisted the claim in trespass. The House of Lords permitted the claim in trespass to proceed to trial despite the absence of any reason to seek compensation. The various judgments in this case do not provide any single reason why this was thought appropriate. Some of the judges may simply have concluded that until the claimants were compensated, there was no reason to stop them from selecting their preferred cause of action (there was no risk of double recovery). Alternatively, it may have been thought legitimate to seek a finding that the action of the officer who shot the deceased was a trespass, and therefore an unlawful interference with the rights of the claimant, so that a declaration was worth pursuing in its own right.[51] This had been the approach taken by a majority of the Court of Appeal. Lord Scott pointed out that the 'vindicatory' role inherent in compensatory damages could not really be said to have been achieved if the very issue urged by the claimants—unlawfulness of the shooting of the deceased, rather than carelessness—had not been tested at trial. In this respect, he had the support of Lord Rodger.

Lumba has effectively ended this discussion. It now seems clear that, in English law, the law of tort will not award substantial damages for a *separate* vindicatory purpose. Lord Scott's remarks should perhaps be read in the context of his evident hostility to exemplary damages,[52] and the explanation of the Privy Council in *Takitoka* that constitutional damages and exemplary damages perform essentially the same function, at least in many cases.

In *Lumba* itself, as we explained in Chapter 2, no additional detention had been caused to the claimants, because they could and would have been detained under a lawful policy,

[50] 'Nominal damages' (a very small amount) might be awarded where a violation of a right did not result in any loss or harm to the claimant; but the idea of 'vindicatory' damages generally implies a substantial award. 'Conventional awards' have also been made, again at a lower level than compensatory awards (see *Rees v Darlington*, Chapter 6). For discussion of various gain-based awards where the claimant's rights have been violated, see the next section of this chapter. These too, of course, may be said to 'vindicate the claimant's right'.

[51] In respect of nominal damages and declarations, as well as 'contemptuous awards', see A. Burrows, Further Reading, Chapter 23.

[52] Apart from Lord Scott's judgment in *Kuddus*, extracted earlier in Section 4.1, note also his article 'Damages' [2007] LMCLQ 465–72.

if such a policy had been followed, and the threshold for exemplary damages had not been passed. Therefore, the question arose whether—in a tort actionable *per se*—substantial damages could be awarded without proof of damage and without an exemplary award. The answer given was no.

Lord Dyson, R (Lumba) v Secretary of State for the Home Department

101 The implications of awarding vindicatory damages in the present case would be far reaching. Undesirable uncertainty would result. If they were awarded here, then they could in principle be awarded in any case involving a battery or false imprisonment by an arm of the state. Indeed, why limit it to such torts? And why limit it to torts committed by the state? I see no justification for letting such an unruly horse loose on our law. In my view, the purpose of vindicating a claimant's common law rights is sufficiently met by (i) an award of compensatory damages, including (in the case of strict liability torts) nominal damages where no substantial loss is proved; (ii) where appropriate, a declaration in suitable terms; and (iii) again, where appropriate, an award of exemplary damages. There is no justification for awarding vindicatory damages for false imprisonment to any of the FNPs.

It must be said that the discussion of this issue was neither detailed nor extensive; but the answer was clear. For thoughtful review and analysis of the present state of play in respect of vindicatory damages, see the works by Witzleb and Carroll (before *Lumba*), and by Barker (after *Lumba*), included in Further Reading.

4.3 GAIN-BASED DAMAGES

Why, in *Kuddus*, did Lords Nicholls and Scott think that exemplary damages might no longer be required to deal with the case where the defendant calculates that he might profit from his tort? One reason they hinted at is the extension of gain-based damages in the law of obligations. The development of 'the law of unjust enrichment' referred to by Lord Nicholls is probably a reference to the increasing availability of gain-based damages for civil wrongs, such as torts and breach of contract.

Here we should note that there is little agreement over appropriate terminology, and not everyone would be happy with the idea of 'gain-based *damages*'. Some would insist that all 'damages' are compensatory. Along these lines, there is a further problem with Lord Nicholls' formulation, since 'unjust enrichment' is generally seen as entirely separate from the law of wrongs (including tort), being concerned with unjust transfers of value which may be made with or without any 'wrong'.

Essentially, 'gain-based' damages are calculated not according to the loss of the claimant, but according to the gain made by the defendant. One form of 'gain-based' award concentrates on stripping defendants of their profits and may be referred to as 'disgorgement damages'. An account of profits (which is clearly available in the action for breach of confidence: see Chapter 14) involves a form of disgorgement. A possibly separate form of gain-based award is referred to as 'restitutionary damages', and this is aimed at reversing 'transfers of value'.[53]

---

[53] J. Edelman, *Gain-Based Damages* (Hart Publishing, 2002) distinguishes between 'disgorgement damages' and 'restitutionary damages', and proposes that both are available for wrongs, including torts.

Two major distinctions must be noted between gain-based damages and exemplary damages. First, gain-based damages are not punitive in nature. On the other hand, accounts of profits generally do seek to *deter*, attacking the profit motive directly. They come close to the second category of exemplary damages, though there the measure of damages is not based upon the profits made. This brings us to the second point, which is that there is a clear measure of gain-based damages. The measure is not the loss suffered by the claimant as in compensatory damages, nor the amount required to 'punish' the defendant or vindicate the strength of the law, as in exemplary damages.[54] In the case of disgorgement (profit-based) damages it is the profit wrongfully (in the case of tort) made by the defendant. In the case of restitutionary damages it is the amount gained through the transfer of value.

The following extract gives a general statement of the kinds of actions in which gain-based damages are available for a tort. The author explains that 'restitutionary damages' are clearly established in torts protecting property rights (in the case of trespass to land, see particularly *Ministry of Defence v Ashman* [1993] 40 EG 144); and he suggests that they should be more widely available on the basis of *deliberate wrongdoing*.

A. Burrows, *Remedies for Torts and Breach of Contract* (3rd edn, Oxford University Press, 2004), 305–6

... The sort of torts for which restitutionary awards can be given are ... not restricted to those in which the plaintiff's property or its proceeds have been acquired.

Taking all three types of restitutionary remedy together (award of money had and received, account of profits, restitutionary damages) the torts for which restitution have been awarded have involved interference with the plaintiff's property, whether that property be real or personal or intellectual. The cases therefore reveal a judicial desire firmly to deter even innocent interference with the plaintiff's property; that is, merely to compensate for any loss caused appears to be regarded as insufficient to deter that interference. This seems sensible. Applying Jackman's theory [(1989) CLJ 302], restitution is justified as a means of deterring harm to the 'facilitative institution' of private property.

A subsidiary feature exhibited in a few of the account of profits cases (eg for passing off and infringement of trademark) is that the tort must be committed deliberately if restitution is to be awarded. It can be strongly argued that this category should be expanded so that restitution should be awarded to reverse gains made by, eg deliberately inducing a breach of contract or a deliberate libel. Given the established categories referred to by Burrows, was Lord Nicholls hinting at a more general role for gain-based damages in *intentional* torts? If so, why did he refer to 'unjust enrichment' (which denotes a wrongful *transfer of value*)?

On the whole, Lord Nicholls appears to have recognized that some role could still be played by exemplary damages; and that this would be dependent on showing 'outrageous' conduct. However, he doubted whether either of Lord Devlin's two categories could be justified. He may have thought that the profit motive in itself (as opposed to outrageous conduct in pursuit of profit) was properly dealt with through the measure of gain-based damages.

54 For a recent illustrative case of trespass to land where a judge's gain-based and exemplary awards were *both* upheld by the Court of Appeal (albeit with reduction to the exemplary component), see *Ramzan v Brookwide Ltd* [2011] EWCA Civ 985. Contrast the refusal of the English courts to award both exemplary and vindicatory damages (earlier). Trespass to land in general is dealt with in Chapter 17.

Whether this is right depends partly on how widely such damages are available for torts in general. Perhaps Lord Nicholls would have liked to expand their availability: see also Chapter 17. We face a particular difficulty in this area: different judges have different ideas about the desirable pattern of available remedies, as do different commentators. This leads people, including judges, to categorize the available remedies in very different ways, despite overlap in the language used.

Gain-based Damages and Non-proprietary Torts

The extent of availability of gain-based damages in tort was addressed in *Devenish Nutrition v Sanofi-Aventis (France) and Others* [2008] EWCA Civ 1086. This was a case of breach of statutory duty (Chapter 16), the defendants having entered into agreements among suppliers of vitamins which contravened Article 81 of the EC Treaty. The European Commission had imposed fines on the sellers, and the action was brought by a claimant who (as a result of the illegal agreement) had bought vitamins at inflated prices. Compensatory damages were clearly available in principle, but had the claimants suffered loss, given that it had at least arguably been able to pass on the inflated price to consumers? It would be difficult to establish whether this had affected sales, and thus profits, for example. The claimants sought an account of profits.

The Court of Appeal held that such a remedy was not available in respect of an action for breach of a statutory duty. Its availability was confined to certain actions, particularly those interfering with the proprietary rights of the claimant (such as trespass to land and goods, or interferences with intellectual property rights). This was despite the fact that in *AG v Blake* [2001] 1 AC 268, an account of profits had been awarded in respect of a breach of contract. Longmore LJ added that before *Blake*, an account of profits 'had always been available where equitable rights (for example a breach of confidence) had been infringed', and that the action in *Blake* itself was justified partly because it was 'closely akin to a claim for breach of a fiduciary obligation' (at [145]). Besides, a gain-based award should not be made where compensatory damages provide an adequate remedy.

The reasoning in *Devenish Nutrition* has been criticized by Odudu and Virgo, 'Remedies for Breach of Statutory Duty' (2009) CLJ 32–4. The authors suggest that there may be cases where it is appropriate for an account of profits to be awarded for non-proprietary torts including breach of a statutory duty, for example where there have been no enforcement proceedings and there is a public interest in the account of profits and its deterrent function. They also argue that even if no account of profits can be awarded, this does not affect the alternative avenue of a claim based in unjust enrichment. Here, passing on of loss to third parties does not destroy the claim. This last point is flatly contradicted by remarks of Longmore LJ:

Longmore LJ, *Devenish Nutrition v Sanofi-Aventis SA (France) & Others*

[147] … If however the claimant has in fact passed the excessive price on to its own purchasers and not absorbed the excessive price itself, there is no very obvious reason why the profit made by the defendants (albeit undeserved and wrongful) should be transferred to the claimant without the claimant being obliged to transfer it down the line to those who have actually suffered the loss. Neither the law of restitution nor the law of damages is in the business of transferring monetary gains from one undeserving recipient to another undeserving recipient even if the former has acted illegally while the latter has not.

Gain-based Damages Contrasted with Damages in Lieu of an Injunction

A distinction needs to be drawn between gain-based damages, particularly an account of profits, and the kind of award that may be made 'in lieu of an injunction' (see particularly Chapter 10, in connection with nuisance; Chapter 17, in connection with trespass to land). The latter sort of award may well incorporate an amount to reflect a hypothetical bargain between reasonable people in the position of the parties; and this may include a share of the profits expected to be made (see the discussion in *Tamares (Vincent Square) v Fairpoint* [2007] EWHC 212 (Ch)). This however is not a 'disgorgement' remedy (the defendant's full profits are not paid over to the claimant),[55] nor does it seek to reverse a transfer of value. Such remedies are awarded only if it has been decided *not* to award an injunction, and so the court is scarcely likely to seek to deter the defendants' activities: that would be self-contradictory. Rather, the goal is to arrive at an appropriate amount of damages to reflect the fact that the defendant has interfered with the claimant's rights but in circumstances where there are insufficient grounds to prohibit the defendant's actions (or sufficient grounds not to do so).

The distinction between these two sorts of award was underlined by the Court of Appeal in the following case, which also seemed to reiterate that a gain-based award may not be appropriate at all in connection with some actions in tort.

Forsyth-Grant v Allen [2008] EWCA Civ 505

This action concerned a nuisance which interfered with the claimant's right to light. The defendants had constructed two semi-detached houses, and the claimant argued that these interfered with light to her hotel. She was successful in her claim, but the judge declined to order an account of profits. The Court of Appeal agreed.

Patten J, *Forsyth-Grant v Allen* [2008] EWCA Civ 505 (giving the judgment of the court)

32. An actionable nuisance does not involve the misappropriation of the claimant's rights in the same way, even as in a case of trespass, let alone as in a case of conversion or copyright or trademark infringement. The essence of the tort is that the claimant's rights to the reasonable enjoyment of her property have been infringed by the use which the defendant makes of his own land. On the face of it, this should not entitle the claimant, in my judgment, to more than compensation for the loss which she has actually suffered; but the highest that it could be put on the authorities is that the claimant can, in appropriate cases, obtain an award calculated by reference to the price, which the defendant might reasonably be required to pay for a relaxation of the claimant's rights so as to avoid an injunction. This, as already explained, falls a long way short of being awarded the whole profit for the development, which is far in excess and completely unrelated to the measure of loss suffered by the claimant. The decision in the *Stoke on Trent* case[56] supports this approach.

---

[55] See also R. Cunnington, 'The Assessment of Gain-based Damages for Breach of Contract' (2008) 71 MLR 559–86.

[56] This is a reference to *Stoke-on-Trent v Wass Ltd* [1988] 1 WLR 1406, listed by Burrows (see Further Reading), Chapter 17 as one of three notable 'anti-restitutionary' decisions. Nominal damages were awarded, and a claim for gain-based damages rejected, by the Court of Appeal. The claim in *Wass* was in nuisance.

33. Mr Ley referred us to a passage in Lord Keith's speech in *Attorney General v Guardian Newspapers Ltd* [1990] 1 AC 109, but that was also an action for breach of confidence where equity has always asserted a jurisdiction to order an account of profits; it is not authority for the making of such an order in a case of nuisance. It seems to me that the judge would have been entitled to reject the claim for an account of profits outright, simply on the basis that it was not an available remedy in an action for nuisance; but even if that is wrong, his acceptance that one needs to show exceptional circumstances is not, in my judgment, open to criticism.

Another case underlining that there is a distinction between a reasonable licence fee and a gain-based award is *Bocardo v Star Energy UK Onshore Ltd* [2010] UKSC 35 (discussed in Chapter 17).

5. DAMAGES UNDER THE HUMAN RIGHTS ACT

There has been considerable progress in recent years in identifying the correct approach to assessment of damages in civil actions under the HRA. As we have seen, these are not actions in tort, but they nevertheless give rise to a liability which operates in parallel with—and sometimes as an alternative to—the law of tort, and which may provide a remedy in circumstances where tort would not. We have dealt with the challenge which this sometimes poses to the boundaries drawn to the law of tort itself (Chapter 3); earlier in this chapter, we have seen that in an HRA action, vindication of rights is not always thought to require a monetary remedy: a declaration of violation is considered adequate. Here we are concerned with the quantum of damages. We will not give separate consideration here to 'right to life' claims, which were discussed in relation to the Fatal Accidents Act earlier in this chapter.

We extracted the early case of *Greenfield* in Section 4.2 of this Chapter. As Lord Bingham there pointed out, domestic courts are required by section 8(4) of the HRA to have regard to the principles applied in the award of damages by the European Court of Human Rights in Strasbourg. Lord Bingham dismissed any contrast between 'principles' (as used in the section), and 'practice' of the Strasbourg Court. It is clear that domestic courts will model their awards on the quantum awarded in similar cases. This means paying attention to all the facts, and attempting to place the violation on a scale of seriousness by reference to Strasbourg cases. That in itself is different from the general approach of the law of tort, which has regard to the claimant's losses when assessing compensatory damages. However, the matter is more complicated than this. There is some variation in the value of money in different jurisdictions where the Convention applies, and this will affect the appropriate award of damages. Equally, attention needs to be given to the date at which awards in previous cases were made, both because the value of money changes, and because Strasbourg practice too is likely to alter over time.

Practice has of course developed since *Greenfield*. Examples where domestic courts have awarded damages under the HRA include *OOO v Commissioner of Police for the Metropolis* [2011] EWHC 1246 (QB). Here, a failure to investigate on the part of the police amounted to a violation of Articles 3 and 4 (inhuman treatment and slavery). However, the breach was in the nature of a failure to protect, rather than direct perpetration of harm; and the failure extended the claimants' suffering by a relatively short period. Positioning this case relative to others in Strasbourg, the amount awarded was £5,000 to each claimant.

In *R (Waxman) v Crown Prosecution Service* [2012] EWHC 133 (Admin), Moore-Bick LJ awarded £3,500 in respect of a failure to prosecute an individual who was harassing the claimant. This substantially affected the claimant's well-being; but did not leave the claimant as vulnerable to abuse as some cases considered in Strasbourg. It was placed on a scale of seriousness, and this yielded the proper award of damages.

In both of these examples, the awards are relatively modest; but they are still substantial. Importantly, in neither case is it likely that an action in tort would succeed at all, given the principles which we have reviewed in *Greenfield*. The cases concerned damages for delay in parole board hearings in relation to convicted prisoners, under Article 5(4) ECHR. Because the claimants remained lawfully detained, neither action would have given rise to an award of damages for false imprisonment (Chapter 2). Though the two cases were factually different, the approach taken by the Court of Appeal was nevertheless difficult to reconcile. The Supreme Court provided the necessary guidance.

R (Faulkner) v Secretary of State for Justice; R (Sturnham) v Parole Board and another [2013] UKSC 23

This decision on joined appeals to the Supreme Court marks an important stage in the unfolding domestic jurisprudence on HRA damages. To some extent, it qualifies Lord Bingham's remarks in *Greenfield*. The cases concerned damages for delay in parole board hearings in relation to convicted prisoners, under Article 5(4) ECHR. Because the claimants remained lawfully detained, neither action would have given rise to an award of damages for false imprisonment (Chapter 2). Though the two cases were factually different, the approach taken by the Court of Appeal was nevertheless difficult to reconcile. The Supreme Court provided the necessary guidance.

In the *Faulkner* case, there had been a delay of around 10 months; and the board would probably have directed the prisoner's conditional release. There was therefore a deprivation of 'conditional liberty' for 10 months, though within the context of a lawful custodial sentence. In such circumstances, the Supreme Court ruled that damages will typically be appropriate. However, the sum of £10,000 awarded by the Court of Appeal was too high; and was reduced to £6,500. Even so, this award to a convicted prisoner is higher than the damages awarded to each of the bereaved parents in the case of *Rabone*. Most importantly, the case departs from tort principles in that a substantial award is made where no damages at all would be offered by the law of tort.

In the *Sturnham* case, there had been no deprivation of conditional liberty, because the board probably would not have ordered release. Nevertheless, there would still be a modest award for the 'anxiety and distress' associated with a delay of several months in a parole hearing. The judge's award of £300 would be reinstated. While this is a modest sum, it is nevertheless an award of damages in circumstances far removed from those which would give rise to compensation in tort.

Consistently with *Greenfield*, the Supreme Court explained that the requirement in section 8(4) HRA, to give effect to 'principles' developed in Strasbourg, is to be broadly read. It is the *practice* of Strasbourg awards which takes priority. In fact, statements of 'principle' in that court are rare, and to be regarded with caution. At present, courts should be guided 'primarily by any clear and consistent practice of the European court'.

Importantly, Lord Reed suggested that the present state of affairs is merely a stage in the development of HRA remedies, through which they will eventually become naturalized. This qualifies the statement of Lord Bingham that courts 'should look to Strasbourg and not to domestic precedents'. The special role of an international court was identified and recognized; and it was underlined that ultimately, what is required by the Convention is the existence of a *domestic* remedy. This need not exactly replicate the *international* remedy,[57] and over time there may even be no need to look to Strasbourg to assess quantum in areas where domestic precedent has been established. Illustrating the last point, the decision in *Sturnham* will now itself be the starting point when assessing Article 5(4) cases (see the following extract). The following guidance appeared at the end of Lord Reed's judgment.

Lord Reed, *R (Faulkner) v Secretary of State for Justice*

100. … the following guidance should be followed in any future cases where it is necessary to cite substantial numbers of Strasbourg decisions on the application of article 41 with a view to identifying the underlying principles. That exercise will not of course be necessary in relation to any future case on article 5(4), which should take the present judgment as its starting point.

101. First, the court should be provided with an agreed Scott schedule, that is to say a table setting out the relevant information about each of the authorities under a series of columns. The information required is as follows:

1. The name and citation of the case, and its location in the bound volumes of authorities.

2. The violations of the Convention which were established, with references to the paragraphs in the judgment where the findings were made.

3. The damages awarded, if any. It is helpful if their sterling equivalent at present values can be agreed.

4. A brief summary of the appellant's contentions in relation to the case, with references to the key paragraphs in the judgment.

5. A brief summary of the respondent's contentions in relation to the case, again with references to the key paragraphs.

102. Secondly, the court should be provided with a table listing the authorities in chronological order.

103. Thirdly, it has to be borne in mind that extracting principles from a blizzard of authorities requires painstaking effort. The submissions should explain the principles which counsel maintain can be derived from the authorities, and how the authorities support those principles. Otherwise, to adapt Mark Twain's remark about life, the citation of authorities is liable to amount to little more than one damn thing after another; or even, to borrow a well-known riposte, the same damn thing over and over again.

Apart from the practical guidance issued to legal advisors, this is an important addition to our understanding of the relationship between international and domestic courts in this context, in which the role of the domestic courts is to extract guidance from the 'blizzard of authorities' emerging from Strasbourg—while setting relatively little store by any attempt to state general principles in the latter court.

[57] For discussion of this issue after *Greenfield*, see Steele, Further Reading.

6. THE FUNDING OF LITIGATION

Undergraduate law courses do not traditionally spend much time considering the way that litigation is funded. But the enormous changes that have been made in respect of the funding of civil litigation in recent years—culminating in significant legislation coming into force in 2013—have a direct impact on the themes of this chapter.

A wide-ranging review of civil litigation costs and funding was led by Lord Justice Jackson. His Final Report was published in January 2010.[58] Following a period of consultation, the Ministry of Justice announced in 2011 its intention to implement the proposed reforms as a package by 2013. This has been achieved through Part 2 of the Legal Aid, Sentencing and Punishment of Offenders Act 2012 (LASPO), and this came into effect in April 2013. The key provisions are sections 44–6; and sections 56–60. The reforms mark an end to recoverable success fees and after the event (ATE) insurance premiums, in return for 'one way costs shifting' (from losing defendants, but not from losing claimants) in personal injury actions, and an increase in general damages.

Background to the 2013 Reforms

The general presumption is that costs of civil litigation will be awarded in the cause, which is to say that the losing party would in most cases reimburse the costs of the winning party. Solicitors who wish to stay in business will in most instances be unwilling to take a case for claimants who have no prospect of paying their costs in the event of failure.[59] Historically therefore, personal injuries claims have often been funded by trades unions, or state-funded through legal aid. Alternatively, claimants with first party insurance may be 'funded by' their insurance company—which is to say that it is really the insurer who is seeking indemnification from a potential wrongdoer.[60] But successive governments determined that the burden of legal aid is simply too great for the state to continue to fund civil claims.

Lord Bingham, *Callery v Gray*
[2002] UKHL 28; [2002] 1 WLR 2000

1 My Lords, for nearly half a century, legal aid provided out of public funds was the main source of funding for those of modest means who sought to make or (less frequently) defend claims in the civil courts and who needed professional help to do so. By this means access to the courts was made available to many who would otherwise, for want of means, have been denied it. But as time passed the defects of the legal aid regime established under the Legal Aid and Advice Act 1949 and later statutes became more and more apparent. While the scheme served the poorest well, it left many with means above a low ceiling in an unsatisfactory position, too well off to qualify for legal aid but too badly off to contemplate incurring the costs of contested litigation. There was no access to the courts for them.

---

[58] *Review of Civil Litigation Costs: Final Report* (TSO, 2010) ('Jackson Report').

[59] If a claim *settles* the situation is still more unpredictable, since the terms of the settlement may or may not include full costs.

[60] Examples are *Stovin v Wise*, where a motor insurer tried to displace liability to the local authority, rather than to another motor insurer; and *Murphy v Brentwood*, where a buildings insurer sought to displace liability, also to a local authority.

Moreover, the effective immunity against adverse costs orders enjoyed by legally-aided claimants was always recognised to place an unfair burden on a privately-funded defendant resisting a legally-aided claim, since he would be liable for both sides' costs if he lost and his own even if he won. Most seriously of all, the cost to the public purse of providing civil legal aid had risen sharply, without however showing an increase in the number of cases funded or evidence that legal aid was directed to cases which most clearly justified the expenditure of public money.

2 Recognition of these defects underpinned the Access to Justice Act 1999 which, building on the Courts and Legal Services Act 1990, introduced a new regime for funding litigation, and in particular personal injury litigation with which alone this opinion is concerned. … The 1999 Act and the accompanying regulations had (so far as relevant for present purposes) three aims. One aim was to contain the rising cost of legal aid to public funds and enable existing expenditure to be refocused on causes with the greatest need to be funded at public expense, whether because of their intrinsic importance or because of the difficulty of funding them otherwise than out of public funds or for both those reasons. A second aim was to improve access to the courts for members of the public with meritorious claims. It was appreciated that the risk of incurring substantial liabilities in costs is a powerful disincentive to all but the very rich from becoming involved in litigation, and it was therefore hoped that the new arrangements would enable claimants to protect themselves against liability for paying costs either to those acting for them or (if they chose) to those on the other side. A third aim was to discourage weak claims and enable successful defendants to recover their costs in actions brought against them by indigent claimants. Pursuant to the first of these aims publicly-funded assistance was withdrawn from run-of-the-mill personal injury claimants. The main instruments upon which it was intended that claimants should rely to achieve the second and third of the aims are described by my noble and learned friend: they are conditional fee agreements and insurance cover obtained after the event giving rise to the claim.

…

The Solution: Its Components

The solution adopted by the Courts and Legal Services Act 1990 remains essential background to the 2013 reforms. It permitted lawyers to charge on a **no win no fee** or **conditional fee** basis—an arrangement that was unlawful at common law. Such arrangements remain unlawful outside the conditions set by relevant legislation; but the permissible arrangements were broadened in 2013 to incorporate 'Damages-Based Agreements' (explained later).

Providing for enforceable conditional fee agreements (CFAs) was not sufficient in itself to secure broad access to justice. The funding regime developed in the 1990s incorporated two additional features.

Fee Uplifts

Lawyers accepting work on a conditional fee basis are taking a risk. If they lose the claim, and costs are awarded in the cause, they will be paid nothing. To make this risk worthwhile, the legislation allowed fee uplifts. The lawyer gained nothing for those claims that are lost; but gained extra fees (above the value of the time spent on the case) for those that were won. Claimant lawyers needed to assess risks appropriately over time.

Since the maximum permissible 'success fee' (uplift) was set at 100 per cent, fees could in some cases be demanded which were double the value of the work actually undertaken. The burden of this inflated fee was initially placed on claimants, the 'success fee' being reclaimed out of damages. In some instances, this might make the action much less worthwhile, and in a personal injury action might lead to significant under-compensation. By section 58A Access to Justice Act 1999, there was a significant change in the CFA regime. The burden of the success fee was placed upon losing defendants.

Behind these provisions was a deliberate strategy, aiming to displace the costs of litigation *from* the state (via legal aid), *to* losing defendants. This policy goal was bluntly spelt out by Lord Hoffmann in the following case concerned not with personal injury but with breach of confidence.

Lord Hoffmann, *Campbell v MGN (No 2)*
[2005] UKHL 61; [2005] 1 WLR 3394

16 ... there is no doubt that a deliberate policy of the 1999 Act was to impose the cost of all CFA litigation, successful or unsuccessful, upon unsuccessful defendants as a class. Losing defendants were to be required to contribute to the funds which would enable lawyers to take on other cases which might not be successful but would provide access to justice for people who could not otherwise have afforded to sue. In some kinds of litigation, such as personal injury actions, the funds provided by losing defendants were intended to be in substitution for funds previously provided by the state in the form of legal aid.

Given that the goal is to displace risks, from the taxpayer to losing defendants, it is worth noting that a good proportion of losing defendants will be public authorities, or others (such as NHS Trusts) funded at public expense. Ultimately, concerns grew that the costs of litigation were falling on such bodies, or upon insurers (and thus upon those paying insurance policies). The European Court of Human Rights in *MGN Ltd v UK* (2011) 53 EHRR 5 did not agree that the recoverable fee uplift in *Campbell v MGN* was a proportionate restriction on the defendant's freedom of speech, and found a violation of Article 10 ECHR. In that case, the uplift was 100 per cent. Privacy cases are to have their own funding regime, and they are therefore outside the ambit of the 2013 reforms. The issue of compatibility of the costs regime with the ECHR was considered again by the Supreme Court in a case not involving freedom of speech, in *Lawrence v Fen Tigers (No 3)* [2015] UKSC 50, as we will see below.

ATE Insurance

The second additional problem was that, if costs are awarded in the cause, a losing claimant can presume that he or she will be ordered to *pay the winning defendant's costs*. Few claimants in a personal injury action will have the means to do this. Therefore, an essential component of the funding arrangements was after the event (ATE) insurance. This insurance is taken out after the accident or injury, generally at the time of making a claim. In return for a premium, the ATE insurer will pay the defendant's costs if the claim fails. ATE policies are negotiated by claimants' solicitors, rather than by claimants themselves. Initially, ATE premiums were, like success fees, payable by a winning claimant. Through section 29 Access to Justice Act 1999, ATE premiums too became payable by losing defendants.

The implications proved troubling. Whereas the possibility of recoverable success fees aimed to transfer the costs of litigation from the state to losing defendants, the recoverability of ATE premiums from losing defendants meant that the claimant paid neither costs nor insurance premiums, win or lose; while claimants' solicitors were indemnified provided they did not take more unsuccessful than successful claims. Nor was their use confined to personal injury. The problem was the lack of any incentive on claimants and their solicitors to keep costs to a reasonable level; and the lack of any control over costs on the part of defendants. These problems emerged very strongly in case law concerned with recovery of ATE premiums; and the combined effect of recoverable success fees and ATE premiums was a major factor in the most recent reforms. The following case therefore continues to provide important background to the current regime.

Callery v Gray [2002] UKHL 28; [2002] 1 WLR 2000

This was a small-scale road accident case involving minor injuries. There was a very low (even tiny) risk that the claim would be resisted. The claimant entered into a CFA with solicitors, agreeing a fee uplift of 60 per cent despite the straightforward nature of the work. He also paid an ATE insurance premium of £350 to cover the possibility of failure (and therefore of paying costs), even though this possibility was remote. The defendant quickly admitted liability and agreed to pay both damages, and reasonable costs, but then argued that the costs claimed were excessive. The 60 per cent uplift was too high, and there was no need to take out ATE insurance at such an early stage, when there was no reason to think that the claim would be resisted.

A district judge in costs-only proceedings ruled that a success fee of 40 per cent (but not 60 per cent) was reasonable, and that the costs of the insurance premium could also be recovered. This decision was upheld on appeal to a judge. The Court of Appeal ([2001] 1 WLR 2112) agreed that it was reasonable to take out ATE insurance on first consulting a solicitor in respect of a modest claim of this nature, and provided the premium was reasonable this would be recoverable even if there was an early settlement in respect of liability.[61] However, the maximum allowable success fee was 20 per cent. Recoverable costs were reduced accordingly.

The House of Lords declined to interfere with the judgment of the Court of Appeal, noting that that court had 'front-line responsibility for making the new system work fairly and effectively' (Lord Bingham at [5]). However, the House noted certain problems associated with the risk-free environment enjoyed by claimants under the new arrangements. Lord Hoffmann described the claim in issue as being 'as certain of success as anything in litigation can be' (at [21]), and noted that the Court of Appeal called it a 'very, very low risk case'. A success fee of 20 per cent, and the early decision to take out ATE insurance, could be justified only by taking a 'global' view (taking into account the policy of the changes), and not by reference to the risks of the claim in question. The difficulties were identified by various members of the House.

The following extract is illustrative.

---

[61] The reasonableness of the particular premium was confirmed by the Court of Appeal in a second judgment, arrived at with the benefit of further evidence: [2001] 1 WLR 2142.

Lord Hoffmann, *Callery v Gray*
[2002] 1 WLR 2000

24 The second argument was that by agreeing to a success fee at the first meeting, the client so to speak insures himself against having to pay a higher one later if his case turns out to be more difficult than at first appeared. (This is very similar to the argument for an early ATE insurance, which I shall come to later.) At first sight, therefore, one could say that agreeing an immediate success fee is no more than economically rational behaviour on the part of any client and that the fee should therefore be recoverable as an expense reasonably incurred.

25 The difficulty is that while, in principle, it may be rational to agree a success fee at the earliest moment, it is extremely difficult to say whether the actual "premium" paid by the client was reasonable or not. This is because the client does not pay the "premium", whether the success fee is agreed at an earlier or later stage. The transaction therefore lacks the features of a normal insurance, in which the transaction takes place against the background of an insurance market in which the economically rational client or his broker will choose the cheapest insurance suited to his needs. Since the client will in no event be paying the success fee out of his pocket or his damages, he is not concerned with economic rationality. He has no interest in what the fee is. The only persons who have such an interest are the solicitor on the one hand and the liability insurer who will be called upon to pay it on the other. And their interest centres entirely upon whether the agreed success fee will or will not exceed what the costs judge is willing to allow.

Although the House was willing to accept the Court of Appeal's judgment, Lords Hoffmann and Scott rather doubted whether further time and experience would really assist in the judgment of a 'reasonable' success fee (uplift) for routine cases, because of the absence of any real market in respect of costs and ATE insurance; and because the judgment of 'reasonableness' was now being conducted in 'global' terms, rather than by reference to the issues in the particular case.

Rogers v Merthyr Tydfil County Borough Council [2006] EWCA Civ 1134 further illustrates the problems. This was a 'slipping and tripping' accident where the 11-year-old claimant had fallen on broken glass in a play area, and sued the local authority.

The action was initially resisted, but liability was eventually conceded and damages were assessed at £3,105 plus interest. Costs were assessed at £16,821.30, clearly much higher than the value of the claim. Included in these costs was an ATE premium of £5,103 (again, higher than the value of the claim). A 100 per cent success fee was also upheld: the evidence was that the claimant's legal advisers lost 70 per cent of 'slipping and tripping' cases that they brought to trial, so the risks were high. The size of the ATE premium was explained partly by the degree of likelihood of failure, and partly by the fact that the insurance cover operated through a 'three-stage' premium. The size of the premium increased at each stage, if the claim had not settled. A smaller total premium could have been paid at the start to cover the whole risk; but of course if the advisers habitually adopted that sort of policy for their clients, very low-risk claims which did settle immediately (such as the claim in *Callery v Gray*, above), would be more costly to insure.

A higher premium reflects a greater risk of failure. A high premium would, in an ordinary market, focus the mind of the purchaser on whether it is worth paying that premium (and thus, whether it is worth taking the risk of failure). But this is no ordinary market, and the high premium has no effect at all on the claimant's decision, because the claimant is relieved of the risk of failure. Provided legal advisers were willing to accept a 70 per cent failure rate, they would persist with weak claims and the insurance premium would do nothing to stop this. The premium would however add considerably to the costs of public authority defendants who are faced with many unmeritorious claims. Could they afford not to settle these claims?[62]

In the period since the 2013 reforms, a number of cases are of course still being concluded which were funded through the 1999 regime. One of these, *Lawrence v Fen Tigers (No 3)* [2015] UKSC 50, starkly illustrates the problems. The claimants successfully brought an action in nuisance against the defendants, funded by a CFA. We extract the Supreme Court's decision in the nuisance action in Chapter 10. The claimants took out an ATE policy; and if they won the case they were liable under the CFA to pay a 100 per cent success fee on top of base costs. At trial, an injunction was ordered together with damages of £20,750. By then, the claimant had incurred costs exceeding £827,600. The judge ordered the second and third defendants to pay 60 per cent of the claimant's costs, including £312,000 in respect of the success fee and ATE premium. Further costs were incurred through appeals to the Court of Appeal and Supreme Court. The defendants argued that the costs regime infringed Article 6 ECHR (access to a court) and Article 1 of Protocol 1 ECHR (the right to enjoy property). The question divided the Supreme Court but, by a majority, it was concluded that the situation in *Campbell* could be distinguished, and that the regime was broadly compatible with the ECHR.

Lord Neuberger and Lord Dyson MR, *Coventry v Lawrence (No 3)*

42 The submissions of Mr McCracken can be summarised as follows. The system set out in the CPD was incompatible with article 6 and A1P1 of the Convention in that it unjustifiably interfered with the article 6 and A1P1 Convention rights of "non-rich" respondents who unsuccessfully contested litigation instituted by appellants who had the benefit of CFA agreements and ATE insurance.

43 The system had a number of shortcomings which were described as "flaws" by Jackson LJ in his Review of Civil Litigation which were summarised by the ECtHR at paras 207–210 of its judgment in *MGN v United Kingdom* 53 EHRR 195. The flaws were (i) the lack of focus of the regime and the lack of any qualifying requirements for appellants who would be allowed to enter into a CFA ; (ii) the absence of any incentive for appellants to control the incurring of legal costs and the fact that judges assessed costs only at the end of the case when it was too late to control costs that had been spent; (iii) the "blackmail" or "chilling" effect of the regime which drove parties to settle early despite good prospects of a defence; and (iv) the fact that the regime gave the opportunity to "cherry pick" winning cases to conduct on CFAs. At para 217, the court concluded that:

"the depth and nature of the flaws in the system … are such that the court can conclude that the impugned scheme exceeded even the broad margin of appreciation to be accorded to the state in respect of general measures pursuing social and economic interests."

[62] For critical discussion of these issues from a member of the judiciary, see P. Kennedy, 'Is This the Way We Want to Go?' (2005) JPIL 117.

44 These flaws were regarded by the ECtHR as sufficiently serious to lead it to conclude that the system was incompatible with article 10 of the Convention. Mr McCracken submits that the same reasoning necessarily requires the court to hold that the system was also incompatible with article 6 and A1P1.

45 The system was arbitrary. It singled out from the class of unsuccessful litigants a subset of those who happened to have been opposed by CFA/ATE-funded litigants and imposed on that subset the burden of funding other unsuccessful cases which did not involve them at all.

46 The real vice of the system lay in the CPD. CPD 11.7 based the assessment of CFA uplifts and ATE premiums exclusively on the ex ante perspective of the CFA/ATE party; and CPD 11.9 expressly disallowed any reduction on the basis that the overall total of base costs and uplifts appeared to be disproportionate. Decisions on uplift therefore disregarded the financial circumstances of the payer, the importance to the payer of fighting the case and the reasonableness of his decision to fight.

Even in reaching their conclusion that the scheme did not violate ECHR rights, the majority recognized serious shortcomings in the scheme:

Lords Neuberger and Dyson, *Coventry v Lawrence (No 3)*

83 To summarise. It was undoubtedly a feature of the 1999 Act scheme that the costs awarded to successful appellants who had the benefit of CFAs could be very high indeed. For that reason, it had the potential to place respondents under considerable pressure to settle before even more costs were incurred. This is the third flaw identified by the ECtHR in *MGN v United Kingdom* 53 EHRR 195 and the second of Lord Neuberger PSC's four unique and regrettable features. We accept that, in a number of individual cases, the scheme might be said to have interfered with a defendant's right of access to justice. But for the reasons stated earlier … , it is necessary to concentrate on the scheme as a whole. The scheme as a whole was a rational and coherent scheme for providing access to justice to those to whom it would probably otherwise have been denied. It was subject to certain safeguards. The government were entitled to a considerable area of discretionary judgment in choosing the scheme that it considered would strike the right balance between the interests of appellants and respondents whilst at the same time securing access to justice to those who would previously have qualified for legal aid. It had to find a solution to the problem created by the withdrawal of legal aid. The government has now produced three different schemes. Each has produced considerable criticism. As already indicated, once civil legal aid was constrained to the extent that it was in 1999, it became impossible to come up with a solution which would meet with universal approval. This is relevant to the question whether the 1999 Act scheme struck a fair balance between the interests of different litigants.

Jackson LJ, for his part, has recently stated that '[b]etween April 2000 and April 2013 the CFA regime was an instrument of injustice and, on occasion, oppression': Lord Justice Jackson, 'Fixing and Funding the Costs of Civil Litigation' (2015) CJQ 260, 264; Lord Mance in *Coventry v Lawrence (No 3)* described it as 'unfairly discriminatory' ([117]). These problems form the background to the most recent reforms.

The 2013 Reforms

The problems just discussed led to a review of the entire funding regime. Introducing his *Review of Civil Litigation Costs: Final Report* in 2010, Jackson LJ said that:

In some areas of civil litigation costs are disproportionate and impede access to justice. I therefore propose a coherent package of interlocking reforms, designed to control costs and promote access to justice.[63]

That package has largely remained intact in its implementation, which has been achieved simultaneously through legislation; through changes to the civil procedure rules; and in the case of an increase in general damages, through action of the courts themselves. Between them, the changes mark significant evolution in civil litigation funding.

The key implementing legislation is LASPO 2012: Part 2 of the statute proceeds by amending key provisions of the Courts and Legal Services Act 1990. Here we summarize the main changes.

No Win No Fee Agreements: CFAs and DBAs (sections 44, 45 LASPO)

In addition to conditional fee agreements (CFAs), introduced earlier, the legislation allows for damages-based agreements (DBAs, sometimes called 'contingency fees'). In both sets of arrangements, the lawyer's payment is conditional on the case being successful. If the case is lost, the lawyer is not paid. If the case is won, the lawyer is paid either the normal fee plus an uplift or success fee (in the case of CFAs); or a percentage of the damages recovered (in the case of DBAs). The maximum payment that a lawyer can recover from a claimant's damages through a DBA is capped at 25 per cent of damages (excluding damages for future care and loss) in personal injury actions; at 35 per cent of damages in employment tribunal cases (the context where contingency fees have previously been recoverable in English courts); and at 50 per cent of damages in all other cases. The recognition of 'contingency fees' (as opposed to conditional fees) is an important moment. There have been concerns about such fees, since they reduce the amount of damages remaining to the successful claimant, and might appear to encourage negotiation of higher settlements, as well as enabling lawyers to acquire fees which are unrelated to the level of work undertaken. They have been associated in the minds of English lawyers with the US legal system, though some doubt has been cast on these reasons for hostility.[64] The embrace of contingency fees crosses a watershed in our system of civil litigation. Recognizing this, the legislation places safeguards on their operation, particularly for the benefit of personal injury claimants. Such claimants will have a particular need for their damages, for example to cover living expenses and care costs. Typically, their injuries will also not be covered by first party insurance.

Changes to CFAs (section 44 LASPO)

The previous arrangements meant that the winning party's 'success fee' was payable by the losing party in addition to the ordinary legal costs of the winning party. From 1 April 2013,

---

[63] Foreword.
[64] See the study by R. Moorhead, 'An American Future?' (2010) 73 MLR 752.

the 'success fee' is no longer payable by the losing side; if such a fee is charged, it will be paid by the winning party, typically out of damages recovered. The 'success fee' can be up to 100 per cent of basic fee—this remains unchanged from when CFAs were first introduced in the 1990s. However, in personal injury cases, the success fee that the lawyer may charge must not exceed 25 per cent of the damages, and this must exclude damages for future care and loss. This is intended to ensure that any damages for future care and loss are protected in their entirety (though we have addressed, in earlier sections, some serious problems arising in the calculation of those losses).

DBAs (section 45 LASPO; section 58AA Courts and Legal Services Act 1990)

Successful claimants using DBAs will recover their costs (lawyers' fees) from defendants in the usual way, but the claimant must pay from damages any shortfall between the solicitors' costs paid by the losing defendant and the agreed DBA fee. So far as lawyers are concerned, their fee is *restricted* to the DBA fee: if the DBA fee is less than the solicitors' costs would be in the absence of a DBA, a losing defendant will simply pay less. In November 2014, the Ministry of Justice announced that the Civil Justice Council would take a close look at technical revisions to the regulations for DBAs. Jackson LJ has argued however that this working group has been told not to consider 'hybrid DBAs', otherwise described as 'no win—low fee' agreements. This in his opinion is an error, as lawyers may be more inclined to work with the possibility of a low fee, than with the possibility of no fee at all: Jackson LJ, 'Fixing and Funding the Costs of Civil Litigation' (2015) CJQ 260.

Legal Expenses Insurance: BTE and ATE

Before the Event (BTE) Insurance

Before the event (BTE) insurance is taken out before an actionable event has occurred. BTE insurance is often purchased as an add-on to existing insurance policies (usually motor or home insurance) although it is available as a stand-alone product. Many consumers who purchase BTE insurance are unaware of the coverage it provides and may not make use of it. Because it is taken out when litigation is merely a 'risk', it operates more like normal insurance than ATE, and is less costly. The promise of BTE insurance is explored by R. Lewis, 'Litigation Costs and Before-the-Event Insurance: the Key to Access to Justice?' (2011) 74 MLR 272.

After the Event (ATE) Insurance

We have seen that after the event (ATE) insurance was a crucial part of the pre-2013 regime. Though it still exists, it is made much less attractive by the 2013 changes, and is no longer a key part of the solution. ATE insurance is taken out before an actionable event has occurred. ATE insurers undertake to pay the defendant's costs in the event that the claimant loses. Because it is bought when litigation is imminent, the risk tends to be high, and the insurance tends to be expensive. As we have seen, the cost has not typically fallen on claimants, win or lose. Rather, it was (under the previous arrangements) recovered from defendants in cases which defendants lost. This too necessarily increases the premium; it is only sometimes recovered. It seems that the premium typically ranged from 30 per cent to 50 per cent of the level of costs incurred; and ATE was therefore implicated in the situation where costs exceeded the claim itself. Crucially, it also contributed to the 'risk-free' environment for claimants.

Jackson LJ, *Review of Civil Litigation Costs: Final Report* (2010), Chapter 9, 4.4

... Any person who finds a willing insurer can take out ATE insurance, whether that person is rich or poor, human or corporate, deserving or undeserving. Furthermore, the protection which a claimant derives from ATE insurance is total. The claimant is not required to make a modest contribution towards adverse costs ... even if he can afford to do so.

In almost all cases, ATE insurance premiums are no longer recoverable if the insurance is taken out after 1 April 2013. ATE insurance remains available, but premiums are payable at the litigant's expense. For *personal injury claims only*, qualified one way costs shifting (QOCS) is the replacement solution. It is designed to protect claimants, while still on balance benefiting defendants as a class.[65] This further underlines the recognized vulnerability of personal injury claimants.

Increase in General Damages

We saw earlier in this chapter that a 10 per cent increase in non-pecuniary general damages has been introduced by the courts. This applies to all tort cases, however funded: *Simmons v Castle* [2012] EWCA Civ 1288. In *Summers v Bundy* [2016] EWCA Civ 126; [2016] PIQR Q6, the Court of Appeal clarified that courts have no discretion in whether to apply the uplift, which had been wrongly disapplied in a claim brought by a legally aided claimant.

Sanctions under Part 36 of the Civil Procedure Rules (section 55 LASPO; Offers to Settle in Civil Proceedings Order 2013)

Under Part 36 of the Civil Procedure Rules, an additional amount must now be paid by a defendant who does not accept a claimant's offer to settle where the court gives judgment that is at least as advantageous as an offer the claimant made to settle the claim. This additional sanction is calculated as 10 per cent of damages where damages are in issue, and 10 per cent of costs for non-damages claims; but is subject to a maximum of around £75,000.

Referral Fees Ban in Personal Injury Cases (sections 57, 59 LASPO)

From 1 April 2013, the payment and receipt of referral fees in personal injury cases is prohibited. 'Referral fees' are payments made by solicitors to third parties for client referrals or introductions. Lord Justice Jackson thought these were unnecessary, since claimants would have little difficulty finding legal representation without such fees. They were also expensive, so that the ban on such fees would reduce costs. His views on this were particularly strong, though such fees have also been defended (Higgins, Further Reading).

---

[65] For review of ATE and BTE insurance, and of insurance in general, in civil litigation, see R. Merkin and J. Steele, *Insurance and the Law of Obligations*, Chapter 13.

Jackson LJ, *Review of Civil Litigation Costs: Final Report*

4.11 … In my view, it is offensive and wrong in principle for personal injury claimants to be treated as a commodity. BTE insurers should not be in the position of auctioning off the personal injury claims of those whom they insure. It is equally unacceptable for claims management companies to buy in personal injury claims from other referrers and then sell them on at a profit. Indeed the very language of the claims management industry characterises personal injury claims as a commodity. Strong cases ready to be pursued are described as "*oven ready*".

4.12 The practice is, in my view, even more abhorrent when the referrer not only demands a referral fee from the solicitor but also takes a slice of the claimant's damages (without having added any value to the case). I am aware of one claims management company which charges its clients a fee of £379 out of damages received.

Costs Protection in Personal Injury Claims: Qualified One Way Costs Shifting (QOCS)

A new costs protection regime has been introduced for personal injury claims (including clinical negligence), which aims to replace the old recoverable ATE premium while not exposing personal injury claimants to inappropriate risk. This regime limits the circumstances under which a claimant might have to pay costs to the other side, and is called 'qualified one way costs shifting' (QOCS). It has been introduced by changes to the Civil Procedure Rules. Evidence to the Jackson review suggested that compensators as a whole (an interesting notion, which suggests the true structure of tort law) would be better off if they *gave up* the right to recover costs when they won, provided they did not pay success fees and ATE premiums when they lost (or, importantly, when they reached a settlement). And of course, the need for recoverable success fees and ATE premiums recedes in a context where the claimant is not generally at risk of paying a winning defendant's costs. The very existence of QOCS as a solution illustrates that defendants in personal injury actions are a class or group of repeat players, who will win and lose over time: it is on this basis that they may win more than they lose through such a change.

There are exceptions to the protection of personal injury claimants through QOCS. The exceptions generally fall into two categories: behavioural (where claimants have acted fraudulently, frivolously, or unreasonably); and financial (can the claimant afford the costs?). Where the lines are drawn will be important; but clarity too is important in this context. It must be clear to potential claimants what would take them outside the protection of QOCS.

Third Party Funding

Another element of the present changes in the funding of civil litigation is the growing use of third party funding. The £70 million claim in *Moore Stephens v Stone & Rolls Ltd* [2009] UKHL 39, was funded by third parties. The Jackson Report described the market as 'still nascent'; but noted that a voluntary code (of self-regulation) had been made available since publication of the Interim Report.[66] In *Excalibur Ventures v Texas Keystone Inc* [2016]

[66] Jackson Report, Chapter 10. For an introduction (written by a litigation funder before the Report) see S. Dunn, 'Paying for Personal Injury Claims—What are the Options for Clients and their Representatives?' (2009) JPIL 218–23. See also Mulheron and Cashman, Further Reading.

EWCA Civ 1144, third parties who had funded hopeless claims were held liable for costs on the indemnity basis:

Tomlinson LJ, *Excalibur Ventures v Texas Keystone*

23 The argument for the funders boiled down in essence to the proposition that it is not appropriate to direct them to pay costs on the indemnity basis if they have themselves been guilty of no discreditable conduct or conduct which can be criticised. Even on the assumption that the funders were guilty of no conduct which can properly be criticised, and I accept that they did nothing discreditable in the sense of being morally reprehensible or even improper, this argument suffers from two fatal defects, both of which were identified by the judge. First, it overlooks that the conduct of the parties is but one factor to be taken into account in the overall evaluation. Second, it looks at the question from only one point of view, that of the funder. As the judge pointed out at para 125, it ignores the character of the action which the funder has funded and its effect on the defendants.

24 The argument is yet further flawed in that it assumes that the funder is responsible only for his own conduct. This too is incorrect. As the judge pointed out at para 60, where conduct comes into consideration in this context, the successful party is afforded a more generous basis for assessing which of his costs should be paid by his opponent because of the way in which the latter, *or those in his camp*, have acted. Thus as the judge pointed out at para 118, a litigant may find himself liable to pay indemnity costs on account of the conduct of those whom he has chosen to engage—e.g. lawyers, or experts, which experts may themselves have been chosen by the lawyers, or the conduct of those whom he has chosen to enlist, e.g. witnesses, even though he is not personally responsible for it. The position of the funder is directly analogous. The funder is seeking to derive financial benefit from pursuit of the claim just as much as is the funded claimant litigant, and there can be no principled reason to draw a distinction between them in this regard. I also agree with Mr Waller that the analysis here is not dependent upon rules of agency—expert and factual witnesses are not agents of the party on whose behalf they give evidence any more than they are agents of the funder. The principle is a broader principle of justice. Deployment of lawyers, experts and other witnesses is a necessary part of bringing the claim to a successful conclusion for the benefit of the litigant, and it is equally a necessary part of bringing it to a successful conclusion for the benefit of the funder. The funder chooses which claims to back, whereas, as the judge rightly observed at para 125, a defendant does not choose by whom to be sued, or in what manner. The judge continued:

"If, then, the funder's witnesses turn out to be liars or the litigation is conducted unreasonably, so that the court awards costs on an indemnity scale, it is just and equitable that the funder should pay on that scale."

I agree. I can see no principled basis upon which the funder can dissociate himself from the conduct of those whom he has enabled to conduct the litigation and upon whom he relies to make a return on his investment.

Fixed Costs

The 'fixed costs' regime previously introduced for road traffic claims up to £10,000—which are of course subject to compulsory insurance—has been extended to claims in relation to employers' liability and public liability. Only the first of these is covered by compulsory insurance, though liability insurance is generally present also for the latter risk. At the same time, the upper limit to which the fixed costs apply has been raised to £25,000, in a measure clearly aimed at controlling costs and increasing the efficiency of the most common types of claims. In November 2016, it was announced that Lord Justice Jackson has been commissioned to undertake a review of fixed recoverable costs, to be completed by 31 July 2017. This will signal the extension of fixed costs, Jackson LJ previously suggesting their use for claims up to £250,000.

7. CONCLUSIONS

i. This chapter has been concerned both with monetary remedies, and with the costs of delivering the law of tort. Both of these are, in many ways, at the core of the subject. The general principle of tort damages is that they compensate the claimant in full for their wrongful losses. The detailed application of this principle is, however, far from straightforward. Among the reasons for this are the need to anticipate what would have happened, had it not been for the tort; and, in the case of a claimant with continuing needs, the need to anticipate what the costs of care and support will be. It must be admitted that in the face of these difficulties, there is no way to be sure of what is a correct award; and periodical payments while solving this problem raise other difficulties, particularly when it comes to protecting the value of the payments.

ii. As with many other aspects of the law of tort, the HRA offers a new set of challenges. In this instance, the HRA raises the question of whether tort's available remedies demonstrate that it is serious about vindicating rights. For the most part, tort damages are more generous than HRA damages; but HRA damages cover a wider scope. The ability of a wider range of relatives to bring actions in respect of wrongful death under the HRA is one illustration; another is the availability of damages for anxiety and distress caused by rights violations under the HRA, in circumstances where tort, since *Lumba*, will offer only nominal damages, if any at all. The question which arises, as in other aspects of the law, is whether the HRA is inclined to influence the law of tort into expanding its remedies; or whether it encourages the courts to play safe with tort remedies, on the basis that rights are now adequately protected elsewhere.

iii. Some of the most significant recent developments in the law of tort have not been at the level of legal principle, but in relation to the funding of civil litigation. Responding to the removal of civil legal aid from almost all areas, the reforms of 1999 introduced a range of measures which, in hindsight, imposed on some losing defendants the burden of crushing costs awards, reflecting 'success fees' and ATE insurance premiums charged to the winning claimant. A set of reforms in 2013 has attempted to redress the balance, but at the price of greater risks for claimants and for their lawyers. The reform of civil litigation costs and funding is still work in progress, and has a greater influence on the shape of the law than any individual development of legal principle is likely to have.

FURTHER READING

Atiyah, P., *The Damages Lottery* (Oxford: Hart Publishing, 1997).

Barker, K., 'Private and Public: The Mixed Concept of Vindication in Torts and Private Law', in S. Pitel, J. Neyers and E. Chamberlain (eds), *Tort Law: Challenging Orthodoxy* (Hart Publishing, 2013).

Beever, A., 'The Structure of Aggravated and Exemplary Damages' (2003) 23 OJLS 87–110.

Cane, P., *Atiyah's Accidents, Compensation and the Law* (8th edn, Cambridge: Cambridge University Press, 2013).

Cunnington, R., 'The Assessment of Gain-based Damages for Contract' (2008) 71 MLR 559–86.

Edelman, J., *Gain-Based Damages* (Oxford: Hart Publishing, 2002).

Edelman, J., 'In Defence of Exemplary Damages'; in C. Rickett (ed.), *Justifying Private Law Remedies* (Oxford: Hart Publishing, 2008).

Harris, D., Campbell, D., and Halson, R., *Remedies in Contract and Tort* (2nd edn, Cambridge: Cambridge University Press, 2002).

Higgins, A., 'Referral Fees—The Business of Access to Justice' (2012) 32 LS 109.

Hurst, P., 'The New Costs Rules and Practice Directions' (2013) CJQ 153.

Law Commission, *Aggravated, Exemplary and Restitutionary Damages* (Law Com Report No 247, London: HMSO, 1997).

Lewis, R., 'Insurance and the Tort System' (2005) 25 LS 85.

Lewis, R., 'The Politics and Economics of Tort Law: Judicially Imposed Periodical Payments of Damages' (2006) 69 MLR 418.

Merkin, R., and Steele, J., *Insurance and the Law of Obligations* (Oxford University Press, 2013), Chapter 13.

Mulheron, R., and Cashman, P., 'Third-party Funding: a Change in the Landscape' (2008) 27 CJQ 312–41.

Mulheron, R., 'The Damages-based Agreements Regulations 2013: Some Conundrums in the 'Brave New World' of Funding' (2013) 32 CJQ 241.

Ramsey J., 'Implementation of the Costs Reforms' (2013) 32 CJQ 112.

Rotherham, C., 'The Conceptual Structure of Restitution for Wrongs' (2007) 66 CLJ 172.

Rotherham, C., 'Gain-based Relief in Tort After AG v Blake' (2010) 126 LQR 102.

Sarathy, G., '*Coventry v Lawrence*: Bad Law Makes Hard Cases?' (2015) CJQ 295.

Scott, Lord, 'Damages' [2007] LMCLQ 465–72.

Steele, J., 'Damages in Tort and under the Human Rights Act: Remedial or Functional Separation?' (2008) 67 CLJ 606–34.

Varuhas, J., 'A Tort-based Approach to damages under the Human Rights Act' (2009) 72 CLJ 750–82.

Walmsley, P., 'The Discount Rate: Is It Time for the Lord Chancellor to Loosen the Straightjacket of *Wells v Wells*?' (2014) JPIL 25.

Witzleb, N., and Carroll, R., 'The Role of Vindication in Torts Damages' (2009) 17 Tort L Rev 16.

9

VICARIOUS LIABILITY AND NON-DELEGABLE DUTIES

CENTRAL ISSUES

i) Vicarious liability is a form of secondary liability, imposed on one person for the tort of another. The tortfeasor remains potentially liable, so that a claim may in principle be brought against either party; but typically, the vicariously liable party is better able to satisfy the judgment.

ii) Vicarious liability depends on two factors: first, the relationship between tortfeasor and defendant; and second, the connection between this relationship, and the tort committed. Both tests have been extensively redefined in recent years.

iii) Vicarious liability for the tort of an employee has long been recognized. It is now also recognized, however, that some relationships falling short of employment will suffice. If the person committing the tort is classified as an 'independent contractor' or regarded as part of an 'independent business', there will be no vicarious liability. However, there are various ways in which there may nevertheless be liability when an independent contractor acts tortiously: for example, through imposition of a **'non-delegable duty'**.

iii) Turning to the necessary connection between the parties' relationship, and the tort, the question is now whether there was a sufficiently **close connection** between the tort, and the employment or other relationship. This test has displaced the narrower question of whether the tort was committed **in the course of employment.**

iv) Under some circumstances, parties are subject to **non-delegable duties** to another. This means that although *tasks* creating certain risks can appropriately be delegated to others, *duties* in respect of those risks cannot. This is different from vicarious liability because it gives rise to liability for the breach of one's own duty, even if the fault is that of another. It is a form of primary (or 'personal') liability. The UK Supreme Court has now recognized that such a duty may be owed by a school to its pupils.

v) There are also some more straightforward ways in which primary liability may be imposed on a person whose independent contractor has committed a tort. For example, carelessly selecting or (if relevant) failing to supervise a contractor or employee may involve a breach of one's own duty of care. This should be kept distinct from vicarious liability.

1. VICARIOUS LIABILITY

This section of the chapter explores vicarious liability. In Section 1.1, we begin by identifying the nature of vicarious liability, and outline the existence of two requirements of sufficient relationship, and sufficient connection with the tort. In Section 1.2, we turn to possible justifications for this form of liability, and explain the direct importance of such justifications as the law currently stands. In Section 1.3, we address the relationship criterion; and in Section 1.4 we explore the notion of 'close connection', and how it has emerged and developed over recent years, permitting a general expansion in the realm of vicarious liability.

1.1 NATURE AND STRUCTURE

Vicarious liability operates most often in the employment context and (now) extends to some analogous relationships. Under this principle, an employer will be liable for the tort of his or her employee, provided that tort is sufficiently connected with the individual's employment. Significantly, it is now recognized that vicarious liability may also operate even where the parties' relationship falls short of a relationship of employment, provided the core features of the employment relationship of relevance to vicarious liability are present: the relationship is described as 'akin to employment'.[1] The principle is not confined to negligence but is general: it extends both to intentional torts and to statutory liability. Other instances of vicarious liability also exist. An example is liability within a partnership for the torts of a partner.[2]

It is sometimes said that another instance of vicarious liability is the liability of a principal for the torts of his or her agent. An 'agent' in this context generally means someone who is vested with 'authority' (though this may only be ostensible) to enter into legal relations on the part of the principal. Although strict liability for the torts of an agent undoubtedly does exist, it has been doubted whether this form of strict liability is genuinely a form of 'vicarious' liability.[3]

Secondary Liability

Attempts have been made to explain the doctrine of vicarious liability by suggesting that the tort is really that of the vicariously liable party, which is to say (in an employment context) the 'employer'.[4] It is suggested however that the better view is that the employee commits a tort; but the employer is liable.[5] That is the view taken in recent decisions of the UK Supreme Court.

---

[1] Section 1.4.
[2] Partnership Act 1890, s 10.
[3] C. Beuermann, 'Dissociating the Two Forms of So-Called 'Vicarious Liability', in S. Pitel, J. Neyers and E. Chamberlain (eds), *Tort Law: Challenging Orthodoxy* (Hart Publishing, 2013).
[4] This idea is discussed by G. Williams, 'Vicarious Liability: Tort of the Master or Tort of the Servant?' (1956) 72 LQR 522; see also R. Stevens, 'Vicarious Liability or Vicarious Action?' (2007) 123 LQR 522.
[5] This was clearly stated by the House of Lords in *Dubai Aluminium v Salaam* [2003] 2 AC 366 and reiterated by Lord Nicholls in *Majrowski v Guy's and St Thomas's NHS Trust* [2006] UKHL 34. It is consistent with the decision of the House of Lords in *A v Hoare* [2008] UKHL 6; [2008] 1 AC 844.

Vicarious liability is essential to the liability in tort of corporations. In *Various Claimants v Catholic Child Welfare Society* [2012] UKSC 56, [34], Lord Phillips remarked that 'in the majority of modern cases, the defendant is not an individual but a corporate entity. In most of them vicarious liability is likely to be the basis on which the defendant was sued'. The point is that a corporate defendant can commit most torts only through others. Its liabilities are usually secondary. On some, defined occasions, the acts of an individual may instead be 'attributed to' the company. This may be the case for example where a company's officers act 'as' the company. The point is that in cases of vicarious liability, the torts of the employee are not attributed to the company, and that the restrictive rules on attribution do not apply. In the case of an intentional tort, this may make all the difference to whether the company can recover its liabilities from its insurance company, for insurance policies will generally not respond to cover harms, or liabilities arising from harms, intentionally caused by the assured. That is outside the purpose of insurance generally, and may also be contrary to public policy.[6]

**Lord Sumption, *Woodland v Swimming Teachers Association*
[2013] UKSC 66**

3 In principle, liability in tort depends on proof of personal breach of duty. To that principle, there is at common law only one true exception, namely vicarious liability. Where a defendant is vicariously liable for the tort of another, he commits no tort himself and may not even owe the relevant duty, but is held liable as a matter of public policy for the tort of the other ...

1.2 JUSTIFICATIONS FOR VICARIOUS LIABILITY

Justifications have become particularly important in the 'new ballgame'[7] of vicarious liability. That is because the Supreme Court in *Various Claimants* declared that the first requirement for establishing vicarious liability—that there is a sufficient relationship between tortfeasor and potentially vicariously liable party—will be assessed in relation to the underlying rationale for such liability.

In the next extract, we see how Lord Phillips framed the relevant justifications in *Various Claimants v Catholic Child Welfare Society* [2012] UKSC 56. The Supreme Court here accepted the existence of a range of policy concerns ([35]), despite the apparent identification of an overriding concern with compensation ([34]).

Lord Phillips, *Various Claimants v Catholic Child Welfare Society*

34 ... The policy objective underlying vicarious liability is to ensure, in so far as it is fair, just and reasonable, that liability for tortious wrong is borne by a defendant with the means to compensate the victim. Such defendants can usually be expected to insure against the risk of

6 These issues are explored by R. Merkin and J. Steele, *Insurance and the Law of Obligations*, Chapters 10 and 11.
7 An expression used by Ward LJ in *E v English Province of Our Lady of Charity* [2012] EWCA Civ 938, [60].

such liability, so that this risk is more widely spread. It is for the court to identify the policy reasons why it is fair, just and reasonable to impose vicarious liability and to lay down the criteria that must be shown to be satisfied in order to establish vicarious liability. Where the criteria are satisfied the policy reasons for imposing the liability should apply. As Lord Hobhouse of Woodborough pointed out in the *Lister case* [2002] 1 AC 215, para 60, the policy reasons are not the same as the criteria. One cannot, however, consider the one without the other and the two sometimes overlap.

35 The relationship that gives rise to vicarious liability is in the vast majority of cases that of employer and employee under a contract of employment. The employer will be vicariously liable when the employee commits a tort in the course of his employment. There is no difficulty in identifying a number of policy reasons that usually make it fair, just and reasonable to impose vicarious liability on the employer when these criteria are satisfied: (i) the employer is more likely to have the means to compensate the victim than the employee and can be expected to have insured against that liability; (ii) the tort will have been committed as a result of activity being taken by the employee on behalf of the employer; (iii) the employee's activity is likely to be part of the business activity of the employer; (iv) the employer, by employing the employee to carry on the activity will have created the risk of the tort committed by the employee; (v) the employee will, to a greater or lesser degree, have been under the control of the employer.

More recently, in *Cox v Ministry of Justice* [2016] UKSC 10; [2016] AC 660, the Supreme Court doubted the significance of the first and fifth factors.

Lord Reed JSC, *Cox v Ministry of Justice*

20 The five factors which Lord Phillips PSC mentioned in para 35 are not all equally significant. The first—that the defendant is more likely than the tortfeasor to have the means to compensate the victim, and can be expected to have insured against vicarious liability—did not feature in the remainder of the judgment, and is unlikely to be of independent significance in most cases. It is, of course, true that where an individual is employed under a contract of employment, his employer is likely to have a deeper pocket, and can in any event be expected to have insured against vicarious liability. Neither of these, however, is a principled justification for imposing vicarious liability. The mere possession of wealth is not in itself any ground for imposing liability. As for insurance, employers insure themselves because they are liable: they are not liable because they have insured themselves. On the other hand, given the infinite variety of circumstances in which the question of vicarious liability might arise, it cannot be ruled out that there might be circumstances in which the absence or unavailability of insurance, or other means of meeting a potential liability, might be a relevant consideration.

21 The fifth of the factors—that the tortfeasor will, to a greater or lesser degree, have been under the control of the defendant—no longer has the significance that it was sometimes considered to have in the past, as Lord Phillips PSC immediately made clear....

It is suggested that in downplaying the first of Lord Phillips' points, the Supreme Court rejected one of the primary reasons why vicarious liability is necessary. If this factor did not feature very much in the remainder of Lord Phillips' judgment, this is perhaps because it forms part of an overarching rationale, rather than providing a means of distinguishing between different cases. In any event, the expectation that the defendant is more likely than the tortfeasor to be able to compensate the victim of tort—partly because of the greater capacity to insure—has played a significant role in proposed justifications for the existence of the principle. Certainly, it need not be the sole reason, and indeed the effect of justifications for vicarious liability is often seen as cumulative:

P. S. Atiyah, *Vicarious Liability in the Law of Tort* (Butterworths, 1967), at 15

In a complex modern society the justification for a particular legal principle may frequently have to be sought in many considerations. None of them taken by itself may be a sufficient reason for the principle, but the combined effect of all of them may be overwhelming.

Of course this means that in any particular case where some of the factors put forward in justification are present and others are not, some sort of balancing operation needs to be made, but this is itself a familiar part of the legal process.

Justice Arguments

At first sight, it is strange to offer arguments of justice for holding someone liable for the torts of another. But there are respectable justice arguments to this effect. In particular, it is said that the defendant should take the *risk of* harm, either because she or he takes the *benefit* of the activity that creates that risk, or because of his or her role in creating the risk.[8] This argument can be described as a theory of enterprise risk, of a moral rather than an economic sort. That is to say, the enterprise should take on the risks it creates and from which it benefits; it is not fair and just that these risks should be passed to others. This justice argument does not depend on saying that there is anything 'wrong' with creating the risk. Further, this approach can be used to justify 'normal' risks inherent in an enterprise, and does not require that the defendant should have 'enhanced' those inherent risks in any way.[9] As Lord Toulson put it in *Mohamud v Wm Morrison Supermarkets plc* [2016] UKSC 11; [2016] AC 677 (para [40]), 'The risk of an employee misusing his position is one of life's unavoidable facts', and there is no need to examine retrospectively the degree to which the employee would have been considered to present a risk.

An alternative, *economic* variant of 'enterprise risk' is sometimes encountered. The idea here is that the costs of an enterprise ought to be 'internalized' in order to stimulate the most *efficient* level of risk-taking. If the enterprise is able to place the risks on another, then it will be tempted to take risks which are not socially efficient, because they come at no cost. This economic variant has not been fully addressed in the recent case law on vicarious liability. It is the moral version that has been emphasized.

This justification seems not to explain why there is *no* vicarious liability for the torts of independent contractors. Liability whenever I 'benefit from' a risk would be very

---

[8] This resembles the fairness argument for strict liability under *Rylands v Fletcher*, which is debated in Chapter 11. *Rylands* itself was a case of negligence on the part of contractors (rather than employees).

[9] Lord Nicholls has clearly embraced this principle in *Dubai Aluminium v Salaam* [2003] 2 AC 366; *Majrowski v Guy's and St Thomas's Hospital Trust* [2006] UKHL 34.

far-reaching since I benefit from many risks. One answer to this is that independent contractors, being independent and working for their own profit, form their own separate 'enterprise': 'it is the contractor who is the *entrepreneur*'.[10] To develop this point, those who are not considered part of the defendant's business may, though not independent contractors themselves, be judged to be part of the business of another. In other words, although enterprise risk *could* justify imposing broad vicarious liability, there are reasons why we might choose to draw the line here. Glanville Williams adds a practical argument, that liability for contractors would simply be inconvenient. It would multiply the number of parties against whom an action may be brought and increase expense and uncertainty.

In the context of modern employment relationships, many non-employees are not really 'entrepreneurs'. For example, some are part of a shifting and informal workforce: see the discussion by E. McKendrick, 'Vicarious Liability and Independent Contractors—A Reexamination' (1990) 53 MLR 770. This altered context has been recognized by the courts in the development of vicarious liability to extend beyond the employment relationship. In *Mohamud v Wm Morrison Supermarkets plc* [2016] UKSC 11; [2016] AC 677, Lord Dyson suggested that changes in the type of relationship to which vicarious liability is now recognized to apply 'have been a response to changes in the legal relationships between enterprises and members of their workforces and the increasing complexity and sophistication of the organization of enterprises in the modern world'. None of this undermines enterprise risk justifications; rather, it shows how important such justifications may be in considering the appropriate response to current changes.[11] Courts have ceased to assume that if someone performing work for another is not strictly their employee, they should necessarily be defined as an 'independent contractor' for purposes of vicarious liability: see further Section 1.4.

Incentive and Deterrence Arguments

The argument from deterrence is that the employer has the *opportunity* to increase standards of safety, for example through better procedures for selecting employees and for their supervision. Therefore, it is best if there is an *incentive* for him or her to do so, through liability for the employee's tort.

It is sometimes said that this argument does not explain why liability is justified in cases where the accident was unavoidable, in that all due care has been applied in selection of employee, maintenance of equipment, and so on. But this criticism is misplaced. Modern theories of regulation suggest that better outcomes will be achieved not by setting fixed standards, but by offering incentives through which the enterprise may *improve* safety standards. The deterrence theory is better expressed as an *incentive* theory: vicarious liability gives employers incentives to find ways to improve safety standards beyond those set by the standard of the 'reasonable person':

---

[10] Y. B. Smith (1923) 23 Col L Rev 444, 461; quoted by G. Williams, 'Liability for Independent Contractors' (1956) CLJ 180, at 196.

[11] For a similar problem caused by complex *corporate* structures (making it more difficult to identify a solvent responsible party), see H. Collins, 'Ascription of Legal Responsibility to Groups in Complex Patterns of Economic Integration' (1990) 53 MLR 731–84.

McLachlin J, *Bazley v Curry*
[1999] 2 SCR 534

Beyond the narrow band of employer conduct that attracts direct liability in negligence lies a vast area where imaginative and efficient administration and supervision can reduce the risk that the employer has introduced into the community.

Equally, and for the same reasons, the idea that an employer is in the best position to 'control' risks is not simply a covert reference to employer's 'fault'. Indeed any such reference would be most unhelpful as it would blur the distinction between vicarious and 'primary' liability. Rather, the incentive argument is general and prospective: liability on employers creates incentives to think up good ways of minimizing risks.

Loss Spreading/Deep Pockets Arguments

The third set of justifications for vicarious liability focuses on the need to compensate victims of tortious conduct. Generally, the most promising route for compensation is through the liability of the employer. At its most basic, this is no more than a deep pockets argument: where funds are available, the best solution is to attach liability to the person with the ability to pay. Introducing *insurance* into the equation makes this into a more modern argument: the risk of harm should be managed by the defendant and spread through a risk-bearing community, not placed entirely upon the vulnerable claimant. This justification was described by Atiyah in 1967 as the dominant justification for vicarious liability among North American writers; and Atiyah himself concluded that the loss-spreading argument was broadly sound:

P. S. Atiyah, *Vicarious Liability in the Law of Tort*, at 26

... it seems that in general the policy of placing the liability for the torts of the servants on their employers is broadly a sound one. It is sound simply because, by and large, it is the most convenient and efficient way of ensuring that persons injured in the course of business enterprises do not go uncompensated. Of course if all workmen insured themselves against third party risks, and if wages and salaries were slightly increased in order to allow workmen to do this, we could get on pretty well without vicarious liability at all. But this would not be so efficient or convenient a way of doing things simply because it would involve an enormous number of insurance policies instead of relatively few, with consequent increase in insurance costs... .

These issues about the practicality, rather than the existence of insurance appear to have been overlooked by the Supreme Court in *Cox v Ministry of Justice*, extracted above.

In recent case law a 'pure' loss-spreading argument has typically not been accepted. Rather, loss-spreading has been combined with the first, justice-based form of justification explored above. This approach—of combining the two—was propounded by the late John Fleming (*Law of Torts*, 9th edn, Law Book Company, 1998, 409–10) and endorsed by the Supreme Court of Canada in *Bazley v Curry*. It is almost the reverse of Atiyah's position since he doubted whether vicarious liability was in fact the most *equitable* means of spreading losses, even though he accepted that it was a convenient and efficient one. He doubted its fairness because risks often are contributed to by many people: there is no single 'risk creator'.[12] As we have seen, the Supreme Court in *Cox v Ministry of Justice* has set greater store by equity, than by loss-spreading; but this was a departure from the earlier judgment in *Various Claimants*, where both were treated as significant.

In conclusion, vicarious liability is best justified at the intersection of all three of the reasons above. Judgments often contain references to (apparently) different concerns, such as loss spreading and also 'fairness'. These justifications are not necessarily in conflict. In *Viasystems v Thermal Transfer* [2006] 2 WLR 428, Rix LJ used judicial shorthand to encapsulate this when he said that vicarious liability applies where it is 'fair, just, and convenient' for it to do so.

1.3 THE TWO LIMBS

It has long been recognized that there are two limbs to determining whether a party is vicariously liable; but the nature of each of these, and their interaction, have been progressively redefined. The first requires examination of the relationship between the defendant and the tortfeasor. Previously, in an employment-type case, it would have been asked whether there was a contract of employment; but the test is no longer so confined. The second requires assessment of the link between *this relationship*, and the tort committed: is there a sufficiently *close connection?* Previously, it would have been asked whether the tort was committed 'in the course of employment' (an expression which itself gave rise to plenty of case law). The 'course of employment' remains relevant in the sense that it is *sufficient* for the tort to be committed in the course of employment; but of course, this is no longer the sole means of showing the connection. A further change in the law is that there is now recognized to be a 'synthesis' between these two limbs:

**Lord Phillips, *Various Claimants v Catholic Child Welfare Society*
[2012] UKSC 56; [2013] 2 AC 1**

21. ... At para 37 of his judgment in this case, Hughes LJ rightly observed that the test requires a synthesis of two stages: (i) The first stage is to consider the relationship of D1 and D2 to see whether it is one that is capable of giving rise to vicarious liability. (ii) Hughes LJ identified the second stage as requiring examination of the connection between D2 and the act or omission of D1. This is not entirely correct. What is critical at the second stage is the connection that links *the relationship between D1 and D2* and the act or omission of D1, hence the synthesis of the two stages.

1.4 RELATIONSHIP BETWEEN TORTFEASOR AND DEFENDANT: FOR WHOSE TORTS?

In a case involving employment, it has traditionally been asked whether the person committing the tort was an 'employee' of the defendant. If not an employee, the person concerned

[12] P.S. Atiyah, *Vicarious Liability in the Law of Tort*, at 26.

would be an 'independent contractor'. These were the two available categories. This division remains significant, but it is no longer necessary to seek a formal relationship of 'employment', for all purposes, between the parties. Rather, the question is whether the relationship has the features which justify vicarious liability on the part of employers. Even if a tortfeasor is not an employee, their relationship may nevertheless be 'akin to employment', sufficient to give rise to vicarious liability. Such individuals are more akin to employees than to 'independent contractors'. Independent contractors have been defined not merely as non-employees, but as parties who are risk-bearers in their own right.

Employee or 'Contractor'?

Even before the most recent developments, the question of who counts as an 'employee' was not decided by reference to any single authoritative test. In the following extract, Denning LJ explains that the traditional test for employment was one of **control**; that there are nevertheless many cases where the relationship is said to be one of employment despite the absence of control, for example where the employee is skilled,[13] and that an alternative question is how far the individual is 'integrated into' the business of the 'employer'. Such discussions retain some significance in determining the nature of a relationship.

Terminological note: a contract of service is the sort of contract that is entered into between employer and employee; a **contract for services** is the sort of contract entered into when appointing an independent contractor. The distinction retains some significance even though the law has extended vicarious liability beyond the classic 'contract of service'.

Denning LJ, Stephenson, Jordan and Harrison Ltd v Macdonald & Evans [1952] 69 RPC 10

[This case] raises the troublesome question: What is the distinction between a contract of service and a contract for services? The test usually applied is whether the employer has the right to control the manner of doing the work.... But in *Cassidy v. The Ministry of Health* [1951] 2 K.B. 343, Somervell, L.J., at pp. 352–3, pointed out that that test is not universally correct. There are many contracts of service where the master cannot control the manner in which the work is to be done, as in the case of a captain of a ship. Somervell, L.J., went on to say that "One perhaps cannot get much beyond this 'Was the contract a contract "of service" within the meaning which an ordinary person would give under the words'." I respectfully agree. As my Lord has said it is almost impossible to give a precise definition of the distinction. It is often quite easy to recognise a contract of service when you see it, but very difficult to say wherein the difference lies. A ship's master, a chauffeur, and a reporter on the staff of a newspaper are all employed under a contract of service; but a ship's pilot, a taxi-man, and a newspaper contributor are employed under a contract for services. One feature which seems to me to run through the instances is that, under a contract of service, a man is employed as part of the business and his work is done as an integral part of the business; whereas under a contract for services his work, although done for the business, is not integrated into it but is only accessory to it.

13 This has been very important in respect of medical staff. In *Cassidy v Ministry of Health* [1951] 2 KB 343, vicarious liability of hospital authorities for their staff was established. Earlier in *Gold v Essex County Council* [1942] 2 KB 293, the Court of Appeal had resorted to the idea of a 'non-delegable duty' in respect of such staff (see Section 2); this is no longer necessary.

The integration test expressed in this passage did not displace the control test altogether. In *Ready Mixed Concrete v Ministry of Pensions and National Insurance* [1968] 2 QB 497, where the court was required to categorize an individual as an employee or contractor for the purposes of deciding obligation to pay national insurance contributions, MacKenna J argued that the control test was still the dominant test, but was not sufficient. Even if there is sufficient control, it must still be asked whether the terms of the contract as a whole were *consistent with* treating it as a 'contract of service'. For example:

MacKenna J, at 520–1

If a man's activities have the character of a business, and if the question is whether he is carrying on the business for himself or for another, it must be relevant to consider which of the two owns the assets ("the ownership of the tools") and which bears the financial risk ("the chance of profit," "the risk of loss"). He who owns the assets and takes the risk is unlikely to be acting as an agent or a servant.

'Dual Employment'

What happens when the employee of one enterprise is 'hired' by another enterprise for a particular task (or for a period of time), and commits a tort while so engaged? Cases answering this question have helped to reshape vicarious liability itself.

Mersey Docks and Harbour Board v Coggins [1947] AC 1 remains a significant decision. The harbour authority (the 'Board') was the general employer of a crane operator. The Board let the crane—with its operator—to a firm of stevedores. The terms of the let provided that the crane operator would be the servant of the stevedores. Through negligent operation of the crane, injury was caused to a third party.

The House of Lords held that in these circumstances, the Board remained the employer of the crane operator. The agreement as to employment between the parties was not conclusive. The crane operator would only be regarded as employed by the stevedores if there was *clear evidence* that the employment *had been transferred* (Lord Macmillan, at 13).

Lord Porter, at 17

Many factors have a bearing on the result. Who is paymaster, who can dismiss, how long the alternative service lasts, what machinery is employed, have all to be kept in mind. The expressions used in any individual case must always be considered in regard to the subject matter under discussion but amongst the many tests suggested I think that the most satisfactory, by which to ascertain who is the employer at any particular time, is to ask who is entitled to tell the employee the way in which he is to do the work upon which he is engaged. If someone other than his general employer is authorized to do this he will, as a rule, be the person liable for the employee's negligence. But it is not enough that the task to be performed should be under his control, he must also control the method of performing it. It is true that in most cases no orders as to how a job should be done are given or required: the man is left to do his own work in his own way. But the ultimate question is not what specific orders, or whether any specific orders, were given but who is entitled to give the orders as to how the work should be done. Where a man driving a mechanical device, such as a crane, is sent to perform a task, it is easier to infer that the general employer continues to control the method of performance since it is his crane and the driver remains responsible to him for its safe keeping. In the present case if the appellants' contention were to prevail, the crane driver would change his employer each time he embarked on the discharge of a fresh ship. Indeed, he might change it from day to day, without any say as to who his master should be and with all the concomitant disadvantages of uncertainty as to who should be responsible for his insurance in respect of health, unemployment and accident. I cannot think that such a conclusion is to be drawn from the facts established. I would dismiss the appeal.

In *Denham v Midland Employers' Mutual Assurance Ltd* [1955] 2 QB 437, the Court of Appeal emphasized that transfer of employment for different purposes may raise different issues. In this case, a 'borrowed' worker had been killed through the negligence of employees of the 'borrowing' company, Le Grands. Once Le Grands had compensated the widow of the deceased, should it be indemnified by its employers' liability insurer, on the basis that the deceased was, at the time, employed by Le Grands? Or should it be indemnified by its public liability insurer, whose policies excluded liability to employees? The Court of Appeal held that the contract of employment remained with the permanent employer, and it was therefore the public liability insurer who should indemnify Le Grands. But it was clear that all three judges in the Court of Appeal believed that Le Grands had 'control' over the work performed by the deceased and would have been vicariously liable for any torts he committed in the course of 'employment' with them. Transfer of employment for the purpose of vicarious liability is not dependent upon a new contract of service which would be recognized for all purposes.

The approach taken in *Denham* has influenced the more recent case law in respect of vicarious liability. Most significantly, tests applicable to one question (who should pay for the torts of a particular individual in particular circumstances?) may be different from the tests applicable in answering a different question (is the same individual an employee?).

Viasystems v Thermal Transfer [2006] 2 WLR 428 (CA)

The full significance of this decision has only gradually emerged:

Ward LJ, *E v English Province of Our Lady of Charity*
[2012] EWCA Civ 938

60   … this decision of the Court of Appeal … will, I believe, come to be seen as something of a William Ellis moment where, perhaps unwittingly, their Lordships picked up the ball and ran with it thereby creating a whole new ballgame—vicarious liability even if there is strictly no employer/employee relationship.

In both *E*, and *Various Claimants*, the approach taken in *Viasystems* was taken up and developed. In *Viasystems* itself, the claimants had contracted with the first defendants to install air conditioning. The first defendants subcontracted ducting work to the second defendants. The second defendants hired a fitter and his mate from the third defendants, to work under the supervision of an employee of the second defendants. The fitter's mate negligently crawled through a duct, fractured a fire protection sprinkler system, and caused severe flooding to the factory. Which defendant would be considered his employer for the purposes of vicarious liability?

May LJ

16 ... The inquiry should concentrate on the relevant negligent act and then ask whose responsibility it was to prevent it.

18 The relevant negligent act was Darren Strang crawling through the duct. This was a foolish mistake on the spur of the moment. I have said that a central question is: who was entitled, *and perhaps in theory obliged,* to give orders as to how the work should or should not be done? Here there is no suggestion, on the facts found by the judge, that either Mr Horsley or Mr Megson had any real opportunity to prevent Darren's momentary foolishness.... Vicarious liability is liability imposed by a policy of the law upon a party who is not personally at fault. So the core question on the facts of this case is who was entitled, and in theory, if they had had the opportunity, obliged, so to control Darren as to stop him crawling through the duct. In my judgment, the only sensible answer to that question in this case is that both Mr Megson and Mr Horsley were entitled, and in theory obliged, to stop Darren's foolishness. Mr Megson was the fitter in charge of Darren. Mr Horsley was the foreman on the spot. They were both entitled and obliged to control Darren's work, including the act which was his negligence.

According to this approach, the test for employment is the entitlement to control. May LJ adds that there is (perhaps) an implied *obligation* to control. This idea of 'obligation' might give the false impression (firmly rejected by May LJ in the sentences that followed) that the liability of the employer is in some sense dependent on a *failure* to control. The test for employment in respect of a particular act is capacity to control. Capacity to control indicates (even if rather roughly) the party on whom it is fair and useful to impose vicarious liability. But liability itself flows from a breach of duty by the employee.

May LJ concluded that both second and third defendants could be said to have an entitlement (and perhaps an obligation) to control Darren's actions. In principle therefore, they should both be regarded as employers. Before this case, there had long been an assumption that there could not be dual employment in respect of a single act. May LJ explained that this assumption stemmed from certain observations made by Littledale J in the case of *Laugher v Pointer* (1826) 5 B & C 547, and that there was no *binding* authority against dual employment for the purposes of vicarious liability. May LJ also pointed out that *Laugher* was decided at a time when the policy of the law was to avoid liability on the part of multiple parties. Given statutory provisions in the Law Reform (Contributory Negligence) Act 1945 and the Civil Liability (Contribution) Act 1978, this is clearly no longer the case. Since both defendants had sufficient control over the negligent party to be regarded as his employer, both would be vicariously liable. Their contribution under the Civil Liability (Contribution) Act 1978 was determined to be equal, a division regarded as inevitable given that neither employer could be said to be at fault.[14]

While agreeing that dual employment was established in this case, Rix LJ argued that 'control', though important, was not sufficient to act as a sole test for employment. Other

[14] Concerning the role of 'fault' in the contribution legislation, see Chapter 7.

'structural and practical considerations' might also be relevant. In this context, he suggested, one needs to ask:

> 79 ... whether or not the employee in question is so much part of the work business or organisation of both employers that it is just to make both employers answer for his negligence. What has to be recalled is that the vicarious liability in question is one which involves no fault on the part of the employer. It is a doctrine designed for the sake of the claimant imposing a liability incurred without fault because the employer is treated by law as picking up the burden of an organisational or business relationship which he has undertaken for his own benefit.

Rix LJ therefore emphasized the underlying policy rationale of vicarious liability. Most presciently, he emphasized that the crucial issue is the *relationship* undertaken by the employer for his or her own benefit, and the obligations that may flow from this.

The two different approaches in *Viasystems* (control, and integration) were further considered in *Hawley v Luminar* [2006] EWCA Civ 18. A nightclub door steward, hired to keep order at the defendant's nightclub, punched the claimant and knocked him to the ground. He suffered severe brain damage. The defendant nightclub proprietor did not hire its own door staff directly, but contracted with ASE (now in liquidation),[15] to provide appropriate staff. Was Warren, who delivered the punch, to be regarded as an employee of Luminar (for whose purposes he was kept order); of ASE (who contracted directly with him and with Luminar); or of both? The Court of Appeal held that it was Luminar—in whose business he was engaged at the time of the tort—who should be regarded as his sole employer.

Hallett LJ argued first that Luminar did not need to rely on the 'skill and expertise' of ASE in providing qualified door staff. They would be well capable of recruiting such staff themselves, and used the services of ASE 'partly as a device to get round employment laws' (at [74]). This approach has clear resonances with Ewan McKendrick's arguments for a more flexible and issue-specific approach to the definition of an employee.[16] Second, although ASE had 'undertaken to provide door staff who knew how to behave':

> ... we find it impossible to accept the further argument that responsibility for controlling this sort of behaviour fell to ASE's staff, their head doorman and the area manager. (at [75])

Rather, 'detailed control' of the door staff was exercised by Luminar's management.

Further, Warren was present at the club, 'decked out' in Luminar uniform and taking instructions from Luminar's management, for two years. To customers and passers-by, he would be taken to be an employee of Luminar.

---

15 Where the employer is in liquidation a claim may be brought against its insurer pursuant to the Third Parties (Rights against Insurers) Act 1930. In this case, important issues arose in respect of the liability of ASE's insurers; these issues concerned the meaning of 'accidental injury'. Was the injury inflicted on the claimant an 'accidental injury', covered by the policy? If not, the insurer would not be liable under the Act. The Court of Appeal decided that the injury was 'accidental' for these purposes. It was perhaps not 'accidental' from the point of view of Warren; but it was 'accidental' from the point of view of the assured party, ASE. The tortfeasor and the employer are treated as separate party for this purpose (interpretation of the insurance policy), even though the vicariously liable employer 'stands in the shoes of' the employee for other purposes (such as contribution: Chapter 7).

16 E. McKendrick, 'Vicarious Liability and Independent Contractors—A Reexamination' (1990) 53 MLR 770.

Whether the test applied was control (the approach of May LJ in *Viasystems*), or the wider question of whether Warren was 'embedded in' the business of Luminar (Rix LJ), the answer was the same: 'there has been effectively and substantially a transfer of control and responsibility from ASE to Luminar'.

Lord Phillips remarked in *Various Claimants* that this case could have been approached as a case of dual employment.

'Akin to Employment'

The approach in *Denham* and *Viasystems* suggests that the category of 'employee' is defined partly by reference to the purpose of the legal rule being applied. In *E v English Province of Our Lady of Charity* [2012] EWCA Civ 938,[17] Ward LJ suggested that in *Viasystems*, 'function triumphed over form' ([60]). In relation to the first limb, the question is subsequently not whether the tortfeasor is an employee, but whether he or she is more *akin to* an employee, or to an independent contractor. In that particular case, a Roman Catholic priest was closer in his relationship to a religious trust standing in place of the bishop to an employee, than to an independent contractor. The diocesan trust, not the priest, was the 'risk bearer'.

This result was approved by the Supreme Court in the following significant case. The Supreme Court acknowledged the influence of the Court of Appeal's analysis in *E*.

Various Claimants v Catholic Child Welfare Society [2012] UKSC 56; [2013] 2 AC 20

This case raised a question about the sharing of responsibility for acts of sexual abuse perpetrated by members of a religious teaching order. It had been determined at first instance and by the Court of Appeal that the diocesan bodies which were responsible under statute for management of the school at which the abuse took place were vicariously liable for acts of abuse which were perpetrated by various members of the order. The issue before the Supreme Court, where the tort claimants themselves played no part, was whether liability was to be shared between these bodies, and the defendant institute, which was a lay Roman Catholic order. So far as the claimants were concerned, liability on the part of the diocesan bodies sufficed. The Supreme Court concluded that although the abusers were not employees of the institute, the institute was nevertheless jointly vicariously liable with the diocesan bodies. The following passage sets out their conclusions as to the first limb.

Lord Phillips (with whom all members of the Supreme Court agreed), *Various Claimants v Catholic Child Welfare Society*

56 In the context of vicarious liability the relationship between the teaching brothers and the institute had many of the elements, and all the essential elements, of the relationship between employer and employees. (i) The institute was subdivided into a hierarchical structure and conducted its activities as if it were a corporate body. (ii) The teaching activity of the brothers was undertaken because the provincial directed the brothers to undertake it. True it is that the brothers entered into contracts of employment with the Middlesbrough

[17] The case is also often known as *JGE v English Province of Our Lady of Charity*.

defendants, but they did so because the provincial required them to do so. (iii) The teaching activity undertaken by the brothers was in furtherance of the objective, or mission, of the institute. (iv) The manner in which the brother teachers were obliged to conduct themselves as teachers was dictated by the institute's rules.

57 The relationship between the teacher brothers and the institute differed from that of the relationship between employer and employee in that: (i) The brothers were bound to the institute not by contract, but by their vows. (ii) Far from the institute paying the brothers, the brothers entered into deeds under which they were obliged to transfer all their earnings to the institute. The institute catered for their needs from these funds.

58 Neither of these differences is material. Indeed they rendered the relationship between the brothers and the institute closer than that of an employer and its employees.

59 Hughes LJ held [2010] EWCA Civ 1106 at [54] that the brothers no more acted on behalf of the institute "than any member of a professional organisation who accepts employment with that status is acting on behalf of the organisation when he does his job". I do not agree with this analysis. The business of the institute was not to train teachers or to confer status on them. It was to provide Christian teaching for boys. All members of the institute were united in that objective. The relationship between individual teacher brothers and the institute was directed to achieving that objective.

60 For these reasons I consider that the relationship between the teaching brothers and the institute was sufficiently akin to that of employer and employees to satisfy stage 1 of the test of vicarious liability.

61 There is a simpler analysis that leads to the conclusion that stage 1 was satisfied. Provided that a brother was acting for the common purpose of the brothers as an unincorporated association, the relationship between them would be sufficient to satisfy stage 1, just as in the case of the action of a member of a partnership. Had one of the brothers injured a pedestrian when negligently driving a vehicle owned by the institute in order to collect groceries for the community few would question that the institute was vicariously liable for his tort.

It has been argued that the final point made by Lord Phillips in relation to what he called a 'simpler' analysis goes too far. While there is plainly vicarious liability within a partnership, this is enshrined in statute and it cannot be too readily concluded that vicarious liability arises in the same way between members of any unincorporated association: P Morgan, 'Vicarious Liability on the Move' (2013) 129 LQR 139.

More generally, it will be seen how far function has floated free of form in the first limb. The reasons which justify vicarious liability for the torts of employees also yield the answers to the question whether a relationship is sufficiently close. That means that the test for a relationship akin to employment in relation to vicarious liability is a specific and 'tort-focused' enquiry. Employment for one purpose is not necessarily employment for another purpose.

In the next case extracted, a later Supreme Court applied the approach in *Various Claimants* in a very different context.

Cox v Ministry of Justice [2016] UKSC 10; [2016] AC 660

The claimant was injured while working as the catering manager in a prison. Her injury was caused through the negligence of a prisoner who was working on prison service pay. The

Supreme Court resolved that the Ministry of Justice was vicariously liable for the torts of the prisoner. The approach in *Various Claimants* was not confined to some special category of case, for example cases involving sexual abuse of children ([29]); and there was nothing in the particular nature of the relationship here which would lead *Various Claimants* to be distinguished. It is in no sense essential to the operation of vicarious liability that the defendant should seek to make a profit; nor do the interests of the defendant and the perpetrator have to be 'in alignment'.

Lord Reed:

32 In the present case, the requirements laid down in the *Christian Brothers* case [2013] 2 AC 1 are met. The prison service carries on activities in furtherance of its aims. The fact that those aims are not commercially motivated, but serve the public interest, is no bar to the imposition of vicarious liability. Prisoners working in the prison kitchens, such as Mr Inder, are integrated into the operation of the prison, so that the activities assigned to them by the prison service form an integral part of the activities which it carries on in the furtherance of its aims: in particular, the activity of providing meals for prisoners. They are placed by the prison service in a position where there is a risk that they may commit a variety of negligent acts within the field of activities assigned to them. That is recognised by the health and safety training which they receive. Furthermore, they work under the direction of prison staff. Mrs Cox was injured as a result of negligence by Mr Inder in carrying on the activities assigned to him. The prison service is therefore vicariously liable to her.

33 A number of arguments were advanced against that conclusion on behalf of the Ministry of Justice. First and foremost, it was argued, on a number of grounds, that the relationship between the prison service and prisoners working in a prison is fundamentally different from that between a private employer and its employees. The primary purpose of the prison service, in setting prisoners to work in prison, is not to advance any business or enterprise of the prison, but to support the rehabilitation of the prisoners as an aim of penal policy. It does not seek to make a profit, but acts in the public interest. Unlike employees, the prisoners have no interest in furthering the objectives of the prison service. Even in the *Christian Brothers* case the interests of the institute and the brothers were in alignment.

34 I am unable to accept this argument. It is true that the prison service seeks to rehabilitate prisoners, and that setting them to work is one of the means by which it attempts to achieve that objective. Rehabilitation is, however, not its only objective: it has also been an aim of penal policy since at least the 19th century to ensure, as it was put in the 1991 White Paper Custody, Care and Justice: The way ahead for the Prison Service in England and Wales (1991) (Cm 1647), para 7.22:

"that convicted prisoners contribute to the cost of their upkeep by helping with the running and maintenance of the prison and by providing goods and services in prison industries and on prison farms."

More importantly, when prisoners work in the prison kitchen, or in other workplaces such as the gardens or the laundry, they are integrated into the operation of the prison. The activities assigned to them are not merely of benefit to themselves: a benefit which is, moreover, merely potential and indirect. Their activities form part of the operation of the prison, and are of direct and immediate benefit to the prison service itself.

1.5 FROM 'COURSE OF EMPLOYMENT' TO 'CLOSE CONNECTION'

If it is established that the relationship between defendant and tortfeasor is sufficient to satisfy the first limb, it is still necessary to ask whether the particular tort committed is sufficiently closely connected to that relationship for vicarious liability to be justified. This statement of the second stage for establishing vicarious liability has only recently emerged. Traditionally, courts approached the question by asking whether the tort was committed 'in the course of employment'. This was also referred to as 'the Salmond test'.

Sir John Salmond, *Torts* (1st edn, 1907), at 83

A master is not responsible for a wrongful act done by his servant unless it is done in the course of employment. It is deemed to be so done if it is either (a) a wrongful act authorised by the master, or (b) a wrongful and unauthorised *mode* of doing some act authorised by the master.

In *Lister v Hesley Hall* [2002] 1 AC 215, a decision of the House of Lords, Lord Millett pointed out that Salmond's statement is not beyond criticism. For one thing, the possibility in (a) is not an example of vicarious liability at all: if the tort is authorized, it is the tort of the master and not of the servant, so that there is simply no need for vicarious liability to apply. A second problem is that the possibility in (b) is not easily applied to a case like *Lister*, where the tortfeasor carries out assaults for his own personal gratification. In *Lister*, Lords Steyn, Clyde, and Millett all attached importance to a further element of Salmond's exposition (at 83–4):

But a master, as opposed to the employer of an independent contractor, is liable even for acts which he has not authorised, provided they are so connected with acts which he has authorised that they may rightly be regarded as modes—although improper modes—of doing them.

They used this to justify a new approach, placing less emphasis on the idea of 'unauthorized modes of performing a duty', and more emphasis on the idea of '**close connection**' with the employment. In subsequent case law, the meaning of this change has been developed further. To understand the origins of the change, we need to consider the decision of the Supreme Court of Canada in *Bazley v Curry*, which has influenced the development of English law.

Bazley v Curry (1999) 2 SCR 534

The defendant Children's Foundation operated residential care facilities for emotionally troubled children. One of the Foundation's employees used his position to abuse children, and was ultimately convicted of sexual abuse of children including the respondent.

At first instance, Lowry J attempted to apply the Salmond test. The employees carried out intimate duties such as bathing the children and putting them to bed. He held that abusing a child during these activities could be said to be an unauthorized mode of doing the relevant authorized act. Thus, the Foundation was vicariously liable. The British Columbia Court of Appeal upheld the decision but on different grounds. Understandably, they felt that the Salmond test applied only very awkwardly to such a case. In the Supreme Court, McLachlin J agreed, adding that the decided case law was of little help. There was a need to return to first principles.

McLachlin's judgment outlines the most general issues (articulating the *policy concerns* that govern the whole of vicarious liability) and moves to the more specific (given these concerns, what *factors* help to decide the right outcome in a given case?).

[29] … two fundamental concerns underlie the imposition of vicarious liability: (1) provision of a just and practical remedy for the harm; and (2) deterrence of future harm. While different formulations of the policy interests at stake may be made (for example, loss internalization is a hybrid of the two), I believe that these two ideas usefully embrace the main policy considerations that have been advanced.

…

[34] The policy grounds supporting the imposition of vicarious liability—fair compensation and deterrence—are related. The policy consideration of deterrence is linked to the policy consideration of fair compensation based on the employer's introduction or enhancement of a risk. The introduction of the enterprise into the community with its attendant risk, in turn, implies the possibility of managing the risk to minimize the costs of the harm that may flow from it.

…

[37] … the policy purposes are served only where the wrong is so connected with the employment that it can be said that the employer has introduced the risk of the wrong (and is thereby fairly and usefully charged with its management and minimization). The question in each case is whether there is a connection or nexus between the employment enterprise and that wrong *in a material way*, not simply *to a material extent*. The Supreme Court of Canada set out some factors which would help future courts to apply this rather complex test. In terms of fair allocation of the risk and/or deterrence.

The aim is for vicarious liability to be both 'fair' and 'useful'. The relevant test for when this will be so is closeness of connection. This in turn is explained in terms of 'introduction of risk'. However, introduction of risk is not a simple idea. The connection between employment and risk must be 'salient', and the employment of the tortfeasor must have made a 'material contribution' to the risk. The question here is whether the employment enhanced the risk *in a material way*, not simply *to a material extent*. The Supreme Court of Canada set out some factors which would help future courts to apply this rather complex test. In particular:

… (3) In determining the sufficiency of the connection between the employer's creation or enhancement of the risk and the wrong complained of, subsidiary factors may be considered. These may vary with the nature of the case. When related to intentional torts, the relevant factors may include, but are not limited to, the following:

(a) the opportunity that the enterprise afforded the employee to abuse his or her power;

(b) the extent to which the wrongful act may have furthered the employer's aims (and hence be more likely to have been committed by the employee);

(c) the extent to which the wrongful act was related to friction, confrontation or intimacy inherent in the employer's enterprise;

(d) the extent of power conferred on the employee in relation to the victim;

(e) the vulnerability of potential victims to wrongful exercise of the employee's power.

Since, in this case, the wrongful acts were related to intimacy which was inherent in the employer's enterprise, and given the power of the employee over the very vulnerable victim, vicarious liability for the intentional acts of abuse could be justified.

McLachlin J then considered whether there should be an exemption from these general rules where the defendant is a non-profit organization.[18] She rejected an argument that it would not be 'fair' to place responsibility on the defendant organization because of its valuable work, which was done for the benefit of the community. Liability may be fair, she said, from the point of view of the vulnerable victim, 'as between him and the institution that enhanced the risk'. This focuses upon a comparison between the victim, and the employer who introduced the risk. Second, McLachlin J argued that deterrence (or incentive) arguments were equally valid for non-profit organizations. Third, and finally, she addressed the general loss distribution arguments:

[53] The third argument, essentially a variation on the first, is that vicarious liability will put many non-profit organizations out of business or make it difficult for them to carry on their good work.... In sum, attaching liability to charities like the Foundation will, in the long run, disadvantage society.

McLachlin J rejected this distributive argument, arguing that it smacks of 'crass and unsubstantiated utilitarianism' (at [54]). Yet, 'utilitarian' argument *in combination with fairness* was earlier treated as a persuasive reason for making a blameless defendant liable. This tends to illustrate Atiyah's point that where not all the justifying factors are present, there will be difficult questions of balance.

The English Case Law from *Lister* to *Various Claimants*

Lister v Hesley Hall [2001] UKHL 22; [2002] 1 AC 215

The claimants had been resident in a boarding house attached to a school owned and managed by the defendants. The warden of the boarding house, who was employed by the defendants, systematically abused children within his care. A claim that there was primary liability on the part of the defendants for their own negligence in the selection or supervision of the warden was rejected at first instance. The first instance judge also rejected a claim that the defendants could be vicariously liable for the acts of abuse committed by the warden, holding that these could not be said to come within the Salmond test for 'course of employment'. The judge nevertheless held that the defendants could be vicariously liable for the warden's *failure to report* his own acts and/or to report the harm suffered by the children, since his duties included these aspects of their welfare. This was, clearly, an artificial argument designed to evade the restrictions of the Salmond test. The Court of Appeal rejected

---

[18] Non-state non-profit defendants may raise different issues from public authority defendants, particularly if one focuses on *distributive justifications*.

it and held that there was no vicarious liability at all in this case. Both courts were bound by the earlier decision in *Trotman v North Yorkshire County Council* [1999] LGR 584 (CA).

In *Trotman*, the deputy headmaster of a special school sexually assaulted a pupil with whom he shared a bedroom on a foreign holiday. Butler-Sloss LJ applied the Salmond test, and concluded that the assault could not be said to be a mode of carrying out the teacher's duties. Rather, it was 'a negation of the duty of the council to look after children for whom it was responsible' (at 591).

The House of Lords in *Lister* overruled *Trotman v North Yorkshire CC* and held the defendants vicariously liable. Influenced by *Bazley v Curry*, the judgments set vicarious liability in a new direction by rephrasing the test for 'course of employment' in terms of 'close connection'. That test has been further developed in subsequent decisions. Although the decision was unanimous, there are important variations between the judgments. Lord Steyn's may be called the leading judgment in that Lord Hutton concurred with his reasoning as did Lord Hobhouse with the addition of some further observations. (As we will see some of these further observations tend to cloud the general picture.) Lord Millett's judgment has been the most influential, and is incompatible with that of Lord Hobhouse.

Lord Steyn, *Lister v Hesley Hall*

17 It is easy to accept the idea that where an employee acts for the benefit of his employer, or intends to do so, that is strong evidence that he was acting in the course of his employment. But until the decision of the House of Lords in *Lloyd v Grace, Smith & Co* [1912] AC 716 it was thought that vicarious liability could only be established if such requirements were satisfied. This was an overly restrictive view and hardly in tune with the needs of society. In *Lloyd v Grace, Smith & Co* it was laid to rest by the House of Lords. A firm of solicitors were held liable for the dishonesty of their managing clerk who persuaded a client to transfer property to him and then disposed of it for his own advantage. The decisive factor was that the client had been invited by the firm to deal with their managing clerk. This decision was a breakthrough: it finally established that vicarious liability is not necessarily defeated if the employee acted for his own benefit. On the other hand, an intense focus on the connection between the nature of the employment and the tort of the employee became necessary.

The Relevant Test?

Lord Steyn was directly influenced by *Bazley v Curry*. He did not state in very clear terms what the content of the 'close connection' case would be; but he did state that the warden's acts of abuse were 'inextricably interwoven' with his duties. In *Lister* the defendants ran the school on a commercial basis, but there is no indication that this was considered relevant.

Lord Hobhouse rejected the approach in *Bazley v Curry*. His expression of the relevant test seems to depart in certain important respects from the idea that in vicarious liability, the employee commits a tort but on grounds of justice and practicality, liability is imposed on the employer. Lord Hobhouse said that *the defendant itself* owed a duty to the children to guard their welfare since it had *assumed responsibility to them*. Hence the relationship between defendant (school) and claimant (child) is all-important. This duty the school had 'entrusted to' the warden, taking into account the terms of his employment. Thus, the *duty breached* is owed by the school: '[T]he employers' liability to the plaintiff is also that of a tortfeasor' (at 55). This interpretation makes *Lister* a case of liability for the breach of a primary duty owed by the school, through the conduct of the employee to whom that duty had been entrusted. If we want to maintain any clarity in this area of law, this is better not referred to as 'vicarious liability'. It is essentially a non-delegable duty of the sort recognized by the UK Supreme Court in *Woodland v Essex*, extracted in the next section.

Lord Millett's approach was broader than the one adopted by the Supreme Court of Canada in *Bazley* and did not require close analysis of the precise duties of the employee. Instead he embraced the idea of liability for risks that are reasonably incidental to employment. Lord Millett's approach is drawn directly from ideas of loss distribution and enterprise risk, and has been very influential in subsequent case law.

Which Tort?

Which tort formed the basis of liability in *Lister v Hesley Hall*? Clearly, the warden's acts amounted to a deliberate assault or 'trespass to the person' (Chapter 2). Lord Millett made clear (para [84]) that on his approach, where the employer 'stands in the shoes' of the tortfeasor, the employer's vicarious liability is *liability for the assaults*, and not for a negligent failure to take care of the boys. Lord Hobhouse as we have explained regarded the duty in this case as owed by the employer, and it seems that this must be a duty to take proper care of the vulnerable children. On his approach, *Lister* would be a case in negligence, despite the deliberate nature of the acts that breached the duty. Lord Steyn's judgment is quite unclear on this point, although he did expressly reserve judgment (at [29]) on the question of whether there might be an alternative action for the warden's failure to report his own wrongdoing and its effect on the children. This alternative action would, clearly, be in negligence.

The House of Lords seems not to have considered that the identification of the relevant tort would affect the limitation period which would apply to the action (Chapter 7). Subsequently, the fundamental importance of this issue (which tort?) became obvious. The House of Lords has now removed this difficulty, in *A v Hoare*. But at the same time, it has also made clear that on facts like those in *Lister* the most appropriate action is in respect of the abuse itself, and is therefore an action in trespass for which the employer may be vicariously liable.

Developing the *Lister* Test

In *Dubai Aluminium v Salaam* [2003] 2 AC 366, the House of Lords adopted a passage (at [65]) in Atiyah's *Vicarious Liability* (p 171), which had also been cited by Lord Millett in *Lister v Hesley Hall* (at [107]):

The master ought to be liable for all those torts which can fairly be regarded as reasonably incidental risks to the type of business he carries on.

In the case of criminal wrongdoing, there is vicarious liability if *the risk of wrongdoing can fairly be said to be reasonably incidental to the employer's business*. This is drawn directly from the 'enterprise risk' justification, and is not qualified by the artificial idea of 'material contribution to risk' employed in the Canadian decision of *Bazley v Curry*. In *Dubai Aluminium* itself, vicarious liability extended to a firm of solicitors where a fraud was committed by one individual partner. This was not an employment case since a partner is not an employee, partnership representing a special form of relationship defined in the Partnership

Act 1890. Nevertheless, the applicable principles are the same as those applying to employees: the question is whether the fraud was perpetrated 'in the ordinary course of the firm's business'.[19]

The Developing Law: Close Connection between What and What?

The cases above did not focus particularly clearly on the question of *what* must be connected to the tort. In the most recent cases, a significant development has been elaboration of this point. It is now recognized that while acts done in the course of employment (the traditional test) will trigger vicarious liability, beyond this, the relevant connection is between *the relationship between tortfeasor and defendant, and the commission of the tort.*

Various Claimants v Catholic Child Welfare Society

Lord Hope has said that the growing recognition of widespread sexual abuse of children 'has presented the law of vicarious liability, once relatively well settled, with new challenges'.[20] The response to that challenge is particularly exemplified by the Supreme Court's decision in *Various Claimants*. We have already extracted this case, and outlined its context, in relation to the first limb. Earlier, we explained how the Supreme Court identified the relationship between the two limbs. The following extract relates to the close connection test at the second limb.

Lord Phillips, *Various Claimants v Catholic Child Welfare Society* [2012] UKSC 56; [2013] 2 AC 1

86 Starting with the Canadian authorities a common theme can be traced through most of the cases to which I have referred. Vicarious liability is imposed where a defendant, whose relationship with the abuser put it in a position to use the abuser to carry on its business or to further its own interests, has done so in a manner which has created or significantly enhanced the risk that the victim or victims would suffer the relevant abuse. The essential closeness of connection between the relationship between the defendant and the tortfeasor and the acts of abuse thus involves a strong causative link.

87 These are the criteria that establish the necessary "close connection" between relationship and abuse. I do not think that it is right to say that creation of risk is simply a policy consideration and not one of the criteria. Creation of risk is not enough, of itself, to give rise to vicarious liability for abuse but it is always likely to be an important element in the facts that give rise to such liability.

This case

88 In this case both the necessary relationship between the brothers and the institute and the close connection between that relationship and the abuse committed at the school have been made out.

[19] Here the firm of solicitors had settled the claim against them and therefore *sought* a finding of vicarious liability; this would enable them to pursue other participants in the fraud for a contribution (Chapter 7).
[20] Lord Hope, 'Tailoring the Law on Vicarious Liability' (2013) LQR 514.

89 The relationship between the brothers and the institute was much closer to that of employment than the relationship between the priest and the bishop in *E's case* [2013] QB 722. The institute was subdivided into a hierarchical structure and conducted its activities as if it were a corporate body. The brothers were subject to the directions as to their employment and the general supervision of the provincial, their superior within that hierarchical structure. But the relationship was not simply one akin to that of employer and employee. The business and mission of the institute was the common business and mission of every brother who was a member of it.

90 That business was the provision of a Christian education to boys. It was to achieve that mission that the brothers joined and remained members of the institute.

91 The relationship between the institute and the brothers enabled the institute to place the brothers in teaching positions and, in particular, in the position of headmaster at St William's. The standing that the brothers enjoyed as members of the institute led the managers of that school to comply with the decisions of the institute as to who should fill that key position. It is particularly significant that the institute provided the headmasters, for the running of the school was largely carried out by the headmasters. The brother headmaster was almost always the director of the institute's community, living on the school premises. There was thus a very close connection between the relationship between the brothers and the institute and the employment of the brothers as teachers in the school.

92 Living cloistered on the school premises were vulnerable boys. They were triply vulnerable. They were vulnerable because they were children in a school; they were vulnerable because they were virtually prisoners in the school; and they were vulnerable because their personal histories made it even less likely that if they attempted to disclose what was happening to them they would be believed. The brother teachers were placed in the school to care for the educational and religious needs of these pupils. Abusing the boys in their care was diametrically opposed to those objectives but, paradoxically, that very fact was one of the factors that provided the necessary close connection between the abuse and the relationship between the brothers and the institute that gives rise to vicarious liability on the part of the latter.

93 There was a very close connection between the brother teachers' employment in the school and the sexual abuse that they committed, or must for present purposes be assumed to have committed. There was no Criminal Records Bureau at the time, but the risk of sexual abuse was recognised, as demonstrated by the prohibition on touching the children in the chapter in the rule dealing with chastity. No doubt the status of a brother was treated by the managers as an assurance that children could safely be entrusted to his care. The placement of brother teachers in St William's, a residential school in the precincts of which they also resided, greatly enhanced the risk of abuse by them if they had a propensity for such misconduct.

94 This is not a borderline case. It is one where it is fair, just and reasonable, by reason of the satisfaction of the relevant criteria, for the institute to share with the Middlesbrough defendants vicarious liability for the abuse committed by the brothers. I would allow this appeal.

In *Mohamud v Wm Morrison Supermarkets plc* [2016] AC 677, counsel for the claimant sought to persuade the Supreme Court to depart from the 'close connection' test, and to adopt a test based upon whether a reasonable observer would have considered the employee to be acting in the capacity of a 'representative of' the employer at the time the tort was committed. The Supreme Court defended the 'close connection' test, but at the same time, reversing the Court of Appeal, found it sufficiently flexible for the claimant to succeed.

Mohamud v Wm Morrison Supermarkets plc [2016] UKSC 11; [2016] AC 677

The claimant asked at the sales kiosk of a supermarket petrol station whether he could print some documents stored on a USB stick. He was subjected to racist, abusive and violent language by an employee of the defendant. The employee then followed the claimant to his car and subjected him to a violent physical attack. The motive was assumed to be racist and unconnected to the interests of the defendant employer. The Supreme Court argued that there was a close connection between the employment of the tortfeasor, and the attack on the claimant. Responding to enquiries was part of the employee's work, and there was an 'unbroken sequence of events' between his initial (albeit racist and abusive) response, and the physical assault. His conduct was thus sufficiently connected with the role entrusted to him.

Lord Toulson JSC traced this approach to the early days of vicarious liability, and to a number of eighteenth-century judgments of Holt CJ. Lord Toulson cited a number of decisions of Holt CJ in relation to negligence; fires; and deceit; and continued:

Lord Toulson JSC, *Mohamud v Wm Morrison Supermarkets plc*

15 Holt CJ gave the same explanation for the development of the principle in *Sir Robert Wayland's Case* (1707) 3 Salk 234:

"the master at his peril ought to take care what servant he employs; and it is more reasonable that he should suffer for the cheats of his servant than strangers and tradesmen."

'At his peril' is the language used to denote strict liability, for example under *Rylands v Fletcher* (Chapter 11): the risk that the employee is not honest more justly falls on the employer than on strangers.

On this basis, employers take the risk, so to speak, that the employees to whom they entrust work may prove to be 'bad eggs', so long as their wrongdoing is sufficiently closely connected to the jobs they are hired to do. Moreover, this is thought to express social justice; although the nature of the justice thereby achieved is not much spelled out beyond the sentiment of Holt CJ expressed above.

How did these principles apply to the present case?

Toulson CJ

The present case

47 In the present case it was Mr Khan's job to attend to customers and to respond to their inquiries. His conduct in answering the claimant's request in a foul-mouthed way and ordering him to leave was inexcusable but within the field of activities assigned to him. What happened thereafter was an unbroken sequence of events. It was argued by the respondent and accepted by the judge that there ceased to be any significant connection between Mr Khan's employment and his behaviour towards the claimant onto the forecourt. I disagree for two reasons. First, I do not consider that it is right to regard him as having metaphorically taken off his uniform the moment he stepped from behind the counter. He was following up on what he had said to the claimant. It was a seamless episode. Secondly, when Mr Khan followed the claimant back to his car and opened the front passenger door, he again told the claimant in threatening words that he was never to come back to petrol station. This was not something personal between them; it was an order to keep away from his employer's premises, which he reinforced by violence. In giving such an order he was purporting to act about his employer's business. It was a gross abuse of his position, but it was in connection with the business in which he was employed to serve customers. His employers entrusted him with that position and it is just that as between them and the claimant, they should be held responsible for their employee's abuse of it.

Too much might be made of the notion of an 'unbroken sequence of events' in the above extract, with its possible implication of a causal link. The connection intended is evaluative: the key point is that the employee's actions continued to be connected with his employment, and were judged not to have become entirely personal despite his 'gross abuse' of his position.

2. NON-DELEGABLE DUTIES

A 'non-delegable duty' cannot be passed on by entrusting its performance to others, whether employees or contractors. If the duty is breached, then even if the defendant has taken all due care, liability will attach to the defendant not vicariously, but as tortfeasor. The duty may be breached with or without fault on anyone's part.

The most well-established non-delegable duties in English tort law are those owed by an employer to his or her employees. At common law, these include duties to provide a safe place and system of work, with competent staff and safe equipment: *Wilsons and Clyde Coal v English* [1938] AC 57; *McDermid v Nash Dredging* [1987] AC 906. According to Williams,[21] these duties owe their origin to a gap in the protection offered by vicarious liability. Under the 'doctrine of common employment' (which has not formed any part of English law since the last traces of it were abolished in 1948),[22] it was considered that an employee could not be liable for careless injury to an employee of the same master. There could be no vicarious liability for servants' failure to discharge their duties to fellow employees in respect of safety. It has been convincingly suggested that outside the tort of negligence, such duties pose little or no problem. It is only the familiarity of the fault standard in negligence which makes them appear anomalous.[23] Perhaps then we should understand as chiefly applicable to negligence the problem pointed out by Williams, namely that there are no clear principles on which to determine which duties are delegable, which non-delegable. Williams traces this problem to the following statement of Lord Blackburn:

Lord Blackburn, *Dalton v Angus* **(1881) 6 App Cas 740, at 829**

a person causing something to be done, the doing of which casts on him a duty, cannot escape from the responsibility attaching on him of seeing that duty performed by delegating it to a contractor.

21 'Liability for Independent Contractors' (1956) CLJ 180.
22 Law Reform (Personal Injuries) Act 1948.
23 R. Stevens, 'Non-delegable Duties and Vicarious Liability' in J. Neyers et al, *Emerging Issues in Tort Law* (Hart Publishing, 2007) 331–68.

Glanville Williams, 'Liability for Independent Contractors' (1956) CLJ 180, at 181

… [Lord Blackburn's] doctrine of the nondelegability of the legal duty cannot have been intended to apply to every duty. He did not, however, say to which duties it did apply. The use made of the dictum in later cases has advanced it to the rank of one of the leading sophistries in the law of tort. Since the judge is left to determine, within the limits of precedent, whether a particular duty is non-delegable or not, the dictum gives him freedom to decide the case as he wishes, while presenting him with a verbal "reason" that conceals his real motivation; and sometimes perhaps it operates as a hypnotic formula inducing the judge to think that he is required to reach a particular conclusion when in fact he is not.

A sceptical view of non-delegable duties as a mere 'device' may be reinforced by the case of *Honeywill & Stein v Larkin* [1934] 1 KB 191, which stated that a person undertaking an 'extra-hazardous activity' will be subject to a non-delegable duty. In that case, it was held that the act of taking a photograph in a theatre with magnesium powder amounted to such an 'extra hazardous' or dangerous act, that the person hiring the photographer could be liable where the act was done without due care. Williams argued that this decision was justified neither in terms of principle, since there was nothing so special about this undertaking that would truly set it apart as exceptional, nor in terms of policy. For the most part, cinema owners would be expected to carry insurance policies covering fire, so that the need for liability was not established.

In *Biffa Waste* [2008] EWCA Civ 1238, which was concerned with welding activities at a recycling plant, *Honeywill* was confined to its facts:

85 At the beginning of this judgment we described the bases of liability in question in this appeal as exceptional. Indeed, in our judgment, the principle in *Honeywill* is anomalous. It is important that it is understood that its application is truly exceptional.

Woodland v Swimming Teachers' Association [2013] UKSC 66

The decision of the UK Supreme Court in this case, recognizing a new non-delegable duty on the part of schools towards pupils in relation to certain activities outside their immediate control and away from school premises, is highly significant.

The claimant, a child, had suffered very severe injuries during a swimming lesson arranged by her school. The lessons were conducted on premises not controlled by the school; and were provided not by school staff but by professional swimming instructors who were independent contractors. Litigation was initially commenced against the swimming instructors, and it appears that there was an admission of liability. Interim payments were made. However, a change of liability insurer on the part of the instructors led to withdrawal of the admission, so that liability became contested some years after the liability question appeared to have been settled.[24] It was against this background that the claimants decided to commence an action against the education authority. Since the authority neither employed the swimming teachers whose negligence is in issue, nor controlled the premises on which the lessons took place, the claimants argued that a non-delegable duty was owed. On this preliminary issue, the Supreme Court ruled for the claimant.

---

[24] The process of litigation is set out by the Court of Appeal in *Woodland v Stopford and Others* [2011] EWCA Civ 266, and described as 'deeply depressing'.

The judgment of Lord Sumption JSC contains an appraisal of the existing authorities on non-delegable duties, and a restatement of the applicable principles. Lord Sumption was concerned solely with what he identified as a particular category of non-delegable duty, which he identified as having its origins in the law of nuisance.[25]

Lord Sumption JSC, *Woodland v Swimming Teachers Association* [2013] UKSC 66

7 The second category of non-delegable duty is, however, directly in point. It comprises cases where the common law imposes a duty on the defendant which has three critical characteristics. First, it arises not from the negligent character of the act itself but because of an antecedent relationship between the defendant and the claimant. Second, the duty is a positive or affirmative duty to protect a particular class of persons against a particular class of risks, and not simply a duty to refrain from acting in a way that foreseeably causes injury. Third, the duty is by virtue of that relationship personal to the defendant. The work required to perform such a duty may well be delegable, and usually is. But the duty itself remains the defendant's. Its delegation makes no difference to his legal responsibility for the proper performance of a duty which is in law his own. In these cases, the defendant is assuming a liability analogous to that assumed by a person who contracts to do work carefully. The contracting party will normally be taken to contract that the work will be done carefully by whomever he may get to do it: see *Photo Production Ltd v Securicor Transport Ltd* [1980] AC 827, 848 (Lord Diplock). The analogy with public services is often close, especially in the domain of hospital treatment in the National Health Service or education at a local education authority school, where only the absence of consideration distinguishes them from the private hospital or the fee-paying school performing the same functions under contract. In the law of tort, the same consequence follows where a statute imposes on the defendant personally a positive duty to perform some function or to carry out some operation, but he performs that duty by entrusting the work to some one else for whose proper performance he is legally responsible. In *Morris v C W Martin & Sons Ltd* [1966] 1 QB 716, 725–728, Lord Denning MR analysed the liability of a non-contractual bailee for reward in similar terms, as depending on his duty to procure that proper care was exercised in the custody of the goods bailed.

The existing relationship referred to in this extract was identified as generally arising from an 'assumption of responsibility', 'imputed to the defendant by virtue of his relationship with the defendant' (11]). Assumptions of responsibility in general are explored in relation to duties of care in negligence in Chapter 6. Lord Sumption expressed the general principles on which a non-delegable duty will be said to arise in the following terms:

Lord Sumption, *Woodland v Swimming Teachers Association*

In what circumstances will a non-delegable duty arise?

22 The main problem about this area of the law is to prevent the exception from eating up the rule. Non-delegable duties of care are inconsistent with the fault-based principles

---

25 See further the discussion of non-delegable duties and *Rylands v Fletcher* in Chapter 11.

on which the law of negligence is based, and are therefore exceptional. The difference between an ordinary duty of care and a non-delegable duty must therefore be more than a question of degree. In particular, the question cannot depend simply on the degree of risk involved in the relevant activity. The ordinary principles of tortious liability are perfectly capable of answering the question what duty is an appropriate response to a given level of risk.

23 In my view, the time has come to recognise that Lord Greene MR in *Gold's case* [1942] 2 KB 293 and Denning LJ in *Cassidy's case* [1951] 2 KB 343 were correct in identifying the underlying principle, and while I would not necessarily subscribe to every dictum in the Australian cases, in my opinion they are broadly correct in their analysis of the factors that have given rise to non-delegable duties of care. If the highway and hazard cases are put to one side, the remaining cases are characterised by the following defining features: (1) The claimant is a patient or a child, or for some other reason is especially vulnerable or dependent on the protection of the defendant against the risk of injury. Other examples are likely to be prisoners and residents in care homes. (2) There is an antecedent relationship between the claimant and the defendant, independent of the negligent act or omission itself, (i) which places the claimant in the actual custody, charge or care of the defendant, and (ii) from which it is possible to impute to the defendant the assumption of a positive duty to protect the claimant from harm, and not just a duty to refrain from conduct which will foreseeably damage the claimant. It is characteristic of such relationships that they involve an element of control over the claimant, which varies in intensity from one situation to another, but is clearly very substantial in the case of schoolchildren. (3) The claimant has no control over how the defendant chooses to perform those obligations, ie whether personally or through employees or through third parties. (4) The defendant has delegated to a third party some function which is an integral part of the positive duty which he has assumed towards the claimant; and the third party is exercising, for the purpose of the function thus delegated to him, the defendant's custody or care of the claimant and the element of control that goes with it. (5) The third party has been negligent not in some collateral respect but in the performance of the very function assumed by the defendant and delegated by the defendant to him.

It is plain that these principles are capable of expanding the liability of public authorities beyond accepted bounds—running contrary to familiar policy objectives outlined in Chapter 6. Lord Sumption recognized the issue, defending the development of non-delegable duties but emphasizing the need to control them:

Lord Sumption, *Woodland v Swimming Teachers Association*

25 The courts should be sensitive about imposing unreasonable financial burdens on those providing critical public services. A non-delegable duty of care should be imputed to schools only so far as it would be fair, just and reasonable to do so. But I do not accept that any unreasonable burden would be cast on them by recognising the existence of a non-delegable duty on the criteria which I have summarised above.

Finally, Lord Sumption and the other members of the Supreme Court concluded that for present purposes, it could be accepted that a non-delegable duty was owed.

Armes v Nottinghamshire County Council [2016] 2 WLR 1455

The application of *Woodland* was considered by the Court of Appeal in *Armes v Nottinghamshire County Council* [2015] EWCA Civ 1139.[26] The case raised the question of whether a non-delegable duty was owed by a local authority to a child in care who had been placed with foster carers, where those carers were abusive. Members of the Court agreed that no such duty was owed, but differed in their reasoning. Tomlinson LJ and Burnett LJ focused primarily on the nature of the duties, and concluded that the local authority has a duty to protect a child from harm; and a statutory duty to provide accommodation and maintenance. For Tomlinson LJ, the statutory duty was performed, not delegated, when the child was placed with a family, so that there was no relevant non-delegable duty in this case. Burnett J emphasized that the authority was under a positive duty to protect, rather than a negative duty not to assault, and it made little sense to speak of delegating such a negative duty. It was significant that no case could be found in which there was a non-delegable duty in relation to an assault, and the position against such duties which was taken by the High Court of Australia in *NSW v Lepore* (2003) 195 ALR 412 was considered 'powerful persuasive authority' ([35]).[27] As Burnett LJ put it:

> **34** I find it very difficult to imagine circumstances in which a court could conclude that there was no vicarious liability for an assault but then go on to fix a defendant with liability for breach of a non-delegable duty not to assault the claimant. If, applying the principles summarized in the *Catholic Church Welfare Society* case (with their carefully calibrated policy considerations), there is no vicarious liability for an assault upon a child in care, I do not consider that the common law should impose liability via this different route.

Black LJ on the other hand determined the case primarily on the basis that it would not be 'fair, just and reasonable', as prescribed by Lord Sumption in *Woodland*, to impose such a duty and, in fact, that it may be contrary to the interests of many children in care, weighing against the placing of children with families, rather than in the Council's own care.

3. OTHER PRIMARY DUTIES: CARE IN SELECTION AND SUPERVISION

There are certain circumstances in which a duty is clearly owed to exercise care in the selection of contractors. As an example, an occupier may discharge its duty to keep visitors reasonably safe by entrusting work to competent contractors, provided reasonable care is taken to select the contractor: Occupiers' Liability Act 1957, section 2(4)(b), extracted in Chapter 12. The benefit of this provision will also be lost if the occupier does not take reasonable steps (*if any such steps are reasonably required*) to check that the contractor's work is appropriately done. In *Gwilliam v West Herts Hospital NHS Trust* [2003] QB 443, the Court of Appeal decided that this duty was merely 'illustrative' of a general obligation to

---

26 At the time of going to press, this decision was subject to an appeal to the Supreme Court. Readers should carefully check for updates.

27 For an argument which would justify strict liability in *Lepore*, see C Beurmann, 'Conferred Authority Strict Liability and Institutional Child Sexual Abuse' (2015) 37 *Syd L Rev* 113.

exercise due care in the selection and (where appropriate) the supervision of contractors. In that case, there was a duty to select competent contractors for the supply and operation of a 'Splat-wall' at a fund-raising event. In *Bottomley v Todmorden Cricket Club* [2003] EWCA Civ 1575, the Court of Appeal said that the same duty to select contractors with care arose at common law, so that it also applied to a case brought in negligence.

Duties to Supervise Employees

Even where injury is caused through the tortious conduct of an *employee*, there may be scope for liability of the employer in accordance with a primary duty. Sometimes, such primary liability may simply be an alternative to vicarious liability. However, breach of a primary duty to select and supervise employees with care may become important, for example, if the injury is not caused 'in the course of employment', so that it is outside the reach of vicarious liability.

4. CONCLUSIONS

i. The law of vicarious liability has undergone significant change and expansion since the decision in *Lister v Hesley Hall*. In the current law, there is a greater emphasis on policy concerns both in determining whether the relationship between tortfeasor and defendant is sufficiently close to give rise to vicarious liability (the first limb); and in addressing the question of whether the tort is sufficiently close to the employment or other relationship (the second limb). Therefore, the *function* of vicarious liability is treated as directly related to the 'tests' to be applied. Curiously perhaps, the courts have begun to create and develop workable tests despite lack of full agreement as to what the underlying functions are. There are at least a recognized and familiar set of functions which, in combination if not individually, are understood to have justified expansion in the law.

ii. Where the second 'limb' of vicarious liability is concerned, commitment to the 'close connection' test has been maintained in the face of recent challenge. Interestingly, the test has not only been defended in functional terms, but also by reference to a sense of 'fairness' which can be traced at least to the eighteenth century. Overall, vicarious liability is set on a trajectory of expansion which is justified by a range of different considerations; but there are of course still cases which will result in no liability. Doubtless, the location of the boundary between liability and no liability will continue to provide challenges.

iii. The development of a new instance of 'non-delegable duty' in relation to a school and its pupils is also striking, and defining the boundaries and rationale of this duty will again no doubt make for interesting case law in future. At present, the limits of the non-delegable duty are uncertain and debatable. It is possible that the UK Supreme Court will follow the High Court of Australia in confining the newly recognized category of duty to cases of negligence rather than intentional wrongdoing; or it may be that the decisive factor will be identified as lying in assumption of responsibility (itself a difficult concept to pin down, as we saw in Chapter 6); or—as will now be familiar from other areas of the law of tort—in the specific policy issues arising in a particular context. In any event, while vicarious liability has recently coalesced around some relatively easily stated tests, notwithstanding the complexity of their underlying rationale, it is likely that the development of non-delegable duties following *Woodland* will prove to be highly context-specific.

FURTHER READING

Atiyah, P. S., *Vicarious Liability in the Law of Tort* (London: Butterworths, 1967).

Beuermann, C., 'Vicarious Liability and Conferred Authority Strict Liability' (2013) 20 Torts LJ 265.

Brodie, D., 'Enterprise Liability: Justifying Vicarious Liability' (2007) 27 OJLS 493–508.

Giliker, P., 'Non-delegable Duties and Institutional Liability for Hospital Staff: Fair, Just and Reasonable?' (2017) JPN, forthcoming.

Giliker, P., 'Vicarious Liability Beyond the Contract of Service' (2012) 28 PN 291.

Hope, Lord, 'Tailoring the Law on Vicarious Liability' (2013) 129 LQR 514.

McKendrick, E., 'Vicarious Liability and Independent Contractors—A Reexamination' (1990) 53 MLR 770.

Morgan, P., 'Recasting Vicarious Liability' (2012) 71 CLJ 615.

Morgan, P., 'Vicarious Liability on the Move' (2013) 129 LQR 139.

Morgan, P., 'Certainty in Vicarious Liability: A Quest for a Chimaera?' (2016) CLJ 202.

Morgan, P., 'Fostering, Vicarious Liability, Non-Delegable Duties, and Intentional Torts' (2016) 132 LQR 399.

Murphy, J., 'The Liability Bases of the Common Law Non-Delegable Duties—A Reply to Christian Witting' (2007) 30 UNSWLJ 86–102.

O'Sullivan, J., 'The Sins of the Father—Vicarious Liability Extended' (2012) 71 CLJ 485.

Vines, P., 'Schools' Responsibility for Teachers' Sexual Assault: Non-delegable Duty and Vicarious Liability' [2003] MULR 22.

Williams, G., 'Liability for Independent Contractors' [1956] CLJ 180.

Witting, C., 'Breach of the Non-Delegable Duty: Defending Limited Strict Liability in Tort' (2006) 33 UNSWLJ 33–60.

Yap, P. J., 'Enlisting Close Connections: A Matter of Course for Vicarious Liability?' (2008) 28 LS 197–214.

PART V

NUISANCE AND DUTIES RELATING TO LAND

This Part of the book is concerned with duties imposed upon occupiers of land. Private nuisance is a tort with a lengthy history, which remedies interferences with the use and enjoyment of neighbours' land. It is certainly stricter than the tort of negligence, and typically deals with rather different interferences. In recent years, the trend has been for the ambit of the tort to be confined, minimizing overlap with negligence but allowing clearer recognition of a distinct and stricter liability. Separate from private nuisance is an action in public nuisance, which is a criminal offence but may be actionable as a tort in certain circumstances. This action focuses not on use and enjoyment of land but on interference with the life and health of the public. Public nuisance has been close to absorption into private nuisance, but the Court of Appeal has affirmed its continuing relevance to claims for personal injury where public health is affected, which are beyond the reach of private nuisance.

Rylands v Fletcher is an action of strict liability applying to one-off escapes from the defendant's land. It overlaps uncomfortably with the tort of negligence and perhaps as a result it has proved difficult to retain the separate identity of this cause of action. This certainly does not indicate that strict liability has no place in modern tort law (as the following Parts of the book attest). *Rylands* itself may be seen as a variation on the theme of liability for the acts of contractors, described in terms of 'non-delegable duties' (explored in Chapter 9).

Private nuisance and *Rylands* liability both involve duties owed by occupiers to people who are outside the land they occupy. In Chapter 12, we explore the rather different duties owed by occupiers to those who enter on to their land, whether 'visitor' or 'trespasser'. These duties are now defined by statute and are analogous to negligence duties. They are however distinct in that they relate specifically to the state of the premises, rather than to activities carried out; and there are some variations from the usual approach to negligence duties. Warnings, for example, may be required where there is a hazard due to the state of the premises. Courts have been eager to keep the duties of occupiers within limits, and this is an area where the idea of individual responsibility on the part of risk-takers has been particularly emphasized. Starting with responsibility on the part of adults in respect of risks that they ought to appreciate, the courts have now extended the same thinking to children, arguing that occupiers should not have to bear liability for all dangers present on land.

10

NUISANCE

CENTRAL ISSUES

i) There are two forms of action in nuisance, namely **public** and **private** nuisance. A private nuisance may be defined as an unreasonable interference with use and enjoyment of land or with some right over, or in connection with it. Public nuisance by contrast is a crime and is actionable by the Attorney-General in the public interest. It extends to a far wider range of interests than private nuisance, including especially public health.

ii) The basis of liability in private nuisance is not straightforward. But, despite some confusing dicta in cases where nuisance and negligence overlap, the tort is clearly very different from negligence. The main concern is not the quality of the defendant's conduct unless this is relevant for some particular reason (for example, in the defence of statutory authority). The main concern is the reasonableness and lawfulness of interference with the claimant's interests in land. A nuisance is an unlawful interference with such interests.

iii) Cases of overlap between negligence and nuisance have caused particular difficulty. One category of overlap arises where actual damage is caused by a nuisance which has not been created by the defendant, but which has arisen on land occupied by the defendant. Beyond this, higher court decisions have minimized the overlap between negligence and nuisance, by removing cases of personal injury from the whole area of private nuisance, and by ensuring that only those with an interest in land may bring an action.

iv) The relationship between private and public interests has always been a key concern surrounding nuisance, and it is now even more pertinent. The influence of the Human Rights Act 1998 has of course added a new element to such issues. In addition, the Supreme Court has recently considered the role of community or public interest in nuisance actions, particularly in relation to remedies.

1. PRIVATE NUISANCE

1.1 MAKING SENSE OF PRIVATE NUISANCE

Private nuisance has a longer history than negligence, and this gives rise to certain challenges in interpreting and applying the law. It could be said that through recent higher court activity, the ambit of nuisance is becoming clearer, but narrower. Nuisance as we describe it here is separate from the tort of negligence, and to a large extent conceptually independent of it.

1.2 THE BASIS OF LIABILITY: PLACING PRIVATE NUISANCE ON THE 'MAP' OF TORT LAW

A Basic Statement of Actionability in Nuisance

'Private nuisance may be described as unlawful interference with a person's use or enjoyment of land, or some right over, or in connection with it.'

The above statement was adopted by Scott LJ in *Read v Lyons* [1945] KB 216, at 236 and approved in a number of other cases. However, it is declared to be a *description* (rather than a definition). With nuisance it is often necessary to turn to previous decisions, rather than to abstract definitions, to settle the detailed question of whether any particular interference is actionable.

Placing Private Nuisance on the Tort Map

Protected Interests and Relevant Conduct

Remembering the way that we 'mapped' tort law in Chapter 1, we see that the description above shows that nuisance is different from negligence in more than one way. It is different from negligence because the definition of **protected interests** in nuisance is both narrower (relating only to interests in or rights over land) and within that field in some senses broader (including losses that would be regarded as intangible and probably some that would be regarded as purely economic in negligence terms).

In terms of **relevant conduct**, there is no requirement that the conduct of the defendant should be careless, although it is often said that reasonableness of conduct plays a part and we will explore whether and when this is so. In some instances, nuisances can arise from perfectly careful, deliberate behaviour. As Lord Goff clearly put it in a key modern case:

Cambridge Water v Eastern Counties Leather plc
[1994] 2 AC 264, at 299

... if the user is reasonable, the defendant will not be liable for subsequent harm to his neighbour's enjoyment of land; but if the user is not reasonable, the defendant will be liable, even though he may have used reasonable care and skill to avoid it.

Although 'conduct' need not be unreasonable in the sense of lack of due care or falling short of a standard, it is clear that there must be some element of 'unreasonableness' before the interference can fulfil the definition of a nuisance. In the above statement, Lord Goff describes the applicable idea of reasonableness through the terminology of 'reasonable user' of the land. Unfortunately, the precise *meaning* of 'reasonable user' has remained rather unclear, as has its range of applicability. This can be traced to some large ambiguities in the important case of *St Helen's v Tipping*, which is extracted later in the present chapter.

Lord Goff also suggested that 'liability for nuisance has generally been regarded as strict' (*Cambridge Water*, above, at 299). In fact, most writers avoid describing it in quite that way. Fleming, for example, categorizes nuisance with 'Miscellaneous' torts, rather than under the category of 'Strict Liability': John G. Fleming, *The Law of Torts* (9th edn, Law Book Company, 1998). Nevertheless, with the support of Lord Goff's statement above, we can say that conduct need not be faulty in all cases of nuisance. In fact, we can go further and suggest that lack of care is only relevant to nuisance actions of particular kinds, and then for particular reasons. Nuisance is, typically, 'stricter than' negligence.

'Continuing' Nuisances

It is also important to notice that nuisances may be, and often are, *continuing*. The core concern is with deliberate activities causing interference, rather than with momentary carelessness causing loss. Dealing with a continuing nuisance requires looking to the future, while negligence cases by contrast invite a retrospective outlook. The key question in cases of continuing nuisance is whether there should be an injunction to stop the unreasonable interference; it is normally thought that only in rare instances would damages be awarded 'in lieu' of the injunction in such a case, although damages may also be sought to compensate for past interference. The overlap between nuisance and negligence is largely confined to cases where the interference amounts to damage of a relevant sort and *has already occurred*. In cases of continuing nuisance where the claimant seeks an *injunction* to prevent the nuisance, there is no question of foreseeability, which is so central to negligence.

Lord Goff, *Cambridge Water*, at 300

... we must be on our guard, when considering liability for damages in nuisance, not to draw inapposite conclusions from cases concerned only with a claim for an injunction. This is because, when an injunction is claimed, its purpose is to restrain further action by the defendant which may interfere with the plaintiff's enjoyment of his land, and ex hypothesi the defendant must be aware, if and when an injunction is granted, that such interference may be caused by the act which he is restrained from committing. It follows that these cases provide no guidance on the question whether foreseeability of harm of the relevant type is a prerequisite of the recovery of damages for causing such harm to the plaintiff.

In the case of continuing nuisances, it is especially clear that a state of affairs may amount to a nuisance even if all due care is taken in the course of the activity which gives rise to it. In *Rushmer v Polsue and Alfieri*, Cozens-Hardy LJ imagined a noise nuisance from the operation of a steam-hammer: 'it would be no answer to say that the steam-hammer is of the most modern approved pattern and is reasonably worked' ([1906] 1 Ch 234, at 251). This comment was expressly approved by Lord Loreburn LC on appeal ([1907] AC 121, at 123). Many of the modern cases analysed in this chapter reaffirm the point.

In summary, nuisance requires that the interference must be judged to be 'unreasonable', and this incorporates assessment of all the circumstances. However, there is no general requirement that *conduct* should be unreasonable. In particular, lack of due care will not be essential.

1.3 ELEMENTS OF ACTIONABILITY

Interference

Our basic description of nuisance above referred to unreasonable interference with the use and enjoyment of land, or with some right over, or in connection with the use and enjoyment of, land. In itself, this does not describe the types of interference which may be involved. In *Hunter v Canary Wharf*, Lord Lloyd said that:

Private nuisances are of three kinds. They are (1) nuisance by encroachment on a neighbour's land; (2) nuisance by direct physical injury to a neighbour's land; and (3) nuisance by interference with a neighbour's quiet enjoyment of his land.

It has been suggested that the last of Lord Lloyd's three categories, 'quiet enjoyment'—complaints about discomfort or inconvenience typically caused by noise, dust, vibration, or smell—make up the bulk of nuisance cases (Buckley, *The Law of Nuisance*, 2nd edn, p 23—see Further Reading to this chapter). As Lord Lloyd explains, nuisance also incorporates cases of physical encroachment (for example by tree roots) and cases of actual physical damage to land. Acid smuts, for example, may affect one's enjoyment of a property; may damage one's trees; or may even damage one's health. It is well established that the first two of these are actionable as nuisances; but the decision in *Hunter v Canary Wharf* heavily qualifies the way that nuisance will approach the third.

There is also another category of case not mentioned by Lord Lloyd, namely interferences with specific rights over land, such as easements. These too are actionable as nuisances: see for example *Colls v Home and Colonial Stores Ltd* [1904] AC 179, concerning interference with light.[1] In *Midtown v City of London Real Property Co Ltd* [2005] EWHC 33, the claimants established that they had acquired a right to light by prescription pursuant to section 3 of the Prescription Act 1832: a right to light to a building is absolute and indefeasible if it 'shall be naturally enjoyed therewith for a period of twenty years without obstruction' (*Midtown* at [6]). In this particular case, the interference amounted to a nuisance.[2]

In the absence of a positive right (such as the right to light acquired by prescription), the mere presence of a building on the defendants' land would not generally amount to a nuisance. Ordinarily, there will need to be some sort of 'emanation' from the defendant's land, as explained in the following extract:

Hunter v Canary Wharf
[1997] AC 655

Lord Goff, at 684–6

… in the absence of an easement, more is required than the mere presence of a neighbouring building to give rise to an actionable private nuisance. Indeed, for an action in private

---

[1] In this case, the interference fell short of a nuisance.

[2] See also *Regan v Paul Properties* [2006] EWCA Civ 1391; [2006] 3 WLR 1131 (below), another actionable interference with right to light which resulted in an injunction.

nuisance to lie in respect of interference with the plaintiff's enjoyment of his land, it will generally arise from something emanating from the defendant's land. Such an emanation may take many forms—noise, dirt, fumes, a noxious smell, vibrations, and suchlike. Occasionally activities on the defendant's land are in themselves so offensive to neighbours as to constitute an actionable nuisance, as in *Thompson-Schwab v. Costaki* [1956] 1 W.L.R. 335, where the sight of prostitutes and their clients entering and leaving neighbouring premises were held to fall into that category. Such cases must however be relatively rare. In one New Zealand case, *Bank of New Zealand v. Greenwood* [1984] 1 N.Z.L.R. 525, the glass roof of a verandah which deflected the sun's rays so that a dazzling glare was thrown on to neighbouring buildings was held, prima facie, to create a nuisance; but it seems that the effect was not merely to reflect the sunlight but to deflect it at such an angle and in such a manner as to cause the dazzling glare, too bright for the human eye to bear, to shine straight into the neighbouring building ... such a case can be distinguished from one concerned with the mere presence of a building on neighbouring land. At all events the mere fact that a building on the defendant's land gets in the way and so prevents something from reaching the plaintiff's land is generally speaking not enough for this purpose.

Lord Goff (and Lord Hoffmann) offered inconclusive remarks on the question of whether interference with television reception—which was the subject of the comments above—could ever amount to a nuisance in English law.[3] If it is so capable, it will be on the basis that there is a substantial interference with 'an important incidence of ordinary user of property'.

Unreasonableness of Interference

In order to be actionable as a nuisance, the relevant interference must also be judged to be 'unreasonable'. 'Unreasonableness' is one of the key concepts in nuisance law. Unfortunately, it is also one of the key puzzles. Some cases discuss the issues in terms of whether the defendant's use of land constitutes a 'reasonable user'. The meaning of *'reasonable user'* is introduced here through two influential nineteenth-century cases.

Bamford v Turnley (Court of Exchequer Chamber, 1862: 3 B & S 66; 31 LJQB 286; 6 LT 721; 9 Jur NS 377; 10 WR 803; 122 ER 27)

The plaintiff complained of interference from smoke and smell arising from the burning of bricks by the defendant. On the basis of *Hole v Barlow* (1858, 6 WR 619; 140 ER 1113), Lord Cockburn CJ directed 'that if the jury thought that the spot was convenient and proper, and the burning of bricks was, under the circumstances, a reasonable use by the defendant of his own land, the defendant would be entitled to a verdict'. It will be seen that this statement incorporated both reasonable user, and the appropriateness of the locality in which the offending activity was carried out. The jury found for the defendant, and the plaintiff appealed to the Court of Exchequer Chamber. By a majority, the Court of Exchequer Chamber allowed the plaintiff's appeal. The main majority judgment dealt narrowly with the correctness of *Hole v Barlow*, which was disapproved as unsupported by prior authority.

---

[3] In the older case of *Bridlington Relay v Yorkshire Electricity Board* [1965] Ch 436, such interference was not recognized as capable of amounting to a nuisance. The House of Lords in *Hunter* accepted that circumstances may have changed since 1965, but did not decide the point since the existence of the building, as we have seen, was not actionable in the absence of an easement.

But it is the separate concurring judgment of Bramwell B that is most often referred to and that continues to inspire most comment. It proposes a potential compromise which has continued to return to the agenda.

Bramwell B, *Bamford v Turnley* (1862)

… those acts necessary for the common and ordinary use and occupation of land and houses may be done, if conveniently done, without subjecting those who do them to an action. This principle would comprehend all the cases I have mentioned, but would not comprehend the present, where what has been done was not the using of land in a common and ordinary way, but in an exceptional manner—not unnatural or unusual, but not the common and ordinary use of land.

Then can this principle be extended to, or is there any other principle that will comprehend, the present case? I know of none. It is for the defendant to show it. There is an obvious necessity for such a principle as I have mentioned. It is as much for the benefit of one owner as of another, for the very nuisance the one has complained of as the result of his neighbour's ordinary use of his neighbour's land, he himself will create in the ordinary use of his own, and the reciprocal nuisances are of a comparatively trifling character. The convenience of such a rule may be indicated by calling it a rule of give and take, live and let live. But none of the above reasoning is applicable to such a case of nuisance as the present. …

But it is said that, temporary or permanent, it is lawful, because it is for the public benefit. In the first place, that law, to my mind, is a bad one which, for the public benefit, inflicts loss on an individual without compensation. But, further, with great respect, I think this consideration misapplied in this and in many other cases. The public consists of all the individuals of it, and a thing is only for the public benefit when it is productive of good to those individuals on the balance of loss and gain to all; so that if all the loss or all the gain were borne and received by one individual, he or the whole would be a gainer. But wherever this is the case, wherever a thing is for the public benefit, properly understood, the loss of all the individuals of the public who lose will bear compensation out of the gains of those who gain. It is for the public benefit there should be railways, but it would not be unless the gain of having the railway was sufficient to compensate the loss occasioned by the use of the land required for its site, and accordingly no one thinks it would be right to take an individual's land, without compensation, to make a railway … So in like way in this case: a money value indeed cannot easily be put on the plaintiff's loss, but it is equal to some number of pounds or pence—£10, £50, or what not. Unless the defendant's profits are enough to compensate this, I deny it is for the public benefit he should do what he has done. If they are, he ought to compensate.

The only objection I can see to this reasoning is, that by injunction or abatement of a nuisance a man who would not accept a pecuniary compensation might put a stop to works of great value, and much more than enough to compensate him. This objection, however, is of small practical importance. It may be that the law ought to be amended, and some means provided to legalise such cases, as I believe is the case in some foreign countries giving compensation; but I am clearly of opinion, that though the present law may be defective, it would be made worse, and be unjust and inexpedient, if it permitted such power of inflicting loss and damage on individuals without compensation, as is claimed by the argument for the defendants. …

Bramwell B divided the cases of amenity nuisance into two. First were those where the inconvenience arose from the 'common and ordinary' use of land. Here, the law of nuisance applies a principle of 'give and take' in a situation understood as one of general reciprocity. As one facet of this, the locality is important. It is appropriate to ask whether the offending use of land is conducted in a suitable location. Second, there are other cases which would fall outside this principle of 'give and take'. In these cases, the defendant's activities go beyond the 'common and ordinary' use of land, even though they are not in any sense 'unnatural or unusual'. Here, it would be no answer to the claim that the activity in question was for the public benefit. On the contrary, the argument that something was for the public benefit would be *believed* only if the activity was still considered worthwhile after the payment of compensation to those whose interests in land were thereby compromised. Only if it remained worthwhile to the defendant in these circumstances could it be said that the activity was of benefit overall.

This idea is often referred to as the principle of 'internalization of costs': those who undertake costly activities should be forced to take into account their *true* costs. Bramwell's overtly economic approach continues to inspire interest. Although it appears to be based in welfare economics rather than in fairness or equity, its outcomes have resonances with more recent approaches to compensation for losses imposed upon individuals by activities that are justified in the public interest (see Section 1.7, Remedies). Bramwell also even suggests, in effect, that a change in the law to allow greater availability of damages in lieu of an injunction would encourage productive activities and enhance economic efficiency. Here, he proposes a constructive compromise which he says would enhance the public interest. It is essentially the same solution proposed by a number of judges and commentators in more recent years (see Section 1.7; and S. Tromans, 'Nuisance—Prevention or Payment?' [1982] CLJ 87), and now authoritatively accepted by the Supreme Court in *Coventry v Lawrence* [2014] UKSC 13. For a study which places Bramwell's approach in the context of its time, see A. W. B. Simpson, *Leading Cases in the Common Law* (Oxford University Press, 1995), chapter 7, 'Victorian Judges and the Problem of Social Cost', p 175.

St Helen's Smelting Co v Tipping (1865) 11 HL Cas 642, HL(E)

In a case which symbolizes the historic conflict between landed and industrial interests, and which appeared likely to bring to a head the question of public interest or at least local prosperity as against established property rights, the plaintiff brought an action in respect of the damage allegedly being caused to his property by copper smelting works on neighbouring land. He had purchased what is described in the judgment of Lord Westbury LC as an 'estate of great value' in June 1860; the particular smelting works in question had commenced later in the same year. However, he had purchased the estate in an area in which the industrial smelting of copper was a well-established activity, and he almost certainly had full knowledge of the defendant's plans at the time of the purchase: it has been suggested that the negotiated price was affected by the construction of the smelting works (Simpson, *Leading Cases in the Common Law*, p 184).

Having succeeded in this action, Tipping later applied successfully for an injunction to restrain the smelting works: *Tipping v St Helen's Smelting Co* (1865) [LR] 1 Ch App 66. The equitable remedy was granted,[4] notwithstanding that Tipping's predecessor in title had sold the neighbouring land to the defendants with full knowledge of their plan to construct copper smelting works.

---

[4] The importance of the 'equitable' nature of the injunctive remedy is that it is available at the discretion of the court, and not as of right: see Section 1.7, Remedies.

The extract that follows is one of the most cited passages in nuisance law, so that its ambiguities are highly significant.

Lord Westbury LC, at 650–2

... my Lords, in matters of this description it seems to me that it is a very desirable thing to mark the difference between an action brought for a nuisance upon the ground that the alleged nuisance produces material injury to the property, and an action brought for a nuisance on the ground that the thing alleged to be a nuisance is productive of sensible personal discomfort. With regard to the latter, namely, the personal inconvenience and interference with one's enjoyment, one's quiet, one's personal freedom ..., whether that may or may not be denominated a nuisance, must undoubtedly depend greatly on the circumstances of the place where the thing complained of actually occurs. If a man lives in a town, it is necessary that he should subject himself to the consequences of those operations of trade which may be carried on in his immediate locality, which are actually necessary for trade and commerce, and also for the enjoyment of property, and for the benefit of the inhabitants of the town and of the public at large ...

But when an occupation is carried on by one person in the neighbourhood of another, and the result of that trade, or occupation, or business, is a material injury to property, then there unquestionably arises a very different consideration. I think, my Lords, that in a case of that description, the submission which is required from persons living in society to that amount of discomfort which may be necessary for the legitimate and free exercise of the trade of their neighbours, would not apply to circumstances the immediate result of which is sensible injury to the value of the property ...

[... the only ground on which Your Lordships are asked to set aside the verdict is that] ... the whole neighbourhood where these copper smelting works were carried on, is a neighbourhood more or less devoted to manufacturing processes of a similar kind, and therefore it is said, that inasmuch as the this copper smelting is carried on in what the Appellant contends is a fit place, it may be carried on with impunity, although the result may be the utter destruction, or the very considerable diminution, of the value of the plaintiff's property.... The word 'suitable' unquestionably cannot carry with it this consequence, that a trade may be carried on in a particular locality, the consequence of which trade may be injury and destruction to the neighbouring property ...

The House of Lords was asked to set aside the judgment of the courts below on the important, but narrow ground that the neighbourhood was one devoted to manufacturing processes. This has become known as an issue concerning the **'locality'** or **'character of the neighbourhood'**. The *St Helen's* case seems to lay down that the 'character of the neighbourhood' is relevant only to certain cases of nuisance, namely those which relate to 'amenity' nuisance, or (mere) interference with 'comfort and convenience'. The difficulty is that Lord Westbury was not consistent in identifying the features of this case which made the locality principle inapplicable. The interference is variously described in the extract above as causing 'material injury to the property'; 'sensible injury to the value of the property', and 'considerable diminution of the value of the property'. The first of these seems to suggest physical damage; the others do not.

Even so, the case is usually understood as dividing cases of material *physical* damage to property (which was present in this case in the form of damage to trees), from cases falling short of that.[5] Even if this was the distinction intended by Lord Westbury (and as we have seen his language was by no means clear), then no particular reason was given for dividing material physical damage from other interferences in this way. Many amenity nuisances are capable of persisting in the long term, and permanent and severe interference with personal comfort, or even with quiet enjoyment, is easily capable of affecting the market value of property. Perhaps this is a point more readily appreciated in the context of the modern domestic housing market, than in the context of competing productive economic uses of land. The status of Tipping's estate was itself ambiguous: it was a working farm; but it also provided a gentleman's residence.

Whatever the true interpretation of the *St Helen's* case, it represents a compromise solution. It places the dividing line in a different position from that proposed by Bramwell B in *Bamford v Turnley*, and unfortunately (since it is the leading authority in this field) it lacks reasoned justifications for doing so.

In the earlier case, Bramwell B wanted the principle of 'give and take' (which would encompass the locality rule) to be confined to cases where land was used in a 'common and ordinary' way. Beyond this, the convenience of the location and the reasonableness of the activity could not, in his view, justify an interference which would otherwise amount to a nuisance. *Bamford v Turnley* itself was a case of nuisance through interference with comfort and enjoyment, but the locality rule did not apply. So some amenity nuisances, on his approach, were *outside* the rule of 'give and take'.

In the *St Helen's* case, it was suggested that in cases of 'material injury to property', there was no place for the locality rule to operate, since no location could be regarded as 'convenient' for an activity having such effects. This much is narrowly compatible with the decision in *Bamford v Turnley*. But in placing the line here, Lord Westbury appears to have meant that *all* cases falling short of 'material injury to property', *are* subject to the locality rule, notwithstanding the fact that the nature of the activity was quite beyond what was common and ordinary. This means that the ambiguous meaning of 'material injury to property' is exceedingly important.

Although Lord Westbury's comments are particularly directed at the locality principle, it is typically assumed that the 'reasonable user' test as a whole is applicable only to amenity nuisances; and then to all such nuisances. An example of this understanding is the following statement of Lord Hoffmann in *Wildtree Hotels v Harrow LBC* [2001] 2 AC 1, concerning claims for damage caused by noise, dust, or vibration:

Being things 'productive of material physical discomfort' within the meaning of Lord Westbury's dichotomy in *St Helen's Smelting v Tipping . . .* , the claim is subject to the principle that a reasonable use of land, with due regard to the interests of the neighbours, is not actionable (at 12).

In the context of building works, Lord Hoffmann went on to explain that '[a]ctionability at common law therefore depends upon showing that the works were conducted without reasonable consideration for the neighbours' (at 13). Building works—in their nature typically both necessary and temporary—are thus subject to questions of 'reasonable consideration'.

---

[5] See for example *Halsey v Esso Petroleum* [1961] 1 WLR 683.

Summary: Unreasonableness and Reasonable User

Our general statement of private nuisance referred to 'unreasonable interference'. The idea of 'reasonable user' introduces slightly different terminology, focusing on the defendant's use of the land, rather than the effect on the claimant. Because of the accepted interpretation of *St Helen's v Tipping*, 'reasonable user' applies to those nuisances falling short of 'material physical damage'.

Reasonable user is not the same as reasonable conduct, since some activities in some places are destined to be judged unreasonable no matter how carefully they are carried out. On the other hand, the idea of 'give and take' means that some activities are protected unless they are carried on without due regard for one's neighbours. We noted the example of reasonable building works. In such cases, there will be attention to methods employed, times of operation, precautions taken, and so on. These are similar to negligence questions surrounding breach of duty, but they are aspects of a different enquiry.

This illustrates a general point about the nature of 'reasonableness' in nuisance. We noted at the start of this section that the crucial question is whether the interference is to be judged unreasonable, *not* whether the defendant's activity is carried out with due care. Nevertheless, there have been cases where the nature of the defendant's activities has been influential, and occasionally decisive, in the balancing exercise. And there are other cases where the nature of the claimant's interests has been a crucial element. The next section considers some 'special' issues in the broader reasonableness enquiry.

Unreasonableness: Special Considerations

Sensitivity

In the case of 'amenity' type nuisances, in which there is interference with personal comfort or convenience, private nuisance will not protect unduly sensitive claimants. Private nuisance protects only *ordinary* use and enjoyment of land. This principle was expressed by Knight-Bruce V-C in *Walter v Selfe* (1851) 4 De G & Sm 315, at 322 as cited, for example, in *Vanderpant v Mayfair Hotel Co Ltd* [1930] 1 Ch 138:

Luxmoore J, at 165

[I]t is necessary to determine whether the act complained of is an inconvenience materially interfering with the ordinary physical comfort of human existence, not merely according to elegant or dainty modes and habits of living, but according to plain and sober and simple notions obtaining among English people: see *Walter v. Selfe* and the remarks of Knight Bruce V.-C.

But what of cases of actual physical damage? In *Robinson v Kilvert* (1889) 41 Ch D 88, the idea that nuisance would not protect those making particularly sensitive use of property applied in a case of actual physical damage. Hot, dry air in a cellar caused damage to paper stored by the plaintiff, the defendant's tenant, on the floor above. Ordinary paper would not have been damaged. The action in nuisance failed. The defendant could not, by choosing a particularly sensitive use of the premises, prevent the defendant from making use of the cellar in a reasonable way, nor convert that use into a nuisance. Cotton LJ put it in the following way (at 94):

If a person does what in itself is noxious, or which interferes with the ordinary use and enjoyment of a neighbour's property, it is a nuisance. But no case has been cited where

> the doing something not in itself noxious has been held a nuisance, unless it interferes with the ordinary enjoyment of life, or the ordinary use of property for the purposes of residence or business. It would, in my opinion, be wrong to say that the doing something not in itself noxious is a nuisance because it does harm to some particular trade in the adjoining property, although it would not prejudicially affect any ordinary trade carried on there, and does not interfere with the ordinary enjoyment of life. Here it is shewn that ordinary paper would not be damaged by what the Defendants are doing, but only a particular kind of paper, and it is not shewn that there is heat such as to incommode the workpeople on the Plaintiff's premises. I am of opinion, therefore, that the Plaintiff is not entitled to relief on the ground that what the Defendants are doing is a nuisance.

Even so, in cases of physical damage, the remoteness rules applicable in nuisance are similar to those in negligence. In particular, if the claimant's sensitivity affects only the *extent* of damage suffered, then the defendant must compensate to the full extent of the loss. The Canadian case of *McKinnon Industries v Walker* [1951] 3 DLR 577 illustrates this well. Emissions from the defendant's factory foreseeably damaged the plaintiff's plants. These happened to be valuable orchids, thus increasing the sum payable in damages. The plaintiff's sensitivity had not caused the defendant's activities to constitute a nuisance, but had merely increased the size of the losses suffered.

In *Network Rail Infrastructure v Morris* [2004] EWCA Civ 172, the claimant sought damages in nuisance in respect of electromagnetic interference caused by Railtrack's signalling system, to electric guitar music played in his recording studio. The Court of Appeal observed that application of the approach in *Robinson v Kilvert* in such a case would be difficult, since use of sensitive equipment is now widespread. Lord Phillips thought that the balance to be struck would be a matter of reasonableness (which, as we have already said, is the traditional underlying test, of which *Robinson v Kilvert* is only an example). He also noted (at [19]) that foreseeability is now recognized to be a vital ingredient in the tort of nuisance. Foreseeability was not established on the facts of the case.

Although Lord Phillips noted that the tort of private nuisance has 'moved on' since cases such as *Robinson v Kilvert*, Buxton LJ went further, arguing that:

> **35** … it is difficult to see any further life in some particular rules of the law of nuisance, such as for instance the idea of "abnormal sensitiveness" drawn from *Robinson v Kilvert*…. That rule was developed at a time when liability in nuisance … was thought to be strict.

He went on to argue that the 'general view of the law of nuisance' had been changed by the judgment of Lord Cooke in *Delaware Mansions v Westminster City Council* [2002] 1 AC 321 (a case of encroaching tree roots), and that questions of reasonableness would now be considered in terms of 'foreseeability'.

It is suggested, however, that key recent decisions such as *Cambridge Water* and *Hunter v Canary Wharf* do not mitigate the strictness of nuisance liability. Quite the contrary: they underline its strictness, while also restricting its scope. *Delaware Mansions* concerned the duty of an occupier (there the Highway Authority) to compensate a neighbour for reasonable repair costs when a nuisance (in the form of *physical damage*) was created by trees on the defendant's land. In this sort of case, in accordance with cases such as *Goldman v Hargrave* and *Leakey v National Trust* (below), it has long been recognized that foreseeability, and the definition of *reasonable steps to abate a nuisance*, are relevant. This does not mean that more typical forms of nuisance are to be approached in terms closer to negligence. There is little justification for treating *Delaware Mansions* as marking a major reorientation in the law of nuisance, akin to *Donoghue v Stevenson* in the tort of negligence (proposed by Buxton LJ at [35]).

Malice

Turning from claimant's use, to defendant's use, bad motive on the part of the defendant will sometimes tip the balance decisively in the claimant's favour. In *Christie v Davey* [1893] 1 Ch 316, the defendant deliberately created a noise nuisance, solely in retaliation against his neighbours, the plaintiffs. The plaintiffs provided music lessons from the semi-detached house which shared a party wall with the defendant's house. Since there was no legitimate reason for the noise interference from the defendants, in contrast with the innocent (if perhaps raucous) activities of the plaintiffs, the defendant would be restrained from continuing.

North J, *Christie v Davey*, at 326–7

If what has taken place had occurred between two sets of persons both perfectly innocent, I should have taken an entirely different view of the case. But I am persuaded that what was done by the Defendant was done only for the purpose of annoyance, and in my opinion it was not a legitimate use of the Defendant's house to use it for the purpose of vexing and annoying his neighbours … This being so, I am bound to give the Plaintiffs the relief which they ask.

Christie v Davey was followed in *Hollywood Silver Fox Farm v Emmett* [1936] 2 KB 468. Here the plaintiff kept silver foxes. The defendant arranged for guns to be fired near to his boundary with the plaintiff's land, and as near to the vixens' pens as possible, solely in order to prevent successful breeding of the animals. Macnaghten J awarded damages, and an injunction to prevent such behaviour during the foxes' breeding season. In doing so, he had to contend with the next case, which has inspired much comment and more confusion over the years.

Bradford Corporation v Pickles [1895] AC 587

Between the two authorities of *Christie v Davey* (1893) and *Hollywood Silver Fox Farm* (1936), an opposite result was obtained in the very different case of *Bradford Corporation v Pickles*. The plaintiffs in this case supplied water to the city of Bradford. Some of it derived from a spring known as Many Wells, situated on land owned by the Corporation. Pickles owned land above Many Wells. His land acted as a sort of natural reservoir for subterranean water which flowed in undefined channels. The water flowed naturally from Pickles' land, to Many Wells. It was common ground that neither party had any legal interest over the water itself. In 1892, Pickles began work on his land which would divert water from its natural route, and would eventually diminish the supply of water to Many Wells. The Corporation claimed that these works were done 'maliciously', to deprive them of water, and sought an injunction.

In refusing the injunction, the House of Lords regarded the matter as resolved by the decision in *Chasemore v Richards* ((1859) 7 HLC 349): there is no ownership in underground water percolating in undefined channels.[6] Rather, a property owner such as Pickles has the right to divert or appropriate such water from beneath his own land. A neighbouring owner has no right to prevent this. In trying to avoid the impact of *Chasemore v Richards*, the Corporation relied on two matters. The first was a point of statutory interpretation which will not affect us. But second, they claimed that Pickles' motive was 'malicious', and that he had therefore acted in excess of his rights. The members of the House were not persuaded by Pickles' own explanation of his acts (that he was seeking to work minerals under his land), and they seem to have concluded that he was seeking to extract an inflated price for his land. As it happens, they were not persuaded that this motive could be described as 'malicious'. But more importantly, they did not consider that motive, malicious or not, was in any sense relevant to the case.

Lord Halsbury LC, at 594–5

The only remaining point is the question of fact alleged by the plaintiffs, that the acts done by the defendant are done, not with any view which deals with the use of his own land or the percolating water through it, but is done, in the language of the pleader, "maliciously." I am not certain that I can understand or give any intelligible construction to the word so used. Upon the supposition on which I am now arguing, it comes to an allegation that the defendant did maliciously something that he had a right to do. If this question were to have been tried in old times as an injury to the right in an action on the case, the plaintiffs would have had to allege, and to prove, if traversed, that they were entitled to the flow of the water, which, as I have already said, was an allegation they would have failed to establish.

This is not a case in which the state of mind of the person doing the act can affect the right to do it. If it was a lawful act, however ill the motive might be, he had a right to do it. If it was an unlawful act, however good his motive might be, he would have no right to do it. Motives and intentions in such a question as is now before your Lordships seem to me to be absolutely irrelevant ... So, here, if the owner of the adjoining land is in a situation in which an act of his, lawfully done on his own land, may divert the water which would otherwise go into the possession of this trading company, I see no reason why he should not insist on their purchasing his interest from which this trading company desires to make profit.

Lord Macnaghten, at 601

He [Pickles] prefers his own interests to the public good. He may be churlish, selfish, and grasping. His conduct may seem shocking to a moral philosopher. But where is the malice? Mr. Pickles has no spite against the people of Bradford. He bears no ill-will to the corporation. They are welcome to the water, and to his land too, if they will pay the price for it. So much perhaps might be said in defence or in palliation of Mr. Pickles' conduct. But the real answer to the claim of the corporation is that in such a case motives are immaterial. It is the act, not the motive for the act, that must be regarded. If the act, apart from motive, gives rise merely to damage without legal injury, the motive, however reprehensible it may be, will not supply that element.

[6] *Chasemore v Richards* is discussed by Joshua Getzler, *A History of Water Rights at Common Law* (Oxford University Press, 2004), 302–25.

'Nuisance' was mentioned only once in the judgment of the House of Lords, and then as providing an analogy (Lord Watson, at 508). Macnaghten J further pointed out (at 476) that in *Allen v Flood* [1898] AC 1, 101, decided soon after *Bradford v Pickles*, Lord Watson had explained that 'No proprietor has an absolute right to create noises upon his land, because any right which the law gives him is qualified by the condition that it must not be exercised to the nuisance of his neighbours or of the public.' One interpretation then is that some of the rights enjoyed by property owners are qualified by the need not to create a nuisance, whereas others are not. One must be careful how much noise one makes, but need not be careful about how much percolating underground water one extracts.

However, a more satisfactory way of dividing noise nuisances from the activities of a land-owner such as Pickles is to suggest that to deprive one's neighbours of water flowing in unde-fined channels, rather than (for example) to subject them to insufferable amounts of noise, is not capable of amounting to a nuisance at all. This time we do not focus exclusively on the defendant, but pay attention also to the claimant. There is no right (absolute or qualified) to receive percolating groundwater, whereas there is a right of quiet enjoyment of one's property. The latter right is, of course, only a relative one, dependent on showing that any interference is unreasonable in the relevant sense. In the same way, there is a right to receive one's groundwa-ter in an uncontaminated form, but this right is qualified by the need to show that any interfer-ence with it is a nuisance, or within the rule in *Rylands v Fletcher* (*Ballard v Tomlinson* (1885) 29 Ch D 115, as interpreted by the House of Lords, and not the Court of Appeal, in *Cambridge Water v Eastern Counties Leather plc* [1994] 2 AC 264). On this interpretation, it is because of the absence of any right to receive groundwater that there is no space for the tort of nuisance to operate, if the only damage suffered is the absence of the resource itself.

It is true that the House of Lords focused on the motive of Pickles in particular, rather than on the nature of the damage suffered by the plaintiff, perhaps because this was the only ground on which the plaintiffs could seek to distinguish *Chasemore v Richards* (1859) 7 HL Cas 349. But the remarks quoted above are consistent with the present interpretation. See for example Lord Halsbury's statement about what would have been needed to be proved in an action upon the case: 'If this question were to have been tried in old times as an injury to the right in an action on the case, the plaintiffs would have had to allege, and to prove . . . that they were entitled to the flow of water, which, as I have already said, they would have failed to establish'. The interpretation is further supported by his comments at 592:

[I]t is necessary for the plaintiffs to establish that they have a right to the flow of water, and that the defendant has no right to do what he is doing.

As Lord Macnaghten put it in the extract earlier, Pickles' acts gave rise to 'damage without legal injury', and this remains true whatever the motive. If so, Macnaghten J was correct to distinguish *Bradford v Pickles* in the *Hollywood Silver Fox Farm* case, for it has no applica-tion to cases of noise nuisance.

Planning Permission and the Character of the Neighbourhood

Inevitably, the law of nuisance raises questions about the boundaries between private law, and the planning process through which certain uses of land must be authorized. It is clear that the grant of planning permission does not operate in the same way as 'statutory author-ity', which is a recognized defence to nuisance (and is considered with other defences in Section 1.6).

Coventry v Lawrence [2014] UKSC 13; [2014] 2 WLR 233

In 2006, the claimants bought a house situated close to a sports stadium used for various motor sports, and a further track used for motocross. These uses were the subject of planning permission. The claimants complained about the noise generated by the use of the defendants' land for motorsports, and the local planning authority served 'abatement notices' requiring noise reduction works to be carried out. Those works having been completed, the planning authority took no further action. The claimants commenced proceedings in nuisance. The Court of Appeal[7] considered that this was a case where, as in *Gillingham v Medway (Chatham) Dock Co Ltd* [1993] QB 343, the noise was such an established part of the 'character of the locality' that it should be taken into account when assessing whether the interference constituted a nuisance. The Supreme Court disagreed, deciding that the approach in *Gillingham* was incorrect. This was by no means the only important aspect of the tort of private nuisance determined by the Supreme Court in a complex decision: see particularly the discussion in Section 1.6 (Defences), and Section 1.7 (Remedies). In certain other aspects of its decision, and particularly its approach to remedies, the Supreme Court accorded considerably more weight to 'public interest' factors than have previously been admitted in cases of private nuisance.

Lord Neuberger, *Coventry v Lawrence* [2014] UKSC 13

94 … I consider that the mere fact that the activity which is said to give rise to the nuisance has the benefit of a planning permission is normally of no assistance to the defendant in a claim brought by a neighbour who contends that the activity causes a nuisance to her land in the form of noise or other loss of amenity.

95 A planning authority has to consider the effect of a proposed development on occupiers of neighbouring land, but that is merely one of the factors which has to be taken into account. The planning authority can be expected to balance various competing interests, which will often be multifarious in nature, as best it can in the overall public interest, bearing in mind relevant planning guidelines. Some of those factors, such as many political and economic considerations which properly may play a part in the thinking of the members of a planning authority, would play no part in the assessment of whether a particular activity constitutes a nuisance—unless the law of nuisance is to be changed fairly radically. Quite apart from this, when granting planning permission for a change of use, a planning authority would be entitled to assume that a neighbour whose private rights might be infringed by that use could enforce those rights in a nuisance action; it could not be expected to take on itself the role of deciding a neighbour's common law rights.

96 However, there will be occasions when the terms of a planning permission could be of some relevance in a nuisance case. Thus, the fact that the planning authority takes the view that noisy activity is acceptable after 8.30 am, or if it is limited to a certain decibel level, in a particular locality, may be of real value, at least as a starting point as Lord Carnwath JSC says in para 218 below, in a case where the claimant is contending that the activity gives rise to a nuisance if it starts before 9.30 am, or is at or below the permitted decibel level. While

---

[7] *Lawrence v Fen Tigers Ltd* [2012] EWCA Civ 26; [2012] 1 WLR 2127.

the decision whether the activity causes a nuisance to the claimant is not for the planning authority but for the court, the existence and terms of the permission are not irrelevant as a matter of law, but in many cases they will be of little, or even no, evidential value, and in other cases rather more.

The conclusion that planning permission cannot be taken to authorize a nuisance, even by changing the character of the neighbourhood, is consistent with another significant conclusion, namely that when assessing the character of the neighbourhood, the court must *ignore* the defendant's activities, *to the extent that they are a nuisance* ([65]). An element of circularity in this approach was admitted ([72]) (how is one first to judge whether the activities amount to a nuisance?); but Lord Neuberger thought the alternative was that the defendants could 'invoke their own wrong' against the claimants. On this approach, the grant of planning permission should make no difference.

It is suggested that Lord Neuberger's approach, though it is now authoritative, may actually go too far in discounting the effects of planning permission. He dismissed the potential distinction between 'strategic' and 'non-strategic' planning permission as a 'recipe for uncertainty' ([91]). Notably Lord Carnwath—whose judgment in the Court of Appeal in *Barr v Biffa Waste Services Ltd* [2012] EWCA Civ 312; [2013] QB 455 was approved by Lord Neuberger—took a different view, considering that some grants of planning permission were of such scope that they could not be ignored in assessing the character of the neighbourhood. And while Lord Neuberger's judgment generally gained the agreement of his colleagues, Lord Carnwath's remarks (below) were also supported by Lord Clarke: as Lord Carnwath has shown, the facts of such cases are so varied that it is difficult to lay down hard and fast rules' ([169]).

Lord Carnwath, *Coventry v Lawrence*

222 In agreement with Peter Gibson LJ in *Wheeler* [1996] Ch 19, 35, I think there should be a strong presumption against allowing private rights to be overridden by administrative decisions without compensation. The public interest comes into play in the limited sense accepted by Lord Westbury in *St Helen's Smelting Co v Tipping* 11 HL Cas 642, 650, as discussed above, that is in evaluating the pattern of uses "necessary ... for the benefit of the inhabitants of the town and of the public at large", against which the acceptability of the defendant's activity is to be judged. Otherwise its relevance generally in my view should be in the context of remedies rather than liability.

223 I would accept however that in exceptional cases a planning permission may be the result of a considered policy decision by the competent authority leading to a fundamental change in the pattern of uses, which cannot sensibly be ignored in assessing the character of the area against which the acceptability of the defendant's activity is to be judged. I read Staughton LJ's use of the word "strategic" as equivalent to Peter Gibson LJ's reference to "a major development altering the character of a neighbourhood with wide consequential effects such as required a balancing of competing public and private interests before permission was granted". For this reason, in my view (differing respectfully from Lord Neuberger PSC on this point) the reasoning of the judge in *Gillingham* can be supported. Similarly, the Canary Wharf development was understandably regarded by Lord Cooke as strategic in the same sense. But those projects were exceptional both in scale and the nature of the planning judgments which led to their approval. By contrast, in neither *Wheeler v JJ Saunders Ltd* nor

Watson v Croft Promosport Ltd did the relevant permissions result in a significant change in the pattern of uses in the area, let alone one which could be regarded as strategic; and for the reasons noted above neither decision could be regarded as reflecting a considered assessment by the authorities concerned of the appropriate balance between public and private interests.

In both of these paragraphs, Lord Carnwath refers to the question of *compensation*. These references are important to the question of remedies for nuisance, and particularly the question of when damages are available in place of an injunction, which was one of the most important aspects of the decision in *Lawrence*. It is considered in Section 1.7. But it is worth noting at this stage that the Supreme Court recommended a much greater flexibility in remedy than has hitherto been recognized in the law of nuisance. Plainly, one question raised if courts are to disregard planning permission is whether activities will be permitted by the planning process only to be stopped by the common law? This was the very move attempted by the planning authority itself in *Gillingham*, and the answer was 'no'. The answer since given however is, 'sometimes, yes', and *Watson v Croft Promo-Sport* [2009] EWCA Civ 15 was one such case. Since *Coventry* will mean that planning permission will not protect against liability in nuisance even where it is 'strategic' in nature, it is significant that the approach in *Watson* was disapproved and that damages will now more often be awarded 'in lieu'.

1.4 CONNECTION WITH THE NUISANCE: WHO MAY BE SUED?

What is the necessary relationship between the defendant and the nuisance? The simplest cases are those where the occupier of land on which a nuisance originates is also the creator of the nuisance. Equally, the case law has treated as without difficulty those cases where the nuisance is created by the servant or agent of the occupier. Tenants and licensees raise different issues, and are considered separately below. But what of other cases where the occupier does not create the nuisance? Some such cases bring into question the nature of the overlap between nuisance and the tort of negligence.

Occupiers Who do not Create the Nuisance (Nonfeasance)

Some occupiers clearly benefit from states of affairs which were created by someone else (typically a previous occupier). In the terms used in *Sedleigh-Denfield v O'Callaghan* [1940] AC 880 (extracted below), such nuisances may be 'adopted' by the occupier. As defined by that case, all that is required for 'adoption' is that the occupier should make some use of whatever constitutes the nuisance. This will be sufficient even if the nuisance was initially created through the act of a trespasser, as in *Sedleigh-Denfield* itself. But falling short of this, there are many other states of affairs which arise on land and where the occupier, though he may not positively adopt the nuisance, is the party in a position to do something to prevent the nuisance from arising or continuing. Although these may arise through the actions of third parties, they may equally arise through natural processes affecting the land. Should there be an action against such an occupier?

If there is such an action, then there will be a *positive duty to act* in order to prevent damage to another. Successive decisions have determined that there is scope for positive duties as regards nuisances arising on land, even where the occupier is not the originator. The content of these duties requires that the occupier should take 'reasonable steps' to abate the nuisance. This sounds very much like negligence, and the language of negligence has been applied (see *Goldman v Hargrave*, Section 1.4). But what should we make of this? It is true that in a case of nuisance, we do not usually ask whether there is a 'duty', nor concentrate on the nature of the steps taken or not taken by the defendant, as is done in the cases extracted below. On the other hand, these cases are not typical of negligence analysis either. They recognize *positive* duties to take action, which are rare in negligence; and the standard applied is *subjective*, whereas the typical negligence standard is of course *objective*. Despite the terms used in *Goldman v Hargrave*, the more recent cases are clearly treated as cases of nuisance.

Sedleigh-Denfield v O'Callaghan [1940] AC 880

Sedleigh-Denfield v O'Callaghan holds the key to understanding many of the more recent cases on the positive duties of an occupier. In this case, a pipe was laid on the defendants' land without their knowledge or consent, by a trespasser.[8] The occupiers subsequently became aware of the existence of the pipe, which had the function of draining their fields. A grating was placed on the pipe, but because of its position it did not adequately prevent the pipe from becoming blocked. During a heavy rainstorm, the pipe became blocked and the water over-flowed on to the plaintiff's neighbouring land. The House of Lords held that the defendants had sufficient connection with the nuisance to be treated as both adopting it, and continuing it. These terms are explained in the extract from the judgment of Viscount Maugham below. Either ground was sufficient for the defendants to be held liable in nuisance.

Viscount Maugham, at 894–5

The statement that an occupier of land is liable for the continuance of a nuisance created by others, e.g., by trespassers, if he continues or adopts it—which seems to be agreed—throws little light on the matter, unless the words "continues or adopts" are defined. In my opinion an occupier of land "continues" a nuisance if with knowledge or presumed knowledge of its existence he fails to take any reasonable means to bring it to an end though with ample time to do so. He "adopts" it if he makes any use of the erection, building, bank or artificial contrivance which constitutes the nuisance. In these sentences I am not attempting exclusive definitions....

My Lords, in the present case I am of opinion that the respondents both continued and adopted the nuisance. After the lapse of nearly three years they must be taken to have suffered the nuisance to continue; for they neglected to take the very simple step of placing a grid in the proper place which would have removed the danger to their neighbour's land. They adopted the nuisance for they continued during all that time to use the artificial contrivance of the conduit for the purpose of getting rid of water from their property without taking the proper means for rendering it safe.

Lord Atkin, at 896–7

... For the purpose of ascertaining whether as here the plaintiff can establish a private nuisance I think that nuisance is sufficiently defined as a wrongful interference with another's

---

[8] This was a rather unusual trespasser: Middlesex County Council laid the culvert for the benefit of another neighbouring occupier.

enjoyment of his land or premises by the use of land or premises either occupied or in some cases owned by oneself. The occupier or owner is not an insurer; there must be something more than the mere harm done to the neighbour's property to make the party responsible. Deliberate act or negligence is not an essential ingredient but some degree of personal responsibility is required, which is connoted in my definition by the word "use." This conception is implicit in all the decisions which impose liability only where the defendant has "caused or continued" the nuisance. We may eliminate in this case "caused." What is the meaning of "continued"? In the context in which it is used "continued" must indicate mere passive continuance. If a man uses on premises something which he found there, and which itself causes a nuisance by noise, vibration, smell or fumes, he is himself in continuing to bring into existence the noise, vibration, etc., causing a nuisance. Continuing in this sense and causing are the same thing. It seems to me clear that if a man permits an offensive thing on his premises to continue to offend, that is, if he knows that it is operating offensively, is able to prevent it, and omits to prevent it, he is permitting the nuisance to continue; in other words he is continuing it.

A useful definition of adopting and continuing is spelt out in Viscount Maugham's judgment. However, given our interest in the similarities and differences between nuisance and negligence, it is also instructive to note the observations of Lord Atkin. In particular, Lord Atkin specifies here that the action in nuisance does not require any degree of negligence, but that it does require some degree of 'personal responsibility'. In other words, in addition to the question of whether the interference amounts to a 'nuisance' (is it an unreasonable interference?), there is the further and separate question of whether there is a sufficient link between the occupier of land, and the nuisance, to justify liability on the part of the occupier. As Lord Atkin says, if the occupier *creates* the nuisance then there is of course an adequate link. In the particular case of *Sedleigh-Denfield*, knowledge of the nuisance (or, as Viscount Maugham put it, 'presumed knowledge') together with the opportunity to take steps to abate the nuisance amounted to sufficient connection.

Since a 'very simple step' would have sufficed to abate the nuisance in *Sedleigh-Denfield* itself, the case did not test the question of what the *content* of the positive duty might be. Questions about the content of the duty were considered in the case of *Goldman v Hargrave*.

Goldman v Hargrave [1967] 1 AC 645

The decision of the Privy Council in *Goldman v Hargrave* does not use the kind of language that is typical of nuisance cases. Indeed in specifying that there must be breach of a 'duty of care' Lord Wilberforce appears to imply that this is a case of negligence properly so called. However, it is suggested that the references to 'negligence' in this case should be read as referring above all to the quality of the actions of the defendant. We should be careful how we read Lord Wilberforce's remark that this is a case 'where liability, if it exists, rests upon negligence and nothing else'. Lord Wilberforce expressly pointed out (at 656) that the Privy Council would decide the case without answering the 'disputable question' of categorization. His comments should not be taken to mean that this was a case in the *tort* of negligence. *Goldman v Hargrave* was a decision on appeal from the High Court of Australia. A giant redgum tree on the defendant's property was struck by lightning and caught fire. The blaze was impossible to deal with while the tree was standing, so it was cut down, and the defendant cleared a space around the tree. From the following day, the defendant did nothing to extinguish the fire, preferring to let it burn itself out. It was found that the defendant could have extinguished the fire by spraying it with water either immediately after the tree was felled, or on the following day. A change in the weather caused the fire to flare up and spread to the plaintiff's land, after which it could not be stopped. The Court of Western Australia found that there was no action available either in nuisance, or in *Rylands v Fletcher*. On appeal, the High Court of Australia held that the appellant was under a duty to use reasonable care once the tree was felled in order to stop the fire from causing damage to his neighbours. The appeal raised the question of whether the principle in *Sedleigh-Denfield* would apply to nuisances arising naturally. But it also raised questions about the *content* of the positive duty.

Lord Wilberforce, at 656–7 (giving the judgment of the Board)

... the case is not one where a person has brought a source of danger onto his land, nor one where an occupier has so used his property as to cause a danger to his neighbour. It is one where an occupier, faced with a hazard accidentally arising on his land, fails to act with reasonable prudence so as to remove the hazard. The issue is therefore whether in such a case the occupier is guilty of legal negligence, which involves the issue whether he is under a duty of care, and, if so, what is the scope of that duty. Their Lordships propose to deal with these issues as stated, without attempting to answer the disputable question whether if responsibility is established it should be brought under the heading of nuisance or placed in a separate category. As this Board has recently explained in *Overseas Tankship (U.K.) Ltd. v. Miller Steamship Co. Pty. Ltd. (The Wagon Mound No. 2)* [1966] 3 WLR 498), the tort of nuisance, uncertain in its boundary, may comprise a wide variety of situations, in some of which negligence plays no part, in others of which it is decisive. The present case is one where liability, if it exists, rests upon negligence and nothing else; whether it falls within or overlaps the boundaries of nuisance is a question of classification which need not here be resolved.

What then is the scope of an occupier's duty, with regard to his neighbours, as to hazards arising on his land? With the possible exception of hazard of fire, to which their Lordships will shortly revert, it is only in comparatively recent times that the law has recognised an occupier's duty as one of a more positive character than merely to abstain from creating, or adding to, a source of danger or annoyance. It was for long satisfied with the conception of separate or autonomous proprietors, each of whom was entitled to exploit his territory in a "natural" manner and none of whom was obliged to restrain or direct the operations of nature in the interest of avoiding harm to his neighbours....

Lord Wilberforce reviewed the older case law including *Giles v Walker* (1890) 24 QBD 656, and rejected a suggested distinction between the present case (natural hazard) and the case of *Sedleigh-Denfield v O'Callaghan* (nuisance created by a third party). He concluded (at 661) that:

> On principle ..., their Lordships find in the opinions of the House of Lords in *Sedleigh-Denfield v O'Callaghan* ... support for the existence of a general duty upon occupiers in relation to hazards occurring on their land, whether natural or man-made.

Later, he considered the *content* of the occupier's duty to neighbours (at 663):

> So far it has been possible to consider the existence of a duty, in general terms. But the matter cannot be left there without some definition of the scope of his duty. How far does it go? What is the standard of the effort required? What is the position as regards expenditure? It is

not enough to say merely that these must be "reasonable," since what is reasonable to one man may be very unreasonable, and indeed ruinous, to another: the law must take account of the fact that the occupier on whom the duty is cast has, ex hypothesi, had this hazard thrust upon him through no seeking or fault of his own. His interest, and his resources, whether physical or material, may be of a very modest character either in relation to the magnitude of the hazard, or as compared with those of his threatened neighbour. A rule which required of him in such unsought circumstances in his neighbour's interest a physical effort of which he is not capable, or an excessive expenditure of money, would be unenforceable or unjust. One may say in general terms that the existence of a duty must be based upon knowledge of the hazard, ability to foresee the consequences of not checking or removing it, and the ability to abate it. And in many cases, as, for example, in Scrutton L.J.'s hypothetical case of stamping out a fire, or the present case, where the hazard could have been removed with little effort and no expenditure, no problem arises. But other cases may not be so simple. In such situations the standard ought to be to require of the occupier what it is reasonable to expect of him in his individual circumstances. Thus, less must be expected of the infirm than of the able-bodied: the owner of a small property where a hazard arises which threatens a neighbour with substantial interests should not have to do so much as one with larger interests of his own at stake and greater resources to protect them: if the small owner does what he can and promptly calls on his neighbour to provide additional resources, he may be held to have done his duty: he should not be liable unless it is clearly proved that he could, and reasonably in his individual circumstance should, have done more. . . . Their Lordships therefore reach the conclusion that the respondents' claim for damages, on the basis of negligence, was fully made out.

Leakey & Others v National Trust [1980] QB 485

The plaintiffs' two houses had been built at the foot of a large mound of earth, 'The Burrow Mump', which was owned and occupied by the defendants. Due to natural weathering and the particular steepness of the relevant banks of the Mump, soil and debris had fallen on the houses over a number of years. After a hot summer and a wet autumn in 1976, the plaintiffs drew the defendants' attention to a large crack in the soil above their houses. Some time later, there was a fall of soil and tree roots on to the plaintiffs' property, and the plaintiffs brought an action in nuisance seeking orders for the abatement of the nuisance and damages.

The Court of Appeal reaffirmed the proposition in *Goldman v Hargrave* that the occupier of land owes positive duties to a neighbour in respect of a nuisance arising on his land through the operation of natural forces, and confirmed that this proposition formed part of English law. It also reaffirmed that the duty as outlined in *Goldman v Hargrave* was subjective, so that the steps which ought reasonably to be taken would vary depending on the resources of the defendant. Such questions, according to Megaw LJ, could be addressed in a broad and general way, and would not require long enquiry into the exact resources available to the parties.

Megaw LJ dealt briefly with the question of the cause of action:

Megaw LJ, at 514–15

. . . The plaintiffs' claim is expressed in the pleadings to be founded in nuisance. There is no express reference to negligence in the statement of claim. But there is an allegation of a breach of duty, and the duty asserted is, in effect, a duty to take reasonable care to prevent part of the defendants' land from falling on to the plaintiffs' property. I should, for myself, regard that as being properly described as a claim in nuisance. But even if that were, technically, wrong, I do not think that the point could or should avail the defendants in this case. If it were to do so, it would be a regrettable modern instance of the forms of action successfully clanking their spectral chains; for there would be no conceivable prejudice to the defendants in this case that the word "negligence" had not been expressly set out in the statement of claim.

Megaw LJ also suggested that the case of *Sedleigh-Denfield v O'Callaghan* marked a turning point in the law, and that:

That change in the law, in its essence and in its timing, corresponds with, and may be viewed as being a part of, the change in the law of tort which achieved its decisive victory in *Donoghue v. Stevenson* [1932] A.C. 562: though it was not until eight years later, in the House of Lords decision in *Sedleigh-Denfield v. O'Callaghan* [1940] A.C. 880, that the change as affecting the area with which we are concerned was expressed or recognised in a decision binding on all English courts: and, even then, the full, logical effect of the decision in altering what had hitherto been thought to be the law was not immediately recognised. But *Goldman v. Hargrave* has now demonstrated what that effect was in English law.

The 'change' with which Megaw LJ is concerned is the recognition of positive duties to act consequent on the occupation of property, and requiring reasonable steps to be taken to prevent harm to one's neighbours. And yet, positive duties to act are no less controversial in the tort of negligence than they have been in nuisance. Megaw LJ may or may not be correct to say that the developments in *Sedleigh-Denfield* and *Goldman v Hargrave* were encouraged by the development of the tort of negligence, but it cannot be assumed that an analysis of those cases in terms of negligence alone would necessarily have led to the decisions as they were reached.

Writing in 1989, Conor Gearty suggested that cases such as *Sedleigh-Denfield*, which concerned indirectly caused physical damage to property, were historically more appropriately categorized as aspects of the newly emerging tort of negligence, rather than of nuisance (Gearty, Further Reading). In key cases such as *Cambridge Water* and *Hunter v Canary Wharf*, the House of Lords has re-emphasized the independence of nuisance from negligence. Arguably, there is now more confidence in the general irrelevance of the defendant's conduct to the majority of nuisance actions, and nuisance exists more securely as an independent action. This being so, there may be less 'strategic' need to evacuate the cases of overlap studied here from the tort of nuisance, and it is suggested that the continuation of the *Sedleigh-Denfield* line of cases is now too well established as an aspect of nuisance to make such a move desirable.

Holbeck Hall Hotel Ltd v Scarborough BC [2000] QB 836

The developments in *Leakey* were tested again before the Court of Appeal in this coastal erosion case. The defendant owned the undercliff between the grounds of the plaintiffs' hotel, and the sea. There had been two landslips on the defendants' land below the hotel in the 1980s, and investigations had therefore been conducted, leading to some remedial works. In 1993, a major landslip caused loss of support to the hotel and grounds and the hotel itself had to be demolished. This case raised questions about the content and extent of the 'measured duty of care' which had not arisen in any significant form in the previous case law.

The Court of Appeal determined that *Sedleigh-Denfield* and *Leakey* applied to a case of loss of support, and considered whether the defendants 'ought to have known' of the danger to the plaintiffs' land, and thus whether a measured duty of care arose. Further, if such a duty did arise, what was the extent of that duty?

In determining whether the 'measured duty of care' arose, Stuart-Smith LJ drew a distinction between *patent* dangers and defects (which can easily be observed), and *latent* dangers and defects. In respect of latent defects, no duty arose to conduct investigations. The emphasis was on 'knowledge' and (through the idea of 'presumed knowledge') on what 'should have been seen'.

Stuart-Smith LJ, *Holbeck Hall Hotel v Scarborough BC*

42. The duty arises when the defect is known and the hazard or danger to the claimants' land is reasonably foreseeable, that is to say it is a danger which a reasonable man with knowledge of the defect should have foreseen as likely to eventuate in the reasonably near future. It is the existence of the defect coupled with the danger that constitutes the nuisance; it is knowledge or presumed knowledge of the nuisance that involves liability for continuing it when it could reasonably be abated....if the defect is latent, the landowner or occupier is not to be held liable simply because, if he had made further investigation, he would have discovered it....

On these particular facts,

43 ....it is in my view clear that Scarborough did not foresee a danger of anything like the magnitude that eventuated. It was common ground that the G.E.N. report gave no clue of such an eventuality; and it seems clear that they could not have appreciated the risk without further investigation by experts.

Stuart-Smith LJ then drew a distinction between the measured duty of care, and 'most cases where physical injury either to the person or the property of the claimant is reasonably foreseeable' (at 44). In the normal run of such cases, he pointed out, there will be liability for all damage of the type that was foreseeable, notwithstanding the extent.[9] The measured duty of care, on his analysis, operates in a way which is contrary to this usual remoteness rule, for it places limits on the *extent* of damage for which the defendant is potentially liable. It does this because of the special subjective nature of the duty. Stuart-Smith LJ particularly highlighted one sentence from the judgment of Lord Wilberforce in *Goldman v Hargrave* quoted earlier in this section, namely that: '*One may say in general terms that the existence of a duty must be based upon knowledge of the hazard, ability to foresee the consequences of not checking or removing it, and the ability to abate it*' (Lord Wilberforce at 663, quoted by Stuart-Smith LJ at 46).

---

[9] This is the consequence of *The Wagon Mound*: see Chapter 3.

In conclusion:

49. ... I do not think justice requires that a defendant should be held liable for damage which, albeit of the same type, was vastly more extensive than that which was foreseen or could have been foreseen without extensive further geological investigation; and this is particularly so where the defect existed just as much on the plaintiffs' land as on their own. In considering the scope of the measured duty of care, the courts are still in relatively uncharted waters. But I can find nothing in the two cases where it has been considered, namely *Goldman's* case [1967] 1 A.C. 645 and *Leakey's* case [1980] Q.B. 485 to prevent the court reaching a just result.

The content of the 'measured duty of care' has also been considered by the Court of Appeal more recently. In *Lambert v Barratt Homes* [2010] EWCA Civ 681, the Court of Appeal found that a judge had failed to consider the scope of the duty owed by a local authority to abate a 'natural nuisance'. While here, the defendant was under a duty to cooperate and to allow access to its land to allow remedial works to be completed, it was not under a duty to carry out those works nor to pay for them to be undertaken. The existence of a negligent party, in this case a developer, was a consideration, since the defendants by contrast were 'not in the slightest degree responsible for' the cause of the flooding. Although the local authority could be expected to have funds 'far in excess of those available to the individual respondents', this was not a reason to place the burden of paying for prevention with them. Somewhat controversially, the Court of Appeal also noted that the claim was brought by insurers of the claimants, and saw 'no reason to ignore' the possibility of their obtaining the necessary funds from their insurers ([22]).

This last statement was questioned, and to some extent criticized, in the case of *Vernon Knights Associates v Cornwall Council* [2013] EWCA Civ 950. In this case, there had been a breach of the measured duty of care when a highway authority failed to implement its own drains maintenance system in order to alleviate flooding of the claimants' land. It was therefore a very different case from *Lambert*. Determining the content of the relevant duty was said to involve a 'somewhat daunting multifactorial assessment' ([50]).

Jackson LJ, *Vernon Knights Associates v Cornwall Council*

49 Where then does the law now stand in relation to the liability of land owners for nonfeasance in respect of natural nuisance? I would not presume to paraphrase the vast body of learning which has accumulated on this topic. Nevertheless I extract from the authorities discussed above the following principles which are relevant to the determination of this appeal:

(i) A landowner owes a measured duty in both negligence and nuisance to take reasonable steps to prevent natural occurrences on his land from causing damage to neighbouring properties.

(ii) In determining the content of the measured duty, the court must consider what is fair, just and reasonable as between the two neighbouring landowners. It must have regard to all the circumstances, including the extent of the foreseeable risk, the available preventive measures, the costs of such measures and the resources of both parties.

(iii) Where the defendant is a public authority with substantial resources, the court must take into account the competing demands on those resources and the public purposes for which they are held. It may not be fair, just or reasonable to require a public authority to expend those resources on infrastructure works in order to protect a few individuals against a modest risk of property damage.

Jackson LJ confessed to 'some doubt as to whether the availability of insurance is a relevant consideration', as he thought had been proposed in *Lambert*; whereas Sir Stanley Burnton expressed stronger doubts, suggesting that 'the availability of insurance is not normally relevant to a duty in tort', and that he could 'think of no case in which a claim in tort has been rejected on the ground that it is a subrogated claim' ([70]). However, it may be noted that the resources of both claimant and defendant were recognized as a proper part of the multi-factorial assessment to be undertaken. Further, as explored in Chapter 11, the *general* pattern of insurance of recognized risks—rather than the presence of a subrogated insurer in a particular case—has been taken into account in considering the extent of strict liability for damage done by escape of dangerous things from land ('*Rylands v Fletcher* liability'). In the case in hand, however, these issues did not need to be resolved: the defendants had failed to make use of an existing installation, and the Court of Appeal considered this to be a case where the measured duty had been breached.

Nonfeasance and Statute

Marcic v Thames Water Utilities Ltd [2004] 2 AC 42, reversing Court of Appeal ([2002] EWCA Civ 64; [2002] 2 WLR 932)

Here the Court of Appeal made surprising use of the *Leakey* line of cases in order to hold a sewerage undertaker liable in nuisance for external flooding by foul water suffered by the plaintiff's property. (The court would also have awarded a remedy under the Human Rights Act 1998 (HRA), had the remedy in nuisance not been sufficient.) The decision was surprising because it was contrary to previous case law determining the liability of sewerage undertakers; and because of the way in which the court interpreted the burden of proving 'fairness' for the purposes of the measured duty of care. The court proposed that the burden of proving that the duty was discharged (which in this instance would be the case if their system of priorities was 'fair') lay on the defendants. Ordinarily, it is of course for the claimant to show that a duty has been breached. Indeed, the Court of Appeal suggested that the taking of 'reasonable steps' to alleviate a nuisance was a *defence* to an action in nuisance. It is clear from the cases reviewed earlier that the subjective content of the measured duty of care is relevant to whether duties arise and are breached, rather than to whether defences are made out in order to rebut some form of presumed liability.

Still more surprising was the content of the 'measured duty' in this case. The flooding of Mr Marcic's property could be alleviated only by acquiring land and building more sewers. In holding that the positive duty under *Leakey* could compel a defendant to take such steps, the Court of Appeal discovered a far more onerous positive duty than has previously been associated with the 'measured duty of care'. The estimated cost of £1,000 million to alleviate the flooding problems of all those in the same position as the plaintiff ([2002]

EWCA Civ 64, at [3]) is a significant investment even for a trading company of the size of the defendants.[10]

The House of Lords reversed the Court of Appeal's decision. The *Leakey* line of cases did nothing to alter the position in respect of sewerage undertakers stated by Denning LJ in *Pride of Derby and Derbyshire Angling Association v British Celanese Ltd* [1953] Ch 149, which was itself based on consideration of the *Sedleigh-Denfield* case:

Denning LJ, at 190, quoted by Lord Hoffmann, *Marcic v Thames Water Utilities*, at [55]

... they [the plaintiffs] have a perfectly good cause of action for nuisance, if they can show that the defendants created or continued the cause of the trouble; and it must be remembered that a person may "continue" a nuisance by adopting it, or in some circumstances by omitting to remedy it: see *Sedleigh-Denfield v. O'Callaghan*.

This liability for nuisance has been applied in the past to sewage and drainage cases in this way: when a local authority take over or construct a sewage and drainage system which is adequate at the time to dispose of the sewage and surface water for their district, but which subsequently becomes inadequate owing to increased building which they cannot control, and for which they have no responsibility, they are not guilty of the ensuing nuisance. They obviously do not create it, nor do they continue it merely by doing nothing to enlarge or improve the system. The only remedy of the injured party is to complain to the Minister.

The House of Lords added that there were good reasons for the common law not to interfere further than this with the activities of sewerage undertakers through the law of nuisance, in particular that the issues had been allocated by statute to an independent regulator with elaborate powers of enforcement.[11] The existence of the statutory scheme was said to exclude the operation of the tort of nuisance, although we may assume from the approval of Denning LJ's statement in the *Pride of Derby* case that the common law is only excluded so far as it relates to cases where the sewerage undertaker has taken over sewers built by another, and where the sewers have become inadequate due to increased demand. This was the situation in *Marcic* itself.

Lord Nicholls, *Marcic v Thames Water Utilities*

34 In my view the cause of action in nuisance asserted by Mr Marcic is inconsistent with the statutory scheme. Mr Marcic's claim is expressed in various ways but in practical terms it always comes down to this: Thames Water ought to build more sewers. This is the only way Thames Water can prevent sewer flooding of Mr Marcic's property. This is the only way because it is not suggested that Thames Water failed to operate its existing sewage system properly by not cleaning or maintaining it. Nor can Thames Water control the volume of water entering the sewers under Old Church Lane. Every new house built has an absolute right to connect. Thames Water is obliged to accept these connections: section 106 of the 1991 Act. A sewerage undertaker is unable to prevent connections being made to the existing system, and the ingress of water through these connections, even if this risks overloading the existing sewers. But, so Mr Marcic's claim runs, although Thames Water was operating its existing system properly, and although Thames Water had no control over the volume of water entering the system, it was within Thames Water's power to build more sewers, as the company now has done, to cope with the increased volume of water entering

10 Annual profits were estimated at £344 million. Having said that, it appears that by the time the case reached the House of Lords, there had been a change in priorities, and the required work had been carried out.

11 Water Industry Act 1991.

the system. Mr Marcic, it is said, has a cause of action at law in respect of Thames Water's failure to construct more sewers before it eventually did in June 2003.

35 The difficulty I have with this line of argument is that it ignores the statutory limitations on the enforcement of sewerage undertakers' drainage obligations. Since sewerage undertakers have no control over the volume of water entering their sewerage systems it would be surprising if Parliament intended that whenever sewer flooding occurs, every householder whose property has been affected can sue the appointed sewerage undertaker for an order that the company build more sewers or pay damages. On the contrary, it is abundantly clear that one important purpose of the enforcement scheme in the 1991 Act is that individual householders should not be able to launch proceedings in respect of failure to build sufficient sewers. When flooding occurs the first enforcement step under the statute is that the director, as the regulator of the industry, will consider whether to make an enforcement order. He will look at the position of an individual householder but in the context of the wider considerations spelled out in the statute. Individual householders may bring proceedings in respect of inadequate drainage only when the undertaker has failed to comply with an enforcement order made by the Secretary of State or the director. The existence of a parallel common law right, whereby individual householders who suffer sewer flooding may themselves bring court proceedings when no enforcement order has been made, would set at nought the statutory scheme. It would effectively supplant the regulatory role the director was intended to discharge when questions of sewer flooding arise.

36 For this reason I consider there is no room in this case for a common law cause of action in nuisance as submitted by Mr Marcic and held by the Court of Appeal.

There will be more to say concerning the House of Lords' handling of the HRA claim in this case, in Section 2 of this chapter. However, for the moment it is worth considering whether the House of Lords was too sceptical about the ability of a court to consider the fairness of the situation as it affected the claimant. For all that the Court of Appeal required a very significant investment by the defendants, that investment had somehow become possible by the time of the action in the House of Lords, and the remedial action had been carried out. Furthermore, the Director had stated in the process of consultation that the *Marcic* case had concentrated *his* mind on the need for 'robust and rational prioritisation schemes' (Lord Nicholls, at [28]), so that it contributed to the formulation of a new and perhaps more defensible approach. Lord Nicholls further admitted in his judgment that '[i]n Mr Marcic's case, matters plainly went awry' (at [43]). Without recourse to the courts, whether through the nuisance claim or the HRA claim, would 'fairness' have received such an emphasis in the new priorities adopted? A critique of the treatment of the statutory scheme in *Marcic* can be found in M. Lee, 'Occupying the Field: Tort and the Pre-Emptive Statute', in T. T. Arvind and J. Steele (eds) *Tort Law and the Legislature* (Hart Publishing, 2013). At the most general level, the comments may also be contrasted with recent cases emphasizing the independence of nuisance, and regulatory schemes, in relation to planning permission in particular (Section 1.3).

In *Dobson v Thames Water* [2007] EWHC 2021, Ramsey J distinguished *Marcic*, and held that an action in nuisance is potentially available if a claimant can show *negligence* in the day-to-day operation of a sewerage system, provided that action does not 'conflict with' the statutory scheme. Lack of care may therefore take the interference outside the protection of *Marcic* and of *Leakey*, particularly if the alleged negligence attaches to 'operational' issues such as the maintenance of a sewage plant, rather than 'policy'-based decisions such as the setting of priorities for spending. Conflict with the statutory scheme is much less likely in these circumstances. In this case, the claimants complained of smells and mosquitoes emanating from a water treatment plant which, they argued, was not carefully run. Such a claim was arguable since it would not fall foul of the considerations that were decisive against the *Marcic* claim. In the short extract below, Ramsey J identifies the concerns which were decisive in *Marcic*, all of which were arguably inapplicable on the assumed facts of this case.

Ramsey J, *Dobson v Thames Water* [2007] EWHC 2021

142. In *Marcic* Lord Nicholls emphasised the "no fault" position in which Thames Water found itself. At para 34 he said "*it is not suggested that Thames Water failed to operate its existing sewage system properly by not cleaning or maintaining it*" and was "*unable to prevent connections being made to the existing system … even if this risks overloading the existing sewers.*" In those circumstances, he said at para 35 that proceedings would "*set at nought the statutory scheme*" and "*effectively supplant the regulatory role*" of Ofwat. Again Lord Hoffmann at para 53 referred to the same lack of a failure by Thames Water and at para 63 referred to the distinction where the exercise involved "*capital expenditure of a statutory undertaking*" as to which the statutory scheme not the court can make the relevant decisions. Otherwise as he said at para 70 the courts would "*subvert the scheme of the 1991 Act.*"

143. There are, in my judgment, two aspects to the reasoning. First, there is the emphasis on absence of fault. Secondly, there is the concept of an inconsistent court process which conflicts with the statutory scheme. If there is fault in the form of negligence and if there is a different cause of action which is not inconsistent and does not conflict then I consider there is nothing to preclude a claim being made on that basis. Policy matters are likely to lead to such inconsistency and conflict whilst operational matters are less likely to do so. It must be a question of fact and degree. Where an allegation is tantamount to requiring major plant renewal that will fall on one side of the line whilst an allegation that a filter should be cleaned will lie on the other side. The mere fact that the effect of the cause of action is to enforce the duty in s. 94(1) does not in itself preclude the cause of action. [Emphasis in original]

Common law remedies may be available then, even if the duty which is thereby enforced appears to be the same as a statutory duty. This is consistent with the position in relation to negligence in the sphere of statutory duties, discussed in Chapter 6, Section 3.[12] The important issue is conflict with the statutory scheme. Overlap without conflict is acceptable. Significant issues surrounding the remedies that might arise if such a nuisance was established were subject to appeal, and are considered in Section 2.2 of this chapter.

Nuisance Created by Tenants and Licensees

Baxter v Camden LBC (No 2) [2001] 1 AC 1

Here, the council had divided a house into three dwellings, and the plaintiffs were tenants of the middle floor. The tenant complained to the council that she suffered serious interference in her enjoyment of the flat as a result of the normal day-to-day noise generated by her neighbours. Although this noise was not unusual, its effect was made worse by the

[12] See particularly our discussion of *Stovin v Wise* [1996] AC 923.

poor sound insulation installed during conversion of the premises. She brought proceedings both on the basis of breach of the covenant of quiet enjoyment in her tenancy, and for nuisance. Her claim for breach of covenant was dismissed because the problem that arose was a result of the state of the premises at the time they were let. The claim in nuisance was also dismissed:

Lord Hoffmann, *Baxter v Camden LBC (No 2)*, at 15–16

I turn next to the law of private nuisance. I can deal with this quite shortly because it seems to me that the appellants face an insuperable difficulty. Nuisance involves doing something on adjoining or nearby land which constitutes an unreasonable interference with the utility of the plaintiff's land. The primary defendant is the person who causes the nuisance by doing the acts in question. As Sir John Pennycuick V-C said in *Smith v Scott* [1973] Ch 314, 321:

> "It is established beyond question that the person to be sued in nuisance is the occupier of the property from which the nuisance emanates. In general, a landlord is not liable for nuisance committed by his tenant, but to this rule there is, so far as now in point, one recognised exception, namely, that the landlord is liable if he has authorised his tenant to commit the nuisance."

What is the nuisance of which the appellants complain? The sounds emanating from their neighbours' flats. But they do not allege the making of these sounds to be a nuisance committed by the other tenants....

... If the neighbours are not committing a nuisance, the councils cannot be liable for authorising them to commit one. And there is no other basis for holding the landlords liable. They are not themselves doing anything which interferes with the appellants' use of their flats. Once again, it all comes down to a complaint about the inherent defects in the construction of the building. The appellants say that the ordinary use of the flats by their neighbours would not have caused them inconvenience if they had been differently built. But that, as I have said more than once, is a matter of which a tenant cannot complain.

As explained here, the lessor is liable for nuisances created by a tenant only if he or she has authorized that nuisance. If the tenant does not create a nuisance, then the landlord does not authorize a nuisance, and so cannot be liable. As Lord Millett put it, at 22:

> The logic of the proposition is obvious. A landlord cannot be liable to an action for authorising his tenant to do something that would not be actionable if he did it himself.

Authorizing a nuisance, rather than creating it by bad design of the premises let, therefore appears to be the only basis on which a landlord will be liable for noise nuisance resulting from the activities of tenants. In fact, the result does not seem to be entirely compelled by logic, as Lord Millett suggests. The House of Lords adopts quite a narrow formulation, particularly when compared with the decision of the Court of Appeal in *Lippiatt*, concerning the congregation of people likely to commit a nuisance upon one's land (below).

In the slightly earlier case of *Hussain v Lancaster City Council* [2000] QB 1, the Court of Appeal also emphasized that the landlord's liability for nuisances caused by the tenant are limited. In this case, the acts of the tenants certainly constituted a nuisance. They carried out a series of acts including racial harassment of neighbours and acts of vandalism against their properties. The council, as landlords, were subject to actions in negligence and nuisance for failing to control the acts of the tenants. Both claims failed. In respect of the action in nuisance, Hirst LJ concluded that the acts of the tenants 'did not involve the tenants' use of the tenants' land and therefore fell outside the scope of the tort' (at 23). This seems to be a reference to the fact that they left their own homes in order to carry out their actions, although this reasoning will be hard to reconcile with the law on licensees (below). Giving what appeared to be a separate sufficient reason for the decision, Hirst LJ added that accord-ing to *Smith v Scott* [1973] Ch 314, a similar case involving nuisances created (on that occa-sion foreseeably) by council tenants, the only grounds for holding a landlord liable for the nuisances of his or her tenant is that the landlord authorized the nuisance. The liability of landlords for nuisances created by tenants was also considered in *Lawrence v Fen Tigers (No 2)* [2015] AC 106, Lord Neuberger suggesting that for a landlord to be liable, they 'must either participate directly in the commission of the nuisance, or they must be taken to have authorized it by letting the property' (at para [11]). In *Cocking v Eacott* [2016] EWCA Civ 140; [2016] 3 WLR 125, Voss LJ summarized the position, namely that for liability (at para [17]):

> there had to be actual, active or direct participation by the landlord or his agents, and the fact that a landlord does nothing to stop or discourage a nuisance cannot amount to participating in it.

Licensees

In *Lippiatt v S. Gloucestershire CC* [2000] QB 51, travellers had congregated on the defend-ant council's land, on one edge of a road. The plaintiffs were tenant farmers of land situated on either side of the road. They complained that the travellers frequently trespassed on their land and carried out various acts amounting to a nuisance, including obstruction, fouling with rubbish and excrement, theft, and actual damage. The first instance judge, Judge Weeks QC, had struck out the statement of claim on the basis that it could not succeed following the newly decided *Hussain* case: the nuisance, he concluded, had not arisen from the licensees' use of the council's land. The Court of Appeal ruled however that the action should not be struck out. The Court therefore had to suggest that this case was at least arguably distin-guishable from the *Hussain* case.

Evans LJ seemed to suggest that the nuisance was not that of the tenants or licensees in carrying out the acts, but that of the council in allowing the licensees to congregate. The question of whether the council authorized or adopted the nuisance therefore need not arise. But if this is what justifies the potential liability in *Lippiatt*, why could the same argu-ment not be used against the council in *Hussain*—that they ought to have taken steps to have evicted the tenants? Perhaps the answer is that the eviction of tenants with a right to occupation, by a housing authority with obligations to provide housing, is a more complex operation which involves many different agencies. Some reasons of this sort were discussed in *Hussain* as militating against the success of an action in nuisance. The same distinction also seems implicit in *Lippiatt*: he proposed that the offenders were either licensees or trespassers, and 'could be moved on'.

In *Cocking v Eacott* [2016] EWCA Civ 140; [2016] 3 WLR 125, the distinction between a tenancy and a licence was crucial to liability. The distinction was explained on the basis that a landlord, unlike a licensor, has ceased to be in occupation of the land: it is the tenant who is the occupier.

Lady Justice Arden, *Cocking v Eacott*
[2016] EWCA Civ 140

34. A landlord who has granted a tenancy is not in general liable in nuisance if his tenant commits that tort. Mrs Waring let her daughter into her property and allowed her and her dog to live there without executing a tenancy. The dog's persistent barking caused a nuisance to the neighbours. Mrs Waring now accepts that the barking amounted to a nuisance: she seeks only to argue that she should not be liable for the tort of her daughter and that she should be in the same position as if she had granted a tenancy.

35. In my judgment, in agreement with Vos and McFarlane LJJ, that argument is wrong in law and the appeal should be dismissed. I agree with the judge that Mrs Waring was liable in law for the nuisance caused by her daughter's dog because as licensor she is to be treated as in occupation of the property. She is not in the same position as a landlord who has parted with possession of the property.

1.5 WHO MAY SUE?

The question of who may sue in private nuisance goes to the very heart of the tort, for it is related to the question of which interests it protects. In the case of *Hunter v Canary Wharf*, the House of Lords has affirmed that nuisance is to be regarded as a tort against property, and not a tort against the person.

Hunter v Canary Wharf [1997] AC 655

The plaintiffs lived in London's Docklands area, which was designated by the Secretary of State as an urban development area and enterprise zone. The consequence of this was that the normal planning process was suspended. It amounted in effect to a general grant of planning permission. Some of the plaintiffs were property owners or leaseholders; others were mere occupiers. The latter group included children. In the first of two actions, the plaintiffs claimed for damages in negligence and nuisance in respect of interference with television reception following the construction of the 'Canary Wharf' tower (250 metres high and over 50 metres square). In the second action, the plaintiffs claimed damages for negligence and nuisance in respect of deposits of dust on their properties and homes caused by the construction of a link road. At first instance, the judge ruled that interference with television reception could amount to a nuisance, but that to claim in private nuisance it was necessary to have a right to exclusive possession of property. The Court of Appeal unanimously reversed these two rulings. The appeal to the House of Lords concerned two points relating to private nuisance. First, could interference with television signals amount to a private nuisance? On this aspect of the case, see the extract in Section 1.3 of this chapter. Second, were all of the plaintiffs entitled to sue in nuisance? We will concentrate here on this crucial second point.

Lord Goff, at 687

Right to sue in private nuisance

... In the two cases now under appeal before your Lordships' House, one of which relates to interference with television signals and the other to the generation of dust from the construction of a road, the plaintiffs consist in each case of a substantial group of local people. Moreover they are not restricted to householders who have the exclusive right to possess the places where they live, whether as freeholders or tenants, or even as licensees. They include people with whom householders share their homes, for example as wives or husbands or partners, or as children or other relatives. All of these people are claiming damages in private nuisance, by reason of interference with their television viewing or by reason of excessive dust.

...

Lord Hoffmann, at 704–8

... the concept of nuisance as a tort against land has recently been questioned by the decision of the Court of Appeal in *Khorasandjian v. Bush* [1993] Q.B. 727. ... Dillon L.J. brushed *Malone v. Laskey* [1907] 2 K.B. 141 aside. He said, at p. 734:

"To my mind, it is ridiculous if in this present age the law is that the making of deliberately harassing and pestering telephone calls to a person is only actionable in the civil courts if the recipient of the calls happens to have the freehold or a leasehold proprietary interest in the premises in which he or she has received the calls."

This reasoning, which is echoed in some academic writing and the Canadian case of *Motherwell v. Motherwell*, 73 D.L.R. (3d) 62 which the Court of Appeal followed, is based upon a fundamental mistake about the remedy which the tort of nuisance provides. It arises, I think, out of a misapplication of an important distinction drawn by Lord Westbury L.C. in *St. Helen's Smelting Co. v. Tipping* (1865).

Lord Hoffmann quoted from Lord Westbury's judgment in *St Helen's Tipping* and continued:

St. Helen's Smelting Co. v. Tipping was a landmark case. It drew the line beyond which rural and landed England did not have to accept external costs imposed upon it by industrial pollution. But there has been, I think, some inclination to treat it as having divided nuisance into two torts, one of causing "material injury to the property," such as flooding or depositing poisonous substances on crops, and the other of causing "sensible personal discomfort" such as excessive noise or smells. In cases in the first category, there has never been any doubt that the remedy, whether by way of injunction or damages, is for causing damage to the land. It is plain that in such a case only a person with an interest in the land can sue. But there has been a tendency to regard cases in the second category as actions in respect of the discomfort or even personal injury which the plaintiff has suffered or is likely to suffer. On this view, the plaintiff's interest in the land becomes no more than a qualifying condition or springboard which entitles him to sue for injury to himself.

If this were the case, the need for the plaintiff to have an interest in land would indeed be hard to justify. The passage I have quoted from Dillon L.J. (*Khorasandjian v. Bush* [1993] Q.B.

727, 734) is an eloquent statement of the reasons. But the premise is quite mistaken. In the case of nuisances "productive of sensible personal discomfort," the action is not for causing discomfort to the person but, as in the case of the first category, for causing injury to the land. True it is that the land has not suffered "sensible" injury, but its utility has been diminished by the existence of the nuisance. It is for an unlawful threat to the utility of his land that the possessor or occupier is entitled to an injunction and it is for the diminution in such utility that he is entitled to compensation.

I cannot therefore agree with Stephenson L.J. in *Bone v. Seale* [1975] 1 W.L.R. 797, 803 804 when he said that damages in an action for nuisance caused by smells from a pig farm should be fixed by analogy with damages for loss of amenity in an action for personal injury. In that case it was said that "efforts to prove diminution in the value of the property as a result of this persistent smell over the years failed." I take this to mean that it had not been shown that the property would sell for less. But diminution in capital value is not the only measure of loss. It seems to me that the value of the right to occupy a house which smells of pigs must be less than the value of the occupation of an equivalent house which does not. In the case of a transitory nuisance, the capital value of the property will seldom be reduced. But the owner or occupier is entitled to compensation for the diminution in the amenity value of the property during the period for which the nuisance persisted. To some extent this involves placing a value upon intangibles. But estates agents do this all the time. The law of damages is sufficiently flexible to be able to do justice in such a case: compare *Ruxley Electronics and Construction Ltd. v. Forsyth* [1996] A.C. 344.

There may of course be cases in which, in addition to damages for injury to his land, the owner or occupier is able to recover damages for consequential loss. He will, for example, be entitled to loss of profits which are the result of inability to use the land for the purposes of his business. Or if the land is flooded, he may also be able to recover damages for chattels or livestock lost as a result. But inconvenience, annoyance or even illness suffered by persons on land as a result of smells or dust are not damage consequential upon the injury to the land. It is rather the other way about: the injury to the amenity of the land consists in the fact that the persons upon it are liable to suffer inconvenience, annoyance or illness.

It follows that damages for nuisance recoverable by the possessor or occupier may be affected by the size, commodiousness and value of his property but cannot be increased merely because more people are in occupation and therefore suffer greater collective discomfort. If more than one person has an interest in the property, the damages will have to be divided among them. If there are joint owners, they will be jointly entitled to the damages. If there is a reversioner and the nuisance has caused damage of a permanent character which affects the reversion, he will be entitled to damages according to his interest. But the damages cannot be increased by the fact that the interests in the land are divided; still less according to the number of persons residing on the premises.

. . .

Once it is understood that nuisances "productive of sensible personal discomfort" (*St. Helen's Smelting Co. v. Tipping*, 11 H.L.Cas. 642, 650) do not constitute a separate tort of causing discomfort to people but are merely part of a single tort of causing injury to land, the rule that the plaintiff must have an interest in the land falls into place as logical and, indeed, inevitable.

Is there any reason of policy why the rule should be abandoned? Once nuisance has escaped the bounds of being a tort against land, there seems no logic in compromise limitations, such as that proposed by the Court of Appeal in this case, requiring the plaintiff to have been resid-ing on land as his or her home. This was recognised by the Court of Appeal in *Khorasandjian v. Bush* [1993] Q.B. 727 where the injunction applied whether the plaintiff was at home or not. There is a good deal in this case and other writings about the need for the law to adapt to modern social conditions. But the development of the common law should be rational and coherent. It should not distort its principles and create anomalies merely as an expedient to fill a gap.

The perceived gap in *Khorasandjian v. Bush* was the absence of a tort of intentional harass-ment causing distress without actual bodily or psychiatric illness. This limitation is thought to arise out of cases like *Wilkinson v. Downton* [1897] 2 Q.B. 57 and *Janvier v. Sweeney* [1919] 2 K.B. 316. The law of harassment has now been put on a statutory basis (see the Protection from Harassment Act 1997) and it is unnecessary to consider how the common law might have developed. But as at present advised, I see no reason why a tort of intention should be subject to the rule which excludes compensation for mere distress, inconvenience or dis-comfort in actions based on negligence: see *Hicks v. Chief Constable of the South Yorkshire Police* [1992] 2 All E.R. 65. The policy considerations are quite different. I do not therefore say that *Khorasandjian v. Bush* was wrongly decided. But it must be seen as a case on intentional harassment, not nuisance.

So far as the claim is for personal injury, it seems to me that the only appropriate cause of action is negligence. It would be anomalous if the rules for recovery of damages under this head were different according as to whether, for example, the plaintiff was at home or at work. It is true, as I have said, that the law of negligence gives no remedy for discomfort or distress which does not result in bodily or psychiatric illness. But this is a matter of general policy and I can see no logic in making an exception for cases in which the discomfort or distress was suffered at home rather than somewhere else.

Lord Cooke of Thornden (dissenting on the issue of who can sue in nuisance), at 711–12

... Naturally I am diffident about disagreeing in any respect with the majority of your Lordships, but such assistance as I may be able to give in your deliberations could not consist in mere conformity and deference; and, if the common law of England is to be directed into the restricted path which in this instance the majority prefer, there may be some advantage in bringing out that the choice is in the end a policy one between compet-ing principles ...

At 713–14

Malone v. Laskey, a case of personal injury from a falling bracket rather than an interference with amenities, is not directly in point, but it is to be noted that the wife of the subtenant's manager, who had been permitted by the subtenant to live in the premises with her husband, was dismissed by Sir Gorell Barnes P., at p. 151, as a person who had "no right of occupation in the proper sense of the term" and by Fletcher Moulton L.J. as being "merely present." My Lords, whatever the acceptability of those descriptions 90 years ago, I can only agree with the Appellate Division of the Alberta Supreme Court in *Motherwell v. Motherwell*, at p. 77, that they are "rather light treatment of a wife, at least in today's society where she is no longer considered subservient to her husband." Current statutes give effect to current perceptions by according spouses a special status in respect of the matrimonial home, as by enabling the court to make orders regarding occupation (see in England the Family Law Act 1996, sections 30 and 31).

The status of children living at home is different and perhaps more problematical but, on consideration, I am persuaded by the majority of the Court of Appeal in *Khorasandjian v. Bush* [1993] Q.B. 727 and the weight of North American jurisprudence to the view that they, too, should be entitled to relief for substantial and unlawful interference with the amenities of their home. Internationally the distinct interests of children are increasingly recognised. The United Nations Convention on the Rights of the Child, ratified by the United Kingdom in 1991 and the most widely ratified human rights treaty in history, acknowledges children as fully-fledged beneficiaries of human rights. Article 16 declares, inter alia, that no child shall be subjected to unlawful interference with his or her home and that the child has the right to the protection of law against such interference. International standards such as this may be taken into account in shaping the common law.

The point just mentioned can be taken further. Article 16 of the Convention on the Rights of the Child adopts some of the language of article 12 of the Universal Declaration of Human Rights and article 8 of the European Convention for the Protection of Human Rights and Fundamental Freedoms (1953) (Cmd. 8969). These provisions are aimed, in part, at protecting the home and are construed to give protection against nuisances.... The protection is regarded as going beyond possession or property rights: see *Harris, O'Boyle and Warbrick, Law of the European Convention on Human Rights* (1995), p. 319. Again I think that this is a legitimate consideration in support of treating residence as an acceptable basis of standing at common law in the present class of case.

At 717–18

The preponderance of academic opinion seems also to be against confining the right to sue in nuisance for interference with amenities to plaintiffs with proprietary interests in land. Professor John G. Fleming's condemnation of a "senseless discrimination"—see now his 8th ed., p. 426—has already been mentioned. His view is that the wife and family residing with a tenant should be protected by the law of nuisance against forms of discomfort and also personal injuries, "by recognising that they have a 'right of occupation' just like the official tenant." *Clerk & Lindsell on Torts*, 17th ed., pp. 910–911, para. 18–39, is to the same effect, as is *Linden, Canadian Tort Law*, 5th ed. (1993), pp. 521–522; while *Winfield & Jolowicz on Tort*, 14th ed. (1994), pp. 419–420 and *Markesinis & Deakin, Tort Law*, 3rd ed. (1994), pp. 434–435 would extend the right to long-term lodgers. *Salmond & Heuston on the Law of Torts*, 21st ed. (1996), p. 63, n. 96 and the New Zealand work *Todd, The Law of Torts in New Zealand*, 2nd ed. (1997), p. 537 suggest that the status of spouses under modern legislation should at least be enough; and the preface to the same edition of *Salmond & Heuston* goes further, by welcoming the decision in *Khorasandjian v. Bush* [1993] Q.B. 727 as relieving plaintiffs in private nuisance cases of the need to show that they enjoyed a legal interest in the land affected.

My Lords, there is a maxim communis error facit jus. I have collected the foregoing references not to invoke it, however, but to suggest respectfully that on this hitherto unsettled issue the general trend of leading scholarly opinion need not be condemned as erroneous. Although hitherto the law of England on the point has not been settled by your Lordships' House, it is agreed on all hands that some link with the land is necessary for standing to sue in private nuisance. The precise nature of that link remains to be defined, partly because of the ambiguity of "occupy" and its derivatives. In ordinary usage the verb can certainly include "reside in," which is indeed the first meaning given in the *Concise Oxford Dictionary*.

In logic more than one answer can be given. Logically it is possible to say that the right to sue for interference with the amenities of a home should be confined to those with proprietary interests and licensees with exclusive possession. No less logically the right can be accorded to all who live in the home. Which test should be adopted, that is to say which should be the governing principle, is a question of the policy of the law. It is a question not capable of being answered by analysis alone. All that analysis can do is expose the alternatives. Decisions such as *Malone v. Laskey* [1907] 2 K.B. 141 do not attempt that kind of analysis, and in refraining from recognising that value judgments are involved they compare less than favourably with the approach of the present-day Court of Appeal in *Khorasandjian* and this case. The reason why I prefer the alternative advocated with unwonted vigour of expression by the doyen of living tort writers is that it gives better effect to widespread conceptions concerning the home and family.

Of course in this field as in most others there will be borderline cases and anomalies wherever the lines are drawn. Thus there are, for instance, the lodger and, as some of your Lordships note, the au pair girl (although she may not figure among the present plaintiffs). It would seem weak, though, to refrain from laying down a just rule for spouses and children on the ground that it is not easy to know where to draw the lines regarding other persons.... Occupation of the property as a home is, to me, an acceptable criterion, consistent with the traditional concern for the sanctity of family life and the Englishman's home—which need not in this context include his workplace. As already mentioned, it is consistent also with international standards.

Commentary

The key judgments in *Hunter v Canary Wharf* have been extracted at some length because of their central importance to the development of the tort of private nuisance, and because of the importance of the variations between them. The majority of the House of Lords resoundingly affirmed that private nuisance was a tort against land and not against the person. The argument that nuisance might be 'modernized' by developing it to protect certain personal interests was rejected. The House of Lords preferred such personal rights to be protected by other means which may be more appropriately designed for the task.

The interpretation of nuisance as exclusively a tort against land resolved the question of who could sue in nuisance; but it also had far-reaching implications for the way that damages are assessed in cases of amenity nuisance (see Lord Hoffmann, earlier), and indeed for the range of injuries for which damages are recoverable in a nuisance action. In particular, it is clear that nuisance will not provide damages for personal injury per se. Although the majority judgments extracted above are generally notable for their logic and coherence, they are not altogether above criticism. In particular, as regards Lord Goff's refusal to treat the home as a special case, it may be objected that there are substantial grounds for doing exactly this: see Article 8 of the European Convention on Human Rights (ECHR), increasingly important in domestic law since enactment of the Human Rights Act 1998 (HRA). Seen in this light, their Lordships' concerns over how one should interpret the interests of the 'au pair girl' for these purposes would simply come down to a question about what counts as a home. This may not be an easy question to answer, but it surely does not require rejection of the whole concept of the home as having special status. Lord Cooke made a broader point about the status both of the home and of children in international human rights instruments in the course of his dissenting judgment.

It is suggested that Lord Cooke is right to say that it is policy, rather than logic, that compels the majority view in *Hunter*. The question is not only the historical one of what nuisance has in the past been able to protect, but the more forward-thinking question of whether nuisance is really adequate to the task of protecting an expanded range of interests. We may accept or reject the policy behind the decision even if we do not accept that the logic is inescapable. In rejecting the idea of a 'substantial link' with the land as giving sufficient standing to sue, Lord Goff suggested that such a change (as he saw it) in the tort of nuisance 'would transform it from a tort to land to a tort to the person, in which damages could be recovered in respect of something less serious than personal injury and the criteria for liability were founded not upon negligence but upon striking a balance between the interests of neighbours in land'. The question remains: is there justification for giving these interests extra protection in tort law, because of their status as events in the home?

Lord Hoffmann's judgment goes furthest in its drive to divorce nuisance from the sorts of personal interest typically protected through the tort of negligence. He explains that cases of nuisance causing personal discomfort do not constitute a 'separate tort' of causing discomfort to people but are still concerned only with the protection of interests in land. From here, he concludes that damages will not be increased 'merely' because more people are on the land, and therefore more people suffer personal discomfort. On the other hand, the 'size, commodiousness, and value' of the property will have an impact on the damages awarded, because the damage to the amenity of the land is valued at a greater sum. This thinking was applied in the case of *Dennis v Ministry of Defence*, which could be seen as a sort of latter-day *St Helen's v Tipping*. We consider *Dennis* later. Lord Hoffmann's approach suggests that it is quite right to award much more substantial damages for noise nuisance to a family or even a single person occupying an exceptionally valuable estate (as in *Dennis*), than to a similar or larger family living in an ordinary dwelling. The 'loss of amenity in the property' will be valued at a much higher sum.

The effect of this reasoning is illustrated by *Raymond v Young* [2015] EWCA Civ 456; [2015] HLR 41. Here there had been a very lengthy history of nuisances committed by a neighbour against the occupiers and former occupiers of a farm, stretching back forty years. The occupiers of the farm were granted an injunction, but this was personal and given the history, it was not likely that a purchaser of the farm would be confident that the nuisances would stop. Thus, there was a diminution in the value of the farm and damages could be awarded *in addition to* the injunction. However, the first instance judge had gone wrong in that he had *also* awarded damages for loss of amenity and distress, in nuisance and under the Protection from Harassment Act 1997. As the Court of Appeal explained, nuisance damages treat loss of amenity in terms of loss of amenity *value*, and this was therefore double counting:

Patten LJ, *Raymond v Young*

After quoting from the judgment of Lord Hoffmann in *Hunter v Canary Wharf* extracted above, Patten LJ continued:

27 The issue in *Hunter* was whether a claim in private nuisance could be maintained by occupiers of flats whose television reception had been interfered with by the construction of the Canary Wharf Tower but who did not have a lease or other right to exclusive possession of their own properties. But I read the passage I have quoted as an endorsement of the principle that damages for what is commonly described as loss of amenity are damages for the diminution in the value of the right to occupy the affected property and not merely damages for the personal distress or inconvenience suffered by the individuals concerned. They are intended to and do compensate the claimant landowners for the distress and loss of amenity which they experience as a result of the nuisance but only in terms of the consequent loss in the use value of their property. For this reason, as Lord Hoffmann explains, the damages are not increased simply because the property is occupied by more than one person.

28 It must, I think, also follow from this that it is not appropriate to make separate awards of damages for distress in cases of nuisance. The consequences in terms of personal distress or discomfort which the claimant may experience as a result of the nuisance are, as I have said, simply part of the assessment of the claimant occupier's loss of amenity …

In the Docklands litigation, *Hunter v Canary Wharf* was the decisive blow to the claimants as a whole. Although some claimants did possess interests of the kind that may be protected by private nuisance, the low amenity value of their interests in land ensured that there would be little benefit in pursuing the actions. This was succinctly expressed by the European Commission on Human Rights in *Khatun v UK* (1998) 26 EHRR CD212, an action brought by disappointed Docklands claimants:

This decision meant that legal aid would be discharged on cost benefit grounds. The predicted value of the collective claim was so low that any pursuit of such claim in the UK courts would be futile.

In *Khatun*, the European Commission on Human Rights dismissed the application, finding no arguable breach of Article 14 ECHR (discrimination on grounds, in this instance, of poverty); of Article 8 (interference with home, family, or private life); nor of Article 13 (no effective remedy in domestic law).

So far as **personal injury** is concerned, we should be careful how we state the conclusion to be drawn from *Hunter v Canary Wharf*. It is clear that no damages will be awarded in respect of personal injury as such. Private nuisance will not operate as an alternative to negligence in this respect. However, it should be clear enough that an activity whose effects cause personal injury on the property—perhaps from noxious fumes, for example—is capable of amounting to a nuisance because the amenity value of premises is inevitably affected by such a state of affairs. Although injured persons will not have an action in their own right as a consequence of being injured, there will presumably be grounds for an action in nuisance either for an injunction, or for damages in respect of the loss of amenity value, just as there would be for other interference with comfort and enjoyment. Indeed, invasions which threaten actual personal injury should logically be subject to increased damages as there is serious loss of amenity. (See further L. Crabb, 'The Property Torts' (2003) 11 Tort L Rev 104–18; and our discussion of *Dobson v Thames Water*, later in this chapter.)

1.6 DEFENCES

Prescription

In principle, the right to commit a nuisance may be obtained by prescription. However, it is necessary that the interference should amount to a nuisance throughout the whole prescriptive period of 20 years. In *Sturges v Bridgman* (1879) 11 Ch D 852, the plaintiff began a conflicting use of the land some time during the period that was claimed to give rise to the right by prescription. As there was no nuisance prior to this, then the time period began to run only when the plaintiff initiated his use of the land.

Coming to the Nuisance?

It is well established that the defendant cannot argue, by way of defence, that the claimant 'came to the nuisance'. Being there first is not a sufficient reason to allow a defendant to create an interference with the claimant's enjoyment of land. Allowing such a defence would entitle a defendant to 'tie up' the potential uses of neighbouring land. *Sturges v Bridgman* (above) is itself a leading authority for this proposition, which has been reaffirmed by the Supreme Court in *Coventry v Lawrence* [2014] UKSC 13. However, the latter decision appears to have introduced qualifications to this simple statement, in circumstances where the defendant's pre-existing use would not otherwise be a nuisance. This is the other side of certain points noted earlier about the decision in *Lawrence*, particularly that a *nuisance* must be ignored in considering the 'character of the neighbourhood'. This is another area where the Supreme Court could be said to have at least 'suggested' a change in the law, by qualifying the status of 'coming to the nuisance', though only where the claimant's actions have changed the use of his or her land. This aspect of the decision is hedged with many qualifications.

Lord Neuberger, *Coventry v Lawrence*

56 … where a claimant builds on, or changes the use of, her land, I would suggest that it may well be wrong to hold that a defendant's pre-existing activity gives rise to a nuisance provided that (i) it can only be said to be a nuisance because it affects the senses of those on the claimant's land, (ii) it was not a nuisance before the building or change of use of the claimant's land, (iii) it is and has been, a reasonable and otherwise lawful use of the defendant's land, (iv) it is carried out in a reasonable way, and (v) it causes no greater nuisance than when the claimant first carried out the building or changed the use. (This is not intended to imply that in any case where one or more of these requirements is not satisfied, a claim in nuisance would be bound to succeed.)

…

58 Accordingly, it appears clear to me that it is no defence for a defendant who is sued in nuisance to contend that the claimant came to the nuisance, although it may well be a defence, at least in some circumstances, for a defendant to contend that, as it is only because the claimant has changed the use of, or built on, her land that the defendant's pre-existing activity is claimed to have become a nuisance, the claim should fail.

Contributory Negligence and *Volenti non fit Injuria*[13]

The wording of the Law Reform (Contributory Negligence) Act 1945 is certainly sufficiently broad to apply to nuisance. However, in the light of the principle that 'coming to the nuisance' is no defence, the applicability of this defence is likely to be limited. Similarly, the defence of *volenti non fit injuria* is theoretically applicable to nuisance but there would perhaps be a need for some active steps on the part of the claimant, encouraging the creation of the nuisance. It is especially hard to imagine a case of *continuing* nuisance in which the defence of *volenti* is made out. Even in *Gillingham v Medway (Chatham) Dock Co Ltd* ([1993] QB 343, extracted earlier in Section 1.3), where a local authority had granted planning permission, the authority was not prevented from changing its mind about the desirability of the defendant's activity. The case was decided on other grounds. This was, however, a case of public nuisance brought for the protection of the rights of local residents, and not ostensibly to protect the plaintiff's own interests.

Statutory Authority

Direct authorization by statute is an important defence to an action in private nuisance. A starting point in determining the limits to this defence is the statement of Lord Blackburn in *Geddis v Proprietors of the Bann Reservoir* (1878) 3 App Cas 430, at 455–6: 'no action will lie for doing that which the legislature has authorized, if it be done without negligence'. Certainly, negligence in the conduct of an authorized activity is likely to take it out of the scope of the defence.

An alternative formulation is the statement of Viscount Dunedin in *Manchester Corporation v Farnworth* [1930] AC 171, at 183: where the 'making or doing' of any thing has been expressly or impliedly authorized by statute, there can be no action in nuisance 'if the nuisance is the inevitable result of the making or doing so authorised'. This suggests that the defence of statutory authority protects only those nuisances which are an 'inevitable' result of the activity authorized. In the leading case of *Allen v Gulf Oil* [1981] AC 1013, the statement of Viscount Dunedin was quoted with approval.

Lord Wilberforce, *Allen v Gulf Oil*
[1981] AC 1013

… The respondent alleges a nuisance, by smell, noise, vibration, etc. The facts regarding these matters are for her to prove. It is then for the appellants to show, if they can, that it was impossible to construct and operate a refinery upon the site, conforming with Parliament's intention, without creating the nuisance alleged, or at least a nuisance. Involved in this issue would be the point discussed by Cumming-Bruce L.J. in the Court of Appeal, that the establishment of an oil refinery, etc. was bound to involve some alteration of the environment and so of the standard of amenity and comfort which neighbouring occupiers might expect. To the extent that the environment has been changed from that of a peaceful unpolluted countryside to an industrial complex (as to which different standards apply—*Sturges v. Bridgman* (1879) 11 Ch.D. 852) Parliament must be taken to have authorised it. So far, I venture to think, the matter is not open to doubt. But in my opinion the statutory authority extends beyond merely authorising a change in the environment and an alteration of standard. It confers immunity against proceedings for any nuisance which can be shown (the burden of so showing being upon the appellants) to be the inevitable result of orecting a refinery upon the site—not, I repeat, the existing refinery, but any refinery—however carefully and with however great a regard for the interest of adjoining occupiers it is sited, constructed and operated. To the extent and only to the extent that the actual nuisance (if any) caused by the actual refinery and its operation exceeds that for which immunity is conferred, the plaintiff has a remedy.

From this statement, we can see that the defendant will not succeed with this defence if the claimant can show *either* that the works in question could have been differently sited within the terms of the statute, and thus the nuisance could have been avoided (as in *Metropolitan Asylum District v Hill*, 6 App Cas 193); *or* that the works were not 'carefully' constructed and operated, and that due care could have avoided the nuisance. In *Allen v Gulf Oil* itself, the statute was specific about the siting of the refinery; *and* no lack of due care was apparent in its construction and operation. Thus the nuisance was an inevitable consequence of the authorized activities, and the defence succeeded.

Allen v Gulf Oil also raised the question of 'implied' authorization. It was held that the defendants could rely on the defence of statutory authorization even though the statute in question, the Gulf Oil Refining Act 1965, expressly authorized only the acquisition of the specific land and the construction of a refinery upon it. It did not expressly authorize the *operation* of the refinery. As Lord Diplock put it (at 1014):

Parliament can hardly be supposed to have intended the refinery to be nothing more than a visual adornment to the landscape in an area of natural beauty. Clearly the intention of Parliament was that the refinery was to be operated as such; and it is perhaps relevant to observe that in *Metropolitan Asylum District v. Hill*, 6 App. Cas. 193, all three members of this House who took part in the decision would apparently have reached the conclusion that the nuisance caused by the small-pox hospital could not have been the subject of an action, if the hospital had been built upon a site which the board had been granted power by Act of Parliament to acquire compulsorily for that specific purpose.

Relationship between Statutory Authorization and Planning Permission

In an earlier section of this chapter (1.3), we saw that planning permission is not a defence in the same way as statutory authority. Local planning authorities do not have authority to override private rights. However, planning permission may nevertheless determine the outcome of the case, if it is interpreted as changing the 'character of the neighbourhood'.

Public Interest?

Public interest in the activities of the defendant is not generally considered to be a defence to an action in nuisance. In *Dennis v MOD* (further discussed below in respect of remedies), Buckley J reviewed the authorities in the following terms:

Dennis v Ministry of Defence [2003] EWHC 793 (QB)

[30] This case raises an important and problematic point of principle in the law of nuisance. Namely, whether and in what circumstances a sufficient public interest can amount to a defence to a claim in nuisance. In several cases the point has arisen in a less dramatic form than here. For example, the local cricket club case: *Miller v Jackson* [1977] QB 966, [1977]

3 All ER 338 and *Kennaway v Thompson* [1981] QB 88, [1980] 3 All ER 329 in which the Court of Appeal affirmed the principle in *Shelfer v City of London Electric Lighting Company* [1894] 1 Ch 287, namely, the fact that the wrong doer is in some sense a public benefactor has never been considered a sufficient reason to refuse an injunction. (See Lindley LJ. At 315/6). Clerk and Lindsell concludes that public interest is "not in itself a defence, but a factor in assessing reasonableness of user". 18th Edition para 19.72. Fleming The Law of Torts 9th Edition at 471 points out that some weight is accorded to the utility of the defendant's conduct, but suggests that the argument "must not be pushed too far." He cites Bohlen Studies 429:

"If the public be interested let the public as such bear the costs."

He points out this can be achieved by holding the defendant liable and leaving him to include the cost in charges to the public, or by statutory authority with provision for compensation. The former suggestion, of course, would only apply to a service provider capable of raising charges.

Buckley J clearly considered the meagre case law not to determine the answer to his simple question of whether the public interest could amount to a defence. Indeed, the case of *Miller v Jackson* [1977] QB 966 appears to be unique in stating clearly that the public interest—in preserving the playing of cricket on village greens—outweighed the private interests of neighbours such that they could have no action in nuisance. Buckley J considered whether he should give effect to the public interest by holding that it afforded a defence in itself, or by varying the remedy that could be awarded. He preferred to take the latter course. There was a nuisance; but damages should be awarded in lieu of an injunction. This was a controversial course to take, but in view of the absence of authority concerning the status of public interest, there was no 'uncontroversial' path available to resolve this case. Effectively the same solution has now been adopted by the Supreme Court in *Coventry v Lawrence*. Because of the solution adopted, it is further explored in respect of 'Remedies', below.

1.7 REMEDIES

Broadly speaking, there are three remedies for nuisance. These are abatement, injunction, and damages.

Abatement

Abatement is a form of self-help. It justifies the claimant in entering on to land from which a nuisance emanates, in order to prevent its continuation. The following statement from the case of *Burton v Winters* [1993] 1 WLR 1077 gives an indication of the types of case in which abatement will be appropriate:

Lloyd LJ, at 1081

[T]he courts have confined the remedy by way of self-redress to simple cases such as an overhanging branch, or an encroaching root, which would not justify the expense of legal proceedings, and urgent cases which require an immediate remedy.

Abatement is regarded by the courts with some caution. This is not surprising, given the possible adverse consequences of self-help, especially in the context of neighbour disputes. Indeed in *Burton v Winters* itself, the plaintiff had been committed to prison for two years for breaching the terms of an injunction which prevented her from damaging the defendants' garage. She had earlier been denied a mandatory injunction requiring the demolition of the garage, even though the court had granted a declaration that it encroached upon her land. The Court of Appeal denied her claim that abatement was an appropriate remedy in such a case.

Injunctions

In cases of continuing nuisance, the majority of claimants will seek an injunction. As already indicated, the continuing nature of many nuisances, and therefore the appropriateness of seeking injunctive relief, is one of the factors marking a distinction between negligence and nuisance. An injunction is an equitable remedy and as such is not available as of right. Rather, it is within the discretion of the court whether to award an injunction, and on what terms. This gives considerable flexibility. Rather than prohibiting the defendant's activities, the court may for example set limits to the times during which the activity may continue, or even order that certain technical alterations are made to ameliorate the nuisance. Mandatory injunctions (which require the defendant to take positive steps) are less often used, and their terms must be very clearly expressed: a recent example is *Regan v Paul Properties* (below). The degree to which courts are ready to award injunctions to protect rights from being violated, rather than leaving those rights unprotected or allowing them to be 'converted into money' through an award of damages instead, raises very important questions. It is also worth noting however that injunctions are personal and that, in the case of a continuing nuisance, a court may take the view that damages are required *in addition to* an injunction, not only because of past interference and injury (below), but also to reflect a continued risk that the value of the property will be affected. Purchasers may not be confident that the nuisance has come to an end or may fear the need to seek their own injunction, affecting the purchase price of the property: see the judgment of the Court of Appeal in *Raymond v Young* [2015] EWCA Civ 456; [2015] HLR 41.

Damages for Past Injury and Interference

Some cases of nuisance do not have any continuing element, but are actions in respect of damage or interference that has already been suffered. Furthermore, even in cases of continuing nuisance there will typically be some element of past interference. In these cases, claimants may be awarded damages to compensate for injury in the usual way. However, it should be noted that the comments of Lord Hoffmann in *Hunter v Canary Wharf* (extracted in Section 5.1) regarding the nature of the interests protected by the tort of nuisance may have invalidated some of the existing case law on the assessment of damages. In particular, he disapproved of the approach of Stephenson LJ in *Bone v Seale* [1975] 1 WLR 797, which suggested that the court should draw analogies with personal injury awards in negligence when compensating for a nuisance by smell. The sums awarded in cases of amenity nuisance must, according to Lord Hoffmann's approach, reflect instead the diminution of amenity value (though this may be temporary) in the property affected.

Damages in Lieu of Injunction

The Chancery Amendment Act of 1858 ('Lord Cairns' Act') gave courts the power to award damages for future interference in lieu of an injunction. However, the power to do this has typically been restrictively interpreted by the courts themselves. Until the decision of the Supreme Court in *Coventry v Lawrence*, courts have mostly regarded themselves as bound by the criteria set out by A. L. Smith LJ in the case of *Shelfer v City of London Electric Lighting Co* [1895] 1 Ch 287, at 322–3:

In my opinion, it may be stated as a good working rule that—

(1) If the injury is small,

(2) And is one which is capable of being estimated in money,

(3) And is one which can adequately be compensated by a small money payment,

(4) And the case is one in which it would be oppressive to the defendant to grant an injunction:—

then damages in substitution for an injunction may be given.

These conditions focus on the interests of the claimant, rather than on extraneous grounds such as the social utility of the defendant's activities. A. L. Smith LJ also suggested that particular conduct on the part of the defendant (amounting to 'reckless disregard for the plaintiff's rights') might militate against the award of damages in lieu, even if all four of the conditions above were satisfied.

There are well-known older cases in which the presumption in favour of an injunction as opposed to damages, and indifference to issues of public interest, appears to have had striking effects. In *Manchester Corporation v Farnworth* [1930] AC 171, the House of Lords said it would disregard the effect of an injunction on Manchester's electricity supply. On the other hand, the demanding nature of the *Shelfer* criteria (bearing in mind that *all* of them should be satisfied) could incline a court against the award of any relief at all, given that the injunction, as an equitable remedy, is not available 'as of right'.

That point was made by Millett LJ in the following extract. The case was concerned not with nuisance but with the award of damages in lieu of an injunction where there had been breach of a restrictive covenant.

Millett LJ, *Jaggard v Sawyer*
[1995] 1 WLR 269

At 286

It has always been recognised that the practical consequence of withholding injunctive relief is to authorise the continuance of an unlawful state of affairs. If, for example, the defendant threatens to build in such a way that the plaintiff's light will be obstructed and he is not restrained, then the plaintiff will inevitably be deprived of his legal right. This was the very basis upon which before 1858 the Court of Chancery had made the remedy of injunction available in such cases. After the passing of Lord Cairns's Act many of the judges warned that the jurisdiction to award damages instead of an injunction should not be exercised as a matter of course so as to legalise the commission of a tort by any defendant who was willing and able to pay compensation.

...

At 287-8

Nevertheless references to the "expropriation" of the plaintiff's property are somewhat overdone, not because that is not the practical effect of withholding an injunction, but because the grant of an injunction, like all equitable remedies, is discretionary. Many proprietary rights cannot be protected at all by the common law. The owner must submit to unlawful interference with his rights and be content with damages. If he wants to be protected he must seek equitable relief, and he has no absolute right to that. In many cases, it is true, an injunction will be granted almost as of course; but this is not always the case, and it will never be granted if this would cause injustice to the defendant. Citation of passages in the cases warning of the danger of "expropriating" the plaintiff needs to be balanced by reference to statements like that of Lord Westbury L.C. in *Isenberg v. East India House Estate Co. Ltd.*(1863) 3 De G. J. & S. 263, 273 where he held that it was the duty of the court not

"by granting a mandatory injunction, to deliver over the defendants to the plaintiff bound hand and foot, in order to be made subject to any extortionate demand that he may by possibility make, but to substitute for such mandatory injunction an inquiry before itself, in order to ascertain the measure of damage that has been actually sustained."

If the effect of granting an injunction *as between the parties* would be oppressive, then an injunction may be declined. The *Shelfer* criteria, Millett LJ explained, were not to be strictly construed, but were illustrative of the general approach to be taken. On the other hand, Bingham LJ cautioned that the test of 'oppressiveness' is a demanding one. It was not equivalent to the 'balance of convenience', which compares the impact on claimant and defendant of the different forms of relief.

Coventry v Lawrence [2014] UKSC 13

We visited *Coventry v Lawrence* in relation to planning permission and the character of the neighbourhood, earlier in this chapter. Arguably, the more significant aspect of the decision is its conclusions on remedies. To one degree or another, all members of the Supreme Court agreed that courts should approach the choice of injunction or damages in a far more flexible and open way than implied by the *Shelfer* criteria, which are not to be slavishly followed. The Supreme Court also took a further significant step and declared that both the public interest, and the interests of third parties where relevant, may also be directly relevant when considering whether to award an injunction or damages in lieu: the issues are not confined to those concerning the wrong of one party to another. Illustrating the significance of these moves, the Court disapproved the approach to remedies taken by the Court of Appeal in the recent decision in *Watson v Croft Promo-Sport* [2009] EWCA Civ 15, both because it had emphasised the 'exceptional' nature of an award of damages in lieu of an injunction; and because it had rejected as irrelevant an argument that public interest favoured the continuation of racing at the defendants' site, suggesting that only in a 'marginal case where the damage to the claimant is minimal' could the public interest be let in.

No Strict Adherence to Shelfer

Whilst Lord Neuberger was markedly less scathing about strict adherence to the *Shelfer* criteria than was Lord Sumption, it was nonetheless clear that in the opinion of all five justices, the *Shelfer* criteria should no longer be strictly applied. Lord Neuberger said that (i) an almost mechanical application of the *Shelfer* criteria, and (ii) an approach in which damages should be applied only in 'exceptional' circumstances, 'are each simply wrong in principle, and give a serious risk of going wrong in practice' ([119]). Lord Sumption's remarks underlined the significance of the issue for nuisance as a whole: the court's discretion as to remedies 'could save the law from anomaly and incoherence' ([157]), which would otherwise be the effect of issuing injunctions to prevent authorized activities. The overall question so far as Lord Sumption was concerned was 'how is one to reconcile public and private law in the domain of land use where they occupy much the same space?' Adherence to the *Shelfer* criteria, in his view, is produced by 'an unduly moralistic approach to disputes', in which the possibility of one party effectively purchasing another's rights is given too much emphasis ([160]). The following observations go further than the other judges were prepared to go, although all agreed that, as Lord Carnwath put it, 'the opportunity should be taken to signal a move away from the strict criteria derived from *Shelfer*' ([239]).

Lord Sumption, *Coventry v Lawrence*

161 In my view, the decision in *Shelfer* [1895] 1 Ch 287 is out of date, and it is unfortunate that it has been followed so recently and so slavishly. It was devised for a time in which England was much less crowded, when comparatively few people owned property, when conservation was only beginning to be a public issue, and when there was no general system of statutory development control. The whole jurisprudence in this area will need one day to be reviewed in this court. There is much to be said for the view that damages are ordinarily an adequate remedy for nuisance and that an injunction should not usually be granted in a case where it is likely that conflicting interests are engaged other than the parties' interests. In particular, it may well be that an injunction should as a matter of principle not be granted in a case where a use of land to which objection is taken requires and has received planning permission. However, at this stage, in the absence of argument on these points, I can do no more than identify them as calling for consideration in a case in which they arise.

So far as the role of public interest is concerned, the change in approach is equally marked.

Lord Neuberger, *Coventry v Lawrence*

124 As for the second problem, that of public interest, I find it hard to see how there could be any circumstances in which it arose and could not, as a matter of law, be a relevant factor. Of course, it is very easy to think of circumstances in which it might arise but did not begin to justify the court refusing, or, as the case may be, deciding, to award an injunction if it was otherwise minded to do so. But that is not the point. The fact that a defendant's business may have to shut down if an injunction is granted should, it seems to me, obviously be a relevant fact, and it is hard to see why relevance should not extend to the fact that a number of the defendant's employees would lose their livelihood, although in many

cases that may well not be sufficient to justify the refusal of an injunction. Equally, I do not see why the court should not be entitled to have regard to the fact that many other neighbours in addition to the claimant are badly affected by the nuisance as a factor in favour of granting an injunction.

Together, these various observations constitute a far-reaching shift, from a focus on the two parties and primarily upon the interests of the claimant; to a balanced exercise in which damages are not 'exceptional' and the interests of other parties, and indeed the public, are also relevant to the choice of remedy. Only Lord Sumption expressed the view that damages should *ordinarily* be sufficient in a case of nuisance.

Though certainly striking, these changes did not emerge without preceding discussion, judicial and academic. Lord Carnwath in a brief discussion neatly brought some key issues together.

Lord Carnwath, *Coventry v Lawrence*

240 As has been seen, Peter Gibson LJ in *Wheeler* [1996] Ch 19 saw more flexible remedial principles as a possible answer to the public interest aspect of cases such as *Gillingham* [1993] QB 343, rather than creating an exception to the law of nuisance. Commenting on the restrictive view taken by the Court of Appeal in *Watson*, Maria Lee has said:

> "The fact that something should go ahead in the public interest does not tell us where the costs should lie; we need not assume that injured parties should bear the burden associated with broader social benefits ... The continued strength of private nuisance in a regulatory state probably depends on a more flexible approach to remedies." ("Tort Law and Regulation: Planning and Nuisance" (2011) 8 JPL 986, 989–990.)

I agree.

Before *Coventry v Lawrence*, the clearest instance of an English court recognizing public interest issues as affecting the choice of remedy was the first instance decision of Buckley J in *Dennis v Ministry of Defence* [2003] EWHC 793 (QB). That case involved the public interest in defence of a realm, and raised the matter of public interest in a very direct manner. Given that the *Shelfer* criteria were not fulfilled, and given that there was a substantial noise nuisance, was the court bound to award an injunction? Buckley J relied on human rights arguments, by reference to the Court of Appeal's decision in *Marcic v Thames Water*[14] in concluding that although the flying of Harrier jets at RAF Wittering had constituted a nuisance, it should be permitted to continue but that damages should be paid. It is interesting that the Supreme Court has now felt able to resolve the underlying issue—of the general relevance of public interest in the law of nuisance—by adapting remedies, without reference to the HRA or to Convention rights. This may be an illustration of the general point, that domestic courts are now less inclined to 'use' Convention arguments to produce desired results.

---

[14] [2002] EWCA Civ 64; [2002] 2 WLR 932 (Court of Appeal, reversed on appeal to House of Lords [2003] UKHL 66; [2003] 3 WLR 1603).

Buckley J, Dennis v Ministry of Defence

Human Rights

[63] Following the implications of *S v France* as identified in *Marcic* and, with respect, with which I agree, I would hold that a fair balance would not be struck in the absence of compensation. I would thus award damages under s 8 [Human Rights Act 1998] in respect of arts 8 and 1 [ECHR]. I would hold, as I believe is implicit in the decision in *S v France*, that the public interest is greater than the individual private interests of Mr and Mrs Dennis but it is not proportionate to pursue or give effect to the public interest without compensation for Mr and Mrs Dennis. I do not accept Mr Elvin's submissions to the effect that the Claimants are not called upon to bear an individual burden. The facts are that the MOD has operated its schemes for purchase of property or grants for double-glazing in the locality generally, but Walcot Hall could not be included. But in any event the local inhabitants constitute a very small proportion of the tax paying community at large. The same imbalance would apply even if one considered all RAF airfields. I have no evidence on this, but it must be the case. In my view, common fairness demands that where the interests of a minority, let alone an individual, are seriously interfered with because of an overriding public interest, the minority should be compensated. To its credit the MOD appears to accept that principle since it operates the voluntary schemes to which I have referred.

Assessment of Damages

An issue left relatively open by the Supreme Court in *Coventry v Lawrence* was the approach to assessing damages in lieu of an injunction, though it was clear that such damages will more readily be awarded. Clearly this is therefore now a pressing issue, both in the *Coventry* case itself, and generally. There was some inconclusive discussion of recent authorities, most particularly concerning the question of whether *more than compensatory damages* should be awarded; and whether these should be 'gain-based'. As Lord Carnwath said, 'the issues are complex on any view' ([248]).

Such questions were considered by Gabriel Moss QC at first instance in the case of *Tamares (Vincent Square) v Fairpoint Properties* [2007] EWHC 212 (Ch); [2007] 1 WLR 2176. Here, it was agreed by the parties that the amount payable in damages could in principle be greater than the value of the lost amenity of the claimant, because the damages ought to compensate for the lost opportunity of an injunction. This was a right to light case between two commercial parties. In these circumstances, the guiding principle was that the court should find what would be a 'fair' result of a hypothetical negotiation between the parties. This hypothetical negotiation would be imagined as being conducted by 'hypothetical reasonable commercial people' and, in accordance with the Court of Appeal's approach in *Lunn Poly Ltd v Liverpool and Lancashire Properties* [2006] EWCA Civ 430, it ought in most cases to be approached as though taking place at the time of the breach. Another guiding principle, given that an injunction had been refused, was that the amount should not be so large that the development, or relevant part of it, would be deterred had such a sum been payable. It is by no means clear that such an assumption could be made in future where the Supreme Court's 'open' approach in *Coventry* is followed: the award of damages will no longer depend on showing there were strong reasons against awarding an injunction.

On the other hand, the approach in *Tamares* suggests that it should be accepted that the owner of the right had a good bargaining position in the hypothetical deal, and so the owner of the right would ordinarily expect to receive some part of the *profit* from the relevant part of the development. This is not, therefore, simple compensation for lost amenity, but compensation for loss of an injunction and an element of damages calculated on the basis of the defendant's likely gain. On the other hand, this was expressed in terms of 'compensation' (for the lost right to stop the interference). It is not a 'disgorgement' remedy of the sort that is intended to strip a defendant of its profits. A remedy of the latter type may appear illogical in a case where the injunctive remedy has been refused on application of the *Shelfer* criteria,[15] for different reasons, it may also appear illogical on the new, more flexible approach, if it is thought that the balance of interests comes down in favour of damages rather than injunction. In *Forsyth-Grant v Allen* [2008] EWCA Civ 505, discussed in Chapter 8, no account of profits was awarded in respect of a nuisance involving interference with the claimant's right to light. These issues remain to be resolved.

2. NUISANCE AND THE HUMAN RIGHTS ACT 1998

2.1 THE CONVENTION RIGHTS AND THEIR STATUS

Private nuisance was one of the first torts to test the impact of the HRA. The impact of that Act was discussed in a general sense in Chapter 1, where the statute was extracted. Here, we remind ourselves of the key provisions.

By section 6 of the HRA, it is unlawful for a public authority—which is defined to include a court—to act incompatibly with a Convention right. It has been generally concluded that this will not mean that new causes of action will arise at common law, but it may mean that existing actions (like private nuisance) may be interpreted differently in light of the Convention rights (see Chapter 1, and further discussion in Chapter 14).

By sections 7 and 8 of the HRA, actions may be brought against a public authority, seeking damages for unlawful acts (in violation of a Convention right). This is not an action in tort, but the existence of remedies under section 8 may influence the development of tort actions (see particularly Chapter 6, Section 3). Of course, such actions are available only against defendants who fit the definition of 'public authorities'.

The following two Articles of the Convention are the most relevant to actions in private nuisance.

Human Rights Act 1998 (c. 42)

Schedule 1 The Articles

Part I The Convention

Rights and Freedoms

Article 8

Right to respect for private and family life

1 Everyone has the right to respect for his private and family life, his home and his correspondence.

[15] The relationship between the *Tamares* approach, and the famous case of *Wrotham Park v Parkside Homes* [1974] 1 WLR 798 (breach of covenant) on the one hand, and 'disgorgement' remedies on the other, is touched upon by Ralph Cunnington in "The Assessment of Gain-Based Damages for Breach of Contract' (2008) 71 MLR 559–86, 563.

2 There shall be no interference by a public authority with the exercise of this right except such as is in accordance with the law and is necessary in a democratic society in the interests of national security, public safety or the economic well-being of the country, for the prevention of disorder or crime, for the protection of health or morals, or for the protection of the rights and freedoms of others....

...

Part II The First Protocol

Article 1

Protection of property

Every natural or legal person is entitled to the peaceful enjoyment of his possessions. No one shall be deprived of his possessions except in the public interest and subject to the conditions provided for by law and by the general principles of international law.

The preceding provisions shall not, however, in any way impair the right of a State to enforce such laws as it deems necessary to control the use of property in accordance with the general interest or to secure the payment of taxes or other contributions or penalties.

2.2 APPLICATIONS

In Section 1.5 of this chapter, we extracted the House of Lords' decision in *Hunter v Canary Wharf*. That case reaffirmed that nuisance is a tort against land and not against the person, and declined to support any 'modernization' of the tort so as to protect those occupying property as a home. Their Lordships considered that such a move would lead to incoherence in the law, and would also be unnecessary. We noted the dissent of Lord Cooke, which was supported in part by the existence of international human rights documents affirming rights specific to the home. With the enactment of the HRA, would the restrictions to the tort of nuisance stated by *Hunter v Canary Wharf* begin to create difficulties?

In *McKenna & Others v British Aluminium* [2002] Env LR 30, Neuberger J declined to strike out actions in nuisance and in *Rylands v Fletcher* which were brought on behalf of children with no proprietary interests in their home. The general nature of their complaints concerned pollution and annoyance from neighbouring industrial activities. (There were additional actions on behalf of adults with proprietary interests, and there were also actions in negligence brought on behalf of all of the claimants, and the striking out action did not apply to these.)

Neuberger J concluded that, in the absence of the HRA, the actions both in nuisance and (by analogy) in *Rylands v Fletcher*, would clearly have failed and would have been struck out. This would have been the effect of the decision in *Hunter v Canary Wharf*, extended to *Rylands v Fletcher* on the authority of *Cambridge Water v Eastern Counties Leather plc*. The relationship between nuisance, and the action in *Rylands v Fletcher*, is considered in the next chapter. For now, we are interested in the way that Neuberger J addressed the impact of the HRA on what was a clear, recent, and binding authority of the House of Lords.

Neuberger J clearly considered that the common law as stated in *Hunter* might be inconsistent with the rights stated in Article 8.1 of the Convention.

Neuberger J, at 17–18

There is obviously a powerful case for saying that effect has not been properly given to Article 8.1 if a person with no interest in the home, but who has lived in the home for some time and had his enjoyment of the home interfered with, is at the mercy of the person who owns the home, as the only person who can bring proceedings. I think it also questionable that it would be Article 8 compliant if, in such a case, damages are limited, as Lord Lloyd of Berwick indicated [in *Hunter v Canary Wharf*, 698H–699A]. If the law is as he stated, then in practice an infant or other person with no interest in the home, has no claim in his own right to [t]use damages. In any event those damages would be calculated so as, in many people's eyes, not to satisfactorily reflect the damage he has suffered in his home.

Subsequently, the issue raised by *McKenna* was considered in slightly different circumstances by the Court of Appeal in *Dobson v Thames Water* [2009] EWCA Civ 28. Here, the defendant was a 'public authority' within the terms of the HRA, and the issue was now expressed, not in terms of whether tort should adapt, but in terms of the availability of a separate remedy under section 8 of the HRA for violation of the occupier's Article 8 right. There was no appeal from the judge's finding, extracted in Section 1.4 of this chapter, to the effect that there could be liability for 'negligent' nuisances which fell outside *Marcic*. But there was an appeal in respect of the available remedies. The judge had been asked to rule on a number of questions of principle, and two were particularly relevant to the present discussion.

First, some of the claimants in *Dobson* were children. If their parents had legal interests in the home and could therefore obtain damages in nuisance, could there still be a separate award to an occupying child, under Article 8 ECHR? The judge answered this question by reference to the claim by one of the children, Thomas Bannister. His conclusion was:

Ramsey J, *Dobson v Thames Water* [2007] EWHC 2021

209 ... when the court awards damages for nuisance to those with a legal interest that will usually afford just satisfaction to partners and children but ... there may be circumstances where they will not. In the case of Thomas Bannister, he lives in the same household as his parents who will receive damages for the loss of amenity of their property. There is nothing in the claim to show that such damages received by the household would not afford just satisfaction as they did for Mrs Dennis or would have done for Mr Marcic. I conclude that these damages would afford Thomas Bannister just satisfaction.

The point made here is that although Thomas Bannister as a mere occupier does not have the right to sue in private nuisance, it is likely that the sum payable to other members of the household in a successful nuisance action would suffice to afford 'just satisfaction', which is the goal of damages under both the ECHR and the HRA.[16] The Court of Appeal had sympathy with this view, but thought the state of the law too uncertain to say quite so much. Rather, they emphasized that even under the approach in *Hunter v Canary Wharf*, the impact of the nuisance upon those occupying the land, 'although not formally the measure of common law damages for loss of amenity, will in practice be relevant to the assessment of

[16] For discussion of the controversies surrounding this interpretation of damages under the HRA, see J. Steele, 'Damages in Tort and under the Human Rights Act: Remedial or Functional Separation?' (2008) 67 CLJ 606–34.

damages in such cases' (at [35]). Section 8(3) of the HRA requires a court to take into account any remedy granted 'in relation to the act in question'. This is not confined to remedies awarded to the person alleging infringement of his or her rights.

Waller LJ, *Dobson v Thames Water* [2009] EWCA Civ 28

45 ... The vital question will be whether it is *necessary* to award *damages* to another member of the household or whether the remedy of a declaration that Article 8 rights have been infringed suffices, alongside the award to the landowner, especially when no pecuniary loss has been suffered. If, for the reasons explained above, ... the effects of the odour and mosquitoes upon Thomas Bannister personally were in practice taken into account in determining the diminution in the amenity value of the property, and therefore in determining the amount of damages awarded to his parents in nuisance, we would regard that as a highly significant consideration when determining whether an award of damages was necessary to afford Thomas just satisfaction under Article 8. In any event the fact of an award to his parents, if made, and its amount, must be a circumstance relevant to whether an award is necessary.

46 ... For the reasons given, it may very well be that a declaration is sufficient in his case, but it will depend on the judge's findings in relation to his parents and to any particular consideration affecting Thomas. Even if it is thought that necessity be shown, the fact of any award to his parents, and its amount will be relevant as to quantum. It should be noted that in any event damages if awarded on such issues are not substantial.

It is noted here that monetary remedies under the HRA are in these circumstances unlikely to be 'substantial'. This is underlined by the Court of Appeal's approach to the second question of principle. That is, could those claimants who had a legal interest in their homes, and who therefore qualified for damages in nuisance, also claim additional damages for violation of their own Article 8 rights? As the Court of Appeal pointed out, this question was drafted on the basis that there might be a 'top-up' award of damages, over and above the compensatory damages awarded by the tort of nuisance. This, they pointed out, was 'highly improbable, if not inconceivable', given the comments above (at [50]). 'Just satisfaction' was unlikely ever to require a top-up award to someone who had already received an award of damages in nuisance in respect of 'injury to the amenity value of the home'.

The difference in outlook between *McKenna* and *Dobson* lies in the realization that damages awarded under the HRA, being modelled on Strasbourg awards, are considerably less generous than are damages in tort. There is no requirement to remodel tort law to provide tort's generous remedies in a case of violation of Convention rights. There is a chance that a claimant may succeed in establishing a violation of his or her rights, which is not 'satisfied by' an award in nuisance. But if so, the remedy is likely to be a declaration of violation, and perhaps, though rarely, a modest award of damages.

The decision of the European Commission of Human Rights in *Khatun v UK* (1998) 26 EHRR CD12 also appears to limit the role of the Convention where nuisances are concerned. The Commission rejected as inadmissible the claims of 181 applicants, arising from the same interferences as *Hunter v Canary Wharf*. In particular, the Commission said that it could not rule that a fair balance had not been struck between the competing interests of the individuals, and of the community as a whole. This was partly because the regeneration of Docklands was carried out in pursuit of a legitimate and important aim. Not every case in which regeneration is claimed to give rise to interference with Article 8 rights will necessarily be safe from a claim based on interference with Convention rights. The Commission noted that neither personal injury nor depreciation in the value of property was complained of in these particular cases; that the period of interference was limited to three and a half years; and that there was no attempt on the applicants' part to prevent the alleged nuisance whilst it was happening.

Changes in the Relationship between Private Right and Public Interest?

As we noted above, the compromise between public and private interests arrived at in the first instance decision of *Dennis v MOD* was based in part on *obiter dicta* of the Court of Appeal in *Marcic*, and appealed to the new status of Convention rights. We also noted however that in *Coventry v Lawrence*, the Supreme Court reached a similar accommodation without reference to the Convention. The House of Lords in *Marcic* itself in any event showed little inclination to support the route taken by the Court of Appeal in relation to Convention rights.

Marcic v Thames Water Utilities Ltd [2003] UKHL 66; [2004] 2 AC 42: Human Rights Act Elements

Extracts from the judgment in Section 1.4 of this chapter dealt with the claim in nuisance. In addition, since the defendant could be treated as a 'public authority' for the purposes of section 6 of the Act, there was scope for a separate claim for damages under section 8. This claim had succeeded before the first instance judge, Sir Richard Havery QC. The Court of Appeal did not disagree with his analysis, although the damages they awarded for nuisance afforded just satisfaction for the infringement and they therefore commented only briefly on this aspect of the case. The House of Lords rejected the claim for damages under the Act for infringement of Convention rights, just as they had rejected the claim in nuisance. The extracts below deal with the HRA claim. As with the claim in nuisance, the statutory context was treated as decisive.

Lord Nicholls

The claim under the Human Rights Act 1998

37 I turn to Mr Marcic's claim under the Human Rights Act 1998. His claim is that as a public authority within the meaning of section 6 of the Human Rights Act 1998 Thames Water has acted unlawfully. Thames Water has conducted itself in a way which is incompatible with Mr Marcic's Convention rights under article 8 of the Convention and article 1 of the First Protocol to the Convention. His submission was to the following effect. The flooding of Mr Marcic's property falls within the first paragraph of article 8 and also within article 1 of the First Protocol. That was common ground between the parties. Direct and serious interference of this nature with a person's home is prima facie a violation of a person's right to respect for his private and family life (article 8) and of his entitlement to the peaceful enjoyment of his possessions (article 1 of the First Protocol). The burden of justifying this interference rests on Thames Water. At the trial of the preliminary issues Thames Water failed to discharge this burden. The trial judge found that the system of priorities used by Thames Water in deciding whether to carry out flood alleviation works might be entirely fair. The judge also said that on the limited evidence before him it was not possible to decide this issue, or to decide whether for all its apparent faults the system

fell within the wide margin of discretion open to Thames Water and the director: [2002] QB 929, 964, para 102.

38 To my mind the fatal weakness in this submission is the same as that afflicting Mr Marcic's claim in nuisance: it does not take sufficient account of the statutory scheme under which Thames Water is operating the offending sewers. The need to adopt some system of priorities for building more sewers is self-evident. So is the need for the system to be fair. A fair system of priorities necessarily involves balancing many intangible factors. Whether the system adopted by a sewerage undertaker is fair is a matter inherently more suited for decision by the industry regulator than by a court. And the statutory scheme so provides. Moreover, the statutory scheme provides a remedy where a system of priorities is not fair. An unfair system of priorities means that a sewerage undertaker is not properly discharging its statutory drainage obligation so far as those who are being treated unfairly are concerned. The statute provides what should happen in these circumstances. The director is charged with deciding whether to make an enforcement order in respect of a sewerage undertaker's failure to drain property properly. Parliament entrusted this decision to the director, not the courts.

39 What happens in practice accords with this statutory scheme. When people affected by sewer flooding complain to the director he considers whether he should require the sewerage undertaker to take remedial action. Before doing so he considers, among other matters, the severity and history of the problem in the context of that undertaker's sewer flooding relief programme, as allowed for in its current price limits. In many cases the company agrees to take action, but sometimes he accepts that a solution is not possible in the short term.

40 So the claim based on the Human Rights Act 1998 raises a broader issue: is the statutory scheme as a whole, of which this enforcement procedure is part, Convention-compliant? Stated more specifically and at the risk of over-simplification, is the statutory scheme unreasonable in its impact on Mr Marcic and other householders whose properties are periodically subjected to sewer flooding?

41 The recent decision of the European Court of Human Rights, sitting as a Grand Chamber, in *Hatton v United Kingdom* (Application No 36022/97) The Times, 10 July 2003 confirms how courts should approach questions such as these. In *Hatton's* case the applicants lived near Heathrow airport. They claimed that the Government's policy on night flights at Heathrow violated their rights under article 8. The court emphasised "the fundamentally subsidiary nature" of the Convention. National authorities have "direct democratic legitimation" and are in principle better placed than an international court to evaluate local needs and conditions. In matters of general policy, on which opinions within a democratic society may reasonably differ widely, "the role of the domestic policy maker should be given special weight": see paragraph 97. A fair balance must be struck between the interests of the individual and of the community as a whole.

42 In the present case the interests Parliament had to balance included, on the one hand, the interests of customers of a company whose properties are prone to sewer flooding and, on the other hand, all the other customers of the company whose properties are drained through the company's sewers. The interests of the first group conflict with the interests of the company's customers as a whole in that only a minority of customers suffer sewer flooding but the company's customers as a whole meet the cost of building more sewers. As already noted, the balance struck by the statutory scheme is to impose a general drainage obligation on a sewerage undertaker but to entrust enforcement of this obligation to an

independent regulator who has regard to all the different interests involved. Decisions of the director are of course subject to an appropriately penetrating degree of judicial review by the courts.

43 In principle this scheme seems to me to strike a reasonable balance. Parliament acted well within its bounds as policy maker. In Mr Marcic's case matters plainly went awry. It cannot be acceptable that in 2001, several years after Thames Water knew of Mr Marcic's serious problems, there was still no prospect of the necessary work being carried out for the foreseeable future. At times Thames Water handled Mr Marcic's complaint in a tardy and insensitive fashion. But the malfunctioning of the statutory scheme on this occasion does not cast doubt on its overall fairness as a scheme. A complaint by an individual about his particular case can, and should, be pursued with the director pursuant to the statutory scheme, with the long stop availability of judicial review. That remedial avenue was not taken in this case.

44 I must add that one aspect of the statutory scheme as presently administered does cause concern. This is the uncertain position regarding payment of compensation to those who suffer flooding while waiting for flood alleviation works to be carried out....

45 It seems to me that, in principle, if it is not practicable for reasons of expense to carry out remedial works for the time being, those who enjoy the benefit of effective drainage should bear the cost of paying some compensation to those whose properties are situated lower down in the catchment area and who, in consequence, have to endure intolerable sewer flooding, whether internal or external. As the Court of Appeal noted, the flooding is the consequence of the benefit provided to those making use of the system: [2002] QB 929, 1001, para 113. The minority who suffer damage and disturbance as a consequence of the inadequacy of the sewerage system ought not to be required to bear an unreasonable burden. This is a matter the director and others should reconsider in the light of the facts in the present case.

46 For these reasons I consider the claim under the Human Rights Act 1998 is ill-founded. The scheme set up by the 1991 Act is Convention-compliant. The scheme provides a remedy for persons in Mr Marcic's unhappy position, but Mr Marcic chose not to avail himself of this remedy.

47 Accordingly this appeal should be allowed. Save as to costs, the order of the Court of Appeal should be set aside and the order of the trial judge varied so as to answer all the preliminary issues in the negative. As to costs, the House gave leave to Thames Water to appeal on terms that the existing costs orders in the courts below remain undisturbed and that Thames Water pay Mr Marcic's costs in the House in any event.

Commentary

When considering compatibility with Convention rights, the House of Lords declined to consider the acts of the defendants as sewerage undertakers, but focused instead on the sufficiency of the statutory scheme as a whole. Although it was considered by Lord Nicholls that in this case 'matters plainly went awry', the existence of a statutory scheme for complaints and enforcement under the Water Industry Act 1991 in effect shielded the water company itself from action under the HRA. Furthermore, the statutory scheme was considered to be Convention-compliant despite concerns, again expressed by Lord Nicholls (at [44]), surrounding the availability of compensation to those suffering external flooding. It was also emphasized that the appropriate route for challenging the operation of the scheme was by judicial review as against the director, *not* in common law (or under the HRA) directly against the sewerage undertaker.

The members of the House of Lords placed considerable emphasis upon the then very recent decision of the Grand Chamber of the Court of Human Rights in *Hatton v UK* ((2003) 37 EHRR 28). This, they argued, showed that in arriving at a fair balance between the interests of people whose homes and property are affected by an activity, and the interests of other people (and the public) in the activity in question, national institutions have a broad discretion in choosing the appropriate machinery and the appropriate solution to achieve this balance.

The precise use made of *Hatton* is not beyond dispute. It is true that the Grand Chamber decided that the national authority should be left a choice in the means by which it achieved a balance between different interests. Nevertheless, the Grand Chamber did still address the *substantive* question of whether or not the solutions in question had achieved a fair balance. It did not confine itself to the procedural question of whether appropriate machinery exists for determining what the appropriate balance might be.

123 ... While the State is required to give due consideration to the particular interests the respect for which it is obliged to secure by virtue of Art.8, it must in principle be left a choice between different ways and means of meeting this obligation. The Court's supervisory function being of a subsidiary nature, it is limited to reviewing whether or not the particular solution adopted can be regarded as striking a fair balance.

Furthermore, the *Hatton* case was not a situation in which priorities needed to be set for the use of resources, so that some needs would go entirely unmet. Rather, it was a case of serious disagreement over what *level* of protection against noise from night flying was acceptable. It was thus the *substance* of the regime adopted, in terms of how it measured noise disturbance and what criteria were set for its control, that was challenged:

Hatton v UK (2003)
37 EHRR 28

125 ... [The Court] notes the dispute between the parties as to whether aircraft movements or quota counts should be employed as the appropriate yardstick for measuring night noise. However, it finds no indication that the authorities' decision to introduce a regime based on the quota count system was as such incompatible with Art.8.

In considering whether an appropriate balance had been struck, the court also stated that it was relevant to consider the impact upon the applicants' interests. For example:

127 ... The Court also notes that the applicants do not contest the substance of the Government's claim that house prices in the areas in which they live have not been adversely affected by the increase in night noise. The Court considers it reasonable, in determining the impact of a general policy on individuals in a particular area, to take into account the individuals' ability to leave the area.

It was relevant that the applicants' interests were not entirely disregarded, and it was also relevant that they may not be so adversely affected as first appeared, if they were able to move out of the area. None of this is quite the same as saying that a fair mechanism for deciding priorities will suffice, or that it is sufficient to entrust the decision to a regulator. The truth is that the House of Lords preferred that the issues concerning Article 8 be considered in a public law context, if necessary through judicial review, and not through an action in the tort of nuisance.

There is also a question over the proper role of the 'margin of appreciation' in a *national* (as opposed to an international) court. Hart and Wheeler, for example, suggest in their analysis of *Hatton v UK* that a national court should be less deferential when asked to rule on similar issues: 'Night Flights and Environmental Human Rights' (2004) 16 JEL 132–9, at 138.

Balancing Rights

We will see in later chapters—particularly Chapters 13 and 14—that courts are often required not only to balance Convention rights against other kinds of interests (such as public interest), but also to balance Convention rights against one another. Interferences with use and enjoyment of land may engage either Article 8 (private and family life), or Article 1 Protocol 1 (enjoyment of possessions); but the interferences themselves may also be connected to exercise of Convention rights. A case raising issues of this sort in relation to nuisance was *Olympic Delivery Authority v Persons Unknown* [2012] EWHC 1012 (Ch), in which the claimant Authority was an exclusive licensee of a site to be developed as the Olympic basketball facility. A protest group named 'Save Leyton Marsh' deliberately prevented the claimants from gaining access to the site. Although the protest engaged Convention rights to freedom of expression and protest (Articles 10 and 11), these were not unqualified rights; and a balancing exercise was required:

Arnold J, *Olympic Delivery Authority v Persons Unknown* [2012] EWHC 1012 (Ch)

24 In those circumstances, it seems to me that the approach laid down by Lord Steyn where both Article 8 and Article 10 ECHR rights are involved in *Re S* [2004] UKHL 47, [2005] 1AC 593 at [17] is applicable in the present case. Here we are concerned with a conflict between the ODA's rights under Article 1 of the First Protocol, and the protesters' rights under Articles 10 and 11. The correct approach, therefore, is as follows. First, neither the ODA's rights under Article 1 of the First Protocol, nor the protesters' rights under Articles 10 and 11 have precedence over each other. Secondly, where the values under the respective Articles are in conflict, an intense focus on the comparative importance of the specific rights being claimed in the individual case is necessary. Thirdly, the justifications for interfering with or restricting each right must be taken into account. Finally, the proportionality test, or ultimate balancing test, must be applied to each.

Approaching the matter in this way, an injunction restraining the nuisance was an appropriate remedy. This illustrates that private law remedies may themselves fall to be assessed and framed in terms of their impact on Convention rights. Injunctions in particular, since they inherently involve a balancing of interests, lend themselves to consideration in terms of the balance they strike between Convention rights, which falls to be assessed in terms of the proportionality of its effects.

3. PUBLIC NUISANCE

3.1 GENERAL STATEMENT: VARIETIES OF PUBLIC NUISANCE

Public nuisance is a crime at common law. Although it no doubt provides a very useful tool for the prosecutor, it has been doubted whether it is an appropriate element in modern criminal law. Historically, it has been broad, impressionistic, and even more indistinct in its boundaries than the tort of private nuisance.

Prior to *Rimmington and Goldstein* (below), the most authoritative definition of the **crime** of public nuisance was as follows:

Archbold's Criminal Pleading, Evidence and Practice (Sweet & Maxwell, 2005), para 31.40

A person is guilty of a public nuisance (also known as common nuisance), who (a) does an act not warranted by law, or (b) omits to discharge a legal duty, if the effect of the act or omission is to endanger the life, health, property, morals or comfort of the public, or to obstruct the public in the exercise or enjoyment of rights common to all her Majesty's subjects.

So broad is the potential scope of this definition, J. R. Spencer in his much-cited study of public nuisance ('Public Nuisance—A Critical Examination' [1989] CLJ 55) wondered whether there was really much need for any other criminal law at all. He concluded however that a trimmed-down version of public nuisance would have a valuable gap-filling role for use against behaviour which seriously threatens public health or the environment, but which fails to fit with the definition of more specific crimes.

In *R v Rimmington and Goldstein* [2005] UKHL 63; [2006] 1 AC 459, two appellants challenged their convictions of offences of public nuisance, arguing (amongst other things) that the offence was so loosely defined that it violated Article 7 ECHR:

Article 7 No punishment without law

1. No one shall be held guilty of any criminal offence on account of any act or omission which did not constitute a criminal offence under national or international law at the time when it was committed. Nor shall a heavier penalty be imposed than the one that was applicable at the time the criminal offence was committed.

The House of Lords determined that the crime of public nuisance was tolerably clear, provided the reference to 'public morals' was removed from the standard definition. Thus the ambit of the offence has been reduced. Equally, the House proposed that a common law offence should only very rarely be used where statutory offences were applicable to the same conduct.[17]

---

[17] The defendants also escaped conviction because there was not a sufficient 'public' dimension to their acts, or in other words no 'common injury'. One had sent offensive racist literature through the post to

Lord Bingham of Cornhill, *R v Rimmington and Goldstein*
[2006] 1 AC 459

30 There is in my opinion considerable force in the appellants' second contention under this head. Where Parliament has defined the ingredients of an offence, perhaps stipulating what shall and shall not be a defence, and has prescribed a mode of trial and a maximum penalty, it must ordinarily be proper that conduct falling within that definition should be prosecuted for the statutory offence and not for a common law offence which may or may not provide the same defences and for which the potential penalty is unlimited. . . . I would not go to the length of holding that conduct may never be lawfully prosecuted as a generally-expressed common law crime where it falls within the terms of a specific statutory provision, but good practice and respect for the primacy of statute do in my judgment require that conduct falling within the terms of a specific statutory provision should be prosecuted under that provision unless there is good reason for doing otherwise.

31 It follows from the conclusions already expressed in paras 29 to 30 above that the circumstances in which, in future, there can properly be resort to the common law crime of public nuisance will be relatively rare. It may very well be, as suggested by J R Spencer in his article cited in para 6 above, at p 83, that "There is surely a strong case for abolishing the crime of public nuisance". But as the courts have no power to create new offences (see para 33 below), so they have no power to abolish existing offences. That is a task for Parliament, following careful consideration (perhaps undertaken, in the first instance, by the Law Commission) whether there are aspects of the public interest which the crime of public nuisance has a continuing role to protect. It is not in my view open to the House in resolving these appeals to conclude that the common law crime of causing a public nuisance no longer exists.

The end result of *Rimmington and Goldstein* is that the crime of public nuisance is more closely defined, and less flexible.

For tort lawyers, the issues that arise from public nuisance are narrower and somewhat more controllable, even if they are the product of historical accident and therefore do not conform to tidy categorization (F. Newark, 'The Boundaries of Nuisance' (1949) 65 LQR 480). From the tort lawyer's point of view, it is convenient to divide public nuisances into three types, which are important to tort law for different reasons:

1. 'amalgamated' private nuisances, affecting large numbers of people;

2. nuisances that affect a sufficient class of people, and are actionable by an individual suffering 'special damage';

3. cases relating to the highway.

3.2 AMALGAMATED PRIVATE NUISANCES

The first category consists of those public nuisances which could be said to be made up of a series of private nuisances. Where a sufficiently substantial number of people suffer relevant interferences, then the interferences will amount to a 'public' nuisance. This type of 'public'

prominent people; the other had posted salt to a friend in New York as a practical joke, and this had caused an anthrax alert when it spilt out of the envelope at a sorting office.

nuisance, which is public because of the numbers of people involved, was summed up in *AG v PYA Quarries* [1957] 2 QB 169, at 187:

Romer LJ

Some public nuisances (for example, the pollution of rivers) can often be established without the necessity of calling a number of individual complainants as witnesses. In general, however, a public nuisance is proved by the cumulative effect which it is shown to have had on the people living within its sphere of influence. In other words, a normal and legitimate way of proving a public nuisance is to prove a sufficiently large collection of private nuisances.

In such a case, the action is brought by the Attorney General, but the case is one of 'amalgamated' private nuisances. Some cases brought in public nuisance therefore provide important authority concerning the principles of private nuisance. An example is *Gillingham v Medway Chatham Dock Co* ([1993] QB 343, extracted in Section 1.3), which also exemplifies that local authorities may bring such actions pursuant to section 222 of the Local Government Act 1972.

AG v PYA Quarries is also a leading authority on the question of what constitutes a sufficient 'class' of people for the purposes of an action in public nuisance, a question of importance to both this and the next category of public nuisance.

Romer LJ, at 184

It is clear ... that any nuisance is "public" which materially affects the reasonable comfort and convenience of life of a class of Her Majesty's subjects. The sphere of the nuisance may be described generally as "the neighbourhood"; but the question whether the local community within that sphere comprises a sufficient number of persons to constitute a class of the public is a question of fact in every case. It is not necessary, in my judgment, to prove that every member of the class has been injuriously affected; it is sufficient to show that a representative cross-section of the class has been so affected for an injunction to issue.

Denning LJ, at 191

So here I decline to answer the question how many people are necessary to make up her Majesty's subjects generally. I prefer to look to the reason of the thing and to say that a public nuisance is a nuisance which is so widespread in its range or so indiscriminate in its effect that it would not be reasonable to expect one person to take proceedings on his own responsibility to put a stop to it, but that it should be taken on the responsibility of the community at large.

3.3 INDIVIDUALS SUFFERING 'SPECIAL DAMAGE'

Cases of 'amalgamated private nuisance', and therefore of overlap between private and public nuisance, are however the exception and not the rule. The second (and more typical) sort of public nuisance concerns interference with the 'comfort and convenience' of a class of Her Majesty's subjects. Public nuisance is thus broader in its coverage than private nuisance, for it encompasses damage to a far wider range of interests. Again, public nuisances of this type are actionable by the Attorney General in civil proceedings (in addition to criminal proceedings), where injunctions may be awarded. A public nuisance which affects the comfort or convenience of a sufficient class may also be actionable by an individual seeking damages. In order to recover compensation in an action for public nuisance, the individual will need to show that he or she has suffered 'special damage'.

In *Colour Quest Ltd v Total Downstream UK plc* [2009] EWHC 540 (Comm), the defendants Total raised among many other arguments the proposition that the second form of nuisance (affecting a class of Her Majesty's subjects) was not actionable by a claimant whose right to the enjoyment of his land (a private nuisance notion) had been affected. David Steel J rejected this argument, emphasizing as he did so that claims in private and public nuisance though entirely different were not mutually exclusive (at [432]–[433]):

David Steel J, *Colour Quest v Total Downstream UK plc* [2009] EWHC 540 (Comm)

432 It follows that a collection of private nuisances can constitute a public nuisance: but it does not follow either that in consequence the claim in private nuisance is subsumed or that a public nuisance involving interference with health or comfort cannot be freestanding. . . .

434 It is accordingly difficult to discern any difficulty in categorizing the incident at Buncefield as a public nuisance. . . . The explosion was caused by negligence. A very large number of people were affected. Those who had an interest in land suffered private nuisance. The explosion endangered the health and comfort of the public at large. Subject to establishing a loss which was particular, substantial and direct . . . there is a claim in public nuisance.

Special Damage

Special damage must be 'particular, direct, and substantial' (*Benjamin v Storr* (1873–74) LR 9 CP 400, Brett J; Buckley, *The Law of Nuisance*, 2nd edn, pp. 74–5). A very broad range of damage is actionable, including purely financial losses. In *Tate and Lyle v GLC* [1983] 2 AC 509, the defendants caused siltation of the River Thames and an obstruction to the public right of navigation. There was no damage to any property owned by the defendants, but they were put to particular expense in dredging the river around their jetties in order to continue their business. While such a claim would surely fail in negligence, the costs incurred were sufficient to represent a special damage for the purposes of public nuisance.

It has long been assumed that damages for personal injury, as well as for pure economic loss, were recoverable in public nuisance. This assumption was challenged in the *Corby Group Litigation* before the Court of Appeal [2008] EWCA Civ 463. The claimants in this significant litigation were born between 1986 and 1999 with deformities of the upper limbs, which they blamed on the manner in which Corby Borough Council had set about the reclamation of a large area of contaminated land which had been acquired from the British Steel Corporation. The defendant council argued that the House of Lords in the two key cases of *Hunter v Canary Wharf* (concerning private nuisance) and *Transco v Stockport* (concerning liability in *Rylands v Fletcher*) had accepted the arguments of

Professor Newark, 'The Boundaries of Nuisance' (1949) 65 LQR 480, to the effect that personal injury damages were not recoverable in any part of the law of nuisance. This depended on acceptance of Professor Newark's argument that public nuisance was not in its origins separate from private nuisance, but was properly seen as a part of the same branch of law, protecting interests in property, not in the person.[18] The Court of Appeal concluded that in neither of the two cases referred to was there an implied reversal of the 'long-established principle that damages for personal injury can be recovered in public nuisance'. In fact, the House of Lords had not even criticized that principle in either of the two cases (*Corby Group Litigation*, at [22]). That was enough to dispose of the council's argument, since earlier cases in which damages for personal injury were awarded for public nuisance were therefore binding upon the Court of Appeal. However, Dyson LJ (with whom Ward LJ and Smith LJ agreed) went on to explain that as a matter of principle, he was not in any event convinced that the argument was correct. He went on to deploy a range of evidence to counteract the defendants' reliance on a single, albeit very influential, piece of academic opinion.

Dyson LJ, *Corby Group Litigation* [2008] EWCA Civ 463

27. It seems to me that it is at least arguable that Professor Newark was wrong to describe a public nuisance as a "tort to the enjoyment of rights in land". The definition of the crime of public nuisance says nothing about enjoyment of land and some public nuisances undoubtedly have nothing to do with the interference with enjoyment of land. As Lord Bingham said, the ingredients of the crime and the tort are the same. A public nuisance is simply an unlawful act or omission which endangers the life, safety, health, property or comfort of the public. As was said in *Salmond and Heuston on the Law of Torts* (21st edition 1986): "Public and private nuisances are not in reality two species of the same genus at all. There is no generic conception which includes the crime of making a bomb-hoax and the tort of allowing one's trees to overhang the land of a neighbour".

28. Professor Newark's response seems to be that, because we are mortals and earthbound, the personal injuries we suffer as a result of a public nuisance must necessarily occur while we are exercising rights in land (p 489). In a sense this is true, if the phrase "exercising rights in land" is given the generous interpretation for which Professor Newark contends, i.e. the liberty to exercise rights over land "in the amplest manner". It can be said that a person who suffers personal injury must be in some physical place when the injury is caused and, unless he is a trespasser, he is exercising a right over land when he is in that place, even if only as a licensee.

29. But even if that is true, it does not follow that the right which is interfered with in a public nuisance case is properly to be regarded as a right to enjoy property. The essence of the right that is protected by the tort of private nuisance is the right to enjoy one's property. It does not extend to a licensee: see *Hunter*. The essence of the right that is protected by the crime and tort of public nuisance is the right not to be adversely affected by an unlawful act or omission whose effect is to endanger the life, safety, health etc of the public. This view is reflected in the *American Law Institute, Restatement of the Law, Second, Torts 2d* (1979) chapter 40

[18] Indicating just how long the assumption has been in existence, Professor Newark traced the 'heresy' of recoverability of personal injury damages in public nuisance to what he called 'an incautious *obiter dictum* which let fall in the Common Pleas in 1535' (Newark, 'The Boundaries of Nuisance' (1949) 65 LQR 480, at 481).

para 821B (h) which states: "Unlike a private nuisance, a public nuisance does not necessarily involve interference with use and enjoyment of land".

30. In these circumstances, it is difficult to see why a person whose life, safety or health has been endangered and adversely affected by an unlawful act or omission and who suffers personal injuries as a result should not be able to recover damages. The purpose of the law which makes it a crime and a tort to do an unlawful act which endangers the life, safety or health of the public is surely to protect the public against the consequences of acts or omissions which do endanger their lives, safety or health. Ono obvious consequence of such an act or omission is personal injury. The purpose of this law is not to protect the property interests of the public. It is true that the same conduct can amount to a private nuisance and a public nuisance. But the two torts are distinct and the rights protected by them are different.

31. On the other hand, I acknowledge that Professor Newark's article presents a powerful argument in support of the proposition that personal injury damages should only be recoverable in negligence and that it is an argument which the House of Lords may accept.

Conclusion

32. For the reasons that I have given, I do not consider that it is open to this court to decide that damages for personal injury are not recoverable in public nuisance. The fact that the law may be developed by the House of Lords deciding to accept Professor Newark's thesis is not a reason for this court not to apply the law as it now stands.

Despite the similarity in name, the Court of Appeal therefore regards public nuisance as an entirely different tort from private nuisance, with different origins and protecting against a different range of interferences.

Subsequently, at trial of a number of issues of principle relating to the litigation, Akenhead J determined that—subject to proof of causation—the council would be liable in public nuisance ([2009] EWHC 1944 (TCC)). The case subsequently settled. Importantly though, he also held that there were breaches of the duty of care in negligence, and of statutory duty in the form of section 33 of the Environmental Protection Act 1990.

3.4 STRUCTURES ADJOINING OR OVERHANGING THE HIGHWAY

A number of authorities concern dangerous structures adjoining or overhanging the highway. These authorities appear to conflict concerning the relevant standard of liability. In *Tarry v Ashton* [1876] 1 QBD 314, the defendant was considered to be under a 'non-delegable duty of care' to repair a lamp overhanging the highway, and was therefore liable to the plaintiff for personal injuries suffered even though she had recently paid reputable contractors to repair the lamp. Perhaps the defendant could reasonably be expected to have been aware of the continuing hazard presented by the lamp. If so, then the later case of *Wringe v Cohen* [1940] 1 KB 229 went further, in that there was liability for artificial structures adjoining the highway whether the defendant could reasonably have known of their condition, or not. By contrast, in *Noble v Harrison* [1926] 2 KB 332, a landowner was found to be not liable when a branch from one of his trees damaged the plaintiff's vehicle, on the basis that the defect in the tree was not reasonably discoverable. On the face of it, a different standard of liability will apply depending on whether the damage is caused by an artificial structure (*Wringe* v *Cohen*), or by a natural feature (*Noble v Harrison*). This scarcely seems defensible, and it has been proposed (Buckley, *The Law of Nuisance*, 2nd edn, p 84) that the interpretation in *Wringe v Cohen* does not represent the law. To accept this would also bring the interpretation concerning structures overhanging the highway into line with the law of nuisance more generally concerning hazards which are not originated by the occupier. It was the view of A. L. Goodhart, writing in 1930, that the following broad and simple conclusion could be drawn in respect of both public and private nuisance:

A. L. Goodhart, 'Liability for Things Naturally on the Land' (1930) 4 CLJ 13, at 30

The correct principle seems to be that an occupier of land is liable for a nuisance of which he knows, or ought to know, whether that nuisance is caused by himself, his predecessor in title, a third person or by nature. Whether a natural condition is or is not a nuisance is, of course, a question of fact. Is the injury caused by the natural condition more than a reasonable neighbour can be asked to bear under the rule of 'live and let live'? In other words, the ordinary rules of nuisance apply in the case of natural conditions. As we must all bear with our neighbour's piano-playing so we must also submit to his thistle down. This does not mean that we have no remedy if he introduces a large orchestra, or if he allows his tree, even of natural growth, to remain in a dangerous condition along the highway.

This statement was endorsed as correct so far as public nuisance is concerned by Kennedy LJ in the public nuisance case of *Wandsworth LBC v Railtrack plc* [2001] EWCA Civ 1236; [2002] 2 WLR 512, at [9]. It is also consistent with the approach of the Court of Appeal in *Mistry v Thakor* [2005] EWCA Civ 953. The claimant was seriously injured while walking along a public highway in Leicester, when two 50-kilogram pieces of concrete cladding fell from a building owned by the defendants. The difficult questions involved in this case—which was accepted to be a case of public nuisance—concerned the knowledge which it was reasonable to impute to the owners, given that they had contracted a surveyor to comment on the state of the building. In its discussion of these issues, the court accepted implicitly that constructive knowledge of the defect (knowledge that a reasonably careful owner would have had) was required for liability to be established. Here, the primary responsibility was that of the surveyor, but lack of care on the part of the owners meant that they too bore some of the responsibility. This was assessed at 20 per cent.

4. THE ENVIRONMENTAL TORT(S)?

On a number of occasions, we have mentioned the potential 'environmental protection' function of both public and private nuisance; and we have also explored cases (such as *Marcic* and *Hatton*) which involve, even if tangentially, the question of environmental rights. Because of the subject matter of the nuisance actions—polluted water, noise, smells, acid smuts, damaged trees, and so on—actions in nuisance are generally recognized to have played some part in the battle against pollution, particularly before the emergence of that range of measures which can be loosely referred to as 'environmental law'. Even so, the actions in nuisance suffer from a number of limitations which have meant that the tort actions covered here and in the subsequent chapter will never be a central plank in environmental protection. Some of these are practical, concerning means of enforcement and the essentially reactive nature of an action in common law. Others are a question of more fundamental principle.

Private nuisance is concerned with protection of rights over land. Environmental law is usually thought to concern a more general public interest in protection of the environment. The question therefore is simple—how can the protection of certain selected private interests be an effective means of securing environmental protection? To the extent that the interests of property owners overlap with environmental interests, this could be described as coincidental. Nevertheless, such overlap undoubtedly exists in numerous cases of pollution, for example. Many aspects of this overlap are considered by contributors to Lowry and Edmunds, *Environmental Protection and the Common Law* (Hart Publishing, 2000). We will see later that some commentators would go further than this, and argue that property rights have much more than a coincidental relationship with environmental protection.

Public nuisance raises a rather different issue, since it is undoubtedly concerned with public health. Public health was a precursor of environmental law and in many respects overlaps with it, but it is still a relatively limited concern when compared with environmental protection in its broadest and most developed modern guise. For example, in the case of statutory nuisances under the Environmental Protection Act 1990 (sections 79–82), the historical link to public health is considered to give rise to certain limitations in the environmental protection function of the statutory nuisance provisions. Even so, the *Corby Group Litigation* seems to illustrate the continued scope for common law in this respect. However, as Akenhead J pointed out, the results of a trial of this sort do not equate to the findings of a free and open enquiry:

Akenhead J, *Corby Group Litigation* [2009] EWHC 1944 (TCC)

2. It must be borne in mind that this trial has not as such been an open-ended inquiry in which the Court in an inquisitorial manner seeks to determine unilaterally what happened and what caused the birth defects. The Claimants have pleaded what their case is and it is that case which they have to establish broadly upon a balance of probabilities and which CBC has to meet. Thus, the Court is restricted to the evidence put before it. For instance, neither party has provided evidence to demonstrate whether there was statistically an increase in miscarriages or stillbirths during the period over which the Claimants were conceived and there has been no comparison with what had occurred over the previous years in Corby or since so far as the incidence of birth defects, miscarriages and stillbirths were concerned; that might have been of assistance to support either side's position. I suggested at an earlier procedural meeting that the parties might consider whether such evidence might be adduced. Further examples are Messrs Cropley and Palmer who were senior engineers and who were dismissed by CBC in early 1997; they were heavily involved in many of the projects about which criticism is made in these proceedings; neither party saw fit to call either of these people. Furthermore, although many thousands of pages of contemporary documents have been produced, many documents have not been; for instance, CBC has had a large number of documents destroyed accidentally; consequently, there are large gaps in the documentation. It would be wrong to speculate as to evidence which was not put before the Court. I must decide this case based on the evidence adduced by the parties.

As noted earlier, there continues to be lively disagreement about the degree to which the action in private nuisance, in particular, can play a part in environmental protection.

Some commentators argue that the protection of property rights by affected individuals is an effective means of attaining environmental protection (see for example E. Brubaker, *Property Rights in the Defence of Nature* (Earthscan, 1995)). This challenges the prevailing orthodoxy, that environmental law must entail the deterrence of private pollution through public law means. Other commentators argue that nuisance is potentially an effective means of attaining an *efficient* level of environmental protection, which is argued to be the only appropriate measure. (The latter argument is derived in part from Ronald Coase's classic essay, 'The Problem of Social Cost' (1960) 3 JLE 1.) And there is also a contrary and subtle argument that philosophically speaking, environmental protection is misunderstood if it is cast primarily as a welfare-based public interest issue. Rather, environmental law should be understood precisely through a modified concept of property rights which recognizes the intrinsic rather than the purely instrumental value of natural resources (S. Coyle and K. Morrow, *Philosophical Foundations of Environmental Law* (Hart Publishing, 2004)).

The problem is that the law of nuisance as it stands does not entirely fit either of the last two conceptual arguments in favour of its use in environmental protection. As regards Coyle and Morrow's argument, we have seen that the primary focus of contemporary nuisance law is on 'use and enjoyment' of land, rather than on intrinsic value. And as regards the argument that nuisance may provide a distinct and independent property-based system for achieving optimum environmental protection, we have seen that the case law on nuisance is pervasively influenced by questions of public interest, by ideas of welfare quite independent of the satisfaction of individual preferences, and of course by deference to legislative intent. To borrow the words of David Campbell, 'Of Coase and Corn: A (Sort Of) Defence of Private Nuisance' (2000) 63 MLR 197–215, nuisance does not in its current form provide any sort of 'bright-line' method of attaining environmental protection, independent of perceived judgments of public interest for resolving environmental issues. (Campbell suggests that nuisance ought to be reformed in order to do just this. In effect, he suggests that judgments as to public interest should be removed from the ambit of nuisance so that through the claims of those with property rights it may better perform its role of enhancing welfare, including environmental protection. This is of course a deeply controversial proposition.)

There are also limitations which are more practical than principled. The expensive and unpredictable process of common law litigation, dependent on open-textured notions such as 'reasonableness' and on the resolve, resources, and qualifying property rights of affected parties, is not in itself the most effective way to achieve fundamental environmental improvements. Even in the apparent heyday of the nuisance actions, the nineteenth century, our focus on decided cases such as *St Helen's v Tipping* may be misleading, for that case has been described as an isolated instance of a sufficiently determined litigant: see further J. P. S. McLaren, 'Nuisance Law and the Industrial Revolution—Some Lessons from Social History' (1983) 3 OJLS 155; J. P. S. McLaren, 'The Common Law Nuisance Actions and the Environmental Battle—Well-Tempered Swords or Broken Reeds?' (1972) 10 Osgoode Hall LJ 505; A. W. B. Simpson, 'Victorian Judges and the Problem of Social Cost', in *Leading Cases in the Common Law* (1995). On the other hand, recent work by Ben Pontin has uncovered a different story, suggesting that genuine social progress may have been achieved through nineteenth-century tort litigation.[19] In more recent work, Pontin has argued that the injunctive

[19] B. Pontin, 'The Secret Achievements of Nineteenth Century Nuisance Law' (2007) 19 Environmental Law and Management 271–4, 276–90, discussing the background to and after-effects of *AG v Birmingham Corporation* (1858) 4 K & J 528.

remedies at the disposal of the courts led to far more positive results than has been acknowledged, with potential lessons for the development of modern law.[20] That being the case, what message might this give for today's courts, given the newly increased flexibility of remedy outlined in Section 1.7?

5. CONCLUSIONS

i. Despite its long historic roots, nuisance retains a useful role within the law of torts. Arguably, this is largely because of the work that has been done to distinguish its principles from those of the tort of negligence. Nuisance typically covers different situations from those with which negligence is concerned, principally those involving continuing states of affairs where there is a conflict between different uses of land. Here, the distinct nature of nuisance principles is at its clearest. This distinctness is reflected also in its remedies, where injunctions play a major role.

ii. Key issues of concern in the modern law of nuisance include the approach to calculation of damages, and the role of public interest in assessing both the existence of a nuisance, and the appropriate remedy. In relation to the first of these, calculation of damages, the character of nuisance as a tort against land is strongly represented by the way in which damages for loss of amenity are calculated with reference to the value of the land. This has led to the frustration of some attempts to use private nuisance as a means of protecting the rights of occupants against pollution and other harms, since damages are not sensitive to the number of people occupying the land and are available only to those with a formal interest in the land. This takes seriously the role of property in the tort of private nuisance. By way of partial contrast, there has been more recognition in recent years that public interest plays an important role in the tort of private nuisance. *Coventry v Lawrence* marks a sea change in the way that decisions about injunctive remedies are to be made, leaving greater scope for interests beyond those of the parties to litigation to be considered and recognizing that those interests, and the conflicts between neighbours typically represented by private nuisance, are always set in the context of a much broader web.

FURTHER READING

Ashworth, A., 'Public Nuisance: Elements of Offence' (2006) Crim LR 153.

Beever, A., *The Law of Private Nuisance* (Hart, 2013).

Buckley, R. A., *The Law of Nuisance* (2nd edn, London: Butterworths, 1991).

Campbell, D., 'Of Coase and Corn: a (Sort of) Defence of Private Nuisance' (2000) 63 MLR 197.

Coase, R., 'The Problem of Social Cost' (1960) 3 JLE 1.

Crabb, L., 'The Property Torts' (2003) 11 Tort L Rev 104–18.

[20] B. Pontin, 'The Common Law Clean Up of the "Workshop of the World": More Realism About Nuisance Law's Historic Environmental Achievements' (2013) 40 Journal of Law and Society 173.

DeMerieux, M., 'Deriving Environmental Rights from the European Convention on Human Rights and Fundamental Freedoms' (2001) 3 OJLS 521.

Gearty, C., 'The Place of Private Nuisance in a Modern Law of Tort' (1989) 48 CLJ 214–42.

Getzler, J., A History of Water Rights at Common Law (Oxford: Oxford University Press, 2004).

Goodhart, A. L., 'Liability for Things Naturally on the Land' (1930) 4 CLJ 13.

Hart, D., and Wheeler, M., 'Night Flights and Strasbourg's Retreat from Environmental Human Rights' (2004) 16 JEL 100–39.

Hilson, C., 'Let's Get Physical' (2009) 29 JEL 33–57.

Jolowicz, J. A., 'Damages in Equity—A Study of Lord Cairns' Act' [1975] CLJ 224.

Lee, M., 'What is Private Nuisance?' (2003) LQR 298–325.

Lee, M., 'Tort Law and Regulation: Planning and Nuisance' (2011) 8 JPL 986.

Lee, M., 'Occupying the Field: Tort and the Pre-emptive Statute', in T. T. Arvind and J. Steele (eds), Tort Law and the Legislature: Common Law, Statute and the Dynamics of Legal Change (Hart Publishing, 2013).

Lee. M., 'The Public Interest in Private Nuisance: Collectives and Communities in Tort' (2015) CLJ 74.

Lees, E., 'Lawrence v Fen Tigers: Where Now for Nuisance?' (2014) Conv 449.

Lowry, J., and Edmunds, R., Environmental Protection and the Common Law (Oxford: Hart Publishing, 2000).

McLaren, J. P. S., 'The Common Law Nuisance Actions and the Environmental Battle—Well-Tempered Swords or Broken Reeds?' (1972) 10 Osgoode Hall LJ 505.

McLaren, J. P. S., 'Nuisance Law and the Industrial Revolution—Some Lessons from Social History' (1983) 3 OJLS 155.

Miller, C., 'Environmental Rights in a Welfare State? A Comment on DeMerieux' (2003) 23 OJLS 111–25.

Morrow, K., 'The Rights Question: the Initial Impact of the HRA on Domestic Law Relating to the Environment' (2005) JPEL 1010–21.

Murphy, J., The Law of Nuisance (Oxford University Press, 2010).

Newark, F. H., 'The Boundaries of Nuisance' (1949) 65 LQR 480.

Ogus, A. I., and Richardson, G. M., 'Economics and the Environment—A Study of Private Nuisance' [1977] CLJ 248.

Pontin, B., 'Tort Law and Victorian Government Growth: The Historiographical Significance of Tort in the Shadow of Chemical Pollution and Factory Safety Regulation' (1998) 18 OJLS 661–80.

Pontin, B., 'Nuisance Law and the Industrial Revolution: A Reinterpretation of Doctrine and Institutional Competence' (2012) 75 MLR 1010.

Simpson, A. W. B., 'Victorian Judges and the Problem of Social Cost', in Leading Cases in the Common Law (Oxford: Oxford University Press, 1995).

Spencer, J., 'Public Nuisance—A Critical Examination' [1989] CLJ 55.

Steele, J., 'Private Law and the Environment: Nuisance in Context' (1995) 15 LS 236.

Taggart, M., *Private Property and the Abuse of Rights in Victorian England* (Oxford: Oxford University Press, 2002).

Wilde, M., 'Nuisance Law and Damages in Lieu of an Injunction: Challenging the Orthodoxy of the *Shelfer* Criteria', in S. Pitel, J. Neyers, and E. Chamberlain (eds), *Tort Law: Challenging Orthodoxy* (Hart Publishing, 2013).

11

RYLANDS V FLETCHER AND STRICT LIABILITY

CENTRAL ISSUES

i) The 'rule in *Rylands v Fletcher*' appears to determine that there is liability for damage done by the escape of dangerous things accumulated on one's land, regardless of fault. The rule applies only if those things were accumulated for one's own purposes, and were not accumulated in the course of a 'natural' use of land. The strictness of the rule is mitigated by a number of defences and criteria, some of which appear incompatible with the underlying logic of the rule itself.

ii) The zone of application of *Rylands v Fletcher* has been in decline pretty much since its inception. Yet the existence of strict liability for dangerous activities (including 'accumulations') is far from being outdated. Despite the apparent conflict in principle between negligence and strict liability, in practice the greater problem is not so much conflict, but overlap. Arguably, the tort of negligence can adapt to impose liability in situations far removed from cases of individual fault, including the situations covered by *Rylands v Fletcher*. This

was the move made by the Australian High Court, in *Burnie Port Authority v General Jones Pty Ltd*. In the English courts, *Rylands* has been described as one of the source authorities for a non-delegable duty based on the relationship between neighbouring occupiers; but without discussion of whether negligence on the part of contractors should therefore be a pre-requisite of liability.

iii) The growth both of strict liability statutes, and of negligence liability divorced from fault, underline that areas of strict liability are entirely acceptable to contemporary thinking. But the growth of these alternative methods of imposing strict liability have left the rule itself exposed as arbitrary, limited, and in this sense archaic. Studying the limited role of *Rylands v Fletcher* is a good way of approaching the subtle relationship between negligence and strict liability; and also allows us to question the underlying purposes of strict liability in tort (see also Chapters 9 and 15).

1. INTRODUCTION

In England and Wales, the 'rule in *Rylands v Fletcher*' is now treated as a branch of the tort of private nuisance. In Australia, the rule has been largely absorbed into negligence, which now provides an alternative route to liability without personal fault where some hazardous activities are concerned. In the United States, a specific and limited principle of strict liability has evolved in respect of 'dangerous' activities. This has clearly developed from the rule in *Rylands v Fletcher* but it is not confined by the limits associated with nuisance, particularly in respect of the types of damage that are recoverable. In Scotland, the rule does not apply: *RHM Bakeries (Scotland) Ltd v Strathclyde Regional Council*, 1985 SLT 214, at 217. *Rylands* deals with 'isolated escapes', and furthermore it deals with cases of actual damage, rather than general 'interference'. As such it provides a direct alternative to negligence in some circumstances. In terms of long-term survival, that has been its problem. In *Northumbrian Water v Sir Robert McAlpine* [2014] EWCA Civ 685; [2014] Env LR 28, a case argued in nuisance, the Court of Appeal confirmed that a defendant will not be liable for an isolated escape 'unless the case can be brought within the rule in *Rylands v Fletcher*': *Rylands* is a branch of nuisance, but it is a distinct branch.

This chapter falls into three parts. The first part considers the case of *Rylands v Fletcher* itself and the origins of the rule. The second identifies the elements of the rule so far as this can be done despite the confused case law. The third part turns to the categorization and boundaries of the rule today. Here we extract the major English cases of *Cambridge Water Company v Eastern Counties Leather plc*, and *Transco v Stockport MBC*, which treat *Rylands* as an aspect of nuisance; and (by contrast) the Australian High Court's decision in *Burnie Port Authority v General Jones Pty Ltd*, which deals with a very similar problem through the tort of negligence.

2. ORIGINS OF THE RULE: *RYLANDS & ANOTHER V FLETCHER*

Rylands & Another v Fletcher (Court of Exchequer Chamber LR 1 Ex 265 (1866); House of Lords LR 3 HL 330 (1868))

The plaintiffs were tenants of land on which they worked a mine. Their workings extended (under licence) through underground shafts to an area beneath neighbouring land. The defendants were neighbouring mill owners. They arranged for the construction of a reservoir in connection with the operation of their mill. There were old shafts under the reservoir, and these shafts connected with the plaintiffs' mine shafts.

The reservoir was not strong enough to bear the pressure of water when filled. As a consequence, it burst downwards and the water flooded the plaintiffs' mineshafts. The action proceeded on the basis that there had been no negligence on the part of the defendants themselves. They had employed a competent engineer and competent contractors. However, it was also stated that reasonable and proper care had not been used by those individuals employed in the planning and construction of the reservoir. The majority of the Court of Exchequer held that the failure of due care on the part of those employed to construct the reservoir did not, in the absence of any notice to the defendants, affect the defendants with any liability. The plaintiffs appealed to the Court of Exchequer Chamber.

Court of Exchequer Chamber

Blackburn J (reading the judgment of the court)

The plaintiff, though free from all blame on his part, must bear the loss, unless he can establish that it was the consequence of some default for which the defendants are responsible. The question of law therefore arises, what is the obligation which the law casts on a person who, like the defendants, lawfully brings on his land something which, though harmless whilst it remains there, will naturally do mischief if it escape out of his land. It is agreed on all hands that he must take care to keep in that which he has brought on the land and keeps there, in order that it may not escape and damage his neighbours, but the question arises whether the duty which the law casts upon him, under such circumstances, is an absolute duty to keep it in at his peril, or is, as the majority of the Court of Exchequer have thought, merely a duty to take all reasonable and prudent precautions, in order to keep it in, but no more. If the first be the law, the person who has brought on his land and kept there something dangerous, and failed to keep it in, is responsible for all the natural consequences of its escape. If the second be the limit of his duty, he would not be answerable except on proof of negligence, and consequently would not be answerable for escape arising from any latent defect which ordinary prudence and skill could not detect.

Supposing the second to be the correct view of the law, a further question arises subsidiary to the first, viz., whether the defendants are not so far identified with the contractors whom they employed, as to be responsible for the consequences of their want of care and skill in making the reservoir in fact insufficient with reference to the old shafts, of the existence of which they were aware, though they had not ascertained where the shafts went to.

We think that the true rule of law is, that the person who for his own purposes brings on his lands and collects and keeps there anything likely to do mischief if it escapes, must keep it in at his peril, and, if he does not do so, is prima facie answerable for all the damage which is the natural consequence of its escape. He can excuse himself by shewing that the escape was owing to the plaintiff's default; or perhaps that the escape was the consequence of vis major, or the act of God; but as nothing of this sort exists here, it is unnecessary to inquire what excuse would be sufficient. The general rule, as above stated, seems on principle just. The person whose grass or corn is eaten down by the escaping cattle of his neighbour, or whose mine is flooded by the water from his neighbour's reservoir, or whose cellar is invaded by the filth of his neighbour's privy, or whose habitation is made unhealthy by the fumes and noisome vapours of his neighbour's alkali works, is damnified without any fault of his own; and it seems but reasonable and just that the neighbour, who has brought something on his own property which was not naturally there, harmless to others so long as it is confined to his own property, but which he knows to be mischievous if it gets on his neighbour's, should be obliged to make good the damage which ensues if he does not succeed in confining it to his own property. But for his act in bringing it there no mischief could have accrued, and it seems but just that he should at his peril keep it there so that no mischief may accrue, or answer for the natural and anticipated consequences. And upon authority, this we think is established to be the law whether the things so brought be beasts, or water, or filth, or stenches.

The case that has most commonly occurred, and which is most frequently to be found in the books, is as to the obligation of the owner of cattle which he has brought on his land, to prevent their escaping and doing mischief. The law as to them seems to be perfectly settled from early times; the owner must keep them in at his peril, or he will be answerable for the natural consequences of their escape …

Blackburn J continued his analysis of the law relating to escaping cattle and continued (at 282):

As has been already said, there does not appear to be any difference in principle, between the extent of the duty cast on him who brings cattle on his land to keep them in, and the extent of the duty imposed on him who brings on his land, water, filth, or stenches, or any other thing which will, if it escape, naturally do damage, to prevent their escaping and injuring his neighbour, and the case of *Tenant v. Goldwin* (1 Salk. 21, 360; 2 Ld. Raym 1089; 6 Mod. 311), is an express authority that the duty is the same, and is, to keep them in at his peril.

Commentary

The rule as stated by Blackburn J does not require that any negligence should be established on anyone's part. Rather, his rule of liability requires the following elements:

(a) a person brings something on his or her land and collects and keeps it there;

(b) this is done for his or her own purposes;

(c) the thing in question is likely to do mischief if it escapes;

(d) the damage done is a natural consequence of the escape.

Blackburn J expressly differentiated this 'true rule of law', from the alternative possibility that liability in the case might have rested upon proof of negligence. As Blackburn J explained, if liability did rest upon negligence, then a subsidiary question would arise, namely 'whether the defendants are not so far identified with the contractors whom they employed, as to be responsible for their lack of care or skill'.

In effect, this alternative is the route adopted by the High Court of Australia in *Burnie Port Authority v General Jones Pty Ltd* ((1992–94) 179 CLR 520), recognizing a 'non-delegable duty' on the part of the occupier to ensure that dangerous works are conducted with reasonable care. The main difference between these two approaches appears to be simple. On the Australian analysis, negligence, negligence on the part of the contractors needs to be established; in *Rylands v Fletcher*, there need be no negligence at all.[1]

The High Court of Australia doubted whether this difference is really so great in practical terms, arguing that negligence would be found on pretty much all those sets of facts where *Rylands* would be available. As we will see later, this depends on a particular interpretation of the tort of negligence as it applies between neighbouring occupiers. The High Court recognized both that there is a special relationship between neighbouring occupiers giving rise to positive duties relating to dangerous activities; and that varying degrees of care would be demanded within the tort of negligence, depending on the degree of danger involved in a particular use of land.

There is now some indication that in English law also, *Rylands* liability is seen as based not on the hazardous nature of the accumulation itself, but on the relationship between

[1] It appears, though, that the contractors were negligent in *Rylands* itself.

defendant and claimant as occupiers of adjacent land. In *Woodland v Swimming Teachers Association*,[2] Lord Sumption JSC explained that there were two distinct categories of case in which non-delegable duties are said to arise. The first comprises 'the creation of hazards in a public place, generally in circumstances which apart from statutory authority would create a public nuisance' ([6]). The second category 'arises not from the negligent character of the act itself but because of an antecedent relationship between the defendant and the claimant' ([7]). Lord Sumption went on to associate *Rylands v Fletcher* not with the first, but with the second category of case:

Lord Sumption, *Woodland v Swimming Teachers Association* [2013] UKSC 66

8 This characterization of non-delegable duties originated in the law of nuisance, and in a number of seminal judgments of Lord Blackburn in the late nineteenth century. It was implicit in the famous judgment of the Exchequer Chamber in *Rylands v Fletcher* (1866) LR 1 Ex 265, delivered by Blackburn J and subsequently affirmed by the House of Lords (1868) LR 3 HL 330, that the duty of the defendant to prevent the escape of water from his reservoir was non-delegable, for on the facts it was due to the operations of an independent contractor ...

9 *Rylands v Fletcher* and *Dalton v Henry Angus & Co* might have been explained by reference to the hazardous character of the operation carried out by the defendant's contractor, and sometimes have been, notably by the Court of Appeal in *Honeywill & Stein Ltd v Larkin Bros (London's Commercial Photographers) Ltd* [1934] 1 KB 191. But it is clear from Lord Blackburn's observations that the essential point about them was that there was an antecedent relationship between the parties as neighbouring landowners, from which a positive duty independent of the wrongful act itself could be derived. The duty was personal to the defendant, because it attached to him in his capacity as the occupier of the neighbouring land from which the hazard originated.

Lord Sumption did not, however, comment on the absence of any apparent need to show negligence on the part of the contractor in *Rylands v Fletcher* itself. It has generally been thought not that *Rylands* provides a route for finding the occupier liable for the negligence of a contractor, but that it provides a route for finding that there is potential liability where an accumulation leads to an escape, irrespective of any negligence at all.

The apparent contradiction between negligence liability, and the rule in *Rylands v Fletcher*, therefore deserves a little thought. The manner in which the rule was stated by Blackburn J seems designed to appeal to a simple sense of fairness: the thing that escapes is accumulated for D's own purposes; therefore D, and not C, must take the consequences should that thing escape. Negligence liability, as stated in *Donoghue v Stevenson*, also had simple intuitive appeal. So how can both make sense in terms of intuitive fairness?

Perhaps the answer lies in the idea of 'keeping things in at one's peril'. We do not primarily regard the damage as the result of an isolated event, namely the escape. Rather, we see it as the result of a risk that is created by an activity on one's land. As already mentioned, this is critically different from most nuisance cases, where the interference is a result—sometimes an inevitable result—of the conflict between two uses of land. *The rule in Rylands v Fletcher*

---

[2] Also extracted and discussed in Chapter 9.

differs from both negligence and nuisance in suggesting that the risks in question may legitimately be run. It does not suggest that the accumulation of a dangerous thing per se amounts to an actionable nuisance. However, the risks associated with an accumulation may not be placed altogether upon an innocent claimant. Rather, the risks are run 'at the peril of' the person who accumulates a dangerous thing for their own purposes. In a sense then, the defendant 'insures' the neighbouring occupier against risk.[3]

We will see later that this idea of 'insuring' against harm was diluted from the start, in particular through the development of broad defences relating to the manner of the escape itself (which should really have been irrelevant in most circumstances). But we should also notice that the apparent contrast with negligence may not be real given the ability of negligence to adapt to different circumstances. In particular, the degree of care that would be undertaken by a prudent person in the exercise of a dangerous calling may bring the negligence duty very close to the duty in *Rylands v Fletcher*, at least in its diluted form. The following extract expresses the issue very clearly.

E. R. Thayer, 'Liability Without Fault' (1916) 29 Harv L Rev 801–15, at 805–6

How powerful a weapon the modern law of negligence places in the hands of the injured person, and how little its full scope has been realized until recently, is well shown by the law of carrier and passenger. The futility of degrees of care in general has long been recognized; but in the case of public service companies the habit of taking as if the carrier owed some special degree of care other than that of the ordinary prudent man has persisted and is common today. Clear-headed judges, however, have pointed out that the distinction is illusory. The ordinary prudent man would never take human beings into his keeping in conditions where they trusted utterly in him, and where life and limb was the stake, without qualifying himself in advance in all practicable ways for so dangerous a business and without using all available precautions in carrying it on. In such a business the highest care is thus nothing more than ordinary care under the circumstances; and it may be conjectured that in the case of carrier and passenger there is little difference, as a practical matter, between the results reached by the law of negligence and the doctrine of *Rylands v Fletcher*. Few cases are likely to arise in which a railroad company would escape today, except where the accident was caused by the unforeseeable intervention of some natural force or human being. Yet those are the very things which excuse him also under *Rylands v Fletcher*.

This stringent liability of the carrier is not due to his public calling, but to the nature of the agencies he uses, the helplessness of the passengers, and the peril to life and limb. . . . And in these respects the parallel between the carrier and the defendant in a case like *Rylands v Fletcher* is close. In each case the defendant has chosen to create a condition dangerous to others unless kept in control. In each case the plaintiff has no means of protecting himself and is left helpless and forced to look to the plaintiff for protection. In the one case as in the other the argument is overwhelming that ordinary prudence requires the defendant not only to take every precaution to inform himself of the dangers of his enterprise before undertaking it, and to guard against such dangers in construction, but also to use unremitting diligence in maintenance and inspection. And so great are the resources of modern science that an

---

[3] This was the approach taken by Pollock: F. Pollock, 'Duties of Insuring Safety: The Rule in *Rylands v Fletcher*' (1886) 2 LQR 52. See also J. Steele and R. Merkin, Further Reading, for discussion in the particular context of liability for fire.

accident occurring without the intervention of a new unforeseeable agency will make a hard case for the defendant. There may, of course, be facts which will entitle him to prevail, but they are most unlikely. It will be a strange case where the accident was due to conditions existing when the defendant did the responsible act, or where new forces operated which should have been foreseen, and yet the defendant was free from blame in failing to guard against them. A proper study of the plaintiff's case with expert assistance will be likely to disclose the elements of liability under the modern law of negligence in the vast majority of cases where, assuming the rule in *Rylands v Fletcher*, the defendant would not be excused in view of *Nicholls v Marsland and Box v Jubb*.

The idea of 'keeping things in at one's peril', softened by a range of defences, could be comprehended from the vantage point of the tort of negligence, according to Thayer's analysis.

The House of Lords (1868) LR 3 HL

The judgment of Blackburn J was approved by the House of Lords. Of the two judges named in the Report, Lord Cairns added some comments about non-natural user. The non-natural user criterion has subsequently been taken to be an additional requirement for the application of the rule. (The absence of a named third judge in the report simply adds to the mystery of *Rylands v Fletcher*, since it seems to underline the fact that the case was seen by its authors as relatively inconspicuous and unproblematic.)[4]

Lord Cairns LC, at 383

My Lords, the principles on which this case must be determined appear to me to be extremely simple. The Defendants, treating them as the owners or occupiers of the close on which the reservoir was constructed, might lawfully have used that close for any purpose for which it might in the ordinary course of the enjoyment of land be used; and if, in what I may term the natural user of that land, there had been any accumulation of water, either on the surface or underground, and if, by the operation of the laws of nature, that accumulation of water had passed off into the close occupied by the Plaintiff, the Plaintiff could not have complained that that result had taken place. If he had desired to guard himself against it, it would have lain upon him to have done so, by leaving, or by interposing, some barrier between his close and the close of the Defendants in order to have prevented that operation of the laws of nature.

As an illustration of that principle, I may refer to a case which was cited in the argument before your Lordships, the case of *Smith v Kenrick* in the Court of Common Pleas (7 C. B. 515).

On the other hand if the Defendants, not stopping at the natural use of their close, had desired to use it for any purpose which I may term a non-natural use, for the purpose of introducing into the close that which in its natural condition was not in or upon it, for the purpose of introducing water either above or below ground in quantities and in a manner not the result of any work or operation on or under the land,—and if in consequence of their doing so, or in consequence of any imperfection in the mode of their doing so, the water came to escape and to pass off into the close of the Plaintiff, then it appears to me that that which the

Defendants were doing they were doing at their own peril; and, if in the course of their doing it, the evil arose to which I have referred, the evil, namely, of the escape of the water and its passing away to the close of the Plaintiff and injuring the Plaintiff, then for the consequence of that, in my opinion, the Defendants would be liable. As the case of *Smith v. Kenrick* is an illustration of the first principle to which I have referred, so also the second principle to which I have referred is well illustrated by another case in the same Court, the case of *Baird v. Williamson* (15 C. B. (N. S.) 317), which was also cited in the argument at the Bar.

My Lords, these simple principles, if they are well founded, as it appears to me they are, really dispose of this case.

The same result is arrived at on the principles referred to by Mr. Justice *Blackburn* in his judgment, in the Court of Exchequer Chamber ... [Lord Cairns here quotes a passage from Blackburn J's judgment, extracted above, and expresses his agreement with it.]

Lord Cranworth

... I come without hesitation to the conclusion that the judgment of the Exchequer Chamber was right. The Plaintiff had a right to work his coal through the lands of Mr. *Whitehead*, and up to the old workings. If water naturally rising in the Defendants' land (we may treat the land as the land of the Defendants for the purpose of this case) had by percolation found its way down to the Plaintiff's mine through the old workings, and so had impeded his operations, that would not have afforded him any ground of complaint. Even if all the old workings had been made by the Plaintiff, he would have done no more than he was entitled to do; for, according to the principle acted on in *Smith v. Kenrick*, the person working the mine, under the close in which the reservoir was made, had a right to win and carry away all the coal without leaving any wall or barrier against *Whitehead's* land. But that is not the real state of the case. The Defendants, in order to effect an object of their own, brought on to their land, or on to land which for this purpose may be treated as being theirs, a large accumulated mass of water, and stored it up in a reservoir. The consequence of this was damage to the Plaintiff, and for that damage, however skilfully and carefully the accumulation was made, the Defendants, according to the principles and authorities to which I have adverted, were certainly responsible.

Commentary

Lord Cranworth reiterated clearly that negligence or lack of care was not required for the application of the principle of liability, despite the apparent negligence of the contractors in the case itself. But it was the judgment of Lord Cairns that added the criterion of *non-natural user*. As Lord Cairns put it, the defendants would have been entitled to use the land for any purpose 'for which it might in the ordinary course of the enjoyment of land be used', and the plaintiffs would have been unable to seek redress for any damage that might flow from that 'ordinary' use in the absence of negligence. But if the defendants made a *non-natural* use of the land (as here), then the defendants were to be treated as doing so 'at their own peril'.

Unfortunately, it will be apparent that Lord Cairns' judgment here contains more than one formulation of this additional criterion of liability, since it refers first to the 'ordinary' use of the land, and second to a distinction between 'natural' and 'non-natural' use. More unfortunately, in discussion of 'non-natural' use he makes some reference to 'that which in its natural condition was not in or upon it'. In the article extracted below, Professor Newark traces different meanings of 'non-natural' as used in the judgment of Lord Cairns, and outlines a major change in the more recent case law beginning with *Rickards v Lothian* in 1913.

F. Newark, 'Non-Natural User and Rylands v Fletcher' (1961) 24 MLR 557–71, at 570–1

Lord Cairns had dealt with three distinct conceptions, and he kept them distinct, but it was his fault to introduce the word "natural" into each. The first is a reference to an escape "by the laws of nature." Here he meant no more than that the dangerous agent moved on to the plaintiff's close in consequence of a natural force, *e.g.*, gravity, and was not propelled thither by act of the defendant. The second is a reference to "the user of land in the ordinary course of enjoyment" which he equates with "natural user." But his very next words show that the was referring to *a user of land which caused the dangerous agent to escape*, as in the *Smith v Kenrick* type of case. And thirdly he refers to "non-natural use" which is artificially introducing the dangerous agent on to the land.

Shortly, what has happened by the time of *Rickards v Lothian* in 1913 is that "ordinary" which had been used as a synonym for "natural" in Lord Cairns' second conception (*viz*, the user which caused the dangerous agent to escape) had been transferred to the third conception which relates to the introduction of the dangerous agent on the land, so that whereas Lord Cairns asserted that bringing the dangerous agent on to the land was necessarily "non-natural use" we are now led to believe that it is only "non-natural" if it is "not ordinary." And the result as applied in the modern cases is, we believe, one which would have surprised Lord Cairns and astounded Blackburn J.

Now however the non-natural user criterion has become the main mechanism for setting some appropriate limits to the rule, and it does so quite independently of the idea of natural in the sense of 'natural condition'. Its content may now (belatedly) be in the process of developing in a manner uncluttered by confusion over the origins, purpose, and nature of the rule. But because of other limitations to the rule (particularly in the form of defences, but also through the close association with other forms of nuisance) this development is probably too late to convert *Rylands v Fletcher* into a workable rule of strict liability.

We will revisit non-natural user and its most recent interpretation in Section 4 of this chapter. For now, we will simply note that one of Lord Cairns' formulations of the rule—the reference to 'ordinary use'—is similar to the expression used by Bramwell B in *Bamford v Turnley* (1862) 122 ER 27, where he summarized a range of cases that was subject to the principle of 'give and take' in the tort of private nuisance. Lord Bramwell's judgment in *Bamford v Turnley* was extracted in Chapter 10. Bramwell B was the single dissenting judge in *Fletcher v Rylands* in the Court of Exchequer, who would have awarded damages to the plaintiff Fletcher, and who was supported on appeal both by the Court of Exchequer Chamber and by the House of Lords. In a footnote to Newark's article extracted above ('Non-Natural User and *Rylands v Fletcher*', at n 53), the author suggests that the similarity between natural user in *Rylands*, and ordinary user in *Bamford v Turnley*, is merely superficial. No comparison could have been intended because (he argues) it would surely otherwise have been mentioned. But as we will see the version of the 'non-natural user' criterion which has been accepted, with variations, since *Rickards v Lothian* in 1913 is precisely an ordinary user test. Recent interpretations of the non-natural user criterion, to be found in Lord Goff's judgment in *Cambridge Water*, and in the judgments of both Lord Bingham and Lord Hoffmann in *Transco v Stockport MBC* (extracted in Section 4.1), turn on 'ordinary' user and certainly bear comparison with Bramwell B's analysis in *Bamford v Turnley*.

3. ELEMENTS OF ACTIONABILITY

A general principle of strict liability for hazardous activities has never developed in English law. Ironically perhaps, it is in the United States that a general principle of strict liability for ultra-hazardous acts has been adopted, despite the 'initially cool reception' given to *Rylands v Fletcher* itself (Fleming, *The Law of Torts*, 9th edn, p. 370; Rest. (Torts) 2d §519). The components of the rule as stated by Blackburn J have been read as strict requirements. In addition, a number of other limitations to the rule have become apparent. As we have seen, these include the requirement (added by Lord Cairns, but reinterpreted over the years) that the defendant's user of the land should be 'non-natural'; but also include a range of defences not mentioned in *Rylands v Fletcher* itself.

Courts have struggled to reconcile the action in *Rylands*, with negligence liability, and this makes it hard to give a wholly consistent account of the case law. This struggle began straight away with cases such as *Jones v Festiniog Railway* ((1868) LR 3 QB) and *Nicholls v Marsland* ((1868) 2 Ex D 1), both of which are discussed later in this chapter.

Accumulation of Something Likely to do Mischief

The defendant must have 'accumulated' something on his or her land; and that thing must be something that, in the words of Blackburn J, is 'likely to do mischief if it escapes'. The thing may be brought on to the land by the defendant. Alternatively, it may come on to the land by a natural process, provided that some action of the defendant has caused it to gather or accumulate. For example, the defendant may have constructed a reservoir that will fill with rainwater, or may have dammed a stream to create a lake. An entirely natural accumulation will not fulfil the requirements of *Rylands v Fletcher*. Thus, *Rylands v Fletcher* itself distinguished the earlier case of *Smith v Kendrick* ((1849) 7 CB 515), in which the accumulation of water was natural. It should be noted however that a case like *Smith v Kendrick* will now be interpreted in terms of a 'measured duty of care' in nuisance within the terms of *Leakey v National Trust* [1980] QB 485 (Chapter 10).

In *Giles v Walker* (1890) 24 QBD 656, a defendant had neglected to mow thistles which had seeded naturally upon his land, thus causing damage to his neighbour when thistle-down was blown on to the neighbour's land. The very brief judgment in *Giles v Walker* did not mention *Rylands v Fletcher*, but its implication was that the rule does not apply to natural accumulations. So far as reported, this is the leading judgment in full:

Lord Coleridge CJ

I never heard of such an action as this. There can be no duty as between adjoining occupiers to cut the thistles, which are the natural growth of the soil. The appeal must be allowed.

Giles v Walker was overruled in *Leakey*, in consequence of the recognition of a positive duty to take reasonable steps to protect one's neighbour. The degree to which positive duties have overtaken the rule in *Rylands v Fletcher* is a question to which we return later.

The additional idea that the things accumulated are 'likely to do mischief' if they escape draws attention to the likely consequences should such an escape occur. Thus an element of foreseeability has been present in *Rylands v Fletcher* from the start, even if it was not expressed in these terms. Because of more recent controversies, we should note that it is foreseeability of danger, not foreseeability of escape specifically, which is implicit in Blackburn J's statement.

Escape

Rylands liability requires an escape. This is one of the most artificial elements of the rule, and the retention of this requirement illustrates clearly that the rule has not developed into a general principle of strict liability.

Viscount Simon, *Read v Lyons* [1947] AC 156, at 168

"Escape," for the purpose of applying the proposition in *Rylands v. Fletcher*, means escape from a place where the defendant has occupation of or control over land to a place which is outside his occupation or control. Blackburn J. several times refers to the defendant's duty as being the duty of "keeping a thing in" at the defendant's peril and by "keeping in" he does not mean preventing an explosive substance from exploding but preventing a thing which may inflict mischief from escaping from the area which the defendant occupies or controls.

An event which occurs entirely within the confines of the defendant's land will therefore not satisfy the criterion. As a result, there was no 'escape' for the purposes of the rule when there was an explosion in a munitions factory, no dangerous thing thus escaping from the defendant's premises. This decisive aspect of *Read v Lyons* was described by Fleming as having in itself ended the possibility of a general rule based on *Rylands v Fletcher*:

J. Fleming, *The Law of Torts* (9th edn, NSW: Law Book Company, 1998)

The most damaging aspect of the decision in *Read v Lyons* was that it prematurely stunted the development of a general theory of strict liability for ultra-hazardous activities.

Application to Cases of Fire

It has sometimes been wondered whether cases of fire damage are special, and more inclined to give rise to strict liability. One reason for this has been the authority of *Musgrove v Pandelis* [1919] 2 KB 43, where a fire began in the engine of a motorcar stored in a garage, and spread to neighbouring property. The occupier of the garage was liable for damage caused by the fire despite a lack of negligence. In the case of *Stannard v Gore*, however, the Court of Appeal interpreted more recent decisions of the House of Lords as setting out general criteria for the operation of liability under *Rylands*, so that there could be no exception for cases of fire. *Musgrove* is unlikely now to be followed, as it was interpreted as—at best—confined to its facts (as those facts appeared in 1919), and there was at least a suspicion that the decision in inconsistent with the principles set out more recently in *Transco v Stockport*. Most importantly perhaps, strict liability under *Rylands v Fletcher* for damage by fire will be limited by the requirement that it is the *fire itself* which must have been accumulated by the defendant. It is not sufficient to show that an accumulation of flammable material has led to the escape of fire, since the material has in that case not 'escaped'.

Ward LJ, *Stannard v Gore*
[2012] EWCA Civ 1248

48 Cases of fire damage are likely to be very difficult to bring within the rule because (1) it is the "thing" which had been brought onto the land which must escape, not the fire which was started or increased by the "thing". (2) While fire may be a dangerous thing, the occasions when fire as such is brought onto the land may be limited to cases where the fire has been deliberately or negligently started by the occupier or one for whom he is responsible. Is this not a relic of the *ignis suus* rule? (3) In any event starting a fire on one's land may well be an ordinary use of the land.

According to Ward LJ, *Musgrove v Pandelis* should 'therefore simply be relegated to a footnote in the history of *Rylands v Fletcher*'. Etherton LJ went further, and suggested that the decision in *Musgrove* was simply unsustainable after *Transco*.

An extra dimension in fire cases is provided by the continued existence of the following statutory provision, itself re-enacting a 1707 provision:

Fires Prevention (Metropolis) Act 1774, section 86

No action, suit, or process whatsoever shall be had, maintained, or prosecuted against any person in whose house, chamber, stable, barn or other building, or on whose estate any fire shall accidentally begin, nor shall any recompense be made by such person for any damage suffered thereby, any law, usage or custom to the contrary notwithstanding.

One question that has arisen is whether this provision should be interpreted as prohibiting liability for fire in the absence of negligence under *Rylands v Fletcher*. The answer to that question is not so important in practice after *Stannard v Gore*, since the Court of Appeal there decided that liability for fire does not arise under *Rylands* unless the fire is either negligently or deliberately started in any event. But it is worth noting Lewison LJ's analysis of the history of the section, from which he concluded that it ought to be interpreted as restricting liability under *Rylands v Fletcher* in fire cases; while Ward LJ and Etherton LJ were each content to accept an earlier analysis of the provision as simply clarifying a point of interpretation in the old law of *ignis suus*, namely when will a fire be regarded as that of the occupier of land on which it starts?[5] On that interpretation, it had no application to *Rylands*, which represented a separate strand of strict liability. Part of the significance of this lies in

---

[5] This was the interpretation of A. Ogus, 'Vagaries in Liability for Escape of Fire' (1969) 27 CLJ 104.

the important role played by insurance in the 1774 legislation as a whole, as well as in its predecessor.[6] As we will see, the general approach in the most recent *Rylands* cases is one of caution in creating liability for commonly insured risks.

Who can Sue and for What Damage?

Personal Injury

When Lord Macmillan said, in *Read v Lyons* (earlier) that the rule would not allow recovery for personal injuries, his comments were against the run of authority. They were based on an analysis of the origins of the action in nuisance, and not on the later case law. Later, in *Hale v Jennings* [1938] 1 All ER 579, the Court of Appeal said that the rule applied where personal injuries were caused by a fairground 'Chair-o-Plane' becoming detached and striking the plaintiff. There was no discussion of the personal injury point. Rather, the court was concerned with the question of whether the Chair-o-Plane was dangerous in itself, or whether the defendant should be exonerated because of the 'fooling about' of one of its customers. In *Perry v Kendricks* [1956] 1 WLR 85, Parker LJ thought that on the balance of authority, it was not open to the Court of Appeal to exclude personal injury from the ambit of the rule. In particular, the Court of Appeal would be bound by its earlier decision in *Musgrove v Pandelis* [1919] 2 KB 43. But *Musgrove v Pandelis* was a case of property damage, and not of injury to the person. The Court of Appeal had there considered the important distinction between physical damage (in that case, to chattels), and damage to proprietary interests, and decided that *Rylands* liability was not confined to the latter.

Now, however, the incorporation of *Rylands v Fletcher* into nuisance, coupled with the decision in *Hunter v Canary Wharf* ([1997] AC 655, Chapter 10), determines clearly that personal injuries will not be compensated under the rule.[7] The same developments also suggest that only those in occupation of land will be able to claim in *Rylands*, but there is much less clarity concerning the nature of the occupation that will suffice. In *Shiffman v Order of St John* [1936] 1 All ER 557, Atkinson J remarked that damages *might* be recoverable under the rule when children were injured by the fall of a flagpole erected by the defendants.[8] Dealing with the occupancy issue, he stated that: 'if it fell it was certain to fall on land of which [the defendants] were not in occupation and on which the public had a right to be.' This kind of 'licence' to be present he thought would be sufficient. More significantly perhaps, in *Charing Cross Electricity Supply Company v Hydraulic Power Company* [1914] 3 KB 772, the Court of Appeal clearly stated that the rule in *Rylands v Fletcher* applied even where the plaintiff suffered injury on a site occupied under licence, and not under any right of property in the soil. The damage suffered there was damage to a pipe (a chattel) laid under (not on) the highway. Notably, the Court of Appeal in the *Charing Cross* case clearly considered liability under *Rylands v Fletcher* to be a species of nuisance, since they assumed that it came within the terms of a clause of the relevant act which saved actions in respect of nuisances arising from the defendants' exercise of their powers (London Hydraulic Power Act 1884, section 17).

---

[6] These issues are explored by J. Steele and R. Merkin, 'Insurance Between Neighbours: *Stannard v Gore* and Common Law Liability for Fire' (2013) 25 JEL 305.

[7] This was clearly stated by the House of Lords in *Transco v Stockport*.

[8] These hypothetical remarks were no part of the *ratio* of the case, which was not decided on the basis of *Rylands v Fletcher* although in it is sometimes assumed that it was (see for example *Transco v Stockport*, at [35]).

'Pure' Economic Loss

In D. Pride & Partners v Institute for Animal Health [2009] EWHC 655 (QB), Tugendhat J ruled that the 'exclusionary rule' which rendered the economic losses pleaded in that case irrecoverable in negligence, applies just as well to actions in private nuisance and in Rylands v Fletcher. The particular 'exclusionary rule' in issue was the one which in Chapter 6 we described as relating to 'category A' economic losses: losses suffered through damage to the property of another. Tugendhat J pointed out that the extension of this rule to Rylands v Fletcher could not be in doubt, since one of the originating authorities on which it is based—Cattle v Stockton Waterworks Co (1875) LR 10 QB 453—was itself a claim argued in Rylands v Fletcher. The leading judgment in Cattle was by Blackburn J himself.

Defences

Consent

It seems to be accepted that consent on the part of the claimant to the accumulation may give rise to a defence, although this does not seem entirely consistent with the purpose of the rule, unless the 'consent' is something closer to shared benefit. In the multi-faceted case of Colour Quest v Total Downstream UK plc [2009] EWHC 540 (Comm), it was accepted that consent does generally amount to a defence to Rylands liability, but this consent was vitiated where there was negligence. In this instance, there was alleged to be negligence both in the accumulation (there was no safe system in place), and in the escape (a fuel tank was carelessly overfilled, leading to a major explosion). David Steel J added that there was no basis for excluding an action in Rylands in a case where negligence is present, but this is another way in which the strictness of Rylands as compared to the action in negligence is restricted.

Vis Major/Act of God; Act of a Stranger

These defences relate to the means by which the escape occurs. Any defence based on the idea that the defendant was not 'to blame' for the way in which an escape occurred will undercut the impact of the rule, which is calculated to place the risk of an escape—and the burden of keeping the thing safe—upon the person who accumulates it.

If these defences are broadly applied, this will further illustrate that Rylands has not been wholeheartedly applied by the courts. An early example is the case of Nicholls v Marsland (1868) 2 Ex D 1, in which 'exceptionally heavy rain' was held to take the escape beyond the reach of the rule in Rylands v Fletcher. A modern court could choose to differ from its nineteenth-century counterpart on the basis that the occurrence of 'exceptional' conditions is now rather more predictable than once was the case. Lord Hoffmann, in Transco v Stockport MBC (at [32]), cites Carstairs v Taylor (1871) LR 6 Ex 217 as evidence that 'act of God' is interpreted broadly. Here, a rat gnawed through a gutter box, causing a flood. There was no liability on the part of the occupier. However, Lord Hobhouse correctly pointed out in response to Lord Hoffmann (Transco, at [59]) that apart from Kelly CB, the other judges in that case distinguished Rylands v Fletcher, so that it is not strong authority on the content of the defence of act of God. Bramwell B, for example, distinguished Rylands on the basis that in Carstairs v Taylor, the accumulation (of rainwater in guttering) was made as much for the benefit of the plaintiff as for that of the defendant. Thus it was not made by the defendant 'for his own purposes'.

Further, in the case of 'act of a stranger', Lord Hoffmann suggests that it is sufficient to show that the escape had been caused by a vandal, for example, and is not attributable to the defendant (*Rickards v Lothian* [1913] AC 263). However, the discussion in *Shiffman v Order of St John* (earlier in this section) suggests that a *foreseeable* act of vandalism would not trigger the defence. And in *Perry v Kendricks* (where the defence was decisive), the court did indeed emphasize the *unforeseeable* nature of the intervention. Some acts of vandalism being quite foreseeable, and the kind of thing that should be guarded against, this interpretation would place some positive duties upon the defendant to 'keep the thing in', even if it falls short of imposing a duty to insure against damage. In *Hale v Jennings* [1938] 1 All ER 579, it was emphasized that the dangerous thing (a fairground 'Chair-o-Plane') was likely to produce the very danger that occurred, where a customer loosened the chair through his own fault did not absolve the defendants from liability under *Rylands v Fletcher*, since it was within the foreseeable risk associated with the operation of the equipment.

The fact remains that under a serious rule of strict liability a defendant could not expect to enjoy broad defences concerning operation of nature and acts of third parties.

Statutory Authority

Significant issues also arise in respect of the defence of statutory authority. We considered this defence in the chapter earlier, concerning nuisance. But the issues are subtly different in respect of *Rylands v Fletcher*. The normal case of private nuisance concerns ongoing activities. In some cases, inevitable interferences arise from those activities. Since those interferences are an inevitable aspect of the authorized activity, a finding of nuisance would contradict the statute. The defence of statutory authority in private nuisance is therefore close to being a logical necessity, although its application to specific circumstances is of course a matter of debate. But in the context of liability under *Rylands v Fletcher*, the escape itself is generally accidental and not an 'inevitable' aspect of the authorization. Authorization for an accumulation clearly authorizes the *risk* of an escape, but this does not compel the view that there should be no liability when an escape actually occurs.

In *Transco*, as we shall see later, Lord Hoffmann has suggested that statutory authority removes liability for escapes in the absence of negligence. In support of this interpretation, Lord Hoffmann quotes from the advice given by Blackburn J himself to the House of Lords in *Hammersmith and City Railway Co v Brand* 1869 [LR] 4 HL, and refers also to Lord Blackburn's statement in *Geddis v Proprietors of the Bann Reservoir* 1878 3 App Cas 430: '. . . no action will lie for doing that which the legislature has authorized, if it be done without negligence, although it does occasion damage to anyone; but an action does lie for doing that which the legislature has authorized, if it be done negligently'.

Neither of these cases concerned the rule in *Rylands v Fletcher* directly. Nevertheless, the statements are very general. Should we take it that they were meant to encompass liability under *Rylands*? It appears that Blackburn J himself *did* consider that the defence applies to *Rylands v Fletcher* in the manner stated in *Brand* and *Geddis*. In *Jones v Festiniog Railway* (1868 [LR] 3 QB), Blackburn and Lush JJ applied the newly formulated rule in *Rylands v Fletcher* to a case of damage caused by sparks emitted from locomotives. In order to hold that there was liability in *Rylands* despite statutory authorization for the operation of the railroad, they clearly thought they first had to hold that as a matter of statutory interpretation, authorization for the running of a railroad did not include authorization for the running of locomotives specifically. These were not essential to the purpose of the enterprise so authorized. Although the plaintiffs in that case were successful, the judges clearly thought that if the accumulation was expressly permitted, then this would be enough to oust the strict liability rule.

This state of affairs seriously restricts the practical ambit of *Rylands v Fletcher*. It also further illustrates that the courts have never really accepted that the rule in *Rylands v Fletcher* has the purpose of internalizing risks.

Sellers LJ, *Dunne v NW Gas Board*
[1964] 2 QB 806, 834

It is not easy to contemplate a case where the inevitable result of doing what a statute required would result in damage except directly to property interfered with, but it could be contemplated, as here, that the result might do so. Gas, water and electricity all are capable of doing damage, and a strict or absolute liability for any damage done by them would make the undertakers of these services insurers.

Sellers LJ clearly thought that this possibility amounted to a conclusive argument *against* the application of the rule. But there is an argument that the undertakers of public services *should be* the insurers of damage done by their activities. Obviously, there may be arguments either way as to whether this is desirable or not. But the evident surprise of the Court of Appeal that such a thing might be suggested illustrates a general lack of clarity about the purpose of the rule. It is not simply that there is disagreement over the purpose of the rule; it is more that the history of the rule is marred by an absence of concern with questions of purpose and rationale.

Remoteness

Foreseeability of some kind is inherent in the rule as initially stated. The decision in *Cambridge Water* (extracted and discussed in Section 4.1) employed an historical analysis to interpret *Rylands* as an aspect of the law of nuisance, and thus determined that the normal rules on remoteness of damage, as expressed in *The Wagon Mound*, apply also to *Rylands v Fletcher*. Not only must the accumulated thing be liable to do mischief if it escapes, but the eventual damage must in a relevant sense be foreseeable. On the rather peculiar facts of *Cambridge Water* itself, the absence of foreseeability in respect of the claimants' damage was plain; but that damage was unforeseeable in a number of different ways.

Non-natural User

In the most recent cases, the idea of 'non-natural user', derived from the judgment of Lord Cairns, has received more direct and sustained consideration. We noted earlier that in his article 'Non-natural User and *Rylands v Fletcher*', Newark argued that Lord Cairns had used the expression in a number of different ways, but that its essence as he used it lay in the contrast between 'natural' and 'artificial' uses of the land. That meaning has now been confined to history, being described by Lord Goff as being 'redolent of a different age' (*Cambridge*

Water v Eastern Counties Leather plc). It is in *Rickards v Lothian* [1913] AC 263, and specifically in the following statement, that the origins of the modern approach to non-natural user are now recognized to lie:

Lord Moulton's idea that the use should not be merely 'ordinary' is the basis for the reasoning in recent case law, where Lord Bingham has suggested that the terminology of 'ordinary user' is preferable to that of 'natural user' (*Transco v Stockport*, extracted later in this chapter, at [11]). But there has been general rejection of the other element in Lord Moulton's statement, that use 'for the general benefit of the community' should be sufficient to make out the defence.

The newer interpretations of non-natural user, based on Lord Moulton's statement, are further considered later in this chapter.

4. CATEGORIZATION AND BOUNDARIES

4.1. THE ENGLISH APPROACH: A SPECIES OF NUISANCE

After much conflicting and inconclusive case law, two House of Lords decisions have considered and retained the rule: *Cambridge Water v Eastern Counties Leather plc* [1994] 2 AC 264, and *Transco v Stockport MBC* [2003] UKHL 61; [2004] 2 AC 1. These cases have considered the categorization of the rule, and have clarified the contents of the applicable tests of foreseeability and of natural user, respectively.

Cambridge Water v Eastern Counties Leather plc: Foreseeability and Non-natural User

The defendants (ECL) were leather manufacturers operating from a site on an industrial village in Sawston, near Cambridge. In the course of their business, they used a chlorinated solvent, perchloroethene (PCE). Quantities of PCE were stored in drums on their premises. The plaintiffs (CWC) owned a borehole at Sawston Mill, from which they extracted water. This water was supplied to domestic users. The borehole was 1.3 miles from the defendants' premises. At the time that the plaintiffs bought Sawston Mill, the presence of PCE in a public water supply was not a matter for concern. Subsequently, pursuant to a European Council Directive (80/778/EEC), the Department of the Environment set a standard for the presence of PCE among other compounds in water intended for domestic use. The water from Sawston Mill was subsequently tested, and it was found that the concentrations of PCE in the water were many times higher than the permitted levels. In 1983, the plaintiffs ceased extracting water from Sawston Mill. They initiated a complex investigation, which traced the PCE levels in the water to the defendants' operations.

Lord Goff discussed the applicability and interpretation of the remoteness criterion in nuisance and continued:

Cambridge Water Co v Eastern Counties Leather plc
[1994] 2 AC 264

Lord Goff of Chieveley

Foreseeability of damage under the rule in *Rylands v. Fletcher*

[Lord Goff quoted from the passage of Blackburn J's judgment extracted in Section 2 above and continued:]

In that passage, Blackburn J. spoke of "anything *likely* to do mischief if it escapes;" and later he spoke of something "which he *knows* to be mischievous if it gets on his neighbour's [property]," and the liability to "answer for the natural *and anticipated* consequences." Furthermore, time and again he spoke of the strict liability imposed upon the defendant as being that he must keep the thing in at his peril; and, when referring to liability in actions for damage occasioned by animals, he referred, at p. 282, to the established principle that "it is quite immaterial whether the escape is by negligence or not." The general tenor of his statement of principle is therefore that knowledge, or at least foreseeability of the risk, is a prerequisite of the recovery of damages under the principle; but that the principle is one of strict liability in the sense that the defendant may be held liable notwithstanding that he has exercised all due care to prevent the escape from occurring.

There are however early authorities in which foreseeability of damage does not appear to have been regarded as necessary: see, e.g., *Humphries v. Cousins* (1877) 2 C.P.D. 239. Moreover, it was submitted by Mr. Ashworth for C.W.C. that the requirement of foreseeability of damage was negatived in two particular cases, the decision of the Court of Appeal in *West v. Bristol Tramways Co.* [1908] 2 K.B. 14 and the decision of this House in *Rainham Chemical Works Ltd. v. Belvedere Fish Guano Co. Ltd.* [1921] 2 A.C. 465.

I feel bound to say that these two cases provide a very fragile base for any firm conclusion that foreseeability of damage has been authoritatively rejected as a prerequisite of the recovery of damages under the rule in *Rylands v. Fletcher*. Certainly, the point was not considered by this House in the *Rainham Chemical* case. In my opinion, the matter is open for consideration by your Lordships in the present case. . . .

The point is one on which academic opinion appears to be divided. . . . However, quite apart from the indications to be derived from the judgment of Blackburn J. in *Fletcher v. Rylands*, L.R. 1 Ex. 265 itself, to which I have already referred, the historical connection with the law of nuisance must now be regarded as pointing towards the conclusion that foreseeability of damage is a prerequisite of the recovery of damages under the rule. I have already referred to the fact that Blackburn J. himself did not regard his statement of principle as having broken new ground; furthermore, Professor Newark has convincingly shown that the rule in *Rylands v. Fletcher* was essentially concerned with an extension of the law of nuisance to cases of isolated escape. Accordingly since, following the observations of Lord Reid when delivering the advice of the Privy Council in *The Wagon Mound (No. 2)* [1967] 1 A.C. 617, 640, the recovery of damages in private nuisance depends on foreseeability by the defendant of the relevant type of damage, it would appear logical to extend the same requirement to liability under the rule in *Rylands v. Fletcher*.

Even so, the question cannot be considered solely as a matter of history. It can be argued that the rule in *Rylands v. Fletcher* should not be regarded simply as an extension of the law of nuisance, but should rather be treated as a developing principle of strict liability from which can be derived a general rule of strict liability for damage caused by ultra-hazardous operations, on the basis of which persons conducting such operations may properly be held strictly liable for the extraordinary risk to others involved in such operations. As is pointed out in *Fleming on the Law of Torts*, pp. 327–328, this would lead to the practical result that the cost of damage resulting from such operations would have to be absorbed as part of the overheads of the relevant business rather than be borne (where there is no negligence) by the injured person or his insurers, or even by the community at large. Such a development appears to have been taking place in the United States, as can be seen from section 519 of the *Restatement of the Law (Second) Torts 2d*, vol. 3, pp. 34–36. The extent to which it has done so is not altogether clear; and I infer from section 519, and the Comment on that paragraph, that the abnormally dangerous activities there referred to are such that their ability to cause harm would be obvious to any reasonable person who carried them on.

I have to say, however, that there are serious obstacles in the way of the development of the rule in *Rylands v. Fletcher* in this way. First of all, if it was so to develop, it should logically apply to liability to all persons suffering injury by reason of the ultra-hazardous operations; but the decision of this House in *Read v. J. Lyons & Co. Ltd* [1947] A.C. 156, which establishes that there can be no liability under the rule except in circumstances where the injury has been caused by an escape from land under the control of the defendant, has effectively precluded any such development.... there is much to be said for the view that the courts should not be proceeding down the path of developing such a general theory. In this connection, I refer in particular to the Report of the Law Commission on Civil Liability for Dangerous Things and Activities (1970) (Law Com. No. 32). In paragraphs 14–16 of the Report, the Law Commission expressed serious misgivings about the adoption of any test for the application of strict liability involving a general concept of "especially dangerous" or "ultra-hazardous" activity, having regard to the uncertainties and practical difficulties of its application. If the Law Commission is unwilling to consider statutory reform on this basis, it must follow that judges should if anything be even more reluctant to proceed down that path.

Like the judge in the present case, I incline to the opinion that, as a general rule, it is more appropriate for strict liability in respect of operations of high risk to be imposed by Parliament, than by the courts. If such liability is imposed by statute, the relevant activities can be identified, and those concerned can know where they stand. Furthermore, statute can where appropriate lay down precise criteria establishing the incidence and scope of such liability.

It is of particular relevance that the present case is concerned with environmental pollution. The protection and preservation of the environment is now perceived as being of crucial importance to the future of mankind; and public bodies, both national and international, are taking significant steps towards the establishment of legislation which will promote the protection of the environment, and make the polluter pay for damage to the environment for which he is responsible—as can be seen from the W.H.O., E.E.C. and national regulations to which I have previously referred. But it does not follow from these developments that a common law principle, such as the rule in *Rylands v. Fletcher*, should be developed or rendered more strict to provide for liability in respect of such pollution. On the contrary, given that so much well-informed and carefully structured legislation is now being put in place for this purpose, there is less need for the courts to develop a common law principle to achieve the same end, and indeed it may well be undesirable that they should do so.

Having regard to these considerations, and in particular to the step which this House has already taken in *Read v. J. Lyons & Co. Ltd.* [1947] A.C. 156 to contain the scope of liability under the rule in *Rylands v. Fletcher*, it appears to me to be appropriate now to take the view that foreseeability of damage of the relevant type should be regarded as a prerequisite of liability in damages under the rule. Such a conclusion can, as I have already stated, be derived from Blackburn J.'s original statement of the law; and I can see no good reason why this prerequisite should not be recognised under the rule, as it has been in the case of private nuisance. . . . It would moreover lead to a more coherent body of common law principles if the rule were to be regarded essentially as an extension of the law of nuisance to cases of isolated escapes from land, even though the rule as established is not limited to escapes which are in fact isolated. I wish to point out, however, that in truth the escape of the P.C.E. from E.C.L.'s land, in the form of trace elements carried in percolating water, has not been an isolated escape, but a continuing escape resulting from a state of affairs which has come into existence at the base of the chalk aquifer underneath E.C.L.'s premises. Classically, this would have been regarded as a case of nuisance; and it would seem strange if, by characterising the case as one falling under the rule in *Rylands v. Fletcher*, the liability should thereby be rendered more strict in the circumstances of the present case.

The facts of the present case

Turning to the facts of the present case, it is plain that, at the time when the P.C.E. was brought onto E.C.L.'s land, and indeed when it was used in the tanning process there, nobody at E.C.L. could reasonably have foreseen the resultant damage which occurred at C.W.C.'s borehole at Sawston.

. . .

Natural use of land

I turn to the question whether the use by E.C.L. of its land in the present case constituted a natural use, with the result that E.C.L. cannot be held liable under the rule in *Rylands v. Fletcher*. In view of my conclusion on the issue of foreseeability, I can deal with this point shortly.

The judge held that it was a natural use. He said:

"In my judgment, in considering whether the storage of organochlorines as an adjunct to a manufacturing process is a non-natural use of land, I must consider whether that storage created special risks for adjacent occupiers and whether the activity was for the general benefit of the community. It seems to me inevitable that I must consider the magnitude of the storage and the geographical area in which it takes place in answering the question. Sawston is properly described as an industrial village, and the creation of employment is clearly for the benefit of that community. I do not believe that I can enter upon an assessment of the point on a scale of desirability that the manufacture of wash leathers comes, and I content myself with holding that this storage in this place is a natural use of land."

It is a commonplace that this particular exception to liability under the rule has developed and changed over the years. It seems clear that, in *Fletcher v. Rylands*, L.R. 1 Ex. 265 itself, Blackburn J.'s statement of the law was limited to things which are brought by the defendant onto his land, and so did not apply to things that were naturally upon the land. Furthermore, it is doubtful whether in the House of Lords in the same case Lord Cairns, to whom we owe the expression "non-natural use" of the land, was intending to expand the concept of natural use beyond that envisaged by Blackburn J. Even so, the law has long since departed from any such simple idea, redolent of a different age; and, at least since the advice of the Privy Council delivered by Lord Moulton in *Rickards v. Lothian* [1913] A.C. 263, 280, natural use has been extended to embrace the ordinary use of land.... *Rickards v. Lothian* itself was concerned with a use of a domestic kind, viz. the overflow of water from a basin whose runaway had become blocked. But over the years the concept of natural use, in the sense of ordinary use, has been extended to embrace a wide variety of uses, including not only domestic uses but also recreational uses and even some industrial uses.

It is obvious that the expression "ordinary use of the land" in Lord Moulton's statement of the law is one which is lacking in precision. There are some writers who welcome the flexibility which has thus been introduced into this branch of the law, on the ground that it enables judges to mould and adapt the principle of strict liability to the changing needs of society; whereas others regret the perceived absence of principle in so vague a concept, and fear that the whole idea of strict liability may as a result be undermined. A particular doubt is introduced by Lord Moulton's alternative criterion—"or such a use as is proper for the general benefit of the community." If these words are understood to refer to such matters as, for example, the provision of services; indeed the same idea can, without too much difficulty, be extended to, for example, the provision of services to industrial premises, as in a business park or an industrial estate. But if the words are extended to embrace the wider interests of the local community or the general benefit of the community at large, it is difficult to see how the exception can be kept within reasonable bounds. A notable extension was considered in your Lordships' House in *Read v. J. Lyons & Co. Ltd.* [1947] A.C. 156, 169–170, *per* Viscount Simon, and p. 174, *per* Lord Macmillan, where it was suggested that, in time of war, the manufacture of explosives might be held to constitute a natural use of land, apparently on the basis that, in a country in which the greater part of the population was involved in the war effort, many otherwise exceptional uses might become "ordinary" for the duration of the war. It is however unnecessary to consider so wide an extension as that in a case such as the present. Even so, we can see the introduction of another extension in the present case, when the judge invoked the creation of employment as clearly for the benefit of the local community, viz. "the industrial village" at Sawston. I myself, however, do not feel able to accept that the creation of employment as such, even in a small industrial complex, is sufficient of itself to establish a particular use as constituting a natural or ordinary use of land.

Fortunately, I do not think it is necessary for the purposes of the present case to attempt any redefinition of the concept of natural or ordinary use. This is because I am satisfied that the storage of chemicals in substantial quantities, and their use in the manner employed at E.C.L.'s premises, cannot fall within the exception.... It may well be that, now that it is recognised that foreseeability of harm of the relevant type is a prerequisite of liability in damages under the rule, the courts may feel less pressure to extend the concept of natural use to circumstances such as those in the present case; and in due course it may become easier to control this exception, and to ensure that it has a more recognisable basis of principle. For these reasons, I would not hold that E.C.L. should be exempt from liability on the basis of the exception of natural use.

Commentary

Foreseeability

The decisive finding of the House of Lords in this case was that reasonable foreseeability is an essential element of liability in *Rylands v Fletcher*, just as it is in nuisance. There were several stages in the reasoning that led to this conclusion.

First, Blackburn J's own statement of the rule incorporated the idea that the substance accumulated is 'likely' to do damage if it escapes. Although there is some case law which does not require that there should be foreseeability, this case law is limited and offers a 'fragile basis' for an argument against a foreseeability requirement. Second, *Rylands v Fletcher* is accepted to be a branch of nuisance, relating to isolated escapes. Therefore, the development of a remoteness rule for nuisance in the form of reasonable foreseeability, as explained in *The Wagon Mound (No 2)*, could not have been intended to bypass *Rylands v Fletcher*. Here Lord Goff leans heavily on Professor Newark's classic article, 'The Boundaries of Nuisance' (1949) 65 LQR 480, as revealing the true historical basis of *Rylands v Fletcher*. This element of the reasoning in *Cambridge Water* has been extremely important, for example in the *Transco* decision.

Third, Lord Goff rejected an invitation to develop the principle in *Rylands* beyond its narrow confines and to see it as part of a developing principle of strict liability for ultra-hazardous operations, in which case he might be free to dispense with the 'reasonable foreseeability' criterion. His rejection of this invitation was supported by three separate reasons:

(a) If there is to be a principle of strict liability for ultra-hazardous activities, why would this be limited to cases of escape, as *Rylands v Fletcher* has been? Here of course it may be objected that *Read v Lyons* (1947) AC 156 could be overruled, if it was thought that a broadened principle would be desirable. But the difficulty remains that there is no clear principled basis to the rule which would set alternative limits to it.

(b) The Law Commission considered a general principle of strict liability for dangerous activities in 1970, and rejected the idea of statutory development (*Report of the Law Commission on Civil Liability for Dangerous Things and Activities* (Law Com Report No 32, 1970)). Therefore the common law should be still more wary.

(c) The case is one of environmental pollution, and it is wise for the common law not to become too involved in this specialized and evolving area.

On the face of it, this third reason may be the weakest. Judges sometimes underestimate the extent to which Parliament works around rules of common law and takes a lead from the principles which are embedded in that law. On the other hand, Lord Goff's words of caution are not without justification. In particular, the evolution of environmental law involves considerable change having an impact on a wide variety of interests. Statutory liabilities generally take effect *prospectively*, and those whose interests are affected may be given fair warning of change to come.

When it came to addressing the facts of the case however, it is not entirely clear which type of foreseeability Lord Goff had in mind, since it is not clear which particular element of the facts made the damage in a relevant sense unforeseeable. In a brief statement on the subject, Lord Goff refers to 'foreseeability of damage'. He does not explicitly require that the escape should be foreseeable. Should we conclude that the escape need not be foreseeable? Not necessarily. Damage may be unforeseeable *because* the escape is unforeseeable. Capturing this ambiguity, two different potential meanings of foreseeability in the context of this case are identified in the following extract.

David Wilkinson, 'Cambridge Water Company v Eastern Counties Leather plc: Diluting Liability for Continuing Escapes' (1994) 57 MLR 799–811, at 803–4

... **Consider the following options.**

- Strict liability means that liability is limited to foreseeable damage and, in determining what damage is foreseeable, the escape itself is not to be assumed. On this view, a defendant would be liable for only that damage caused by the escape which a reasonable bystander would have anticipated. The foreseeability of the escape itself is an integral part of foreseeability of damage. If no escape is foreseeable then, as a matter of logic, no damage of any kind is foreseeable. We may refer to this view as 'full foreseeability.'

- Strict liability means that liability is limited to foreseeable damage and, in determining what damage was foreseeable, the escape is to be assumed (whether or not it was foreseeable). On this view, a defendant would be liable for all damage caused by the escape that a reasonable bystander, upon being informed of the escape, would have anticipated. The foreseeability of the escape is irrelevant to the foreseeability of damage. We may refer to this as 'semi-foreseeability'. ...

- Strict liability means that foreseeability is irrelevant to liability. On this view, a defendant would be liable for all damage caused by the escape, whether or not foreseeable. This view is no longer tenable in the light of the present case.

It seems likely that Lord Goff had in mind the reasons given by the first instance judge, Kennedy J, for saying that the damage was unforeseeable for the purposes of an action in either nuisance or negligence. The appeal to the House of Lords concerned the question of whether absence of foreseeability *also* ruled out an action in *Rylands v Fletcher*. The reasons given by Kennedy J were summarized by Lord Goff (at 292) in his judgment as follows. The reasons are multiple, reflecting the facts of this particular case:

Lord Goff
[1994] 2 AC 264, at 292

However, as the judge found, a reasonable supervisor at ECL would not have foreseen, in or before 1976, that such repeated spillages of small quantities of solvent would lead to any environmental hazard or damage—ie that the solvent would reach the aquifer or that, having done so, detectable quantities would be found down-catchment. *Even if he had foreseen that solvent might enter the aquifer, he would not have foreseen that such quantities would produce any sensible effect upon water taken down-catchment, or would otherwise be material or deserve the description of pollution.* ... The only harm that could have been foreseen from a spillage was that somebody might have been overcome by fumes from a spillage of a significant quantity.'

[Emphasis added]

If we do, as Wilkinson proposes, 'presume the escape', it was therefore not reasonably foreseeable in this case that the type of damage in question would be done. This 'additional' aspect of unforeseeability mentioned by Kennedy J and repeated by Lord Goff, italicized in the extract above, could be referred to as 'semi-foreseeability' in Wilkinson's sense. Therefore, *both* forms of unforeseeability were present in *Cambridge Water*, and it is not possible to be entirely clear which one was decisive. 'Semi-foreseeability' would be more consistent with the general purpose of the rule in *Rylands v Fletcher*, than would full foreseeability.

The House of Lords in the later case of *Transco v Stockport MBC* gave a far clearer account of the foreseeability criterion and even appeared to treat the issue as clearly settled. Their interpretation does not require foreseeability of escape. Lord Bingham said that the foreseeability criterion will be satisfied 'however unforeseeable the escape', provided that the defendant ought to have recognized the risk of damage (at [10]); and Lord Hoffmann said (at [33]) that under *Rylands v Fletcher*, 'the defendant will be liable even if he could not reasonably have foreseen that there would be an escape'. As explained earlier, this interpretation is the most appropriate to the strict liability rule.

Non-natural User

Lord Goff added some comments on non-natural user, though they did not form part of the decision.

Lord Goff generally accepted that the principle of 'natural' user can be equated with 'ordinary' user. He was also clear that being 'for the general benefit of the community' is not sufficient to create an 'ordinary' user of land, and in this respect he disagreed with the first instance judge. Even though the defendant's activities were generally beneficial in providing local employment, this could not be a reason for defining their use as a 'natural' one. But he thought that there was some room for ambiguity in the space between these two clear cases, since some uses which are for the benefit of a *local* community will be thought to amount to a natural user: 'If these words [referring to the 'benefit of the community'] are understood to refer to a local community, they can be given some content . . .'. Here, Lord Goff seems to have been thinking of accumulations which are of general or reciprocal benefit to all. Potential claimants may gain directly from the accumulation, or may have made similar accumulations of their own, as in the provision of domestic water supplies.

In any case, Lord Goff made very clear that the storage of chemicals in drums, no matter how appropriate that storage might be in the precise location stored, was not in his opinion capable of amounting to a 'natural user'. Neither appropriateness of the location, nor general public interest (for example, in providing local employment), were relevant tests to apply for the purposes of this criterion.

Transco plc v Stockport Metropolitan Borough Council [2003] UKHL 61; [2004] 2 AC 1

The House of Lords was invited by counsel to follow the Australian lead, and to declare *Rylands v Fletcher* to have been absorbed by negligence. It declined to do so. The 'non-natural user' criterion was unanimously thought not to be satisfied where the use in question was provision of a domestic water supply to a block of flats. Additional reasons for rejecting the claim were offered by Lord Bingham (there was no accumulation of a 'dangerous' thing) and Lord Scott (there was no relevant escape). Lord Hoffmann's judgment merits separate consideration because it grapples with the boundaries of the strict liability rule, through the non-natural user criterion, not only through analysis of the case law, but also in policy terms.

The facts of the case are briefly summarized in the extract from Lord Bingham's judgment.

Lord Bingham of Cornhill

2 … The salient facts appear to me to be these. As a multi-storey block of flats built by a local authority and let to local residents, Hollow End Towers was typical of very many such blocks throughout the country. It had been built by the respondent council. The block was supplied with water for the domestic use of those living there, as statute has long required. Water was carried to the block by the statutory undertaker, from whose main the pipe central to these proceedings led to tanks in the basement of the block for onward distribution of the water to the various flats. The capacity of this pipe was much greater than the capacity of a pipe supplying a single dwelling, being designed to meet the needs of 66 dwellings. But it was a normal pipe in such a situation and the water it carried was at mains pressure. Without negligence on the part of the council or its servants or agents, the pipe failed at a point within the block with the inevitable result that water escaped. Since, again without negligence, the failure of the pipe remained undetected for a prolonged period, the quantity of water which escaped was very considerable. The lie and the nature of the council's land in the area was such that the large quantity of water which had escaped from the pipe flowed some distance from the block and percolated into an embankment which supported the appellant Transco's 16-inch high-pressure gas main, causing the embankment to collapse and leaving this gas main exposed and unsupported. There was an immediate and serious risk that the gas main might crack, with potentially devastating consequences. Transco took prompt and effective remedial measures and now seeks to recover from the council the agreed cost of taking them.

…

The future development of *Rylands v Fletcher*

…

10 It has from the beginning been a necessary condition of liability under the rule in *Rylands v Fletcher* that the thing which the defendant has brought on his land should be "something which … will naturally do mischief if it escape out of his land" (LR 1 Ex 265, 279 per Blackburn J), "something dangerous … ", "anything likely to do mischief if it escapes", "something … harmless to others so long as it is confined to his own property, but which he knows to be mischievous if it gets on his neighbour's" (LR 3 HL 330, 340, per Lord Cranworth). The practical problem is of course to decide whether in any given case the thing which has escaped satisfies this mischief or danger test, a problem exacerbated by the fact that many things not ordinarily regarded as sources of mischief or danger may none the less be capable of proving to be such if they escape. … Bearing in mind the historical origin of the rule, and also that its effect is to impose liability in the absence of negligence for an isolated occurrence, I do not think the mischief or danger test should be at all easily satisfied. It must be shown that the defendant has done something which he recognised, or judged by the standards appropriate at the relevant place and time, he ought reasonably to have recognised, as giving rise to an exceptionally high risk of danger or mischief if there should be an escape, however unlikely an escape may have been thought to be.

11 ... I think it clear that ordinary user is a preferable test to natural user, making it clear that the rule in *Rylands v Fletcher* is engaged only where the defendant's use is shown to be extraordinary and unusual. This is not a test to be inflexibly applied: a use may be extraordinary and unusual at one time or in one place but not so at another time or in another place (although I would question whether, even in wartime, the manufacture of explosives could ever be regarded as an ordinary user of land, as contemplated by Viscount Simon, Lord Macmillan, Lord Porter and Lord Uthwatt in *Read v J Lyons & Co Ltd* [1947] AC 156, 169–170, 174, 176–177, 186–187). I also doubt whether a test of reasonable user is helpful, since a user may well be quite out of the ordinary but not unreasonable, as was that of *Rylands, Rainham Chemical Works* or the tannery in *Cambridge Water*. Again, as it seems to me, the question is whether the defendant has done something which he recognises, or ought to recognise, as being quite out of the ordinary in the place and at the time when he does it. In answering that question, I respectfully think that little help is gained (and unnecessary confusion perhaps caused) by considering whether the use is proper for the general benefit of the community. In *Rickards v Lothian* itself, the claim arose because the outflow from a wash-basin on the top floor of premises was maliciously blocked and the tap left running, with the result that damage was caused to stock on a floor below: not surprisingly, the provision of a domestic water supply to the premises was held to be a wholly ordinary use of the land. An occupier of land who can show that another occupier of land has brought or kept on his land an exceptionally dangerous or mischievous thing in extraordinary or unusual circumstances is in my opinion entitled to recover compensation from that occupier for any damage caused to his property interest by the escape of that thing, subject to defences of Act of God or of a stranger, without the need to prove negligence.

The present appeal

...

13 It is of course true that water in quantity is almost always capable of causing damage if it escapes. But the piping of a water supply from the mains to the storage tanks in the block was a routine function which would not have struck anyone as raising any special hazard. In truth, the council did not accumulate any water, it merely arranged a supply adequate to meet the residents' needs. The situation cannot stand comparison with the making by Mr Rylands of a substantial reservoir. Nor can the use by the council of its land be seen as in any way extraordinary or unusual. It was entirely normal and routine. Despite the attractive argument of Mr Ian Leeming for Transco, I am satisfied that the conditions to be met before strict liability could be imposed on the council were far from being met on the facts here.

Lord Hoffmann

...

The social background to the rule

28 Although the judgment of Blackburn J [in *Fletcher v Rylands*] is constructed in the traditional common law style of deducing principle from precedent, without reference to questions of social policy, Professor Brian Simpson has demonstrated in his article "Legal Liability for Bursting Reservoirs: The Historical Context of *Rylands v Fletcher*" (1984) 13 J Leg Stud 209 that the background to the case was public anxiety about the safety of reservoirs, caused in particular by the bursting of the Bradfield Reservoir near Sheffield on

12 March 1864, with the loss of about 250 lives. The judicial response was to impose strict liability upon the proprietors of reservoirs. But, since the common law deals in principles rather than ad hoc solutions, the rule had to be more widely formulated.

29 It is tempting to see, beneath the surface of the rule, a policy of requiring the costs of a commercial enterprise to be internalised; to require the entrepreneur to provide, by insurance or otherwise, for the risks to others which his enterprise creates. That was certainly the opinion of Bramwell B, who was in favour of liability when the case was before the Court of Exchequer: (1865) 3 H & C 774. He had a clear and consistent view on the matter: see *Bamford v Turnley* (1862) 3 B & S 62, 84–85 and *Hammersmith and City Railway Co v Brand* (1867) LR 2 QB 223, 230–231. But others thought differently. They considered that the public interest in promoting economic development made it unreasonable to hold an entrepreneur liable when he had not been negligent.... On the whole, it was the latter view—no liability without fault—which gained the ascendancy. With hindsight, *Rylands v Fletcher* can be seen as an isolated victory for the internalisers. The following century saw a steady refusal to treat it as laying down any broad principle of liability. I shall briefly trace the various restrictions imposed on its scope.

Restrictions on the rule

...

(f) Non-natural user

36 The principle in *Rylands v Fletcher* was widely expressed; the essence was the escape of something which the defendant had brought upon his land. Not surprisingly, attempts were immediately made to apply the rule in all kinds of situations far removed from the specific social problem of bursting reservoirs which had produced it. Leaks caused by a rat gnawing a hole in a wooden gutter-box (*Carstairs v Taylor* LR 6 Ex 217) were not at all what Blackburn J and Lord Cairns had had in mind. In some cases the attempt to invoke the rule was repelled by relying on Blackburn J's statement that the defendant must have brought whatever escaped onto his land "for his own purposes". This excluded claims by tenants that they had been damaged by escapes of water from plumbing installed for the benefit of the premises as whole. Another technique was to imply the claimant's consent to the existence of the accumulation. But the most generalized restriction was formulated by Lord Moulton in *Rickards v Lothian* [1913] AC 263, 280....

37 The context in which Lord Moulton made this statement was a claim under *Rylands v Fletcher* for damage caused by damage to stock in a shop caused by an overflow of water from a wash-basin in a lavatory on a floor above. To exclude domestic use is understandable if one thinks of the rule as a principle for the allocation of costs; there is no enterprise of which the risk can be regarded as a cost which should be internalised. That would at least provide a fairly rational distinction. But the rather vague reference to "the ordinary use of the land" and in particular the reference to a use "proper for the general benefit of the community" has resulted in the rule being applied to some commercial enterprises but not others, the distinctions being sometimes very hard to explain.

38 In the *Cambridge Water Co* case [1994] 2 AC 264, 308–309 Lord Goff of Chieveley noted these difficulties but expressed the hope that it would be possible to give the distinction "a more recognisable basis of principle". The facts of that case, involving the storage of substantial quantities of chemicals on industrial premises, were in his opinion "an almost

classic case of non-natural use". He thought that the restriction of liability to the foreseeable consequences of the escape would reduce the inclination of the courts to find other ways of limiting strict liability, such as extension of the concept of natural use.

Where stands the rule today?

39 I pause at this point to summarise the very limited circumstances to which the rule has been confined. First, it is a remedy for damage to land or interests in land. As there can be few properties in the country, commercial or domestic, which are not insured against damage by flood and the like, this means that disputes over the application of the rule will tend to be between property insurers and liability insurers. Secondly, it does not apply to works or enterprises authorised by statute. That means that it will usually have no application to really high risk activities. As Professor Simpson points out (1984) 13 J Leg Stud 225 the Bradfield Reservoir was built under statutory powers. In the absence of negligence, the occupiers whose lands had been inundated would have had no remedy. Thirdly, it is not particularly strict because it excludes liability when the escape is for the most common reasons, namely vandalism or unusual natural events. Fourthly, the cases in which there is an escape which is not attributable to an unusual natural event or the act of a third party will, by the same token, usually give rise to an inference of negligence. Fifthly, there is a broad and ill-defined exception for "natural" uses of land. It is perhaps not surprising that counsel could not find a reported case since the second world war in which anyone had succeeded in a claim under the rule. It is hard to escape the conclusion that the intellectual effort devoted to the rule by judges and writers over many years has brought forth a mouse.

Is it worth keeping?

40 In *Burnie Port Authority v General Jones Pty Ltd* (1994) 179 CLR 520 a majority of the High Court of Australia lost patience with the pretensions and uncertainties of the rule and decided that it had been "absorbed" into the law of negligence. Your Lordships have been invited by the respondents to kill off the rule in England in similar fashion. It is said, first, that in its present attenuated form it serves little practical purpose; secondly, that its application is unacceptably vague ("an essentially unprincipled and ad hoc subjective determination" said the High Court (at p 540) in the *Burnie* case) and thirdly, that strict liability on social grounds is better left to statutory intervention.

41 There is considerable force in each of these points. It is hard to find any rational principle which explains the rule and its exceptions.... And the proposition that strict liability is best left to statute receives support from the speech of Lord Goff of Chieveley in the *Cambridge Water* case ...

...

43 But despite the strength of these arguments, I do not think it would be consistent with the judicial function of your Lordships' House to abolish the rule. It has been part of English law for nearly 150 years and despite a searching examination by Lord Goff of Chieveley in the *Cambridge Water* case [1994] 2 AC 264, 308, there was no suggestion in his speech that it could or should be abolished. I think that would be too radical a step to take.

44 It remains, however, if not to rationalise the law of England, at least to introduce greater certainty into the concept of natural user which is in issue in this case. In order to do so, I think it must be frankly acknowledged that little assistance can be obtained from the kinds of user which Lord Cairns must be assumed to have regarded as "non-natural" in *Rylands v Fletcher* itself.... Whatever Blackburn J and Lord Cairns may have meant by "natural", the law was set on a different course by the opinion of Lord Moulton in *Rickards v Lothian* [1913] AC 263 and the question of what is a natural use of land or, (the converse) a use creating an increased risk, must be judged by contemporary standards.

45 Two features of contemporary society seem to me to be relevant. First, the extension of statutory regulation to a number of activities, such as discharge of water (section 209 of the Water Industry Act 1991) pollution by the escape of waste (section 73(6) of the Environmental Protection Act 1990) and radioactive matter (section 7 of the Nuclear Installations Act 1965). It may have to be considered whether these and similar provisions create an exhaustive code of liability for a particular form of escape which excludes the rule in *Rylands v Fletcher.*

46 Secondly, so far as the rule does have a residuary role to play, it must be borne in mind that it is concerned only with damage to property and that insurance against various forms of damage to property is extremely common. A useful guide in deciding whether the risk has been created by a "non-natural" user of land is therefore to ask whether the damage which eventuated was something against which the occupier could reasonably be expected to have insured himself. Property insurance is relatively cheap and accessible, in my opinion people should be encouraged to insure their own property rather than seek to transfer the risk to others by means of litigation, with the heavy transactional costs which that involves. The present substantial litigation over £100,000 should be a warning to anyone seeking to rely on an esoteric cause of action to shift a commonplace insured risk.

47 In the present case, I am willing to assume that if the risk arose from a "non-natural user" of the council's land, all the other elements of the tort were satisfied....

48 The damage which eventuated was subsidence beneath a gas main: a form of risk against which no rational owner of a gas main would fail to insure. The casualty was caused by the escape of water from the council's land. But the source was a perfectly normal item of plumbing. The pipe was, it is true, considerably larger than the ordinary domestic size. But it was smaller than a water main. It was installed to serve the occupiers of the council's high rise flats; not strictly speaking a commercial purpose, but not a private one either.

49 In my opinion the Court of Appeal was right to say that it was not a "non-natural" user of land. I am influenced by two matters. First, there is no evidence that it created a greater risk than is normally associated with domestic or commercial plumbing.... I agree with my noble and learned friend, Lord Bingham of Cornhill, that the criterion of exceptional risk must be taken seriously and creates a high threshold for a claimant to surmount. Secondly, I think that the risk of damage to property caused by leaking water is one against which most people can and do commonly insure. This is, as I have said, particularly true of Transco, which can be expected to have insured against any form of damage to its pipe. It would be a very strange result if Transco were entitled to recover against the water authority for similar damage emanating from its high-pressure main.

...

Lord Hobhouse of Woodborough

52 I consider that the rule is, when properly understood, still part of English law and does comprise a useful and soundly based component of the law of tort as an aspect of the law of

private nuisance. It derives from the use of land and covers the division of risk as between the owner of the land in question and other landowners. It is not concerned with liability for personal injuries which is covered by other parts of the law of torts (*Read v J Lyons & Co Ltd* [1947] AC 156) and which does not rise for discussion in this case.....

54 The salient features of the rule are easily identified: the self interest of the landowner, his conduct in bringing or keeping on his land something dangerous which involves a risk of damaging his neighbours' property, the avoidance of such damage by ensuring that the danger is confined to his own property and liability to his neighbours if he fails to do so, subject to a principle of remoteness. The subsequent complications and misunderstandings have arisen, not from the original rule and its rationale, but from additional criteria, often inappropriately expressed, introduced in later cases.

The principle

55 The principle which the rule reflects is also easily apparent. It is that the law of private nuisance recognises that the risk must be borne by the person responsible for creating it and failing to control it. It reflects a social and economic utility. The user of one piece of land is always liable to affect the users or owners of other pieces of land. An escape of water originating on the former, or an explosion, may devastate not only the land on which it originates but also adjoining and more distant properties. The damage caused may be very serious indeed both in physical and financial terms. There may be a serious risk that if the user of the land, the use of which creates the risk, does not take active and adequate steps to prevent escape, an escape may occur. The situation is entirely under his control: other landowners have no control. In such a situation, two types of solution might be adopted. One would be to restrict the liberty of the user of the land, the source of the risk, to make such use of his land as he chooses. The other is to impose a strict liability on the landowner for the consequences of his exercising that liberty. The rule adopts the second type of solution ... It is a coherent principle which accords with justice and with the existing legal theory at the time.

56 This approach was entirely in keeping with the economic and political culture of the 19th century, laissez faire and an understanding of the concept of risk. During the 20th century and particularly during the second half, the culture has changed. Government has increasingly intervened to limit the freedom of a landowner to use his land as he chooses, e g through the planning laws, and has regulated or forbidden certain dangerous or anti-social uses of land such as the manufacture or storage of explosives or the emission of noxious effluents. Thus the present state of the law is that some of the situations where the rule in *Rylands v Fletcher* applies are now also addressed by the first type of solution. But this does not deprive the rule of its utility.... As Lord Goff pointed out in *Cambridge Water* [1994] 2 AC 264, the occasions where *Rylands v Fletcher* may have to be invoked by a claimant may be reducing but that is not to say that it has ceased to be a valid part of English law. The only way it could be rendered obsolete is by a compulsory strict public liability insurance scheme for all persons using their land for dangerous purposes. However this would simply be to re-enact *Rylands v Fletcher* in another guise.

57 *Rylands v Fletcher* was unremarkable in the mid 19th century since there was then nothing peculiar about strict liability. There were many other fields in which strict liability existed, for example conversion. For those following a "common" calling, such as common carriers or common inn-keepers, liability was also strict. Although the origins were already present in the 19th century in the defence of "inevitable accident" in trespass cases, it was only later that the generalised criterion of negligence was developed, culminating in *Donoghue v Stevenson* [1932] AC 562. That is a fault—i e, breach of a duty of care—not a risk concept. But, where the situation arises as between landowners and arises from the dangerous use of his land by one of them, the risk concept remains relevant. He who creates the relevant risk and has, to the exclusion of the other, the control of how he uses his land, should bear the risk. It would be unjust to deny the other a risk based remedy and introduce a requirement of proving fault.

Comments

Although there were no dissenting judgments, the members of the House of Lords varied widely in their emphasis and in their reasons for retaining the rule in *Rylands v Fletcher*. Lord Bingham clarified the content of the rule, suggesting that the mischief or danger test should be hard to satisfy, and that it is preferable to refer to 'ordinary' rather than to 'natural' user. On the other hand, he made it clear that 'ordinary' is not a synonym for 'reasonable'; that a perfectly reasonable use of land may well be judged 'non-natural'; and that public utility will (additionally) be no defence. Although Lord Bingham thought that the conditions of the rule should be hard to fulfil, he also thought that there are circumstances in which it is still justified. Specifically, he mentioned the facts of *Cambridge Water*, had there been foreseeability of damage, as well as the older cases of *AG v Cory Brothers* [1921] 1 AC 521, and *Rainham Chemical Works v Belvedere Fish Guano Ltd* [1921] 2 AC 465. In these cases, he suggested that strict liability is 'just'. While he considered that any *extension* of the principle in *Rylands* would be better left to legislation, he made the point that to abrogate the existing rule may well be to 'falsify' the assumption on which various statutory strict liabilities had been enacted, and that this step should therefore be avoided. It is clear from Lord Bingham's judgment that personal injury damages will not be available in *Rylands v Fletcher*. He also thought there had been no relevantly hazardous accumulation of a 'dangerous' thing on these specific facts.

Lord Hobhouse appeared to be the most enthusiastic of their Lordships about the retention of strict liability under *Rylands v Fletcher*. He defended the justice and coherence of the rule in *Rylands*, arguing that the many confusions concerning its extent are created by later cases, and are not aspects of the original rule. However, this does not deal with the question of why there should be rather arbitrary limitations (especially the requirement of an escape) inherent in a rule that is supposedly based on defensible principles. Lord Hobhouse implies that strict liability was a more familiar and widely accepted principle of liability at the time of the decision in *Rylands v Fletcher* than it is today. His historical account here differs, at least in its emphasis, from that of A. W. B. Simpson, who has suggested that fault was already on the ascendant at the time that *Rylands* was decided, and who has proposed that the decision was primarily a reaction to the problem of bursting reservoirs.

A. W. B. Simpson, 'Bursting Reservoirs and Victorian Tort Law: *Rylands and Horrocks v Fletcher*', in Simpson, *Leading Cases in the Common Law* (Oxford: Oxford University Press, 1996), 195–226, at 197–8; by permission of Oxford University Press

Writers on the common law have long regarded *Rylands v Fletcher* as an anomalous decision. Back in the nineteenth century Pollock criticised it in his treatise on the law of torts; Holmes had considerable difficulty fitting it into his general theory of tort law. A commonly held view used to be that the original common law proceeded on the basis that a man acted at his peril, but this harsh doctrine was progressively relaxed in the nineteenth century with the reception of the principle of liability only for negligent conduct. The law was thus moralized, and *Rylands v Fletcher* can only be explained as an atavistic decision, a throwback or a survival of more primitive times. This picture of legal development would today not be accepted by serious legal historians, but the alternative story still leaves much to be explained. It goes like this. Before the nineteenth century, questions of fault, contributory fault, assumption of risk, standards of appropriate behaviour, causation, and so forth, certainly arose in litigation. But there was virtually no law about them. They were treated as jury questions, to be handled in the main by lay common sense. The trial judge might well give the jury some guidance, but what he said was not subject to review and did not feature in law reports or legal treatises. What happened in the nineteenth century was the creation of law on issues where there had been none before. But on this view *Rylands v Fletcher* still appears puzzling, for it was decided at the end of a period in which the negligence principle had been steadily gaining ground through the extension of the tort of negligence.

The numerous judges who were involved in the case must have been aware that, if tort law was to incorporate two different principles of liability, there was a need to explain the relationship between them. Only two of them attempted to do so. One was Bramwell B., who favoured strict liability in his dissenting opinion in the Court of Exchequer, and the other was Blackburn J.... Bramwell B dealt with the problem very briefly, but thought that in collision cases the negligence principle had to apply as a matter of logic, and this because of a problem over causation ... Blackburn J, the judge most closely associated with the so-called rule in *Rylands v Fletcher*, offered a much more radical theory. It was that the *primary* principle of tort law was that of strict liability. The negligence principle applied only as an exception in situations in which people had, by implication, agreed that it should—the theory of assumption of risk....

Blackburn's theory was not very convincing, but his contention that strict liability was the norm was stated in an opinion agreed by Willes, Keating, Mellor, Montague Smith, and Lush JJ ... It seems as if Willes J and his colleagues were persuaded in *Rylands v Fletcher* that strict liability was the basic common law rule, and fault liability the exception. This, viewed at least from a modern perspective, seems to reverse the natural order of things, and certainly nothing of the sort had ever been said in the nineteenth century before this.

The way in which the rule in *Rylands v Fletcher* was restrictively interpreted in early cases such as *Carstairs v Taylor* (1871) LR 6 Ex 217, *Nicholls v Marsland* (1868) 2 Ex D 1, and even *Jones v Festiniog Railway* (1868) [LR] 3 QB, suggests that many nineteenth-century courts did not find the idea of strict liability in this particular context as natural and comfortable as Lord Hobhouse implies. If they had, then a more robust rule, and a clearer rationale, would surely have developed in the years immediately following the decision in *Rylands v Fletcher* itself.

Lord Hoffmann's Interpretation

Lord Hoffmann's general interpretation of the rule, or what is left of it, is almost as negative as the majority judgment in *Burnie Port Authority v General Jones Pty* (1994) 179 CLR 520 (extracted later in this chapter); but for different reasons. Like the High Court of Australia, Lord Hoffmann contends that the rule in *Rylands* is now of very limited application. However, he concludes that this is the case not because of the ability of negligence to apply on the same facts, but because the most exceptional or dangerous uses of land are now dealt with via statute. In many cases, the relevant 'accumulation' will today be permitted by statute, giving rise to a defence of statutory authority. In Lord Hoffmann's analysis, the recognition of this defence is one of the key reasons why claims under *Rylands v Fletcher* are now so rarely successful. In other cases, there will be a statutory regime of *liability* in force, which will displace the common law rule, and frequently exceed it, Lord Hoffmann offers a number of examples. In these instances, the relevant liability is strict, and excludes defences such as 'act of God' or of a third party.[9] In the particular case before the House, Lord Hoffmann points out (at [42]) that the claimant gas company would have been barred, by statute, from claiming if the leak had been from water mains belonging to a water authority (Water Industry Act 1991, section 209(3)(b)). This provision governs the distribution between two public utilities of a particular sort of risk, and also precludes expensive transaction costs involved in litigation between these utilities at the expense of users. By extension, Lord Hoffmann considered that this was a reason why litigation was also inappropriate between the gas supplier and the local authority. The gas company would be imprudent not to seek insurance against the possibility of damage caused by flooding. A first party insurance solution was regarded as preferable by Lord Hoffmann, primarily because of the lower transaction costs.

But Lord Hoffmann's preoccupation with distributive questions went further than this. Importantly, he suggested that the ambit of the rule in *Rylands v Fletcher*, and particularly the non-natural user criterion, should itself now be understood in terms of insurability. If an occupier of land can reasonably be expected to insure against the kind of danger posed by the defendant's use of land, then that use should on his analysis be seen as a 'natural user'. It appears to be only those risks that are *not* readily insurable by those exposed to them that will count as 'non-natural' (or extraordinary) uses.

This approach identifies a reason of policy which might both justify the retention of the rule, and at the same time be used to keep it within ascertainable limits, without heavy reliance on artificial concepts such as 'escape'. We should notice that this solution is in an important respect more restricted in its scope than the Australian approach, which recognized a strict form of liability between neighbours, via the tort of negligence. In the Australian approach outlined later, the activity carried on by the defendant occupier must be shown to be hazardous. However, many hazardous activities, which might fit the definition in *Burnie Port Authority*, are also insurable. The Australian approach places the burden of insurable losses on the defendant so long as they arise from a relevantly hazardous activity, and of course provided a relevant standard of care has been breached. Lord Hoffmann would place the burden of insuring against such losses on the claimant, provided the risk is readily insurable.

The question of whether a user is non-natural therefore becomes one of who should pay for insurance to cover the risk that the activity creates. On Lord Hoffmann's approach, the far lower transaction costs associated with insuring against one's own losses, when compared with the costs of litigation, suggest that first party insurance is to be preferred where this is possible. It can readily be seen why this might be appropriate as between two public

[9] In *Cordin v Newport CC* (23/01/2008, QBD (TCC)), Judge Graham Jones made precisely this point. The defendant council was liable in *Rylands v Fletcher* for flooding of the claimants' land when water escaped from a reservoir; but there was also liability under the Water Resources Act 1991, s 209. As is often the case, the problem with *Rylands* here is not that it imposes strict liability, but that it does not add to the other potential sources of liability.

utilities, or between a public utility and a local authority, as in *Transco* itself. But is it generally a sound means of distinguishing natural from non-natural user, and therefore for establishing and rationalizing the boundary between strict liability and negligence? Here we should note again that ever since its inception, *Rylands* has been a rule in search of a robust rationale.

It is suggested that more empirical information would be required before reaching a conclusion on this. For example, we might ask what is the most *efficient* allocation of the burden of insurance, drawing attention to the importance of risk-rating. How can insurers establish the appropriate *cost* of insurance, if they deal only with those who are *exposed to* risk? In most such situations, the risk-creator has the fullest information about the risk. This may be adapted to a point about coverage. Will a potential claimant have sufficient knowledge to ensure that they *seek* insurance? The issue of insurability also raises an issue of fairness, which was mentioned by Lord Hobhouse in the extract earlier. Who ought to bear the *cost* of insurance? In the circumstances of *Rylands v Fletcher* liability, many claimants and defendants will be linked only by physical neighbourhood, and not (for example) by contractual or quasi-contractual relationships such as employment or consumer-producer relationships; nor will they have an immediate correspondence in interests. Here, there is no direct way in which the cost of insurance (if imposed primarily on defendants) will be passed to the group of potential claimants; nor will it be shared directly with prospective claimants in renewed premiums, as in motor insurance. It makes sense in this context to discuss the *fairness* of the burden of insurance, and on whom it should fall. However, this analysis does not fit so well where the defendant is a public utility or public authority, and this underlines the significance of Lord Hoffmann's observations concerning the vital importance of statutory intervention into most cases of dangerous accumulation. In *Cordin* (n 9 in this chapter), the judge discussed Lord Hoffmann's approach in *Transco* but decided not to be guided by considerations of insurability. His reasons were that (a) the House of Lords had not been unanimous as to its relevance; (b) in the case of flooding, the claimants' loss may turn out not to be commercially insurable; and (c) the correct approach was really a matter for Parliament, which had decided to impose strict liability through the Water Resources Act 1991, section 209.

At a much more general level, Lord Hoffmann's approach is important because it gives reasons based in distributive concerns, for limiting the ambit of the strict liability rule. It therefore directly counters any suggestion that the principle of strict liability ought to be developed further into a general principle relating to dangerous activities, and it gives some distributive reasons why 'internalization' through liability may not be the appropriate way forward. Thus, even if we move our discussion to distributive questions Lord Hoffmann's approach suggests that the 'internalizers' should not be allowed to have things all their own way. In this, he continues an academic discussion that he initiated in *Wildtree Hotels* [2011] 2 AC 1, concerning a particular and long-lived economic interpretation of private nuisance.

We introduced the decision in *Stannard v Gore* in relation to the 'escape' of fire, in Section 3 of this chapter. *Transco v Stockport* was held there to provide an authoritative approach to *Rylands v Fletcher* in all contexts, including cases of fire. Further, Ward LJ echoed Lord Hoffmann's remarks about commonplace insured risks and the questionable value of resolving questions about the allocation of such risks through liability principles. As in *Transco*, the insurance status of the particular claimant was not the prime consideration: liability would not depend on whether the parties happened to be insured; but whether it was appropriate to impose strict liability was a question influenced by the general pattern of insurance:

Ward L.J, *Stannard v Gore*
[2012] EWCA Civ 1248

50 Fire cases and this appeal must be judged in accordance with the test to be derived from *Transco*. . . . Applying those principles I reach the following conclusions:

(1) The "thing" brought onto Wyvern's premises was a large stock of tyres.

(2) Tyres, as such, are not exceptionally dangerous or mischievous.

(3) There is no evidence that Mr Stannard recognised nor ought he reasonably to have recognised that there was an exceptionally high risk of danger or mischief if the tyres, as such, should escape.

(4) The tyres did not escape. What escaped was the fire, the ferocity of which was stoked by the tyres which were burning on, and remained burning on, Wyvern's premises. The Recorder was wrong to conclude it was the escape of fire that brought the case within *Rylands v Fletcher* principles.

(5) In any event, keeping a stock of tyres on the premises of a tyre-fitting business, even a very large stock, was not for the time and place an extraordinary or unusual use of the land. Here again the Recorder erred.

(6) Therefore *Rylands v Fletcher* liability is not established and, no negligence having been proved, the claim must fail.

(7) The moral of the story is taken from the speech of Lord Hoffmann: make sure you have insurance cover for losses occasioned by fire on your premises.

Stannard, therefore, provides further evidence of the impact of the decision in *Transco*, and the continuation of its reasoning.

4.2 AUSTRALIAN HIGH COURT: NON-DELEGABLE DUTIES IN NEGLIGENCE

The High Court of Australia decided the following case very soon after the House of Lords' decision in *Cambridge Water v Eastern Counties Leather plc*. While the House of Lords as we have seen decided to treat *Rylands* liability as an aspect of the tort of nuisance, the High Court of Australia decided that *Rylands*-type cases should generally be dealt with by the tort of negligence. The High Court's conclusion that there was liability *in negligence* on the facts of *Burnie Port Authority* illustrates both that the tort of negligence is not always permeated by a concern with personal 'fault'; and that the idea of fault is so adaptable that it may sometimes impose stringent duties on individuals, dependent on the activity being carried out. Whose duty was it to take care, and what degree of care was required? Since the duty was non-delegable, it amounted to a positive duty to take action. On the other hand, the content of the duty relates to 'taking care'; it takes the *form* of a duty to *ensure that care is taken*. The High Court recognized that the *standard* of care would be variable, depending on the hazardous nature of the activity. We have already noted, in Section 1 of this chapter, that in *Woodland v Swimming Teachers Association*, the UK Supreme Court has recognized an extension of non-delegable duties of care and has described *Rylands* liability itself as based upon the special relationship between neighbouring occupiers. But it has not used that insight in order to absorb *Rylands* into the tort of negligence, as the Australian High Court did.

Burnie Port Authority had retained an independent contractor to carry out building work. This work involved welding in close proximity to cartons of Isolite, a highly flammable substance. Through the contractors' negligence, a fire started which spread to premises occupied by the plaintiff, ruining a quantity of the plaintiffs' frozen vegetables. This case recalls the facts of *Rylands v Fletcher* itself, where there had been negligence on the part of the contractors employed to construct the reservoir.

Burnie Port Authority v General Jones Pty Limited
(1994) 179 CLR 520; 120 ALR 42 (High Court of Australia)

Mason CJ, Deane, Dawson, Toohey, and Gaudron JJ at 549–52

Conclusion

Once it is appreciated that the special relationship of proximity which exists in circumstances which would attract the rule in *Rylands v Fletcher* gives rise to a non-delegable duty of care and that the dangerousness of the substance or activity involved in such circumstances will heighten the degree of care which is reasonable, it becomes apparent, subject to one qualification, that the stage has been reached where it is highly unlikely that liability will not exist under the principles of ordinary negligence in any case where liability would exist under the rule in *Rylands v Fletcher*....

At 556

The qualification mentioned in the preceding paragraph is that there may remain cases in which it is preferable to see a defendant's liability in a *Rylands v Fletcher* situation as lying in nuisance (or even trespass) and not in negligence.... It follows that the main consideration favouring preservation of the rule in *Rylands v Fletcher*, namely, that the rule imposes liability in cases where it would not otherwise exist, lacks practical substance. In these circumstances, and subject only to the above-mentioned possible qualification in relation to liability in nuisance, the rule in *Rylands v Fletcher*, with all its difficulties, uncertainties, qualifications and exceptions, should now be seen, for the purposes of the common law of this country, as absorbed by the principles of ordinary negligence. Under those principles, a person who takes advantage of his or her control of premises to introduce a dangerous substance, to carry on a dangerous activity, or to allow another to do one of those things, owes a duty of reasonable care to avoid a reasonably foreseeable risk of injury or damage to the person or property of another. In a case where the person or property of the other person is lawfully in a place outside the premises that duty of care both varies in degree according to the magnitude of the risk involved and extends to ensuring that such care is taken.

The present case

... Fortunately, our conclusion that the rule in *Rylands v Fletcher* has been absorbed by the principles of ordinary negligence makes it unnecessary to attempt to derive from the decided cases some basis in principle for answering the question whether the welding activities in the circumstances of the present case were or were not a "non-natural" or "special" use of the Authority's premises. The critical question for the purposes of applying the principles of ordinary negligence to the circumstances of the present case is whether the Authority took advantage of its occupation and control of the premises to allow its independent contractor to introduce or retain a dangerous substance or to engage in a dangerous activity on the premises. The starting point for answering that question must be a consideration of what relevantly constitutes a dangerous substance or activity. . . .

At 559

. . . the overall work which the independent contractor was engaged to carry out on the premises was a dangerous activity in that it involved a real and foreseeable risk of a serious conflagration unless special precautions were taken to avoid the risk of serious fire. It was obvious that, in the event of any serious fire on the premises, General's frozen vegetables would almost certainly be damaged or destroyed. In these circumstances, the Authority, as occupier of those parts of the premises into which it required and allowed the Isolite to be introduced and the welding work to be carried out, owed to General a duty of care which was non-delegable in the sense we have explained, that is to say, which extended to ensuring that its independent contractor took reasonable care to prevent the Isolite being set alight as a result of the welding activities. It is now common ground that W. & S. did not take such reasonable care.

It follows that the Authority was liable to General pursuant to the ordinary principles of negligence for the damage which General sustained.

Commentary

The solution adopted by the High Court of Australia was to 'absorb' *Rylands* to negligence, by recognizing a non-delegable duty of care in circumstances such as these. The idea of a non-delegable duty has certain advantages over the rule in *Rylands v Fletcher*. It can be explained in principled terms, through the ideas of dangerousness, proximity, and dependence, rather than through apparently arbitrary 'rules' relating to (for example) accumulation and escape. And it is clearly not limited to protection of interests in land. However, this solution depends on accepting some controversial ideas about the position now reached in the tort of negligence, particularly in recognizing non-delegable duties in a broadened range of circumstances.[10]

A crucial aspect of the majority judgment in *Burnie Port Authority* is its description of the occupier as being in a position of 'control', while the occupier of neighbouring premises is in a 'position of special vulnerability and dependence', so that the relationship is cast in terms of a 'special relationship of proximity'. We have already seen (in Chapter 6, Section 2) that at the time of *Burnie Port Authority*, the High Court of Australia was willing to take a freer view of 'proximity' in the duty of care than its English counterpart. In fact, as we also noted there, the High Court has more recently *disapproved* the central role previously attributed to proximity.[11] Yet without this specific proposition, would there be any force in the assertion that *Rylands* liability is unnecessary, since negligence will be an appropriate action in the

[10] Note that it is also quite possible that the majority of the High Court would revert to nuisance law if faced with facts closely analogous to *Cambridge Water*. But how would they decide such a nuisance case without reference to the specific requirements of an action in *Rylands v Fletcher*, now that they have concluded that the action is too ambiguous to be applied?

[11] See our discussion of economic loss cases in Chapter 6, Section 2.

same circumstances? On this point, the High Court relied upon a rationalization of positive duties offered by Mason J in the case of *Kondis v State Transport Authority* (1984) 152 CLR 672. But it also broadened it. *Kondis* was a case concerning the non-delegable duty of an employer towards an employee, in circumstances where an independent contractor had been negligent. Mason J's analysis was aimed at providing reasons which might support the established proposition that the employer is under a non-delegable duty to provide a safe system of work to employees. These justifying reasons turned on the employer's position of control, and the employee's special position of dependence or vulnerability. Mason J explained that the employment relationship was one of a series of relationships which were recognized as giving rise to positive duties. A further example, as can be seen from the extract above, was provided by occupiers and their invitees. In the UK, no such rationalization has been attempted, and it is doubtful whether the *Kondis* interpretation would be easily accepted. Even if it was accepted, it is still more doubtful whether it could be relied upon in order to allow recognition of a 'special relationship', based on control and dependence, between neighbours where one is carrying out a hazardous operation.

Through its use of positive duties to ensure that care is taken, the *Burnie* case accepts that there is nothing outdated about a rule whose effect is to impose liability in the absence of personal fault. Indeed, it suggests that the negligence principle has adapted over the years to the point that those conducting particular activities have a duty to ensure that a high level of care is taken to protect certain others against the risk of harm. But it also suggests, in effect, that it is too late for *Rylands v Fletcher* to be developed in such a way as to provide a coherent rule of strict liability. Whether it is right to say that negligence can adapt to provide sufficient coverage of all those areas where stricter standards of liability at common law are justified depends on recognizing that standards of care are highly flexible according to the danger posed by one's activities. It also depends on recognizing occupation of neighbouring land as giving rise to one of a group of relationships involving special, positive duties of care. Nevertheless, the revised rule in *Rylands v Fletcher* has been confined to protection of a narrow range of interests associated with nuisance, and itself now lacks the adaptability associated with the tort of negligence. Quite possibly, the new acceptance of non-delegable duties on the part of the UK Supreme Court in *Woodland v Swimming Teachers Association* (extracted in Chapter 9, and earlier in this chapter) will in time lead to new directions in strict liability, one of whose forebears will be *Rylands v Fletcher*.

5. CONCLUSIONS

i. The 'rule in *Rylands v Fletcher*' is by no means the only instance of strict liability in the law of tort, and we have seen that it is very rarely successfully argued. At the same time, it is one of the most studied branches of the law of tort. The reason for this may very well be that it is so close to the tort of negligence in its concern with one-off events which cause damage. In this, it forms a distinct branch of the tort of nuisance; so that it is no longer recognized as extending to personal injury.

ii. Despite the many restrictions that have been placed on the operation of the rule, its core analysis retains appeal and in this sense provides a rival analysis to the negligence parable in *Donoghue v Stevenson*. Rather than asking whose duty it was to avoid harm (what steps should have been taken?), *Rylands* asks *at whose risk* an accumulation was made. This concern with identifying allocation of risk can be seen not only in other areas of strict liability (such as Consumer Protection, Chapter 15); but also in the tort of negligence itself (recall our discussion of Remoteness of Damage, in Chapter 3). In retreating from applying the rule, courts have nevertheless retained it; and if there is to be an expansion in the realm of non-delegable duties in the tort of negligence, one of the ancestors of any such development will be this action, which is now recognized—and duly confined—as simply a branch of nuisance.

FURTHER READING

Abraham, K., 'Rylands v Fletcher: Tort Law's Conscience', in R. Rabin and S. Sugarman (eds), *Torts Stories* (Foundation Press, 2003).

Dyson, M. (ed), *Regulating Risk Through Private Law* (Intersentia, 2017).

Heuston, R. V. F., and Buckley, R. A., 'The Return of *Rylands v Fletcher*' (1994) 110 LQR 506–9.

Keating, G., 'Rediscovering *Rylands*: An Essay for Bob Rabin' (2012) 61 De Paul L Rev 543.

Law Commission, *Civil Liability for Dangerous Things and Activities* (Law Com Report No 32, London: HMSO, 1970).

Molloy, R. J., '*Fletcher v Rylands*—A Reexamination of Juristic Origins' (1942) 9 U Chi L Rev 266.

Murphy, J., 'The Merits of *Rylands v Fletcher*' (2004) 24 OJLS 643–69.

Newark, F. H., 'The Boundaries of Nuisance' (1949) 65 LQR 480.

Newark, F. H., 'Non-Natural User and *Rylands v Fletcher*' (1961) 24 MLR 557–71.

Nolan, D., 'The Distinctiveness of *Rylands v Fletcher*' (2005) 121 LQR 421.

Simpson, A. W. B., 'Bursting Reservoirs and Victorian Tort Law: *Rylands and Horrocks v Fletcher*', in Simpson, *Leading Cases in the Common Law* (Oxford: Oxford University Press, 1995); previously published in a slightly different version as 'Legal Liability for Bursting Reservoirs: The Historical Context of *Rylands v Fletcher*' (1984) 13 JLS 209.

Stallybrass, W. T. S., 'Dangerous Things and Non-Natural User of Land' [1929] CLJ 376.

Steele, J., and Merkin, R., 'Insurance Between Neighbours: *Stannard v Gore* and Common Law Liability for Fire' (2013) JEL 305.

Thayer, E. R., 'Liability Without Fault' (1916) 29 Harv L Rev 801–15.

Wilkinson D., '*Cambridge Water Company v Eastern Counties Leather plc*: Diluting Liability for Continuing Escapes' (1994) 57 MLR 781–99.

12

LIABILITY FOR
DANGEROUS PREMISES

CENTRAL ISSUES

i) This chapter concerns damage which arises out of dangers encountered on premises. The duties we consider here are different from the duties in private and public nuisance (Chapter 10) and under the rule in *Rylands v Fletcher* (Chapter 11), in that they are owed to parties who are present on the premises, and not to neighbouring occupiers or (for example) users of the highway.

ii) The duties in question concern dangers encountered on the premises. Historically, different duties were owed at common law, depending on the classification of the person who brought the claim. The relevant duties and liabilities have now been codified by two pieces of legislation. The first, the Occupiers' Liability Act 1957 ('the

1957 Act') applies to 'visitors'. Visitors are (very broadly speaking) parties who have a right or a permission to be present. The second, the Occupiers' Liability Act 1984 ('the 1984 Act'), applies to most other entrants on to the premises, including trespassers.

iii) In their content, the duties under the 1957 and 1984 Acts are similar to negligence duties. Indeed the occupier's duties to visitors and licensees were among the examples of duties to take care mentioned by Lord Atkin in *Donoghue v Stevenson* (Chapter 3). On the other hand, it is unusually clear in the case of the occupier's liabilities that some positive duties (for example, to repair fences or to provide appropriate warnings) are intended.

1. OCCUPIERS' LIABILITY UNDER STATUTE

1.1 PRELIMINARIES

When are the Occupiers' Liability Acts Engaged?

Does the Injury or Damage Occur on Premises Occupied by the Defendant?

In order to decide whether a particular set of facts gives rise to an 'occupiers' liability' claim, the first question is whether this is a case where personal injury or property damage is suffered *while the claimant or the claimant's property is on premises occupied by the defendant*.[1] If the only injury or damage done is suffered *outside* those premises, then the case is not one of occupiers' liability. On such facts, there may of course be an action in negligence; in nuisance if there is an unreasonable interference with the claimant's interests in land (Chapter 10); or in *Rylands v Fletcher* if damage is done by escape of a dangerous thing (Chapter 11).

Does the Damage Arise from the State of the Premises?

If the injury or damage is suffered on the premises, we must ask whether the injury or damage arises from a danger associated with the state of the premises.

The duties set out in the Occupiers' Liability Acts have been understood as 'occupancy duties' (concerned solely with the state of the premises), to be contrasted with 'activity duties' (concerned with conduct or activities carried out on the premises). Despite the broad wording of both Occupiers' Liability Acts (1957 Act, section 1(1); 1984 Act, section 1(1)(b), 'dangers due to the state of the premises or to things done or omitted to be done on them'), the Court of Appeal has held in *Fairchild v Glenhaven Funeral Services Ltd* [2002] 1 WLR 1052, at [113]–[131],[2] and in *Bottomley v Todmorden Cricket Club* [2003] EWCA Civ 1575, at [31], that only dangers associated with the state of the premises are within the scope of the Acts. This distinction has been used to exclude liability under the Acts (rather than in negligence at common law) in recent cases such as *Poppleton v Trustees of Portsmouth Youth Activities Committee* [2008] EWCA Civ 646. Here the claimant was engaged in an inherently risky activity (use of a climbing wall) and he attempted a very dangerous manoeuvre which was beyond his level of competence. The severe injuries he sustained were not attributable to the state of the premises.[3] Similarly, in *Yates v National Trust* [2014] EWHC 222 (QB), [2014] PIQR P6, the claimant was seriously injured while hired by independent contractors to work as a tree surgeon on the defendants' land. He alleged that the defendants had taken no steps to ensure that their contractors' working methods were competent and safe. Nicol J held that no duty under the Occupiers' Liability Act 1957 was owed, as the dangers were due to the activities carried out, and not to the state of the premises.

[1] The 1957 Act covers both personal injury and property damage; property damage is excluded from the operation of the 1984 Act.

[2] Although there was an appeal to the House of Lords in *Fairchild* [2002] UKHL 22; [2003] 1 AC 32, that appeal did not concern the occupiers' liability issue.

[3] At first instance, the judge had held that there was a duty to warn the claimant that the matting provided would not keep him safe from injury if he fell heavily on to it. The Court of Appeal disagreed, but thought that such a duty would in any event not arise within the Occupiers' Liability Acts because there was no defect in the property of which to warn.

The same distinction between activity and occupancy duties was observed by the Court of Appeal in the case of a trespasser (in that particular instance, a burglar) in *Revill v Newbery* [1996] QB 567. Since that case involved an activity (shooting a shotgun through the closed door of a shed) rather than a state or condition of the premises, it was dealt with as a case in negligence.

However, it is significant that in *Revill v Newbery* the provisions of the 1984 Act were still treated as relevant to the court's understanding of the negligence duty. A similar move was made in the more recent decision of *Everett v Comojo* [2011] EWCA Civ 13, in relation to visitors rather than trespassers. Here, guests at a members-only night club were stabbed by another guest. Since the attacker could not be found, a claim was brought against the night-club itself. The Court of Appeal pointed out that this was a case of an alleged *positive* duty, to prevent deliberate acts of a third party. Common law has only reluctantly admitted such duties, as we saw in Chapter 3. However, the Court found it relevant that the defendant was recognized to owe certain positive duties to the claimants as its visitors. Similarly, occupiers of premises may owe duties *at common law* to protect visitors against the deliberate acts of third parties on the premises. Not only the existence, but also the content and extent of such duties, would be influenced by—even modelled upon—the 'common duty of care' set out in the 1957 Act, which is a duty to take such steps as are reasonable to ensure that the visitor is reasonably safe.

Smith LJ, *Everett v Comojo*
[2011] EWCA Civ 13; [2012] 1 WLR 150

35 Lord Faulks urged the court to say that any such duty (including the standard of care) should be narrowly drawn. I think that he had in mind the kind of definition which the court applied in the *Dorset Yacht* case where a high degree of foreseeability of the kind of harm in question was to be required before there could be liability. I am not prepared to say that, as between the managers of a nightclub and guests, there should be a higher degree of foreseeability than is required under the common duty of care in the Occupiers' Liability Act 1957. The degree of proximity (including the economic relationship) between the two is so close that I do not think any special rule of foreseeability is required in the interests of fairness, justice and reasonableness. I think that that was the kind of duty which the Australian judge had in mind in the passage from *Chordas*'s case 91 ALR 149 quoted earlier. That is also the clear intention of the Canadian Occupiers Liability Act. It follows that I do not think that the judge misdirected himself when he adopted the *Chordas* decision as the basis of the duty.

36 The common duty of care is an extremely flexible concept, adaptable to the very wide range of circumstances to which it has to be applied. It can be applied to the static condition of the premises and to activities on the premises. It can give rise to vicarious liability for the actions of an employee of the occupier who, for example, might have created a temporary tripping or slipping hazard. I think that it is appropriate (fair, just and reasonable) that it should govern the relationship between the managers of an hotel or nightclub and their guests in relation to the actions of third parties on the premises. I do not think it possible to define the circumstances in which there will be liability. Circumstances will vary so widely. However, I think it will be a rare nightclub that does not need some security arrangements which can be activated as and when the need arises. What they need to be will vary. One can think of obvious examples where liability will attach. In a nightclub where experience has shown that entrants quite often try to bring in offensive weapons it may be necessary to arrange for

everyone to be searched on entry. In a nightclub where outbreaks of violence are not uncommon, liability might well attach if a guest is injured in an outbreak of violence among guests and there is no one on hand to control the outbreak. It may be necessary for the management of some establishments to arrange for security personnel to be present at all times within areas where people congregate. On the other hand, in a respectable members-only club where violence is virtually unheard of no such arrangements would be necessary. The duty on management may be no higher than that staff be trained to look out for any sign of trouble and to alert security staff.

In the present case, there had been no breach of the relevant duty. However, the very recognition of such a duty in this case is significant. The 'common duty of care' here is interpreted as having a far wider application than the content of the statutory provisions themselves. Perhaps then statutory duties have come to influence the common law in relation to duties between occupier and visitor (or in *Revill v Newbery*, trespasser). Another interpretation is that the statutory language has been too restrictively interpreted in earlier cases, so that the statutory duty itself should be interpreted as applicable to all cases where the duty owed arises out of the relationship between an occupier, and an entrant onto land or premises,[4] irrespective of whether the harm is caused by the state of premises, or something done on those premises. The Court of Appeal appears at times to have spoken in terms of the *same* duty—the common duty of care—in these different contexts; but the more general run of authority suggests that the duties at common law and under statute are better seen as analogous, rather than one and the same.

Whose Responsibility to Guard against the Risks?

It is true that some fairly technical questions arise in interpreting the statutory liabilities. But the underlying question of whose obligation it is to take precautions in respect of dangers is of great social importance. For many years, the obvious need in this area was for a greater awareness of the duties of occupiers, particularly in respect of children. Under *Addie v Dumbreck* [1929] AC 358, the only duty owed to a trespasser (even a child) was the duty not deliberately or recklessly to *cause* harm. In that case, a 4-year-old child was killed when he fell through the unprotected cover of a mill wheel. Despite knowledge on the part of the defendants that young children trespassed on their premises, no duty was owed in respect of this glaring hazard. The 1984 Act was a response to the House of Lords' later inconclusive efforts to set out the contents of a more humane duty towards trespassers in another case involving a child: *British Railways Board v Herrington* [1972] AC 877. Although the members of the House were agreed that a duty was owed to the child in that case, there was considerable variation in the formulation of the duty itself and of the circumstances in which it arose. The Law Commission proposed clarifying legislation which became the 1984 Act (Law Com No 75, Cmnd 6428, 1976).

In more recent years, the chief concern has changed. There is perceived to be a risk of over-protection and (therefore) of over-deterrence. In a number of recent cases, the House of Lords and Court of Appeal have emphasized that not all hazards are the responsibility of occupiers.

---

[4] For an argument that the distinction between acts and omissions is far more important than the distinction between 'activity and occupancy', and that the relationship between occupier and entrant onto land is crucial in determining whether positive duties to keep safe will arise, see S. Bailey, 'Occupiers' Liability: The Enactment of "Common Law" Principles', in T. T. Arvind and J. Steele (eds), *Tort Law and the Legislature* (Hart, 2013), 207.

Occupiers of land, including especially those whose land provides important public amenity, should not be compelled to over-prioritize safety in the face of obvious hazards. Safety is of course important, but as Lord Scott of Foscote has put it, this 'is no reason for imposing a grey and dull safety regime on everyone' (*Tomlinson v Congleton BC* [2003] UKHL 47, at [94]). The common thread of these cases is rejection of the idea that competent adults must be, in effect, prevented from running risks that they can easily appreciate for themselves.

These developments are at least in tune with the sentiments behind the Social Action, Responsibility and Heroism Act, discussed in Chapter 3. It is quite possible that this statute will be relevant in an occupiers' liability case, section 2 stating that '[a] court must have regard to whether the alleged negligence or breach of statutory duty occurred when the person was acting for the benefit of society or any of its members'. Given the emphasis already placed on social utility and the responsibility of claimants in the occupiers' liability context, the best guess is that this will, or would, make little difference to the approach already taken by the courts, particularly when assessing whether the risk was one against which protection should have been offered.

1.2   WHO IS AN OCCUPIER?

Under both statutes, the duties are owed by an 'occupier'. There is no statutory definition of 'occupier', and the meaning of the term is to be deduced from case law (1957 Act, section 2(1). 'Occupation' is a matter not of ownership but of effective control. There may be more than one occupier of premises, as the next case illustrates.

Wheat v Lacon [1966] AC 552

The defendant brewers were the owners of a public house. The running of the business was entrusted to a manager, employed under a service agreement. The manager and his wife lived on the first floor of the premises.

The plaintiff and her husband were staying on the first floor as paying guests of the manager's wife. The plaintiff's husband suffered a fatal fall while on his way downstairs to buy drinks from the bar. It was found that the accident was caused by a handrail which was too short, in combination with absence of proper lighting on the stairs. Were the defendant brewers liable as 'occupiers'?

The House of Lords found that the defendants were 'occupiers' of the first floor of the premises, and owed the common duty of care under the 1957 Act. However, they had not breached this duty. The defendant brewers, and their manager, could both be occupiers of the premises simultaneously. Although they might be in occupation of different parts of the premises, in this case *both* parties were occupiers of the first floor. The relevant duties owed under the Act would depend upon the 'circumstances' of the occupation:

Lord Denning, at 580–1

In the light of these cases, I ask myself whether the brewery company had a sufficient degree of control over the premises to put them under a duty to a visitor. Obviously they had complete control over the ground floor and were "occupiers" of it. But I think that they had also sufficient control over the private portion. They had not let it out to Mr. Richardson by a demise. They had only granted him a licence to occupy it, having a right themselves to do repairs. That left them with a residuary degree of control which was equivalent to that retained by the Chelsea Corporation in *Greene's* case [1954] 2 Q.B. 127. They were in my opinion "an occupier" within the Act of 1957. Mr. Richardson, who had a licence to occupy, had also a considerable degree of control. So had Mrs. Richardson, who catered for summer guests. All three of them were, in my opinion, "occupiers" of the private portion of the "Golfer's Arms." There is no difficulty in having more than one occupier at one and the same time, each of whom is under a duty of care to visitors. . . .

What did the common duty of care demand of each of these occupiers towards their visitors? Each was under a duty to take such care as "in all the circumstances of the case" is reasonable to see that the visitor will be reasonably safe. So far as the brewery company are concerned, the circumstances demanded that on the ground floor they should, by their servants, take care not only of the structure of the building, but also the furniture, the state of the floors and lighting, and so forth, at all hours of day or night when the premises were open. But in regard to the private portion, the circumstances did not demand so much of the brewery company. They ought to see that the structure was reasonably safe, including the handrail, and that the system of lighting was efficient. But I doubt whether they were bound to see that the lights were properly switched on or the rugs laid safely on the floor. The brewery company were entitled to leave those day-to-day matters to Mr. and Mrs. Richardson. They, too, were occupiers. The circumstances of the case demanded that Mr. and Mrs. Richardson should take care of those matters in the private portion of the house. And of other matters, too.

. . . So far as the handrail was concerned, the evidence was overwhelming that no one had any reason before this accident to suppose that it was in the least dangerous. So far as the light was concerned, the proper inference was that it was removed by some stranger shortly before Mr Wheat went down the staircase. Neither the brewery company nor Mr and Mrs Richardson could be blamed for the act of a stranger.

Premises that are empty are not necessarily 'unoccupied' for these purposes. In *Harris v Birkenhead Corporation* [1976] 1 All ER 341, the local authority made a compulsory purchase order and served notices on the tenant and owner of a house requiring them to surrender occupation of the premises. The local authority was treated as 'occupier' of the premises from the time that they were vacated, even though they had taken no further positive steps and had no physical 'presence' on the property. It was through their lawful actions that the property had become vacant, and they therefore exercised control over the premises.

Contractors who are engaged in carrying out work on premises may attain sufficient control over the site to be treated as 'occupiers'. This may lead to a situation of dual occupation: see Lord Goff, *Ferguson v Welsh* [1987] 1 WLR 1553, below.

1.3 THE DUTY OWED TO 'VISITORS' UNDER THE OCCUPIERS' LIABILITY ACT 1957

Occupiers' Liability Act 1957

Preliminary

1—(1) The rules enacted by the two next following sections shall have effect, in place of the rules of the common law, to regulate the duty which an occupier of premises owes to his visitors in respect of dangers due to the state of the premises or to things done or omitted to be done on them.

(2) The rules so enacted shall regulate the nature of the duty imposed by law in consequence of a person's occupation or control of premises and of any invitation or permission he gives (or is to be treated as giving) to another to enter or use the premises, but they shall not alter the rules of the common law as to the persons on whom a duty is so imposed or to whom it is owed; and accordingly for the purpose of the rules so enacted the persons who are to be treated as an occupier and as his visitors are the same (subject to subsection (4) of this section) as the persons who would at common law be treated as an occupier and as his invitees or licensees.

(3) The rules so enacted in relation to an occupier of premises and his visitors shall also apply, in like manner and to the like extent as the principles applicable at common law to an occupier of premises and his invitees or licensees would apply, to regulate—

(a) the obligations of a person occupying or having control over any fixed or moveable structure, including any vessel, vehicle or aircraft, and

(b) the obligations of a person occupying or having control over any premises or structure in respect of damage to property, including the property of persons who are not themselves his visitors.

(4) A person entering any premises in exercise of rights conferred by virtue of—

(a) section 2(1) of the Countryside and Rights of Way Act 2000, or

(b) an access agreement or order under the National Parks and Access to the Countryside Act 1949,

is not, for the purposes of this Act, a visitor of the occupier of the premises.

Extent of occupier's ordinary duty

2.—(1) An occupier of premises owes the same duty, the "common duty of care", to all his visitors, except in so far as he is free to and does extend, restrict, modify or exclude his duty to any visitor or visitors by agreement or otherwise.

(2) The common duty of care is a duty to take such care as in all the circumstances of the case is reasonable to see that the visitor will be reasonably safe in using the premises for the purposes for which he is invited or permitted by the occupier to be there.

(3) The circumstances relevant for the present purpose include the degree of care, and of want of care, which would ordinarily be looked for in such a visitor, so that (for example) in proper cases—

(a) an occupier must be prepared for children to be less careful than adults; and

(b) an occupier may expect that a person, in the exercise of his calling, will appreciate and guard against any special risks ordinarily incident to it, so far as the occupier leaves him free to do so.

(4) In determining whether the occupier of premises has discharged the common duty of care to a visitor, regard is to be had to all the circumstances, so that (for example)—

(a) where damage is caused to a visitor by a danger of which he had been warned by the occupier, the warning is not to be treated without more as absolving the occupier from liability, unless in all the circumstances it was enough to enable the visitor to be reasonably safe; and

(b) where damage is caused to a visitor by a danger due to the faulty execution of any work of construction, maintenance or repair by an independent contractor employed by the occupier, the occupier is not to be treated without more as answerable for the danger if in all the circumstances he had acted reasonably in entrusting the work to an independent contractor and had taken such steps (if any) as he reasonably ought in order to satisfy himself that the contractor was competent and that the work had been properly done.

(5) The common duty of care does not impose on an occupier any obligation to a visitor in respect of risks willingly accepted as his by the visitor (the question whether a risk was so accepted to be decided on the same principles as in other cases in which one person owes a duty of care to another).

(6) For the purposes of this section, persons who enter premises for any purpose in the exercise of a right conferred by law are to be treated as permitted by the occupier to be there for that purpose, whether they in fact have his permission or not....

...

Implied Term in Contracts

5.—(1) Where persons enter or use, or bring or send goods to, any premises in exercise of a right conferred by contract with a person occupying or having control of the premises, the duty he owes them in respect of dangers due to the state of the premises or to things done or omitted to be done on them, in so far as the duty depends on a term to be implied in the contract by reason of its conferring that right, shall be the common duty of care.

To Whom is the Duty Owed?

The 1957 Act replaces the various duties owed by occupiers at common law with a single statutory duty, the common duty of care (section 2(1)). The duty is owed to all those who would have been classed either as invitees, or as licensees, at common law.

Lord Denning, *Roles v Nathan*
[1963] 1 WLR 1117, at 1122

[The 1957 Act] has been very beneficial. It has rid us of those two unpleasant characters, the invitee and the licensee, who haunted the courts for years, and it has replaced them by the attractive character of the visitor, who has so far given no trouble at all.

An **invitee** was a person who has been invited on to the premises. A **licensee** was some-one who merely had permission to enter the premises. This permission did not need to be express. Whether an individual had an 'implied' licence to be present was a question of fact.

In addition to those counting as invitees or licensees, section 1(6) adds to the category of 'visitors' all those who enter premises **in the exercise of a right conferred by law.** Section 5 provides that where a person enters premises **under the terms of a contract,** a term will (if necessary) be implied into the contract that the common duty of care is owed.

There have been some uncertainties in the relevant classification of visitors to whom the common duty of care is owed, and we now consider some of these uncertainties.

Implied Licences

When is it to be *implied* that a party has permission to enter on to the premises? This has become much less of an issue since the introduction of clear duties to non-visitors under the 1984 Act. However before the decision in *Herrington* (earlier), when very few duties were owed to trespassers, courts were perhaps over-eager to think of reasons why permission to enter could be implied. Children became the main beneficiaries of implied licences (though see *Lowery v Walker* [1911] AC 10 for a case where adults were treated as implied licensees, since the occupier had done nothing over a period of many years to deter people from walking across his land). In *Cook v Midland Great Western Railway Co of Ireland* [1909] AC 229, the House of Lords was prepared to accept that children who entered on to the defendant's land without permission and played on a railway turntable might be treated as doing so with the 'leave and licence' of the defendants, given their knowledge that children often came on to the land, and given that the turntable was likely to be very attractive to children. This case was later described by Devlin J as the 'classic case' of an *allurement to children* (*Phipps v Rochester* [1955] 1 QB 450, at 462). As we will see in Section 1.4 below, it is in respect of children that a duty to provide protection to non-visitors is now most likely to be established under the 1984 Act. That being so, implied licences are not regularly discussed in recent case law.

Purpose of the Visit

A person may have permission to enter premises for one reason, yet cease to be classed as a visitor if he or she exceeds the terms of that permission. This was confirmed by the House of Lords in the case of *Tomlinson v Congleton* [2003] UKHL 47; [2004] 1 AC 46, in which the claimant suffered catastrophic injuries through diving in shallow water in a lake where swimming was not permitted. His head had struck the sandy bottom of the lake, and he had broken his neck. The claimant's advisers conceded that he was, at the time of his injury, a trespasser. There was some controversy in the House of Lords over whether that concession was correctly made, partly because the claimant's argument was precisely that more steps should have been taken to *prevent him* from swimming. It was accepted by the majority of judges (with the disagreement of Lord Scott, at [91]) that he was indeed a trespasser. But it was also accepted that this would not be the decisive factor in this case, which was treated as involving an obvious hazard. Neither visitors nor trespassers need to be warned of obvious hazards (see for example *Darby v National Trust*, below, and *Poppleton v Trustees of Portsmouth Youth Activities Committee*, earlier). The absence of duty to warn of obvious hazards may also be relevant in respect of children, as we will see.

Lord Hoffmann, *Tomlinson v Congleton*
[2003] UKHL 47; [2004] 1 AC 46

7 …. The council … said that once he entered the lake to swim, [the claimant] was no longer a "visitor" at all. He became a trespasser, to whom no duty under the 1957 Act is owed. The council cited a famous bon mot of Scrutton LJ in *The Carlgarth* [1927] P 93, 110: "When you invite a person into your house to use the staircase, you do not invite him to slide down the banisters". This quip was used by Lord Atkin in *Hillen v ICI (Alkali) Ltd* [1936] AC 65, 69 to explain why stevedores who were lawfully on a barge for the purpose of discharging it

nevertheless became trespassers when they went on to an inadequately supported hatch cover in order to unload some of the cargo. They knew, said Lord Atkin, at pp 69–70, that they ought not to use the covered hatch for this purpose; "for them for such a purpose it was out of bounds; they were trespassers". So the stevedores could not complain that the barge owners should have warned them that the hatch cover was not adequately supported. Similarly, says the council, Mr Tomlinson became a trespasser and took himself outside the 1957 Act when he entered the water to swim.

8 Mr Tomlinson's advisers', having reflected on the matter, decided to concede that he was indeed a trespasser when he went into the water. Although that took him outside the 1957 Act, it did not necessarily mean that the council owed him no duty.

...

13 ... I have ... come to the conclusion that the concession was rightly made. The duty under the 1984 Act was intended to be a lesser duty, as to both incidence and scope, than the duty to a lawful visitor under the 1957 Act. That was because Parliament recognised that it would often be unduly burdensome to require landowners to take steps to protect the safety of people who came upon their land without invitation or permission. They should not ordinarily be able to force duties upon unwilling hosts. In the application of that principle, I can see no difference between a person who comes upon land without permission and one who, having come with permission, does something which he has not been given permission to do. In both cases, the entrant would be imposing upon the landowner a duty of care which he has not expressly or impliedly accepted. The 1984 Act provides that even in such cases a duty may exist, based simply upon occupation of land and knowledge or foresight that unauthorised persons may come upon the land or authorised persons may use it for unauthorised purposes. But that duty is rarer and different in quality from the duty which arises from express or implied invitation or permission to come upon the land and use it.

14 In addition, I think that the concession is supported by the high authority of Lord Atkin in *Hillen v ICI (Alkali) Ltd* [1936] AC 65. There too, it could be said that the stevedores' complaint was that they should have been warned not to go upon the hatch cover and that logically this duty was owed to them, if at all, when they were lawfully on the barge.

...

The categorization of the claimant as a trespasser in *Tomlinson v Congleton* influenced another appellant to make a similar concession in *Rhind v Astbury Water Park* [2004] EWCA Civ 756. This was another case of catastrophic injuries suffered in shallow water, though this time there was a concealed hazard. The appellant accepted on the basis of *Tomlinson v Congleton* that when he had entered the water contrary to express prohibition, he had become a trespasser and any duty owed would be under the 1984 Act. This was eventually decisive, since a 1984 Act duty is only owed if the occupier has knowledge which ought to alert him to the existence of the danger. That was not the case in *Rhind*, where there was a concealed hazard of which the occupier was not aware.

It should also be noted that the duty owed under the 1957 Act is only a duty to keep the visitor safe *for the purposes for which he is invited or permitted by the occupier to be there* (section 2(1)). This will often reinforce the effect of the above cases, since the duty will not extend to prohibited activities unless (for example) the prohibition is not sufficiently clear.

Users of Rights of Way

Persons who are using a right of way are not owed a duty under the 1957 Act, since they do not come within any of the categories above: *Holden v White* [1982] QB 679 (private rights of way); *Greenhalgh v BRB* [1969] 2 QB 286 (public rights of way). Users of **private** rights of way are expressly included within the provisions of the 1984 Act (below). Users of **public** rights of way, however, seem to enjoy no protection under either statute.

Those who enter premises under the 'right to roam' provisions of the Countryside and Rights of Way Act 2000, or via an access agreement under the National Parks and Access to the Countryside Act 1949, are excluded from the 1957 Act (sections 1(4)(a) and (b) respectively). We consider duties owed to non-visitors when we turn to the 1984 Act, below.

The Content of the 'Common Duty of Care' under the 1957 Act

The duty owed by the occupier is to 'take such care as in all the circumstances of the case is reasonable to see that the visitor will be reasonably safe in using the premises for the purposes for which he is invited or permitted by the occupier to be there ... ' (section 2(2)).

This is clearly a negligence-type duty, since it turns on acting reasonably. However, it is also clearly a duty to *take steps*, and this is obviously capable of including positive elements in the form of obligations to repair, fence, warn, and so on. Equally, it is an 'objective' duty, focused on whether the premises are 'reasonably safe'. The existence of some reasonably foreseeable risk of harm does not show that the premises were not reasonably safe. In *Rochester Cathedral v Debell* [2016] EWCA Civ 1094, the claimant was injured after tripping over a small lump of concrete 'protruding from the base of a traffic bollard' in a cathedral precinct. A first instance judge awarded damages; but the Court of Appeal emphasized that 'not all foreseeable risks give rise to the duty to take remedial action' (para [25]). The question was not simply whether there was a foreseeable danger, but 'whether the piece of concrete created a danger of a kind which the Cathedral authorities were required to address' (para [26]). Applying this test, there was no such duty in this case.

Warnings

The occupier may be able to discharge the common duty of care by issuing an appropriate warning. However, it is important to note that a warning does not discharge the duty *unless* it is sufficient to keep the visitor reasonably safe (section 2(4)(a)). For example, a sign may warn of a dangerous bridge, but does the sign also make clear where a safe crossing point may be found? (*Roles v Nathan* [1963] 1 WLR 1117, at 1124.) In *Intruder Detection & Surveillance v Fulton* [2008] EWCA Civ 1009, a householder had not discharged his duty to contractors who came to his house to set up a burglar alarm system, though he had clearly warned them that there were no banisters on the first floor landing. These had been temporarily removed by other contractors in the process of renovation. No amount of warning could make the task safe, because the risk of falling through momentary error was so great.[5] Notably these were not 'experts' in respect of the particular danger concerned.

[5] This decision seems harsh to the occupier given that the contractors had persuaded him to let them in and do the work despite the danger: he had not expected them at that particular time. It should be noted that these were contribution proceedings brought by the injured man's employer against the occupier, and the employer was held to take a greater share of the blame for having failed to ensure a safe place and system of work—a recognized non-delegable duty (Chapter 9).

It should also be emphasized that the duty is to ensure that *the visitor* is safe, not that the *premises* are safe. Thus, an effective warning must be sufficient for the particular claimant to be made reasonably safe. In the case of children (unless perhaps there is a reasonable expectation that they will be accompanied), a warning may need to be much clearer. Conversely, in *Roles v Nathan*, the particular visitors in question were specialists and, given this (particularly in the light of section 2(3)(b)), the warning that was given sufficed.

Importantly, recent cases have emphasized that there is no duty to warn adults, at least,[6] of dangers that are obvious. In *Staples v West Dorset District Council* [1995] PIQR 439, the claimant fell on 'the Cobb' at Lyme Regis. The Cobb is an obviously slippery algae-covered surface (which is frequently drenched with seawater). The Court of Appeal rejected an argument that the claimant should have been warned of the danger.

A further illustration of the application of this reasoning is *Edwards v Sutton LBC* [2016] EWCA Civ 1005: there was no duty to warn a cyclist of the low parapet along a narrow bridge, since the low parapet was clearly visible and the danger of toppling over was obvious.

In *English Heritage v Taylor* [2016] EWCA Civ 448, the first instance judge had been entitled to find that the danger posed by a steep drop below an 'informal path' taken by the claimant was *not* obvious, so that the duty to take reasonable steps was owed. The Court found it necessary to add the following comments, to avoid any broader interpretation of the case, and to seek to meet the argument that a duty to warn of such dangers at heritage sites, principally ancient castles, would be both onerous and undesirable. It may be wondered however whether the insistence that steps taken need only be those that are 'reasonable'—including on aesthetic grounds—will offer much guidance to occupiers of such sites:

The Master of the Rolls, *English Heritage v Taylor* [2016] EWCA Civ 448; [2016] PIQR P14

Conclusion

28 Mr O'Sullivan says that the Recorder's finding against the defendant is extremely important. He says that, as with many public organisations which have large areas of land and premises open to the public, it has acted (as an occupier) in a way consistent with the principle that adult visitors do not require warnings of obvious risks except in cases where they do not have a genuine and informed choice. He also says that, if we dismiss this appeal, organisations like English Heritage will be under pressure to adopt an unduly defensive approach to their guardianship of historic sites which are part of our precious heritage and this will lead to an unwelcome proliferation of unsightly warning signs. This is contrary to the public interest. The courts should be astute to avoid such a consequence. Moreover, a decision in favour of the claimant in the present case will fuel the popular conception that this country is in the grip of a compensation culture.

29 I do not accept these *in terrorem* arguments. First, the decision that I have reached in this case is a straightforward application of the principle to which I have referred at [28] above. There is no basis for interfering with the Recorder's finding that the sheer drop from the grass pathway into the moat was not an obvious danger.

6 We consider children separately later.

30 Secondly, I accept that questions of whether a danger is obvious may not always be easy to resolve. In some cases, this may present an occupier of land with a difficulty. But there are many areas of life in which difficult borderline judgments have to be made. This is well understood by the courts and is taken into account in deciding whether negligence or a breach of s.2 of the Act has been established. In this context, it is highly relevant that the common duty of care is to take such care "as in all the circumstances is reasonable" to see that the visitor is "reasonably" safe in using the premises for the purpose for which he is invited or permitted by the occupier to be there. The court is, therefore, required to consider all the circumstances. These will include how obvious the danger is and, in an appropriate case, aesthetic matters. If an occupier is in doubt as to whether a danger is obvious, it may be well advised to take reasonable measures to reduce or eliminate the danger. But the steps need be no more than reasonable steps. That is why the decision in this case should not be interpreted as requiring occupiers like English Heritage to place unsightly warning signs in prominent positions all over sensitive historic sites. They are required to do no more than take reasonable steps. The Recorder found the existence of a breach of the common duty of care on a very specific basis, namely the failure to provide a sign warning of a sheer drop which was not obvious.

31 I have added these concluding comments because it is important that the significance of this decision should not be misunderstood. But for the reasons that I have given, I would dismiss this appeal.

'Specialists'

To paraphrase section 2(3)(b), an occupier can expect a specialist (a 'person in the exercise of his calling') to guard against risks ordinarily associated with his job. This is provided the occupier 'leaves him free to do so'. In *Roles v Nathan* [1963] 1 WLR 1117, two chimney sweeps were given appropriate information about a defective boiler. The occupier was not liable for their deaths because, had they heeded the warnings given and acted will due care, they could have made themselves safe. It does not follow from section 2(3)(b) that *no duty at all* is owed in respect of 'ordinary' risks of specialized work. In *Salmon v Seafarer Restaurants* [1983] 1 WLR 1264, a fireman was injured when attending a fire started through the negligence of the occupier's employees. Woolf J (giving judgment for the Court of Appeal) pointed out that 'when [the firefighters] attend they will be at risk even though they exercise all the skill of their calling'. Section 2(3)(b) only provides that the occupier may expect the specialist to exercise a level of care appropriate to his or her calling. If the visitor exercises such skill and care and the risk nevertheless remains, then this subsection gives no reason to deny compensation to the injured party. This case can be clearly contrasted with *Roles v Nathan*, where the evidence was that the sweeps did not act with appropriate regard for their own safety, and did not heed clear warnings.

Children

Section 2(3)(a) states the converse rule, that occupiers must be prepared for children to be *less* careful than adults when it comes to their own safety. Pre-1957 Act case law is often referred to in interpreting this section, but this case law is inconsistent.

In *Glasgow Corporation v Taylor* [1922] 1 AC 44, the defendants were occupiers of a Botanical Garden to which children (including unaccompanied children) had free access. The plaintiff's son, who was 7 years old, went to the garden unaccompanied and died when he ate the berries of a poisonous shrub. Since the child was entitled to be present in the relevant part of the gardens, which was much frequented by children, and since there was ready access to the tree, the House of Lords held on a preliminary issue that there was a good cause for trial. The berries could constitute a hidden danger as against a child. This case indicates that the idea of an 'allurement' or 'trap' for children may have some use where children are present with permission, and is not limited to cases of 'implied licence'.

A continuing puzzle, mentioned but not resolved in *Glasgow Corporation v Taylor*, concerns the degree to which occupiers are obliged to make their premises safe for *unaccompanied* children. Smaller children are of course expected to be less careful than older ones; but by the same token adults are expected to supervise those small children to a greater extent. The degree of parental supervision that is considered appropriate may well be expected to change over time, although it is also not surprising that in the days when (it appears) children as young as 4 were left to wander public parks alone,[7] the courts refused to impose on occupiers the duties that parents did not (or could not)[8] fulfil.

Devlin J attempted to set out a workable approach to such cases in *Phipps v Rochester Corporation* [1955] 1 QB 450 (a pre-1957 Act case in which he treated a 5-year-old child wandering on to an unfenced 'building site' near to his home as an implied licensee). His approach to the content of the duty owed requires an interpretation of where 'prudent people' will allow their children to go unaccompanied:

At 471

[The occupier's] duty is to consider with reasonable care whether there are on his premises, so far as he knows their condition, any dangers that would not be obvious to the persons whom he has permitted to use them; and if there are, to give warning of them or to remove them. If he rightly determines a danger to be obvious, he will not be liable because some individual licensee, albeit without negligence in the special circumstances of his case, fails to perceive it . . . .

I think that it would be an unjustifiable restriction of the principle if one were to say that although the licensor may in determining the extent of his duty have regard to the fact that it is the habit, and also the duty, of prudent people to look after themselves, he may not in that determination have a similar regard to the fact that it is the habit, and also the duty, of prudent people to look after their little children. If he is entitled, in the absence of evidence to the contrary, to assume that parents will not normally allow their little children to go out unaccompanied, he can decide what he should do and consider what warnings are necessary on that basis. He cannot then be made liable for the exceptional child that strays, nor will he be required to prove that any particular parent has been negligent.

The result of this was that if the child was so young that a degree of supervision by an adult ought to be expected, then the only required warnings are those that would be needed to

[7] Apart from *Glasgow Corporation v Taylor*, see *Hastie v Edinburgh Magistrates*, 1907 SC 1102 (4-year-old fell into a lake); *Stevenson v Glasgow Corporation*, 1908 SC 1034 (small child fell into a river in a public park). In *Thomas v BRB* [1976] 1 QB 912, a 2-year-old had wandered from her own garden while her mother was in and out of the house and it was inherent to her claim that the railway line should have been properly fenced off. See also *Bourne Leisure v Marsden*, below: small children will occasionally stray.

[8] Absence of a 'nurse' for the children—mentioned in *Hastie v Edinburgh Magistrates*—is of course some indication that the children were not those of well-off families.

alert a guardian to the danger. The relevant danger in *Phipps* (a trench in the ground) being obvious to an adult, there was no breach of the occupier's duty. This was not a case where fencing the entire area was regarded as feasible or necessary, and this distinguishes it from cases where children wander onto the railway, for example.

Bourne Leisure v Marsden [2009] EWCA Civ 671

In this case the Court of Appeal had cause to revisit the issues raised in *Phipps v Rochester*, and derived important principles from that case. The claimants had taken their small children to a holiday park. The children had briefly evaded the attention of their mother who was talking to another holiday-maker, and the older child (who was 2 years of age) had drowned in a pond. There was a path to the pond, which was fenced, but the child was able to climb over the fence. The Court of Appeal held that there had been no breach of duty under the 1957 Act. It would be impracticable to fence every source of hazard, and clearer information about the location of hazards would have made no difference. The court made plain that their decision did not imply fault on the part of the parents. But unless there is a reason to expect unaccompanied children to encounter a danger, there is no duty to warn of dangers that would be obvious to *a parent or guardian*. The Court of Appeal here reinforced the message which is one of the themes of recent case law in the area: some tragic accidents simply occur without culpability.

Duty of Visitors in General to be Careful

Apart from the specific references in section 2(3) to children and experts, there is also a general reference to 'the degree of care, and of want of care, which would ordinarily be looked for in such a visitor'. In *Tacagni v Cornwall* [2013] EWCA Civ 702, a claim failed where a pedestrian had been 'out late at night, having had a few drinks, on an unlit road, without a torch and in new and uncomfortable flip flops'. In finding the council partly to blame for injury to the claimant, the judge had 'left out of account, in considering whether Penwith were in breach of duty, a highly material factor, namely what degree of care could be expected of an ordinary visitor' (Lewison LJ, [4]). However, in *AB v Pro-Nation Ltd* [2016] EWHC 1022 (QB), it was relevant when judging the safety of a staircase to bear in mind that it was located in licensed premises. Referring to section 2(3) of the Act, the judge noted the claimant's argument 'that one of the purposes for entering the Pulse Bar was to consume alcohol and that therefore the Defendant should have had regard to the possibility that visitors were under the influence of alcohol when using the staircase: the staircase ought to be safe for use by visitors who had been drinking.' That point appears to have been accepted. The claimant had lost his footing after drinking around six or seven pints of beer: this was momentary carelessness and not a suitable case for a finding of contributory negligence; but it was also to be expected given the purpose of his visit.

Dangers Created by Independent Contractors

According to section 2(4)(b) of the 1957 Act, an occupier is not liable 'without more' for dangers created by independent contractors in the execution 'of any work of construction, maintenance or repair'. In *Ferguson v Welsh* (below) this was interpreted by the House of Lords as extending to demolition work. To benefit from the protection of this provision, the occupier must have acted reasonably in entrusting the work to a contractor and must also have taken reasonable steps to ensure *both* that the contractor was competent, *and* that the work had been 'properly done'. It should be remembered that these are ways in which the occupier may *discharge* the common duty of care, since they amount to reasonable steps to keep the visitor safe. Under what circumstances will an occupier still be liable under the Act for harm done by an independent contractor on the premises? This has become a vexed question.

In *Ferguson v Welsh* [1987] 1 WLR 1553, a district council contracted with a company (S) to carry out demolition work on their premises. The council prohibited subcontracting of the work without permission. S nevertheless did subcontract the work to two brothers (W) who adopted unsafe working practices. The plaintiff (F) was offered a job by the W brothers, and while assisting with the demolition was seriously injured. Judgment was given against the W brothers. The appeal to the House of Lords concerned the possible liability of the council as occupier.

The House of Lords determined that the council had not breached its duty under the 1957 Act in this case. However, Lord Keith's interpretation of the potential duties was broad. Lords Brandon and Griffiths concurred with Lord Keith, but Lords Oliver and Goff added some qualifications. As we will see later, more recent cases in the Court of Appeal are hard to reconcile with Lord Keith's expansive view of the duties under the 1957 Act, and are more consistent with the views of Lords Oliver and Goff.

Lord Keith thought that the council should be treated as having 'invited' F on to the premises, since it had put S into occupation of the premises and 'put him [S] into a position to invite the W brothers and their employees onto them' (at 1559). This is questionable, since there was a prohibition on subcontracting without permission. Lord Goff by contrast thought it possible that F might be a visitor in respect of S, but a trespasser in respect of the council, although he was prepared to accept that F was a visitor for the sake of argument.

Second, Lord Keith decided that the injury to F arose out of a danger that fell within the scope of the 1957 Act. This was expressly doubted by Lord Goff, who thought that F's injury 'arose not from the state of the premises but from the manner in which he carried out his work on the premises'. Lord Keith on the other hand said that the 'dangers' covered by the Act are 'not only ... dangers due to the state of the premises but also known dangers due to things done or omitted to be done on them' (at 1559).

Third, Lord Keith interpreted the occupiers' duties under section 2(4)(b) quite broadly. Considering this provision, Lord Keith said:

At 1560–1

It would not ordinarily be reasonable to expect an occupier of premises having engaged a contractor whom he has reasonable grounds for regarding as competent, to supervise the contractor's activities in order to ensure that he was discharging his duty to his employees to observe a safe system of work. In special circumstances, on the other hand, *where the occupier knows or has reason to suspect that the contractor is using an unsafe system of work*, it might well be reasonable for the occupier *to take steps to see that the system was made safe*.

The crux of the present case therefore, is whether the council knew or had reason to suspect that Mr. Spence, in contravention of the terms of his contract, was bringing in cowboy operators who would proceed to demolish the building in a thoroughly unsafe way. The thrust of the affidavit evidence admitted by the Court of Appeal was that Mr. Spence had long been in the habit of sub-contracting his demolition work to persons who proceeded to execute it by the unsafe method of working from the bottom up. If the evidence went the length of indicating that the council knew or ought to have known that this was Mr. Spence's usual practice, there would be much to be said for the view that they should be liable to Mr. Ferguson. No responsible council should countenance the unsafe working methods of cowboy operators.

[Emphasis added]

Lord Keith here speculates that *if* an occupier has 'reasonable grounds to suspect' unsafe working practices, they *may have* a duty to *supervise* the contractor's activities. Lord Oliver (at 1562), while agreeing that there was no breach of duty in this case, emphasized that he did not think any such duty of supervision, if it arose, would arise out of the defendant's status as occupier. More would be required than that:

It is possible to envisage circumstances in which an occupier of property engaging the services of an independent contractor to carry out work on his premises may, as a result of his state of knowledge and opportunities of supervision, render himself liable to an employee of the contractor who is injured as a result of the defective system of work adopted by the employer. But I incline to think that his liability in such case would be rather that of joint tortfeasor than of an occupier.

Similarly, Lord Goff (at 1564) thought that Lord Keith's approach threatened to impose too extensive a duty on occupiers.

More recently, in *Fairchild v Glenhaven* [2001] EWCA Civ 1881; [2002] 1 WLR 1052, the Court of Appeal has set out a restricted approach to the coverage of the two Occupiers' Liability Acts. In particular, the Court of Appeal has ruled that the 1957 Act and the 1984 Act are confined to 'occupancy duties', and do not extend to dangers arising out of *activities* carried out on the premises. This is inconsistent with Lord Keith's view that the injury to F in *Ferguson v Welsh* arose out of a danger that was within the scope of the duties under the 1957 Act.

The distinction in *Fairchild* was reaffirmed by the Court of Appeal in *Bottomley v Todmorden Cricket Club* [2003] EWCA Civ 1575:

Brooke LJ

42 It appears ... that some confusion lingers over the effect of the decision of this court in *Fairchild v Glenhaven Services Ltd.* Of course, there may be many occasions when an occupier may be legally liable in negligence in respect of the activities which he permits or encourages on his land. This liability stems from his 'activity duty'. He may also be legally liable for the state of his premises, and this liability stems from his 'occupancy duty'. *Fairchild* was a rare case in which it was necessary to make a distinction between the two, and this court held that an employee of a very well-known firm of contractors was owed no occupancy duty by the CEGB in the early 1950s as occupiers of the power station in which the claimant contracted mesothelioma during the contract works.

43 It was unnecessary for the House of Lords in *Ferguson v Welsh* [1987] 1 WLR 1553 to get themselves involved in this arcane debate.

In *Bottomley v Todmorden*, the defendant cricket club had arranged for a two-man stunt team named 'Chaos Encounter' to conduct a pyrotechnic display at an annual fundraising event. The members of Chaos Encounter (who did not appeal a finding of liability against them) had invited the claimant to assist, and he was injured. The Court of Appeal found that this was a case where the occupier was liable because it had failed to exercise reasonable care to select competent and safe 'contractors' (albeit unpaid on this occasion). However, this liability was in negligence, and *not* under the 1957 Act (at [48]–[49]). Brooke LJ argued that the duty passed the *Caparo* test and that it was 'fair, just, and reasonable'.

In *Bottomley*, it was made clear that the duty to select a competent contractor also exists in the tort of negligence. It was this duty which was breached by the cricket club. Similarly, in *Gwilliam v West Herts Hospital NHS Trust* [2002] EWCA Civ 1041; [2003] QB 443, it was held that the duty also arose within the 1957 Act, but outside the specific area of works of 'construction, maintenance, or repair'. Section 2(4)(b) is merely illustrative of a broader principle.

Exclusion of Liability, and Defences

A Note about Notices

We have already seen that occupiers may provide warnings—sometimes in the form of notices—which if sufficient to keep the visitor safe may discharge the common duty of care. Notices may have more than one function, however. Of course, they may seek to exclude visitors altogether ('Keep Out'), or they may set out the limits of permission ('No swimming'). In either case, they may be relevant in defining the status of the claimant as visitor or non-visitor (*Tomlinson v Congleton*, earlier in this chapter). Some notices, however, go further, and seek to exclude liability for injury or damage done ('the occupier accepts no liability for any injury suffered on the premises', or more simply, 'Enter at your own risk'). It is wise to keep in mind all three of these potential uses of a notice. In terms of their legal implications, they need separate consideration. Here we consider the last variation.

Exclusion of Liability

How far is the occupier able to exclude or limit liability for injury or damage under the 1957 Act? Even in the absence of a contract, such notices are governed by the Unfair Contract Terms Act 1977 and the Consumer Rights Act 2015. Which statute applies seems to depend on whether the visitor is a 'consumer'. Neither statute applies where the visit is purely recreational (or, in the case of the 1977 Act, educational), unless it falls within the business purposes of the occupier—eg, if the occupier makes money from recreational visitors.

Unfair Contract Terms Act (UCTA) 1977

1 Scope of Part I

(1) For the purposes of this Part of this Act, "negligence" means the breach—

(a) of any obligation, arising from the express or implied terms of a contract, to take reasonable care or exercise reasonable skill in the performance of the contract;

(b) of any common law duty to take reasonable care or exercise reasonable skill (but not any stricter duty);

(c) the common duty of care imposed by the Occupiers' Liability Act 1957 or the Occupiers' Liability Act (Northern Ireland) 1957.

...

(3) In the case of both contract and tort, sections 2 to 7 apply (except where the contrary is stated in section 6(4)) only to business liability, that is liability for breach of obligations or duties arising—

(a) from things done or to be done by a person in the course of a business (whether his own business or another's); or

(b) from the occupation of premises used for business purposes of the occupier;

and references to liability are to be read accordingly but liability of an occupier of premises for breach of an obligation or duty towards a person obtaining access to the premises for recreational or educational purposes, being liability for loss or damage suffered by reason of the dangerous state of the premises, is not a business liability of the occupier unless granting that person such access for the purposes concerned falls within the business purposes of the occupier.

2 Negligence liability

(1) A person cannot by reference to any contract term or to a notice given to persons generally or to particular persons exclude or restrict his liability for death or personal injury resulting from negligence.

(2) In the case of other loss or damage, a person cannot so exclude or restrict his liability for negligence except in so far as the term or notice satisfies the requirement of reasonableness.

(3) Where a contract term or notice purports to exclude or restrict liability for negligence a person's agreement to or awareness of it is not of itself to be taken as indicating his voluntary acceptance of any risk.

[(4) This section does not apply to—

(a) a term in a consumer contract, or

(b) a notice to the extent that it is a consumer notice,

(but see the provision made about such contracts and notices in sections 62 and 65 of the Consumer Rights Act 2015).][9]

11 The "reasonableness" test

(1) In relation to a contract term, the requirement of reasonableness for the purposes of this Part of this Act ... is that the term shall have been a fair and reasonable one to be included having regard to the circumstances which were, or ought reasonably to have been, known to or in the contemplation of the parties when the contract was made.....

The Act expressly extends to liability under the 1957 Act (section 1(1)(c)). The provisions of section 2 apply *only* to 'business liability' (section 1(3)), which is defined by reference

---

[9] These words were added by the Consumer Rights Act 2015.

to the use of the premises for business purposes (section 1(3)(b)). If people gain access to the property for educational or recreational purposes, any resulting liability is *not* business liability, *unless* those educational or recreational purposes fall within the business purposes of the occupier. However, by amendment to section 2, if the claimant enters the premises pursuant to a consumer contract; or if the notice is a 'consumer notice', UCTA 1977 will not apply, and the relevant law will instead be found in the Consumer Rights Act 2015. The critical question will be what is a consumer notice? The answer can only be gleaned from the latter Act. By section 76(2), the definition of 'consumer' and of 'trader' will be the same in both parts of the Act. Therefore, all that is required is that the individual be 'acting for purposes that are wholly or mainly outside that individual's trade, business, craft or profession'—that is, that they are *not* traders, professionals etc for the purpose of their visit. There is no need for the visitor to be intending to enter into a contractual relationship as 'consumer' when they enter the premises. However, by section 66(4), purely recreational visits are again outside the provisions below.

Consumer Rights Act (CRA) 2015

Part 1 CONSUMER CONTRACTS FOR GOODS, DIGITAL CONTENT AND SERVICES

. . .

2 Key definitions

(1) These definitions apply in this Part (as well as the definitions in section 59).

(2) *"Trader"* means a person acting for purposes relating to that person's trade, business, craft or profession, whether acting personally or through another person acting in the trader's name or on the trader's behalf.

(3) *"Consumer"* means an individual acting for purposes that are wholly or mainly outside that individual's trade, business, craft or profession.

. . .

Part 2 UNFAIR TERMS

61 Contracts and notices covered by this Part

(1) This Part applies to a contract between a trader and a consumer.

(2) This does not include a contract of employment or apprenticeship.

(3) A contract to which this Part applies is referred to in this Part as a *"consumer contract"*.

(4) This Part applies to a notice to the extent that it—

(a) relates to rights or obligations as between a trader and a consumer, or

(b) purports to exclude or restrict a trader's liability to a consumer.

(5) This does not include a notice relating to rights, obligations or liabilities as between an employer and an employee.

(6) It does not matter for the purposes of subsection (4) whether the notice is expressed to apply to a consumer, as long as it is reasonable to assume it is intended to be seen or heard by a consumer.

(7) A notice to which this Part applies is referred to in this Part as a *"consumer notice"*.

(8) In this section *"notice"* includes an announcement, whether or not in writing, and any other communication or purported communication.

62 Requirement for contract terms and notices to be fair

(1) An unfair term of a consumer contract is not binding on the consumer.

(2) An unfair consumer notice is not binding on the consumer.

(3) This does not prevent the consumer from relying on the term or notice if the consumer chooses to do so.

(4) A term is unfair if, contrary to the requirement of good faith, it causes a significant imbalance in the parties' rights and obligations under the contract to the detriment of the consumer.

(5) Whether a term is fair is to be determined—

  (a) taking into account the nature of the subject matter of the contract, and

  (b) by reference to all the circumstances existing when the term was agreed and to all of the other terms of the contract or of any other contract on which it depends.

(6) A notice is unfair if, contrary to the requirement of good faith, it causes a significant imbalance in the parties' rights and obligations to the detriment of the consumer.

(7) Whether a notice is fair is to be determined—

  (a) taking into account the nature of the subject matter of the notice, and

  (b) by reference to all the circumstances existing when the rights or obligations to which it relates arose and to the terms of any contract on which it depends.

(8) This section does not affect the operation of—...

  (d) section 65 (exclusion of negligence liability).

65 Bar on exclusion or restriction of negligence liability

(1) A trader cannot by a term of a consumer contract or by a consumer notice exclude or restrict liability for death or personal injury resulting from negligence.

(2) Where a term of a consumer contract, or a consumer notice, purports to exclude or restrict a trader's liability for negligence, a person is not to be taken to have voluntarily accepted any risk merely because the person agreed to or knew about the term or notice.

(3) In this section *"personal injury"* includes any disease and any impairment of physical or mental condition.

(4) In this section *"negligence"* means the breach of—

  (a) any obligation to take reasonable care or exercise reasonable skill in the performance of a contract where the obligation arises from an express or implied term of the contract,

  (b) a common law duty to take reasonable care or exercise reasonable skill,

(c) the common duty of care imposed by the Occupiers' Liability Act 1957 or the Occupiers' Liability Act (Northern Ireland) 1957, or

(d) the duty of reasonable care imposed by section 2(1) of the Occupiers' Liability (Scotland) Act 1960.

66 Scope of section 65

…

(4) Section 65 does not apply to the liability of an occupier of premises to a person who obtains access to the premises for recreational purposes if—

(a) the person suffers loss or damage because of the dangerous state of the premises, and

(b) allowing the person access for those purposes is not within the purposes of the occupier's trade, business, craft or profession.

It appears that UCTA 1977 will now apply *only* if the person entering the premises is *not* a consumer. Therefore, the provisions of UCTA in relation to occupiers' liability appear to apply only to those entering in the exercise of a trade, craft or profession. For others, the provisions of CRA 2015 will be relevant.

Business Liability and Trader-Consumer Liability

Under UCTA 1977, in cases of business liability, it is not possible to exclude or restrict liability for personal injury or death (section 2(1)). In the case of other damage (and property damage is covered by the 1957 Act), any attempt to exclude or restrict liability is subject to the test for reasonableness set out in section 11. Under CRA 2015, similar provisions apply to prevent exclusion of liability for personal injury or death where a trader is dealing with, or giving a notice to, a consumer (section 65). In the case of other damage, the test for fairness set out in section 62 will apply.

Other Cases

In other cases, section 2 and (therefore) section 11 of UCTA do not apply; nor do sections 62 and 65 CRA 2015. At common law, before the enactment of UCTA, occupiers were regarded as free to exclude their liability to visitors provided they took reasonable steps to bring the exclusion of liability to the attention of the visitor. Since the occupier was free to grant or withhold permission to enter the premises, he or she should also be free to set the conditions of entry (*Ashdown v Williams* [1957] 1 QB 409). It is assumed that the position remains the same for occupiers whose occupation is not caught by the definition of 'business occupation' (above) or (where applicable) who are not traders dealing with consumers. Jones argues that several qualifications are needed to this general assumption (M. Jones, *Textbook on Tort*, 8th edn, chapter 6, pp. 308–11). In particular, it is doubtful whether the reasoning in *Ashdown* is applicable to those who enter premises in exercise of a 'right conferred by law' (section 1(6)); it is possible that exclusion clauses should be ineffective against children (unless perhaps it is reasonable to expect them to be supervised by an adult—see earlier); and there is an argument that the duty owed to non-visitors is unexcludable (see later) so that it should also apply against visitors if all other liability is excluded.

Other Defences

Although the 1957 Act does not mention contributory negligence, it is clear that the provisions of the Law Reform (Contributory Negligence Act) 1945 are relevant to liabilities arising under both Occupiers' Liability Acts. For that reason, the partial defence of contributory negligence is available in actions under these statutes (see Chapter 5).

Section 2(5) of the 1957 Act specifically refers to risks which are 'willingly accepted' by the visitor, amounting to a statutory form of the general defence of *volenti non fit injuria* or willing acceptance of risk (Chapter 5). It is made clear in section 2(5) that the principles to be applied are the same as those applied at common law. We touch on some controversies with *volenti* in respect of non-visitors, later.

1.4 THE DUTY OWED TO 'NON-VISITORS' UNDER THE 1984 ACT

Occupiers' Liability Act 1984

1 Duty of occupier to persons other than his visitors

(1) The rules enacted by this section shall have effect, in place of the rules of the common law, to determine—

(a) whether any duty is owed by a person as occupier of premises to persons other than his visitors in respect of any risk of their suffering injury on the premises by reason of any danger due to the state of the premises or to things done or omitted to be done on them; and

(b) if so, what that duty is.

(2) For the purposes of this section, the persons who are to be treated respectively as an occupier of any premises (which, for those purposes, include any fixed or movable structure) and as his visitors are—

(a) any person who owes in relation to the premises the duty referred to in section 2 of the Occupiers' Liability Act 1957 (the common duty of care), and

(b) (those who are his visitors for the purposes of that duty.

(3) An occupier of premises owes a duty to another (not being his visitor) in respect of any such risk as is referred to in subsection (1) above if—

(a) he is aware of the danger or has reasonable grounds to believe that it exists;

(b) he knows or has reasonable grounds to believe that the other is in the vicinity of the danger concerned or that he may come into the vicinity of the danger (in either case, whether the other has lawful authority for being in that vicinity or not); and

(c) the risk is one against which, in all the circumstances of the case, he may reasonably be expected to offer the other some protection.

(4) Where, by virtue of this section, an occupier of premises owes a duty to another in respect of such a risk, the duty is to take such care as is reasonable in all the circumstances of the case to see that he does not suffer injury on the premises by reason of the danger concerned.

(5) Any duty owed by virtue of this section in respect of a risk may, in an appropriate case, be discharged by taking such steps as are reasonable in all the circumstances of the case to give warning of the danger concerned or to discourage persons from incurring the risk.

(6) No duty is owed by virtue of this section to any person in respect of risks willingly accepted as his by that person (the question whether a risk was so accepted to be decided on the same principles as in other cases in which one person owes a duty of care to another).

[(6A) At any time when the right conferred by section 2(1) of the Countryside and Rights of Way Act 2000 is exercisable in relation to land which is access land for the purposes of Part I of that Act, an occupier of the land owes (subject to subsection (6C) below) no duty by virtue of this section to any person in respect of—

(a) a risk resulting from the existence of any natural feature of the landscape, or any river, stream, ditch or pond whether or not a natural feature, or

(b) a risk of that person suffering injury when passing over, under or through any wall, fence or gate, except by proper use of the gate or of a stile.

(6B) For the purposes of subsection (6A) above, any plant, shrub or tree, of whatever origin, is to be regarded as a natural feature of the landscape.

(6C) Subsection (6A) does not prevent an occupier from owing a duty by virtue of this section in respect of any risk where the danger concerned is due to anything done by the occupier—

(a) with the intention of creating that risk, or

(b) being reckless as to whether that risk is created.]

(7) No duty is owed by virtue of this section to persons using the highway, and this section does not affect any duty owed to such persons.

(8) Where a person owes a duty by virtue of this section, he does not, by reason of any breach of the duty, incur any liability in respect of any loss of or damage to property.

(9) In this section—

"highway" means any part of a highway other than a ferry or waterway;

"injury" means anything resulting in death or personal injury, including any disease and any impairment of physical or mental condition; and

"movable structure" includes any vessel, vehicle or aircraft.

[1A Special considerations relating to access land]

[In determining whether any, and if so what, duty is owed by virtue of section 1 by an occupier of land at any time when the right conferred by section 2(1) of the Countryside and Rights of Way Act 2000 is exercisable in relation to the land, regard is to be had, in particular, to—

(a) the fact that the existence of that right ought not to place an undue burden (whether financial or otherwise) on the occupier,

(b) the importance of maintaining the character of the countryside, including features of historic, traditional or archaeological interest, and

(c) any relevant guidance given under section 20 of that Act.]

To Which Parties is the Duty Owed?

Subject to the exclusion in section 1(7) of persons using the highway, the duty under the 1984 Act is capable of being owed to all those who are not visitors under the 1957 Act. Duties to people who enter in accordance with the 'right to roam' provisions of the Countryside (Rights of Way) Act 2000 are subject to special conditions.

When is the Duty Owed?

It has been said that the duty under the 1984 Act is a 'lesser duty, as to both incidence and scope' (Lord Hoffmann, *Tomlinson v Congleton*, at [13]). Not every non-visitor is owed a duty on every occasion. The criteria relevant to establishing *whether a duty arises* on a specific occasion are set out in section 1(3) of the 1984 Act. These provisions have no direct counterpart in the 1957 Act, since the common duty of care under that Act is always owed to visitors.

According to section 1(3)(a), no duty will arise unless the occupier is aware of the danger *or has reasonable grounds to believe* that it exists. Similarly, according to section 1(3)(b), no duty will be owed to the non-visitor unless the occupier knows *or has reasonable grounds to believe* that the non-visitor is in (or likely to come into) the vicinity of the danger. Having 'reasonable grounds to believe' involves a subjective element: what knowledge did the occupier actually have?

In *Donoghue v Folkestone Properties* [2003] QB 1008, the claimant (a professional diver) chose to dive from a slipway into a harbour after midnight in midwinter. He struck his head on a grid-pile under the water and broke his neck, becoming tetraplegic. At first instance, the judge held that the defendants knew that substantial numbers of people used the slipway for diving into the harbour and that the gridpiles constituted a danger at certain states of the tide. Since these constituted a concealed danger, this was the sort of risk against which the occupier ought to offer some protection. Therefore, the defendants had a duty at least to place a warning notice on the slipway, since this would have deterred the claimant from diving. This was not a case, it might be noted, where the claimant had full knowledge of the risk involved.

The Court of Appeal reversed the judge's finding of liability, on the basis that the condition in section 1(3)(b) was not satisfied. Although the occupier was aware that people did use the slipway *at certain times*, they had no relevant knowledge of the likely presence of an individual at the actual time and place of the accident. A duty may thus be owed in the summer, but not in the winter. It should be noticed that although diving into a harbour in midwinter is not ordinarily to be expected, offering protection to winter visitors might not impose any additional burdens. A permanent notice, for example, would deter both summer and winter visitors. Lord Phillips suggested that if the council had displayed a notice during the summer, but taken it down during the winter, they would not have been in breach of a duty (at [56]). He concluded that a council which offered no protection at all could not therefore be in breach during the winter, either.

In *Rhind v Astbury Water Park* [2004] EWHC Civ 756 the position was more straightforward in that the defendant occupier was not in possession of any information which would have indicated the presence of the hidden danger—in this case, a submerged fibreglass container resting on the bottom of a lake. For that reason, the claim was dismissed on an application of section 1(3)(a). This illustrates the less onerous nature of the 1984 Act duties. In principle there is no obligation to check for hidden dangers in the water if swimming is prohibited. If the claimant had been a visitor, there would have been a duty to take positive steps of just this sort in order to ensure that he was reasonably safe.

There is a further important condition in section 1(3)(c). A duty will be owed only if the risk is one against which the occupier *may reasonably be expected to offer the non-visitor some protection*. It is important to note that this requires an examination of what is reasonable in relation to the *specific* trespasser. In *Ratcliff v McConnell*, the Court of Appeal emphasized that the claimant was an adult and could reasonably be expected to appreciate obvious risks which would be less obvious to a child. The Court of Appeal drew attention to the earlier case of *McGinlay (or Titchener) v BRB* [1983] 1 WLR 1427, a case under the Occupiers' Liability (Scotland) Act 1960. Here, a 15-year-old child had been considered sufficiently mature to appreciate the dangers of slipping through the gaps in a fence and wandering on to a railway line.

Obvious Dangers

The 1984 Act duty will not generally be owed in respect of obvious dangers (*Donoghue v Folkestone*, at [33]–[35]). If there are reasons to expect the presence of a *child* trespasser, however, then the same danger may give rise to a duty, unless the child should be mature enough to appreciate the danger.

In *Young v Kent County Council* [2005] EWHC 1342, the presence of children on a school roof was to be expected, even though the roof was clearly out of bounds. The child claimant was present at the school while attending a youth club, and it was known that children had gone on to the roof from time to time. On this occasion, the child was retrieving a football. Insufficient measures were taken to prevent access to the roof:

Morison J

33 ... the danger of serious injury to a child, albeit a trespasser, was or should have been apparent to the school, and the prevention of accident was cheap. In my view, any school such as this one ought to have carried out a risk assessment of their premises and, if they had done so, they would have come to the conclusion that there was a risk of children getting onto the roof and suffering injury or death, and their failure to fence off the access point was negligent. Having invited children onto their property, they did owe a duty to ensure that the wandering child, the non-visitor, the trespasser, was not allowed to encounter this danger. In my judgment, the defendants were in breach of their duty under the 1984 Act.

Interestingly, although the risk of harm from going on to the roof was not treated as sufficiently obvious to the 12-year-old claimant to come into the category of risks against which no protection is required, the claimant was still seen as sufficiently careless for his damages to be reduced by 50 per cent on account of contributory negligence. This was largely because of his behaviour while on the roof, where he jumped on a skylight. The school's duty was to take reasonable steps to deter him from going on to the roof at all.

Subsequently in *Keown v Coventry Healthcare Trust* [2006] 1 WLR 953, the Court of Appeal applied both the reasoning and the spirit of *Tomlinson v Congleton* [2004] 1 AC 46 to a case involving injury to an 11-year-old child. The distinction between adults and children is one of 'fact and degree' where their understanding of risk is concerned (at [12]). The claimant had fallen while climbing the outside of a fire escape on the defendant's hospital grounds, but the fire escape *was* not faulty and the child should have appreciated the risk. Therefore there was no danger due to the state of the premises for the purposes of section 1(1)(a). Longmore LJ distinguished *Young*, arguing that in that case it was the 'brittle sky-lights' which made the roof dangerous premises in that case. It could not have been that the child did not understand the risk, because he was thought to be contributorily negligent. The same sort of approach was adopted in *Baldacchino v West Wittering* [2008] EWHC 3386 (QB), where the claimant was 14.

The thinking in *Keown* and *Baldacchino* may represent a hardening in attitude towards risk-taking claimants including 'older' children. But the attitude to claimants and protec-tiveness toward defendants who have custody of significant public amenities tend to run together. Part of the point behind the decision in *Baldacchino* is that the seafront cannot be made a risk-free area, without excluding people from it altogether.

The Content of the Duty

The content of the duty in section 1(4) is stated in very similar terms to the common duty of care under the 1957 Act. The sole difference is that under the 1984 Act, reasonable steps must be taken to ensure that the entrant does not 'suffer injury', while the 1957 Act obliges the occupier to take reasonable steps to ensure that the visitor is 'safe'. The difference reflects the exclusion from the 1984 Act of liability for property damage (section 1(8)).

Warnings/Discouragement

As with the 1957 Act, the duty may in appropriate cases be discharged by a relevant warning (section 1(5)). However, we have already seen that there is no duty to warn a visitor of risks that are obvious (*Staples v West Dorset*, Section 1.3 of this chapter). Clearly, the same is true of trespassers: *Ratcliff v McConnell*, below, at [27]; *Tomlinson v Congleton*; *Darby v National Trust*; *Baldacchino v West Wittering* (above).

It should be noted that in the 1984 Act, in addition to warnings, it may also be sufficient to discharge the duty if an occupier has taken reasonable steps to 'discourage persons from incurring the risk'.

Ratcliff v McConnell [1999] 1 WLR 670

The plaintiff, a 19-year-old student, chose to climb the fence of his college swimming pool at night, and execute a running dive into the water. He was very seriously injured. The college had fenced the pool in order to discourage swimming, and employed security guards to patrol the campus. The Court of Appeal held that there was no obligation to warn an adult trespasser of the obvious dangers of diving into a pool. It is well known that pools vary in their depth and configuration and that diving without checking the depth is dangerous. There was no hidden danger, and the existence of a slope between the deep end and the shallow end did not constitute such a hidden danger or trap (at [37]). There was no need to post more specific notices than those prohibiting swimming. Further, the steps taken by the college to discourage use were sufficient, even though there was some evidence of sporadic night-time use of the pool prior to the claimant's accident. The col-lege did not have to punish offenders to emphasize the rules in order to satisfy their duty under the 1984 Act: such a suggestion 'goes far beyond discouragement' (at [47]). Further, the Court of Appeal thought it clear that in this case the claimant had 'willingly accepted the risk' (at [47]): see later.

Exclusion and Defences

Exclusion of Liability

The Unfair Contract Terms Act 1977 (UCTA) has not been amended to refer to the duty owed by occupiers under the 1984 Act. While there was some doubt over whether UCTA extended to the common law duty of humanity under *Herrington*,[10] it is clear that sections 2 and (therefore) 11 UCTA do *not* apply to the duty under the 1984 Act. The position may be very different if trespassers satisfy the definition of 'consumers' under CRA 2015. Given the brevity of that definition, extracted above, it seems possible that they would; so that notices directed at trespassers could be 'consumer notices'. If this is the case then trespassers could be protected by the provisions of CRA 2015. Outside such cases, are we to conclude, as with the exclusion of non-business liability under the 1957 Act, that occupiers are entirely free (in accordance with *Ashdown v Samuel Williams*) to exclude liability? Before the 1984 Act, John Mesher suggested that since the reasoning in *Ashdown* turned on the occupier's ability to lay down criteria governing entry on to the premises, this reasoning cannot be extended to trespassers ([1979] 43 Conv 58, 63). Though he was writing of the *Herrington* duties, the reasoning is just as apposite now that the 1984 Act is in place. Should the duty therefore be regarded as an 'unexcludable minimum'? After all, such duties are owed only where it is 'reasonable in all the circumstances of the case' to offer the entrant some protection. Alternatively, if the 1984 Act can be excluded, is the *Herrington* duty still unexcludable as it is a duty of 'common humanity'?

Volenti/Willing Acceptance of Risk

Section 1(6) of the 1984 Act clearly states that the question of willing acceptance of risk is to be considered on the same principles as in other cases. In Chapter 5, we investigated the limited applicability of the *volenti* defence, at least so far as negligence is concerned. It was emphasized that *knowledge* of the risk is not the same as *willing acceptance* of the risk. However, in the case of occupiers' liability to trespassers under the 1984 Act, courts seem to have thought it sufficient to show that the claimant had full knowledge of and appreciated the risk; and that he or she had decided to enter the premises (or engage in prohibited use of the premises) notwithstanding the existence of that risk. This appears to have been the approach in both *McGinlay (or Titchener) v BRB* [1983] 3 All ER 770 and *Ratcliff v McConnell* (above).

The approach of the House of Lords in *McGinlay v BRB* has been criticized. As Jaffey points out in the article extracted below, the case law on *volenti non fit injuria* is divided as to whether a real agreement to exempt the defendant from liability is required and, if it is, whether such an agreement can realistically be implied when the claimant only encounters the danger *after* the relevant negligence. Jaffey points out that in *McGinlay* the House of Lords appeared to say that such an agreement was required, in a case when realistically, any such agreement was in the realms of fiction.

---

[10] J. Mesher, 'Occupiers, Trespassers, and the Unfair Contract Terms Act 1977' [1979] 43 Conv 58, argued at 63 that UCTA did not extend to this duty.

A. J. E. Jaffey, 'Volenti Non Fit Injuria' (1985) 44 CLJ 87, at 90–1

... The main ground of the decision was that, having regard to the plaintiff's knowledge of the danger and her knowledge that she should keep a proper lookout for trains, and the other circumstances of the case, the Railways owed her no duty to do more than they had done to maintain the fence. Alternatively, even if the defendants would otherwise have been in breach of their duty to the plaintiff, they were protected by s 2(3) of the [Occupiers' Liability (Scotland) Act], which provides:

Nothing in the foregoing provisions of this Act shall be held to impose on an occupier any obligation to a person entering on his premises in respect of any risks which that person has willingly accepted as his; and any question whether a risk was so accepted shall be decided on the same principles as in other cases in which one person owes to another a duty to take care.

Lord Fraser, with whose judgment all the other members of the House of Lords agreed, said that this section merely put into words the principle *volenti non fit injuria* [[1983] 1 WLR 1427, at p. 1434]. The result of such a defence, he said, would be that whether the respondents would otherwise have been in breach of their duty to the appellant or not, the appellant had exempted them from any obligation towards her. He referred to Salmond and Heuston [*The Law of Torts,* 18th edn, 467] for this formulation. To exempt someone from an obligation surely requires some agreement with, or promise to, that person by which he is released or excused from an obligation to which he would otherwise be subject. Indeed, in the passage referred to by Lord Fraser Salmond and Heuston speak of the agreement of the plaintiff, express or implied, to exempt the defendant. ... It is hard to see however how the plaintiff's entering on the land with full knowledge of the danger can amount to an agreement with, or promise to, the defendant. At what moment were the Railways relieved of their obligations in relation to the safety of the plaintiff? At the moment when she passed through the gap in the fence or a split second before that? We are clearly in the realms of fiction if a person's conduct in voluntarily taking a known risk is treated as an implied agreement with the person who created the danger.

Contributory Negligence

This defence is clearly available in principle in actions under the 1984 Act, but there is reduced scope for its applicability given the prerequisites for the existence of a duty. For a case where the defence did operate, see *Young v Kent County Council* [2005] EWHC 1342. This case involved a child who was old enough to be regarded as contributorily negligent (he should have realized it was dangerous to jump on a skylight), but young enough to need protection from his own decision to go into a prohibited area (the roof).

Specific Users

Users of Public Rights of Way

We noted earlier that users of public rights of way are excluded from protection under the 1984 Act. If the right of way is adopted as a highway maintainable at public expense, there is a duty on the relevant highway authority (not the occupier whose land is crossed by the highway) to maintain it (Highways Act 1980, section 41). There would of course remain the possibility that the user of a public right of way will be owed a duty at common law, through the tort of negligence. Section 1(7) expressly preserves any existing duties.

As explained by F. R. Barker and N. D. M. Parry, 'Private Property, Public Access and Occupiers' Liability' (1995) 15 LS 335, the difficulty with any such negligence duty is that the occupier of land has traditionally been subject to no *positive* obligations (giving rise to liability for *failures to repair*) in respect of public rights of way: this is the rule in *Gautret v Egerton* (1867) LR 2 CP 371. Barker and Parry explain that this general approach was challenged in the case of *Thomas v British Railways Board* [1976] 1 QB 912, in which a 2-year-old child crossed through a gap where a stile had been on a public footpath and wandered on to a railway line. She was still on the footpath when she was struck by a train. In *Thomas*, the Court of Appeal decided that the defendants owed a duty of care which had been breached through failure to replace the missing stile.[11] However, Barker and Parry also concede that there are several problems with attempting to develop a consistent approach based on *Thomas*. One such problem is that in *Thomas*, the Court of Appeal was influenced by the House of Lords' then-recent judgment in *BRB v Herrington* [1972] AC 877, and perhaps reasoned by analogy with the 'duty of common humanity'. As the authors point out, *Herrington* was afflicted by serious ambiguity and this is why it was superseded by legislation. Users of the highway were deliberately and expressly omitted from coverage under the resulting 1984 Act. It might therefore be bizarre to resurrect *Herrington*, with all its uncertainties, to cover an expressly excluded group, although there have been other suggestions that *Herrington* duties may survive, for example if the 1984 Act duty is validly excluded. A further significant problem is that in the case of *McGeown v Northern Ireland Housing Executive* [1995] 1 AC 233, the House of Lords held (while not discussing *Thomas*) that an occupier could not be liable to the user of a public right of way for negligent nonfeasance (including failure to repair), explicitly affirming the rule in *Gautret v Egerton* (1867) LR 2 CP 371. If this means that *Thomas* is wrongly decided, then it means that a 2-year-old child wandering through a broken stile or fence on a footpath is owed no duty, while a 2-year-old or even 12-year-old child wandering through a broken fence into an area where she is not allowed to be will (if the knowledge conditions are satisfied) be quite likely to be owed a duty (see *Young v Kent CC*, discussed earlier).

Access Land

The Countryside (Rights of Way) Act 2000 (CROW) introduced an important public 'right to roam' on certain land (referred to as 'access land'). Through amendments to the 1957 and 1984 Acts, CROW introduced specific limitations on the duties that may arise in respect of 'access land'. Individuals exercising the 'right to roam' are excluded from the definition of visitor in the 1957 Act (section 1(4)(a)), and new provisions in the 1984 Act add particular conditions governing the question of whether a duty is owed. We should also note section 12(1):

Countryside (Rights of Way) Act 2000

12 (1) The operation of section 2(1) in relation to any access land does not increase the liability, under any enactment not contained in this Act or under any rule of law, of a person interested in the access land or any adjoining land in respect of the state of the land or of things done or omitted to be done on the land.

[11] It was found that such a young child, who had left her garden nearby, would not have climbed a stile.

2. CONCLUSIONS

i.   While applying the provisions of the two Occupiers' Liability Acts, the courts are undeniably concerned to strike the right balance between protection of the safety of visitors to premises, and avoidance of unfair and onerous duties on occupiers of land. Recent cases emphasize the free choice of claimants (and of those others who may wish to make the same sort of choice in the future), but they are also preoccupied with certain 'collective' questions. In particular, there is a concern with public amenity and its continued availability. Occupiers' liability therefore naturally raises the sorts of issue that have become associated with 'compensation culture', and the case of *Tomlinson v Congleton* has become a key illustration of the way that courts are capable of raising such issues for themselves. Occupiers' liability is concerned not just with the narrow application of statutory provisions, but with the distribution of risks associated with premises.

ii   The statutory provisions allow this balance to be struck in a number of ways. One way in which courts have struck the balance in recent years is through restriction of occupiers' liability to 'occupancy', rather than 'activity' duties. Others include the redefinition of a visitor who strays beyond the purpose of their visit as a trespasser; and, importantly, the recognition that obvious dangers require no warning. Overall, visitors and trespassers are owed only a duty to take such steps as will make them 'reasonably' safe, and this permits the courts to develop a distinctive notion of what level of expectation is reasonable. Trespassers, for their part, are owed duties only in respect of hazards of which occupiers are or should be aware, and only if the occupier should be aware of their presence. While it remains true therefore that occupiers owe enhanced duties as a consequence of their occupation of premises, these duties are by no means unrestricted, and the boundaries of such duties are carefully defined with their consequences in mind.

FURTHER READING

Bailey, S., 'Occupiers' Liability: the Enactment of 'Common Law' Principles', in T. T. Arvind and J. Steele (eds), *Tort Law and the Legislature* (Hart, 2013), 207.

Barker, F. R., and Parry, N. D. M., 'Private Property, Public Access and Occupiers' Liability' (1995) *15 LS* 335.

Buckley, R. A., 'The Occupiers' Liability Act 1984—Has Herrington Survived?' [1984] *Conv* 413.

Goodhart, A. L., 'The *Herrington Case*' (1972) 88 LQR 310.

Jaffey, A. J. E., 'Volenti non fit injuria' [1985] CLJ 87.

Jones, M., 'The Occupiers Liability Act 1984' (1984) 47 MLR 713.

Law Commission, *Report on Liability for Damage or Injury to Trespassers and Related Questions of Occupiers' Liability* (Law Com Report No 75, Cmnd 6428, 1976).

Law Reform Committee, *Third Report* (Cmnd 9305, 1954).

Mesher, J., 'Occupiers, Trespassers, and the Unfair Contract Terms Act 1977' [1979] 43 Conv 58–60.

Morgan, J., 'Tort, Insurance, and Incoherence' (2004) 67 MLR 384.

North, P. M., *Occupiers' Liability* (London: Butterworths, 1971).

Stevens-Hoare, M., and Higgins, R., 'Roam Free?' (2004) NLJ 1846.

PART VI

DEFAMATION
AND PRIVACY

In this Part, we consider two closely related areas where the new European flavour of English tort law has been notable. In relation to defamation, a domestic reform agenda has also developed apace, and there has been a decision to shift the balance more decisively in favour of freedom of expression than the Convention would require. Nevertheless, the resulting law plainly builds upon developments achieved by the courts, which were in turn inspired or enabled by the new status of Convention rights. Both areas continue to raise the issue of how to 'balance' competing rights and interests, which has become familiar through adapting English law to better incorporate Convention rights.

In Chapter 13, we consider the actions in defamation, which have been a part of the English law of tort for centuries. These actions protect reputation, and it has long been recognized that in awarding remedies for defamatory statements the law of tort has a potentially restrictive effect on the exercise of free speech. Many aspects of defamation law have appeared to favour the claimant over the maker of a statement. The Defamation Act 2013 makes the most far-reaching statutory intervention into the law of defamation to date, but does not attempt to sweep away the common law and start entirely afresh. The Act attempts to 'rebalance' and to simplify the law, and to control its potential misuse.

Chapter 14 traces the emergence and development of a new cause of action, which is generally described as a tort. This action protects the claimant's reasonable expectation of privacy against interference in the form of publication. The action emerged in response to the enactment of the Human Rights Act 1998. Underlining the novelty of this development, the courts accept that the 'very content' of the tort is provided by the Convention rights to privacy and freedom of expression in Articles 8 and 10. Concepts of balance and of proportionality are inherent to deliberation over these remedies.

An interesting question concerns the apparently conflicting directions taken by the law in these two related areas. Defamation, as much as privacy, can be seen as striking a balance between Article 8 and Article 10 rights. Yet the reform agenda in relation to defamation has been focused on the protection of free expression; while the developing law of privacy is one manifestation of a wider concern with protecting individuals from the worst excesses of (generally) the press. Putting both together, the question that emerges is whether the law can influence the conditions for a press that is both free, and responsible, while also balancing the rights in reputation and privacy on the one hand, and expression on the other. That is no small question.

13

DEFAMATION

CENTRAL ISSUES

i) Common law has provided powerful protection to reputation through the torts of libel and slander. **Slanders** are generally transitory in form while **libels**, broadly, are more permanent in form. Both of these torts protect a claimant's interest in reputation against defamatory 'statements' (which need not take the form of words). Neither tort requires any particular state of mind on the part of the defendant, except in special circumstances (for example, where the statement is one of opinion, not of fact, in which case lack of honest belief must generally be shown). Libel and slander are therefore torts of strict liability which in special circumstances become dependent on 'malice'.

ii) It has long been recognized that the protection thus afforded to reputation can conflict with freedom of expression. This has been the chief reason for gradual modification in the law of defamation. In the courts, the relationship between the protected interest in **reputation** and the competing interest in **freedom of expression** had begun to change before the most recent legislative intervention in the Defamation Act 2013. Freedom of expression had begun to be understood in terms of the public interest in receiving and

imparting information in the context of a democratic society. This approach was clearly influenced by the European Convention on Human Rights. After the Human Rights Act, freedom of expression could no longer be regarded as a residual personal right (if it ever was), but was interpreted as a positive right reinforced by the public interest.

iii) Recent statutory intervention through the Defamation Act 2013 intervenes more decisively in an attempt to achieve a new balance between reputation, and freedom of expression, while also simplifying applicable legal principles. In key areas, the position reached by the common law has been abolished and replaced by simpler provisions which strengthen protection for freedom of expression. The statutory approach is motivated by concern with the adverse consequences of defamation law to date, and not directly with the need to address Convention rights, though these rights have underpinned the changes in domestic law which inform it. In virtually all respects, the new legislation shifts the balance in favour of protecting speech; yet at the same time, it has been recognized at least in theory that reputation too is within the protection of Article 8 of the Convention. Equally significant are statutory attempts to constrain potential misuses of the law of defamation, for example by stifling 'libel tourism', by restricting the role of juries, and by clarifying the responsibilities of those operating websites. Since the previous edition, particularly important questions have arisen concerning the application of the new requirement of 'serious harm' under section 1 of the Defamation Act 2013.

1. COMMON LAW AND 2013 REFORMS

The Defamation Act 2013 (the 2013 Act) is by no means the first statutory intervention into the law of defamation, but it is the most far-reaching. Lobbying groups have been notably successful in bringing about their desired changes, and the Act has been described as 'the culmination of a phenomenally successful political campaign'.[1] Many of its provisions replace elements of common law as well as certain provisions of earlier statutes. However, the 2013 Act still does not attempt to sweep away all aspects of common law and start afresh. Rather, it builds on the work of the courts in recent years, albeit with some notable additions.

There are three distinct reasons why common law remains important in the law as it currently stands. First, the 2013 Act came into force on 1 January 2014, and by section 16 of the Act, most of its provisions are expressed to be inapplicable to actions which accrued—or in some instances statements which were made—before that date. For these cases, the pre-Act law continues to apply. Second, by no means all elements of the law are altered by the statute. Even where the statute does apply, there are areas where the common law continues to be definitive or partially definitive. Examples are the distinction between 'fact' and 'opinion' used in section 3 of the 2013 Act, which is not defined in the statute, so that courts will need to apply earlier decisions on this point; and the meaning of a 'defamatory statement', to which section 1 of the Act makes important additions without altering the basic definition. In these areas, the applicable principles are derived from a combination of statute and common law. Third, even where common law has been replaced, the new provisions generally state a revised version of the position arrived at by the courts. At times, the statute deliberately reflects recent decisions of the courts, and the Explanatory Notes published with the statute at many points make this apparent, although litigation around section 1(1) indicates that results could diverge further than expected from the common law position (see Section 4.2). Parliament in this instance seems to have been content to work in partnership with the courts, adopting judicial innovations and leaving considerable discretion on some key points—such as the 'public interest' defence—to the courts. In an area of law so dominated by ideas of 'balance', it is also highly likely that some decisions concerning the common law were themselves influenced by the developing reform agenda. Apart from these points, when it comes to *understanding* the law, the position reached prior to the Act is of course often essential background, and will be referred to where it is both helpful, and feasible to do so.

The new statutory provisions are extracted and discussed throughout this chapter, rather than in a separate section. This reflects the fact that the present law is derived from an amalgamation of common law and statutory principles. Nevertheless, even those approaching

---

[1] A. Mullis and A. Scott, 'Tilting at Windmills: the Defamation Act 2013' (2014) 77 MLR 87, 87.

the area for the first time may find useful a brief overview of the major changes wrought by the 2013 Act.

Defamation Act 2013: Key Provisions

In outline, notable contributions made by Defamation Act 2013 are as follows.

1. Introduction of a 'serious harm' criterion, aimed at preventing trivial claims (section 1(1)).

2. A new requirement in the case of bodies trading for profit that a statement is not actionable unless it is likely to cause 'serious financial loss' (section 1(2)).

3. Replacement of the common law defence of 'justification' with a slightly simpler, but otherwise similar defence which is now named 'truth' (section 2).

4. Replacement of the common law defence of 'fair comment' with a simplified defence named 'honest opinion', in which the problematic concept of 'malice' plays no part (section 3).

5. Replacement of the ground-breaking defence of 'Reynolds privilege' with a new defence of 'publication on a matter of public interest', which helps to realize the radical nature of the 'privilege' (section 4).

6. Clarification of the potential liabilities of website operators for defamatory statements posted on their websites by others (section 5).

7. Creation of a new category of privileged statements in scientific and academic journals (section 6).

8. Reform of the 'single publication rule' to protect further publications of the same statement, for example through internet archives (section 8).

9. Restriction on actions against persons not domiciled in the UK or an EU member state: this is an attempt to tackle 'libel tourism' (the bringing of actions in UK courts in order to benefit from the claimant-friendly law that has existed in this jurisdiction) (section 9).

10. Additional protection to 'secondary' publishers (those who do not originate a statement) (section 10).

11. Curtailment of jury trials in defamation actions: trial is now to be without a jury unless the court orders otherwise (section 11).

12. The availability of new powers for courts deciding defamation actions: to order a summary of its judgment to be printed (section 12); or a statement to be removed; or distribution to cease (section 13).

In this chapter, we set out to explore the law as it stands, incorporating the statutory provisions and common law where it is still relevant, or essential to grasping the present law. The 2013 Act aims to 'rebalance' the law of defamation.[2] In the next section, before addressing the details of the law, we begin by considering what exactly is being 'balanced'?

---

[2] See for example Ministry of Justice, *Complaints about defamatory material posted on websites: Guidance on Section 5 of the Defamation Act 2013 and Regulations* (January 2014), para 1: 'The purpose of the Defamation Act 2013 is to rebalance the law on defamation and to provide more effective protection for freedom of speech while at the same time ensuring that people who have been defamed are also entitled to protect their reputation.'

2. THE COMPETING INTERESTS: EXPRESSION AND REPUTATION

Libel and slander have a long history—far longer, for example, than negligence. Protection of reputation through civil law was well established by the start of the sixteenth century,[3] and significantly predates the recognition of 'human rights' in any form. Even so, in modern times the law of defamation has openly reflected the tension between freedom of expression, and protection of reputation. This tension has affected the manner in which the torts are defined; the defences and remedies available; and the funding of litigation. After the Human Rights Act 1998 (HRA), reputation and freedom of expression have competed in a new context. The most recent statutory reforms swing the balance further towards freedom of expression, and are particularly aimed at avoiding a 'chilling effect' on speech. Although the influence of Convention rights on the legislation is implicit and indirect, consideration of these rights has helped to shape the judge-made developments which are in many respects continued by the legislation. We begin by examining the rival interests in expression and reputation and the changing nature of their recognition in law. Freedom of expression is much more easily mapped onto the European Convention on Human Rights (ECHR) than reputation; but recent developments have found a place for reputation also within the range of protected Convention rights.

2.1 FREEDOM OF EXPRESSION

Why Protect Expression?

There is more than one possible reason for protecting freedom of expression. As we will see, the choice of rationale has a practical impact on the law of defamation, and the evolution of its principles.

David Feldman, *Civil Liberties and Human Rights in England and Wales* (2nd edn, Oxford: Oxford University Press, 2002), 762–6; by permission of Oxford University Press

THE IMPORTANCE OF FREEDOM OF EXPRESSION

The liberty to express one's self freely is important for a number of reasons, which help to shape the development and application of the law on freedom of expression. First, self-expression is a significant instrument of freedom of conscience, personal identity, and self-fulfilment. From the point of view of civil liberties, this is probably the most important of the justifications which can be offered for free speech.

...

The freedom to choose between values, to have fun through communication, to identify and be identified with particular values or ideas, and to live one's life according to one's choice, is the essence of liberty. Freedom of expression has an important role to play here.…

[3] The first known action in slander is said by Warren and Brandeis to have been recorded in 1356: 'The Right to Privacy' (1890) 4 *Harvard Late Review*, at 198.

The second justification concerns the contribution of communication to the growth of knowledge and understanding. Freedom of expression enables people to contribute to debates about social and moral values. It is arguable that the best way to find the best or truest theory or model of anything is to permit the widest possible range of ideas to circulate. The interplay of these ideas, challenging each other and allowing the strengths and weaknesses of each to be exposed, is more likely than any alternative strategy to lead to the best possible conclusion. This treats freedom of expression as an instrumental value, advancing other goods (the development of true or good ideas) with a consequential benefit for the individual and society.

This is the basis on which freedom of expression appealed to John Milton, in *Aeropagitica*, and to the utilitarian mind of John Stuart Mill, who gave the most famous, and most convincing, justification for freedom of speech in *On Liberty*. Mill argued on utilitarian grounds that there was a distinction in principle between facts and opinion. When dealing with opinions, all should be freely expressed, subject to any restrictions necessary to protect against identifiable harm…. Assertions of fact, on the other hand, could by definition be either true or false. There would be good reason to allow free expression of the truth, as this would lead to advances in knowledge and material improvements in society, but this does not justify permitting free expression of falsehoods. However, it is not always possible to say whether an assertion is true or false, and many benefits may flow from allowing statements of fact to be asserted so that they may be tested…. on a rule-utilitarian analysis the benefits of a general principle permitting freedom of expression are held to outweigh the disbenefits resulting from particular aspects of the rule. It is therefore preferable to permit freedom to express opinions and facts, even if untrue, rather than to adopt a general rule which permits censorship and coercion in relation to expression….

A third justification for free expression is that it allows the political discourse which is necessary in any country which aspires to democracy…. A democratic rationale for freedom of expression makes perfect sense if applied to a society in which the operative model of democracy is one in which the people have the right to participate directly in day-to-day governmental decision making, or to have their views considered in the choice of policies by government. It works less well if the prevailing model is one in which the people merely choose a government, which is then free to get on with the job of governing…. The representative system, such as we have in the UK, would offer less support to free-expression rights than a participatory system.

In this extract, David Feldman outlines three justifications for freedom of expression.[4] He suggests that from a 'civil liberties' point of view—which in this context is concerned chiefly with personal freedom and autonomy—the first justification is the most important. Recent judgments in defamation cases consider freedom of expression in much more 'instrumental' terms than this, appealing more to the *public* interest in freedom of expression and to the goals that it serves. That reading of freedom of expression is consistent with the concerns which have led to the Defamation Act 2013. The second and third justifications outlined by Feldman, both of which are concerned with the public interest, are of growing influence. Here is a judicial example:

---

[4] He continues by identifying two further, less influential justifications: forcing the development of a capacity for tolerance, and fostering artistic and scholarly endeavour.

Lord Nicholls, *Reynolds v Times Newspapers*
[2001] 2 AC 127, at 200

The high importance of freedom to impart and receive information and ideas has been stated so often and so eloquently that this point calls for no elaboration in this case. At a pragmatic level, freedom to disseminate and receive information on political matters is essential to the proper functioning of the system of parliamentary democracy cherished in this country. This freedom enables those who elect representatives to Parliament to make an informed choice, regarding individuals as well as policies, and those elected to make informed decisions.

Lord Nicholls appears to embrace the argument from democracy, while Feldman (at the end of the extract above) was rather sceptical of its value in a representative democracy such as that of Britain. For Lord Nicholls, political representatives will be inclined to act more appropriately if the public is better informed, and they may even be influenced by public debate. The judgments in *Reynolds* were clearly influenced by Article 10 of the ECHR, and by the HRA which was then on the verge of commencement. Although the decision in *Reynolds* has been superseded by section 4 of the Defamation Act 2013, that provision effectively continues the work begun by the courts, though with greater clarity as to the working concepts, and without the awkward categorization as a 'privilege'.[5] Though the legislation is not motivated by a wish to reflect the requirements of the Convention, the influence of Convention rights in the law on which the statute builds is clear. The legislation sets out to strike a fresh balance; but the tools used to achieve that are largely modelled on the concepts developed by the courts under the influence of Convention jurisprudence.

Freedom of Expression: The Legal Provisions

European Convention for the Protection of Human Rights and Fundamental Freedoms, 1950 ('the Convention')

Article 10 Freedom of Expression

1. Everyone has the right to freedom of expression. This right shall include freedom to hold opinions and to receive and impart information and ideas without interference by public authority and regardless of frontiers . . . .

2. The exercise of these freedoms, since it carries with it duties and responsibilities, may be subject to such formalities, conditions, restrictions or penalties as are prescribed by law and are necessary in a democratic society, in the interests of national security, territorial integrity or public safety, for the prevention of disorder or crime, for the protection of health or morals, for the protection of the reputation or rights of others, for preventing the disclosure of information received in confidence, or for maintaining the authority and impartiality of the judiciary.

This provision is one of the 'Convention rights' annexed to the HRA. We have analysed the way in which the 'Convention rights' are treated in the HRA in Chapters 1 and 10.

---

[5] See Section 5, 'Defences'.

Section 6 of the HRA, extracted in Chapter 1, has been of particular importance for the law of defamation. This section states that it is unlawful for a public authority (which is defined to include a court) to act in a way that is incompatible with a Convention right. As a consequence of section 6, any court must ensure that its decisions are compatible with the relevant Convention rights, including those in Article 10. In Chapter 1 we considered whether this introduces 'horizontal effect' into the HRA, affecting the rights and obligations between citizens, rather than just the rights of citizens against the state. Judicial development in defamation law since enactment suggests an element of 'indirect' horizontal effect. 'Indirect' horizontal effect influences the interpretation of existing causes of action, rather than the creation of new actions.

The right to freedom of expression protected by the HRA is specifically the 'Convention right' expressed in Article 10. Therefore, we must examine the terms of Article 10 itself.

Article 10: Essential Features

Certain important features of this Article should be highlighted. First, the right is very broadly expressed and includes expression of information, opinions, and ideas. Second, the Article is concerned not only with *imparting* information, opinions, and ideas, which is probably the most natural meaning of the term 'expression', but also with *receiving* them. Third, states may legitimately restrict the right defined in Article 10(1), as described in Article 10(2). Among the legitimate aims are penalties designed to protect *reputation*. However, it is equally important that any such restrictions must be *prescribed by law*, and that they should be *'necessary in a democratic society'*. The European Court of Human Rights has on more than one occasion found that English defamation law violated Article 10 because it failed to comply with these qualifications to Article 10(2) (*Tolstoy Miloslavsky v UK* (1995) 20 EHRR 442; *Steel and Morris v UK* (2005) 41 EHRR 403).

The 'Chilling Effect'

The prospect of an action in defamation may have unhealthy deterrent effects, inhibiting publication not only of falsehoods but also of some worthwhile and important material. This prospect is captured in the idea of a 'chilling effect'. The expression originated in the United States and was imported into English law in *Derbyshire v Times Newspapers* [1993] AC 534, through reference to the Supreme Court's decision in *New York Times v Sullivan* 376 US 254 (1964).[6] It is another way of referring to a 'deterrent'.

Reference to the chilling effect has become an established aspect of judicial and political discussion of defamation. The risk of 'chilling' has been exacerbated by certain features of the law.[7] By definition, the chilling effect is important chiefly from the point of view of 'functional' justifications for freedom of expression: the danger is that the public will remain uninformed of potentially important issues, and the quality of debate will be adversely affected.[8]

---

[6] See also Section 5.4 of this chapter.

[7] Examples we will see in this chapter are the burden of proving truth; the scale of possible damages; the absence of financial support for defendants; and the general costs of litigation including especially the risk of disproportionate costs where the claimant enters into a conditional fee agreement.

[8] For confirmation of the chilling effect in the media, see E. Barendt, L. Lustgarten, K. Norrie, and H. Stephenson, *Libel and the Media: The Chilling Effect* (Oxford: Clarendon Press, 1997).

2.2 REPUTATION

As we noted above, defamation actions protect reputation. Historically, defamation has been almost unique in protecting personal reputation,[9] but developments in the tort of malicious falsehood have created greater potential overlap.

There is no Convention *right* which is expressly dedicated to protecting reputation. However, we have seen that protection of reputation is stated to be a legitimate reason to restrict freedom of expression, so long as the restrictions are necessary and prescribed by law (Article 10(2)). On its own, this would appear to reverse the traditional common law hierarchy of interests:

Peter Cane, *The Anatomy of Tort Law* (Oxford: Hart Publishing, 1997), 134

... in traditional English tort law, reputation is more highly prized than (the countervailing interest in) freedom of speech and information, and such protections for the latter as are recognised are embodied in defences to a claim for defamation rather than in the definition of the wrong of defamation.

It is now clear however that 'reputation' is also within the protection set out by Article 8 ECHR.[10] The implication is that at least some defamation actions should raise very similar issues to the privacy actions discussed in Chapter 14, and in particular a balance between rights needs to be struck in both areas. Since the previous edition of this work, this has become more securely recognized.

Lord Phillips, *Flood v Times Newspapers* [2012] 2 AC 273

The balancing act and human rights

44. ... The decisions to which I have referred contain frequent emphasis on the importance of freedom of speech and, in particular, the freedom of the press. That importance has been repeatedly emphasised by the European Court of Human Rights when considering article 10 of the Convention for the Protection of Human Rights and Fundamental Freedoms. There is, however, a conflict between article 10 and article 8, and the Strasbourg court has recently recognised that reputation falls within the ambit of the protection afforded by article 8: see *Cumpănă and Mazăre v Romania* (2004) 41 EHRR 200 (GC), para 91 and *Pfeifer v Austria* (2007) 48 EHRR 175, paras 33, 35. In *Reynolds* Lord Nicholls, at p 205, described adjudicating on a claim to *Reynolds* privilege as "a balancing operation". It is indeed. The importance of the public interest in receiving the relevant information has to be weighed against the public interest in preventing the dissemination of defamatory allegations, with the injury that this causes to the reputation of the person defamed.

[9] Corporations have been able to sue in defamation in the same way as individuals, but this is qualified by s 1(1) Defamation Act 2013, requiring the likelihood of 'serious financial harm.' Another tort which protects personal reputation is malicious prosecution (Chapter 2).

[10] Apart from the case next extracted and Strasbourg authorities referred to there, see also *Cliff v Slough BC* [2010] EWCA Civ 1171.

45 There is a danger in making an exact comparison between this balancing exercise and other situations where article 8 rights have to be balanced against article 10 rights. Before the development of Reynolds privilege, the law of defamation, as developed by Parliament and the courts, already sought to strike a balance between freedom of expression and the protection of reputation. Thus a fair and accurate report of court proceedings is absolutely privileged. Publication is permitted even though this may involve publishing allegations that are clearly defamatory. The balance in respect of the reporting of such proceedings is heavily weighted in favour of freedom of speech. The public interest in favour of publication is firmly established. The judge has, however, jurisdiction to make an anonymity order, thereby tilting the balance back. Decisions in relation to the exercise of this power cannot be automatically applied to a situation where the publication of defamatory allegations has no statutory protection. In the former case one starts with a presumption in favour of protected publication; in the latter one starts with a presumption against it.

A key point made by Lord Phillips in this extract is that there are different ways to strike a 'balance'. In privacy actions, the question of balance is often directly before the courts as they determine whether or not to issue an injunction. In defamation, the 'balance' sought by the law may be achieved by a pattern of legal principles which strike the overall balance between reputation and freedom of expression. Even so, it remains a challenge to explain why the structure and principles of the two areas of law remain so different, outside certain areas. In particular, injunctions to restrain publication are a key remedy in privacy actions, but are rarely used until after a full trial in defamation actions. Equally, the reform debate has been almost entirely dominated by freedom of expression rather than reputation: how can it be clearly decided whether the correct balance has been struck, if only one side of the balance is being considered?

Two distinct ways of addressing this issue are possible. One is to suggest that at the level of individual interests, the significance of reputation is not to be underestimated: it is an essential aspect of human well-being.[11] Another is to suggest that whatever the public and social reasons for protecting freedom of expression, similar arguments can also be made for protection of reputation. Both of these are captured by Mullis and Scott,[12] who suggest that:

The task of designing any libel regime must involve reaching an appropriate accommodation between individual rights and social interests in both freedom of expression and reputation.

This means accepting that there is a social or 'public' value to reputation, just as there is to freedom of expression. Indeed, precisely this was suggested by Lord Nicholls in the leading (though now superseded) case of *Reynolds v Times Newspapers*:

Lord Nicholls, *Reynolds v Times Newspapers*, at 201

Reputation is an integral and important part of the dignity of the individual. It also forms the basis of many decisions in a democratic society which are fundamental to its well-being: whom to employ or work for, whom to promote, whom to do business with or to vote

[11] W. Howarth, 'Libel: Its Purpose and Reform' (2011) 74 MLR 845;

[12] A. Mullis and A. Scott, 'The Swing of the Pendulum: Reputation, Expression and the Re-centring of English Libel Law', in D. Capper (ed.), *Modern Defamation Law: Balancing Reputation and Free Expression* (QUB, 2012).

for. Once besmirched by an unfounded allegation in a national newspaper, a reputation can be damaged forever, especially if there is no opportunity to vindicate one's reputation. When this happens, society as well as the individual is the loser. For it should not be supposed that protection of reputation is a matter of importance only to the affected individual and his family. Protection of reputation is conducive to the public good. It is in the public interest that the reputation of public figures should not be debased falsely. In the political field, in order to make an informed choice, the electorate needs to be able to identify the good as well as the bad. Consistently with these considerations, human rights conventions recognise that freedom of expression is not an absolute right. Its exercise may be subject to such restrictions as are prescribed by law and are necessary in a democratic society for the protection of the reputations of others.

The crux of this appeal, therefore, lies in identifying the restrictions which are fairly and reasonably necessary for the protection of reputation.

3. LIBEL, SLANDER, AND MALICIOUS FALSEHOOD

3.1 LIBEL AND SLANDER

Libel and slander are separate torts. At common law, a libel is a defamatory statement in permanent or semi-permanent form.[13] The written word may be a libel, while the spoken word is, at common law, capable of amounting to a slander. The practical difference between the two is that libel is actionable per se or without proof of damage. Slander, at common law, is actionable only if 'special damage' is shown.

A number of exceptions apply. Some of these specify that certain statements, not easily defined as permanent in form, may amount to libels. Others remove the special damage requirement from certain forms of slander.

Statements that are Potential 'Libels' by Statute

By section 4(1) of the Theatres Act 1968, the publication of defamatory words in the course of a theatrical performance amounts to a libel.

By section 166 of the Broadcasting Act 1990, publication of defamatory words, pictures, gestures, and other 'statements' broadcast on *radio or television* amounts to a libel.

Slanders that are Actionable without Proof of Damage

There are two surviving exceptions to the general rule that slander is actionable only on proof of special damage. Two other exceptions, one statutory and one arising at common law, were abolished by **section 14 of the Defamation Act 2013**.[14]

1. Imputation of a criminal offence punishable with imprisonment. This exception is recognized at common law.

---

[13] In *Monson v Tussauds* [1894] 1 QB 671, a defamatory waxwork image of the plaintiff (placed close to the famous 'Chamber of Horrors') was treated as a potential libel.

[14] These were imputations of unchastity of a woman or girl under Slander of Women Act 1891; and imputation of certain (generally contagious) diseases, at common law.

2. By section 2 of the Defamation Act 1952:

> In an action for slander in respect of words calculated to disparage the plaintiff in any office, profession, calling, trade or business held or carried on by him at the time of the publication, it shall not be necessary to allege or prove special damage, whether or not the words are spoken of the plaintiff in the way of his office, profession, calling, trade or business.

3.2 MALICIOUS FALSEHOOD

We outlined the tort of malicious falsehood in Chapter 2. It is very different from defamation in that it requires the claimant to show a **false statement**; **made with malice**; **and** (unless section 2 of the Defamation Act 1952 applies) **special damage**. This may make the action considerably less attractive to claimants than the actions in defamation, which universally presume falsehood and require no malice (unless to displace certain defences). But it remains significant that defamation is not the only route to protection of reputation—and, most particularly, of *trading* reputation.

4. ELEMENTS OF A CLAIM IN DEFAMATION

Unless the action is one in which special damage must be shown, at common law the claimant in a defamation action has needed to prove only the following:

> The defendant has published a statement; with defamatory meaning; referring to the claimant.

This states only three requirements. However, **section 1 of the Defamation Act 2013** (extracted at Section 4.2) makes two very significant additions, one general, the other specific to corporations trading for profit. This is one of the most important provisions of the Act: it sets the tone for other provisions, by establishing that a defamatory statement is actionable only if it is likely to cause **serious harm** to reputation. Second, in the case of a body trading for profit, this must take the form of **serious financial loss**. For other claimants, the likely harm may be to reputation pure and simple.

Here, we consider these four elements: defamatory meaning; 'serious harm' (in general, and in relation to bodies that trade for profit); publication; and reference to the claimant. Even if the claimant can show all of these elements, the defendant may nevertheless be able to establish one of the defences described in the following section. If the action is for a slander which is not actionable per se, then the claimant will also need to show that special damage was caused by the statement.

4.1 DEFAMATORY MEANING
A Basic 'Definition'

The basic definition of a 'defamatory' meaning is still derived from common law. Section 1 adds that statements with such a meaning are actionable only if 'serious harm' is likely.

Lord Atkin, *Sim v Stretch*
[1936] 2 All ER 1237

Judges and textbook writers alike have found difficulty in defining with precision the word "defamatory." The conventional phrase exposing the plaintiff to hatred, ridicule and contempt is probably too narrow. The question is complicated by having to consider the person or class of persons whose reaction to the publication is the test of the wrongful character of the words used. . . . I propose in the present case the test: *would the words tend to lower the plaintiff in the estimation of right-thinking members of society generally?* Assuming such to be the test of whether words are defamatory or not there is no dispute as to the relative functions of judge and jury, of law and fact. It is well settled that the judge must decide whether the words are capable of a defamatory meaning. That is a question of law: is there evidence of a tort? If they are capable, then the jury is to decide whether they are in fact defamatory.

[Emphasis added]

Lord Atkin's encapsulation is still the leading statement of 'defamatory meaning'. There is an objective element to the idea of defamatory meaning because it refers to *right-thinking members of society*. If the only people who would think ill of the claimant as a result of the statement are not 'right-thinking', then in principle there is no defamatory meaning, even if the opinion of such people is important to the claimant. Such a case was *Byrne v Dean* [1937] 1 KB 818. Here the claimant was a member of a golf club. Someone informed the police that there were gambling machines on club premises, and they were removed. An anonymous poem was pinned to the wall implying that the mystery informant was the claimant.

This, according to the majority of the Court of Appeal, could not be defamatory:

Slesser LJ, at 834

In no case as it seems to me can it be said that merely to say of a man that he has given information which will result in the ending of a criminal act is in itself defamatory where he is doing no more than reporting to the police that which if known by the police might well end in the discovery of an illegal act . . .

This 'objective' element has its limits, however. For example in *John v MGN* [1997] QB 586 it was considered defamatory to allege that the plaintiff was suffering from an eating disorder. Logically, 'right-thinking people' might be expected to meet such information with sympathy rather than criticism. The 'right-thinking' person, we might conclude, is taken to be morally upstanding, but not necessarily entirely rational.

The Defamatory Meaning

Statements are inherently ambiguous and few, if any, succeed in conveying the same meaning to all those who read, see or hear them. Even so, defamation generally requires that ultimately, a 'single meaning' is attached to the statement.[15] This is where the subtleties begin.

---

[15] The impact of this is modified in some respects by s 5(2) Defamation Act 2013 (and its predecessor): not every possible imputation need be true, providing additional (unproved) imputations do not seriously harm the claimant's reputation.

The claimant is required to specify a defamatory meaning which is conveyed as the 'natural and ordinary' meaning of the statement. It does not need to be shown that this is the meaning intended by the defendant. As was made clear in *Sim v Stretch* (above), provided the meaning is *capable of being conveyed by the statement*, then whether the meaning was in fact defamatory is a question of fact which has been a question for the jury. Equally, if the statement has a defamatory meaning, then a defendant who wishes to assert truth must ensure that the 'justification' offered is sufficient to deal with that defamatory meaning.[16] It is not good enough to show that the words are true on the face of them, if they are held to carry a different meaning which is defamatory of the claimant.[17]

'True' and 'False' Innuendo

Generally, with the exception of 'true' innuendo, both parties will propose the meaning that they consider to be the 'natural and ordinary' meaning of the words used. This is a rather misleading phrase. The 'natural and ordinary meaning' can often involve an element of 'reading between the lines'. This is referred to as an 'innuendo'. There are two sorts of innuendo. The 'false' innuendo is a matter of implication from the words themselves, and is an aspect of their ordinary meaning. The 'true' innuendo is a meaning available only to those who have knowledge of certain additional facts, outside the statement itself. We will consider each in turn.

False Innuendo

As Lord Devlin explained in *Lewis v Daily Telegraph*, the difference between literal meaning and false innuendo is a matter of degree.

Lewis v Daily Telegraph
[1964] AC 234, at 278

A derogatory implication may be so near the surface that it is hardly hidden at all or it may be more difficult to detect. If it is said of a man that he is a fornicator the statement cannot be enlarged by innuendo. If it is said of him that he was seen going into a brothel, the same meaning would probably be conveyed to nine men out of ten. But the lawyer might say that in the latter case a derogatory meaning was not a necessary one because a man might go to a brothel for an innocent purpose. An innuendo pleading that the words were understood to mean that he went there for an immoral purpose would not, therefore, be ridiculous. To be on the safe side, a pleader used an innuendo whenever the defamation was not absolutely explicit. That was very frequent, since scandalmongers are induced by the penalties for defamation to veil their meaning to some extent. Moreover, there were some pleaders who got to think that a statement of claim was somehow made more forceful by an innuendo, however plain the words. So rhetorical innuendoes were pleaded, such as to say of a man that he was a fornicator meant and was understood to mean that he was not fit to associate with his wife and family and was a man who ought to be shunned by all decent persons and so forth. Your Lordships were told, and I have no doubt it is true, that before 1949 it was very rare indeed to find a statement of claim in defamation without an innuendo paragraph.

[16] *Substantial* justification will generally be sufficient, as we will see.
[17] Subject to s 5(3) Defamation Act 2013.

An example of an alleged 'false innuendo' is *Sim v Stretch* (extracted earlier). The defendant Sim had sent a telegram to the plaintiff, concerning a housemaid named Edith, which was received at the village shop (and which was therefore 'published' to a third party). The telegram read:

Edith has resumed her service with us today. Please send her possessions and the money you borrowed also her wages to Old Barton.

Taking exception to this, the plaintiff argued:

By the said words the defendant meant and was understood to mean that the plaintiff was in pecuniary difficulties, that by reason thereof he had been compelled to borrow and had in fact borrowed from the said housemaid, that he had failed to pay the said housemaid her wages and that he was a person to whom no one ought to give any credit.

The House of Lords was doubtful whether the words could carry this meaning, but did not decide this point, since they concluded that even if the meaning was established, such a meaning was not capable of being defamatory. Right-thinking people would think nothing of borrowing from a servant. It was an almost daily occurrence, according to Lord Atkin. The point here is that the pleaded meaning is simply a matter of *implication from the words* used. It is a false innuendo.

If the words used are considered 'incapable' of the meaning alleged by the claimant, then the claim will fail. This was the case in *Lewis v Daily Telegraph* [1964] AC 234.

The defendant newspapers had published stories reporting (truthfully) that the City of London Fraud Squad was inquiring into the affairs of a company. Since the literal meaning of the story (existence of an investigation) was true, the plaintiff sought to argue that the articles suggested, by implication, that there was not only suspicion (this too could perhaps be justified), but also guilt.

Lord Devlin, *Lewis v Daily Telegraph*
[1964] AC 234, at 285–6

It is not … correct to say as a matter of law that a statement of suspicion imputes guilt. It can be said as a matter of practice that it very often does so, because although suspicion of guilt is something different from proof of guilt, it is the broad impression conveyed by the libel that has to be considered and not the meaning of each word under analysis. A man who wants to talk at large about smoke may have to pick his words very carefully if he wants to exclude the suggestion that there is also a fire; but it can be done. One always gets back to the fundamental question: what is the meaning that the words convey to the ordinary man: you cannot make a rule about that. They can convey a meaning of suspicion short of guilt; but loose talk about suspicion can very easily convey the impression that it is a suspicion that is well founded.

In the libel that the House has to consider there is, however, no mention of suspicion at all. What is said is simply that the plaintiff's affairs are being inquired into. That is defamatory, as is admitted, because a man's reputation may in fact be injured by such a statement even though it is quite consistent with innocence. I dare say that it would not be injured if everybody bore in mind, as they ought to, that no man is guilty until he is proved so, but unfortunately they do not. It can be defamatory without it being necessary to suggest that the words contained a hidden allegation that there were good grounds for inquiry. A statement that a woman has been raped can affect her reputation, although logically it means that she is innocent of any impurity: *Yousoupoff v. Metro-Goldwyn-Mayer Pictures Ltd* I(1934) 50 T.L.R. 581, C.A.]. So a statement that a man has been acquitted of a crime with which in fact he was never charged might lower his reputation. Logic is not the test. But a statement that an inquiry is on foot may go further and may positively convey the impression that there are grounds for the inquiry, that is, that there is something to suspect. Just as a bare statement of suspicion may convey the impression that there are grounds for belief in guilt, so a bare statement of the fact of an inquiry may convey the impression that there are grounds for suspicion. I do not say that in this case it does; but I think that the words in their context and in the circumstances of publication are capable of conveying that impression. But can they convey an impression of guilt? Let it be supposed, first, that a statement that there is an inquiry conveys an impression of suspicion; and, secondly, that a statement of suspicion conveys an impression of guilt. It does not follow from these two suppositions that a statement that there is an inquiry conveys an impression of guilt. For that, two fences have to be taken instead of one. While, as I have said, I am prepared to accept that the jury could take the first, I do not think that in a case like the present, where there is only the bare statement that a police inquiry is being made, it could take the second in the same stride. If the ordinary sensible man was capable of thinking that where ever there was a police inquiry there was guilt, it would be almost impossible to give accurate information about anything: but in my opinion he is not. I agree with the view of the Court of Appeal.

'True' Innuendo

In some cases, the defamatory meaning complained of can be understood *only* if certain additional facts—not mentioned in the statement—are known. If so, this is a case of 'true' innuendo. In such cases, the claimant must make clear the additional facts that are relevant when pleading the defamatory meaning. An example is *Tolley v Fry* [1931] AC 333. The defendants had advertised their 'Fry's Chocolate Creams' with a cartoon representing the plaintiff, a well-known amateur golfer, and a verse which referred to him by name. His likeness was being exploited in order to promote the goods of another, without permission and without reward, and the case is therefore often cited as an early example of 'appropriation of personality'. In this particular case however, the plaintiff was able to claim successfully in libel. The necessary additional fact providing the innuendo was that earning money from golf or from associated activities or sponsorship, including advertising, was inconsistent with his status as an amateur golfer. This case contains both 'false' and 'true' innuendo.

Viscount Hailsham, at 337

He did not complain of the caricature or the words as being defamatory in themselves; but the innuendo alleged that the "defendants meant, and were understood to mean, that the plaintiff had agreed or permitted his portrait to be exhibited for the purpose of the advertisement of the defendants' chocolate; that he had done so for gain and reward; that he had prostituted his reputation as an amateur golf player for advertising purposes, that he was seeking notoriety and gain by the means aforesaid; and that he had been guilty of conduct unworthy of his status as an amateur golfer."

In *Hough v London Express* [1940] 2 KB 507, it was made clear that in the case of a true innuendo, there is no need to show that any person who knows the relevant facts actually understands the article to be defamatory, or believes the defamatory meaning to be true.

4.2 SERIOUS HARM

Defamation Act 2013

Section 1. – Serious harm

1. A statement is not defamatory unless its publication has caused or is likely to cause serious harm to the reputation of the claimant.

2. For the purposes of this section, harm to the reputation of a body that trades for profit is not "serious harm" unless it has caused or is likely to cause the body serious financial loss.

Section 1 is a very important provision. During the legislative process, it seemed clear that its aim is to remove the temptation to bring 'trivial' claims in defamation, and that in this respect it built upon progress made by the courts themselves. As one would expect from such a core provision, it has quickly needed to be interpreted by the courts; and the question that has arisen is the extent to which the section departs from the position reached by common law immediately before enactment. The test in section 1(1) is whether there is likely to be serious harm to the *reputation* of the claimant; it seems clear that there is no need to show that tangible loss of income, for example, is likely to follow, and the section therefore does not contradict the law's position that reputation is an interest worthy of protection in its own right. It is still correct to say that it is actionable 'per se' (without proof of tangible loss). There is an equally significant additional requirement in section 1(2), which certainly adds to the requirements of the common law, namely that where a body that trades for profit is concerned, there will be 'serious harm' *only* if the statement is likely to cause 'serious financial loss.' Again, the provision requires only that the loss is *likely*.

Section 1(1)

Section 1(1) appears to continue the work of the courts in a number of its decisions concerning common law. So for example the 'Explanatory Notes' refer to the decisions in *Thornton v Telegraph Media Group Ltd* [2010] EWHC 1414, which suggested that a 'threshold of seriousness' must be passed before a statement can be actionable; and *Jameel v Dow Jones & Co* [2005] EWCA Civ 75, where the Court of Appeal ruled that there must be a 'real and substantial tort' before a claim in defamation can be brought. In the latter case, publication in the UK had been so limited that it would be an abuse of process to bring legal proceedings: the article had been published to only five people in England and Wales, and only two of these were truly independent of the claimant. After these decisions, the courts stated the position at common law with greater confidence: it was said that the advantage sought by the claimant from the action must be 'worth the candle' (*Jameel*) or, as Tugendhat J put it in *Euromoney Institutional Investor v Aviation News* [2013] EWHC

1505 (QB), 'worth the expenditure of costs and other resources that would be involved if the action were to proceed' ([143]).[18]

Since the commencement of section 1(1), the focus has changed, and the question has become whether section 1(1) requires the claimant to show on the balance of probabilities that serious harm to reputation has in fact been caused (or is likely to be caused). This would be a departure from the common law with far reaching effects. Rather than focusing merely on *seriousness* of the libel, avoiding trivial claims, this test would focus on *proof* that harm has or will occur. This has not previously been required at common law, and may prove problematic for reasons pointed out by Warby J in *Ames v Spamhaus Project Ltd* [2015] EWHC 127 (QB):

> **55** … there may be circumstances in which one would naturally expect to see tangible evidence that a statement had caused harm to reputation, but as practitioners in this field are well aware, it is generally impractical for a claimant to seek out witnesses to say that they read the words complained of and thought the worse of the claimant.

To date, the most significant decision to interpret section 1(1) is *Lachaux v Independent Print Ltd* [2015] EWHC 2242. At the time of going to press, a reserved judgment of the Court of Appeal in this case is awaited. For the time being however, the judgment of Warby J settles that section 1(1) does substitute 'a new and stiffer statutory test requiring consideration of actual harm' [para 50], which places a higher hurdle in the way of would-be claimants:

> **45** In my judgment … in enacting section 1(1) Parliament intended to do more than just raise the threshold for defamation from a tendency to cause "substantial" to "serious" reputational harm. The intention was that claimants should have to go beyond showing a tendency to harm reputation. It is now necessary to prove as a fact on the balance of probabilities that serious reputational harm has been caused by, or is likely to result in future from, the publication complained of.

This is, indeed, a significant change, and since it is also recommended by Warby J that the issues generally be tried as a preliminary issue, the change may—inadvertently no doubt—risk increasing the cost of libel actions in the courts. However, Warby J emphasized that in the case of a serious allegation, it may be possible to satisfy section 1(1) by inference:

> **57** Much that is said on the claimant's behalf on this aspect of the matter seems to me to be based on a false premise, namely that on this approach it will in all cases be necessary for a claimant to adduce evidence to prove that the publication complained of is defamatory of him or her. As recognised in *Cooke's case* [2015] 1 WLR 895 and *Ames's case* [2015] 1 WLR 3409, however, the serious harm requirement is capable of being satisfied by an inferential case, based on the gravity of the imputation and the extent and nature of its readership or audience. Suppose a well-known public figure complains of national media publication of a grave imputation, such as conspiracy to murder or serious sexual crime. They could hardly be required to call witnesses who read the words to say they thought the worse of the claimant

---

18 In *Euromoney*, the question was whether to allow amendment of the claim.

in order to establish a claim. In such a case the common law rules for the objective assessment of the meaning and defamatory tendency of words are plainly unaffected, as is the single meaning rule.

In other words, evidence of serious harm will not be required in *every* case of libel. It remains to be seen under what circumstances the gravity of the allegation will be sufficient to raise an inference of serious harm; but in *Lachaux* itself, the inference was drawn in relation to an individual who had only visited the UK a handful of times and was known only to a few hundred people. It has been suggested that the judgment is 'overall helpful to claimants where there has been substantial publication'.[19]

Section 1(2)

The provision in section 1(2) is important in its own right. The provision was not originally part of the Government's Defamation Bill, but was added to the Bill by the opposition and, eventually, accepted by the Government. The Explanatory Notes hint that the subsection merely states what would in any case be the position if applying the 'special damage' criterion to bodies trading for profit: such bodies, the Notes suggest, 'are in practice likely to have to show actual or likely financial loss' for the general test to be satisfied. However, it appears that the subsection achieves reform on an issue which has previously divided the judiciary; namely whether it is right to allow a trading corporation to bring an action in defamation for damage to reputation, in the absence of proof of any likely *financial* impact on the company itself. It is not necessarily the case that 'serious harm' would have been understood to require likely financial impact in the absence of section 1(2). This is illustrated by the discussion in *Jameel v Wall Street Journal* [2006] UKHL 44, where a majority of the House of Lords declined to follow the path preferred by Lord Hoffmann and Baroness Hale, namely to require a trading corporation to show 'special damage'. As Lord Hoffmann put it ([91]):

> ... a commercial company has no soul and its reputation is no more than a commercial asset, something attached to its trading name which brings in customers. I see no reason why the rule which requires proof of damage to commercial assets in other torts, such as malicious falsehood, should not also apply to defamation.

The majority in *Jameel* saw the matter differently. Lord Hope thought it unsatisfactory to single out trading companies for separate treatment compared to other bodies such as trade unions and charities. That however is the move now made by the legislation. Lord Hope also drew attention to the potentially 'incalculable' damage that can be done to corporate reputation. And indeed, the statutory provision does not take the route of requiring 'special damage' to be proved. Rather, it requires only that the statements are *likely* to cause damage. The relevant damage that is likely however must be 'serious' *financial* loss.

The first judicial consideration of section 1(2) came in *Brett Wilson LLP v Persons Unknown* [2015] EWHC 2628 (QB), a case which is also distinctive for an award of damages (in addition to injunctions) against unknown defendants—those responsible for running the 'solicitorsfromhell.com' website. Clearly, the purpose of an award that is highly

[19] H. Tomlinson and L. Skinner, '*Lachaux v Independent Print*—"Serious Harm" under the Defamation Act 2013 and the Drawing of Inferences' (2015) 26 Ent L R 294.

unlikely ever to be satisfied is vindicatory. As in *Lachaux*, Warby J held that the requirement of serious financial harm could also be satisfied by inference in a suitable case. The claimant alleged that it was inevitable that a number of prospective clients who read the website either had decided or would decide not to instruct the firm; and stated a belief that there had been a noticeable drop in conversion of enquiries to instruction in the past six months. No figures could be provided to establish the relevant damage; but these assertions were found, in the circumstances, to suffice.[20]

4.3 PUBLICATION

If the defamatory statement is made available to any party other than the subject of the defamation, then in principle it is 'published'. This requirement has been judged to be met even if it is made available to only one person, such as the person at the village shop who took the telegram in *Sim v Stretch*. In *Huth v Huth* [1915] 3 KB 32, there was held to have been no publication where a butler opened a letter addressed to the subject of the alleged libel, because he was not authorized to do so. This amounts to a remoteness rule. Foreseeability has been held to be the test for 'remoteness' in defamation, in respect of the consequences of publication and republication: *Slipper v BBC* [1991] 1 All ER 165. However, as we have seen, the development of a 'substantial harm' criterion—both at common law and in section 1—means that a defamation action is now likely to be struck out if publication is very limited. There was a change of emphasis even before the 2013 Act.

Modern forms of publication have global reach and given that English libel law has had some very tempting features for those shopping around for a forum,[21] it is important to note that the courts had begun, before the 2013 Act, to require substantial publication *in this jurisdiction*. On the other hand, it should be remembered that publication to one person may in some circumstances be expected to lead to much broader circulation, especially if that person is a journalist: this was the case in *Haji-Ioannou v Dixon* [2009] EWHC 178, where the claim was not struck out. In *Al-Amoudi v Brisard* [2006] EWHC 1062 (QB), Gray J held that publication on the internet does not give rise to any presumption that publication has been made to a substantial number of people: the burden is on the claimant to show that the statement complained of has actually been accessed and read.[22]

Reform of the Republication Rule

Particular controversy has surrounded the **republication rule**, particularly where this applies to the inclusion of previous news stories in a newspaper's internet archive. It is in the nature of such archives that items are transferred to them without alteration. In *Loutchansky v Times Newspapers (Nos 2–5)* [2002] QB 783, the Court of Appeal determined that there is a new publication of statements included in the archive on each occasion that the statement is accessed. This was an application of *Duke of Brunswick v Harmer* (1849) 14 QB 185, where the delivery of a copy of a newspaper 17 years after its first publication

[20] See further H. Tomlinson QC, 'Brett Wilson LLP v Persons Unknown, corporate damages and injunction against unknown operators of website' (2016) Ent L Rev 22.

[21] The defendant has the burden of showing truth and the level of available damages is high. The republication rule described below, but now controlled by s 8 Defamation Act 2013, has also had an impact.

[22] A defence based on lack of substantial publication was therefore not struck out: the defendants argued that the statement complained of, published on the internet, had only been downloaded in the UK by lawyers and associates of the claimant.

amounted to a new publication. It contrasts with the US 'single publication' rule, which was applied to websites in *Firth v State of New York NY Int 88* (2002). The impact was to deprive newspapers of the intended protection of the '*Reynolds* defence', though this defence has itself now been superseded by the clearer and simpler provisions in section 4 of the Defamation Act 2013. Nevertheless, because the Court of Appeal suggested that a notice could be attached to the material warning against treating it as the truth, and that this would be effective against libel actions, the European Court of Human Rights in *Times Newspapers v UK* [2009] EMLR 14 dismissed an application by Times Newspapers alleging that its Article 10 rights had been violated by the Court of Appeal's decision in *Loutchansky*. *The Times* alleged that the decision would have an inevitable 'chilling effect' on the availability of valuable archive material. The European Court of Human Rights noted that the applicants had, subsequent to the Court of Appeal's ruling, attached a notice to the relevant material within the archive:

"This article is subject to High Court libel litigation between [G.L.] and Times Newspapers. It should not be reproduced or relied on without reference to Times Newspapers Legal Department."

The court agreed that the approach to internet archives involved an issue which engaged Article 10. But it went on to conclude that the interference with freedom of expression imposed through the libel action was proportionate to the legitimate goal of protecting the reputation of GL: the domestic courts' ruling was a 'justified and proportionate' restriction on the applicant's freedom of expression.

The republication rule has now been controlled—and its effect reversed—by section 8 of the Defamation Act 2013, thus exceeding the protection of speech required by the ECHR. Whether the Court of Appeal was correct in its supposition that the notice would afford the required protection will not be relevant in future. But at the same time, it is reasonable to ask whether it is better that an internet archive now need not warn readers that questions have been raised about the truth of statements made in the archived reports: this is the consequence of the legislation.

Defamation Act 2013

8 Single publication rule

(1) This section applies if a person—

   (a) publishes a statement to the public ("the first publication"), and

   (b) subsequently publishes (whether or not to the public) that statement or a statement which is substantially the same.

(2) In subsection (1) "publication to the public" includes publication to a section of the public.

(3) For the purposes of section 4A of the Limitation Act 1980 (time limit for actions for defamation etc) any cause of action against the person for defamation in respect of the subsequent publication is to be treated as having accrued on the date of the first publication.

(4) This section does not apply in relation to the subsequent publication if the manner of that publication is materially different from the manner of the first publication.

(5) In determining whether the manner of a subsequent publication is materially different from the manner of the first publication, the matters to which the court may have regard include (amongst other matters)—

    (a) the level of prominence that a statement is given;

    (b) the extent of the subsequent publication.

(6) Where this section applies—

    (a) it does not affect the court's discretion under section 32A of the Limitation Act 1980 (discretionary exclusion of time limit for actions for defamation etc), and

    (b) the reference in subsection (1)(a) of that section to the operation of section 4A of that Act is a reference to the operation of section 4A together with this section.

Section 4A of the Limitation 1980, which is referred to in the section above, sets the limitation period for actions in defamation at one year from publication, although this is subject to the court's discretion to allow a later claim under section 32A (a discretion which is rarely exercised).[23] The effect of section 8 therefore is to attack the single publication rule indirectly, rather than through a conceptual change in what counts as a 'publication'. A subsequent publication will not be able to give rise to a new cause of action if it falls outside the limitation period running from the first publication, unless of course the court exercises its discretion to extend the period. Courts will doubtless have regard to the purpose of the statute in deciding whether to extend the period or not. However, there are still potential exceptions. In particular, if the *manner* of republication is different, then the limitation period may begin afresh: in effect, this will be treated as a new publication. Thus the section continues to strike a balance, and does not permit an extensive publication to masquerade as equivalent to a very limited earlier one.

Repetition

Another important feature of the English approach to publication is the **repetition rule.** Subject to comments concerning secondary parties below, any person who is involved in the dissemination of statements can be said to be 'publishing' those statements even if they do not explicitly adopt the statement as correct, and will therefore be vulnerable to an action in defamation. There is no need to show that the defendant is the *originator of* the statement, in the sense of being the first to make it. To repeat a rumour, even while disowning it, is capable of amounting to a libel or slander. The impact of this rule has now been considerably softened where allegations on a matter of **public interest are neutrally reported without adoption.** This was achieved initially at common law (*Al-Faqih v HH Saudi Research and Marketing (UK) Ltd* [2001] EWCA Civ 1634; *Charman v Orion* [2007] EWCA Civ 972); but has once again been more securely set out by the 2013 Act, section 4(3) (Section 5, Defences).

Protection of Secondary Parties

'Secondary' parties (printers, newsagents, and so on) were, at common law, open to defamation actions even where they had not failed to exercise due care. There was heated

---

[23] For limitation periods in general, see Chapter 7.

debate about the extent to which they were protected by a defence of 'innocent dissemination', particularly in the Court of Appeal in *Goldsmith v Sperrings* [1977] 1 WLR 478, but by section 1 of the Defamation Act 1996, a new statutory defence was introduced for those who play a secondary role in publication of defamatory material, provided they take appropriate care. Before this defence has any part to play, however, the defendant needs to be a 'publisher' of the statement in the first place, and this requires some active part to be played—as we will see. Now, by **section 10 of the Defamation Act 2013**, there is additional protection to secondary publishers, but this is a supplement to the existing statutory protection and does not replace it. These provisions are explored in relation to Defences, below.

4.4 REFERENCE TO THE CLAIMANT

A statement need not mention the claimant by name in order to be understood as referring to him or her. Reference to the claimant can also occur by implication. This implication may, as with meaning, depend on knowledge of special facts, provided *some* people are aware of those facts. Such people may make up a relatively small group. In *Hough v London Express* [1940] 2 KB 507, the plaintiff was the wife of a boxer (Frank Hough). The defendant newspaper published an article describing the words of an entirely different woman, who was described as his wife. The defamatory meaning depended on knowledge that the plaintiff lived with Frank Hough as his wife. This additional fact *not only* supplied the defamatory meaning (that she lived as his wife, but was not), but was also needed in order to establish that the words referred, by implication, to the plaintiff.

Reference to the claimant may be entirely accidental. At common law, this was no defence. Now, sections 1 and 4 of the Defamation Act 1996 provide potential defences for some (but not all) defendants involved in a publication who had no grounds for believing that the statement was defamatory of the claimant. These provisions are further explored under Defences.

Can a statement made about a *group* of people be defamatory of any member of that group? The answer is that it can, and that there really are no special rules of thumb which apply in 'group defamation' cases. The overriding question, as in any case of defamation where a person is not explicitly named, is whether the statement 'pointed to' or would be taken to refer to the individual (*Knupffer v London Express Newspapers* [1944] 1 AC 116; *Riches v Mirror Group Newspapers* [1986] QB 256).

5. DEFENCES

5.1 THE MEANING OF 'MALICE'

The defence of qualified privilege is defeated on proof of 'malice'. For cases applying the law as it stood before the Defamation Act 2013, the same is true of the defence of 'fair comment'.[24] It is therefore useful to have in mind the leading statement of 'malice' in this context, which derives from a case on qualified privilege. There has been some debate

---

[24] Under the 2013 Act, the relevant defence is 'honest opinion', and malice plays no part: the key question is whether the opinion is honestly held (see Section 5.3).

whether malice has the same meaning in fair comment, but that question will now lose its significance after the 2013 reforms.

Lord Diplock, *Horrocks v Lowe*
[1975] AC 135, at 149–50

... in all cases of qualified privilege there is some special reason of public policy why the law accords immunity from suit—the existence of some public or private duty, whether legal or moral, on the part of the maker of the defamatory statement which justifies his communicating it or of some interest of his own which he is entitled to protect by doing so. If he uses the occasion for some other reason he loses the protection of the privilege. So, the motive with which the defendant on a privileged occasion made a statement defamatory of the plaintiff becomes crucial. The protection might, however, be illusory if the onus lay on him to prove that he was actuated solely by a sense of the relevant duty or a desire to protect the relevant interest. So he is entitled to be protected by the privilege unless some other dominant and improper motive on his part is proved. "Express malice" is the term of art descriptive of such a motive. Broadly speaking, it means malice in the popular sense of a desire to injure the person who is defamed and this is generally the motive which the plaintiff sets out to prove. But to destroy the privilege the desire to injure must be the dominant motive for the defamatory publication; knowledge that it will have that effect is not enough if the defendant is nevertheless acting in accordance with a sense of duty or in bona fide protection of his own legitimate interests.

The motive with which a person published defamatory matter can only be inferred from what he did or said or knew. If it be proved that he did not believe that what he published was true this is generally conclusive evidence of express malice, for no sense of duty or desire to protect his own legitimate interests can justify a man in telling deliberate and injurious falsehoods about another, save in the exceptional case where a person may be under a duty to pass on, without endorsing, defamatory reports made by some other person.

According to Lord Diplock, 'malice' is concerned either with knowing publication of falsehood; or (in the alternative) with desire to injure the claimant provided this is the dominant motive for the publication. Either form will do.

5.2 TRUTH (PREVIOUSLY JUSTIFICATION)

The actions in defamation are designed to penalize falsehood, and true accusations are treated as lowering reputation only to its rightful level. If the truth of the defamatory meaning can be established, then the motive of the defendant in publishing the statement is entirely irrelevant. This was true at common law, and continues to be the case now under the newly stated defence of 'truth'. This principle of defamation law though long-cherished could be questioned once reputation is defined as within Article 8: why should the 'balance' always lie on the side of publication, in the case of trivial but damaging truths? That question dominates the law of privacy, but the structure of defamation law seems to offer no place for it.

The statutory defence of truth now *replaces* the common law defence of 'justification'. However, the Explanatory Notes published with the statute explain (at para 16) that the section 'is intended broadly to reflect the current law while simplifying and clarifying certain elements'. Equally, para 18 explains that '[i]n cases where uncertainty arises the current case law would constitute a helpful but not binding guide to interpreting how the new statutory defence should be applied'. It is plain that the new provision is not regarded as constituting an entirely fresh start.

Defamation Act 2013

2. — Truth

(1) It is a defence to an action for defamation for the defendant to show that the imputation conveyed by the statement complained of is substantially true.

(2) Subsection (3) applies in an action for defamation if the statement complained of conveys two or more distinct imputations.

(3) If one or more of the imputations is not shown to be substantially true, the defence under this section does not fail if, having regard to the imputations which are shown to be substantially true, the imputations which are not shown to be substantially true do not seriously harm the claimant's reputation.

(4) The common law defence of justification is abolished and, accordingly, section 5 of the Defamation Act 1952 (justification) is repealed.

To benefit from the defence of truth, the defendant need not have known nor cared whether the allegation was true, and (with one exception) may even have acted out of spite toward the claimant. The exception arises under section 8 of the Rehabilitation of Offenders Act 1974: where a person has a 'spent' conviction for an offence, and where the alleged defamation is a statement referring to the claimant's guilt in respect of that offence, the defence of truth will be lost if 'malice' is proved.[25]

On the other hand, the very fact that truth is merely a defence, and that falsehood plays no part in the *definition* of a defamatory statement, complicates this simple picture. The burden of establishing truth continues to fall on the defendant rather than the claimant.

Truth and Defamatory Meaning

We have already seen that the claimant must set out the defamatory meaning of the words complained of. In doing this, the claimant is able to gain an element of control over litigation. Although the defendant is free to choose which defamatory meaning he or she will seek to show to be true, nevertheless this must be sufficient to remove the 'sting' of the allegation. At common law, it was said that 'the justification must be as wide as the charge'.[26]

25 Subsections 16(1)–(3).

26 Since the Court of Appeal's decision in *Lucas-Box v News Group Newspapers Ltd* [1986] 1 WLR 147, defendants have been required to set out precisely what meaning they intend to justify; just as the meaning contended for by the claimant must be *capable of being conveyed* by the statement, so also must the meaning argued (and justified) by the defendant pass the same test.

According to section 2(1) of the Defamation Act 2013, the *imputation conveyed* must be shown to be 'substantially true'. The test of 'substantial truth' (or previously, justification) was itself developed at common law, but is now clearly a part of the statutory definition of the defence.

Further help is at hand for defendants in the form of section 2(3) of the Defamation Act 2013, which replaces section 5 of the Defamation Act 1952. The essential point of section 5, and of the new subsection, was simple:

Lord Denning, *Moore v News of the World Ltd*
[1972] 1 QB 441, at 448

... a defendant is not to fail simply because he cannot prove every single thing in the statement to be true.

Section 2(3) applies where there is more than one defamatory imputation, just as section 5 did before it. Before section 5 was applied, the court had to decide that the defamatory allegations in question were 'distinct'—which was taken to mean, that they do not have a 'common sting'. The new subsection does not use the word 'distinct'. Nevertheless, it does operate where there is more than one 'imputation'; and it seems this will be taken to have much the same meaning as the idea of distinct allegations. Indeed, the Explanatory Notes make plain that this is the intention: the new provisions 'are intended to have the same effect as those in s 5 of the 1952 Act' (para 17).

Assuming that the approach under the new provision will be the same, if the allegations *do* have a '**common sting**', the situation is both simpler, and much more beneficial to defendants: they may justify any of the allegations, using evidence drawn from any source including other parts of the same publication. These cases do not require the protection of section 2(3) and do not fall within it.

If the allegations are **distinct**, then section 2(3) comes into play. This section provides that a defendant who can justify only one of the allegations may still argue that the remaining charge is insignificant—that is to say, that it does not materially injure the claimant's reputation once the truth of the justified charge is taken into account. Alternatively, damages may be paid in respect of the remaining charge. Given that one allegation has been justified, these damages (depending of course on the nature of the two allegations) may be relatively moderate.

5.3   HONEST OPINION (PREVIOUSLY FAIR COMMENT)

Section 3 of the Defamation Act 2013 replaces the common law defence of 'fair comment', with a defence named 'honest opinion'. Earlier, in *Joseph v Spiller* [2010] UKSC 53, the Supreme Court had suggested that the existing defence be renamed 'honest comment'. The statutory provision is a more decisive move in the same direction, and clearly settles some debated aspects of the law. It does not include the common law requirement that the opinion must relate to a matter of 'public interest', though this requirement had in any case been exceedingly readily fulfilled; nor does it depend upon 'malice'.

Defamation Act 2013

3. — Honest opinion

(1) It is a defence to an action for defamation for the defendant to show that the following conditions are met.

(2) The first condition is that the statement complained of was a statement of opinion.

(3) The second condition is that the statement complained of indicated, whether in general or specific terms, the basis of the opinion.

(4) The third condition is that an honest person could have held the opinion on the basis of—

(a) any fact which existed at the time the statement complained of was published;

(b) anything asserted to be a fact in a privileged statement published before the statement complained of.

(5) The defence is defeated if the claimant shows that the defendant did not hold the opinion.

(6) Subsection (5) does not apply in a case where the statement complained of was published by the defendant but made by another person ("the author"); and in such a case the defence is defeated if the claimant shows that the defendant knew or ought to have known that the author did not hold the opinion.

In addition, section 3(7) defines 'privileged statements' by reference to other statutory provisions; while section 3(8) abolishes the common law defence of fair comment and, accordingly, section 6 of the Defamation Act 1952.

The protection offered to opinion or comment has been an important defence at common law and many judicial (and other) statements have supported its existence in a robust and general form. In *Slim v Daily Telegraph* [1968] 2 QB 157, Lord Denning captured the protective judicial approach towards statements of opinion as follows:

… the right of fair comment is one of the essential elements which go to make up our freedom of speech. We must ever retain this right intact. It must not be whittled down by legal refinements.

It has not been possible to keep the defence entirely clear of legal refinements. Principally, this is because it is necessary to distinguish a comment or opinion from a statement of fact (a point on which common law will continue to be authoritative notwithstanding the change in terminology); and because there are some limits beyond which the defence will not operate.

Why give Special Protection to Comment?

The particularly strong protection offered to comment, as opposed to fact, can be explained through two linked ideas.

1. Free Expression of Opinions is Essential to Debate, and Free and Lively Debate is Essential to Democracy and the Emergence of Truth

There is clearly some judicial support for this approach:

Scott LJ, *Lyon v Daily Telegraph*
[1943] KB 746, at 752

The reason why, once a plea of fair comment is established, there is no libel, is that it is in the public interest to have a free discussion of matters of public interest.

Similarly, the following statement was quoted with approval by Lord Nicholls, in *Albert Cheng v Tse Wai Chun Paul* [2000] 4 HKC 1, at 14:[27]

J. G. Fleming, *The Law of Torts* (9th edn, NSW: Law Book Company, 1998), 648

… untrammelled discussion of public affairs and of those participating in them is a basic safeguard against irresponsible political power. The unfettered preservation of the right of fair comment is, therefore, one of the foundations supporting our standards of personal liberty.

2. Misguided Comment or Opinion is Less Dangerous than Inaccurate Statements of Fact

The theory adopted by common law appears to be that people in general will not be misled by what is evidently mere opinion. There is therefore less *need* to penalize comment than fact: it is less dangerous both to reputation, and to truth, because the reader is 'free' to assess the opinions offered (and will not be unduly influenced by them). This presumes a fairly robust and healthy level of public debate and fits well with the broadly instrumental, 'democratic' justifications for freedom of speech identified at the start of this chapter. That being so, it is no surprise to see this approach reflected in Lord Nicholls' brief remarks on the subject in *Reynolds*:

Lord Nicholls, *Reynolds v Times Newspapers Ltd*
[2001] 2 AC 127, at 201

… [r]eaders and viewers may make up their own minds on whether they agree or disagree with defamatory statements which are recognisable as comment and which, expressly or impliedly, indicate in general terms the facts on which they are based.

Applying these two justifications for the defence, one would expect its boundaries to be set by reference to *the impact of the publication upon the reader*, rather than by judging fairness in the light of the defendant's intentions. But there has been an element of inconsistency in the case law, which the new statutory provision may help to resolve.

[27] Lord Nicholls was sitting in this case as a member of the Hong Kong Court of Final Appeal.

The Ingredients of Honest Opinion

1. No Public Interest Criterion

At common law, comment had to be on a matter of 'public interest'. However, the classic exposition of 'public interest' in the particular context of 'fair comment', to be found in the case of *London Artists v Littler* [1969] 2 QB 375, ensured that most issues except those which can be described as genuinely 'private' would fall within the definition of 'public interest' for the fair comment defence. In *London Artists* itself, the subject of the comment was the running of a West End play. The removal of the 'public interest' criterion might therefore be seen as chiefly a clarification.

2. The 'Opinion' Must Be Genuine Opinion as Opposed to Imputation of Fact

Section 3(2) (extracted earlier) sets out the first 'condition' for protection, namely that the statement must be a statement of opinion. This is intended to 'reflect the current law'.[28] In judging whether a statement is opinion or fact the *form* in which it is expressed is not decisive. An assertion that a work of art is 'rubbish' takes the form of a fact, but clearly expresses an opinion. As with defamatory meaning, the question is how the words complained of would be *understood*; and the Explanatory Notes suggest that 'the assessment is on the basis of how the ordinary person would understand it'. In *Yeo v Times Newspapers Ltd* [2014] EWHC 2853 (QB); [2015] 1 WLR 971, applying the common law rather than the statutory test, it was emphasized that the 'subject matter and context of the words may be an important indicator of whether they are fact or opinion' ([88]). In this case, which involved criticism of the conduct of a Parliamentary Select Committee chairman, it was also said that the political context of the speech meant that it was more likely that an ordinary reader would understand the words as stating opinion rather than fact. Defences of justification, *Reynolds* privilege, and honest comment, all succeeded in this case.

3. Indication of the Factual Basis for the Opinion

Section 3(3) provides that the comment must implicitly or explicitly indicate—whether in general or specific terms—the 'basis' of the opinion (which is to say, the facts upon which it is based). This reflects the common law, most particularly as it was clarified by the decision of the Supreme Court in *Joseph v Spiller* [2010] UKSC 53; [2011] 1 AC 852: courts should not seek too specific an indication of the facts which form the basis for the opinion stated.

Lord Phillips PSC, *Joseph v Spiller*
[2010] UKSC 53; [2011] 1 AC 852

98 ... There is no case in which a defence of fair comment has failed on the ground that the comment did not identify the subject matter on which it was based with sufficient particularity to enable the reader to form his own view as to its validity. For these reasons, where adverse comment is made generally or generically on matters that are in the public domain I do not consider that it is a prerequisite of the defence of fair comment that the readers should be in a position to evaluate the comment for themselves.

...

101 There are a number of reasons why the subject matter of the comment must be identified by the comment, at least in general terms. The underlying justification for the creation of the fair comment exception was the desirability that a person should be entitled to express his view freely about a matter of public interest. That remains a justification for the defence, albeit that the concept of public interest has been greatly widened. If the subject matter of the comment is not apparent from the comment this justification for the defence will be lacking. The defamatory comment will be wholly unfocused.

102 It is a requirement of the defence that it should be based on facts that are true. This requirement is better enforced if the comment has to identify, at least in general terms, the matters on which it is based. The same is true of the requirement that the defendant's comment should be honestly founded on facts that are true.

103 More fundamentally, even if it is not practicable to require that those reading criticism should be able to evaluate the criticism, it may be thought desirable that the commentator should be required to identify at least the general nature of the facts that have led him to make the criticism. If he states that a barrister is "a disgrace to his profession" he should make it clear whether this is because he does not deal honestly with the court, or does not read his papers thoroughly, or refuses to accept legally aided work, or is constantly late for court, or wears dirty collars and bands.

104 Such considerations are, I believe, what Mr Caldecott had in mind when submitting that a defendant's comments must have identified the subject matter of his criticism if he is to be able to advance a defence of fair comment. If so, it is a submission that I would endorse. I do not consider that Lord Nicholls[29] was correct to require that the comment must identify the matters on which it is based with sufficient particularity to enable the reader to judge for himself whether it was well founded. The comment must, however, identify at least in general terms what it is that has led the commentator to make the comment, so that the reader can understand what the comment is about and the commentator can, if challenged, explain by giving particulars of the subject matter of his comment why he expressed the views that he did. A fair balance must be struck between allowing a critic the freedom to express himself as he will and requiring him to identify to his readers why it is that he is making the criticism.

The Supreme Court's conclusion in *Joseph v Spiller* was accepted and adopted by the legislature in framing section 3(3). It is worth noting that, long before the decision in *Joseph v Spiller*, it was clear that if the facts on which the comment is based are *generally known to the public*, then the defendant need not set them out explicitly in the publication. Rather, such facts must be sufficiently 'indicated'. The following leading case remains significant in interpreting the law.

Kemsley v Foot [1952] AC 345

The defendant had published an article attacking the conduct of a newspaper, under the title 'Lower than Kemsley'. There was no other reference in the article to Kemsley, who was proprietor of an entirely separate newspaper. Kemsley brought an action in libel on the basis that the article, through its title, attacked his reputation. The House of Lords decided

[29] Lord Phillips is referring here to one aspect of the judgment of Lord Nicholls in *Cheng v Tse Wai Chun Paul* (2000) 10 BHRC 525.

that a sufficient 'substratum of fact' was present in the statement made. The *fact* referred to by implication was that Kemsley was responsible for the press of which he was proprietor. This was well known, and did not have to be spelt out explicitly. The *criticism* was that the Kemsley press was 'low'. This might be fact or comment, but in any case it was not (as the plaintiffs contended) pure comment made without reference to relevant facts. The defence could therefore go before the jury.

The next important question was whether the defendant needs to show the *truth* of all facts used as the basis of the comment. Here, the House of Lords in *Kemsley* provided defendants with significant leeway.

Lord Porter, *Kemsley v Foot*
[1952] AC 345, at 357–8

... As I hold, any facts sufficient to justify [the] statement would entitle the defendants to succeed in a plea of fair comment. Twenty facts might be given in the particulars and only one justified, yet if that one fact were sufficient to support the comment so as to make it fair, a failure to prove the other nineteen would not of necessity defeat the defendants' plea. The defendant only needs to prove a sufficiently solid foundation for the comment.

4. Could an Honest Person Have Held the Opinion?

Section 3(4) requires that an 'honest person' could have held the opinion *either* (a) 'on the basis of facts that existed at the time the statement complained of was published'; *or* (b) on the basis of anything asserted as a fact in a privileged statement published before the statement complained of.

It is plain that the hallmark of 'honest opinion' is not the reasonableness of the opinion, but the possibility that **an honest person might hold it**. There is a degree of objectivity therefore (the standard relates to what view an honest person could take). However, the standard will protect a wider range of statements than a 'reasonableness' criterion would achieve, since opinions which are not 'reasonable' may nevertheless be honestly held. Nevertheless, an honest person must have some basis on which to form an opinion. The statute sets out the basis on which such an honest opinion might be formed. The first limb, (a), refers to 'facts that existed' at the time of the statement. It may be assumed that this will apply only to *true* facts since they could not otherwise be said to 'exist'; and that reflects the prior common law. On the other hand, it would appear that it does not now matter whether or not the maker of the statement was *aware of* the facts, since what matters is whether an honest person *could* form the opinion on the basis of those facts.

The second limb, (b), applies to facts asserted in privileged statements.

5. Did the Defendant Honestly Hold the Opinion?

Section 3(5) provides that the defence of honest opinion will be defeated if the claimant shows 'that the defendant did not hold the opinion'. It is in this way that the statute avoids the concept of 'malice' altogether: publishing an opinion that is not genuinely held is the replacement idea, avoiding the need to consider the difficult question of *motive*.

Before the 2013 Act, the notion of honesty had been distanced from the notion of fairness or reasonableness. Notable is the following statement of Lord Porter.

Lord Porter, *Turner v MGM*
[1950] 1 All ER 449

To a similar effect were the words of LORD ESHER, M.R. (20 Q.B.D. 281), in *Merivale v. Carson* which are so often quoted:

" … would any fair man, however prejudiced he may be, however exaggerated or obstinate his views, have [written] this criticism… ?"

I should adopt them except that I would substitute "honest" for "fair" lest some suggestion of reasonableness instead of honesty should be read in.

The intention was to enhance the protection offered by the defence. What though of those who publish the opinions of others? The 2013 Act deals with this through a separate subsection, section 3(6): if the defendant publishes a statement of opinion made by another, the test is whether the defendant *knew or ought to have known'* that the *author* did not hold the opinion. In other words, a publisher of someone else's statements is protected unless there is reason to think the statement-maker was not honest. This is a new and simpler way of approaching an old problem. Previously, the House of Lords in *Telnikoff v Matusevitch* [1992] 2 AC 343 had dealt with the issue by applying an objective test to the published comment: could an honest person have held the views expressed? Now, a reasonableness test is applied to the defendant in relation to the publication of another's views.

6. From 'Malice' to Honesty

At the start of this section on defences, we outlined the general test for 'express malice', derived from *Horrocks v Lowe*. *Horrocks v Lowe* itself concerned qualified privilege, but it was often assumed that the test would be the same in fair comment. In *Cheng v Tse Wai Chun* [2000] 4 HKC 1,[30] Lord Nicholls proposed that malice may operate quite differently in the two defences. His approach in that case may be seen as the background to the new statutory approach, in which 'malice' does not feature at all. His analysis may therefore also offer some clues as to how the new provisions will operate. In particular, while intent to injure, ill will, or spite, will certainly suffice to lose the protection of qualified privilege, Lord Nicholls doubted whether this should be the case in 'fair comment' (as it was then called). In particular, 'intent to injure' is not inconsistent with the *purpose* for which the defence of fair comment exists, since many (if not most) contributors to the debate have an ulterior motive of some kind.

---

[30] This decision is binding in Hong Kong law, but not in English law. An extract is set out here because Lord Nicholls' assessment of the case law is drawn from the English authorities; because Lord Nicholls was the chief architect of the *Reynolds* privilege which also sidestepped issues of malice; and because it has been referred to in numerous subsequent decisions in England, as well as in the Explanatory Notes to the 2013 Act.

Lord Nicholls, *Cheng v Tse Wai Chun*
[2000] 4 HKC 1

The purpose and importance of the defence of fair comment are inconsistent with its scope being restricted to comments made for particular reasons or particular purposes, some being regarded as proper, others not. Especially in the social and political fields, those who make public comments usually have some objective of their own in mind, even if it is only to publicise and advance themselves. They often have what may be described as an 'ulterior' object. Frequently their object is apparent, but not always so. They may hope to achieve some result, such as promoting one cause or defeating another, elevating one person or denigrating another. In making their comments they do not act dispassionately, they do not intend merely to convey information. They have other motives.

The presence of these motives, and this is of crucial importance for present purposes, is not a reason for excluding the defence of fair comment. The existence of motives such as these when expressing an opinion does not mean that the defence of fair comment is being misused. It would make no sense, for instance, if a motive relating to the very feature which causes the matter to be one of public interest were regarded as defeating the defence. On the contrary, this defence is intended to protect and promote comments such as these. Liberty to make such comments, genuinely held, on matters of public interest lies at the heart of the defence of fair comment. That is the very object for which the defence exists. Commentators, of all shades of opinion, are entitled to 'have their own agenda'. Politicians, social reformers, busybodies, those with political or other ambitions and those with none, all can grind their axes. The defence of fair comment envisages that everyone is at liberty to conduct social and political campaigns by expressing his own views, subject always, and I repeat the refrain, to the objective safeguards which mark the limits of the defence.

...

Spiteful comments

One particular motive calls for special mention: spite or ill-will. This raises a difficult point. I confess that my first, instinctive reaction was that the defence of fair comment should not be capable of being used to protect a comment made with the intent of injuring another out of spite, even if the person who made the comment genuinely believed in the truth of what he said. Personal spite, after all, is four square within the popular meaning of malice....

On reflection I do not think the law should attempt to ring-fence comments made with the sole or dominant motive of causing injury out of spite or, which may come to much the same, causing injury simply for the sake of doing so. In the first place it seems to me that the postulate on which this problem is based is a little unreal. The postulate poses a problem which is more academic than practical. The postulate is that the comment in question falls within the objective limits of the defence. Thus, the comment is one which is based on fact; it is made in circumstances where those to whom the comment is addressed can form their own view on whether or not the comment was sound; and the comment is one which can be held by an honest person. This postulate supposes, further, that the maker of the comment genuinely believes in the truth of his comment. It must be questionable whether comments, made out of spite and causing injury, are at all likely to satisfy each and every of these requirements. There must be a query over whether, in practice, there is a problem here which calls for attention....

The final paragraph depends on 'honest belief' being part of the test for fairness. That is, broadly, how the law has now been settled.

5.4 PUBLICATION ON A MATTER OF PUBLIC INTEREST

Defamation Act 2013

---

4. Publication on matter of public interest

(1) It is a defence to an action for defamation for the defendant to show that—

(a) the statement complained of was, or formed part of, a statement on a matter of public interest; and

(b) the defendant reasonably believed that publishing the statement complained of was in the public interest.

(2) Subject to subsections (3) and (4), in determining whether the defendant has shown the matters mentioned in subsection (1), the court must have regard to all the circumstances of the case.

(3) If the statement complained of was, or formed part of, an accurate and impartial account of a dispute to which the claimant was a party, the court must in determining whether it was reasonable for the defendant to believe that publishing the statement was in the public interest disregard any omission of the defendant to take steps to verify the truth of the imputation conveyed by it.

(4) In determining whether it was reasonable for the defendant to believe that publishing the statement complained of was in the public interest, the court must make such allowance for editorial judgement as it considers appropriate.

(5) For the avoidance of doubt, the defence under this section may be relied upon irrespective of whether the statement complained of is a statement of fact or a statement of opinion.

(6) The common law defence known as the Reynolds defence is abolished.

Section 4 states a new defence of publication on a matter of public interest. The defence will succeed provided the subject matter of the publication is a public interest matter, and the publisher 'reasonably believed' that publication was in the public interest whether the allegation was true or false. The defence has its origins in common law and particularly in the innovative decision of the House of Lords in *Reynolds v Times Newspapers* [2001] 2 AC 127. Some consideration of its history is essential to understanding the provision itself, not least because the courts are required to 'make such allowance for editorial discretion' as they think appropriate. The development of the defence remains in the hands of the courts.

The House of Lords described the defence it had created in *Reynolds* as a form of 'privilege'; and attempted to define it in line with existing common law privileges requiring a 'duty' to convey information, and a corresponding 'interest' in receiving that information.[31] It was pointed out by critics that the resemblance was weak, and that it was a poor form of privilege which offered protection only once all the circumstances had been weighed: traditionally, a

---

[31] *Adam v Ward* [1917] AC 309.

'privilege' provides the maker of a statement with certainty that it is safe to do so, on a particular occasion. The legislation improves on the common law position by reclassifying the defence as, simply, protecting publication that is in the public interest, thus removing the difficult connection to privilege. The components of the defence are also somewhat simplified and clarified. The *Reynolds* defence has, therefore, broken free from the sources from which it developed. The exercise in judicial development of the law has at the same time been vindicated: plainly here judicial activism has been accepted by the legislature, which has stepped in to complete its achievements. Legislation has been needed to achieve a degree of simplification where the courts had not, at least so far, been able to reach agreement on the radical nature of the decision.[32]

In order to understand the legislative provision (section 4), we should consider its precursor in *Reynolds*.

Reynolds v Times Newspapers Ltd [2001] 2 AC 127

Lord Nicholls identified the subject matter of the claim at 191:

> Mr Reynolds pleaded that the sting of the article was that he had deliberately and dishonestly misled the Dáil on Tuesday, 15 November 1994 by suppressing vital information. Further, that he had deliberately and dishonestly misled his coalition cabinet colleagues, especially Mr Spring, the Tánaiste (deputy prime minister) and minister for foreign affairs, by withholding this information and had lied to them about when the information had come into his possession.

The material differences between English and Irish editions of the newspaper and the version of the story carried by each played a part in the newspaper's failure to persuade the House of Lords that it should benefit from a qualified privilege in this case.

The Context of *Reynolds*: Political Speech

The newspaper advanced a case that English law should *recognize and protect a general category of 'political speech'*, subject to proof of malice. This suggestion was explicitly related to the historic decision of the US Supreme Court in *Sullivan v New York Times* 376 US 254 (1964). *Sullivan*, and its invocation of the 'chilling effect', had been relied on some years earlier by the House of Lords when it determined, in *Derbyshire v Times Newspapers* [1993] AC 534, that an elected entity such as a local authority would be unable to sue for defamation. With the HRA on the verge of commencement, the defendants sought to extend this invocation of *Sullivan* to achieve more general protection for political speech. As we have seen, the statutory language now adopted is more general, referring to 'public interest'; and the position in this jurisdiction is very different from that adopted in the US.

In *Sullivan*, the US Supreme Court recognized that 'political speech' must be protected against the threat of defamation actions. The case was brought by an elected official who argued that he was accused in an advertisement (by implication, since he was not named in the publication) of violent intimidation of civil rights protesters. The Supreme Court held

[32] In *Jameel v Wall Street Journal* (below), Lord Hoffmann and Baroness Hale suggested that the *Reynolds* defence be simply recognized as a public interest defence; but the courts as a whole had not been ready for this move.

that in the absence of a relevant state of mind on the part of the defendants, this publication could not be the subject of libel proceedings.

The relevant state of mind which would take the publication outside the protection of the *Sullivan* defence was similar to 'malice', as that expression is used in *Horrocks v Lowe*. It would not be essential (although it would be sufficient) to show actual spite or ill will. Rather, intentional deceit (knowing publication of lies), or reckless disregard for truth, would suffice. Unusually, this state of mind would have to be shown with 'convincing clarity', and not simply on the balance of probabilities.[33] In effect, this amounted to a 'qualified privilege' for political speech, and this is what was contended for by the newspaper's lawyers in *Reynolds*.

Rejecting the newspaper's argument, the House of Lords pointed out that the idea of 'political speech' was inherently difficult to define and that it could lead to overly narrow protection.[34] The privilege that was recognized in *Reynolds* was in one sense broader, in that it could arise in respect of any matter of *public interest*. However, in other respects it was much narrower and more uncertain than the rule argued for by the defendants. The House of Lords did not offer unqualified protection to all public interest publications, subject to malice. Instead, a more modest but still controversial adaptation of the common law was undertaken, developing the duty-interest version of the qualified privilege defence so that it would cover certain publications made to the world at large. A new and very different sort of 'duty-interest' privilege was recognized, in which the relevant interest is explicitly the *public* interest in receiving information irrespective of its truth or falsity. Now, through legislation, the link with privilege has been broken: it can be seen as merely a stage in the development of the public interest defence.

The *Reynolds* privilege left many important decisions over proper journalistic conduct to the courts and, unlike *Sullivan*, it (effectively) focused on the *conduct* of the defendant. This was a relatively novel departure for defamation law, which was not typically concerned with negligence-type standards.

Lord Nicholls, *Reynolds v Times Newspapers*
[2001] 2 AC 127

… At 204–5
Conclusion

My conclusion is that the established common law approach to misstatements of fact remains essentially sound. The common law should not develop "political information" as a new "subject matter" category of qualified privilege, whereby the publication of all such information would attract qualified privilege, whatever the circumstances. That would not provide adequate protection for reputation. Moreover, it would be unsound in principle to distinguish political discussion from discussion of other matters of serious public concern. The elasticity of the common law principle enables interference with freedom of speech to be confined to what is necessary in the circumstances of the case. This elasticity enables

[33] Loveland points out that the majority of the Supreme Court will not have trusted the Alabama courts with the 'balance of probabilities' test in such cases: I. Loveland, *Political Libels* (Hart Publishing, 2000).

[34] In the United States, the boundaries of the *Sullivan* privilege have been elastic and it has been interpreted as including actions brought by 'public', not just 'political' figures.

the court to give appropriate weight, in today's conditions, to the importance of freedom of expression by the media on all matters of public concern.

Depending on the circumstances, the matters to be taken into account include the following. The comments are illustrative only. 1. The seriousness of the allegation. The more serious the charge, the more the public is misinformed and the individual harmed, if the allegation is not true. 2. The nature of the information, and the extent to which the subject matter is a matter of public concern. 3. The source of the information. Some informants have no direct knowledge of the events. Some have their own axes to grind, or are being paid for their stories. 4. The steps taken to verify the information. 5. The status of the information. The allegation may have already been the subject of an investigation which commands respect. 6. The urgency of the matter. News is often a perishable commodity. 7. Whether comment was sought from the plaintiff. He may have information others do not possess or have not disclosed. An approach to the plaintiff will not always be necessary. 8. Whether the article contained the gist of the plaintiff's side of the story. 9. The tone of the article. A newspaper can raise queries or call for an investigation. It need not adopt allegations as statements of fact. 10. The circumstances of the publication, including the timing.

This list is not exhaustive. The weight to be given to these and any other relevant factors will vary from case to case. Any disputes of primary fact will be a matter for the jury, if there is one. The decision on whether, having regard to the admitted or proved facts, the publication was subject to qualified privilege is a matter for the judge. This is the established practice and seems sound. A balancing operation is better carried out by a judge in a reasoned judgment than by a jury. Over time, a valuable corpus of case law will be built up.

Broadly, the newspaper was entitled to publish unproven allegations where there is a *duty* to do so, and a corresponding public *right to know* the information. The most significant, and most obvious criticism levelled at *Reynolds* is that this test would do little to foster an editor's 'confidence' in publishing any given story. Later courts attempted to grapple with this problem; and section 4 continues their work.

Jameel v Wall Street Journal [2006] UKHL 44; [2007] 1 AC 359

The message conveyed by the majority of judges in this case is that the spirit of *Reynolds* was to enhance the protection of responsible journalism. The ten factors offered by Lord Nicholls were indicative; and the relationship with common law privilege not to be taken too seriously. No list of factors appears in the statutory provision.

The *Wall Street Journal* reported that the Saudi authorities were cooperating with the United States in the investigation of terrorism, and that the accounts of a number of Saudi companies had been frozen in order to pursue this goal. Some of those companies were named in the article, and it was claimed that the articles were thereby defamatory of the claimants. The first instance judge and the Court of Appeal accepted that the subject matter of the report was of sufficiently weighty public interest to come within the ambit of the *Reynolds* privilege, but concluded that it was not essential to the proper reporting of this story that individuals should be named. This being the case, the naming of the claimants' company could *not* be covered by the privilege. The House of Lords disagreed, and expressed a variety of strong views on the need to protect **responsible journalism**.

Lord Bingham and Lord Hope took the most traditional view, proposing that a reciprocity between 'duty' and 'interest' remained essential to the operation of the privilege. Lord

Scott thought that the *Reynolds* privilege had involved 'moulding' of previous common law authorities, and expressed full agreement with Lord Hoffmann. Lord Hoffmann and Baroness Hale were ready to drop the reference to a 'privilege', and admit that *Reynolds* really created a new public interest defence—precisely the step now taken by the legislature. Lord Hoffmann and Baroness Hale were critical of the way that lower courts were failing to recognize the revolutionary spirit of *Reynolds*. It was a **different jurisprudential creature** than common law qualified privilege (Baroness Hale, at [146]).

Lord Hoffmann, *Jameel v Wall Street Journal* [2016] UKHL 44

46 Although Lord Nicholls uses the word 'privilege' it is clearly not being used in the old sense. It is the material which is privileged, not the occasion on which it is being published. There is no question of the privilege being defeated by proof of malice because the propriety of the conduct of the defendant is built into the conditions under which the material is privileged....

56 In *Reynolds*, Lord Nicholls gave his well-known non-exhaustive list of ten matters which should in suitable cases be taken into account. They are not tests which the publication has to pass. In the hands of a judge hostile to the spirit of *Reynolds*, they can become ten hurdles at any of which the defence may fail. That is how Eady J treated them. The defence, he said, can be sustained only after 'the closest and most rigorous scrutiny' by the application of what he called 'Lord Nicholls' ten tests'. But that, in my opinion, is not what Lord Nicholls meant....

The European Court of Human Rights dismissed an application against the UK by the *Wall Street Journal*, the defendants in the action brought by Jameel: *Wall Street Journal Europe SPRL v UK* (2009) 48 EHRR SE19. Although the first instance judge had held against the claimants could not be said to be 'victims' for the purposes of an action under the Convention.[35] Nor could the presumption of falsity, which was retained by the House of Lords for corporations by a majority in *Jameel*, be said to violate Article 10 in and of itself. It is recognized that when applying *Reynolds*—and by necessary implication its statutory successor—regard must be had not only to Article 10, but also to the potential for Article 8 to be engaged. In *Yeo v Times Newspapers Ltd* [2014] EWHC 2853 (QB), Warby J concluded that Article 8 was not engaged, since the allegedly defamatory comments involved did not touch on the 'private and family life' of the claimant, only on his public, political role. Thus, the emphasis was appropriately on protection of Article 10.

Flood v Times Newspapers [2012] UKSC 11

Reversing a decision of the Court of Appeal, the Supreme Court in this case decided that a publication containing allegations of corruption on the part of C, a serving police officer, were protected by *Reynolds* privilege. The decision to print the story and to name the officer concerned were decisions that could be made by 'responsible journalists'. Lords Mance and Dyson particularly emphasized that decision-making by editors and journalists merits respect and should be given weight.

---

[35] Article 35(3) and (4) ECHR.

Lord Mance, *Flood v Times Newspapers*
[2012] UKSC 11

137 The courts … give weight to the judgment of journalists and editors not merely as to the nature and degree of the steps to be taken before publishing material, but also as to the content of the material to be published in the public interest. The courts must have the last word in setting the boundaries of what can properly be regarded as acceptable journalism, but within those boundaries the judgment of responsible journalists and editors merits respect. This is, in my view, of importance in the present case.

A draft Defamation Bill was before Parliament at the time of the decision in *Flood*. Illustrating the reciprocal influence of courts and legislature in reforming this area, the remarks in *Flood* are now directly reflected in section 4(4) Defamation Act. In *Pinard-Byrne v Linton* [2015] UKPC 41; [2016] EMLR 4, the Privy Council reaffirmed that a responsible editor will take steps to investigate or 'verify' the truth of the allegations being made. For the *Reynolds* defence to succeed:

38 … There must be a public interest in the publication of the details of the allegations of crime or professional misconduct and there must be verification because the need for verification provides real protection for the individual concerned …

Section 4

We extracted section 4 at the start of this section. It not only simplifies and recategorizes the law, but also makes reasonable belief on the part of the publisher the decisive factor. Respect for editorial judgment is expressly part of the judgment as to reasonableness. It therefore makes a clean break from any link to privilege, and from any idea that Lord Nicholls might have been setting out a 'checklist' of considerations to be fulfilled in every case. It also makes no reference to 'malice', which ordinarily is decisive in depriving a defendant of a defence of qualified privilege, but again this does no more than formalize the common law position. Now, such matters will be relevant only to the extent that they affect the 'reasonableness' of the belief that publication is in the public interest. The language of 'responsible journalism' is avoided, and indeed the *Reynolds* defence itself did not only benefit newspapers: for example it was applied to the publication of a book in the case of *Charman v Orion* [2007] EWCA Civ 972.

Reportage

A particular line of authority developed before the 2013 Act under the auspices of the *Reynolds* privilege establishing that where the 'public interest' in publication derived not from the *content* of an allegation, but from the fact that it had been made, then one of Lord Nicholls' ten factors—whether the defendant had taken steps to verify the allegation—would be inapplicable (*Roberts v Gable* [2008] QB 502). This 'reportage' category did not include reports which adopted the allegations as *true* (as in *Galloway v Telegraph Group* [2006] EWCA Civ 17, where the allegations were embraced 'with relish and fervour' and were also embellished). The approach to reportage in these cases has been adopted in section 4(3) of the Defamation Act 2013, extracted earlier in this section.

5.5 INNOCENT DEFAMATION; DISTRIBUTORS AND INTERMEDIARIES

Innocent Defamation

'Innocence' in respect of a defamatory statement was no defence at common law. The Defamation Act 1996 introduced two defences of use to those who are not at fault in the publication of a defamatory statement. The first, in section 1, benefits only those who are not in the position of 'author, editor, or publisher' of a statement, and requires reasonable care to be taken. 'Publisher' for these purposes is a narrower category than the class of people 'publishing' a statement at common law (see *Bunt v Tilley*, later in this section), and is defined in the section itself. This section is intended to assist those with a 'secondary' role in the publication.

Defamation Act 1996

1 Responsibility for publication

(1) In defamation proceedings a person has a defence if he shows that—

  (a) he was not the author, editor or publisher of the statement complained of,

  (b) he took reasonable care in relation to its publication, and

  (c) he did not know, and had no reason to believe, that what he did caused or contributed to the publication of a defamatory statement.

(2) For this purpose "author", "editor" and "publisher" have the following meanings, which are further explained in subsection (3)—

  "author" means the originator of the statement, but does not include a person who did not intend that his statement be published at all;

  "editor" means a person having editorial or equivalent responsibility for the content of the statement or the decision to publish it; and

  "publisher" means a commercial publisher, that is, a person whose business is issuing material to the public, or a section of the public, who issues material containing the statement in the course of that business.

(3) A person shall not be considered the author, editor or publisher of a statement if he is only involved—

  (a) in printing, producing, distributing or selling printed material containing the statement;

  (b) in processing, making copies of, distributing, exhibiting or selling a film or sound recording (as defined in Part I of the Copyright, Designs and Patents Act 1988) containing the statement;

  (c) in processing, making copies of, distributing or selling any electronic medium in or on which the statement is recorded, or in operating or providing any equipment, system or service by means of which the statement is retrieved, copied, distributed or made available in electronic form;

  (d) as the broadcaster of a live programme containing the statement in circumstances in which he has no effective control over the maker of the statement;

  (e) as the operator of or provider of access to a communications system by means of which the statement is transmitted, or made available, by a person over whom he has no effective control.

Section 1 only benefits those who have no reason to believe that the publication is defamatory and who take reasonable care. Once put on notice that the publication contains defamatory material, the protection of section 1 ceases to operate (section 1(1)(c)).

The Defamation Act 2013 has added further protection for 'secondary' publishers, as they might loosely be called. Section 10 applies to the same categories of publisher as the provision just extracted:

Defamation Act 2013

10. Action against a person who was not the author, editor etc

(1) A court does not have jurisdiction to hear and determine an action for defamation brought against a person who was not the author, editor or publisher of the statement complained of unless the court is satisfied that it is not reasonably practicable for an action to be brought against the author, editor or publisher.

(2) In this section *"author", "editor"* and *"publisher"* have the same meaning as in section 1 of the Defamation Act 1996.

This relatively simple provision only protects secondary publishers if it happens not to be reasonably practicable to proceed against the author, editor or (primary) publisher; this is aimed at removing the temptation to proceed against 'soft targets' in the distribution process and thus to contribute to the chilling effect; but its protection is naturally contingent on circumstance.

Section 5 is a more complex provision.

5. Operators of websites

(1) This section applies where an action for defamation is brought against the operator of a website in respect of a statement posted on the website.

(2) It is a defence for the operator to show that it was not the operator who posted the statement on the website.

(3) The defence is defeated if the claimant shows that—

(a) it was not possible for the claimant to identify the person who posted the statement,

(b) the claimant gave the operator a notice of complaint in relation to the statement, and

(c) the operator failed to respond to the notice of complaint in accordance with any provision contained in regulations.

(4) For the purposes of subsection (3)(a), it is possible for a claimant to "identify" a person only if the claimant has sufficient information to bring proceedings against the person.

(5) Regulations may—

(a) make provision as to the action required to be taken by an operator of a website in response to a notice of complaint (which may in particular include action relating to the identity or contact details of the person who posted the statement and action relating to its removal);

(b) make provision specifying a time limit for the taking of any such action;

(c) make provision conferring on the court a discretion to treat action taken after the expiry of a time limit as having been taken before the expiry;

(d) make any other provision for the purposes of this section.

(6) Subject to any provision made by virtue of subsection (7), a notice of complaint is a notice which—

(a) specifies the complainant's name,

(b) sets out the statement concerned and explains why it is defamatory of the complainant,

(c) specifies where on the website the statement was posted, and

(d) contains such other information as may be specified in regulations.

(7) Regulations may make provision about the circumstances in which a notice which is not a notice of complaint is to be treated as a notice of complaint for the purposes of this section or any provision made under it.

(8) Regulations under this section—

(a) may make different provision for different circumstances;

(b) are to be made by statutory instrument.

…

(10) In this section "regulations" means regulations made by the Secretary of State.

(11) The defence under this section is defeated if the claimant shows that the operator of the website has acted with malice in relation to the posting of the statement concerned.

(12) The defence under this section is not defeated by reason only of the fact that the operator of the website moderates the statements posted on it by others.

Plainly, the section aims to offer appropriate protection to the operators of websites, who may well fulfil the definition of a 'publisher' at common law. That definition is not altered, instead, new provisions are introduced specifically to deal with the distinctive issues that may arise.[36] Regulations have been issued to clarify the process required of both complainants and website operators in relation to potentially defamatory material posted on websites;[37] these are accompanied by Guidance.[38] The pre-Act law illustrates the difficulties, and also shows how the courts had attempted to achieve appropriate solutions from case to case.

Godfrey v Demon Internet [2001] QB 201

Demon Internet was an Internet Service Provider (ISP), providing subscribers with access to (amongst other things) bulletin boards. The claimant put Demon on notice of a defamatory statement posted on the board, and requested its removal. Demon did not remove the posting. Morland J held that the ISP had 'published' the statement:

… every time one of the defendants' customers accesses [the bulletin] and sees that posting defamatory of the plaintiff there is a publication to that customer.

[36] For an enquiry into the issues, see S. Hedley, 'The Internet: Making a Difference?', in D. Capper, *Modern Defamation Law: Balancing Reputation and Free Expression* (QUB, 2012)

[37] The Defamation (Operators of Websites) Regulations 2013 (SI 2013 No 3028).

[38] MoJ, *Complaints about defamatory material posted on websites: Guidance on Section 5 of the Defamation Act 2013 and Regulations* (January 2014).

Having been put on notice, Demon could not benefit from the protection of section 1 of the Defamation Act 1996. An operator in the position of Demon could now benefit from the protection of section 10 or section 5 of the Defamation Act 2013, if it was practicable to bring an action against other appropriate parties (section 10) or if those parties were identifiable (section 5).

Bunt v Tilley [2006] EWHC 407

This case also concerned an ISP, but the case was crucially different from *Godfrey*. First, the defendants appear to have played a much more passive role in publication. Therefore, they did not satisfy the *threshold* test of having 'published a defamatory statement' which, quite independently of section 1 of the Defamation Act 1996, is a prerequisite of a successful action in defamation. Second, no adequate steps were taken by the claimant to put them on notice of the defamatory contents for the purposes of section 1 of the Defamation Act 1996. And third, the defendants were protected by the Electronic Commerce (EC Directive) Regulations 2002, regulation 13. As a result, there was no liability on the part of the ISPs.

For present purposes, it is particularly important to notice the first of these distinctions. There is no need to bring into play the section 1 defence if the defendant has not passed the threshold test of 'publishing' the defamatory statement as a matter of common law. 'Publication' for these purposes requires some element of knowledge. There is of course no need to know that the statement *is defamatory* (this is the very point of section 1). But the defendant should at least intend a publication:

Eady J, *Bunt v Tilley*
[2006] EWHC 407 (QB)

22 I have little doubt . . . that to impose legal responsibility upon anyone under the common law for the publication of words it is essential to demonstrate a degree of awareness or at least an assumption of general responsibility, such as has long been recognised in the context of editorial responsibility. As Lord Morris commented in *McLeod v St. Aubyn* [1899] AC 549, 562:22:

"A printer and publisher intends to publish, and so intending cannot plead as a justification that he did not know the contents. The appellant in this case never intended to publish."

In that case the relevant publication consisted in handing over an unread copy of a newspaper for return the following day. It was held that there was no sufficient degree of awareness or intention to impose legal responsibility for that 'publication'.

While not concluding that there was any error of analysis in this case, the Court of Appeal in *Tamiz v Google* (below) has nevertheless set some limits to the degree to which the idea of 'publication' can be used to prevent liability on the part of operators of other types of website.

In *Metropolitian International Schools Ltd v Designtechnica Corp, Google UK Ltd, Google Inc* [2009] EWHC 1765, [2009] EMLR 27, Eady J ruled that an internet search engine provider is not to be regarded as 'publishing' the material which is located by an internet search, including 'snippets' which appear in response to the search. Google, in this case, merely facilitated the discovery of potentially defamatory material by making automatic search in response to search terms entered by internet users. Even once notification of libellous material is given, the search results cannot be 'taken down': the search engine can only respond by blocking particular URLs or web addresses. The defendant in this instance could not be fixed with liability for the period after which it had been notified because it was, during this period, attempting to block the web addresses in question. Its position was therefore different from the position of internet service providers who fail to respond to complaints and remove defamatory material of which they have been notified (as in *Godfrey v Demon Internet*, above).

Tamiz v Google Inc [2013] EWCA Civ 68

Without suggesting that these decisions were incorrect, the Court of Appeal differed from Eady J (the judge below) in relation to whether Google could be described as the 'publisher' of certain statements posted on its 'Blogger' service. While the defendant was not considered to be a publisher of those statements before the claimant's complaint, it was arguable that it could be said to have become a secondary publisher of the material during the period (which in this instance was five weeks) between notification, and removal of the material. In this instance, the 'Blogger' site would be treated as akin to an 'enormous bulletin board' provided by the defendant—the posts on that board were not akin to 'graffiti' left on the defendant's wall. The case was not so similar to *Bunt v Tilley* as to call for similar conclusions. It was also arguable that the protection of section 1 of the Defamation Act 1996 would in any event be lost, because the defendant may have had cause to believe that defamatory allegations had been made (section 1(1)(c)).

Nevertheless, the Court of Appeal found a different route to striking out the action. Given the relatively short period of time during which the posts were available after the defendants received the complaint, there would not be held to have been a 'real and substantial tort'. The comments would have 'receded into history' and any damage to the claimant's reputation would be 'trivial': 'the game would not be worth the candle'. As already explained, this test has now been subsumed for future cases into the 'serious harm' test in section 1(1).

Offers to Make Amends

Any defendant may respond to an action in defamation by 'offering to make amends'. The appropriate contents of such an offer, and its implications, are explained in sections 2 to 4 of the Defamation Act 1996. As stated by Lord Judge LCJ in *KC v MGN Ltd (Costs)* [2013] EWCA Civ 3: 'The objective, to the advantage of both sides, is vindication without litigation.' 'Amends' for these purposes must include a suitable apology and correction, together with appropriate damages. Damages should be agreed. If an offer to make amends is accepted, but no agreement is reached as to damages, then damages will be assessed by a court on broadly the same basis as in defamation generally. However, the offer to make amends will be taken into account and a suitable discount applied.[39] The only *defence* to flow from these

[39] *Nail v News Group Newspapers* [2005] 1 All ER 1040.

provisions is provided by section 4 of the Defamation Act 1996. By this section, it will be a defence to an action in defamation to show that an offer to make amends has been made, provided the defendant had no grounds for believing that the statement made was defamatory of the claimant.

Defamation Act 1996

4 Failure to accept offer to make amends

...

(2) The fact that the offer was made is a defence (subject to subsection (3)) to defamation proceedings in respect of the publication in question by that party against the person making the offer....

(3) There is no such defence if the person by whom the offer was made knew or had reason to believe that the statement complained of—

(a) referred to the aggrieved party or was likely to be understood as referring to him, and

(b) was both false and defamatory of that party;

but it shall be presumed unless the contrary is shown that he did not know and had no reason to believe that was the case.

(4) The person who made the offer need not rely on it by way of defence, but if he does he may not rely on any other defence.

On the face of it, section 4(3) is similar to section 1 and appears to be concerned with failure to exercise due care in publication. But in *Milne v Express Newspapers* [2005] 1 WLR 772, the Court of Appeal made clear that this is not the correct interpretation. Rather, by subsection (3) the defence is lost only if there is a state of mind akin to malice under *Horrocks v Lowe*. If the defendant makes a publication *knowing or having reason to believe* that the statement is false and defamatory, then this is equivalent to knowledge of falsity, or recklessness as to truth, as required by malice. The required state of mind for section 4 is therefore quite different from due care under section 1.

5.6 PRIVILEGE

Some statements are recognized to be so important that they ought to be made with full confidence that they are beyond the reach of an action in defamation. In other words, these statements are to be protected *regardless of truth or falsity*. Such statements are protected by privilege.

Absolute and Qualified Privilege

There are two levels of privilege in English law. Statements that attract 'absolute privilege' cannot be the subject of proceedings in defamation no matter what the motive of the speaker. Statements that attract 'qualified privilege' can only be the subject of proceedings in defamation if it can be shown that they were made with 'express malice'.

Absolute Privilege

In some situations, being able to speak freely is of such public importance (or, in the case of judicial proceedings, potentially defamatory statements are so unavoidable a part of the procedure), that no action in defamation is possible, no matter what the motive of the speaker. Key examples of 'absolute privilege' are statements in Parliament; statements made in the course of judicial proceedings; and fair and accurate reports of judicial proceedings (Defamation Act 1996, section 14; amended by section 7 of the Defamation Act 2013).

Qualified Privilege

Statutory qualified privilege: section 15 of the Defamation Act 1996 specifies that the reports and other statements mentioned in Schedule 1 to the Act are protected by qualified privilege. The Schedule is lengthy and may be directly consulted by those who are curious to see these listed. Some additions are made by Defamation Act 2013, section 7. More notable however is the separate section 6.

Defamation Act 2013

6. Peer-reviewed statement in scientific or academic journal etc

(1) The publication of a statement in a scientific or academic journal (whether published in electronic form or otherwise) is privileged if the following conditions are met.

(2) The first condition is that the statement relates to a scientific or academic matter.

(3) The second condition is that before the statement was published in the journal an independent review of the statement's scientific or academic merit was carried out by—

(a) the editor of the journal, and

(b) one or more persons with expertise in the scientific or academic matter concerned.

(4) Where the publication of a statement in a scientific or academic journal is privileged by virtue of subsection (1), the publication in the same journal of any assessment of the statement's scientific or academic merit is also privileged if—

(a) the assessment was written by one or more of the persons who carried out the independent review of the statement; and

(b) the assessment was written in the course of that review.

(5) Where the publication of a statement or assessment is privileged by virtue of this section, the publication of a fair and accurate copy of, extract from or summary of the statement or assessment is also privileged.

(6) A publication is not privileged by virtue of this section if it is shown to be made with malice . . . .

This section creates an entirely new qualified privilege, and does not mirror any judicial developments. Rather, it reflects the concerns of lobbyists, particularly 'Sense about Science', though it is not confined to scientific publications. The concerns that gave rise to the reform were affected by litigation brought by the British Chiropractic Association against a science writer, Simon Singh.[40] Though ultimately unsuccessful, the litigation underlined the vulnerability of *individual* writers on scientific matters, since the claimants had chosen not to proceed against the Guardian newspaper in which the article was published. Oddly perhaps, the new section would not have protected the writer in that case, since it applies only to peer reviewed statements in certain journals.

Qualified privilege at common law: the leading statement of qualified privilege at common law, outside the area defined by *Reynolds v Times Newspapers*, is the following:

Lord Atkinson, *Adam v Ward*
[1917] AC 309

A privileged occasion is … an occasion where the person who makes a communication has an interest or a duty, legal, social, or moral, to make it to the person to whom it is made, and the person to whom it is so made has a corresponding interest or duty to receive it. This reciprocity is essential.

Leaving aside the many variations of common law privilege and concentrating on this short but widely accepted statement of principle, we can see that Lord Atkinson emphasizes *both sides* of a relationship. The *giver of the statement* must be under a duty, which may be legal, social, or moral, to make the statement to the relevant person (and not more widely). The person who receives it must have a corresponding *interest or duty* in receiving it. Lord Atkinson goes so far as to underline that *the reciprocity is essential*. With this in mind, it is clear that the form of privilege recognized in *Reynolds v Times Newspapers* is a striking departure for common law. Section 4 of the Defamation Act 2013, as we have seen, breaks the link between the defence derived from *Reynolds* (now, the public interest defence), and qualified privilege, thus clarifying the nature of *Reynolds*.

6. JURISDICTION

Section 9 of the Defamation Act 2013 limits the jurisdiction of the courts of England and Wales to hear defamation claims. The provision is directly aimed at curtailing 'libel tourism', which is to say the bringing of actions in English courts where neither the publication, nor the defendant, is strongly linked to the jurisdiction. This phenomenon had been encouraged by the pro-claimant features of English libel law. For reasons of EU and international law however, the impact of the section is limited by the need to exclude actions against persons domiciled in a range of jurisdictions. The restrictions apply even where the claimant is domiciled in England and Wales.

9. Action against a person not domiciled in the UK or a Member State etc

(1) This section applies to an action for defamation against a person who is not domiciled—

   (a) in the United Kingdom;

(b) in another Member State; or

(c) in a state which is for the time being a contracting party to the Lugano Convention.

(2) A court does not have jurisdiction to hear and determine an action to which this section applies unless the court is satisfied that, of all the places in which the statement complained of has been published, England and Wales is clearly the most appropriate place in which to bring an action in respect of the statement.

Note that England and Wales must be *clearly* the most appropriate place for the action. It is apparently not enough for it to be one appropriate forum amongst others.

7. PARTIES WHO CANNOT SUE IN DEFAMATION

In *Derbyshire v Times Newspapers* [1993] AC 534, the House of Lords accepted that open criticism of a directly elected body such as a local authority was so important that such a body should not be entitled to bring an action in defamation. The case incorporated a relatively early recognition of the 'chilling effect' in English courts. The prohibition in *Derbyshire* did not extend to individual politicians. Equally, the local authority retained the right to bring an action in malicious falsehood where, as we have seen, the rules strike a different balance between claimant and defendant, requiring falsehood, actual damage, and inappropriate motive to be established by the claimant.

Lord Keith, at 547–8

There are ... features of a local authority which may be regarded as distinguishing it from other types of corporation, whether trading or non-trading. The most important of these features is that it is a governmental body. Further, it is a democratically elected body, the electoral process nowadays being conducted almost exclusively on party political lines. It is of the highest public importance that a democratically elected governmental body, or indeed any governmental body, should be open to uninhibited public criticism. The threat of a civil action for defamation must inevitably have an inhibiting effect on freedom of speech. ... What has been described as "the chilling effect" induced by the threat of civil actions for libel is very important. Quite often the facts which would justify a defamatory publication are known to be true, but admissible evidence capable of proving those facts is not available. This may prevent the publication of matters which it is very desirable to make public.

Lord Keith in this case (decided before the HRA was enacted) expressed the view that English law had had no need for the assistance of the European Convention in protecting freedom of expression.

In *Goldsmith v Bhoyrul* [1998] QB 459, the principle against local authorities suing in defamation was extended to cover *political parties* standing for election. So far, however, this is as far as the restriction has developed. Certainly, an *individual* seeking election may sue for defamation. In *Culnane v Morris and Naidu* [2005] EWHC 2438, an election candidate for the British National Party brought an action in defamation arising from statements in an election leaflet circulated on behalf of the Liberal Democrat candidate. Eady J had to interpret section 10 of the Defamation Act 1952, which provides:

10 Limitation on privilege at elections

A defamatory statement published by or on behalf of a candidate in any election to a local government authority or to Parliament shall not be deemed to be published on a privileged occasion on the ground that it is material to a question in issue in the election …

In *Plummer v Charman* [1962] 1 WLR 1469, the Court of Appeal had concluded from this section that the *only* defences available where statements are made in an election campaign were justification (now truth) and fair comment (now honest opinion)—in other words, and despite the title to the section, that *no* privilege could attach to them. Eady J used the author-ity of the HRA to depart from this interpretation and to understand the words as provid-ing that no *special or additional* privilege attaches to election material because of its status. Therefore, the defendant could attempt an argument that the statements made were within the protection of qualified privilege.

8. REMEDIES

Superficially at least, libel damages appear very generous, given that the injury suffered by the claimant is typically intangible and in some instances no quantified loss is established at all. Such damage is to some extent 'presumed' on the claimant's behalf; although the operation of this principle is altered by section 1 of the Defamation Act 2013 and particu-larly by the requirement that bodies trading for profit must be likely to suffer serious finan-cial harm, for a statement to be actionable by them.

There are significant contrasts between the calculation of defamation damages and of damages in cases of personal injury. As we saw in Chapter 8, awards in respect of non-pecuniary loss in personal injury cases are 'conventional', and all parties are able to ascer-tain in advance what a 'typical' award for a given injury is likely to be. Defamation awards are not (or have not been until recently) subject to convention in the same way. They are also typically 'at large'. They were generally assessed by the jury, though juries are no longer likely to appear in many—if any—defamation actions (section 11).

In a series of cases through the 1990s, the Court of Appeal took action to restrain the level of damages awarded in defamation cases. The tactics of interpretation employed by the Court of Appeal were controversial, but in any event the consequence was that juries were given considerably more guidance than was previously the case. As with many other provisions of the 2013 Act, section 11 may be loosely seen as a continuation of the work of the judiciary.

In *John v MGN* [1997] QB 587, at the culmination of this judicial reform process, Sir Thomas Bingham MR explained that before the Court of Appeal took action, the jury had been 'in the position of sheep loosed on an unfenced common, with no shepherd' (at 608). They lacked guidance, and not unexpectedly had no instinctive sense of where to pitch their award. The stages in the Court of Appeal's campaign against this state of affairs were as follows.

1. In *Sutcliffe v Pressdram* [1991] 1 QB 153, the Court of Appeal resolved that the jury had clearly not understood the value of money when it made its award of £600,000 to the wife of a convicted murderer. *Private Eye* magazine had suggested that she benefited from her husband's crimes by selling her story to a newspaper. In future, juries should

have more guidance on the real value of the sums awarded. However, the Court of Appeal had no choice but to remit the case for a new trial.

2. By the time of *Rantzen v MGN* [1994] QB 670, the Court of Appeal had acquired a new power under section 8 of the Courts and Legal Services Act 1990 to replace a jury award which was considered to be excessive. It recognized that the jury award of £250,000 might not fit the existing definition of 'excessive', and (referring to *Pepper v Hart*) it was clear that there was no intention to change the definition of this word on the part of the legislature. But the Court of Appeal nevertheless decided—appealing to Article 10 ECHR—that it had a *duty* to interpret section 8 as broadening its powers of intervention in the sense of lowering the threshold of intervention. This case was decided some years before the HRA and this interpretation required the Court of Appeal to misapply some observations of Lord Goff in *AG v Guardian (No 2)* [1990] 1 AC 109 where he had said that there was no difference between common law, and Article 10. What he meant by this was that there was no need for change. It is a big step from this to hold that statutory provisions *must* be reinterpreted specifically in order to protect Article 10 rights (or, more strongly still since this is before the HRA, to protect the UK from litigation on the basis of a violation of Article 10).

Now that there would be awards arrived at by the Court of Appeal, rather than simply by juries, juries should in future have these judicial awards referred to them for attention. However, the corpus of Court of Appeal awards built up slowly, and the Court of Appeal grew impatient.

3. In *John v MGN* [1997] QB 586, the Court of Appeal took two further decisive steps. First, reversing its own conclusion in both *Sutcliffe* and *Rantzen*, the court decided that juries should have the level of non-pecuniary awards in personal injury actions brought to their attention. Second, counsel for both parties would be invited to suggest an appropriate level of damages. This would not lead to a bidding war, because counsel would learn to be realistic:

Lord Bingham, at 616

The plaintiff will not wish the jury to think that his main object is to make money rather than clear his name. The defendant will not wish to add insult to injury by underrating the seriousness of the libel. So we think the figures suggested by responsible counsel are likely to reflect the upper and lower bounds of a realistic bracket. The jury must of course make up their own mind and must be directed to do so. They will not be bound by the submission of counsel or the indication of the judge. If the jury make an award outside the upper or lower bounds of any bracket indicated and such award is the subject of appeal, real weight must be given to the possibility that their judgment is to be preferred to that of the judge.

Some forceful doubts about the step taken in *John* were set out by Lord Hoffmann in the following appeal from the Jamaican Court of Appeal. This Privy Council decision was an appeal on Jamaican law so that it is binding only in Jamaican law, and the comments did not quite amount to formal disapproval of the approach in *John*. Equally, of course, the 2013 reforms in effect remove the jury from defamation trials. Even so, the principles set out by Lord Hoffmann are of general interest as they draw attention to the need to protect reputation in the first place—a need too readily forgotten perhaps in the journey to better protection of free speech. Lord Hoffmann's remarks place some traditional arguments about defamation awards in a modern social and legal context.

The Gleaner v Abrahams
[2004] 1 AC 628

49 Reference to awards in personal injuries cases ... was advocated as a legitimate comparison by Diplock LJ in *McCarey v Associated Newspapers Ltd (No 2)* [1965] 2 QB 86, 109–110 but rejected by Lord Hailsham of St Marylebone LC in *Broome v Cassell & Co Ltd* [1972] AC 1027, 1070–1071 and by the Court of Appeal in *Rantzen's* case [1994] QB 670, 695. In *John v MGN Ltd* [1997] QB 586, the Court of Appeal reversed itself and since then juries have regularly been told to have regard to awards of general damages (for pain, suffering and loss of amenity) in personal injury actions. These are themselves conventional figures: the current scale was fixed by the Court of Appeal in *Heil v Rankin* [2001] QB 272 and runs to a maximum of £200,000 for the most catastrophic injuries. As a result, Eady J said in *Lillie v Newcastle City Council* [2002] EWHC 1600 (QB) at [1547]–[1551] that there is now a ceiling of £200,000 for compensatory damages in libel cases.

50 Their Lordships express no view on the current practice in England. But the matter is clearly one on which different opinions may be held. The arguments in favour of comparison tend to stress the moral unacceptability of treating damage to reputation as having a higher "value" than catastrophic damage to the person. It is however arguable that the assessment of general damages in both personal injury and libel cases is far more complicated than trying to "value" the damage: an exercise which everyone agrees to be impossible on account of the incommensurability of the subject matter. Other factors enter into the calculation. Personal injury awards are almost always made in actions based on negligence or breach of statutory duty rather than intentional wrongdoing. Furthermore, the damages are almost always paid out of public funds or by insurers under policies which are not very sensitive to the claims records of individual defendants. The cost is therefore borne by the public at large or large sections of the public such as motorists or consumers. The exemplary and deterrent elements in personal injury awards are minimal or non-existent. On the other hand, the total sums of compensation paid for personal injury are very large. They have an effect on the economy which libel damages do not. The amounts of the awards in personal injury actions therefore depend to some extent upon what society can afford to pay victims of accidents over and above compensation for the actual financial loss they have suffered. As Lord Woolf MR said of general damages in personal injury cases in *Heil v Rankin* [2001] QB 272, 297, para 36: "Awards must be proportionate and take into account the consequences of increases in the awards of damages on defendants as a group and society as a whole."

51 Once it is appreciated that the awards are not paid by individual defendants but by society as a whole or large sections of society, there are also considerations of equity between victims of personal injury which influence the level of general damages. Compensation, both for financial loss and general damages, goes only to those who can prove negligence and causation. Those unable to do so are left to social security: no general damages and meagre compensation for loss of earnings. The unfairness might be more readily understandable if the successful tort plaintiffs recovered their damages from the defendants themselves but makes less sense when both social security and negligence damages come out of public funds. So any increase in general damages for personal injury awarded

by the courts only widens the gap between those victims who can sue and those who cannot.

... **53** Few of these considerations of equity and policy apply to awards in defamation cases. On the other hand, defamation cases have important features not shared by personal injury claims. The damages often serve not only as compensation but also as an effective and necessary deterrent. The deterrent is effective because the damages are paid either by the defendant himself or under a policy of insurance which is likely to be sensitive to the incidence of such claims. Indeed, the effectiveness of the deterrent is the whole basis of Lord Lester's argument that high awards will have a "chilling effect" on future publications. Awards in an adequate amount may also be necessary to deter the media from riding roughshod over the rights of other citizens. In *Kiam's* case Sedley LJ said, at p 304, para 75:

"in a great many cases proof of a cold-blooded cost-benefit calculation that it was worth publishing a known libel is not there, and the ineffectiveness of a moderate award in deterring future libels is painfully apparent ... Judges, juries and the public face the conundrum that compensation proportioned to personal injury damages is insufficient to deter, and that deterrent awards make a mockery of the principle of compensation."

...

55 In addition, as this case amply illustrates, there are other differences between general damages in personal injury cases and general damages in defamation actions. One is that the damages must be sufficient to demonstrate to the public that the plaintiff's reputation has been vindicated. Particularly if the defendant has not apologised and withdrawn the defamatory allegations, the award must show that they have been publicly proclaimed to have inflicted a serious injury. As Lord Hailsham of St Marylebone LC said in *Broome v Cassell & Co Ltd* [1972] AC 1027, 1071, the plaintiff "must be able to point to a sum awarded by a jury sufficient to convince a bystander of the baselessness of the charge".

56 A second difference is that in an action for personal injury it is usually not difficult for the plaintiff to prove that his injury caused inability to work and consequent financial loss. Loss of earnings is therefore recoverable as special damage and ordinarily, in cases of grievous injury, constitutes by far the greater part of the award. Likewise, the expenses of care, nursing and so forth are recoverable as special damage. They do not constitute a factor in the assessment of general damages. In defamation cases, on the other hand, it is usually difficult to prove a direct causal link between the libel and loss of any particular earnings or any particular expenses. Nevertheless it is clear law that the jury are entitled to take these matters into account in the award of general damages. The strict requirements of proving causation are relaxed in return for moderation in the overall figure awarded. In the present case, in which Mr Abrahams was unable to find any remunerative employment for five years, loss of earnings must have played a significant part in the jury's award.

Lord Hoffmann here underlines a traditionally recognized distinction between the functions of defamation damages, and of damages for personal injury. Personal injury damages are almost solely compensatory: they seek to make good what has been lost.[41] Defamation damages on the other hand have multiple roles to play. Certainly, they may seek to **compensate**

[41] For refinements and qualifications to this statement see Chapter 8.

for hurt feelings and lost opportunities. But they are also aimed at **vindication** of the claimant's good reputation (in other words at repairing the damage suffered),[42] and also at **deterrence**. Equally, they are more frequently inflated by an element of **aggravation**: the injury to the claimant is made worse by the conduct of the defendant after the complaint of defamation is made. For example, in *Sutcliffe v Pressdram, Private Eye* responded to the initiation of proceedings by publishing further allegations about the plaintiff. In *John v MGN*, having initially offered a limp apology, the defendants responded aggressively with further allegations. Defamation awards are capable of being increased by an award of **exemplary damages**, most particularly where the defendant *calculated* that he or she could profit from publication of a defamatory statement. This was held to be the case in *John* itself, where the defendant newspaper was treated as having decided that it could achieve higher sales figures through carrying an ill-researched and sensationalist story concerning the plaintiff's alleged eating disorder, irrespective of its truth or falsity. By section 34 of the Crime and Courts Act 2013, exemplary damages cannot be awarded against a relevant publisher found liable in a relevant claim if it was a member of an approved regulator at the time of the events giving rise to the claim, but there are exceptions concerned with the reasonableness of the regulator's decision whether or not to award a penalty. By section 41, 'relevant publishers' are those who publish news-related material written by different authors and subject to editorial control. Claims for exemplary damages against the press will, so far as approved regulators emerge, therefore be subject to the provisions of this statute.

The deterrence argument mentioned above brings us to a less traditional aspect of Lord Hoffmann's defence of defamation damages. The **economic impact** of defamation damages is, he contends, also different from the impact of personal injury damages. On the one hand, there is no real harm in having high awards, since there is little impact on the economy as a whole: defamation proceedings tend to be 'one-off' affairs between the parties and do not engage a broad sector of the economy.[43] Equally, the award is likely to succeed in having considerable **deterrent effect**, according to Lord Hoffmann. *Either* the defendant will not have insured against this form of liability at all, *or* any relevant insurance contract will provide for penalties in the event of a claim being made.

How does Lord Hoffmann's argument in favour of a separation between libel and personal injury damages stand up to scrutiny, particularly having regard to the new status of Article 10 in English law? It can of course be pointed out by a critic of libel awards that the UK has twice been found to have violated Article 10 on the grounds of disproportionate awards of damages. On the other hand, in neither of these cases (*Tolstoy Miloslavsky v UK*; *Steel and Morris v UK*) was there a media defendant—both awards were made against *individuals*. In the case of *Steel and Morris*, the disproportion in the award was expressly identified as flowing, at least partly, from a comparison with the *defendant's means*. Disproportion is only partly a question of relationship between award and injury suffered. Thus, an award might arguably be 'proportionate' if it is based on the amount needed to *deter* future interference with the reputation of the claimant or of others, particularly where the defendant is in no sense 'impecunious'. Indeed, high awards (particularly those which treat persistence in a defence or course of conduct as grounds for aggravated damages) could be seen as an

---

[42] Note, on this point, the award of damages against 'persons unknown' in *Brett Wilson LLP v Persons Unknown* [2015] EWHC 2628 (QB). Given that the damages were unlikely ever to be paid, the purpose is clearly vindicatory.

[43] This omits the non-economic social harm of the chilling effect; but Lord Hoffmann seems to have considered the 'chilling' of bad journalism to be quite beneficial.

aspect of a broader goal, to encourage apologies and discourage extended litigation. This is underlined by sections 2–4 of the Defamation Act 1996, introducing provisions relating to offers to make amends.

John had some real effect in scaling down the larger defamation awards, but those awards remain high in comparison with general damages for personal injury. In *Tierney v Newsgroup Newspapers Ltd* [2006] EWHC 3275, Eady J remarked as follows:

> Libel damages have been scaled down in recent years so that it is widely reckoned that the maximum possible award would be in the order of £215,000 for the most serious libels, taking into account inflation and the impact on personal injury awards of the Court of Appeal's decision in *Heil v Rankin* [2001] QB 272.

Injunctions

There is a long-standing principle that courts will be very reluctant to grant injunctions to restrain publication in advance of full trial of a defamation action, which is to say on an 'interim' basis. At common law, interim injunctions have not been granted unless the defendant has *no realistic chance* of succeeding in a defence: *Bonnard v Perryman* [1891] 2 Ch 269. What then is the impact of section 12 of the HRA in a defamation action? This question is particularly pressing given the growing influence of the action to restrain publication of *private* information (Chapter 14). As we noted at the start of this chapter, protection of reputation is one of the reasons why freedom of expression may legitimately be restricted within the terms of Article 10 of the Convention. But equally, reputation is an aspect of privacy, which is protected by Article 8. As Ward LJ expressed the matter in *Roberts v Gable* [2007] EWCA Civ 721; [2008] QB 502, the *Reynolds* defence sought to balance these two rights: 'responsible journalism is the point at which a fair balance can be held between freedom of expression on matters of public concern and the reputation of the individual harmed by that disclosure, the vital balance between article 10 and article 8 of the Convention'.

Section 12 of the HRA is extracted in Chapter 1.

If a court is considering whether to restrain publication, section 12(3) requires that the applicant should be 'likely' to succeed in its application at trial, before such restraint can be granted. Even taking into account section 12(4), this would (if applied to defamation) *dilute* the protection afforded to free speech at common law, since *Bonnard v Perryman* requires that the claimant, to obtain such an injunction, needs to show that the defendant has no realistic prospect of success. Clearly, this is much more demanding than the 'likelihood' test.

In *Greene v Associated Newspapers* [2004] EWHC 2322, the Court of Appeal concluded that, despite its general wording, section 12(3) had no application to an action in defamation. A section concerned with protecting 'freedom of expression' could not have been intended to *reduce* the protection afforded to freedom of expression, and it would be absurd to replace the *Bonnard v Perryman* approach with the weaker 'likelihood' test. Prior to *Greene*, the role of section 12 had been considered in respect of actions for *breach of confidence* (*Cream Holdings v Banerjee* [2005] 1 AC 253). Here, section 12(3) introduces the vexed question of balance between rights under Articles 8 (privacy) and 10 (expression). In *Greene*, the Court of Appeal's conclusion in respect of defamation was that *even if* reputation is regarded as protected within the terms of Article 8 (as it now is), defamation actions nevertheless raise distinct issues when it comes to remedies. A reputation can be repaired by an award of damages, while confidentiality is destroyed for good once the information is published. There needs to be a very strong reason for prior restraint in an action for defamation.

The boundaries between claims to protect against damaging and untrue allegations of fact, and claims to protect against publication of true but private information, is an uncertain one and many claims are likely to arise which involve elements of both. The law is currently more prepared to restrain publication which, while truthful, interferes with privacy (it is none of the public's business to know), than to restrain publication which is untruthful and damages reputation. The potential for overlap is illustrated by the case of *Lord Browne of Madingley v Associated Newspapers* [2007] EWCA Civ 295; [2008] QB 103, where the claimant sought to prevent publication of material relating both to his intimate life and to his business interests. In practice, the reputational issues are inclined to blend into questions of legitimate public interest, which are considered in determining the claim for an injunction on the basis of invasion of privacy.

New Remedies and the 2013 Act

The 2013 Act introduces new remedies through sections 12 and 13. Section 12 is aimed at vindicating reputation without inflating the cost of defamation actions, and in this sense it is in the same spirit as sections 2–4 of the Defamation Act 1996 (offers to make amends). By section 12, the court may order the defendant to publish a summary of its judgment, where it has decided in favour of the claimant. The details of the summary and its publication should be agreed by the parties but in default of that, they are to be determined by the court. Section 13 is more complex, and is necessitated partly by the protection offered to those who are not 'publishers' by section 10. The section enables the court to order those distributing a defamatory publication to stop doing so, which is a significant provision since in some instances section 10 will preclude an action against them.

13. Order to remove statement or cease distribution etc

(1) Where a court gives judgment for the claimant in an action for defamation the court may order—

(a) the operator of a website on which the defamatory statement is posted to remove the statement, or

(b) any person who was not the author, editor or publisher of the defamatory statement to stop distributing, selling or exhibiting material containing the statement.

(2) In this section *"author"*, *"editor"* and *"publisher"* have the same meaning as in section 1 of the Defamation Act 1996.

(3) Subsection (1) does not affect the power of the court apart from that subsection.

It has been suggested by Mullis and Scott (Further Reading) that it is the failure to think further about new types of remedy, focused on correction and vindication other than upon large awards of damages, which is the major disappointment of the legislative reforms. Their point is that the cost of current proceedings is a potential barrier to claimants and defendants alike, and that rebalancing of defamation should not necessarily be all about deterring its use.

9. CONCLUSIONS

i. The law of defamation inevitably raises the question of how to balance freedom of expression, against protection of reputation. That question has been expressed over the years in relation to the defamation actions in a variety of different contexts. It is given a new dimension by the integration of Articles 8 and 10 ECHR into English law through the Human Rights Act 1998; but it also underlies all of the provisions of the Defamation Act 2013, most of which seek to build upon the emerging balance achieved by the courts in recent years.

ii. It is particularly clear that the legislation builds on the work of the courts in relation to the defences of honest opinion and of public interest reporting. The latter defence is a reworking of the ground-breaking decision in *Reynolds v Times Newspapers*, which adopts the core principles of that decision but breaks the link with privilege which was the basis on which the House of Lords was able to justify that development. Thus, defamation provides a striking example both of judicial development of new legal principles, and of cooperation between legislature and the courts in developing a new balance in a politically, as well as ethically sensitive area. However, the legislature has also been able to develop the law in directions that would not have been open to the courts alone, for example by all but abolishing trial by jury in cases of defamation, and by the introduction of new remedies designed to reduce the 'chilling effect' of this area of law.

iii. One pressing question has emerged concerning the interpretation of s1 of the Defamation Act 2013. Was this intended simply to define the level of seriousness required for an actionable defamation, or was it intended that defamation claimants must now prove on balance of probabilities that harm to reputation has flowed, or is likely to flow, from the defamatory statement? The trial of this question as a preliminary issue is capable of extending the length of defamation trials. To date, the latter interpretation has been adopted, but at the same time, courts have recognized that in appropriate cases, the requirement may be satisfied by inference. The views of appeal courts on this question are currently awaited.

FURTHER READING

Balin, R., Handman, L., and Reid, E., 'Libel Tourism and the Duke's Manservant—An American Perspective' (2009) EHRLR 303–31.

Barendt, E., *Freedom of Speech* (2nd edn, Oxford: Oxford University Press, 2005), chapters 1–2 and 6.

Bosland, J., Kenyon, A. T., and Walker, S., 'Protecting Inferences of Fact in Defamation Law: Fair Comment and Honest Opinion' (2015) 74 CLJ 234–60.

Dunlop, R., 'Article 10, The Reynolds Test and the Rule in the Duke of Brunswick's Case—The Decision in *Times Newspapers v UK*' (2006) EHRLR 327.

Groppo, M., 'Serious Harm: A Case Law Restrospective and Early Assessment' (2016) 8 Journal of Media Law 1.

Howarth, D., 'Libel: Its Purpose and Reform' (2011) 74 MLR 845.

Loveland, I., *Political Libels* (Oxford: Hart Publishing, 2000).

Mitchell, P., *The Making of the Modern Law of Defamation* (Oxford: Hart Publishing, 2005).

Mullis, A., and Scott, A., 'Tilting at Windmills: The Defamation Act 2013' (2014) 77 MLR 87.

Steyn, Lord, '2000–2005: Laying the Foundations of Human Rights Law in the United Kingdom' (2005) 4 EHRLR 349.

Trindade, F., 'Malice and the Defence of Fair Comment' (2001) 117 LQR 169.

14

PRIVACY

CENTRAL ISSUES

i) This chapter describes the emergence of a new action to protect privacy, and its later development. The tools for achieving this development were provided by the Human Rights Act 1998, and this is important to the way in which the law has developed as elements of Convention jurisprudence have been deeply absorbed into English law.

ii) The starting point has been and still is that English law recognizes no general tort of invasion of privacy. Since the Human Rights Act 1998, courts have consistently said that they recognize privacy as an 'underlying value' of English law. Even so, it has been clearly stated that recognition of an underlying value is different from recognition of a legal principle which can be applied in concrete situations (Lord Hoffmann, *Wainwright v Home Office* [2004] 2 AC 406, at [31]).

iii) From the equitable action for **breach of confidence**, an action for *unjustified publication of private information* has emerged. After some uncertainty, the courts have now defined this as a tort. Interim injunctions to restrain publication are available in many

cases, in marked contrast with the position in defamation (Chapter 13), and courts also recognize that 'disgorgement damages' (where defendants are required to repay profits made from the wrong) are often appropriate. Although the substantive requirements of this action have changed, the equitable remedies remain in place.

iv) In recent years, controversy has centred around the injunctive remedies available to protect privacy, and especially their interaction with internet publication; and the element of secrecy involved with 'super-injunctions'. At the same time however, evidence of gross illegal violations of personal privacy on the part of the press, and the continuing difficulties of restraining on-line publications, have created a new impetus to attempt to achieve a responsible press. This is a counterpoint to the developments towards enhanced freedom of expression that are evident in defamation reform, and raises the question of how far it is possible to control the press without compromising its independence.

1. A NEW PROTECTED INTEREST AT COMMON LAW?

When we considered defamation, in Chapter 13, we noted that the actions in libel and slander have protected reputation for centuries, and we moved to the well-recognized potential for conflict between protection of reputation and the interest in freedom of expression. Protection of 'privacy', to the extent that tort law attempts it, will also lead to questions of conflict with freedom of expression. But there has been a prior difficulty to resolve. This difficulty is that privacy was not traditionally recognized as a protected interest in its own right in English tort law. It remains the case that privacy is protected only in a specific way, through the tort of misuse of private information.

Privacy, in this respect, has appeared to be different from reputation. Now, however, the position is quite different. As we saw in Chapter 13, English courts have increasingly described the protection of reputation as falling within the Article 8 'Privacy' right, and the categorization of reputation in at least some instances in terms of Article 8 is beginning to seem important in the present 'rebalancing' of the law. In both areas of law, the move to a balance based on equality between the rights is a significant development. The expanding protection of privacy in its own right has been notable; but where reputation is concerned, the trend has been to restrict its protection in order to safeguard speech. It is possible that over time, the two will come to resemble each other more closely.

In the past, English law undoubtedly left some claimants without a cause of action where it could be said that their privacy, private space, or 'right to be let alone' has been interfered with. A key example (although the outcome might be different today)[1] is *Kaye v Robertson* [1991] FSR 62. The claimant (an actor) was lying unconscious in hospital when journalists broke into his room and took photographs. The defendant's newspaper sought to publish these as part of an 'exclusive interview'. Members of the Court of Appeal made plain that they wished there was a suitable tort through which to restrain publication. In the circumstances, they employed the action in malicious falsehood in order to award an interim injunction. The 'falsehood', clearly, was the claim that the plaintiff had granted an interview; the 'actual damage' required was (less convincingly) that he could not benefit by granting an exclusive interview to any other newspaper.[2] The plaintiff in *Kaye v Robertson* did not try to argue his case in terms of breach of confidence. As we will see later, at the time of the decision it would have been thought that this action depended on a relationship of confidentiality which did not exist between the parties.

A few years later, in *Spencer v UK* (1998) 25 EHRR CD105, the European Commission was persuaded that there was no gap in English law in such cases (publication of unauthorized photographs taken through intrusion into private places). The applicant's privacy rights could have been protected in English law, had they argued their case in terms of breach of confidence. In fact, this argument—that privacy *was* protected in domestic law through the action for breach of confidence—was not very clearly supported by the case law

---

[1] Because of developments in the action to protect private information: see *Campbell v MGN* [2004] 2 AC 457, and other cases, discussed later.

[2] This tends to devalue the claimant's complaint since it implies that his right to remain free from interference is of value to him only because he could profit in the future from publicity. Publicity rights and values of privacy overlap in cases such as this, but in principle they are distinct.

at the time of *Spencer v UK*. The decisive change was to follow in *Douglas v Hello!* [2001] QB 967, which recognized that there is an action to restrain publication of unauthorized photographs where there is a reasonable expectation of privacy. The decision is extracted in Section 4 of this chapter.

But this does not mean that privacy is now protected at common law in any general way. In *Peck v UK* [2003] EMLR 15, a decision of the European Court of Human Rights, the applicant had been recorded on CCTV in a public street shortly after attempting suicide. The recording was then released to, and pictures from it were broadcast by, a number of news agencies. The European Court of Human Rights held that the claimant's Article 8 right to privacy had been violated. Although the plaintiff was in a public place, namely the street, he could not have anticipated the breadth of publication that ensued. The UK was in violation of Article 13, which requires a remedy in domestic law where substantive Convention rights have been violated. In *Wainwright v Home Office* [2004] 2 AC 406, Lord Hoffmann denied that *Peck* showed the need for a general 'privacy tort'. Rather, he said that it showed the need for specific *legislative* control of the use of CCTV footage.

In *Wainwright v Home Office* [2004] 2 AC 406 itself, the House of Lords declined to develop existing law in order to provide any remedy to individuals who had been subjected to intrusive and inappropriately conducted strip searches on a visit to prison. The House of Lords doubted whether this indicated a gap in the protection of Convention rights; but the European Court of Human Rights has ruled that it did.

2. 'PRIVACY': ONE RIGHT OR FOUR PROTECTED INTERESTS?

The idea that a general 'right to privacy' can be identified 'immanent in'[3] existing law, and (furthermore) that this right ought to be recognized specifically through creation of a dedicated privacy *tort*, dates to a seminal law review article published in 1890 by Warren and Brandeis, 'The Right to Privacy' (1890) 4 Harv L Rev 193. Warren and Brandeis surveyed a range of actions available in English law, and argued that underlying these was a right to 'privacy'. Social conditions required that privacy be recognized and given protection through the law of tort. The authors' chief *concern* (no different from the concern in much more recent case law such as *Von Hannover v Germany* [2004] ECHR 294), was with the conduct of the press, and this provided the personal motivation for their article.[4] Their *method* was to suggest that privacy interests should and could be protected in the same way as the familiar interests in physical integrity and personal property. The 'privacy right' is derived from an analogy with *trespass* torts.

[3] This means (simply) that the right can be derived from the legal material itself and without having to seek a justification elsewhere.

[4] Warren felt that his wife had been harassed by the press, which was printing too many details of parties at their home. The last straw was intrusive coverage into the wedding of their daughter. Speaking of the Warrens' daughter, and given the extraordinary influence of the Warren and Brandeis article, William Prosser later suggested that hers was the original 'face that launched a thousand law suits' (Prosser, 'Privacy', at 423).

S. D. Warren and L. D. Brandeis, 'The Right to Privacy' (1890) 4 Harv L Rev 193, 193–6

That the individual shall have full protection in person and in property is a principle as old as the common law; but it has been found necessary from time to time to define anew the exact nature and extent of such protection. Political, social, and economic changes entail the recognition of new rights, and the common law, in its eternal youth, grows to meet the demands of society. Thus, in very early times, the law gave a remedy only for physical interference with life and property, for trespasses vi et armis . . . . Later, there came a recognition of man's spiritual nature, of his feelings and his intellect. Gradually the scope of these legal rights broadened; and now the right to life has come to mean the right to enjoy life,—the right to be let alone; the right to liberty secures the exercise of extensive civil privileges; and the term 'property' has grown to comprise every form of possession—intangible, as well as tangible.

. . . This development of the law was inevitable. The intense intellectual and emotional life, and the heightening of sensations which came with the advance of civilization, made it clear to men that only a part of the pain, pleasure and profit of life lay in physical things. Thoughts, emotions, and sensations demanded legal recognition, and the beautiful capacity for growth which characterizes the common law enabled the judges to afford the requisite protection, without the interposition of the legislature.

Recent inventions and business methods call attention to the next step which must be taken for the protection of the person, and for securing to the individual what Judge Cooley calls the right "to be let alone". [Cooley on Torts, 2d ed., p. 29] Instantaneous photographs and newspaper enterprise have invaded the sacred precincts of private and domestic life; and numerous mechanical devices threaten to make good the prediction that "what is whispered in the closet shall be proclaimed from the house-tops." . . . the question of whether our law will recognize and protect the right to privacy in this and in other respects must soon come before our courts for consideration.

Of the desirability—indeed of the necessity—of some such protection, there can be no doubt. The press is overstepping in every direction the obvious bounds of propriety and of decency.... The intensity and complexity of life, attendant upon advancing civilization, have rendered necessary some retreat from the world, and man, under the refining influence of culture, has become more sensitive to publicity, so that solitude and privacy have become more essential to the individual; but modern enterprise and invention have, through invasions upon his privacy, subjected him to mental pain and distress, far greater than could be inflicted by mere bodily injury....

From this extract we can see the method at work in the essay (as well as its polemical style). Remedies for invasion of a right to privacy should emerge as an extension from, and be closely modelled upon, the protection of property (tangible and intangible), of confidence, and of reputation. The reason why it should so emerge is that it is now needed.

In the United States, the arguments of Warren and Brandeis were spectacularly successful (although there is some question whether the exceptions to the right to privacy have swallowed up the rule, at least where *publication* of private information is concerned).[5] After

---

[5] G. Phillipson, 'Judicial Reasoning in Breach of Confidence Cases Under the Human Rights Act: Not Taking Privacy Seriously' (2003) EHRLR 53, cites D. Zimmerman, 'Requiem for a Heavyweight: A Farewell to Warren and Brandeis's Privacy Tort' (1983) 68 Cornell L Rev 291. Zimmerman suggests that the defence

an initial rejection in the New York case of *Roberson v Rochester Folding Box Co* 171 NY 538, 64 NE 442 (1902), Warren and Brandeis' thesis was accepted by the Supreme Court of Georgia in *Pavesich v New England Life Insurance Co* 122 Ga 190, 50 SE 68 (1905) (where the defendant had used the name and image of the plaintiff to advertise their products), and an enforceable right to privacy was recognized. This acceptance rapidly spread to other state jurisdictions. In an equally influential later article, William Prosser explained that in accepting the existence of a right of privacy, the courts had been little concerned to explore what privacy actually *was*.

William Prosser, 'Privacy' (1960) 48 Cal L Rev 383, at 386–9

In nearly every jurisdiction[6] the first decisions were understandably preoccupied with the question whether the right of privacy existed at all, and gave little or no consideration to what it would amount to if it did. It is only in recent years, and largely through the legal writers, that there has been any attempt to inquire what interests are we protecting, and against what conduct. Today, with something over three hundred cases in the books, the holes in the jigsaw puzzle have been largely filled in, and some rather definite conclusions are possible.

What has emerged from the decisions is no simple matter. It is not one tort, but a complex of four. The law of privacy comprises four distinct kinds of invasion of four different interests of the plaintiff, which are tied together by the common name, but otherwise have almost nothing in common except that each represents an interference with the right of the plaintiff, in the phrase coined by Judge Cooley, "to be let alone." Without any attempt to exact definition, these four torts may be described as follows:

1. Intrusion upon the plaintiff's seclusion or solitude, or into his private affairs.
2. Public disclosure of embarrassing private facts about the plaintiff.
3. Publicity which places the plaintiff in a false light in the public eye.
4. Appropriation, for the defendant's advantage, of the plaintiff's name or likeness.

It should be obvious at once that these four types of invasion may be subject, in some respects at least, to different rules; and that when what is said as to any one of them is carried over to another, it may not be at all applicable, and confusion may follow.

Whereas Warren and Brandeis had sought to show that there was a distinctive privacy right underlying a range of case law (which was capable of protection at common law), Prosser set out to divide that case law into a number of categories which, he said, protected slightly *different* interests, even if these protected interests could still (in his view) properly be regarded as aspects of a broader notion of privacy. He did not seek to show *why* these privacy interests are worth protecting, or what the broader idea of privacy (if any) might consist in. He was concerned however about the propensity for the action(s) in privacy to avoid and override important restrictions—such as the defence of truth in defamation actions—which had evolved in the established torts. Such was the influence of Prosser's

of 'newsworthiness' has effectively destroyed the protection sought by Warren and Brandeis against unwelcome intrusion and publication. A broader line is drawn around press freedom in the United States than in England.

6 Prosser is here referring to *state* jurisdictions within the United States.

arguments that they provided the model for revising the outline of privacy torts in the Second US Restatement (Torts).

In England, Prosser's arguments have been taken to demonstrate that there is no identifiable core to the right of 'privacy' which would make it capable of protection as a general interest. An important example is Lord Hoffmann's view in *Wainwright v Home Office* [2004] 2 AC 406:

18 The need in the United States to break down the concept of invasion of privacy into a number of loosely-linked torts must cast doubt upon the value of any high-level generalisation which can perform a useful function in enabling one to deduce the rule to be applied in a concrete case. English law has so far been unwilling, perhaps unable, to formulate such a high level principle.... In The Poverty of Principle (1980) 96 LQR 73, Raymond Wacks turned the tables on the arguments of Warren and Brandeis, suggesting that in some instances the attempt to define a range of existing actions as really to do with privacy not only has been overdone, but also has led to real confusion. He pointed out that in certain decisions of the US Supreme Court,[7] privacy had become synonymous with autonomy itself,[8] a much larger and more fundamental value which surely could not be sensibly used as a protected right or interest for the purposes of tort law, without further definition. The common law simply did not need the general idea of privacy.

Wacks suggested abandoning appeal to the 'abstract' idea of privacy, and advocated protection of 'personal information' which he thought was at the core of privacy interests. This sort of thinking (avoiding broad general principles and allowing evolution of existing actions in order to meet current needs) is the most comfortable for common lawyers.[9] Equally, Article 8 is perhaps the most diverse and elusive[10] of Convention rights, and even if more general protection was desired, it is not clear what form this could or should take.

English courts have stated that they will not create new torts in order to give direct effect to Convention rights. Even so, existing causes of action have absorbed a new right or interest (in privacy) which is *not* an offshoot of existing ideas of property. English common law is not doing precisely what Warren and Brandeis suggested over 100 years ago, deriving a new idea of property *from existing common law cases* in the light of changing needs. Instead, it is giving effect to a Convention right. The absorption of Article 8 (and Article 10) into this area of law is now clearly established.

3. ARTICLE 8 ECHR AND THE HUMAN RIGHTS ACT 1998

This section considers the tools which have been used in the emergence of a tort of misuse of private information, and absorption of privacy rights to common law.

---

7 Particularly regarding sexual freedom and obscene material.

8 This was only one of seven ways that Wacks suggested privacy had become irretrievably confused with other issues; it may however be the most important.

9 For an exploration of privacy which is not derived from notions of property or equity, see D. Feldman, 'Secrecy, Dignity, or Autonomy? Views of Privacy as a Civil Liberty' (1994) 47 CLP 41.

10 *Malcolm v Secretary of State for Justice* [2011] EWCA Civ 1538, [26] (freedom of a prisoner to exercise in open air).

3.1 ARTICLE 8, EUROPEAN CONVENTION ON HUMAN RIGHTS

Article 8 Right to respect for private and family life

1. Everyone has the right to respect for his private and family life, his home and his correspondence.

2. There shall be no interference by a public authority with the exercise of this right except such as is in accordance with the law and is necessary in a democratic society in the interests of national security, public safety or the economic well-being of the country, for the prevention of disorder or crime, for the protection of health or morals, or for the protection of the rights and freedoms of others.

The most authoritative interpretation of the obligations imposed by Article 8 in relation to publication is provided by the following case, which has influenced the reasoning in domestic cases very directly.[11] Though in some respects this case sets a very demanding standard, in other respects (particularly as regards the content of Article 8), the guidance it offers is limited.

Von Hannover v Germany [2004] ECHR 294

In this case, the European Court of Human Rights confirmed that Article 8 imposes *positive* obligations upon States to ensure that rights to privacy are respected. Prior to this decision, there was no definitive statement to this effect,[12] although to a large extent English courts anticipated it through their interpretation of the Human Rights Act 1998 (HRA) (later in this chapter).

German law has accorded considerable protection to privacy interests. It has done so through interpretation of Article 1 (relating to the dignity of the human being) and Article 2 (relating to free development of personality) of the Basic Law (*Grundgesetz*). In this case, however, the applicant challenged the restrictions on protection of privacy which operate in German law in respect of 'figures of contemporary society'. It is clear that these restrictions aimed to protect the competing public interests in expression and information. That being so, the applicant was challenging the way that German law struck the balance between protection of individual privacy and protection of a public interest in information where the everyday (unexceptional) behaviour of public figures is concerned. While the Court in this instance held that the balance had not been correctly struck, in a more recent decision concerning further complaints by the same applicant, it has accepted the approach now taken by the German courts.

The Applicant's Case

The applicant, Princess Caroline of Monaco, wished to prevent publication of certain photographs. The photographs showed her pursuing a range of 'ordinary' activities. All were

---

[11] See the discussion of *McKennitt v Ash* and *PJS v News Group Newspapers*, later in this section.

[12] See G. Phillipson, 'Transforming Breach of Confidence? Towards a Common Law Right of Privacy under the Human Rights Act' (2003) 66 MLR 726–58.

taken in places where, to one extent or another, the public had access. The photographs were interpreted by the German courts as being in no sense derogatory (although one showed her tripping and falling at the beach). However, they were taken without permission and on 'unofficial' occasions when she had no wish to be photographed. The German courts ruled that most of the photographs could be published. Princess Caroline was a 'figure of contemporary society *par excellence*' (even though she had no official state functions), and in German law she therefore had to tolerate publication of photographs in which she appeared *in a public place* even if they showed scenes from her daily life. Her interests were outweighed by the need to inform. It was thought however that one of the photographs should not be published as it violated her rights under the Basic Law (as explained above). It showed her at the far end of a restaurant garden, and this counted as a 'secluded place' whereas the interior of a restaurant did not. In the garden, she could have assumed that she was 'not exposed to public view'.

Princess Caroline applied to the European Court of Human Rights, arguing that her rights under Article 8 had been violated. The Court found in her favour.

The general principles governing the protection of private life and the freedom of expression

56 In the present case the applicant did not complain of an action of the State, but rather of the lack of adequate State protection of her private life and her image.

57 The court reiterates that although the object of Article 8 is essentially that of protecting the individual against arbitrary interference by the public authorities, it does not merely compel the State to abstain from such interference: in addition to this primarily negative undertaking, there may be positive obligations inherent in an effective respect for private or family life. These obligations may involve the adoption of measures designed to secure respect for private life even in the sphere of the relations of individuals between themselves …

58 That protection of private life has to be balanced against the freedom of expression guaranteed by Article 10 of the Convention. In that context the Court reiterates that the freedom of expression constitutes one of the essential foundations of a democratic society … In that connection the press plays an essential role in a democratic society. Although it must not overstep certain bounds, in particular in respect of the rights and reputations of others, its duty is nevertheless to impart—in a manner consistent with its obligations and responsibilities—information and ideas on all matters of public interest… Journalistic freedom also covers possible recourse to a degree of exaggeration, or even provocation …

59 Although freedom of expression also extends to the publication of photos, this is an area in which the protection of the rights and reputation of others takes on particular importance. The present case does not concern the dissemination of ideas, but of images containing very personal or even intimate information about an individual. Furthermore, photos appearing in the tabloid press are often taken in a climate of continual harassment which induces in the person concerned a very strong sense of intrusion into their private life or even of persecution.

60 In the cases in which the Court has had to balance the protection of private life against the freedom of expression it has always stressed the contribution made by photos or articles in the press to a debate of general interest… The Court thus found, in one case, that the use of certain terms in respect of an individual's private life was not justified by considerations of

public concern and that those terms did not [bear] on a matter of general importance ... and went on to hold that there had not been a violation of Article 10. In another case, however, the Court attached particular importance to the fact that the subject in question was a news item of major public concern and that the published photographs did not disclose any details of [the] private life of the person in question [*Krone-Verlag*] and held that there had been a violation of Article 10.... .

Application of these general principles by the Court

...

63 The Court considers that a fundamental distinction needs to be drawn between reporting facts—even controversial ones—capable of contributing to a debate in a democratic society relating to politicians in the exercise of their functions, for example, and reporting details of the private life of an individual who, moreover, as in this case, does not exercise official functions. While in the former case the press exercises its vital role of watchdog in a democracy by contributing to 'imparting information and ideas on matters of public interest' [*Observer and Guardian v UK*] it does not do so in the latter case.

69 The Court considers that everyone, even if they are known to the general public, must be able to enjoy a legitimate expectation of protection of and respect for their private life ...

Conclusion

76 As the Court has stated above, it considers that the decisive factor in balancing the protection of private life against freedom of expression should lie in the contribution that the published photos and articles make to a debate of general interest. It is clear in the instant case that they made no such contribution since the applicant exercises no official function and the photos and articles related specifically to details of her private life.

77 Furthermore, the Court considers that the public does not have a legitimate interest in knowing where the applicant is and how she behaves generally in her private life even if she appears in places that cannot always be described as secluded and despite the fact that she is well known to the public.

Even if such a public interest exists, as does a commercial interest of the magazine in publishing these photos and these articles, in the instant case those interests must, in the Court's view, yield to the applicant's right to the effective protection of her private life.

78 Lastly, in the Court's opinion the criteria established by the domestic courts were not sufficient to ensure the effective protection of the applicant's private life and she should, in the circumstances of the case, have had a 'legitimate expectation' of protection of her private life.

Conclusions from *Von Hannover*

The largest contribution of *Von Hannover* to general Convention jurisprudence was its clear recognition of positive obligations on the State to secure privacy in dealings between private parties, and particularly in actions against the press. Domestic legal systems must be able to handle the balancing issue that is explained in *Von Hannover*, where Article 8 rights conflict with Article 10 rights, in such a case.

Some important guidance on this balancing exercise is offered by the Court. In particular, the Court reiterates that the key purpose of the Article 10 right is instrumental: freedom of expression is vital to the flourishing of a democratic society and is a key component in the sort of society that will uphold the other rights and freedoms in the Convention (at [58]). This is compatible with the explanation of Article 10 that we said, in Chapter 13, was adopted in the recent English case law on defamation. In privacy cases, the right of the public to be informed is in potential conflict with the right of an individual to enjoy their privacy. In the *Von Hannover* case, the Court made clear that unless there is a distinct public interest reason for revealing private information (and it seems *particularly photographs*), it will be inappropriate to *allow publication*. Much positive action to secure privacy *will be in restraint of freedom of expression*, and the state is generally obliged *not* to act in such a way as to restrict expression. However, there is no substantial difference in the weight that is accorded to the two rights in privacy, and in freedom of expression. *States cannot evade the need to balance the rights by according priority to freedom of expression; nor by doing nothing.*

The European Court also emphasized an important difference between **the public interest** (in being informed) which often underlies the Article 10 right, and a **public preference** for certain types of reporting, which makes a particular sort of publication commercially successful: this distinction can clearly be seen in the Supreme Court's decision in *PJS v News Group Newspapers* [2016] AC 1081, and numerous other decisions of the UK courts. The Court clearly did not endorse the views of the German Federal Constitutional Court that 'entertainment in the press is neither negligible nor entirely worthless and therefore falls within the scope of application of fundamental rights'. A report must be demonstrated to serve a particular purpose, if it is to outweigh an individual's right to privacy. Provided the publication itself is 'low-grade', then it seems that even a relatively anodyne publication (with minor impact on privacy) should be restrained. An alternative reading of the *Von Hannover* case is possible, which would place more emphasis on 'harassment' of the Princess through a course of conduct which deprived her of her private life. But this is hard to sustain given the nature of the conclusions reached and especially the identification of the *contribution made by the photos to public debate* as the 'decisive factor'.

Certain other findings of the European Court are also of importance. In particular, the Court emphasized that even a 'public figure' still has an expectation of privacy. This is so not only where the claimant is best described as a 'celebrity' but even when they have some constitutional significance. Privacy is also not to be defined in exclusively spatial terms, limiting protection to areas where the public has no access. The individual claimant does not need to be in a secluded *place*, in order to benefit from the protection of Article 8. Both of these principles are consistent with English law as it has recently developed.[13]

The Court states that its conclusions on release of information are strengthened by consideration of the *manner in which the photographs were acquired*—that is to say, through covert means, without permission, and as part of a campaign amounting to 'harassment'.[14]

---

[13] As to the first see *HRH Prince of Wales v Associated Newspapers* [2006] EWCA Civ 1776)—the heir to the throne has a reasonable expectation of privacy in his diaries. As to the second, see *Campbell v MGN* (extracted below)—photographs taken in the street may be the subject of an injunction if there is a reasonable expectation of privacy.

[14] See M. A. Sanderson, 'Is Von Hannover v Germany a Step Backwards for the Substantive Analysis of Speech and Privacy Interests?' [2004] EHRLR 631–44. Sanderson argues that the low-grade nature of the

More recent decisions of the Court have clarified that publication of photographs may be regarded as violations of Article 8 even in the absence of intrusion or harassment in the sense of a media campaign;[15] and in *McKennitt v Ash* [2006] EWCA Civ 1714; [2008] QB 73, the Court of Appeal considered and rejected an argument that intrusion and harassment were crucial to the holding in *Von Hannover*. In English law then, the *Von Hannover* approach guides courts in balancing the rights of parties even in cases which are far from intrusion or harassment.

Further clarification can be gleaned from a more recent decision in relation to a complaint by the same applicant.

Von Hannover v Germany [2012] EMLR 16

This decision also concerned a photograph of Princess Caroline and her husband, in a public place. The German courts had changed their approach in response to the earlier *Von Hannover* decision, abandoning the category of public figures who would enjoy only limited privacy protection and introducing a concept of 'graduated' protection. Each photo should be assessed and the court should decide whether there was a sufficient interest in publishing it, very much in line with the European Court's approach in the earlier *Von Hannover* decision. Indeed, the overriding test applied was whether the publication contributed meaningfully to public debate. While a number of photographs were subject to injunctions in the national courts to prohibit publication, a final photograph was regarded differently: the German Federal Court decided that publication should be permitted. This was because the photograph was looked at together with an accompanying story touching on the ill health of Prince Rainier III of Monaco (the first applicant's father) during the time of the skiing holiday depicted. This, the Federal Court of Justice determined, was 'an event of contemporary society' that the press was entitled to report; and the photograph—of the applicants in a public street in St Moritz during their holiday—was sufficiently linked to the story. Taking both together, the publication was permitted.

The decision of the Grand Chamber in this case appeared more deferential to the national court than its earlier *Von Hannover* decision; but this doubtless reflects the changes made to balancing rights in the national courts. Provided the balancing exercise between Articles 8 and 10 is carried out in conformity with the criteria in the Court's case law, the Grand Chamber considered that there would need to be strong reasons for the Court to substitute its own view: there is a 'margin of appreciation' in respect of actual balance struck.[16] Since there was no basis on which to criticize the criteria applied, no violation of Article 8 was established.

Two questions may be asked. First, how strong were the reasons for including a photograph to accompany the story? It seems that there was a sufficient 'link' between the picture and the contribution made by the story to satisfy the German court: the two looked at together had a sufficient 'public interest' quality. It would have reached a different position had the article been 'merely a pretext' for publishing a photograph of a prominent person. In the English case of *Campbell v MGN*, it might appear that a rather

publications dominated the decision in *Von Hannover*, so that the Court never analysed the nature of the privacy interest very closely.

[15] *Sciacca v Italy* (2005) 43 EHRR 330.

[16] Compare the perception of some senior English judges that too much control of the relevant balance was being exercised by Strasbourg: J. Steele, Further Reading.

stricter approach was taken to publication of a photograph to accompany a legitimate story: some other photograph of the claimant could have been used to 'brighten up' the story, rather than one taken without permission in the street. But the photograph in *Campbell* was more intrusive and taken on an occasion that the claimant would have reasonably wished to keep private. All of the facts are relevant when balancing Article 8 and 10 rights and interests.

A second question surrounds the circumstances in which the photograph was taken, and the relevance of these circumstances, and this reflects our discussion of the first *Von Hannover* decision (above). The applicants in this and the earlier case described a general atmosphere of harassment which deprived them of a private life. In this instance, the photograph had indeed been taken without knowledge or permission. Both the national court and the Grand Chamber appear to have accepted that the circumstances in which a photograph is taken will be a factor to weigh in the balance. Here, however, the applicants had brought no evidence to suggest that the means used were illegal or surreptitious, and there were no grounds on which to explore the issue further. The case illustrates nevertheless that the circumstances of the photograph will be among the relevant factors in the overall balance between Articles 8 and 10. Complaints about publication and about intrusion shade into one another, and not only where photographs are concerned, as is well illustrated by the question posed by the appeal in *PJS v News Group Newspapers* [2016] AC 1081: is it legitimate to control print publication in national newspapers, when the relevant information is already available via social media and elsewhere on the internet? In holding that it was, the Supreme Court emphasized the greater intrusion into privacy associated with unrestrained print publication:

**Lord Neuberger, *PJS v News Group Newspapers Ltd*
[2016] AC 1081**

61 The significance of intrusion, as opposed to confidentiality, ...was well explained in the judgment of Eady J in *CTB's* case [2011] EWHC 1326, where he refused an application by a newspaper to vary an interlocutory injunction because of what he referred to as widespread coverage on the Internet. At para 24 he said that:

... it is fairly obvious that wall-to-wall excoriation in national newspapers ... is likely to be significantly more intrusive and distressing for those concerned than the availability of information on the Internet or in foreign journals to those, however many, who take the trouble to look it up.

As he went on to say in para 24, in a case such as this, for so long as the court is in a position to prevent some of that intrusion and distress, depending upon the individual circumstances, it may be appropriate to maintain that degree of protection.

3.2 THE HUMAN RIGHTS ACT 1998

Before the decision of the European Court of Human Rights in the first *Von Hannover* decision, English courts had already concluded that they were required to balance the rights in Articles 8 and 10 as a matter of English law, as a consequence of the Human Rights Act 1998

(HRA). This section considers the relevant provisions of the HRA. In the next section, we turn to the case law.

Section 6

Section 6 of the HRA is extracted in Chapter 1.

We have touched on the general implications of this provision in Chapters 1, 10, and 13. The general issue in respect of privacy actions is whether the Convention rights will have any effect in **actions between private parties**. Sections 7 and 8 (also extracted in Chapter 1) ensure that the Convention rights can be the basis of an action in their own right in 'vertical' cases, which is to say where the individual or other private party brings an action against a public authority. Any impact on actions between private parties is described as **horizontal effect**.

Actions relating to privacy have made a particular contribution to the understanding of horizontal effect. The HRA does not enable courts to create entirely new causes of action between private parties. The following comments from *Campbell v MGN* are reasonably conclusive on this point.[17]

Campbell v MGN
[2004] 2 AC 457

Lord Hoffmann

49 ... Even now the equivalent of Article 8 has been enacted as part of English law, it is not directly concerned with the protection of privacy against private persons or corporations. It is, by virtue of section 6 of the 1998 Act, a guarantee of privacy only against public authorities. Although the Convention, as an international instrument, may impose upon the United Kingdom an obligation to take some steps (whether by **statute** or otherwise) to protect rights of privacy against invasion by private individuals, it does not follow that such an obligation would have any counterpart in domestic law.

Baroness Hale

132 ... The 1998 Act does not create any new cause of action between private persons. But if there is a cause of action applicable, the court as a public authority must act compatibly with both parties' Convention rights....

Section 6 does not entitle courts to *create new torts*; but on the other hand, existing causes of action should be interpreted with regard to the Convention rights. That then is the formal position. In reality, recent changes have gone further than this. This was achieved principally through interpretation of section 12, rather than section 6, though the duty in section 6 is also frequently mentioned.

---

[17] See also Lord Steyn, '2000–2005: Laying the Foundations for Human Rights Law' (2005) 4 EHRLR 349.

Section 12

Section 12 is concerned with the Convention right to freedom of expression. But it is through consideration of this section that equal weight has been given to other Convention rights, including privacy. The impact of section 12 in this area of private law has been much greater than a surface reading would lead us to expect.

Section 12 of the HRA is extracted in Chapter 1.

The section requires that particular regard be had to the Article 10 right *in any case where a remedy is being considered* which may interfere with the Article 10 right. In *Douglas v Hello!*, it was pointed out that because regard must be had to freedom of expression *in any* such case (and not just in cases brought against public authorities), Article 10 must *necessarily have some horizontal effect*. Perhaps surprisingly, this section was also the vehicle through which Article 8 rights were given horizontal effect in that particular case. Having regard to the Article 10 right must involve having regard to the *restrictions* on the right outlined in Article 10(2), since these are an inherent part of the definition of the Convention right to freedom of expression. We extracted Article 10 in Chapter 13 (Defamation). Here is a reminder of the way the restrictions to the right operate.

Article 10.2

The exercise of [freedom of expression], since it carries with it duties and responsibilities, may be subject to such formalities, conditions, restrictions or penalties as are prescribed by law and are necessary in a democratic society, in the interests of national security, territorial integrity or public safety, for the prevention of disorder or crime, for the protection of health or morals, *for the protection of the reputation or rights of others, for preventing the disclosure of information received in confidence, or for maintaining the authority and impartiality of the judiciary.*

[Emphasis added]

In this way, section 12 gives limited horizontal effect not only to Article 10 rights, but also to all those other rights by which they are expressly qualified: *Douglas v Hello!* [2001] QB 967.

Equality between the Rights

On the face of it, section 12(4) gives priority to freedom of expression, since a court must have 'particular regard' to it. Since the section is primarily concerned with remedies, it might be assumed that it works against the availability of injunctions. An injunction was initially sought in *Douglas v Hello!* and importantly, this interpretation (giving priority to freedom of expression) was rejected. The restrictions in Article 10(2) are an inherent part of the definition of the Convention right to freedom of expression. Hence, the right and its restrictions should be given the same 'particular' consideration. This element of the Court of Appeal's approach—**equality between rights**—is consistent with the *Von Hannover* decision as outlined above,[18] and was strongly re-emphasized by the Supreme Court in *PJS v News Group Newspapers* [2016] AC 1081. Equality between rights is in marked contrast

[18] As we will see, equality between the rights was not so clearly recognized in *A v B plc* [2003] QB 195, for example, but it was endorsed by the House of Lords in *Campbell v MGN* [2004] UKHL; [2004] 2 AC 457.

with US law, which gives priority to freedom of expression, a contrast noted by Sedley LJ in *Douglas v Hello!* [2001] QB 967:

135 … The European Court of Human Rights has always recognised the high importance of free media of communication in a democracy, but its jurisprudence does not—and could not consistently with the Convention itself—give article 10(1) the presumptive priority which is given, for example, to the First Amendment in the jurisprudence of the United States' courts. Everything will ultimately depend on the proper balance between privacy and publicity in the situation facing the court.

Section 12(4)(b) also requires a court when considering freedom of expression to have regard to 'any relevant privacy code'.

Whatever judicial creativity can be observed in the earlier cases explored in the next section of this chapter, a recent Joint Committee of the House of Commons and House of Lords rejected criticisms from 'elements of the media' that the law in this area is 'judge-made' (hence, open to attack as undemocratic).

Joint Committee on Privacy and Injunctions, Session 2010–2012, Report (HL 273, HC 1443, 27 March 2012)

40. The laws around privacy already have statutory foundation. They have developed following the passing of the Human Rights Act 1998, which Parliament enacted in full knowledge that the common law would gradually develop a right to privacy in UK law. During the passage of the Human Rights Bill through the House of Lords the then chairman of the Press Complaints Commission, the Rt Hon Lord Wakeham, moved an amendment which aimed "to stop the development of a common law of privacy". The amendment was withdrawn. Replying to the debate on it the Lord Chancellor, the Rt Hon Lord Irvine of Lairg, said—

"I repeat my view that any privacy law developed by the judges will be a better law after incorporation of the convention because the judges will have to balance and have regard to articles 10 and 8, giving article 10 its due high value. What I have said is in accord with European jurisprudence."

In other words, the developments in the domestic courts charted here were more or less as anticipated; though perhaps the depth of influence of the Convention rights has exceeded expectations. The same point was made by Lord Neuberger in *PJS*:

Lord Neuberger, *PJS v News Group Newspapers* [2016] AC 1081

71 In the light of the facts as they currently appear and the law as it has now been developed, it appears to me that the interlocutory injunction sought by PJS should be granted. The courts exist to protect legal rights, even when their protection is difficult or unpopular in some quarters. And if Parliament takes the view that the courts have not adapted the law to fit current realities, then, of course, it can change the law, for instance by amending section 12 of the 1998 Act.

4. DEVELOPMENT OF THE NEW TORT

4.1 DISCLOSURE OF PRIVATE 'INFORMATION'

Following the HRA, spectacular developments in protection of privacy have taken place through development of the action for breach of confidence. Historically, this action has not been categorized as a tort. Rather, obligations of confidence have been recognized in equity, binding the recipient of information as a matter of conscience:

> 65 ... If information is accepted on the basis that it will be kept secret, the recipient's conscience is bound by that confidence, and it will be unconscionable for him to break his duty of confidence by publishing the information to others ...

Brooke LJ, *Douglas v Hello!*
[2001] QB 967

After some uncertainty, it is now clear that the new action is to be described as a tort, even though its origins lie in the action for breach of confidence, and in the enactment of the Human Rights Act. While the word 'tort' has been used in a number of cases, including *McKennitt v Ash*, it was only in *Vidal-Hall v Google Inc* [2015] EWCA Civ 311 that categorization became essential: this decision is extracted below. In order to understand the emergence of the new tort, some selected aspects of the large case law on breach of confidence are covered here. These are the aspects which are needed if we are to reach an understanding of the process by which privacy is emerging as a protected interest.

The Previously Existing Law: What is (or was) 'Breach of Confidence'?

It is true to say that even before the HRA came into force in October 2000, the action for breach of confidence was in a process of development and had been identified as having the potential to protect some aspects of privacy.[19] We can identify three requirements of the action for breach of confidence.

1. The information in question must have the 'necessary quality of confidentiality'.
2. The recipient of the information must be under an obligation of confidence.
3. The interest in confidentiality will be balanced against any public interest in disclosure.

The 'Necessary Quality of Confidentiality'

The action certainly protected commercial confidences or 'trade secrets'. In *Attorney-General v Guardian* [1987] 1 WLR 1248, it was found to extend to state secrets (and therefore prevented the defendant newspaper from publishing extracts from the book *Spycatcher*), but in such cases a positive public interest in protecting the confidence needed to be shown.

---

[19] *Hellewell v Chief Constable of Derbyshire* [1995] 1 WLR 804 per Laws LJ; W. Wilson, 'Privacy, Confidence and Press Freedom: A Study in Judicial Activism' (1990) 53 MLR 43, commenting on *Stephens v Avery* [1988] Ch 449.

It was important that the protected information must not be already in the public domain; and that it was not merely trivial. 'Confidence' extended to some information of a personal or sexual nature either within marriage (*Argyll v Argyll* [1967] Ch 302), or (more controversially) outside it (*Stephens v Avery* [1988] Ch 449). In the latter case, Sir Nicolas Browne-Wilkinson V-C held that personal information could be subject to a duty of confidence sufficient to give rise to an action to restrain its publication, even though the only relationship between the parties, at the time of disclosure, had been one of friendship.[20]

The Obligation of Confidence

It was for a long time considered essential that the information should have been conveyed to its recipient *subject to an obligation of confidence*. This was indeed the foundation of the action. Whereas 'confidentiality' is a quality of information, 'confidence' is a quality of the relationship between confider and the person confided in. This obligation would be binding on the conscience of the recipient and would provide a prima facie reason (subject to other considerations such as public interest, below) for protecting the confidence. Such an obligation, once established, could bind a third party (such as a newspaper) coming into possession of the information with notice of it. The duty might be express (for example a contractual term), or implied from the nature of the relationship within which the information was divulged.

In the more recent case law, it has been clearly stated that this sort of duty is no longer a *requirement* of the action for breach of confidence. The absence of any need for a distinct duty of confidence was described by Lord Hoffmann in *Campbell v MGN* [2004] 2 AC 457 at [48] as 'firmly established'. The question is whether this requirement ended with the Court of Appeal's ground-breaking decision in *Douglas v Hello!*, or before.

The following passage from the House of Lords' decision in *A-G v Guardian (No 2)* [1990] 1 AC 109, 281 has been widely quoted in recent cases. It shows that a **relationship** of confidence was no longer required in all cases even *before* the HRA. An obligation of confidence could arise where the information had not been deliberately divulged to the recipient at all.

Lord Goff of Chieveley, Attorney-General v Guardian (No 2) [1990] 1 AC 109, 281

I realise that, in the vast majority of cases, in particular those concerned with trade secrets, the duty of confidence will arise from a transaction or relationship between the parties—often a contract, in which event the duty may arise by reason of either an express or an implied term of that contract. It is in such cases as these that the expressions "confider" and "confidant" are perhaps most aptly employed. But it is well settled that a duty of confidence may arise in equity independently of such cases; and I have expressed the circumstances in which the duty arises in broad terms, not merely to embrace those cases where a third party receives information from a person who is under a duty of confidence in respect of it, knowing that it has been disclosed by that person to him in breach of his duty of confidence, but also to include certain situations, beloved of law teachers—where an obviously confidential document is wafted by an electric fan out of a window into a crowded street, or where an

[20] The information here was not trivial. It related to a lesbian affair conducted by the plaintiff with a woman who had then, perhaps as a consequence, been murdered by her husband.

obviously confidential document, such as a private diary, is dropped in a public place, and is then picked up by a passer-by.... I have however deliberately avoided the fundamental question whether, contract apart, the duty lies simply "in the notion of an obligation of conscience arising from the circumstances in or through which the information was communicated or obtained" (see *Moorgate Tobacco Ltd v Philip Morris Ltd (No 2)* (1984) 156 CLR 414, 438 ...).

Much has been made of this passage, yet it does not alter the classification of breach of confidence as an action arising **in equity**, out of obligations of confidence that are binding on the conscience of the defendant.[21] The recent developments outlined below undoubtedly take a further decisive step, protecting information *simply because of its private nature*. It may be this further step away from obligations binding in conscience that explains Lord Nicholls' decision (otherwise unexplained) to describe the action as a tort in *Campbell v MGN* [2004] 2 AC 457.

Public Interest in Disclosure

It was certainly realized before the HRA that public and private interests would have to be balanced when deciding whether to grant injunctions. Equally, it was realized that the 'public interest' in disclosure may engage Article 10 of the Convention. The 'public interest' in disclosure may be based on the need to disclose wrongdoing if that is indicated by the information concerned: 'there is no confidence in iniquity'.[22] Alternatively, there may be some other sort of public interest in disclosure. For example in *W v Egdell* [1990] Ch 359, a doctor who suspected that his patient should not be released on parole because he posed a *danger to public safety* was justified in releasing details from a medical report—ordinarily subject to confidentiality—to relevant parties. In *Attorney-General v Guardian (No 2)* [1990] 1 AC 109, Lord Goff stated the general (pre-HRA) position like this:

... although the basis of the law's protection of confidence is that there is a public interest that confidences should be preserved and protected by the law, nevertheless that public interest may be outweighed by some other countervailing public interest which favours disclosure. This limitation may apply, as the learned judge pointed out, to all types of confidential information. It is this limiting principle which may require a court to carry out a balancing operation, weighing the public interest in maintaining confidence against a countervailing public interest favouring disclosure.

Like the other elements listed above, the required balancing process has been transformed by the adaptation of the action to deal directly with privacy.

The traditional action for breach of confidence still exists, and it concerns information that was imparted subject to a duty of confidence (with the variations deriving from *A-G v Guardian Newspapers* referred to above). Alongside this has emerged a transformed action, in which the remedy for breach of confidence has become inhibited by a very different balancing process, based on the competing interests in privacy and expression. This second action has now broken away to be recognized as a tort, and is the subject of the remainder of this section. However, there are of course hybrid cases in which information has been

[21] See for example the discussion of breach of confidence in Sarah Worthington, *Equity* (Clarendon Press, 2003), chapter 5.

[22] *Fraser v Evans* [1969] 1 QB 349; Brooke LJ *Douglas v Hello!* at [65].

imparted subject to a duty of confidentiality (such as the duty implied in employment), and it is also information in which there is a reasonable expectation of privacy. In *HRH Prince of Wales v Associated Newspapers* [2006] EWHC 522 (Ch); [2008] Ch 57, the Court of Appeal explained that in such a case, the balance between Article 8 and Article 10 must be addressed, but the defendant has a more difficult task because it is not sufficient that publication of the material itself should be in the public interest; since there is also a legitimate public interest in confidences being kept, there must be shown to be a public interest in revealing the information which outweighs the importance of preserving confidentiality. This appears to mean that in an action which combines both privacy and a duty of confidence, the defendant must work harder to show that the balance favours publication.

The New Law: An Action in Respect of *Private* Information

The new case law stemming from *Douglas v Hello!* protects information *having a necessary quality of privacy*, against publication. There is no longer any need to show that the defendant is *bound in conscience* to keep the information private. Such cases are not 'breach of confidence' cases, since no confidence between the parties need be shown. They are to do with protection against (or remedies for) publication of *private information*. In *Vidal-Hall v Google*, the Court of Appeal had to decide whether this action should now be classified as a tort.

Lord Dyson MR and Sharp LJ, *Vidal-Hall v Google*
[2015] EWCA Civ 311

17 The issue of classification or nomenclature has been the subject of some discussion in the cases, and amongst academics. So far as we are aware however with the possible exception, on the defendant's case, of *Douglas v Hello! Ltd (No 3)* this is the first case in which the classification question has made a difference. Put shortly, if a claim for misuse of information is not a tort for the purposes of service out of the jurisdiction, but is classified as a claim for breach of confidence, then on the authority of the *Kitechnology* [1995] FSR 765, which is binding on us, the claimants will not be able to serve their claims for misuse of private information on the defendant.

18 Although the issue as framed in this appeal in one sense is a narrow one, it is none the less appropriate to look at it in the broader context. Fifteen years have passed since the coming into force of the Human Rights Act 1998 in October 2000, which incorporates into our domestic law the Convention for the Protection of Human Rights and Fundamental Freedoms. And it is a decade now since the seminal decision of the House of Lords in *Campbell v MGN Ltd* [2004] 2 AC 457. The problem the courts have had to grapple with during this period has been how to afford appropriate protection to privacy rights under article 8 of the Convention, in the absence (as was affirmed by the House of Lords in *Wainwright v Home Office* [2004] 2 AC 406) of a common law tort of invasion of privacy.

19 We were taken to a number of cases by Mr White to establish what is in fact an uncontroversial proposition—that the gap was bridged by developing and adapting the law of confidentiality to protect one aspect of invasion of privacy, the misuse of private information. This addressed the tension between the requirement to give appropriate effect to the right to respect for private and family life set out in article 8 of the Convention and the common law's perennial need (for the best of reasons, that of legal certainty) to appear not to be doing anything for the first time (to which Sedley LJ pointed in one of the earliest cases in which this issue was addressed: *Douglas v Hello! Ltd* [2001] QB 967, para 111...

20 Thus, in *A v B plc* [2003] QB 195, para 4 Lord Woolf CJ, giving the judgment of the court, said that articles 8 and 10 of the Convention provided new parameters within which the courts would decide actions for breach of confidence, and that the court could act in a way that was compatible with Convention rights, as it was required to do under section 6 of the 1998 Act, by absorbing the rights which articles 8 and 10 protect into the long established action for breach of confidence.

21 However, a number of things need to be said. First, there are problems with an analysis which fails to distinguish between a breach of confidentiality and an infringement of privacy rights protected by article 8, not least because the concepts of confidence and privacy are not the same and protect different interests. Secondly, as has been consistently emphasised by the courts, we are concerned with a developing area of the law. Although the process may have started as one of absorption (per Lord Woolf CJ) it is clear that, contrary to the submissions of the defendant, there are now two separate and distinct causes of action: an action for breach of confidence; and one for misuse of private information. Thirdly, it is also the case that the action for misuse of private information has been referred to as a tort by the courts.

Illustrating how far the law has developed, in *PJS v News Group Newspapers*, Lord Mance simply and consistently referred to avoidance of 'tortious invasion of privacy rights'.

The action to protect private information is now interpreted as having the following *two* requirements:

The Claimant Must Have Had a 'Reasonable Expectation of Privacy' in the Information (or Images) in Question

This is the test adopted by the majority of judges in *Campbell v MGN* [2004] 2 AC 457, and it has been consistently applied and interpreted by the courts.

The Court Must Balance the Interest in Keeping the Information Private Against the Interest in Revealing the Information

This now clearly involves interpretation of competing Convention rights (and potentially other interests too), in the light of provisions of the HRA. Article 10(2), as explained earlier, is the source of this balancing exercise. The right to freedom of expression in Article 10 is inherently qualified by other rights and interests. Further, Article 10 is interpreted chiefly in terms of *public interest* in disclosure. This is essential because in many but not all cases, the person who wishes to publicize the information will be a media defendant, and their 'personal' interest may be regarded as chiefly commercial. The applicable approach is now closely modelled on the European Court of Human Rights' judgment in *Von Hannover*. *Defendants must show convincing reasons why there is a proportionate reason of public interest to justify publication in the face of a reasonable expectation of privacy.*

Douglas v Hello! [2001] QB 967

A celebrity couple (Michael Douglas and Catherine Zeta-Jones) entered into a contract with *OK!* magazine, giving the magazine exclusive rights to publish photographs of the couple's wedding. All employees and guests at the wedding were explicitly instructed that no photography was allowed, except by the official photographer. Somehow, someone at the wedding took photographs and these fell into the hands of *OK!* magazine's rival, *Hello!*, which planned to publish them. Importantly, it was not clear whether these photographs were taken by somebody who had been invited to the wedding; by an employee; or by an intruder. Had they been taken by an intruder, then it could not be said that the photographs in question were taken *in breach of an obligation of confidence*; there would have been no relationship at all. It was this possibility which led the Court of Appeal to consider whether the publication of the photographs could instead be restrained on the basis that they were *private*.

Although the loss suffered by *OK!* was purely commercial in nature, the couple themselves also lost the opportunity to *control* the published images of this private event, despite their best efforts (see the contractual right of veto referred to at [140] below), and this could be described in terms of 'privacy'. It should be noted that this was an 'interim' action in which the claimants sought to prevent publication pending the full hearing on the merits. The Court of Appeal discharged the injunctions, but the claimants, and *OK!* magazine whose contractual rights to print the photographs were rendered less valuable, sought damages and these claims were assessed by the Court of Appeal in *Douglas v Hello! (No 3)* [2006] QB 125. In this later decision, the Court of Appeal accepted that the law in this area had moved so rapidly that it could now be seen that an injunction for the benefit of the Douglases should have been maintained in the present case.[23] This does not alter the far-reaching significance of this case. In fact, it shows how clearly the changes outlined by the Court of Appeal have been recognized within a short space of time.

Of the three judgments, that of Sedley LJ contains the clearest statement that information will now be protected on the basis that it is *private*.

Sedley LJ

110 ... The courts have done what they can, using such legal tools as were to hand, to stop the more outrageous invasions of individuals' privacy; but they have felt unable to articulate their measures as a discrete principle of law. Nevertheless, we have reached a point at which it can be said with confidence that the law recognises and will appropriately protect a right of personal privacy.

111 The reasons are twofold. First, equity and the common law are today in a position to respond to an increasingly invasive social environment by affirming that everybody has a right to some private space. Secondly, and in any event, the Human Rights Act 1998 requires the courts of this country to give appropriate effect to the right to respect for private and family life set out in article 8 of the European Convention for the Protection of Human Rights and Fundamental Freedoms. The difficulty with the first proposition resides in the common law's perennial need (for the best of reasons, that of legal certainty) to appear not to be doing anything for the first time. The difficulty with the second lies in the word "appropriate". But the two sources of law now run in a single channel because, by virtue of section 2 and section 6 of the Act, the courts of this country must not only take into account jurisprudence of both the Commission and the European Court of Human Rights which points to a positive institutional obligation to respect privacy; they must themselves act compatibly with that and the other Convention rights. This, for reasons I now turn to, arguably gives the final impetus to the recognition of a right of privacy in English law.

...

[23] *OK!* lost their claim based on breach of confidence, but succeeded on appeal to the House of Lords.

126 What a concept of privacy does ... is accord recognition to the fact that the law has to protect not only those people whose trust has been abused but those who simply find themselves subjected to an unwanted intrusion into their personal lives. The law no longer needs to construct an artificial relationship of confidentiality between intruder and victim: it can recognise privacy itself as a legal principle drawn from the fundamental value of personal autonomy.

The above paragraphs of Sedley LJ's judgment are clearly ground-breaking in that they recognize privacy itself as the basis of a cause of action, independent of the requirement for a relationship of confidence or trust. On his analysis, the HRA had given the final push to a change that had already been slowly taking shape. Now, since *Wainwright* and *Campbell*, we can clearly see that English law still recognizes no *general* action to protect privacy. But in some actions to restrain publication, privacy is protected in its own right.

Equally significant were the more detailed elements of Sedley LJ's judgment, considering the way in which privacy would need to be balanced against freedom of expression when considering remedies. Here he considered the relevant approach to a claim for an injunction to restrain publication. But first, Sedley LJ analysed the provisions of the HRA. His analysis is a defining moment in that it recognizes horizontality, *and* equity between rights. It does so through interpretation of section 12.

133 Two initial points need to be made about section 12 of the Act. First, by subsection (4) it puts beyond question the direct applicability of at least one article of the Convention as between one private party to litigation and another—in the jargon, its horizontal effect. Whether this is an illustration of the intended mechanism of the entire Act, or whether it is a special case (and if so, why), need not detain us here. The other point, well made by Mr Tugendhat, is that it is "the Convention right" to freedom of expression which both triggers the section (see section 12(1)) and to which particular regard is to be had. That Convention right, when one turns to it, is qualified in favour of the reputation and rights of others and the protection of information received in confidence. In other words, you cannot have particular regard to article 10 without having equally particular regard at the very least to article 8 ... The approach in this paragraph was cited with approval by both Lord Hope (in the majority) and Lord Hoffmann (dissenting) in *Campbell v MGN*, below.

Having concluded that Articles 8 and 10 were both given a degree of horizontal effect by section 12 of the HRA, Sedley LJ went on to consider how the two should be balanced given the nature of the rights themselves, and given the terms of section 12.

136 ... It will be necessary for the court, in applying the test set out in section 12(3), to bear in mind that by virtue of section 12(1)(4) the qualifications set out in article 10(2) are as relevant as the right set out in article 10(1). This means that, for example, the reputations and rights of others—not only but not least their Convention rights—are as material as the defendant's right of free expression. So is the prohibition on the use of one party's Convention rights to injure the Convention rights of others. Any other approach to section 12 would in my judgment violate section 3 of the Act.[24] Correspondingly, as Mr Tugendhat submits, "likely" in

24 Section 3 provides that 'So far as it is possible to do so, primary legislation and subordinate legislation must be read and given effect in a way that is compatible with the Convention rights.' The only legislation being interpreted in this case was of course the HRA itself.

section 12(3) cannot be read as requiring simply an evaluation of the relative strengths of the parties' evidence. If at trial, for the reasons I have given, a minor but real risk to life, or a wholly unjustifiable invasion of privacy, is entitled to no less regard, by virtue of article 10(2), than is accorded to the right to publish by article 10(1), the consequent likelihood becomes material under section 12(3). Neither element is a trump card. They will be articulated by the principles of legality and proportionality which, as always, constitute the mechanism by which the court reaches its conclusion on countervailing or qualified rights. It will be remembered that in the jurisprudence of the Convention proportionality is tested by, among other things, the standard of what is necessary in a democratic society. It should also be borne in mind that the much-quoted remark of Hoffmann LJ in *R v Central Independent Television plc* [1994] Fam 192, 203 that freedom of speech "is a trump card which always wins" came in a passage which expressly qualified the proposition (as Lord Hoffmann has since confirmed, albeit extrajudicially, in his 1996 Goodman Lecture) as lying "outside the established exceptions, or any new ones which Parliament may enact in accordance with its obligations under the Convention". If freedom of expression is to be impeded, in other words, it must be on cogent grounds recognised by law.

The following paragraph gives a useful summary of the entire reasoning process where the privacy action is concerned:

137 Let me summarise. For reasons I have given, Mr Douglas and Ms Zeta-Jones have a powerful prima facie claim to redress for invasion of their privacy as a qualified right recognized and protected by English law. The case being one which affects the Convention right of freedom of expression, section 12 of the Human Rights Act 1998 requires the court to have regard to article 10 (as, in its absence, would section 6). This, however, cannot, consistently with section 3 and article 17, give the article 10(1) right of free expression a presumptive priority over other rights. What it does is require the court to consider article 10(2) along with 10(1), and by doing so to bring into the frame the conflicting right to respect for privacy. This right, contained in article 8 and reflected in English law, is in turn qualified in both contexts by the right of others to free expression. The outcome, which self-evidently has to be the same under both articles, is determined principally by considerations of proportionality.

Having outlined the method by which Article 8 rights may be both recognized as protected in an action to restrain publication, and qualified by the right to freedom of expression, Sedley LJ went on to decide that in this particular case, an interim injunction to restrain publication would **not** be granted.

144 In the present case, and not without misgiving, I have concluded that, although the first two claimants are likely to succeed at trial in establishing a breach of their privacy in which "Hello!" may be actionably implicated, the dominant feature of the case is that by far the greater part of that privacy has already been traded and falls to be protected, if at all, as a commodity in the hands of the third claimant. This can be done without the need of an injunction, particularly since there may not be adequate countervailing redress for the defendants if at trial they stave off the claim for interference with contractual relations. The retained element of the first two claimants' privacy is not in my judgment—though I confess it is a close thing—sufficient to tilt the balance of justice and convenience against such liberty as the defendants may establish, at law and under article 10, to publish the illicitly taken photographs.

Sedley LJ considered that the interests of the claimants were predominantly commercial. For that reason, he mentions an important remedy which we touched on in Chapter 8: the 'account of profits'. This remedy is thought to provide a significant deterrent effect because rather than seeking to compensate the claimant for their losses, it requires the defendant to pay back (or 'disgorge') the profits they have wrongfully acquired in breach of equitable obligation. In principle, it therefore removes the profit motive. Although the boundaries between equity and common law are both fluid and questionable,[25] the account of profits has traditionally been seen as an *equitable* remedy, particularly appropriate in cases where the balance has come down against the grant of an interim injunction.[26] Apart from its deterrent effect, the remedy will often provide appropriate compensation.

Typically however, *privacy* (as opposed to *commercial confidence*) may not be sufficiently compensated by an account of profits. Although the account of profits is a powerful remedy, in such cases it falls far short, in terms of its value to the claimant, of an injunction. The reason why Sedley LJ thought the balance was a 'close thing' in this case was that there was still, despite the commercial context of the agreements, a small element of retained privacy. This retained element of privacy may have come down to the ability to choose which photographs were released. If so, this was outweighed by the interest in freedom of expression. In *Douglas v Hello! (No 3)* (extracted later in this section) it was said that this retained element of privacy, small though it is, should have been protected through an injunction. Following *Von Hannover v Germany*, it was clear that where *publication of the photographs was not required on the basis of any public interest argument*, there was nothing to put into the balance on the side of Article 10. The small element of retained privacy was therefore sufficient.

Many cases have followed. There has been a clear trend towards requiring convincing reasons for publication, in circumstances where there is a 'reasonable expectation of privacy', and towards more direct reliance on the reasoning in the first *Von Hannover* decision. The Convention rights in Articles 8 and 10 are now accepted to provide 'the very content of the domestic tort'.[27] Given the considerable amount of case law that has built up, we can only cover some aspects of the developing law. Here we consider cases involving intimate details, often of a sexual nature; cases involving photographs; the nature of the balance to be struck between Article 8 and Article 10; and cases involving children.

Intimate Details

Although publications revealing intimate details are often 'trivial' in tone, the harm done should not be assumed to be trivial or even simple.[28] The difficulty is that there is a ready audience—and market—for such revelations.

25 Sarah Worthington, *Equity*, chapters 1 and 10.

26 Worthington, *Equity*, pp. 140–3. The availability of profits-based 'disgorgement' damages for tort is discussed by James Edelman, *Gain-Based Damages* (Hart Publishing, 2002). The Court of Appeal in *Douglas v Hello! (No 3)* clearly thought the remedy was available and it is unlikely this would depend on categorization as tort or equitable wrong. See N. Witzleb, 'Monetary Remedies for Breach of Confidence in Privacy Cases' (2007) 27 LS 430–64.

27 Lord Woolf, *A v B plc* [2002] EWCA Civ 337. This statement is often referred to by subsequent courts as a reason for departing from Lord Woolf's own reasoning and turning to *Von Hannover* for guidance instead.

28 For exploration of the complex harms and motives which may confront the law see J. Richardson, 'If I Cannot Have Her Everybody Can: Sexual Disclosure and Privacy Law', in J. Richardson and E. Rackley (eds), *Feminist Perspectives on Tort Law* (Routledge, 2012).

A v B plc [2003] QB 195

A v B plc was an early exercise in providing guidelines for the award of interim injunctions after *Douglas v Hello!* In hindsight, Lord Woolf's approach does not appear true to the 'presumptive equality between rights' set out in *Douglas v Hello!* and reaffirmed in numerous cases. A review serves to illustrate how far the law has moved.

The claimant in this case, a married professional footballer, sought injunctions against a newspaper, in order to prevent disclosure of sexual relationships he had had with the second defendant and another woman. He also sought an injunction against the second defendant, preventing her from disclosing her 'kiss and tell' story to anyone 'with a view to its publication in the media'. He obtained these injunctions at first instance, but they were discharged by the Court of Appeal.

In *A v B*, Lord Woolf explained his general conclusion that the injunction should be discharged:

> **44** ... The degree of confidentiality to which A was entitled, notwithstanding that C and D did not wish their relationship with A to be confidential, was very modest.

Lord Woolf's approach in this case no longer represents the law and would not pass the test of compatibility with the *Von Hannover* decision, for at least two reasons.[29]

First, in para [11(v)], Lord Woolf asserted that there is no need to show an identifiable public interest in publication, in order to engage Article 10: restraining publication is a restriction of free speech per se and requires justification. This is directly opposed to the approach taken in *Von Hannover*, which held that the state must act to prevent even fairly anodyne photographs from being published, if there was a reasonable expectation of privacy in relation to them, and unless there was a distinct countervailing interest in expression attached to their publication.

Second, Lord Woolf treated *understandable* interest on the part of the public as equivalent to *legitimate* interest. This seems to mean that voyeurism—at least where celebrities are concerned—weighs in the balance in favour of publication, no matter how lurid the reporting concerned.[30] He added to this that courts should not be the arbiters of taste. But the decision in *Von Hannover* requires a specific public interest in disclosure. Subsequently, courts have appealed directly to *Von Hannover* and, while not attempting to be 'arbiters of taste', they have nevertheless protected the expectation of privacy in sexual relationships—even if these are adulterous, unconventional, or based on a commercial transaction—and have demanded positive reasons to justify publication where there is some reasonable expectation of privacy. There has been a decisive shift therefore in the way that privacy in sexual relationships is protected.

A key illustration of how the law had changed on this issue is *Mosley v News Group Newspapers Ltd* [2008] EWHC 1777 (QB); [2008] EMLR 20. Here the defendants published sensational stories in their newspaper and on the internet based on clandestine recordings of sexual encounters between the claimant and a number of women, who were paid for their participation.

[29] For further discussion see G. Phillipson, 'Judicial Reasoning in Breach of Confidence Actions Under the Human Rights Act: Not Taking Privacy Seriously?' (2003) EHRLR Supp. 54.
[30] The style of reporting was described as a matter of taste not law, and a question for the Press Complaints Commission and the customers of the newspaper concerned, not for the courts.

Eady J awarded damages against the defendant for the invasions of privacy involved in the publications. His starting point was that there is a reasonable expectation of privacy in sexual activity between consenting adults in private, provided there is no serious breach of the criminal law: 'people's sex lives are essentially their own business.' Not only did this apply to encounters in the nature of an orgy, it could also apply where the transaction is purely commercial in nature (though in this instance, the evidence suggested the relationships were not purely commercial, and all the participants felt betrayed by the woman who had passed information and images to the newspaper). Clearly the public (or a section of it) was interested in the stories, but in order to justify publication, the defendants had to show a real reason why the public interest in publication outweighed the expectation of privacy already established. The newspaper attempted an argument based on the need to reveal that a person with a position of public importance (within the FIA) had conducted what they described as 'Nazi themed' orgies. Eady J examined this proposed public interest justification and determined that the orgies were not 'Nazi themed'. They only had a normal sado-masochistic flavour. Eady J's dismissal of the newspaper's claims is based on rejection of moralism: the revelation of 'unconventional' activities is not sufficient to engage legitimate public interest. The direct contrast with *A v B* on this issue is clear.

Eady J, *Max Mosley v News Group Newspapers*

The Nazi and concentration camp theme

123 ... since I have concluded that there was no such mocking behaviour and not even, on the material I have viewed, any evidence of imitating, adopting or approving Nazi behaviour, I am unable to identify any legitimate public interest to justify either the intrusion of secret filming or the subsequent publication.

"Depravity and adultery"

124 I need to consider, therefore, whether the residual S and M behaviour and other admitted aspects of what took place on March 28 could be said in themselves to be matters of legitimate journalistic investigation or public interest. Mr Warby described it as immoral, depraved and to an extent adulterous. Everyone now, thanks to the News of the World, probably holds an opinion on that, but even if there was adultery and even if one happens to agree that it was "depraved", it by no means follows that they are matters of genuine public interest, as that is understood in the case law.

125 The modern approach to personal privacy and to sexual preferences and practices is very different from that of past generations. First, there is a greater willingness, and especially in the Strasbourg jurisprudence, to accord respect to an individual's right to conduct his or her personal life without state interference or condemnation. It has now to be recognised that sexual conduct is a significant aspect of human life in respect of which people should be free to choose. That freedom is one of the matters which Art.8 protects: governments and courts are required to afford remedies when that right is breached.

126 Secondly, as Lord Nicholls at [17]–[18] and Lord Hoffmann at [50] observed in *Campbell* in 2004, remedies should be available against private individuals and corporations (including the media) because, absent any serious element of public interest, they are obliged to

respect personal privacy as much as public bodies. It is not merely state intrusion that should be actionable....

127 Thirdly, it is not for the state or for the media to expose sexual conduct which does not involve any significant breach of the criminal law. That is so whether the motive for such intrusion is merely prurience or a moral crusade. It is not for journalists to undermine human rights, or for judges to refuse to enforce them, merely on grounds of taste or moral disapproval. Everyone is naturally entitled to espouse moral or religious beliefs to the effect that certain types of sexual behaviour are wrong or demeaning to those participating. That does not mean that they are entitled to hound those who practise them or to detract from their right to live life as they choose.

128 It is important, in this new rights-based jurisprudence, to ensure that where breaches occur remedies are not refused because an individual journalist or judge finds the conduct distasteful or contrary to moral or religious teaching. Where the law is not breached, as I said earlier, the private conduct of adults is essentially no one else's business. The fact that a particular relationship happens to be adulterous, or that someone's tastes are unconventional or "perverted", does not give the media *carte blanche*.

The key then is that to outweigh a reasonable expectation of privacy, the revelation must contribute to debate. It is not enough that there is a ready audience for it.

Having concluded that the claimant's Article 8 rights had been violated, a substantial award of damages was made, but no additional exemplary damages were included. The reason for this was that the action is closely modelled on the jurisprudence of the Strasbourg court. Strasbourg awards do not include an award of exemplary damages, and to do so would not be consistent with 'proportionality'.[31] While some in the media claimed that 'judge-made law' was now working too hard in favour of privacy and neglecting freedom of expression,[32] a Joint Committee of both Houses of Parliament concluded, after hearing evidence, not only that the courts were now striking a 'better' balance between privacy and free speech, but also that the levels of damages awarded had been 'too low to act as a deterrent': courts should be given the power to award exemplary damages for privacy violations, if necessary through legislation.[33]

The question of damages for invasions of privacy was visited again in the case of *Gulati and others v MGN Ltd* [2015] EWCA Civ 1291. This was a test case in which substantial damages awards made to a number of victims of 'phone hacking' by journalists were challenged on appeal. The highest award was £80,000, and others stood at £40,000, and it was argued that these were too high; and that they did not stand comparison with Strasbourg awards; further that they should be comparable to such awards, because of the influence of the Convention in developing the action to protect private information. Citing the comments of Lord Hoffmann in relation to libel damages in *The Gleaner*, extracted in Chapter 13, the Court of Appeal concluded that English law offered the appropriate guidance in this case—there was no need to reach results which were similar to Strasbourg awards:

---

[31] Touching on these issues, see K. Hughes, *Horizontal Privacy* (2009) 125 LQR 244–7. For discussion of other non-compensatory damages see N. Witzleb, 'Justifying Gain-based Remedies for Invasion of Privacy' (2009) OJLS 1–39.

[32] Most notably, on the part of Paul Dacre, Editor in Chief of Associated Newspapers, Speech to the Society of Editors, November 2008.

[33] Joint Committee on Privacy and Injunctions, 2012, para 134.

Arden LJ, *Gulati v MGN Ltd*
[2015] EWCA Civ 1291

88 … English law has only recently recognised a civil wrong for intrusions of privacy. Initially the law of confidence was expanded by reference to the values to be found in articles 8 and 10 of the Convention. However an action for breach of confidence did not completely coincide with a right of action for pursuing private information in violation of article 8: see *Vidal-Hall* [2015] 3 WLR 409, para 21. In *Vidal-Hall*, para 51, this court took the important step of holding that, in so far as a claim was based on the use of private information, the legal wrong was the tort of misuse of private information for the purposes at least of service out of the jurisdiction, rather than breach of confidence.

89 The court, when making an award for misuse of private information is not proceeding under either section 8 of the Human Rights Act 1998 or article 41 of the Convention. The question of the measure of damages is more naturally a question for English domestic law. I give two reasons for this. First, the conditions of the tort are governed by English law and not the Convention. That again makes it more appropriate for English domestic law to assess the measure of damages. Moreover, if damages awarded for misuse of private information within the law were excessive, there would be appropriate ways for the national authorities to reduce them. They would not have to wait to be given a lead by the Strasbourg court. Second, national courts are intrinsically better able to assess the adequacy of an award in their jurisdiction than an international body. This is one of the bases in which the Strasbourg court is likely to recognise that there is a margin of appreciation in its jurisprudence.

In a passage which helps to underline the significance of privacy and the need for press regulation, the Court of Appeal was clear in its condemnation of the defendants' conduct. The following paragraph answered the defendants' argument that where there were multiple claims, the court should 'step back', and look at the awards in their entirety. The Court saw no reason why the awards should be 'scaled back' on this basis.

Arden LJ, *Gulati v MGN*

106 Indeed, so far as I can see, there were no mitigating circumstances at all. The employees of MGN instead repeatedly engaged in disgraceful actions and ransacked the claimants' voicemail to produce in many cases demeaning articles about wholly innocent members of the public in order to create stories for MGN's newspapers. They appear to have been totally uncaring about the real distress and damage to relationships caused by their callous actions. There are numerous examples in the articles of the disclosure of private medical information, attendance at rehabilitation clinics, domestic violence, emotional calls to partners, details of plans for meeting friends and partners, finances and details of confidential employment negotiations, which the judge found could not have been made if the information had not been obtained by hacking or some other wrongful means. The disclosures were strikingly distressing to the claimants involved.

PJS v News Group Newspapers Ltd [2016] UKSC 26; [2016] AC 1081

The decision of the Supreme Court in *PJS* decisively affirms the developments above. The claimant, a well-known figure in the music industry and partner of a well-known musician with whom he had two children, sought to restrain 'kiss and tell' revelations concerning his extra-marital sexual activities in a national newspaper. An interim injunction was awarded, but the newspaper sought its discharge: information about the identity of the claimant and his partner, and information about his activities, had already been printed in other jurisdictions, and were available on the internet to those who sought them. The Supreme Court maintained the injunctions. The Court emphasized that 'tortious interference with privacy', as Lord Mance described it, was quite different from breach of confidence. Privacy may well continue to be worth protecting even when certain details have been shared with some readers: confidentiality, by contrast, tends to be lost on publication.

In addition, the Supreme Court strongly defended the importance of privacy in relation to adulterous sexual relationships; the need for there to be some convincing public interest reason for publication where a reasonable expectation of privacy existed; and the need to take into consideration the privacy interests of children where revelations about their parents are threatened. We deal with the first two of these here; and the issue of children separately below.

In the following extract, Lord Mance explains that the Court of Appeal had erred in suggesting that section 12 enhances the weight to be given to freedom of expression:

Lord Mance, *PJS v News Group Newspapers*

19 There is, as all members of the Supreme Court conclude, a clear error of law in the Court of Appeal's reasoning in relation to section 12. For reasons given in para 20 below, it consists in the self-direction [2016] EWCA Civ 393 at [40] that section 12 enhances the weight which article 10 rights carry in the balancing exercise. …

20 The Court of Appeal's initial self-direction is … contrary to considerable authority, including authority at the highest level, which establishes that, even at the interlocutory stage, (i) neither article has preference over the other, (ii) where their values are in conflict, what is necessary is an intense focus on the comparative importance of the rights being claimed in the individual case, (iii) the justifications for interfering with or restricting each right must be taken into account and (iv) the proportionality test must be applied …

The Justices concluded that the Court of Appeal had gone wrong, not only in regarding section 12 as elevating the importance of freedom of expression, but in considering that the defendant's planned revelations were supported by any public interest argument at all:

ii) *The reference to a limited public interest*

21 The Court of Appeal in my opinion also erred in the reference it made, at three points in its judgment (paras 13, 30 and 47), to there being in the circumstances even a limited public interest in the proposed story and in its introduction of that supposed interest into a balancing exercise: para 47(v). In identifying this interest, the Court of Appeal relied upon a point made by an earlier Court of Appeal in the *Hutcheson* case [2012] EMLR 2 (and before that by Tugendhat J in the *Terry* case [2010] 2 FLR 1306), namely that the media are entitled to criticise the conduct of individuals even where there is nothing illegal about it. That is obviously so. But criticism of conduct cannot be a pretext for invasion of privacy by disclosure of alleged sexual infidelity which is of no real public interest in a legal sense. It is beside the point that the claimant and his partner are in other contexts subjects of public and media attention factors without which the issue would hardly arise or come to court. It remains beside the point, however much their private sexual conduct might interest the public and help sell newspapers or copy.

...

24 In these circumstances, it may be that the mere reporting of sexual encounters of someone like the claimant, however well known to the public, with a view to criticising them does not even fall within the concept of freedom of expression under article 10 at all. But, accepting that article 10 is not only engaged but capable in principle of protecting any form of expression, these cases clearly demonstrate that this type of expression is at the bottom end of the spectrum of importance (compared, for example, with freedom of political speech or a case of conduct bearing on the performance of a public office). For present purposes, any public interest in publishing such criticism must, in the absence of any other, legally recognised, public interest, be effectively disregarded in any balancing exercise and is incapable by itself of outweighing such article 8 privacy rights as the claimant enjoys.

In the final paragraph above, Lord Mance questions whether Article 10 is engaged at all in the absence of a public interest reason for publication. But even setting this aside, there was no relevant public interest which was *capable* of being weighed in the balance. There was simply nothing to weigh against the claimant's privacy. A general approach to such cases was set out:

32 ... Every case must be considered on its particular facts. But the starting point is that (i) there is not, without more, any public interest in a legal sense in the disclosure or publication of purely private sexual encounters, even though they involve adultery or more than one person at the same time, (ii) any such disclosure or publication will on the face of it constitute the tort of invasion of privacy, (iii) repetition of such a disclosure or publication on further occasions is capable of constituting a further tort of invasion of privacy, even in relation to persons to whom disclosure or publication was previously made—especially if it occurs in a different medium ...

Photographs

Campbell v MGN [2004] UKHL 22; [2004] 2 AC 457

In this case, the House of Lords had its first opportunity to consider the developments charted earlier in this section. The claimant, Naomi Campbell, was a renowned model, who had publicly stated that she did not take drugs. This was untrue, and it was common ground that this untruth put factual reporting of her drug addiction into the public domain: there is a public interest, engaging Article 10, in correcting untrue information, especially where the speaker is a role model. The defendant newspaper published articles which not only disclosed her drug addiction, but also detailed her self-help treatment through 'Narcotics Anonymous'. The reports gave details of group meetings and showed photographs of her in the street leaving the meetings.

By a majority (Lords Hope and Carswell and Baroness Hale), the House of Lords awarded modest damages. Lords Nicholls and Hoffmann dissented. The reasons for the narrowness of the majority do not relate to the most general questions about privacy and confidence, and the authoritative statements on these topics can be drawn from all five judgments. Significantly, these confirm the steps taken in *Douglas v Hello!* All five judges were agreed that certain elements of the reports—the bare fact of addiction for example—were justified in the public interest. The difference of view was whether any of the remaining details were themselves sufficient to warrant an award of damages, or whether they should be regarded as within the area of journalistic discretion.

The issues must be approached in two stages, reflecting the two criteria for the new action that we outlined earlier. First, did the information have the necessary quality of privacy? Second, if the claimant's interest in privacy was weighed against the public interest in disclosure (protected by Article 10), where did the balance lie? Importantly, all the judges agreed that there was presumptive equality between these rights, *even* in a case between private individuals. Despite the prohibition on new causes of action, the House of Lords therefore endorsed the horizontal effect of Convention rights *within* causes of action as explained by Sedley LJ in *Douglas v Hello!* If anything, it was the two dissenting judges who most clearly endorsed the idea that the action for breach of confidence has been transformed and that it now recognized privacy as a protected interest.

Lord Nicholls (dissenting)

13 The common law or, more precisely, courts of equity have long afforded protection to the wrongful use of private information by means of the cause of action which became known as breach of confidence. A breach of confidence was restrained as a form of unconscionable conduct, akin to a breach of trust. Today this nomenclature is misleading. The breach of confidence label harks back to the time when the cause of action was based on improper use of information disclosed by one person to another in confidence. To attract protection the information had to be of a confidential nature. But the gist of the cause of action was that information of this character had been disclosed by one person to another in circumstances "importing an obligation of confidence" even though no contract of non-disclosure existed: see the classic exposition by Megarry J in *Coco v A N Clark (Engineers) Ltd* [1969] RPC 41, 47–48. The confidence referred to in the phrase "breach of confidence" was the confidence arising out of a confidential relationship.

14 This cause of action has now firmly shaken off the limiting constraint of the need for an initial confidential relationship. In doing so it has changed its nature. In this country this development was recognised clearly in the judgment of Lord Goff of Chieveley in *Attorney General v Guardian Newspapers Ltd (No 2)* [1990] 1 AC 109, 281. Now the law imposes a "duty of confidence" whenever a person receives information he knows or ought to know is fairly and reasonably be regarded as confidential. Even this formulation is awkward. The continuing use of the phrase "duty of confidence" and the description of the information as "confidential" is not altogether comfortable. Information about an individual's private life would not, in ordinary usage, be called "confidential". The more natural description today is that such information is private. The essence of the tort is better encapsulated now as misuse of private information.

15 In the case of individuals this tort, however labelled, affords respect for one aspect of an individual's privacy. That is the value underlying this cause of action. An individual's privacy can be invaded in ways not involving publication of information. Strip searches are an example. The extent to which the common law as developed thus far in this country protects other forms of invasion of privacy is not a matter arising in the present case. It does not arise because, although pleaded more widely, Miss Campbell's common law claim was throughout presented in court exclusively on the basis of breach of confidence, that is, the wrongful *publication* by the "Mirror" of private *information*.

...

Given that the claimant had put her drug addiction into the public domain (by lying), Lord Nicholls expressly doubted (at [26]) whether further information about her treatment retained 'the character of private information'. However, he continued:

28 ... I would not wish to found my conclusion solely on this point. I prefer to proceed to the next stage and consider how the tension between privacy and freedom of expression should be resolved in this case, on the assumption that the information regarding Miss Campbell's attendance at Narcotics Anonymous meetings retained its private character. At this stage I consider Miss Campbell's claim must fail. I can state my reason very shortly. On the one hand, publication of this information in the unusual circumstances of this case represents, at most, an intrusion into Miss Campbell's private life to a comparatively minor degree. On the other hand, non-publication of this information would have robbed a legitimate and sympathetic newspaper story of attendant detail which added colour and conviction. This information was published in order to demonstrate Miss Campbell's commitment to tackling her drug problem. The balance ought not to be held at a point which would preclude, in this case, a degree of journalistic latitude in respect of information published for this purpose.

...

Lord Hoffmann (dissenting)

61 That brings me to what seems to be the only point of principle which arises in this case. Where the main substance of the story is conceded to have been justified, should the newspaper be held liable whenever the judge considers that it was not necessary to have published some of the personal information? Or should the newspaper be allowed some margin of choice in the way it chooses to present the story?

62 In my opinion, it would be inconsistent with the approach which has been taken by the courts in a number of recent landmark cases for a newspaper to be held strictly liable for exceeding what a judge considers to have been necessary. The practical exigencies of journalism demand that some latitude must be given. Editorial decisions have to be made quickly and with less information than is available to a court which afterwards reviews the matter at leisure. And if any margin is to be allowed, it seems to me strange to hold the "Mirror" liable in damages for a decision which three experienced judges in the Court of Appeal have held to be perfectly justified.

Baroness Hale

156 ... The editor accepted that even without the photographs, it would have been a front page story. He had his basic information and he had his quotes. There is no shortage of photographs with which to illustrate and brighten up a story about Naomi Campbell. No doubt some of those available are less flattering than others, so that if he had wanted to run a hostile piece he could have done so. The fact that it was a sympathetic story is neither here nor there. The way in which he chose to present the information he was entitled to reveal was entirely a matter for him. The photographs would have been useful in proving the truth of the story had this been challenged, but there was no need to publish them for this purpose. The credibility of the story with the public would stand or fall with the credibility of "Mirror" stories generally.

157 The weight to be attached to these various considerations is a matter of fact and degree. Not every statement about a person's health will carry the badge of confidentiality

or risk doing harm to that person's physical or moral integrity. The privacy interest in the fact that a public figure has a cold or a broken leg is unlikely to be strong enough to justify restricting the press's freedom to report it. What harm could it possibly do? Sometimes there will be other justifications for publishing, especially where the information is relevant to the capacity of a public figure to do the job. But that is not this case and in this case there was, as the judge found, a risk that publication would do harm. The risk of harm is what matters at this stage, rather than the proof that actual harm has occurred. People trying to recover from drug addiction need considerable dedication and commitment, along with constant reinforcement from those around them. That is why organisations like Narcotics Anonymous were set up and why they can do so much good. Blundering in when matters are acknowledged to be at a "fragile" stage may do great harm.

Douglas v Hello! (No 3)

In *Douglas v Hello!* as we have seen, the Court of Appeal refused to grant interlocutory injunctions against publication of the photographs. However, there was a strong expectation that damages would be awarded.

In *Douglas v Hello! (No 3)* [2006] QB 125, the case returned to the Court of Appeal. A number of issues arose. Some of them relate to claims not by the couple themselves, but by *OK!* magazine. The arguments of *OK!* magazine, whose contractual interests were affected by the unauthorized publication of photographs by *Hello!*, are entirely related to commercial interests and some of the issues (particularly as regards the level of *intention* required) have been discussed in Chapter 2. *OK!*'s claim was dismissed by the Court of Appeal but succeeded on appeal to the House of Lords. The privacy claim was not subject to an appeal, and the Court of Appeal provided important clarification on a number of issues. The court's conclusions are further evidence of the rapid change in the law affecting this area.

The judgment of the court was delivered by Lord Phillips MR. We will focus on four issues.

The Existence of a Privacy Interest

92 We should make clear at the outset that the only issue on liability was whether the photographs published by Hello! infringed rights of confidence or privacy enjoyed by the Douglases. As the judge recorded, Hello! did not seek to argue that it was in the public interest that they should publish the unauthorised photographs or that their article 10 rights of freedom of expression outweighed any rights of confidence or privacy that the Douglases enjoyed.

…

95 Applying the test propounded by the House of Lords in *Campbell v MGN Ltd* [2004] 2 AC 457, photographs of the wedding plainly portrayed aspects of the Douglases' private life and fell within the protection of the law of confidentiality, as extended to cover private or personal information.

What had, at the time of *Douglas v Hello!*, been a complex question of law—was there a privacy interest in the photographs at all?—had now become straightforward. There certainly was such an interest.

Balancing and the Award of an Injunction

It will be plain from para [92] of Lord Phillips' judgment (above) that following the decision in *Von Hannover*, and provided the required element of privacy is established, it will now be appropriate to weigh an interest in freedom of expression against the privacy interest of the claimant *only if there is a positive public interest reason supporting disclosure*. The general public interest in press freedom or absence of censorship will not be enough (or, to put it another way, there is no such general public interest).[34] Therefore in this case, nothing at all seems to have gone into the balance on the side of Article 10. This approach is inspired by *Von Hannover* and marks a significant change from the judgment of Sedley LJ in *Douglas v Hello!*, which was dominated by questions of balance. Indeed, without such questions of balance, there would have been no discussion of section 12, and therefore no horizontal effect for the Article 8 privacy right in the first place!

The discharge of the interlocutory injunction

251 We turn to an issue upon which we were not addressed, but which we believe justifies revisiting. It is the decision of this court in November 2000 [2001] QB 967 to lift the interlocutory injunction granted by Hunt J, restraining Hello! from publishing the unauthorised photographs. In our view, in the light of the law as it can now be seen to be, that decision was wrong, and the interlocutory injunction should in fact have been upheld.

252 The reasons given by the three members of this court for concluding that an interlocutory injunction was inappropriate were slightly different. Brooke LJ considered that it was no more than arguable that the Douglases "had a right to privacy which English law would recognise", and that their claim based on privacy was "not a particularly strong one" (paras 60 and 95). Although Sedley LJ thought that the Douglases had "a powerful prima facie claim to redress for invasion of their privacy", he considered that "by far the greater part of that privacy has already been traded and falls to be protected, if at all, as a commodity in the hands of [OK!]": paras 137 and 144. Keene LJ, at para 171, was primarily influenced by the point that the "court in exercising its discretion at this interlocutory stage must still take account of the widespread publicity arranged by the [Douglases] for this occasion".

253 In our view, these analyses, and indeed the decision to discharge the injunction, did not give sufficient weight to ... the strength of the Douglases' claim for an injunction restraining publication of the unauthorised photographs. Although Sedley LJ took the view that they had a strong case in this connection, it would appear that Brooke and Keene LJJ were more doubtful. The Court of Appeal did not have the benefit of the reasoning in the House of Lords in *Campbell v MGN Ltd* [2004] 2 AC 457 or, even more significantly for present purposes, the reasoning of the European Court of Human Rights in *Von Hannover v Germany* 40 EHRR 1. Had the court had the opportunity to consider those two decisions, we believe that it would have reached the conclusion that the Douglases appeared to have a virtually unanswerable case for contending that publication of the unauthorised photographs would infringe their privacy.

254 Of course, even where a claimant has a very strong case indeed for contending that publication of information would infringe his privacy, there may be good reasons for refusing an interlocutory injunction. In the present case, however, we find it difficult to see how

[34] In *Von Hannover*, for example, the European Court of Human Rights rejected the view of the German Federal Constitutional Court that there was a lightweight but potentially useful category of journalism which could be called 'infotainment'.

it could be contended that the public interest (as opposed to public curiosity) could be involved over and above the general public interest in a free press. Particularly so, as it was clearly the intention of the Douglases and OK! to publish a large number of (much clearer) photographs of the same event. The fact that the Douglases can be fairly said to have "traded" their privacy to a substantial extent as a result of their contract with OK! does not undermine the point that publication of the unauthorised photographs would infringe their privacy.

A Claim in Confidence by OK! Magazine?

The Court of Appeal also decided that a claim in confidence by OK! magazine, on the basis that the publication breached a duty of confidence owed to them, could not succeed. It was inconsistent with the couple's claim that they had a retained right of privacy in the photos. The idea that these two positions are inconsistent was rejected by a majority of the House of Lords. Lord Hoffmann thought there could be commercial confidence in any material in which people were willing to pay for exclusive rights. In this instance, we should 'keep our minds on the money'.

Lord Hoffmann, Douglas v Hello! and Others (No 3) [2007] UKHL 21

118 ... your Lordships should not be concerned with Convention rights. "OK!" has no claim to privacy under article 8 nor can it make a claim which is parasitic upon the Douglases' right to privacy. The fact that information happens to have been about the personal life of the Douglases is irrelevant. It could have been information about anything that a newspaper was willing to pay for. What matters is that the Douglases, by the way they arranged their wedding, were in a position to impose an obligation of confidence. They were in control of the information.

...

124 ... Some may view with distaste a world in which information about the events of a wedding, which Warren and Brandeis in their famous article on privacy ... regarded as a paradigm private occasion, should be sold in the market in the same way as information about how to make a better mousetrap. But being a celebrity or publishing a celebrity magazine are lawful trades and I see no reason why they should be outlawed from such protection as the law of confidence may offer.

The 'Ultimate Balance'

The *Campbell* approach to balancing the demands of Articles 8 and 10 was summarized by Lord Steyn in the case of *Re S* [2005] 1 AC 594, in terms of four propositions:

17 ... First, neither article has *as such* precedence over the other. Secondly, where the values under the two articles are in conflict, an intense focus on the comparative importance of the specific rights being claimed in the individual case is necessary. Thirdly, the justifications for interfering with or restricting each right must be taken into account. Finally, the proportionality test must be applied to each. For convenience I will call this the ultimate balancing test.

This approach to the balancing process has now become well established. As we have seen, it was approved and applied by the Supreme Court in *PJS v News Group Newspapers*. Just as the Grand Chamber in the second *Von Hannover* decision said that states have a considerable 'margin of appreciation' in their decision as to where the balance falls, so also the Court of Appeal has made plain that appellate courts should be slow to interfere with first instance decisions, provided they are reached on the correct principles (*AAA v Associated Newspapers* [2013] EWCA Civ 554).

Children

In *Murray v Big Pictures Ltd* [2008] EWCA Civ 446, the Court of Appeal was willing to accept as arguable a claim for damages in respect of publication of a photograph taken in a public street and showing the author J. K. Rowling together with her family, including her 19-month-old son. The child might well have a 'reasonable expectation of privacy' in this sort of context, and it was wrong to suggest that the parents were merely bringing a claim on their own account, in the name of the child. In making the judgment in respect of rights violations, all would depend upon the circumstances of the case. But in this case, there were reasons which made the claim arguable. This case combines the issue of photographs and the issue of children.

Sir Anthony Clarke MR, *Murray v Big Pictures (UK) Ltd*

17 It may well be that the mere taking of a photograph of a child in a public place when out with his or her parents, whether they are famous or not, would not engage article 8 of the Convention. However, as we see it, it all depends upon the circumstances. We will return to the context below but it seems to us that the judge's approach depends too much upon a consideration of the taking of the photograph and not enough upon its publication. This was not the taking of a single photograph of David in the street. On the claimant's case, which must be taken as true for present purposes, it was the clandestine taking and subsequent publication of the photograph in the context of a series of photographs which were taken for the purpose of their sale for publication, in circumstances in which BPL did not ask David's parents for their consent to the taking and publication of his photograph. It is a reasonable inference on the alleged facts that BPL knew that, if they had asked Dr and Mrs Murray for their consent to the taking and publication of such a photograph of their child, that consent would have been refused.

18 Moreover, on the assumed facts, this was not an isolated case of a newspaper taking one photograph out of the blue and its subsequent publication. This was at least arguably a very different case from that to which Baroness Hale of Richmond referred in her now well known example, in *Campbell v MGN Ltd* [2004] 2 AC 457, para 154, of Ms Campbell being photographed while popping out to buy the milk. The correspondence to which we have referred shows that a news agency, a freelance photographer and two newspapers had photographers outside the Murrays's house in the period before publication of the photograph and a schedule exhibited to the particulars of claim shows that this was not an isolated event.... Since the whole point of putting the photograph on the website in order to sell the right to publish it was because of the media interest, including interest in David as JK Rowling's child, on the material available it seems to us to be likely that BPL was fully aware of the potential value of taking and publishing such photographs. The photograph could, after all, have been published with David's features pixelated out if BPL

had wished. In these circumstances the parents' perception that, unless this action succeeds, there is a real risk that others will take and publish photographs of David is entirely understandable.

Similarly, in *Weller v Associated Newspapers* [2015] 1 WLR 1541; [2016] 1 WLR 1541, the Court of Appeal upheld the award of an injunction to restrain publication of photographs of the children of a musician on a family outing with their father. The children had not courted publicity nor had their parents sought to bring them into the public eye beyond speaking about them; nor did they perform any public functions; and the photographs and article related sole to details of their private life, with the sole purpose of satisfying public curiosity. Nevertheless, the interests of the child though important are not uniquely significant. In *AAA v Associated Newspapers Ltd* [2013] EWCA Civ 554, the child's expectation of privacy was a highly significant factor, but other factors also weighed in the balance. In this case, the child's father was not the mother's partner, but a well-known politician who had previously fathered another child as a result of an extra-marital relationship. The mother had shown at least an ambivalent attitude to making known the paternity of the claimant; and the story was considered to have a public interest element to it because of its reflection on a public figure.

A contrasting case in respect of its outcome is *K v News Group Newspapers* [2011] EWCA Civ 439. Here the Court of Appeal did reverse a first instance decision, on the basis that it had not given sufficient weight to the interests of children affected by stories about an extra-marital affair. Particular weight ought to have been attached to their interests, irrespective of their father's actions. Crucial differences appear to have been that the affair here remained essentially private despite being known amongst work colleagues; and that the story had no great public interest significance, being of interest purely because the claimant was relatively well known.

In *PJS v News Group Newspapers*, the privacy interests of children whose father was the subject of 'kiss and tell' stories were seen as important by all members of the Supreme Court, and were particularly emphasized by Baroness Hale

Baroness Hale, *PJS v News Group Newspapers* [2016] UKSC 26

72 I agree that this appeal should be allowed and the interim injunction restored for the reasons given by Lord Mance JSC. I wish only to add a few words about the interests of the two children whom PJS has with YMA. It is simply not good enough to dismiss the interests of any children who are likely to be affected by the publication of private information about their parents with the bland statement that these cannot be a trump card. Of course they cannot always rule the day. But they deserve closer attention than they have so far received in this case, for two main reasons. First, not only are the children's interests likely to be affected by a breach of the privacy interests of their parents, but the children have independent privacy interests of their own. They also have a right to respect for their family life with their parents. Secondly, by section 12(4)(b), any court considering whether to grant either an interim or a permanent injunction has to have particular regard_ to any relevant privacy code. It is not disputed that the Independent Press Standards Organisation Editors Code of Practice, which came into force in January, is a relevant

Code for this purpose. This, as Lord Mance JSC has explained, at para 36, provides that "editors must demonstrate an exceptional public interest to over-ride the normally paramount interests of children under 16".

4.2 INJUNCTIONS

Given the onward march of the privacy action detailed in Section 4.1, in recent years the most significant controversies have concerned the power of the injunctive remedies to which it gives rise. While the law continues to move forwards, official statistics suggest that use of the courts to obtain privacy injunctions has been in decline. It is not only the capacity of claimants to secure injunctions and prevent publication, but also the attachment of anonymity and in some instances wider confidentiality to proceedings which has caused the greatest concern. Whilst anonymized injunctions themselves may be seen as an exception to 'open justice' in the UK, more criticism flowed from 'super-injunctions', where even the *existence* of the injunction may not be revealed. Whilst the expression is sometimes loosely used, there is a formal definition:

Ministry of Justice, *Statistics on Privacy Injunctions January to June 2013*, Glossary

Super-injunction

A particular type of privacy injunction which restrains a person from publishing information which concerns the applicant (the person seeking to obtain the injunction) and is said to be confidential or private, and publicizing or informing others of the existence of the injunction and the court proceedings.

This type of injunction threatens to violate principles of 'open justice' because even the *existence* of the injunction is not revealed. There has been unease that the use and development of law is hidden from public view. The case which brought the existence of super-injunctions to public attention was *LNS/John Terry v Persons Unknown* [2010] EWHC 119 (QB), in which the injunction was discharged. This was not, however, the first instance of a super-injunction being awarded.

Legitimate concerns about the need for open justice led to the establishment of a Committee on Super-Injunctions, chaired by Lord Neuberger, which reported in May 2011. The Report concluded that such injunctions were and should be rare; that the need to derogate from 'open justice' had to be justified by the claimant and that this was a 'heavy burden'; that principles of necessity and proportionality were to be applied; and that the use of super-injunctions should be kept to an absolute minimum. However, where the conditions were met, courts should grant the remedy in order to protect legitimate interests. The Committee also proposed that *statistics* on privacy injunctions and super-injunctions should be published, so that there is public knowledge of the extent of the remedies awarded, and of the nature of the confidentiality being applied. The most recent report published in March 2016 identified there were only two new applications for privacy injunctions during the period July to December 2015. However, the decision of the Supreme Court in *PJS v News Group*

Newspapers Ltd [2016] UKSC 26 has been controversial, and has undoubtedly returned privacy injunctions to public attention.

5. INTRUSION

Not all invasions of privacy involve *publication*, whether of photographs or of information. While breach of confidence has not previously been recognized as a tort, there are certain other actions which clearly are torts and may serve in the protection of privacy. These include trespass (Chapters 2 and 17), nuisance (Chapter 10), and the action in *Wilkinson v Downton* (Chapter 2).

The judgment of the House of Lords in *Wainwright v Home Office* [2004] 2 AC 406 is a major obstacle to development of a general tort capable of dealing with 'intrusion'. In this case, the claimants had been subjected to a humiliating strip search on a visit to prison. This search was found to have been in contravention of the applicable Prison Rules; however, there was no finding of any particular intent to humiliate the claimants, nor even to breach the rules. The searches were aimed at identifying whether visitors were carrying drugs.

The case was decided after the decision of the Court of Appeal in *Douglas v Hello!*, but before the decision of the House of Lords in *Campbell* and (notably) before the Court of Human Rights' decision in *Von Hannover*.

Lord Hoffmann, *Wainwright v Home Office*

31   There seems to me a great difference between identifying privacy as a value which underlies the existence of a rule of law (and may point the direction in which the law should develop) and privacy as a principle of law in itself. The English common law is familiar with the notion of underlying values—principles only in the broadest sense—which direct its development. A famous example is *Derbyshire County Council v Times Newspapers Ltd* [1993] AC 534, in which freedom of speech was the underlying value which supported the decision to lay down the specific rule that a local authority could not sue for libel. But no one has suggested that freedom of speech is in itself a legal principle which is capable of sufficient definition to enable one to deduce specific rules to be applied in concrete cases. That is not the way the common law works.

32   Nor is there anything in the jurisprudence of the European Court of Human Rights which suggests that the adoption of some high level principle of privacy is necessary to comply with article 8 of the Convention. The European Court is concerned only with whether English law provides an adequate remedy in a specific case in which it considers that there has been an invasion of privacy contrary to article 8(1) and not justifiable under article 8(2). So in *Earl Spencer v United Kingdom* 25 EHRR CD 105 it was satisfied that the action for breach of confidence provided an adequate remedy for the Spencers' complaint and looked no further into the rest of the armoury of remedies available to the victims of other invasions of privacy. Likewise, in *Peck v United Kingdom* (2003) 36 EHRR 719 the court expressed some impatience, at paragraph 103, at being given a tour d'horizon of the remedies provided and to be provided by English law to deal with every imaginable kind of invasion of privacy. It was concerned with whether Mr Peck (who had been filmed in embarrassing circumstances by a CCTV camera) had an adequate remedy when the film was widely published by the media. It came to the conclusion that he did not.

33 Counsel for the Wainwrights relied upon Peck's case as demonstrating the need for a general tort of invasion of privacy. But in my opinion it shows no more than the need, in English law, for a system of control of the use of film from CCTV cameras which shows greater sensitivity to the feelings of people who happen to have been caught by the lens. For the reasons so cogently explained by Sir Robert Megarry V-C in *Malone v Metropolitan Police Comr* [1979] Ch 344, this is an area which requires a detailed approach which can be achieved only by legislation rather than the broad brush of common law principle.

34 Furthermore, the coming into force of the Human Rights Act 1998 weakens the argument for saying that a general tort of invasion of privacy is needed to fill gaps in the existing remedies. Sections 6 and 7 of the Act are in themselves substantial gap fillers; if it is indeed the case that a person's rights under article 8 have been infringed by a public authority, he will have a statutory remedy. The creation of a general tort will, as Buxton LJ pointed out in the Court of Appeal [2002] QB 1334, 1360, para 92, pre-empt the controversial question of the extent, if any, to which the Convention requires the state to provide remedies for invasions of privacy by persons who are not public authorities.

35 For these reasons I would reject the invitation to declare that since at the latest 1950 there has been a previously unknown tort of invasion of privacy.

The suggestion in para [34] that the HRA provides the remedies that tort might otherwise be stretched to supply is now quite a familiar part of the judicial landscape: it was used by the House of Lords to prevent extension of the tort of misfeasance in a public office to cases not involving material damage, but 'only' interference with constitutional rights, in *Watkins v Home Secretary* (Chapter 2), and it was emphasized again as a reason against a new 'liability principle' in cases of police negligence in *Van Colle* (Chapter 6). But the argument in this instance could be said to overlook the development of the action to restrain publication of private information beginning with *Douglas v Hello!*, which has grown out of the positive duty on states to secure Article 8 rights of all its citizens against interference from non-state actors. Lord Hoffmann's point is consistent and clear: there is no general common law action to protect privacy, though the HRA may provide such an action against state authorities.

Lord Hoffmann went on to explain that even if section 8 of the HRA had been in force at the time of the strip search in question, it should not necessarily be assumed that damages would have been available in this case. Retaining the traditional tort law perspective, he felt that here too, intention might be relevant. In *Wainwright v UK* (26 September 2006) [2008] 1 PLR 398, the European Court of Human Rights held however that the UK was in violation of the applicants' rights under Article 8 of the Convention, and also under Article 13 (failure to provide an adequate domestic remedy).

6. CONCLUSIONS

i. As in the case of defamation, the story of tort law where protection of privacy is concerned has been one of real interaction between common law, and Convention rights. The development of a tort of misuse of private information is the most strikingly novel feature of tort law in the last ten years. The mechanism for creating such a development in the courts has been use of the existing cause of action for breach of confidence; but this has been achieved by using enactment of the Human Rights Act 1998 as the occasion for deep entrenchment of Articles 8 and 10 in English law. The result is not just a 'transformed' action for breach of confidence, but a new cause of action protecting privacy, which is now recognized as a tort.

ii. The development of a tort of misuse of private information has inevitably led the courts into controversial areas, since it is often (though not always) the press whose intention to publish information is restricted by the new action. Key to the operation of the new action is the balancing of privacy rights (protected by Article 8) against freedom of expression (protected by Article 10). Freedom of expression has no presumptive priority, and while in principle both weigh equally in the scales, the courts have followed the lead of the European Court of Human Rights. Provided there is a reasonable expectation of privacy, the courts will require some reason of public interest in favour of publication, if anything at all is to be placed in the balance against a privacy right. Where the reason for publication is merely satisfaction of public curiosity about private lives, the balance will, simply, fall in favour of privacy.

iii. At the same time, the behaviour of sections of the UK's press in recent years has served to underline the need for effective regulation—a course which continues to prove elusive. The case of *Gulati v MGN* gave some insight into this behaviour and its effects on individuals. For the time being, though the costs of privacy actions are undoubtedly prohibitive for all but the wealthiest claimants, the legal principles developed by the courts offer claimants a potentially powerful arsenal. At least, that is the theory. As is illustrated by the case of Max Mosley, privacy is a vulnerable commodity, and it can be formidably difficult to overcome the interests of the press in seeking publication of what will arouse the curiosity of the public, no matter how different this may be from the legal approach to 'public interest'. Some have argued that in the age of the internet, the Supreme Court judgment in *PJS*, similarly, is merely a holding back of the tide of publication, given the intervention of the internet. Just as the interests of the press in publication of sensationalist stories helps to explain the development of the action for privacy, the same interests also indicate the problems that lie in the way of any effective control through the law.

FURTHER READING

Feldman, D., 'Secrecy, Dignity, or Autonomy? Views of Privacy as a Civil Liberty' (1994) 47 CLP 41.

Feldman, D., 'The Developing Scope of Article 8 of the European Convention on Human Rights' [1997] EHRLR 265–74.

Fenwick, H., and Phillipson, G., 'The Doctrine of Confidence as a Privacy Remedy in the Human Rights Act Era' (2000) 63 MLR 663–93.

Gomery, G., 'Whose Autonomy Matters? Reconciling the Competing Claims of Privacy and Freedom of Expression' (2007) LS 404–29.

Markesinis, B., 'Our Patchy Law of Privacy: Time to do Something About It' (1990) 53 MLR 802.

Moreham, N. A., 'Privacy in the Common Law: A Doctrinal and Theoretical Analysis' (2005) 121 LQR 628–56.

Moreham, N., 'The Right to Respect for Private Life in the European Court of Human Rights: A Reexamination' (2008) 52 EHRLR 44–79.

Morgan, J., 'Privacy, Confidence, and Direct Effect: "Hello" Trouble' (2003) 62 CLJ 44–73.

O'Callaghan, P., *Refining Privacy in Tort Law* (Springer, 2012).

Phillipson, G., 'Judicial Reasoning in Breach of Confidence Cases Under the Human Rights Act: Not Taking Privacy Seriously?' [2003] EHRLR (Supp) 53–72.

Phillipson, G., 'Transforming Breach of Confidence?: Towards a Common Law Right of Privacy Under the Human Rights Act' (2003) 66 MLR 726–58.

Phillipson, G., 'Privacy', in D Hoffman (ed.), *The Impact of the Human Rights Act on Private Law* (Cambridge, 2011).

Richardson, J., 'If I Cannot Have Her Everyone Can', in J. Richardson and E. Rackley, *Feminist Perspectives on Tort Law* (Routledge, 2012).

Sanderson, M. A., 'Is *Von Hannover v Germany* a Step Backwards for the Substantive Analysis of Speech and Privacy Interests?' [2004] EHRLR 631–44.

Toulson, R. G., and Phipps, C. M., *Confidentiality* (2nd edn, London: Sweet & Maxwell, 2006).

Wacks, R., 'The Poverty of Privacy' (1980) 96 LQR 73.

Warbrick, C., 'The Structure of Article 8' [1998] EHRLR 32–44.

Wilson, W., 'Privacy, Confidence and Press Freedom: A Study in Judicial Activism' (1990) 53 MLR 43.

Witzleb, N., 'Monetary Remedies for Breach of Confidence in Privacy Cases' (2007) 27 LS 430.

Witzleb, N., 'Justifying Gain-Based Remedies for Invasion of Privacy' (2009) OJLS 1–39.

PART VII

STRICTER LIABILITIES

We have already explored a number of torts which are 'stricter' than negligence. Examples include nuisance, the action in *Rylands v Fletcher*, and the defamation torts. 'Strict' and 'not strict' are not simple categories. Further, it is not only the applicable criteria of liability, but also the available defences, which affect the strictness of these actions. It makes sense, therefore, to ask not only *whether* liability is or is not 'strict', but also *in what way* it is strict.

In this final Part of the text, we collect together a number of actions which are towards the stricter end of the scale. These causes of action further illustrate that the boundaries between fault-based liability, and strict liability, may be surprisingly difficult to pin down. Furthermore, the goals of these various forms of strict liability are varied. Here too, the diversity of torts should not be underestimated.

In Chapter 15, we explore statutory strict liability for damage done by defective products. Here, the strictness of the statutory liability is affected fundamentally by interpretation of the key 'development risks' defence, and of the central notion of defectiveness. The goal of this strict liability is an allocation of risks between manufacturer and consumer, and in this respect it represents a compromise. A principled analysis can take us only so far.

In Chapter 16, we turn to the action for breach of statutory duty. This action will not always give rise to strict liability, because the nature of the duty is defined by the statute in question. But in some instances, liability has been stricter than any addressed so far. Some Health and Safety regulations applying to employers have even been regarded as imposing 'absolute' liability. Section 69 of the Enterprise and Regulatory Reform Act 2013 has brought about a major change in this established field of strict liability, removing civil liability altogether from health and safety regulations and statutes unless further regulations are passed to the contrary. The stated intention is to replace strict liability with a negligence standard in this area. Since health and safety constitutes the most established category of actionable breaches of statutory duty at common law, this may affect the position of the chapter in future.

Finally in Chapter 17 we return to common law duties. We explored trespass to the person in Chapter 2 along with the intentional torts, but we noted that there was a strong element of strictness about those torts. Here we consider a range of proprietary torts which form other branches of trespass, and where the strictness of liability has not been diluted in the same way. Trespass to land and goods imposes strict liability in respect of certain interferences with proprietary rights. The protection offered is partly dependent on the remedies available, and here we revisit and develop some of the issues concerning compensatory and non-compensatory remedies in Chapter 8. If trespass torts protect rights, what range of remedies is available and appropriate? Finally we turn to the tort of conversion. The action for conversion is different from the trespass torts in that it protects not possession but title, or the right to possess, and responds to actions which are inconsistent with ownership. This tort is therefore uniquely close to the law of property, even in comparison with other torts that protect proprietary rights.

15

PRODUCT LIABILITY

CENTRAL ISSUES

i) Part I of the Consumer Protection Act 1987 introduces a form of strict liability for harm done by defective products. The statute gives effect to an EEC Directive, and it bears the marks of political compromise. The central justification of the Directive is that it apportions risks associated with products between consumers and producers. It is one element in a broader European regime of product safety.

ii) The key requirement of liability under the Consumer Protection Act 1987 and under the Directive is that harm must be caused by a 'defect' in the product; and a producer of goods may be exonerated if the state of knowledge at the time did not make it possible for the defect to be discovered. It was argued from the inception of the Directive that these key features would make the statutory liability little different from negligence; but the case law to date suggests that the statutory liability is in some respects easier to establish than liability in negligence.

1. DEFECTIVE PRODUCTS AND THE STANDARD OF LIABILITY

The unified tort of negligence emerged in a case of product liability. In *Donoghue v Stevenson*, the plaintiff claimed that she had consumed part of a bottle of ginger beer; that a decaying snail floated out of the bottle; and that she suffered personal injury in the form of gastro-enteritis, and 'shock'. The basis of her claim in tort was that the snail was present through the *negligence* of the manufacturer; and that this negligence led to consequential harm in the form of personal injury.

The key significance of *Donoghue* was that it recognized a general legal relationship that is separate from contract. This legal relationship was marked by proximity or 'neighbourhood' between the defendant (whose alleged negligence created the risk of harm), and the plaintiff (who as ultimate consumer of the product was exposed to that risk). According to Lord Atkin, this relationship gave rise to a duty to take reasonable steps to protect the consumer from harm. The duty owed by the manufacturer to the consumer (provided that consumer is relevantly 'proximate' within the terms of the neighbour principle) is a duty *to take care*; and liability is restricted to *consequential harm*.

The Consumer Protection Act 1987 creates *additional* liability on the part of manufacturers where damage is caused by a defect in a product.[1] Like the action in negligence, liability under this Act only extends to *consequential damage* (in the form of damage to property or personal injury). There is no liability under the Act for damages assessed by reference to the purchase price or value of the product, or for damage done to the product itself. Unlike negligence, damage to what may be broadly called 'commercial' property is not covered under the Act (section 2(3)). It is 'consumer protection' legislation. On the other hand, personal injury is covered by the Act in all contexts.

Liability under the Consumer Protection Act 1987 is defined without reference to fault. The statute was intended to give effect to Directive 85/374/ EEC, on the approximation of the laws, regulations and administrative provisions of the Member States concerning liability for defective products (the 'Directive on Product Liability').[2] The Preamble to this Directive explicitly states that the relevant liability is 'without fault'. Accordingly, there is no need to show lack of care—or other wrongful conduct—on the part of the manufacturer.

But the statute does not create liability for all injuries caused by products. Liability under the Act requires that injury or damage is caused by **a defect in a product**. By section 3(1) of the Act, a 'defect' is defined in terms of the legitimate expectations of 'persons in general'. The key distinction between liability based on fault at common law, and 'strict' liability under the Consumer Protection Act 1987, lies in the difference between **showing negligence**—for example in the design, manufacture, or marketing of the product (the position at common law); and **showing defectiveness in the product** (the position under the Consumer Protection Act 1987). It has been argued that this distinction may prove to be very fine or even insignificant; but the (relatively sparse) case law indicates that there is a distinction in effect nonetheless.[3]

Importantly, a controversial defence (**the development risks defence**) was included in both the Directive (where it was said to be at the discretion of Member States) and the Consumer Protection Act 1987. The effect of this defence is to further narrow the distinction between common law and statutory product liability. Broadly speaking, the impact of the defence is that the consumer takes the risk of defects which could not have been discovered at the time of manufacture, because scientific knowledge at the time did not permit the relevant risk to be known.[4] The exact breadth and meaning of this defence is very important to the nature of the liability introduced by the Consumer Protection Act 1987: 3.5.

---

[1] It is additional because other potential actions against the producer, including the action in negligence, are expressly preserved by s 2(6).

[2] There had already been discussion in the UK concerning strict liability for products, prompted largely by the failure of tort law to compensate the victims of Thalidomide. This was a drug prescribed during the 1960s to pregnant women in order to combat morning sickness, but which led to significant birth defects. In the UK, the issue of strict liability for defective products was for a time treated as part of a wider debate over compensation for disability and disease. That being so, the Directive (and the Consumer Protection Act 1987) have been criticized as introducing a mere sectoral solution to the problem of compensation. It is restricted to products, and even then only to defective ones: see J. Stapleton, *Product Liability* (Butterworths, 1994) and J. Stapleton, 'Product Liability Reform—Real or Illusory?' (1986) 6 OJLS 392–422.

[3] See in particular our discussion of *A v National Blood Authority* [2001] 3 All ER 289, later in this chapter.

[4] Defects which could not be discovered for reasons unconnected with lack of knowledge (for example, because there is no known *method for detection*) are not within the defence.

1.1 FROM NEGLIGENCE TO DEFECTIVENESS: ALLOCATION OF RISKS

The Directive on Product Liability is expressly concerned with the apportionment of risks associated with products. The Directive was the subject of extended political negotiation between Member States, and the apportionment of risks it incorporates is in effect a compromise. Broadly, producers take the risks of defectiveness, whether these risks are produced by lack of care or not; while consumers take the risks associated with non-defective products (subject of course to liability in contract and in tort).

The effect of the development risks defence (Section 3.5) is to introduce a major qualification to this basic apportionment. In the case of a defect which in the relevant sense could not have been discovered by the manufacturer (an undiscoverable defect), the risk will not lie on the manufacturer.

The development risks defence has the potential, depending on its interpretation, to undermine the strictness of the product liability regime.[5] The EC Commission has justified the defence as protecting socially desirable *innovation*:

Commission of the European Communities, *Third Report on the application of Council Directive 85/374/EEC* (the 'Product Liability Directive') 14 September 2006

The DRC[6] was defined in order to establish a satisfactory compromise between the need to stimulate innovation on the one hand and consumers' legitimate expectations for safer products on the other. The crucial argument of the current debate on the DRC is that removing the clause would stifle innovation.

The findings presented in this report[7] seem to indicate that the often-used argument of the Development Risk Clause being a significant factor in achieving the Directive's balance between the need to preserve incentives to innovation and consumer's interests is well-founded and is based on the following:

- the DRC protects incentives to innovate in reducing the innovation-related risks, by not diverting resources from R & D to insurance policies and by pushing firms to align to state of the art knowledge;
- the DRC is probably one key factor in determining the relative stability of product liability costs in European industry and keeping litigation at a reasonable level;
- in a strict liability regime, companies in high-tech/high risk sectors would find it very difficult to obtain a reasonable insurance policy which covers their developmental risks.

The combination of these factors lead Fondazione Rosselli to conclude that the costs of letting the producers innovate within a strict liability environment would be extremely high, and would affect consumers in the long term. In effect, both the Lovells and the Rosselli studies conclude that such a defence should be maintained.

---

[5] See the articles extracted and referred to in our analysis of the statutory provisions, later.

[6] The 'Development Risk Clause' (the clause of the Directive that sets out the development risk defence: Directive on Product Liability, Art 7(e)).

[7] The Fondazione Roselli Report (published in 2004), carried out for the European Commission.

It seems that companies in 'high tech/high risk sectors' effectively *do not* operate in a 'strict liability regime' under the Directive (see the third bullet point in the extract above). We give fuller consideration to this state of affairs when we consider Defences, in Section 3.

2. THE BROADER CONTEXT: THE LIMITED IMPACT OF THE CONSUMER PROTECTION ACT 1987

Analysis of statutory strict liability for harm done by products is of course very instructive from the point of view of the general law of tort. There are interesting parallels between the statutory liability, and common law liabilities based on negligence and on strict liability. But in some respects, a focus on the terms of the Consumer Protection Act 1987 is misleading. There are two broad reasons for saying this.

2.1 CLOSENESS TO NEGLIGENCE

First, there are relatively few successful product liability claims under the Act which would not also succeed at common law. Indeed, there still appear to be more books and articles written about the statute than there are successful claims under it.[8] Of course, this is partly because of the definition of 'defect' and the inclusion of a number of significant defences, including the important 'development risks defence', which we have already noted and which will be explored in the following section. But there are other significant reasons too, which have received less emphasis.

Causation

Whether an action in respect of harm caused by a product is brought at common law or under statute, and whatever the standard of liability, the claimant must show that the injury suffered was caused by the defect (under statute) or the negligence (at common law). Either way, proving causation will be far from straightforward in many cases where the mechanics of cause and effect are disputed and (particularly) where the major evidence is epidemiological. Among such cases are many pharmaceutical claims.

In an action for product liability at common law or under statute the claimant (or claimants) must show not only that the injury was caused by negligence or a defect; *but also* that the particular product causing the harm was manufactured by the defendant, and not by some other manufacturer. We saw the impact of some such problems—and the ways in which common law moves to some extent to accommodate them—in Chapter 4.

The issue of causation is sometimes linked to problems relating to 'defectiveness'. In *XYZ v Schering* [2002] EWHC 1420, a number of women brought actions against the manufacturers of 'third-generation' combined oral contraceptives. The claimants argued that these products were 'defective' within the terms of the Consumer Protection Act 1987, and that the defects in question had caused them to suffer cardio-vascular injuries such as deep vein thrombosis and pulmonary embolism. The claims failed. Mackay J held that the claimants

---

[8] The Directive is harmonizing legislation and there is also European case law to draw upon. However, D. Fairgrieve and G. Howells (Further Reading) report low take-up of the Directive in all countries with the exception of Austria, where previous protection was less strong.

had not established on the balance of probabilities that the contraceptives had increased their risk of sustaining these injuries, when compared with the risks associated with the previous generation of combined oral contraceptives. Only the *excess* risk associated with the new product would be unknown to the women, who were otherwise treated as making an informed choice to use this method of contraception (combined oral contraceptives). Thus, the products were not 'defective': the available evidence could not be said to establish that the risk of injury was enhanced by the defect. The same evidence would have been relevant to proof of causation, had the claims not failed at this initial hurdle.

In a far simpler case, it has proved possible to conclude that an injury was caused by a defect on the basis that the only serious alternative explanation could be discounted. In *Ide v ATB Sales* [2008] EWCA Civ 424; [2009] RTR 8, the Court of Appeal upheld a judge's decision to this effect. The claimant had been seriously injured while riding his Marin mountain bike off-road, and brought an action against the defendant importers (see later in this chapter for the range of defendants who may be liable under the Act). The left handlebar had snapped. The defendants argued that the rider had through his own actions caused the crash and that this had caused the handlebars to break. Having analysed the evidence and rejected this theory, the judge had been entitled to conclude that a defect had caused the crash. Since this was liability under the Consumer Protection Act, there was no need to discover or specify *what* defect had caused the handlebars to snap; it was enough that the only real alternative explanation had been discounted. A contrasting decision is *McGlinchey v General Motors UK Ltd* [2012] CSIH 91, an appeal to the Inner House of the Court of Session in Scotland. Here a car had rolled down a steep hill and injured its owner. The first instance court had rejected as implausible the only two causes of the accident proposed to it, namely a defect in the handbrake, and user error in failing to engage the handbrake. The Inner House decided that having rejected the possibility of failure to engage the handbrake—on the basis that the car otherwise would have rolled down the steep hill much sooner—the court was nevertheless not obliged to accept that there had been a defect in the handbrake. Other possibilities—including wear and tear—existed. It was always the duty of the court to decide whether a cause was probable on the balance of probabilities, even if the other implausible explanations had been eliminated. In *Hufford v Samsung* [2014] EWHC 2956 (TCC), it was emphasized that the burden of proving that the damage was caused by a defect remained on the claimant, even if the defect in question did not need to be identified with a great deal of specificity. Here, there was no reason to prefer the claimant's argument, that a defect in a fridge freezer had led to a fire, over the defendant's—namely, that the fire had started outside the fridge freezer, in a pile of combustible material.

Funding and Access to Justice

Liability rules will only have an impact if potential claimants have access to justice. On the other hand, in a regime of conditional fees, as we explained in Chapter 8, it is possible for speculative claims to be initiated. The importance of funding is illustrated by the case of *Paul Sayers and Others v SmithKline Beecham plc & Others* [2004] EWHC 1899 (QB) (the 'MMR/MR Vaccine Litigation'). Actions were brought on behalf of a number of claimants, who suffered from autism and whose families blamed that condition on vaccines manufactured by the defendants. It was clear that there would be significant difficulties in proving causation,[9] and the Legal Services Commission withdrew funding from the action. The

---

[9] Numerous studies have been conducted and none have shown a connection between the MMR/MR vaccines and autism.

claimants were therefore exposed to an order of costs against them, should they lose, and their actions were discontinued.

2.2 REGULATION OF PRODUCT SAFETY

The second general reason why it is misleading to consider 'product liability' in isolation is that the Directive is only one element in a European strategy for increasing product safety. Indeed in 2005, the UK responded to revisions in the EC Directive on General Product Safety with the General Product Safety Regulations 2005, incorporating new powers of recall on the part of regulators, and duties of notification on the part of producers.[10] To the extent that product liability is intended to achieve a measure of deterrence, it therefore overlaps with a developing regulatory regime.

Addressing this topic in the context of the law of tort takes product liability out of its broader context, of enhancing safety. Even so, we can appreciate an underlying theme of consumer safety law: how can we enhance safety and compensate the victims of product defects, without stifling innovation and thereby denying society the benefits of new products, and of economic development? Even simpler products may entail inherent dangers and some such products are wanted nevertheless. In the next extract, the last two points are brought together.[11]

Chris Hodges, 'Approaches to Product Liability in the Member States', in D. Fairgrieve (ed.), *Product Liability in Comparative Perspective*, at 201

The level of product liability claims in Europe has consistently remained far lower than that which has been produced in the USA by their procedural rules and constitutional climate, given in particular their different situation in relation to availability of healthcare and insurance. It is widely recognised that the overheated liability system in the USA produces economic results that encourage lawyer-led litigation and in which lawyers can reap very substantial and disproportionate rewards. The impact of reforms to European rules on access to justice, class actions, funding mechanisms and damages should be carefully considered so as to avoid these American problems. Existing variations in national rules on litigation procedure and funding constitute significant barriers to consumers in bringing claims and confusion to all litigants and non-national lawyers in understanding some national systems.

The function of a product liability mechanism is primarily to pay adequate compensation to those to whom claimable harm is caused. . . . A further function is to impose a deterrent on producers to take care that their products are designed, manufactured and labelled so as to minimise the safety risks of use. Deterrence is of limited value as a mechanism of behavioural control since it acts *post facto* whereas the considerable corpus of regulatory controls may be expected to be of greater impact in acting preventatively. . . .

---

[10] D. Fairgrieve and G. Howells, 'General Product Safety—a Revolution Through Reform?' (2006) 69 MLR 59–69; P. Cartwright, 'Enforcement, Risk and Discretion: The Case of Dangerous Consumer Products' (2006) 26 LS 524–43.

[11] See for example *Sam Bogle v McDonald's Restaurants* (Section 3.4): hot tea and coffee in container with a removable lid not 'defective'.

3. LIABILITY UNDER THE CONSUMER PROTECTION ACT 1987

The Consumer Protection Act 1987 was enacted to give effect—as the UK was required to do—to the Product Liability Directive. Despite the breadth and depth of the academic literature surrounding the legislation, it appears that the first cases applying the Act were decided some 12 years after the statute came into effect: *Abouzaid v Mothercare* (strap of 'cosytoes' hitting child in the eye: defective); *Richardson v LRC* (2000) 59 BMLR 185 (failed condom: not defective); *A v National Blood Authority* [2001] 3 All ER 289 (blood products infected with hepatitis C virus: defective). By then, the UK legislation had already survived a challenge to the European Court of Justice in *CEC v UK* [1997] 3 CMLR 923, though without wholehearted vindication of the UK wording.

3.1 THE LIABILITY UNDER THE ACT AND WHO IS LIABLE: SECTION 2

Section 2(1) of the Act states the basic liability introduced by the statute. Section 2(2) states the parties who will be thereby be liable.

Consumer Protection Act 1987

2 Liability for defective products

(1) Subject to the following provisions of this Part, where any damage is caused wholly or partly by a defect in a product, every person to whom subsection (2) below applies shall be liable for the damage.

(2) This subsection applies to—

   (a) the producer of the product;

   (b) any person who, by putting his name on the product or using a trade mark or other distinguishing mark in relation to the product, has held himself out to be the producer of the product;

   (c) any person who has imported the product into a member State from a place outside the member States in order, in the course of any business of his, to supply it to another.

(3) Subject as aforesaid, where any damage is caused wholly or partly by a defect in a product, any person who supplied the product (whether to the person who suffered the damage, to the producer of any product in which the product in question is comprised or to any other person) shall be liable for the damage if—

   (a) the person who suffered the damage requests the supplier to identify one or more of the persons (whether still in existence or not) to whom subsection (2) above applies in relation to the product;

   (b) that request is made within a reasonable period after the damage occurs and at a time when it is not reasonably practicable for the person making the request to identify all those persons; and

(c) the supplier fails, within a reasonable period after receiving the request, either to comply with the request or to identify the person who supplied the product to him.

...

(5) Where two or more persons are liable by virtue of this Part for the same damage, their liability shall be joint and several.

(6) This section shall be without prejudice to any liability arising otherwise than by virtue of this Part.

3.2 WHAT IS A PRODUCT?

Primarily, liability is placed on *producers*. However, certain other parties may be liable under particular circumstances. These include 'own-branders' (who are effectively holding themselves out as producers), and parties who import the products from outside the Member States. As an alternative, the claim may be made against a supplier who does not identify who the producer is.

1(2)(c) ... "product" means any goods or electricity and (subject to subsection (3) below) includes a product which is comprised in another product, whether by virtue of being a component part or raw material or otherwise; ... By section 2(3) (above), faulty component parts are treated as being separate products, and the party who is potentially liable if those components are defective is the producer (or importer, and so on) of those components, rather than of the product in which they are incorporated. *However*, the manufacturer of a component part will not be liable for damage done *to the larger product in which it is incorporated*: see section 5(2) extracted below, refining the definition of 'damage' recoverable under the Act.

3.3 DAMAGE

5 Damage giving rise to liability

(1) Subject to the following provisions of this section, in this Part "damage" means death or personal injury or any loss of or damage to any property (including land).

(2) A person shall not be liable under section 2 above in respect of any defect in a product for the loss of or any damage to the product itself or for the loss of or any damage to the whole or any part of any product which has been supplied with the product in question comprised in it.

(3) A person shall not be liable under section 2 above for any loss of or damage to any property which, at the time it is lost or damaged, is not—

(a) of a description of property ordinarily intended for private use, occupation or consumption; and

(b) intended by the person suffering the loss or damage mainly for his own private use, occupation or consumption.

(4) No damages shall be awarded to any person by virtue of this Part in respect of any loss of or damage to any property if the amount which would fall to be so awarded to that person, apart from this subsection and any liability for interest, does not exceed £275.

(5) In determining for the purposes of this Part who has suffered any loss of or damage to property and when any such loss or damage occurred, the loss or damage shall be regarded as having occurred at the earliest time at which a person with an interest in the property had knowledge of the material facts about the loss or damage.

(6) For the purposes of subsection (5) above the material facts about any loss of or damage to any property are such facts about the loss or damage as would lead a reasonable person with an interest in the property to consider the loss or damage sufficiently serious to justify his instituting proceedings for damages against a defendant who did not dispute liability and was able to satisfy a judgment.

(7) For the purposes of subsection (5) above a person's knowledge includes knowledge which he might reasonably have been expected to acquire—

(a) from facts observable or ascertainable by him; or

(b) from facts ascertainable by him with the help of appropriate expert advice which it is reasonable for him to seek;

but a person shall not be taken by virtue of this subsection to have knowledge of a fact ascertainable by him only with the help of expert advice unless he has failed to take all reasonable steps to obtain (and, where appropriate, to act on) that advice.

(8) Subsections (5) to (7) above shall not extend to Scotland.

Clearly, some parts of this section (subsections (5)–(7)) are important in defining the date of damage for the purposes of determining when the limitation period will begin to run: see further Section 3.6 of this chapter.

The types of 'damage' recoverable under the Act are broadly similar to the types of damage recoverable through the tort of negligence. There must be damage either to the person or to *property other than the product itself*. Defectiveness in the product is not enough in itself; nor is harm to the property that is claimed to be defective.[12] By section 5(2), as already noted, a component part is not treated as having caused damage if it merely damages the product into which it is incorporated. Importantly, by section 5(3) only *consumer* property is protected. Damage to property not intended for private or family use (broadly, commercial property) is not recoverable under the Act.

3.4 THE CRUCIAL CONCEPT: DEFECTIVENESS

As we have already discussed, 'defect' is the central criterion for liability under the statute. 'Defectiveness' plays an equivalent role to 'negligence' at common law.

[12] For the position in negligence see *Murphy v Brentwood* [1991] 1 AC 398; *Muirhead v Industrial Tank Speciality Ltd* [1986] QB 507.

3 Meaning of "defect"

(1) Subject to the following provisions of this section, there is a defect in a product for the purposes of this Part if the safety of the product is not such as persons generally are entitled to expect; and for those purposes "safety", in relation to a product, shall include safety with respect to products comprised in that product and safety in the context of risks of damage to property, as well as in the context of risks of death or personal injury.

(2) In determining for the purposes of subsection (1) above what persons generally are entitled to expect in relation to a product all the circumstances shall be taken into account, including—

(a) the manner in which, and purposes for which, the product has been marketed, its getup, the use of any mark in relation to the product and any instructions for, or warnings with respect to, doing or refraining from doing anything with or in relation to the product;

(b) what might reasonably be expected to be done with or in relation to the product; and

(c) the time when the product was supplied by its producer to another;

and nothing in this section shall require a defect to be inferred from the fact alone that the safety of a product which is supplied after that time is greater than the safety of the product in question.

By section 3(1), the key question in respect of defectiveness is whether the safety of the product is not such as persons generally are entitled to expect.

It should be noted that in making a judgment as to defectiveness, 'all the circumstances' are to be taken into account (section 3(2)). The listed factors are merely illustrative. Section 3(1) differs very slightly from the wording of the Directive itself:

Directive on Product Liability

Article 6

1. A product is defective when it does not provide the safety which a person is entitled to expect, taking all circumstances into account ...

The language in the Directive is ambiguous, since it does not make clear whether the test is what 'a person' who is *consuming* the product is entitled to expect; or what 'a person' who is representative of the general public is entitled to expect. The UK legislation adopts the latter interpretation.

Defectiveness vs Negligence

Before the Act came into effect, there was some difference of view about the difference that the move to a defectiveness test would make. Christopher Newdick argued that 'defect' would be easier to establish than negligence. (He reserved his criticism for the development risks defence.)

C. Newdick, 'The Development Risk Defence of the Consumer Protection Act 1987' (1988) 47 CLJ 455–76

The European Directive on Product Liability introduces a new regime of strict product liability to the member states of the Community. Those injured by products may recover by showing that the product is 'defective', *i.e.*, that it 'does not provide the safety that a person is entitled to expect…'. The advantage of this approach for the individual is likely to be that liability turns on the existence of a defect alone. Unlike the law of Negligence, no question of foresight of the danger, or of the precautions taken to avoid it, arises for consideration. Strict product liability depends on the condition of the product, not the fault of its maker or supplier.

Jane Stapleton, on the other hand, argued that the concept of 'defectiveness' would itself not operate significantly differently from the 'negligence' standard. She further argued that a special strict liability regime for *products* was in any case anomalous and unjustified.

J. Stapleton, 'Products Liability Reform: Real or Illusory?' (1986) 6 OJLS 392–422, at 420–1

The assumption that stricter liability for products will be provided by the new Directive is unwarranted. On examination, its central concepts such as cost-benefit assessments and the development risk defence are not only inconsistent with the theoretical arguments used to justify the reform but they are also so poorly thought out that it is debatable whether the liability foreshadowed in the Directive will have a significantly wider scope than the current negligence regime.

Even if there are cases in which the new law will provide a remedy where there would have been none under negligence,[13] the reform can be criticised for generating … unattractive anomalies in the remedies available to classes of the disabled. Despite trenchant academic criticism the current vogue for *ad hoc* solutions such as products liability reform seems to survive…

Although the volume of case law considering 'defectiveness' is still relatively modest, it has generally become clear that there is scope for a claimant to succeed under the Act, where a claim in negligence would fail. 'Defectiveness' is likely to be easier to prove than negligence in the simpler, more mechanical cases. These are also the cases least likely to attract the development risks defence. It remains true that (as Stapleton argued) the regime is not a full strict liability regime, even for damage done by products. It only applies in cases of 'defect'. But this should not be too surprising: it is normal for 'strict' liabilities to be strict in some ways, and not in others, and that is illustrated throughout this text.

The interpretation of defectiveness is therefore crucial, and if the definition of defect should prove to be capricious or anomalous, the regime that results will be defensible (if at all) only on the basis that it is a 'compromise'.

We therefore turn to the UK case law on the issue of defectiveness.

---

[13] Stapleton noted here that the Directive does have some unequivocal advantages for certain claimants—notably in the extended definition of 'producers' in Article 3.

Iman Abouzaid v Mothercare (UK) Ltd (21 December 2000, CA)

The claimant was helping his mother to attach a 'cosytoes', manufactured by the defendants, to his younger brother's pram. An elastic strap snapped out of his grasp and a metal buckle on the end of the strap struck him in the eye. His vision in that eye was very substantially impaired. The Court of Appeal held that the injury was caused by a defect in the product. No 'development risks' defence could arise because a simple test could have shown that the risk existed at the time the goods were manufactured. The risk was in no sense outside the reach of established knowledge at that time, even if it had not been explicitly recognized. By contrast, a claim in negligence at common law would fail, largely because the risk of injury was small, and a reasonable manufacturer may well have failed to recognize it.

Tesco Stores v Connor Frederick Pollock [2006] EWCA Civ 393

The claimant, aged 13 months, had swallowed dishwasher powder from a plastic bottle bought from Tesco (the first defendant), becoming seriously ill. The powder was Tesco's own brand (see section 2(2)(b)), but the bottle had been manufactured by the second defendant. The case against the defendants was that the bottle was too easily opened. It was supposed to have a 'child resistant' cap, but the claimant managed to open it. Evidence showed that the 'squeeze and turn' cap required considerably less resistance to open than would be required by a cap which met the British Standard for such lids (although in principle, it required more force than a child of 13 months would be *expected* to be able to apply). There was no legal requirement that all dishwasher powder should be sold in containers with caps which met the British Standard. The question was, rather, whether the cap could be opened sufficiently easily for it to be described as 'defective', within the terms of section 3(1) of the Act, extracted earlier. Did it provide the level of safety that persons generally would be entitled to expect? The Court of Appeal decided that it did. The product was not defective.

Laws LJ

18 What, on the facts here, were 'persons generally entitled to expect' of the safety features of this cap and bottle? In my judgment they were entitled to expect that the bottle would be more difficult to open than if it had an ordinary screwtop. Anything more specific, as a test of public expectation, runs into the difficulties which I have just described. Here, the bottle was more difficult to open than an ordinary screwtop, though not as difficult to open as it would have been if the British Standard torque measure had been complied with. There was, in my judgment, no breach of the 1987 Act.

In this case, there was some scepticism that the young claimant could genuinely have opened the screw top (and therefore some suspicion that the bottle had been left open by an adult), although on balance this matter was settled in favour of the claimant to the satisfaction of the first instance judge. It could be argued that the resistance required to open this cap, being significantly more than a small child would be expected to be able to apply, was sufficient to avoid being held to be 'defective'. But is it really sufficient to say—as Laws LJ did at [18]—that the *only* reasonable expectation of people generally is that a 'child resistant cap' will be 'more difficult to open' than an ordinary screwtop? This is surely expecting too little, since it means (literally) that *any* extra resistance is enough. This is not, it is suggested, what people could legitimately expect of a 'child resistant cap'. On the other hand, the actual resistance of the cap in this particular case could have been held to be within the legitimate expectations of the public. It remained something of a mystery how this particular child had managed to open it.

An earlier case which indicates that consumer **responsibility** is relevant to the fair apportionment of risk is *Sam Bogle and Others v McDonald's Restaurants* [2002] EWHC 490 (QB). Each of the claimants (most of them children) were injured by spillage of hot tea and coffee served at McDonald's restaurants. The claims call to mind a widely known American case in which a claimant secured substantial damages for scalding injuries sustained when hot coffee sold at a McDonald's 'drive thru' restaurant spilt on to her lap. In *Bogle v McDonald's* by contrast, the defendants were held not to be liable either in negligence, or under the Consumer Protection Act 1987.

The claim under the Act turned on the heat of the drinks and the design of their container, the lid of which was to be removed for drinking. Later, a differently designed cup was introduced, allowing the coffee to be drunk through a spout. (In this regard note the terms of section 3(2) extracted earlier: the introduction of a safer product at a later date does not by itself mean that the product which caused the harm was defective. But note also that people may prefer *not* to drink tea and coffee through a spout.)

The most sophisticated judicial analysis of 'defectiveness' to date was attempted in *A v National Blood Authority*. Here we consider the issues surrounding 'defectiveness' in this case. In the next section, we consider its implications for the 'development risks defence'.

A and Others v National Blood Authority and Another [2001] 3 All ER 289 (Burton J)

The claimants had all contracted Hepatitis C from blood transfusions. They brought actions against the defendants as suppliers of the relevant blood products. At the time that the transfusions were carried out, the defendants and the medical profession were well aware that there was a risk of infection by Hepatitis C through blood products. This knowledge was not shared with the general public. There was an actual expectation of 'clean blood'. An actual expectation is not however sufficient; section 3(1) refers to the level of safety that people are *entitled* to expect—not the level that they *do* expect. Further, there was no available test that could be used to check individual units of blood for the virus, and therefore the risk of infection was unavoidable. Therefore, it was assumed that an action could only be brought under the Consumer Protection Act 1987, and that no action could be brought at common law.[14]

The chief question for the court was whether the blood products, some of which were unavoidably infected by the Hepatitis C virus, were 'defective'. If they were, a subsidiary question was whether the 'development risks defence' could be applied. There was no way of finding the defect. It was held that the infected blood products were defective, and that the development risks defence was not made out. The claimants were successful.

A curious feature of this case was that the judge, Burton J, dispensed with any reference to the Consumer Protection Act 1987 in respect of the primary issues, surrounding defectiveness and the development risks defence. Instead, he referred directly to the corresponding Articles of the Directive (Articles 6 and 7(1)(e) respectively). His reason for this was that the

[14] Could an action have been brought on the basis of a *failure to advise*? The problem with such a claim would lie in causation, if the defendants could argue that the transfusions were emergency treatment and that they would have been accepted even if the risk was known. The test of causation under the Consumer Protection Act 1987 is simpler: did the defect cause the harm?

European Court, in *CEC v UK* [1997] 3 CMLR 923, had recently confirmed that the courts of the UK should interpret the Consumer Protection Act 1987 in accordance with the wording of the Directive.

Burton J, *A v National Blood Authority*

21 Although the United Kingdom Government has not amended s4(1)(e) of the CPA so as to bring it in line with the wording of the directive, there is thus binding authority of the Court of Justice that it must be so construed. Hence . . . the major discussions in this case, and all the areas of most live dispute, have concentrated entirely upon the wording of arts 6 and 7(e) of the directive, and not upon the equivalent sections of the CPA, to which I shall make little or no further reference.

This approach—bypassing the wording of the CPA itself—has not been adopted in other cases that have analysed the meaning of 'defect', or the development risks defence. It is hard to capture the dense reasoning in this case, but we can point out some crucial elements in the finding that the blood was 'defective'.

1. Although the medical profession was aware of the unavoidable risk that blood would be infected, the public generally was not aware of this risk. This in itself was not decisive, because Article 6 (like section 3) refers to what people were *entitled* to expect. The public's expectation of 'clean blood' was not unreasonable, even though the medical profession knew it to be unattainable. Members of the public were 'entitled', given the information made publicly available, to expect clean blood. Therefore, although the products made by the defendants were no worse—in terms of the risks of infection—than any blood supplied at the time could have been, they were still 'defective' on the 'expectation' test.

2. Unavoidability of the risk was not relevant to the test for 'defectiveness' (at [63]). Although it has been queried how any issue could be excluded from the expression '*all* the circumstances' (which is used in both the Act and the Directive), Burton J pointed out that avoidability was not relevant to the purpose of the Directive—which was to apportion liability for defects to producers, subject to the defences available. Avoidability, then, was not part of the definition of a 'defect'. In support of the judge's interpretation, it can be said that avoidability is in no way similar to the kinds of considerations listed in Article 6 and section 3(2), all of which are likely to affect the safety, in practice, of the product (who is going to use it and when? What instructions are provided?). Avoidability does not go to safety.

3. Burton J held that the infected bags of blood were **non-standard products** (also referred to in the judgment as 'lemons' (at [65])). The importance of this in respect of 'defectiveness' was as follows:

The defendants argued that all bags of blood carried the same *risk* of infection. Since there was no test for determining which were the infected bags, they were all to be regarded as equally dangerous. The bags were a standard product. Where a standard product carries an inherent risk, but is still regarded as worthwhile and desirable, the standard product cannot be regarded as defective. This would be true of alcohol for example, or tobacco, whose risks are inherent and cannot realistically be described in terms of 'defects'. Similarly, many drugs have known potential side-effects. All packs of aspirin, for example, carry the same risk of causing internal bleeding, and a pack of aspirin which does turn out to have this effect on a consumer cannot be described as defective. Any pack of aspirin has the potential to do this.

The judge dismissed this argument on two grounds:

1. The infected bags were not the same as the other bags. The injury was not caused simply by a difference in the reaction of the patient: some of the bags were infected ('non-standard'), the others were not. The infected bags were a non standard product.

2. Even in the case of a standard product (such as a normal pack of aspirin), adverse side-effects are only acceptable if they are made known. (We may now add to this that they need not be made known if they are obvious—following subsequent cases such as *Bogle v McDonald's* (discussed earlier in this section), and applying the spirit of *Tomlinson v Congleton* [2004] 1 AC 46.)

Burton J, A v National Blood Authority
[2001] 3 All ER 289

[66] ... I am quite clear that the infected blood products in this case were non-standard products (whether on the basis of being manufacturing or design defects does not appear to me to matter). Where, as here, there is a harmful characteristic in a non-standard product, a decision that it is defective is likely to be straightforward, and I can make my decision accordingly. However, the consequence of my conclusion is that 'avoidability' is also not in the basket of circumstances, even in respect of a harmful characteristic in a standard product. So I shall set out what I consider to be the structure for consideration under art 6. It must be emphasised that safety and intended, or foreseeable, use are the lynch-pins: and, leading on from these, what legitimate expectations there are of safety in relation to foreseeable use....

[67] The first step must be to identify the harmful characteristic which caused the injury (art 4). In order to establish that there is a defect in art 6, the next step will be to conclude whether the product is standard or non-standard. This will be done (in the absence of admission by the producer) most easily by comparing the offending product with other products of the same type or series produced by that producer. If the respect in which it differs from the series includes the harmful characteristic, then it is, for the purpose of art 6, non-standard. If it does not differ, or if the respect in which it differs does not include the harmful characteristic, but all the other products, albeit different, share the harmful characteristic, then it is to be treated as a standard product.

Non-standard products

[68] The circumstances specified in art 6 may obviously be relevant—the product may be a second—as well as the circumstances of the supply. But it seems to me that the primary issue in relation to a non-standard product may be whether the public at large accepted the nonstandard nature of the product—ie they accept that a proportion of the products is defective (as I have concluded they do not in this case). That, as discussed, is not of course the end of it, because the question is of legitimate expectation, and the court may conclude that the expectation of the public is too high or too low. But manifestly questions such as

warnings and presentations will be in the forefront. However, I conclude that the following are not relevant: (i) avoidability of the harmful characteristic—ie impossibility or unavoidability in relation to precautionary measures; (ii) the impracticality, cost or difficulty of taking such measures; and (iii) the benefit to society or utility of the product (except in the context of whether—with full information and proper knowledge—the public does and ought to accept the risk).

Burton J also added some comments relating to *standard* products:

[73] I can accept that resolution of the problem of the defective standard product will be more complex than in the case of a non-standard product. This trial has been in respect of what I am satisfied to be a non-standard product, and I see, after a three-month hearing, no difficulty in eliminating evidence of avoidability from art 6. It may be that, if I am right in my analysis, and if it is followed in other cases, problems may arise in the consideration of a standard product on such basis, but I do not consider any such problems will be insurmountable if safety, use and the identified circumstances are kept in the forefront of consideration. Negligence, fault and the conduct of the producer or designer can be left to the (limited) ambit of art 7(e) ... This approach leaves all questions of conduct to the 'development risks defence'. The statutory product liability was clearly interpreted as a strict liability regime, albeit one that is relatively confined in scope. On the other hand, because the court laid such emphasis on the fact that knowledge of the risks concerned was not shared with the public, the burden placed on producers of medical products may not be very difficult to avoid. Advice as to risks may be sufficient to avoid the judgment of defectiveness, by altering legitimate expectations of safety.

3.5 DEFENCES

The following defences are available *in addition to* the possibility that the product was not defective (Section 3). The most important defence as we have said is the 'development risks' defence, in section 4(1)(e).

4 Defences

(1) In any civil proceedings by virtue of this Part against any person ("the person proceeded against") in respect of a defect in a product it shall be a defence for him to show—

(a) that the defect is attributable to compliance with any requirement imposed by or under any enactment or with any Community obligation; or

(b) that the person proceeded against did not at any time supply the product to another; or

(c) that the following conditions are satisfied, that is to say—

   (i) that the only supply of the product to another by the person proceeded against was otherwise than in the course of a business of that person's; and

   (ii) that section 2(2) above does not apply to that person or applies to him by virtue only of things done otherwise than with a view to profit; or

(d) that the defect did not exist in the product at the relevant time; or

(e) that the state of scientific and technical knowledge at the relevant time was not such that a producer of products of the same description as the product in question might be expected to have discovered the defect if it had existed in his products while they were under his control; or

(f) that the defect—

    (i) constituted a defect in a product ("the subsequent product") in which the product in question had been comprised; and

    (ii) was wholly attributable to the design of the subsequent product or to compliance by the producer of the product in question with instructions given by the producer of the subsequent product.

(2) In this section the relevant time in relation to electricity, means the time at which it was generated, being a time before it was transmitted or distributed, and in relation to any other product, means—

    (a) if the person proceeded against is a person to whom subsection (2) of section 2 above applies in relation to the product, the time when he supplied the product to another;

    (b) if that subsection does not apply to that person in relation to the product, the time when the product was last supplied by a person to whom that subsection does apply in relation to the product.

Notice that under section 4(1)(d), the producer will be exonerated if it can establish that the defect was not present at the relevant time (which is, broadly, the time of first supply). This defence was successfully relied upon in *Terence Piper v JRI (Manufacturing) Ltd* [2006] EWCA Civ 1344, where it was held that an artificial hip was probably damaged at the time of surgery, and was not defective when supplied. On the other hand, undue fragility in a product may itself amount to a 'defect'. By section 6(4), the partial defence of contributory negligence (as set out in the Law Reform (Contributory Negligence) Act 1945) is applicable to actions under the Consumer Protection Act.

Section 4(1)(e): The Development Risks Defence

As we have seen, the incorporation of the development risks defence has been controversial. Its effect is that a producer of goods only takes the risk of defects that could have been discovered at the relevant time. The risk that defects will be discovered later falls on the consumer. Why is this? The key idea is 'apportionment of risk', and the preamble to the Directive makes this plain:

Directive 85/374/EEC of 25 July 1985, Preamble

Whereas liability without fault on the part of the producer is the sole means of adequately solving the problem, peculiar to our age of increasing technicality, of a fair apportionment of the risks inherent in modern technological production;

...

Whereas a fair apportionment of risk between the injured person and the producer implies that the producer should be able to free himself from liability if he furnishes proof that as to the existence of certain exonerating circumstances....

This does not get us very far however, because it simply states that the burden of risk should be apportioned 'fairly'. It is hard to know how to ascertain fairness as between two faultless parties. Such questions, one would have thought, could only be resolved by looking more broadly at the opportunities to manage or minimize unknown risks,[15] and (equally import-antly) to the distribution of the *benefits* with which the risks are accompanied. This is the sort of idea which is expressed by Jane Stapleton in terms of 'enterprise liability'; the enter-prise which benefits from the risks, and has the greatest potential control over those risks, ought to be liable if the risks materialize.[16] The development risks defence, in *any* form, undercuts this goal, as it also undercuts the goal of deterrence.

As we saw in the introductory section to this chapter, the newest justification for the defence turns on encouragement to innovation and the wish not to stifle productive risks. In other words, deterrence *of beneficial risk-creation* is not desired.

Apart from the general controversy surrounding the very existence of the defence, there is also a more particular controversy surrounding the way in which the UK has transposed the Directive in this respect. The UK wording departs from the wording of the Directive, and it appears to most commentators that the defence as expressed in the UK legislation is capable (depending on its application) of exonerating more producers than is envisaged by the Directive. The relevant forms of wording are as follows.

Consumer Protection Act 1987

Section 4(1)(e)

... the state of scientific and technical knowledge at the relevant time was not such that a producer of products of the same description as the product in question might be expected to have discovered the defect if it had existed in his products while they were under his control ...

Directive on Product Liability 1985

Article 7

The producer shall not be liable as a result of this Directive if he proves:

...

(e) that the state of scientific and technical knowledge at the time when he put the product into circulation was not such as to enable the existence of the defect to be discovered; ...

Broadly, there are two criticisms of the UK's particular version of the development risks defence, compared with the version in the Directive.

1. There is claimed to be a substantial difference between what a producer might be *expected* to discover, as in the Act; and what it would be *possible* to discover, given the existing state of knowledge, as in the Directive. It is argued by some that the former sets a standard of reasonable expectation, and is therefore quite similar to negligence.

15 This depends on the idea that although the specific danger is unknown, the general risk that the prod-uct will contain dangers is known. But of course as we get further from known dangers, the risks become harder to quantify.

16 Jane Stapleton, 'Product Liability Reform—Real or Illusory?' (1986) 6 OJLS 392–422.

2. The UK wording seems to suggest that the relevant knowledge (when judging whether it would have been possible to recognize the defect) is knowledge of *producers in the industry*. The wording in the Directive seems to encompass scientific knowledge *wherever* it was being developed.

There has been some support for the UK's interpretation of the development risks defence. For example Christopher Newdick suggested at the time of enactment that the version adopted by the UK simply expressed more clearly what would be the inevitable content of the test.

C. Newdick, 'The Development Risk Defence of the Consumer Protection Act 1987' (1988) 47 CLJ 455–76, at 459–60

There are two reasons for thinking that the government may be right. First, when a court assesses the relevant state of scientific and technical knowledge, it will not require the defendant to prove, conclusively and absolutely, a worldwide absence of knowledge of the defect. It would be impracticable to insist on proof that all the libraries of the world had been scoured and all the unpublished theses in universities, in every language, had been read. More probably, the court will make a judgment on the basis of expert evidence. . . .

Secondly, it is conceivable that the plaintiff could present information which revealed the existence of the defect, but which could not reasonably be expected to have been known to the producer . . . There is no doubt that the development risk defence in this form sits uneasily in a measure designed to introduce strict product liability. In effect it relieves the producer of liability when he had not been negligent in failing to discover the defect. This apparent contradiction of purpose is the unavoidable result of the inclusion of the defence in the Product Liability Directive.

CEC v UK [1997] 3 CMLR 923

Given the difference in wording between Article 7(e) of the Directive, and section 4(1)(e) of the Consumer Protection Act (extracted above), the European Commission took the view that the UK had not properly transposed the Directive. It therefore began infringement proceedings against the UK.

Before the European Court of Justice, the Commission failed to prove its case. On the narrowest point, the Commission agreed that some aspects of the wording were inconsistent with the Directive; but pointed out that the Commission had failed to refer to any UK case law which showed that section 4(1)(e) would actually be *interpreted* so as to depart from the Directive.[17]

More importantly for the general interpretation of the Directive throughout the Member States, the Court of Justice also commented on the defence itself. The Court specified that the relevant state of knowledge for the purposes of Article 7(e) was the objective state of knowledge, not the knowledge to be expected of a producer in the particular industry. However, most controversially, the Court accepted the analysis of Advocate General Tesauro which preceded the judgment, to the effect that the relevant knowledge must be 'accessible'. This

[17] Necessarily, since there would appear to have been *no* UK case law applying the Act at the relevant time.

seemed to go some way towards accepting that the UK approach represented the *proper* interpretation of the Directive.

Opinion of Mr Advocate General Tesauro

A number of key points can be extracted from the Advocate General's quite lengthy opinion, as follows.

1. The defence does not help a defendant who is able to show simply that the risk was unknown *among producers of the product in question*. The defence only applies where the risk genuinely cannot be discovered in the light of existing knowledge. Existing knowledge for these purposes includes knowledge among those at the forefront of research. Indeed, even one 'isolated opinion' will do (subject to 'accessibility', see later in this chapter). This is partly because it is an objective of the strict liability regime to encourage investment in research and development relating to risks.[18]

2. The 'development risks defence' *only* assists a defendant in respect of *risks* which cannot be discovered. It does not apply where the risk is known, but no methodology has been developed for identifying the defect in a particular product, or for removing it. It does not assist a defendant in respect of risks which cannot be *avoided*, either because no method for doing so has been discovered, or because that method is too expensive to be applied. This is because the defence is a narrow exception to the general allocation of risk to producers rather than consumers. It is up to producers to manage, internalize, or (so far as possible) avoid risks that were—in the objective sense—'known' or 'knowable' at the time of manufacture. The decision as to defect in *A v National Blood Authority* (see Section 3.4) is compatible with this.

3. Most controversially from the point of view of those who support strict liability, the Advocate General accepted the UK's position that knowledge must be in some sense **accessible** if it is to defeat the defence. This does not mean that the producer *ought to have discovered it* in the full negligence sense. But the Advocate General does suggest that research published only in Manchuria, for example, may not be regarded as sufficiently accessible to defeat the defence against a European producer. The producer is expected to *find* developing knowledge; but there is a limit to this expectation. Knowledge that is not accessible at all is (in effect) not there to be found.

Judgment of the European Court of Justice (Wathelet J)

25 Several observations can be made as to the wording of Article 7(e) of the Directive.

26 First, as the Advocate General rightly observes in paragraph 20 of his Opinion, since that provision refers to 'scientific and technical knowledge at the time when the producer put the product into circulation', Article 7(e) is not specifically directed at the practices and safety standards in use in the industrial sector in which the producer is operating, but, unreservedly, at the state of scientific and technical knowledge, including the most advanced level of such knowledge, at the time when the product in question was put into circulation.

---

18 On the other hand it has been argued that this incentive to research can be overdone, so that it begins to stifle innovation: see Chris Hodges, 'Development Risks: Unanswered Questions', extracted later.

27 Second, the clause providing for the defence in question does not contemplate the state of knowledge of which the producer in question actually or subjectively was or could have been apprised, but the objective state of scientific and technical knowledge of which the producer is presumed to have been informed.

28 However, it is implicit in the wording of Article 7(e) that the relevant scientific and technical knowledge must have been accessible at the time when the product in question was put into circulation.

29 It follows that, in order to have a defence under Article 7(e) of the Directive, the producer of a defective product must prove that the objective state of scientific and technical knowledge, including the most advanced level of such knowledge, at the time when the product in question was put into circulation was not such as to enable the existence of the defect to be discovered. Further, in order for the relevant scientific and technical knowledge to be successfully pleaded as against the producer, that knowledge must have been accessible at the time when the product in question was put into circulation. On this last point, Article 7(e) of the Directive, contrary to what the Commission seems to consider, raises difficulties of interpretation which, in the event of litigation, the national courts will have to resolve, having recourse, if necessary, to Article 177 of the EC Treaty.

...

32 The Commission takes the view that inasmuch as section 4(1)(e) of the Act refers to what may be expected of a producer of products of the same description as the product in question, its wording clearly conflicts with Article 7(e) of the Directive in that it permits account to be taken of the subjective knowledge of a producer taking reasonable care, having regard to the standard precautions taken in the industrial sector in question.

33 That argument must be rejected in so far as it selectively stresses particular terms used in section 4(1)(e) without demonstrating that the general legal context of the provision at issue fails effectively to secure full application of the Directive. Taking that context into account, the Commission has failed to make out its claim that the result intended by Article 7(e) of the Directive would clearly not be achieved in the domestic legal order.

...

37 ... the Court has consistently held that the scope of national laws, regulations or administrative provisions must be assessed in the light of the interpretation given to them by national courts (see, in particular, Case C-382/92 *Commission v United Kingdom* 1994 ECR I-2435, paragraph 36). Yet in this case the Commission has not referred in support of its application to any national judicial decision which, in its view, interprets the domestic provision at issue inconsistently with the Directive.

38 Lastly, there is nothing in the material produced to the Court to suggest that the courts in the United Kingdom, if called upon to interpret section 4(1)(e), would not do so in the light of the wording and the purpose of the Directive so as to achieve the result which it has in view and thereby comply with the third paragraph of Article 189 of the Treaty (see, in particular, Case C-91/92 *Faccini Dori v Recreb* 1994 ECR I-3325, paragraph 26). Moreover, section 1(1) of the Act expressly imposes such an obligation on the national courts.

Not surprisingly, the interpretation of the defence in the decision above has been criticized from very different perspectives.

Chris Hodges, 'Development Risks: Unanswered Questions' (1998) 61 MLR 560, at 569

At first sight, the test in the defence seems to be whether the defect could have been discovered by any human, using, it is implied, all available powers of logic, data and techniques. Relevant techniques might include the most sophisticated information technology, computing, testing and monitoring in use. Clearly, if this analysis is correct, the standard set by the defence is very high. It would only succeed in very rare circumstances, if ever. It requires all producers to adopt the very highest standard of methodology. Given that many innovations are discovered by small and medium enterprises, is it reasonable to expect all enterprises to adopt the same highest possible standard, irrespective of resources and cost?

These considerations undermine the credibility of this defence. The charge against the wording of the defence in the Directive is, therefore, that it is not capable of being interpreted in practice. It is unworkable on a literal reading and requires interpretation if it is to reflect the policy of protecting innovation …

M. Mildred and G. Howells, 'Comment on "Development Risks: Unanswered Questions"' (1998) 61 MLR 570, at 572

The existence of powerful computerised databases will allow the producer to satisfy itself of the nature of published knowledge in the various fields of knowledge before putting a product into circulation. Since they will be available without regard to the industrial sector within which the producer works there is no reason to confine discoverability by accessibility to a particular sector. There is no doubt that this will be a burden to producers but the very title of the Consumer Protection Act 1987 shows that the interests of the producer (which Hodges sets out to defend) are by no means paramount. The producer is, of course, undertaking innovation for competitive and economic advantage just as much as, if not more than, for philanthropic purposes.

Does the motive of the producer make a difference? 'Risky' products may of course be produced by non-profit-making organizations (as in *A v National Blood Authority*) but for the most part it is true that innovation is carried out in pursuit of profit—as indeed products such as hot tea and coffee are made available through the market. Beneficial products are still beneficial no matter what the incentive for producers to make them available, or to develop them. Should profit motive make a difference? If so, does this leave a major gap in justification for strict liability?

A v National Blood Authority: Development Risks Issues

Here we return to the leading UK case, *A v National Blood Authority*, and turn our attention to its treatment of the development risks defence.

For the reasons we explained earlier, Burton J referred directly to the Directive, rather than to the Act, when interpreting both 'defectiveness', and 'development risks'. His interpretation drew upon the Advocate General's opinion in *CEC v UK*, extracted above. In particular, he explained that the development risks defence does not assist a defendant where the *method for identifying and removing* the defect is unknown, provided the risk of that defect *is* known. Given that the risk of infection with Hepatitis C was clearly recognized, this finding was itself sufficient to dispose of the defence in this case. However, Burton J added a gloss regarding non-standard products (such as the bags of infected blood in this case). That is, non-standard products will very rarely attract the development risks defence. If they do so at all, they will do so only once, until the first non-standard product or 'lemon' is discovered.

Burton J, *A v National Blood Authority*

[75] The purpose of the directive, from which art 7(e) should obviously not derogate more than is necessary (see Recital 16) is to prevent injury, and facilitate compensation for injury. The defendants submit that this means that art 7(e) must be construed so as to give the opportunity to the producer to do all he can in order to avoid injury: thus concentrating on what can be done in relation to the particular product. The claimants submit that this will rather be achieved by imposing obligation in respect of a known risk irrespective of the chances of finding the defect in the particular product, and I agree.

[76] The purpose of art 7(e) was plainly not to discourage innovation, and to exclude development risks from the directive, and it succeeds in its objective, subject to the very considerable restrictions that are clarified by European Commission v UK: namely that the risk ceases to be a development risk and becomes a known risk not if and when the producer in question (or, as the CPA inappropriately sought to enact in s 4(1)(e) a producer of products of the same description as the product in question) had the requisite knowledge, but if and when such knowledge were accessible anywhere in the world outside Manchuria. Hence it protects the producer in respect of the unknown (inconnu). But the consequence of acceptance of the defendants' submissions would be that protection would also be given in respect of the known.

[77] The effect is, it seems to me, not, as the BGH[19] has been interpreted as concluding (or perhaps as it did conclude, but if it did then I would respectfully differ) that non-standard products are incapable of coming within art 7(e). Non-standard products may qualify once—ie if the problem which leads to an occasional defective product is (unlike the present case) not known: this may perhaps be more unusual than in relation to a problem with a standard product, but does not seem to me to be an impossible scenario. However, once the problem is known by virtue of accessible information, then the non-standard product can no longer qualify for protection under art 7(e).

The decision in *A v National Blood Authority* has been subjected to some academic criticism (from different perspectives) by C. Hodges, 'Compensating Patients' (2001) 117 LQR 528; and G. Howells and M. Mildred, 'Infected Blood: Defect and Discoverability. A First Exposition of the EC Product Liability Directive' (2002) 65 MLR, 95. Counsel for the claimants and defendants offer some reflections on the case in M. Brooke and I. Forrester, 'The Use of Comparative Law in *A & Ors v National Blood Authority*', in D. Fairgrieve (ed.),

[19] This is a reference to the 'German bottle case' of 9 May 1995, NJW 1995, 2162 (German Federal Supreme Court, 'BGH'). A mineral water bottle with a hairline crack was defective, and the development risks defence was not made out, even though the producer applied the latest technology in its production process.

Product Liability in Comparative Perspective (Cambridge University Press, 2005). The chapter includes a postscript by the judge, Sir Michael Burton. The decision is more strongly criticized by J. Stapleton, 'Bugs in Anglo-American Product Liability', in the same collection (at pp. 325–90). In Stapleton's view, the judge tried too hard to give the Directive 'work to do', and to avoid the conclusion that the Directive (and the Consumer Protection Act 1987) were 'not only … toothless but pointless.' An alternative reading is that the judgment was thereby true to the objectives of the legislation. On the other hand, the treatment of 'non-standard products' in *A v National Blood Authority* has been met with some considerable doubt and this issue remains to be further explored—if indeed any suitable cases make their way to court.

3.6 LIMITATION PERIOD
Limitation Act 1980

11A Actions in respect of defective products

(1) This section shall apply to an action for damages by virtue of any provision of Part I of the Consumer Protection Act 1987.

(2) None of the time limits given in the preceding provisions of this Act shall apply to an action to which this section applies.

(3) An action to which this section applies shall not be brought after the expiration of the period of ten years from the relevant time, within the meaning of section 4 of the said act of 1987; and this subsection shall operate to extinguish a right of action and shall do so whether or not that right of action had accrued, or time under the following provisions of this Act had begun to run, at the end of the said period of ten years.

(4) Subject to subsection (4) below, an action to which this section applies in which the damages claimed by the plaintiff consist of or include damages in respect of personal injuries to the plaintiff or any other person or loss of or damage to any property, shall not be brought after the expiration of the period of three years from whichever is the later of—

    (a) the date on which the cause of action accrued; and

    (b) the date of knowledge of the injured person or, in the case of loss of or damage to property, the date of knowledge of the plaintiff or (if earlier) of any person in whom his cause of action was previously vested.

(5) If in a case where the damages claimed by the plaintiff consist of or include damages in respect of personal injuries to the plaintiff or any other person the injured person died before the expiration of the period mentioned in subsection (4) above, that subsection shall have effect as respects the cause of action surviving for the benefit of his estate by virtue of section 1 of the Law Reform (Miscellaneous Provisions) Act 1934 as if for the reference to that period there were substituted a reference to the period of three years from whichever is the later of—

    (a) the date of death; and

    (b) the date of the personal representative's knowledge.

Claims under the Consumer Protection Act 1987 are not within the operation of section 33 of the Limitation Act 1980, which confers a discretion on the court in certain cases of personal injury to allow extension to the limitation period.[20]

Horne-Roberts v SmithKline Beecham [2001] EWCA Civ 2006; [2002] 1 WLR 1662

In this case, the claimant had brought an action for damages under the Consumer Protection Act 1987 in respect of injuries that he argued were caused by a vaccine. The batch number of the vaccine was identified, but was wrongly attributed to another producer. It was in fact produced by SmithKline Beecham. The error came to light in August 2000, the action having been commenced (against the wrong party) in August 1999. The vaccine was administered in June 1990, so that by this time the action was outside the ten-year limitation period set out in section 11A of the Limitation Act 1980 (above).

The Court of Appeal held that the claimant could substitute a different defendant pursuant to section 35 of the Limitation Act 1980, and the Civil Procedure Rules, rule 19.5, even when the ten-year period had expired. For the purposes of this rule (and of section 35), claims under the Consumer Protection Act 1987 are to be treated in the same way as claims in contract and tort. But the limitation periods applied to common law actions in contract and tort are *procedural*: generally (and with the exception of the action in conversion) the expiry of the limitation period bars the *remedy*, but does not extinguish the *right*. There was a powerful argument that the variation of defendant in this case should not be permitted, because the Directive on Product Liability itself states that after the ten-year period has expired, the *right to an action* is extinguished. The long-stop provision is not a merely procedural bar.

Article 11

Member states shall provide in their legislation that the rights conferred upon the injured person pursuant to this Directive shall be extinguished upon the expiry of a period of ten years from the date on which the producer put into circulation the actual product which caused the damage, *unless the injured person has in the meantime instituted proceedings against the producer.*

[Emphasis added]

Section 11A(3) of the Consumer Protection Act 1987 also expressly states that the section operates to *extinguish* the right of action.

The Court of Appeal seems to have thought that in a case where by mistake proceedings had been instituted against the wrong producer, the final proviso of Article 11 (italicized above) would be satisfied: this *is* a case where the injured party had 'instituted proceedings against the producer' (albeit the wrong producer).[21] That being so, the time limit for claims under the statute set out in section 11A was to be treated for these purposes as a normal time limit, and the claim was not extinguished.

[20] Section 33 applies only to claims which are within s 11; and s 11A states that the preceding sections (including therefore s 11) do not apply to claims under the Consumer Protection Act 1987.

[21] If this seems to be a stretch to benefit the claimant, it may indicate that courts in personal injuries actions are very used to operating a discretion to permit claims outside the limitation period.

In *O'Byrne v Aventis Pasteur MSD Ltd* (Case C-127/04, 9 February 2006), the European Court of Justice (ECJ) appeared to have conceded that the issue of substitution of defendants was an issue of *procedural law*, and was therefore a matter for the national court, preserving the authority of *Horne-Roberts v SKB*.[22] Unfortunately however, the ECJ added a rider to the effect that Articles 1 and 3 of the Directive must be taken to state exhaustively the category of defendants against whom actions can be brought. It seems highly unlikely that this was meant to contradict the general finding that the question was one for national courts. But the comments could not be said to be completely clear. That being so, the House of Lords in *O'Byrne v Aventis Pasteur SA* [2008] UKHL 34; [2008] 4 All ER 881 determined that the issue must be referred to the ECJ for a second time, in order to obtain a clear statement of the position where a claimant by mistake names the wrong producer on their initial claim, but does so within the limitation period.

The possible and likely meanings of the ECJ's remarks in its first ruling in *O'Byrne* have been analysed by Geraint Howells: '*O'Byrne v Aventis Pasteur SA*—how many trips to Luxembourg are necessary?' (2009) JBL 97–101. Howells draws attention to the delays and difficulties which have, in this argument over a preliminary legal issue, been placed in the way of a brain-damaged claimant, and underlines that this sort of effect was not the intention of the harmonized limitation period. Howells particularly draws attention to the nature of the compromise effected by the Directive, including as it does a development risks defence for producers of products such as these.

On 2 December 2009, in *Aventis Pasteur v O'Byrne* (Case–358/08); [2010] 1 WLR 1375, the ECJ made its second ruling on the limitation question in respect of these proceedings. The Court ruled that although the ten-year limitation period is to be regarded as strict, there are certain relevant exceptional circumstances where substitution of defendant could take place outside that period. One such exception is where the party proceeded against is in effect the same party as the producer. Another is where the claimant cannot reasonably be expected to know who the producer is. In these circumstances, in accordance with Article 3(3) of the Directive, the supplier may be treated as the producer, unless the supplier informs the claimant of the identity of the producer once proceedings are commenced.

The case returned to the UK's highest court, by now the UK Supreme Court, in *O'Byrne v Aventis-Pasteur* [2010] UKSC 23; [2010] 1 WLR 1412. The Supreme Court interpreted the ECJ's decision as requiring the national court to consider not only whether the manufacturer wholly owned the distributor, as it did here, but whether it had *controlled* the distributor: the core of the ECJ's ruling was that a producer could not be sued after expiry of the limitation period. Unanimously, the Supreme Court allowed the appeal, ruling that the claim was out of time.

4. CONCLUSIONS

i. The Consumer Protection Act 1987 appears to enact a clear form of strict liability, in which defectiveness of products is the key determinant of liability for harm those products cause, rather than reasonableness of conduct on the part of a manufacturer. The reality, however, is more complex. In many respects, liability under the statute resembles the tort of negligence more closely than might be expected, and issues

[22] See however the note by C. Hodges, 'Product Liability: Suppliers, Limitation and Mistake' (2006) 122 LQR 393, arguing that *Horne-Roberts* is wrong or the UK has not properly transposed the Directive.

of causation and proof remain important. The key dilution of the strictness of the regime comes, however, in the form of the 'development risks defence'. The consumer takes some of the risks of defective products, to the extent that they could not have been discovered at the time of manufacture given the state of scientific knowledge at that time. The exact parameters of the defence are of course important; but its very existence illustrates that liability under the Act performs an allocation of risk. Not all risks of defectiveness have been placed with manufacturers; and in this respect, something akin to the fault standard in negligence continues to operate. In fact, there has been relatively little take-up of the Act, and negligence frequently continues to be argued alongside it.

FURTHER READING

Clark, A., *Product Liability* (London: Sweet & Maxwell, 1989).

Fairgrieve, D. (ed.), *Product Liability in Comparative Perspective* (Cambridge: Cambridge University Press, 2005).

Fairgrieve, D., and Howells, G., 'Rethinking Product Liability: A Missing Element in the European Commission's Third Review of the Product Liability Directive' (2007) 70 MLR 962.

Goldberg, R., *Causation and Risk in the Law of Torts: Scientific Evidence and Medicinal Product Liability* (Oxford: Hart Publishing, 1999).

Hodges, C., 'Development Risks: Unanswered Questions' (1998) 61 MLR 560.

Hodges, C., 'Approaches to Product Liability in the EU and Member States', in D. Fairgrieve (ed.), *Product Liability in Comparative Perspective* (Cambridge: Cambridge University Press, 2005).

Hodges, C., 'Product Liability: Suppliers, Limitation and Mistake' (2006) 122 LQR 393.

Howells, G., *Comparative Product Liability* (Aldershot: Dartmouth, 1993).

Mildred, M., and Howells, G., 'Comment on "Development Risks: Unanswered Questions"' (1998) 61 MLR 570.

Newdick, C., 'The Future of Negligence in Product Liability' (1987) 103 LQR 288–310.

Newdick, C., 'The Development Risk Defence of the Consumer Protection Act 1987' (1988) 47 CLJ 455–76.

Stapleton, J., 'Product Liability Reform—Real or Illusory?' (1986) 6 OJLS 392–422.

Stapleton, J., *Product Liability* (London: Butterworths, 1994).

Stapleton, J., 'Bugs in Anglo-American Product Liability', in D. Fairgrieve (ed.), *Product Liability in Comparative Perspective* (Cambridge: Cambridge University Press, 2005) 295–333.

Whittaker, S., *Liability for Products: English Law, French Law, and European Harmonization* (Oxford: Oxford University Press, 2005).

16

BREACH OF STATUTORY DUTY

CENTRAL ISSUES

i) If a statute imposes a duty but does not specify a civil remedy, an action in tort may sometimes be available to remedy harm caused by a breach of the duty. This action in tort will be an action for 'breach of statutory duty'. The duty is defined by statute; but the action is brought at common law.

ii) Historically, the action for breach of statutory duty has been very significant in the context of industrial safety.

Outside that area it has been more restricted in scope, and the trend has been to adopt an approach which restricts it further. However, legislation enacted in 2013 will have a major impact on future claims for damages for breach of health and safety statutes and regulations, dramatically reducing recovery in the most significant area in which it has previously been available.

1. TORT AND LEGISLATION: THE DISTINCTIVENESS OF THE TORT OF 'BREACH OF STATUTORY DUTY'

The tort action for breach of statutory duty is a hybrid between statute (defining the duty) and common law (determining whether the breach is actionable).

Lord Wright, *London Passenger Transport Board v Upson*
[1949] AC 155, at 168

... a claim for damages for breach of a statutory duty intended to protect a person in the position of the particular plaintiff is a specific common law right which is not to be confused in essence with a claim for negligence. The statutory right has its origin in the statute, but the particular remedy of an action for damages is given by the common law in order to make effective, for the benefit of the injured plaintiff, his right to the performance by the defendant of the defendant's statutory duty.

2. THE QUESTION OF INTERPRETATION: DOES THE BREACH GIVE RISE TO LIABILITY AT COMMON LAW?

The authorities in this area are dominated by questions of parliamentary intent and its interpretation. While the general opinion seems to be that the area is confused and unpredictable, the majority of cases can be understood in terms of two contrasting approaches to parliamentary intent. The second, and less restrictive, has been widely applied in 'health and safety' cases. It is here however that recent legislative intervention will now restrict the operation of the tort.

Two Potential Approaches

Lord Simonds, *Cutler v Wandsworth Stadium Ltd*
[1949] AC 398, at 169

The only rule which in all the circumstances is valid is that the answer must depend on a consideration of the whole Act and the circumstances, including the pre-existing law, in which it was enacted.

'What did Parliament intend (or not intend)?' is potentially a very open-ended question. In order to answer it, it is not enough simply to study the statute in its context. We also need to know roughly what we are looking for.

What are We Looking For?

The following two distinct approaches are present in the case law explored in this chapter.[1]

Interpretive Approach 1: we are looking for legislative intent to create the cause of action

On this approach, the cause of action in tort for breach of statutory duty depends on there being an intention, on the part of the legislature, *to create* such a common law right of action.

If no intention to create the right of action can be identified, no right of action will be held to exist. If this is what we are looking for, then there is a single question of statutory interpretation:

Did Parliament intend there to be a right of action at common law?

Interpretive Approach 2: we are looking for legislative intent to benefit the claimant

On this approach, the cause of action in tort for breach of statutory duty depends on there being an intention, on the part of the legislature, to *benefit* the claimant or a limited class of people including the claimant.

---

[1] Our coverage is of course selective. For more extensive examination of the action and its development see K. Stanton, *Breach of Statutory Duty in Tort* (2nd edn, Sweet & Maxwell, 1986).

Here, the right of action arises at common law, in order to give effect to the statutory duty.[2] If this is the correct analysis, there are two questions of statutory interpretation. Both are different from the single question above:

(a) Did Parliament enact the duty with the intention of benefiting the claimant?; and

(b) Is there any reason to think that Parliament intended to exclude the right of action, which is available at common law as a means of enforcing the duty?

Interpretive question (b) will be triggered if (for example) the statute provides for an alternative means of enforcement, such as a criminal penalty. But in principle, this is only one example of the circumstances in which the court may conclude that Parliament intended there not to be a right of action.

It should be obvious that *both* these approaches involve interpretation of parliamentary intention. It is easy to see why they can be and often are understood in terms of the relevant *presumption* that applies. The first approach typically starts with a presumption that there is *no* right of action where a statutory duty is breached, unless there is good reason to think that Parliament intended to create such an action. The second approach involves a presumption that there *is* a right of action, but *only* if (a) is satisfied: the statutory duty seems designed to benefit the claimant or a class including the claimant. Another way of looking at (b) is that common law provides a remedy to support Parliament's actions, and this is not inconsistent with Parliament's intentions. Though this may seem a manipulation of Parliament's silence on the question of civil remedies, it should be remembered that the courts have approached industrial safety legislation in particular in this way for well over a century, with the full knowledge of Parliament, and that successive statutes introducing safety duties will have been enacted on the clear assumption that they would give rise to actions in tort. Very simple statutory language could have been included to reverse the courts' approach in this regard.

Outside health and safety legislation, however, there is a strong trend towards the first interpretive approach, and this has led to *restriction* in availability of the action for breach of statutory duty. In *Peter Campbell v Gordon Joiners Ltd* [2016] UKSC 38, this difference of approach was a central issue.

3. INJURIES AT WORK

We start our extracts with a defining case of civil liability for breach of industrial safety legislation. It exemplifies the second approach introduced in Section 2, in which the right of action is presumed to arise at common law, *provided* the legislature intended to confer a benefit.

Groves v Winborne (Lord) [1898] 2 QB 402

The plaintiff was a boy employed in the defendant's Iron Works. By section 5 of the Factory and Workshop Act 1878, certain dangerous machinery had to remain fenced. Relevant machinery was left unfenced, and the plaintiff's arm was caught in the cog-wheels of a steam winch. He was so badly injured that his forearm had to be amputated. There was clearly a

---

[2] 'Benefit' to the claimant may certainly include protection from harm (*Groves v Winborne* (later in this section)); it may also perhaps include the conferral of rights whose invasion is actionable per se (*Cullen v RUC*, Lords Bingham and Steyn, dissenting (Section 6)).

breach of section 5. The duty imposed by this section was not subject to reasonable care or to any questions of practicability or efficiency. It was an 'absolute' duty.

The Court of Appeal held that the defendant was liable in damages to the plaintiff. The key difficulty of interpretation arose from the fact that the statute provided sanctions for a breach of duty, in the form of fines and penalties. Should these penalties be taken to show that Parliament wished to exclude the action at common law which would otherwise arise from breach of the statutory duty?

A. L. Smith LJ, *Groves v Wimborne* [1898] 2 QB 402, at 406–7

The Act in question, which followed numerous other Acts in pari materia, is not in the nature of a private legislative bargain between employers and workmen, as the learned judge seemed to think, but is a public Act passed in favour of the workers in factories and workshops to compel their employers to do certain things for their protection and benefit. The first question is what duty is imposed by that Act upon the occupiers of factories and workshops with regard to the fencing of machinery. By s. 5 it is enacted that "with respect to the fencing of machinery the following provisions shall have effect." Then by sub-s. 3 of the section, as amended by the Factory and Workshop Act, 1891, s. 6, sub-s. 2, "All dangerous parts of the machinery, and every part of the mill gearing shall either be securely fenced, or be in such position or of such construction as to be equally safe to every person employed in the factory as it would be if it were securely fenced"; and by sub-s. 4, "All fencing shall be constantly maintained in an efficient state while the parts required to be fenced are in motion or use for the purpose of any manufacturing process", and "a factory in which there is a contravention of this section shall be deemed not to be kept in conformity with this Act." In the present case it is admitted that machinery on the defendant's premises which came within these provisions was not fenced as required by the Act, and that injury was thereby occasioned to the plaintiff, a boy employed on the works. On proof of a breach of this statutory duty imposed on the defendant, and injury resulting to the plaintiff therefrom, prima facie the plaintiff has a good cause of action. I leave out of the question for a moment the provisions of ss. 81, 82, and 86 of the Act. Could it be doubted that, if s. 5 stood alone, and no fine were provided by the Act for contravention of its provisions, a person injured by a breach of the absolute and unqualified duty imposed by that section would have a cause of action in respect of that breach? Clearly it could not be doubted. That being so, unless it appears from the whole "purview" of the Act, to use the language of Lord Cairns in the case of *Atkinson v. Newcastle Waterworks Co.* (1877) 2 Ex D 441, that it was the intention of the Legislature that the only remedy for breach of the statutory duty should be by proceeding for the fine imposed by s. 82, it follows that, upon proof of a breach of that duty by the employer and injury thereby occasioned to the workman, a cause of action is established. The question therefore is whether the cause of action which prima facie is given by s. 5 is taken away by any provisions to be found in the remainder of the Act. It is said that the provisions of ss. 81, 82, and 86 have that effect, and that it appears thereby that the purview of the Act is that the only remedy, where a workman has been injured by a breach of the duty imposed by s. 5, shall be by proceeding before a court of summary jurisdiction for a fine under s. 82, which fine is not to exceed £100. In dealing with the question whether this was the intention of the Legislature, it is material, as Kelly C.B. pointed out in giving judgment in the case of *Gorris v. Scott* (1874) LR 9 Ex 125, to consider for whose benefit the Act was passed, whether it was passed in the interests of the public at large or in those of a particular class of persons.

In its day, the huge practical significance of *Groves v Wimborne* was that it provided a remedy to an employee injured at work which could not at that time have been achieved through any other action in tort. The statutory duty was imposed directly upon the employer and was absolute in nature. Therefore, even if a fellow employee was directly responsible for removing the fencing which had at one time been present, the employer could not escape liability by invoking the 'doctrine of common employment'.[3] *Groves v Wimborne* opened up an important gap in the protection given to employers by that doctrine, and was compatible with the general legislative effort to protect the safety of workers. The approach in this case was subsequently applied in many others.[4]

The existence of the action has been deeply embedded in the health and safety area, where many statutory provisions designed to ensure safety have also given rise to civil liability. The standard of care applicable to any such action is as defined in the statute, though this question can of course throw up difficult arguments when it comes to interpretation. But the picture changed quite radically in 2013, reversing the trajectory of over 100 years of legal development from the time of *Groves v Wimborne*.

The majority of today's many health and safety regulations are governed by the Health and Safety at Work etc. Act 1974 (HSWA 1974), although there are also a number of other individual statutes in force. Until 2013, section 47(2) of this statute specified that breach of regulations made under the statute were actionable unless the regulation expressly provided to the contrary. Now however, section 47(2) has been amended. The statutory change goes further than altering the impact of regulations made under HSWA, and affects other health and safety legislation also.

Enterprise and Regulatory Reform Act 2013

69 Civil liability for breach of health and safety duties

(1) Section 47 of the Health and Safety at Work etc. Act 1974 (civil liability) is amended as set out in subsections (2) to (7).

(2) In subsection (1), omit paragraph (b) (including the *"or"* at the end of that paragraph).

(3) For subsection (2) substitute—

"(2)   Breach of a duty imposed by a statutory instrument containing (whether alone or with other provision) health and safety regulations shall not be actionable except to the extent that regulations under this section so provide.

(2A)   Breach of a duty imposed by an existing statutory provision shall not be actionable except to the extent that regulations under this section so provide (including by modifying any of the existing statutory provisions).

(2B)   Regulations under this section may include provision for—

(a)   a defence to be available in any action for breach of the duty mentioned in subsection (2) or (2A);

---

[3]   This doctrine held that an employee could not bring an action in respect of the tort of a fellow employee (of the same master). The doctrine no longer exists in any form. See further Chapter 5, in respect of *volenti non fit injuria* (willing acceptance of risk).

[4]   See in particular the decision of the House of Lords in *Butler v Fife Coal Co Ltd* [1912] AC 149.

(b) any term of an agreement which purports to exclude or restrict any liability for such a breach to be void."

…

It is clear both from the Explanatory Notes and preceding policy documents that the intention is to ensure that employees have remedies only where the employer can be said to have been negligent; it achieves this in the first instance by removing civil liability altogether from certain health and safety statutes and regulations. To which such provisions does the section then apply?

The new section 47(2) removes civil liability—unless and until provided to the contrary—from 'health and safety regulations'. By section 15 of the HSWA 1974, 'health and safety regulations' are defined as regulations that are passed under the framework of that Act. This is therefore a far-reaching change, removing civil liability altogether for the time being, and strict liability it would seem in the long run, from numerous widely used regulations.[5] An example is the Provision and Use of Work Equipment Regulations 1998, which have not only generated many damages claims each year, but have been the subject of interpretation in the House of Lords on a number of occasions, most recently in *Smith v Northamptonshire County Council* [2009] UKHL 27. In such cases, the key question has been whether the cause of the injury suffered by the claimant falls within the parameters of the strict—or even absolute—safety duties set out in the various regulations. So in *Smith*, the question was whether a ramp used on a regular basis by an employee to help a patient from her house to a vehicle was judged not to be 'work equipment'. If so, there would be liability if this equipment should prove to be faulty, irrespective of the cause of its defectiveness. In this instance, it was not held to be work equipment, and so liability was avoided.[6] Section 69 represents a sea change in this area of law.

Arguably, in terms of the principles being set out the still more far-reaching provision is the new section 47(2A). This affects legislation other than HSWA 1974 itself, some of it very long-standing. Its ambit depends upon the meaning of an 'existing statutory provision'; and this phrase is defined in section 53(1) of the HSWA as referring to the statutes listed in Schedule 1. The list includes some of the most significant and long-established legislation in this area, including the Factories Act 1961, interpreted by the Supreme Court in *Baker v Quantum Clothing Group Ltd* [2011] UKSC 17 and the direct descendant of a number of earlier statutes. While civil liability under HSWA is a relatively new phenomenon which has advanced in response to European law, civil liability for breach of duties set out in these other statutes is far older and is the consequence of developments in the national courts. Altogether, section 69 significantly reduces—to the point of reversing—the significance of *Groves v Wimborne* in its primary zone of application after 115 years of undiminished influence.

Some reasons for this change are indicated in the Explanatory Notes to the legislation. The aim is to avoid over-application of health and safety measures because of a perception that civil liability will be imposed for 'technical breaches' (by which it appears is meant, breaches

---

[5] For a sense of how widely the regulations are the subject of court decisions, readers may glance at M. Jones (ed.), *Clerk and Lindsell on Torts* (20th edn, Sweet & Maxwell, 2010), chapter 13. Of course these will be the tip of the iceberg as more claims will be settled.

[6] For discussion see N. Tomkins, 'Work Equipment and Duties on Employees' (2010) Journal of Personal Injury Law 1–9.

not involving fault.) At first reading in the House of Lords, the provision was removed from the Bill. In an instructive debate, it was pointed out that the strict liability provisions generally avoided costly litigation over whether there had been any lack of care. Equally, strict liability could be argued to be fair in this context because the employer generally has greater access to evidence which would be relevant to the negligence standard. In these respects, a shift back to negligence is a retrograde step. However, the provision was reinstated by the House of Commons, and passed through the Lords at the second attempt.

The remaining question is of course how much difference in practice this large change in applicable principles will make. On the face of it, it completely alters the landscape of civil liability in the employment context, and it seems likely that its influence will indeed be profound. However, there are some potential avenues to civil liability which may take on new importance after section 69. First, it has been pointed out that the Employers' Liability (Defective Equipment) Act 1969, which has not been much needed given the development of civil liability under HSWA regulations, remains good law. This statute is unaffected because it is not 'health and safety' legislation as defined in HSWA. It imposes liability on employers where equipment is faulty through the negligence of others.[7] Second, the employer's non-delegable duties to employees (to provide a safe place and system of work, safe staff and equipment) are likely to become increasingly important. These duties, outlined in Chapter 9 and most famously embodied in the decision in *Wilson and Clyde Coal v English* [1937] 3 All ER 628, impose strict liability at common law, but rest ultimately on the negligence of someone employed by the defendant.

A third possibility is that the tort of negligence itself may provide the route to a relatively strict form of liability in this context, by operating in combination with the regulations themselves.[8] The regulations have not been repealed, but set out duties which are the subject of criminal penalties. An argument has been put that at least where those regulations set out tests turning on what is 'reasonably practicable', they should be relevant to understanding what will amount to 'reasonable care', because a reasonable employer would not breach these duties. This is a route to 'reinvigorating the common law', in combination with the regulations, and the possibilities are illustrated by the Supreme Court's decision in *Kennedy v Cordia* [2016] UKSC 6; [2016] 1 WLR 597. Here, the Supreme Court emphasized the existence of duties to conduct risk assessments *at common law*, as well as under applicable regulations. Conducting such risk assessments is part of the actions of a reasonable employer. It is possible that constructive action by the courts will once again come to determine whether injured employees can recover damages in civil claims where evidence of 'carelessness' in the usual sense is lacking. It is indeed a case of 'back to the future'.

A further possibility is that UK law may now be in conflict with European obligations, in failing to give effect to Directive 89/391 on the introduction of measures to encourage improvements in the safety and health of workers [1989] OJ L183/1, which inspired the broadening of civil liability under HSWA. There would in theory be two routes to liability here, though of course both are of value only while the UK retains membership of the EU. The first is that the Directive might have 'direct effect', so that a claim could be made directly by the injured worker who ought to have been benefited. This route, however, would be effective only in cases where the employer is an 'emanation of the state'. The second

7 N. Tomkins, 'Civil Health and Safety Law After the Enterprise and Regulatory Reform Act 2013' (2013) JPIL 203.

8 We explored the capacity of the tort of negligence to produce relatively strict forms of liability in Chapter 11.

possibility in theory is that an employee could bring an action against the UK on the basis that it had failed to implement a Directive and that this failure had caused the individual loss. This is known as a 'Francovich action' (*Francovich v Italy* [1995] ICR 722). Although different views have been expressed,[9] the difficulty facing both possibilities is that it is by no means clear that the Directive requires civil liability to be in place; and the Regulations are still supported by criminal sanctions. If a particular sort of remedy is not required by the Directive, then neither route will bear fruit.

4. GENERAL EVOLUTION

In some contexts, the law has developed away from the position stated in *Groves v Wimborne*. In this section we examine the courts' evolving approach to interpretation of legislative intent.

Sanctions and Other Means of Enforcement

The Court of Appeal in *Groves v Wimborne* gave due weight to the existence of a *statutory sanction*, but decided that the existence of a modest fine did not displace the civil action. The role of sanctions and alternative remedies is often considered with reference to the following judicial comment. (The case from which this comment is derived had nothing to do with the action for breach of statutory duty in tort. It was concerned with the status of a lease under which the statutory manner of paying rent had not been complied with. The question was whether an alternative way of paying the rent was good enough to safeguard the rights of a successor to the lessee.)

Doe d Bishop of Rochester v Bridges
[1824–1834] All ER 167 (1831)

… Where an Act creates an obligation, and enforces the performance in a specified manner, we take it to be a general rule that performance cannot be enforced in any other manner. If an obligation is created, but no mode of enforcing its performance is ordained, the common law may, in general, find a mode suited to the particular nature of the case.

This statement has been taken to suggest that there cannot be an action for breach of statutory duty if some other means of enforcement of the duty exists. In *Cutler v Wandsworth Stadium* [1949] AC 398, Lord Simonds referred to the above passage from *Doe v Bridges*. But he also relied upon *Groves* and the subsequent case of *Black v Fife Coal Co Ltd* [1912] AC 149, acknowledging that the existence of a penalty was not *decisive*.

In *Cutler*, Lord Simonds also stated a *positive* presumption flowing from the *absence* of any other means of enforcement:

---

[9] Compare the analysis by Tomkins (n 7) with the doubts expressed by Limb and Cox, 'Section 69 of the Enterprise and Regulatory Reform Act 2013—plus ça change?' (2014) JPIL 1.

Lord Simonds, *Cutler v Wandsworth Stadium*, at 170

... if a statutory duty is prescribed but no remedy by way of penalty or otherwise for its breach is imposed, it can be assumed that a right of civil action accrues to the person who is damnified by the breach. For, if it were not so, the statute would be but a pious aspiration.

This presumption too may be rebutted in a suitable case.

The Importance of Statutory Interpretation in Groves v Wimborne

On the second interpretive approach outlined above, the *starting* point should be the purpose of the statute. Was the statute intended to benefit the claimant (or a class of people including the claimant)? *Cutler v Wandsworth* itself is a good illustration of this.

Cutler v Wandsworth Stadium [1949] AC 398

The plaintiff was a bookmaker. He brought an action against the occupier of a licensed dog-racing track for failing to provide him with space on the track where he could carry out book-making, in accordance with section 11(2)(b) of the Betting and Lotteries Act 1934. Criminal penalties were specified for failure to comply with this provision. The House of Lords held that no civil action was available on the part of the plaintiff in respect of a breach of this duty.

Lord Simonds, *Cutler v Wandsworth Stadium*, at 409

... I have no doubt that the primary intention of the Act was to regulate in certain respects the conduct of race tracks and in particular the conduct of betting operations thereon. If in consequence of those regulations being observed some bookmakers will be benefited, this does not mean that the Act was passed for the benefit of bookmakers in the sense in which it was said of a Factory Act that it was passed in favour of the workmen in factories. I agree with Somervell LJ that where an Act regulates the way in which a place of amusement is to be managed, the interests of the public who resort to it may be expected to be the primary consideration of the legislature. If from the work of regulation any class of persons derives an advantage, that does not spring from the primary purpose and intention of the Act.

In more recent years, parliamentary intention has been interpreted in a different way. Here we extract two very significant cases. The approach taken in the second of these, *Ex p. Hague*, is clearly incompatible with the *Groves* case, although the actual outcome could be reconciled with it. The first of the two, extracted next, is more subtle. Is it compatible with *Groves*, or not?

Lonrho v Shell Petroleum (No 2) [1982] AC 173

Lonrho invested considerable sums in the construction and operation of an oil pipe-line to take oil from Mozambique to Southern Rhodesia. The pipeline was completed in January 1965. In November 1965 the government of Southern Rhodesia declared unilat-eral independence. Measures were put in place prohibiting trade with Southern Rhodesia, including the supply of oil. Lonrho argued that Shell and others had continued to supply oil to Southern Rhodesia although this was prohibited. If so, this would be in breach of the Southern Rhodesia (Petroleum) Order 1965, and a criminal offence. Lonrho further argued that they suffered financial loss through this breach of the Order on the part of Shell, since their actions enabled the regime in Rhodesia to resist international pressure, prolonging the need for sanctions and causing Lonrho to make significant losses. Here, we extract the part of Lord Diplock's judgment which deals with the action for breach of statutory duty.[10]

Lord Diplock, *Lonrho v Shell Petroleum (No 2)*
[1982] AC 173, at 185–6

The sanctions Order … creates a statutory prohibition upon the doing of certain classes of acts and provides the means of enforcing the prohibition by prosecution for a criminal offence which is subject to heavy penalties including imprisonment. So one starts with the presumption laid down originally by Lord Tenterden C.J. in *Doe d. Murray v. Bridges* (1831) 1 B. & Ad. 847, 859, where he spoke of the "general rule" that "where an Act creates an obligation, and enforces the performance in a specified manner … that performance cannot be enforced in any other manner"—a statement that has frequently been cited with approval ever since, including on several occasions in speeches in this House. Where the only manner of enforcing performance for which the Act provides is prosecution for the criminal offence of failure to perform the statutory obligation or for contravening the statutory prohibition which the Act creates, there are two classes of exception to this general rule.

The first is where upon the true construction of the Act it is apparent that the obligation or prohibition was imposed for the benefit or protection of a particular class of individuals, as in the case of the Factories Acts and similar legislation. As Lord Kinnear put it in *Butler (or Black) v. Fife Coal Co. Ltd.* [1912] A.C. 149, 165, in the case of such a statute:

> There is no reasonable ground for maintaining that a proceeding by way of penalty is the only remedy allowed by the statute … We are to consider the scope and purpose of the statute and in particular for whose benefit it is intended. Now the object of the present statute is plain. It was intended to compel mine owners to make due provision for the safety of the men working in their mines, and the persons for whose benefit all these rules are to be enforced are the persons exposed to danger. But when a duty of this kind is imposed for the benefit of particular persons there arises at common law a correlative right in those persons who may be injured by its contravention.

The second exception is where the statute creates a public right (i.e. a right to be enjoyed by all those of Her Majesty's subjects who wish to avail themselves of it) and a particular member of the public suffers what Brett J. in *Benjamin v. Storr* (1874) L.R. 9 C.P. 400, 407, described as "particular, direct, and substantial" damage "other and different from that which was common to all the rest of the public." Most of the authorities about this second exception deal not with public rights created by statute but with public rights existing at common law, particularly in respect of use of highways. *Boyce v. Paddington Borough Council* [1903] 1 Ch. 109 is one of the comparatively few cases about a right conferred upon the general public by statute. It is in relation to that class of statute only that Buckley J.'s oft-cited statement

---

[10] See also Chapter 2 for discussion of the case in relation to civil conspiracy.

at p. 114 as to the two cases in which a plaintiff, without joining the Attorney-General, could himself sue in private law for interference with that public right, must be understood. The two cases he said were: '... first, where the interference with the public right is such as that some private right of his is at the same time interfered with ... and, secondly, where no private right is interfered with, but the plaintiff, in respect of his public right, suffers special damage peculiar to himself from the interference with the public right.' The first case would not appear to depend upon the existence of a public right in addition to the private one, while to come within the second case at all it has first to be shown that the statute, having regard to its scope and language, does fall within that class of statutes which creates a legal right to be enjoyed by all of Her Majesty's subjects who wish to avail themselves of it. A mere prohibition upon members of the public generally from doing what it would otherwise be lawful for them to do, is not enough.

My Lords, it has been the unanimous opinion of the arbitrators with the concurrence of the umpire, of Parker J., and of each of the three members of the Court of Appeal that the sanctions Orders made pursuant to the Southern Rhodesia Act 1965 fell within neither of these two exceptions. Clearly they were not within the first category of exception. They were not imposed for the *benefit or protection* of a particular class of individuals who were engaged in supplying or delivering crude oil or petroleum products to Southern Rhodesia. They were intended to put an end to such transactions. Equally plainly they did not create any public right to be enjoyed by all those of Her Majesty's subjects who wished to avail themselves of it. On the contrary, what they did was to withdraw a previously existing right of citizens of, and companies incorporated in, the United Kingdom to trade with Southern Rhodesia in crude oil and petroleum products. Their purpose was, perhaps, most aptly stated by Fox L.J.:

"I cannot think that they were concerned with conferring rights either upon individuals or the public at large. Their purpose was the destruction, by economic pressure, of the U.D.I. regime in Southern Rhodesia; they were instruments of state policy in an international matter."

At first sight, Lord Diplock appears to have adopted a general presumption *against* a civil right of action. But on inspection, this presumption is not general at all, but is *specific* to cases where another means of enforcing the duty (including a criminal penalty) is contained in the statute. The entire discussion in this extract therefore fits into question (b) in the second interpretive approach set out in Section 2.

Even here, where a statutory means of enforcement (a criminal sanction) exists, Lord Diplock went on to explain that there are two ways in which the presumption against a common law action for breach of statutory duty might be rebutted. The first of these exceptions is where the obligation is imposed for the benefit or protection of a particular class of individuals. This would clearly include a case like *Groves*. But if *Groves v Winborne* is correct, then Lord Diplock has his rules and exceptions the wrong way around. The *general rule* should be that there is an action for breach of a duty, if that duty is intended to benefit the claimant: the possible *exception* is that if there is a statutory penalty, it should be considered whether Parliament intended this to be the only means of enforcement.

Lord Diplock's approach is inclined to *broaden* the scope of the action. If 'conferring a benefit' is an exception to the general rule, then how is the intention of Parliament to be further considered? There seems to be no room for an exception to this exception. It is probably Lord Diplock's interpretation which has led to the impression (otherwise plainly untrue) that the presumptions applying in *Groves* do not involve interpretation of the will of Parliament, but give rise to automatic liability (see the argument put for the plaintiff in *Ex p. Hague*, below).

The second of Lord Diplock's exceptional categories is much more difficult to interpret, but it turns on the *creation of legal rights to be enjoyed by all of Her Majesty's subjects*. It is notoriously unclear what Lord Diplock had in mind here, not least because the case he cites (*Benjamin v Storr*) is a case of public nuisance, not of breach of statutory duty.[11] All things considered, we should not struggle unduly with this category, which has not developed since *Lonrho*.[12]

The following case more clearly shows a departure from the approach in *Groves v Wimborne*, but it does not seek to cast doubt upon that case itself.

R v Deputy Governor of Parkhurst, ex p. Hague [1992] 1 AC 58

The plaintiffs, who were lawfully detained in prison, argued that they had been subjected to treatment which was in breach of Prison Rules. In the case of Hague (the first plaintiff), it was alleged that he was segregated from other prisoners in breach of the Rules, and that this breach was subject to an action for breach of statutory duty.[13]

The crucial question is set out in the following passage:

Lord Jauncey

Mr. Sedley for Hague submitted that there had been a breach of the prison rules which sounded in damages. In a carefully reasoned argument to which I hope that I do justice in paraphrasing he argued that a breach of statutory duty unaccompanied by a statutory remedy or penalty affords a right of action to a person injured thereby where the plaintiff belongs to a class which the statutory provision was intended to protect, and the breach has caused the plaintiff damage of a kind against which the provision was intended to protect him. In support of this proposition he relied on *Groves v. Lord Wimborne* [1898] 2 Q.B. 402 and *Cutler v. Wandsworth Stadium Ltd.* [1949] A.C. 398. Where such a situation existed, as it did in the present case, no question of legislative intent arose....

Mr. Laws on the other hand maintained that the first question to be considered was what rights, if any, Parliament intended to confer in passing the statute and that matters such as availability of other remedies merely assisted the resolution of that question and were not in themselves decisive. He also relied on *Groves v. Wimborne* and *Cutler v. Wandsworth Stadium Ltd.* Mr. Laws argued that the Secretary of State had no power under section 47 of the Prison Act 1952 to make rules which conferred private rights on individuals.

[11] It is important to notice that one of Lord Diplock's more puzzling pronouncements—that 'a mere prohibition on members of the public generally . . . is not enough' *relates specifically to this narrow category of case*. Lord Diplock does *not* say here that failure to abide by a prohibition imposed on the general public cannot ever amount to a breach of duty; nor even that it cannot ever give rise to an action for breach of statutory duty. He simply says that such a prohibition will not suffice to create legal rights on the part of the public generally (whatever that might mean).

[12] The authors of the leading work on breach of statutory duty say that 'little is known' about this category, and that 'No action has been successfully based on these words since they were uttered' (Stanton et al, *Statutory Torts*, 2.024, p. 38).

[13] The prisoners also brought actions for false imprisonment (see Chapter 2). These actions also failed: the change in conditions of imprisonment could not make their imprisonment unlawful.

These possible approaches, set out by rival counsel, almost precisely reflect the two interpretive approaches we outlined at the start of this section. However there is one crucial difference, which is that the argument put for Hague implies that no reference to Parliamentary intention is required in a case where the statute confers a benefit, and there is no penalty or other means of enforcement specified in the statute. This would make the action for breach of statutory duty *automatic* in such a case. As we have explained, any such implication is at odds with the reasoning in *Groves*.

In the event, this ambitious argument backfired. Throughout his judgment, Lord Jauncey took it that *any* reference in the authorities to statutory intention disproved the approach urged by the plaintiffs, and proved the approach urged by the defendants. Every authority consulted referred, of course, to the importance of parliamentary intention; and Lord Jauncey did not distinguish which *sort* of intention (to create a right of action, or to benefit the claimant) was required.

Lord Jauncey concluded with an approach that is at odds with *Groves v Wimborne*:

At 170

My Lords, I take from these authorities that it must always be a matter for consideration whether the legislature intended that private law rights of action should be conferred upon individuals in respect of breaches of the relevant statutory provision. The fact that a particular provision was intended to protect certain individuals is not of itself sufficient to confer private law rights of action upon them, something more is required to show that the legislature intended such conferment.

The Prison Act 1952 is designed to deal with the administration of prisons and the management and control of prisoners. It covers such wide-ranging matters as central administration, prison officers, confinement and treatment of prisoners, release of prisoners on licence, provision and maintenance of prisons and offences. Its objects are far removed from those of legislation such as the factories and coal mines Acts whose prime concern is to protect the health and safety of persons who work therein. Section 47 empowers the Secretary of State to make rules in relation to many of the matters with which the Act is concerned and is in the following terms, inter alia:

"(1) The Secretary of State may make rules for the regulation and management of prisons, remand centres, detention centres and Borstal institutions respectively, and for the classification, treatment, employment, discipline and control of persons required to be detained therein."

I find nothing in any of the other sections of the Act to suggest that Parliament intended thereby to confer on prisoners a cause of action sounding in damages in respect of a breach of those provisions. To give the Secretary of State power in section 47 to confer private law rights on prisoners would therefore be to allow him to extend the general scope of the Act by rules.

Lord Jauncey says here that the crucial issue is always whether the legislature intended that private rights of action should be conferred. But in both *Groves* and *Lonrho*, and also other decisions quoted by Lord Jauncey such as *Black v Fife*, the question is whether the duty seeks to confer, not a right of action, but *a benefit* (which in the safety legislation takes the form of *protection from harm*) upon the claimant. Lord Jauncey here takes the step from the second rights on prisoners would therefore be to allow him to extend the general scope of the Act interpretive approach we outlined at the start of this section, to the first. In later decisions, at least outside the health and safety field, it has consistently been said that the crucial question is *whether the legislature intended to confer a right of action*.

As for *Hague* itself, the selection of interpretive approach might have been decisive, if it had been found that the legislature *did* intend to benefit prisoners through the relevant Prison Rule (by setting limits to acceptable treatment). But the purpose of the relevant Prison Rule as the House of Lords interpreted it was not, in any event, to benefit the prisoner:

Lord Bridge, at 160

The purpose of the rule, apart from the case of prisoners who need to be segregated in their own interests, is to give an obviously necessary power to segregate prisoners who are liable for any reason to disturb the orderly conduct of the prison generally. The rule is a purely preventive measure.

In later case law, *Ex p. Hague* has been explained as a case where the relevant Rules were 'regulatory in character'. Therefore, like *Lonrho*, the case could have been disposed of simply by saying that the purpose of the statutory duty was not to benefit the plaintiff. The status of this and the following case, and the continuing relevance of *Groves v Wimborne*, were brought into issue in *Campbell v Peter Gordon Joiners Ltd* [2016] UKSC 38, extracted in Section 6.

5. FURTHER RESTRICTIONS: 'SOCIAL WELFARE' LEGISLATION AND 'PUBLIC LAW DUTIES'

X v Bedfordshire CC [1995] 2 AC 633

This was a defining case in respect of the duty of care in negligence in the context of statutory *powers* (Chapter 6). It was an equally important case in respect of the action for breach of statutory duty.

The appeals heard together by the House of Lords comprised two cases raising child protection matters; and three cases raising issues of educational malpractice. The applicable child protection legislation involved statutory duties, as well as statutory powers. It was therefore argued that in the child protection cases, there was (in addition to the negligence action) an action for breach of a statutory duty. This, like the negligence claim, was rejected.

Lord Browne-Wilkinson, *X v Bedfordshire CC,* at 731–2

The principles applicable in determining whether such statutory cause of action exists are now well established, although the application of those principles in any particular case remains difficult. The basic proposition is that in the ordinary case a breach of statutory duty does not, by itself, give rise to any private law cause of action. However a private law cause of action will arise if it can be shown, as a matter of construction of the statute, that the statutory duty was imposed for the protection of a limited class of the public and that Parliament intended to confer on members of that class a private right of action for breach of the duty.... Although the question is one of statutory construction and therefore each case turns on the provisions in the relevant statute, it is significant that your Lordships were not referred to any case where it had been held that statutory provisions establishing a regulatory system or a scheme of social welfare for the benefit of the public at large had been held to give rise to a private right of action for damages for breach of statutory duty. Although regulatory or welfare legislation affecting a particular area of activity does in fact provide protection to those individuals particularly affected by that activity, the legislation is not to be treated as being passed for the benefit of those individuals but for the benefit of society in general. Thus legislation regulating the conduct of betting or prisons did not give rise to a statutory right of action vested in those adversely affected by the breach of the statutory provisions, i.e. bookmakers and prisoners: see *Cutler's* case [1949] A.C. 398; *Reg. v. Deputy Governor of Parkhurst Prison, Ex parte Hague* [1992] 1 A.C. 58. The cases where a private right of action for breach of statutory duty have been held to arise are all cases in which the statutory duty has been very limited and specific as opposed to general administrative functions imposed on public bodies and involving the exercise of administrative discretions.

Lord Browne-Wilkinson followed the *Ex p. Hague* approach, and thought this consistent with all of the previous case law (including *Groves v Wimborne*). Indeed, he seems to go even further, clearly stating (as Lord Jauncey did not) that there is a presumption *against* a right of action, and that it must be established that Parliament intended such a right to exist, if the action is to succeed. Equally clearly, we can see from the final paragraph above that Lord Browne-Wilkinson thought that the statutory duties arising in a 'scheme of social welfare' are not generally of a type that would give rise to an action in tort. They are too broad and imprecise, and their aim is to benefit the public at large, rather than a specified class of individuals.

Later in his judgment, Lord Browne-Wilkinson applied this general approach to the cases in hand. The right of action was denied, because the duties in question *were not of the right sort*. In particular, they rely upon the exercise of discretion or judgment. Although they are intended to protect children such as the plaintiffs, they are no more than 'public law duties', and their enforcement should be at public law.

The restrictive approach in *X v Bedfordshire* where social welfare legislation is concerned has been adopted by later courts, for example in *O'Rourke v Camden* [1998] AC 188: the duty under section 63(1) of the Housing Act 1985 to provide temporary accommodation to homeless individuals was enforceable only through judicial review. It was in the nature of a public law duty, and the availability of judicial review ensured that the duty would not be reduced to a 'toothless regime' or 'pious aspiration' in the absence of a damages remedy.

The question of who the duty was intended to benefit has also been used to limit civil liability for breach of statutory duty. In *Jain v Trent Strategic Health Authority* [2009] UKHL 4, the House of Lords interpreted the relevant duties as being for the benefit of people who were residents in care homes—so that breach of the duties was not actionable by the owner of a home. In *Merelie v General Medical Council* [2009] EWHC 1165 (QB), Cranston J said that duties under the Dentists Act 1984 were imposed for the benefit of patients, not primarily of dentists, so that the claimant (a dentist) could not rely on a breach of the statutory duty as the basis for her action. It was also relevant that she could have chosen to bring an action for judicial review: there was no absence of a remedy, but the appropriate remedy for breach of this sort of duty lay at public law. Other significant recent cases where an argument based on breach of statutory duty was quickly dismissed because the approach to 'public law duties' is now so well established are *Mitchell v Glasgow City Council* [2009] UKHL 11 (statutory duties on local authorities as social landlords are not actionable at private law as they are solely public law duties—the issue here being control of another tenant) and, very similarly, *X & Y v London Borough of Hounslow* [2009] EWCA Civ 286. There has been no deviation from the restrictive approach in *X v Bedfordshire* where such duties are concerned; the temptation to extend this restrictive approach to other sorts of statutory duty has become an issue.

6. RECENT CASES: WHICH APPROACH?

Civil Liberties

Cullen v Chief Constable of the Royal Ulster Constabulary [2003] UKHL 39; [2003] 1 WLR 1763

The claimant was arrested on suspicion of an offence of withholding information relating to the murder of a police officer. He later pleaded guilty to an offence. While being questioned, his right of access to a solicitor was deferred four times. Such deferrals were permitted by the Northern Ireland (Emergency Provisions) Act 1987, but in contravention of that Act, no reasons for the deferrals were given. The claimant brought an action for damages in respect of the failure to give reasons.

The majority of the House of Lords (Lords Hutton, Millett, and Rodger) held that the claimant had no right of action for breach of statutory duty. There was a joint dissent by Lords Bingham and Steyn. This dissent distinguished *Ex p. Hague* and *X v Bedfordshire*. The 1987 Act should be taken to *confer a right* on individuals in the position of the claimant; and there were no grounds for displacing the presumption that an action would therefore lie at private law. This general approach, which starts with the purpose and nature of the legislation and identifies it as conferring a benefit in the nature of a right upon the claimant, is compatible with *Groves v Wimborne* and the second interpretive approach outlined earlier.

The decision of the majority may or may not have been directly influenced by the presumption against actionability expressed in *X v Bedfordshire*. No presumption against the right of action was explicitly invoked, but the majority concluded that the duty was a 'public law' duty, and the appropriate means of enforcing the duty was through an application for judicial review.[14] It is possible that a different conclusion would have been drawn if the claimant had suffered tangible loss or injury (see Lord Rodger at [86]).

Campbell v Peter Gordon Joiners Ltd [2016] UKSC 38

This case directly raised the correct approach to take in cases of breach of statutory duty. It also concerned the independently important question of whether there is a common law remedy for an injured employee where there has been a breach of the employer's duty to insure its liabilities to him. This duty is contained in the Employers' Liability (Compulsory

---

[14] As the dissenting judges pointed out, this may not be a very practicable remedy in the circumstances: 'There are formidable problems in a detainee applying for judicial review when he has been denied access to a solicitor' (at [20]).

Insurance) Act 1969. The action was not brought against the company, which was insolvent. In the absence of a relevant insurer, the action was brought instead against a director of the company on the basis that he had failed to insure. The primary duty to insure is contained in section 1(1) of the 1969 Act; criminal penalties are set out in section 5, and include penalties on directors and others.

Employers' Liability (Compulsory Insurance) Act 1969

1. Insurance against liability for employees

(1) Except as otherwise provided by this Act, every employer carrying on any business in Great Britain shall insure, and maintain insurance, under one or more approved policies with an authorised insurer or insurers against liability for bodily injury or disease sustained by his employees, and arising out of and in the course of their employment in Great Britain in that business …

…

5. Penalty for failure to insure

An employer who on any day is not insured in accordance with this Act when required to be so shall be guilty of an offence and shall be liable on summary conviction to a fine not exceeding level 4 on the standard scale; and where an offence under this section committed by a corporation has been committed with the consent or connivance of, or facilitated by any neglect on the part of, any director, manager, secretary or other officer of the corporation, he, as well as the corporation shall *be deemed to be guilty of that offence and shall be liable to be proceeded against and punished accordingly.*

Lord Carnwath, *Campbell v Peter Campbell Joiners* [2016] UKSC 38

12 For my part I find it unnecessary in this appeal to engage in discussion of the extent to which Lord Diplock's formulation has been modified by later authorities. I would only observe that the statements of Lord Browne-Wilkinson and Lord Jauncey referred to by Lord Brodie were made in the context of cases concerning liability of public authorities, which may

on directors, the duty itself was imposed not on them, but on the company.

The issues divided the Supreme Court. The majority judgment of Lord Carnwath took an approach based on close reading of the statutory language. In doing so, he did not go so far as to accept some observations of the court below, to the effect that *Groves v Wimborne* no longer represents the modern law, and that Lord Diplock's presumptions in *Lonrho* had been modified by later authorities including *X v Bedfordshire* and *ex p Hague.* Neither however did he completely dismiss them; rather, he was 'content to assume' that *Lonrho* remained a reliable guide. The dissenting judges, however, roundly dismissed the observations, pointing out that the later authorities dealt specifically with public law duties: Lord Toulson regarded the suggestion as 'startling'. Despite the majority's assumption that *Lonrho* still offered a reliable guide, their approach was based on close reading in order to glean Parliamentary intent. The essential difficulty, for the majority, was that despite the imposition of a penalty raise rather different issues. I am content to assume (without deciding) that Lord Diplock's words remain a reliable guide at least in relation to statutory duties imposed for the benefit of employees. I would also proceed on the basis (agreeing in this respect with Sir John Megaw in *Richardson's* case [1995] QB 123, 135C–D) that the duty of the employer under section 1 of the 1969 Act was imposed for the benefit of the employees, in the sense indicated by Lord Diplock.

13 This however is not enough for Mr Campbell. The essential starting point for Lord Diplock's formulation is an obligation created by statute, binding in law on the person sought to be made liable. There is no suggestion in that or any other authority that a person can be made indirectly liable for breach of an obligation imposed by statute on someone else. It is no different where the obligation is imposed on a company. There is no basis in the case law for looking through the corporate veil to the directors or other individuals through whom the company acts. That can only be done if expressly or impliedly justified by the statute.

Dealing with a fairness-based argument of Lord Drummond Young in the court below, Lord Carnwath continued:

18 With respect to him, I do not find these observations helpful in resolving the issue before us, which depends not on general questions of fairness, but on the interpretation of a particular statutory scheme in its context. The fact that the company can only act through its officers tells one nothing about their potential liability to third parties for its acts or failures. The judgment of Atkin LJ to which he refers affirms the rule (supported by reference to a statement of Lord Buckmaster in *Rainham Chemical Works Ltd v Belvedere Fish Guano Co Ltd* [1921] 2 AC 465, 476) that directors are not in general liable for the tortious actions of the company. The scope of a potential common law claim against a director for ordering or procuring such a tortious act is not in issue in this case, which turns entirely on alleged liability under the statute. This requires the court to pay due respect to the language and structure used by Parliament, rather than to preconceptions of what its objectives could or should have been.…

In para [12], Lord Carnwath does lay to rest the particularly suspect reasoning of Stuart-Smith LJ in the earlier, similar case of *Richardson v Pitt-Stanley* [1985] QB 123. Here, Stuart-Smith LJ had argued that the purpose of the 1969 Act was not solely to benefit employees, but also to benefit employers: insurance is generally intended to benefit the assured. This missed the point that the statute was one of *compulsory* insurance, to avoid the problem of uncompensated injuries to employees. Here, Lord Carnwath (like the dissenting judges) prefers the interpretation of Megaw LJ, who dissented in that case. However, Lord Carnwath's approach to statutory interpretation leads to the same result: there is no personal duty on the director, despite the imposition of criminal penalties where there is a failure to insure.

The minority judges, Lord Toulson and Baroness Hale, rejected this approach as unduly formalistic, and gave stronger support to the continuing authority of *Groves v Wimborne* and *Lonrho*. Their favoured approach was based on a purposive, rather than detailed reading of the statutory language. As with *Groves* and *Lonrho*, the intention to benefit the claimant was decisive.

Lord Toulson, *Campbell v Peter Gordon Joiners Ltd* [2016] AC 1513

29 In his dissenting judgment in *Richardson v Pitt-Stanley* [1995] QB 123, 135, Sir John Megaw ... said:

"With great respect, I find it difficult to believe that the parliamentary draftsman would have intended to make provision that there should be no civil right or remedy by using the formula of section 1 of the Employers' Liability (Compulsory Insurance) Act 1969 , 'shall insure', followed by section 5 'shall be guilty of an offence'; as contrasted with the formula of declaring an act or omission to be unlawful and then separately providing a criminal penalty for the breach."

I agree.

30 The approach which commends itself to the majority concentrates on the form of the language. It is argued that the structure of the Act is such that the only duty created by it is explicitly placed on the company by section 1(1) , and that the mechanism by which a director or other officer of the company is deemed to be guilty of a breach of that duty is consistent with and supports that proposition. I have set out the alternative approach, which looks at the function and substantive effect of the deeming provision in real terms. The choice between a formal approach and a functional approach in the interpretation and application of statutory language is an aspect of the choice between formalism and realism which has been a fruitful subject since as long ago as the publication of *Holmes's The Common Law* in 1881. In deciding which approach is preferable, the context matters. The present context is legislation for the protection of a vulnerable group, a company's employees. In that context I regard the functional approach as more appropriate. I cannot improve on Lord Drummond Young's pithy statement, in his dissenting opinion in this case 2015 SLT 134, para 47 that "in the context of legislation aimed at employee protection the formalist approach is "excessively conceptual; it focuses on differences of structure that do not reflect the basic objectives of the statute".

...

It is interesting that Lord Toulson sees in the dispute about statutory duties a much wider debate between 'formalism', and 'realism'; should courts look at the form of statutory language, or at the intended and actual effect of the law? He went further, and acknowledged that the role of the courts in this context cannot be simply confined to interpreting statutory language; courts must take some responsibility for making decisions that the legislature has not debated:

35 As Lord Kinnear's statement indicates, the cause of action is at common law (except in cases where a statute expressly creates a civil right of action). The cause of action which was held to exist in *Groves v Lord Wimborne* [1898] 2 QB 402 was created by the court. It was founded on a statute but it was the court that determined that breach of the provisions of the Act should be actionable at the suit of the injured party for whose protection the provisions were intended. The conventional jurisprudence is that the court's function is to ascertain as a matter of interpretation whether Parliament intended that there should be civil liability, but that understates the role of the courts in cases where the legislation is silent on the point. In such cases "the judges face hieroglyphs without a Rosetta Stone", to

borrow a metaphor of Judge Richard Posner writing extrajudicially (*Divergent Paths—The Academy and the Judiciary*, Harvard University Press (2016), p 172). Judge Posner candidly and correctly states that the judges' role in such cases is the active role of filling gaps left by the legislature.

The decision of the majority contrasts with the position in relation to compulsory motor insurance. In *Monk v Warbey* [1935] 1 KB 75, the owner of a car had lent it to a friend, who was not covered by a policy of liability insurance. The friend through his negligence caused injuries to the plaintiff. Because the driver of the car was uninsured and could not meet the claim for damages, the plaintiff brought an action against the car owner, based on his breach of statutory duty:

Road Traffic Act 1930, section 35(1)[15]

… it shall not be lawful for any person to use, or to cause or permit any other person to use, a motor vehicle on a road unless there is in force in relation to the user of the vehicle … a policy of insurance … in respect of third party risks .…

This claim for breach of statutory duty was successful. The Court of Appeal perceived that the purpose of the Act was to ensure that judgments in relation to personal injury sustained on the roads could be met. This being so, the Road Traffic Act is to be treated as relating to health and safety.[16] The minority in *Campbell* felt that the Employers' Liability (Compulsory Insurance) Act 1969 should be treated in the same way. But the majority distinguished *Monk v Warbey* on the rather formalistic basis that the statutory duty is differently worded.

7. THE AMBIT OF THE TORT

Once it is shown that the duty is actionable, the duty itself is defined by the statute, and this will determine the relevant liability standard. This may be strict, or it may be dependent on a failure to take reasonable care. The Law Reform (Contributory Negligence) Act 1945 applies to actions for breach of statutory duty, so that damages may be reduced to reflect relative fault on the part of the claimant.

Damage of the Type the Duty was Intended to Prevent

In the much-cited case of *Gorris v Scott* (1874) LR 9 Exch 125, it was emphasized that the only recoverable damage in an action for breach of statutory duty is damage of the sort that the duty was designed to prevent. Here, the defendant ship owner was under a statutory duty to keep cattle penned when in transit on board his ship. The reason for this duty was the avoidance of disease. The claimant's sheep were left unpenned, in breach of the duty, but they did

---

[15] The equivalent provision is now s 143 of the Road Traffic Act 1988.

[16] This is reinforced by the decision in *Bretton v Hancock* [2005] EWCA Civ 404; (2005) RTR 22. The statutory duty under s 143 Road Traffic Act 1988 does not exist for the purpose of reimbursing economic losses in the form of liability through contribution (Chapter 7).

not catch a disease—they were swept overboard. There was no liability, because it was not the purpose of the statute to protect from this sort of danger.

8. THE EFFECT ON NEGLIGENCE ACTIONS

There is some risk that the restrictive approach to the action for breach of statutory duty might have a knock-on effect in the tort of negligence. But it is important to recognize that in cases of negligence, the duty arises at common law *as a consequence of the relationship between the parties*, as interpreted through the test in *Caparo v Dickman*: there is foreseeability and proximity, and the imposition of a duty is 'fair, just, and reasonable'.

The applicable rules and the relationship between common law and statutory duty were considered by the Court of Appeal in *Rice v Secretary of State for Trade and Industry* [2007] EWCA Civ 289; [2007] ICR 1469. In this case, the Harbour Board owed statutory duties in respect of those employed at the docks, and for some periods also acted as their employer. The statutory duties owed were not themselves actionable in private law, but the relationship between the parties—itself partly defined by the statutory duties—was such as to give rise to a duty at common law in respect of their health and safety. They had been offered no safety protection at all while unloading asbestos in hessian sacks.[17]

9. CONCLUSIONS

i.   The action for breach of statutory duty raises questions about the partnership between courts and legislature. For over a hundred years, courts have developed remedies at common law for employees who have been injured by breaches of statutory duty. Typically, this has meant adding a right to compensation to existing criminal penalties. In a radical move, Parliament in 2013 removed civil liability from the majority of health and safety statutes and regulations, thus markedly confining the significance of this action.

ii. Outside the area of liability to employees, a more restrictive approach has been seen in recent years. Arguably, this is confined to cases where there is a broad, public duty which cannot be said to benefit a specified class of individuals. However, the right approach to interpreting statutory language and Parliamentary intent continues to trouble the courts, leading to a divided Supreme Court in the recent case of *Campbell v Peter Gordon Joiners*. The minority judgment of Lord Carnwath suggests a connection between the dispute in these cases, and much broader issues about formalist and realist approaches to adjudication. Overall, there is no doubt that Parliamentary intention is fundamental to the action for breach of statutory duty; the dispute is over which sort of intention is required, and how closely—or purposively—statutory language needs to be read in order to derive the answer.

[17] The case proceeded to trial, where breach of duty and causation of damage (mesothelioma) were successfully established: *Rice v Secretary of State for Business Enterprise and Regulatory Reform* [2008] EWHC 3216 (QB).

FURTHER READING

Foster, N., 'Private Law and Public Goals: The Continuing Importance of the Action for Breach of Statutory Duty' (delivered to the 'Obligations IV' conference, Singapore, 23–25 July 2008; <http://works.bepress.com/neil-foster/11>).

Limb, P., and Cox, J., 'Section 69 of the Enterprise and Regulatory Reform Act 2013—plus ça change?' (2014) JPIL 1.

Matthews, M. H., 'Negligence and Breach of Statutory Duty' (1984) 4 OJLS 429.

Roy, A., 'Without a safety net: litigating employers' liability claims after the Enterprise Act' (2015) JPIL 15

Stanton, K., *Breach of Statutory Duty* (London: Sweet & Maxwell, 1986).

Stanton, K., 'New Forms of the Action for Breach of Statutory Duty' (2004) 120 LQR 324–41.

Stanton, K., Skidmore, P., Harris, M., and Wright, J., *Statutory Torts* (London: Sweet & Maxwell, 2003).

Tomkins, N., 'Civil Health and Safety Law after the Enterprise and Regulatory Reform Act 2013' (2013) JPIL 203

Williams, G., 'The Effect of Penal Legislation in the Law of Tort' (1960) 23 MLR 233.

17

TRESPASS TO LAND AND GOODS, AND CONVERSION

CENTRAL ISSUES

i) The torts in this chapter all protect proprietary rights, but they do so in different ways. The trespass torts protect
against direct interferences with land
and goods possessed by the claimant.
Conversion on the other hand protects
against interferences with goods (but
not land) which are actually inconsistent with the claimant's right of possession. In effect, a conversion amounts to
a denial of the claimant's right.

ii) Conversion occupies a unique place
in English law. It is a tort, but its

functions overlap strongly with
property law. This unique position
is reflected in all aspects of the tort
but most particularly in the available
remedies. These remedies include
recovery of the chattel in some cases
(though not as of right), and damages
based both on value of the goods (if
not recovered), and on consequential
loss. Though sidelined in the majority of tort courses, conversion is a
hard-working tort of broad commercial significance.

1. TRESPASS TO LAND

Trespass to land is constituted by a direct and unjustifiable interference with the possession of land.

The specific interest protected by trespass to land will be more clearly grasped if we compare it with the action in private nuisance (Chapter 10). **Private nuisance** protects against
unlawful interference with the **use and enjoyment of land**. It is actionable only by a person
with title to the land, in the form of a *right to exclusive possession*. This may be the freeholder,
or the leaseholder, or someone who holds a right to exclusive possession through statute.
Although injunction is usually the preferred remedy in a case of continuing nuisance, where
damages are assessed they are assessed by reference to diminution in the amenity value of
the land.[1] Interference must be shown to be 'unreasonable', and this may involve a balancing

---

[1] *Hunter v Canary Wharf* [1997] AC 655.

exercise taking into account the interests of the claimant and the activity of the defendant. Some interferences are not actionable, on the basis of a principle of 'live and let live'.

Trespass to land on the other hand protects against interference with the possession of land itself. It is actionable by anyone with the right to possession, even if this falls short of a right to *exclusive* possession. It is actionable for example by a mere licensee, who would not be able to bring an action in private nuisance. Invasions are actionable without reference to 'reasonableness', and there is no question of permitting minor invasions on a principle of 'live and let live'. This would be incompatible with the rights to possession which are protected by the tort. Although *reasonableness* is no defence, a defendant may escape liability by showing *justification*. As with the other trespass torts examined in Chapter 2, justification may be established in the form of emergency or self-defence, for example.

1.1 NON-DELIBERATE TRESPASS TO LAND

In Chapter 2, we explained that the torts which together constitute trespass to the person are now regarded as 'intentional', even though the form of intention required is not closely related to culpability. It is the *direct physical contact with the person of the claimant* that must be intended, and not any wrongfulness or harm. Equally, in the case of trespass to land, no wrongfulness nor actual harm need be intended. Trespass liability is 'strict'. But does the incursion on to the claimant's land need to be intentional?

League Against Cruel Sports v Scott [1986] QB 240

The claimants owned various parcels of unfenced moorland, over which they did not allow hunting. After several incursions on to their land by the hunt, including incursion by hounds, the claimants brought an action in trespass against the defendants, who were joint masters of the hunt. They claimed not only damages but also a declaration of unlawfulness and an injunction to prevent future trespasses.

The claim was successful. Damages were awarded, together with an injunction.

Park J, *League Against Cruel Sports v Scott*
[1986] 1 QB 240

Mr. Blom-Cooper submits that intention, wilfulness, and indeed any concept of fault liability do not constitute an element in the tort of trespass to land. When hounds enter or cross forbidden land the only question is whether such intrusion is voluntary or involuntary. The only defences recognised by law to an action for trespass are inevitable accident and necessity.

...

... I am, however, unable to spell out from the authorities cited by Mr Blom-Cooper the proposition that he has advanced. I have, therefore, come to the conclusion that, before a master of hounds may be held liable for trespass on land by hounds, it has to be shown that he either intended that the hounds should enter the land, or by negligence he failed to prevent them from doing so.

In my judgment the law as I take it to be may be stated thus: where a master of staghounds takes out a pack of hounds and deliberately sets them in pursuit of a stag or hind, knowing that there is a real risk that in the pursuit hounds may enter or cross prohibited land, the master will be liable for trespass if he intended to cause hounds to enter such land, or if by his failure to exercise proper control over them he caused them to enter such land.

…

Further, if it is virtually impossible, whatever precautions are taken, to prevent hounds from entering league land, such as Pitleigh for example, yet the master knowing that to be the case, nevertheless persists in hunting in its vicinity, with the result that hounds frequently trespass on the land, then the inference might well be drawn that his indifference to the risk of trespass amounted to an intention that hounds should trespass on the land.

The master's negligence, or the negligence of those servants or agents or followers of the hunt for whose conduct he is responsible, has also to be judged in the light of all the circumstances in which the trespass in question occurred.

Trespass to land requires the defendant to enter the land either intentionally or through *carelessness*. Here, the idea of 'involuntary' (as opposed to merely mistaken) entry is quite plausible: the land was unfenced, and some of the incursions were by hounds rather than people.[2]

We discovered in Chapter 2 that since *Letang v Cooper* [1965] 1 QB 232, trespass to the person has been confined to *intentional* acts. For example, in the tort of battery, only if physical contact is intended is there an action in trespass to the person. Cases of *careless* contact are to be governed only by the principles of the tort of negligence. This reasoning has not been replicated in respect of trespass to land.

Remedies

As with trespass to the person, the claimant may seek an injunction to prevent continuing or future interference; compensatory damages in respect of past interference and any consequential damage caused; and a declaration that the trespass is unlawful.

In *Anchor Brewhouse Developments Ltd v Berkley House Ltd* (1987) 38 BLR 87, Scott J granted an injunction where the jib of a crane on the defendant's land trespassed over the property of the plaintiffs. Scott J recognized that the grant of an injunction here would allow the plaintiff to seek extortionate payments for the right to 'use' their space to complete construction works, but considered himself bound to award the injunction. More recent cases have not taken such an uncompromising view about appropriate remedies.

In *Jaggard v Sawyer* [1995] 1 WLR 269, the Court of Appeal pointed out that the injunctive remedy is an *equitable* remedy which is always within the discretion of the court. Although damages in lieu of an injunction may only be awarded where relevant criteria are fulfilled, there is always an option for the court to award no remedy at all. The injunction is not available 'as of right'.

We extracted *Jaggard v Sawyer* in Chapter 10, Section 1.7 (Nuisance), where we also discussed the '*Shelfer* criteria' for award of damages in lieu of an injunction. Here, it is worth noting Millett LJ's comments on the approach in *Anchor Brewhouse*:

---

[2] Another hypothetical instance of 'involuntary' entry is where the defendant is involved in a traffic accident and is thrown on to the claimant's land.

Millett LJ, *Jaggard v Sawyer*
[1995] 1 WLR 285

In *Anchor Brewhouse Developments Ltd. v. Berkley House (Docklands Developments) Ltd.* . . . Scott J. granted an injunction to restrain a continuing trespass. In the course of his judgment, however, he cast doubt on the power of the court to award damages for future trespasses by means of what he described as a "once and for all payment." This was because, as he put it, the court could not by an award of damages put the defendant in the position of a person entitled to an easement; whether or not an injunction were granted, the defendant's conduct would still constitute a trespass; and a succession of further actions for damages could accordingly still be brought. This reasoning strikes at the very heart of the statutory jurisdiction; it is in marked contrast to the attitude of the many judges who from the very first have recognised that, while the Act[3] does not enable the court to license future wrongs, this may be the practical result of withholding injunctive relief. . . . It is in my view fallacious because it is not the award of damages which has the practical effect of licensing the defendant to commit the wrong, but the refusal of injunctive relief. Thereafter the defendant may have no right to act in the manner complained of, but he cannot be prevented from doing so. The court can in my judgment properly award damages "once and for all" in respect of future wrongs because it awards them in substitution for an injunction and to compensate for those future wrongs which an injunction would have prevented. . . .

The choice is not only between injunction and damages; if damages are not appropriate, there is still a choice between injunction, and nothing. As we saw in Chapter 8, when assessing damages in lieu of an injunction, the court will ask what reasonable parties would have bargained for. This is clearly illustrated by the decision of the Supreme Court in *Star Energy UK Onshore Ltd v Bocardo* [2010] UKSC 35. Here there was a trespass, which the judge found did not disturb the claimant's use and enjoyment of land 'one iota'. Rights to search for and get oil from a natural underground reservoir had been granted to the defendants pursuant to statute; but they committed a trespass to the extent that they did not obtain access rights for their pipelines beneath the claimants' land. The claimants had 'title' to the substrata. The wells extended from about 800 feet to 2,800 feet below the surface, and therefore were 'far from being so deep as to reach the point of absurdity' ([27]). Were they however 'in possession' of the substrata so that they could claim in trespass?

Lord Hope of Craighead, *Bocardo v Star Energy*
[2010] UKSC 35

31 As Aikens LJ said in the Court of Appeal [2010] Ch 100, para 66, it is difficult to say that Bocardo has actual possession of the strata below the Oxted Estate as it has done nothing to reduce those strata into its actual possession. But he held that Bocardo, as the paper title owner to the strata and all within it (other than any gold, silver, saltpetre, coal and petroleum which belong to the Crown at common law or by statute), has the prima facie right to possession of those strata so as to be deemed to be in factual possession of them. I think that he was right to conclude that this was the effect of Slade J's dictum. As the paper title carries

---

[3] Chancery Amendment Act 1858, or 'Lord Cairns's Act', which permitted courts of Chancery to award damages. The Common Law Procedure Act 1854 permitted courts of common law to award injunctions.

with it title to the strata below the surface, Bocardo must be deemed to be in possession of the subsurface strata too. There is no one else who is claiming to be in possession of those strata through Bocardo as the paper owner.

There was, therefore, a trespass in this case; but how should damages be calculated? The statutory scheme set out a power of compulsory acquisition; and the correct approach was to apply general principles of compulsory acquisition law to the assessment of damages. Any value to the claimant's rights which was attributable to the scheme itself (the extraction of oil) had to be discounted. The relevant licence fee that would have been payable under the statutory scheme was assessed at £82.50. However, the Court of Appeal had concluded that if negotiating a licence, the parties would have been aware that lawyers are expensive and the defendants would have been generous to the claimants, settling for a fee of £1,000. This is very considerably lower than 9 per cent of the value of oil extracted which had been awarded by the first instance judge (£621,180, plus interest). The Supreme Court preferred the approach of the Court of Appeal, Lord Brown describing the £1,000 award as 'positively generous' ([92]). The statutory framework plainly had a decisive influence over the remedy awarded. The case nevertheless underlines that a trespass may be committed where there is no disturbance to the claimant's use and enjoyment of the land; and that a trespass which does not cause any loss may be thought to require damages on the basis of a reasonable user fee.

The right to bring an action in trespass in relation to drilling below property has been significantly adjusted by statute, in order to facilitate 'fracking'.[4] The rights created (and taken away) are very broadly defined:

Infrastructure Act 2015

43 Petroleum and geothermal energy: right to use deep-level land

(1) A person has the right to use deep-level land in any way for the purposes of exploiting petroleum or deep geothermal energy.

(2) Land is subject to the right of use (whether for the purposes of exploiting petroleum or deep geothermal energy) only if it is—

   (a) deep-level land, and

   (b) within a landward area.

...

(4) Deep-level land is any land at a depth of at least 300 metres below surface level.

Gain-based Damages

There are cases of trespass where a gain-based award of damages has been made. In *Penarth Dock v Pounds* [1963] 1 Lloyd's Rep 359, Lord Denning assessed damages against defendants who had trespassed by refusing to remove their pontoon from the plaintiffs' dock. The

---

[4] For critical discussion of the steps taken to ease the way to 'fracking' generally, see E. Stokes, 'Regulatory Domain and Regulatory Dexterity: Critiquing the UK Governance of "Fracking"' (2016) 79 MLR 961.

plaintiffs had not suffered any loss, and Lord Denning awarded damages 'reversing the gain' that the defendants had made. This benefit though was not in the form of positive profits, but of expenses saved. It represented a rental value of the property. Similarly in *MOD v Ashman* [1993] 40 EG 144, a tenant wrongfully refused to quit when given notice to do so. A majority of the Court of Appeal awarded damages for this trespass to land which were not based on loss to the plaintiffs, but on 'the value of the benefit which the occupier has received'. Hoffmann LJ clearly said that this was a claim for restitution.

The continuing difficulty is how to determine when gain-based damages will be considered appropriate, since it seems increasingly clear that damages in lieu of an injunction are to be regarded as different and in a sense compensatory, even if the appropriate sum to compensate the claimant's lost opportunity to bargain may include a share of profits (see the discussion in Chapter 8). At present, there is no agreed means of distinguishing between an *Ashman*-type case (where a restitutionary award was made) and cases where a compensatory award will be appropriate. A clue may be that damages in lieu are by definition awarded only if an injunction is refused. This may provide a contrast with the wrongful refusal to quit in *Ashman*: where there are damages in lieu, the court has decided that the balance comes down in favour of permitting the trespass. This is different from those cases where the full benefit of the wrong ought to be removed from the defendant.

In *Horsford v Bird* [2006] UKPC 3, the Privy Council made an award of damages in lieu of an injunction where the respondent had encroached on to the appellant's land, constructing a boundary fence in such a position that he effectively added 455 square feet of the appellant's garden to his own. Assessing damages, the question the Privy Council asked itself was what the appellant might reasonably have sought from the defendant as the price of the land that had been annexed by the respondent. What makes the damages awarded slightly hard to categorize is that the Privy Council considered the *value to the respondent* of enlarging the plot in this way, arriving at a sum which was double the market value of the piece of land as an undeveloped plot. This is still, it is suggested, a compensatory measure, where the value to the trespassing party affects the amount that has been lost through his failure to bargain, because it affects the likely outcome of the hypothetical negotiation.[5]

Again, it is important to note that this was a case where the judge had already decided not to grant a mandatory injunction, requiring the respondent to remove his swimming pool and boundary wall. In principle, the decision to deny an injunction should be reached only in the restricted circumstances set out in Chapter 10 (the *Shelfer* criteria), including a condition that the interference suffered by the claimant should be appropriately 'compensated' (the word used in *Shelfer*) by a 'small' money payment—although as we saw in Chapter 10, members of the Supreme Court have expressed a view that in the context of nuisance, at least, the criteria should not be slavishly followed and may be regarded as somewhat out of date (*Coventry v Lawrence* [2014] UKSC 13). In addition, the Privy Council awarded a sum representing a percentage of the capital value of the land on a yearly basis up to the date on which the initial judgment was given (a period of over eight years). This part of the award was explicitly described as 'compensatory'.

[5] It is however described by James Edelman as 'the value obtained by a trespasser from the free use of the land'; J. Edelman, 'Restitutionary Damages for Torts' (2006) 122 LQR 391, 392. The compensatory interpretation proposes that the value to the trespasser is a relevant factor in determining what value is lost through the wrong, in the sense that it could otherwise have been gained in a bargain with the defendant. In itself this might sound an inappropriate analysis: refusal of the injunction is the essential background which makes it respectable.

2. WRONGFUL INTERFERENCE WITH GOODS: THE TYPES AND THE LEGISLATION

Torts (Interference with Goods) Act 1977

1 Definition of "wrongful interference with goods"

In this Act "wrongful interference", or "wrongful interference with goods", means—

(a) conversion of goods (also called trover),

(b) trespass to goods,

(c) negligence so far as it results in damage to goods or to an interest in goods,

(d) subject to section 2, any other tort so far as it results in damage to goods or to an interest in goods

[and references in this Act (however worded) to proceedings for wrongful interference or to a claim or right to claim for wrongful interference shall include references to proceedings by virtue of Part I of the Consumer Protection Act 1987 [or Part II of the Consumer Protection (Northern Ireland) Order 1987] (product liability) in respect of any damage to goods or to an interest in goods or, as the case may be, to a claim or right to claim by virtue of that Part in respect of any such damage].

The Torts (Interference with Goods) Act 1977 made a number of changes to the common law, as well as codifying the law in some respects. Although it abolished the action in detinue,[6] it did not create any new actions nor did it greatly simplify the law.

As can be seen from section 1 of the Act, a range of distinct actions at common law continues to protect interests in goods, and these actions are referred to as instances of 'wrongful interference with goods'. This includes negligence in relation to goods. For recent analysis of the whole field, contending that the area has come to be divided into intentional interferences in which liability is strict (trespass and conversion); and non-deliberate interferences in which liability is fault-based (negligence); see Simon Douglas, *Liability for Wrongful Interferences with Chattels* (Hart Publishing, 2011). The account in this chapter offers a more traditional picture, in which the law has not evolved to such a coherent position, particularly where trespass and conversion are concerned.

The traditional view is that **trespass to goods** involves direct and unjustified interference with goods, which are in the possession of the claimant. Examples include poisoning or beating animals, or scratching the paintwork of a vehicle. It is accepted that the criterion of 'directness' arose out of historical contingency, rather than logic or principle.[7]

A. Hudson, 'Trespass to Goods', in N. E. Palmer and E. McKendrick (eds), *Interests in Goods* (2nd edn, London: Lloyds of London Press, 1998)

Trespass [to goods] bears the marks of its early origins. It is constituted by a direct, immediate and unjustified interference with the possession of the chattels of another.

---

[6] By s 2(1), extracted below.

[7] For an account see Douglas, Chapter 6.

Conversion by contrast involves actions which are inconsistent with the claimant's title to the goods. We define conversion more fully in the next section.

Trespass to goods is like all forms of trespass in its limitation to *direct* interferences[8] (though it has been suggested that the tort has more recently evolved to replace the 'direct-ness' criterion with a requirement of 'intention' (Douglas, 105–11)). Since many (though not all) cases of trespass to goods involve damage, negligence frequently presents an alterna-tive action, which is not confined to direct interference nor, of course, to intentional inter-ferences. Therefore, the practical importance of trespass to goods is quite restricted, even though it may cover a wider range of interferences than conversion. Illustrating its potential breadth is the suggestion in *Rugby Football Union v Viagogo Ltd* [2011] EWHC 764 (QB), that boarding a bus without any intention of buying a ticket may be a trespass to goods ([10]).

3. CONVERSION

3.1 GENERAL DEFINITION AND DISTINCTIVE FEATURES

A 'conversion' is a deliberate dealing with a chattel in a manner that is seriously inconsist-ent with the claimant's title.

Distinctive Features

1. Although the defendant's dealing with the chattel must be deliberate, the interference with the claimant's title need not be. Liability is strict, and may catch even an entirely honest defendant (see further Section 3.2).[9]

2. As with any tort, the nature of the protected interest should be reflected in the rem-edies available. In an appropriate case, a court may in its discretion order the return of a converted chattel to the claimant. But this remedy is not available *as of right* even where the defendant retains possession of the goods. In this and certain other ways, conversion suffers from inconsistency. It is accused of performing too many roles, none of them wholly satisfactorily. In particular, it has been argued that the process of returning goods to those who have the appropriate interest in them ought to be achieved through the law of property, *not* through the law of obligations.[10]

Andrew Tettenborn, 'Conversion, Conversion, Tort and Restitution', in N. Palmer and E. McKendrick, *Interests in Goods*, at 825

… the nub of the problem is that no-one has ever sat down seriously to consider what conversion is *for*. True, it is classified as a tort: but that is only for historical reasons and for lack of anywhere else to file it. In fact it is trying to do not one, but three very

---

[8] For example, Hudson (earlier) explains that putting poison in an animal's mouth may be trespass to the animal, but putting poison in its *feed* is only trespass to the feed.

[9] See also the exploration by Douglas: conversion is *both* strict, *and* dependent on intention.

[10] Tony Weir, *Casebook on Tort* (9th edn, Sweet & Maxwell, 2000); Nick Curwen, 'The Remedy in Conversion: Confusing Property and Obligation' (later in this chapter); A. Tettenborn, 'Damages in Conversion' (later in this chapter).

different jobs at the same time; it is (1) standing in as a kind of surrogate *vindication*, allowing owners to get back their property or its value from a wrongful possessor (call this the 'recovery function'); (2) acting to compensate owners for losses caused by past misdealings with their property (tort proper); and (3) on occasion reversing unjust enrichment arising from the property or its proceeds which have got into the wrong hands (restitution).

Tettenborn suggests that the three functions of conversion need to be kept distinct, in order to avoid falling into error, and indeed to avoid hardship to 'innocent' converters caught by the strictness of its liability.

The third function specified by Tettenborn in this extract is restitution. It is in the nature of conversion that the defendant often has an opportunity to *use* the chattel in a productive way,[11] and in this sense may be 'unjustly enriched.' The relationship between conversion, and 'unjust enrichment', is awkward, because conversion (like all torts) is a 'wrong', while 'unjust enrichment' need not involve a wrong at all, but seeks to correct transfers which should not have occurred. This issue arises particularly in respect of available 'remedies' (later in this chapter).[12]

3.2 STANDARD OF LIABILITY

Liability in conversion is strict, in that there need not be any knowledge of inconsistency with the claimant's rights. In fact, there need not be any knowledge of the claimant's rights at all, and conversion may be committed through entirely faultless conduct. Nevertheless, intention *to assert dominion over the goods* is required.

To explain this further, we need to explore the role of 'deliberate dealing', which formed a part of our general definition in Section 3.1.

Lord Nicholls' Analysis of 'Deliberate Dealing' in *Kuwait Airways*

In the next extract, Lord Nicholls identifies three elements in the general definition of a 'conversion'.

Lord Nicholls, *Kuwait Airways v Iraqi Airways Co (Nos 4 and 5)* [2002] 2 AC 883

39. ... Conversion of goods can occur in so many different circumstances that framing a precise definition of universal application is well nigh impossible. In general, the basic features of the tort are threefold. First, the defendant's conduct was inconsistent with the rights of the owner (or other person entitled to possession). Second, the conduct was deliberate, not accidental. Third, the conduct was so extensive an encroachment on the rights of the owner

---

[11] Though not, of course, in the case of a conversion by destroying or losing the chattel: see Section 3.4 for an outline of relevant behaviour towards a chattel that may amount to conversion.

[12] Not everyone agrees there can be 'remedies' for unjust enrichment. Peter Birks argued that correction of an unjust transfer should not be described as a remedy, but as the vindication of a right.

as to exclude him from use and possession of the goods. The contrast is with lesser acts of interference. If these cause damage they may give rise to claims for trespass or in negligence, but they do not constitute conversion.

Peter Cane has suggested that some trouble is potentially caused by the way that Lord Nicholls expressed the second general feature of conversion: the dealing with the goods must be 'deliberate, not accidental'.

Lord Nicholls' requirement for deliberate dealing refers to the *quality of the dealing with the defendant's goods*. It is this, not anything else, which must be deliberate rather than accidental. Thus, the taking of someone else's goods by mistake (or 'accidentally'), *may* amount to a conversion. For example, if I take your goods believing them to be mine, I have done so 'by accident'; yet at the same time I 'deliberately' act so as to assert dominion over the goods. This means essentially that I treat them as my own. In such a case, I am particularly likely to treat them as my own, because I think that they *are* my own. This example shows that dealing may be both deliberate and accidental, in different senses.

Therefore, Lord Nicholls did create scope for confusion when he used the word 'accidental' in contrast to 'deliberate'. An accidental taking of the claimant's chattel may still be a conversion, provided I intend to exercise dominion over it.

The opposite sort of case may also exist. This is where the *taking or possession* of the chattel is deliberate, but the defendant does *not* intend to exercise dominion over it. This is not a conversion, though it may well be a trespass. Lord Nicholls also emphasized this point in the *Kuwait Airways* case. He described the lack of intent as relevant to the question whether the owner is excluded from possession at all.

Lord Nicholls, *Kuwait Airways v Iraqi Airways Co (Nos 4 and 5)* [2002] UKHL 19; [2002] 2 AC 883

14 Whether the owner is excluded from possession may sometimes depend upon whether the wrongdoer exercised dominion over the goods. Then the intention with which acts were done may be material. The ferryman who turned the plaintiff's horses off the Birkenhead to Liverpool ferry was guilty of conversion if he intended to exercise dominion over them, but not otherwise: see *Fouldes v Willoughby*. . . .

In *Fouldes v Willoughby* (1841) 8 M & W 540, referred to by Lord Nicholls, the plaintiff had paid for his two horses to be transported across the River Mersey on the Birkenhead ferry. The defendant ferryman refused to transport them. He removed them from the ferry and turned them loose. This was not a conversion:

Lord Abinger, *Fouldes v Willoughby*

It is a proposition familiar to all lawyers, that a simple asportation of a chattel, without any intention of making any further use of it, although it may be a sufficient foundation for an action of trespass, is not sufficient to establish a conversion. I had thought that the matter had been fully discussed, and this distinction established, by the numerous cases which have occurred on this subject . . . I think that the learned judge was wrong, in telling the jury that the simple fact of putting these horses on the shore by the defendant, amounted to a conversion of them to his own use. In my opinion, he should have added to his direction, that it was for them to consider what was the intention of the defendant in so doing. If the object, and whether rightly or wrongly entertained is immaterial, simply was to adduce the plaintiff to go on shore himself, and the defendant, in furtherance of that object, did the act in question, it was not exercising over the goods any right inconsistent with, or adverse to, the rights which the plaintiff had in them....

This is an example where there is no conversion because the defendant does not mean by his actions to assert ownership or a right to possession over the horses. This case illustrates the importance of intention to the tort of conversion.[13]

But does this mean, as Lord Nicholls proposes, that the intention of the defendant is relevant to the question of *whether the claimant was deprived of his or her right to possession at all*? Peter Cane has argued that Lord Nicholls was *not* correct in this respect.

Peter Cane, 'Causing Conversion' (2002) 118 LQR 544, at 546

An obvious problem with this definition[14] is that it turns independent elements of the Clerk and Lindsell definition into interdependent elements. Under the definition, 'inconsistent dealing' (exercising dominion) is one element of conversion, and depriving the owner of possession is another. The concept of possession relates to a physical state of affairs, and the defendant's state of mind is irrelevant to whether the defendant's conduct has deprived the owner of, or excluded the owner from, possession.

The Clerk and Lindsell definition referred to by both Lord Nicholls and Peter Cane was as follows:

In order to constitute a conversion, it is necessary either that the party taking the goods should intend some use to be made of them, by himself or by those for whom he acts, or that, owing to his act, the goods are destroyed or consumed, to the prejudice of the lawful owner. As an instance of the latter branch of this definition, suppose, in the present case, the defendant had thrown the horses into the water, whereby they were drowned, that would have amounted to an actual conversion; or as in the case cited in the course of argument, of a person throwing a piece of paper into the water for, in these cases, the chattel is changed in quality, or destroyed altogether. But it has never yet been held that the single act of removal of a chattel independently of any claim over it, either in favour of the party himself or anyone else, amounts to a conversion of the chattel. In the present case, therefore, the simple removal of the horses by the defendant for a purpose wholly unconnected with any least denial of the right of the plaintiff to the possession and enjoyment of them, is no conversion....

---

13 It also illustrates the distinction between conversion, and trespass to goods. If trespass to goods had been pleaded, there would have been a good chance of success. There was a direct and probably unjustified interference with the goods; but no intention on the part of the defendant to treat the goods as his own.

14 Peter Cane is referring here to the threefold general definition of conversion offered by Lord Nicholls, and extracted above.

Clerk and Lindsell on Torts (17th edn, London: Sweet & Maxwell, 1995), 636, para 13–12[15]

... conversion is an act of deliberate dealing with a chattel in a manner inconsistent with another's right whereby that other is deprived of the use and possession of it.

It is suggested that Cane's criticism on this point does not hit home. What conversion protects is the **right to possession** and not simple physical possession, as Cane implies. Otherwise, the action of the ferryman in *Foulkes v Willoughby*—which deprived the claimant of physical possession—would have been a conversion. Dealing is *only* inconsistent with rights to possession if the dealing 'means' that the defendant has dominion over the goods. The 'defendant's state of mind' may be irrelevant, as Cane says, to whether the owner is excluded from *physical* possession. But it is *not* irrelevant to the prior requirement, that the manner of dealing should be (in the words of the Clerk and Lindsell definition) 'inconsistent with another's right'.[16]

This point about intention and the definition of conversion was important to the decision in *Kuwait Airways* itself. The facts of the case also demonstrate that intention can often be construed from actions. For example, someone who repaints a chattel in their own colours, or improves it in some way, is almost certainly asserting 'dominion' over it.

Kuwait Airways Corporation v Iraqi Airways Corporation (Nos 4 and 5) [2002] UKHL 19; [2002] 2 AC 883

In August 1990, Iraq invaded Kuwait, and passed resolutions proclaiming the integration of Kuwait into Iraq. The defendant was ordered by the Iraqi government to fly ten of the claimant's passenger aircraft to Iraq. These were incorporated into the defendant's fleet and used for its own flights. On 11 January 1991, the claimant issued a writ claiming the delivery up of its aircraft with consequential damages for the defendant's unlawful interference with them, alternatively consequential damages in the amount of the value of the aircraft, relying on section 3 of the Torts (Interference with Goods) Act 1977, and common law.

No state recognized the sovereignty of Iraq over the territory of Kuwait. Military action was commenced against Iraq. In the conflict, the subsequent fortunes of the aircraft themselves were mixed. Four of the ten were destroyed by bombing. These planes, stationed at Mosul, are referred to as 'the Mosul four'. The remaining six planes were evacuated to Iran between 15 January and 4 February 1991 (shortly after the writ was issued). These are 'the Iran six'. They were returned by Iran to the claimant in 1992, on payment by Iran of US$20 million.

Not surprisingly, the applicable law for this case was a real issue. The writ was issued before the enactment of the Private International Law (Miscellaneous Provisions) Act 1995. That Act would require that the law of the jurisdiction in which the tort was committed would be applied. Therefore, this case would now be approached entirely as a matter of Iraqi law. But before that, common law required that a 'double actionability rule' should be applied. This required that the acts must be tortious according to the law of *both* Iraq and England. The House of Lords disregarded the 'repugnant' Iraqi Resolution 369 which purported to

---

[15] See now the 21st edition, 2014, 17-07, where the extracted wording is retained.

[16] See also Section 3.3 of this chapter on the nature of 'possession' at law.

extinguish Kuwait as an independent state. Disregarding this Resolution, the acts would amount to 'usurpation' (the relevant wrong under Iraqi law). The remaining questions (in which we are interested here) are whether the acts were *also* tortious under English law (this section); and what damages could be claimed (Section 3.5).

In this case, restoration of the aircraft was not in issue. The Mosul four could not be restored because they had been destroyed. The Iran six had already been reclaimed, but the claimant had paid $20 million to a third party in order to retrieve them.[17]

The main judgment in the case was delivered by Lord Nicholls, Lord Scott dissented in part. The other Lords agreed with Lord Nicholls, though with some additional comments.

We have already extracted some of the crucial elements of Lord Nicholls' judgment so far as they relate to the general requirements of the tort of conversion. In due course (when we consider remedies) we will extract some important comments relating to causation and damages. These were the most difficult issues in the case. The conclusion that the acts of the defendant did in fact amount to a conversion was relatively brief:

Lord Nicholls, *Kuwait Airways v Iraqi Airways (Nos 4 and 5)*

43 Here, on and after 17 September 1990 IAC was in possession and control of the ten aircraft. This possession was adverse to KAC. IAC believed the aircraft were now its property, just as much as the other aircraft in its fleet, and it acted accordingly. It intended to keep the goods as its own. It treated them as its own. It made such use of them as it could in the prevailing circumstances, although this was very limited because of the hostilities. In so conducting itself IAC was asserting rights inconsistent with KAC's rights as owner. This assertion was evidenced in several ways. In particular, in September 1990 the board of IAC passed a resolution to the effect that all aircraft belonging to the (dissolved) KAC should be registered in the name of IAC and that a number of ancillary steps should be taken in relation to the aircraft. In respect of nine aircraft IAC then applied to the Iraqi Directorate of Air Safety for certificates of airworthiness and reregistration in IAC's name. IAC effected insurance cover in respect of five aircraft, and a further four after the issue of the writ. Six of the aircraft were overpainted in IAC's livery. IAC used one aircraft on internal commercial flights between Baghdad and Basra and for training flights. The two Boeing 767s were flown from Basra to Mosul in mid-November 1990.

44 Mance J concluded that in these circumstances IAC had wrongfully interfered with all ten aircraft. In the Court of Appeal Brooke LJ said, at pp 915C–D, para 74:

"The board resolution makes it completely clear that as soon as RCC Resolution 369 came into effect IAC resolved to treat these ten aircraft as their own and to exercise dominion over them in denial of KAC's rights, and this continuing usurpation and conversion of KAC's aircraft subsisted right up to the issue of the writ in this action by which KAC demanded the return of all these aircraft."

I agree. IAC's acts would have been tortious if done in this country.

The crucial thing is that IAC was (as Lord Nicholls put it) 'asserting rights inconsistent with KAC's rights as owner', and this was evidenced in various ways. In this case, which did not involve actual taking by the defendant, the *meaning* of the defendant's possession of the

---

[17] Neither Iran nor Iraq could be sued in tort, because of the doctrine of state immunity.

aircraft was particularly significant. It was irrelevant that IAC believed itself to *be* the lawful owner of the aircraft, under Iraqi law.

In *Kuwait Airways*, the defendant was liable because it 'manifested' an 'assertion of rights or dominion over the goods'.

3.3 WHICH GOODS CAN BE 'CONVERTED'?

Only chattels (not land) may be 'converted'. Furthermore, only 'tangible' property (things with physical form that may be 'touched') can be converted. Although the latter distinction has been criticized as outdated and arbitrary,[18] it was confirmed by the House of Lords in *OBG v Allan* [2007] UKHL 21; [2008] 1 AC 1. Here, invalidly appointed receivers of a company were not liable in conversion for interfering with the contractual interests of the company (by bringing those contracts to an end and seeking settlements against contracting parties). On the other hand, a *share certificate*, for example, *is* tangible property, as also is a cheque, so that these chattels may be converted. Bearing in mind that consequential losses are recoverable (and potentially disgorgement damages and restitution too), the commercial significance of the tort of conversion is considerable, even despite the decision not to extend it to 'intangibles'.[19]

The issue of intangible property divided the House of Lords in *OBG v Allan*. Lord Nicholls and Baroness Hale were of the view that the law should be modernized and the action extended to intangibles: the restriction to tangible property reflected the era in which the tort developed. The majority considered that this would fundamentally alter the basis of the tort, and that it would be far more than the 'modest but principled extension' which Lord Nicholls considered it to be (at [233]). They also proposed a number of reasons why the change would not be for the better. In the extracts below, Lord Hoffmann points out that while title to goods has traditionally been strongly protected by the common law, purely economic interests continue to be protected only in narrowly defined circumstances; to allow strict liability to extend into a domain where even intention is not generally sufficient would be illogical and dangerous (see further Chapter 2; Chapter 6). This reasoning has been criticized by Green and Randall, *The Tort of Conversion*, on the basis that the reasons for limiting recovery for pure economic losses (including multiplicity of claimants) do not apply. In the extract below, Lord Brown gives an example of the uncertainties to which the defendants would be exposed on the facts of the case in hand.[20]

OBG v Allan
[2007] UKHL 21

Lord Hoffmann

99 By contrast with the approving attitude of Cleasby B [in *Fowler v Hollins* (1872) LR 7 QB 616)] to the protection of rights of property in chattels, it is a commonplace that the law has always been very wary of imposing any kind of liability for purely economic

---

[18] Green and Randall, *The Tort of Conversion* (2009), Chapter 5.

[19] An example of a case of conversion of a cheque is *International Factors Ltd v Rodriguez* [1979] QB 351.

[20] The majority's view is criticized by Sarah Green, 'To Have and to Hold? Conversion and Intangible Property' (2008) 71 MLR 114–31.

loss. The economic torts which I have discussed at length are highly restricted in their application by the requirement of an intention to procure a breach of contract or to cause loss by unlawful means. Even liability for causing economic loss by negligence is very limited. Against this background, I suggest to your Lordships that it would be an extraordinary step suddenly to extend the old tort of conversion to impose strict liability for pure economic loss on receivers who were appointed and acted in good faith. Furthermore, the effects of such a change in the law would of course not stop there. *Hunter v Canary Wharf Ltd* [1997] AC 655, 694 contains a warning from Lord Goff of Chieveley (and other of their Lordships) against making fundamental changes to the law of tort in order to provide remedies which, if they are to exist at all, are properly the function of other parts of the law.

100 As to authority for such a change, it hardly needs to be said that in English law there is none. I need go no further than Halsbury's Laws of England, 4th ed reissue vol 45(2) (1999), para 547, which says "The subject matter of conversion or trover must be specific personal property, whether goods or chattels." The Law Revision Committee was invited, in 1967, to consider whether any changes are desirable in the law relating to conversion and detinue. In its 18th Report (Conversion and Detinue) in 1971 (Cmnd 4774) the committee treated them both as confined to wrongful interference with chattels. They made various recommendations for changes in the law but none for the extension of conversion to intangible choses in action. On the contrary, the Torts (Interference with Goods) Act 1977, which was passed as a result of their recommendations, defined wrongful interference with goods to include conversion of goods (section 1) and defined goods in section 14(1) to include "all chattels personal other than things in action and money".

...

Lord Brown

321 In common with Lord Hoffmann and Lord Walker I too would regard the expansion of the tort of conversion to cover the appropriation of things in action, as proposed by Lord Nicholls, to involve too radical and fundamental a change in the hitherto accepted nature of this tort (see particularly the Torts (Interference with Goods) Act 1977) to be properly capable of achievement under the guise of a development of the common law. Lord Nicholls suggests that this would represent merely "a modest but principled extension of the scope of the tort". I see it rather differently, as no less than the proposed severance of any link whatever between the tort of conversion and the wrongful taking of physical possession of property (whether a chattel or document) having a real and ascertainable value. Indeed, I respectfully question whether such a proposed development in the law ought in any event to be welcomed. I recognise, of course, that the tort has long since been extended to encompass a variety of documents, not merely documents of title and negotiable instruments but also any business document which in fact evidences some debt or obligation. But to my mind there remains a logical distinction between the wrongful taking of a document of this character and the wrongful assertion of a right to a chose in action which properly belongs to someone else. One (the document) has a determinable value as at the date of its seizure. The other, as so clearly demonstrated by this very case (OBG), does not. It is one thing for the law to impose strict liability for the wrongful taking of a valuable document; quite a different thing now to create strict liability for, as here, wrongly (though not knowingly so) assuming the right to advance someone else's claim.

Similar issues were more recently considered by the Court of Appeal in *Your Response Ltd v Datateam Media Ltd* [2014] EWCA Civ 281. The claim was for sums due under a contract for management of an electronic database, in which the data manager argued that it held rights (in the form of a lien) over the database pending payment of its fees, so that it was entitled to withhold data until payment. The key issue of law was whether it is possible to exercise a lien over intangible property. The judge held that such a lien is possible, based upon the analogy between electronic data, and traditional book-keeping. But as the Court of Appeal pointed out, he was not asked to consider the case of *OBG v Allan*.

In the Court of Appeal, the claim was dismissed. A common law lien permitted a bailee in possession of goods to refuse to redeliver them to the bailor until paid (*Tappenden v Artus* [1964] 2 QB 185). This however required 'actual possession of goods'. For this reason, the court considered whether it is possible to have 'actual possession of' an intangible. Following *OBG v Allan*, the starting point was that 'the essence of conversion is a wrongful interference with the possession of tangible property'; and that common law draws a sharp distinction between tangible and intangible property. Four arguments were made against this conclusion (set out at [18]), but all were rejected. For our purposes the most significant was the second:

Moore-Bick LJ, *Your Response v Datateam Business Media Ltd*

18. Mr. Cogley put forward four separate arguments in opposition to that analysis. The first was that the database in the present case should be regarded as a physical object, because it exists in a physical form on the data manager's servers. The second was that the essence of possession is physical control coupled with an intention to exclude others and that a person can properly be said to possess something if he is able to exercise complete control over access to it. An example might be the possession of goods in a warehouse to which there is only one key. The third was that a database can be regarded as a document and can be treated as if it were one for all purposes. The fourth was that there is a distinction to be drawn between choses in action, properly so called, and other kinds of intangible property, such as an electronic database, to which the principles enunciated on *OBG v Allan* do not apply.

The second argument identified by Moore-Bick LJ suggests that 'possession' should be approached in terms of 'practical control', so as to include intangibles. This was however rejected.

23. Although an analogy can be drawn between control of a database and possession of a chattel, I am unable to accept Mr. Cogley's argument. It is true that practical control goes hand in hand with possession, but in my view the two are not the same. Possession is concerned with the physical control of tangible objects; practical control is a broader concept, capable of extending to intangible assets and to things which the law would not regard as property at all. The case of goods stored in a warehouse, the only key to which is held by the bailee, does not in my view undermine that distinction, because the holder of the key has physical control over physical objects. In the present case the data manager was entitled, subject to the terms of the contract, to exercise practical control over the information constituting the database, but it could not exercise physical control over that information, which was intangible in nature. For the same reason the withholding of the database by the data manager could not, even if wrongful, constitute the tort of conversion.

As to the fourth argument, the Court of Appeal reiterated the traditional common law position that there is no 'tertium quid' or third kind of property, distinct from chattels on the one hand, and 'choses in action' on the other. Moore-Bick LJ, for his part, thought the case for changing this position and recognizing 'a third category of intangible property', to be 'powerful', referring to the arguments of Green and Randall. But he also considered that it would be inconsistent with the decision in *OBG v Allan* to develop the law in this way ([27]). The other two judges agreed that this step could not be taken by the Court of Appeal; but also doubted that it should be taken.

3.4 WHAT INTEREST IN THE CHATTELS MUST THE CLAIMANT HAVE?

Sarah Worthington, *Personal Property Law: Text and Materials* (Oxford: Hart Publishing, 2000), 574

... a claimant wishing to sue in conversion must have the right to possession at the time the conversion takes place. If the claimant cannot show this, then the action will fail. However, the claimant does not have to show that he has the ultimate or the best right to possession; all he has to show is that he has a better right than the defendant. It follows that bailees and 'finders' may be able to sue in conversion if the bailed or found property is taken from them by someone with no better right to it than they have.

What is a 'Right to Possession'?

The legal concept of 'possession' is not the same as the lay meaning of 'possession'. Rights to possess a chattel may vary depending on the purpose of possession, and may be relative to the rights of others. (See also Green and Randall, Chapter 4.)

F. H. Lawson and B. Rudden, *The Law of Property* (3rd edn, Oxford: Clarendon Press, 2002), 64–5

Where chattels are concerned, the law's approach reduces costs in the resolution of disputes by protecting possession without requiring the person so protected to prove ownership. It is up to the defendant to justify the taking or detention of the thing. The presumption also imposes a respect for possession, however it was obtained. If someone finds a ring, or a thief steals a bicycle, each is protected against anyone who takes it without consent—except, of course, the person who had prior possession and who lost the ring or had the bicycle stolen and so on.

In more technical language, we may say that there are rights to possess and rights which flow from having acquired possession. For the first phrase English (and American) law tends to use the word 'title': your title to some asset indicates your right to possess it. It is possible for there to be two or more titles to a thing, one being stronger than another. If you make a ring from your own hair, there is no doubt whatever that it is yours and that you have a better right to it than anyone else. If you lose it, you can claim it from the finder. But in the absence of any claim by you, the finder is treated as having a title good against everyone. You have a better right to possess the thing than does the finder, but the finder has a better right to possess it than does anyone else.

The Relative Nature of Possessory Rights

Lawson and Rudden make clear that a finder—or even a thief—may acquire rights to possess a chattel, good against everyone except the person who lost the goods.

Parker v British Airways Board [1982] QB 1004

A passenger found a gold bracelet in an executive lounge occupied by the defendant. He handed it to an employee of the defendant and requested that it should be returned to him, if the owner could not be found. It was not claimed, and the defendant sold it for £850.

The passenger successfully sued the defendant in conversion, and recovered £850 as damages.

Donaldson LJ, *Parker v British Airways Board* [1982] QB 1004

…

Rights and obligations of the finder

1 The finder of a chattel acquires no rights over it unless (a) it has been abandoned or lost and (b) he takes it into his care and control.

2 The finder of a chattel acquires very limited rights over it if he takes it into his care and control with dishonest intent or in the course of trespassing.

3 Subject to the foregoing and to point 4 below, a finder of a chattel, whilst not acquiring any absolute property or ownership in the chattel, acquires a right to keep it against all but the true owner or those in a position to claim through the true owner or one who can assert a prior right to keep the chattel which was subsisting at the time when the finder took the chattel into his care and control.

4 Unless otherwise agreed, any servant or agent who finds a chattel in the course of his employment or agency and not wholly incidentally or collaterally thereto and who takes it into his care and control does so on behalf of his employer or principal who acquires a finder's rights to the exclusion of those of the actual finder.

5 A person having a finder's rights has an obligation to take such measures as in all the circumstances are reasonable to acquaint the true owner of the finding and present whereabouts of the chattel and to care for it meanwhile.

Theft

Despite the proviso expressed by Donaldson LJ in the extract above, that a finder who acts with dishonest intent will acquire only very limited rights over a chattel, claimants who have (on the balance of probabilities) acquired title through *theft* have nevertheless been successful in actions to recover stolen property from the police (provided the police have no statutory powers to retain them): *Costello v Chief Constable of Derbyshire Constabulary* [2001] 1 WLR 1437; *Gough v Chief Constable of West Midlands Police* [2004] EWCA Civ 206. The claimants in these cases would not of course be able to retain the goods if the lawful owner of the goods could be found.

3.5 WHAT AMOUNTS TO A CONVERSION?

Andrew Tettenborn, 'Damages in Conversion—The Exception or The Anomaly?' (1993) 52 CLJ, at 129–30

Put shortly D commits conversion against P where, without legal justification, he does any of (i) to (vii) below in relation to a thing belonging to P:

(i) Being in possession of the thing, he fails on demand to return it to P.

(ii) He takes it, whether from P or from a third party.

(iii) He receives it from a third party T who has no title to it.

(iv) He physically transfers it to T, eg by sale or gift, or otherwise acts so as to destroy P's title to it.

(v) He destroys it.

(vi) Being a bailee, he wrongfully loses it or allows it to be destroyed.

(vii) Having obtained it lawfully, he wrongfully keeps or uses it.

There are two further important points on liability in conversion generally. First, it must be borne in mind that liability is prima facie strict, so that in any of the above situations D is liable in damages whether or not he knew the goods he was dealing with were P's or that he was otherwise infringing P's rights. Secondly, it should be remembered that dealings with another's goods may involve D in two or more acts of conversion. In any such case, P can (subject to the law of limitation of actions) rely on any individual conversion that he may choose.

3.6 WHAT ARE THE REMEDIES?
Return of Goods

One would have thought, since conversion protects rights of possession, that the return of goods would, where this is possible, be available as of right. But this is not the case. Where the defendant is still in possession of the 'converted' goods, the claimant may seek their return. But the limited scope for recovery as a remedy shows that conversion, being merely a tort, provides only a clumsy and limited mechanism for enforcing (or vindicating) proprietary rights.[21]

[21] On the other hand, the claimant is freed from the need to *prove ownership*. As Tettenborn points out, the compromise action in conversion may actually work better in some respects than the pure property action that exists in most civilian legal systems: 'Conversion, Tort and Restitution', Section 3.1 in this chapter, at 826.

Historical Origins

At common law, recovery of goods *could* sometimes be achieved through the action in detinue. But even detinue carried an alternative in the form of damages. Recovery of goods could not be achieved through the action on the case which began as 'trover', and became conversion.

Nick Curwen, 'The Remedy in Conversion: Confusing Property and Obligation' (2006) 26 LS 570, at 571–2

The failure of the common law to develop an effective action for the recovery of goods has both stunted the growth of a distinct law of property in relation to goods and distorted the principles of the law of tort. The problem goes back to the earliest days of the common law. Detinue was an ancient action brought for the recovery of goods. The remedy was an order that the defendant must return the goods or pay their full value to the claimant. The claim was proprietary in nature, a demand for recovery, but the remedy was personal rather than real because the defendant had the option of paying damages in lieu of restitution.

... Trover was an action in trespass on the case for the conversion of goods ... Brian Simpson[22] ... relates that in the sixteenth century it was not possible for two types of action to exist on the same set of facts so pleaders had to frame their action so as to avoid any suggestion that detinue was the appropriate action. If detinue lay, that prevented an action in conversion. In the early cases, going back to the late fifteenth century, it was held that if the defendant changed the nature of the goods then that changed the property in them. This development enabled the new action to replace completely detinue but at the expense of perpetrating an obvious fiction.

Eventually the rule against overlapping actions disappeared and it was accepted that the claimant did not lose property in the goods until the defendant had satisfied the court order by paying the full value of them to the claimant. But the fiction had done its work and the action remained in essence a tort remediable at common law by compensation. In effect, the claimant was forced to waive their proprietary claim and sue for damages. There was no scope, as in detinue, for ordering restitution in specie or, in the alternative, paying damages.

The extract above explains how the modern tort of conversion emerged. Further confusion was introduced by abolishing detinue, and shifting some of its (already compromised) functions to the tort of conversion. This was achieved by the Torts (Interference With Goods) Act 1977.

Torts (Interference With Goods) Act 1977

2 Abolition of detinue

(1) Detinue is abolished.

(2) An action lies in conversion for loss or destruction of goods which a bailee has allowed to happen in breach of his duty to his bailor (that is to say it lies in a case which is not otherwise conversion, but would have been detinue before detinue was abolished).

---

[22] A. W. B. Simpson, 'The Introduction of the Action on the Case for Conversion' (1959) 75 LQR 364.

3 Form of judgment where goods are detained

(1) In proceedings for wrongful interference against a person who is in possession or in control of the goods relief may be given in accordance with this section, so far as appropriate.

(2) The relief is—

(a) an order for delivery of the goods, and for payment of any consequential damages, or

(b) an order for delivery of the goods, but giving the defendant the alternative of paying damages by reference to the value of the goods, together in either alternative with payment of any consequential damages, or

(c) damages.

...

By section 3(1), the court *may* order delivery up (section 3(1)(a)). If the court does not order delivery up, the claimant may choose between the other remedies; but if (b) is selected, the *defendant* may elect whether to return the goods, or pay their value.

Damages

Damages are available both:

1. where the defendant retains the chattel, but an order for recovery is not made; and

2. where the defendant no longer retains the chattel.

In either case, the basic measure has generally been accepted to be *the value of the goods at the date of conversion*; damages in respect of consequential loss will also be available where appropriate. However, the judgment in *Kuwait Airways* may signal a change to come.

In either case, title to the goods is extinguished when the award of damages is satisfied (or payment made in satisfaction of a final settlement): section 5 of the Torts (Interference with Goods) Act 1977.

In a case where the defendant refuses to return the goods, then the value of the goods may be an appropriate measure. But it has been argued that a measure of damages that reflects the *value of the goods* rather than the loss caused to the claimant—particularly given that consequential losses are recoverable in any event—is unfair to 'honest converters' who do not retain the goods. It has been argued that beyond the action against converters who *retain* the chattel (Section 3), damages assessed by reference to the value of the goods cannot generally be justified. As with other torts, compensatory damages should be assessed by reference to *what the claimant has lost*. On the other hand, the full measure of damages related to the value of the goods might be justified in particular circumstances, for example if the converter is dishonest.[23]

The general measure of damages, and the case for treating dishonest converters differently, were discussed in the case of *Kuwait Airways*. We now turn to the important issues in that case surrounding damages.

[23] A. Tettenborn, 'Damages in Conversion—The Exception or the Anomaly?' (1993) 52 CLJ 128–47.

Kuwait Airways: Damages Issues

We set out the facts of *Kuwait Airways* earlier (see Section 3.2). As we saw, there was no possibility of recovering the aircraft themselves in that case. Some had been destroyed, others had been recovered by the claimant from a third party (Iran) for a large payment.

The Basic Measure of Damages in Conversion

As we said earlier, the basic measure of damages in conversion is usually based on the value of the converted goods at the date of conversion. After a wide review of the authorities, Lord Nicholls decided that the 'value measure' is intended to reflect the claimant's loss. This is controversial in itself. He then went on to say that, sometimes, the claimant's loss is not properly reflected in the value measure; and that when this is the case, the court should assess damages according to *the loss suffered*.

Lord Nicholls, *Kuwait Airways v Iraqi Airways (Nos 4 and 5)* [2002] 2 AC 883

67 ... The fundamental object of an award of damages in respect of this tort, as with all wrongs, is to award just compensation for loss suffered. Normally ("prima facie") the measure of damages is the market value of the goods at the time the defendant expropriated them. This is the general rule, because generally this measure represents the amount of the basic loss suffered by the plaintiff owner. He has been dispossessed of his goods by the defendant. Depending on the circumstances some other measure, yielding a higher or lower amount, may be appropriate. The plaintiff may have suffered additional damage consequential on the loss of his goods. Or the goods may have been returned.

68 This approach accords with the conclusion of the Law Reform Committee in its 18th report (Conversion and Detinue) (1971) (Cmnd 4774) that the general rule as respects the measure of damages for wrongful interference should be that the plaintiff is entitled to recover the loss he has suffered. The committee considered this conclusion was "right in principle", and added, in paragraph 91:

"In many cases the value of the chattel itself will either represent this loss or form an important element in its calculation; but consideration of the value of the chattel should not be allowed to obscure the principle that what the plaintiff is entitled to recover is his true loss."

Causation

Where the 'Iran six' were concerned, significant questions arose surrounding the operation of causal tests. The defendants had used the planes and treated them as their own. However, even if the defendants had not put the aircraft to use (or transported them to Iran for safe keeping), the claimants would still not have had possession of the planes. The initial taker was the state of Iraq. Could it then be said that the defendant had not 'caused' the loss of the planes? Lord Nicholls rejected this argument.

80 The existing principle of strict liability as described above is deeply ingrained in the common law. It has survived at least since the days of Lord Mansfield in *Cooper v Chitty* (1756) 1 Burr 20. The hardship it may cause to those who deal innocently with a person in possession of goods has long been recognised. Blackburn J noted this in the leading case of *Fowler v Hollins* (1875) LR 7 HL 757, 764. The hardship arises especially for innocent persons who no longer have the goods. There has been some statutory amelioration of the principle, in the Factors Acts and elsewhere, but in general the principle endures.

81 Consistently with this principle, every person through whose hands goods pass in a series of conversions is himself guilty of conversion and liable to the owner for the loss caused by his misappropriation of the owner's goods. His liability is not diminished by reason, for instance, of his having acquired the goods from a thief as distinct from the owner himself. In such a case, it may be said, looking at the successive conversions overall, the owner is no worse off as a result of the acts of the person who acquired the goods from the thief. Such a person has not "caused" the owner any additional loss.

82 In one sense this is undoubtedly correct. The owner had already lost his goods. But that is really nothing to the point for the purposes of assessing damages for conversion. By definition, each person in a series of conversions wrongfully excludes the owner from possession of his goods. This is the basis on which each is liable to the owner. That is the nature of the tort of conversion. The wrongful acts of a previous possessor do not therefore diminish the plaintiff's claim in respect of the wrongful acts of a later possessor. Nor, for a different reason, is it anything to the point that, absent the defendant's conversion, someone else would wrongfully have converted the goods. The likelihood that, had the defendant not wronged the plaintiff, somebody would have done so is no reason for diminishing the defendant's liability and responsibility for the loss he brought upon the plaintiff.

83 Where, then, does this leave the simple "but for" test in cases of successive conversion? I suggest that, if the test is to be applied at all, the answer lies in keeping in mind, as I have said, that each person in a series of conversions wrongfully excludes the owner from possession of his goods. The exclusionary threshold test is to be applied on this footing. Thus the test calls for consideration of whether the plaintiff would have suffered the loss in question had he retained his goods and not been unlawfully deprived of them by the defendant. The test calls for a comparison between the owner's position had he retained his goods and his position having been deprived of his goods by the defendant. Loss which the owner would have suffered even if he had retained the goods is not loss "caused" by the conversion. The defendant is not liable for such loss.

...

85 For these reasons I consider KAC's claims in respect of the Iran Six do not fail at the threshold stage. Had KAC not been unlawfully deprived of its goods by IAC KAC would not have suffered any of the heads of loss it is now claiming. Had KAC retained possession of the Iran Six, the aircraft would not have been evacuated to Iran.

As we can see from the last sentence of this extract (and also from para [83]), the question is not, 'would the claimant have been deprived of possession "but for" the acts of the defendant?'; it is rather, 'would the claimant have suffered any of these heads of loss, had the claimant retained possession?' The 'but for' test does not apply in the same way in conversion as it does in any other tort. But to apply it in the usual manner would be inconsistent with the logic of the tort.

Remoteness of Damage

The remaining extracts propose certain distinctions between 'honest' and 'dishonest' converters of goods, in respect of assessment of damages.

A significant issue arose concerning the extent of damages for which the defendants would be liable in respect of the conversion of the Iran six, since the claimants used the temporary unavailability of this part of its fleet (which had not been destroyed) as the occasion for substantial restructuring with new aircraft. As we learned in Chapter 3, rules of 'remoteness of damage' ask which losses are fairly attributable to the tort of the defendant.

100 Expressed in terms of the traditional guideline principles, the choice is between confining liability for consequential loss to damage which is "foreseeable", as distinct from damage flowing "directly and naturally" from the wrongful conduct. In practice, these two tests usually yield the same result. Where they do not, the foreseeability test is likely to be the more restrictive. The prevalent view is that the more restrictive test of foreseeability is applicable to the torts of negligence, nuisance, and *Rylands v Fletcher*: see the two *Wagon Mound* cases [1961] AC 388 and [1967] 1 AC 617 and *Cambridge Water Co v Eastern Counties Leather plc* [1994] 2 AC 264. The Court of Appeal recently applied this test to the tort of conversion, apparently without any contrary argument, in *Saleslease Ltd v Davis* [1999] 1 WLR 1664, although the members of the court differed in the application of the principle to the facts of the case.

101 In contrast, the less restrictive test is applicable in deceit. The more culpable the defendant the wider the area of loss for which he can fairly be held responsible: see the discussion by my noble and learned friend Lord Steyn in *Smith New Court Securities Ltd v Scrimgeour Vickers (Asset Management) Ltd* [1997] AC 254, 279–285.

102 This bifurcation causes difficulty with the tort of conversion. Dishonesty is not an essential ingredient of this wrong. The defendant may be a thief, or he may have acted wholly innocently. Both are strictly liable. But it seems to me inappropriate they should be treated alike when determining their liability for consequential loss. Parliament, indeed, has recognised that for some purposes different considerations should apply to persons who steal goods, or knowingly receive stolen goods, and persons who can show they bought the goods in good faith. . . .

103 I have already mentioned that, as the law now stands, the tort of conversion may cause hardship for innocent persons. This suggests that foreseeability, as the more restrictive test, is appropriate for those who act in good faith. Liability remains strict, but liability for consequential loss is confined to types of damage which can be expected to arise from the wrongful conduct. You deal with goods at the risk of discovering later that, unbeknown to you, you have not acquired a good title. That is the strict common law principle. The risk is that, should you not have acquired title, you will be liable to the owner for the losses he can expect to have suffered as a result of your misappropriation of his goods. That seems the preferable approach, in the case of a person who can prove he acted in the genuine belief the goods were his. A person in possession of goods knows where and how he acquired them. It is up to him to establish he was innocent of any knowing wrongdoing. This is the approach Parliament has taken in section 4 of the Limitation Act 1980.

104 Persons who knowingly convert another's goods stand differently. Such persons are acting dishonestly. I can see no good reason why the remoteness test of "directly and naturally" applied in cases of deceit should not apply in cases of conversion where the defendant acted dishonestly.

Lord Nicholls here introduces a division in the remoteness test applying to consequential losses in conversion. The 'negligence' measure (foreseeability) applies to innocent conversion. The 'intentional' measure (directness) applies to dishonest conversion. The same principles ought, if correct, to apply in other torts (such as battery, considered in Chapter 2) which may be committed either culpably (with intent as to the wrongful element), or not.

Gain-based Awards

The claimants in this case had not argued for a gain-based award. But Lord Nicholls gave a clear signal that he might have made such an award, if pleaded. There were two different elements to his discussion of a gain-based award. The first relates to restitution for unjust enrichment; the second to 'user damages' for the tort.

Unjust Enrichment

79 ... Vindication of a plaintiff's proprietary interests requires that, in general, all those who convert his goods should be accountable for *benefits* they receive. They must make restitution to the extent they are unjustly enriched. The goods are his, and he is entitled to reclaim them and any benefits others have derived from them. Liability in this regard should be strict subject to defences available to restitutionary claims such as change of position: see *Lipkin Gorman v Karpnale Ltd* [1991] 2 AC 548. Additionally, those who act dishonestly should be liable to make good any *losses* caused by their wrongful conduct. Whether those who act innocently should also be liable to make good the plaintiff's losses is a different matter. A radical reappraisal of the tort of conversion along these lines was not pursued on these appeals. So I shall say nothing more about it.

As Lord Nicholls says, this suggestion is 'radical'. It is more far-reaching than an adjustment to the measure of damages. It treats the *basis* of the claim in conversion as being unjust enrichment, requiring restitution; with an additional liability (for losses caused) which could potentially be applied to dishonest converters only. This hints at a radical reappraisal of the action in conversion. Loss-based damages would be *additional* to restitution; and they may be available only in cases of dishonest conversion.

'User Damages'

Here, Lord Nicholls said that he might have made an award of damages based on the benefit derived by the defendants from 'use' of the aircraft.

The Iran Six: "user damages"

87 I have noted that the fundamental object of an award of damages for conversion is to award just compensation for loss suffered. Sometimes, when the goods or their equivalent are returned, the owner suffers no financial loss. But the wrongdoer may well have benefited from his temporary use of the owner's goods. It would not be right that he should be able to keep this benefit. The court may order him to pay damages assessed by reference to the value of the benefit he derived from his wrongdoing. I considered this principle in *Attorney General v Blake* [2001] 1 AC 268, 278–280. In an appropriate case the court may award damages on this "user principle" in addition to compensation for loss suffered. For

instance, if the goods are returned damaged, the court may award damages assessed by reference to the benefit obtained by the wrongdoer as well as the cost of repair.

88 Recognition that damages may be awarded on this principle may assist in making some awards of damages in conversion cases more coherent. For example, I respectfully think this is the preferable basis for the award of damages in *Solloway v McLaughlin* [1938] AC 247 in respect of Solloway's misappropriation of the 14,000 shares deposited with him by McLaughlin. McLaughlin suffered no financial loss from the misappropriation, because equivalent shares were returned to McLaughlin when he closed his account. But Solloway profited by the fall in the value of the shares by selling them when they were deposited with him and repurchasing them at the lower market price obtaining when McLaughlin closed his account.

...

The damages discussed in this passage might, if they had been awarded, have been described in different ways. It is clear that they are *damages*, since Lord Nicholls uses that term. They are distinct from the award of 'restitution for unjust enrichment' described above. Equally, it is clear that they are a response to the defendant's tort. They are damages for a wrong (a tort), calculated on the basis of benefits to the defendant, not on the basis of financial loss suffered by the claimant (see para [87]: 'the owner suffers no financial loss. But the wrongdoer may well have benefited … ').

Beyond this, it is rather hard to categorize what is meant by 'user damages'. Perhaps Lord Nicholls is referring to the same sort of 'restitutionary damages' available in the trespass case of *MOD v Ashman*, which quantify the value of having use of the property. If that is the case, the reference to *A-G v Blake* in the extract above is not helpful. In that case, Lord Nicholls deliberately avoided describing the award as 'restitutionary'. An award based on 'benefits' in the form of 'profits' as in *Blake* (if that is what Lord Nicholls had in mind) might be described as *disgorgement damages*, rather than 'user damages'.

'Disgorgement' is generally thought to be available only in cases of *dishonest* wrongdoing. Was this a case of dishonest conversion, or not? IAC well knew the history of ownership of the aircraft, and it knew that the aircraft had been seized through an act of war. This was certainly not a case of 'accidental' conversion. But when discussing the applicable Iraqi law of usurpation, Lord Nicholls made clear that he did *not* think this was a case of 'bad faith', which was relevant to Iraqi law.

Lord Nicholls, *Kuwait Airways*

48 … IAC acted in the belief that RCC Resolution 369 gave it a good title. This also was common ground. (In this regard, and to this extent, the existence of this decree will be recognisod by an English court. This is not giving effect to Resolution 369. This is doing no more than accept the existence of this decree as the explanation for IAC's state of mind.)

If the test for 'good faith' in usurpation (in Iraqi law) is similar to the idea of 'honesty' which might be applied in the tort of conversion, then there would be no dishonesty on the part of the defendants in this case. IAC honestly believed they had a good claim in law to the aircraft. But if *that* is the case, the 'user damages' discussed by Lord Nicholls should have been *restitutionary* damages, not disgorgement damages. And in that case, the references to *A-G v Blake* are not helpful.

4. CONCLUSIONS

i. The actions reviewed in this chapter are relatively little studied by undergraduate law students, but retain their significance in practice. Their applicable principles are very different from negligence; but in the retention of strict liability, trespass to land and goods appear to have diverged also from their close relatives, the torts collected in Chapter 2 as aspects of trespass to the person. Comparing them will show how important it is to ask *what* must be intended and, indeed, what *aspect* of liability is strict, when comparing one form of liability with another. Even where, as here, liability attaches to *faultless* action, there may still be an element of intention—such as the 'deliberate dealing' with goods in conversion.

FURTHER READING

Curwen, N., The Remedy in Conversion—Confusing Property and Obligation' (2006) 26 LS 570.

Douglas, S., *Liability for Wrongful Interferences with Chattels* (Oxford: Hart Publishing, 2011).

Edelman, J., 'Gain-Based Damages and Compensation', in A. Burrows and Lord Rodger (eds), *Mapping the Law* (Oxford: Oxford University Press, 2006) 141.

Green, S., 'Conversion and Theft—Tangibly Different?' (2012) 128 LQR 564.

Green, S., and Randall, J., *The Tort of Conversion* (Oxford: Hart Publishing, 2009).

Hickey, R., 'Stealing Abandoned Goods: Possessory Title and Proceedings for Theft' (2006) 26 LS 584.

Samuel, G., 'Wrongful Interference with Goods' (1982) 31 ICLQ 357.

Simpson, A. W. B., 'The Introduction of the Action on the Case for Conversion' (1959) 75 LQR 364.

Skene, L., 'Property Interests in Human Bodily Material' (2012) 20 Med L Rev 227.

Tettenborn, A., 'Damages in Conversion—The Exception or the Anomaly?' (1993) 52 CLJ 128–47.

Tettenborn, A., 'Conversion, Tort and Restitution', in N. Palmer and E. McKendrick (eds), *Interests in Goods* (2nd edn, London: Lloyds of London Press, 1998).

Wall, J., 'The Legal Status of Body Parts: a Framework' (2011) 31 OJLS 783.